MUSEUM ADMINISTRATION

MUSEUM ADMINISTRATION

LAW AND PRACTICE

Second edition

WALTER G. LEHMANN

ROWMAN & LITTLEFIELD
Lanham • Boulder • New York • London

Acquisitions Editor: Charles Harmon
Acquisitions Assistant: Erinn Slanina
Sales and Marketing Inquiries: textbooks@rowman.com

Credits and acknowledgments for material borrowed from other sources, and reproduced with permission, appear on the appropriate pages within the text.

Published by Rowman & Littlefield
An imprint of The Rowman & Littlefield Publishing Group, Inc.
4501 Forbes Boulevard, Suite 200, Lanham, Maryland 20706
www.rowman.com
86-90 Paul Street, London EC2A 4NE

Interior design: Scott S. Tully

British Library Cataloguing in Publication Information Available

Library of Congress Cataloging-in-Publication Data

Names: Lehmann, Walter G., 1962- author.
Title: Museum administration : law and practice / Walter G. Lehmann.
Description: Second edition. | Lanham : Rowman & Littlefield, [2022] | Includes bibliographical references and index.
Identifiers: LCCN 2021053602 (print) | LCCN 2021053603 (ebook) | ISBN 9781538166352 (cloth) | ISBN 9781538166369 (epub)
Subjects: LCSH: Museums--Law and legislation--United States. | LCGFT: Textbooks.
Classification: LCC KF4305 .L444 2022 (print) | LCC KF4305 (ebook) | DDC 344.73/093--dc23/eng/20211109
LC record available at https://lccn.loc.gov/2021053602
LC ebook record available at https://lccn.loc.gov/2021053603

TABLE OF CONTENTS

Charles Willson Peale (American 1741—1827) was an American painter, soldier, scientist, inventor, politician, naturalist, and the brother and father of several other noted American artists. He is also credited with founding the first museum in the United States. The Artist in His Museum *(1822) is a full-length self-portrait of Peale depicted lifting a curtain and inviting the viewer into his "cabinet of curiosities."*

INTRODUCTION: WHAT IS "MUSEUM LAW"?

Museums must comply with a myriad of laws regulating virtually every aspect of their organization and operations. In his seminal 1983 essay "Vincible Ignorance: Museums and the Law," Stephen Weil referred to "the inexorable advance of a mass of regulation" that threatened to overwhelm museum directors.[NOTE 1] Reflecting the optimism of the Reagan era, Weil looked forward to a time when the tide of excessive regulation would be turned back. Sadly, since that time the "inexorable advance" of regulation bemoaned by Weil has continued to grow exponentially, with no sign of any respite in sight.

While some of these laws apply to businesses in general and some apply to all kinds of nonprofit charitable organizations, others are entirely unique to the museum community. As Weil explained, there is no one field of museum law. Rather, the practice of museum law involves the application of legal principles derived from many different areas of the law to the day-to-day management and administration of museum organizations.

There are over 35,000 museums in the United States alone. These organizations run the gamut from major cultural institutions such as the Metropolitan Museum of Art, the Getty Museum and the like, to small one-room historical societies and virtual (online) museums. Museum professionals at organizations large and small routinely encounter a wide range of legal issues while carrying out their administrative duties.

While the day-to-day responsibility for identifying and addressing institutional legal concerns tends to fall with the museum's director,[NOTE 2] increasingly other museum professionals are expected to be familiar with legal issues within their area of expertise—registrars with intellectual property law, human resource directors with employment law, development officers with regulations on fundraising and charitable giving, and facilities managers with Americans with Disabilities (ADA) requirements, for example.

These museum professionals have a seemingly impossible task. They are charged with the responsibility of ensuring not only that the museum adheres to all applicable legal requirements, but that they do so in furtherance of their institution's mission and in strict compliance with a growing body of professional ethical codes and best practices.

Despite this growing need for legal guidance and knowledge, access to legal counsel remains limited for most museums. Only museum professionals at the largest and wealthiest museums have in-house legal counsel at their disposal, with approximately fifty museums in the United States currently possessing in-house legal staff. [NOTE 3] Most museums, even larger institutions such as the Cleveland Museum of Art and the Minneapolis Institute of Art, rely either exclusively or primarily on outside and *pro bono* legal counsel for their museum-related legal needs. Legal professionals frequently serve on museum boards, and while some may have expertise in areas of law relevant to museums (employment law, for example) and a few may have experience with laws affecting nonprofit organizations in general, only a small handful of attorneys are familiar with the broad range and scope of museum practices, procedures and ethical codes. [NOTE 4]

Out of necessity, then, many museum professionals typically rely on information gleaned from colleagues, professional conferences, and free legal resources such as blogs, list-serves, and the like, to assess the legal sufficiency of their management decisions. While such efforts at "self-education" are laudable and completely understandable given the position in which museum professionals are placed, it nonetheless can result in needless exposure to risk when the law is misunderstood, misapplied, or simply overlooked. It also explains the often extremely conservative "black letter" approach to certain aspects of the law at many of our cultural institutions, as well as a "wild west" attitude about compliance with legal requirements in other contexts.

LAW VS. ETHICS

What makes museum law practice unique—and infinitely interesting—is the central role played by each museum's unique institutional culture and by the many ethical codes and best practices promulgated by the museum profession to guide museum practice. While lawyers generally approach legal issues from a minimalist "enforcement" perspective ("what does the law require"?), museum professionals must also consider their particular institutional mission and internal policies as well as the guidelines and codes of ethics promulgated by applicable museum professional organizations ("what does the museum profession expect?") and the views of the public which they serve.

Institutional and professional practices of cultural organizations often impose requirements that are distinct from applicable legal standards. [NOTE 5] In some cases ethical codes may impose a "higher" standard, but often they simply impose a different one. Ideally, by adhering to institutional policies, generally accepted professional "best practices" and ethical codes, the integrity of the institution and its reputation in the eyes of the public are preserved. Having said that, museum professionals should not hesitate to question the efficacy of ethical codes, particularly when they are promulgated in response to unwanted media attention and public scrutiny. [NOTE 6]

LEGAL THINKING VS. MUSEUM THINKING

The differing perspectives of lawyers and museum professionals can be described as "legal thinking" versus "museum thinking." What may be considered the right outcome from a legal standpoint may not necessarily reflect the values a given cultural institution wants to uphold.[NOTE 7] Due to the fact that museums ultimately exist to serve the public, this difference is often manifested as a conflict between private rights and public access, and between private ownership and the public trust. In certain contexts, the notion of exclusive rights and private ownership run counter to the museum's obligations as a trustee of a charitable trust. In other contexts, the museum must weigh its obligations to the public at large with its obligations to private individuals, cultural communities, or other stakeholders.

The approach a museum takes in managing its affairs depends primarily on the nature of the institution and its values. The way in which a museum's policies and practices reflect institutional values is sometimes referred to as the museum's "institutional tone." The degree to which a museum is willing to take risks—both legal and ethical—is a key component of this institutional tone. Some institutions take the approach that their mission is to reflect the general norms of the society in which they operate. Others feel that their primary responsibility is to question established practices. Either approach is perfectly reasonable: the point is that it is essential for museum professionals—and legal counsel—to clearly understand their museum's values and to keep these in mind when managing that institution.

At its heart, applying legal principles and ethical codes in any given situation is a process of assessing and managing risk. The museum manager is responsible for applying legal and ethical principles to minimize the risk that the museum's actions will infringe on another's rights or otherwise create legal or reputational liability for the institution. While no museum professional is expected to become an expert on the law, it is crucial for museum professionals to be able to identify potential legal and ethical pitfalls and know when it is appropriate to seek professional advice.

Today, there is a growing understanding of the relevance of law in cultural institutions and efforts to provide museum professionals with access to legal and ethical resources. A growing number of colleges and universities are offering undergraduate and graduate programs and degrees in museum studies, many of which include courses that address the legal and ethical aspects of museum administration. Many law schools now offer courses in art and museum law, although the content of these courses varies widely and tends to focus on discrete aspects of an art and museum law practice, such as intellectual property, business transactions, nonprofit organizations, or laws affecting the art markets and cultural property. Professional development programs, such as the Getty Leadership Institute, are also increasingly available to museum professionals.

Museum professionals need not become lawyers to accomplish their jobs, but they do need enough training to enable them to identify the potential legal issues involved in the situations they face daily. They need to know how to respond to those issues and to know when to seek the advice of experienced legal counsel. That is the primary goal of this book—to provide a comprehensive but concise introduction to the wide range of legal and ethical issues facing museums. While the book is principally designed as a textbook for use in connection with museum studies programs and law school courses on art and museum topics, it is also intended to be a useful resource for museum professionals and practicing lawyers alike.

To that end, this book utilizes a "casebook" approach to museum administration law and practice, incorporating relevant court decisions and other primary source materials to illustrate the application of legal and ethical concepts to real-life museum scenarios. The book begins with a discussion of issues relating to museum organization and governance. Laws relating to museum personnel and museum facilities are also covered, as are museum intellectual property, museum collections and funding for museums. Readers will gain a working knowledge of basic legal concepts and how these concepts arise in the museum setting. The legal issues faced by museums—particularly in the areas of tax law, labor law and intellectual property—are rapidly changing. It is hoped that this book will provide a foundation on which museum professionals—lawyers and non-lawyers alike—can build as they pursue what will undoubtedly be a challenging but hopefully rewarding career in museum administration.

Walter G. Lehmann
December 2019

NOTES:

NOTE 1: Stephen E. Weil, "Vincible Ignorance: Museums and the Law" in *Beauty and the Beasts*, Smithsonian Books, 1983, pp. 133-42.

NOTE 2: Weil. Museum boards are charged with setting policy and overseeing core museum functions, but as a practical matter the museum director must both provide guidance to the board and to staff regarding potential legal issues.

NOTE 3: When Weil wrote his article "Vincible Ignorance" in 1983, he noted that there were "scarcely half-a-dozen museums in the United States" with in-house legal counsel. At that time, the Smithsonian Institution had a staff of eight lawyers. The Smithsonian legal department alone now has a total of 13 full-time lawyers, with additional legal staff in other departments.

NOTE 4: Pro bono legal advice is typically provided as a result of a relationship with a museum board member who is a member of a local law firm. While understandable from a practical perspective, this form of legal representation is not ideal for a number of reasons, not least of which are the potential for conflicts of interest, hesitation by staff to avoid over-burdening the attorney providing pro bono advice, and the simple fact that such legal representation is often provided by attorneys who have little or no experience working in or with cultural institutions.

NOTE 5: For a discussion of the relationship between legal standards and ethical codes, see Maria C. Malaro, "Why Ethics?" in *Museum Governance: Mission, Ethics, Policy*, Smithsonian Institution Press, 1994, at pp. 16-21.

NOTE 6: There are situations where professional ethical codes have clearly been adopted in an attempt to insulate cultural institutions from criticism from the media and the public for perceived "unethical practices." The consequences of such "fig leaf" ethical codes are often not thoroughly considered and can do more harm than good.

NOTE 7: The outcome in *Christophe Bruchell v. Mass MOCA* is a good example of the difference between legal thinking and cultural institution thinking. In that case, which involved the scope of the Visual Artists Rights Act, the District Court determined that Mass MOCA had the right to display an unfinished work of art despite the fact that the work was not fully realized by the artist. Immediately after the verdict in Mass MOCA's favor was announced, the museum's director decided not to display the work in deference to the concerns of the artist and respect for artistic integrity in general. 565 F. Supp. 2d 245 (D. Mass. 2008).

MUSEUM ADMINISTRATION:

LAW AND PRACTICE

Walter G. Lehmann

CHAPTER 1:
MUSEUM ORGANIZATION AND GOVERNANCE

In this chapter we consider the definition of "museum" and the museum as a legal entity. We examine museum organizational structures, including public, private and quasi-governmental or hybrid organizations. We also look at museum governance, including the role of museums boards, museum policies and procedures, as well as oversight of museums by the state attorney general through the federal tax code and other regulatory means.

WHAT IS A MUSEUM?

The word "museum" is derived from Latin and originates from the Greek "musaem" or "mouseion," used to describe a shrine or temple to the Muses. The term was first applied to the Mouseion at Alexandria, an institution founded by Ptolemy I Soter or perhaps Ptolemy II Philadelphus as a venue for music and poetry, a library, and a school of philosophy. These "temples of the Muses" were primarily educational, much like modern colleges and universities.

The Musaeum or Mouseion at Alexandria was an institution devoted to the study of music, poetry and the arts and included a philosophical school and the famous Library of Alexandria. It did not have a collection of works of art; rather it brought together some of the best scholars of the Hellenistic world, analogous to a modern university. This original Musaeum was the source for the modern usage of the word museum.

Today the word "museum" refers to a wide variety of organizations focused on experiential learning through the collection, exhibition and scholarly research of objects and ideas. Some museums are primarily collecting institutions, while others merely exhibit the collections owned by others. Museums may occupy physical space or exist solely in the digital realm as a "virtual" museum.

The International Council of Museums (ICOM) is an association of museums from around the world. ICOM currently defines a museum as "a nonprofit, permanent institution in the service of society and its development, open to the public, which acquires, conserves, researches, communicates and exhibits the tangible and intangible heritage of humanity and its environment for the purposes of education, study and enjoyment." ICOM is in the process of reviewing and revising this definition to reflect the changing role of museums in the 21st Century. A proposed new definition of "museum" is included in the first set of Cases and Other Readings below.

The American Alliance of Museums (AAM) is an association of American museums of all kinds—from art museums to zoos. According to AAM, "the common denominator " shared by all museums is "making a unique contribution to the public by collecting, preserving, and interpreting things of this world."

The Museum and Library Services Act, which established the Institute of Museum and Library Services (IMLS), describes a museum as "a public or private nonprofit agency or institution organized on a permanent basis for essentially educational or aesthetic purposes, which, utilizing a professional staff, owns or utilizes tangible objects, cares for them, and exhibits them to the public on a regular basis."

These are just some of the ways to define a museum.

CASES AND OTHER READINGS

Reading Note: The International Council of Museums (ICOM) is composed of member museums from around the world. An ICOM committee proposed the following new definition of a "museum" for consideration at the 2019 annual meeting. The proposal was tabled and as of this writing has not been adopted by the organization.

ICOM'S NEW ALTERNATIVE MUSEUM DEFINITION

Following the processes of active listening, collecting, and collating alternative definitions through its standing committee on Museum Definition, Prospects and Potentials (MDPP), the Executive Board of ICOM, at its 139th session in Paris on 21-22 July 2019, selected the below as a new alternative museum definition for a vote to be included in the ICOM Statutes instead of the current museum definition:

"Museums are democratising, inclusive and polyphonic spaces for critical dialogue about the pasts and the futures. Acknowledging and addressing the conflicts and challenges of the present, they hold artefacts and specimens in trust for society, safeguard diverse memories for future gen-

erations and guarantee equal rights and equal access to heritage for all people. Museums are not for profit. They are participatory and transparent, and work in active partnership with and for diverse communities to collect, preserve, research, interpret, exhibit, and enhance understandings of the world, aiming to contribute to human dignity and social justice, global equality and planetary wellbeing."

Reading Note: The Institute of Museum and Library Services (IMLS) provides grants and other support to American museums and libraries. The eligibility criteria for museums applying for IMLS grants suggests what kinds of organizations IMLS considers to be "museums."

IMLS GRANT APPLICATIONS: ELIGIBILITY CRITERIA: MUSEUMS (EXCERPT)

To be eligible as a museum, you must:

- be either a unit of State or local government or a private nonprofit organization that has tax-exempt status under the Internal Revenue Code;
- be located in one of the 50 States of the United States of America, the District of Columbia, the Commonwealth of Puerto Rico, Guam, American Samoa, the Virgin Islands, the Commonwealth of the Northern Mariana Islands, the Republic of the Marshall Islands, the Federated States of Micronesia, or the Republic of Palau; and
- qualify as one of the following:
    1. a museum [NOTE 1] that, using a professional staff, [NOTE 2] is organized on a permanent basis for essentially educational or aesthetic purposes; owns or uses tangible objects, either animate or inanimate; cares for these objects; and exhibits these objects to the general public on a regular basis through facilities that it owns or operates. [NOTE 3]
    2. a public or private nonprofit agency which is responsible for the operation of a museum may apply on behalf of the museum.

Please note that a museum located within a parent organization that is a State or local government or multipurpose not-for-profit entity, such as a municipality, university, historical society, foundation, or cultural center, may apply on its own behalf if the museum: (1) is able to independently fulfill all the eligibility requirements listed above; (2) functions as a discrete unit within the parent organization; (3) has its own fully segregated and itemized operating budget; and (4) has the authority to make the application on its own. When any of the last three conditions cannot be met, a museum may only apply through its parent organization.

IMLS may determine that a nonprofit organization that is affiliated with a museum is eligible for this program where the organization can demonstrate that it has the ability to administer the project and can ensure compliance with the terms of these guidelines and the applicable law, including the Assurances and Certifications. The applicant organization must submit an agreement from the museum that details the activities that the applicant and museum will perform and binds the museum to the statements and assurances made in the grant application.

Prospective applicants that cannot fulfill all of these requirements should contact IMLS to discuss their eligibility before applying. IMLS may require additional supporting documentation from the applicant to determine the museum's autonomy.

Note: Special conditions of eligibility apply to the Museum Grants for African American History and Culture program, the National Leadership Grants for Museums program, and the Native American/Native Hawaiian Museum Services Program. Please see the individual guidelines for these programs for specific eligibility requirements.

NOTES:

NOTE 1: Museums include, but are not limited to, aquariums, arboretums, art museums, botanical gardens, children's/youth museums, general museums (those having two or more significant disciplines), historic houses/sites, history museums, natural history/anthropology museums, nature centers, planetariums, science/technology centers, specialized museums (limited to a single distinct subject), and zoological parks.

NOTE 2: An institution uses a professional staff if it employs at least one professional staff member, or the full-time equivalent, whether paid or unpaid, primarily engaged in the acquisition, care, or exhibition to the public of objects owned or used by the institution.

NOTE 3: An institution exhibits objects to the general public if such exhibition is a primary purpose of the institution. An institution that exhibits objects to the general public for at least 120 days a year is deemed to exhibit objects to the general public on a regular basis.

An institution that exhibits objects by appointment may meet the requirement to exhibit objects to the general public on a regular basis if it can establish, in light of the facts under all the relevant circumstances, that this method of exhibition does not unreasonably restrict the accessibility of the institution's exhibits to the general public.

An institution that does not have as a primary purpose the exhibition of objects to the general public but that can demonstrate that it exhibits objects to the general public on a regular basis as a significant, separate, distinct, and continuing portion of its activities, and that it otherwise meets the museum eligibility requirements, may be determined to be eligible as a museum under these guidelines. For more information, please see 45 C.F.R. Chapter XI, Subchapter E (Institute of Museum and Library Services).

Reading Note: The American Alliance of Museums (AAM) is an association of American museums of all types. Among other things, the AAM provides accreditation for museums that meet the association's professional and ethical standards. AAM's criteria for participating in its accreditation program gives some insight into what AAM considers the fundamental elements of a "museum."

AMERICAN ALLIANCE OF MUSEUMS, ACCREDITATION ELIGIBILITY

To participate in the Alliance's Accreditation Program, a museum must:

- Be a legally organized nonprofit institution or part of a nonprofit organization or government entity
- Be essentially educational in nature
- Have a formally stated and approved mission
- Use and interpret objects or a site for the public presentation of regularly scheduled programs and exhibits
- Have a formal and appropriate program of documentation, care, and use of collections or objects
- Carry out the above functions primarily at a physical facility or site
- Have been open to the public for at least two years
- Be open to the public at least 1,000 hours a year
- Have accessioned 80 percent of its permanent collection
- Have at least one paid professional staff with museum knowledge and experience
- Have a full-time director to whom authority is delegated for day-to-day operations
- Have the financial resources sufficient to operate effectively
- Demonstrate that it meets the Core Standards for Museums
- Successfully complete the Core Documents Verification Program

STUDY QUESTIONS

- How has the definition of "museum" changed over time? What does this say about the role these organizations play in our society? Does the definition change depending on cultural norms and applicable legal regimes? How does ICOM's proposed new definition reflect these changes? ICOM's Extraordinary General Assembly (EGA), which took place on September 7, 2019, in Kyoto, Japan, postponed the vote on the new museum definition. Why do you think the new ICOM definition was controversial?
- List some key elements of a museum. What factors distinguish museums from other entities?

- How does the definition of "museum" reflect legal and ethical notions behind the purpose of these organizations and how they operate?
- What purpose do these definitions serve? In what ways are they similar? Different?
- Do any of these definitions (or parts of them) appear to be arbitrary?
- Some definitions, such as those of ICOM, define which organizations may participate in professional organizations, as members or otherwise. Other definitions, such as those of IMLS and AAM, establish eligibility for certain benefits or status. Describe these distinctions. Are there others?
- The IMLS Eligibility Criteria includes special restrictions when a museum is part of another entity—what concerns do these restrictions address?

MUSEUM ORGANIZATION AND GOVERNANCE

Museums may be organized as governmental agencies, nonprofit organizations, or for-profit entities. Museum assets, including collections, can be publicly or privately owned. Funding for museum administration, operations and programming may be derived from a single public or private source or a variety of public and private sources. Museum governance is the aggregate of a museum's culture, methods, processes, systems, and controls for providing direction to the affairs of the museum and executing that direction (including the museum's mission and purpose). How a museum is organized plays a crucial role in its governance.

Although rare, there are some for-profit museums. They are organized like other for-profit businesses and managed solely or primarily for the benefit of the museum's owners or shareholders.

Governmental museums are typically organized through a governmental charter or other implementing statute or law. They may require that board members be appointed by a governmental body, such as a state legislature or a municipality, and include other statutory requirements concerning the governance of the organization. Some museums—the Smithsonian is perhaps the best example—are organized in a way that combines both governmental and private nonprofit elements. Such hybrid public/private or "quasi-governmental" organizations present a unique set of governance issues. Public history museums such as state and local historical societies, are often governmental or quasi-governmental organizations.

In some cases, a museum may be part of another institution—a college or university, for example. These "embedded" museums must at times deal with conflicts arising from being

SMITHSONIAN INSTITUTION

APRIL 2020

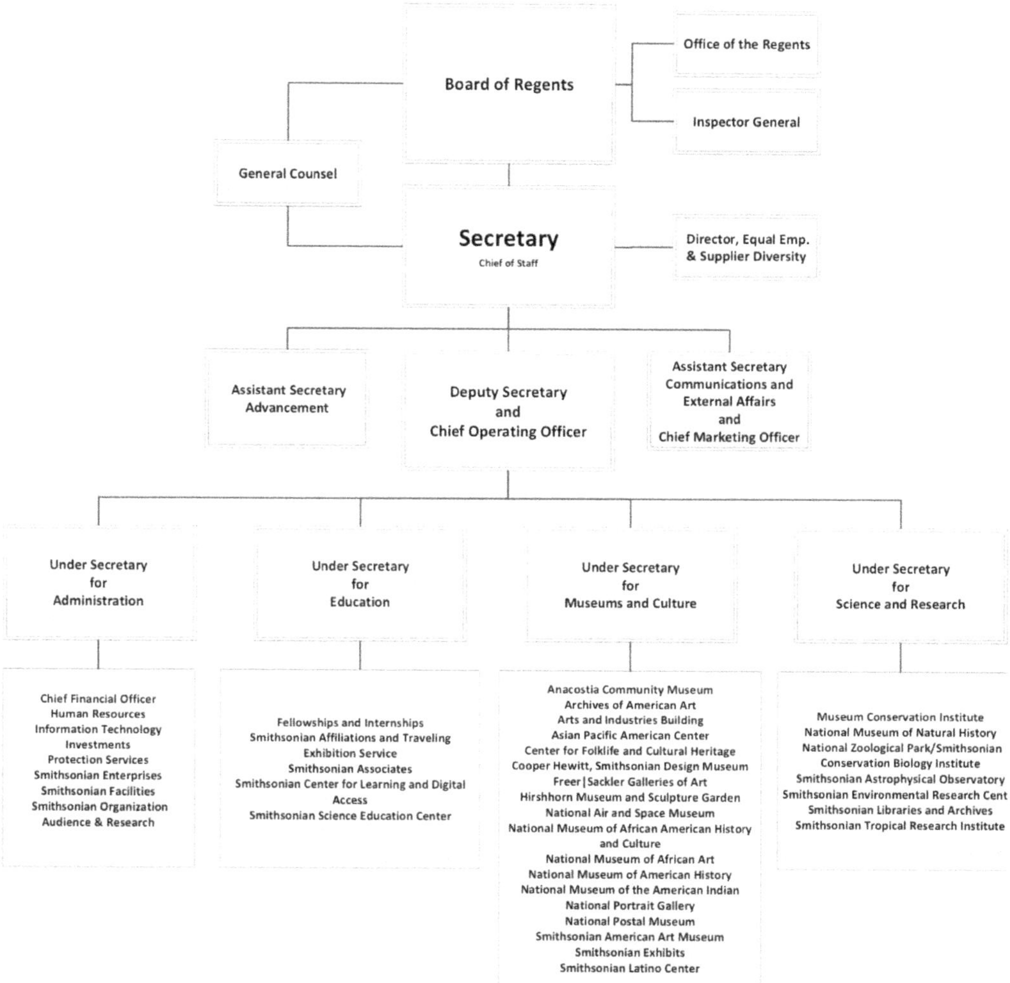

Founded in 1846 with funds from an Englishman, the Smithsonian is the world's largest museum, education and research complex. It is governed by a Board of Regents which includes the Vice President of the United States, the Chief Justice of the Supreme Court, three U.S. Senators, three members of the U.S. House of Representatives, and nine citizens.

---

part of an organization which may have practices and priorities that are not completely aligned with those of the museum community.

In America, the majority of museums are organized as private, nonprofit organizations. For this reason, our discussion will focus mainly on the private nonprofit museum.

Museums are regulated under applicable federal, state, and local laws, through a variety of professional ethical codes, and by internal organizational policies and practices. Unlike for-profit entities whose primary purpose is to provide a financial return to its shareholders, the purpose of a private nonprofit museum is typically summarized in a mission statement drafted and adopted by its governing board. The mission statement encapsulates the essential purpose of the organization and establishes the parameters for articulation of the museum's goals and values.

Most private nonprofit museums are organized through state charitable corporation statutes as public charities. As such, they share attributes of both business corporations and traditional trusts. These museums are considered "charitable trusts" in the sense that they hold their assets, including their collections, in trust for the benefit of the public. This charitable trust relationship imposes restrictions on museum governance and the management of its collections. As charitable corporations, museums generally have a corporate organizational structure established through the adoption of articles of incorporation and bylaws. These organizational documents may be supplemented by written policies and procedures relating to specific aspects of the museum's day-to-day administration and management.

Museums are typically governed by a board of directors, sometimes referred to as "trustees." Board members are responsible for establishing the museum's governance policies and procedures and for ensuring the sustainability and relevance of the organization. The selection and tenure of board members, as well as voting procedures, committee assignments, and designation of board officers (chair, vice chair, secretary, treasurer, etc.) as well as other core governance procedures, are set out in the museum's bylaws.

The board members of private nonprofit museums are fiduciaries of the museum as a charitable trust. The members of the board as trustees have legal control over the museum's assets and must manage those assets for the benefit of the beneficiaries of the trust—in this case the public. The museum's assets must only be used to carry out the stated purpose of the trust.

To prevent an abuse of a trustee's authority over a trust and its assets, the law imposes certain fiduciary duties on trustees. Trustees may be held legally liable for conduct which falls below these minimum standards.

As trustees, members of the museum board owe three basic fiduciary duties: the duties of obedience, care and loyalty to the institution. The duty of obedience requires museum trustees to govern the museum according to its mission and to adopt policies and select goals and priorities that are not only consistent with the mission but are also wise in light of the museum's resources.

The duty of care requires museum trustees to exercise good faith and a reasonable amount of diligence and care—that of a "prudent person"—in managing the museum and its assets. The museum board may delegate responsibilities and decision-making authority to the museum director and staff, but they must exercise oversight and cannot delegate complete control over the management of the museum. Management decisions must be based on appropriate investigation and gathering of the facts and due consideration of those facts. Decision-making should be based on facts, not arbitrary reasons, and adequate records of the decision and the decision-making process should be kept.

The duty of loyalty requires a museum trustee to act only for the good of the organization and its public beneficiaries. As such, the interests of the museum must always come before a board member's personal interests or those of a third party. Trustees must avoid even the appearance of favoring a person or entity other than the organization and any other improprieties. To ensure this, museum trustees should establish a written policy for addressing conflicts of interests. A typical conflict of interest policy requires trustees to disclose any potential conflicts of interest and to recuse themselves from any board discussions and decisions relating to those potential conflicts. The conflict-of-interest policy also establishes procedures for decision making by the "non-conflicted" trustees.

The State Attorney General has the primary responsibility for the oversight of charitable organizations, including museums, which are organized in that state. Generally speaking, only the State Attorney General has the ability to enforce laws against charitable organizations. Put another way, only the State Attorney General has "standing" to bring a lawsuit alleging mismanagement of a charity, but the Attorney General cannot be compelled to do so. If the State Attorney General becomes aware that a charity is violating its fiduciary duties, he or she may investigate and could bring a suit against the charity.

In the case of the Evergreen Aviation and Space Museum (see Cases and Other Readings below) for example, the Washington State Attorney General was informed by a whistle-blower that the organization, which was run by a board composed of members of a for-profit company, made a substantial loan to the for-profit company. The Attorney General's ensuing investigation turned up a number of other issues relating to the museum board's fiduciary duties and conflicts of interest. The Attorney General summarized its findings in an audit report and recommended changes to the organization governance structure to address its concerns.

What if the State Attorney General declines to take legal action against a charity that is violating the law? Can an individual or a group have "standing" to sue a charity? As exemplified by the Mary Baker Eddy case (included in the Cases and other Readings below), courts have recognized "standing" for certain private individuals and entities in specific situations on a case-by-case basis. The courts have created a variety of tests for determining when these private parties have standing to bring a legal action against a charitable organization in lieu of the Attorney General. In some states, legislative changes now allow private lawsuits against charities under limited circumstances. These laws are sometimes referred to as "private attorney general" statutes. Needless to say, the issue of standing often arises in cases involving allegations of mismanagement of charities by their boards of trustees.

In addition to applicable legal duties, the conduct of museum trustees may also be governed by ethical codes and professional guidelines. Some of these apply to nonprofit organizations generally, while others are specific to the museum community.

There are several principal museum associations. The International Council of Museums (ICOM) represents the international museum community. In the United States, the American Alliance of Museums (AAM) is the main museum association with members from all types of museums—from art museums to zoos. AAM grants accreditation to museums that meet certain minimum standards and follow accepted practices. It also issues guidance on all aspects of museum administration and management. AAM may deny accreditation or reaccreditation to museums which do not meet its standards and may sanction museums for violating its ethical codes. The AAM's "Ethics Standards and Professional Practices" are summarized on its website. The Association of Art Museum Directors (AAMD) is a membership organization composed of the directors of American art museums. AAMD also issues guidance on a variety of administration and management issues relevant to its member museums. AAMD also can enforce its standards by denying membership to the director of a non-compliant museum. AAMD's "Professional Practices for Art Museums" can be found on its website. The American Association for State and Local History (AASLH) represents state and local historical societies throughout the United States. It also promulgates ethical codes and professional guidelines for its member organizations. These are compiled on its website as AASLH's Statement of Professional Standards and Ethics. In addition to these main museum associations, there are numerous associations representing a variety of museum professionals in specific fields—curators, registrars, development officers, and the like.

As noted above, museums are generally organized under state incorporation statutes as charitable organizations. Most states also require charities operating within their state to register with a state charities board and to comply with state-imposed laws regulating charities operating within their jurisdiction. In some jurisdictions, charitable organizations may be entitled to beneficial tax-treatment including not having to pay sales tax on purchases or property tax on charity-owned real estate.

Nonprofit organizations, including museums, may apply for federal tax-exempt status from the IRS by submitting an application form ("Form 1023") and providing information about the organization's mission, finances, bylaws and policies. The principal advantage of obtaining "tax-exempt" status from the IRS is that individual donors to tax-exempt organizations may be able to deduct the value of their donation on their personal tax returns. For the charity, "tax-exempt" status may allow the organization to avoid paying federal tax on revenue related to furthering its mission. These issues will be discussed in more detail in chapter 6.

To qualify for tax-exempt status under federal law, the entity must be organized for a charitable purpose which may be scientific, educational or religious. Most museums seek tax-exempt status as educational institutions. Supporting or affiliated nonprofit organizations ("friends' groups") may also seek to qualify as tax-exempt organizations.

There must be no private benefit: qualifying tax-exempt organizations must be operated such that no part of its net earnings "inures to the benefit of" any private shareholder or individual. The organization's insiders (those who govern or otherwise exercise control over the organization) are held to a "reasonableness" standard with respect to this prohibition on private inurement. Common private inurement problems include excessive compensation, excessive payments for services performed by insiders, high rents, favorable loans, and preferential services performed by the organization for particular beneficiaries.

An otherwise tax-exempt organization may face tax liability for revenue-generating activities that do not further its charitable purpose—this is known as "unrelated business income tax" or UBIT. A tax-exempt organization may also face tax liability in situations where the IRS determines that there has been an "excess benefit" to an organization insider in violation of the ban on private inurement. In extreme cases of organizational mismanagement or malfeasance, the IRS may revoke the offending organization's tax-exempt status.

Organizations that qualify for tax-exempt status are required to file with the IRS an annual informational tax return referred to as Form 990. The 990 requires documentation regarding the nonprofit's organizational structure, personnel, finances, charitable activities, and policies. Tax-exempt organizations including museums must make their 990 annual returns and exemption applications filed with the IRS available for public inspection and copying upon request. In addition, the IRS also makes these documents available.

STUDY QUESTIONS

- In what ways does the form of the museum organization—as a nonprofit corporation or as a charitable trust, for example—affect its governance and operation?
- Where a museum is part of another entity—such as a governmental body or another institution (a college or university for example)—what potential governance issues can you identify?
- Identify the principal museum associations and their constituent members.

Reading Note: The Mary Baker Eddy case reprinted below focuses on the issue of "special interest standing" to enforce a charitable trust. Following investigation by the New Hampshire Director of Charitable Trusts (part of of the State Attorney General's office), the trustees of a charitable trust entered into a stipulation agreement regarding the ongoing management of the trust. A beneficiary of the trust sought "special interest standing" to review and potentially object to an annual accounting filed by the trustees pursuant to the stipulation agreement, and to request the appointment of an independent trustee. The Court reviewed various formulations of the special interest standing doctrine and applied its preferred test to the facts presented.

IN RE TRUST OF MARY BAKER EDDY

The Supreme Court of New Hampshire 7th Circuit Court-Dover Probate Division
No. 2018-0309. Argued: February 14, 2019, Opinion Issued: June 14, 2019

DONOVAN, J.

The Second Church of Christ, Scientist, Melbourne (Australia) appeals an order of the Circuit Court (*King*, J.), denying it standing to request affirmative relief and enforce certain charitable trusts created by the will of Mary Baker Eddy. We affirm.

I. FACTUAL AND PROCEDURAL BACKGROUND

***Mary Baker Eddy** (1821-1910) was an influential American author, teacher, and religious leader, noted for her groundbreaking ideas about spirituality and health, which she named Christian Science.*

The relevant facts follow. Mary Baker Eddy founded the Church of Christian Science and, upon her death in 1910, her will established two testamentary trusts, known as the Clause VI Trust and Clause VIII Trust. The Clause VI Trust bequeathed to the "Christian Science Board of Directors of The Mother Church" $100,000 in trust "for the purpose of providing free instruction for indigent, well educated, worthy Christian Scientists." Clause VIII of Mrs. Eddy's will devised "all the rest, residue and remainder of [her] estate . . . to The Mother Church—The First Church of Christ, Scientist, in Boston, Massachusetts, in trust," for certain "general purposes." She directed, *inter alia*, that "such portion of the income of [her] residuary estate as may be necessary shall be used for the purpose of keeping in repair the church building" and her former home in Boston and that "the balance of said income, and such portion of the principal as may be deemed wise," shall be used "for the purpose of more effectually promoting and extending the religion of Christian Science as taught by [Mrs. Eddy]."

In previous litigation concerning these trusts, we upheld the validity of the trusts and established that the bequest in Clause VIII was to be held in trust for two purposes, church building repair and "promoting and extending the religion of Christian Science as taught by [Mrs. Eddy]." *Glover v. Baker*, 76 N.H. 393, 400-01 (1912); *see also Fernald v. Church*, 77 N.H. 108, 109 (1913). The Massachusetts Supreme Judicial Court reached a similar conclusion in *Chase v. Dickey*, 99 N.E. 410 (Mass. 1912), wherein the court held that the construction of the Clause VIII Trust manifests a purpose to make the promotion and extension of the religion of Christian Science the "dominating and real residuary purpose" of Mrs. Eddy. *Chase*, 99 N.E. at 415. As a result of this litigation, court oversight of the trusts commenced, and annual accounts for both trusts, and requests for appointments of trustees, have been filed in the Concord Probate Court (now, Circuit Court) for over one hundred years.

The trustees of the Clause VIII Trust were comprised of the Board of Directors of the Mother Church and Josiah Fernald, the administrator of Mrs. Eddy's estate, until Mr. Fernald's death in 1949. At that time, Judge Lord of the probate court, in a letter to the trustees, concluded that it was "not necessary to fill the vacancy [of Mr. Fernald]" and that the "five members of the Christian Science Board of Directors who are the surviving trustees . . . shall constitute the sole trustees" of the Clause VIII Trust. Since the 1949 letter, the trustees of the Clause VIII Trust have all been members of the Mother Church Board of Directors.

In 1993, following an investigation by the New Hampshire Director of Charitable Trusts (DCT) into a five million dollar loan from the Clause VIII Trust to the Mother Church to be used to fund a failed television venture, the Probate Court (*Cushing*, J.) approved a stipulation between the DCT and the trustees of the Clause VIII Trust. The stipulation provided, *inter alia*, that: (1) the Mother Church agreed to repay the loan to the Clause VIII Trust; (2) the Clause VIII Trust income was to be used to repair the church, with any available, remaining income to be applied to the promotion and extension of Christian Science, at the discretion of the trustees; (3) further loans from the trust were prohibited; and (4) the principal of the Clause VIII Trust could only be invaded with court approval. The current litigation commenced in 2015, when Second Church, an alleged qualified beneficiary of the Clause VIII Trust, sought to review, and potentially object to, the annual accounting filed by the trustees. Although the DCT assented to Second Church's motion, the trustees objected on the basis that Second Church, as a "branch church," lacked standing to sue. Second Church responded by arguing that it had standing under the special interest doctrine. The court scheduled a hearing to address the issue of standing. However, the court did not rule on Second Church's motion or the standing issue because the parties agreed at the hearing that Second Church would withdraw its motion and the DCT, Second Church, and the trustees would cooperate to resolve concerns raised by Second Church and the DCT.

Notably, prior to the court's scheduling order, the DCT had not responded to the concerns voiced by Second Church. Thereafter, the DCT filed a memorandum in April 2016 asserting that Second Church did not have special interest standing, especially in light of the DCT's "plan to review the Clause VIII Trust's decision making concerning its distributions." In his memorandum, the DCT recognized that prior litigation had arisen from the "tension" between the two beneficial purposes of the Clause VIII Trust, namely: (1) repair of the Mother Church building(s); and (2) "promoting and extending the religion of Christian Science." The DCT also acknowledged the tension between the 1912 decision in *Chase*, 99 N.E. at 415, that devoted the Clause VIII Trust distributions primarily to promoting and extending the religion of Christian Science, and the court's approval of the 1993 stipulation prioritizing distributions for church repairs. The DCT further opined that "[b]ecause the trustees of the Clause VIII Trust are also the Board of Directors of the Mother Church, they have embedded conflicting fiduciary obligations." In light of these concerns, the DCT outlined a review plan that he intended to undertake with the trustees, which included a "review [of] the distributions made from the Clause VIII [Trust]." The DCT concluded that because his office had, and continued to take, an active role in monitoring the Clause VIII Trust, "special interest standing is not warranted."

Thereafter, following the DCT's objection to the trustees' accounts filed in 2016, the DCT and trustees reached an agreement and the trustees filed a motion, assented-to by the DCT, to, among other things, approve an amended account. Second Church moved for authorization to file an *amicus curiae* brief voicing its continuing concerns. The trial court issued an order requiring the trustees to file accounts audited by an independent auditor. The court also denied Second Church's motion, but indicated that Second Church should share information with the DCT who, by statute, represents their interests in this matter. *See* RSA [New Hampshire Revised Statutes Annotated] 564-B:4-405© (2007).

Subsequently, the trustees submitted an assented-to motion to, *inter alia*, amend the 1993 order. Second Church, again, sought to submit a brief as *amicus curiae*. The trustees objected. Second Church filed a responsive pleading as well as a status report and a request for time to conduct discovery, despite the fact that its standing to participate in this matter had not yet been determined. The court scheduled a hearing for November 2017. Prior to the hearing, the trustees filed a memorandum concerning the issue of standing. Second Church responded by moving for the appointment of an independent trustee and filing a memorandum on standing.

In March 2018, the trial court issued an order finding that Second Church failed to satisfy its burden to demonstrate that it had standing. We note that in making this determination, the trial court did not identify the standard by which it decided the standing issue—i.e., whether the trial court considered the challenge to Second Church's standing as a motion to dismiss.

In its order, the trial court acknowledged the general rule that when a trust is determined to be charitable, it becomes the duty of the attorney general to ensure that the rights of the public in the trust are protected and that the trust is properly executed. *See Petition of Burnham*, 74 N.H. 492, 494 (1908). The court further noted that New Hampshire law is unclear as to whether a possible beneficiary of a charitable trust, like Second Church here, has standing. Looking to other jurisdictions for guidance, the trial court determined that most jurisdictions have ruled that a possible beneficiary is generally not entitled to sue for enforcement of the trust. *See Alco Gravure, Inc., v. Knapp Foundation*, 479 N.E.2d 752, 755 (N.Y. 1985); *see also State ex rel. Nixon v. Hutcherson*, 96 S.W.3d 81, 83-84 (Mo. 2003). However, the trial court also found that courts have recognized an exception to this rule "where an individual seeking enforcement of the trust has a 'special interest' in continued performance of the trust distinguishable from that of the public at large." *Hooker v. Edes Home*, 579 A.2d 608, 612 (D.C. 1990).

After considering how other courts have applied the doctrine of special interest standing, the trial court applied a five-factor test, often referred to as the Blasko test. *See* Mary Grace Blasko, Curt S. Crossley, David Lloyd, *Standing to Sue in the Charitable Sector*, 28 U.S.F. L. Rev. 37, 61 (1993) (hereinafter, "Blasko"). The test is based upon a comprehensive survey of case law and it sets forth five factors to determine whether a plaintiff's interest is distinct enough from the public at large to justify conferring standing upon the plaintiff in order to enforce a charitable trust. *See generally id.* The factors are: (1) the extraordinary nature of the acts complained of and the remedies sought; (2) the presence of bad faith; (3) the attorney general's availability and effectiveness; (4) the nature of the benefitted class and its relationship to the charity; and (5) the social desirability of conferring standing. *Id.* at 61.

Applying the Blasko test, the trial court found that none of the factors weighed in favor of granting Second Church standing. Second Church filed a motion for reconsideration, which the trial court denied. This appeal followed.

II. ANALYSIS OF SECOND CHURCH'S CLAIMS

On appeal, Second Church argues that, even though the trial court properly adopted the Blasko test, it misapplied the factors. Second Church asserts that, under the Blasko test, as one of a limited number of potential beneficiaries under the trusts, it has a "special interest" in the Clause VIII Trust sufficient to justify standing. Moreover, Second Church contends that the trial court improperly reached its decision without the development of a factual record, while also faulting Second Church for not developing sufficient facts to demonstrate standing. Although the DCT agrees with Second Church that we should "recognize the standing of certain persons or entities that have a special interest in a particular charitable trust to enforce that trust," both the DCT and the trustees maintain that the trial court properly determined that Second Church lacks special interest standing. We agree with the DCT and the trustee.

A. Standing Issue

We generally will not disturb the circuit court's decree unless it is unsupported by the evidence or plainly erroneous as a matter of law. *In re Estate of Locke*, 148 N.H. 754, 755 (2002); *see also* RSA 567-A:4 (2007). In this case, the parties dispute the applicable standard of review. Second Church argues that we should review the trial court's application of the special interest standing factors *de novo*. The DCT argues that the question of whether to adopt special interest standing is a question of law which we review *de novo*. However, the trustees and the DCT further argue that we should not disturb the trial court's standing determination unless it is plainly erroneous as a matter of law.

Because the trial court did not clarify how it reviewed the pleadings in determining that Second Church lacked standing, and there was no discovery or evidentiary hearing, we assume without deciding that the trial court viewed the challenge to Second Church's standing as a motion to dismiss.[NOTE 1] When a motion to dismiss "challenges the plaintiff's standing to sue, the trial court must look beyond the plaintiff's unsubstantiated allegations and determine, based on the facts, whether the plaintiff has sufficiently demonstrated his right to claim relief." *Ossipee Auto Parts v. Ossipee Planning Board*, 134 N.H. 401, 403-04 (1991). Nonetheless, in this case, the material facts are not disputed; only their legal effect stands in dispute. *See Appeal of N.H. Right to Life*, 166 N.H. 308, 311 (2014). The issue of standing is, therefore, a question of law, which we review *de novo*. *Id.*

The general rule is that potential trust beneficiaries, in suits involving charitable trusts, may not bring an action to enforce the terms of such a trust. *See Restatement (Third) of Trusts* § 94 cmt. *g* at 8-9 (2011). Instead, the attorney general (or the DCT, as his representative) has the statutory power and duty to represent the public in the enforcement and supervision of charitable trusts. *See* RSA 564-B:4-405(c); RSA 7:20 (2013); *Attorney Gen. v. Rochester Trust Co.*, 115 N.H. 74, 76 (1975) (the attorney general has the duty to protect the rights of the public in charitable trusts); *Concord Nat. Bank v. Haverhill*, 101 N.H. 416, 419 (1958); *Restatement (Third) of Trusts*, *supra* at 4. As another court has framed the issue:

> Principally, the rationale for vesting exclusive power in a public officer stems from the inherent impossibility of establishing a distinct justiciable interest on the part of a member of a large and constantly shifting benefited class, and the recurring burdens on the trust res and trustee of vexatious litigation that would result from recognition of a cause of action by any and all of a large number of individuals who might benefit incidentally from the trust.

Hooker, 579 A.2d at 612. Nonetheless, the Restatement as well as other jurisdictions have recognized an exception to this rule when a clearly identified class "has a justiciable interest in enforcement of the trust." *Id.*; *see Alco Gravure*, 479 N.E.2d at 755-56 (concluding that plaintiffs had standing where they were a well-defined class of potential beneficiaries challenging the dissolution of the charitable corporation); *Restatement (Third) of Trusts*, *supra* § 94 cmt. *g* at 8-9.

Although we have yet to determine whether a potential beneficiary of a charitable trust has standing, our law supports the concept of conferring standing upon a third party if it establishes that it has a special interest. For instance, we have previously noted that "[w] hile the Attorney General . . . represents the public in the enforcement and supervision of charitable trusts, this [representation] does not preclude other interested parties from presenting their views particularly where they are acting for the benefit of the charitable trust as a whole." *Concord Nat. Bank*, 101 N.H. at 419. RSA 564-B:4-405(c) also implicitly allows special interest standing by providing that "[t]he settlor of a charitable trust or the director of charitable trusts, *among others*, may maintain a proceeding to enforce the trust." RSA 564-B:4-405(c) (emphasis added). Moreover, the comments to the Uniform Trust Code, upon which the New Hampshire Trust Code is based, *see* RSA ch. 564-B (2007 & Supp. 2018), contemplate that certain others may have standing based upon their special interest in the charity. *See* Unif. Trust Code § 405, Comment (2006) ("The grant of standing to the settlor does not negate the right of the state attorney general or *persons with special interests* to enforce either the trust or their interests." (emphasis added)); *see also* Unif. Trust Code, *supra* § 413, Comment ("[A] petition requesting a court to enforce a charitable trust or to apply cy pres may be maintained by . . . the state attorney general, or by a person having a special interest in the charitable disposition.").

Accordingly, we recognize the doctrine of special interest standing in matters involving charitable trusts. We must next determine how to apply this doctrine. Second Church argues that the trial court correctly adopted the Blasko five-factor test. Second Church further argues that the presence of any one factor by itself is sufficient to conclude that it has a special interest. *See* Blasko, *supra* at 61.

The trustees advocate for a more stringent test, which follows the test approved by the American Law Institute (ALI), that proposes five factors similar to the Blasko factors but requires a private party to satisfy all of the factors to demonstrate special interest standing. *See Restatement of the Law Charitable Nonprofit Organizations* § 6.05 (Tent. Draft No. 2, 2017) (approved May 22, 2017). The trial court considered this test but applied the Blasko test upon determining that the flexibility of the Blasko test better suits the pursuit of a just outcome. The DCT argues that the trial court properly adopted and applied the Blasko test.

We look to other jurisdictions for guidance on the application of the special interest standing doctrine. *See N.H. Right to Life v. Dir., N.H. Charitable Trusts Unit*, 169 N.H. 95, 103 (2016) (looking to the decisions of other jurisdictions interpreting similar acts for guidance). The Arizona Court of Appeals adopted a modified version of the five-factor balancing test described by Blasko, giving special emphasis to the nature of the benefitted class and its relationship to the trust, the nature of the remedy requested, and the effectiveness of attorney general enforcement of the trust. *Schalkenbach Foundation v. Lincoln*, 91 P.3d 1019, 1026 (Ariz. Ct. App. 2004). In *Alco Gravure*, the New York Court of Appeals considered similar, albeit fewer, factors to determine whether the plaintiffs had a "special interest" in charitable funds and could maintain a suit. *Alco Gravure*, 479 N.E.2d at 755-56. There, the court focused on the well-defined class of beneficiaries and the fact that they were challenging the dissolution of the charitable corporation, as opposed to the ongoing administration of the corporation, to conclude that the plaintiffs had standing. *Id.*

Similarly, in *Hooker*, the District of Columbia Court of Appeals considered the nature of the class and the nature of the challenge to the trustees' acts in deciding whether to apply the special interest exception. *Hooker*, 579 A.2d at 614, 616-17 (concluding that the class of elderly, indigent women, who are eligible potential residents of a Trust-operated home, had standing to challenge the trustees' decision to put into effect a "major change from the manner in which the trust had been administered in the past"). The Supreme Court of Missouri likewise recognized that "[a] person . . . may have standing if he or she is entitled to a preference under the terms of the trust or if the person is a member of a small class of identifiable beneficiaries." *State ex rel. Nixon*, 96 S.W.3d at 84. The court also acknowledged that a person may establish standing if he or she "is entitled to receive a benefit under the trust that is not merely the benefit to which members of the public in general are entitled." *Id.* at 84-85 (quotation omitted) (concluding that the plaintiffs could not establish standing when they failed to meet the burden of "showing a clear, identifiable, and present claim to any benefits" from the trust).

After review of the factors that other jurisdictions consider relevant to a special interest standing determination, we agree with the trial court that the Blasko test is preferable because it provides a court with the flexibility to consider a variety of factors. Although Blasko suggests that "[t]he presence of any one . . . factor[] by itself can lead a court to decide that the plaintiff has a special interest in a charity," the article notes that, "[i]f a combination of elements is present, then a court can balance them against one another and reach a decision." Blasko, *supra* at 61. Depending upon the circumstances, some factors may carry more weight than others and, in New Hampshire, when evaluating whether a party has standing to sue, we generally focus upon whether the party suffered a legal injury against which the law or policy was designed to protect. *See Petition of Lath*, 169 N.H. 616, 620 (2017).

Accordingly, because of the various interests that must be considered to determine special interest standing in the context of charitable trust matters, we conclude that a balancing test of all five Blasko factors best comports with New Hampshire law. We thus address each factor in turn.

i. The Extraordinary Nature of the Acts Complained of and the Remedy Sought

As to the first factor, the trial court found that Second Church's request for an independent trustee, among other remedies, seeks to undo prior court orders and suggests remedies despite Second Church's "informative and thorough *amicus* submissions that the Court assumes the DCT has reviewed." The trial court therefore determined that Second Church merely disagreed with the DCT's judgment, and this disagreement is not sufficient to justify standing. Second Church argues that the trial court erred by: (1) focusing on the requested relief, rather than the extraordinary nature of the acts alleged by Second Church; and (2) failing to recognize that the bad acts committed by the trustees are extraordinary while the requested remedy is not.

Blasko recognized that "courts seem to be influenced from the outset by the nature and extent of the remedy requested." Blasko, *supra* at 62. When a requested remedy could be "highly intrusive in the administration of the trust," it is likely to weigh against a finding of standing. *See Schalkenbach Foundation*, 91 P.3d at 1027-28. When trustees seek to fundamentally change the charitable bequest by dissolving the nonprofit corporation or closing the facility created by the trust, and the plaintiffs seek to stop this action, then the plaintiffs are more likely to establish standing. *See Hooker*, 579 A.2d at 616- 17; *Alco Gravure*, 479 N.E.2d at 755.

To begin, we need not decide whether the trial court should have considered the extraordinary nature of the bad acts, because, upon our *de novo* review, we consider them now, and we conclude that Second Church has not demonstrated that the trial court's failure to consider the extraordinary acts is sufficient, by itself, to constitute reversible error. *See Gallo v. Traina*, 166 N.H. 737, 740 (2014). Accordingly, we examine the requested remedy in relation to the nature of the alleged bad acts.

Second Church alleges that the trustees engaged in self-dealing and have an embedded conflict due to their dual role as trustees and members of the board of directors of the Mother Church. Furthermore, Second Church alleges, among other things, that the trustees have improperly favored the Mother Church when distributing the Clause VIII trust assets. Second Church, therefore, seeks the "relief of having an independent trustee appointed to the Clause [VIII] [T]rust."

We find *Schalkenbach Foundation* to be instructive under these circumstances. *Schalkenbach Foundation*, 91 P.3d at 1027. In *Schalkenbach Foundation*, the appellants alleged that the Foundation had been systematically diverting funds from their approved purpose to improper uses, which the court found implied a request to remedy the situation by the appellants' participation in and influence of the daily operations of the Foundation. *Id.* at 1027-28. The appellants specifically requested, among other things, to "replace the Foundation's officers and directors with persons interested in carrying out the terms of the charitable trust." *Id.* at 1021. The court concluded that the remedies that the appellants wished to impose were "highly intrusive in the administration of the trust, which could open the Foundation to further litigation by other potential or disappointed beneficiaries." *Id.* at 1028.

Similarly, here, because Second Church seeks the appointment of an independent trustee to oversee the administration of the trust, including the distribution of funds, this request would influence the daily operations of the trust and the ongoing administration of the trust. Consequently, this remedy could expose the charity to vexatious litigation by Second Church or other disappointed beneficiaries that would still be concerned with the distribution of funds even after the appointment of an independent trustee.

Moreover, Second Church's requested remedy is unnecessary under the circumstances because the trial court has already taken steps to address the alleged bad acts. Notably, in its March 2018 order, the trial court acknowledged the embedded conflict and imposed certain conditions that addressed this conflict, including, *inter alia*, requiring the trustees to furnish to the DCT a schedule of recipients of the Clause VIII distributions. The March 2018 order also partially amended the 1993 order "to the extent it gave priority to church repair." Therefore, in relation to the nature of the trustees' alleged bad acts, the appointment of an independent trustee would be unnecessary under these circumstances. Accordingly, this factor weighs against standing.

ii. Presence of Bad Faith

As to the second factor, Second Church argues that the evidence that the trustees acted in bad faith is substantial. Blasko notes that the presence of fraud or other deliberate misconduct is not a factor which courts necessarily discuss when evaluating a plaintiff's special interest, but it is nevertheless an element which influences their decisions. Blasko, *supra* at 64. "When alleging fraud . . . the plaintiff must specify the essential details of the fraud, and specifically allege the facts of the defendant's fraudulent actions. It is not sufficient for the plaintiff merely to allege fraud in general terms." *Lamprey v. Britton Constr.*, 163 N.H. 252, 262-63 (2012) (quotation omitted) (standard for withstanding a motion to dismiss when alleging fraud).

Second Church specifically contends that the trustees acted in bad faith when they distributed the Clause VIII funds solely to the Mother Church. However, as the DCT counters, Second Church fails to consider the 1993 order which required the trustees to make distributions of the Clause VIII Trust's income primarily to repair the mother church. Second Church also asserts that after being ordered by the trial court to submit independent audits on the accounts, the trustees submitted non-independently prepared unaudited financial statements and, given the existence of the embedded conflict, this conduct represented a clear example of bad faith. The trial court found that the accounts were accepted for several years by the then-DCT and were implicitly approved by the court. The trial court acknowledged that, by doing so, the trustees committed misconduct. However, the court further found that Second Church's allegations were insufficient to demonstrate outright fraud or bad faith. We agree.

Second Church's allegations do not demonstrate that this conduct amounts to bad faith or fraud that directly injures Second Church. *See* Blasko, *supra* at 64-65. The assertion that the conduct represented bad faith merely because of an embedded conflicting fiduciary obligation is insufficient. *See Lamprey*, 163 N.H. at 256 (explaining that the threshold inquiry on a motion to dismiss involves testing the facts alleged against the applicable law, and that we need not accept allegations that are mere conclusions of law).

Second Church further relies upon *Matter of Green Charitable Trust*, 431 N.W.2d 492 (Mich. Ct. App. 1988), to argue that the trustees' mismanagement is sufficient to confer standing. In *Green Charitable Trust*, named beneficiaries of a charitable trust and the state attorney general brought petitions against the trustees alleging that the trustees mismanaged the sale of property owned by the charitable trust. *Green Charitable Trust*, 431 N.W.2d at 494-95, 505-06. The court upheld the trial court's finding that the trustees violated their fiduciary duty to the beneficiaries by mismanaging the sale of the property and having a conflict of interest in representing both the buyer and seller of the property. *Id.* at 497, 504.

Green Charitable Trust is inapposite to the circumstances here. First, standing was not at issue in *Green Charitable Trust*. Second, here Second Church is a *potential* beneficiary, whereas, in *Green Charitable Trust*, the *named* charitable trust beneficiaries together with the attorney general challenged the actions of the trustees. *Id.* at 494-95. Thus, the reasoning in *Green Charitable Trust* does not provide support for Second Church's assertion that the trustees' alleged mismanagement demonstrates bad faith sufficient to weigh in favor of standing. Moreover, Second Church's allegations of mismanagements—that Mother Church received all distributions, the trustees failed to restore the priorities of the Clause VIII Trust after the 1993 order, and the trustees failed to have independent audits of the accounts—are insufficient to demonstrate bad faith that weighs in favor of granting it standing.

In sum, while Second Church's allegations may demonstrate misconduct, they fail to demonstrate fraud or bad faith. Thus, we agree with the trial court that this factor is neutral and neither weighs against nor in favor of conferring standing.

iii. Attorney General's Availability and Effectiveness

Second Church next argues that the DCT has not been effective in policing the trustees' misconduct. The trustees disagree and argue that the DCT has been available and effective in enforcing the trusts. The trustees further contend that this finding is the most important Blasko factor to consider when deciding whether to grant special interest standing.

As we previously discussed, the DCT is empowered to represent the public and potential beneficiaries of New Hampshire charitable trusts. *See* RSA 564-B:4-405(c). When assessing this factor under the Blasko test, "the nature and level of the attorney general's involvement can profoundly influence a court's decision to grant or deny standing." Blasko, *supra* at 67. "[W]here the attorney general is heavily involved in charities regulation, courts generally will take a dim view of private parties attempting to step into the attorney general's role to seek enforcement of charitable fiduciary duties." *Id.* at 70.

Under this factor, we consider whether the attorney general is able to enforce the trust or whether the lack of enforcement is due to a conflict of interest, ineffectiveness, or lack of resources. *Schalkenbach Foundation*, 91 P.3d at 1028 (attorney general's decision not to enforce the trust was not influenced by lack of resources and there was no evidence of neglect of the public interest; thus, this factor weighed against a finding of special interest standing).

Second Church alleges that the DCT allowed the trust to "fall into the exclusive control of the conflicted . . . trustees," participated in the crafting of the 1993 order that "turned the Trust priorities upside down," and sat idly by as the trustees diverted "some $26 million in funds to their preferred Mother Church." We disagree with Second Church's characterization of the DCT's oversight. As the trial court noted, during the long history of the trusts, the DCT's performance of his duties has been mixed and arguably deficient.

However, the record also demonstrates that during the pendency of the present dispute, the DCT has been an active participant, has acknowledged the embedded conflict with the trustees, and suggested measures to mitigate the effect of that conflict. For instance, during a motions hearing, the trustees acknowledged that the DCT had certain objections to the accounts filed in 2016 and that the two parties then proceeded to work together to resolve those concerns. In addition, in the DCT's memorandum concerning the standing of Second Church, he recognized the "embedded conflicting fiduciary obligations," while also asserting a plan to, *inter alia*, review the trustees' process for making distributions and review the trustees' resolution regarding the conflicting fiduciary obligations.

Nonetheless, Second Church maintains that the DCT is ineffective in addressing the embedded conflict with the trustees and, therefore, allowing Second Church to intervene as a party familiar with the trusts "is the best, and perhaps only, way to protect the Trust assets." Second Church relies upon the reasoning in *Holt v. College of Osteopathic Physicians and Surgeons*, 394 P.2d 932 (Cal. 1964), in which the court noted that "[t]he administration of charitable trusts stands only to benefit if in addition to the Attorney General other suitable means of enforcement are available." *Holt*, 394 P.2d at 936. In *Holt*, minority trustees brought suit against the charitable corporation and the majority trustees alleging that the defendant trustees acted contrary to the charitable purposes of the college. *Id.* at 934. The attorney general filed an answer concluding that the suggested changes to the operation of the college would not be detrimental to the public interest and did not warrant legal action by its office to prevent such changes. *Id.* The attorney general also claimed not to have information that the trust assets were being diverted from their charitable purpose, which, as the court noted, illustrated the concern that the attorney general "may not be in a position to become aware of wrongful conduct or to be sufficiently familiar with the situation to appreciate its impact." *Id.* at 935-36. The court held that the attorney general applied the wrong test in deciding not to take legal action because the assets of the college could only be used for the purposes for which they were received in trust, not in any manner that was not detrimental to the public interest. *Id.* at 936.

Second Church's reliance on *Holt* is misplaced. First, the plaintiffs in *Holt* were minority trustees, whereas here, the appellant is a *potential* beneficiary. *See id.* at 934. Second, the attorney general in *Holt* applied the wrong test when determining whether to take legal action, while here, the record demonstrates that the attorney general is actively involved in overseeing the administration of the trust. Second Church fails to demonstrate that it is better suited or more qualified than the attorney general to ensure the proper enforcement of the trust. Despite Second Church's assertion that it is "extensively familiar" with the relationships among the Mother Church, the Christian Science Publishing Society, and the Clause VIII Trust, Second Church does not allege or explain, not only how it is familiar with the trust, but also how any "familiar[ity]" with the trusts places it in a better position than the DCT. Moreover, Second Church does not allege that it has access to documents and information that the DCT does not have. In fact, Second Church's pleadings to the trial court indicate that it relied upon documents it received from the DCT as factual support for its allegations regarding the trustees' actions and the trustees' relationship with the DCT.

Second Church also alleges that "[g]iven the number of questionable acts taken by the . . . Trustees, it may be that there are simply too many aspects of the administration of the Clause [VIII] Trust for the DCT to effectively police." To support this contention, Second Church asserts that it wrote a letter in January 2017 alerting the DCT of potential mismanagement of trust assets, and Second Church believes that the DCT has not acted on that information. However, as mentioned above, the DCT has been actively involved in this matter and has taken steps to address the embedded conflict. The trial court's March 2018 order also ensures the continued involvement of the DCT by requiring the trustees to submit to the DCT "along with the annual audited accounts, a schedule of recipients of Clause VIII distributions and provide affidavit(s), under oath, that these distributees are in fact 'third party recipients' and not affiliated with the Mother Church." The DCT's reluctance to agree with Second Church to seek the appointment of an independent trustee is not sufficient to support Second Church's allegation that the attorney general is not involved or is ineffective.

Thus, we agree with the trial court that this factor does not weigh in favor of granting standing to Second Church. In addition, we iterate the trial court's encouragement of Second Church to continue to share information and its concerns with the DCT.

iv. Nature of the Benefitted Class and its Relationship to the Charity

Second Church argues that it is part of a defined class of entities that bears a special relationship to the charity. Courts have found special interest standing where the class of entities is "sharply defined and its members are limited in number." *Hooker*, 579 A.2d at 614. "[A] plaintiff should have a direct and defined interest, distinct from that of the general public, in the enforcement of the charitable obligations at issue to claim a 'special interest' in the charity." Blasko, *supra* at 70.

Second Church contends that it is a branch church, one of 1,400 Christian Science churches, that is defined by its unique connection to the Mother Church. Second Church relies upon several cases to argue that other courts have "granted special interest standing to more attenuated persons." For instance, Second Church relies upon *Y.M.C.A. of City of Washington*, where members of a local branch brought suit claiming that the YMCA breached a charitable trust by allowing the local branch building to deteriorate and by closing it. *Y.M.C.A. of City of Washington v. Covington*, 484 A.2d 589, 591 (D.C. 1984). In holding that the plaintiffs had special interest standing, the District of Columbia Court of Appeals concluded that the members of the branch received a particular benefit from this local branch and the closing of the building injured them in particular. *Id.* at 592. Similarly, in *Alco Gravure*, the plaintiffs—a corporate employer whose employees were intended beneficiaries of the Foundation, and two individual employees of the corporate plaintiff—constituted a class of potential beneficiaries of the Foundation. *Alco Gravure*, 479 N.E.2d at 753-54 ("The Foundation's primary purpose was . . . to assist employees of the founder's corporations and their families."). The plaintiffs were entitled to a preference in the distribution of the defendants' funds and were therefore challenging the dissolution of the Foundation and the complete elimination of their status as preferred beneficiaries of the funds. *Id.* at 754-56. The court found that the plaintiffs had special interest standing because the class of beneficiaries was both well-defined and entitled to a preference in the distribution of the defendants' funds. *Id.* at 755. The court also granted standing because it found that the policy reasons for limiting standing did not apply to the circumstances in that case. *Id.* at 756. Specifically, the court concluded that "the present action concerns not the ongoing administration of a charitable corporation, but the dissolution of that corporation and the complete elimination of the individual plaintiffs' status as preferred beneficiaries of the funds." *Id.*

The cases relied upon by Second Church concern plaintiffs that comprise a sharply defined set of potential beneficiaries with a greater interest in the charitable trust and corporation than the general public. Second Church fails to demonstrate that it is in such a class. The income from the Clause VIII Trust is to be utilized for the purpose of promoting and extending the religion of Christian Science. This broad language dispels any notion that the distribution of the income is limited to a small, identifiable class. The trust was intended to benefit more than just the branch churches. Moreover, Second Church is not alleging a harm directly related to its church, but rather is challenging ongoing administration that could impact all of the potential beneficiaries. Thus, the class of potential beneficiaries is not sharply defined. Because Second Church is not in a small, well-defined class, we agree with the trial court that "the potential for vexatious litigation is heightened."

We are not persuaded by Second Church's attempt to alleviate this concern by arguing that the appointment of an independent trustee "will likely eliminate the need for the special interest standing it seeks." Accordingly, this factor weighs against standing.

v. Subjective Factors and Social Desirability

Second Church next argues that it is socially desirable to grant it standing. Blasko describes this factor as somewhat of a catch-all factor, applying to "those cases where there seemed to have been an egregious wrong which would otherwise go uncorrected." Blasko, *supra* at 75.

The trial court found that although it remained "concerned about the embedded conflict," it did not find Second Church's claim that it "is 'well positioned to monitor and enforce the terms of the Trusts' due to its status as a branch church and knowledge of the religion ... [to] weigh[] heavily in its determination of standing." We agree. The DCT has acknowledged the conflict and is actively involved in the oversight of the trust, and Second Church has been encouraged to share its perspective with the DCT. Importantly, under RSA 7:20, the DCT "shall have and exercise all the common law and statutory rights, duties, and powers of the attorney general in connection with the supervision, administration, and enforcement of charitable trusts." *See also* RSA 7:19-:32-a (2013 & Supp. 2018).

Consequently, after considering all of the factors together, we conclude that Second Church has failed to demonstrate that it has a special interest in the Clause VIII Trust sufficient to grant it standing to petition for the appointment of an independent trustee to the trust.

B. PROCEDURAL ISSUE

Finally, Second Church argues, in passing, that the trial court erred when it denied it standing on a limited record. Specifically, Second Church asserts that the trial court erred by "effectively" requiring that it "prove each Blasko factor by a preponderance of the evidence" without the benefit of discovery and without holding an evidentiary hearing. However, the record does not show either that the trial court used a preponderance of the evidence standard when it applied the Blasko factors or that Second Church complained to the trial court about its inability to obtain discovery.[NOTE 2] *See Halifax-American Energy Co. v. Provider Power, LLC*, 170 N.H. 569, 574 (2018). Similarly, there is no evidence in the record that Second Church requested an evidentiary hearing or argued to the trial court that it erred by not holding one. *See id.* Accordingly, we decline to address these arguments because Second Church did not provide the trial court with an opportunity to address them.

Because we conclude that Second Church lacks standing, we need not address its argument requesting the appointment of an independent trustee. We reiterate the trial court's sentiment that Second Church is encouraged to share its perspective and concerns with the DCT, and, when appropriate, seek to file as *amicus curiae* with the trial court.

Affirmed.

LYNN, C.J., and HICKS, BASSETT, and HANTZ MARCONI, JJ., concurred.

NOTES:

NOTE 1: We note that the plainly erroneous language derives from case law and RSA 567-A:4. RSA 567- A:4 states, in relevant part: "The findings of fact of the judge of probate are final unless they are so plainly erroneous that such findings could not be reasonably made." Our case law has somewhat altered this standard and provides that "[w]e will not disturb the probate court's decree unless it is unsupported by the evidence or plainly erroneous as a matter of law." *In re Estate of Locke*, 148 N.H. at 755.

In this case, because there was no evidentiary hearing, the trial court did not necessarily find any facts and it would be inappropriate to defer to its factual findings or rulings of law. Nonetheless, the trustees and the DCT, at oral argument, advocated for a plainly erroneous standard because the trial court judge had presided over this case for several years and had the benefit of having the entire probate record before him when deciding the issue of standing. Although this is true, we have the majority of the record before us, and, because the material facts are not in dispute, *de novo* review is more appropriate.

NOTE 2: We observe that the material facts are largely undisputed. In addition, the record indicates that Second Church sought additional time to obtain discovery from the DCT and the Mother Church. Second Church never sought the trial court's permission or authorization to either engage in or compel discovery and, thus, did not raise this argument before the trial court.

STUDY QUESTIONS

- What was the underlying issue in the *Mary Baker Eddy* case and what was the attorney general's role in resolving it?
- Why did the Second Church petition the court for "special interest standing"?
- The court reviewed the factors that other jurisdictions consider in making a "special interest standing" decision and agreed with the trial court that the Blasko test was preferable—why? Summarize the five Blasko factors and how they were applied in this case.

Reading Note: In the Evergreen Aviation and Space Museum case, the Washington State Attorney General was informed by a whistle-blower that the organization, which was run by a board composed of members of a for-profit company, made a substantial loan to the for-profit company. The Attorney General's ensuing investigation turned up a number of other issues relating to the museum board's fiduciary duties and conflicts of interest. The Attorney General summarized its findings and recommendations in an audit report reprinted below.

The Hughes H-4 Hercules (also known as the Spruce Goose) as seen inside its current resting place, the main building of the Evergreen Aviation & Space Museum near McMinneville, OR.

EVERGREEN AVIATION AND SPACE MUSEUM AND THE CAPTAIN MICHAEL KING SMITH EDUCATIONAL INSTITUTE

Washington State Attorney General, Public Audit Report, Dept. of Justice, Civil Enforcement Division, March 20, 2014, DOJ File No. 137300/XCT0045-12

Dear Board of Directors:

This letter constitutes the final report of our investigation into the Evergreen Aviation and Space Museum and the Captain Michael King Smith Educational Institute ("Museum") as a nonprofit charitable organization governed by ORS Chapter 128. Despite serious concerns about the operation and future of the Museum, the Department of Justice (the "Department") is not pursuing any enforcement actions at this time. Based on the findings and conclusions detailed below, however, the Department recommends substantial changes to the Museum's governance and oversight (some of which the Museum has implemented during this audit), including a review of the Museum's articles, bylaws, and operations, an overhaul of the executive committee and board, the adoption of a "whistleblower" protection policy, and implementation of budgetary reforms.

This report is based on the records provided by the Museum, interviews with former employees, current employees, volunteers, counsel, documents and testimony presented at the property tax trial before the Oregon Tax Court, and the Department's own research. This report is the public record of our investigation and should be shared with all board directors for the organization.

I. INTRODUCTION

The Attorney General is responsible for supervising charitable organizations holding or soliciting assets in Oregon. See ORS 180.060(1)(d) and (6), ORS 128.610 et seq., and

ORS Chapter 65. This responsibility includes the power and duty to investigate whether charitable organizations are carrying out their charitable mission or breaching any fiduciary duties arising under statutory or common law. ORS 128.680. The Charitable Activities Section of the Oregon Department of Justice ("Department") performs these duties on behalf of the Attorney General.

In October 2012, the Department opened an investigation into the Museum in response to a confidential complaint regarding a conflict-of-interest transfer of more than $700,000 from the Museum to a for-profit Evergreen International Aviation entity. [NOTE 1] During the investigation, the Museum confirmed that it had "loaned" $725,000 to an Evergreen for-profit company, although the loan was repaid with interest shortly after the Department's inquiry. As a result of concerns about this transaction, the Department continued its investigation into the Museum's general operations and governance.

In any investigation of a charitable entity, the Department's overriding goals are to protect charitable assets and preserve valuable community resources. During our review, the Department expressed concerns that Evergreen's deteriorating financial condition, evident from media and other public sources, posed risks to the Museum's assets and operations. With Evergreen's closure and bankruptcy those concerns have manifested into tangible and serious consequence for the Museum, including increased costs, a loss of a major source of support, and changes in board composition.[NOTE 2]

The Museum was built and exists as the result of Mr. Smith's efforts and funding. Through the companies and private foundation he controls, Mr. Smith has likely spent over $150 million dollars on the construction of the buildings that house the Museum and waterpark. The Department is concerned that aspects of the Museum's structure and operations place the viability of the Museum at risk. As described in more detail below, the risk factors include a pattern of activity that jeopardizes the Museum's tax-exempt status and a precarious financial structure. The Museum does not separately own its buildings and land but has depended on the free lease of buildings, land, and numerous exhibit items from Evergreen and Mr. Smith's private foundation, thereby making it difficult for the Museum to operate as an independent institution whose fate is separate from that of these entities.

In response to the Department's investigation, the Museum's board adopted significant governance reforms. These reforms represent a substantial and appropriate step toward better governance. While we believe the enactment of such reforms is an important and necessary step in the Museum's development, the board will face challenges in their implementation and in safeguarding the Museum's future. This report is intended to help the board understand the Department's concerns about past operations and governance with the goal of helping the board avoid similar problems in the future. In addition, this report describes the legal framework in which charitable, tax-exempt organizations operate because that framework should guide the board's decisions in exercising its fiduciary obligations to the Museum.

II. SUMMARY OF FINDINGS AND CONCLUSIONS

The Department's investigation revealed significant governance issues arising from an overly close relationship between the Museum, on the one hand, and Evergreen and Mr. Smith on the other. Although the Museum declined to provide certain documents and did not allow interviews of Museum staff persons involved in the transaction giving rise to the investigation, the Department was able to identify areas of concern:

1. Members of the Museum's board appear to have failed in their duties to the Museum. The Evergreen executives serving on the board appear to have breached their fiduciary duties by failing to act in the best interests of the Museum. It appears that other board members have failed to be engaged or exercise active oversight, largely deferring to Mr. Smith's plans and decisions for the Museum;

2. Some specific transactions suggest that charitable assets may have been mismanaged; and

3. The overall activities of the Museum raise significant questions about whether the Museum is properly pursuing a tax-exempt purpose or whether the Museum is properly reporting to the IRS taxable "unrelated business income."

The Department considered potential enforcement actions including removal of Museum directors and actions against individuals to recover diverted charitable assets and damages for other losses. The Department ultimately decided against pursuing either of these options for a number of reasons. First, the Museum has adopted significant governance changes in response to this investigation, we have made additional suggestions in this report, and other changes are occurring as the result of Evergreen's bankruptcy. The existing board deserves an opportunity to implement their changes, consider our additional suggestions, respond to recent and evolving events, and demonstrate its ability to pursue the independent interests of the Museum. Enforcement action is not the ideal method to effectuate such change, given these other options.

Second, a number of the potentially improper financial transactions reported to the Department happened many years ago and the lapse of time would pose significant impediments to pursuing them. With respect to two more recent loan transactions discussed below, in one case the Museum has been repaid and in the other the Museum may be repaid by Mr. Smith personally. In light of the potential but uncertain impact on the Museum from Evergreen's bankruptcy and the uncertain outcome of discussions between Mr. Smith and the Museum regarding his continued support, we believe the appropriate course of action is for the Department to continue to monitor these matters.

Third, the Department has concerns about certain tax issues discussed below, which are best addressed by the Internal Revenue Service (IRS). The Department intends to relay our concerns to the IRS.

III. INVOLVED ORGANIZATIONS AND PARTIES

The Museum's history and operations are intertwined with a number of related parties and entities. An understanding of these relationships is important background in assessing the Museum's operations and future and in conveying the Department's concerns.

The Museum "campus" as many people refer to it consists of the Aviation museum building, the Space museum building, the theater building which houses a large screen theater and administrative offices for the Museum and Evergreen, the Wings & Waves waterpark, the newly finished chapel, and a Boy Scout campground. A section in front of and in between the aviation building and waterpark is now fenced off for the construction of a five-story hotel to be called the Red Hawk Lodge, although we understand construction has been suspended for the time being. In addition, there is a vineyard in front of the museum buildings and recently an Evergreen 747 was moved and parked in front of the museum buildings with plans to repurpose it as a youth hostel somewhere on the campus. The Museum campus is on the north side of Highway 18 in McMinnville.

Directly across the street from the Museum campus, on the south side of Highway 18, are a number of buildings owned and operated by the Evergreen International Aviation for-profit companies. Evergreen International Aviation is a privately owned company, founded and owned primarily by Mr. Smith.[NOTE 3] The company has a number of affiliates or subsidiaries, including Evergreen Vintage Aircraft Inc., Evergreen Agricultural Enterprises, Inc., Evergreen Trade, Inc., Ventures Acquisition Co., LLC, and Evergreen Holdings, Inc., [NOTE 4] which we will refer to interchangeably and collectively as "Evergreen."

While the Museum's campus and displays are impressive, in fact, the Museum owns relatively little of what the public sees. The Museum's assets consist largely of the Spruce Goose (the H-4 Hercules aircraft designed and flown by Howard Hughes), a limited number of exhibits, leasehold improvements, and office equipment. The buildings and land on which it operates are owned by other entities. The aviation museum, theater, and waterpark buildings and land are owned by Evergreen. The space museum building and land are owned by the Michael King Smith Foundation ("MKS Foundation"), a charitable trust created by Mr. Smith in 2006.[NOTE 5] The land on which the chapel, Boy Scout camp, and winery are located is owned by Evergreen.[NOTE 6] The Museum operates the buildings and programs at all these facilities pursuant to written lease agreements with Evergreen or MKS Foundation. Under the leases, the Museum pays no rent, but is responsible for all operational costs including utilities, maintenance, and repairs.[NOTE 7]

IV. THE MUSEUM

A. Formation

The Museum was incorporated by Captain Michael K. Smith, the oldest son of Mr. Smith, in 1991 as a public benefit nonprofit corporation with members and named the Evergreen Museum. In the beginning, the Museum operated out of Evergreen hangar space on the south side of Highway 18. Its collection consisted primarily of items owned by Mr. Smith and his son. Though it was open to the public, relatively few people knew of its existence.

In 1992, Evergreen acquired the Spruce Goose from the Aero Club of Southern California. The Spruce Goose was purchased through a stock purchase agreement, promissory note, and security agreement executed by Mr. Smith on behalf of Evergreen. Evergreen immediately assigned the contractual rights and obligations to the Museum. The Spruce Goose was disassembled and moved to Oregon in 1993 and its segments placed in temporary hangars until a permanent structure could be built. In 1993, the Museum also changed its name to Evergreen Airventure Museum. After plans for reassembly and construction stalled, the aviation building, where the Spruce Goose is displayed, opened in June 2001. In 1999, the Museum's name was changed to The Captain Michael King Smith Evergreen Aviation Educational Institute. The Museum adopted its current name in 2009.

B. Dependence on Evergreen

In many respects, the opening of the aviation museum building and the public display of the reassembled Spruce Goose represented the real launch of the Museum. In September 2000, as the Museum was preparing for the opening of the aviation building and poised for significant growth, Mr. Smith hired attorney William Schaub to serve as the Museum's Executive Director.

The Department interviewed Mr. Schaub about the Museum's governance and operations during the period he served as Executive Director. Mr. Schaub served in that capacity from September 2000 to November 2003.[NOTE 8] Although Mr. Schaub's tenure and the related events were some time ago, the Department believes this historical perspective is informative to all involved. It is important for the Museum board to recognize situations in which the Museum's relationship to Evergreen may have interfered with the Museum's obligations to operate independently from Evergreen and recognize situations that require additional investigation by the board.

When he was hired, Mr. Schaub understood that his efforts were to focus on making the Museum more independent from Evergreen and Mr. Smith, which included obtaining public charity status for the Museum, which was then classified as a private foundation. Although construction of the aviation building was being completed around the Spruce Goose, the aviation building was neither constructed nor owned by the Museum. As indicated previously, Evergreen owns the land and the aviation building. The Museum's revenue for 2000, including donations, was around $300,000.[NOTE 9] The Museum staff consisted of five employees who were housed at the Evergreen premises. Evergreen paid Mr. Schaub's salary for the first year and continued to pay part of his salary thereafter. In addition, Museum employee benefits were paid through Evergreen throughout Mr. Schaub's tenure.

According to Mr. Schaub and others, the Museum was treated and operated as if it was a division of Evergreen.[NOTE 10] This culture was epitomized by the practice of Evergreen holding daily management meetings which Museum representatives were required to attend, along with representatives from Evergreen's various for-profit companies. The Museum's participation in Evergreen management meetings continued throughout the Department's investigation and after we raised concerns about the practice. The Department has been informed that the practice ended in October 2013, just before the closure of Evergreen was announced.

The Evergreen overlay was further reflected in the Museum's board composition. Throughout the Museum's existence, Evergreen executives have had an ongoing presence on the Museum board and substantial influence over Museum business, particularly because the board met infrequently, leaving Evergreen executives to participate in and direct its daily operations. Museum staff and volunteers consistently perceived and portrayed the role of the Evergreen executives as relaying or carrying out directives from Mr. Smith.

The reality is that the Museum exists because of Evergreen and Mr. Smith. As a result, Evergreen and Mr. Smith exerted tremendous control over the Museum. Mr. Schaub reported examples of Evergreen's control or influence during his tenure (2000-2003) including the following:

- Evergreen and/or Mr. Smith personally owned at least one-third of the planes exhibited at the Museum and an exhibit outlining the history of Evergreen was installed at Mr. Smith's direction. Evergreen planes were prominently displayed, and the Museum facility was routinely used to woo Evergreen business contacts and vendors. As part of Mr. Smith's personal purchase of a helicopter collection, he obligated the Museum staff to construct a reproduction of an antique plane for the seller of the helicopter collection.
- Mr. Schaub reported that Evergreen employees would regularly appear on the Museum's books and payroll as the Museum's accounting system was connected to and/or operated by Evergreen.
- The Museum owned the rights to the Spruce Goose name for licensing purposes. Evergreen used the Spruce Goose name on its wine and retained all proceeds. Mr. Schaub's efforts to get a licensing agreement in place with the Museum were rebuffed. In 2004, after Mr. Schaub's employment

had been terminated, the Museum did execute a two-year licensing agreement with Evergreen which provided for one-year renewals by mutual agreement. It is not known if any payments were made to the Museum under the agreement or whether the licensing agreement was renewed.

- At Mr. Smith's insistence, an ice cream parlor was installed in the Museum facility for the benefit of his minor grandchildren and was done without any board review or approval. Mr. Smith refused to execute a lease for the space and Museum staff operated the ice cream parlor for two years, with all proceeds distributed to the family. The ice cream parlor is no longer in operation.

- Mr. Schaub and others reported that Evergreen periodically removed and scrapped donations, exhibit materials and the like without consulting with Museum staff.

- Mr. Schaub and others reported that Evergreen executives and/or Mr. Smith were involved with, directed, and interfered with daily operations at the Museum. They could and would take employees and volunteers away from tasks, summon them to their offices, and redirect them to other matters.

- Mr. Smith repeatedly represented to Mr. Schaub that Evergreen and/or Mr. Smith would cover all of the Museum's expenses prior to the opening of the aviation building as a donation and that once the opening occurred and the Museum could support itself going forward, it would start with a clean slate. Yet after the aviation building was opened, Evergreen required the Museum to pay $483,000 to reimburse Evergreen for covering the Museum's payroll in prior periods and to pay $140,000 to Hoffman and Benge for outstanding construction bills related to the aviation building. When Museum staff protested, they were variously informed that the Evergreen was carrying a "note" in excess of $500,000 which no one had ever seen, were informed the board approved the payment when no board minutes existed reflecting any discussion on the topic, and told that the Museum would simply be shut down if it did not pay the money. Mr. Schaub indicated the unexpected depletion of more than $600,000 from the Museum's funds significantly impacted their planned marketing, educational, and exhibit programs. (The Museum's IRS 990PF from 2003 reflects the Museum's repayment of significant indebtedness to unidentified parties).

- Mr. Schaub reported that Mr. Smith decided that the Museum should begin paying rent for the space they occupied at Evergreen (before the aviation building was completed) and insisted on $17,500/month, though Mr. Schaub obtained information indicating that the fair market rent for the space was closer to $3,300/month. Mr. Schaub insisted the matter be presented to the board for review. Before the board could review the matter, a $17,500 line item was inserted in the Museum's accounting ledger. This was eventually reversed without board intervention. (Financial statements provided to this office indicate that in 2004-2006, after Mr. Schaub was no longer employed by the Museum, the Museum leased warehouse and office space from a related party, variously identified as Venture Holdings, Inc. and Ventures Acquisition Co., LLC, for $17,500 per month. In 2006 alone, the Museum paid $210,000 in connection with this lease).

C. Efforts at Independence

1. Board Involvement

Mr. Schaub indicated he worked hard at recruiting Museum board members to improve its profile, independence, and expertise. He felt he made significant strides on that front. The earliest board minutes the Department obtained are from January 2002. The board met five times in 2002 and four times in 2003 (though one meeting appears to have been an executive committee meeting for which there are no minutes). The minutes reflect the board was engaged and focused on how to promote and grow the Museum. Discussions were held about developing an endowment, promotional efforts with the board of tourism and others, the need for fundraising and control of expenditures, and opportunities for acquisitions and exhibits.

Certain entries in the Museum's minutes are noteworthy. In 2002, the board commented that no more funds should be expended on capital projects until the funds were actually raised and that it would be important to have final drawings and preferably models prepared to show potential donors in fundraising efforts. The board contributed ideas regarding contacts for fundraising, promotional efforts, and exhibits.

In the May 30, 2002 meeting, it appears there were some questions raised about a "loan" from Evergreen that was reflected in the financial report. The minutes described the "loan" as relating to expenditures Evergreen fronted when the Museum was unable to pay its own expenses and though it's not entirely clear from the minutes, this would seem to relate to Evergreen's claim for reimbursement as described by Mr. Schaub. The board's response was to indicate that a reserve fund should be established. The general impression from the minutes is that the board was only informed about the loan after the fact; the board had an appropriate awareness that such transactions are not advisable, and wanted to institute plans to avoid similar situations in the future.

Starting in 2004, the board began meeting less often. In 2004, there was one executive committee meeting and two full board meetings. In 2005, there were two executive committee meetings and two full board meetings. Thereafter, the board met once a year and there are no minutes for any executive committee meetings.

2. Voting Members

The Museum's governing documents with respect to the voting rights of members and handling of related issues are troubling. Mr. Schaub reported that updating the Museum's articles and bylaws to include voting members was part of the Museum's overall transition from a private foundation to a public charity. He reports this change was discussed repeatedly with Mr. Smith and the board tasked him with drafting new governing documents.

At the March 28, 2002 board meeting, the final version of the amended articles and bylaws were presented to and approved by the board. Changes in the March 2002 governing documents included increasing the minimum size of the board, giving members voting rights to elect and remove directors and approve amendments to governing documents, increasing the number of board meetings to at least 4 times a year, requiring an annual meeting of the members, and establishing a number of committees.

After board approval of the amendments to the articles and bylaws, a member meeting was held on November 2, 2002 at the Museum and ballots were mailed to members. Mr. Schaub and others attended the member meeting and recall that Mr. Smith and other Evergreen executives were also present, although this was disputed. The board met on November 7, 2002, a few days after the membership meeting. Yet the board minutes make no mention of the recently held member meeting or election. Moreover, at the November 7, 2002 board meeting, a new director was nominated by Mr. Schaub and Mr. Smith and voted onto the board by the other directors. There appears to be a complete disconnect between the member meeting, the board meeting, and the new articles and bylaws.

In 2003, the March 2002 amended articles and bylaws were submitted to the IRS as part of the Museum's request to change its tax-exempt status from a private foundation to a public charity. Mr. Schaub also filed the March 2002 amended articles and bylaws with the Oregon Secretary of State ("SOS") in 2003.

Another annual members meeting was scheduled for November 28, 2003. Ballots were prepared and mailed to members beforehand, though the member meeting did not take place. Mr. Schaub's employment was terminated on November 6, 2003 and thereafter, Mr. Smith, in his stated capacity as chairman of the Museum board, sent a letter to the Oregon SOS stating that the 2002 amended articles and bylaws did not have the proper approval of the Museum's board, that their filing was a mistake, and that the Museum wanted to withdraw the filing.[NOTE 11] Mr. Smith's retraction letter and accompanying documents were also attached to the Museum's 2004 Form 990, which asked if the organization had made any changes to its governing documents. There is no record in the Museum minutes that the board ever voted to rescind the amended articles or bylaws that they approved in March 2002.[NOTE 12] Despite the rescission, on its 2008-2010 Forms. 990, the Museum reported it had members with voting rights.

The Museum has not offered an explanation as to how the Board could approve amendments to articles and bylaws that contained voting membership provisions in 2002, submit those amended documents to the IRS in 2003 in connection with its request to be reclassified as a public charity, send ballots to members in 2002 and 2003, subsequently conclude that the decision to allow members voting rights was invalid, and then drop the project to substantively update the organization's governing documents, which was not pursued again until the Department began this investigation. The handling of the membership issue raises concerns because once a nonprofit corporation opts to have voting members any decision to terminate their voting rights must be approved by the members.

D. Continued Expansion and Evergreen Control

After the construction and opening of the aviation building, the construction of the theater building, the space building, and waterpark quickly followed. The board seemed to have little to no input on those matters. Although the Museum did not own any of the land on which the buildings were constructed, it seems that it was always understood that the Museum would assume responsibility for operating the buildings once completed and adapt its programs accordingly.

The first mention of the theater building in the board minutes was in August 2002 where it was reported that the board was updated regarding prospective plans for a facility designed to play IMAX films and informed. that Mr. Smith would look into obtaining a market analysis to determine if the theater would be beneficial and financially feasible. If any such analysis was done, it was not reported in any subsequent minutes. The next mention of the theater building was in the August 2004 minutes, when the final design plans were presented to the board. There was no discussion of budget, costs, projected income or the role of the Museum with the IMAX.

Nonetheless, the August 2004 minutes reflect that the board was engaged in making the IMAX a success, using it as a launching pad for further promotion of the Museum, and a fundraising opportunity. The IMAX theater opened in April 2007. Evergreen originally leased the equipment from IMAX, but in 2010, the Museum entered into a sublease, signed by John Irwin on behalf of the Museum and Blythe Berselli on behalf of Evergreen. Both individuals were employed by Evergreen and on the board of the Museum at the time. The Museum minutes do not reflect any discussion or independent review regarding the sublease or financial impact to the Museum.

Over time, the Museum determined that operating the IMAX system was not financially viable and decided to switch to a digital format. In 2012, the Museum entered into a negotiated settlement with IMAX to terminate the agreement, which involved a significant payment to IMAX. Museum counsel recently informed the Department that Evergreen, not the Museum, paid IMAX under this negotiated settlement.

Construction of the Space building began in 2006 and is located on land owned by the MKS Foundation. At the 2008 board meeting, held shortly before the Space building's opening, Ms. Berselli reported that the Museum had entered into a $2.5 million contract with Kansas Cosmosphere for the construction and installation of certain exhibits at the Space building, that the Museum had paid $1.64 million on the contract but was unable to pay the balance, and that it had been determined it was best to allow the MKS Foundation to assume all rights and liabilities under the contract, but allow the Museum to use the displays in the Space building.

The Museum's 2007 audited financial statement described the agreement as creating joint ownership of the exhibits and gallery in proportion to the ratio each organization bore under the Cosmosphere contract. No prior board minutes contain any discussion of the Cosmosphere contract with the Museum and the 2008 minutes do not reflect any meaningful discussion by the board before it voted to ratify the assignment. It appears that as result of its obligations under the Cosmosphere contract, the Museum was unable to pay all of its ongoing administrative and operating expenses, which Evergreen covered or contributed to. Over time, the Museum's debt to Evergreen for these ongoing administrative expenses approached $1 million; the Museum was able to pay off this debt fully by 2012, but there was no mention of this arrangement or liability in any of the board minutes.

At the 2008 board meeting, the board was also presented with a five-year, $0 rent lease between the Museum and the MKS Foundation for the Space building. Ms. Berselli then presented a proposal, to sublease part of the Space building to Evergreen Agriculture for retail space, which included a wine bar, at a rate of $1.50 per square foot for an initial term of 3 years. Again, the minutes do not reflect any discussion by the board before it approved both transactions.

Though the board minutes do not reflect any discussions about long-term plans to construct and operate the waterpark and hotel, such plans were in the works no later than 2009. In order to begin construction, Evergreen had to obtain Yamhill County voter approval to annex the land into the urban growth boundary. The matter was placed on the ballot in May 2009 and passed. In the lead-up to the vote, the development plans were described as building a 50,000-square-foot water park and a 80- to 90-room resort lodge. At the October 2009 board meeting, Evergreen's president informed the Museum board that Hoffman Construction had been commissioned to build the waterpark, which would be the Museum's next activity. At the 2010 board meeting, Hoffman Construction gave an update on the waterpark construction and explained that it was being built first because of its ability to generate revenue. Ms. Berselli indicated the focus of the waterpark would be education and explained that the MKS Foundation would own the waterpark, but the Museum would operate it. Plans for the lodge were also outlined and included a 54-room Northwest style facility with a restaurant, spa/exercise facility, wine bar, and 8-9 rooms for student housing.

The waterpark opened in June 2011. The Museum entered into a month-to-month lease agreement with the MKS Foundation regarding the operation of the waterpark. Like the other lease agreements, the Museum pays $0 rent, but is responsible for paying maintenance and utilities. John Irwin, who also was an officer of Evergreen at the time, signed the lease on behalf of the Museum. There is no evidence from the documents provided to the Department that the lease was presented to the Museum board for review or approval.

In November 2012, the News-Register reported that construction on a chapel, campground, Boy Scout memorial, and adventure park behind the aviation building had commenced. Since the Department initiated this review, Evergreen has completed construction of the chapel and the Museum has entered into a lease to operate it. When asked why the Museum would build a chapel, Mr. Wood has responded "Because Del Smith wanted it."[NOTE 13] More recently, the Museum has reported that the chapel will be used not only for weddings and special events, but as a nondenominational sanctuary for staff, volunteers, and community members.

An Evergreen 747 was recently moved over to the Museum campus and the Department was informed that the plan is to convert it into student housing akin to a youth hostel. Construction of the lodge was underway, but is reportedly now on hold. Mr. Smith and Evergreen representatives have indicated that there are long-term plans to establish an orphanage on the property, though the Department has not seen any formal plans to that effect. It is not known what role, if any, the Museum will have in operating the youth hostel and lodge though Mr. Wood has promoted the lodge in various articles in his capacity as Executive Director of the Museum and has been involved in promoting the Museum in connection with finding potential lenders for the lodge.

E. 2012 Transfer of Funds

As indicated above, the Department's investigation was prompted by a report, subsequently confirmed by the Museum, that substantial funds were transferred from the Museum's account to Evergreen. Although Evergreen repaid the funds with interest after the Department initiated this review, additional facts regarding the transaction bear discussion.

The Museum's former Financial Director, Ms. Mery, was interviewed in the presence of Museum counsel about this specific transaction in December 2012, immediately before she left the Museum's employment and moved out-of-state. The former Financial Director was helpful and forthcoming. She explained that she was contacted by John Irwin, then president of Evergreen and the Museum's treasurer, on October 2, 2012 and asked how much cash the Museum had on hand. She reported that the Museum had $750,000 in its winter savings.[NOTE 14] She indicated the Museum needed the funds to cover payroll and the negotiated settlement with IMAX. Mr. Irwin indicated Evergreen may need $400,000 to make an interest payment on its debt. The following day, Mr. Irwin contacted Ms.

Mery again and requested the Museum's bank balance and indicated that Evergreen would need all of the funds, but would repay it in three days. Ms. Mery expressed skepticism regarding repayment, noting she was aware of Evergreen's financial condition.[NOTE 15]

Ms. Mery refused to make the transfer. As a result, on October 3rd Mr. Irwin and Ms. Berselli, both Evergreen executives and Museum board members, who also had signing authority on the Museum accounts, went to the bank themselves and wired $725,000 from the Museum's account to Evergreen. After the transfer had been made, Ms. Mery was told to work with Evergreen counsel to work out the terms of a note for the funds. Although Mr. Irwin originally told Ms. Mery that repayment would be made in three days, Evergreen counsel informed her that the repayment term was 30 days and suggested the note have a 15-day repayment term, given the dispute. Yet, within the hour, Ms. Mery received a fully executed 30-day promissory note, signed by Mr. Irwin, on behalf of the Museum, and Ms. Berselli, on behalf of Evergreen. The promissory note is dated October 4, 2012, and includes 9.0% interest. When asked about this transaction, Mr. Wood acknowledged that he had not been consulted beforehand and was not particularly pleased with how it had been handled, but indicated he never had any serious concerns about the impact on the Museum. Mr. Woods was confident that Mr. Smith and/or Evergreen would ultimately do right by the Museum, given their long-term investment in and commitment to the Museum.

Ms. Mery reported that after the transfer, the Museum lacked the funds to meet its upcoming payroll mid-month and contacted Evergreen for repayment and/or assistance. On October 10th Evergreen transferred $125,000 to the Museum to help cover its payroll. The Museum was also instructed to renegotiate the payment terms of its settlement with IMAX. The Museum was due to pay the settlement in full on or by November 19th but Ms. Berselli informed Ms. Mery that the Museum would not be able to do so because the promissory note from Evergreen would not be paid by then. Ms. Berselli then directly renegotiated payment terms with IMAX to extend the settlement payments until August 2013.

On October 19, 2012, the Department issued its first letter to the Museum inquiring about the transaction. The Museum, through counsel, responded by letter dated October 29, 2012 that the note had been paid in full as of that date. The letter also asserted that the transaction was good for the Museum as it received 9.0% interest, which far exceeded any interest it would have otherwise earned, that the Museum was never in financial stress as a result of the loan since it had roughly $12 million in assets, that the Museum would not exist but for the support of Evergreen, and that this was the only time the Museum has ever loaned money to Evergreen. On November 9, 2012, the Museum board met and passed a resolution ratifying the $725,000 transaction, finding the transaction was fair to and benefitted the Museum and was appropriate under the circumstances, particularly in light of the long history of support received from Evergreen.[NOTE 16]

F. Contract to Purchase Airplanes from Evergreen

In the course of its investigation, the Department also reviewed a transaction involving a Museum contract to purchase $500,000 in equipment from Evergreen (the "Airplane Contract"). In its review, the Department learned that in May 2012, Mike Hines, then President of Evergreen Trade who also serves on the Museum board, presented Mr. Wood with a $500,000 contract for the purchase of a DC-9 and a 747 cutaway from Evergreen for use as Museum exhibits. Mr. Smith had seen a 747 cutaway exhibit overseas and believed the Museum should have a similar exhibit. There was no independent review by the board or input from other Museum staff regarding the purchase, including whether or not the Museum could afford the purchase and whether such an exhibit fit within the Museum's priorities. The agreement was signed by Mike Hines on behalf of Evergreen. Mr. Wood signed the agreement on behalf of the Museum.

When presented with the Airplane Contract, Mr. Wood indicated that $500,000 was a significant amount of money and that the Museum did not have the funds. Mr. Wood reported he was told by the Evergreen executive(s) that he need not worry about the figure because the Museum was not going to pay anything on the contract anyway. He asked for clarification and was just told the Museum would not have to pay it. Mr. Wood felt he had no real choice but to sign the contract under the circumstances.

Ms. Mery, the former Financial Director of the Museum, stated she did not "book" the Airplane Contract on the Museum ledger before leaving the Museum in December 2012. When she learned of the contract, she raised questions about it because both she and the curator would ordinarily review and approve such contracts before they were executed. Ms. Mery reported she was aware of rumors circulating among employees and volunteers that Mr. Hines had purchased a group of DC-9s for Evergreen at $5,000 or $7,000 apiece. She asked for verification of the $500,000 value, but never received it.[NOTE 17] At one point during her inquiries, Evergreen indicated it would add value to the contract by constructing part of the exhibit for the plane and Ms. Mery asked that this provision be put in writing, which was never done.

Because Ms. Mery indicated the contract had never been booked on the Museum's ledger, the Department was under the impression there had been no financial impact from the contract. Before the Department interviewed Mr. Wood, Museum counsel also informed the Department that the contract had been rescinded. However, when the Department interviewed Mr. Wood in July 2013, he disclosed that the Museum had paid approximately $250,000 to Evergreen on the contract because the contract has been booked in the accounting system. He assumed that Ms. Mery had done that, though he didn't know why; Mr. Wood did not book the contract or direct anyone to do so. However, Ms. Mery was very clear and adamant that she had not done this. Mr. Wood was aware that payments were being made, but did not raise the issue. From his perspective, the Museum regularly owed Evergreen money each month because of shared administrative expenses and he did not pursue it further.

The Department asked for any documents regarding the rescission and payments. The Museum provided redacted minutes from the meeting of the board's newly formed Governance Committee, which is comprised of three independent directors without financial ties to Evergreen. (The formation of this committee is one of the changes implemented by the Museum since the Department's review was initiated, discussed in further detail below). The June 2013 minutes reflect that when Mr. Wood was asked about the contract, he informed the Governance Committee that the Museum no longer wanted the DC-9 because a more historically significant plane, a VC-9 ("Air Force Two") was available for $25,000 plus $30,000 in shipping costs, that the 747 cutaway was too expensive for the Museum, and that he preferred the entire agreement be rescinded; The committee was informed by Mr. Irwin that approximately $250,000 had been paid on the contract and that Evergreen could repay that amount by the end of the year. A formal agreement to rescind the transaction was executed in July 2013 and, in August 2013, Evergreen executed an unsecured promissory note payable to the Museum for $249,673, which sum was due on or before December 31, 2013, with interest accruing at the federal short-term interest rate. Shortly before the bankruptcy filings, Evergreen informed the Museum that it would not be able to pay the promissory note.

G. Museum Revenue and Support

A chart summarizing the Museum's revenue streams, based on its Forms 990 and financial statements, is marked Exhibit 1 and attached hereto. The Museum's financial situation is unusual in a number of respects. While the physical facilities of the Museum are massive compared to organizations such as OMSI and Portland Art Museum, its yearly revenue has generally been less than half that of those organizations.

In addition, the Museum engages in very little traditional fundraising. A relatively small proportion of its revenues are from donations. In recent years, donated income ranged from a high of 23% in 2009 to as little as 7% in 2012. Instead, the Museum relies heavily on admission fees at its various facilities as well as special events, gift shop sales, and food sales to generate revenue. In particular, the Museum saw a dramatic increase in revenue following the opening of the Wings and Waves Waterpark in June 2011.

Admission fees to the aviation and space building generate roughly $2 million annually. Membership fees have steadily increased, but in recent years, have stabilized at approximately $300,000. In 2011, the Wings and Waves Waterpark alone generated $2.6 million for half a year's operations. Another area of growth for the Museum has been the special events and cafe, which operates food concession for visitors and caters special events at the Museum. Revenue from special events and the cafe have increased to approximately $600,000 and $1,000,000, respectively. Meanwhile, theater revenue has steadily declined from its initial peak of more than $500,000.[NOTE 18]

Some of these revenue streams may be construed as unrelated business income for which the entity must pay taxes ("UBIT"). Yet the Museum has reported minimal amounts of UBIT. The Museum appears to take a different position from other museums regarding UBIT. Portland Art Museum and OMSI report virtually all of their special event revenue and substantial portions of their gift shop revenue on their Forms 990-T. In contrast, the Museum has not reported any income from the leases for the Evergreen wine bars, special events, the arcade in the waterpark, or the waterpark in general. The Museum: reports minimal amounts of UBIT for the theater operations and gift shop sales.

The waterpark is the single greatest source of revenue for the Museum. The waterpark is not separately incorporated or otherwise organized. It is not owned by the Museum, even though it is operated by the Museum. Since its initial opening, the facility has been altered to include more educational exhibits, to limit film screenings to educational material, and to eliminate the arcade, but it is unclear how operating a waterpark furthers the charitable mission of the Museum. The Museum has not sought formal legal advice or a private letter ruling from the IRS that the waterpark qualifies as an exempt activity. The Museum did obtain a single page memo from its accounting firm, which also serves as Evergreen's accounting firm, that summarily states the waterpark does not constitute UBIT.[NOTE 19] The memo was obtained in February 2012, approximately eight months after the waterpark had been opened and was being operated by the Museum.

H. Accomplishments and Future, Long-Term Plans for the Museum

The facilities used by the Museum are impressive. The Museum has developed a remarkably committed and high caliber army of volunteers and has retained a dedicated Executive Director and staff who work diligently to help the Museum succeed. The Museum has developed a successful relationship with the McMinnville school district and provides tremendous support to the school district, its teachers, and students. The Museum unquestionably expends significant effort and resources on educational endeavors throughout the region and is generous in its efforts to support education and veterans.

When asked to describe the long term plans for the Museum, Mr. Wood candidly stated that there are long-term plans for the Museum and they were known only to Mr. Smith. Mr. Wood's personal goals for the Museum were to continue to grow the Museum so that it could reach more and more students and offer more and more educational opportunities at all levels. Mr. Wood's commitment to education and belief in its ability to improve the lives of everyone, particularly the young, was readily apparent and obviously heartfelt.

V. CHANGES IMPLEMENTED AT THE MUSEUM

During the course of the Department's review, the Museum implemented a number of changes.

In November 2012, the Museum's board established a Governance Committee comprised of three long time board members who were not employed by or otherwise financially affiliated with Evergreen to review and approve or reject any transaction between the Museum and Evergreen or any other conflict-of-interest transaction and to work with the Museum's counsel in responding to the Department's investigation. The Governance Committee was further authorized and charged with determining whether any additional changes should be implemented by the Museum to improve the independent governance of the Museum.

In November 2012, the Governance Committee adopted a new banking policy providing that any transfers from the Museum to Evergreen must be approved by the Museum's Director of Finance and a disinterested board director. The Museum distributed the revised banking policy internally and to the Museum's bank. In March 2013, the Museum moved its bank account to another institution and eliminated Evergreen employees as authorized signers on the new account. The Governance Committee further refined the banking policy to require the approval of an authorized signer and disinterested board member for transfers exceeding $100,000 and for transfers in any amount to Evergreen. This policy was also distributed internally and to the financial institution.

In June 2013, the Museum adopted new bylaws and policies recommended by the Governance Committee. The changes included the following:

- The board will continue to be comprised of at least 3 directors with no maximum number set. At least two-thirds of the board members must be independent directors, i.e., have no affiliation with or economic interest in Evergreen or Mr. Smith, was adopted.
- The board will meet at least twice a year. A quorum continues to be one-third of the board and action requires the vote of a majority present.
- The composition of the Executive Committee ("EC") was altered to require 9 members, at least 5 of which must be independent. The Museum indicated that at this time, the remaining 4 EC members will continue to be Evergreen executives, to wit, Ms. Berselli, Mr. Irwin, Mr. Hines, and Mr. Smith.
- The EC will meet at least four times per year. The EC cannot take any action unless a quorum is present and the majority present consists of independent directors.
- The independent members of the EC will review and approve or reject all conflict-of interest transactions.
- No Evergreen employee, director or officer shall be an authorized signer on the Museum's bank accounts.

- An Audit Committee will be formed and will review and approve the Museum's Form 990. The majority of the Audit Committee members will be independent directors.
- The inter-company ledger account between the Museum and Evergreen will be zeroed out and closed by December 31, 2013.
- New Museum employees will receive training on Oregon law regarding nonprofit governance, management, and conflicts of interest within 90 days of hiring.
- New board directors will receive training on fiduciary duties under Oregon law, conflicts of interest, and good governance practices within 90 days of joining the board.
- The Museum will continue to employ the same financial auditor as Evergreen to prepare its audited financial statements because it is cost-effective.
- The new Finance Director of the Museum (to be hired) will not have any professional or economic relationship with Evergreen.

The Museum was insistent throughout the Department's review that altering the board composition to eliminate or reduce the number of Evergreen executives, particularly from the EC, was not an acceptable option. However, with the recent closure of Evergreen and the bankruptcy proceedings, the composition of the board and EC is already changing.

VI. RECENT DEVELOPMENTS

In November 2013, the Department received the Museum's 2012 IRS Form 990, which indicates that the Museum's financial health is deteriorating. The Museum's prior Forms 990 had not shown any operating losses and its 2011 Form 990 showed that its revenues exceeded expenses by more than $1.4 million. However, at the end of 2012, the Museum reported a loss of over $400,000. Between 2011 and 2012, it appears the Museum's personnel costs increased by approximately $800,000 and advertising and promotional costs increased by nearly $900,000. It appears the increased costs for advertising may be the result of the MKS Foundation paying for such expenses in 2011 but not subsidizing those costs to the same degree in 2012.

The Museum counsel also informed the Department in November 2013 that due to Evergreen's inability to cover its mortgage on the theater building, the Museum would temporarily rent the theater building for $50,000 a month while it explored its options. The Evergreen mortgage on the theater building is secured not only by that property, but also by the aviation building and Evergreen's default on the theater building mortgage raises issues with respect to the Museum's continued access to both facilities.

Also in November 2013, Museum counsel informed the Department that Evergreen will be unable to pay the $250,000 promissory note it issued in connection with the rescission of the 747 cutaway contract. Payment on the note was due on or before December 31, 2013. Though the Museum was exploring the possibility of accepting the Evergreen 747 currently parked in front of the Museum and the 747 cutaway located out-of-state in lieu of payment, those items are encumbered by liens.

These recent developments highlight concerns about whether the Museum's operations are sustainable and about its capacity to withstand financial setbacks. It will be necessary for the board to seriously evaluate its finances going forward and not to simply rely upon the fact that it reports having positive net worth. Unless the Museum receives substantial donations in the near future, the Museum does not appear to be in a position to incur additional expenses and expand its displays. Instead, the board will likely be faced with difficult decisions about how to maintain its core programs.

Making those decisions will require the board to evaluate fully the true costs of its various activities. To the extent that expenses associated with the Museum's activities, such as advertising and promotion, have been paid for by MKS Foundation, Mr. Smith or Evergreen, it may be difficult to develop accurate financial reports and projections for particular programs unless past support from other sources is factored into consideration. For example, it does not appear that revenues from the theater are sufficient to justify a monthly expenditure of $50,000 to rent the theater facility.

The board should also consult with the Museum's accountants to evaluate the accuracy of the information the Museum has provided to the IRS about its activities and governance. Focusing on the Forms 990 the organization has submitted for years 2008-2012, some of the reported information appears inconsistent or questionable when compared to the information gathered in the course of the Department's investigation.

VII. LEGAL ISSUES

A. Tax-Exempt Status

1. Private Benefit/Inurement

Tax-exempt organizations must be organized and operated exclusively for religious, educational, or charitable purposes and no part of their earnings can inure to the benefit of private individuals.[NOTE 20] The term "exclusively" has not been interpreted to mean solely, but the presence of a single nonexempt purpose, if substantial, will destroy the organization's exemption regardless of the number or importance of its exempt purposes. *American Campaign Academy v. Commissioner*, 92 TC 1053, 1065 (1989). Prohibited private inurement or benefits can take many forms such as advantage, profit, privilege, gain or interest. *Id.* Factors suggesting private benefit include "control by the founder over the entity's funds, assets, and disbursements; use of entity monies for personal expenses; payment of salary or rent to the founder without any accompanying evidence or analysis of the reasonableness of the amounts; and purported loans to the founder showing a ready private source of credit." *Rameses School of San Antonio, Texas v. Commissioner*, T.C. Memo 2007-85 at 7 (U.S. Tax Ct 2007).

A tax-exempt organization is not prohibited from entering into agreements or transactions with its founder, directors or officers, but any transaction in which a private individual appears to receive a disproportionate benefit in the exchange raises concerns about private inurement. Making unsecured loans at below-market rate is a form of private inurement. *Lowry Hospital Association v. Commissioner*, 66 T.C. 850 (1976). Indeed, the mere fact the tax-exempt organization acts as a source of loan credit to a private individual can constitute private inurement. *Easter House v. US.*, 12 Cl. Ct 476,488 (1987).

A number of the transactions described in this report raise concerns about whether they might constitute private inurement. When donors donate to tax exempt organizations, they agree to relinquish control over those donations. The fact Mr. Smith and/or Evergreen donated or invested sums far in excess of any benefits received does not negate the private inurement that may have occurred.

2. Nonexempt Activities

A tax-exempt organization jeopardizes its tax-exempt status "if it operates a trade or business as a substantial part of its activities even though the organization has certain exempt purposes and its profits do not inure to the benefit of individual members of the organization." Marilyn E. Phelan, *Nonprofit Organizations: Law and Taxation* § 7.33 (2011); see also, *Indiana Retail Hardware Association v. US.*, 366 F2d 998 (Cl Ct 1966). Substantial profits, use of commercial pricing structures, and competition with for-profit entities in the same field are seen as hallmarks of substantial involvement in nonexempt activities. Though there is no specific or easy mathematical test for ascertaining what constitutes a substantial involvement in nonexempt activities, some legal scholars have stated that nonexempt activities should not exceed 15% of the total activities. Phelan, *Nonprofit Organizations: Law and Taxation* § 7.33 at fn. 3.

A tax-exempt organization is required to report and pay tax on its unrelated business income ("UBIT"). UBIT is business income is that derived from a trade or business, regularly carried on, that is not substantially related to the charitable, educational, or other purpose that is the basis of the organization's exemption. The Museum appears to engage in extensive unrelated business activities. The special events, certain theater movies, gift store sales, and waterpark operations could potentially qualify as UBIT. And as of 2011, those figures far exceed 15% and would seemingly demonstrate that a substantial part of the Museum's activities are dedicated to nonexempt activity.

B. Board Fiduciary Duties

It is generally recognized that well-governed charitable organizations are more likely to comply with tax laws, safeguard charitable assets, and fulfill their charitable missions. In recognition of this dynamic, the IRS has published recommendations for charitable organization which can be found on its website: http://www.irs.gov/Charities-&-Nonprofits/Governance-of-Charitable Organizations-and-Related-Topics.

The IRS recommendations include having independent board members who represent a broad public interest and are informed and active in overseeing the organization's operations and finances. Similarly, Independent Sector, a coalition of nonprofit leaders, convened a Panel on the Nonprofit Sector to prepare guidelines for good governance. The publication entitled Principles for Good Governance and Ethical Practices: A Guide for Charities and Foundations (2007) sets forth 33 principles, which includes the recommendation that a substantial majority of the board of a public charity, generally meaning at least two-thirds, should be independent members. The Museum's new bylaws conform to this recommendation. This principle and recommended practice is in furtherance of the board members' duty of loyalty to the nonprofit. The IRS reviews board composition of charitable organizations to assess the potential for insider transactions and misuse of charitable assets.

Under state law, board directors have fiduciary duties to the organization they serve—the duties of care, loyalty, and obedience. The duty of care requires a director to perform his duties in good faith and with the care an ordinarily prudent person in a like position would exercise under similar circumstances. This requires the director to actively participate in the management of the organization. Though a director is not required to make the "right" decision at all times, he is required to make informed decisions, including making reasonable inquiries when appropriate. The duty of loyalty requires a director to act solely in the best interests of the organization. Thus, decisions regarding the organization's funds and assets must promote the organization's public purposes rather than private interests. Conflict-of-interest transactions should be closely scrutinized and the directors should understand the public will be skeptical of any such arrangement. Organizations should adopt written conflict-of-interest policies and use them.

Charitable organizations cannot loan money to its officers or directors. ORS 65.364. The duty of obedience requires a director to adhere to the organization's governing documents and mission and to comply with all relevant state and federal laws, including IRS rules and regulations for tax-exempt entities.

1. Evergreen Executives Serving on Museum Board

It appears that the Evergreen executives who also served as Museum directors have at times acted in the best interests of Evergreen, not the Museum. But when acting as directors of the Museum, they owed their fiduciary duties to the Museum, not Evergreen or Mr. Smith. The $725,000 transfer and the $500,000 contract are examples of such conduct.

While the $725,000 transfer was characterized as a loan, the money was taken without regard to the impact on the Museum because Evergreen needed it for purposes it never disclosed to the Department. The Department does not know what, if any, explanation for the loan was given to the board.[NOTE 21] The transfer was imprudent and reckless on the part of the Museum. The Museum transferred virtually all of its cash to a company with a CCC credit rating that was reportedly in violation of its financial covenants and struggling to make an upcoming interest payment. The loan agreement included no security or guarantees and the interest rate bore no relation to the economics of the transaction. Though the Museum indicated it had roughly $12 million in assets and was never at risk in the transaction, that statement does not comport with the reality that the Museum's Finance Director had to obtain funds from Evergreen to cover its immediate payroll and was told to renegotiate the IMAX settlement because the Museum would not be repaid in 30 days. The $12 million figure cited by the Museum encompasses exhibits such as the Spruce Goose and restricted funds and inappropriately downplays the risks associated with the transfer of most of its liquid assets.

In the $500,000 Airplane Contract, Evergreen executives who are also Museum directors appear to have insisted on a transaction the Museum could not afford. Their reasons for doing so are not known, but they do not appear to have been for the Museum's benefit. Despite the fact Mr. Wood was told the Museum would not actually have to pay anything on the contract and that Ms. Mery did not book the contract in the Museum's accounting system, Evergreen obtained $250,000 from the Museum for the contract during the Department's active investigation. Arid when the transaction was rescinded in response to the Department's inquiry, the Museum was not repaid, but was given an unsecured promissory note, which Evergreen has now acknowledged that it cannot pay. The Museum's ability to recover the funds or to otherwise be made whole is uncertain in light of the bankruptcy proceedings.

2. Board as a Whole

In recent years up until the Department's review, it appears the disinterested directors have exercised little oversight of the management or direction of the Museum, have not actively participated in the decisions regarding its future, or sought to be informed about such issues.[NOTE 22] The failure to act and to be informed can be as damaging to an organization as an affirmative breach. The failure to be engaged enables affirmative breaches to occur and problems that could have been resolved or averted through active oversight can develop into crises from which it may be difficult to recover.

In recent years, board minutes do not reflect any substantive discussions about whether or why the Museum should lease or assume responsibility for the theater, the waterpark, the chapel or lodge under construction. The board appears to have had no input on the recruiting and hiring of any of its executive directors. All of the Museum's executive directors have been persons known by Mr. Smith and presented to the board.

Both the Evergreen executives and the board have failed to exercise appropriate care in handling conflict-of-interest transactions. The board's ratification of the $725,000 transfer and the insistence that the persons involved in the transaction remain on the board are also troubling. Conflicted board directors will not be held liable for an insider transaction if the transaction was fair to the nonprofit at the time it was entered into or if it was approved by a majority of disinterested directors with knowledge of all material facts. It appears to the Department that the transaction would not be deemed fair to the Museum when considered at the time of its execution.[NOTE 23]

Though the board did respond by removing Evergreen executives as signatories on Museum accounts, one might have expected a stronger reaction from an active and independent board upon learning that $725,000, virtually all the Museum's cash, was withdrawn from the Museum's accounts without the board's prior knowledge or consent and loaned to a company that by all public reports was in serious financial distress. For example, the board might have launched its own independent investigation or removed the person involved in the withdrawal from the board. Instead, the board ratified the transaction and insisted that the Evergreen executives responsible for the transaction maintain key roles on the Museum's Executive Committee.

The Airplane Contract and the board's rescission of the contract are similarly problematic. The original transaction does not appear to have been in the Museum's best interests. Even if the property was worth $500,000 or more, its purchase was a significant unbudgeted expenditure. The rescission does not appear fair to the Museum since it has not been made whole. It is unclear whether the board had all the relevant facts surrounding the execution of the agreement—i.e., that the Museum was told it would not actually have to pay on the contract and that the Museum Finance Director did not book the contract in the Museum's ledger—when it approved the rescission and accepted the unsecured promissory note. And approximately three months after executing the promissory note, Evergreen informed the Museum it would not be able to pay the note. The Evergreen executives on the board should have foreseen such a possibility when the terms of the rescission were discussed and disclosed that. The Museum is now in the difficult position of waiting for resolution of the bankruptcy proceedings.[NOTE 24]

These two transactions were opportunities for the board to embrace their role as directors, fully investigate what has occurred, and take definitive corrective action.

VIII. CONCLUSIONS

The Department has serious concerns regarding the operations and future of the Museum.

As discussed above, based on the information provided to us, the Department is of the opinion that members of the board of directors, to varying degrees, have failed to adhere to the standards expected of charitable fiduciaries, although as previously expressed, we do not believe enforcement action is appropriate under the circumstances. In response to the Department's investigation, the board began taking preliminary steps toward greater independence from Evergreen, and as the result of Evergreen's bankruptcy, by necessity, the Museum will be required to become even more independent. In addition, significant issues such as the full impact of bankruptcy proceedings, the Museum's tax-exempt status, and potential liability for UBIT and property tax have yet to be determined. The Museum now faces unique challenges. The board should be given an opportunity to pursue the independent interests of the Museum pursuant to its revised governance structure and current economic realities. The board will have to devote significant effort for the Museum to continue and we feel they should be given the opportunity to succeed.

Since the initiation of this review, the Museum has started to separate certain internal operations from Evergreen, such as ending the use of a linked accounting system. In addition, they have made the governance changes discussed above. Those efforts should continue. The Department believes the following additional changes would be beneficial.

- Review and address the 2002 articles and bylaws which provided for voting members.
- The Museum has indicated it plans to develop an Audit Committee to review the organization's Form 990 on a prospective basis. Once formed, the committee should also evaluate the accuracy of the Museum's prior filings and file amendments if appropriate or have its accounting firm undertake such a review.
- Reconstitute the executive committee to be comprised completely of disinterested directors, save and except for Mr. Smith, should he wish to continue serving on the board.
- Recruit additional board members and diversify its composition to include those with expertise in nonprofit matters, fundraising, and museum operations.
- Engage an independent law firm or expert in charitable taxation to assist the Museum's review of whether its operation of the waterpark, special events, and chapel constitute unrelated business income activities and whether these activities jeopardize the Museum's tax-exempt status.

- The reconstituted board should re-evaluate whether the Museum should operate the theater, waterpark, and chapel and whether it is consistent with its mission and its financial capacity.
- Adopt a "whistleblower" protection policy and develop methods by which Museum staff and volunteers can feel comfortable reporting concerns to one or more designated independent board directors.
- Substantially increase the focus on fundraising and donor development and engage in long-term strategic planning.
- Implement budgetary restrictions so that expenditures are not made or committed to absent a specific funding plan and make increased use of financial information and budgets in the board's decision making.
- Join the American Alliance of Museums and employ the guidelines and ethical rules promulgated by the organization.
- Continue the development of more specific policies and training documents and expand board training to include existing as well as new members. The Department has been informed that the development of training materials referenced in counsel's June 2013 letter are underway, but not yet complete.
- The board should immediately inform the Department about any litigation or bankruptcy filings associated with the Evergreen which impacts the Museum.

Charitable fiduciaries commit to operating their organization for exclusively charitable purposes and are required to operate within a legal framework that ensures a lack of private inurement and proper taxation of commercial activities. Some of the actions described in this report raise concerns about whether the organization is operating in accordance with IRS requirements for a 501(c)(3) public charity. Because that is a matter of federal tax law, the Department will refer this matter to the IRS for review.

The Department hopes the Museum can learn from this review and improve its governance and operations to ensure its long-term future.

ELLEN F. ROSENBLUM
Attorney General

NOTES:

NOTE 1: For the purposes of this report, we will use the term "Museum" to refer to the nonprofit organization and will use the term "Evergreen" to refer to Evergreen International Aviation and its various for-profit affiliates and subsidiaries.

NOTE 2: In November 2013, Evergreen announced that it was closing, although Mr. Delford Smith, the primary owner of Evergreen and financial supporter of the Museum, initially disputed that the closure was permanent.

On December 19, 2013, creditors filed a petition in New York seeking to force certain Evergreen companies, namely Evergreen International Airlines, Inc., Evergreen International Aviation, Inc., and Evergreen Holdings, Inc., into bankruptcy. On December 31, 2013, other Evergreen entities filed a voluntary petition for Chapter 7 bankruptcy in Delaware. The New York bankruptcy petition has been dismissed, but the petitioners in that action have filed adversary proceedings in the Delaware bankruptcy. Between the Evergreen petition and the adversary proceeding, all Evergreen entities appear to be encompassed by the Delaware bankruptcy proceeding.

NOTE 3: Bankruptcy filings indicate that a small percentage of the company is owned by a trust for the benefit of Mr. Smith's surviving son, Mark Smith.

NOTE 4: Evergreen Helicopter, Inc. was sold to Erickson Air-Crane, Inc. in March 2013 to generate funds to repay Evergreen debts.

NOTE 5: MKS Foundation is a private foundation for which Mr. Smith is the sole trustee. It has 501(c)(3) tax-exempt status.

NOTE 6: Ownership is stated as reflected in recorded county property tax records. According to county tax officials, deeds have been executed conveying the land on which the waterpark, Boy Scout camp, and chapel are located to MKS Foundation for $0, but the county has not processed the deeds due to delinquent property taxes totaling just over $1 million. The Museum and the county are currently in litigation over whether the property qualifies for exemption from property taxes. Assuming recognition of the noted conveyances, all of the Museum campus is owned by MKS Foundation, except for the aviation building, theater building, and the site designated for the lodge, which continue to be owned by Evergreen.

NOTE 7: There appears to be some uncertainty regarding past lease arrangements for the theater building, the occupancy of which was shared with Evergreen. Museum counsel has recently advised that the lease agreement for the theater building included in the Museum's property tax application may have been an unexecuted draft. In any event, as of November 2013, the Museum no longer occupies that space rent-free. The Museum has agreed, at least temporarily, to pay $50,000 a month to rent the theater building.

NOTE 8: Mr. Schaub's employment was terminated by the Museum, which resulted in subsequent litigation between the parties. In connection with this employment dispute, the trial court granted summary judgment in favor of the Museum and other defendants. The lawsuit was resolved through a confidential settlement after Mr. Schaub appealed. The Department reviewed some of the trial court pleadings, including affidavits and deposition excerpts, as some of the allegations in the proceeding concerned management of the Museum and its governing documents. The Museum declined to voluntarily produce the deposition transcripts or to make Evergreen executives who are board members available for interviews to enable the Department to more fully evaluate the organization's past governance and history.

NOTE 9: The Department does not have access to the Museum's Form 990PF for the years 2000 and 2001 or to financial statements for years prior to 2004. The revenue figure is based on the October 2000 Management Review Report, which reported revenue, including donations, totaling $297,800 through September 2000.

NOTE 10: The attitude that the Museum is one of the Evergreen companies is also reflected in recent comments by Mr. Smith to the media. In response to an inquiry regarding the petition to force Evergreen into bankruptcy, Mr. Smith was quoted as saying, "The trading company is doing very well, the museum's doing very well, the ground handling company is doing very well, . . . We're just going to shut that airline down and we'll crank it up when the military has a need." Richard Read, Creditors Try to Force Evergreen International Airlines into Involuntary Chapter 7 Bankruptcy, Oregonian, Dec. 19, 2013.

NOTE 11: Although Mr. Smith identifies himself as Chairman of the Board in the 2003 retraction letter, the position of Chairman was only created as part of the 2002 amendments he asserted were invalid.

NOTE 12: Museum counsel has advised the Department that despite the lack of any record in the board minutes, the board did in fact vote to rescind the 2002 amended articles and bylaws in the November 2003 meeting, although we were not provided with any documentation to supplement the minutes provided. Museum counsel states that the vote to approve the 2002 amended articles and bylaws was invalid because the board thought the documents had been reviewed by the Museum's New York counsel, when that was not the case.

NOTE 13: Molly Walker, *New Evergreen Chapel to Hold First Memorial Service*, News-Register, Oct. 11, 2013.

NOTE 14: The Museum has significant seasonal fluctuation in its attendance and revenue and relies on its savings from summer revenue to carry it through the winter.

NOTE 15: The Department has not requested or obtained any internal financial information for Evergreen, a privately-held for-profit company. Nonetheless, information regarding Evergreen's financial condition has been publicly reported. In October 2012, Standard & Poor's Rating Services placed Evergreen on CreditWatch with negative implications because of the company's liquidity problems and weak performance, gave it a credit rating of CCC, and noted that it had an interest payment due October 31st. It further stated that Evergreen was in violation of its interest coverage and leverage covenants, but had obtained a waiver from its lenders. At that same time, there were a number of articles published regarding lawsuits filed against Evergreen for breach of contract and/or failure to pay vendors.

NOTE 16: Neither the note, nor the resolution describes Evergreen's purpose in requesting the loan. Reuters reported that Evergreen made its October 31st interest payment and as a result, S&P did not immediately downgrade Evergreen's credit rating; although it was subsequently downgraded in January 2013.

NOTE 17: The Museum produced to the Department a summary desktop appraisal obtained by Evergreen dated November 6, 2012, six months after the contract was entered into. The appraisal valued a 747 cutaway exhibit at $760,000, using a cost approach. The appraisal did not include inspection of the actual 747 being sold, which is believed to be at an Evergreen facility out-of-state. So far as the Department is aware, no Museum staff has seen the actual plane that is the subject of the contract. The appraisal contains no details or breakdown describing how the figure was calculated. An internal cost summary prepared by Evergreen valued the 747 cutaway at $691,100, including costs for transportation and exhibit installation.

NOTE 18: The fact that the Museum currently enjoys minimal occupancy overhead has allowed it to maintain its operations. If the Museum were required to pay more in rent, it is doubtful it could remain in operation without significant changes to its revenue streams. Moreover, it is not clear that increased revenues from the waterpark will result in greater financial stability for Museum programs. The Museum's 2012 Form 990 raises serious questions about the sustainability of the Museum's existing operations. While the Museum's 2011 Form 990 showed its revenues exceeded its expenses by $1.4 million, its 2012 Form 990 indicates its expenses are increasing even more rapidly than revenue and the Museum reported a loss of more than $400,000 last year.

NOTE 19: The memo identified three other amusement parks or recreational facilities that operate as charitable tax-exempt entities—Oaks Park Association, Gilroy Gardens Family Theme Park, and Sports Outdoor and Recreation Park. These entities are distinguishable from the Museum. Oaks Park was established in 1905 and is of historic interest. See the National Amusement Park Historical Association, www.napha.org. Gilroy Gardens operates as a supporting organization to the City of Gilroy, which owns most of the land and assets used for the park. Interestingly, the CPA's memo omits any discussion of Gilroy Garden's troubled financial history prior to its sale to the City, which may have been a relevant to the board's consideration of the risks of expanding its operations to include a waterpark. Sports Outdoor and Recreation Park was specifically created and designed for the physically and cognitively disabled. We believe it would have been appropriate for the board to request more information about whether the listed examples were, in fact, closely comparable to the Museum's waterpark.

NOTE 20: Additionally, 501(c)(3) organizations are prohibited from intervening or participating in political campaigns on behalf of candidates, engaging in substantial lobbying or political activity, and having purposes that are contrary to public policy, *American Campaign Academy v. Commissioner*, 92 TC 1053, 1065 (1989), none of which are relevant to this review.

NOTE 21: It is of great concern to the Department that in the existing Museum culture, it may be that no reason whatsoever need be given for such transactions and the impact on the Museum bears no weight. In discussing the $725,000 transaction, the Museum's Executive Director recently said, "When the guy that owns your building asks you to loan some money, you do," Richard Read, *Aviation Museum Mired in Dubious Loan History*, Statesman Journal, Dec. 22, 2013.

NOTE 22: In describing the failure of the board of directors as a whole, we are referring to the board and directors as a collective entity. Board composition has changed over time and we do not have detailed information about each individual board member's participation or the information that they specifically considered in guiding their actions. Nonetheless, when viewed as a whole and based on the information presented to the Department, it does not appear the directors have exercised meaningful oversight.

NOTE 23: Based on the Museum's refusal to allow the Department to interview certain persons associated with the Museum, it is unclear whether the disinterested directors were given all the relevant facts regarding the transaction when they were asked to ratify it, including information about the scope of Evergreen's indebtedness, and whether their ratification was meaningful or reflected the due diligence that is expected of charitable fiduciaries.

NOTE 24: The Department believes that, in the interim, the Museum has received the VC-9, though we do not know what costs the Museum incurred or what commitments were made as part of the transaction.

STUDY QUESTIONS

- The *Audit Report on the Evergreen Aviation Museum* recounts a wide range of issues raised in the management of a private museum. What does the Audit Report tell us about the role of the Attorney General in the oversight of charities? Why did the Attorney General conduct an audit of the Evergreen Museum?
- Diagram the relationships between the for-profit and nonprofit entities in the *Evergreen Museum* case study.
- Summarize the key governance issues raised in the *Evergreen Museum* Audit Report. What legal lines were crossed? What ethical guidelines were breached? How should the museum's management have done things differently to avoid these problems? What steps should the Evergreen Museum take to prevent these problems from occurring again?
- Why did the Attorney General decide not to exercise its authority to remove board members?
- What role did the board have in correcting the problems at the Museum? What solutions did it propose?
- What does the *Evergreen Museum* Audit Report tell us about the need for legal and ethical guidance in managing museums? What issues are unique to museums? What issues involve nonprofits generally? What issues apply to any type of business entity?
- What role did tax law play in the *Evergreen Museum* case study?

CHAPTER 2
MUSEUM PERSONNEL

In this chapter we explore issues relating to the management of museum staff. We start with reviewing staff roles and responsibilities. We then turn to basic employment law concepts, hiring and firing practices, and employee handbooks; employment laws including requirements under the Fair Labor Standards Act and employees/independent contractor classification; and laws relating to employment discrimination, occupational safety, immigration, and unionization. Finally, we look at how these legal issues apply to museum volunteers and interns.

MUSEUM STAFF ROLES AND RESPONSIBILITIES

In the broadest sense, the term "museum personnel" is comprised of everyone who assists the museum in carrying out its mission. This includes members of the museum board, executive level staff, departmental staff, interns (paid and unpaid) and volunteers. It also includes employees who are hired to carry out the terms of a particular grant, as well as independent contractors who are hired to work on a specific project.

Museum personnel are the lifeblood of the museum. They can also be the bane of a museum manager's existence. No other area of museum administration is so fraught with potential pitfalls and litigation risks. While the roles and responsibilities of museum staff are often highly specialized, the legal issues are not unique. In almost all circumstances, employment laws apply equally to museums as to other nonprofit organizations and to businesses generally. It is important to keep in mind that museum personnel need to be treated in the same way as employees in any business context would be treated.

Employment law is a complex and rapidly changing area of the law. Employment law disputes can present substantial financial as well as reputational risks for the museum. As a result, when faced with employment-related disputes, it is not unusual for museum administrators to seek outside legal counsel from experienced employment law attorneys. Even at museums which have in-house legal staff, it is not unusual to outsource all but the most basic employment law matters. Establishing policies and procedures, and applying them consistently, is essential to the sound management of museum personnel.

Museums are staffed with people with a wide variety of experience and skills. The composition of the staff depends on the museum's mission and organizational structure, as well as the institution's size and budget. Larger museums are like colleges and universities in the sense that they employ people with a wide range of educational backgrounds and professional skills—from custodians with little formal education to curators with Ph.Ds. Those who work in museums are often willing to trade higher levels of compensation which might be available in the for-profit world for the mission-based and (sometimes) more relaxed, congenial world typical of nonprofit organizations. However, lax management practices, less transparency, and a "non-profit mentality" can lead to serious employment problems. In smaller organizations, staff may find that they are expected to be "jacks-of-all-trades" responsible for a wide variety of responsibilities. For some this is attractive, but for others it can also become problematic if expectations are not properly managed.

Executive-level staff may include the museum's director, who may also serve on the museum's board, and other members of the senior management team with expertise in finance, fundraising, human resources, and exhibitions and programming. Additional positions typically depend on the museum's particular mission and programming goals and may include curators; registrars; conservators; museum educators; exhibit designers; print publication editors; marketing managers; communications, marketing, IT experts; fundraising and development staff; facilities maintenance personnel; art preparators and handlers; security guards; gallery attendants; and front-line customer service staff.

The roles and responsibilities associated with a position are often specified in a job description. The job description is useful when hiring new employees and during regular performance reviews, although additional responsibilities may be added during the course of employment. Particularly within smaller institutions, staff members often wear multiple hats, and oversee various parts of the museum's administration and business. Often roles develop and change overtime as the museum's needs change. As a result, it is sometimes difficult to maintain accurate job descriptions.

As a result of the often-complex division of responsibilities in museums, the interaction between board members and staff, and between staff themselves, can pose difficult legal and ethical issues. Varying levels of influence, and professional codes of conduct, among other things, can pose troubling questions about appropriate behavior. In these situations, respect for reporting hierarchies and spheres of influence are paramount. The *Evergreen* case reprinted in chapter 1 included several examples of undue influence by board members.

Under the doctrine of respondeat superior, the employer can be held liable for the tortious actions of its employees while they are acting within the scope of their employment. The doctrine applies to employees, including interns and volunteers, but it does not apply to independent contractors. (Some jurisdictions may impose liability for the acts of independent contractors by statute.) The tortious conduct must be one which is a foreseeable consequence or risk of the employment. In addition, many employment statutes may also hold an organization liable for the unlawful or negligent actions of its employees. A museum's bylaws may also indemnify employees, including board members, for liability resulting from actions taken within the scope of the employee's job. These risks can be managed by purchasing insurance. The museum's insurance policies should be reviewed periodically to ensure that it provides adequate coverage.

An employee handbook detailing the museum's employment policies, procedures and expectations should be compiled and regularly updated to reflect changes in applicable laws and the museum's own practices. A well-written employee handbook can help to avoid conflicts and misunderstandings. The employee handbook sets the tone for the employment relationship. It can also help create a structured work-environment and enhance loyalty to the organization. At a minimum, the museum's employee handbook should include an overview of the organization, hiring and firing procedures, standards of conduct (including policies on reporting workplace harassment, etc.), an explanation of compensation and benefits, procedures for performance review and promotions, vacation and leave policies, and policies regarding the use of company equipment, communications, and social media.

Unless the museum is prepared to be bound by them, rigid procedures for terminating employment such as notice requirements and specific compensation in case of termination, should be avoided. If the museum does not follow the procedures stated in the handbook, the museum can be subject to legal liability. Disclaimers, including that the terms of the employee handbook do not form a contractual relationship, may be advisable. A copy of the handbook should be given to each employee when they are hired, and the employee should sign an acknowledgement that they have received and reviewed it.

Before hiring a new employee, it is important to draft a clear and accurate job description. In some cases, certain steps are required with respect to posting job opportunities and soliciting applications. After interviewing and narrowing the field of qualified candidates, background and reference checks of the finalist should be conducted. As the *Ahmed* case included in the readings below shows, such checks can disclose important information which can be used to disqualify a potential candidate. Once a candidate has been selected, the museum should present an offer letter setting out the terms of employment. Generally speaking, only senior-level employees enter into a written employment contract. Most employees are hired on an "employment-at-will" basis. (The concept of employment at will is discussed in detail below.)

An offer letter is a good way of memorializing the expectations of the museum and the employee. The letter may contain the job description, compensation, applicable benefits, and other provisions applicable to the job. The offer letter may be contingent on completion of a background or reference check. The museum should be careful that the offer letter does not inadvertently undermine the employee-at-will relationship. Statements that may create an expectation of employment for a specific term or on a permanent basis should be avoided. Adding a statement that nothing in the offer letter is intended to alter the "at-will" status of the employment is a good idea.

As part of the hiring process, it is also good practice to have the new employee sign a confidentiality agreement and acknowledge the museum's conflicts of interest policy and other relevant policies. The museum should, at a minimum, conduct annual performance reviews with each employee. That is a good time to also review the museum's employment policies and procedures contained in the employee handbook. A record of each performance review should be kept in the employee's file.

Many legal disputes—discrimination, retaliation, contract, or tort law claims—are triggered by firing an employee. It is important to follow consistent procedures throughout the employment relationship to ensure that the museum does not face undue liability for terminating the employment relationship. In addition to conducting regular performance reviews, human resources staff should promptly investigate complaints about employee behavior.

Where problems are evident, except in extremely egregious circumstances, progressive levels of discipline to allow an opportunity for the employee to correct the problematic behavior should be favored over summarily firing the offending employee. Interviews with the employee should always be conducted in front of a witness and documented. If the employee's behavior does not change, the employee may be given the opportunity to resign or be terminated, depending on the situation and applicable state laws for unemployment compensation. If a severance agreement is offered, it should be drafted in consultation with an attorney familiar with applicable state and federal employment laws and the policies and practices of the museum.

EMPLOYMENT LAWS

Employment is highly regulated on the federal, state, and local level. Laws governing employment are complex and rapidly changing. Employment laws for the most part do not distinguish between for-profit and nonprofit entities. It bears repeating that museums are not exempt from employment laws and that issues relating to employment represent the single largest source of liability for museums. Although termed "employment" or "labor" laws, in many cases these laws apply either directly or by analogy not only to salaried and hourly employees, but also to volunteers and interns. These laws may also apply to workers found to be misclassified as "independent contractors."

Fundamental to employment law is the concept of "employment-at-will." Absent a written employment contract, and subject to specific restrictions and exemptions contained in applicable employment laws and regulations, employees serve at the whim of their employer and may be fired with or without cause at any time. A written employment contract is a binding agreement between the employer and the employee, the terms of which govern the rights and obligations of each party to the contract. A written employment contract may alter the "employment-at-will" status of the employee and govern termination rights and other aspects of the employment relationship. While it is unusual for most museum employees to have employment contracts, in some cases upper-level managers including the museum director may have an employment contract spelling out the terms of their employment. More common is the use of offer letters even for lower-level employees. To preserve the "at will" status of an employee, care must be taken to ensure that the offer letter does not become a binding contract.

On the federal level, basic wage and hour regulations are set out in the Fair Labor Standards Act (FLSA). The FLSA sets federal minimum wages and overtime compensation as well as establishing other employment rights and protections. Most states and local governments have similar laws applying to employment within their jurisdiction, although the minimum wage may be higher than the federal base.

Certain nonprofit organizations—currently those that generate income of less than $500,000 per year—may be exempt from FLSA wage and hour laws. The income threshold generally does not include donations and other nonbusiness-related proceeds. However, individual employees at such organizations involved in interstate commerce, or in commercial activities such as managing the museum shop, may still be covered under FLSA. And importantly, state wage and hour laws may still apply. For these reasons, museums should exercise extreme caution when relying on the nonprofit exemption.

FLSA establishes two classes of employees: those who are "exempt" and those who are "non-exempt." Non-exempt employees are protected by FLSA regulations, while certain exempt employees may not be entitled to FLSA protection. Employees may be paid a salary or a commission for their services or may be paid based on the number of hours worked. Contrary to common belief, the exempt and non-exempt classes of employees do not directly equate to salaried versus hourly wage compensation, although an employee who receives an hourly wage cannot be considered exempt under any circumstances.

The basis for determining whether an employee is exempt or non-exempt depends on the type of work the employee does and the way it is performed. In addition, there is a federal salary threshold to qualify as an exempt employee. With few exceptions, to be exempt an employee must earn at least the federal salary threshold (as of January 1, 2020, the threshold is $35,568 per year or $684 per week) and be paid on a salary basis and perform exempt job duties. Executive, supervisory, professional, and outside sales positions are typically considered exempt employees.

Employees who earn less than the federal salary threshold, and those who either are paid on an hourly basis or who do not perform exempt job duties, are non-exempt employees and are subject to FLSA rules and regulations. Non-exempt employees must be paid the applicable minimum wage and are entitled to "time and a half" for work over forty hours per week. Other rules and regulations under FLSA also apply to non-exempt employees. Exempt employees are not entitled to overtime compensation, even if they work more than forty (40) hours per week. The practice of paying "comp time"—that is, giving paid time off to non-exempt employees rather than pay overtime—is no longer allowed under FLSA. States may have additional requirements and state labor laws should always be consulted.

Museum jobs often evolve depending on the changing needs of the organization, the skills of the employee, and other factors. It is not unusual for a museum employee's actual work responsibilities to change dramatically over time. For this reason, it is important to perform a regular audit of the museum's job descriptions to ensure that they accurately reflect each employee's actual duties and their exempt/non-exempt status.

Depending on the size of the organization and the status of the employee, the provision of certain benefits, including health insurance, may also be required. Obviously, compliance with a myriad of federal and state employment compensation requirements can be extremely difficult. Some museums employ payroll companies to handle withholdings and other issues relating to employment compensation. Others handle compensation in house. The museum's human resources manager is usually responsible for handling most employment-related issues, including pay and benefits.

WHO IS AN EMPLOYEE?

A business with employees (including a museum) must withhold income, FICA (social security) and Medicare taxes, and pay unemployment tax on wages paid to its employees. Many states have laws affecting minimum wage, overtime, child labor and exempt employees.

Staff at the Cleveland Museum of Art install a new exhibition.

A museum does not need to withhold these taxes and pay unemployment tax for workers who are properly classified as independent contractors. Independent contractors provide services to an employer in exchange for compensation but are not considered employees for the purpose of FLSA and other employment laws. Since they are not considered employees, independent contractors are generally not entitled to receive health insurance and other employment benefits typically provided to employees. The independent contractor, not the museum, is responsible for paying any income, social security, Medicare, and unemployment taxes which may become due.

Classification of a worker as an independent contractor depends on the relationship and degree of control the employer exercises over the worker. The more independence the worker has in performing the work, the more likely he or she will be considered an independent contractor. The determination as to whether a worker is an employee or an independent contractor is an objective regulatory test. In fact, the understanding between the parties and the nature of their contractual relationship bears no relevance to the classification of a worker as an employee or an independent contractor. Just because a worker has signed a written agreement stating that he or she is an independent contractor does not mean that the worker has been properly classified as an independent contractor.

The Internal Revenue Service (IRS) 20-factor test may help in determining whether a worker can be considered an independent contractor for tax-withholding purposes. The IRS factors are organized into three general categories: behavioral control, financial control, and the relationship between the parties. When working with independent contractors, it is essential to document the factors used in making the determination that a given worker is an independent contractor. The IRS provides guidance on applying the 20-factor test on its website. (See *Determining Independent Contractor Status.*) It also provides specific guidance on determining employee/independent contractor status for nonprofit organizations including museums. (See *Exempt Organizations and Independent Contractors.*) In certain cases, the IRS issues determination letters to provide guidance to businesses making independent contractor determinations.

In addition to the issue of tax-withholding, the classification of an independent contractor affects the obligation to comply with minimum wage and overtime laws. The Fair Labor Standards Act (FLSA) does not cover independent contractors. State laws may also exempt independent contractors from state labor laws. As a result, there is a business incentive to classify workers as independent contractors. The factors considered in assessing FLSA compliance are similar to, but not the same as, the IRS 20-factor test. Like the IRS, the Department of Labor provides a number of guides on its website. (See for example *Fair Labor Standards Fact Sheet #13.*) A business that misclassifies its workers as independent contractors for compensation purposes risks having to reimburse those workers for unpaid wages.

The misclassification of employees as independent contractors can expose the employer museum to liability, including the obligation to withhold income, and to pay FICA (social security), Medicare taxes and unemployment taxes, as well as potential penalties.

Disputes involving the question whether an independent contractor is properly classified typically arise in situations where the employer dismisses a worker presumed to be an independent contractor, and the worker then files for unemployment compensation. This is what happened in the *Mattatuck Museum* case included in the readings below. In these "disgruntled" worker cases, the business may be found liable for misclassifying its workers and failing to comply with withholding and the minimum wage and overtime requirements under the FLSA or equivalent state statutes.

When hiring an independent contractor, it is important to enter into a written agreement. At a minimum, the independent contractor agreement should include a description of the services that will be provided, a payment schedule, a defined term after which the agreement expires, and procedures for terminating the agreement before the term ends (in case things don't work out). If the independent contractor is being hired in a capacity in which intellectual property may be created, the independent contractor agreement should also include a "work-for-hire" provision (see Chapter 5 for a more detailed discussion). While a written independent contractor agreement can help to substantiate the worker's status as an independent contractor, the agreement is not a substitute for conducting the employment relationship in a manner that meets the independent contractor test, including the degree of control exercised over the worker.

CASES AND OTHER READINGS

Reading Note: In addition to exhibiting art and historical objects, the Mattatuck Museum in Waterbury, Connecticut, offered a variety of instructional art courses. An instructor, who had taught several art courses at the museum, was fired, and applied for unemployment compensation benefits. The museum contested the instructor's claim, arguing that she had been hired as an independent contractor and not as an employee. The case is an example of an employee misclassification claim.

MATTATUCK MUSEUM-MATTATUCK HISTORICAL SOC'Y V. ADMINISTRATOR, UNEMPLOYMENT COMPENSATION ACT

679 A.2d 347 (Conn. 1996)

Opinion: Appeal by the plaintiff from a decision by the employment security board of review affirming an award of unemployment compensation benefits to the defendant Karen Perrella, brought to the Superior Court in the judicial district of Waterbury and tried to the court, Cone, J.; judgment dismissing the appeal, from which the plaintiff appealed. Affirmed.

BERDON, J.

The dispositive issue raised in this appeal is whether, for the purposes of eligibility for unemployment compensation benefits, the provision of art courses by the plaintiff, Mattatuck Museum-Mattatuck Historical Society, constitutes an activity within its usual course of business. The plaintiff appeals from the judgment of the trial court in which the court held that the employment security board of review (board) had properly concluded that the plaintiff had failed to prove that the claimant, Karen Perrella, was employed as an independent contractor under the provisions of the Unemployment Compensation Act (act). We affirm the judgment of the trial court.

The Mattatuck Historical Society operates the Mattatuck Museum. For simplicity, we refer solely to the Mattatuck Museum as the plaintiff. Perrella was named as a defendant in the administrative appeal to the Superior Court. [Connecticut] General Statutes § 31-222 et seq.

The following facts relevant to this appeal are undisputed. The plaintiff operates largely as an exhibition hall for regional historic artifacts and art. According to its own literature, however, the plaintiff also offers several artistic programs, including lectures, workshops, and arts and crafts courses, which are the subject of this appeal.

A variety of instructional art courses were offered by the plaintiff. The classes were held at the museum and taught by individuals hired by the plaintiff. Enrollment was open to the general public, and registration fees for the courses were discounted for museum members. In an effort to publicize the courses, the plaintiff prepared and distributed brochures describing the nature of the courses being offered, course schedules, and the cost of enrollment.

Perrella contacted the plaintiff to express her interest in teaching art courses, and was employed in January, 1989. Between 1989 and 1990, Perrella taught several courses, including watercolor, portraiture, pastels and oil painting, sculpture, and children's workshops.

In August, 1990, however, the plaintiff terminated Perrella's services. Subsequently, Perrella filed for unemployment compensation benefits. The plaintiff contested Perrella's claim, arguing that she had been employed as an independent contractor. The named defendant, the administrator of the act (administrator), applying General Statutes § 31-222 (a)(1)(B) (ii), found Perrella to be an employee of the plaintiff and thus eligible for unemployment compensation benefits. The plaintiff appealed the administrator's decision to an appeals referee, who determined that an employment relationship existed because, pursuant to § 31-222 (a)(1)(B) (ii) (II), the plaintiff's art courses were within its "usual course of business." After unsuccessful appeals to the board and then to the Superior Court, the plaintiff appealed to the Appellate Court, and we transferred the appeal to this court pursuant to Practice Book § 4023 and General Statutes § 51-199 (c).

General Statutes § 31-222 (a)(1)(B) provides in relevant part:

"Any service performed . . . after December 31, 1977, including service in interstate commerce, by . . . (ii) any individual who, under either common law rules applicable in determining the employer-employee relationship or under the provisions of this subsection, has the status of an employee. Service performed by an individual shall be deemed to be employment subject to this chapter irrespective of whether the common law relationship of master and servant exists, unless and until it is shown to the satisfaction of the administrator that (I) such individual has been and will continue to be free from control and direction in connection with the performance of such service, both under his contract for the performance of service and in fact; and (II) such service is performed either outside the usual course of the business for which the service is performed or is performed outside of all the places of business of the enterprise for which the service is performed; and (III) such individual is customarily engaged in an independently established trade, occupation, profession or business of the same nature as that involved in the service performed. . . ."

In his decision, the appeals referee determined in relevant part: "The museum seeks to distance itself from the art courses through a claim that these courses are not the usual work of a museum. It, however, is unsuccessful.

"The museum began a program of art study prior to those which the claimant taught. It determined a need within the community and responded. These then became part of the museum's normal business as they are offered continually to the public. Other evidence is supplied by the course offerings. Members are provided a discounted fee. This is obviously to encourage membership, a fee situation. This furthers the museum's program and mission and closely ties the art courses to the museum."

The board concluded that the plaintiff failed to satisfy any of the prongs of the ABC test provided in § 31-222 (a)(1)(B), discussed hereinafter. Because we conclude, like the trial court, that prong B of the test has not been satisfied, we need not reach the question of whether the board's additional determinations with respect to prongs A and C were correct.

We first consider the appropriate standard of review for the question presented. "To the extent that an administrative appeal, pursuant to General Statutes § 31-249b, concerns findings of fact, a court is limited to a review of the record certified and filed by the board of review. The court must not retry facts nor hear evidence.... If, however, the issue is one of law, the court has the broader responsibility of determining whether the administrative action resulted from an incorrect application of the law to the facts found or could not reasonably or logically have followed from such facts. Although the court may not substitute its own conclusions for those of the administrative board, it retains the ultimate obligation to determine whether the administrative action was unreasonable, arbitrary, illegal or an abuse of discretion...." (Citations omitted.) *United Parcel Service, Inc. v. Administrator,* 209 Conn. 381, 385-86, 551 A.2d 724 (1988). In this case, therefore, we must determine whether, in light of the evidence presented, the board's finding that the provision of art courses was within the plaintiff's usual course of business was unreasonable, arbitrary or an abuse of discretion.

An individual may receive unemployment compensation benefits if he or she was an "employee" within the meaning of the act. In addition to defining the employer-employee relationship pursuant to the common law, § 31-222 (a)(1)(B) provides that individuals who perform services for others are presumed to be employees, unless the recipient of the services (enterprise) satisfies the statutory exclusion, which is popularly known as the "ABC test." In order for an enterprise to demonstrate that an individual was not an employee, and that the enterprise therefore has no liability for unemployment taxes under the act, the enterprise must prove that the individual satisfies each of the three prongs of the ABC test. This test is conjunctive; failure to satisfy any one of the prongs will render the enterprise subject to the act. *Latimer v. Administrator*, 216 Conn. 237, 247, 579 A.2d 497 (1990). Under the ABC test, an individual will not be considered an employee if: "[A] such individual has been and will continue to be free from control and direction in connection with the performance of such service, both under his contract for the performance of service and in fact; and [B] such service is performed either outside the *usual course of the business* for which the service is performed or is performed outside of all the places of business of the enterprise for which the service is performed; and [C] such individual is customarily engaged in an independently established trade, occupation, profession or business of the same nature as that involved in the service performed. . . ." (Emphasis added.) General Statutes § 31-222 (a)(1)(B) (ii) (I) (II) and (III).

At issue in this appeal is prong B of the test: whether the provision of art courses falls outside the plaintiff's "usual course of business." Resolution of this question requires that the phrase "usual course of business" be defined. This court has not previously defined this phrase expressly for the purposes of unemployment compensation. See *Daw's Critical Care Registry, Inc. v. Dept. of Labor*, 42 Conn. Sup. 376, 401-402, 622 A.2d 622 (1992), aff'd, 225 Conn. 99, 622 A.2d 518 (1993) (characterizing Connecticut precedent relating to prong B of ABC test as limited). Nevertheless, we find guidance in the plain language of the statute and the precedents of those states that have analyzed the meaning of this term.

Prong B is also satisfied if it is proven, in the alternative, that the service "is performed outside of all the places of business of the enterprise for which the service is performed . . . ." General Statutes § 31-222 (a)(1)(B) (ii) (II). The plaintiff does not make this claim because Perrella's services were performed on-site at the museum.

In making our determination, we take as our starting point the fact that the act is remedial and, consequently, should be liberally construed in favor of its beneficiaries. *Taminski v. Administrator*, 168 Conn. 324, 328, 362 A.2d 868 (1975). Indeed, the legislature underscored its intent by expressly mandating that the act "shall be construed, interpreted and administered in such manner as to presume coverage, eligibility and non-disqualification in doubtful cases." General Statutes § 31-274 (c).

Our analysis commences with a review of the text of the act. "In interpreting the language of a statute, the words must be given their plain and ordinary meaning and their natural and usual sense unless the context indicates that a different meaning was intended. . ..

When the language is plain and unambiguous, we need look no further than the words themselves because we assume that the language expresses the legislature's intent . . . Indeed, [a] basic tenet of statutory construction is that when a statute . . . is clear and unambiguous, [generally] there is no room for construction. . . ." (Citations omitted; internal quotation marks omitted.) *Oller v. Oller-Chiang*, 230 Conn. 828, 848, 646 A.2d 822 (1994).

First, it must be determined for whose "business" the service was performed—that is, for museums in general or specifically for the business of the plaintiff's museum. The plaintiff focuses on that which is outside the usual course of business for museums generally. It argues that, because the dictionary defines "museum" as "an institution devoted to the procurement, care, and display of objects of lasting interest or value"; Webster's Third New International Dictionary; art courses are outside the *usual course of its business*. This argument, however, ignores the plain language of prong B, which requires inquiry into "the business for which the service is performed. . . ." (Emphasis added.) General Statutes § 31-222 (a)(1)(B) (ii) (II). Prong B does not refer to the type of business, but, rather, to the specific business activities engaged in by the enterprise. Accordingly, with respect to this prong, we examine the particular activities engaged in by the plaintiff.

We next define the term "usual." The plaintiff argues that "usual" does not mean "if you do it, it is within your usual course of business." We agree. To define the term in such a manner would include every relationship, including bona fide independent contractors, within the purview of the act. Indeed, the administrator does not argue for such a definition. Rather, the administrator asserts, and we agree, that "usual," in accordance with its common usage, simply means that an activity is performed by the enterprise on a regular or continuous basis. In the terms of § 31-222 (a)(1)(B) (ii) (II), if the activity is not performed on a regular or continuous basis, then the employer has satisfied prong B because the activity is "outside the usual course of the business" of the enterprise.

The term "usual" is defined as "such as accords with usage, custom, or habit: of the character or amount in common use . . . commonly or ordinarily employed . . . such as occurs in ordinary practice or in the ordinary course of events." Webster's Third New International Dictionary.

We note that there may be some situations, for example, those involving start-up businesses or new ventures of established businesses, in which the activity in question has not been performed for a sufficient duration to be deemed to be performed on a regular or continuous basis. In such cases, a better indication of whether the activity is in the "usual course of business" may be whether the enterprise holds itself out to the public or other interested entities as performing the activity. See *Hart v. Johnson*, 68 Ill. App.3d 968, 976, 386 N.E.2d 623 (1979).

The plaintiff further argues that the offering of art courses was outside its "usual course of business" because the services provided by Perrella as compared to its other activities were de minimis with respect to the revenue generated from or resources devoted to the art courses. Prong B, however, does not compel an inquiry into the substantiality or extent of a particular business activity in relation to other activities conducted by the enterprise. We agree that the mere fact that an enterprise undertakes an activity as an isolated instance does not render that activity within its "usual course of business." If, however, an enterprise undertakes an activity, not as an isolated instance but as a regular or continuous practice, the activity will constitute part of the enterprise's usual course of business irrespective of its substantiality in relation to the other activities engaged in by the enterprise.

In sum, prong B requires the finder of fact to determine whether the activity performed is within the "usual course of business" of the specific business at issue. In our view, "usual course of business," as used in § 31-222 (a)(1)(B) (ii) (II), means that the enterprise performs the activity on a regular or continuous basis, without regard to the substantiality of the activity in relation to the enterprise's other business activities.

This definition of "usual course of business," as used in prong B of the ABC test, is in accord with the precedent of other states. In *Bigfoot's, Inc. v. Board of Review of the Industrial Commission of Utah*, 710 P.2d 180, 180-81 (Utah 1985), the Supreme Court of Utah considered whether the performance of entertainers was within the usual course of business of the plaintiff's bar for the purposes of unemployment compensation. During a fifteen month period, the bar engaged numerous bands to perform at its place of business with the expectation that the bands would attract customers and increase business. Id., 181. The court reasoned that because it was "usual and customary" for the plaintiff's bar to provide entertainment, the employment of entertainers was within its "usual course of business." Id.

For slightly different reasons, in *Yurs v. Director of Labor*, 94 Ill. App.2d 96, 103, 235 N.E.2d 871 (1968), the Appellate Court of Illinois concluded that an organist was an employee of a funeral home within the terms of Illinois' Unemployment Compensation Act. Between 1959 and 1962, the organist performed at nearly 285 funeral services, and the music was included in the "package price" of each service. Id., 102, 104. Concluding that the funeral home was required to pay unemployment compensation taxes, the court stated: "The frequency of the inclusion of music in the funeral services indicated that it was a usual part of the services offered by [the] plaintiffs. . . . It cannot be said under these circumstances that the furnishing of music was not in aid of and a part of [the] plaintiffs' business." Id., 104.

Accordingly, we concur in the trial court's judgment that the board did not act unreasonably or arbitrarily in concluding that the offering of art courses was within the plaintiff's "usual course of business." The referee found that the plaintiff offered the art courses on a regular and continuous basis. The record reflects the fact that the plaintiff had employed instructors to teach art courses for several years. Perrella approached the plaintiff with her resume because she knew that it offered art courses to the general public. Moreover, the plaintiff held itself out to the public as offering art courses. The plaintiff produced and distributed brochures announcing the courses, class hours, location, registration fees, and the instructors' names. Indeed, the brochure listed Perrella as a member of its "faculty," from which the general public could infer that the art courses were a regular part of the plaintiff's business. Furthermore, the appeals referee found that the plaintiff discounted the art courses for members in an effort to bolster its membership. We therefore conclude that substantial evidence exists in the record for the board to have determined that the provision of art courses was within the plaintiff's usual course of business and that the trial court properly so held.

STUDY QUESTIONS

- What was the employment law issue in the Mattatuck Museum case? Why was the museum the plaintiff, and what were they contesting?
- Did the court apply federal or state law in their determination of the employment status of the art instructor? The court refers to an "ABC test"—describe the three factors of that test. Why was the second factor—whether the museum offered art instruction as part of its "usual course of business"—essential to the outcome of this case?
- In what way does the structure of the employment relationship, including employee control, nature of the business, and the employee's other activities, define the nature of the employee relationship?
- The court cites *CCNV v. Reid* in explaining the factors involved in employee classification. That case is also important for its conclusions on copyright ownership and is included in the readings in chapter 4.

Reading Note: The DeCordova and Dana Museum case reprinted below also deals with the classification of employees. Like the Mattatuck Museum, the DeCordova Museum offered art instruction, in this case a formal school of art which had its own administrative and teaching staff but was part of the museum's overall organizational structure. The museum sought a determination from the court on whether it was obligated to make contributions to the Massachusetts unemployment compensation fund on behalf of its art instructors.

DECORDOVA AND DANA MUSEUM AND PARK V. DIRECTOR OF THE DIVISION OF EMPLOYMENT SECURITY

370 Mass. 175 (1976)

PETITION filed in the District Court of Central Middlesex on July 31, 1973, for review of a decision of the board of review in the Division of Employment Security.

WILKINS, J.

We must decide whether the DeCordova and Dana Museum and Park (DeCordova) must make contributions to the unemployment compensation fund, maintained under the Massachusetts Employment Security Law (G. L. c. 151A), with respect to the services of those of its employees who work exclusively in DeCordova's school of art. DeCordova is a nonprofit corporation which maintains an arts center in Lincoln, consisting of a museum, a park, and a school of art. The school of art has its own administrative and teaching staff and functions separately from DeCordova's other programs but as a unit within DeCordova's organizational structure. DeCordova claims that employment in its school of art is not "employment" as defined in G. L. c. 151A, Section 4A, inserted by St. 1971, c. 940, Section 4.

The basic controversy turns on whether persons working in the school of art are "in the employ of a religious, charitable, educational or other organization, other than a school which is not an institution of higher education." G. L. c. 151A, Section 4A (f). The parties agree that the school is not an institution of higher education. DeCordova argues that, therefore, services for such a school are excluded from "employment" covered under the Employment Security Law. The Director of the Division of Employment Security (Director) argues that employees working for the school of art are in the employ of DeCordova and that DeCordova is not an exempt school. We conclude that this awkwardly drafted statute requires DeCordova to treat employees working for its school of art as engaged in employment covered by the Employment Security Law.

DeCordova and Dana Museum and Park is a 30-acre sculpture park and contemporary art museum on the shore of Flint's Pond in Lincoln, Massachusetts. Established in 1950, it is the largest park of its kind in New England encompassing 30 acres, 20 miles northwest of Boston.

DeCordova's appeal has arrived here as a result of the following events. The Director concluded that DeCordova's school employees were engaged in "employment" under G. L. c. 151A, Section 4A, interpreting the exemption for services in the employ of a school as applicable only to organizations operating a primary, elementary, or secondary school, "the attendance at which is required by law and therefore, compulsory." DeCordova appealed to the board of review (board) in the Division of Employment Security. The board found that teachers are required to enter into teaching agreements with DeCordova and that the right to terminate a teacher's employment rests ultimately with the director of DeCordova and its board of directors. On the other hand, the board of review found that the school of art was functionally separate from DeCordova's other programs. Not relying on the reason advanced by the Director in support of his decision, a majority of the three-person board ruled that the services performed by the staff of the school of art constituted employment, "not in the employ of a school, but in the employ of the appellant organization, a nonprofit educational organization within the meaning of [Section 4A (f)]." The board, therefore, affirmed the Director's decision. The decision of the board was affirmed in turn on DeCordova's appeal to the District Court of Central Middlesex. See G. L. c. 151A, Sections 12 and 42. DeCordova then appealed directly to this court, as provided in G. L. c. 151A, Section 42.

We agree with DeCordova that the question before us is solely a question of law. There are no findings of fact made by the board which preclude DeCordova from seeking our independent judgment on the application of Section 4A (f) to its circumstances. The facts are not in dispute.

Our function is to discern the legislative intent in the language of Section 4A (f). Literally, Section 4A (f), which is set forth in full in the margin,[NOTE 1] includes within covered employment any service performed in the employ of an organization unless that organization is a school below college level. Employment by DeCordova obviously is employment by an organization, and DeCordova as an organization is not a school below college level.

DeCordova responds to this literal application of Section 4A (f) by contending that it should not be required to contribute solely because it maintains a museum as well as a school of art. It argues that employees of an identical school of art, standing alone as an employer, would not be engaged in employment under the statute and that the Legislature could not have intended to require different treatment of services for two otherwise similar schools. DeCordova stresses that it operates a school of the type defined in Section 4A (f) and that the word "organization" in Section 4A (f) does not require that the organization be a legal entity. DeCordova undertakes to support this position by the legislative history of Section 4A (f).

Section 4A was added to G. L. c. 151A by St. 1971, c. 940, an act the heading of which states that it further regulates "the provisions of the employment security law in order to conform with the requirements of the federal law. . . ." An introductory clause states that the purpose of St. 1971, c. 940, is "to immediately make necessary changes in the employment security law in order to conform with federal law. . . ." From this language and the provisions of the act, a legislative intent to adjust the Massachusetts law to meet Federal requirements is apparent. There is no indication that the Legislature intended any other broadening of the scope of the coverage of the law.[NOTE 2]

The 1970 amendments to the Federal law encouraged States to make services in the employ of most charitable organizations subject to the State unemployment system for the first time.[NOTE 3] However, certain services in the employ of charitable organizations do not have to be covered by a State's law. See Int. Rev. Code of 1954, Section 3309(b). Among these services are services performed "in the employ of a school which is not an institution of higher education." Int. Rev. Code of 1954, Section 3309(b) (3).

Statute 1971, c. 940, adopted all the permissible Federal exceptions concerning employees of charitable organizations. All of them, except the exemption involved here, were added to G. L. c. 151A, Section 6, which lists services which are not included within "employment." St. 1971, c. 940, Section 8. A number of the services exempted by G. L. c. 151A, Section 6, are defined in terms of the nature of the service performed and not in terms of the nature of the employer. We think that some significance can be derived from the fact that the exception in Section 3309(b) (3) for services "in the employ of a school which is not an institution of higher education" is absent from the listing of exempt services in Section 6.

The Legislature undertook to exclude from "employment" services in the employ of a school below college level in the section which otherwise extended coverage to educational institutions and other charitable organizations. It merged the language of Section 3306(c) (8)—"service performed in the employ of a religious, charitable, educational, or other organization described in section 501(c) (3) . . ."—with the language from Section 3309(b) (3)—"in the employ of a school which is not an institution of higher education"—to produce Section 4A (f). This blending of themes was not accomplished without some discord, but we think it significant that the word "organization" in Section 4A (f) incorporates the Federal tax meaning of the word "organization" as appearing in Section 501 of the Code. Such an organization must be formally organized, at least to the extent of having its own articles of organization.[NOTE 4] See Int. Rev. Code of 1954, Section 501 (c) (3); Treas. Reg. Section 1.501(c) (3)-1 (a), (b) (1939). Cf. *Faulkner v. Commissioner*, 112 F.2d 987, 989 (1st Cir. 1940).

The use of the term "organization" in Section 4A (f) supports the Director's interpretation of Section 4A (f). A school below college level the employees of which are to be exempt from coverage must be an organization which exists as such under Federal tax law. The employees working in DeCordova's school of art are employees of an organization (DeCordova) described in Section 501(c) (3) of the Code and exempt from income tax under Section 501(a) of the Code. However, that organization is not a school. We will adhere to the meaning for Federal tax purposes of language incorporated in a State statute where no contrary legislative intent is apparent. See *B. W. Co. v. State Tax Comm'n*, ante, 18, 22-23 (1976); *Forte Inv. Fund v. State Tax Comm'n*, 369 Mass. 786, 788 (1976).

Other considerations which might be guides in determining the meaning of this language tend, on balance, to support our conclusion that employees of the school of art are covered. By deciding that those employees are within the act we eliminate the possibility that the Commonwealth's plan might be found to be underinclusive and thus fail to achieve approval by the Federal government. Our decision conforms to the mandate of G. L. c. 151A, Section 74, as appearing in St. 1949, c. 290, that the Employment Security Law "shall be construed liberally in aid of its purpose, which purpose is to lighten the burden which now falls on the unemployed worker and his family." On the other hand, we recognize that neither the State nor Federal law requires that all employees of a single employer be treated similarly, as either covered or not covered. See G. L. c. 151A, Section 4A (d) and (e) and Section 8; Int. Rev. Code of 1954, Section 3306(c) (5), (10), (13), (15), and (17). We further recognize that a corporate reorganization may produce the tax result for which DeCordova argues here and that the different treatment of employees of DeCordova's school of art and those of a similar school, having no other activities, has no strong support in terms of public policy.

Judgment affirmed.

NOTES:

NOTE 1: General Laws c. 151A, Section 4A (f), reads as follows: "[The term 'employment' shall include any service performed] . . . (f) in the employ of a religious, charitable, educational or other organization, other than a school which is not an institution of higher education,—only if the service is excluded from 'employment' as defined in the Federal Unemployment Tax Act solely by reason of section 3306 (c) (8) of that act and is not excluded from 'employment' under section six."

NOTE 2: The Employment Security Amendments of 1970 made extensive changes in the Federal unemployment tax provisions. Act of August 10, 1970, Pub. L. No. 91-373, 84 Stat. 695, amending Int. Rev. Code of 1954, Sections 3301-3311. A State unemployment law may be approved and certified by the Secretary of Labor as meeting Federal requirements (Int. Rev. Code of 1954, Section 3304[a] and [c]), and, if so certified, any employer making contributions under such a State law is entitled to a stated credit against his Federal tax. Int. Rev. Code of 1954, Section 3302(a), (b), (c). Statute 1971, c. 940, was a timely response to the deadline for compliance with the changes in the Federal law. Int. Rev. Code of 1954, Section 3304(c). See Act of August 10, 1970, Pub. L. No. 91-373, Section 142(i), 84 Stat. 708.

NOTE 3: State coverage of employment by such organizations was encouraged by conditioning Federal approval of the State law on a broadening of coverage to provide benefits for most employees of most charitable organizations. See Act of August 10, 1970, Pub. L. No. 91-373, Section 104, 84 Stat. 697, amending Int. Rev. Code of 1954, Section 3304(a) (6), which, through Section 3309(a)(1)(A), requires States to pay unemployment compensation with respect to services excluded from the Federal tax by Section 3306(c) (8) (i.e., "services performed in the employ of a religious, charitable, educational, or other organization described in section 501[c][3] which is exempt from income tax under section 501[a]").

NOTE 4: The reference to "other organization" in Section 4A (f) is meaningful only if one understands that in its historical and statutory context it means any other organization "described in section 501(c) (3) which is exempt from income tax under section 501(a)." Int. Rev. Code of 1954, Section 3306(c) (8). Unless the "organization" under Section 4A (f) is an "organization" described in Section 501(c) (3), service in the employ of the organization could not be "excluded from 'employment' as defined in the Federal Unemployment Tax Act solely by reason of section 3306 (c) (8)," as required by the last clause in Section 4A (f).

STUDY QUESTIONS

- The DeCordova and Dana Museum operates an art school as well as a museum and a sculpture park. Why did the museum bring this lawsuit against the state government?
- Identify the "awkwardly drafted" statutory language that the court was tasked with interpreting in this case.
- How did the museum and the Director of the Division of Employment Security differ in their interpretion of this provision of the statute? What are the implications of these differing interpretations?
- The court choose to take a narrow view of the exception from coverage for employees under the statute. What did the court conclude? What policy does this interpretation advance?
- What are the implications for the museum? The court alludes to a remedy for the museum—how could its organizational structure be changed to accomplish the outcome the museum is seeking?
- How do the *Mattatuck* and *DeCordova* cases differ—for example, employee/employer relationship vs. entity organizational structure?

EMPLOYMENT DISCRIMINATION AND OTHER EMPLOYMENT LAWS

Another significant body of employment law involves employment discrimination. An employer, including a museum, may not make its hiring, promotion or firing decisions based on age, race, gender, religion, national origin, or other factors that federal, state or local laws recognize as protected. For example, the Age Discrimination in Employment Act (ADEA) prohibits employers with more than twenty employees from discriminating against workers or job applicants aged forty or older. Other federal and state laws protect certain categories of employees, including those with physical and mental disabilities, sexual orientation, and marital status, among others. Both the *Ahmed* case and the *Torres* complaint included in the readings below involve alleged violations of federal and state employment discrimination laws. *Ahmed* involved a claim of discrimination in hiring. The plaintiff in *Torres* was a gay man who was HIV positive; he claimed that he was forced to resign from a job he had held for ten years due to the hostile workplace created by his new boss.

Another set of laws—generally referred to as "whistleblower" laws—prohibit retaliation, including firing an employee, for carrying out a public policy such as informing governmental authorities of unsafe conditions or illegal activities by the employer. Employers who violate these anti-discrimination laws may be held liable for monetary damages and may even be required to reinstate a terminated employee and pay back wages.

Other employment laws require certain employers to provide unemployment and workers' compensation insurance. These laws vary by state. Under certain circumstances, an employee who loses their job may be entitled to receive compensation through the state's unemployment insurance program. As discussed in the previous section and the *Mattatuck* and *DeCordova* cases reprinted above, application of these laws often involves the classification of workers as employees or independent contractors.

Workers who are injured on the job may be entitled to compensation for their injuries under state workers' compensation laws. Workers' compensation laws are designed to pay the expenses of employees who are harmed while performing job-related duties. Employees who qualify can recover lost wages, medical expenses, disability payments, and costs associated with rehabilitation and training. Employers are required to maintain workers' compensation insurance coverage for their employees.

Federal and state laws, including the Occupational Safety and Health Act (OSHA) and state equivalents, regulate certain aspects of the employer's workplace to ensure workers' safety. Museum collections, facilities and certain employment activities may raise OSHA compliance issues. Museum collections may be a source of toxic or hazardous materials—taxidermy specimens for example may contain high levels of arsenic which was often used as a preservative. Museum buildings, particularly historic structures, may be the source of lead paint, asbestos and other hazardous materials. Some museums, such as the underground mine museum discussed in the *National Coal Museum* case reprinted below, present inherent risks and may be regulated by specific occupational or other safety laws. And certain activities, such as using power tools to build exhibition cases for example, may pose serious risks of personal injury. Museums should conduct routine safety audits and comply with OSHA and other applicable workplace safety regulations.

Federal immigration and labor laws present challenges to museums interested in hiring foreign workers. There are several government agencies involved with granting permission for foreign workers to work in the United States. First, employers must seek certification through the U.S. Department of Labor. Once the application is approved, the employer must petition the U.S. Citizen and Immigration Services for a visa. Applicants must establish that they are admissible to the U.S. under provisions of the Immigration and Nationality Act (INA). (8 U.S.C. ch. 12 (§§ 1101, 1151–1157, 1181–1182, 1201, 1254–1255, 1259, 1322, 1351.) There are a number of different categories under which a foreigner can apply to enter the United States to work with a museum. For example, there are special visas, referred to as O-1B visas, which allow artists with extraordinary abilities to work in the U.S. for a period of up to three years. Immigration is a complex and changing area of the law. Suffice it to say that museums should seek specialized legal counsel to deal with issues involving foreign workers.

Increasingly museum staff are seeking to unionize parts of the museum workforce. Employees at the New Museum voted to unionize in 2019. Since then, numerous museums have faced efforts to unionize parts of their workforce, including the Guggenheim and the Whitney museums in New York City. As of this writing, employees at the Brooklyn Museum were also seeking to hold a vote to unionize.

There are many laws and court decisions that govern the creation and operation of unions. The main source of law regarding unions is federal law, as most unions are national organizations. The most important federal laws governing unions include: the National Labor Relations Act (NLRA) (29 U.S.C. § 151–169), which guarantees basic rights of private sector employees to organize trade unions, engage in collective bargaining, and enjoy other rights including striking if necessary; the Labor Management Relations Act (also known as the Taft-Hartley Act) (9 U.S.C. ch. 7 §§ 141-197), which added a list of prohibited actions by unions, or "unfair labor practices," to the NLRA; and the Labor-Management Reporting and Disclosure Act (29 U.S.C. ch. 11 §§ 401-531), which regulates labor unions internal affairs.

In addition to federal law, there are state laws governing unions. Some states have passed "right to work" laws or "open shop" laws, which give employees the right to work without joining a union or paying union dues. As with immigration, unions present complex legal issues and require experienced legal advice.

CASES AND OTHER READINGS

Reading Note: Tarek Ahmed, a software engineer who had worked as an independent contractor for the American Museum of Natural History, applied for a full-time position as a software developer at the museum. Ultimately the museum refused to hire him and terminated its contract with his company. The software engineer filed suit against the museum alleging numerous violations of federal and New York state anti-discrimination laws.

AHMED V. AMERICAN MUSEUM OF NATURAL HISTORY

U.S. District Courty, Southern District of New York,
17cv2095 (DLC)
Opinion and Order, October 9, 2018

DENISE COTE, District Judge:

Plaintiff Tarek Ahmed, a software developer who worked under contract for defendant the American Museum of Natural History (the "Museum"), alleges that the Museum and Samuel Tran, his supervisor at the Museum, retaliated against him in violation of Title VII of the Civil Rights Act of 1964, 42 U.S.C. § 2000a et seq. ("Title VII"), the New York State Human Rights Law, N.Y. Executive Law § 290 et seq. ("NYSHRL"), and the New York City Human Rights Law, N.Y.C. Admin. Code § 8-101 et seq. ("NYCHRL"). The defendants have moved for summary judgment. For the reasons below, the motion is granted.

BACKGROUND

The following facts are undisputed or taken in the light most favorable to the plaintiff, unless otherwise noted. Ahmed has been a software developer and engineer since 1997. Ahmed worked on and off as an independent contractor for a software company called Door3 from 2008 to the beginning of 2016. Around December 2013, the Museum engaged Door3 to design and implement new software for the Museum's ticketing kiosks, website, and mobile applications. Around July 2014, Ahmed joined this effort as an independent contractor for Door3. The software program Ahmed was working on, Tessitura, went live in May 2015, after which the Museum continued to engage Door3 to troubleshoot various software bugs and deployment issues until the Fall of 2015.

Ahmed left Door3 in early 2016, and in January 2016, reached out to the Museum's Director of Digital Technology to inform her that he was looking for work. It turned out that at that time, the Museum had decided to dedicate approximately $25,000 to improve Tessitura. In March 2016, Ahmed, through the new company he formed, TEK, Inc., contracted with the Museum pursuant to a Vendor Agreement to "provide technical consulting, development services, quality assurance testing and deployment implementation support for the Museum's ticket application." The Vendor Agreement stated that TEK, Inc. was being engaged in its capacity as an independent contractor and set a completion date of April 30, 2016. Ahmed signed the Vendor Agreement as President of TEK, Inc.

Defendant Tran, Director of System Administration in the Information Technology Department at the Museum, oversaw management of certain IT infrastructure, e.g., servers and storage devices, and managed the virtualization services. Tran was one of Ahmed's supervisors at the Museum. Juan Montes, the Museum's Chief Information Officer, served as Tran's direct supervisor and oversaw the Museum's technical operations. Ahmed was also supervised by Susan Weisbrod, the Tessitura Project Manager at the Museum, and was expected to update Weisbrod on the status of his work at least twice a week.

Ahmed was also required to work physically at the Museum every day with the laptop and desk purchased for or assigned to him by Tran. According to Ahmed, he was also expected to be at the Museum while the Museum was open and the other members of the IT staff were present and to attend certain employee-only meetings with other Museum employees. While Ahmed was not required to report when he arrived or ask permission to leave, he felt that if he was absent without an explanation, he would have faced consequences.

Some of Ahmed's tasks under his agreement with the Museum were to fix a Tessitura application bug; complete school group ticketing enhancements, insert e-commerce reporting, and encapsulate and streamline the application deployment process. Satisfied with the work, the Museum engaged TEK, Inc. with three successive scopes of work after April 2016: (1) a project beginning in May 2016 to enhance the software in the Museum's in-house ticketing kiosk; (2) a project beginning in June 2016 to upgrade the ticketing software and develop software to sell tickets to an upcoming film festival online; and (3) a project beginning in August 2016 to upgrade the new software and provide school group fixes/enhancements, and add accessibility enhancements. There were times, however, when plaintiff performed projects on an ad hoc basis that were not contained in the scope of work to which he had agreed with the Museum.

In the Spring of 2016, the Museum began discussions regarding establishing a full-time software developer position at the Museum. Ahmed indicated his interest in the position in or about April 2016. On or around June 23, 2016, Montes and Tran approached Ahmed to ask whether he wanted the position, and he answered affirmatively. Human Resources ("HR") required a formal process to be followed to hire a new employee. Tran enlisted Ahmed's help to draft certain portions of the job description by providing a list of what technologies would be necessary for the position. The written job description required a Bachelor's Degree in Computer Science, Information Technology, or a related field. The Museum's management approved hiring someone for the position on July 18, 2016.

On July 21, 2016, Ahmed submitted the first of two applications for the position. In the first application, Ahmed did not enter a school or any details, but entered "Bachelor's" under "Educational Institutions/Degree Type" with no graduation date. On the resume he submitted, Ahmed incorrectly stated that he received a B.S. in "Computer Science" from Long Island University ("LIU") in 1997 and graduated summa cum laude. The resume also erroneously indicated that Ahmed had performed services under his TEK, Inc. business since 2015 and that he worked for a website, Bunk1.com, from 2000-2005.

Tran viewed Ahmed's application and was concerned it was incomplete. Tran advised Ahmed that HR would look at his application closely, and it needed to be filled out completely and as accurately as possible. Tran advised Ahmed about a prior candidate who had applied for a job, but had placed inaccurate information in his application. The Museum rescinded the job offer even though the candidate had moved a great distance to work for the Museum.

On August 1, 2016, Ahmed submitted a second cover letter, application, and resume to replace his first set of materials. He did so because he was concerned he would fail a background check on the basis of the first set of materials. In this second application, Ahmed changed the education section of the application to read, "Long Island University, 1993-1997" with a major in Computer Science, but stated that he did not graduate. On his resume, Ahmed changed his work experience to state that he had worked at TEK, Inc. from 2005 even though TEK, Inc. was incorporated in 2016. Ahmed claims that he did not spend much time on his application because Tran constantly told him that the job was his.

That same day, Tran, who claims that he did not review Ahmed's second set of application materials, selected Ahmed as the final candidate for the software developer position, triggering an automatic email to Ahmed from the Museum, which stated that offers were contingent on a successful reference check and background check.

Meanwhile, Ahmed was instructed to go to the Tessitura conference in Washington, D.C., from August 7-11, 2016 along with other Museum employees. The Museum paid for his attendance and travel expenses. One night, at the conference, Ahmed witnessed Tran, who appeared to be drunk, make sexual advances towards a female coworker. Ahmed proceeded to pull Tran away from the coworker and told him that his behavior was "not cool." The next morning, Ahmed recalls telling Tran that "it really wasn't cool what happened last night" and suggested that Tran apologize to the female co-worker, who "didn't seem like herself." Tran does not remember acting this way on the night in question, or Ahmed's comments to him.

On August 11, when Ahmed returned from the conference, he completed the pre-employment paperwork and returned it to LaToya Young, the Museum's Assistant Director of Employment in the HR Department. The documents included an employee data sheet and background check authorization and release. Young reviewed the documents in her office with Ahmed. Young noticed that Ahmed entered his highest level of education as an Associate's degree from Long Island University, and again, did not include a date of graduation. When Young asked Ahmed about the missing date, Ahmed told her that he was not sure of the date but that it was probably 1995 or 1996. According to Ahmed, Young took it upon herself to write June 1, 1995 onto the employee data form. Young also noticed that, based on his response on the employee data sheet, Ahmed did not meet the Bachelor's degree requirement stated in the job posting. Young submitted Ahmed's materials for a background check pursuant to standard Museum procedure in order to determine his actual academic background.

On August 19, Young along with others in HR received an email from Michael Goun, the Museum's then-Director of Revenue Security and Investigations with the results of the background check conducted by private vendor Intellicorp. The email stated: "Candidate cleared pre-employment screening except for education and prior employments. . . . Education—Long Island University—database used by school unable to confirm Associate's degree." Young then called Ahmed to inform him of the results and that he could either get a copy of the degree itself or a formal letter from his university's Registrar Office stating that he received his degree. When Young contacted LIU directly to inquire about Ahmed's degree, she was told that LIU had never awarded Associate's degrees in Computer Science. That same day, August 19, Ahmed visited LIU to inquire about the Associate's degree. He was told that he did not have enough credits to earn his Associate's degree.[NOTE 1] LIU never conferred an Associate's degree in Computer Science on Mr. Ahmed.

During a telephone conversation with Tran and Montes later that day to discuss Ahmed's application, Young told both of them that she believed that Ahmed misrepresented his educational background on his application materials. Young told Montes and Tran that the normal procedure in this circumstance would be to rescind the job offer. Montes was distressed by the news. Montes informed Young that Ahmed's work was critical to several projects at the Museum and that delaying his hire or rescinding his job offer would be a considerable disadvantage to the Museum. Young relayed that message to her supervisor. Because Montes still wanted to hire Ahmed at this point, Young recommended that Ahmed be interviewed by two members of the HR department for a further credibility analysis.

Following this conversation with Young, Montes and Tran spoke by telephone with Ahmed that day. The content of that conversation is disputed but the parties agree that the clearance issue was discussed. Tran remembers having a conversation with Montes in which Montes informed Tran that he had decided not to continue to pursue Ahmed's hire. Either that Friday, August 19, or the following Monday morning, they called Young back and Montes informed her that he now agreed with her assessment that plaintiff was misrepresenting his educational credentials. By this point, Montes believed that the Museum should revoke the offer of full-time employment.

Three of Ahmed's coworkers have testified that they noticed tension between Tran and Ahmed.[NOTE 2] One colleague testified that he noticed increased tension between Tran and Ahmed during Ahmed's final weeks at the Museum and that he believed this tension began before the Tessitura conference. He also told Ahmed that he believed Tran was trying to derail Ahmed's hire. Another colleague also told Ahmed that she felt Tran may have derailed Ahmed's job offer. She suspected this was because Tran "might have been a little intimidated by Tarek's familiarity and knowledge of" the Tessitura application. A third colleague indicated in testimony that after Ahmed's background check she became aware of "issues" between Ahmed, Tran, and Montes, and felt that they were not getting along well.

On Monday, August 22, Young sent out an email calling off the interviews by the two members of the Museum's Human Resources team. That same day, Ahmed sent an email to Tran and Montes inquiring about his start date, to which Montes responded that he will have an update the following morning. On August 23, Ahmed met with Montes and Tran.

They informed him that the conditional offer of employment was rescinded, but that the Museum would continue to work with him as an independent contractor.

Ahmed tried to resolve the situation by continuing attempts to verify that he had earned an Associate's degree. According to Ahmed, Young told him that all Ahmed needed to clear the background check was a letter from his University indicating that he had the requisite credits for the Associates degree. On September 6, 2016, Ahmed provided Young with a letter from LIU stating: "This is to certify that Tarek Ahmed has completed all requirements for the Associates of Arts degree." Ahmed then emailed the Museum's Chief Digital Officer, to inform her that he had proof of his Associate's degree.

On September 9, Ahmed asked Montes whether he had received anything from HR regarding his job offer and Montes said he had not. Ahmed then sent an email to HR, copying both Montes and Tran, inquiring about the status of his job offer following his production of the LIU letter. According to Ahmed, within a minute or so after Ahmed sent the email, Montes came out of his office and began yelling and screaming at Ahmed. Feeling hostility from both Tran and Montes, Ahmed decided to leave the Museum for the rest of the day.

Upon leaving work, a distressed Ahmed called the Chief Digital Officer to discuss the rescission of his conditional offer. That officer explains that, while she did not think that Ahmed was directing any anger at her, she felt that he was very upset, speaking quickly and loudly. Following their conversation, she expressed concern to Montes that there may be a risk to the Museum because she believed Ahmed had the keys to code and data and, in his discontent, could willfully damage the Museum's digital property. Montes made the decision to terminate the Museum's contract with TEK, Inc. Ahmed does not deny that he was upset and would have sounded so, but explains that the only reason he sounded upset was because he was still on edge from his encounter with Montes less than half an hour prior to the telephone call. That evening, Ahmed received an email from Montes terminating the Museum's contract with TEK, Inc.

Following the termination of the TEK, Inc. contract, around September 14, Ahmed reported for the first time his allegations that Tran had sexually harassed a fellow employee at the August conference. He made this report to the Museum's Senior Director of HR. After an internal investigation, the Museum decided that although Tran should be counseled for drinking too much at the conference, he did not violate the Museum's anti-harassment policy.

Ahmed filed a charge with the Equal Employment Opportunity Commission, and received a right to sue letter on February 23, 2017. On March 23, 2017, Ahmed filed this lawsuit against the Museum and Tran, primarily claiming unlawful retaliation for opposing discrimination on the basis of sex in violation of Title VII, NYSHRL, and NYCHRL. Following discovery, on May 2, 2018, defendants moved for summary judgement.

DISCUSSION

Summary judgment may not be granted unless all of the submissions taken together "show...that there is no genuine dispute as to any material fact and the movant is entitled to judgment as a matter of law." Fed. R. Civ. P. 56(a). "Summary judgment is appropriate when the record taken as a whole could not lead a rational trier of fact to find for the non-moving party." *Smith v. Cty. of Suffolk*, 776 F.3d 114, 121 (2d Cir. 2015) (citation omitted). The moving party bears the burden of demonstrating the absence of a material factual question, and in making this determination, the court must view all facts in the light most favorable to the non-moving party. *Gemmink v. Jay Peak, Inc.*, 807 F.3d 46, 48 (2d Cir. 2015). Once the moving party has asserted facts sufficient to carry its burden of production, "the party opposing summary judgment may not merely rest on the allegations or denials of his pleading; rather his response, by affidavits or otherwise as provided in the Rule, must set forth specific facts demonstrating that there is a genuine issue for trial." *Wright v. Goord*, 554 F.3d 255, 266 (2d Cir. 2009) (citation omitted).

In the context of employment discrimination, "an extra measure of caution is merited" in granting summary judgment because "direct evidence of discriminatory intent is rare and such intent often must be inferred from circumstantial evidence found in affidavits and depositions." *Schiano v. Quality Payroll Sys., Inc.*, 445 F.3d 597, 603 (2d Cir. 2006) (citation omitted). Nonetheless, "a plaintiff must provide more than conclusory allegations to resist a motion for summary judgment." *Holcomb v. Iona Coll.*, 521 F.3d 130, 137 (2d Cir. 2008). Ultimately, as in all cases, the test for summary judgment is whether "a reasonable jury could return a verdict for the nonmoving party." *Nunn v. Mass. Cas. Ins. Co.*, 758 F.3d 109, 114 n.4 (2d Cir. 2014) (citation omitted).

I. Federal and State Retaliation Claims

Title VII makes it unlawful for an employer "to discriminate against any employee or applicant because that individual opposed any practice made unlawful by Title VII." *Hicks v. Baines*, 593 F.3d 159, 164 (2d Cir. 2010) (citation omitted). "This anti-retaliation provision is intended to further the goals of [Title VII] by preventing an employer from interfering (through retaliation) with an employee's efforts to secure or advance enforcement of Title VII's basic guarantees." Id. (citation omitted).

The Supreme Court has explained that a broad interpretation of Title VII's retaliation provision furthers the overall purpose of the statute:

> Title VII depends for its enforcement upon the cooperation of employees who are willing to file complaints and act as witnesses. Interpreting the antiretaliation provision to provide broad protection from retaliation helps ensure the cooperation upon which accomplishment of the Act's primary objective depends.
>
> *Burlington N. & Santa Fe Ry. Co. v. White*, 548 U.S. 53, 67 (2006).

Title VII and the NYSHRL generally "cover 'employees,' not independent contractors." *Eisenberg v. Advance Relocation & Storage, Inc.*, 237 F.3d 111, 113 (2d Cir. 2000). Whether a person is properly considered an "employee" for Title VII purposes is determined through a fact-specific, thirteen-factor test articulated by the Supreme Court in *Community for Creative Non-Violence v. Reid*, 490 U.S. 730 (1989). These factors are:

> the hiring party's right to control the manner and means by which the product is accomplished[;]... the skill required; the source of the instrumentalities and tools; the location of the work; the duration of the relationship between the parties; whether the hiring party has the right to assign additional projects to the hired party; the extent of the hired party's discretion over when and how long to work; the method of payment; the hired party's role in hiring and paying assistants; whether the work is part of the regular business of the hiring party; whether the hiring party is in business; the provision of employee benefits; and the tax treatment of the hired party.

Id. at 751–52. This list of factors is "non-exhaustive." *Salamon v. Our Lady of Victory Hosp.*, 514 F.3d 217, 227 (2d Cir. 2008), as amended (Apr. 22, 2008). The first factor, which examines the "extent to which the hiring party controls the 'manner and means' by which the worker completes her assigned tasks," is the "most important factor in determining the existence of an employment relationship." Id. at 227, 228 (citation omitted). Where the adverse employment action at issue in a Title VII claim is an employer's failure to hire an individual, that individual need not be an employee. 42 U.S.C.A. §2000e-3(a) (prohibiting employers from discriminating against "employees or applicants for employment" because they have opposed unlawful employment practices).

Courts in this Circuit analyze Title VII and NYSHRL retaliation claims under the burden-shifting standard set out in *McDonnell Douglas Corp. v. Green*, 411 U.S. 792, 802 (1973). See *Summa v. Hofstra Univ.*, 708 F.3d 115, 125 (2d Cir. 2013). Under the McDonnell Douglas standard, a plaintiff establishes a prima facie case of retaliation by making "four showings: that (1) she engaged in a protected activity; (2) her employer was aware of this activity; (3) the employer took adverse employment action against her; and (4) a causal connection exists between the alleged adverse action and the protected activity." Id. (citation omitted). "Once the plaintiff has established a prima facie showing of retaliation, the burden shifts to the employer to articulate some legitimate, non-retaliatory reason for the employment action." *Zann Kwan v. Andalex Grp. LLC*, 737 F.3d 834, 845 (2d Cir. 2013). If the defendant articulates a non- retaliatory reason, the plaintiff has the burden to prove that the retaliation was a "'but-for' cause of the adverse action, and not simply a 'substantial' or 'motivating' factor in the employer's decision." Id. Title VII prohibits an employer from "discriminat[ing] against any of [its] employees ... because he has opposed any practice made an unlawful employment practice by this subchapter." 42 U.S.C. § 2000e-3(a). For a plaintiff to establish that he was engaged in protected activity, the first prong of a prima facie case of retaliation, "the plaintiff need only have had a good faith, reasonable belief that he was opposing an employment practice made unlawful by Title VII." *Kessler v. Westchester Cty. Dep't of Soc. Servs.*, 461 F.3d 199, 210 (2d Cir. 2006) (citation omitted). Protected activity need not consist of a formal complaint of discrimination, rather, an "internal complaint to company management" can constitute a protected activity under Title VII. *Kotcher v. Rosa & Sullivan Appliance Ctr., Inc.*, 957 F.2d 59, 65 (2d Cir. 1992).

An adverse employment action in the retaliation context is one that "well might have dissuaded a reasonable worker from making or supporting a charge of discrimination." Burlington, 548 U.S. at 68 (citation omitted). This category of actions is broad and "extends beyond workplace-related or employment- related retaliatory acts and harm." Id. at 67. A plaintiff may demonstrate a causal connection between the protected activity and the adverse employment action (1) indirectly, by showing that the protected activity was followed closely by discriminatory treatment, or through other circumstantial evidence such as disparate treatment of fellow employees who engaged in similar conduct; or (2) directly, through evidence of retaliatory animus directed against the plaintiff by the defendant. Hicks, 593 F.3d at 170 (citation omitted). "An intervening event between the protected activity and the adverse employment action may defeat the inference of causation where temporal proximity might otherwise suffice to raise the inference." *Nolley v. Swiss Reinsurance Am. Corp.*, 857 F. Supp. 2d 441, 461 (S.D.N.Y. 2012), aff'd sub nom. *Nolley v. Swiss Re Am. Holding Corp.*, 523 F. App'x 53 (2d Cir. 2013) (citing cases).

Ahmed's two retaliation claims both stem from the same allegedly protected activity. Ahmed claims that the Museum retaliated against him for his actions and statements at the Tessitura conference, namely pulling Tran away from a female coworker and telling him that his behavior towards her was "not cool" and his reiteration to Tran the following day that "it really wasn't cool what happened last night." It will be assumed for the purposes of the analysis that follows that Ahmed's statements to Tran constituted protected activity.[NOTE 3] Ahmed challenges two adverse employment actions as unlawful retaliation. First, the Museum's failure to hire him for the permanent position and, second, the Museum's termination of his company's contract with the Museum. Both actions constitute materially adverse employment actions and may properly form the basis of retaliation complaints. Both claims fail, however, because Ahmed has not sufficiently demonstrated a causal connection between these actions and the claimed protected activity to raise a question of fact that would permit a rational fact finder to infer the requisite retaliatory motive.

1. Failure to Hire

Ahmed's first claim is that the Museum failed to hire him as a full-time software developer at the Museum in retaliation for his statements and actions opposing Tran's sexual advances towards a female coworker at the Tessitura conference. Because failure-to-hire claims do not require an employment relationship, regardless of whether Ahmed should be considered an employee of the museum for Title VII purposes, he may bring this failure-to-hire claim. Ahmed has not submitted sufficient evidence to satisfy the causation prong of his prima facie case of retaliatory refusal to hire. Ahmed argues that the temporal proximity between his alleged protected activity at the August 7-11 Tessitura conference and the Museum's August 22 decision not to hire him creates an inference of causation and is circumstantial evidence that the Museum's proffered non-discriminatory reason for not hiring him was pretextual.

Undisputed evidence of intervening events rebut any inference of causation created by the short period of time between the protected activity and the decision not to hire Ahmed. While Ahmed was informed of the Museum's decision not to hire him only twelve days after the conference at which the protected activity occurred, between those dates the Museum initiated and received the results of Ahmed's background check, which revealed that his stated educational background could not be confirmed. Young, in the Museum's HR department, had already interviewed Ahmed and she concluded that Ahmed had misrepresented his education. At that point the normal Museum procedure was to rescind the candidate's job offer. These events were entirely unrelated to Ahmed's protected activity, and explain why Ahmed was not hired as a Museum employee.

Ahmed argues that Tran manipulated the Museum into deciding not to hire him. Ahmed's best evidence for this is the series of conversations that occurred between Friday, August 19 and Monday, August 22. In their initial conversation on August 19 about Ahmed's misrepresentation of his educational background, Montes told Young he still wanted to hire Ahmed. But, after Montes and Tran spoke with Ahmed later that day, Montes called Young with Tran on the line either that Friday or early the following Monday and told her that he believed the Museum should not hire Ahmed. After this conversation, Young cancelled the additional HR interviews she had scheduled to determine if Ahmed's job application could be salvaged. Montes and Tran then informed Ahmed that he would not be hired. Ahmed speculates that Tran may have said something to Montes in a separate conversation that influenced Montes and caused him to retract his support of Ahmed's job application. A fact finder may not render a verdict based on speculation.

Speculation is insufficient to permit a rational factfinder to infer a retaliatory motive. There is no evidence that Montes was influenced by anything other than Ahmed's failure to explain to him the discrepancy between his educational credentials as claimed by him and reported by LIU. An employer is entitled to set its own standards for employment, see *Stern v. Trustees of Columbia Univ. in City of New York,* 131 F.3d 305, 313 (2d Cir. 1997), and there can be no dispute that honesty is an entirely valid, non-discriminatory requirement. This duty of honesty regarding educational credentials was particularly important since Ahmed did not even possess the bachelor's degree listed as a prerequisite for the position. Ahmed also points to testimony from co-workers about the strained relationship between Tran and Ahmed as circumstantial evidence of causation. While Ahmed does present evidence that others believed Tran did not want Ahmed to receive the job offer, he puts forward no evidence that Tran's observed animosity towards Ahmed was due to his protected behavior. In fact, one co-worker speculated that Tran was trying to derail Ahmed's job offer because Tran was intimidated by Ahmed's technical prowess and another claimed to have noticed increased tension between the two before the conference at which the protected activity took place. It is unnecessary to resolve, therefore, what portions of this co-worker testimony would be admissible at trial.

Finally, Ahmed attempts to show a causal connection by asserting that he was treated differently from other similarly situated job candidates who fail a background check because he was never provided the opportunity to have a post-background check interview with members of the HR team and generally because other candidates were hired despite misrepresentations regarding their education in their application materials. The parties agree that it is the Museum's practice to examine discrepancies in application materials on a case-by-case basis to determine whether the candidate should be hired. Ahmed argues that the Museum's August 22 cancellation of his additional HR interviews indicates that the Museum departed from its ordinary practices and treated him more harshly than other candidates who were interviewed multiple times by HR and that this difference in treatment is circumstantial evidence of causation. While differential treatment can serve as circumstantial evidence of causation, here, Ahmed has not presented evidence that permits a rational fact finder to conclude that he was treated differently than other candidates. The Museum states that when it discovers discrepancies it seeks to determine whether the applicant deliberately lied on their application or, instead, made a good-faith mistake. It points to examples of at least eight candidates who were not hired since 2012 because their application included discrepancies about educational achievements and asserts that where the Museum ultimately did hire individuals whose applications contained discrepancies, it was after either determining that the individual had a good faith belief that their representation was correct or the applicant corrected the error. In contrast, the Museum explains that after several discussions with Ahmed regarding the educational discrepancies on his application and independently calling LIU to attempt to verify Ahmed's education, Young concluded that she "did not believe Mr. Ahmed to be credible." Ahmed has presented no evidence of a similarly situated job applicant who was treated more generously than he. See *Graham v. Long Island R.R.*, 230 F.3d 34, 39 (2d Cir. 2000).

2. Termination of TEK, Inc. Contract

Ahmed's second retaliation claim arises from the termination of the TEK, Inc. contract. Unlike the failure-to-hire claim, Ahmed's claim that his contract was terminated in retaliation for his protected activity depends on whether Ahmed was an employee of the Museum. The parties dispute whether Ahmed was an independent contractor, working through his company TEK, Inc., or a Museum employee and both sides present evidence regarding the manner and circumstances of his work that speak to the thirteen factors articulated by the Supreme Court in Reid. 490 U.S. 730 (1989). See also *Knight v. State Univ. of New York at Stony Brook*, 880 F.3d 636, 643 (2d Cir. 2018).

Even if Ahmed were able to show that he should be considered a Museum employee, his contract termination claim fails. As with his failure-to-hire claim, the relative temporal proximity between the allegedly protected activity at the August 7-11 conference and the contract termination of September 9 is insufficient to create an inference of causation given intervening events. Ahmed's September 9 call to the Museum's Chief Digital Officer and the security concerns that this telephone call elicited immediately led to the termination of the TEK, Inc. contract. It is undisputed that Ahmed was disturbed in his call to the Officer and that she expressed fear he would damage the Museum's computer system. The undisputed evidence is that Ahmed's heated conversation with the Chief Digital Officer and her concerns regarding security were the cause of the contract termination.

The decision to end TEK, Inc.'s contract was made by Montes after he heard the Chief Digital Officer's security concerns about Ahmed and Ahmed has presented no evidence that either Montes or the Officer knew of his allegedly protected activity. Ahmed has also presented no evidence that Tran played any role in the Museum's decision to terminate the contract. When Montes and Tran told Ahmed on August 23 that he would not be hired, they reiterated that his contract work with the Museum would continue. Here, as in his failure-to-hire claim, any suggestion that Tran improperly influenced the decision to cancel the contract is mere speculation and insufficient to defeat summary judgment.

II. NYCHRL Retaliation Claims

The NYCHRL also makes it unlawful to retaliate against an employee for protected activity. "[T]o prevail on a retaliation claim under the NYCHRL, the plaintiff must show that she took an action opposing her employer's discrimination, and that, as a result, the employer engaged in conduct that was reasonably likely to deter a person from engaging in such action." *Mihalik v. Credit Agricole Cheuvreux N.A., Inc.*, 715 F.3d 102, 112 (2d Cir. 2013). Claims under the NYCHRL must be analyzed "separately and independently from any federal and state law claims, construing the NYCHRL's provisions broadly in favor of discrimination plaintiffs, to the extent such a construction is reasonably possible." Id. at 109 (citation omitted). Under the NYCHRL, "'opposing any practice' can include situations where a person, before the retaliatory conduct occurred, merely made clear her disapproval of the defendant's discrimination by communicating to him, in substance, that she thought his treatment of the victim was wrong." Id. at 112 (citation omitted).

Under the NYCHRL, "[t]he employer may present evidence of its legitimate, non-discriminatory motives to show the conduct was not caused by discrimination, but it is entitled to summary judgment on this basis only if the record establishes, as a matter of law, that discrimination played no role in its actions. Id. at 110 n.8 (citation omitted). "If the plaintiff responds with some evidence that at least one of the reasons proffered by the defendant is false, misleading, or incomplete... such evidence of pretext should in almost every case indicate to the court that a motion for summary judgment must be denied." *Bennett v. Health Mgt. Sys., Inc.*, 936 N.Y.S.2d 112, 124 (1st Dep't 2011).

For the reasons discussed above, the defendants' motion for summary judgment should also be granted as to Ahmed's NYCHRL retaliation claims. While the summary judgment standard for NYCHRL claims is more stringent than that for Title VII and the NYSHRL, plaintiffs must still establish a causal connection between the adverse employment action and the protected activity. As described above, Ahmed has failed to present evidence sufficient to permit a rational factfinder to find such a causal connection and so his NYCHRL claims must also fail.

CONCLUSION

The defendants' May 2, 2018 motion for summary judgment is granted.

NOTES:

NOTE 1: This was apparently a mistake on the part of the LIU registrar, because he later received a letter from LIU indicating that he had completed "all requirements" for an Associate's degree.

NOTE 2: This testimony is recited without analyzing the extent to which it might constitute admissible trial testimony.

NOTE 3: The Second Circuit has held that complaints made to the allegedly discriminating actor about the actor's discriminatory behavior do not satisfy the protected activity requirement when the actions are directed at non-employees. *Wimmer v. Suffolk Cty. Police Dep't*, 176 F.3d 125, 135 (2d Cir. 1999).

STUDY QUESTIONS

- In the Ahmed case, summarize the dispute. What does the plaintiff allege happened? What, in the plaintiff's opinion, was the reason for terminating his employment offer? What facts support the museum's position?
- What is the significance of whether the plaintiff was misclassified as an independent contractor? What factors does the plaintiff cite to establish his claim of "misclassification"?
- What claims does the plaintiff make regarding termination of his service contract?
- The court granted summary judgement for the museum. What was the basis for the court's decision?

Reading Note: The complaint reprinted below details another claim of employment discrimination brought against The American Museum of Natural History based on the actions of its CIO. In this case, the plaintiff, Peter Torres, had worked at the museum for ten years and had been granted workplace accommodations based on his medical condition in 2012. In his complaint, Torres alleges that harassment by his boss, based on his sexual orientation and health status, began in 2016.

TORRES V. THE AMERICAN MUSEUM OF NATURAL HISTORY

U. S. District Court, Southern District of New York, 17 CV 2825

(Filed April 20, 2017)

COMPLAINT

Plaintiff Peter Bryan Torres, by his counsel, The Harman Firm, LLP, alleges for his Complaint against Defendants The American Museum of Natural History and Juan Montes, individually, as follows:

PRELIMINARY STATEMENT

1. Plaintiff Peter Bryan Torres ("Plaintiff" or "Mr. Torres") worked at The American Museum of Natural History ("Corporate Defendant" or the "Museum") as the Administrative Manager for Information Technology & Office of the Chief Information Officer. Juan Montes ("Individual Defendant" or "Mr. Montes") (Individual and Corporate Defendants are hereinafter referred to collectively as "Defendants") is the Museum's Chief Information Officer and Mr. Torres's supervisor at the Museum.

2. Defendants subjected Mr. Torres to severe discrimination and harassment on the basis of his disability (HIV and narcolepsy) and sexual orientation (gay). After learning that Mr. Torres is HIV-positive, Mr. Montes began a campaign of harassment and discrimination against Mr. Torres. Among other things, he refused to touch or come near Mr. Torres, took away Mr. Torres's job responsibilities, screamed at Mr. Torres to "leave his medical shit at home," and made numerous highly offensive and discriminatory comments about Mr. Torres's sexual orientation and HIV status.

3. Plaintiff seeks damages and costs against Defendants for interfering with and retaliating against him for his exercise of his rights under the Family and Medical Leave Act ("FMLA"), 29 U.S.C. §§ 2601 et seq.

4. Plaintiff also seeks damages and costs against Defendants for discriminating against him on the basis of his disability by subjecting him to a hostile work environment and failing to provide him with a reasonable accommodation, in violation of the New York City Human Rights Law ("NYCHRL"), N.Y.C. Admin. Code § 8-101 et seq.

5. Plaintiff also seeks damages and costs against Defendants for subjecting him to a hostile work environment based on his sexual orientation, in violation of the NYCHRL.

6. Plaintiff also seeks damages and costs against Defendants for retaliating against him for his complaints of disability and sexual orientation discrimination and for his request for a reasonable accommodation, in violation of the NYCHRL.

7. Plaintiff also seeks damages and costs against Individual Defendant for intentional infliction of emotional distress, in violation of the New York State common law.

8. Plaintiff also seeks damages and costs against Corporate Defendant for taking unlawful deductions from his paycheck, in violation of the New York State Labor Law ("NYLL"), N.Y. Lab. Law § 193.

JURISDICTION AND VENUE

9. Pursuant to 28 U.S.C. § 1331, this Court has original jurisdiction over Plaintiff's claims arising under the FMLA.

10. Pursuant to 28 U.S.C. § 1332, this Court has supplemental jurisdiction over Plaintiff's NYCHRL, NYLL, and common law claims, as those claims are so related to the federal claims that they form part of the same case or controversy.

11. Pursuant to 28 U.S.C. § 1391(b), venue is proper in the United States District Court for the Southern District of New York, as a substantial part of the events giving rise to these claims occurred within this District.

TRIAL BY JURY

12. Plaintiff respectfully requests a trial before a jury.

PARTIES

13. Plaintiff, at all times relevant hereto, was and is a resident of Hudson County in the State of New Jersey.

14. Upon information and belief, at all times relevant hereto, Corporate Defendant was and is a not-for-profit corporation organized under the laws of the State of New York with its principal place of business located at Central Park West and 79th Street, New York, New York 10024.

15. Upon information and belief, at all times relevant hereto, Individual Defendant was and is Corporate Defendant's Chief Information Officer and a resident of Bronx County in the State of New York.

STATEMENT OF FACTS

16. Mr. Torres is diagnosed with HIV and narcolepsy.
17. Mr. Torres also suffers from a rare genetic mutation which causes his HIV symptoms to be particularly resistant to antiretroviral treatments.
18. Mr. Torres began working at the Museum on or about May 5, 2007.
19. Throughout his employment, Mr. Torres has been an outstanding, dedicated employee who has consistently fulfilled his job responsibilities, earning several promotions and raises over the course of his employment.
20. Mr. Torres's current position at the Museum is Administrative Manager for Information Technology & Office of the Chief Information Officer.
21. Mr. Torres, who is gay, has been out at work throughout his employment; all of his coworkers were aware of his sexual orientation.
22. In and around 2012, Mr. Torres requested a medical accommodation to allow him to continue to perform the essential functions of his job—namely, that he be allowed to arrive at work late and leave early when his medical conditions necessitated.
23. The Museum granted Mr. Torres's request.
24. For the next several years, the accommodation functioned without issue: Mr. Torres's accommodation had no effect on the Museum's business or efficiency, and the Museum had no complaints about Mr. Torres's performance.
25. In and around April 2015, the Museum hired Juan Montes as Chief Information Officer, and Mr. Montes became Mr. Torres's direct supervisor.
26. On or about May 23, 2016, Mr. Torres collapsed in his home around 5:30 p.m. due to HIV-related medical issues and was rushed to the emergency room.
27. Mr. Torres texted his colleagues, including Mr. Montes, around 7:00 p.m. to let them know that he was in the hospital.
28. That same evening, around 10:30 p.m., Mr. Montes called Mr. Torres at the hospital under the pretext that he was concerned for Mr. Torres's health, asking Mr. Torres what was going on.
29. Mr. Torres responded that he was still at the hospital, was scared, and was unsure what was happening, as he was still waiting to see test results.
30. Mr. Montes responded only, "Okay…should I contact HR?"
31. Mr. Torres replied that there was no need to contact HR, as HR was typically only notified about extended absences.

32. Mr. Montes responded, "Oh, okay, no problem, I just wanted to make sure," and ended the conversation.

33. Two days later, Mr. Torres returned to work.

34. Upon Mr. Torres's return to work, he updated Mr. Montes on his health and, in doing so, disclosed his HIV status to Mr. Montes for the first time.

35. Mr. Montes immediately confronted him aggressively, stating, "I should have been told what your medical issues are [referring to Mr. Torres's HIV status and narcolepsy]. I can't have your medical issues interfering with my vision for the Museum."

36. Mr. Montes then told Mr. Torres that he was a "danger" to Mr. Montes and Mr. Montes's children because Mr. Torres is HIV-positive.

37. Mr. Montes informed Mr. Torres that he had gone to HR the previous day and demanded that HR disclose to him Mr. Torres's full medical history, which HR refused to do.

38. Mr. Montes then told Mr. Torres that Mr. Montes "should have been given full disclosure of [Mr. Torres's] medical history upon being offered the position as Chief Information Officer" so that he could "decide whether [he] wanted to work with someone like [Mr. Torres]."

39. Mr. Torres told Mr. Montes that he was taking care of his health, that his medical conditions had never interfered with his work performance, and that he was certainly no "danger" to Mr. Montes or his children.

40. Mr. Montes again responded with vitriol and hostility, telling Mr. Torres, "I don't know that. I don't know anything about it!"

41. In an attempt to show Mr. Montes that he was proactive about managing his HIV treatment, Mr. Torres took out his cellphone to show Mr. Montes a cellphone application, MyChart, that Mr. Torres uses to keep track of his HIV treatment plan, monitor lab test results, and communicate with his doctors.

42. Mr. Montes grabbed Mr. Torres's cellphone out of Mr. Torres's hand and perused Mr. Torres's confidential and private medical history without authorization.

43. Later that day, Mr. Torres learned that Mr. Montes had told the Museum that Mr. Torres was "missing" and that "no one knew where he was" the day after Mr. Torres's hospitalization; Tarek Ahmed, an employee in Mr. Torres's department, asked Mr. Torres, "[Mr. Montes] said you were missing, what happened?"

44. Mr. Torres, surprised, responded, "I wasn't missing, I was in the hospital. When did he tell you that?"

45. Mr. Ahmed told Mr. Torres that Mr. Montes had made the comment the previous day—after Mr. Montes had personally spoken to Mr. Torres while Mr. Torres was in the hospital.

46. Mr. Torres formally complained to HR about the incident with Mr. Montes, specifically citing disability discrimination.

47. Mr. Torres spoke to Kala Harinarayanan, the Museum's Director of Environmental Health and Safety, who said that the Museum would "investigate."

48. The Museum, however, did not begin to investigate Mr. Torres's allegations until March 10, 2017—nearly one year after Mr. Torres's complaint.

49. After learning of Mr. Torres's HIV status, Mr. Montes began a campaign of harassment and discrimination against Mr. Torres and has done everything in his power to pressure Mr. Torres into leaving his position at the Museum.

50. Shortly after learning that Mr. Torres has HIV, Mr. Montes began to take away Mr. Torres's job responsibilities, reassigning Mr. Torres's tasks to less experienced employees.

51. Mr. Montes humiliated, ostracized, and harassed Mr. Torres on a daily basis.

52. Mr. Montes screamed at Mr. Torres to "leave his medical shit at home and out of the office" in reference to Mr. Torres's informing him that he is HIV-positive.

53. After learning of Mr. Torres's HIV status, Mr. Montes refused to speak with Mr. Torres unless absolutely necessary or to reprimand and harass him.

54. While Mr. Montes would make polite conversation with other employees and regularly gave other employees feedback and guidance, he now refused to meet with Mr. Torres or even say good morning to him.

55. If Mr. Montes needed to give instructions or assignments to Mr. Torres, he would go out of his way to avoid speaking to Mr. Torres personally, instead using another employee, such as Mr. Benedetto, to communicate with Mr. Torres.

56. Mr. Montes required Mr. Torres to notify everyone in the department when Mr. Torres needed to miss work due to his medical condition, yet did not require any other employees to do so.

57. Mr. Montes interfered with Mr. Torres's existing medical accommodation by creating burdensome, irregular procedures for Mr. Torres's use of his accommodation.

58. Upon information and belief, Mr. Montes pressured Museum HR into requiring Mr. Torres to submit excessive medical documentation in an effort to set Mr. Torres up so that Mr. Torres's accommodation request would be denied and he could be terminated.

59. Upon receiving the documents, HR (upon information and belief, at Mr. Montes's directive) then required Mr. Torres and his doctors to make extensive changes and edits to the submitted medical documentation before the Museum would accept it.

60. The Museum required Mr. Torres to submit such changes up to four times per month.

61. Even then, Mr. Montes refused to allow Mr. Torres to use his accommodation as agreed; Mr. Montes told Mr. Torres that he could not come in late or leave early because Mr. Torres was "out of sick time," even though Mr. Torres's accommodation consisted of being allowed to come in late or leave early when necessary.

62. At the same time, Mr. Montes allowed other employees to come in late or take time off work for non-medical reasons.

63. For example, he allowed Mike Benedetto, the Museum's Director of Information Technology and Deputy Chief Information Officer, to routinely come in late and to take time off for Boy Scout events.

64. On days that Mr. Torres had a scheduled doctor's appointment or needed to leave work early for medical reasons, Mr. Montes refused to allow him to take a lunch break or even eat at his desk, telling him that he was not allowed to eat lunch—even though Mr. Montes knew that such a restriction could endanger Mr. Torres's health.

65. No other employees in Mr. Torres's department were ever subjected to such a policy.

66. When Mr. Torres needed to arrive late to work for medical reasons, Mr. Montes deducted the time from his wages.

67. Again, to Mr. Torres's knowledge, no other employee in the department ever had their pay docked for leaving early for appointments.

68. In addition, all employees in Mr. Torres's department were allowed to work from home.

69. Mr. Torres's working from home had never previously been a problem, yet Mr. Montes suddenly revoked only Mr. Torres's ability to do so, taking away a right that every other employee enjoyed.

70. Mr. Montes intentionally attempted to sabotage Mr. Torres's work and set him up for termination by giving him unrealistic deadlines and impossible assignments.

71. For example, Mr. Montes claimed that Mr. Torres had mistakenly made travel arrangements and sent him to Syracuse for a meeting that was actually being held in Rochester.

72. Mr. Torres was shocked that he had made such a mistake. Afraid that he would be terminated, he apologized profusely to Mr. Montes and directly contacted the travel agency to find out more details about what had happened.

73. Upon contacting the travel agency, however, the travel agent forwarded Mr. Torres emails from Mr. Montes to the travel agency, in which Mr. Montes had requested that the agency arrange for Mr. Montes to travel to Syracuse.

74. In reality, Mr. Torres had made previous arrangements with the agency for Mr. Montes to travel to Rochester, and Mr. Montes had never traveled to Syracuse at all. The entire trip was a complete fabrication, intended to create an excuse for Mr. Montes to give Mr. Torres negative performance feedback.

75. Mr. Montes conspicuously avoided physical contact with Mr. Torres because of his HIV status.

76. Mr. Montes refused to touch or come near Mr. Torres, keeping his back to the wall and creating as much space as possible when speaking to Mr. Torres.

77. This highly offensive, discriminatory conduct was so obvious that Mr. Torres's coworkers noticed and made comments to Mr. Torres about Mr. Montes's behavior.

78. Sally Holt, an employee in Mr. Torres's department, witnessed Mr. Montes clinging to the wall in an exaggerated manner while speaking to Mr. Torres, as he had begun to do regularly while speaking to Mr. Torres.

79. Ms. Holt asked, "What the hell was that?" in reference to Mr. Montes's behavior.

80. Mr. Torres responded, "He does that whenever he sees me."

81. Mr. Torres's coworkers began to avoid Mr. Torres, as well, due to Mr. Montes's overt discrimination.

82. Mr. Montes would frown, visibly displeased, if anyone attempted to make polite conversation with Mr. Torres.

83. Gradually, Mr. Torres's coworkers began to speak to Mr. Torres in a whisper and cut short any friendly conversations with him, intimidated by Mr. Montes's behavior and open dislike of Mr. Torres.

84. When Mr. Torres sprayed Lysol in his workspace, Mr. Montes profusely thanked him in a sarcastic manner, implying that the air around Mr. Torres was contaminated because Mr. Torres has HIV.

85. Mr. Montes told Mr. Torres that Mr. Montes's brother was gay and that his family had disowned him because of it.

86. Mr. Torres later told Mr. Montes that he found it difficult to speak honestly with Mr. Montes about his disabilities or his sexual orientation, based on Mr. Montes's previous comments about Mr. Montes's brother and about HIV. Specifically, Mr. Torres raised concerns about Mr. Montes's potentially believing offensive, negative stereotypes about gay men who have HIV, namely that they somehow "deserve" or are at "fault" for being HIV-positive.

87. Mr. Montes refused to address Mr. Torres's concerns about discrimination and, in fact, confirmed Mr. Torres's fears, telling Mr. Torres, "You're right. That is how it's perceived."

88. On another occasion, Mr. Montes discouraged Mr. Torres's heterosexual coworkers from attempting to include Mr. Torres in a workplace conversation about celebrity crushes; when Mr. Benedetto mentioned a male athlete, Mr. Montes quickly cut him off, saying, "Hey, Mike, uh-uh," and shaking his head disapprovingly.

89. Before this, Mr. Torres's straight coworkers had always made efforts to include Mr. Torres in such conversations, and Mr. Torres had always been able to discuss his sexual orientation and relationships openly with his colleagues.

90. On June 12, 2016, Mr. Torres's cousin was killed in the mass shooting at the Pulse nightclub in Orlando, Florida.

91. Mr. Montes regularly used the department's expense budget to purchase flowers for other employees, but refused to do so for Mr. Torres.

92. Instead, Mr. Torres's coworkers had to go around the office, collecting money for the flowers.

93. In July 2016, Mr. Montes—who had previously given Mr. Torres only stellar performance reviews—gave him the lowest possible score, citing only "subpar performance."

94. Mr. Torres repeatedly asked Mr. Montes to elaborate on this "subpar performance," yet Mr. Montes refused to do so, telling Mr. Torres that he would "forgive it."

95. Eventually, after Mr. Torres insisted, Mr. Montes cited as the basis for the low score three times that Mr. Torres had arrived late to work.

96. However, each incident was covered by Mr. Torres's medical accommodation, which had been agreed upon with the Museum in 2012 and had functioned without issue for over four years.

97. Mr. Torres explained that the time off had been covered by his existing accommodation, sick leave, and FMLA leave, voicing his concerns that Mr. Montes's negative review was pretext for disability discrimination.

98. Mr. Montes responded only, "But if it were not FMLA days, I could terminate you, right?"

99. Mr. Torres, confused by Mr. Montes's bizarre response, asked what he meant.

100. Mr. Montes said, "If I didn't know about your medical condition, then I could terminate you, right?"

101. Mr. Torres complained to HR and to Mr. Montes, yet nothing was done, and the discrimination and harassment continued unabated.

102. Mr. Torres began to experience severe anxiety and depression related to the ongoing discrimination, including suicidal ideation related to fears of losing his job and health insurance coverage, difficulty sleeping, headaches, a variety of gastrointestinal symptoms including nausea and vomiting blood, loss of appetite, and feelings of shame, hopelessness, and pessimism.

103. In August 2016, Mr. Torres had a seizure as a result of the discriminated-related stress.

104. The seizure caused Mr. Torres to fall and tear multiple ligaments in his knee.

105. The injury was so severe that it necessitated reconstructive surgery, which is still pending.

106. Mr. Torres needed to take time off work due to his injury.

107. When Mr. Torres returned to work in December 2016, he was still recovering from the injury and relied on a cane to walk.

108. Upon seeing this, Mr. Montes openly mocked Mr. Torres, commenting, "Oh my God, now he even has a cane?!"

109. After the Museum failed to respond to Mr. Torres's complaints, Mr. Torres retained counsel.

110. A litigation hold letter was sent to the Museum on or about March 9, 2017.

111. Only thereafter did the Museum commence the "investigation" that it had said would begin in May 2016, nearly a year earlier.

112. The investigation involved a six-hour interview of Mr. Torres.

113. The only result of the Museum's investigation was an email to Mr. Torres from the Museum's HR, telling Mr. Torres that if he did not immediately return to work, the Museum would stop paying him.

114. Far from disciplining Mr. Montes or taking any action to address Mr. Torres's complaints, the Museum's response utterly failed to address the ongoing discrimination harassment in any way whatsoever, yet it simultaneously demanded that he return to the abusive and unabated hostile work environment. As such, Mr. Torres has been constructively terminated from his position at the Museum.

115. Mr. Montes and the Museum have made Mr. Torres's working conditions so difficult and unpleasant that a reasonable person in his shoes would have felt compelled to resign.

CAUSES OF ACTION FIRST CAUSE OF ACTION

Interference in Violation of the FMLA
(Against All Defendants)

116. Plaintiff hereby realleges and incorporates each and every allegation contained in paragraphs 1 through 115 with the same force as though separately alleged herein.

117. The FMLA prohibits an employer from interfering with, restraining, or denying the exercise of (or attempts to exercise) any rights provided by the FMLA.

118. Defendants interfered with Plaintiff's exercise of his rights under the FMLA by refusing to allow him to use leave to which he was entitled under the FMLA.

119. As such, Defendants have violated the FMLA.

120. As a direct and proximate consequence of Defendants' FMLA interference, Plaintiff has suffered, and continues to suffer, substantial damages, including, but not limited to, emotional distress and suffering, all in amounts to be determined at trial.

SECOND CAUSE OF ACTION

Retaliation in Violation of the FMLA
(Against All Defendants)

121. Plaintiff hereby realleges and incorporates each and every allegation contained in paragraphs 1 through 120 with the same force as though separately alleged herein.

122. The FMLA prohibits an employer from retaliating against an employee for having exercised or attempted to exercise any FMLA right.

123. Defendants retaliated against Plaintiff for his exercise of, and his attempts to exercise, his rights under the FMLA by subjecting him to discrimination and harassment and prohibiting him from taking further advantage of his FMLA rights.

124. As such, Defendants have violated the FMLA.

125. As a direct and proximate consequence of Defendants' retaliation, Plaintiff has suffered, and continues to suffer, substantial damages, including, but not limited to, emotional distress and suffering, all in amounts to be determined at trial.

THIRD CAUSE OF ACTION

Disability Discrimination in Violation of the NYCHRL
(Against All Defendants)

126. Plaintiff hereby realleges and incorporates each and every allegation contained in paragraphs 1 through 125 with the same force as though separately alleged herein.

127. The NYCHRL prohibits an employer from discriminating against an employee because of that employee's actual or perceived disability.

128. Defendants discriminated against Plaintiff based on his disability by subjecting him to a hostile work environment, including making discriminatory and harassing comments and treating him less well than other employees.

129. As such, Defendants have violated the NYCHRL.

130. As a direct and proximate consequence of Defendants' disability discrimination, Plaintiff has suffered, and continues to suffer, substantial damages, including, but not limited to, emotional distress and suffering, all in amounts to be determined at trial.

FOURTH CAUSE OF ACTION

Sexual Orientation Discrimination in Violation of the NYCHRL
(Against All Defendants)

131. Plaintiff hereby realleges and incorporates each and every allegation contained in paragraphs 1 through 130 with the same force as though separately alleged herein.

132. The NYCHRL prohibits an employer from discriminating against an employee because of that employee's actual or perceived sexual orientation.

133. Defendants discriminated against Plaintiff based on his sexual orientation by subjecting him to a hostile work environment, including making discriminatory and harassing comments and treating him less well than other employees.

134. As such, Defendants have violated the NYCHRL.

135. As a direct and proximate consequence of Defendants' sexual orientation discrimination, Plaintiff has suffered, and continues to suffer, substantial damages, including, but not limited to, emotional distress and suffering, all in amounts to be determined at trial.

FIFTH CAUSE OF ACTION

Failure to Provide a Reasonable Accommodation in Violation of the NYCHRL (Against All Defendants)

136. Plaintiff hereby realleges and incorporates each and every allegation contained in paragraphs 1 through 135 with the same force as though separately alleged herein.

137. The NYCHRL requires an employer to engage in a mandatory interactive process to identify a reasonable accommodation for an employee with a disability.

138. Defendants failed to provide a reasonable accommodation for Plaintiff's disability by interfering with his use of his existing accommodation and refusing to engage in the mandatory interactive process to identify any other accommodation.

139. As such, Defendants have violated the NYCHRL.

140. As a direct and proximate consequence of Defendants' failure to provide a reasonable accommodation for his disability, Plaintiff has suffered, and continues to suffer, substantial damages, including, but not limited to, emotional distress and suffering, all in amounts to be determined at trial.

SIXTH CAUSE OF ACTION

Retaliation in Violation of the NYCHRL (Against All Defendants)

141. Plaintiff hereby realleges and incorporates each and every allegation contained in paragraphs 1 through 140 with the same force as though separately alleged herein.

142. The NYCHRL prohibits an employer from retaliating against an employee for engaged in protected activity under the NYCHRL.

143. Plaintiff engaged in protected activity under the NYCHRL when he requested a reasonable accommodation and when he properly complained to Defendants of disability and sexual orientation discrimination.

144. Defendants retaliated against Plaintiff by, among other things, subjecting him to further discrimination and harassment, interfering with his use of a reasonable accommodation, and refusing to correct the discriminatory behavior.

145. As such, Defendants violated the NYCHRL.

146. As a direct and proximate consequence of Defendants' retaliation, Plaintiff has suffered, and continues to suffer, substantial damages, including, but not limited to, emotional distress and suffering, all in amounts to be determined at trial.

SEVENTH CAUSE OF ACTION

Intentional Infliction of Emotional Distress
in Violation of the New York State Common Law
(Against Individual Defendant)

147. Plaintiff hereby realleges and incorporates each and every allegation contained in paragraphs 1 through 146 with the same force as though separately alleged herein.

148. Individual Defendant subjected Plaintiff to extreme and outrageous conduct, including near-constant abuse and harassment concerning Plaintiff's disability and sexual orientation.

149. Individual Defendant intended his actions to cause, or disregarded a substantial probability that his actions would cause, severe emotional distress to Plaintiff.

150. As a direct result of Individual Defendant's conduct, Plaintiff has suffered severe emotional distress leading to significant medical and psychological consequences, including a seizure and persistent suicidal ideation.

EIGHTH CAUSE OF ACTION

Unlawful Wage Deductions in Violation of NYLL § 193
(Against Corporate Defendant)

151. Plaintiff hereby realleges and incorporates each and every allegation contained in paragraphs 1 through 150 with the same force as though separately alleged herein.

152. NYLL § 193 prohibits an employer from making any deduction from the wages of an employee unless permitted by law or by the employee.

153. Corporate Defendant deducted Plaintiff's wages for needing to arrive late to work for medical reasons, without Plaintiff's consent.

154. As such, Corporate Defendant has violated the NYLL.

155. As a direct and proximate consequence of Corporate Defendant's NYLL violations, Plaintiff has suffered, and continues to suffer, substantial damages, all in amounts to be determined at trial.

REQUEST FOR RELIEF

WHEREFORE, Plaintiff respectfully requests the following relief:

A. For the first cause of action, damages to be determined at trial;

B. For the second cause of action, damages to be determined at trial;

C. For the third cause of action, damages to be determined at trial;

D. For the fourth cause of action, damages to be determined at trial;

E. For the fifth cause of action, damages to be determined at trial;

F. For the sixth cause of action, damages to be determined at trial;

G. For the seventh cause of action, damages to be determined at trial; and

H. For the eighth cause of action, damages to be determined at trial;

I. For such other and further relief as the Court deems just and proper.

Dated: New York, New York April 19, 2017

By: Walker G. Harman , Jr., Edgar M. Rivera
THE HARMAN FIRM , LLP
Attorneys for Plaintiff

STUDY QUESTIONS

- In the *Torres* complaint, what federal and state employment law violations does the plaintiff allege?
- What accommodations had been made by the museum to address the plaintiff's medical condition? What changed?
- In what ways does the plaintiff allege he was treated differently from other employees?
- Torres states that he filed a complaint with the museum's human resources department. What steps did the HR department take and when?
- Assess the likelihood that the plaintiff will prevail if the case goes to trial. What are the strengths and weaknesses of the plaintiff's case?

- Both the *Ahmed* lawsuit and the *Torres* complaint were brought against the American Museum of Natural History. Compare and contrast the situations in the two cases and assess the working conditions at the museum. What advice can you give the museum to help ensure that these employment disputes do not happen again?

Reading Note: The following case deals with workplace safety in museums. While the health and safety of museum employees are typically regulated by federal and state labor and occupational safety rules, in this case the museum was a former operating coal mine. As such, it presents an interesting twist involving the application of federal mine safety regulations as well as OSHA requirements.

SECRETARY OF LABOR V. THE NATIONAL COAL MUSEUM

OSHRC Docket No. 99-2240 Before: Adm. Law Judge Ken S. Welsch

(August 17, 2001)

DECISION AND ORDER

The National Coal Museum (Museum), a nonprofit corporation, operated a mine museum for public tours in an abandoned underground coal mine in southern Illinois until January 14, 2000. Prior to its closing in January, 2000, the Museum received serious and willful citations on November 29, 1999, after an inspection by the Occupational Safety and Health Administration (OSHA). The Museum timely contested the citations.

The serious citation alleges that the Museum violated § 5(a)(1) (item 1) of the Occupational Safety and Health Act (Act) for failing to examine and inspect the underground intake air courses and seals in their entirety; § 5(a)(1) (item 2) of the Act for failing to equip the hoist skip with a safety catch or equivalent; and 29 C.F.R. § 1910.307(b) (item 3) for having unprotected incandescent light bulbs and electric circuits in the underground tour area. A penalty of $2,100 is proposed for each alleged violation.

The willful citation alleges that the Museum violated § 5(a)(1) (item 1) of the Act for failing to adequately support the roof at numerous locations in the underground travelways. A penalty of $21,000 is proposed.

The hearing was held in Chicago, Illinois, on November 15-17 and December 5-8, 2000. The Museum is represented pro se by its owner, Dr. Christopher Ledvina. At the hearing, the Secretary withdrew item 2 of serious Citation no. 1 (Tr. 31). Also, the parties stipulate that during the applicable period, the Museum employed employees and was in a business which affected commerce within the meaning of the Act (Tr. 20, 32). Jurisdiction and coverage is established.[NOTE 1] The parties filed post-hearing briefs.

The Museum denies the alleged violations, their classifications and the reasonableness of the proposed penalties. The Museum argues that OSHA's jurisdiction was preempted by Federal and state mine laws, pursuant to § 4(b)(1) of the Act. Also, the Museum claims unreasonable inspection by OSHA, in violation of § 8(a) of the Act, and vindictive prosecution.

The Museum's preemption, vindictive prosecution, and unreasonable inspection defenses are rejected. However, based on the record, items 1 and 3 of serious Citation no. 1 are vacated. Item 1 of willful Citation no. 2 is affirmed as serious and a penalty of $5,000 is assessed.

BACKGROUND

On May 7, 1996, the Museum obtained an abandoned underground coal mine in West Frankfort, Illinois. Mine #25 had been owned by the Old Ben Mine Company since 1978 and had produced coal for sale until October, 1994. After acquiring the property, the Museum[NOTE 2] converted the underground coal mine into an exhibition and tourist attraction. The Museum re-opened the underground mine for public tours on August 15, 1996 (Tr. 551, 549, 1411, 1461). When it closed in January, 2000, there were four employees with underground duties and three employees in the office (Tr. 981, 1464).

The Museum's owner and chairman of the board was Dr. Christopher Ledvina.[NOTE 3] Janet Howe, co-founder, was the secretary/treasurer (Tr. 1312). The Museum's superintendent was William Bullock, a former miner with 37 years of coal mine experience (Tr. 982, 984). The Museum employed other experienced miners to maintain the underground facilities, operate the hoist, and act as tour guides (Tr. 981, 1076, 1089, 1334, 1369). The former miners held certificates as hoist operators, mine examiners and mine managers (Tr. 1111). During its peak, the Museum employed approximately 22 employees (Tr. 1464).

Mine #25 covered approximately 18 square miles (Tr. 1141-1142). The Museum's above ground facilities included a parking lot, a large hoist capable of carrying 40 people below ground, and a large metal building which housed the hoist drive mechanism, an old miners' washroom, and a gift store (Exh. R-5; Tr. 65, 1092-1093). The hoist was located at "B" shaft, which also functioned as the air upcast and downcast for the underground mine's ventilation system. "A" shaft functioned as a downcast (Tr. 63, 129, 516-517, 780, 1119).

The underground mine, approximately 600 feet below ground, consisted of a maze of connecting tunnels referred to as passageways, travelways and crosscuts (Exh. C-2; Tr.

1093, 1410). Approximately 68 concrete seals[NOTE 4] had been placed in tunnels around the perimeter to separate the unused areas of the abandoned mine from the Museum. The Museum comprised an area approximately 2,300 feet by 1,000 feet[NOTE 5] (Tr. 503, 890-891, 1087). The public tour area covered approximately 400 feet by 800 feet (Tr. 1101). The tour area had displays showing an actual mine collapse and mine equipment such as the continuous miner (Exh. C-2; Tr. 248, 1095-1098). The tour area started at the hoist in "B" shaft and was identified by yellow ropes, hanging lights and a chainlink screen along the roof (Tr. 57, 248, 1046-1047). In three years of operation, over 70,000 visitors had toured the underground mine (Tr. 1002, 1409).

From the Museum's inception, the State of Illinois, Division of Minerals and Mines, conducted regular inspections of the underground facilities under the Illinois Coal Mining Act (Exh. C-32). State mine inspector Jerry Odle conducted no less than 36 inspections prior to September 20, 1999. During his inspection, Odle prepared written inspection reports and gave copies to the Museum (Exh. R-10; Tr. 494, 536).

During the summer of 1999, the Museum began experiencing financial problems. In an attempt to raise money and awareness, Dr. Ledvina moved into the underground mine for thirty days in August, 1999. The Museum was also seeking financial assistance from the state (Exhs. C-41, C-42; Tr. 1415, 1464). According to Dr. Ledvina, the governor's office became interested and designated a task force to consider state funding. After the state declined, the Museum was visited by the state police, state fire marshals and state department of revenue (Tr. 1380, 1417-1418, 1465-1466).

After an underground inspection on September 20, 1999, state mine inspector Odle issued the Museum an Order to Comply requiring corrections by September 26 in the roof support system and the water pump (Exhs. C-1, C-9). On September 27, Odle issued the Museum a Notice closing the mine to the public until the corrections were made (Exh. C-17). The Museum began some repair work (Tr. 103, 105, 143, 688, 989).

OSHA received a referral on September 30, 1999, from the Illinois Division of Minerals and Mines (Tr. 1163, 1177-1178). On October 1, 1999, OSHA compliance officer (CO) Cynthia Wagner initiated an inspection of the Museum (Tr. 54). CO Wagner, who lacked coal mining experience, was accompanied by state mine inspector Odle (Tr. 55, 109, 113). Superintendent Bullock participated in the opening conference and a portion of the walkaround inspection (Tr. 56, 58). After spending approximately three hours underground, CO Wagner issued the Museum a Notice of Imminent Danger[NOTE 6] identifying as hazards unsafe roof support and the Museum's failure to inspect seals. The Notice of Imminent Danger referenced the state's inspection and closure Notice (Exh. C-3; Tr. 68, 115).

CO Wagner attempted to continue the OSHA inspection on October 6, 1999, but the Museum refused entry to state mine inspector Odle (Tr. 69-70). CO Wagner re-entered the mine on October 7 with OSHA compliance officer Greg Malone, who had previously been an inspector with the Federal Mine Safety and Health Administration (MSHA) (Tr. 71). On October 8, Dr. Ledvina called OSHA and refused entry to further OSHA inspections (Tr. 72). On October 12, the U.S. Magistrate granted OSHA an inspection warrant (Exhs. C-4, C-5). Other entries into the mine were made by OSHA on October 13, October 20, and November 5 (Tr. 75-76, 152, 275, 778). The underground inspections were delayed because of a problem with the hoist[NOTE 7] (Exhs. C-6, C-7; Tr. 353).

OSHA's inspections involved at least three OSHA inspectors, the state mine inspector, and an MSHA inspector. Additionally, OSHA and MSHA inspectors observed activities of employees above ground from the gift store and parking lot during a three-week period when the hoist was not operating (Tr. 153, 474, 1302-1303).

As a result of OSHA's inspections, serious and willful citations were issued to the Museum on November 29, 1999, alleging in part a failure to inspect seals and air courses in their entirety, to protect light bulbs and conduit, and to adequately support the roof. The Museum went out of business on January 14, 2000 (Tr. 1377). During its operation, the Museum had no employees' lost time injuries or injuries to the public (Tr. 705, 1408).

DISCUSSION

In addition to disputing the violations and proposed penalties, the Museum has asserted as affirmative defenses preemption under § 4(b)(1) of the Act, unreasonable OSHA inspection under § 8(a) of the Act, and vindictive prosecution.

A. Preemption under § 4(b)(1) of the Act

The Museum argues that it was exempted from the requirements of the Act because OSHA's jurisdiction was preempted by the Mine Safety and Health Administration (MSHA), and by the Illinois Division of Minerals and Mines' enforcement of the state Coal Mining Act (Museum's Closing Brief, pp. 14-34).

There is no dispute that prior to the Museum obtaining mine #25, it was owned by the Old Ben Coal Company. Old Ben had extracted coal for sale from the mine from 1978 until October 14, 1994. When the mine was owned by Old Ben, it was regularly inspected by MSHA. After the Museum acquired mine #25 on May 7, 1996, it was inspected by Illinois Division of Minerals and Mines until October 20, 1999. The Museum was not inspected by MSHA (Exhs. R-6, R-10, Tr. 494,549, 826, 891, 896).

OSHA's jurisdiction is limited by § 4(b)(1) of the Act, which provides:

> Nothing in this Act shall apply to working conditions of employees with respect to which other Federal agencies and State agencies acting under section 274 of the Atomic Energy Act of 1954, as amended (42 U.S.C. 2021), exercise statutory authority to prescribe or enforce standards or regulations affecting occupational safety and health.

In order to establish preemption under §4(b)(1), the employer must show that an agency other than OSHA possesses the statutory authority to regulate the health and safety of workers and that the other agency has taken action to exercise the authority by promulgating regulations to exempt the particular working conditions. Northwest Airlines, Inc., 8 BNA OSHC 1982 (No. 1367,1980). Even if another agency has exercised authority, OSHA's jurisdiction is preempted only as to those working conditions actually covered by the other agency's regulations. Alaska Trawl Fisheries, Inc., 15 BNA OSHC 1699, 1703-1704 (No. 89-1192, 1992).

To determine whether OSHA's jurisdiction is preempted , the analysis involves: (1) whether the federal or state agency has enforcement authority to regulate the working conditions of employees; (2) whether a regulation has been promulgated by the Federal or state agency; and (3) whether the regulation promulgated covers the specific "working conditions" at issue. Bush & Burchett, Inc., 117 F.3d 932, 936 (6th Cir. 1996).

MSHA Jurisdiction

MSHA's jurisdiction is governed by the Federal Mine Safety and Health Act (FMSHA). The purpose of FMSHA is to provide for the safe working conditions of miners in mines, including underground coal mines. FMSHA at § 802(h)(1) defines a "coal or other mine" to mean:

> (A) an area of land from which minerals are extracted in nonliquid form or, if in liquid form, are extracted with workers underground, (B) private ways and roads appurtenant to such area, and (C) lands, excavations, underground passageways, shafts, slopes, tunnels and workings, structures, facilities, equipment, machines, tools, or other property including impoundments, retention dams, and tailings ponds, on the surface or underground, used in, or to be used in, or resulting from, the work of extracting such minerals from their natural deposits in nonliquid form, or if in liquid form, with workers underground, or used in, or to be used in, the milling of such minerals, or the work of preparing coal or other minerals, and includes custom coal preparation facilities.

To avoid confusion regarding any overlap in jurisdiction, OSHA and MSHA signed an Interagency Agreement on March 29, 1979. In accordance with the Interagency Agreement, OSHA also issued an Instruction CPL 2.42 on March 14, 1980 (Exh. R-8). As stated in the Instruction, the interagency agreement is "designed to clarify situations involving overlapping jurisdiction between MSHA and OSHA with respect to the health and safety of miners." The agreement describes MSHA jurisdiction as promulgating and enforcing "safety and health standards regarding working conditions of employees engaged in underground and surface mineral extraction (mining), related operations, and preparation and milling of the minerals extracted." FMSHA identifies three mining activities, including extracting, milling minerals, and preparing coal or other minerals. *Lancashire Coal Co. v. MSHA*, 968 F.2d 388, 390 (3rd Cir. 1992) (MSHA lacked jurisdiction over an abandoned coal silo).

The Museum did not operate mine #25 for coal extraction, milling, or preparation. The Museum's business did not involve mining coal or other minerals for commercial purposes (Tr. 550, 732, 826, 1100). The pieces of coal that were picked up by tourists from the mine floor or sold in the gift store were not from extraction or milling operations (Tr. 578, 913-914). Such pieces of coal were incidental to the Museum's purpose as a tourist attraction. The Museum's employees were not mining coal. The employees were tour guides (Tr. 250, 1076). The Museum's business was tourism (Tr. 577). The Museum was a nonprofit business, and its funding did not come from the sale of coal (Tr. 19, 37). Its funding came from donations, admissions, memberships, and the gift store (Tr. 1125). Its state permit was to operate a mine museum, not a coal mine (Tr. 1411).

Superintendent Bullock described the Museum as "in the tourism business." He testified that "[w]e were a museum. We would take people underground and show them the underground workings of an actual coal mine" (Tr. 982). The Museum did not refer to or try to comply with MSHA regulations (Tr. 1003).

From its inception, the Museum had been informed that MSHA lacked jurisdiction and would not make inspections (Tr. 6, 828, 878, 990, 1008, 1133-1134, 1332). On November 10, 1999, MSHA specifically wrote the Museum that it had no jurisdiction over mine #25 (Exh. R-7). MSHA had changed mine #25's status to permanently abandoned when the Museum took possession (Exh. R-6; Tr. 827, 898). The Museum was not given a new mine identification number by MSHA (Tr. 878, 1143).

Also, the initial reference to MSHA regulations in the OSHA citations issued to the Museum does not establish preemption. As described by assistant area director Janis Barrier, MSHA standards were identified as the basis for correcting the hazards (Tr. 1211).

OSHA's jurisdiction was not preempted by MSHA. The Museum was not mining coal; it was an exhibition facility for public tours (Tr. 555). The mining of coal had ceased when the Old Ben Mine Company closed its operation.

State Jurisdiction

OSHA's jurisdiction was also not preempted by the Illinois Division of Minerals and Mines' enforcement of the Coal Mining Act. Under § 4(b)(1), OSHA is preempted by state agencies acting under § 274 of the Atomic Energy Act of 1954, as amended (42 U.S.C. 2021). The Illinois Division of Minerals and Mines was not shown to be such a state agency.

Illinois is also not acting under OSHA's state planned system (Tr. 1301). Section 18 of the Act provides that states, if approved, have authority to conduct OSHA inspections. Illinois is within the Federal system and is not a state planned state (29 C.F.R. Part 1952). The state agency did not have authority to regulate employees' safety and health pursuant to § 18 of the Act.

Although the state agency made regular inspections, its state Coal Mining Act is similar to FMSHA in that coverage is limited to the extraction of coal. Section 103 of the Illinois Coal Mining Act defines a "mine and coal mine" to mean:

any area of land and any structures, facilities, machinery, tools, equipment, shafts, slopes, tunnels, excavations, and other property, real or personal, placed upon, under or above the surface of such land by any person, used in, or to be used in, or resulting from, the work of extracting in such area bituminous coal, lignite, or anthracite, from its natural deposits in the earth by any means or method including the method known as carbon recovery, and the work of preparing the coal so extracted, and includes custom coal preparation facilities (Exh. C-32).

As stated, the Museum was not engaged in extracting coal (Tr. 732). The Museum did not record the sale of coal with the state (Tr. 740). As noted by state inspector Odle, Federal MSHA and the Illinois Division of Minerals and Mines inspect the same mines (Tr. 727, 993). When the state agency referred the matter to OSHA, Illinois had decided to stop inspecting the mine (Tr. 671, 683, 686). OSHA's jurisdiction was not preempted by the state agency (Tr. 1210, 1301).

B. Reasonableness of OSHA's Inspection under § 8(a) of the Act

The Museum alleges that OSHA's inspection was unreasonable because of the number of inspectors (OSHA, MSHA, and state) used and the number of days it took to complete the inspection. Such activity disrupted the Museum's business and eventually closed it. The Museum also argues that OSHA's inspection (1) forced Museum employees to enter dangerous areas of the mine, (2) diverted its employees during remediation efforts, (3) was conducted on weekends and overnight, and (4) took photographs underground without permission. The Museum seeks to dismiss the citations.

Section 8(a) of the Act directs that OSHA's inspection be conducted in a reasonable manner, at reasonable times, and within reasonable limits. To establish the affirmative defense, the employer must have evidence of unreasonable conduct by OSHA during the inspection. Hamilton Fixture, 16 BNA OSHC 1073, 1077 (No. 88-1720, 1993). The record must show that OSHA substantially failed to comply with the provisions of § 8(a), and such noncompliance substantially prejudiced the Museum. Gem Industrial, Inc., 17 BNA OSHC 1185 (No. 93-1122, 1995). Evidence that an OSHA compliance officer conducted an inspection to harass an employer can be relevant to a § 8(a) defense. See Quality Stamping Products Co., 7 BNA OSHC 1285, 1287, n. 6 (No. 78-235, 1979).

Based on many years of reviewing OSHA cases, OSHA's inspection of the Museum does at first glance appear excessive as compared to a "typical" OSHA inspection. For this inspection, OSHA used at least three OSHA inspectors, numerous (6-8) MSHA inspectors and a state mine inspector (Tr. 419, 1001). OSHA conducted approximately five underground inspections (October 1, 7, 13, 20 and November 5) and spent an additional three weeks above ground observing employees (Tr. 153, 474, 1302). Also, OSHA issued an imminent danger notice after its first visit to the mine and obtained an inspection warrant after the second underground inspection. Such extensive activity by OSHA is viewed in the context of a small nonprofit employer with less than ten employees operating a public tourist attraction. The Museum had never been previously inspected by OSHA. It had regularly been inspected by the state and was under a state closure Order when OSHA initiated its inspection. OSHA assistant area director Janis Barrier described it as a "unique inspection" (Tr. 1288-1289).

Despite this appearance, OSHA's inspection was not unreasonable under § 8(a) of the Act. OSHA had jurisdiction and had received a valid referral of unsafe conditions underground from the state. OSHA inspectors, who lacked mining experience, needed to rely upon mine inspectors from MSHA and the state for technical assistance (Tr. 1245). Such reliance was reasonable and justified. The delays in OSHA's inspection, in part, were due to the Museum's insistence on an inspection warrant and the failure of the mine hoist to operate. Also, the conditions underground and OSHA's safety concerns, not only for the Museum's employees but also for its own inspectors, made the inspection more complex. There is no showing that OSHA forced any person into dangerous areas. Superintendent Bullock testified that at no time was he told by OSHA to walk under unsupported roof. In fact, OSHA warned him not be expose himself to roof hazards (Tr. 304-305, 1025-1026). Assistant area director Janis Barrier explained that the need for additional inspection days underground was because of OSHA's attempt to ascertain proper abatement methods (Tr. 1245). The Act sets no limitation on the number of days an inspection can take. Also, the alleged violations for the most part were cited under the General Duty Clause at § 5(a)(1) of the Act. These factors made the inspection more difficult, requiring more days and more personnel than other OSHA inspections.

With regard to photographs, the record fails to show that OSHA was advised not to take them. The Museum had no signs posted. Also, OSHA took precautions before taking photographs, including measuring methane levels (Tr. 291).

Any disruption to the Museum's business was not unreasonable. The Museum was already closed to public tours based on the state's closure notice. Other than superintendent Bullock, other Museum employees were not involved in the OSHA inspection. During the initial inspection, Bullock even chose not to participate in a portion of the walk around (Tr. 56).

OSHA's affect on the Museum's time was not unreasonable. Although the hoist operator was required to remain at the hoist while people were underground, OSHA's underground inspections were less than three hours (Tr. 110, 276). The repair work by Museum employees was not hindered. OSHA's inspection was during normal business hours.

Section 8(a) of the Act was not violated. The Museum's real problem was the lack of funds for materials and manpower and not the OSHA inspection (Tr. 439, 1064).

C. Vindictive Prosecution

The Museum alleges that OSHA's inspection was vindictive because it was based on an improperly motivated referral by the Illinois Division of Minerals and Mines. The Museum argues that OSHA's inspection was initiated before it had corrected the conditions noted in the state's Order to comply (Museum's Closing Brief, p. 10). The Museum seeks to dismiss the citations.

"Vindictive prosecution is a prosecution to deter or punish the exercise of a protected statutory or constitutional right." *United States v. Goodwin*, 457 U.S. 368, 372 (1982). There must be a showing that OSHA's action was taken in response to an exercise of a protected right. "If government misconduct is found, the court can dismiss the vindictively motivated charge or the entire action." National Engineering & Contracting Co., 18 BNA OSHC 1075, 1077 (No. 94-2787, 1997) (vindictive prosecution not found despite evidence that OSHA had referred to the employer as a "bad actor" and that OSHA would "play hardball" to "get them"). "In addition to evidence of animus or retaliatory motive," the party "must produce evidence tending to show that it would not have been cited absent that motive." Id. at 1078.

The record in this case does not support a vindictive prosecution defense. The Museum has not identified any protected right it exercised that caused OSHA to conduct its inspection and issue citations. OSHA received the referral from a state agency and it was obligated to investigate the allegations. The Museum's claim relates to the state's motivation in making the referral to OSHA, not OSHA's motivation to inspect. OSHA was required to inspect the Museum based on information of possible safety and health violations. Even an improperly motivated complaint is not in itself sufficient grounds for invalidating the inspection. Quality Stamping Products, 7 BNA 1285, 1287 (No. 78-235, 1979).

The Museum was repeatedly inspected by state mine inspectors and visited by state auditors, state police and the Governor's office. Such state activity was not caused by OSHA. Until the referral, there is no showing that OSHA was even aware of the Museum's activity. There had been no previous OSHA inspections.

OSHA's decision to inspect and prosecute was based upon normal factors ordinarily considered in determining the proper course to pursue. National Engineering, 18 BNA at 1079. For the most part, the conditions cited by OSHA, including the failure to inspect the seals in their entirety and inadequate roof support, are undisputed. The record from the inspection supports a prima facie showing of violative conditions.

Alleged Violations

Serious Citation No. 1
Item 1 - Inadequate Inspections of Seals and Air Course

The citation alleges that the Museum did not examine and inspect in their entirety the northeast, east, and west intake air courses and 57 of the concrete seals. The alleged violation is cited under § 5(a)(1) of the Act. Section 5(a)(1), referred to as the General Duty Clause, requires an employer to furnish employment and a place of employment which is free from recognized hazards that may cause or is likely to cause death or serious physical harm to employees.

To establish a violation of § 5(a)(1), the Secretary must prove that (1) there was an activity or condition in the employer's workplace that constituted a hazard to employees, (2) either the cited employer or its industry recognized that the condition or activity was hazardous, (3) the hazard was causing or likely to cause death or serious physical harm, and (4) there were feasible means to eliminate the hazard or materially reduce it. Waldon Healthcare Ctr., 16 BNA OSHC 1052, 1058 (No. 89-2804, 1993).

"The general duty clause, while intended to protect employees from hazards that have yet to be addressed by standards, is not intended to replace standards as an enforcement mechanism." Waldon Healthcare Ctr., 16 BNA OSHC at 1060. There are no specific OSHA standards involving inspections and examinations of air intake courses and concrete seals in an underground mine (Tr. 1208). Citing the General Duty Clause was appropriate in this case.

The Museum's underground ventilation involved dual intake air courses. Fresh air from outside the mine was drawn through a predetermined course of tunnels in the mine and then returned to the outside (Tr. 256, 515-516). One air course ventilated the perimeter tunnels in front of the concrete seals. A separate air course circulated air through the interior tour area (Tr. 102, 625, 813, 1065).

Fresh air was drawn in through "A" and "B" shafts and exhausted out the "B" shaft (Tr. 129, 1119). A wall in the middle of the "B" shaft allowed fresh air to be drawn down one side and bad air to be exhausted from the other side (Tr. 517). A large exhaust fan, located above "B" shaft, was used to draw fresh air down "A" shaft and the other side of "B" shaft (Tr. 815, 865). For perimeter ventilation, fresh air was drawn down the "A" shaft,[NOTE 8] circulated through the tunnels in front of the concrete seals, and exhausted out the "B" shaft (Tr. 92, 132, 256-257, 516, 521, 637, 1087). For interior ventilation, fresh air was drawn down the intake side of "B" shaft, circulated throughout the tour area, and exhausted through the upcast side of "B" shaft (Tr. 521, 813).

The Museum agrees that at the time of OSHA's inspection, it was not inspecting in its entirety the perimeter air course and all of the concrete seals. Employees were unable to visually inspect at least 40 seals and could not walk the perimeter air course (Tr. 1086). Such inspections and examinations were not possible because of the inadequate roof support in many of the passageways. Instead, the Museum performed air monitoring at designated checkpoints to verify the proper functioning of the air course (Tr. 640, 1024). The Museum's air monitoring results were maintained in a logbook at the facility and were available to OSHA (Tr. 100, 256). Eventually, the Museum contemplated placing new seals in closer to the tour area; thus reducing the ventilation area it had to examine (Tr. 103, 958, 1027).

By failing to physically inspect all of the seals and the perimeter air course, the Secretary is concerned that disruptions in air circulation and unexpected accumulations of water, methane gas or bad air (oxygen deficient atmosphere) around the seals could not be detected and corrected (Tr. 814-815). The purpose of a ventilation system is to allow fresh air to dilute and replace accumulations of bad air and gases such as methane (Tr. 811). The Secretary argues that physical examinations are necessary to verify the adequacy of the ventilation system and the integrity of the seals.

The potential for disruptions in the perimeter air course existed. Dr. Ledvina testified that there had been at least one major roof fall during the Museum's operation and 19 other major roof falls during the history of the mine (Tr. 1487-1488). The underground map identifies the location of 22 roof falls (Exh. C-2; Tr. 895). Superintendent Bullock testified that there were 30 roof falls[NOTE 9] (Tr. 1057). In addition to actual roof falls, the record indicates numerous areas of unsupported or inadequately supported roof.

The record also shows that there was a potential for problems around the seals, including accumulations of methane gas and water. Mines in Illinois, including mine #25, are generally considered "gassy mines" (Tr. 548, 1138). Dr. Ledvina considered "mine #25 above average" in methane gas (Tr. 1142-1143). According to state inspector Odle, the concentration of methane gas behind the seals could be approximately as high as 45 percent, which is not uncommon in old coal mines (Tr. 545). The explosive level of methane gas is between 5 and 15 percent (Tr. 547, 1141). Dr. Ledvina testified that any time the methane level approached 1 percent in front of the seals, "it's time to take immediate corrective action" (Tr. 1141). He stated that during the three years as a museum, there were 3, "possibly 5," occasions when the concentration of methane gas was near or above one percent inside the Museum area. The problem occurred generally when there was low outside barometric pressure (Tr. 1141). State mine inspector Odle testified that in 1998 he detected a level of methane gas exceeding 1 percent at the northeast seal (Tr. 546). He described another incident when the level exceeded 5 percent (Tr. 546-547).

In addition to methane gas, the record reflects accumulations of water in the mine. Water can affect the integrity of the concrete seals. State mine inspector Odle first reported water at the seals on October 21, 1998 (Exh. R-10). In his report dated December 1, 1998, he found water accumulations in front of the #17 and #18 seals in the north which prevented visual examinations of the seals. He noted that the water was possibly destroying the seals. The Museum was directed to pump out the water by January 2, 1999 (Exh. C-33). He also noted water accumulations on September 14, 1999, and October 1, 1999 (Exh. R-10).

A hazard may be recognized by either the individual employer itself or its industry. A hazard is deemed "recognized" when the potential danger of a condition or activity is either actually known to the particular employer or generally known in the industry. Pepperidge Farm Inc., 17 BNA OSHC 1993 (No. 89-0265, 1997). In this case, the Museum knew of the hazards associated with accumulations of methane gas and water and the need to visually inspect the air course and seals. Based on their previous coal mining experience, Dr. Ledvina and superintendent Bullock acknowledged the need to inspect the seals and air courses (Tr. 1087, 1136). The Museum's own plan noted that inspections were required (Exh. C-38).

The hazards were also recognized by the coal mining industry. MSHA and state mining regulations direct mine operators to examine seals and air courses (Tr. 808-809).

MSHA regulations at 30 C.F.R. § 75.364(b) requires examinations for hazardous conditions at least every 7 days in at least one entry of each intake air course, return air course, and seal. Section 75.364(b)(4) provides for examinations "[a]t each seal along return and bleeder air courses[NOTE 10] and at each seal along intake air courses not examined under § 75.360(b)(5)."

The Illinois Coal Mining Act requires at § 6.04 examinations of working places in gassy mines:

> When the mine is to be operated he [examiner] shall examine the prescribed working places of such mine within 4 hours before any workers in such shift, other than the examiner or the examiners designated by the Mine Manager to make the examination, enter the underground areas of the mine. Examine every working place in the mine and make test therein with a permissible flame safety lamp for accumulation of methane and oxygen deficiency in the air therein; examine seals and doors to determine whether they are functioning properly; inspect and test the roof, face and rib conditions in the working areas and on active roadways and travelways; inspect active roadways, travelways, approaches to abandoned working and accessible falls in active sections for explosive gas and other hazards; and inspect to determine whether the air in each split is traveling in its proper course and in normal volume (Exh. C-32).

The same examination is expected for non-coal producing shifts, except if the work is expected to be done on the immediate shaft bottom. See § 6.04(A)(2).

Regulations applicable to operating coal mines are also indicative of the hazards in a mine museum (Tr. 477, 968-969). Dr. Ledvina recognized that the dangers of a coal mine were also present at the Museum (Tr. 38). The hazards caused by disruptions in air flow and the affects on seal integrity are the same whether in an operating coal mine or in a mine used for public tours. The hazards are recognized.

In order to prevail with a § 5(a)(1) violation, the Secretary must also show that the hazards were causing or likely to cause death or serious physical harm, and there were feasible means to eliminate the hazards or materially reduce them. See Fluor Constructors International, Inc., 17 BNA OSHC 1947 (No. 92-2342, 1997). The Secretary must show that the abatement measure would reduce the risk of severe injury from the hazard. The proposed abatement is judged by what a reasonable person familiar with the conditions of the industry would have instituted. *Pratt & Whitney Aircraft v. Secretary of Labo*r, 649 F.2d 96, 106 (2d Cir. 1980).

As recommended abatement, the Secretary's citation directs the Museum to perform the inspections and examinations in their entirety. However, the Secretary acknowledges that such inspections could not be performed until the Museum corrected the inadequate roof support throughout the mine, which is the basis for the Secretary's willful citation (Secretary's Post-Hearing Brief, pp. 33, 35; Tr. 90, 107, 253). By allowing the Museum to first support the roof, the Secretary recognizes that the abatement of making complete inspections was not feasible under the circumstances of this case. Otherwise, the Museum was placed in a "Catch-22" situation.[NOTE 11]

According to the Museum, the seals were not checked after September 30, 1999, because of the state's Order to comply (Tr. 1022, 1492). Pursuant to agreement with state mine inspector Odle, the Museum was permitted to inspect as close as possible to the seals and do air monitoring at checkpoints to ensure no disruptions and proper ventilation (Tr. 511, 640). The Secretary does not dispute that the Museum was performing spot air monitoring. There is no evidence of actual disruptions in air flow or damage to the seals. To reduce the hazard, vent pipes in the seals were opened to relieve water build-up behind the seals and equalize the gas pressure (Tr. 623-624, 1061).

The Illinois Coal Mine Act provides exceptions for inspections of less than the entirety (Tr. 508, 727, 728, 732). State inspector Odle testified that exception to such inspections was provided as common practice by Illinois in cases where a seal becomes inaccessible (Tr. 508-509). Odle authorized the exception to the Museum in order to repair the roof support. MSHA inspector Odum testified that MSHA also recognized exceptions to visually examining seals on rare occasions (Tr. 809-810).

State mine inspector Odle testified that based on his air monitoring, he detected no problems with the Museum's ventilation system (Tr. 729). He found the air courses functioning properly from September 1, 1999, through November 29, 1999 (Tr. 524). On September 14, 1999, inspector Odle did cite in his monthly inspection report the Museum's failure to examine the seals and air courses (Exh. R-10). However, Dr. Ledvina immediately responded to Odle that the examinations were conducted but not recorded. State inspector Odle testified that he never found explosive levels of methane around the seals and was not aware of a seal rupture or failure (Tr. 645). Also, OSHA's air monitoring failed to record any level of methane gas or detect disruptions in the air flow (Tr. 260).

The alleged violation of § 5(a)(1) is not established.

Item 3 - Unprotected Light Bulbs in Tour Area

The citation alleges that unprotected incandescent light bulbs and electrical circuits in the tour area were not safe for Class II, Division 2, hazardous locations. Section 1910.307(b) [NOTE 12] provides that:

> Equipment, wiring methods, and installations of equipment in hazardous (classified) locations are to be intrinsically safe or approved for the hazardous (classified) location, or safe for the hazardous (classified) location.

Under § 1910.399 definitions, Class II, Division 2, is a location in which:

> (a) combustible dust will not normally be in suspension in the air in quantities sufficient to produce explosive or ignitible mixtures, and dust accumulations are normally insufficient to interfere with the normal operation of electrical equipment or other apparatus; or (b) dust may be in suspension in the air as a result of infrequent malfunctioning of handling or processing equipment, and dust accumulations resulting therefrom may be ignitible by abnormal operation or failure of electrical equipment or other apparatus.

Throughout the tour area and along the travelway to "A" shaft, the walkway for tourists was a 4-foot wide mat on the ground. Chain link or wire mesh was secured to the roof to prevent falling dirt or rocks. On both sides of the walkway, rope mesh was used as hand rails. Lights consisting of incandescent 100-watt light bulbs were hung outside the walkway along one side. The light bulbs were spaced approximately 12 feet apart and hung one foot below the roof. There were hundreds of light bulbs in the tour area. The light bulbs were not enclosed or otherwise protected. Flexible romax cable which was not inside metal conduit connected the light bulbs (Exhs. C-29, C-30; Tr. 57, 262, 340, 345-346, 380, 475, 500, 951, 967-968, 1043-1044, 1046, 1049).

OSHA classified the tour area as Class II, Division 2, because of the potential for combustible methane gas or coal dust (Tr. 260, 340, 342). As discussed, coal mines in Illinois are considered "gassy" and methane gas has been detected at mine #25. However, there is no showing that methane gas was ever detected in the tour area (Tr. 1053, 1149). The methane gas detected by state inspector Odle in 1998 was at the northeast seal (Tr. 545-546). The Museum also has never detected methane gas in the tour area (Tr. 1066). During its inspection, OSHA did not find methane gas (Tr. 260, 263, 944).

The Secretary also was concerned for combustible levels of coal dust if there was a roof fall (Tr. 340-341). The record shows that roof falls have occurred at mine #25. Dr. Ledvina acknowledged at least one major roof fall during the Museum's operation (Tr. 1487-1488). Where the roof fall occurred was not identified. Although coal was all around the tour area, OSHA did not monitor for coal dust (Tr, 261, 373).

A Class II, Division 2, hazardous location is based on the potential suspension of combustible dust, not gases such as methane. Also, with the Museum's dual ventilation system, there is no showing of potential methane gas in the tour area. The perimeter air course was designed to remove the methane gas without affecting the tour area (Tr. 582, 639). There was no showing of methane gas or the potential in the tour area.

With regard to coal dust, the record also does not show the potential for the suspension of coal dust in the tour area. The Secretary failed to establish the combustible level of coal dust and show that it was potentially explosive because of unprotected light bulbs. As described by OSHA, coal dust may be ignitable but is not a source of ignition (Tr. 261). The coal dust in mine #25 was not airborne (Tr. 340). OSHA and state mine inspector Odle performed no air monitoring for coal dust (Tr. 261, 373, 622).

The Museum's lighting system was approved by state inspector Odle (Tr. 1063). He did not consider the light bulbs a hazard after at least 36 inspections of the mine. The lights complied with the Illinois Coal Mining Act (Tr. 587, 727). Odle, who has 16 years of coal mining experience, has worked as a state coal mine inspector for 11 years enforcing mine safety standards. He has made over 2,000 mine safety inspections in Illinois (Tr. 489, 490, 492). Based on his experience, Odle opined that "coal dust ignitions were not likely" (Tr. 622). He never detected any problems with the lights (Exh. R-10; Tr. 1063). Because of dampness in the mine, there was an absence of "float dust" (Tr. 622). Superintendent Bullock testified that "mine 25 did not produce float dust" (Tr. 1052). Also, according to MSHA inspector Odum, FMSHA allows bare light bulbs in track mines. See 30 C.F.R. § 75.522.1(a) (Tr. 940-941).

OSHA inspector Leland Darrow, who recommended the citation, was in the mine for less than three hours, which was his total underground coal mine experience (Tr. 274, 350-351). CO Darrow did not know if coal dust would explode if subjected to an ignition source. He performed no tests or sampling to determine if sufficient suspended coal dust was potentially present in the mine (Tr. 373).

MSHA inspector Odum, who accompanied OSHA, identified the hazard of light bulbs was from an employee or machinery inadvertently hitting bulbs and damaging them (Tr. 828-829). He did not identify as a hazard the potential suspension of coal dust. Also, the lights were not subject to employee activity. The lights were located several feet off the walkway. There is no showing that the light bulbs were broken by employees or equipment.

A violation of § 1910.307(b) is not established.

Willful Citation No. 2
Item 1 - Unsupported/Inadequate Roof Support

The citation alleges that the roof was unsupported or inadequately supported along the Main East Travel Way and the Main East Entry. The Secretary alleges a violation of the General Duty Clause at § 5(a)(1) of the Act.

The roof support system at mine #25 was primarily by roof bolts.[NOTE 13] The steel bolts are approximately six feet long. Using a roof bolting machine, the bolts with a 6-inch square bearing plate are screwed tight up against the roof. There were thousands of bolt installations at the mine, many dating to the opening of the mine (Tr. 527-528, 707, 787, 1033, 1082).

There is no dispute that the mine roof in many areas was unsupported (no bolts or other support) or inadequately supported (bearing plate not tight against roof or missing). The Museum recognized that in many locations the roof support system was inadequate (Tr. 67, 84). The Museum's map of the underground mine identifies 17 areas of unsupported roof (Exh. C-2; Tr. 895). Also, the map identifies 22 locations of roof falls (Exh. C-2; Tr. 895). Superintendent Bullock testified that there was one "massive roof fall right before we shut down" and one smaller fall (Tr. 1055). He estimated that there were a total of 30 roof falls (Tr. 1057). Most of the roof falls occurred prior to the Museum's acquisition (Tr. 1487-1488). MSHA inspector Mark Odle testified that on October 20, 1999, the inspection team was unable to examine the seals because of a roof fall in the travelway (Tr. 782).

The record establishes that the inadequate roof support in various areas of the mine was a recognized hazard. State inspector Odle first noted the problem with unsupported roof in his inspection of August 7, 1998 (Exh. R-10). Also, he found during his inspection of September 20, 1999, that the Museum had not corrected the roof support problem in the tour area cited in a July 9 inspection (Exhs. C-9, C-10). On August 7, 1998, October 2, 1998, and November 19, 1998, Odle noted that additional roof support was needed in various locations (Exhs. C-12, C-13, C-14). Copies of Odle's inspection reports were given to the Museum. Superintendent Bullock admitted that if the Museum had the money, it would have re-bolted "every bit of the mine" (Tr. 1063-1064).

The photographs taken during OSHA's inspection show areas of missing bolts, missing plates and where the roof had sloughed14 from under the plate, eliminating contact with the roof (Exhs. C-18 through C-30; Tr. 77, 83-84, 709-710). When the bearing plate is missing or not in contact with the roof, the roof is not adequately supported (Tr. 286, 295, 789). The photographs show bearing plates more than one foot below the roof (Exh. C-18; Tr. 288-289). Also, the roof bolts are shown spaced more than 5 feet apart (Tr. 301, 306). Although providing some support, it is undisputed that such bolts no longer provided adequate roof support (Tr. 77, 715, 729, 786). MSHA inspector Odum opined that the roof bolts had become ineffective or had been dislodged from the roof because of deterioration of the roof over time (Tr. 783-784, 786).

MSHA regulations at 30 C.F.R. § 75.202 provide:

> (a) The roof, face and ribs of areas where persons work or travel shall be supported or otherwise controlled to protect persons from hazards related to falls of the roof, face or ribs and coal or rock bursts.

(b) No person shall work or travel under unsupported roof unless in accordance with this subpart.

Employees' exposure to the inadequate roof support was likely to cause serious injury or death. During OSHA's inspection, Museum employees were underground attempting to repair the water pump and the roof bolter (Tr. 146-147, 403, 543). Although the Museum had employees underground to repair the roof support system, employees were observed working or passing through areas where the roof support was inadequate (Tr. 83, 146-147). Also, the areas of unsupported or inadequately supported roof were located where employees had to travel on a routine basis as part of their remediation activity (Tr. 67, 76, 971). In one instance, superintendent Bullock was observed under an area of unsupported roof (Exh. C-22; Tr. 303-305, 783).

Also, the Museum's roof control plan was the plan approved for the Old Ben Mine Company (Exh. C-38; Tr. 1002). The plan required roof bolts to be placed at 5-foot intervals (Tr. 283, 526-527, 533, 786). The Society of Mining Engineering handbook recommends that roof bolts not be installed any further than 5 feet apart (Tr. 785).

The Museum does not argue that the bolts could not be replaced or tightened. Abatement was feasible.

The record establishes a violation of § 5(a)(1).

Willful Classification for Citation No. 2

The Secretary alleges the lack of adequate roof support in violation of § 5(a)(1) is willful. In order to be considered a willful violation, the violation must be shown to be "one committed with intentional knowing or voluntary disregard for the requirements of the Act, or with plain indifference to employee safety." Conie Construction, Inc., 16 BNA OSHC 1870, 1872 (No. 92-264, 1994). Willful violations require a "heightened awareness" of the relevant standard that demonstrates a voluntary or conscious disregard of its requirements or a plain indifference to employee safety. A showing of "malicious intent" or "venal motive" is not necessary. An employer's intentional disregard or plain indifference to its safety obligations can be established in various ways, including proof of prior citations or showing that an employer harbored a state of mind such that, if he were informed of the applicable requirements, he would not care. Morrison-Knudsen Co./Yonkers Contracting Co., 16 BNA OSHC 1105, 1123 (No. 88-572, 1993).

In this case, the Museum's failure to adequately support the mine roof was not willful. It is undisputed that the Museum was aware the mine's roof was not adequately supported. However, the Museum had not previously been inspected by OSHA. By the time of OSHA's inspection four days later, the Museum was under a state closure Order dated

September 27, 1999, and attempting to comply with the order's requirements, including adequately supporting the roof (Tr. 144).

Although previous state inspections had noted areas of inadequate roof support, the Museum was permitted to continue to operate, and it appears that the conditions noted were corrected. There is no showing prior to the state's closure action that the Museum refused to correct the conditions (Exhs. C-9 through C-16). Inspector Odle testified that he had discussed the roof support with the Museum on several occasions. However, he did not consider the lack of adequate roof support as intentional disregard by the Museum (Tr. 713). The Museum was attempting to make the corrections in good faith with the hope of reopening to the public. Based on the record, the Museum's failure to adequately support the roof was due more to the lack of money and the Museum's confusion regarding the requirements of the various state and federal agencies rather than the Museum's intentional disregard or plain indifference toward employees' safety. Such circumstances in this case do not rise to the level of willful.

A violation is not willful if the employer has made a good faith attempt to correct the condition. The test of good faith for these purposes is objective–whether the employer's belief concerning a factual matter was reasonable under the circumstances. General Motors Corp., Electro-Motive Div., 14 BNA OSHC 2064 (Nos. 82-630, 84-731, 84-816, 1991). The Museum was attempting to comply with the state's Order when OSHA arrived. An employer can make a good faith effort to eliminate a hazard even though its efforts are not entirely effective or complete. Valdak Corp, 17 BNA OSHC 1135, 1139 (No. 93-239, 1995), aff'd. 73 F.3d 1455 (8th Cir. 1996).

Penalty Consideration for Citation No. 2

The Commission is the final arbiter of penalties in all contested cases. In determining an appropriate penalty, the Commission is required to consider the size of the employer's business, history of previous violations, the employer's good faith, and the gravity of the violation. Gravity is the principal factor to be considered.

The Museum was a small employer with less than 10 employees. At the time of OSHA's inspection, the Museum had four employees working in the mine exposed to the unsupported roof. There was also three employees in the office (Tr. 1464). The Museum has no history of prior OSHA violations. The Museum is also entitled to good faith credit in that it was attempting to comply with the state's closure order.

A penalty of $5,000 is reasonable for failing to adequately support the mine roof as required by § 5(a)(1). There were four employees exposed to the condition who were experienced miners (Tr. 725-726). The employees' exposure was incidental to their attempt to correct the inadequate roof support. During its existence, the Museum had no lost time injuries (Tr. 705).

FINDINGS OF FACT AND CONCLUSIONS OF LAW

The foregoing decision constitutes the findings of fact and conclusions of law in accordance with Rule 52(a) of the Federal Rules of Civil Procedure.

ORDER

Based upon the foregoing decision, it is ORDERED that:

Citation No. 1

Item 1, alleged serious violation of § 5(a)(1) of the Act, is vacated and no penalty is assessed.
Item 2, alleged serious violation of § 5(a)(1) of the Act, is withdrawn by the Secretary.
Item 3, alleged serious violation of § 1910.307(b), is vacated and no penalty is assessed.

Citation No. 2

Item 1, alleged willful violation of § 5(a)(1), is affirmed as serious and a penalty of $5,000 is assessed.

/s/ KEN S. WELSCH Judge

Date: August 17, 2001

NOTES:

NOTE 1: Although the Museum is no longer in business, the Secretary has jurisdiction to initiate civil enforcement action because the alleged violations occurred while the Museum was still in business and had employees. Joel Yandell d/b/a Triple L. Tower, 18 BNA OSHC 1623 (No. 94-3080, 1999).

NOTE 2: The Museum also owned the nearby Orient 2 mine which was an above-ground historical mine site (Tr. 121, 1454-1455).

NOTE 3: Dr. Ledvina has a doctorate degree in philosophy and mining engineering. He had worked in the coal mines as a supervisor until a mine accident in 1978 left his lower body paralyzed. He is now in a wheelchair (Tr. 1145-1148). Dr. Ledvina used money received from his Workers' Compensation settlement to start the Museum (Tr. 1435).

NOTE 4: A seal is a wall erected from floor to roof in a tunnel to separate the worked out from the active area of the mine (Tr. 808).

NOTE 5: The Museum's underground area of operation was not large compared to an active coal mine (Tr. 807).

NOTE 6: An imminent danger notice under § 13 of the Act is not a citation. It warns employees of unsafe conditions (Tr. 1216-1217).

NOTE 7: OSHA had information that the hoist problem was rigged by Dr. Ledvina (Tr. 544-545).

NOTE 8: "A" shaft also had a skip hoist and was the emergency escape route (Tr. 57-58).

NOTE 9: According to MSHA inspector Gary Odum, 10 roof falls is a considerable amount but "probably not unlikely. Thirty [roof falls] is probably too many. It's an excessive amount" (Tr. 892).

NOTE 10: Witnesses described the Museum's ventilation system as a bleeder air course which is used to ventilate worked out mine areas (Tr. 638, 876, 1121).

NOTE 11: The Museum could not perform complete inspections because of the roof and it could not fix the roof because of the lack of complete inspections.

NOTE 12: The Secretary has the burden of proving a violation. In order to establish a violation of an occupational safety or health standard, the Secretary has the burden of proving: (a) the applicability of the cited standard, (b) the employer's noncompliance with the standard's terms, (c) employee access to the violative conditions, and (d) the employer's actual or constructive knowledge of the violation (i.e., the employer either knew or, with the exercise of reasonable diligence could have known, of the violative conditions). Atlantic Battery Co., 16 BNA OSHC 2131, 2138 (No. 90-1747, 1994).

NOTE 13: In addition to roof bolts, other roof support systems included placing timbers or a crib (Exhs. C-25, C-28; Tr. 90, 283, 312-313, 793, 797, 803).

NOTE 14: This condition is also referred to as "rib rashing" or "spalling" (Tr. 301, 529).

STUDY QUESTIONS

- How did the Occupational Safety and Health Administration (OSHA) first become involved in inspecting the National Coal Mine Museum? What were the OSHA violations identified in the National Coal Mine case? What purpose do the financial penalties imposed by OSHA for these violations serve?
- The museum's owner represented the museum pro se in the OSHA citation hearing. What procedural and substantive arguments did the museum director make in opposing the citations? Why did the museum director complain about the repeated visits by OSHA inspectors and the delays in their inspections?
- How did the court resolve the conflict between OSHA and the Illinois state mining regulations? Explain the decision reached by the court. What do you think was behind the situation and the court's decision?
- Can you think of other types of museum facilities or museum collections that might present a unique set of occupational hazards for museum employees?

INTERNS AND VOLUNTEERS

Interns and other categories of individuals receiving training in a museum (externs, apprentices, graduate assistants) may also be outside the coverage of federal and state employment compensation laws. As with independent contractors, determining whether a particular intern is exempt involves applying a number of factors. Key to the determination is whether the training is for the benefit of the intern and does not displace the museum's other employees, as well as whether there is an expectation of future employment. Internships may be unpaid or paid. Paid internships may be regulated under the Fair Labor Standards Act (FLSA) and state law and may require the payment of minimum wages and overtime. The law in this area is changing rapidly so extra care should be made to comply with current laws and regulations regarding compensation for interns.

Volunteers who give their time without compensation from the museum may also be exempt from wage and hour laws under FLSA and state equivalents. Among the important factors is whether the volunteer expects to receive any benefits (other than personal pleasure) from performing the activities, and whether the services are the kind typically associated with paid work. In the museum world, people sometimes volunteer (or "intern") with the hope or expectation (or implied or express promise by the museum) that they may be given a paid position at a later date. Performing unpaid services as part of a path to future employment is not volunteering, and the "volunteer" in these situations may be treated as an employee under federal and state labor laws. Some states require written acknowledgement from the volunteer that they are expressly waiving their right to compensation.

Sometimes museum employees also volunteer to do certain things for the museum, such as helping with hosting a fundraising gala for example, which may be outside the scope of the employee's normal duties. These situations raise interesting employee compensation questions. If the employee's volunteer activities are clearly distinct from their paid work responsibilities and there is no coercion involved, there should be no problem—but misunderstandings can and do arise. A non-exempt employee's "volunteer" activities may trigger the obligation to pay overtime and meet other FLSA requirements.

The application of federal and state employment laws to volunteers varies by jurisdiction. Absent a written agreement to the contrary, volunteers are considered "employees-at-will" and can be "fired" at any time. When firing a volunteer, the same procedures to terminate an employment relationship (discussed at the beginning of this chapter) should be followed. As noted above, the wage, hour and other protections in FLSA do not apply to bona fide volunteers. However, if a "volunteer" is deemed to in fact be an employee, they may be entitled to back pay for all of their "volunteer" time. Volunteers are generally not covered by employment anti-discrimination laws, but if the employment relationship has been mischaracterized, the "volunteer" may be entitled to protection under applicable employment discrimination laws as an employee.

Despite their status as non-employees, volunteers can create a hostile work environment or otherwise violate the rights of the museum's employees. For this reason, the museum's anti-discrimination and anti-harassment policies should be applied equally to the museum's volunteers.

For the purposes of the Americans with Disabilities Act (the ADA), volunteers are entitled to "reasonable accommodation" to the same extent as regular employees.

The law is unclear about whether or how employment safety laws, including OSHA, apply to volunteers. When volunteers are engaged in activities that may trigger OSHA concerns, they should be included in OSHA training to the same extent as the museum's regular employees.

The application of state workers' compensation laws to interns and volunteers also varies by jurisdiction. Generally speaking, if the injured worker is a volunteer, the museum is not covered by limits on liability included in workers' compensation laws. Some states allow organizations to specifically include their volunteers under their workers' compensation insurance policy. Museums may also consider additional insurance coverage for their volunteers, particularly if they are engaged in high-risk activities.

People who volunteer at nonprofit organizations, including museums, run the risk that their actions, while well-intentioned, may cause harm to another. If those actions are deemed negligent, the volunteer may face civil liability for damages caused by the negligent conduct. Volunteer protection acts, which limit the liability of nonprofit organizations and their volunteers under specific circumstances, have been enacted on both the federal and state level.

The federal Volunteer Protection Act (VPA) (42 U.S.C. 14501-05), for example, reduces or eliminates tort liability for harm caused by an uncompensated volunteer's acts of ordinary negligence committed within the scope of the volunteer's responsibilities. Protection under VPA does not apply if the volunteer engages in willful or criminal misconduct, gross negligence, reckless misconduct, or a conscious, flagrant indifference to the rights or safety of the individual(s) harmed by the volunteer. The VPA also does not apply if the volunteer causes harm by operating a motor vehicle, vessel, aircraft, or other vehicle for which the state requires its operator to possess an operator's license or maintain insurance.

Immigration laws generally do not apply to volunteers, but if any remuneration or other benefit is received, the museum should collect an I-9 form in the same way it does for its employees.

Volunteers may have access to confidential information such as member and donor lists, and employee medical and personal information. A volunteer may also have potential conflicts of interest. For these reasons, volunteers should be asked to sign the same conflicts disclosures and confidentiality agreements as the museum's regular employees.

In short, except for issues relating to compensation, best practice suggests that volunteers should be treated in the same way as regular museum staff with respect to most employment laws, to the extent that is possible. "Hiring" and "firing" volunteers should be conducted in accordance to established procedures to avoid risks associated with violating federal and state laws, including claims involving misclassification, discrimination, or claims based on contract or tort law. A volunteer handbook, similar to the museum's employee handbook, should be prepared and provided to all volunteers.

CASES AND OTHER READINGS

Reading Note: The case reprinted below involves a group of unpaid interns who worked for the production company that produced the award-winning movie *Black Swan*. The central question in this case is whether the interns should have been classified as employees under the Fair Labor Standards Act, and as such should be entitled to compensation as employees under that Act. While the case involves a for-profit company, it contains lessons for museums and other nonprofits that employ unpaid interns.

GLATT V. FOX SEARCHLIGHT PICTURES

811 F.3d 528 (2015).

Before WALKER, JACOBS, and WESLEY, Circuit Judges.

Plaintiffs, who were hired as unpaid interns, claim compensation as employees under the Fair Labor Standards Act and New York Labor Law. Plaintiffs Eric Glatt and Alexander Footman moved for partial summary judgment on their employment status. Plaintiff Eden Antalik moved to certify a class of all New York interns working at certain of defendants' divisions between 2005 and 2010 and to conditionally certify a nationwide collective of all interns working at those same divisions between 2008 and 2010. The district court (William H. Pauley III, J.) granted Glatt and Footman's motion for partial summary judgment, certified Antalik's New York class, and conditionally certified Antalik's nationwide collective. On defendants' interlocutory appeal, we VACATE the district court's order granting partial summary judgment to Glatt and Footman, VACATE its order certifying Antalik's New York class, VACATE its order conditionally certifying Antalik's nationwide collective, and REMAND for further proceedings.

Black Swan *is a 2010 American psychological horror film based on a production of Tchaikovsky's* Swan Lake *ballet by the prestigious New York City Ballet company. Staring Natalie Portman, Vincent Cassel, Mila Kunis, Barbara Hershey, and Winona Ryder, the film grossed over $329 million worldwide and received five nominations at the 83rd Academy Awards, including Best Picture, Best Director, Best Cinematography, Best Film Editing, and winning Best Actress (for Portman).*

BACKGROUND

Plaintiffs worked as unpaid interns either on the Fox Searchlight-distributed film Black Swan or at the Fox corporate offices in New York City. They contend that the defendants, Fox Searchlight and Fox Entertainment Group, violated the Fair Labor Standards Act (FLSA), 29 U.S.C. §§ 206–07, and New York Labor (N.Y.LL), N.Y. Labor Law § 652, by failing to pay them as employees during their internships as required by the FLSA's and NYLL's minimum wage and overtime provisions. The following background facts are undisputed except where noted.

Eric Glatt

Eric Glatt graduated with a degree in multimedia instructional design from New York University. Glatt was enrolled in a non-matriculated (non-degree) graduate program at NYU's School of Education when he started working on *Black Swan*. His graduate program did not offer him credit for his internship.

From December 2, 2009, through the end of February 2010, Glatt interned in *Black Swan*'s accounting department under the supervision of Production Accountant Theodore Au. He worked from approximately 9:00 a.m. to 7:00 p.m. five days a week. As an accounting intern, Glatt's responsibilities included copying, scanning, and filing documents; tracking purchase orders; transporting paperwork and items to and from the *Black Swan* set; maintaining employee personnel files; and answering questions about the accounting department.

Glatt interned a second time in *Black Swan*'s post-production department from March 2010 to August 2010, under the supervision of Post Production Supervisor Jeff Robinson. Glatt worked two days a week from approximately 11:00 a.m. until 6:00 or 7:00 p.m. His post-production responsibilities included drafting cover letters for mailings; organizing filing cabinets; filing paperwork; making photocopies; keeping the take-out menus up-to-date and organized; bringing documents to the payroll company; and running errands, one of which required him to purchase a non-allergenic pillow for Director Darren Aronofsky.

Alexander Footman

Alexander Footman graduated from Wesleyan University with a degree in film studies. He was not enrolled in a degree program at the time of his *Black Swan* internship. From September 29, 2009, through late February or early March 2010, Footman interned in the production department under the supervision of Production Office Coordinator Lindsay Feldman and Assistant Production Office Coordinator Jodi Arneson. Footman worked approximately ten-hour days. At first, Footman worked five days a week, but, beginning in November 2009, he worked only three days a week. After this schedule change, *Black Swan* replaced Footman with another unpaid intern in the production department.

Footman's responsibilities included picking up and setting up office furniture; arranging lodging for cast and crew; taking out the trash; taking lunch orders; answering phone calls; watermarking scripts; drafting daily call sheets; photocopying; making coffee; making deliveries to and from the film production set, rental houses, and the payroll office; accepting deliveries; admitting guests to the office; compiling lists of local vendors; breaking down, removing, and selling office furniture and supplies at the end of production; internet research; sending invitations to the wrap party; and other similar tasks and errands, including bringing tea to Aronofsky and dropping off a DVD of *Black Swan* footage at Aronofsky's apartment.

Eden Antalik

Eden Antalik worked as an unpaid publicity intern in Fox Searchlight's corporate office in New York from the beginning of May 2009 until the second week of August 2009. During her internship, Antalik was enrolled in a degree program at Duquesne University that required her to have an internship in order to graduate. Antalik was supposed to receive credit for her internship at Fox Searchlight, but, for reasons that are unclear from the record, she never actually received the credit.

Antalik began work each morning around 8:00 a.m. by assembling a brief, referred to as "the breaks," summarizing mentions of various Fox Searchlight films in the media. She also made travel arrangements, organized catering, shipped documents, and set up rooms for press events.

Prior Proceedings

On October 19, 2012, plaintiffs filed their first amended class complaint seeking unpaid minimum wages and overtime for themselves and all others similarly situated. Thereafter, Glatt and Footman abandoned their class claims and proceeded as individuals. After discovery, Glatt and Footman moved for partial summary judgment, contending that they were employees under the FLSA and NYLL. The defendants cross-moved for summary judgment claiming that Glatt and Footman were not employees under either statute. At about the same time, Antalik moved to certify a class of New York State interns working at certain Fox divisions and a nationwide FLSA collective of interns working at those same divisions.

On June 11, 2013, the district court concluded that Glatt and Footman had been improperly classified as unpaid interns rather than employees and granted their partial motion for summary judgment. The district court also granted Antalik's motions to certify the class of New York interns and to conditionally certify the nationwide FLSA collective.

On September 17, 2013, the district court, acting on defendants' motion, certified its order for immediate appeal under 28 U.S.C. § 1292(b). On November 26, 2013, we granted defendants' petition for leave to file an interlocutory appeal from the district court's orders. For the reasons that follow, we vacate the district court's orders and remand.

DISCUSSION

At its core, this interlocutory appeal raises the broad question of under what circumstances an unpaid intern must be deemed an "employee" under the FLSA and therefore compensated for his work. That broad question underlies our answers to the three specific questions on appeal. First, did the district court apply the correct standard in evaluating whether Glatt and Footman were employees, and, if so, did it reach the correct result? Second, did the district court err by certifying Antalik's class of New York interns? Third, did the district court err by conditionally certifying Antalik's nationwide collective?

I. Glatt's and Footman's Employment Status

We review the district court's order granting partial summary judgment to Glatt and Footman de novo. See *Velez v. Sanchez*, 693 F.3d 308, 313–14 (2d Cir.2012). Summary judgment is appropriate only if, drawing all reasonable inferences in favor of the nonmoving party, there is no genuine issue of material fact and the moving party is entitled to judgment as a matter of law. Id. at 314.

With certain exceptions not relevant here, the FLSA requires employers to pay all employees a specified minimum wage, and overtime of time and one-half for hours worked in excess of forty hours per week. 29 U.S.C. §§ 206–07. NYLL requires the same, except that it specifies a higher wage rate than the federal minimum. See N.Y. Labor Law § 652. An employee cannot waive his right to the minimum wage and overtime pay because waiver "would nullify the purposes of the [FLSA] and thwart the legislative policies it was designed to effectuate." *Barrentine v. Arkansas–Best Freight Sys., Inc.*, 450 U.S. 728, 740 (1981) (internal quotation marks omitted); see also *Tony & Susan Alamo Found. v. Sec'y of Labor*, 471 U.S. 290, 302 (1985) (exceptions to coverage under the FLSA affect more people than those workers directly at issue because exceptions are "likely to exert a general downward pressure on wages in competing businesses").

The strictures of both the FLSA and NYLL apply only to employees. The FLSA unhelpfully defines "employee" as an "individual employed by an employer." 29 U.S.C. § 203(e)(1). "Employ" is defined as "to suffer or permit to work." Id. § 203(g). New York likewise defines "employee" as "any individual employed, suffered or permitted to work by an employer." 12 N.Y.C.R.R. § 142–2.14(a). Because the statutes define "employee" in nearly identical terms, we construe the NYLL definition as the same in substance as the definition in the FLSA. See *Zheng v. Liberty Apparel Co.*, 355 F.3d 61, 78 (2d Cir.2003).

The Supreme Court has yet to address the difference between unpaid interns and paid employees under the FLSA. In 1947, however, the Court recognized that unpaid railroad brakemen trainees should not be treated as employees, and thus that they were beyond the reach of the FLSA's minimum wage provision. See *Walling v. Portland Terminal Co.*, 330 U.S. 148 (1947). The Court adduced several facts. First, the brakemen-trainees at issue did not displace any regular employees, and their work did not expedite the employer's business. Id. at 149–50. Second, the brakemen-trainees did not expect to receive any compensation and would not necessarily be hired upon successful completion of the course. See id. at 150. Third, the training course was similar to one offered by a vocational school. Id. at 152. Finally, the employer received no immediate advantage from the work done by the trainees. Id. at 153.

In 1967, the Department of Labor ("DOL") issued informal guidance on trainees as part of its Field Operations Handbook. The guidance enumerated six criteria and stated that the trainee is not an employee only if all of the criteria were met. See DOL, Wage & Hour Div., Field Operations Handbook, Ch. 10, ¶ 10b11 (Oct. 20, 1993), available at http://www.dol.gov/whd/FOH/FOH_Ch10.pdf. In 2010, the DOL published similar guidance for unpaid interns working in the for-profit private sector. This Intern Fact Sheet provides that an employment relationship does not exist if all of the following factors apply:

1. The internship, even though it includes actual operation of the facilities of the employer, is similar to training which would be given in an educational environment;
2. The internship experience is for the benefit of the intern;
3. The intern does not displace regular employees, but works under close supervision of existing staff;
4. The employer that provides the training derives no immediate advantage from the activities of the intern; and on occasion its operations may actually be impeded;
5. The intern is not necessarily entitled to a job at the conclusion of the internship; and
6. The employer and the intern understand that the intern is not entitled to wages for the time spent in the internship.

DOL, Wage & Hour Div., Fact Sheet #71, Internship Programs Under The Fair Labor Standards Act (April 2010), available at http://www.dol.gov/whd/regs/compliance/whdfs71.pdf.

The district court evaluated Glatt's and Footman's employment using a version of the DOL's six-factor test. However, the district court, unlike the DOL, did not explicitly require that all six factors be present to establish that the intern is not an employee and instead balanced the factors. The district court found that the first four factors weighed in favor of finding that Glatt and Footman were employees and the last two factors favored finding them to be trainees. As a result, the district court concluded that Glatt and Footman had been improperly classified as unpaid interns and granted their motion for partial summary judgment.

The specific issue we face—when is an unpaid intern entitled to compensation as an employee under the FLSA?—is a matter of first impression in this Circuit. When properly designed, unpaid internship programs can greatly benefit interns. For this reason, internships are widely supported by educators and by employers looking to hire well-trained recent graduates.[NOTE 1] However, employers can also exploit unpaid interns by using their free labor without providing them with an appreciable benefit in education or experience. Recognizing this concern, all parties agree that there are circumstances in which someone who is labeled an unpaid intern is actually an employee entitled to compensation under the FLSA. All parties also agree that there are circumstances in which unpaid interns are not employees under the FLSA. They do not agree on what those circumstances are or what standard we should use to identify them.

The plaintiffs urge us to adopt a test whereby interns will be considered employees whenever the employer receives an immediate advantage from the interns' work. Plaintiffs argue that focusing on any immediate advantage that accrues to the employer is appropriate because, in their view, the Supreme Court in Portland Terminal rested its holding on the finding that the brakemen trainees provided no immediate advantage to the employer.

The defendants urge us to adopt a more nuanced primary beneficiary test. Under this standard, an employment relationship is created when the tangible and intangible benefits provided to the intern are greater than the intern's contribution to the employer's operation. They argue that the primary beneficiary test best reflects the economic realities of the relationship between intern and employer. They further contend that a primary beneficiary test that considers the totality of the circumstances is in accordance with how we decide whether individuals are employees in other circumstances.

DOL, appearing as amicus curiae in support of the plaintiffs, defends the six factors enumerated in its Intern Fact Sheet and its requirement that every factor be present before the employer can escape its obligation to pay the worker. DOL argues (1) that its views on employee status are entitled to deference because it is the agency charged with administering the FLSA and (2) that we should use the six factors because they come directly from Portland Terminal.

We decline DOL's invitation to defer to the test laid out in the Intern Fact Sheet. As DOL makes clear in its brief, its six-part test is essentially a distillation of the facts discussed in Portland Terminal. DOL Br. at 11–12, 21. Unlike an agency's interpretation of ambiguous statutory terms or its own regulations, "an agency has no special competence or role in interpreting a judicial decision." *State of N.Y. v. Shalala*, 119 F.3d 175, 180 (2d Cir.1997). And as DOL concedes, DOL Br. at 21, this interpretation is entitled, at most, to Skidmore deference to the extent we find it persuasive. See *Skidmore v. Swift & Co.*, 323 U.S. 134, 140 (1944) (the weight given to the Administrator's judgment depends on "all those factors which give it power to persuade"). Because the DOL test attempts to fit

Portland Terminal's particular facts to all workplaces, and because the test is too rigid for our precedent to withstand, see, e.g., Velez, 693 F.3d at 326, we do not find it persuasive, and we will not defer to it.

Instead, we agree with defendants that the proper question is whether the intern or the employer is the primary beneficiary of the relationship. The primary beneficiary test has two salient features. First, it focuses on what the intern receives in exchange for his work. See Portland Terminal, 330 U.S. at 152 (focusing on the trainee's interests). Second, it also accords courts the flexibility to examine the economic reality as it exists between the intern and the employer. See *Barfield v. N.Y.C. Health & Hosps. Corp.*, 537 F.3d 132, 141–42 (2d Cir.2008) (employment for FLSA purposes is "a flexible concept to be determined on a case-by-case basis by review of the totality of the circumstances").

Although the flexibility of the primary beneficiary test is primarily a virtue, this virtue is not unalloyed. The defendants' conception of the primary beneficiary test requires courts to weigh a diverse set of benefits to the intern against an equally diverse set of benefits received by the employer without specifying the relevance of particular facts. Cf. *Brown v. N.Y.C. Dep't of Educ.*, 755 F.3d 154, 163 (2d Cir.2014) ("While our ultimate determination [of employment status] is based on the totality of circumstances, our discussion necessarily focuses on discrete facts relevant to particular statutory and regulatory criteria." (internal citation omitted)).

In somewhat analogous contexts, we have articulated a set of non-exhaustive factors to aid courts in determining whether a worker is an employee for purposes of the FLSA. See, e.g., Velez, 693 F .3d at 330 (domestic workers); *Brock v. Superior Care, Inc.*, 840 F.2d 1054, 1058–59 (2d Cir.1988) (independent contractors). In the context of unpaid internships,[NOTE 2] we think a non-exhaustive set of considerations should include:

1. The extent to which the intern and the employer clearly understand that there is no expectation of compensation. Any promise of compensation, express or implied, suggests that the intern is an employee—and vice versa.

2. The extent to which the internship provides training that would be similar to that which would be given in an educational environment, including the clinical and other hands-on training provided by educational institutions.

3. The extent to which the internship is tied to the intern's formal education program by integrated coursework or the receipt of academic credit.

4. The extent to which the internship accommodates the intern's academic commitments by corresponding to the academic calendar.

5. The extent to which the internship's duration is limited to the period in which the internship provides the intern with beneficial learning.

6. The extent to which the intern's work complements, rather than displaces, the work of paid employees while providing significant educational benefits to the intern.

7. The extent to which the intern and the employer understand that the internship is conducted without entitlement to a paid job at the conclusion of the internship.

Applying these considerations requires weighing and balancing all of the circumstances. No one factor is dispositive and every factor need not point in the same direction for the court to conclude that the intern is not an employee entitled to the minimum wage. In addition, the factors we specify are non-exhaustive—courts may consider relevant evidence beyond the specified factors in appropriate cases.

This flexible approach is faithful to Portland Terminal. Nothing in the Supreme Court's decision suggests that any particular fact was essential to its conclusion or that the facts on which it relied would have the same relevance in every workplace. See Portland Terminal, 330 U.S. at 150–53; see also *Solis v. Laurelbrook Sanitarium & Sch., Inc.*, 642 F.3d 518, 526 n. 2 (6th Cir.2011) ("While the Court's recitation of the facts [in Portland Terminal] included those that resemble the Secretary's six factors, the Court gave no indication that such facts must be present in future cases to foreclose an employment relationship." (internal citation omitted)).

The approach we adopt also reflects a central feature of the modern internship—the relationship between the internship and the intern's formal education. The purpose of a bona-fide internship is to integrate classroom learning with practical skill development in a real-world setting,[NOTE 3] and, unlike the brakemen at issue in Portland Terminal, all of the plaintiffs were enrolled in or had recently completed a formal course of post-secondary education. By focusing on the educational aspects of the internship, our approach better reflects the role of internships in today's economy than the DOL factors, which were derived from a 68–year old Supreme Court decision that dealt with a single training course offered to prospective railroad brakemen.

In sum, we agree with the defendants that the proper question is whether the intern or the employer is the primary beneficiary of the relationship, and we propose the above list of non-exhaustive factors to aid courts in answering that question. The district court limited its review to the six factors in DOL's Intern Fact Sheet. Therefore, we vacate the district court's order granting partial summary judgment to Glatt and Footman and remand for further proceedings. On remand, the district court may, in its discretion, permit the parties to submit additional evidence relevant to the plaintiffs' employment status, such as evidence on Glatt's and Footman's formal education. Of course, we express no opinion with respect to the outcome of any renewed motions for summary judgment the parties might make based on the primary beneficiary test we have set forth.

II. Antalik's Motion to Certify the New York Class

We turn now to the defendants' appeal of the district court's order certifying Antalik's proposed class. We review the district court's class certification ruling for abuse of discretion and the conclusions of law that informed its decision to grant certification de novo. See *Parker v. Time Warner Entm't Co.*, 331 F.3d 13, 18 (2d Cir.2003).

Antalik moved to certify the following class:

All individuals who had unpaid internships between September 28, 2005 and September 1, 2010 with one or more of the following divisions of FEG [Fox Entertainment Group]: Fox Filmed Entertainment, Fox Group, Fox Networks Group, and Fox Interactive Media (renamed News Corp. Digital Media).

Pls.' Mot. For Class Cert. 19, Doc. No. 104.

Antalik bore the burden of showing that her proposed class satisfied Rule 23's requirements of: (1) numerosity; (2) commonality; (3) typicality; and (4) adequacy of representation. See Fed.R.Civ.P. 23(a)(1–4). Because Antalik moved to certify the class pursuant to Rule 23(b)(3), she was also required to show that "questions of law or fact common to class members predominate over any questions affecting only individual members, and that a class action is superior to other available methods for fairly and efficiently adjudicating the controversy." See Fed R. Civ. P. 23(b)(3). "The predominance requirement is satisfied if resolution of some of the legal or factual questions that qualify each class member's case as a genuine controversy can be achieved through generalized proof, and if these particular issues are more substantial than the issues subject only to individualized proof." In re U.S. Foodservice Inc. Pricing Litig., 729 F.3d 108, 118 (2d Cir.2013) (internal quotation marks omitted).

The district court found that common questions pertaining to liability could be answered by evidence tending to show that interns were recruited to help with busy periods, that they displaced paid employees, and that Fox employees overseeing internships did not believe they complied with the law. Because "common questions of liability predominate over individual calculations of damages," the district court concluded that Antalik had satisfied her burden to establish predominance. S.A. 33–34.

On appeal, the defendants argue the district court erred by concluding that Antalik demonstrated predominance because it misconstrued our standards for determining when common questions predominate over individual ones. We agree and therefore vacate the district court's order certifying Antalik's class.[NOTE 4]

Antalik points to evidence, relied on by the district court, suggesting that the defendants sometimes used unpaid interns in place of paid employees. Such evidence is relevant but not sufficient to answer the question of whether each intern was an employee entitled to compensation under the FLSA. As our previous discussion of the proper test indicates, the question of an intern's employment status is a highly individualized inquiry. Antalik's common evidence will not help to answer whether a given internship was tied to an education program, whether and what type of training the intern received, whether the intern continued to work beyond the primary period of learning, or the many other questions that are relevant to each class member's case. Moreover, defendants' undisputed evidence demonstrated that the various internship programs it offered differed substantially across the many departments and four Fox divisions included in the proposed class.

In sum, even if Antalik established that Fox had a policy of replacing paid employees with unpaid interns, it would not necessarily mean that every Fox intern was likely to prevail on her claim that she was an FLSA employee under the primary beneficiary test, the most important issue in each case. Thus, assuming some questions may be answered with generalized proof, they are not more substantial than the questions requiring individualized proof. See, e.g., *Myers v. Hertz Corp.*, 624 F.3d 537, 548 (2d Cir.2010) (district court did not abuse its discretion by denying certification of a class of store managers where determination of whether managers were exempt under the FLSA would be resolved only "by examining the employees' actual job characteristics and duties"); In re Wells Fargo Home Mortgage Overtime Pay Litig., 571 F.3d 953, 958–59 (9th Cir.2009) (district court abused its discretion by certifying a class of mortgage consultants because employer's centralized policy of exempting consultants did not predominate over individual variation in job responsibilities).

Because the most important question in this litigation cannot be answered with generalized proof, we vacate the district court's order certifying Antalik's proposed class and remand for further proceedings consistent with this opinion.[NOTE 5]

III. Antalik's Motion to Conditionally Certify the Nationwide FLSA Collective

Finally, we turn to the defendants' appeal of the district court's order conditionally certifying Antalik's proposed nationwide FLSA collective. Like the district court's certification determination pursuant to Rule 23, we review its decision to conditionally certify an FLSA collective for abuse of discretion. See Myers, 624 F.3d at 554; *Morgan v. Family Dollar Stores, Inc.*, 551 F.3d 1233, 1260 (11th Cir.2008).

The FLSA permits employees to create a collective by opting-in to a backpay claim brought by a similarly situated employee. 29 U.S.C. § 216(b). The unique FLSA collective differs from a Rule 23 class because plaintiffs become members of the collective only after they affirmatively consent to join it. See *Genesis Healthcare Corp. v. Symczyk*, 133 S.Ct. 1523, 1530 (2013). As a result, unlike a Rule 23 class, a conditionally certified FLSA collective does not acquire an independent legal status. Id.

In Myers, we endorsed a two-step process for certifying FLSA collective actions. At step one, the district court permits a notice to be sent to potential opt-in plaintiffs if the named plaintiffs make a modest factual showing that they and others together were victims of a common policy or plan that violated the law. 624 F.2d at 555. At step two, with the benefit of additional factual development, the district court determines whether the collective action may go forward by determining whether the opt-in plaintiffs are in fact similarly situated to the named plaintiffs. Id.

Antalik moved, at step one, to conditionally certify the following nationwide collective:

All individuals who had unpaid internships between September 28, 2008 and September 1, 2010 with one or more of the following divisions of FEG: Fox Filmed Entertainment, Fox Group, Fox Networks Group, and Fox Interactive Media (renamed News Corp. Digital Media).

Pls.' Mot. For Class Cert. 28, Doc. No. 104.

After some discovery had been completed, the district court, relying primarily on its analysis of commonality with respect to Antalik's Rule 23 motion, authorized plaintiffs to send the opt-in notice because Antalik put forth generalized proof that interns were victims of a common policy to replace paid workers with unpaid interns. On defendants' motion for reconsideration, the district court narrowed the opt-in notice to include only those individuals who held unpaid internships between January 18, 2010, and September 1, 2010, because the statute of limitations precluded claims by earlier Fox interns.

We certified for immediate review the question of whether a higher standard, urged by defendants, applies to motions to conditionally certify an FLSA collective made after discovery. We do not need to decide that question, however, because the plaintiffs in Antalik's proposed collective are not similarly situated even under the minimal pre-discovery standard.[NOTE 6] Under the primary beneficiary test we have set forth, courts must consider individual aspects of the intern's experience. None of the common proof identified by Antalik, and relied on by the district court, will address these questions, and all of the issues with respect to the proposed class's range of experience will also be issues for the proposed collective. If anything, Antalik's proposed collective presents an even wider range of experience than her proposed class because it is nationwide in scope, rather than limited to just New York interns.

Accordingly, for substantially the same reasons as with respect to Antalik's Rule 23 motion, we vacate the district court's order conditionally certifying Antalik's proposed nationwide collective action and remand for further proceedings.[NOTE 7]

CONCLUSION

For the foregoing reasons, the district court's orders are VACATED and the case REMANDED for further proceedings consistent with this opinion.

JOHN M. WALKER, JR., Circuit Judge.

NOTES:

NOTE 1: See, e.g., Nat'l Ass'n of Colleges & Emp'rs, Position Statement: U.S. Internships (July 2011), available at http://www . naceweb.org/advocacy/position-statements/ united-states-internships.aspx ("NACE, Position Statement").

NOTE 2: Like the parties and amici, we limit our discussion to internships at for-profit employers.

NOTE 3: See, e.g., NACE, Position Statement (defining the internship as "form of experiential learning that integrates knowledge and theory learned in the classroom with practical application and skills development in a professional setting").

NOTE 4: In light of this disposition, we need not consider defendants' arguments related to commonality. See *Myers v. Hertz Corp.*, 624 F.3d 537, 548 (2d Cir.2010).

NOTE 5: Nevertheless, although the district court's certification order was erroneous in light of the new legal standard we have announced today, we cannot foreclose the possibility that a renewed motion for class certification might succeed on remand under our revised standard.

NOTE 6: "We are not necessarily limited to the certified issue, as we have the discretion to consider any aspect of the order from which the appeal is taken." J.S. ex rel. *N.S. v. Attica Cent. Sch.*, 386 F.3d 107, 115 (2d Cir.2004); accord *Grayson v. K Mart Corp.*, 79 F.3d 1086, 1096 (11th Cir.1996) (same applied to order conditionally certifying a collective).

NOTE 7: Again, we do not foreclose the possibility that a renewed motion for conditional collective certification might succeed on remand under the revised standard. See supra n. 5.

STUDY QUESTIONS

- Who initiated the *Fox Searchlight* lawsuit and why? What were the key differences between the three plaintiffs' situations?
- Did the court conclude that the interns were employees?
- Why did the court refuse to apply the Fair Labor Standards Act (FLSA) factors in this case? What is the "primary beneficiary" test? What factors are involved? Explain the court's reasoning for adopting this test. What is the central feature of the court's "primary benefit" test?
- What liability was imposed on the production company as a result of this ruling?
- How did the court rule on the class action issue? Why?
- Does *Fox Searchlight* apply to nonprofits? Hint—see NOTE 2.

- In 2014, publisher Condé Nast agreed to retroactively pay $5.8m to 7000 former interns who had worked at *Vanity Fair*, *Vogue*, and other magazines to settle a class-action lawsuit accusing the magazine company of underpaying its workers.
- If the defendant in these cases had been a nonprofit museum rather than a for-profit Hollywood movie studio or a New York for-profit publisher, do you think the court would have come to a different result?
- What impact do you think these rulings will have on the availability of internship opportunities at museums and other organizations? What policies and procedures should a museum adopt to ensure that it does not encounter similar problems with its internship programs?

CHAPTER 3:
MUSEUM FACILITIES

In this chapter we consider issues relating to the management of museum facilities. The museum's responsibility for the safety of its visitors (including minors), speech rights on museum property, use of museum facilities by third parties, emergency planning and management, compliance with ADA regulations, and historic preservation laws, are just some of the many issues that can arise in connection with managing museum facilities.

USE OF MUSEUM FACILITIES

Museum facilities represent the physical manifestation of the museum. Many museums are housed in iconic buildings designed by famous architects. Other museums are located in historic structures. Sometimes the building may be an essential part of the museum's collection, such as in the case of historic house museums, for example. Others are built to preserve and display the museum's collections. In any case, museum buildings house museum personnel and collections and provide the platform on which the museum's many and varied activities—exhibitions, programs, fundraising, etc.—take place.

Proper management of museum facilities is an important part of a museum's public trust responsibility. As the American Alliance of Museums (AAM) *Standards Regarding Facilities and Risk Management* state: "Museums care for their resources in trust for the public. It is incumbent upon them to ensure the safety of their staff, visitors and neighbors, maintain their buildings and grounds, and minimize risk to the collections that they preserve for future generations." Assessing and addressing the safety risks to people and collections associated with the operation of museum facilities are just one part of this trust responsibility. Complying with laws regulating the accessibility and use of museum facilities are another. Building construction and maintenance raise additional legal issues. Museums that maintain historic properties—which can be viewed as part of the museum's collections—may also need to consider the impact of historic preservation laws.

MUSEUM VISITORS

Every museum has a duty to protect the people who enter its buildings and grounds. Human beings are remarkably prone to accidents and injury—they are, after all, human. They may slip, trip, or fall, hurting themselves or others, or damaging museum property.

Likewise, museum visitors make up all sectors of the population, from the very young to the very old, and those who, for one reason or another, may be particularly at risk of injury. And museums, which often feature unusual architecture and have high-value objects on display, are ideal places for accidents of all kinds. In fact, the very nature of museums, which encourage people to look at things rather than looking where they are going, is part of the problem. Some museum features or exhibits may also be inherently dangerous or encourage dangerous behavior. The latter are often referred to in the law as "attractive nuisances."

The museum may be held liable for any accidents or injury occurring on its premises. Liability is governed by tort law concepts that vary widely in their scope and application and by jurisdiction. In assessing the legal risks, it is essential to determine the applicable law. Most often legal liability is based on a finding of *negligence*—that is, conduct or conditions that fall below a certain standard established by law for the protection of others. Where there is a reasonable connection between the substandard conduct or conditions and the injury or damage that results, the museum may be found to have been negligent and may be held liable for the resulting injury or damage. The *Alloway* case included in the Cases and Other Readings below involves a claim of negligence by the museum in designing and maintaining an exhibit and in not adequately warning guests about the hazardous conditions.

The standard of conduct or care is generally that of a reasonably prudent person under similar circumstances. A professional with special knowledge or skills may be held to a level of care or skill that an ordinary person with that knowledge or skill would be expected to exercise. For example, a museum director may be held to a level of care or skill that a reasonably prudent museum director would exercise under similar circumstances.

Minors in the museum present a special problem. Often safety measures that may seem reasonably prudent with respect to adult visitors may not be considered sufficient with regard to children. As a result, extra care must be taken in planning programs or exhibits where is it likely that children will be present.

While waivers or disclaimers may be obtained from the parents of minors who visit the museum—particularly for extended visits like summer camps—when faced with an injured plaintiff, courts generally interpret those agreements narrowly, or ignore them altogether. In many states, parents have no legal authority to contract or bargain away their children's rights, including the right to sue for injuries. Settlements of claims involving minors often require court approval. When a parent signs a waiver, there is no judicial supervision. And the statute of limitations for minors may not even begin to run until the child becomes an adult. In a few states, courts have upheld parental waivers where the child is injured in a manner anticipated by the waiver and there is no finding of gross negligence on the part of the host entity. In some jurisdictions this "minority rule" applies only to nonprofit organizations. In any case, under appropriate circumstances a carefully drafted waiver or disclaimer can be helpful in alerting museum visitors to potential risks so that they can take necessary precautions. In some situations, signage may be an appropriate substitute for a written waiver or disclaimer.

The museum may be held indirectly or "vicariously" liable for the negligent acts of board members, staff, and volunteers during the exercise of their employment or museum-related duties. Policies and practices regarding employee and volunteer conduct and behavior can help to minimize risks posed by those acting in an employment or volunteer capacity on behalf of the museum.

Some states have enacted "charitable immunity" laws that limit the liability of certain nonprofit organizations under their jurisdiction. These laws take a variety of forms. In the *Pantano* case reprinted below, the outcome turned on whether the plaintiff was a "direct beneficiary" of the museums charitable activities—if not, the museum would not be held liable for the plaintiff's injuries under New Jersey law.

Generally speaking, the museum would not be held liable for the negligent acts of a *bona fide* independent contractor. Risks can be managed through contractual provisions including indemnification provisions which assign responsibility for any liability that may arise from contracted for goods or services. Independent contractors can be required to obtain insurance coverage and indemnify the museum for any damages resulting from the provision of their services. Insurance policies can and should also be utilized to manage the impact of risks that the museum cannot avoid. Even so, in operating its facilities, museums should attempt to minimize risks whenever possible.

Accidents will happen. However, to minimize potential liability, museums are expected to adopt facilities management practices to reduce risks. The key to these management practices is to anticipate potential risks and to implement practices and procedures which will reduce them to acceptable levels. In some cases, a formal risk assessment is conducted in connection with or by an insurance carrier. With regards to museum exhibits, for example, the nature of the exhibit, the level of access granted to visitors, the characteristics of the visitors, and whether the exhibit involves interactive elements, may all factor into the risk assessment.

Museum professionals may need to seek creative solutions to minimizing risks. Often a barrier or signage which might be appropriate in another setting may conflict with curatorial objectives or an artist's vision for the work on display. At the end of the day, however, professional judgment must outweigh creative whims to preserve the museum's integrity and reputation.

Reading Note: Trip and fall cases are highly fact dependent. In the case reprinted below, the plaintiff, a museum visitor, alleged that she was injured because of the negligent design and maintenance of a science museum exhibit. The appeals court reviewed the trial court's grant of summary judgement for the museum and remanded the case for further proceedings. The case exemplifies how courts apply the standard of care in the museum context.

CHRISTINA ALLOWAY V. THE FRANKLIN INSTITUTE

No. 2840 EDA 2016 (Pa Super. 2017)

Before: GANTMAN, P.J., PANELLA, and STRASSBURGER, JJ.

Memorandum by STRASSBURGER, J.:

Christina Alloway appeals from the August 11, 2016 order granting summary judgment in favor of The Franklin Institute. Upon review, we reverse and remand for further proceedings.

The Franklin Institute is a science museum located in Philadelphia, Pennsylvania. In August 2014, Alloway was a patron of the museum and "sustained an ankle injury as the result of a fall while exiting from the 'Neural Climb' attraction at the Brain Exhibit" at the museum. Trial Court Opinion, 3/17/2017, at 2. "As its name suggests, the 'Neural [C]limb' portion of the Brain Exhibit is an interactive climbing attraction." *Id.* Specifically, Alloway contended that when she "climbed down off of the [B]rain [E]xhibit, she stepped down off of an abnormally large step onto an uneven surface where the padded/spongy floor meets the hard floor and was caused to trip and fall on the uneven/unstable surface of the exhibit." Third Amended Complaint, 5/20/2016, at ¶ 7. According to Alloway, her fall was caused by the negligence of The Franklin Institute's design and maintenance of the exhibit, as well as its failure to warn patrons of the dangerous condition. *Id.* at ¶ 12.

The 18-foot-tall "Neural Climb," which features dynamic lighting and sound effects, is a popular part of the "Your Brain" exhibit at The Franklin Institute in Philadelphia. The "Neural Climb" was the subject of the "slip and fall" case Alloway v. The Franklin Institute.

Thus, in August 2015, Alloway filed a complaint against The Franklin Institute. After several sets of preliminary objections, the pleadings were closed, and the parties conducted discovery. On June 30, 2016, The Franklin Institute moved for summary judgment. Alloway filed a response, and on August 16, 2016, the trial court granted summary judgment in favor of The Franklin Institute and against Alloway. Alloway timely filed a notice of appeal, and both Alloway and the trial court complied with Pa.R.A.P. 1925.

On appeal, Alloway argues that the trial court erred in granting summary judgment where genuine issues of material fact exist. *See* Alloway's Brief at 5. We review such a claim mindful of the following.

> Our standard of review on an appeal from the grant of a motion for summary judgment is well-settled. A reviewing court may disturb the order of the trial court only where it is established that the court committed an error of law or abused its discretion. As with all questions of law, our review is plenary.
>
> In evaluating the trial court's decision to enter summary judgment, we focus on the legal standard articulated in the summary judgment rule. Pa.R.C.P. 1035.2. The rule states that where there is no genuine issue of material fact and the moving party is entitled to relief as a matter of law, summary judgment may be entered. Where the nonmoving party bears the burden of proof on an issue, he may not merely rely on his pleadings or answers in order to survive summary judgment. Failure of a non-moving party to adduce sufficient evidence on an issue essential to his case and on which he bears the burden of proof establishes the entitlement of the moving party to judgment as a matter of law. Lastly, we will review the record in the light most favorable to the non-moving party, and all doubts as to the existence of a genuine issue of material fact must be resolved against the moving party.

Krauss v. Trane U.S. Inc., 104 A.3d 556, 562-63 (Pa. Super. 2014) (quoting *Shepard v. Temple University*, 948 A.2d 852, 856 (Pa. Super. 2008)).

We bear in mind the well-settled law regarding the obligations of a landowner to business invitees. [NOTE 1]

> Pennsylvania courts long have recognized that a land owner owes a duty to business invitees to keep premises safe. "The standard of care a possessor of land owes to one who enters upon the land depends upon whether the person entering is a trespassor, licensee, or invitee." *Carrender v. Fitterer*, 469 A.2d 120, 123 ([Pa.] 1983). In *Carrender*, our Supreme Court explained:
>
> > Possessors of land owe a duty to protect invitees from foreseeable harm. Restatement [(Second) of Torts], §§ 341A, 343 & 343A. With respect to con-

ditions on the land which are known to or discoverable by the possessor, the possessor is subject to liability only if he

"(a) knows or by the exercise of reasonable care would discover the condition, and should realize that it involves an unreasonable risk of harm to such invitee, and

(b) should expect that they will not discover or realize the danger, or will fail to protect themselves against it, and

(c) fails to exercise reasonable care to protect them against the danger."

Restatement, *supra*, § 343. Thus, as is made clear by section 343A of the Restatement,

> "[a] possessor of land is not liable to his invitees for physical harm caused to them by any activity or condition on the land whose danger is known or obvious to them, unless the possessor should anticipate the harm despite such knowledge or obviousness."

Restatement, *supra*, § 343A.

Id. For a danger to be "known," it must "not only be known to exist, but ... also be recognized that it is dangerous and the probability and gravity of the threatened harm must be appreciated." *Id.* at 124 (quoting Restatement (Second) of Torts, § 343A, comment b).

More recently, this Court reiterated that "[t]he duty owed to a business invitee is the highest owed to any entrant upon land. The landowner is under an affirmative duty to protect a business visitor not only against known dangers but also against those which might be discovered with reasonable care." *Campisi v. Acme Markets, Inc.*, 915 A.2d 117, 119 (Pa. Super. 2006) (citation omitted). Further:

> An invitee is entitled to expect that the possessor will take reasonable care to ascertain the actual condition of the premises and, having discovered it, either to make it reasonably safe by repair or to give warning of the actual condition and the risk involved therein. Therefore an invitee is not required to be on the alert to discover defects which, if he were a mere licensee, entitled to expect nothing but notice of known defects, he might be negligent in not discovering. This is of importance in determining whether the visitor is or is not guilty of contributory negligence [NOTE 2] in failing to discover a defect, as well as in determining whether the defect is one which the possessor should believe that his visitor would not discover, and as to which, therefore, he must use reasonable care to warn the visitor.

Restatement (Second) of Torts § 343, comment d.

Reinoso v. Heritage Warminster SPE LLC, 108 A.3d 80, 84–85 (Pa. Super. 2015) (*en banc*).

As the trial court acknowledges, whether The Franklin Institute breached this duty "hinges on whether a finder of fact could find the existence of a latent defect which was or should have been known to the premises owner." *Id.* The trial court concluded that because "Alloway fails to provide technical data regarding a hazardous slant or unevenness, the eventual fact finder's analysis must hinge on more subjective evidence and testimony." *Id.* The trial court went on to conclude that "[w]hile [Mark Harmon, representative of The Franklin Institute,] was willing to concede to the existence of unlevel areas on the exhibit's floor, he stressed that the ground itself was largely uniform in evenness." *Id.* at 6-7. Thus, the trial court concluded there was no defect as a matter of law. Alloway argues that this testimony should be permitted to be weighed by a fact finder.

We review the evidence considered by the trial court, beginning with a review of Alloway's account of the fall. Alloway described the Brain Exhibit as "a dark place, very few lights, with some netting and platforms to climb through." *See* The Franklin Institute's Motion for Summary Judgment, 6/30/2016, at Exhibit D (N.T. (Deposition of Alloway), 6/6/2016, at 24). According to Alloway, she "stepped like [she] would step off of a step, because that is the distance that it looked like to [her]." *Id.* at 28. "The surface was not a hard floor like it looked to be. It's foam and it was uneven." *Id.* at 29. Alloway testified that she fell "[b]ecause the floor was uneven." *Id.* at 32.

In support of its motion for summary judgment, The Franklin Institute provided a diagram of this location and Harmon's testimony. The diagram shows that there was a 1¼ inch slant to the step from which Alloway fell. *See* Memorandum of Law in Support of The Franklin Institute's Motion for Summary Judgment, 6/30/2016, at 19 (showing a diagram of the step where there is a 1¼ inch slant to the step). Additionally, Harmon testified that there are no safety or warning signs about the Neural Climb. *See* The Franklin Institute's Motion for Summary Judgment, 6/30/2016, at Exhibit E (N.T. (Deposition of Harmon), 6/6/2016, at 25). Harmon testified that "[p]retty much every place where you step down is even.... There might be a slight slant." *Id.* at 26. When Harmon was asked whether "there are some exits and entrances into the Neural Climb that ... the flooring underneath would be unlevel," Harmon responded, "Yes. I'll agree to that." *Id.* at 27- 28.

Based on the foregoing, we conclude that there is sufficient evidence, if believed by a fact-finder, to find a defect in the exhibit about which The Franklin Institute knew or should have known. Thus, we hold the trial court erred in granting summary judgment on this basis. [NOTE 3]

We now turn to the trial court's conclusion that even if there was a defect, that defect did not present an unreasonable danger. Trial Court Opinion, 3/17/2017, at 8. The determination of whether a danger is unreasonable is generally left to the fact finder. *See e.g., Zito v. Merit Outlet Stores*, 647 A.2d 573 (Pa. Super. 1994) (holding a jury should determine whether the store laid out displays and aisles in such a way that it could not rely on patrons observing an existing ramp).

The trial court concluded that the name of the exhibit itself, the Neural Climb, together with Alloway's climbing through the exhibit before her final step caused her fall, leads to the conclusion that "a reasonable patron would have been aware of the atypical nature of the exhibit and would have adjusted his or her behavior accordingly." Trial Court Opinion, 3/17/2017, at 8. Once again, we conclude that the extent of Alloway's potential comparative negligence is an issue for a fact finder. According to Alloway, the step "looked like a normal size step down" and she did not realize it was as high as it was and then when she stepped, the "floor was uneven." The Franklin Institute's Motion for Summary Judgment, 6/30/2016, at Exhibit D (N.T. (Deposition of Alloway), 6/6/2016, at 30, 32). Again, these facts, if credited by a fact-finder, could lead to the conclusion that Alloway acted reasonably. *See Jerominski v. Fowler, Dick & Walker*, 93 A.2d 433 (Pa. 1953).

Because "there is evidence that would allow a fact-finder to render a verdict in favor of the non-moving party," we hold the trial court erred by granting summary judgment in favor of The Franklin Institute. *Reinoso*, 108 A.3d at 85 (quoting *Mull v. Ickes*, 994 A.2d 1137, 1139-40 (Pa. Super. 2010)). Thus, we reverse the order of the trial court.

Order reversed. Case remanded for further proceedings. Jurisdiction relinquished.

NOTES:

NOTE 1: In the instant case, the parties do not dispute that Alloway was a business invitee and therefore owed the highest duty of any entrant upon land by The Franklin Institute. *See* Trial Court Opinion, 3/17/2017, at 6 ("That Alloway was a business invitee is not in dispute[.]").

NOTE 2: Comparative negligence is codified in 42 Pa.C.S. § 7102 and provides as follows:

> In all actions brought to recover damages for negligence resulting in death or injury to person or property, the fact that the plaintiff may have been guilty of contributory negligence shall not bar a recovery by the plaintiff or his legal representative where such negligence was not greater than the causal negligence of the defendant or defendants against whom recovery is sought, but any damages sustained by the plaintiff shall be diminished in proportion to the amount of negligence attributed to the plaintiff.

Id. at § 7102(a).

NOTE 3: We recognize that the aforementioned slant and unevenness may appear to be trivial. However, we have held that the triviality of a defect is a question best resolved by a fact finder. *See Reinoso*, 180 A.3d at 87 ("Pennsylvania courts have largely avoided assigning any dividing line between trivial and non-trivial defects[.]").

STUDY QUESTIONS

- In *Alloway* the appeals court reversed the trial court's grant of summary judgement to the museum. What was the basis for the reversal?
- Pennsylvania law distinguishes between three types of visitors—what are they? What obligations does a business owner have to each type?
- What key fact did the court rely on in reversing the trial court's decision?
- What did the *Alloway* court say about the plaintiff's responsibility?

Reading Note: The following case also involves appellate court review of a trial court decision to grant summary judgement in favor of a museum. A visitor slipped on the front steps of the museum while attending a panel discussion at the museum hosted by her employer. The appellate court reviewed New Jersey law which limits liability for charitable organizations under certain circumstances, and remanded the case to the trial court to determine whether the museum would be liable based on the facts of the case.

LOREDANA PANTANO V. NEWARK MUSEUM

DOCKET NO. A-0252-14T1 (N.J. Super. Feb. 11, 2016)
Before Judges Messano, Simonelli and Carroll.

On appeal from the Superior Court of New Jersey, Law Division, Essex County, Docket No. L-94-13.

PER CURIAM

Plaintiff Loredana Pantano appeals from the Law Division's August 15, 2014 order that dismissed her complaint against defendants Newark Museum and Newark Museum Association (collectively, the Museum). The judge concluded that plaintiff's claim was barred by the Charitable Immunity Act (the CIA), N.J.S.A. 2A:53A-7 to -13-1.

The standards we apply on appeal are well-known. "An appellate court reviews an order granting summary judgment in accordance with the same standard as the motion judge." *Bhagat v. Bhagat*, 217 N.J. 22, 38 (2014) (citing *W.J.A. v. D.A.*, 210 N.J. 229, 237-38 (2012); *Henry v. N.J. Dep't of Human Servs.*, 204 N.J. 320, 330 (2010)). We "identify whether there are genuine issues of material fact and, if not, whether the moving party is entitled to summary judgment as a matter of law." Ibid. (citing *Brill v. Guardian Life Ins. Co. of Am.*, 142 N.J. 520, 540 (1995); R. 4:46-2(c)).

> [A] determination whether there exists a "genuine issue" of material fact that precludes summary judgment requires the motion judge to consider whether the competent evidential materials presented, when viewed in the light most favorable to the non-moving party, are sufficient to permit a rational factfinder to resolve the alleged disputed issue in favor of the non-moving party.
> [*Brill*, supra, 142 N.J. at 540.]

We then decide "whether the motion judge's application of the law was correct." *Atl. Mut. Ins. Co. v. Hillside Bottling Co.*, 387 N.J. Super. 224, 231 (App. Div.), certif. denied, 189 N.J. 104 (2006). In this regard, "[w]e review the law de novo and owe no deference to the trial court . . . if [it has] wrongly interpreted a statute." *Zabilowicz v. Kelsey*, 200 N.J. 507, 512 (2009).

I.

We discern the following facts from the motion record. See *Ji v. Palmer*, 333 N.J. Super. 451, 463-64 (App. Div. 2000) (appellate review of the grant of summary judgment is limited to the record that existed before the motion judge). On the morning of February 9, 2012, plaintiff slipped and fell on icy steps at an entrance to the Museum, suffering injuries to her back. [NOTE 1] At the time, plaintiff was employed as an immigration attorney by La Casa de Don Pedro (La Casa), a nonprofit organization located in Newark. Upon arrival at her office that day, plaintiff was told by La Casa's Director of Personal Development to go to the Museum for an educational panel discussion being held as part of La Casa's fortieth anniversary celebration. Plaintiff's co-workers were also instructed by their supervisors to attend the event at the Museum, and a sign was placed on La Casa's office door stating that it would be closed until noon.

La Casa's Director of Program and Fund Development, Carrie Puglisi, testified at her deposition that the event was one of several organized to celebrate and commemorate the organization's history and role in the development of Newark. Staff members were not directly engaged in fundraising, but they were told to mingle with those attending the event, some of whom were contributors to La Casa. The Museum charged La Casa a fee for the use of the facility, specifically an auditorium to be used by the panel and those in attendance.

The Museum is a nonprofit association organized exclusively for charitable, artistic, scientific, educational, historical and cultural purposes, and is exempt from all federal, state and local taxes. It does, on occasion, rent its facilities to the public in order to generate income. On the day of plaintiff's fall, the Museum was closed to the public, and its exhibitions were not open to La Casa's guests.

Plaintiff filed suit alleging the Museum was negligent in its maintenance of the premises. Following discovery, the Museum moved for summary judgment, contending that plaintiff was a direct beneficiary of its charitable endeavors. Plaintiff cross-moved, arguing that she was required to attend the event by her employer, and therefore was not a direct beneficiary of the Museum's benefactions. She also asserted that the Museum was not engaged in any charitable purpose at the time, because it had rented the facility to La Casa in order to generate income.

After considering argument, the judge rendered an oral opinion concluding that "plaintiff was . . . directed to go to the event . . . . And she was told to go there by her boss . . . to be a face of La Casa, to advance La Casa's position among some participants and in the community." The judge noted it was undisputed that the Museum was a charitable institution. She reasoned that the issue was whether or not plaintiff was a "beneficiary under the [CIA]."

The judge rejected the contention that plaintiff was not a beneficiary of the Museum's charitable endeavors because she was required to be there by her employer. The judge reasoned such an argument was "a strained interpretation of what it mean[t] to be a beneficiary of the charitable entit[y's] purposes and benef[actions]." She noted that La Casa itself benefitted from the Museum's charitable endeavors by being permitted to use the facility. The judge granted the Museum's motion, and this appeal followed.[NOTE 2]

Plaintiff contends that she was not a "beneficiary" of the Museum's charitable purposes at the time of her fall because she was on the premises at the direction of her employer. We agree that pursuant to the Court's holding in *Mayer v. Fairlawn Jewish Center*, 38 N.J. 549 (1962), plaintiff was not a "direct recipient of [the Museum's] good works." *Ryan v. Holy Trinity Evangelical Lutheran Church*, 175 N.J. 333, 350 (2003). We therefore reverse.

II.

The grant or denial of a motion seeking immunity under the CIA is a question of law that we review de novo. *Estate of Komninos v. Bancroft Neurohealth, Inc.*, 417 N.J. Super. 309, 318 (App. Div. 2010); *Auerbach v. Jersey Wahoos Swim Club*, 368 N.J. Super. 403, 410 (App. Div.), certif. denied, 180 N.J. 458 (2004). Although the issue before us is discrete, the precise contours of the existing legal landscape are difficult to discern.

In pertinent part, the CIA provides

> No nonprofit corporation, society or association organized exclusively for religious, charitable or educational purposes . . . shall, except as is hereinafter set forth, be liable to respond in damages to any person who shall suffer damage from the negligence of any agent or servant of such corporation, society or association, where such person is a beneficiary, to whatever degree, of the works of such nonprofit corporation, society or association; provided, however, that such immunity from liability shall not extend to any person . . . where such person is one unconcerned in and unrelated to and outside of the benefactions of such corporation, society or association.

[N.J.S.A. 2A:53A-7(a) (emphasis added).]

"The CIA serves two primary purposes. First, immunity preserves a charity's assets. Second, immunity recognizes that a beneficiary of the services of a charitable organization has entered into a relationship that exempts the benefactor from liability." *Kuchera v. Jersey Shore Family Health Ctr.*, 221 N.J. 239, 247 (2015) (citing *O'Connell v. State*, 171 N.J. 484, 496 (2002)).

For purposes of the CIA, the Court has explained

> The established test for determining whether a party is a beneficiary of the works of a charity has two prongs. The first is that the institution pleading the immunity, at

the time in question, "was engaged in the performance of the charitable objectives it was organized to advance." The second is that the injured party must have been a direct recipient of those good works.

[*Ryan*, supra, 175 N.J. at 350 (citations omitted) (quoting *Anasiewicz v. Sacred Heart Church*, 74 N.J. Super. 532, 536 (App. Div.), certif. denied, 38 N.J. 305 (1962)).]

Whatever separates a "beneficiary" from a non-beneficiary for purposes of the CIA, one thing is clear

> In assessing who is a beneficiary of the works of a charity, that notion is to be interpreted broadly, as evidenced by the use of the words "to whatever degree" modifying the word "beneficiary" in the statute. Those who are not beneficiaries must be "unconcerned in and unrelated to" the benefactions of such an organization.

[Id. at 353 (quoting *Gray v. St. Cecilia's School*, 217 N.J. Super. 492, 495 (App. Div. 1987)).]

As to the first prong, we reject plaintiff's argument that the Museum was not engaged in its charitable purposes at the time of her fall because it charged a customary fee for use of the facility. "A qualifying organization does not lose its statutory immunity merely because it charges money for its services, unless it makes a profit or collects fees for services totally unrelated to its organizational pursuits." *Graber v. Richard Stockton Coll. of N.J.*, 313 N.J. Super. 476, 482 (App. Div.) (citations omitted), *certif. denied*, 156 N.J. 409 (1998). The record is quite clear that hosting an educational panel discussion in the auditorium was entirely consistent with the Museum's charitable endeavors. Although we recently characterized the second prong of the test as "distinguish[ing] between 'persons benefiting from the charity,' and persons who contribute to the charity 'by virtue of their attendance or participation,'" *Kain v. Gloucester City*, 436 N.J. Super. 466, 480 (App. Div.) (quoting *Roberts v. Timber Birch-Broadmoore Athletic Ass'n*, 371 N.J. Super. 189, 196 (App. Div. 2004)), *certif. denied*, 220 N.J. 207 (2014), the issue is more complex.

As noted, in this case the judge reasoned that the Museum was engaged in its charitable works by permitting La Casa to utilize the facility, albeit at a modest cost. We have frequently said that "[b]eneficiary status '[does] not depend upon a showing that the claimant personally received a benefit from the works of the charity,' but rather 'whether the institution pleading the immunity . . . was engaged in the performance of the charitable objectives it was organized to advance.'" *Hehre v. DeMarco*, 421 N.J. Super. 501, 508 (App. Div. 2011) (second and third alterations in original) (quoting *Anasiewicz*, supra, 74 N.J. Super. at 536), *certif. denied*, 209 N.J. 99 (2012); accord *Auerbach*, supra, 368 N.J. Super. at 414; *Rupp ex rel. Rupp v. Brookdale Baptist Church*, 242 N.J. Super. 457, 463 (App. Div. 1990).

The Court has recognized that, for purposes of the CIA, a plaintiff is a beneficiary of an entity's good works even though his or her presence on the premises results from a relationship with another person or entity, and not the charity itself. In *Ryan*, supra, for example, the plaintiff, a member of a nonprofit group, The Mothers' Center, that held its weekly meetings at a church that charged a small fee, was injured when struck in the head by a door that came off its hinges. 175 N.J. at 337-39. The Mothers' Center was entitled to immunity under the CIA. Id. at 349.

The Court then considered whether the plaintiff was a beneficiary of the church's charitable works for purposes of the CIA. Id. at 350. The Court concluded: "The Mothers' Center receives benefits through its members. [The plaintiff] was a member of the Mothers' Center and was physically present on the premises of [the church] for the purpose of receiving the benefits conferred by that church on the Mothers' Center and the partakers of its programs." Id. at 353-54. The Court held that the church was immune. Id. at 354.

In *Bieker v. Community House of Moorestown*, 169 N.J. 167, 171 (2001), while the plaintiff was playing basketball in a nonprofit organization's gymnasium, his minor son, who had accompanied his father as a spectator, strayed and was injured. The Court remanded the matter to the trial court to resolve factual questions as to whether the nonprofit was entitled to immunity under the CIA. Id. at 179-80. However, the Court also held, that "[t]he child was plainly a recipient of Community House's 'benefactions,' even if only as a companion of his father and a spectator at his father's basketball game." Id. at 180.

We have reached similar conclusions in a variety of factual circumstances. For example, in *Kain*, supra, 436 N.J. Super. at 471, the plaintiff was injured while chaperoning his sons' Boy Scout troop during a sailing lesson aboard a ship operated by a charitable nonprofit entity. We held that "[i]n his capacity as both a parent and a chaperone for the group receiving the benefit of the educational sail, [the plaintiff] cannot qualify as one 'unconcerned in and unrelated to the benefactions of'" the charitable entity. Id. at 481 (quoting *Ryan*, supra, 175 N.J. at 353).

In *Lax v. Princeton University*, 343 N.J. Super. 568, 569-70 (App. Div. 2001), the plaintiff fell while attending a concert at a hall owned by the university and rented to a nonprofit chamber symphony. Citing the Court's reasoning in *Bieker*, we held that the university was immune under the CIA. Id. at 573. See also *Gray*, supra, 217 N.J. Super. at 493-95 (mother who was on the premises to pick up her son after class was a beneficiary of parochial school's benefactions); *Bixenman v. Christ Episcopal Church Parish House*, 166 N.J. Super. 148, 150-53 (App. Div. 1979) (member of Greek Orthodox parish that paid nominal fee for use of the defendant-church's premises was beneficiary of the defendant-church's "benefactions"); *Pomeroy v. Little League Baseball of Collingswood*, 142 N.J. Super. 471, 475 (App. Div. 1976) (nonprofit baseball league immune for injuries sustained by spectator at game); *Anasiewicz*, supra, 74 N.J. Super. at 537-38 (church was immune for injuries suffered by a non-parishioner guest at wedding).

However, other cases have reasoned that the "[t]he controlling relationship is that between the plaintiff as an individual and the defendant entity." *Auerbach*, supra, 368 N.J. Super. at 414-15; see also *Kasten v. Y.M.C.A.*, 173 N.J. Super. 1, 8 (App. Div. 1980) ("[T]he plaintiff's individual relationship with the defendant charity is controlling.") (citing Mayer, supra, 38 N.J. at 553-54). This is no more apparent than those limited number of reported decisions in which the factual scenario involves a plaintiff who, like plaintiff here, finds herself on the premises of a charitable entity at the command of her employer.

In *Mayer v. Fairlawn Jewish Center*, 71 N.J. Super. 313, 315 (App. Div. 1961), *aff'd* in part, *rev'd* in part on other grounds, 38 N.J. 549 (1962), a case the motion judge found "[did not] have any applicability," an employee of the Development Corporation for Israel, was promoting the sale of bonds at a dinner on the premises of the defendant. In describing the relationship between the plaintiff's employer and the defendant on the night of the accident, we said "that the sale of the bonds and the use of the hall therefor, represented a co-operative effort by [the defendant] and the Development Corporation to achieve a common objective." Id. at 316-17.

In affirming the trial court's rejection of the defendant's asserted immunity, we held

> [The] [p]laintiff was not a member of [the] Center. He had no concern or relation with its benefactions. He was not even a resident of the community. He was "outside" of its "benefactions." His attendance at the Center building on the night of the accident was in the performance of his job for his employer and not as a recipient of [the] Center's beneficence or philanthropy .... To hold that, because of his employment, plaintiff derived an indirect advantage from the activities of [the] Center and that, therefore, he was a beneficiary of the "works" of [the] Center so as to render it free from liability . . . , is to ascribe to the [CIA] a meaning completely foreign to its declared purpose and unwarrantedly to extend its protective scope.

[Id. at 321.]

In affirming this portion of our decision, the Court said

> We desire to emphasize further plaintiff's capacity as an employee of Development Corporation of Israel. Assuming, arguendo, his employer was a recipient of Center's benefactions, Mayer's status on the premises cannot be measured by that of his employer. His rights so far as the statutory immunity is concerned depended upon his own individual relation with the Center. True, he was on the premises under the aegis of his employer, and by virtue of the employer's arrangement became an implied invitee of the Center. But he was there in fulfillment of his function and obligation as an employee to engage in the employer's work at the direction of the employer, and not for the purpose of receiving personally the philanthropy of the Center. Under the circumstances present he was a stranger to the charity and the statute does not stand in the way of recovery.

[*Mayer*, supra, 38 N.J. at 553-54 (emphasis added).]

The *Mayer* Court cited a number of out-of-state decisions in support of its conclusion, and one New Jersey decision, *Rose v. Raleigh Fitkin-Paul Morgan Memorial Hospital*, 136

N.J.L. 553 (E. & A. 1948). In *Rose*, decided before enactment of the CIA, the Court of Errors and Appeals concluded that a private duty nurse who was injured by the negligence of a charitable hospital was not "a participant in the hospital's bounty," because she was paid by her patient, not the hospital, her presence was advantageous to the hospital because of a serious nursing shortage, and she was an invitee of the hospital. Id. at 556-57.

In *Glowacki v. Underwood Memorial Hospital*, 270 N.J. Super. 1 (App. Div. 1994), a pediatric nurse employed by a Philadelphia hospital was dispatched by her employer to assist in the transport of a critically ill baby from a New Jersey hospital and was injured in the process. I d. at 5-6. We dismissed as "without merit" the hospital's argument that it was subject to the CIA's limitation on damages, id. at 12 (citing R. 2:11-3(e)(1)(E)), holding the "[p]laintiff was not a beneficiary within the contemplation of the statute." Ibid. (citing *Mayer,* supra, 71 N.J. Super. at 313; *Mayer,* supra, 38 N.J. at 549).

In *Ryan*, supra, 175 N.J. at 354, the Court summarily rejected the plaintiff's reliance on *Mayer.* Noting that Mrs. Ryan was not employed by the Mothers' Center, and explaining its holding in Mayer, the Court said that Mayer's "rights depended on his individual relation with the [Jewish] Center." Ibid. Mayer was not a beneficiary under the CIA because "[h]e was present on the premises . . . at the direction of his employer and in fulfillment of his function as an employee, not for the purpose of receiving personally the philanthropy of the [Jewish] Center." Ibid. (emphasis added).

In this case, the Museum argues that plaintiff was not on the premises to actually perform any function related to her employment at La Casa. It cites to deposition testimony from Puglisi acknowledging that La Casa's employees were at the Museum to partake in the panel discussion, and they had no particular function to perform. The Museum argues that *Mayer* is therefore distinguishable. We disagree.

The plaintiff in *Mayer* was on the premises "[i]n his official capacity," although it is unclear what functions, if any, he was performing that night at a "dinner held . . . for the promotion of bond sales." *Mayer*, supra, 71 N.J. Super. at 315. There was a charge for tickets to the event, only a minimal portion of which went to the Jewish Center itself, id. at 316, and there is no indication that the plaintiff was actually selling development bonds at the dinner. In other words, we have no reason to believe that he was performing any more specific function on behalf of his employer than plaintiff was performing on behalf of La Casa.

The record is clear. Despite having scheduled appointments at her office on the day in question, plaintiff was ordered to report to the Museum instead and represent her employer at an event celebrating its fortieth anniversary. Ironically, in this case, plaintiff fell on entrance steps to the Museum, i.e., before she was able to perform any function that might have been assigned by her employer. There simply is no support for the Museum's position that plaintiff's status as a non-beneficiary was dependent upon a specific job-related task that she was to perform while on the premises.

Applying the two-prong test for beneficiary status, it is clear that plaintiff suffered her injury while the Museum "'was engaged in the performance of the charitable objectives it was organized to advance.'" *Ryan*, supra, 175 N.J. at 350 (quoting *Anasiewicz*, supra, 74 N.J. Super. at 536). To be a beneficiary under the second prong, the "injured party [must be] a direct recipient" of the Museum's good works. Ibid. (citing *DeVries v. Habitat for Humanity*, 290 N.J. Super. 479, 487-88 (App. Div. 1996), *aff'd* o.b., 147 N.J. 619 (1997)). Only those "'unconcerned in and unrelated to the benefactions of [the] organization'" are "not beneficiaries." Id. at 353.

As the cited cases amply demonstrate, our consideration of whether plaintiff was a direct beneficiary of the Museum's benefactions requires a fact-sensitive analysis. See *DeVries*, supra, 290 N.J. Super. at 488-93 (discussing various factual patterns in determining an injured party's beneficiary status). In *Mayer*, supra, the Court clearly stated that the plaintiff was not a beneficiary of the Jewish Center's benefactions because "he was there in fulfillment of his function and obligation as an employee to engage in the employer's work at the direction of the employer, and not for the purpose of receiving personally the philanthropy of the Center." 38 N.J. at 554. In *Ryan*, supra, the Court implicitly reaffirmed that the employee of a third party who is injured on the premises of a charity is not a beneficiary of that charity, even though the employer itself was receiving the benefactions of the charity. 175 N.J. at 354.

"[A]s an intermediate appellate court, we are bound to follow and enforce the decisions of the Supreme Court." *Kaye v. Rosefielde*, 432 N.J. Super. 421, 470-71 (App. Div. 2013), *rev'd* on other grounds, 223 N.J. 218, 238 (2015). Under existing precedent, plaintiff, as an employee of La Casa who was ordered on the day of her fall to attend the panel discussion at the Museum, was not a direct beneficiary of the Museum's charitable endeavors.

We therefore reverse the order granting summary judgment to the Museum and remand the matter to the Law Division.

NOTES:

NOTE 1: Although not dispositive to the issues raised on appeal, plaintiff received medical treatment through her employer's workers' compensation carrier, which currently has a lien on any recovery.

NOTE 2: We do not have an order denying plaintiff's cross-motion which sought to strike the Museum's affirmative defense that the CIA applied.

STUDY QUESTIONS

- New Jersey law limits the liability of charitable organizations under certain circumstances. What was the key factual issue in the *Pantano* case? Describe the reasoning on which the court's decision to remand the case was based.

- Do you think that charitable immunity laws like the one in Pantano are a good idea? Assess the pros and cons.

- What advice would you give to a museum based on these two trip and fall cases?

- In 2012, the Los Angeles Museum of Art installed a large-scale public art sculpture on its grounds entitled *Levitated Mass*. The artwork by Michael Heizer consists of a 340-ton boulder placed above an inground pedestrian walkway. Transportation of the boulder from a quarry to the museum was a public spectacle: videos are available on LACMA's website and on YouTube. Assess the legal risks associated with *Levitated Mass*. Can you think of other risky museum exhibits or programs?

Levitated Mass, *a massive rock sculpture installed at the Los Angeles County Museum of Art, posed a number of unusual risks.*

MUSEUM FACILITIES AS PUBLIC FORUMS

As public trusts, museums, whether publicly or privately owned, are generally open to the public. They are sometimes the venue for exploring controversial subjects and often encourage a diversity of viewpoints. As such, museums are increasingly becoming a venue for public demonstrations and protests on all kinds of cultural and political issues.

Some protests are targeted at controversial donors, directors, or board members connected to the museum. Others are in reaction to controversial exhibits or programs, or objects contained in the museum's collections. Still others simply seek to use the museum property as a high-profile venue for expressing social or political points of view. To what extent must a museum tolerate such disruptive behavior? And what steps can a museum lawfully take to control protests on the museum's property?

The First Amendment to the United States Constitution states that Congress "will pass no law abridging the freedom of speech." In the First Amendment context, "speech" may consist of words or actions, and is sometimes referred to more broadly as "expression." Prohibitions on flag-burning and other acts of protest may raise First Amendment issues. Whether speech occurring in a museum is protected by the First Amendment depends on the answers to five key questions: Is there state action? Is the speech "protected speech"? Who is speaking? What is the forum and applicable test? And, are the museum's policies clear, objective, and consistently enforced?

Since the First Amendment prohibits the government from restricting speech, it is impossible for a purely private party to violate it: State action is required. The question "is there state action?" depends on whether the museum is a public or private museum. Municipal museums and those that are publicly funded clearly meet the requirement for state action. Museums that receive federal funding—in the form of grants or otherwise—also open themselves up to claims under the First Amendment. A museum that did not accept any government funding would not be subject to the requirements of the First Amendment.

Whether the speech is "protected speech" depends on the type of speech involved. Commercial speech—speech promoting goods or services—receives little or no protection under the First Amendment. As a result, a museum can prohibit or restrict commercial speech on museum property. Someone attempting to place an advertisement for goods or services on museum property, for example, would not be entitled to protection under the First Amendment. Political speech, on the other hand, may be entitled to First Amendment protection depending on the nature of the forum and the applicable test.

First Amendment case law identifies four main types of forums, each of which has its own applicable balancing test. Traditional forums are public spaces, such as streets, parks, sidewalks, and the like. In these public spaces, restrictions on freedom of speech must be applied evenly, without consideration as to the nature of the speech. In the legal parlance, such restrictions must be "content neutral"—that is, the restrictions cannot be based on what is being said (content), but they can regulate how the speech is presented. Reasonable restrictions based on time, place, and manner of the expression are acceptable. Any such restrictions must be narrowly tailored and must serve a compelling state interest. Alternative channels for expression must be provided.

Designated forums are spaces that are intentionally made available for expressive speech. Places such as community centers and public auditoriums are examples of designated forums. While not "public spaces" *per se*, these venues have opened themselves up as public forums and are treated as such. Accordingly, as with traditional public forums, restrictions on expressive speech must be content neutral and narrowly tailored to serve a compelling state interest. Reasonable restrictions may be placed on the time, place, and manner of the speech.

Limited forums are places not ordinarily associated with public speech, such as libraries and museums. Restrictions can be placed on expressive speech in these spaces if such restrictions are reasonable in light of the purpose of the restriction, and the restrictions are neutral with respect to viewpoint. Certain types of speech—such as political protests—can be prohibited as long as those restrictions are implemented in a content-neutral way. In other words, a museum can prohibit political protests on museum property if it prohibits all political protests and not just those expressing viewpoints it disfavors.

Restrictions on expressive speech in non-public forums, such as hospitals, military bases, and jails, are acceptable under the same standards as those for limited forums.

To ensure that restrictions placed on expressive speech in a museum's buildings and grounds are implemented in a consistently objective, unbiased, and neutral manner, the adoption of a policy on viewpoint expression in the museum is advised. The museum may want to consider providing a controlled venue for expressive speech—designating a corner of the lobby, for example. Care should be taken in doing this, however, because once a venue is designated, it will be difficult to change. Guidelines for acceptable subject manner, etc. can be outlined in the museum's public expression policy.

The museum's social media platforms may also function as public forums. The same considerations apply when a museum allows public expression on its social media platforms. The museum should adopt terms of use for its social media accounts for employees, volunteers, and the public, that reflect and are consistent with the museum's policies on public expression.

Museums should be mindful of the fact that while the museum can be an acceptable forum for political activity, including campaign events, the museum risks its tax-exempt status if it is perceived to be engaging in lobbying activities. Renting space to a political candidate may be acceptable if candidates with other views are also able to rent the space on the same terms and conditions. Candidates must be allowed equal time at any political forums or events sponsored by the museum. And any income received by the museum from such a campaign event would likely be subject to unrelated business income tax (UBIT) unless it clearly furthers the museum's mission. More on these issues can be found the discussion of museum funding in chapter 6.

CASES AND OTHER READINGS

Reading Note: The *GeorgiaCarry.Org* case reprinted below involves a museum's ability to prohibit certain types of activities on its property. The court's ruling turns on whether a Georgia law permits a private organization that leases property from a governmental entity to prohibit the carrying of firearms on the leased premises. The court makes clear at the outset that its decision is not based on federal or state constitutional questions, even though the impetus behind bringing the case is the constitutional right to bear arms and, tangentially, the right to freedom of expression.

GEORGIACARRY.ORG, INC. V. ATLANTA BOTANICAL GARDEN, INC.

S18G1149 (Ga. Supreme Ct. 2019)

BETHEL, Justice.

The Atlanta Botanical Garden, Inc. (the "Garden") leases land from the City of Atlanta where the Garden maintains and nurtures an extensive garden complex. The Garden wishes to enforce a policy precluding the possession of firearms by visitors to, and guests of, the Garden, like Phillip Evans. Evans holds a valid weapons carry license under Georgia law and asserts that he is authorized to carry a firearm at the garden under the authority of OCGA [Official Code of Georgia Annotated] § 16-11-127 (c), which provides that license holders "shall be authorized to carry a weapon . . . in every location in this state not [excluded by] this Code section." The Garden counters that it may enforce its policy based on an exception to the general rule found in the same statutory paragraph. Specifically, the Garden claims that it may exclude Evans because it is, in the words of the statute, "in legal control of private property through a lease" and is thus entitled "to exclude or eject a person who is in possession of a weapon . . . on their private property." Id.

As a preliminary matter, it is worth noting that the resolution of this appeal does not turn on an interpretation or understanding of the Second Amendment to the Constitution of the United States [NOTE 1] or of Article 1, Section 1, Paragraph VIII of the Georgia Constitution.[NOTE 2] Nor does this appeal require us to determine whether the statute runs afoul of other provisions of the United States Constitution or the Georgia Constitution regarding property rights. Rather than requiring an analysis of these constitutional issues, this appeal turns only on the proper interpretation of the above-referenced statute.[NOTE 3] We granted certiorari to consider whether OCGA § 16-11-127 (c) permits a private organization that leases property owned by a municipality to prohibit the carrying of firearms on the leased premises. The Court of Appeals determined that it does and affirmed the trial court's grant of summary judgment in favor of the Garden on the petition for declaratory and injunctive relief filed by GeorgiaCarry.Org, Inc. ("GeorgiaCarry") and Evans (collectively, the "Appellants"). See *GeorgiaCarry.org, Inc. v. Atlanta Botanical Garden, Inc.*, 345 Ga. App. 160 (812 SE2d 527) (2018).

Contrary to the rulings below, we determine that for purposes of OCGA § 16-11-127 (c), property may be considered "private" only if the holder of the present estate in the property is a private person or entity. In this case, because the City is a public entity, if it is the holder of the present estate, then the leased premises is not private property within the meaning of the statute because property owned by a municipality is not "private property." If the City thus owns the property, then the Garden has no right to exclude the carrying of firearms on the leased premises because it is not "in legal control of private property through a lease." If, on the other hand, by the terms of the 50-year lease with the City, the Garden holds the present estate in the property, then the property is "private property," the Garden is a "private property owner," and it had the right to exclude Evans from carrying a firearm on the premises. However, because the lease is not in the record on appeal and because this determination requires an examination of its provisions to determine whether it granted an estate to the Garden, summary judgment should not have been granted in favor of the Garden under the theory it asserted in its motion for summary judgment. We therefore reverse the judgment of the Court of Appeals and remand the case for further proceedings.

1. BACKGROUND.

> Summary judgment is proper if the pleadings, depositions, answers to interrogatories, and admissions on file, together with the affidavits, if any, show that there is no genuine issue as to any material fact and that the moving party is entitled to a judgment as a matter of law. OCGA § 9-11-56 (c). Thus, to prevail on a motion for summary judgment, the moving party must demonstrate that there is no genuine issue of material fact so that the party is entitled to judgment as a matter of law. A defendant may do this by either presenting evidence negating an essential element of the plaintiff's claims or establishing from the record an absence of evidence to support such claims. . . . Summary judgments enjoy no presumption of correctness on appeal, and an appellate court must satisfy itself de novo that the requirements of OCGA § 9-11-56 (c) have been met.

(Citations and punctuation omitted.) *Cowart v. Widener*, 287 Ga. 622, 624 (1) (a) (697 SE2d 779) (2010).

The underlying facts of this case are largely undisputed. As the Court of Appeals recounted:

> The Garden is a private, nonprofit corporation that operates a botanical garden complex on property secured through a 50-year lease with the City of Atlanta. [NOTE 4] Evans holds a Georgia weapons carry license and is a member of GeorgiaCarry, a gun-rights organization. In October 2014, Evans twice visited the Garden, openly carrying a handgun in a holster on his waistband. Although no Garden employee objected to [Evans'] weapon on his first visit, he was stopped by a Garden employee during his second visit and informed that weapons were prohibited on the Garden premises, except by police officers. A security officer eventually detained Evans, and he was escorted from the Garden by an officer with the Atlanta Police Department. Evans and GeorgiaCarry subsequently filed a petition in the Fulton County Superior Court, seeking declaratory and injunctive relief on the basis that OCGA § 16-11-127 (c) authorized Evans—and similarly situated individuals—to carry a weapon at the Garden. The trial court dismissed the petition after concluding that the issues were not appropriate for the relief sought, a ruling that the Supreme Court reversed in part on appeal. See *GeorgiaCarry.org v. Atlanta Botanical Garden, Inc.*, 299 Ga. 26 (785 SE2d 874) (2016). On remand, the trial court held that the Garden's property was consid-

ered private under well-established Georgia precedent, allowing the Garden to exclude weapons and, consequently, granted summary judgment to the Garden. [NOTE 5]

GeorgiaCarry, 345 Ga. App. at 161. The Court of Appeals affirmed the trial court's grant of summary judgment in favor of the Garden, and we granted certiorari.

2. HISTORY OF OCGA § 16-11-127 (C).

The current text of OCGA § 16-11-127 (c) was enacted as one of a series of significant revisions to Georgia's weapons possession laws beginning in 2008. Until June 30, 2008, former OCGA § 16-11-127 (a) prohibited individuals from carrying firearms and other prohibited items "at a public gathering." See Ga. L. 2003, p. 423, § 1 (effective June 1, 2003). "Public gatherings" included, but were not limited to, "athletic or sporting events, churches or church functions, political rallies or functions, publicly owned or operated buildings, or establishments at which alcoholic beverages are sold for consumption on the premises." OCGA § 16-11-127 (b) (effective June 1, 2003). The Code section also provided that it did not "otherwise prohibit the carrying of a firearm in any other public place by a person licensed or permitted to carry such firearm[.]" Id.

In 2008, the General Assembly amended this Code section to, among other things, provide that certain government and law enforcement officials were permitted to carry "pistols" in "publicly owned or operated buildings," except that a courthouse security plan could prohibit the carrying of a pistol in a courthouse. Ga. L. 2008, p. 1199, § 4 (effective July 1, 2008). The 2008 law also permitted any "person licensed or permitted to carry a firearm" under state law to carry a firearm, subject to some limitations, "in all parks, historic sites, and recreational areas, including all publicly owned buildings located in such parks, historic sites, and recreational areas and in wildlife management areas . . . and in public transportation[.]" Id. The 2008 law also provided that no person was permitted to carry a firearm into a place prohibited by federal law. Id.

On June 4, 2010, a more sweeping reform to the firearm possession laws, including the provisions of OCGA § 16-11-127, took effect. Except for government buildings, courthouses, jails, prisons, places of worship, state mental health facilities, and areas in and around schools, the new version of OCGA § 16-11-127 (c) permitted "a license holder" and other statutorily authorized persons to carry a weapon "in every location in this state." Ga. L. 2010, p. 963, § 1-3 (effective June 4, 2010). The 2010 law provided that any person who carried a weapon into any of the prohibited locations would be "guilty of carrying a weapon . . . in an unauthorized location" and that such conduct would be "punished as a misdemeanor[.]" Id. The 2010 law also contained the proviso that "private property owners or persons in legal control of property through a lease, rental agreement, licensing agreement, contract, or any other agreement to control access to such property" had the right to "forbid possession of a weapon or long gun on their property." Id.

On July 1, 2014, this Code section was again amended. Among other changes to the state's weapons possession laws that took effect the same day, the proviso in OCGA § 16-11-127 (c) was amended by the General Assembly to insert the word "private" in three instances where it had not previously been included:

> . . . private property owners or persons in legal control of *private* property through a lease, rental agreement, licensing agreement, contract, or any other agreement to control access to such *private* property shall have the right to exclude or eject a person who is in possession of a weapon or long gun on their *private* property[.]

(Emphasis supplied.) Ga. L. 2014, p. 599, § 1-3 (effective July 1, 2014). This is the current text of OCGA § 16-11-127 (c), and it was in effect at the time the Garden prohibited Evans from carrying a firearm onto the premises the Garden leases from the City of Atlanta. [NOTE 6]

The Garden and amici curiae [NOTE 7] have argued throughout this case that, because the Garden has a private property interest—a leasehold—in the premises it leases from the City of Atlanta, that premises is considered "private property" within the meaning of OCGA § 16-11-127 (c) for the duration of the lease. It was on this basis that the Court of Appeals determined that the Garden had the right to exclude Evans from carrying a firearm on the premises. As discussed below, we reject this interpretation of the statute.

3. FOR PURPOSES OF OCGA § 16-11-127 (C), "PROPERTY" IS PUBLIC OR PRIVATE DEPENDING ON THE NATURE OF THE HOLDER OF THE PRESENT ESTATE IN THE PROPERTY.

As we are concerned here with the interpretation of OCGA § 16-11-127 (c), we begin with well-established principles of statutory construction. As we have discussed:

> [A] statute draws its meaning from its text. And because we presume that the General Assembly meant what it said and said what it meant when it comes to the meaning of statutes, we must read the statutory text in its most natural and reasonable way, as an ordinary speaker of the English language would. Important are the common and customary usages of the words, which, in cases like this one, include the usual and customary meaning of terms as used in a legal context. For context, we may look to other provisions of the same statute, the structure and history of the whole statute, and the other law—constitutional, statutory, and common law alike—that forms the legal background of the statutory provision in question.

(Citations and punctuation omitted.) *Fed. Deposit Ins. Corp. v. Loudermilk*, 305 Ga. 558, 562 (1) (826 SE2d 116) (2019).

The key issue in this case is the meaning of the phrase "private property," as it is used four times in the current version of OCGA § 16-11-127 (c). That Code section provides, in relevant part, that

> A license holder[NOTE 8] . . . shall be authorized to carry a weapon ... in every location in this state not [excluded by] this Code section; provided, however, that *private property* owners or persons in legal control of *private property* through a lease, rental agreement, licensing agreement, contract, or any other agreement to control access to such *private property* shall have the right to exclude or eject a person who is in possession of a weapon . . . on their *private property*. . . .

(Emphasis supplied.)

The phrase "private property" is not defined in OCGA § 16-11-127 (c), and the Code does not otherwise provide an applicable definition for that phrase. Thus, we must examine the meaning of those words in their broader context, including other legal authorities which may inform our understanding of the phrase's meaning in this statute. *Loudermilk*, 305 Ga. at 562 (1).

Black's Law Dictionary defines "private" to mean "[o]f, relating to, or involving an individual, as opposed to the public or the government." Black's Law Dictionary 1389 (10th ed. 2014). It likewise defines "private property" to mean "[p]roperty—protected from public appropriation—over which the owner has exclusive and absolute rights." Black's Law Dictionary 1412 (10th ed. 2014). To the extent these definitions are helpful, they suggest two principles pertinent to this case. First, in order for a piece of property to be considered "private," the property must be in private ownership. Second, government ownership of the property means that such property is not "private property."

These principles comport with our decision in *Department of Transportation v. City of Atlanta*, 255 Ga. 124, 132 (3) (b) (337 SE2d 327) (1985), in which we determined that the term "private property," as used in a statute outlining the Department of Transportation's authority to bring condemnation proceedings, "does not include property owned by a government or a government entity," noting that such a reading of the phrase "follows the plain meaning of 'private property.'" We went on to note that "[m]unicipal land . . . is in *all* respects public property." (Emphasis in original.) Id. at 134 (3) (c). Such a reading of the term "private property" is also consistent with a decision of the Court of Appeals in which it determined that the certain property at issue in the case was "public property inasmuch as it [was] owned by [a county housing authority], a public institution." *Vakilzadeh Enters., Inc. v. Housing Auth. of the County of DeKalb*, 271 Ga. App. 130, 131 (608 SE2d 724) (2004).

Moreover, following the 2014 amendment, OCGA § 16-11-127(c) now draws a clear distinction between "private property" and "public property." In the 2014 amendment, which brought the Code section into its current form, the General Assembly limited the right to exclude the carrying of firearms to only those who own or lease "private property." But, as discussed above, that right was not always thus limited. The version of OCGA § 16-11-127 (c) in effect from June 4, 2010, to June 30, 2014, provided that

> private property owners or persons in legal control of *property* through a lease, rental agreement, licensing agreement, contract, or any other agreement to control access to such *property* shall have the right to forbid possession of a weapon or long gun on their *property.*

(Emphasis supplied.) Ga. L. 2010, p. 963, § 1-3.

As the Appellants note and the Court of Appeals acknowledged, with respect to leased property, this language was notably silent as to whether the underlying property being leased was public or private. Thus, a fair reading of the 2010 provision suggests there would have been little need to determine whether the property at issue was public or private as the right to exclude firearms from a leased premises was not dependent on the public or private nature of the property. Accordingly, the Garden's argument that its leasehold interest in the property gives it the right to exclude the possession of firearms on the leased property would be significantly stronger if the version of OCGA § 16-11-127 (c) enacted in 2010 had been in effect at the time the Garden excluded Evans from carrying a firearm on the property. But it was not.

The 2014 amendment to the Code section specified that the right to exclude the carrying of firearms applies only to "private property." To suggest otherwise is to argue that the additional language made no change to the statute's application. Such a reading of course violates a core principle of statutory interpretation that "changes in statutory language generally indicate an intent to change the meaning of the statute." (Citation omitted.) *Jones v. Peach Trader Inc.*, 302 Ga. 504, 514 (III) (807 SE2d 840) (2017). See also *Dept. of Transp.*, 255 Ga. at 132 (3) (b) ("After repeated references to 'property,' or 'any property,' we cannot ignore the legislature's specific use of the adjective 'private' for the first time.")

All parties seem to agree that no reading of OCGA § 16-11-127(c) permits a determination that the City of Atlanta is a "private property owner" under the statute. In light of the dictionary definitions noted above, other interpretations of the statutory phrase "private property" in our applicable decisional law, and the evolution of the text of OCGA § 16-11-127 (c) leading up to the 2014 amendment, they are undoubtedly correct. Even so, the Garden urges this Court to find that its lease with the City of Atlanta makes the Garden "a person in control of private property through a lease" within the meaning of the statute. But the simple fact that a lease is held by a private entity does not answer the question of whether the property in question is "private property."

We note that in support of its holding below, the Court of Appeals relied principally on this Court's statement in *Delta Air Lines, Inc. v. Coleman*, 219 Ga. 12, 16 (1) (131 SE2d

768) (1963) that "private property becomes public property when it passes into public ownership; and public property becomes private property when it passes into private ownership." (Punctuation omitted.) *GeorgiaCarry*, 345 Ga. App. at 162. The Court of Appeals also relied upon two later decisions in support of the broad proposition that the public or private nature of property changes based on the public or private nature of an entity that holds a leasehold interest in it. Id. at 162-163 (citing *Columbus Bd. of Tax Assessors v. Med. Ctr. Hosp. Auth.*, 302 Ga. 358 (806 SE2d 525) (2017) and *Douglas County v. Anneewakee, Inc.*, 179 Ga. App. 270 (346 SE2d 368) (1986)).

As this Court discussed in *Coleman*, under the tax code in effect at the time, all public property was exempt from taxation but remained so only so long as it remained in public ownership. *Coleman*, 219 Ga. at 16. This Court stated that once property was sold to a private owner, "the natural implication is that it goes there with the ordinary incidents of private property and therefore is subject to being taxed." Id. This principle was not limited simply to cases in which a parcel of public property was sold in fee to a private owner who would be subject to ad valorem taxes on the property. The tax code in effect at the time also required "the owner of any *estate* in land less than the fee to return it for taxes and pay taxes on it as on other property." (Emphasis supplied.) Id. As "[a] leasehold is an estate in land less than the fee," this Court determined that the tax code provided that such leasehold was "severed from the fee and classified *for tax purposes* as realty." (Emphasis supplied.) Id. Thus, in *Coleman*, we held that "[w]hen the City of Atlanta conveyed . . . a leasehold *estate* in the land . . . [the City] completely disposed of a distinct *estate* in its land for a valuable consideration, and [the private entity] acquired [the distinct estate] and holds it as a *private owner*." (Emphasis supplied.) Id.

Based on *Coleman* and later property tax cases, the Court of Appeals held that "the leasehold interest held by the Garden, when severed from the fee owned by the City of Atlanta, is classified as private property." Id. at 163. The Garden and amici curiae now urge this Court to affirm that ruling and its application of *Coleman*.

The Court of Appeals was undoubtedly correct that the Garden has property rights in the property it leases from the City of Atlanta. Those are private rights because the Garden is a private entity. But that does not answer the question of whether, by virtue of the rights granted by the lease, the Garden has an "estate" in the property. The Court of Appeals appears to have interpreted *Coleman* to mean that any lease between a public landlord and a private tenant renders the leased property "private property" because such lease creates a private estate in the property. But that does not reflect a correct understanding of the legal concepts relating to leases that underlie *Coleman*.

When a landlord and a tenant enter into a lease for a specified period of time, as the Garden and the City did here, that lease may create one of two types of rights in the property in favor of the tenant. If the lease grants to the tenant "the right simply to possess and enjoy the use of" the property, "no estate passes out of the landlord and the tenant has only a usufruct." OCGA § 44-7-1 (a). "A usufruct has been referred to as merely a license in real property, which is defined as authority to do a particular act or series of acts on land of another without possessing any estate or interest therein." (Citation and punctuation omitted). *Jekyll Dev. Assoc., L.P. v. Glynn County Bd. of Tax Assessors*, 240 Ga. App. 273, 274 (1) (523 SE2d 370) (1999).

However, a lease for a fixed period of time may also create an estate for years. "An estate for years is one which is limited in its duration to a period which is fixed or which may be made fixed and certain." OCGA § 44-6-100. "The grant by one person to another of an estate for years out of his own estate, with reversion to himself, is usually termed a lease." OCGA § 44-6-102. "An estate for years carries with it the right to use the property in as absolute a manner as may be done with a greater estate, provided that the property or the person who is entitled to the remainder or reversion interest is not injured by such use." OCGA § 44-6-103.[NOTE 9] "[I]t is the policy of the law to treat the tenant of any estate for years as the owner, during the life of such estate." *Evans Theatre Corp. v. De Give Inv. Co.*, 79 Ga. App. 62, 67 (52 SE2d 655) (1949) (citing *James G. Wilson Mfg. Co. v. Chamberlain-Johnson-Du Bose Co.*, 140 Ga. 593 (79 SE 465) (1913)). See also *Coleman*, 219 Ga. at 16 (conveyance of leasehold estate "disposed of a distinct estate" in the land which grantee holds "as a private owner."); *Life Chiropractic College, Inc. v. Carter & Assoc., Inc.*, 168 Ga. App. 38, 39 (1) (308 SE2d 4) (1983) (distinguishing between "right of possession" created by usufruct and "proprietary interest" granted by estate for years).

"Because a usufruct is not considered an estate in real property under Georgia law," *Clayton County Board of Tax Assessors v. Aldeasa Atlanta Joint Venture*, 304 Ga. 15, 16 (1) (815 SE2d 870) (2018), the creation of a usufruct in favor of a tenant does not pass any estate out of the hands of the landlord. Thus, during the term of a usufruct, the landlord continues to hold the present estate in the property. By contrast, if the lease creates an estate for years, the present estate in the property passes from the landlord/grantor to the tenant/grantee for the duration of the lease, and the tenant/grantee is treated by our law as the owner of the property for that period of time. *Evans Theatre Corp.*, 79 Ga. App. at 67.

As *Coleman* and its progeny illustrate, this distinction presents itself most readily in the context of property taxation because estates for years are taxable, and usufructs are not. See *Camp v. Delta Air Lines, Inc.*, 232 Ga. 37, 39 (205 SE2d 194) (1974) (citing *Coleman* for the proposition that an estate for years is taxable). See also *Macon-Bibb County Bd. of Tax Assessors v. Atlantic Southeast Airlines, Inc.*, 262 Ga. 119, 119 (414 SE2d 635) (1992) (construing OCGA § 48-5-3 to exclude usufructs from the definition of "taxable property"). *Coleman* itself acknowledges that it was because the lease at issue in that case created an estate—as opposed to a usufruct—that the property interest held by the private entity was taxable. *Coleman*, 219 Ga. at 16-17 (1). But *Coleman* and other tax cases, as well as our modern statutes regarding usufructs and estates for years, illustrate a broader principle—that the grant of an estate transfers ownership of the property to the estate holder during the term of the estate, *Evans Theatre Corp.*, 79 Ga. App. at 67, whereas, the creation of a usufruct does not. The Court of Appeals' analysis and application of *Coleman* and its progeny omits this key distinction.

This leaves the case before us in an interesting posture. The Garden has argued throughout the case that its status as a private entity and its lease with the City make the property at issue "private property" within the meaning of OCGA § 16-11-127 (c). But as we have just discussed, that a lease is held by a private entity does not summarily answer the question of whether the property governed by the lease is "private property." Rather, an examination of the terms of the lease is required in order to determine whether the lease created an estate in the private lessee such that the property has become private property for the term of the lease.

While the Garden's lease with the City may allow the Garden to use and enjoy the leased premises and create for the Garden private property *rights* in the premises, it is not clear whether the provisions of the lease grant an *estate* in the property to the Garden. If the lease does not grant an estate to the Garden, the Garden merely has a usufruct. If that is the case, throughout the term of the Garden's lease with the City, the leased premises has never been anything other than public property because the present estate in the property has always been held by the City of Atlanta, a public entity. See *Dept. of Transp.*, 255 Ga. at 132-133 (3). That a private entity has a lease granting it the right to use and enjoy the public property does not change this essential fact. See OCGA § 44-7-1 (a).

However, it is quite possible that the 50-year lease between the City and the Garden created an estate for years that is presently held by the Garden. Where "the term of a lease is for a period greater than five years, a rebuttable presumption arises that the parties intended to create an estate for years rather than a usufruct." *Eastern Air Lines, Inc. v. Joint City-County Bd. of Tax Assessors*, 253 Ga. 18, 19 (1) (315 SE2d 890) (1984). See also OCGA § 44-7-1 (b) ("All renting or leasing of real estate for a period of time less than five years shall be held to convey only the right to possess and enjoy such real estate, to pass no estate out of the landlord, and to give only the usufruct unless the contrary is agreed upon by the parties to the contract and is so stated in the contract."). In order to resolve whether the presumption is overcome in a given case, the court "must examine the terms of the lease [agreement] and determine what interests the parties intended to convey." *Eastern Air Lines*, 253 Ga. at 19 (1). The "key inquiry turns upon whether various restrictions in the agreement, limiting [the lessee's] use of the premises, sufficiently negate the presumption that this is an estate for years." *Camp v. Delta Air Lines, Inc.*, 232 Ga. 37, 40 (205 SE2d 194) (1974) (finding the use restrictions in a 30-year lease were incompatible with an estate for years and rebutted the presumption that the lease created an estate for years). "An estate for years may be encumbered or somewhat limited without being reduced to a usufruct." *Jekyll Dev.*, 240 Ga. App. at 275 (2). "As in the construction of all agreements, the cardinal rule to be used by the court is that the terms of the instrument itself must be scrutinized to ascertain what interest the parties intended to be conveyed or demised by it." *Allright Parking of Ga., Inc. v. Joint City-County Bd. of Tax Assessors*, 244 Ga. 378, 385 (260 SE2d 315) (1979).

If the lease in fact granted an estate for years to the Garden, the Garden holds the present estate in the property for the duration of the lease—in other words, Georgia law considers the Garden to be the owner of the property during the term of the lease. If that is the case, because the Garden is a private entity, the property is "private" so long as the Garden holds the estate. *Coleman*, 219 Ga. at 16. The Garden would thus be considered a "private property owner" within the meaning of OCGA § 16-11-127 (c).

Employing the distinction between usufructs and estates in land that *Coleman* and our modern property statutes recognize gives full effect to each of the provisions of OCGA § 16-11-127 (c) at issue here. This is critical because courts should "avoid a construction that makes some language surplusage." *Lucas v. Coulter*, 303 Ga. 261, 263 (811 SE2d 369) (2018). By distinguishing between owners and lessees of private property, OCGA § 16-11-127 (c) vests rights to exclude the carrying of firearms in separate classes of persons and entities. The interpretation of the term "private property" we have outlined above means that any private entity that holds the present estate in land (whether in fee or a lesser estate such as an estate in years) is a "private property owner" within the meaning of the statute for the duration of that estate, and the land it owns is "private property" by virtue of that estate. Under OCGA § 16-11-127 (c), such a person can exclude the carrying of firearms on their property.

However, if one private person leases property from another private person and that lease creates only a usufruct, the tenant is not a "private property owner." But that person may be "in legal control of private property through a lease." If so, such tenant would only be permitted to exclude the carrying of firearms on the property if it could show that the property was "private property" due to the private nature of the landlord (not the tenant) and that the tenant was in "legal control" of such property through its lease.[NOTE 10] In such a case, the tenant would have the right under the statute to exclude the carrying of firearms on the leased premises. Thus, proper application of *Coleman* and our statutes regarding usufructs and estates for years avoids the redundancy inherent in the interpretation of OCGA § 16-11-127 (c) adopted by the Court of Appeals and gives distinct effect to each of the provisions of the statute granting rights to owners and lessees of private property. See *Berryhill v. Georgia Cmty. Support & Solutions, Inc.*, 281 Ga. 439, 441 (638 SE2d 278) (2006) ("Courts should give a sensible and intelligent effect to every part of a statute and not render any language superfluous.").

4. CONCLUSION.

Based on the foregoing, we determine that for purposes of OCGA § 16-11-127 (c), property may only be considered "private" if the holder of the present estate in the property is a private person or entity. In this case, because the City is a public entity, if it is the holder of the present estate in the land it leases to the Garden, the leased premises is not "private property" within the meaning of the statute, and the Garden has no right to exclude the carrying of firearms on the leased premises because it is not "in legal control of private property through a lease." By contrast, if by the terms of the 50-year lease, the Garden holds the present estate in the property, the property is "private property," the Garden is a "private property owner," and it had the right to forbid Evans from carrying a firearm on the premises pursuant to OCGA § 16-11-127 (c). This reading of the statute gives full effect to the 2014 amendment to OCGA § 16- 11-127 (c), the distinction the statute draws between "private property owners" and "persons in legal control of private property through a lease," and our existing statutory and case law setting forth the conditions under which a lease is deemed to create an estate in the lessee such that it is the "owner" of the property during the term of the lease.

However, because the lease between the Garden and the City is not in the record and because this question turns on its interpretation, summary judgment in favor of the Garden should not have been granted because the Garden is not entitled to judgment as a matter of law at this point in the proceedings. See OCGA § 9- 11-56 (c). Rather, in order to determine the proper application of OCGA § 16-11-127 (c) to this or any lease of land by a private entity from a governmental entity, the court must determine whether the specific lease in question creates an estate for years or a usufruct. That has not been done in this case and cannot be done on the record before us. We therefore reverse the decision of the Court of Appeals affirming the trial court's grant of summary judgment in favor of the Garden and remand the case for further proceedings.[NOTE 11]

Judgment reversed and case remanded. All the Justices concur, except Melton, C.J., not participating, and Ellington, J., disqualified. PETERSON, Justice, concurring.

There is no responsibility of government more fundamental than the protection of private property; as the Georgia Constitution puts it, "[p]rotection to person and property is the paramount duty of government. . .." Ga. Const. of 1983, Art. I, Sec. I, Par. II. This principle has been crystal-clear since well before the founding of our Republic. See, e.g., 1 William Blackstone, Commentaries on the Laws of England 135 (1765) ("So great moreover is the regard of the law for private property, that it will not authorize the least violation of it; no, not even for the general good of the whole community. . . . [T]he law of the land has postponed even public necessity to the sacred and inviolable rights of private property."); 2 Joseph Story, Commentaries on the Constitution of the United States § 1790 (Thomas M. Cooley ed., 4th ed. 1873) ("One of the fundamental objects of every good government must be the due administration of justice; and how vain it would be to speak of such an administration, when all property is subject to the will or caprice of the legislature and the rulers."); *Lynch v. Household Fin. Corp.*, 405 U. S. 538, 552 (92 SCt 1113, 31 LE2d 424) (1972) ("That rights in property are basic civil rights has long been recognized." (citing John Locke, John Adams, and William Blackstone)).

Our constitutional system of limited government and individual rights depends upon the consistent government protection of private property. As the high court of one of our sister states recently observed, "a government's failure to protect private property rights puts every other civil right in doubt." *AGCS Marine Ins. Co. v. Arlington County*, 800 SE2d 159, 163 (Va. 2017) (citation and punctuation omitted). We made a similar point over a half- century ago: "Private property is the antithesis of Socialism or Communism. Indeed, it is an insuperable barrier to the establishment of either collective system of government." *State Hwy. Dep't v. Branch*, 222 Ga. 770, 772 (152 SE2d 372) (1966).

But today we have decided that, although lessees who hold an estate for years are properly classified under OCGA § 16-11-127 (c) as "private property owners" and thus may still exclude persons carrying firearms, private lessees of public property who hold only a usufruct may no longer choose to exclude persons carrying firearms from their property. For at least most of those whose leases were executed before the effective date of the 2014 amendment that we consider today that amendment retroactively destroyed the property right such lessees had to exclude people carrying firearms. This may be at odds with the Georgia Constitution, which contains a wide range of complementary protections for private property rights. Here are a few of the more explicit protections: Ga. Const. of 1983, Art. I, Sec. I, Par. I ("No person shall be deprived of life, liberty, or property except by due process of law."); Art. I, Sec. I, Par. II ("Protection to person and property is the paramount duty of government and shall be impartial and complete. No person shall be denied the equal protection of the laws."); Art. I, Sec. I, Par. X ("No bill of attainder, ex post facto law, retroactive law, or laws impairing the obligation of contract or making irrevocable grant of special privileges or immunities shall be passed."); Art. I, Sec. III, Par. I (a) ("private property shall not be taken or damaged for public purposes without just and adequate compensation being first paid"). [NOTE 12]

Today, we interpret the 2014 amendment's prohibition on excluding persons carrying firearms as applying to private parties whose lease of public property has conferred on them only a usufruct. This application may run afoul of several of the provisions I identify above (and perhaps some that I have not), but I will focus on what seems to me the most obvious problem—the Constitution's prohibition on retroactive laws found in Article I, Section I, Paragraph X.

"Even when the General Assembly clearly provides that a law is to be applied retroactively, our Constitution forbids statutes that apply retroactively so as to injuriously affect the vested rights of citizens." *Deal v. Coleman*, 294 Ga. 170, 175 (2) (751 SE2d 337) (2013) (citation and punctuation omitted). Such a statute "takes away or impairs vested rights acquired under existing laws or creates a new obligation, imposes a new duty, or attaches a new liability in respect to transactions or considerations already past." *Southern States-Bartow County, Inc. v. Riverwood Farm Homeowners Assn.*, 300 Ga. 609, 612 (797 SE2d 468) (2017) (citation and punctuation omitted). "[T]his principle does not apply with respect to public rights, which are shared by the People in common, and which can be modified by the People—through their elected representatives—as they see fit." *Deal*, 294 Ga. at 179 (2) (a). Nor does it apply to a "mere minimal condition" on a vested right, such as a retroactive impairment that could be avoided by the payment of a tax. See *Southern States*, 300 Ga. at 612-13.

But the amendment destroys a portion of the right to exclude others from one's property, "one of the most essential sticks in the bundle of rights that are commonly characterized as property." *Dolan v. City of Tigard*, 512 U. S. 374, 393 (114 SCt 2309, 129 LE2d 304) (1994) (citation and punctuation omitted); see also *Rabun County v. Mountain Creek Estates, LLC*, 280 Ga. 855, 856-57 (1) (632 SE2d 140) (2006) ("The term property comprehends not only the thing possessed, but also, in strict legal parlance, means the rights of the owner in relation to land or a thing; the right of a person to possess, use, enjoy and dispose of it, and the corresponding right to exclude others from the use." (citation and punctuation omitted)). "Indeed, it is difficult to conceive of any property as private if the right to exclude is rejected." Richard A. Epstein, *Takings, Exclusivity and Speech: The Legacy of PruneYard v. Robins*, 64 U. CHI. L. REV. 21, 22 (1997). Before the amendment, Georgia law respected that right to exclude by providing that "private property owners or persons in legal control of property through a lease, rental agreement, licensing agreement, contract, or any other agreement to control access to such property" had the right to "forbid possession of a weapon or long gun on their property." OCGA § 16-11-127 (c) (2010). The amendment constricted that right to exclude in a significant way.

The property rights conferred by a lease are not merely a public right available to all, but the sort of private, vested rights that the government may not retroactively impair. See *Appalachee Enterprises, Inc. v. Walker*, 266 Ga. 35, 37 (2) (463 SE2d 896) (1995) (statutory provision for extension of land-use covenants unconstitutionally retroactive as applied to developer who purchased lots prior to statutory change); *Todd v. Morgan*, 215 Ga. 220, 221-22 (2) (109 SE2d 803) (1959) (statutory change in conditions under which title to land used to secure debt would revert to grantor violated federal and state constitutional provisions against passage of retroactive laws or laws that impair the obligations of contracts).

And the intrusion that may be authorized by the amendment cannot be said to be a "mere minimal condition." Even though the amendment would not preclude anyone from using their property altogether, the right to exclude other persons, as noted above, is an essential element of property rights. And there is nothing a property owner or lessor can do to avoid the implications of the amendment. Compare *Southern States*, 300 Ga. at 612-13 (statute that "eliminate[s]" right for non-conforming use if land is not actually used for non-conforming purpose within one year is unconstitutionally retrospective in application); with *Hayes v. Howell*, 251 Ga. 580, 583-84 (2) (b) (308 SE2d 170) (1983) (statute that does not divest mineral owner of his rights, but merely conditions their retention by allowing landowner to prevent acquisition via adverse possession by paying taxes on the rights, is constitutional).[NOTE 13]

All of this said, the nature of usufructs has a strange consequence for the constitutionality of the amendment. The amendment was likely unconstitutional in nearly all of its applications the moment that it became effective, because all of the lessees to which it applied had entered into their leases before the effective date. But the amendment has become more constitutional as time has gone by, as leases that conveyed a usufruct expire and are renewed or the property is leased to someone else after the amendment's effective date (which, of course, doesn't raise a retroactivity problem). The amendment became effective about five years ago. Leases for a term less than five years presumptively confer a usufruct; leases for a term longer than five years presumptively confer an estate for years. See OCGA § 44-7-1. Of course, longer-term leases can confer only a usufruct if the parties so agree, and certainly such leases still exist. But there are far fewer leases creating a usufruct that predate the amendment today than there were when the amendment was enacted.

Then-Chief Judge Dillard identified similar constitutional problems below, arguing that the canon of constitutional avoidance offered an additional reason to adopt the construction the Court of Appeals placed on the amendment. See *GeorgiaCarry.Org v. Atlanta Botanical Garden, Inc.*, 345 Ga. App. 160, 166-67 (812 SE2d 527) (2018) (Dillard, C.J., concurring fully and specially). Although obviously I, too, have constitutional concerns, the avoidance canon empowers a court to choose only "between competing plausible interpretations of a statutory text." *Nordahl v. State*, Ga. , (1) (829 SE2d 99) (2019). I join the Court's opinion in full because I have not been able to identify a competing interpretation that I find sufficiently plausible to invoke the canon.

I recognize that the General Assembly enacted the amendment in furtherance of the right to keep and bear arms. This is a right that has been jealously guarded in this state. See, e.g., *Nunn v. State*, 1 Ga. 243, 251 (1846). But each of the branches of state government must protect that right without jeopardizing other equally fundamental rights. It should not go without noting that the consequence of our decision today is that the amendment likely was unconstitutional in almost all of its applications when it first became effective, and probably in some that still remain.

NOTES:

NOTE 1: "A well regulated Militia, being necessary to the security of a free State, the right of the people to keep and bear Arms, shall not be infringed." U.S. Const. amend. II.

NOTE 2: "The right of the people to keep and bear arms shall not be infringed, but the General Assembly shall have the power to prescribe the manner in which arms may be borne." Ga. Const. Art. I, Sec. I, Par. VIII.

NOTE 3: In his concurrence, Justice Peterson identifies some circumstances in which serious questions would arise about the constitutionality of OCGA § 16- 11-127 (c), as applied to the Garden. To decide this appeal, however, we need not—and therefore do not—address those questions.

NOTE 4: While it is uncontested that the Garden and the City entered into a 50- year lease, the remaining terms of the lease are not otherwise presented in the record.

NOTE 5: The Garden's motion was filed as a motion for judgment on the pleadings. It also filed a response to a motion for summary judgment filed by the Appellants. Because that response included an affidavit and exhibits, the trial court issued an order converting the Garden's motion for judgment on the pleadings to a motion for summary judgment and ruled upon it as such. See OCGA § 9-11-12 (c) ("If, on a motion for judgment on the pleadings, matters outside the pleadings are presented to and not excluded by the court, the motion shall be treated as one for summary judgment[.]").

NOTE 6: The General Assembly subsequently amended OCGA § 16-11-127 in 2015, but that change did not alter the language of subsection (c). See Ga. L. 2015, p. 805, § 3 (effective July 1, 2015).

In 2016, the Georgia House of Representatives passed a bill (House Bill 1060) that the Garden contends, had it gone into effect, would have specifically barred entities like the Garden from excluding licensed gun holders. The provisions in the House version of House Bill 1060 to which the Garden points us were removed when the Senate Judiciary Committee (and later the full Senate) adopted a substitute version of the bill. Compare House Bill 1060 (As Passed House) (2016) (available at http://www.legis.ga.gov/Legislation/20152016/159239.pdf) with House Bill 1060 (As Passed Senate) (2016) (available at http://www.legis.ga.gov/Legislation/20152016/160743.pdf). The Senate version of House Bill 1060, which was later agreed to by the House of Representatives, was vetoed by Governor Nathan Deal and did not take effect. See Status History of HB 1060 (2015-2016 Regular Session) (available at http://www.legis.ga.gov/Legislation/en-US/display/20152016/HB/1060).

The Garden apparently notes the history of this 2016 legislative proposal to show that the General Assembly, in 2016, did not believe that the version of OCGA § 16-11-127 (c) that took effect in 2014 would bar organizations such as the Garden from excluding the carrying of firearms on property leased from a government entity. But because "failed legislative proposals are a particularly dangerous ground" on which to rest an interpretation of a statute, see *United States v. Craft*, 535 U. S. 274, 287 (122 SCt 1414, 152 LE2d 437) (2002) (citation and punctuation omitted), we lend little credence to this argument.

NOTE 7: The Court received briefs in support of the Garden filed on behalf of the Metro Atlanta Chamber, the Development Authority of Fulton County, the Joint Development Authority of Metropolitan Atlanta, Invest Atlanta, and Decide DeKalb.

NOTE 8: "license holder" is "a person who holds a valid weapons carry license. OCGA § 16-11-125.1 (3). Weapons carry licenses are issued pursuant to the standards and procedures set forth in OCGA § 16-11-129.

NOTE 9: CGA § 44-6-60 provides that

> An estate in remainder is one limited to be enjoyed after another estate is terminated or at a time specified in the future. An estate in reversion is the residue of an estate, usually the fee left in the grantor and his heirs after the termination of a particular estate which he has granted out of it. The rights of the reversioner are the same as those of a vested remainderman in fee.

NOTE 10: As with many terms in OCGA § 16-11-127 (c), the phrase "legal control of private property through a lease, rental agreement, licensing agreement, contract, or any other agreement to control access to such private property" is not defined. However, we need not construe the meaning of this phrase in this case in light of our determination that the property cannot be considered "private property" if the Garden holds a mere usufruct in it.

NOTE 11: In their briefs before this Court, the Garden and its supporting amici curiae outline a number of economic, fiscal, social, and public safety concerns they contend will result from a decision by this Court in favor of the Appellants in this case. Whatever merit those arguments may have, those arguments are policy arguments, not legal ones. "[S]triking the right balance between competing legitimate policy interests is a political question, and this Court is concerned only with legal questions. As members of this State's judicial branch, it is our duty to interpret the laws as they are written. We leave political questions to the political branches, and the policy arguments in this case are properly directed to the General Assembly." (Citations and punctuation omitted.) *Deal v. Coleman*, 294 Ga. 170, 174 n.11 (751 SE2d 337) (2013).

NOTE 12: Some of these provisions have federal corollaries. Although we may well interpret many of our provisions consistent with the parallel federal provisions, I have previously observed that the text and history of our Takings Clause suggest that it perhaps should not be. See *Diversified Holdings v. City of Suwanee*, 302 Ga. 597, 615 (807 SE2d 876) (2017) (Peterson, J., concurring); see also Maureen E. Brady, *The Damaging Clauses*, 104 VA. L. REV. 341 (2018) (arguing that state constitution takings clauses that prohibit "damaging" or "injuring" property for public use without just compensation should be interpreted more broadly than the federal Takings Clause).

NOTE 13: I do not doubt the General Assembly's authority to prescribe prospectively the terms under which state and local governments may lease their property. But the amendment did not merely affect leases executed following its effective date.

STUDY QUESTIONS

- What was the fundamental issue in the *GeorgiaCarry.Org* case? How did the court rule? What principle of property law was central to the court's interpretation of the statute?

- This case involves the right of a museum to prohibit certain activities on property leased from a governmental entity. Based on the court's ruling, what standard would apply to expressive speech on the museum's premises? What considerations will a museum want to include in a lease?

ONLINE ACTIVITY

- Research and summarize current news articles regarding protests at and against museums.

EMERGENCY AND DISASTER PLANNING AND MANAGEMENT

An important part of museum stewardship involves planning for and responding to the variety of emergencies that can and will occur in museum facilities. Potential emergencies run the gamut from personal injuries to damage to museum collections. The damage may be accidental, or, as exemplified by the *Davis* case included in the reading below, a deliberate act of vandalism. Museums are also "soft targets" which may attract those interested in perpetrating hate crimes or terrorism. Museums should have strong relationships with local law enforcement. FBI and DHS [Department of Homeland Security] support and training may also be advisable.

All museums accredited by the American Alliance of Museums are expected to have a comprehensive emergency and disaster preparedness plan which covers staff, visitors, facilities, and the museum's collections. The emergency and disaster preparedness plan will provide a one-stop guide to museum staff on how to prepare for and respond to an emergency. The plan should be considered a "living document" that is in writing, widely distributed, and reviewed and updated frequently. In drafting the document, inclusion and communication are crucial. Input from all museum departments as well as from external first responders and recovery experts should be incorporated into the plan.

The Brazilian National Museum burning behind the statue of Emperor Pedro II. The building was heavily damaged by a large fire in September 2018 started by an overheated air conditioner. Although some items were saved, it is believed that 92.5% of its archive of 20 million items were destroyed in the fire.

While the protection of museum collections is important, any emergency response plan should always consider the safety of museum visitors and staff first. An effective emergency and disaster response plan will include: first response procedures; evacuation procedures; call rosters including contact information for key museum staff as well as first responders and recovery services; insurance policy information and notification procedures; and museum staff roles and responsibilities in an emergency.

The plan will also contain information about the location and nature of museum collections, although care should be taken to ensure that access to any confidential information about collections—such as storage location and access information—is restricted to those who need to know that information. If the museum collections contain high value objects, information about those collections may need to be kept confidential—otherwise the plan can inadvertently serve as a handy guide to burglarizing the collections.

A thorough emergency management plan will also contain comprehensive appendices addressing procedures and resources for salvaging and conserving specific types of museum collections. Initial conservation steps may spell the difference between saving or losing collections objects, particularly when water damage is involved.

In responding to a museum emergency, notification of the museum's insurance carrier must not be overlooked. To obtain coverage for costs incurred in response to an emergency, it may be necessary to obtain approval from the museum's insurance carrier before engaging response or recovery services. Failing to do so may result in the denial of insurance coverage and can be an expensive mistake.

CASES AND OTHER READINGS

Reading Note: The case reprinted below is an appeal of a criminal conviction for damaging objects in the North Carolina Museum of Art's collection. While the case involves a deliberate act of vandalism, it illustrates some of the risks to which museum collections may be exposed.

STATE OF NORTH CAROLINA V. JOHN ANTHONY DAVIS

86 N.C. App. 25 (N.C. Ct. App. 1987)

Opinion

APPEAL by defendant from Preston, Judge. Judgment entered 22 April 1986 in Superior Court, WAKE County. Heard in the Court of Appeals 4 May 1987.

Chief Judge HEDRICK concurring in the result in part and dissenting in part.

Defendant was indicted in case number 85CRS47980 for a violation of G.S. [North Carolina General Statutes] 14-398, which makes it a Class H felony to "willfully or maliciously or wantonly write upon, cull tear, deface, disfigure, soil, obliterate, break or destroy . . . any . . . object of art or curiosity deposited in a . . . museum . . ." where the amount of damage done exceeds $50.00. Defendant was also indicted, in case number 85CRS47981, for the misdemeanor of willful and wanton damage to real property, a violation of G.S. 14-127. The State contended that defendant, a security guard at the North Carolina Museum of Art, angered by a job demotion, deliberately stopped up a toilet in the women's rest room at the museum, causing it to overflow. According to the State, the water caused damage to floors and carpets in the museum, as well as leaving a tideline on an Eighteenth Century French tapestry stored in the basement of the museum.

Defendant pleaded not guilty and was tried by a jury. During the trial the judge, over defendant's objection, allowed the State's motion for a jury view. The local press was allowed to attend the proceedings held at the museum and individual jurors were allowed to ask questions during the jury view.

Defendant's motion to dismiss the charges was denied and defendant was found guilty by the jury of both charges. Judge Preston consolidated the convictions for judgment and sentenced defendant to three years' imprisonment, suspended on condition of payment of $9,929.65 in restitution to the museum. Defendant appeals.

PARKER, Judge.

Defendant's primary contention on this appeal is that the evidence presented by the State was insufficient to convince a rational trier of fact of defendant's guilt beyond a reasonable doubt and that his motion to dismiss the charges against him should, therefore, have been granted. The well-established test to be applied in ruling on a defendant's motion to dismiss is whether the State has produced substantial evidence of each and every element of the offense charged or a lesser included offense, and substantial evidence that the defendant committed the offense. *State v. Powell*, 299 N.C. 95, 261 S.E.2d 114 (1980). The evidence is to be viewed in the light most favorable to the State, giving the State the benefit of every reasonable inference which can be drawn from the evidence. *State v. McNeil*, 280 N.C. 159, 185 S.E.2d 156 1971).

When so viewed, the evidence presented at trial tended to show that on the date of the alleged offense, 25 May 1985, defendant was employed as a security guard at the N.C. Museum of Art. On that date, which was a Saturday, defendant came on duty at 3:30 p.m. The museum was open on Saturday, and was to be closed on Sunday and Monday for a holiday. At around 3:55 p.m., security guard Jeanette Stewart discovered that a toilet in the women's rest room on the entry level was continuously flushing. The water was just "going around, going down the drain," and was not overflowing onto the floor. Ms. Stewart reported the problem to her supervisor, who told her to periodically check the toilet to make sure it was not overflowing. She checked several times during the remainder of her shift and found the toilet was still flushing but not overflowing. The supervisor decided that, as the water was not overflowing, the toilet could wait until regular museum hours on Tuesday to be repaired. Defendant was informed of the problem with the toilet and of the decision to just let it run until Tuesday.

At 5:30 p.m., the museum closed. Ms. Stewart went off duty and security guard Sandra Roberson reported for duty. The museum building was secured and by 6:20 p.m. defendant and Ms. Roberson were the only people in the museum. At 7:25 p.m., defendant began a routine patrol of the museum. Ms. Roberson remained at the security desk and followed defendant's progress through the museum by monitoring the museum's sophisticated alarm system of motion and heat detectors. Defendant radioed Ms. Roberson from the women's rest room, asked her if she could hear the water running and commented on the amount of water being wasted. Ms. Roberson then noticed that it took a longer time than normal for defendant to get from the women's room to the next motion detector. When defendant returned from his round, he insisted that Ms. Roberson make the following entry in the log exactly as he dictated it: "While on patrol Officer Davis discovered the water overflow in the ladies room. It was discussed earlier with Hann, and he said not to notify engineering staff until Tuesday morning. Per; Ms. Stewart."

At about 9:35 p.m., Ms. Roberson began her patrol. She heard a sound like running water and discovered "a whole lot of damn water coming down" from the balcony of the entry level overlooking the main gallery. Ms. Roberson called maintenance personnel who instructed her on how to turn off the water to the toilet. Museum employees were also called in to help clean up the water. The water had flowed onto several levels of the museum, staining carpets and shorting electrical outlets which burned the carpets and became inoperative. The water also flowed into a basement storage room and onto an Eighteenth Century French tapestry, which was rolled up on the floor. When employees began to arrive to help clean up, defendant signed out and left the museum before his shift was over. Defendant was later asked by his supervisor to fill out a report on the incident. He refused and was discharged.

A maintenance crew dismantling the toilet for repair discovered that the outflow pipe was blocked by an eight-inch stack of paper towels. According to the State's expert witness, the chief engineer at the museum, this stack of towels was sufficient to completely block the outflow pipe. The expert testified that the running toilet flowed at a rate of approximately thirty to sixty gallons of water per minute and that once the outflow pipe became clogged, the water probably began to overflow the toilet in a matter of seconds.

Defendant contended at trial that at the time he made his 7:25 p.m. rounds the toilet was overflowing and the floor drain was handling the water overflow adequately. The chief engineer testified that if the continuously flushing toilet were overflowing, the floor drain could not handle the volume of water.

Defendant was charged with violations of G.S. 14-127 and G.S. 14-398. These statutes read:

14-127. Willful and wanton injury to real property. If any person shall willfully and wantonly damage, injure or destroy any real property whatsoever, either of a public or private nature, he shall be guilty of a misdemeanor and shall be punished by fine or imprisonment or both, in the discretion of the court.

14-398. Theft or destruction of property of public libraries, museums, etc. Any person who shall steal or unlawfully take or detain, or willfully or maliciously or wantonly write upon, cut, tear, deface, disfigure, soil, obliterate, break or destroy, or who shall sell or buy or receive, knowing the game to have been stolen, any book, document, newspaper, periodical, map, chart picture, portrait engraving, statue, coin, medal, apparatus, specimen, or other work of literature or object of art or curiosity deposited in a public library, gallery, museum, collection, fair or exhibition, or in any department or office of State or local government, or in a library, gallery, museum, collection, or exhibition, belonging to any incorporated college or university, or any incorporated institution devoted to educational, scientific, literary, artistic, historical or charitable purposes, shall, if the value of the property stolen, detained, sold, bought or received knowing same to have been stolen, or if the damage done by writing upon, cutting, tearing, defacing, disfiguring, soiling, obliterating, breaking or destroying any such property, shall not exceed fifty dollars ($50.00), be guilty of a misdemeanor and upon conviction shall be fined or imprisoned in the discretion of the court. If the value of the property stolen, detained, sold or received knowing same to have been stolen, or the amount of damage done in any of the ways or manners hereinabove set out, shall exceed the sum of fifty dollars ($50.00), the person committing same shall be punished as a Class H felon.

Clearly, these statutes require, as an essential element of the offenses set forth, a showing that the person charged "willfully" or "wantonly" caused the damage to real property or an object of art. The words "willful" and "wanton" have substantially the same meaning when used in reference to the requisite state of mind for a violation of a criminal statute. *State v. Williams*, 284 N.C. 67, 199 S.E.2d 409 (1973). "Willful" as used in criminal statutes means the wrongful doing of an act without justification or excuse, or the commission of an act purposely and deliberately in violation of the law. *State v. Arnold*, 264 N.C. 348, 141 S.E.2d 473 (1965). "Willfulness" is a state of mind which is seldom capable of direct proof, but which must be inferred from the circumstances of the particular case. Id.

The evidence, when viewed in the light most favorable to the State, was sufficient to allow the jury to infer that defendant put the paper towels in the toilet intending to create a serious water problem. It is not necessary for a person to know that he is breaking the law for an act to be "willful." *State v. Coal Co.*, 210 N.C. 742, 188 S.E. 412 (1936). Further, a person is presumed to intend the natural and foreseeable consequences of his unlawful acts. *State v. Ferguson*, 261 N.C. 558, 135 S.E.2d 626 (1964). Damage to the toilet (as an attached fixture, part of the real property, see generally Annot., 52 A.L.R.2d 222 (1957)) and water damage to the floor of the museum were natural and foreseeable consequences of clogging the constantly-running toilet. Therefore, we affirm the conviction for willful damage to real property in violation of G.S. 14-127.

With respect to the conviction for violation of G.S. 14-398, the evidence was not in our view sufficient to support the necessary finding that defendant's act was the proximate cause of the damage to the tapestry. The State presented no evidence as to the condition of the tapestry immediately before 25 May 1985. A photograph showing the tapestry without the tideline was tendered into evidence, but no witness testified as to when the photograph was made. This photograph was an item in the conservation file containing information on each art object at the museum. The photograph does not depict the linen border which according to the evidence was sewn on in 1978. The most recent condition report in the file was dated January 1980. Further, the evidence was uncontradicted that the tapestry was lying on the floor rolled up in a storage room located directly under the rest room with the malfunctioning toilet. Other objects stored in this room did not get wet. The State's evidence showed that water ran into the room because the seal around the pipe for the floor drain in the rest room had not been properly caulked. This crack permitted water to seep down the outside of the pipe. The record is devoid of any evidence as to when the tapestry was stored in this room and when it was last unrolled prior to 25 May 1985. In our view, considering all the evidence in the light most favorable to the State, the mere fact that this tapestry was wet on 25 May 1985 is not sufficient to support a finding beyond a reasonable doubt that defendant's act in putting the towels in the toilet caused the tideline damage to the tapestry. Evidence as to the condition of the tapestry prior to the flooding was necessary to establish all material elements of the offense. In *In re Meaut*, 51 N.C. App. 153, 275 S.E.2d 200 (1981), respondents were observed throwing rocks at a carload of motor vehicles on a train; when the train stopped two vehicles were damaged. This Court per Judge (now Justice) Whichard stated:

> The testimony of the State's witness tended to show that the train in question was en route fron Rocky Mount to Hope Mills. The witness testified: "I did not personally inspect the cars in Rocky Mount. A member of our department told me that the cars were in good shape when they were in Rocky Mount." This testimony was properly stricken, upon respondents' motion, as hearsay. Without this testimony there was no evidence before the court as to the condition of the automobiles prior to their arrival at the locus in quo, and such evidence was an essential foundation to a permissible inference that the damage resulted from the acts of respondents rather than from some other cause.

51 N.C. App. at 155-56, 275 S.E.2d at 202.

The trial court erred in denying defendant's motion to dismiss the felony charge against him. Our ruling on this issue makes discussion of defendant's assignments of error regarding the proper measure of damage to the tapestry unnecessary as those contentions relate to the felony only.

Defendant also assigns error to the trial court's order allowing a jury view at the art museum and to the court's conduct of the jury view itself. Under G.S. 15A-1229 (a), the decision to permit a jury view is vested in the discretion of the trial judge. The decision will not be disturbed absent an abuse of discretion. See *State v. Wilson*, 313 N.C. 516, 330 S.E.2d 450 (1985). Defendant has shown no abuse of discretion by the trial judge in permitting the view.

Defendant also contends that the order permitting the view was fatally defective as it failed to include an instruction to the officer escorting the jury that no one is to be allowed to communicate with the jury. See G.S. 15A-1229 (a). This contention is without merit. The order was drafted jointly by the district attorney and defense counsel and was entered with only a general objection to the jury view itself. While not reciting the language of the statute verbatim, the order did contain sufficient precautionary language to insure that defendant's right to an impartial jury was not impaired, including orders that the jury be accompanied by two deputies, that the jurors not be allowed to talk among themselves and that no one be allowed to speak with the jury. This order was sufficient to comply with the requirements of G.S. 15A-1229 (a) and the assignment of error is overruled.

Defendant further contends that he was unduly prejudiced by the conduct of the jury view as the press was allowed to be present and the members of the press were introduced to the jury. Criminal trials in North Carolina are open to the press and the public. N.C. Const. art. I, 24. Defendant argues that by allowing the press to attend the jury view and by introducing the members of the press to the jurors, the trial judge unduly prejudiced him by emphasizing the highly publicized nature of the trial and by detracting from the decorum of the proceedings. Although conditions were less than ideal for court proceedings, the trial judge kept the press quiet and away from the jury and gave adequate instructions to the jury concerning the publicity surrounding the trial.

Finally, defendant contends that by allowing individual jurors to ask questions at the jury view, the trial court committed prejudicial error. We disagree. The jurors were allowed to state their questions, which were duly recorded by the court reporter. The questioning was tightly controlled and conducted in such a way as to fully protect defendant's right to a fair trial. The trial judge asked each attorney if there were any objection to the question, and defense counsel never voiced an objection. Defendant has failed to demonstrate any prejudice resulting from the manner in which the jury view was conducted.

In summary, defendant's conviction in 85CRS47980, willful damage to an object of art, is vacated. We find no prejudicial error in defendant's conviction for willful damage to real property, and the case is remanded to the Superior Court for entry of judgment on the misdemeanor conviction.

No. 85CRS47980—reversed.
No. 85CRS47981—no error.

Remanded for entry of judgment.

Judge EAGLES concurs.

Chief Judge HEDRICK concurs in the result in part and dissents in part.

STUDY QUESTIONS

- *Davis* is an appeal from a criminal conviction for deliberately damaging the museum's facilities and collections. Describe the events that led to the criminal case. What criminal statutes were involved? Why did the court reject the felony conviction?
- Although in this case the actions of the security guard were deliberate, it is easy to envision a situation where similar damage occurred accidentally. What museum practices and procedures are raised by the facts of this case? What could the museum have done differently to protect its collections?

JONESTOWN SCIENCE CENTER HYPOTHETICAL DISASTER SCENARIO

It is a busy Saturday at the Jonestown Science Center. After a record snowfall earlier in the week, life in Jonestown is finally getting back to normal. Although a severe winter weather warning is in effect, a large crowd is enjoying a new exhibit about evolution.

Earlier in the day, the Collections Registrar had noticed a lot of ice building up on the downspouts at the rear of the building. After lunch, she goes out to take another look. While looking up at the large icicles by the back door, some of them come loose and fall, knocking her down. Returning from lunch with a wealthy prospective donor, the Development Director finds the Collections Registrar lying unconscious in the parking lot.

Meanwhile, back in the Science Center, the next planetarium show is being announced. As people begin to take their seats, a Volunteer Docent at the front desk receives a phone call from a man who says that he has planted a bomb in the building and says that unless the Science Center closes the evolution exhibit "immediately" he will "torch the building." The Volunteer makes an announcement over the loudspeaker telling everyone to leave the building right away.

As part of the Science Center's "Science Saturday" program, the Curator of Education is demonstrating "Crocodile Chemistry" in the lower level of the building. When he hears the announcement, he panics and knocks over a Bunsen burner, which ignites a pile of paper napkins and the tablecloth, and quickly gets out of control. The room is engulfed in smoke and flames.

During the chaos that ensues, a group of teenage punks enters the Collections Storage area and ransacks several of the collection cabinets. They are seen by another Volunteer Docent carrying some long, thin objects that look like spears out the back door.

The Jonestown Fire Department arrives and quickly puts out the fire, but there is extensive smoke and water damage, particularly in the lower level of the building.

After the Fire Department departs, the weather turns from bad to worse. A freak winter lightning storm hits. Lightning strikes a transformer servicing the building and causes a power outage. Sheets of rain pour down on the roof. Suddenly the Volunteer Coordinator hears a strange cracking noise coming from outside her office. The roof over the front entrance collapses and water and debris pours in through a gaping hole in the ceiling.

The temperature in the building begins to drop toward freezing. The Executive Director locates the Science Center's Disaster and Emergency Planning Handbook and assembles the Disaster Response Team. "What next?" she asks the team members.

STUDY QUESTIONS

- Analyze the Jonestown Science Center Hypothetical Scenario and advise the Executive Director on what she should do to address the situation. Be sure to consider both immediate mitigation steps as well as recommendations for changes in the museum's policies and practices.

ADA COMPLIANCE

The Americans with Disabilities Act (ADA) was enacted in 1990 to ensure that people with disabilities have the same rights and opportunities as everyone else. The ADA can be best understood as both a civil rights law and a building code. The ADA gives civil rights protections to individuals with disabilities like those given to individuals based on race, color, sex, national origin, age, and religion. According to the ADA National Network, the ADA "guarantees equal opportunity for individuals with disabilities in public accommodations, employment, transportation, state and local government services, and telecommunications." In addition to giving a cause of action for civil rights violations, the ADA and its implementing regulations set out standards for constructing, remodeling, and maintaining ADA compliant facilities.

As public trusts, museums have an ethical obligation to provide and maintain access for those with disabilities. The American Alliance of Museum's *Core Standards for Museums* states: "The museum strives to be inclusive and offers opportunities to diverse participation." Similarly, the AAM's *Code of Ethics for Museums* obligates the museum to ensure that "programs are accessible and encourage participation of the widest possible audience consistent with its mission and resources."

Museums also have a legal obligation under the ADA to provide and maintain access to those with disabilities. Museums operated by state and local governments are governed by Title II of the ADA which prohibits discrimination against qualified individuals with disabilities with all programs, activities, and services of public entities.

Private museums are considered "public accommodations" for the purposes of Title III of the Act, which prohibits private places of public accommodations from discriminating against people with disabilities. Title III sets minimum standards for accessibility for alterations and new construction of facilities. These are essentially minimum building design requirements relating to accessibility which should be consulted whenever the museum is considering a building or remodeling project.

Title III also requires public accommodations to remove barriers in existing buildings where it is easy to do so without too much difficulty or expense. It directs businesses to make "reasonable modifications" to facilities and management practices to address accessibility. A reasonable modification may involve making a structural change to an existing premises to afford a person with a disability full enjoyment of the premises. Title III also requires businesses to make "reasonable accommodations" for people with disabilities. A reasonable accommodation may involve a change, exception or adjustment to a rule, policy, or practice.

In addition, Title III also requires that public accommodations take reasonable steps to communicate effectively with people who have speech, vision, or hearing disabilities. This requirement extends not only to physical accommodations but also to interactive displays, audio/visual materials, websites, social media, and the like. A lengthy set of technical guidelines have been developed by federal agencies to assist individuals and entities with understanding their rights and duties under the ADA.

The unique nature of museums and the wide variety of services they provide to the public means that museums must be particularly mindful of ADA compliance issues. Accessibility should be a key consideration in planning and implementing every museum function, from exhibit design to website design, from auditorium seating to museum shop product placement. Policies and procedures regarding service animals and mobility devices should be established and enforced consistently. Audio-visual media should include closed captioning. As technology evolves, best practices regarding accessibility will also change.

The ADA is enforced by the Disability Rights Section of the Civil Rights Division of the Department of Justice. Anyone who believes they or someone else has been discriminated against can file a complaint with the Disability Rights Section in the Department of Justice. The complaint can be filed online at https://www.ada.gov/complaint/ or by mail or fax. Complaints are reviewed by DRS staff and an investigation is opened when warranted. Most ADA complaints are resolved informally through the ADA Mediation Program. Two examples of ADA settlement agreements are included in the Cases and Other Readings below. Settlement agreements are published and made available to the public. They can provide helpful guidance for anticipating ADA compliance issues at museums of all kinds.

Class action lawsuits initiated by a small handful of law firms alleging violations of ADA requirements, particularly with regards to websites, have become increasingly common in recent years. Many of these "trolling" lawsuits are frivolous, but often businesses, including museums, choose to settle rather than incur the legal expenses necessary to defend against them. The best defense against these class action lawsuits is to consistently comply with ADA requirements.

Many museums adopt an ADA policy and appoint a staff member to serve as the ADA compliance officer for the museum. By encouraging visitors to communicate directly with the museum about their accessibility concerns, and by proactively addressing those concerns, museums can avoid having to respond to a formal ADA complaint or defend against a trolling lawsuit.

CASES AND OTHER READINGS

Reading Note: The following is an example of an agreement to resolve an ADA complaint filed against a museum. The Settlement Agreement sets out the deficiencies identified by a Department of Justice investigation and the corrective measures the museum has agreed to take.

SETTLEMENT AGREEMENT BETWEEN THE UNITED STATES OF AMERICA AND THE NATIONAL MUSEUM OF CRIME AND PUNISHMENT UNDER TITLE III OF THE AMERICANS WITH DISABILITIES ACT

(January 2015)

A. BACKGROUND

1. The parties to this Settlement Agreement are the United States of America and the National Museum of Crime and Punishment, which is located in Washington, D.C.

2. This Settlement Agreement ("Agreement") resolves an investigation and compliance review conducted by the United States Department of Justice ("Department") of the National Museum of Crime and Punishment ("NMCP") under Title III of the Americans with Disabilities Act of 1990, as amended, 42 U.S.C. §§ 12181-12189 ("ADA"). Based on the Department's investigation and compliance review, the Department found that the NMCP failed to make all of its exhibits, public programs, and other offerings accessible to individuals with disabilities, and failed to furnish appropriate auxiliary aids and services to ensure effective communication with patrons with disabilities.

3. In order to avoid litigation, the parties agree to the terms of this Agreement. These terms are intended to redress the violations of the ADA that have been identified by the Department.

B. JURISDICTION

4. The NMCP is a privately owned museum dedicated to the history of criminology and penology including the history of crime, law enforcement, forensic science, and crime scene investigation (CSI). It is located at 575 Seventh Street, NW, in Washington, DC.

5. In its facilities, the NMCP operates galleries devoted to staged crime scenes, an interactive crime solving exhibit through forensic science techniques, a mock police station, and authentic artifacts such as an electric chair, a gas chamber, prison art, and a jail cell, as well as a museum shop. The NMCP is a place of public accommodation subject to the requirements of Title III of the ADA [Americans with Disabilities Act] and its implementing regulation. 42 U.S.C. §§ 12181(7), 12182; 28 C.F.R. Part 36.

6. Public accommodations, such as the NMCP, are required to provide full and equal enjoyment of their goods, services, facilities, privileges, advantages, and

accommodations in the most integrated setting appropriate to people with disabilities. 42 U.S.C. §§ 12182(a), (b)(1)(B); 28 C.F. R. §§ 36.201, 36.203(a). Specifically, public accommodations must:

- Ensure that no individual is discriminated against on the basis of disability in the full and equal enjoyment of their goods, services, facilities, privileges, advantages, or accommodations. 42 U.S.C. §§ 12182; 28 C.F.R § 36.201(a);

- Make reasonable modifications in policies, practices, or procedures, when the modifications are necessary to afford goods, services, facilities, privileges, advantages, or accommodations to people with disabilities, unless the public accommodation can demonstrate that making the modifications would fundamentally alter the nature of the goods, services, facilities, privileges, advantages, or accommodations. 42 U.S.C. §§ 12182(b)(2)(A)(ii); 28 C.F.R. § 36.302(a);

- Ensure that no individual with a disability is excluded, denied services, segregated or otherwise treated differently than other individuals because of the absence of auxiliary aids and services, unless the public accommodation can demonstrate that taking those steps would fundamentally alter the nature of the goods, services, facilities, privileges, advantages, or accommodations being offered or would result in an undue burden. 42 U.S.C. § 12182(b)(2)(A)(iii); 28 C.F.R. § 36.303;

- Ensure that all of its newly constructed or altered buildings and facilities, including exhibits, are readily accessible to, and usable by, people with disabilities. 42 U.S.C. § 12183(a); 28 C.F.R. §§ 36.401(a)(1), 36.402 (a)(1).

7. The Attorney General is authorized to conduct periodic compliance reviews of public accommodations under the ADA. 42 U.S.C. § 12188(b)(1)(A)(i); 28 C.F.R. § 36.502(c).

8. The Attorney General is further authorized to commence a civil action in a United States district court when he has reasonable cause to believe there is a pattern or practice of discrimination or discrimination that raises an issue of general public importance, and may seek injunctive relief, monetary damages, and civil penalties. 42 U.S.C. §§ 12188(b)(1)(B), 12188(b)(2); 28 C.F.R. §§ 36.503, 36.504.

C. APPLICABLE STANDARDS

9. The NMCP is housed in a building altered for use as a museum after January 26, 1992. Any alteration to a place of public accommodation, such as the

NMCP, after that date, shall be made so as to ensure that, to the maximum extent feasible, the altered portions of the facility are readily accessible to and usable by people with disabilities. 42 U.S.C. § 12183(a); 28 C.F.R. § 36.402(a)(1).

10. For purposes of this Agreement, the term "*1991 Standards*" means requirements set forth in the ADA Standards for Accessible Design, originally published on July 26, 1991, and republished as Appendix D to 28 C.F.R. Pt. 36. 28 C.F.R. § 36.104.

11. For purposes of this Agreement, the term "*2010 Standards*" means the 2010 ADA Standards for Accessible Design, which consists of Appendices B and D to 36 C.F.R. Pt. 1191 (2009), and the requirements contained in subpart D of 28 C.F.R. Pt. 36.28 C.F.R. § 36.104.

12. The Department began this investigation and conducted architectural surveys of the NMCP before the 2010 Standards took effect. The Department's analysis as to whether the NMCP is in compliance with the ADA is based on the 1991 Standards. As 28 C.F.R. § 36.406(a)(5)(ii) makes clear, the 2010 Standards apply to determine the remedial actions the NMCP must take.

D. FINDINGS BY THE UNITED STATES

13. Beginning in May 2011, the Department, with the cooperation of the NMCP, conducted a compliance review, under Title III and the Department's implementing regulation, 28 C.F.R. Pt. 36, to assess the accessibility of the NMCP to patrons with disabilities.

14. Based on that compliance review, the Department found that the NMCP failed to alter its facilities in a manner that is readily accessible to and usable by people with disabilities. Barriers include, but are not limited to:

    - Protruding objects throughout the facility;
    - Inaccessible routes to certain exhibits;
    - Toilet rooms with inaccessible features such as high thresholds at entry doors and insufficient toe clearance at the designated wheelchair accessible stall.

15. The Department further determined that the NMCP failed to make all of its exhibits, public programs, and other offerings accessible, and failed to furnish appropriate auxiliary aids and services to ensure effective communication with patrons with disabilities in several ways, including but not limited, to the following:

- Auxiliary aids and services are not provided for patrons who are blind or have low vision in all public programs, media, and exhibits;
- Auxiliary aids and services are not provided for patrons who are deaf or hard of hearing in all public programs, media, and exhibits;
- The NMCP website lacks features that allow individuals with disabilities who require assistive technologies to access information, links, ticket purchases, and online shopping. Controls on interactive multimedia exhibits and technologies are not all within the reach range of patrons who use wheelchairs or are of short stature.

16. Based on its investigation and compliance review, the Department made a series of findings regarding the NMCP's lack of accessibility to people with disabilities. These findings are listed in Appendix 1.

E. TERMS OF AGREEMENT

17. The NMCP shall ensure that no individual is discriminated against on the basis of disability in the full and equal enjoyment of its goods, services, facilities, privileges, advantages, or accommodations. 42 U.S.C. §§ 12182 –12183; 28 C.F.R § 36.201(a).

18. The NMCP shall provide full and equal enjoyment of its goods, services, facilities, privileges, advantages, and accommodations in the most integrated setting appropriate to people with disabilities. 42 U.S.C. § 12182(b)(1)(B); 28 C.F.R. § 36.203.

19. The NMCP shall make reasonable modifications in policies, practices, or procedures, when the modifications are necessary to afford goods, services, facilities, privileges, advantages, or accommodations to people with disabilities, unless the NMCP can demonstrate that making the modifications would fundamentally alter the nature of the goods, services, facilities, privileges, advantages, or accommodations. 42 U.S.C. §12182(b)(2)(A)(ii); 28 C.F.R. § 36.302.

20. The NMCP shall furnish appropriate auxiliary aids and services where necessary to ensure effective communication with people with disabilities, unless NMCP can demonstrate that taking those steps would fundamentally alter the nature of the goods, services, facilities, privileges, advantages, or accommodations being offered or would result in an undue burden. 42 U.S.C. § 12182(b)(2)(A)(iii); 28 C.F.R. § 36.303.

21. Within 120 days of the effective date of this agreement, the NMCP shall ensure that its website conforms to the Level AA Success Criteria and Con-

formance Requirements of the Web Content Accessibility Guidelines ("WCAG") 2.0 (Dec. 11, 2008), published by the World Wide Web Consortium ("W3C"), Web Accessibility Initiative ("WAI"), available at www.w3.org/TR/WCAG.

22. The NMCP shall ensure that all of its alterations, additions, and exhibits are readily accessible to, and usable by, people with disabilities and also ensure that it designs, constructs and installs all exhibits in compliance with 42 U.S.C. § 12183(a) and 28 C.F.R. §§ 36.401-406.

23. The NMCP shall maintain in operable working condition those features of its facilities, including exhibits and equipment, required to be accessible by this Agreement or under the ADA. 28 C.F.R. § 36.211.

REMEDIAL MEASURES

24. Within 12 months of the effective date of this Agreement, the NMCP shall complete the remedial measures identified in Appendix 1.

25. Within thirty (30) days of the effective date of this Agreement, the NMCP shall retain a consultant to certify that any alterations or additions to the facilities, including exhibits, comply with the requirements of the ADA and this Agreement. The consultant shall have experience in evaluating compliance with requirements of Title III of the ADA and its implementing regulation, including 42 U.S.C. §§ 12182–12183, 28 C.F.R. Pt. 36. NMCP shall not retain the consultant without having received the prior written approval of the Department.

26. Within thirty (30) days of the effective date of this Agreement, the NMCP shall designate or hire an ADA Compliance Officer and identify this individual to the Department. NMCP shall not designate or hire an ADA Compliance Officer without having received the prior written approval of the Department. No later than sixty (60) days after the selection, the NMCP shall ensure that the ADA Compliance Officer undergoes training on the NMCP's obligations under the ADA and this Agreement, at the expense of the NMCP. The ADA Compliance Officer shall be responsible for handling disability-related complaints from the patrons of the NMCP and for ensuring the NMCP's compliance with the ADA and this Agreement.

27. Within thirty (30) days of the effective date of this Agreement, the NMCP shall develop an ADA Complaint Resolution Policy to address ADA-related complaints and shall provide a written copy of the policy to the Department for review and approval. This policy shall identify the ADA

Compliance Officer, the procedure for filing complaints and the process by which complaints will be investigated and resolved. The NMCP shall implement the policy within thirty (30) days of approval by the Department.

28. Within sixty (60) days of the effective date of this Agreement, the NMCP shall train all supervisors and managers on the NMCP's obligations under the ADA and this Agreement. The NMCP shall ensure that all newly hired supervisors and managers receive this training within thirty (30) days of hire or promotion.

29. The NMCP shall provide a written report annually to the Department on its progress regarding the completion of its obligations under this Agreement, including under Section E. The report shall identify and document (e.g., with copies of construction contracts, photographs and/or design drawings) the revisions that have been made and any training of employees that has occurred (by date and the content of the training), and include copies of any ADA-related policies that the NMCP has adopted. The report shall be provided to the Department annually on the anniversary of the effective date of this Agreement, except that the last report shall be provided three months prior to the expiration of this Agreement.

F. IMPLEMENTATION AND ENFORCEMENT

30. The Department shall have the right, during the course of this Agreement and with seven (7) days notice to the NMCP, to conduct inspections of the NMCP and to request documents or photographs in order to evaluate compliance with this Agreement. The Department shall make every effort to conduct its inspections at times that are agreeable to NMCP so as to cause minimal disruption to its operations.

31. If the Department believes that the NMCP is not in compliance with this Agreement or any requirements contained herein, the Department will notify the NMCP in writing of the alleged noncompliance and attempt to seek a resolution of the matter with the NMCP. If the parties are unable to reach a resolution within thirty (30) days of the date of the Department's written notification, the Department may seek enforcement of the terms of this Agreement and/or the ADA in court. In the event a court determines that the NMCP has failed to comply with any term of this Agreement, such failure to comply shall be treated as a second violation of Title III of the ADA, and the Department may seek, and the court may assess, civil penalties as provided in 42 U.S.C. § 12188(b)(2)(C).

32. In consideration for the Agreement set forth above, the Department will not institute any civil action alleging discrimination based on the allegations raised in Paragraphs 14 -16, except as provided in Paragraph 31 above.

33. The Department's failure to enforce any provision of this Agreement shall not be construed as a waiver by the Department of any right to enforce any provisions.

34. This Agreement shall be binding upon the NMCP, and its agents and employees. In the event the NMCP seeks to transfer or assign all or part of its interests in any exhibition or facility covered by this Agreement, and the successor or assignee intends to carry on the same or similar use of the facility, as a condition of sale, the NMCP shall obtain the written accession of the successor or assignee to any obligations remaining under this Agreement for the remaining term of this Agreement.

35. All notices, demands, or other communications to be provided under this Agreement shall be in writing and delivered by email or overnight delivery to the following persons and addresses (or such other persons and addresses as any party may designate in writing from time to time): (Omitted)

36. This Agreement constitutes the entire Agreement between the parties relating to Department of Justice Case No. 202-16-189, and no other statement, promise or agreement, either written or oral, made by either party or agents of any party, that is not contained in this written Agreement, including Appendix 1, shall be enforceable.

37. If any provision of this Agreement is determined by any court to be unenforceable, the other terms of this Agreement shall nonetheless remain in full force and effect, provided however, that if the severance of any such provision materially alters the rights or obligations of the parties, the Department and the NMCP shall engage in good faith negotiations in order to adopt mutually agreeable amendments to this Agreement as may be necessary to restore the parties as closely as possible to the agreed upon relative rights and obligations.

38. This Agreement does not affect the NMCP's continuing responsibility to comply with all aspects of the ADA not covered by this Agreement.

39. A signatory to this document in a representative capacity for the NMCP represents that he or she is authorized to bind NMCP to this Agreement.

40. The effective date of this Agreement is the date of the last signature below. The Agreement shall remain in effect for three years from the effective date, unless extended by written agreement of the parties.

STUDY QUESTIONS

- What were the accommodation issues at the *National Crime Museum*? What changes was the museum required to make?

Reading Note: The following is an example of an agreement to resolve an ADA complaint filed against a museum. The Settlement Agreement sets out the deficiencies identified by a Department of Justice investigation and the corrective measures the museum has agreed to take.

SETTLEMENT AGREEMENT BETWEEN THE UNITED STATES OF AMERICA AND THE PALM SPRINGS ART MUSEUM

U.S. Department of Justice Complaint #202-12C-523
United States Attorney's Office Matters #2014V02399 and #2016V00356
(March 2018)

A. BACKGROUND

1. The parties to this Settlement Agreement are the United States of America and the Palm Springs Art Museum ("Museum").

2. This Settlement Agreement ("Agreement") resolves two complaints received by the United States Department of Justice, and a United States Attorney's Office ("USAO") investigation and compliance review of the Museum under Title III of the Americans with Disabilities Act of 1990, as amended, 42 U.S.C. §§ 12181–12189 ("ADA"). Based on the USAO's investigation and compliance review, the USAO finds that the Museum had failed to provide appropriate auxiliary aids and services to individuals with hearing disabilities.

3. The investigation commenced when the Department received a complaint dated February 3, 2014, from Museum visitor J.V., who is deaf, alleging the Museum did not have a script of an audio tour for a special exhibit available to provide her full and equal enjoyment of the tour.

4. Subsequently, the Department received a complaint dated January 7, 2015, from Museum visitor D.P., who is hard of hearing, alleging the Museum did not have

a properly functioning assistive listening device to accommodate his hearing loss to allow him full and equal enjoyment of a film offered by the Museum.

B. JURISIDICTION

5. The Museum is a nonprofit corporation that exhibits contemporary, Western, and Native American art, culture, architecture, and natural history. The Museum operates three facilities. The primary facility is located at 300 South Palm Canyon Drive, Palm Springs, California 92262. The Museum also has two additional locations: The Architecture + Design Center located in the Edwards Harris Pavilion at 300 South Palm Canyon Drive, Palm Springs, California 92262, as well as the Palm Springs Art Museum in Palm Desert located at 72-567 Highway 111, Palm Desert, California 92260. All three facilities are subject to the terms of this Agreement.

6. Each Museum facility is a place of public accommodation subject to the requirements of Title III of the ADA and its implementing regulations. 42 U.S.C. §§ 12181(7)(H) & 12182; 28 C.F.R. [Code of Federal Regulations] Part 36. The Museum is a public accommodation as it owns, operates, or leases the three Museum facilities.

7. Public accommodations, such as the Museum, are required to provide full and equal enjoyment of their goods, services, facilities, privileges, advantages, and accommodations in the most integrated setting appropriate to people with disabilities. 42 U.S.C. §§ 12182(a) & (b)(1)(B); 28 C.F.R. §§ 36.201 & 36.203(a). Specifically, a public accommodation must:

    1. Ensure that no individual is discriminated against on the basis of disability in the full and equal enjoyment of its goods, services, facilities, privileges, advantages, or accommodations. 42 U.S.C. §§ 12182; 28 C.F.R. § 36.201(a).

    2. Make reasonable modifications in policies, practices, or procedures, when the modifications are necessary to afford goods, services, facilities, privileges, advantages, or accommodations to people with disabilities, unless the public accommodation can demonstrate that making the modifications would fundamentally alter the nature of the goods, services, facilities, privileges, advantages, or accommodations. 42 U.S.C. § 12182(b)(2)(A)(ii); 28 C.F.R. § 36.302(a).

    3. Ensure that no individual with a disability is excluded, denied services, segregated or otherwise treated differently than other individuals because of the absence of auxiliary aids and services, unless the public accommodation can demonstrate that taking those steps would fun-

damentally alter the nature of the goods, services, facilities, privileges, advantages, or accommodations being offered or would result in an undue burden. 42 U.S.C. § 12182(b)(2)(A)(iii); 28 C.F.R. § 36.303.

8. The Attorney General is authorized to conduct periodic compliance reviews of public accommodations under the ADA. 42 U.S.C. § 12188(b)(1)(A)(i); 28 C.F.R. § 36.502(c).

9. The Attorney General shall investigate alleged violations of Title III of the ADA and may commence a civil action if there is reasonable cause to believe that any person or group of persons has been discriminated against in violation of Title III of the ADA and such discrimination raises an issue of general public importance. 42 U.S.C. § 12188(b)(1)(B); 28 C.F.R. §§ 36.503 & 36.504. Ensuring that persons who are deaf or hard of hearing have access to museum exhibits is an issue of general public importance.

10. As a result of the concerns raised by the USAO, the Museum has engaged in efforts to offer deaf or hard-of-hearing individuals equal access to its exhibits, programs, and activities.

C. DETERMINATIONS BY THE UNITED STATES

11. The USAO determined that the Museum had failed to ensure that people who are deaf or hard of hearing had an equal opportunity to participate in and benefit from services, programs, and activities offered to others without disabilities. The USAO identified various aspects of the Museum that were not in compliance with the ADA and, specifically, with the provisions identified in Paragraph 7 above.

12. The USAO initially identified the following specific violations of the ADA:

    1. The Museum did not provide to Complainant J.V. any captioning, transcripts or other means of effectively communicating the experience and content of the Museum's exhibits and special exhibits. See 28 C.F.R. § 36.303(a), (b) and (c).

    2. The Museum did not have properly functioning assistive listening devices for Complainant D.P. to view a film shown at the Museum. See 28 C.F.R. § 36.303(a), (b) and (c); ADA Standards for Accessible Design at §§ 219 & 706 (Sept. 15, 2010).

13. The USAO further alleges that the Museum had failed to make its exhibits, public programs, and other offerings accessible to deaf or hard-of-hearing individuals in several ways, including but not limited to the following:

1. Failing to provide, or furnishing defective or faulty assistive listening devices;

2. Failing to provide captioning or transcripts for audiovisual exhibits;

3. Failing to make qualified sign language interpreters or other appropriate auxiliary aids or services available for lectures; and

4. Failing to take steps to ensure that effective communication is provided, including adequately training staff and volunteers on how to address questions regarding accessibility services for individuals with hearing disabilities.

D. TERMS OF THE AGREEMENT

14. In order to avoid potential litigation, the parties agree to the terms of this Agreement. These terms are intended to redress only the violations of the ADA that have been identified in this Agreement.

15. In consideration of the terms of this Agreement and the Museum's promises contained in Section D of this Agreement, the United States agrees to close the investigations regarding the allegations contained in Complainant J.V.'s and Complainant D.P.'s complaints. The United States will not institute any civil action except as provided in paragraph 28 below.

16. In return, the Museum shall ensure that no individual is discriminated against on the basis of a hearing disability in the full and equal enjoyment of its goods, services, facilities, privileges, advantages, or accommodations. 42 U.S.C. §§ 12182 & 12183; 28 C.F.R § 36.201(a).

17. The Museum shall provide full and equal enjoyment of its goods, services, facilities, privileges, advantages, and accommodations in the most integrated setting appropriate to individuals who are deaf or hard of hearing. 42 U.S.C. § 12182(b)(1)(B); 28 C.F.R. § 36.203.

18. The Museum shall furnish appropriate auxiliary aids and services where necessary to ensure effective communication with people with hearing disabilities, unless the Museum can demonstrate that taking those steps would fundamentally alter the nature of the goods, services, facilities, privileges, advantages, or accommodations being offered or would result in an undue burden. 42 U.S.C. § 12182(b)(2)(A)(iii); 28 C.F.R. § 36.303.

19. The Museum shall respond to telephone calls from a telecommunications relay service in the same manner it responds to other telephone calls. 28 C.F.R. § 36.303(c)(4).

20. The Museum shall maintain in operable working condition those features of its facilities, including exhibits and equipment, required to be accessible by this Agreement or under the ADA. 28 C.F.R. § 36.211.

SPECIFIC REMEDIAL MEASURES

21. Pursuant to this Agreement, the Museum will ensure that its audiovisual presentations, programs, and other exhibits are accessible, with the provision of appropriate auxiliary aids and services, as set forth in the Paragraphs 22-26.

22. Within four (4) months of the effective date of this Agreement, the Museum agrees to do the following:

    1. Audiovisual Presentations with Uncaptioned AudioTracks
        1. Provide transcripts for any audiovisual programs and computer interactives with uncaptioned audio tracks. The transcript of the audiovisual exhibits will, to the extent feasible, reflect the interaction experienced by visitors who are not deaf or hard of hearing. The availability of this service, as well as how to access it, will be advertised to visitors. See 28 C.F.R. § 36.303.
    2. Uncaptioned Audio-Only Programs
        1. Provide transcripts or wall text for those programs with audio-only tracks; advertise that this service is available; and provide information on how to access it. See 28 C.F.R. § 36.303.
    3. Audiovisual Programs with Uncaptioned Audio Tracks
        1. Provide captions or transcripts for all audiovisual presentations in permanent exhibitions.
        2. Provide captions or transcripts for all temporary audiovisual public programs that are scheduled by the Museum if the Museum has five or more business days to arrange for captions or transcripts.
        3. If captioned versions or transcripts of audiovisual presentations shown during public programs, touring exhibitions and special events are not available, the Museum will advertise that sign language interpreters, oral interpreters, assistive listening devices, or real-time captioning will be made available as soon as practicable and upon no more than five days' advance request. See 28 C.F.R. § 36.303.
        4. For public events that are organized less than two weeks before the event's commencement, the Museum will furnish appropriate auxiliary aids or services to ensure effective communication as required by 28 C.F.R. 36.303(c)(ii), and shall work with the event organizer to ensure that such appropriate auxiliary aids and services are provided.

4. Assistive Listening Systems

    1. Furnish assistive listening devices free of charge to visitors who are hard of hearing. ADA Standards for Accessible Design at §§ 219 & 706 (Sept. 15, 2010).
    2. Provide in each theater and lecture hall in any Museum facility a minimum number of receivers equal to 4% of the total number of fixed seats. Of this number of receivers, 25% must be compatible with a hearing aid. ADA Standards for Accessible Design at § 219.3 (Sept. 15, 2010); see 28 C.F.R. Pt. 36, App. B, at § 219 (July 1, 2015).

5. Signage

    1. Post a minimum of one sign in each Museum at the ticketing desk or booth advertising the availability of auxiliary aids and services. ADA Standards for Accessible Design at §§ 219.10 & 703.7.2.4 (Sept. 15, 2010).
    2. Indicate on the Museum's website that auxiliary aids and services are available and the method by which a visitor should request an aid or service.

ADDITIONAL REMEDIAL MEASURES

23. The Museum shall designate an ADA Compliance Officer and ensure that the ADA Compliance Officer undergoes training on the Museum's obligations under the ADA and this Agreement. The ADA Compliance Officer shall be responsible for handling hearing disability-related complaints from the patrons of the Museum and for ensuring the Museum's compliance with the ADA and this Agreement.

24. Within thirty (30) days of the effective date of this Agreement, to the extent not already undertaken, the Museum shall develop an ADA Complaint Resolution Policy to address ADA-related complaints and shall provide a written copy of the policy to the USAO for review and approval. This policy shall identify the ADA Compliance Officer, the procedure for filing complaints and the process by which complaints will be investigated and resolved. The Museum shall implement the policy within thirty (30) days of approval by the USAO.

25. Within sixty (60) days of the effective date of this Agreement, the Museum shall train all supervisors and managers on the Museum's obligations under the ADA and this Agreement. The Museum shall ensure that all newly hired supervisors and managers receive this training within thirty (30) days of hire or promotion.

26. The Museum shall provide a written report annually to the USAO on its progress regarding the completion of its obligations under this Agreement, including under Section E. The report shall identify and document (e.g., with photographs and/or signed declarations) the revisions that have been made and any training of employees that has occurred (by date and the content of the training), and include copies of any ADA-related policies that the Museum has adopted. The report shall be provided to the USAO annually on the anniversary of the effective date of this Agreement, except that the last report shall be provided three months prior to the expiration of this Agreement.

E. IMPLEMENTATION AND ENFORCEMENT

27. The USAO shall have the right, during the course of this Agreement and with seven (7) days' notice to the Museum, to conduct inspections of the Museum, and to request documents or photographs in order to evaluate compliance with this Agreement. The USAO shall make every effort to conduct its inspections at times that are agreeable to Museum so as to cause minimal disruption to its operations.

28. If the USAO believes that the Museum is not in compliance with this Agreement or any requirements contained herein, the USAO will notify the Museum in writing of the alleged noncompliance and attempt to seek a resolution of the matter with the Museum. If the parties are unable to reach a resolution within thirty (30) days of the date of the USAO's written notification, the USAO may seek enforcement of the terms of this Agreement and/or the ADA in court. In the event a court determines that the Museum has failed to comply with any term of this Agreement, the USAO may seek, and the court may assess, civil penalties as provided in 42 U.S.C. § 12188(b)(2)(C).

29. The USAO's failure to enforce any provision of this Agreement shall not be construed as a waiver by the USAO of any right to enforce any provisions.

30. This Agreement shall be binding upon the Museum, and its agents and employees. In the event the Museum seeks to transfer or assign all or part of its interests in any exhibition or facility covered by this Agreement, and the successor or assignee intends to carry on the same or similar use of the facility, as a condition of sale, the Museum shall obtain the written accession of the successor or assignee to any obligations remaining under this Agreement for the remaining term of this Agreement.

   1. All notices, demands, or other communications to be provided under this Agreement shall be in writing and delivered by email or overnight delivery to the following persons and addresses (or such other persons

and addresses as any party may designate in writing from time to time): (Omitted)

2. This Agreement constitutes the entire Agreement between the parties relating to Department of Justice Case No. 202-12C-523, and USAO Matter Nos. 2014V02399 and 2016V00356 and no other statement, promise or agreement, either written or oral, made by either party or agents of any party, that is not contained in this written Agreement, shall be enforceable.

3. If any provision of this Agreement is determined by any court to be unenforceable, the other terms of this Agreement shall nonetheless remain in full force and effect, provided however, that if the severance of any such provision materially alters the rights or obligations of the parties, the USAO and the Museum shall engage in good faith negotiations in order to adopt mutually agreeable amendments to this Agreement as may be necessary to restore the parties as closely as possible to the agreed upon relative rights and obligations.

4. This Agreement does not affect the Museum's continuing responsibility to comply with all aspects of the ADA not covered by this Agreement.

5. A signatory to this document in a representative capacity for the Museum represents that he or she is authorized to bind the Museum to this Agreement.

6. The effective date of this Agreement is the date of the last signature below. The Agreement shall remain in effect for three years from the effective date, unless extended by written agreement of the parties.

STUDY QUESTIONS

- Who initiated the ADA Complaint against the Palm Springs Museum? What compliance issues were found? What remedial steps was the museum required to make?
- Both the National Crime Museum and the Palm Springs Museum were required to adopt an ADA policy as part of their ADA Settlement Agreements. What would you recommend be included in their new policy?
- Settlement Agreements like those reprinted above are regularly published and made available to the public. What can you learn from reading ADA settlement agreements like these?

HISTORIC PRESERVATION

Many museums are housed in historic buildings. In some cases, the buildings themselves are considered part of the museum's collection. A variety of federal, state, and local laws regulate the use of historic buildings.

The national park system, which was originally established in 1916, was reorganized in the Historic Site Act of 1935 which set as national policy the preservation "for public use historic sites, buildings and objects of national significance." The Act established the Historic American Buildings Survey to document significant historic structures and created the National Historic Landmark program to identify structures of national significance. Today, over 2600 properties have been formally designated as National Historic Landmarks. A complete list of National Historic Landmarks by state can be found on the NPS website—www.nps.gov.

The National Historic Preservation Act (NHPA), enacted in 1966, made sweeping changes to federal historic preservation law. The NHPA established the National Register of Historic Places. It also mandated a regulatory process for reviewing potential impacts to historic properties, commonly referred to as "Section 106 review." The NHPA requires each state to maintain a State Historic Preservation Office (SHPO) to facilitate federal historic preservation efforts. In some states the SHPO office is part of the state's public history function, while in others it is housed in the state's economic development office or within another state government entity.

The National Register of Historic Places is a list of historic properties which meet certain criteria set out in the statute, including age, significance, and integrity. Generally, a building must be at least 50 years old to be listed on the National Register or meet other criteria for significance.

The NHPA establishes a process for listing on the National Register. A nomination application may be submitted to the SHPO office in the state where the property is located by the property owner, historical societies, preservation organizations, governmental agencies, or other individuals or groups. If the application is not made by the owner or

The Custom House in Salem, Massachusetts, is one of 12 historic structures at the Salem Maritime National Historic Site located along the waterfront of Salem Harbor in Salem, Massachusetts. Designated in 1938, Salem Maritime was the first National Historic Site established under the Historic Site Act. The site interprets the Triangle Trade during the colonial period, in cotton, rum, sugar, and slaves; the actions of privateers during the American Revolution; and global maritime trade with the Far East, after independence.

owners of the property, the SHPO notifies the owners and solicits public comments. If the owner(s) object, the property cannot be listed on the National Historic Register, but the SHPO can forward the application to the National Park Service for a Determination of Eligibility (hence the designation "Eligible for Listing on the National Historic Register"). If the owner(s) do not object, the application is then reviewed by the SHPO office and the state's National Register Review Board. Completed nominations are then submitted to the National Park Service Keeper of the National Register for final review and listing on the National Register of Historic Places.

Properties that are designated as National Historic Landmarks may be eligible for federal, state, or local preservation incentives, including grants and tax credits. They may also be subject to preservation easements and to stringent building code requirements. Alterations or improvements to the property may be subject to Section 106 review. The property may also fall under certain state and local regulations as a result of the designation.

The Section 106 review process encourages, but does not mandate, preservation of historic sites. The review process is triggered when a project involves federal property, funds, licenses or permits that directly or indirectly affects a historic property. In such cases, the federal agency (or lead agency) involved in the project must consult with the relevant SHPO office and certain stakeholders to assess whether the property is eligible for registration on the National Register of Historic Places, and if so, to identify any adverse impacts to the historic nature of the property and to develop a mitigation plan to minimize those adverse effects.

In addition to the SHPO office, those entitled to consultation "by right" include federally recognized Indian tribes, relevant local governments, and the applicant of the federal assistance, permit, license, or approval. Other stakeholders with a demonstrated legal, economic, or historic preservation interest in a project may be included by invitation. In some cases, local museums may be involved in the consultation process. The Section 106 process is often part of a larger review of the environmental impacts of a project conducted as part of a National Environmental Policy Act environmental review.

CHAPTER 4:
MUSEUM INTELLECTUAL PROPERTY

In this chapter we focus on intellectual property rights and how they arise in the museum context. We start with a general overview of basic intellectual property law concepts: patents, trade secrets, trademarks, personal rights, moral rights, and copyrights. Then we focus in-depth on the elements of copyright: copyright duration and the limitations and exceptions to copyright, including first sale, public display, and fair use. We apply these principles by considering issues raised by "appropriate art." Finally, we look at museum intellectual property audits and policies.

PART I: INTELLECTUAL PROPERTY RIGHTS

What is "intellectual property"? Property can be tangible or intangible. As the story goes, Sir Isaac Newton was hit on the head by an apple (a tangible thing) and formulated the concept of gravity (an intangible idea) which he then explained in the book *Philosophiae Naturalis Principia Mathematica.* An intangible idea expressed in a tangible form becomes intellectual property. For example, a book is a tangible thing that contains intangible ideas expressed through language and imagery. Inventions, ideas, creative and artistic works—indeed anything that is the product of human thought and creativity that can be expressed in a tangible form—is intellectual property.

Property (real or intellectual) can be privately or publicly owned. In Western societies, it is generally agreed that the individual who creates intellectual property is the exclusive owner of that property (at least initially) and is entitled to certain rights, including the right to prohibit others from using that intellectual property without permission. Underlying the concept of intellectual property as a private right are various notions about the relationship between the person who created the work and the work itself. The four basic theories about intellectual property are: (i) that the creator has certain inalienable natural rights to the results of their creativity (the "Labor" theory); (ii) that a creative work is the progeny or "offspring" of the person who created it (the "Moral" theory); (iii) that the grant of exclusive rights to useful and creative works encourages their creation and benefits society as a whole (the "Utilitarian" theory); and (iv) that the grant of exclusive rights furthers human society and culture (the "Social Planning" theory).

Intellectual property rights are recognized through legal constructs that vary by jurisdiction. In the United States, intellectual property rights are defined and protected through common law jurisprudence, federal or state statutory laws and regulations, private contracts, and through voluntary adopted guidelines and policies. In contrast with other Western countries, apart from certain very limited "moral rights" recognized under the Visual Artists Rights Act, and certain privacy and publicity rights, in the United States intellectual property rights are freely alienable—that is, the creator of a work can sell, assign, or otherwise transfer her rights to her intellectual property. The following discussion of intellectual property rights will focus on intellectual property rights under U.S. law that are applicable to museums.

There are five basic forms of intellectual property: patents, trade secrets, trademarks, copyrights, and personal and reputational rights (rights of privacy and publicity, and moral rights). The basic elements of each type of intellectual property are briefly summarized below. Emphasis will be placed on copyrights because these rights are perhaps the most applicable in the museum context.

(261)

Anno Octavo

Annæ Reginæ.

An Act for the Encouragement of Learning, by Vesting the Copies of Printed Books in the Authors or Purchasers of such Copies, during the Times therein mentioned.

Whereas Printers, Booksellers, and other Persons have of late frequently taken the Liberty of Printing, Reprinting, and Publishing, or causing to be Printed, Reprinted, and Published Books, and other Writings, without the Consent of the Authors or Proprietors of such Books and Writings, to their very great Detriment, and too often to the Ruin of them and their Families: For Preventing therefore such Practices for the future, and for the Encouragement of Learned Men to Compose and Write useful Books; May it please Your Majesty, that it may be Enacted, and be it Enacted by the Queens most Excellent Majesty, by and with the Advice and Consent of the Lords Spiritual and Temporal, and Commons in this present Parliament Assembled, and by the Authority of the same, That from and after the Tenth Day of April, One thousand seven hundred and ten, the Author of any Book or Books already Printed, who hath not Transferred to any other the Copy or Copies of such Book or Books, Share or Shares thereof, or the Bookseller or Booksellers, Printer or Printers, or other Person or Persons, who hath or have Purchased or Acquired the Copy or Copies of any Book or Books, in order to Print or Reprint the same, shall have the sole Right and Liberty of Printing such Book and Books for the Term of One and twenty Years, to Commence from the said Tenth Day of April, and no longer; and that the Author of any Book or Books already Composed and not Printed and Published, or that shall hereafter be Composed, and his Assignee, or Assigns, shall have the sole Liberty of Printing and Reprinting such Book and Books for the Term of Fourteen

6 Ttt 2

The Statute of Anne, also known as the Copyright Act 1710, is an act of the Parliament of Great Britain passed in 1710. It is considered to be the first statute to provide for copyright regulated by the government and courts, rather than by private parties.

PATENTS

Patent rights involve novel inventions. The invention can be a method, process, device, composition, or design. The invention must be useful. Patent rights are recognized and governed by federal statute. There is a formal application and review process after which the patent owner is granted an exclusive monopoly over the exploitation of the invention for a limited period.

Patents are generally not applicable in the museum setting, although it is conceivable that a museum could either create or use a patentable invention. An innovative design for an exhibition case, or an original method for conserving a work of art, for example, may contain patentable elements.

TRADE SECRETS

Trade secrets are ideas or information that is not generally known and that give the owner a competitive advantage. In some cases, trade secrets may also be patentable. To maintain intellectual property rights in trade secrets, they must be treated as confidential and not shared publicly. Trade secret laws seek to protect the commercial value of the ideas or information.

Examples of potential trade secrets in the museum setting include proprietary donor and member lists, confidential relationships with suppliers, and certain types of business methods and practices. Secret formulas and recipes may also be protectable as trade secrets.

TRADEMARKS

Trademarks are words, names, symbols, colors, sounds, or other devices (or combinations thereof) used to identify goods or services and to distinguish them from the goods or services offered by others. A name used to identify a business or organization—Ford Motor Company, for example—may not function as a trademark. The same name used to identify a product or service—"Ford" used to identify cars and trucks manufactured by the Ford Motor Company—does function as a trademark. Domain names are not necessarily trademarks themselves, but they may contain a trademark. A domain name may also function as a trademark depending on the circumstances under which it is used.

Trademark rights give the owner the exclusive right to use the mark in connection with its goods or services. Trademark rights may be protected under common law or by state or federal statutes. To be eligible for protection as a trademark, the mark must be distinctive. Fanciful or arbitrary marks (such as the name "Apple" used to identify computers and smartphones) are favored. Marks which describe the goods or services or use generic terms are generally considered not sufficiently "distinctive" to warrant protection as a trademark. However, a mark may become distinctive as a result of being used in connection with a specific product or service for a long period of time—this is known as "acquired distinctiveness" or "secondary meaning." A mark that lacks distinctiveness may be registered on the Supplemental Register and may acquire distinctiveness over time.

Examples of trademarks in the museum setting include names, logos, or slogans used to identify the museum or its programs, exhibits, and the like. For example, the mark "Andy Warhol" is registered in connection with a variety of goods and services by the Andy Warhol Foundation for the Visual Arts, and the mark "Andy Warhol Museum" is registered as well.

Common law trademark rights arise from long use of a mark in commerce in connection with specific goods or services such that the public has come to associate the mark with a particular source of those goods or services. State registration provides limited protection for trademarks. The Lanham Act governs the registration and protection of trademarks at the federal level.

There is a formal process for registering and maintaining trademarks under federal law. An application for trademark registration may be initiated for a mark before it is used in commerce. Known as an "intent-to-use" (ITU) application, this allows the applicant to "reserve" a trademark for a limited period. Benefits of registering a trademark include protection of the investment in developing a brand and image, constructive notice to potential infringers, and the ability to obtain statutory damages for trademark infringement.

Trademark registration is perpetual so long as the mark is continuously used in connection with the identified goods or services and formalities for maintaining the registration—including periodic renewals with affidavits of continuing use—are followed. The owner of a trademark may sue an unauthorized user for infringing on the owner's trademark rights.

A failure to assert trademark rights against infringers can result in dilution of trademark rights. An example of trademark dilution is when a proprietary trade name becomes a generic term for a product—for example, the use of the trade name "Kleenex" to refer to paper facial tissues. For this reason, trademark owners must actively police the use of their trademarks.

Use of another's trademark in a way that misleadingly suggests or implies endorsement or sponsorship may give rise to a claim of misappropriation. It is common practice for museums to thank their corporate sponsors by displaying their corporate logos in exhibits and the like. To avoid misunderstandings or worse, museums should obtain express permission before using the trademarks of businesses and organizations.

PERSONAL RIGHTS

Personal rights refer to the rights a person has in their own body and the aspects of their being or "personhood"—including their name, appearance, and life experiences. To the extent these rights are intangible they can be considered intellectual property. Personal rights and the laws that protect them vary widely by culture. The law of personal rights is rapidly evolving, in large part due to changes in audio and video recording technology and the growth of social media.

Often personal rights are defined in terms of privacy—that is, the ability to prevent intrusion into one's personal life by governments and other individuals. Privacy rights protect private individuals against unwanted public exposure. In response to unwanted attention by journalists and the publication of personal facts in society columns, Samuel D. Warren and Louis Brandeis wrote a law review article in which they famously described the right of privacy as "the right to be left alone." Increasingly privacy rights have focused on the right to control and exploit one's individual personhood, including "the right to be forgotten."

In the United States, laws regarding privacy rights vary greatly by jurisdiction and are comprised of both statutes and case law. Each state has its own laws on privacy. The basic forms of privacy rights traditionally recognized under U.S. law include: (i) the right to prevent unreasonable intrusion into private aspects of one's life; (ii) the right to prevent damage to one's reputation, either from public disclosure of true but embarrassing facts or from the publication of untrue statements; and (iii) the right to prevent the appropriation of one's name and likeness.

Since the goal of these rights is to prevent intrusion into one's personal life, generally speaking they do not apply in situations where a person is "in the public eye." Public figures—celebrities, politicians, and other people who have become noteworthy, either through their own intentional acts or because they find themselves involved in public events, may not be able to assert privacy rights, at least with respect to their public activities. This is known as the "public figure" exception. People who are not public figures, but who are involved in newsworthy events are sometimes referred to as "limited public figures" meaning their privacy rights with respect to the specific newsworthy event may be restricted or non-existent.

The last form of privacy right referred to above—the right of appropriation—is sometimes alternatively described as a right of publicity—that is, the right to control the commercial use of one's name, appearance, or other personal identifying characteristics. These aspects of "personhood" may have substantial economic value, particularly for celebrities. Indeed, there is an enormous business in the exploitation of celebrity publicity rights. In response, a growing number of states have enacted statutes governing publicity rights. Publicity rights can also be understood in terms of unfair competition or as a form of personal trademark.

Questions regarding the scope of publicity rights—the degree to which such rights can be alienable, whether they survive the death of the person and whether they can be inherited, and to what extent they are limited by the First Amendment and freedom of expression, for example—remain to be tested in the courts. Suffice it to say that privacy rights, including the right of publicity, will increasingly become an important form of intellectual property.

In the museum context, rights of privacy and publicity may arise in a variety of contexts, from the collection and dissemination of personal information and images of donors, visitors, and the like, to the use of recognizable images of people in artistic works, and their public display in the museum.

MORAL RIGHTS

Moral rights involve the relationship between the author of a creative work and the work itself. These rights are predicated on the idea that artistic creations are an extension of the person who created them—somewhat like the paternal relationship between a parent and child (except that the child is the creative work, not another human being). Moral rights seek to preserve the reputation of the artist by granting the artist the right to protect the integrity of the artist's work and to control its exploitation. Moral rights apply to a work regardless of who owns the physical copy of the work or the copyright in the work.

While the concept of moral rights is generally recognized in most European countries (as well as in Canada and Australia), under U.S. intellectual property law, which is focused primarily on economic rights, the concept of moral rights is only recognized in a very limited way. Depending on the jurisdiction, moral rights may include a variety of rights regarding an artist's control over his or her creative work. These rights include: the right of attribution, the right of integrity, the right of display, the right of authentication or right to determine ownership, and the right to share in the proceeds from subsequent sales of the work (the "resale royalty" right). Since moral rights are rights that are inherent in an individual, generally speaking, they cannot be transferred or waived. However, in some jurisdictions moral rights can be inherited. It is not uncommon for an artist's estate to assert moral rights in the artist's work.

In the United States, moral rights are recognized only to a very limited extent: they are protected through judicial interpretation of intellectual property laws and statutorily by the federal Visual Artists Rights Act (VARA), 17 U.S.C. § 106, and in some cases by state law. The moral rights recognized by VARA apply only to certain narrowly delineated types of visual art specified in the statute. These include paintings, drawings, sculptures and still photographs produced for exhibition. Only single copies or signed limited editions of 200 copies or less are covered by the VARA statute. The work must also be of "recognized stature"—a vague concept that has been interpreted by case law. Moral rights under VARA are limited to specific rights granted to the artist with regards to attribution, alteration, or destruction of the protected work. VARA also includes a process by which an artist can waive his or her moral rights. This can only be done in writing though what is known as a "VARA Waiver."

The obligation to pay a "resale royalty"—typically a percentage of the sales price of a work of art—to the artist when a work is resold to a third party, is relatively common in European countries. The idea is to allow the artist (and in some cases the artist's estate or heirs) to share in the increased value of the artwork when it is resold. Attempts have been made to establish a resale royalty right in the United States. California enacted a Resale Royalty Act in 1976, but the law has been deemed unconstitutional because it encroaches on exclusive Congressional authority to enact laws affecting copyright. Legislation to establish a federal resale royalty right is routinely proposed in Congress but to date no action has been taken to establish an American version of the resale royalty right. In large part, the idea of a resale royalty goes against the idea prevalent in the United States that artwork, like other property, should be freely transferable. Developments in digital technology, including the creation of "non-fungible tokens" or NFTs and other technologies which allow artists to track their work, may enable a viable contractual approach to resale royalties.

COPYRIGHTS

Copyright is the exclusive right to reproduce, distribute copies, prepare derivative works, and (for certain works) the right to display or perform the work in public. As such copyright is a form of limited monopoly over the exploitation of a creative work.

In the United States, copyrights are governed by federal law. The United States Constitution gives Congress the power to grant a limited monopoly in creative works. Article I Section 8, Clause 8 of the Constitution authorizes Congress authority "To promote the progress of science and useful arts, by securing for limited times to authors and inventors the exclusive right to their respective writings and discoveries."

The first U.S. copyright statute, enacted in 1790, applied only to maps, charts and books and protection was for only 14 years after publication, with the right to renew for an additional 14 years. Over the past two centuries, copyright protection has greatly expanded. Today statutory copyright protection covers all creative works for extremely long periods of time.

The exclusive right granted by copyright law conflicts with the concepts of freedom of expression recognized in the First Amendment to the Constitution. The impact the expansion of copyright protection has had on cultural institutions including museums cannot be overstated. As a result, the importance of exceptions to copyright protection—most notably the doctrine of "fair use"—have become increasingly important. These exceptions will be explored in greater detail below.

Today U.S. copyright law protects all original works of authorship. Ideas and concepts are not eligible for copyright protection, but the tangible expression of those ideas and concepts may be protected by copyright. For example, the idea for a television show cannot be protected, but a written treatment based on that idea may be copyrightable. To be protected by copyright, the work must be created by a human being—smartphone photos taken by a gorilla, for example, are not protected by copyright.

While the work must be original, the threshold for originality is quite low. A photographic snapshot, for example, may be eligible for copyright protection. The *Bridgeman* case included in the readings below explores this threshold concept of "originality"—in that case, the court concludes that photographic reproductions of two-dimensional works of art, such as those taken by museums to document and catalogue their collections, do not contain sufficient originality to qualify for copyright protection.

Copyright arises on creation. When an idea or concept is fixed in a tangible medium of expression—through writing or other means of recording—that tangible expression may be copyrighted. So, for example, while an oral presentation (a speech for example) would not be subject to copyright, the transcript of the speech or an audio recording of the speech, is eligible for copyright protection. Similarly, a performance would not be protected by copyright, but the play or script on which the performance is based, as well as the audio or video recording of the performance, could be protected by copyright. Under prior copyright laws, certain formalities such as including a copyright notice and registering and renewing copyrights, were required to maintain a copyright. Today no such formalities are required. It is no longer necessary to include a copyright notice, and while there are advantages to registering copyrightable works, registration with the U.S. Copyright Office is no longer required. In short, when you take a photograph with your smartphone or write an email to a friend, your work is automatically entitled to protection under U.S. copyright law.

Certain works are inherently not entitled to copyright protection. Short phrases—slogans for example—are not copyrightable, but they may function as trademarks and be protectable as such. Facts and theories, including data, lack the originality to give rise to copyright protection—but if the data is organized in a specific way, the database as a whole may be protected by copyright. Certain common themes, elements, or modes of expression ("scenes-a-faire") that are indispensable to telling a story are not copyrightable. For example, the use of a flashback to tell a narrator's story would not be a protectible element of an otherwise copyrightable work. Works created by the federal government (but not necessarily those created by state or local governments) are categorically excluded from copyright protection. Federal, state and local statutes and laws are not subject to copyright. Works that are not subject to copyright—either for one of the foregoing reasons, or because the term of copyright in the work has expired—are said to be "in the public domain."

In most cases, the copyright in the work is owned by the author or creator of the work. There are some special situations affecting copyright ownership, however. Copyright in a collaborative work—that is, a work created by two or more people working together—is owned jointly by all of the creators of the work. This is known as "joint copyright ownership." In a joint copyright situation, each of the joint copyright owners has the right to independently exploit the copyright—their only obligation to the other joint copyright owners is to share any revenues resulting from their exploitation of the work. This can be problematic. Imagine a situation where two people collaborate in writing a play, for example. The joint copyright owners would both have the right to perform the play at competing theaters across the street from each other—their only obligation would be to share any profits from their own show with the other copyright owner. To ensure the orderly exploitation of a collaborative work it is usually best to avoid creating a joint copyright by clarifying in writing beforehand who or what entity will control copyright in the work.

The employer/employee relationship also affects copyright ownership. Under U.S. copyright law, a work created by an employee within the scope of his employment is owned by the employer. The key question is whether the work was created as part of the employee's assigned duties. Thus, for example, copyright in a blog post about an item in the museum's collections written by the museum's curator would be owned by the museum, while a post written by the same curator about his son's baseball team would be owned by the curator.

Works created by independent contractors present another copyright ownership issue. Because copyright arises on creation and is owned by the creator, absent a written agreement to the contrary, copyright is owned by the independent contractor. The Supreme Court made this clear in the *Community for Creative Non-Violence* case reprinted in the Cases and Other Readings section below. The court concluded that absent a written "work-for-hire" agreement, the sculptor commissioned to create the work retained copyright ownership in it.

Paying a contractor to create a copyrightable work may create an implied license—that is, the person or entity paying the contractor may have the right to use the work for the purposes for which the work was created—but compensation alone does not result in the transfer of copyright ownership in the work. To acquire copyright in a work created by an independent contractor, it is necessary to have the contractor sign a written agreement that includes specific copyright "work-for-hire" language. The "work-for-hire" language acknowledges that the contractor is creating the work as a work-for-hire under U.S. copyright law and that the person or entity hiring the contractor is the copyright owner. The work-for-hire agreement must be executed prior to creating the work, otherwise in order to transfer ownership, the copyright must be assigned.

Copyright ownership is alienable—that is, it may be transferred by the copyright owner. Any transfer or assignment of copyright must be in writing and signed by the copyright owner. Copyright transfers and assignments may be recorded with the U.S. Copyright Office but there is no requirement to do so. When a copyright owner dies, the copyright becomes part of the owner's estate. Copyrights may be bequeathed and inherited via a specific clause in a will or may pass as part of the assets in the residuary of the estate.

Some copyright owners choose to voluntarily give up all or a portion of their copyright in a work. They do this because they want members of the public to be able to use their work freely without first asking for permission. This can be done by informing the public that the work is free to be used. Essentially the copyright owner is granting a proactive license to use the work consistent with the terms of the license. The Creative Commons (creativecommons.org) is an organization that provides a standardized set of such proactive licenses.

Copyright includes the right to create works that are derived from the original work. These new works are referred to as "derivative works." The extent to which a work is has been "derived from" a copyrighted work, or is itself an independently copyrightable work, is subject to much debate. In *Picket v. Prince*, included in the Cases and Other Readings below, the court was asked to assess whether a guitar which incorporated the musician Prince's famous Glyph symbol into its design, constituted a derivative work.

Since copyright arises on creation, there is no longer any requirement to register a work with the Copyright Office in order to obtain copyright protection. However, there are still advantages to copyright registration. In addition to obtaining a unique identification number for the work, registration puts the public on notice and makes it easier to identify and locate the copyright claimant of a given work in order to request permission. Registration is required before commencing a copyright infringement lawsuit and enables the copyright claimant to assert the Copyright Act's provisions pertaining to statutory damages. Registering a work with the Copyright Office is a relatively simple and inexpensive process which can easily be done online.

CASES AND OTHER READINGS

Reading Note: The *Bridgeman* case reprinted below established an important precedent regarding copyright in two-dimensional art. It is particularly relevant to museums, which use images of paintings and other art in their collections for a variety of purposes. The case explores the threshold requirement of originality, and the court concludes that exact reproductions are not entitled to copyright protection.

BRIDGEMAN V. COREL

25 F. Supp. 2d 421 (1998)

MEMORANDUM OPINION

KAPLAN, District Judge.

Plaintiff The Bridgeman Art Library, Ltd. ("Bridgeman") claims to have exclusive rights in photographic transparencies of a substantial number of well-known works of art located in museums around the world and to have transformed those transparencies into digital images in which it also claims exclusive rights. It contends that defendant Corel Corporation ("Corel") is marketing in the United States and abroad compact disks containing digital images of a significant number of the same works of art which, Bridgeman claims, must have been copied from its transparencies and that Corel thus is infringing its copyrights in the United States, the United Kingdom and Canada. It claims as well that Corel's actions violated Sections 32(1) and 43(a) of the Lanham Act and are actionable at common law.[NOTE 1] The matter now is before the Court on Corel's motion for summary judgment dismissing the complaint and Bridgeman's cross-motion for partial summary judgment.

FACTS

Bridgeman

Bridgeman is an English company which has an office in New York.[NOTE 2] It is in the business of acquiring rights to market reproductions of public domain works of art owned by museums and other collections[NOTE 3] which it obtains either from the owners of the underlying works of art or freelance photographers it hires.[NOTE 4] Bridgeman maintains a library of those reproductions in the form of large format color transparencies and digital files.[NOTE 5] Additionally, Bridgeman attaches a color correction strip to each transparency to ensure that the image is a genuine reflection of the original work as it existed in the circumstances in which it was photographed.[NOTE 6]

Bridgeman distributes its images as transparencies and as digital files on CD-ROM. The high-resolution transparencies are made available to clients through licensing arrangements,[NOTE 7] while the low resolution CD-ROM images generally are provided to Bridgeman's clients without charge as a digital catalog of available transparencies. [NOTE 8]

Corel

Corel is a Canadian corporation engaged chiefly in the creation and marketing of computer software products. Among Corel's products is a set of seven CD-ROMs known as "Corel Professional Photos CD-ROM Masters I-VII" ("Masters CD-ROM").[NOTE 9] This product contains seven hundred digital reproductions of well-known paintings by European masters. Corel maintains that it obtained the images for its Masters CD-ROM from 35 millimeter slides owned by OWI.[NOTE 10] Corel claims that it was told that the slides were created from lithograph images owned by OWI's president, Richard Friedman. [NOTE 11]

Bridgeman's Claim

Bridgeman here claims that Corel has infringed its rights in approximately 120 of its images. Its theory is that (1) the owners of the underlying works of art, all of which it concedes are in the public domain, strictly limit access to those works, (2) Bridgeman's transparencies of those works, from which it prepared its digital images and presumably other reproductions, are "the only authorized transparencies of some of these works of art,"[NOTE 12] and (3) "[b]y inference and logical conclusion, the images in Corel's CD-ROMs must be copies of Bridgeman's transparencies because they have not proved legal [sic] source."[NOTE 13] The alleged infringements are said to have occurred in the United States, Canada and Great Britain.

Bridgeman contends that it enjoys copyright in the allegedly infringed transparencies on a number of theories. First, in 1997, after the dispute with Corel arose, Bridgeman obtained from the Register of Copyrights a certificate of registration for a derivative work entitled Old World Masters I, which consists of digital images and transparencies of all or substantially all of the reproductions allegedly infringed by Corel.[NOTE 14] Second, it contends that its transparencies enjoy copyright protection under the laws of the United Kingdom and Canada as well as the Convention for the Protection of Literary and Artistic Works, popularly known as the Berne Convention.

DISCUSSION

I. Summary Judgment

Under Fed.R.Civ.P. 56(c), summary judgment is appropriate if there is no genuine issue of material fact and the moving party is entitled to a judgment as a matter of law.[NOTE 15] While the burden rests on the moving party to demonstrate the absence of a genuine issue of material fact[NOTE 16] and the Court must view the facts in the light most favorable to the non-moving party,[NOTE 17] a defendant may prevail if it can demonstrate that the plaintiff cannot establish an essential element of its claim.[NOTE 18]

II. The Copyright Claim

United States Infringement

To establish copyright infringement under the Copyright Act of 1976,[19] a plaintiff must establish ownership of a valid copyright and copying.[NOTE 20] Corel contests both elements, alleging that Bridgeman has no valid copyright in its images and, in the alternative, that there is no evidence of copying. The Court therefore addresses each element in turn. A threshold matter, however, is the applicable choice of law for these questions.

1. Choice of Law

Bridgeman argues that its rights are to be determined entirely under British law on the theory that the copying and initial infringement occurred in England.[NOTE 21] The matter is not quite that simple. In view of the United States' accession to the Berne Convention[NOTE 22] and the Universal Copyright Convention ("UCC"),[NOTE 23] a foreign national such as Bridgeman may seek copyright protection under the Copyright Act although the source of its rights lies abroad.[NOTE 24] The Nimmers suggest that, under the Berne Convention's principle of national treatment, the law of the country of the alleged infringement controls.[NOTE 25] The Second Circuit disagrees. The Circuit recently held that the principle of national treatment does not express any choice of law rule. It "simply requires that the country in which protection is claimed must treat foreign and domestic authors alike."[NOTE 26]

The next question, of course, is how to choose the applicable law. *Itar-Tass* says that the Berne Convention itself cannot be the source of law because it is not self-executing.[NOTE 27] And since the Copyright Act has no choice of law provision, the matter is left to federal common law.[NOTE 28] In consequence, the applicable law is not necessarily the same for each element of the copyright claim.[NOTE 29] The Court therefore must determine which law governs copyrightability and the alleged infringements.

As copyright is a form of property, the Court determines the interests of the parties based on "the law of the state with 'the most significant relationship' to the property and the parties."[NOTE 30] According to *Itar-Tass,* relevant factors include the nationality of the authors, the place of initial publication, and the country of origin as determined under the Berne Convention.[NOTE 31]

At issue here are nearly 120 photographs produced either by the museums owning the original works of art or by freelance photographers employed by Bridgeman, which is based in the United Kingdom. Many of the underlying works are in Britain.[NOTE 32] Bridgeman claims to own any literary property in all the photographs although the record arguably supports the view that Bridgeman in some instances is merely an exclusive licensing and sales agent for reproductions owned by the museums that own the original works of art.[NOTE 33] In any case, however, the photographs first were published in the United Kingdom. In these circumstances, the Court concludes that the United Kingdom has the most significant relationship to the issue of copyrightability.

The applicable law for the second element of the copyright claim is simply that of the infringement situs.[NOTE 34] Thus, whether an infringement has occurred in the United States is a matter of United States law.

2. Copyrightability

For the reasons discussed above, whether copyright subsists in Bridgeman's transparencies is a question of United Kingdom law. The result depends upon the Copyright, Designs and Patents Act 1988 (the "UK Act") which renders "*original* literary, dramatic, musical or artistic works" copyrightable.[NOTE 35] To be original, a work "need not be original or novel in form, but it must originate with the author and not be copied from another work."[NOTE 36] That is not to say that the author, in all circumstances, must create the entire work from scratch to be accorded copyright protection. "Protection of a derivative work turns on whether the [author's] skill, judgment and labour transforms the underlying work in a relevant way."[NOTE 37] That is, the originality requirement is not met where the work in question "is wholly copied from an existing work, without any significant addition, alteration, transformation, or combination with other material."[NOTE 38]

This principle is exemplified in the Privy Council's oft quoted observation that although:

> "[i]t takes great skill, judgment and labour to produce a good copy by painting or to produce an enlarged photograph from a positive print, ... no one would reasonably contend that the copy painting or enlargement was an 'original' artistic work in which the copier is entitled to claim copyright. Skill, labor or judgment merely in the process of copying cannot confer originality.... There must in addition be some element of material alteration or embellishment which suffices to make the totality of the work an original work."[note 39]

In light of the originality requirement, Bridgeman's images are not copyrightable under the UK Act. It is uncontested that Bridgeman's images are substantially exact reproductions of public domain works, albeit in a different medium. The images were copied from the underlying works without any avoidable addition, alteration or transformation. Indeed, Bridgeman strives to reproduce precisely those works of art.

Bridgeman, nevertheless, claims that its works are original. It argues first that the variation in medium establishes sufficient variation from the underlying works to support originality.[NOTE 40] The Court is unpersuaded. "[T]he mere reproduction of a work of art in a different medium should not constitute the required originality for the reason that no one can claim to have independently evolved any particular medium.'"[NOTE 41] As discussed above, the law requires "some element of material alteration or embellishment" to the totality of the work. At bottom, the totality of the work is the image itself, and Bridgeman admittedly seeks to duplicate exactly the images of the underlying works.

Plaintiff next argues that its images are original because of the attached color correction bars.[NOTE 42] The Court, however, need not decide whether Bridgeman's images are copyrightable to the extent of this feature. As indicated below, even if the images with color bars attached are copyrightable, they may be infringed only by reproduction of Bridgeman's unique variation, the color bars. As Corel's images do not include correction strips, their significance for copyrightability is academic in this case.

Finally, plaintiff argues that photography requires artistic talent and originality and therefore would have the Court conclude that its transparencies photographs of underlying works of art are original.[NOTE 43] To be sure, much, perhaps almost all, photography is sufficiently original to be subject to copyright. Certainly anyone who has seen any of the great pieces of photography for example, Alfred Eisenstadt's classic image of a thrilled sailor exuberantly kissing a woman in Times Square on V-J Day, the stirring photograph of U.S. Marines raising the American flag atop Mount Surabachi on Iwo Jima, Ansel Adams' work and the portraits of Yousuf Karsh[NOTE 44] must acknowledge that photographic images of actual people, places and events may be as creative and deserving of protection as purely fanciful creations. But one need not deny the creativity inherent in the art of photography to recognize that a photograph which is no more than a copy of the work of another as exact as science and technology permit lacks originality. That is not to say such a feat is trivial, simply not original. The more persuasive analogy is that of a photocopier. Surely designing the technology to produce exact reproductions of documents required much engineering talent, but that does not make the reproductions copyrightable. As the Privy Council said in *Interlego,* "[s]kill, labour or judgment merely in the process of copying cannot confer originality."[NOTE 45]

> "[T]here has been no independent creation, no distinguishable variation from preexisting works, nothing recognizably the author's own contribution" that sets Bridgeman's reproductions apart from the images of the famous works it copied.

[NOTE 46] Consequently, Bridgeman's images lack sufficient originality to be copyrightable under the UK A47.47.tt/ct.[NOTE 47]

3. Proof of Copying

Even if its images were copyrightable, Bridgeman could not make out its claim because it has raised no genuine issue of fact as to infringement. To prove infringement, Bridgeman must prove that Corel actually copied its images and that "the copying is illegal because a substantial similarity exits between the defendant's work and the protectible elements of the plaintiff's work."[NOTE 48]

As direct proof is understandably difficult to acquire, copying generally is established by a showing of access by the defendant and of similarities between the accused and accusing works that are probative of copying.[NOTE 49] There is substantial doubt as to whether plaintiff has made out even a *prima facie* case of access[NOTE 50] and reason to doubt also the similarity of the low resolution Corel CD's and Bridgeman's high resolution transparencies,[NOTE 51] both of which bear on whether there is enough evidence of copying to withstand defendant's motion. In view of the Court's conclusion as to substantial similarity, however, it need not resolve these issues. In the case of derivative works such as Bridgeman's images, copyright protection extends,[NOTE 52] and the similarity to be weighed in determining infringement pertains, only to the original elements contributed by the author.[NOTE 53] Thus, assuming *arguendo* that Bridgeman holds a copyright in its images, similarity would be judged only with respect to those elements materially altering or embellishing the underlying works, the public domain paintings.

Within this limited framework, the Court finds no probative similarities between the parties' images. Plaintiff readily concedes the only similarity between the two sets of reproductions is that "both are exact reproductions of public domain works of art."[NOTE 54] Because, by definition, public domain works are not subjects of copyright, this cannot serve as the requisite similarity for copyright infringement. Even if Bridgeman had a copyright in the one element distinguishable from the underlying works (i.e., the color bars plaintiff attaches to its images), there would be no similarity because Corel's images do not include this feature.

When, as here, the only similarity between two works is with respect to non-copyrightable elements, summary judgment is appropriate.[NOTE 55]

The Canada and United Kingdom Infringement Claims

The alleged copyright infringements which occurred outside of the United States are not actionable under the Copyright Act, as the Act has no extraterritorial operation.[NOTE 56] To the extent such claims arise under the laws of Canada and the United Kingdom, the Court lacks jurisdiction to decide them for the reasons discussed below in Section IV.

III. Lanham Act Claim

The amended complaint next claimed that Corel violated Section 43(a) of the Lanham Act[NOTE 57] because it has falsely described the origin of the images on its CD-ROMs and falsely suggested that Corel's product is connected or associated with or sponsored by Bridgeman or the museums it represents.[NOTE 58] The argument was that the public has come to associate the *Mona Lisa* and other works, images of which are in Bridgeman's collection of reproductions, with Bridgeman or its client museums. *Ergo,* the sale of Corel's reproductions of the *Mona Lisa* and other works, according to Bridgeman, is associated with Bridgeman or its clients.

Section 43(a) comprises two prongs, the first of which[59] protects against infringement of unregistered trademarks and the second of which[NOTE 60] prohibits false advertising.[NOTE 61] Although the amended complaint evidently sought to allege both theories, Bridgeman has focused only on the first and thus has abandoned the second. And there are fundamental problems with Bridgeman's argument.

To begin with, Bridgeman's claim, even at the outset, in substantial measure was that the copying of its images violates the Lanham Act because its images are associated with it or its clients. To the extent that the claim rests on copying *vel non,* it is without merit. The Copyright Act is the only source of protection against the copying, without more, of copyrightable material.[NOTE 62] But this proposition is not necessarily the end of plaintiff's original claim. The Court assumes, without deciding, that one might make a trademark or comparable use of a copyrighted or copyrightable image which itself serves as a trademark and thus entitle the copyright owner to relief under the Lanham Act for reasons going beyond the alleged copying itself. Such an image might be used, for example, in a manner that would engender confusion as to the copyright holder's association with or sponsorship of a product on which the image appeared.[NOTE 63] But Bridgeman has made out no such claim here.

First of all, Bridgeman's answers to defendant's interrogatories substantially narrowed its claim. It specifically asserted that the only basis for its claims of unfair competition and deceptive trade practices was Corel's alleged copying of Bridgeman's images and the sales of the copies at lower prices.[NOTE 64] And even if Bridgeman had not so limited its Lanham Act claim, the claim would have other problems. For one thing, Bridgeman has conceded that the images in question are not trademarks or service marks of its products or those of its client museums.[NOTE 65] In other words, it has admitted formally that the images in question do not serve to identify the source of Bridgeman's products or services. That alone is fatal to its Section 43(a) claim.[NOTE 66]

Next, Bridgeman has failed to allege or offer any evidence of any trademark use by Corel of any of the images at issue. That is to say, there is no suggestion that Corel uses any of the images in a manner intended or likely to be taken as an identifier of the source of Corel's product.[NOTE 67] Bridgeman asserts only that 120 of the 700 images on Corel's CD-ROM are of works of which Bridgeman also distributes images. Given Corel's lack of any trademark use of any of the images, there simply is no possibility of confusion.

Finally, if anything is associated with Bridgeman or its client museums, it is the underlying works of art, not whatever subtle differences may exist between those works and Bridgeman's images of them. Bridgeman is no more able to appropriate to itself exclusive rights to the use of the underlying public domain works via the law of trademarks than it is via the law of copyright.[NOTE 68]

IV. Jurisdiction

Having disposed of plaintiff's Copyright and Lanham Act claims the Court must determine whether it has the power to decide plaintiff's remaining claims and, if so, whether it should exercise that power.

Judicial Power

1. Canada and United Kingdom Infringements

There is no independent basis of federal subject matter jurisdiction over plaintiff's claims of copyright infringement in Canada and the United Kingdom. While Section 1338(a) of the Judicial Code[NOTE 69] confers jurisdiction over matters relating to copyrights and trademarks, it does so only with respect to claims that arise "under any Act of Congress."[NOTE 70] Obviously, then, Section 1338(a) does not create jurisdiction for Bridgeman's claim under the laws of Canada and the United Kingdom. Nor can Bridgeman rely on the Berne Convention and its implementation vehicle, the BCIA. The Berne Convention is a treaty, not an act of Congress. Moreover, the Convention is not self-executing.[NOTE 71]

Section 1331 [NOTE 72] similarly is unavailing as a source of jurisdiction for these claims. Although federal question jurisdiction includes claims arising under treaties, the Berne Convention is not self-executing. In consequence, Bridgeman has no claim arising under the Convention within the meaning of Section 1331.

Absent as well is jurisdiction based on diversity of citizenship under Section 1332.[NOTE 73] Corel is a citizen of Canada; Bridgeman a subject of the United Kingdom. "As the pleadings clearly show, all parties are aliens, and neither the constitutional nor statutory grants of jurisdiction include such a suit."[NOTE 74] That each company does business in New York is immaterial for citizenship and therefore jurisdictional purposes.[NOTE 75]

2. Common Law Unfair Competition

Plaintiff asserts jurisdiction with regard to its common law unfair competition claims under 28 U.S.C. § 1338(b). Section 1338(b) confers jurisdiction over such claims "when joined with a substantial and related claim under the copyright ... or trade-mark laws."[NOTE 76] This jurisdictional base, however, is conditioned on a viable copyright or trademark claim arising under United States law.[NOTE 77] Inasmuch as Bridgeman has no viable claims under the Copyright and Lanham Acts, jurisdiction over its unfair competition claims under Section 1338(b) fails.

Discretionary Jurisdiction

The doctrine of supplemental jurisdiction, now largely codified in 28 U.S.C. § 1367,[NOTE 78] gives federal courts, which have subject matter jurisdiction over federal claims, discretion to decide closely related claims over which there is no independent basis of federal jurisdiction. But once "all bases for federal jurisdiction have been eliminated from a case so that only pendant [sic] state claims remain, the federal court should ordinarily dismiss the state claims."[NOTE 79] When, as here, the federal claim is dismissed early in the litigation process, "the presumption to decline jurisdiction is strong."[NOTE 80]

Conclusion

For the foregoing reasons, defendant's motion for summary judgment dismissing the complaint is granted. The Copyright Act and Lanham Act claims are dismissed on the merits and all other claims for lack of subject matter jurisdiction. Plaintiff's cross motion for partial summary judgment is denied.

SO ORDERED.

NOTES:

NOTE 1: The amended complaint for the first time added Off the Wall, Inc. ("OWI"), allegedly a dissolved California corporation, as a defendant. Sec. Am.Cpt. ¶ 4. OWI never was served. The action has been dismissed as against it pursuant to FED.R.CIV.P. 4(m).

NOTE 2: Eichel Dep. at 3.

NOTE 3: Pooley Dep. at 16.

NOTE 4: Bridgeman Dep. at 23. The photographer attests that the photograph was authorized and that he or she has a copyright in the photograph and then assigns the copyright to Bridgeman. *Id.* at 23, 56.

NOTE 5: Pooley Dep. at 16.

NOTE 6: Eichel Dep. at 29, 30.

NOTE 7: Bridgeman Dep. at 45.

NOTE 8: Eichel Dep. at 35-36. These CD-ROMs are not for sale in the United States, though they are sold in the United Kingdom. *Id.* at 36.

NOTE 9: Smyth Dep. at 2.

NOTE 10: *Id.* at 2-3.

NOTE 11: *Id.* at 3.

NOTE 12: Plaintiff's Memorandum 5 (hereinafter "Pl. Mem.").

NOTE 13: *Id.*

NOTE 14: Am.Cpt.Ex. C.

NOTE 15: *Anderson v. Liberty Lobby, Inc.*, 477 U.S. 242, 106 S. Ct. 2505, 91 L. Ed. 2d 202 (1986).

NOTE 16: *Adickes v. S.H. Kress & Co.*, 398 U.S. 144, 157, 90 S. Ct. 1598, 26 L. Ed. 2d 142 (1970).

NOTE 17: *United States v. Diebold, Inc.*, 369 U.S. 654, 655, 82 S. Ct. 993, 8 L. Ed. 2d 176 (1962).

NOTE 18: *Celotex Corp. v. Catrett,* 477 U.S. 317, 322, 106 S. Ct. 2548, 91 L. Ed. 2d 265 (1986).

NOTE 19: 17 U.S.C. §§ 1-702 (1998).

NOTE 20: *Feist Publications, Inc. v. Rural Telephone Service Co.,* 499 U.S. 340, 361, 111 S. Ct. 1282, 113 L. Ed. 2d 358 (1991); *Repp v. Webber,* 132 F.3d 882, 888 (2d Cir. 1997). As a threshold matter, the protections of the Copyright Act generally extend only to registered copyrights. 17 U.S.C. § 411(a). That same section, however, exempts from the registration requirement Berne Convention works the origin of which is outside the United States. *Id.* Since the origin of Bridgeman's works was Great Britain, *see infra,* registration is not required here.

NOTE 21: Plaintiff's Memorandum Opposing Judgment on the Pleadings 37-40 (hereinafter "Pl. 12(b) (6) Mem.").

NOTE 22: Sept. 9, 1986, 25 U.S.T. 1341.

NOTE 23: Sept. 6, 1952, 6 U.S.T. 2732.

NOTE 24: UCC, Art. II ¶ 1 (Paris Text July 24, 1971); Berne Convention, Art. 2 ¶ 6, Art. 5 ¶ 1 (Paris Text July 24, 1971).

NOTE 25: 4 MELVILLE B. NIMMER AND DAVID NIMMER, NIMMER ON COPYRIGHT § 17.05, at 17-37 (1997) (hereinafter NIMMER). *Accord, e.g., Subafilms, Ltd. v. MGM-Pathe Comm. Co.,* 24 F.3d 1088, 1097 (9th Cir.) (*en banc*), *cert. denied,* 513 U.S. 1001, 115 S. Ct. 512, 130 L. Ed. 2d 419 (1994).

NOTE 26: *Itar-Tass Russian News Agency v. Russian Kurier, Inc.,* 153 F.3d 82, 90 & n. 8 (2d Cir.1998).

NOTE 27: *Id.* (citing Berne Convention Implementation Act of 1988, Pub.L. 100-568, §§ 4(a) (3), 2(2), 3(a) (2), 102 Stat. 2853-54 (1988), (hereinafter "BCIA")).

NOTE 28: *Itar-Tass,* 153 F.3d at 90.

NOTE 29: *Id.* (citing RESTATEMENT (SECOND) OF CONFLICT OF LAWS § 222 (1971)).

NOTE 30: *Id.*

NOTE 31: *Id.* at 90. The Berne Convention defines the country of origin of a particular work as the country in which the work first was published. Berne Convention Art. 5 ¶ 4. Published works are "works published with the consent of their authors, whatever may be the means of manufacture of the copies." *Id.* at Art. 3 ¶ 3. The circuit noted that the law of the country of origin will not always control.

NOTE 32: Over 50 of the underlying works are in the United Kingdom. Fewer than 20 are in each of Italy and France. The remainder are scattered among at least nine countries.

NOTE 33: Pl. 56.1 St. ¶ 19.

NOTE 34: *Itar-Tass,* 153 F.3d at 91 (citing *Lauritzen v. Larsen,* 345 U.S. 571, 583, 73 S. Ct. 921, 97 L. Ed. 1254 (1953)).

NOTE 35: The Copyright, Designs and Patents Act, 1988, ch. 1, § 1(1) (UK) (emphasis added).

NOTE 36: *Interlego AG v. Tyco Industries Inc.,* 25 R.I. 652, 57 A. 867, 1 A.C. 217 (P.C.1989), 3 All E.R. 949, 970 (1988) (appeal taken from Hong Kong).

NOTE 37: 2 MELVILLE B. NIMMER AND PAUL E. GELLER, INTERNATIONAL COPYRIGHT LAW & PRACTICE § 2[3][b], at UK-28 (1998) (citations omitted), (hereinafter "INTERNATIONAL COPYRIGHT LAW").

NOTE 38: *Id.,* § 2[1][b][ii] at UK-19.

NOTE 39: *Interlego,* 3 All E.R. at 971-72.

NOTE 40: Pl. 12(b) (6) Mem. at 8.

NOTE 41: *L. Batlin & Son, Inc. v. Snyder,* 536 F.2d 486, 491 (2d Cir.) (*en banc*) (quoting 1 M. NIMMER, THE LAW OF COPYRIGHT § 10.2, at 94) (1975), *cert. denied,* 429 U.S. 857, 97 S. Ct. 156, 50 L. Ed. 2d 135 (1976).

United States law is persuasive in construing English law for two reasons. First, there is substantial similarity between the originality requirements of the UK Act and the Copyright Act. As does the U.K. Act, the Copyright Act extends protection only to "original works of authorship." 17 U.S.C. § 102(a) (1998). A work is original if it owes its creation to the author and was not merely copied. *Feist Publications,* 499 U.S. at 345, 111 S. Ct. 1282. With respect to derivative works, the originality requirement warrants that there be a distinguishable variation between the work in which copyright is sought and the underlying work. *Batlin,* 536 F.2d at 490-91; *Matthew Bender & Co. Inc. v. West Publishing Inc.,* No. 97-7910, 158 F.3d 674, 1998 WL 764837, at *6-*9 (2d Cir.1998). Important to this calculus is that the demonstration of some physical, as opposed to artistic, skill does not constitute a "distinguishable variation." *Durham Industries, Inc. v. Tomy Corp.,* 630 F.2d 905, 910 (2d Cir.1980) (citing *Batlin,* 536 F.2d at 491).

Second, the Privy Council itself has looked to American law as persuasive authority with respect to copyright originality. *See Interlego,* 3 All ER at 969 (quoting Story, J.).

NOTE 42: Pl. Mem. at 14.

NOTE 43: Tr. at 24-26.

NOTE 44: E.g., portrait of Sir Winston Churchill in YOUSUF KARSH, FACES OF OUR TIME 37 (1971).

NOTE 45: *Interlego,* 3 All ER at 971.

NOTE 46: *Durham Industries, Inc. v. Tomy Corp.,* 630 F.2d 905, 910 (2d Cir.1980).

NOTE 47: For the reasons discussed *supra,* footnote 41, the Court would reach the same result under United States law.

NOTE 48: *Streetwise Maps, Inc. v. Vandam, Inc.,* 159 F.3d 739, 746-47 (2d Cir.1998).

NOTE 49: *Repp v. Webber,* 132 F.3d at 889 (citing *Laureyssens v. Idea Group, Inc.,* 964 F.2d 131, 140 (2d Cir.1992)). Proof of copying is generally adduced in this manner because often, as here, there is no direct evidence of copying.

NOTE 50: Plaintiff initially asked the Court to infer access on the theory that Bridgeman had the only images of the works in question and that the works themselves could not have been photographed anew. Ultimately, however, Bridgeman admitted that it is not the only possible source for 119 of the 120 images. But it still asks that copying of all 120 might be inferred on the basis that the 120th image must have been copied.

NOTE 51: *See Streetwise,* at 746 (noting that at this stage of inquiry, "similarity" relates not only to the copyrightable elements, but to the entire work).

NOTE 52: *See* INTERNATIONAL COPYRIGHT LAW, § 2[3][b] at UK-28.

NOTE 53: *Feist Publications,* 499 U.S. at 361, 111 S. Ct. 1282; *Streetwise,* at 746.

NOTE 54: Pl.Mem. at 27. *See also* Eichel Dep. at 165.

NOTE 55: *Arica Institute, Inc. v. Palmer,* 970 F.2d 1067, 1072 (2d Cir.1992) (citing *Warner Bros. Inc. v. Am. Broadcasting Cos.,* 720 F.2d 231, 240 (2d Cir.1983)).

NOTE 56: *See* 4 NIMMER § 17.02 at 17-20; *accord, Subafilms, Ltd. v. MGM-Pathe Communications Co.,* 24 F.3d 1088 (9th Cir.), *cert. denied,* 513 U.S. 1001, 115 S. Ct. 512, 130 L. Ed. 2d 419 (1994); *Filmvideo Releasing Corp. v. Hastings,* 668 F.2d 91 (2d Cir.1981); *Foster v. WNYC-TV,* 1989 WL 146277, *2 (S.D.N.Y.1989).

NOTE 57: 15 U.S.C. § 1125(a) (1988). Plaintiff has conceded the insufficiency of its claim under Section 32 of the Act. (Pl.12(b) (6) Mem. 24; Pl.Mem. 27)

NOTE 58: Am.Cpt. ¶¶ 26-29.

NOTE 59: 15 U.S.C. § 1125(a) (1) (A).

NOTE 60: *Id.* § 1125(a) (1) (B).

NOTE 61: 4 J. THOMAS McCARTHY, McCARTHY ON TRADEMARKS § 27:9 (1998) (hereinafter McCARTHY ON TRADEMARKS).

NOTE 62: *Kregos v. Associated Press,* 3 F.3d 656, 666 (2d Cir.1993) (state cause of action preempted by federal copyright laws when state law right asserted is equivalent to rights protected under federal law), *cert. denied,* 510 U.S. 1112, 114 S. Ct. 1056, 127 L. Ed. 2d 376 (1994); *G. Ricordi & Co. v. Haendler,* 194 F.2d 914 (2d Cir.1952); *see Sears, Roebuck & Co. v. Stiffel Co.,* 376 U.S. 225, 232-33, 84 S. Ct. 784, 11 L. Ed. 2d 661 (1964); *see Fabrication Enterprises, Inc. v. Hygenic Corp.,* 64 F.3d 53, 58 n. 4, (2d Cir.1995) (Lanham Act does not protect invention, which is the province of patent law); *Duraco Products, Inc. v. Joy Plastic Enterprises, Ltd.,* 40 F.3d 1431 (3d Cir.1994) (same); *Stormy Clime, Ltd. v. ProGroup, Inc.,* 809 F.2d 971, 977-78 (2d Cir.1987) (same).

NOTE 63: *See Mulberry Thai Silks, Inc. v. K & K Neckwear, Inc.,* 897 F. Supp. 789, 792 (S.D.N.Y.1995).

NOTE 64: Fritz Decl.Ex. H, responses to interrogatory nos. 37-38.

NOTE 65: Fritz Decl.Ex. H, response to interrogatory no. 39.

NOTE 66: *See Hughes v. Design Look, Inc.,* 693 F. Supp. 1500, 1505-06 (S.D.N.Y.1988) (estate of Andy Warhol not entitled to Section 43(a) protection for Warhol paintings because the paintings were not used as trademarks); 1 McCARTHY ON TRADEMARKS § 3:4, at 3-12 to 3-13.

NOTE 67: The amended complaint alleges only that Corel sells CD-ROMs under the title "Corel Professional Photos CD-ROM, Masters I-VII" and that the CD-ROMs permit purchasers to download images of the underlying public domain works. (Am.Cpt.preamble) There is no suggestion that any of the disputed images appears on the packaging or in advertising for the product.

NOTE 68: *See Kienzle v. Capital Cities/Am. Broadcasting Co.*, 774 F. Supp. 432, 438-39 (E.D.Mich.1991) (no Section 43(a) protection for matters in the public domain).

NOTE 69: 28 U.S.C. § 1338(a) (1998).

NOTE 70: *Id.*

NOTE 71: *See Itar-Tass*, 153 F.3d at 90. The circuit court noted that the BCIA amended the Copyright Act to provide: "No right or interest in a work eligible for protection under this title may be claimed by virtue of, or in reliance upon, the provisions of the Berne Convention, or the adherence of the United States thereto." 17 U.S.C. §§ 104(c). *See also* BCIA § 2(2) ("The obligations of the United States under the Berne Convention may be performed only pursuant to appropriate domestic law."); Section 3(a) (2) ("The provisions of the Berne Convention ... shall not be enforceable in any action brought pursuant to the provisions of the Berne Convention itself."); Section 3(b) (1) ("The provisions of the Berne Convention ... do not expand or reduce the right of any author of a work, whether claimed under Federal, State, or the common law ... to claim authorship of the work." *See also* 1 NIMMER § 1.12[A] at 1-106, 1-107 (noting that Congress declares in the BCIA that the Berne Convention is not self-executing); *Quantitative Financial Software Ltd. v. Infinity Financial Technology, Inc.*, 1998 WL 427710 (S.D.N.Y. 1998).

NOTE 72: 28 U.S.C. § 1331 (1998).

NOTE 73: 28 U.S.C. § 1332 (1998).

NOTE 74: *Joseph Muller Corporation Zurich v. Societe Anonyme de Gerance et D'Armement*, 451 F.2d 727 (2d Cir.1971), *cert. denied*, 406 U.S. 906, 92 S. Ct. 1609, 31 L. Ed. 2d 816 (1972); *Quantitative Financial Software Ltd.*, 1998 WL 427710; *Lloyds Bank PLC v. Norkin*, 817 F. Supp. 414 (S.D.N.Y.1993).

NOTE 75: Irrelevant as well would be any contention that New York is the principal place of business in the United States. The worldwide principal place of business is determinative of citizenship. *Bailey v. Grand Trunk Lines New England*, 805 F.2d 1097, 1101 (2d Cir.1986), *cert. denied*, 484 U.S. 826, 108 S. Ct. 94, 98 L. Ed. 2d 54 (1987).

NOTE 76: 28 U.S.C. § 1338(b).

NOTE 77: *Historical Truth Productions, Inc. v. Sony Pictures Entertainment, Inc.*, 1995 WL 693189, *14 (S.D.N.Y.1995); *Envirex Inc. v. FMC Corp.*, 1993 WL 572321, *16 n. 1 (E.D.Wis.1993), *aff'd*, 16 F.3d 420 (Fed.Cir.1993).

NOTE 78: 28 U.S.C. § 1367 (1998).

NOTE 79: *Baylis v. Marriott Corp.*, 843 F.2d 658, 665 (2d Cir.1988) (citing *United Mine Workers of America v. Gibbs*, 383 U.S. 715, 725, 86 S. Ct. 1130, 16 L. Ed. 2d 218 (1966)); *Davis v. United Artists, Inc.*, 547 F. Supp. 722, 728 (S.D.N.Y.1982) (court may decline to hear pendant unfair competition claims under § 1338(b) when copyright claim is dismissed).

NOTE 80: *Bill v. Casarona*, 1996 WL 389304, *4 (S.D.N.Y.1996) (citing *Historical Truth Productions, Inc. v. Sony Pictures Entertainment, Inc.*, 1995 WL 693189 (S.D.N.Y.1995)); *Fonar Corp. v. Magnetic Resonance Plus, Inc.*, 920 F. Supp. 508 (S.D.N.Y.1996), *vacated on other grounds*, 105 F.3d 99 (2d Cir.), *cert. denied*, ___ U.S. ____, 118 S. Ct. 265, 139 L. Ed. 2d 191 (1997); *Davis v. United Artists, Inc.*, 547 F. Supp. at 728.

STUDY QUESTIONS

- In the *Bridgeman* case, the court addressed the issue of copyright originality. According to the court, what makes a work sufficiently "original" to be protected by copyright? What sources did the court rely on in making this decision? Does the creator's state of mind—their intentions—determine whether a work is original?

- How did the court address the issue of applicable international law? See NOTE 41.

- After the first *Bridgeman* decision was issued, in the words of Judge Kaplan, the court was "bombarded with additional submissions" from the plaintiff, arguing in part that the court had erred in applying UK copyright law. In a second *Bridgeman* case, 36 F. Supp. 2d 191 (S.D.N.Y. 1999), Judge Kaplan applied US law to the issue of copyrightability, rather than UK law as in the first judgment. Citing *Nimmer on Copyright*, which stated that there "appear to be at least two situations in which a photograph should be denied copyright for lack of originality." Kaplan considered one of those situations, as described by Nimmer, to be directly relevant, namely that "where a photograph of a photograph or other printed matter is made that amounts to nothing more than slavish copying." A slavish photographic copy of a painting thus, according to Nimmer, lacks originality and thus copyrightability under the US Copyright Act.

- Kaplan stated that there is "little doubt that many photographs, probably the overwhelming majority, reflect at least the modest amount of originality required for copyright protection" noting prior caselaw holding that "[e]lements of originality ... may include posing the subjects, lighting, angle, selection of film and camera, evoking the desired expression, and almost any other variant involved." However, Bridgeman had, by its own admission, performed "slavish copying," which did not qualify for copyright protection. "[I]ndeed," Judge Kaplan explained "the point of the exercise was to reproduce the underlying works with absolute fidelity" and noted "[i]t is uncontested that Bridgeman's images are substantially exact reproductions of public domain works, albeit in a different medium."

- Assess the trademark claim made by the plaintiff in *Bridgeman*. Why was it unsuccessful?

- *Bridgeman* involved two-dimensional works of art. In *Ets-Hokin*, 323 F.3rd 763 (2003), the court addressed copyright originality in a photograph of a three-dimensional work: "Specifically, we must decide whether professional photographer Joshua Ets-Hokin's commercial photographs, dubbed "product shots," of the Skyy Spirits vodka bottle merit copyright protection. Given the Copyright Act's low threshold for originality generally and the minimal amount of originality required to qualify a photograph in particular, we conclude that Ets-Hokin's photographs are entitled to copyright protection." How does this case apply in the museum context?

- What concerns do the *Bridgeman* and *Ets-Hokin* cases raise for museums regarding their ability to control images of their collection objects?

Reading Note: Another important threshold issue in copyright protection involves who owns copyright in the creative work. The Supreme Court decision in *Community for Creative Non-Violence* below addresses the concept of copyright "work-for-hire." As a result of this decision, it is now common practice to execute written copyright "work-for-hire" agreements with independent contractors hired to create copyrightable work product.

COMMUNITY FOR CREATIVE NON-VIOLENCE V. REID

490 U.S. 730 (1989)

JUSTICE MARSHALL delivered the opinion of the Court.

In this case, an artist and the organization that hired him to produce a sculpture contest the ownership of the copyright in that work. To resolve this dispute, we must construe the "work made for hire" provisions of the Copyright Act of 1976 (Act or 1976 Act), 17 U.S.C. 101 and 201(b), and in particular, the provision in 101, which defines as a "work made for hire" a "work prepared by an employee within the scope of his or her employment" (hereinafter 101(1)).

I

Petitioners are the Community for Creative Non-Violence (CCNV), a nonprofit unincorporated association dedicated to eliminating homelessness in America, and Mitch Snyder, a member and trustee of CCNV. In the fall of 1985, CCNV decided to participate in the annual Christmastime Pageant of Peace in Washington, D.C., by sponsoring a display to dramatize the plight of the homeless. As the District Court recounted:

"Snyder and fellow CCNV members conceived the idea for the nature of the display: a sculpture of a modern Nativity scene in which, in lieu of the traditional Holy Family, the two adult figures and the infant would appear as contemporary homeless people huddled on a streetside steam grate. The family was to be black (most of the homeless in Washington being black); the figures were to be life-sized, and the steam grate would be positioned atop a platform 'pedestal,' or base, within which special-effects equipment would be enclosed to emit simulated 'steam' through the grid to swirl about the figures. They also settled upon a title for the work—'Third World America'—and a legend for the pedestal: 'and still there is no room at the inn.'" 652 F. Supp. 1453, 1454 (DC 1987). Snyder made inquiries to locate an artist to produce the sculpture. He was referred to respondent James Earl Reid, a Baltimore, Maryland, sculptor. In the course of two telephone calls, Reid agreed to sculpt the three human figures. CCNV agreed to make the steam grate and ped-

In 1985, the Community for Creative Non-Violence (CCNV), a homeless charity in Washington D.C., hired sculptor James Earl Reid to create Third World America, a statue depicting the plight of homeless people, for a Christmas pageant. Both CCNV and Reid claimed copyright in the completed sculpture. In CCNV v. Reid *the Supreme Court considered whether the work was a "work-for-hire" under U.S. copyright law.*

estal for the statue. Reid proposed that the work be cast in bronze, at a total cost of approximately $100,000 and taking six to eight months to complete. Snyder rejected that proposal because CCNV did not have sufficient funds, and because the statue had to be completed by December 12 to be included in the pageant. Reid then suggested, and Snyder agreed, that the sculpture would be made of a material known as "Design Cast 62," a synthetic substance that could meet CCNV's monetary and time constraints, could be tinted to resemble bronze, and could withstand the elements. The parties agreed that the project would cost no more than $15,000, not including Reid's services, which he offered to donate. The parties did not sign a written agreement. Neither party mentioned copyright.

After Reid received an advance of $3,000, he made several sketches of figures in various poses. At Snyder's request, Reid sent CCNV a sketch of a proposed sculpture showing the family in a creche-like setting: the mother seated, cradling a baby in her lap; the father standing behind her, bending over her shoulder to touch the baby's foot. Reid testified that Snyder asked for the sketch to use in raising funds for the sculpture. Snyder testified that it was also for his approval. Reid sought a black family to serve as a model for the sculpture. Upon Snyder's suggestion, Reid visited a family living at CCNV's Washington shelter but decided that only their newly born child was a suitable model. While Reid was in Washington, Snyder took him to see homeless people living on the streets. Snyder pointed out that they tended to recline on steam grates, rather than sit or stand, in order to warm their bodies. From that time on, Reid's sketches contained only reclining figures.

Throughout November and the first two weeks of December 1985, Reid worked exclusively on the statue, assisted at various times by a dozen different people who were paid with funds provided in installments by CCNV. On a number of occasions, CCNV members visited Reid to check on his progress and to coordinate CCNV's construction of the base. CCNV rejected Reid's proposal to use suitcases or shopping bags to hold the family's personal belongings, insisting instead on a shopping cart. Reid and CCNV members did not discuss copyright ownership on any of these visits.

On December 24, 1985, 12 days after the agreed-upon date, Reid delivered the completed statue to Washington. There it was joined to the steam grate and pedestal prepared by CCNV and placed on display near the site of the pageant. Snyder paid Reid the final installment of the $15,000. The statue remained on display for a month. In late January 1986, CCNV members returned it to Reid's studio in Baltimore for minor repairs. Several weeks later, Snyder began making plans to take the statue on a tour of several cities to raise money for the homeless. Reid objected, contending that the Design Cast 62 material was not strong enough to withstand the ambitious itinerary. He urged CCNV to cast the statue in bronze at a cost of $35,000, or to create a master mold at a cost of $5,000. Snyder declined to spend more of CCNV's money on the project.

In March 1986, Snyder asked Reid to return the sculpture. Reid refused. He then filed a certificate of copyright registration for *Third World America* in his name and announced plans to take the sculpture on a more modest tour than the one CCNV had proposed. Snyder, acting in his capacity as CCNV's trustee, immediately filed a competing certificate of copyright registration.

Snyder and CCNV then commenced this action against Reid and his photographer, Ronald Purtee,[NOTE 1] seeking return of the sculpture and a determination of copyright ownership. The District Court granted a preliminary injunction, ordering the sculpture's return. After a 2-day bench trial, the District Court declared that *Third World America* was a "work made for hire" under 101 of the Copyright Act and that Snyder, as trustee for CCNV, was the exclusive owner of the copyright in the sculpture. 652 F. Supp., at 1457. The court reasoned that Reid had been an "employee" of CCNV within the meaning of 101(1) because CCNV was the motivating force in the statue's production. Snyder and other CCNV members, the court explained, "conceived the idea of a contemporary Nativity scene to contrast with the national celebration of the season," and "directed enough of [Reid's] effort to assure that, in the end, he had produced what they, not he, wanted." Id., at 1456.

The Court of Appeals for the District of Columbia Circuit reversed and remanded, holding that Reid owned the copyright because *Third World America* was not a work for hire. 270 U.S. App. D.C. 26, 35, 846 F.2d 1485, 1494 (1988). Adopting what it termed the "literal interpretation" of the Act as articulated by the Fifth Circuit in *Easter Seal Society for Crippled Children & Adults of Louisiana, Inc. v. Playboy Enterprises*, 815 F.2d 323, 329 (1987), *cert. denied*, 485 U.S. 981 (1988), the court read 101 as creating "a simple dichotomy in fact between employees and independent contractors." 270 U.S. App. D.C., at 33, 846 F.2d, at 1492. Because, under agency law, Reid was an independent contractor, the court concluded that the work was not "prepared by an employee" under 101(1). *Id.*, at 35, 846 F.2d, at 1494. Nor was the sculpture a "work made for hire" under the second subsection of 101 (hereinafter 101(2)): sculpture is not one of the nine categories of works enumerated in that subsection, and the parties had not agreed in writing that the sculpture would be a work for hire. *Ibid.* The court suggested that the sculpture nevertheless may have been jointly authored by CCNV and Reid, *id.*, at 36, 846 F.2d, at 1495, and remanded for a determination whether the sculpture is indeed a joint work under the Act, id., at 39-40, 846 F.2d, at 1498-1499.

We granted certiorari to resolve a conflict among the Courts of Appeals over the proper construction of the "work made for hire" provisions of the Act.[NOTE 2] 488 U.S. 940 (1988). We now affirm.

II

A

The Copyright Act of 1976 provides that copyright ownership "vests initially in the author or authors of the work." 17 U.S.C. 201(a). As a general rule, the author is the party who actually creates the work, that is, the person who translates an idea into a fixed, tangible expression entitled to copyright protection. 102. The Act carves out an important exception, however, for "works made for hire." [NOTE 3] If the work is for hire, "the employer or other person for whom the work was prepared is considered the author" and owns the copyright, unless there is a written agreement to the contrary. 201(b). Classifying a work as "made for hire" determines not only the initial ownership of its copyright, but also the copyright's duration, 302(c), and the owners' renewal rights, 304(a), termination rights, 203(a), and right to import certain goods bearing the copyright, 601(b)(1). See 1 M. Nimmer & D. Nimmer, Nimmer on Copyright 5.03 [A], pp. 5-10 (1988). The contours of the work for hire doctrine therefore carry profound significance for freelance creators - including artists, writers, photographers, designers, composers, and computer programmers - and for the publishing, advertising, music, and other industries which commission their works.[NOTE 4]

Section 101 of the 1976 Act provides that a work is "for hire" under two sets of circumstances:

"(1) a work prepared by an employee within the scope of his or her employment; or (2) a work specially ordered or commissioned for use as a contribution to a collective work, as a part of a motion picture or other audiovisual work, as a translation, as a supplementary work, as a compilation, as an instructional text, as a test, as answer material for a test, or as an atlas, if the parties expressly agree in a written instrument signed by them that the work shall be considered a work made for hire."[NOTE 5] Petitioners do not claim that the statue satisfies the terms of 101(2). Quite clearly, it does not. Sculpture does not fit within any of the nine categories of "specially ordered or commissioned" works enumerated in that subsection, and no written agreement between the parties establishes *Third World America* as a work for hire.

The dispositive inquiry in this case therefore is whether *Third World America* is "a work prepared by an employee within the scope of his or her employment" under 101(1). The Act does not define these terms. In the absence of such guidance, four interpretations have emerged. The first holds that a work is prepared by an employee whenever the hiring party[NOTE 6] retains the right to control the product. See *Peregrine v. Lauren Corp.*, 601 F. Supp. 828, 829 (Colo. 1985); *Clarkstown v. Reeder*, 566 F. Supp. 137, 142 (SDNY 1983). Petitioners take this view. Brief for Petitioners 15; Tr. of Oral Arg. 12. A second, and closely related, view is that a work is prepared by an employee under 101(1) when the hiring party has actually wielded control with respect to the creation of a particular work. This approach was formulated by the Court of Appeals for the Second Circuit, *Aldon Accessories Ltd. v. Spiegel, Inc.*, 738 F.2d 548, *cert. denied*, 469 U.S. 982 (1984), and adopted by the Fourth Circuit, *Brunswick Beacon, Inc. v. Schock-Hopchas Publishing Co.*, 810 F.2d 410 (1987), the Seventh Circuit, *Evans Newton, Inc. v. Chicago Systems Software*, 793 F.2d 889, *cert. denied*, 479 U.S. 949 (1986), and, at times, by petitioners, Brief for Petitioners 17. A third view is that the term "employee" within 101(1) carries its common-law agency law meaning. This view was endorsed by the Fifth Circuit in *Easter Seal Society for Crippled Children & Adults of Louisiana, Inc. v. Playboy Enterprises*, 815 F.2d 323 (1987), and by the Court of Appeals below. Finally, respondent and numerous amici curiae contend that the term "employee" only refers to "formal, salaried" employees. See, e. g., Brief for Respondent 23-24; Brief for Register of Copyrights as Amicus Curiae 7. The Court of Appeals for the Ninth Circuit recently adopted this view. See *Dumas v. Gommerman*, 865 F.2d 1093 (1989).

The starting point for our interpretation of a statute is always its language. *Consumer Product Safety Comm'n v. GTE Sylvania, Inc.*, 447 U.S. 102, 108 (1980). The Act nowhere defines the terms "employee" or "scope of employment." It is, however, well established that "[w]here Congress uses terms that have accumulated settled meaning under ... the common law, a court must infer, unless the statute otherwise dictates, that Congress means to incorporate the established meaning of these terms." *NLRB v. Amax Coal Co.*, 453 U.S. 322, 329 (1981); see also *Perrin v. United States*, 444 U.S. 37, 42 (1979). In the past, when Congress has used the term "employee" without defining it, we have concluded that Congress intended to describe the conventional master-servant relationship as understood by common-law agency doctrine. See, e. g., *Kelley v. Southern Pacific Co.*, 419 U.S. 318, 322 -323 (1974); *Baker v. Texas & Pacific R. Co.*, 359 U.S. 227, 228 (1959) (*per curiam*); *Robinson v. Baltimore & Ohio R. Co.*, 237 U.S. 84, 94 (1915). Nothing in the text of the work for hire provisions indicates that Congress used the words "employee" and "employment" to describe anything other than "'the conventional relation of employer and employee.'" *Kelley*, supra, at 323, quoting *Robinson*, supra, at 94; cf. *NLRB v. Hearst Publications, Inc.*, 322 U.S. 111, 124 -132 (1944) (rejecting agency law conception of employee for purposes of the National Labor Relations Act where structure and context of statute indicated broader definition). On the contrary, Congress' intent to incorporate the agency law definition is suggested by 101(1)'s use of the term, "scope of employment," a widely used term of art in agency law. See Restatement (Second) of Agency 228 (1958) (hereinafter Restatement).

In past cases of statutory interpretation, when we have concluded that Congress intended terms such as "employee," "employer," and "scope of employment" to be understood in light of agency law, we have relied on the general common law of agency, rather than on the law of any particular State, to give meaning to these terms. See, e. g., *Kelley*, 419 U.S., at 323 -324, and n. 5; id., at 332 (Stewart, J., concurring in judgment); *Ward v. Atlantic Coast Line R. Co.*, 362 U.S. 396, 400 (1960); *Baker*, supra, at 228. This practice reflects the fact that "federal statutes are generally intended to have uniform nationwide application." *Mississippi Band of Choctaw Indians v. Holyfield*, ante, at 43. Establishment of a federal rule of agency, rather than reliance on state agency law, is particularly appropriate here given the Act's express objective of creating national, uniform copyright law by broadly pre-empting state statutory and common-law copyright regulation. See 17 U.S.C. 301(a). We thus agree with the Court of Appeals that the term "employee" should be understood in light of the general common law of agency.

In contrast, neither test proposed by petitioners is consistent with the text of the Act. The exclusive focus of the right to control the product test on the relationship between the hiring party and the product clashes with the language of 101(1), which focuses on the relationship between the hired and hiring parties. The right to control the product test also would distort the meaning of the ensuing subsection, 101(2). Section 101 plainly creates two distinct ways in which a work can be deemed for hire: one for works prepared by employees, the other for those specially ordered or commissioned works which fall within one of the nine enumerated categories and are the subject of a written agreement. The right to control the product test ignores this dichotomy by transforming into a work for hire under 101(1) any "specially ordered or commissioned" work that is subject to the supervision and control of the hiring party. Because a party who hires a "specially ordered or commissioned" work by definition has a right to specify the characteristics of the product desired, at the time the commission is accepted, and frequently until it is completed, the right to control the product test would mean that many works that could satisfy 101(2) would already have been deemed works for hire under 101(1). Petitioners' interpretation is particularly hard to square with 101(2)'s enumeration of the nine specific categories of specially ordered or commissioned works eligible to be works for hire, e. g., "a contribution to a collective work," "a part of a motion picture," and "answer material for a test." The unifying feature of these works is that they are usually prepared at the instance, direction, and risk of a publisher or producer.[NOTE 7] By their very nature, therefore, these types of works would be works by an employee under petitioners' right to control the product test.

The actual control test, articulated by the Second Circuit in *Aldon Accessories*, fares only marginally better when measured against the language and structure of 101. Under this test, independent contractors who are so controlled and supervised in the creation of a particular work are deemed "employees" under 101(1). Thus work for hire status under 101(1) depends on a hiring party's actual control of, rather than right to control, the product. *Aldon Accessories*, 738 F.2d, at 552. Under the actual control test, a work for hire could arise under 101(2), but not under 101(1), where a party commissions, but does not actually control, a product which falls into one of the nine enumerated categories. Nonetheless, we agree with the Court of Appeals for the Fifth Circuit that "[t]here is simply no way to milk the 'actual control' test of *Aldon Accessories* from the language of the statute." *Easter Seal Society*, 815 F.2d, at 334. Section 101 clearly delineates between works prepared by an employee and commissioned works. Sound though other distinctions might be as a matter of copyright policy, there is no statutory support for an additional dichotomy between commissioned works that are actually controlled and supervised by the hiring party and those that are not.

We therefore conclude that the language and structure of 101 of the Act do not support either the right to control the product or the actual control approaches.[NOTE 8] The structure of 101 indicates that a work for hire can arise through one of two mutually exclusive means, one for employees and one for independent contractors, and ordinary cannons of statutory interpretation indicate that the classification of a particular hired party should be made with reference to agency law.

This reading of the undefined statutory terms finds considerable support in the Act's legislative history. Cf. *Diamond v. Chakrabarty*, 447 U.S. 303, 315 (1980). The Act, which almost completely revised existing copyright law, was the product of two decades of negotiation by representatives of creators and copyright-using industries, supervised by the Copyright Office and, to a lesser extent, by Congress. See *Mills Music, Inc. v. Snyder*, 469 U.S. 153, 159 (1985); Litman, Copyright, Compromise, and Legislative History, 72 Cornell L. Rev. 857, 862 (1987). Despite the lengthy history of negotiation and compromise which ultimately produced the Act, two things remained constant. First, interested parties and Congress at all times viewed works by employees and commissioned works by independent contractors as separate entities. Second, in using the term "employee," the parties and Congress meant to refer to a hired party in a conventional employment relationship. These factors militate in favor of the reading we have found appropriate.

In 1955, when Congress decided to overhaul copyright law, the existing work for hire provision was 62 of the 1909 Copyright Act, 17 U.S.C. 26 (1976 ed.) (1909 Act). It provided that "the word 'author' shall include an employer in the case of works made for hire."[NOTE 9] Because the 1909 Act did not define "employer" or "works made for hire," the task of shaping these terms fell to the courts. They concluded that the work for hire doctrine codified in 62 referred only to works made by employees in the regular course of their employment. As for commissioned works, the courts generally presumed that the commissioned party had impliedly agreed to convey the copyright, along with the work itself, to the hiring party. See, e. g., *Shapiro, Bernstein & Co. v. Jerry Vogel Music Co.*, 221 F.2d 569, 570, *rev'd*, 223 F.2d 252 (CA2 1955); *Yardley v. Houghton Mifflin Co.*, 108 F.2d 28, 31 (CA2 1939), *cert. denied*, 309 U.S. 686 (1940).[NOTE 10]

In 1961, the Copyright Office's first legislative proposal retained the distinction between works by employees and works by independent contractors. See Report of the Register of Copyrights on the General Revision of the U.S. Copyright Law, 87th Cong., 1st Sess., Copyright Law Revision 86-87 (H. R. Judiciary Comm. Print 1961). After numerous meetings with representatives of the affected parties, the Copyright Office issued a preliminary draft bill in 1963. Adopting the Register's recommendation, it defined "work made for hire" as "a work prepared by an employee within the scope of the duties of his employment, but not including a work made on special order or commission." Preliminary Draft for Revised U.S. Copyright Law and Discussions and Comments on the Draft, 88th Cong., 2d Sess., Copyright Law Revision, Part 3, p. 15, n. 11 (H. R. Judiciary Comm. Print 1964) (hereinafter Preliminary Draft).

In response to objections by book publishers that the preliminary draft bill limited the work for hire doctrine to "employees,"[NOTE 11] the 1964 revision bill expanded the scope of the work for hire classification to reach, for the first time, commissioned works. The bill's language, proposed initially by representatives of the publishing industry, retained the definition of work for hire insofar as it referred to "employees," but added a separate clause covering commissioned works, without regard to the subject matter, "if the parties so agree in writing." S. 3008, H. R. 11947, H. R. 12354, 88th Cong., 2d Sess., 54 (1964), reproduced in 1964 Revision Bill with Discussions and Comments, 89th Cong., 1st Sess., Copyright Law Revision, pt. 5, p. 31 (H. R. Judiciary Comm. Print 1965). Those representing authors objected that the added provision would allow publishers to use their superior bargaining position to force authors to sign work for hire agreements, thereby relinquishing all copyright rights as a condition of getting their books published. See Supplementary Report, at 67.

In 1965, the competing interests reached a historic compromise, which was embodied in a joint memorandum submitted to Congress and the Copyright Office,[NOTE 12] incorporated into the 1965 revision bill, and ultimately enacted in the same form and nearly the same terms 11 years later, as 101 of the 1976 Act. The compromise retained as subsection (1) the language referring to "a work prepared by an employee within the scope of his employment." However, in exchange for concessions from publishers on provisions relating to the termination of transfer rights, the authors consented to a second subsection which classified four categories of commissioned works as works for hire if the parties expressly so agreed in writing: works for use "as a contribution to a collective work, as a part of a motion picture, as a translation, or as supplementary work." S. 1006, H. R. 4347, H. R. 5680, H. R. 6835, 89th Cong., 1st Sess., 101 (1965). The interested parties selected these categories because they concluded that these commissioned works, although not prepared by employees and thus not covered by the first subsection, nevertheless should be treated as works for hire because they were ordinarily prepared "at the instance, direction, and risk of a publisher or producer." Supplementary Report, at 67. The Supplementary Report emphasized that only the "four special cases specifically mentioned" could qualify as works made for hire; "[o]ther works made on special order or commission would not come within the definition." *Id.*, at 67-68.

In 1966, the House Committee on the Judiciary endorsed this compromise in the first legislative Report on the revision bills. See H. R. Rep. No. 2237, 89th Cong., 2d Sess., 114, 116 (1966). Retaining the distinction between works by employees and commissioned works, the House Committee focused instead on "how to draw a statutory line between those works written on special order or commission that should be considered as works made for hire, and those that should not." *Id.*, at 115. The House Committee added four other enumerated categories of commissioned works that could be treated as works for hire: compilations, instructional texts, tests, and atlases. *Id.*, at 116. With the single addition of "answer material for a test," the 1976 Act, as enacted, contained the same definition of works made for hire as did the 1966 revision bill, and had the same structure and nearly the same terms as the 1966 bill.[NOTE 13] Indeed, much of the language of the 1976 House and Senate Reports was borrowed from the Reports accompanying the earlier drafts. See, e. g., H. R. Rep. No. 94-1476, p. 121 (1976); S. Rep. No. 94-473, p. 105 (1975).

Thus, the legislative history of the Act is significant for several reasons. First, the enactment of the 1965 compromise with only minor modifications demonstrates that Congress intended to provide two mutually exclusive ways for works to acquire work for hire status: one for employees and the other for independent contractors. Second, the legislative history underscores the clear import of the statutory language: only enumerated categories of commissioned works may be accorded work for hire status. The hiring party's right to control the product simply is not determinative. See NOTE, The Creative Commissioner: Commissioned Works Under the Copyright Act of 1976, 62 N. Y. U. L. Rev. 373, 388 (1987). Indeed, importing a test based on a hiring party's right to control, or actual control of, a product would unravel the "'carefully worked out compromise aimed at balancing legitimate interests on both sides.'" H. R. Rep. No. 2237, supra, at 114, quoting Supplemental Report, at 66.[NOTE 14]

We do not find convincing petitioners' contrary interpretation of the history of the Act. They contend that Congress, in enacting the Act, meant to incorporate a line of cases decided under the 1909 Act holding that an employment relationship exists sufficient to give the hiring party copyright ownership whenever that party has the right to control or supervise the artist's work. See, e. g., *Siegel v. National Periodical Publications, Inc.*, 508 F.2d 909, 914 (CA2 1974); *Picture Music, Inc. v. Bourne, Inc.*, 457 F.2d 1213, 1216 (CA2), *cert. denied*, 409 U.S. 997 (1972); *Scherr v. Universal Match Corp.*, 417 F.2d 497, 500 (CA2 1969), *cert. denied*, 397 U.S. 936 (1970); *Brattleboro Publishing Co. v. Winmill Publishing Corp.*, 369 F.2d 565, 567-568 (CA2 1966). In support of this position, petitioners note: "Nowhere in the 1976 Act or in the Act's legislative history does Congress state that it intended to jettison the control standard or otherwise to reject the pre-Act judicial approach to identifying a work for hire employment relationship." Brief for Petitioners 20, citing *Aldon Accessories*, 738 F.2d, at 552.

We are unpersuaded. Ordinarily, "Congress' silence is just that - silence." *Alaska Airlines, Inc. v. Brock*, 480 U.S. 678, 686 (1987). Petitioners' reliance on legislative silence is particularly misplaced here because the text and structure of 101 counsel otherwise. See *Bourjaily v. United States*, 483 U.S. 171, 178 (1987); *Harrison v. PPG Industries, Inc.*, 446 U.S. 578, 592 (1980).[NOTE 15] Furthermore, the structure of the work for hire provisions was fully developed in 1965, and the text was agreed upon in essentially final form by 1966. At that time, however, the courts had applied the work for hire doctrine under the 1909 Act exclusively to traditional employees. Indeed, it was not until after the 1965 compromise was forged and adopted by Congress[NOTE 16] that a federal court for the first time applied the work for hire doctrine to commissioned works. See, e. g., *Brattleboro Publishing Co.*, supra, at 567-568. Congress certainly could not have "jettisoned" a line of cases that had not yet been decided.

Finally, petitioners' construction of the work for hire provisions would impede Congress' paramount goal in revising the 1976 Act of enhancing predictability and certainty of copyright ownership. See H. R. Rep. No. 94-1476, supra, at 129. In a "copyright marketplace," the parties negotiate with an expectation that one of them will own the copyright in the completed work. *Dumas*, 865 F.2d, at 1104-1105, n. 18. With that expectation, the parties at the outset can settle on relevant contractual terms, such as the price for the work and the ownership of reproduction rights.

To the extent that petitioners endorse an actual control test,[NOTE 17] CCNV's construction of the work for hire provisions prevents such planning. Because that test turns on whether the hiring party has closely monitored the production process, the parties would not know until late in the process, if not until the work is completed, whether a work will ultimately fall within 101(1). Under petitioners' approach, therefore, parties would have to predict in advance whether the hiring party will sufficiently control a given work to make it the author. "If they guess incorrectly, their reliance on 'work for hire' or an assignment may give them a copyright interest that they did not bargain for." *Easter Seal Society*, 815 F.2d, at 333; accord, *Dumas*, supra, at 1103. This understanding of the work for hire provisions clearly thwarts Congress' goal of ensuring predictability through advance planning. Moreover, petitioners' interpretation "leaves the door open for hiring parties, who have failed to get a full assignment of copyright rights from independent contractors falling outside the subdivision (2) guidelines, to unilaterally obtain work-made-for-hire rights years after the work has been completed as long as they directed or supervised the work, a standard that is hard not to meet when one is a hiring party." Hamilton, Commissioned Works as Works Made for Hire Under the 1976 Copyright Act: Misinterpretation and Injustice, 135 U. Pa. L. Rev. 1281, 1304 (1987).

In sum, we must reject petitioners' argument. Transforming a commissioned work into a work by an employee on the basis of the hiring party's right to control, or actual control of, the work is inconsistent with the language, structure, and legislative history of the work for hire provisions. To determine whether a work is for hire under the Act, a court first should ascertain, using principles of general common law of agency, whether the work was prepared by an employee or an independent contractor. After making this determination, the court can apply the appropriate subsection of 101.

B

We turn, finally, to an application of 101 to Reid's production of *Third World America*. In determining whether a hired party is an employee under the general common law of agency, we consider the hiring party's right to control the manner and means by which the product is accomplished.[NOTE 18] Among the other factors relevant to this inquiry are the skill required;[NOTE 19] the source of the instrumentalities and tools;[NOTE 20] the location of the work;[NOTE 21] the duration of the relationship between the parties;[NOTE 22] whether the hiring party has the right to assign additional projects to the hired party;[NOTE

23] the extent of the hired party's discretion over when and how long to work;[NOTE 24] the method of payment;[NOTE 25] the hired party's role in hiring and paying assistants;[NOTE 26] whether the work is part of the regular business of the hiring party;[NOTE 27] whether the hiring party is in business;[NOTE 28] the provision of employee benefits;[NOTE 29] and the tax treatment of the hired party.[NOTE 30] See Restatement 220(2) (setting forth a nonexhaustive list of factors relevant to determining whether a hired party is an employee).[NOTE 31] No one of these factors is determinative. See *Ward*, 362 U.S., at 400; *Hilton Int'l Co. v. NLRB*, 690 F.2d 318, 321 (CA2 1982).

Examining the circumstances of this case in light of these factors, we agree with the Court of Appeals that Reid was not an employee of CCNV but an independent contractor. 270 U.S. App. D.C., at 35, n. 11, 846 F.2d, at 1494, n. 11. True, CCNV members directed enough of Reid's work to ensure that he produced a sculpture that met their specifications. 652 F. Supp., at 1456. But the extent of control the hiring party exercises over the details of the product is not dispositive. Indeed, all the other circumstances weigh heavily against finding an employment relationship. Reid is a sculptor, a skilled occupation. Reid supplied his own tools. He worked in his own studio in Baltimore, making daily supervision of his activities from Washington practicably impossible. Reid was retained for less than two months, a relatively short period of time. During and after this time, CCNV had no right to assign additional projects to Reid. Apart from the deadline for completing the sculpture, Reid had absolute freedom to decide when and how long to work. CCNV paid Reid $15,000, a sum dependent on "completion of a specific job, a method by which independent contractors are often compensated." *Holt v. Winpisinger*, 258 U.S. App. D.C. 343, 351, 811 F.2d 1532, 1540 (1987). Reid had total discretion in hiring and paying assistants. "Creating sculptures was hardly 'regular business' for CCNV." 270 U.S. App. D.C., at 35, n. 11, 846 F.2d, at 1494, n. 11. Indeed, CCNV is not a business at all. Finally, CCNV did not pay payroll or Social Security taxes, provide any employee benefits, or contribute to unemployment insurance or workers' compensation funds.

Because Reid was an independent contractor, whether "Third World America" is a work for hire depends on whether it satisfies the terms of 101(2). This petitioners concede it cannot do. Thus, CCNV is not the author of "Third World America" by virtue of the work for hire provisions of the Act. However, as the Court of Appeals made clear, CCNV nevertheless may be a joint author of the sculpture if, on remand, the District Court determines that CCNV and Reid prepared the work "with the intention that their contributions be merged into inseparable or interdependent parts of a unitary whole." 17 U.S.C. 101.[NOTE 32] In that case, CCNV and Reid would be co-owners of the copyright in the work. See 201(a).

For the aforestated reasons, we affirm the judgment of the Court of Appeals for the District of Columbia Circuit.

It is so ordered.

NOTES:

NOTE 1: Purtee was named as a defendant but never appeared or claimed any interest in the statue.

NOTE 2: Compare *Easter Seal Society for Crippled Children & Adults of Louisiana, Inc. v. Playboy Enterprises*, 815 F.2d 323 (CA5 1987), (agency law determines who is an employee under 101), *cert. denied*, 485 U.S. 981 (1988), with *Brunswick Beacon, Inc. v. Schock-Hopchas Publishing Co.*, 810 F.2d 410 (CA4 1987) (supervision and control standard determines who is an employee under 101); *Evans Newton, Inc. v. Chicago Systems Software*, 793 F.2d 889 (CA7) (same), *cert. denied*, 479 U.S. 949 (1986); and *Aldon Accessories Ltd. v. Spiegel, Inc.*, 738 F.2d 548 (CA2) (same), *cert. denied*, 469 U.S. 982 (1984). See also *Dumas v. Gommerman*, 865 F.2d 1093 (CA9 1989) (a multifactor formal, salaried employee test determines who is an employee under 101).

NOTE 3: We use the phrase "work for hire" interchangeably with the more cumbersome statutory phrase "work made for hire."

NOTE 4: As of 1955, approximately 40 percent of all copyright registrations were for works for hire, according to a Copyright Office study. See Varmer, Works Made for Hire and On Commission, in Studies Prepared [490 U.S. 730, 738] for the Subcommittee on Patents, Trademarks, and Copyrights of the Senate Committee on the Judiciary, Study No. 13, 86th Cong., 2d Sess., 139, n. 49 (Comm. Print 1960) (hereinafter Varmer, Works Made for Hire). The Copyright Office does not keep more recent statistics on the number of work for hire registrations.

NOTE 5: Section 101 of the Act defines each of the nine categories of "specially ordered or commissioned" works.

NOTE 6: By "hiring party," we mean to refer to the party who claims ownership of the copyright by virtue of the work for hire doctrine.

NOTE 7: See Supplementary Report of the Register of Copyrights on the General Revision of the U.S. Copyright Law: 1965 Revision Bill, 89th Cong., 1st Sess., Copyright Law Revision, pt. 6, pp. 66-67 (H. R. Judiciary Comm. [490 U.S. 730, 742] Print 1965) (hereinafter Supplementary Report); Hardy, Copyright Law's Concept of Employment - What Congress Really Intended, 35 J. Copr. Soc. USA 210, 244-245 (1988).

NOTE 8: We also reject the suggestion of respondent and amici that the 101(1) term "employee" refers only to formal, salaried employees. While there is some support for such a definition in the legislative history, see Varmer, Works Made for Hire 130; n. 11, infra, the language of 101(1) cannot support it. The Act does not say "formal" or "salaried" employee, but simply "employee." Moreover, respondent and those amici who endorse a formal, salaried employee test do not agree upon the content of this test. Compare, e. g., Brief for Respondent 37 (hired party who is on payroll is an employee within 101(1) with Tr. of Oral Arg. 31 (hired party who receives a salary or commissions regularly is an employee within 101(1)); and Brief for Volunteer Lawyers for the Arts, Inc., et al. as Amici Curiae 4 (hired party who receives a salary and is treated as an employee for Social Security and tax purposes is an employee within 101(1)). Even the one Court of Appeals to adopt what it termed a formal, salaried employee test in fact embraced an approach incorporating numerous factors drawn from the agency law definition of employee which we endorse. See *Dumas*, 865 F.2d, at 1104.

NOTE 9: The concept of works made for hire first arose in controversies over copyright ownership involving works produced by persons whom all parties agreed were employees. See, e. g., *Colliery Engineer Co. v. United Correspondence Schools Co.*, 94 F. 152 (CC SDNY 1899); *Little v. Gould*, 15 F. Cas. 612 (No. 8,395) (CC NDNY 1852). This Court first took note of the work for hire doctrine in *Bleistein v. Donaldson Lithographing Co.*, 188 U.S. 239, 248 (1903), where we found that an employer owned the copyright to advertisements that had been created by an employee in the course of his employment. *Bleistein* did not, however, purport to define "employee."

NOTE 10: See Varmer, Works Made for Hire 130; Fidlow, The "Works Made for Hire" Doctrine and the Employee/Independent Contractor Dichotomy: The Need for Congressional Clarification, 10 Hastings Comm. Ent. L. J. 591, 600-601 (1988). Indeed, the Varmer study, which was commissioned by Congress as part of the revision process, itself contained separate subsections labeled "Works Made for Hire" and "Works Made on Commission." It nowhere indicated that the two categories might overlap or that commissioned works could be made by an employee.

NOTE 11: See, e. g., Preliminary Draft, at 259 (statement of Horace S. Manges, Joint Committee of the American Book Publishers Council and the American Textbook Publishers Institute) ("There would be a necessity of putting people on the payroll whom the employers wouldn't want to put on the payroll, and where the employees would prefer to work as independent contractors"); *id.*, at 272 (statement of Saul N. Rittenberg, MGM) ("[T]he present draft has given more emphasis to formalism than necessary. If I commission a work from a man, ordering a work specially for my purposes, and I pay for it, what difference does it make whether I put him under an employment contract or establish an independent contractor relationship?"); *id.*, at 260 (statement of John R. Peterson, American Bar Association) ("I don't think there is any valid philosophical or economic difference between the situation in which you have a man on a continuing basis of orders which justifies placing him on your payroll, and the situation in which you give him a particular order for a particular job").

NOTE 12: The parties to the joint memorandum included representatives of the major competing interests involved in the copyright revision process: publishers and authors, composers, and lyricists. See Copyright Law Revision: Hearings on H. R. 4347, 5680, 6831, 6835 before Subcommittee No. 3 of the House Committee on the Judiciary, 89th Cong., 1st Sess., pt. 1, p. 134 (1965).

NOTE 13: An attempt to add "photographic or other portrait[s]," S. Rep. No. 94-473, p. 4 (1975), to the list of commissioned works eligible for work for hire status failed after the Register of Copyrights objected: "The addition of portraits to the list of commissioned works that can be made into 'works made for hire' by agreement of the parties is difficult to justify. Artists and photographers are among the most vulnerable and poorly protected of all the beneficiaries of the copyright law, and it seems clear that, like serious composers and choreographers, they were not intended to be treated as 'employees' under the carefully negotiated definition in section 101." Second Supplementary Report of the Register of Copyrights on the General Revision of the U.S. Copyright Law: 1975 Revision Bill, Chapter XI, pp. 12-13.

NOTE 14: Strict adherence to the language and structure of the Act is particularly appropriate where, as here, a statute is the result of a series of carefully crafted compromises. See *Rodriguez v. Compass Shipping Co.*, 451 U.S. 596, 617 (1981); *United States v. Sisson*, 399 U.S. 267, 291 , 298 (1970).

NOTE 15: In framing other provisions of the Act, Congress indicated when it intended to incorporate existing case law. See, e. g., H. R. Rep. No. 94-1476, p. 121 (1976) ("There is . . . no need for a specific statutory provision concerning the rights and duties of the co-owners [sic] of a work; court-made law on this point is left undisturbed"); S. Rep. No. 94-473, supra, at 104 (same).

NOTE 16: Over the course of the copyright revision process, Congress frequently endorsed a negotiated compromise which years later in 1976 it formally enacted with only minor revisions. See *Mills Music, Inc. v. Snyder*, 469 U.S. 153, 160 -161 (1985).

NOTE 17: Petitioners concede that, as a practical matter, it is often difficult to demonstrate the existence of a right to control without evidence of the actual exercise of that right. See *Murray v. Gelderman*, 566 F.2d 1307, 1310-1311 (CA5 1978).

NOTE 18: See, e. g., *Hilton Int'l Co. v. NLRB*, 690 F.2d 318, 320 (CA2 1982); *NLRB v. Maine Caterers, Inc.*, 654 F.2d 131, 133 (CA1 1981), *cert denied*, 455 U.S. 940 (1982); Restatement 220(1).

NOTE 19: See, e. g., *Bartels v. Birmingham*, 332 U.S. 126, 132 (1947); *Hilton Int'l Co.*, supra, at 320; *NLRB v. A. Duie Pyle, Inc.*, 606 F.2d 379, 382 (CA3 1979); Restatement 220(2)(d).

NOTE 20: See, e. g., *NLRB v. United Ins. Co. of America*, 390 U.S. 254, 258 (1968); *United States v. Silk*, 331 U.S. 704, 717 , 718 (1947); *Dumas*, 865 F.2d, at 1105; Restatement 220(2)(e).

NOTE 21: See, e. g., *United Ins. Co.*, supra, at 258; *Dumas*, supra, at 1105; *Darden v. Nationwide Mutual Ins. Co.*, 796 F.2d 701, 705 (CA4 1986); Restatement 220(2)(e).

NOTE 22: See, e. g., *United Ins. Co.*, supra, at 259; *Bartels*, supra, at 132; Restatement 220(2)(f).

NOTE 23: See, e. g., *Dumas*, supra, at 1105.

NOTE 24: See, e. g., *United Ins. Co.*, supra, at 258; *Short v. Central States, Southeast & Southwest Areas Pension Fund*, 729 F.2d 567, 574 (CA8 1984).

NOTE 25: See, e. g., *Dumas*, supra, at 1105; *Darden*, supra, at 705; *Holt v. Winpisinger*, 258 U.S. App. D.C. 343, 351, 811 F.2d 1532, 1540 (1987); Restatement 220(2)(g).

NOTE 26: See, e. g., *Bartels*, supra, at 132; *Silk*, supra, at 719; *Darden*, supra, at 705; *Short*, supra, at 574.

NOTE 27: See, e. g., *United Ins. Co.*, supra, at 259; *Silk*, supra, at 718; *Dumas*, supra, at 1105; *Hilton Int'l Co.*, supra, at 321; Restatement 220(2)(h).

NOTE 28: See, e. g., Restatement 220(2)(j).

NOTE 29: See, e. g., *United Ins. Co.*, supra, at 259; *Dumas*, supra, at 1105; *Short*, supra, at 574.

NOTE 30: See, e. g., *Dumas*, supra, at 1105.

NOTE 31: In determining whether a hired party is an employee under the general common law of agency, we have traditionally looked for guidance to the Restatement of Agency. See, e. g., *Kelley v. Southern Pacific Co.*, 419 U.S. 318, 323 -324, and n. 5 (1974); id., at 332 (Stewart, J., concurring in judgment); *Ward v. Atlantic Coast Line R. Co.*, 362 U.S. 396, 400 (1960); *Baker v. Texas & Pacific R. Co.*, 359 U.S. 227, 228 (1959).

NOTE 31: Neither CCNV nor Reid sought review of the Court of Appeals' remand order. We therefore have no occasion to pass judgment on the applicability of the Act's joint authorship provisions to this case.

STUDY QUESTIONS

- Copyright arises on creation, but who owns it? Summarize the court's analysis and conclusion in *CCNV v. Reid*. Why did the court treat the base of the sculpture and the sculpture itself differently? If you were commissioning a sculpture from an artist, what would you have done differently?

- As a result of the decision in *CCNV v. Reid* it is now common practice to have independent contractors who are being hired to create original copyrightable works to sign a written "work-for-hire" agreement. To effectively establish copyright ownership in the person or organization commissioning the work, the agreement should include language similar to the following: *As between Company and Contractor, all right, title and interest in and to the Work and in and to the Services and Materials provided by Contractor in connection with this Agreement will at all times belong solely and exclusively to Company. To the extent that any of Contractor's Services and Materials include any original work of authorship entitled to protection under the laws of copyright, the parties acknowledge and agree that (i) Contractor's Services and Materials have been specially ordered and commissioned by Company as a contribution to a collective work, a supplementary work, an audiovisual work, or such other category of work as may be eligible for treatment as a "work made for hire" under the United States Copyright Act; (ii) Contractor is an independent contractor and not an employee, partner, joint author or joint venture with Company or Company's business; and (iii) Company shall be the sole owner of the Work and of Contractor's Services and Materials, any works derived there from, and any work embodying the Contractor's Services and Materials created in connection with this Agreement, pursuant to the United States Copyright Act. To the extent that the Work and Contractor's Services and Materials are not properly characterized as a "work made for hire" Contractor hereby irrevocably grants to Company all right, title and interest in and to the Work and to Contractor's Services and Materials (including but not limited to the copyright therein), and any and all intellectual property embodied therein, in perpetuity throughout the world and in all media.*

Reading Note: Among the bundle of rights that the copyright owner controls are the right to make derivative works—that is, works that are derived from the copyrighted work. In *Pickett v. Prince* reprinted below, the substantive question before the court is what constitutes a "derivative" work—in this case the allegedly infringing work is a guitar which incorporated a copyrighted symbol in its design.

PICKETT V. PRINCE

52 F. Supp. 2d 893 (N.D. Ill. 1999)

MEMORANDUM OPINION AND ORDER

PALLMEYER, District Judge.

> In a case that has spanned five years, two judges, numerous counsel, and lengthy discovery proceedings; has spawned multiple motions and published orders; and has at last teetered to the brink of trial, the parties debate over the use of the Symbol that has come to identify Defendant,[NOTE 1] the Artist formerly known as Prince. Indeed, Defendant may as well have had this protracted litigation in mind when he lyrically asked: "Why do we scream at each other. This is what it sounds like. When doves cry."[NOTE 2]

Plaintiff filed this suit against Defendant in 1994, alleging infringement of Plaintiff's copyright in a Symbol-shaped guitar (the "Symbol-guitar") that Plaintiff allegedly designed. Because it is undisputed that Defendant designed the Symbol itself, the central issue for the court is whether Plaintiff has an enforceable copyright in the Symbol-guitar as a derivative work. Although both parties recognize the derivative work issue as dispositive, Plaintiff contends that Defendant is barred from raising it by an earlier decision made by Judge Shadur. In July 1997, Defendant brought counterclaims for copyright infringement against Plaintiff. Judge Shadur dismissed those counterclaims on December 18, 1997 on the grounds that the statute of limitations had expired. *See Pickett v. Prince,* No. 94 C 4740, 1997 WL 790599 (N.D.Ill. Dec. 18, 1997). Defendant moved the court for reconsideration, which was denied by Judge Shadur on May 7, 1998. *See Pickett v. Prince,* 5 F. Supp. 2d 595 (N.D.Ill.1998). When the validity of Plaintiff's copyright was raised in the parties' pre-trial materials on March 15, 1999, this court invited a motion for summary judgment. The matter is now fully briefed. For the reasons discussed below, the court grants the motion and dismisses the case.

The unpronounceable symbol (later dubbed "Love Symbol #2")

FACTUAL BACKGROUND

The facts relevant to this motion are largely undisputed.[NOTE 3] Defendant is a well-known recording artist, performer, and songwriter of popular music.[NOTE 4] Around 1990, Defendant created and began using a symbol (the "First

Symbol") based solely on the male and female signs.[NOTE 5] The First Symbol appeared on the cover of the "Graffiti Bridge" album, which was released on August 21, 1990. (Def.Aff. ¶ 2, Ex. A to Defendant's Memorandum of Law in Support of Summary Judgment Submitted Pursuant to Elisabeth Schoening, a freelance artist, to embellish the symbol (the "Embellished Symbol" or "Symbol") for the release of a single entitled "7" by combining the First Symbol with a drawing of the number "7" (reproduced at the end of this opinion as Figure 1). (*Id.* ¶ 4; Schoening Aff. ¶¶ 3-4, Ex. C to Def. Motion.) The Symbol was included on Defendant's "Androgynous" album, which was released on October 13, 1992. (Def.Aff.¶ 5.) In December 1992, Defendant adopted the Symbol as his name.[NOTE 6]

It is fair to say that the Symbol is recognized throughout the United States and around the world as designating Defendant. Defendant has incorporated the Symbol into a variety of items he uses in performance, ranging from his clothing, jewelry, stage props, and musical instruments. Notably, Kenneth Yould, an industrial art designer, designed a musical percussion instrument for Paisley Park Enterprises, Inc., Defendant's company, back in 1991. (Yould Dep., at 9-12, Ex. H to Def. Motion.) The instrument, called a Tamboracca, was a hexagon-shaped instrument that integrated the First Symbol into its design (reproduced at the end of this opinion as Figure 2). (*Id.*) In the latter part of 1991, Mr. Yould also designed a guitar in the shape of the First Symbol. (*Id.* at 25.) This design was later modified in late 1992 to include the Embellished Symbol. (*Id.* at 36.) Apparently, Mr. Yould did not register copyrights in the two musical instruments.[NOTE 7] Defendant did not obtain a copyright in the Symbol itself until June 27, 1997. (*See* Copyright Registration, Ex. F to Def. Motion.)

Plaintiff is a well-known guitar maker and self-proclaimed fan of Defendant. As an expression of his admiration for Defendant, Plaintiff created a guitar in the shape of the Symbol sometime in 1993 (reproduced at the end of this opinion as Figure 3), with hopes that he would be able to sell it to Defendant, thereby enhancing his own reputation as a guitar maker. *Pickett,* 1997 WL 790599, at *2. Plaintiff claims that he showed the guitar to Defendant in 1993, but Defendant denies that he ever encountered either Plaintiff or the Symbol-guitar. While the parties dispute whether such a meeting ever took place, it is uncontested that Defendant did not purchase Plaintiff's Symbol-guitar. Plaintiff's disappointment must have turned to indignant rage when he later learned that Defendant was actually performing on tour during April 1993 with a Symbol-shaped guitar. Plaintiff filed his original, *pro se* complaint claiming fraud and consumer fraud on May 24, 1994, and in his Second Amended Complaint on September 10, 1996, he alleged copyright infringement of his rights in the guitar. He does not claim to own a copyright in the Symbol itself.

It is undisputed that Plaintiff had seen the Symbol on Defendant's album covers before he conceived of the idea to design the Symbol-shaped guitar. (Pickett Dep., at 42-43, Ex. E to Def. Motion.) His copyright applications with the U.S. Copyright Office for the guitar are consistent with that fact. On August 27, 1996, Plaintiff filed a copyright application, which described the guitar as a three-dimensional sculptural work. (Guitar Copyright Registration, Ex. M to Def. Motion.) In a Supplementary Registration filed on February 3, 1999, he amplified the copyright to identify the guitar as based on or incorporating elements of the pre-existing "two-dimensional graphic symbol of Prince Rogers Nelson." (*Id.*) In other words, the guitar is a derivative work based on and incorporating Defendant's now copyrighted Symbol.[NOTE 8] It is also undisputed that he never received permission from Defendant to use the Symbol in his work. Defendant urges that Plaintiff's failure to do so renders his own copyright invalid.

Plaintiff challenges this interpretation of the law and contends that even if Defendant's interpretation is correct, the law of this case bars Defendant from making this argument. Specifically, Plaintiff points to counterclaims that Defendant filed on July 7, 1997 for copyright infringement against Plaintiff. The counterclaims alleged that Plaintiff violated Defendant's exclusive right "to reproduce the copyrighted work" and "to prepare derivative works based upon" the Symbol. *See* 17 U.S.C. §§ 106(1)-(2). Defendant claimed that "Plaintiff's Guitar and Plaintiff's designs for his Guitar are unauthorized derivative works" and that "Plaintiff's copyright registration for Plaintiff's Guitar does not grant Plaintiff a copyright in said Guitar because Plaintiff did not have the Artist's permission to create Plaintiff's Guitar as a derivative work from the Artist's copyrighted Embellished Symbol." (Def. Amended Answer to Pl. Second Amended Counterclaim ¶¶ 13, 28.)

Judge Shadur found that the statute of limitations had run, making the counterclaims stale and unenforceable. *See Pickett,* 1997 WL 790599, at *6. Under Judge Shadur's calculations, which relied on the three-year statute of limitations in the Copyright Act, 17 U.S.C. § 507(b), any counterclaims of copyright infringement had to be asserted by July 5, 1997 since the complaint had been served on July 5, 1994. *Id.* at *2. Defendant, however, first tendered his counterclaims to the court on July 7, 1997. After dismissal of the counterclaims, Defendant moved for reconsideration on the grounds that Judge Shadur had miscalculated the last filing date. Defendant agreed that the statute of limitations on Defendant's counterclaims lapsed on July 5, 1997, but pointed out that July 5, 1997 was a Saturday. Under Rule 6(a), Defendant argued, he had until the next court business day, Monday, July 7, 1997, to file his counterclaims. *See* FED.R.CIV.P. 6(a). Although Judge Shadur indicated that Defendant's calculation was correct, he ultimately concluded that the "argument fails as a matter of law because it simply comes too late." *Pickett,* 5 F. Supp. 2d at 596. Judge Shadur indicated that the right time to have advocated the present contention was when Plaintiff's motion for summary judgment on the counterclaims was fully briefed and submitted to the court, and not after the ruling had been made. *Id.* Failure to raise the argument earlier therefore constituted a forfeiture of that argument. *Id.*

The case was reassigned to this court in October 1998, and the court set a March 22, 1999 trial date. On March 15, 1999, the parties appeared before the court for a final pre-trial conference. In his final pretrial submissions, Defendant challenged the validity of Plaintiff's copyright on the ground that Plaintiff did not have authorization to incorporate the Symbol into his derivative work. Recognizing the issue as a question of law, the court requested that the parties brief the following issues: (1) whether Plaintiff's copyright infringement claim fails as a matter of law because his derivative work relied on unauthorized use of the Symbol, and (2) whether Judge Shadur's dismissal of the counterclaims as time-barred precludes Defendant from raising the issue of validity as a defense. The court discusses the procedural question first because if Plaintiff is correct that Defendant is barred from raising the validity defense, the court need not reach that issue.

DISCUSSION

I. Summary Judgment Standard

The court may invite the appropriate party to move under Rule 56 when it thinks the case is ripe for summary disposition, as happened here. *See* 10A CHARLES A. WRIGHT, ARTHUR R. MILLER & MARY KAY KANE, FEDERAL PRACTICE & PROCEDURE: Civil 3d § 2720 (1998). Summary judgment is proper "if the pleadings, depositions, answers to interrogatories, and admissions on file, together with the affidavits, if any, show that there is no genuine issue as to any material fact and that the moving party is entitled to a judgment as a matter of law." FED.R.CIV.P. 56(c). In ruling on a motion for summary judgment, the court must view the evidence and draw all reasonable inferences in the nonmovant's favor. *Anderson v. Liberty Lobby, Inc.,* 477 U.S. 242, 255, 106 S. Ct. 2505, 91 L. Ed. 2d 202 (1986). The party that bears the burden of proof on a particular issue at trial may not rest on the pleadings, but must affirmatively demonstrate, by specific factual allegations, that there is a genuine issue of material fact that requires trial. *Celotex Corp. v. Catrett,* 477 U.S. 317, 324, 106 S. Ct. 2548, 91 L. Ed. 2d 265 (1986). Here, both parties agree that the dispositive issue for purposes of the motion is one of law: the validity of Plaintiff's copyright. Before reaching that issue, the court first addresses the effect of Judge Shadur's dismissal of Defendant's counterclaims.

II. Dismissal of Counterclaims

Plaintiff contends that Defendant lost his right to challenge the validity of Plaintiff's derivative work because Judge Shadur dismissed his counterclaims. Defendant counters that while Defendant may have lost a remedy against Plaintiff, he did not lose the right to argue that Plaintiff has no remedy against him because his copyright is invalid and unenforceable.

Though both parties' briefs reflect careful research, neither party has located case law that addresses the issue squarely. That is, none of the cases cited by the parties (nor any located by the court) present a situation where a defendant's counterclaims were dismissed as time-barred and the defendant later tried to raise the issue at the heart of the counterclaims as a defense to the plaintiff's claims.

To the extent that Plaintiff argues that the law of the case doctrine prevents this court from now allowing Defendant to go forward with making counterclaims alleging copyright infringement, the court agrees. The law of the case doctrine, as most commonly defined, "posits that when a court decides upon a rule of law, that decision should continue to govern the same issues in subsequent stages in the same case." *Christianson v. Colt Indus. Operating Corp.*, 486 U.S. 800, 816, 108 S. Ct. 2166, 100 L. Ed. 2d 811 (1988) (quoting *Arizona v. California*, 460 U.S. 605, 618, 103 S. Ct. 1382, 75 L. Ed. 2d 318 (1983)); *see also Avitia v. Metropolitan Club of Chicago, Inc.*, 49 F.3d 1219, 1227 (7th Cir. 1995). The Seventh Circuit has held that a variant of the doctrine applies in the present situation, where a case was reassigned from one judge to another in the same court. *Best v. Shell Oil Co.*, 107 F.3d 544, 546 (7th Cir. 1997). Arriving at that conclusion, however, does not get this matter much closer to resolution—Defendant is not trying to revive his dismissed counterclaims, and the court would not entertain such an effort.

What is not so clear is whether the dismissal of the counterclaims means that Defendant has forfeited his ability to assert that Plaintiff unlawfully created his guitar, even by way of defense, as Plaintiff contends. After reviewing the case law and statutory language and employing common sense, the court respectfully rejects Plaintiff's estoppel argument.

Analysis begins with the Copyright Act. Section 106 of that Act sets forth six exclusive rights of copyright (the "bundle of rights") enjoyed by the copyright holder, including the right to: (1) reproduce the copyrighted work, (2) prepare derivative works based upon the copyrighted work, (3) distribute copies of the copyrighted work, (4) publicly perform the copyrighted work, (5) display the copyrighted work, and (6) in the case of sound recordings, perform such by means of a digital audio transmission. 17 U.S.C. § 106. Anyone who violates any of the exclusive rights of the copyright owner by unlawfully using or unlawfully authorizing the use of the protected work is an infringer. *Sony Corp. v. Universal City Studios, Inc.*, 464 U.S. 417, 432, 104 S. Ct. 774, 78 L. Ed. 2d 574 (1984). Defendant's earlier counterclaims were based on his exclusive right to "reproduce the copyrighted work" (the Symbol) and to "prepare derivative works based upon the copyrighted work." According to Plaintiff, once Defendant's counterclaims were dismissed, he could no longer assert those rights against Plaintiff in any manner, whether by way of an infringement claim or as a defense to Plaintiff's claims. In other words, "[a]bsent the ability to sue a particular infringer for a specific act of copyright infringement, a copyright owner's bundle of rights... is lost against that particular infringer." (Mr. Pickett's Memorandum in Support of Copyright Validity (hereinafter "Pl. Memo"), at 11.)

In Plaintiff's view, section 103 of the Copyright Act supports his position. Under section 103, a derivative work is separately and independently copyrightable and is entitled to independent copyright protection, even as against the creator of the original work. 17 U.S.C. § 103(a). Protection for the derivative work extends only to the new material contributed by its author. 17 U.S.C. § 103(b). Plaintiff argues that section 103 does not recognize any defenses to a claim of infringement of the derivative work by the creator of the original, and "Defendant cannot resurrect his lost [section] 106 rights in a [section] 103 setting." (Pl. Memo, at 11.) Plaintiff thus submits that Defendant may contest the scope of Plaintiff's derivative work under section 103, but may not raise the issue of invalidity or lack of authorization of the derivative work.

The court is not persuaded that dismissal of Defendant's counterclaims on timeliness grounds means that Defendant may not raise a defense based on facts that were central to his counterclaims. The Supreme Court has recognized that statutes of limitation "are by definition arbitrary, and their operation does not discriminate between the just and the unjust claim...." *Chase Sec. Corp. v. Donaldson,* 325 U.S. 304, 314, 65 S. Ct. 1137, 89 L. Ed. 1628 (1945). Though only a "working hypothesis," the Court has articulated that as a matter of constitutional law, statutes of limitations "go to matters of remedy, not to destruction of fundamental rights." *Id.* Likewise, the Seventh Circuit has interpreted Supreme Court holdings that Congress and the states have the power to expand statutes of limitations retroactively, as happened in *Chase Securities,* to imply that "limitations periods are not generally to be viewed as affecting substantive rights." *Banas v. American Airlines,* 969 F.2d 477, 485 (7th Cir.1992) (citing *Campbell v. Holt,* 115 U.S. 620, 6 S. Ct. 209, 29 L. Ed. 483 (1885); *Chase Sec. Corp. v. Donaldson,* 325 U.S. 304, 65 S. Ct. 1137, 89 L. Ed. 1628 (1945); *International Union of Elec., Radio & Machine Workers Local 790 v. Robbins & Myers, Inc.,* 429 U.S. 229, 97 S. Ct. 441, 50 L. Ed. 2d 427 (1976)). [NOTE 9]

Relying on the Supreme Court's language in *Chase,* Defendant argues that the passage of time, which may prevent Defendant from asserting a legal claim and seeking remedies against Plaintiff, does not convert Plaintiff's unlawful use of a copyright to a lawful one. The court agrees. Nothing in the case law definitively holds that a time-barred cause of action destroys the right to raise the facts central to that action as a defense, where the defending party does not seek any affirmative remedy. Neither could an adverse ruling due to an expired statute of limitations excuse Plaintiff from proving essential elements of his claim (i.e., that he had a valid copyright), as will be discussed further below. The court does not find any support for Plaintiff's contentions outside the area of copyright law, either. For example, a criminal defendant whose section 1983 claim for an unlawful search becomes time-barred does not lose his right to allege a Fourth Amendment violation as a defense in his later trial. Nor would the fact that the statute of limitations had expired on a trespass claim bar a landowner from raising an injured party's unauthorized entry on land as a defense to a tort claim.

The court additionally rejects Plaintiff's contention that the issues of invalidity and authorization have been decided in a previous stage of the lawsuit. Judge Shadur never addressed the merits of the counterclaims; he dismissed those claims only because the statute of limitations had expired. Whether such a decision is deemed "on the merits" or "procedural" does not affect the fact that Judge Shadur never resolved the substantive merit of Defendant's counterclaims that Plaintiff's creation of a derivative work violated Defendant's own copyright. The only issue that was decided at that earlier stage of the lawsuit was whether the statute of limitations had expired on the counterclaims.

Moreover, accepting Plaintiff's "bundle of rights" argument would lead to an anomalous result. Defendant points out that Plaintiff's complaint challenges Defendant's use of a guitar that resembles Plaintiff's because that guitar, like Plaintiff's, derives from the Symbol. Thus, as described by Defendant, Plaintiff's theory appears to be that merely because Defendant did not bring suit against him promptly, Plaintiff "inherits all the exclusive rights, including the right to sell his guitar depicting Defendant's copyrighted Symbol and the exclusive right to prepare derivative works based on the Symbol-shaped guitar." (Defendant's Reply in Support of His Motion for Summary Judgment (hereinafter "Def. Reply"), at 15.) The court agrees with that characterization of Plaintiff's position and also finds it untenable. If Plaintiff's argument is accepted, Defendant has basically waived his exclusive right to prepare derivative works based on his copyrighted work, and Plaintiff himself now has the exclusive right to prepare derivative works based on a Symbolshaped guitar. To this court's knowledge, no court has ever found that to be so, and nothing in the language of the Copyright Act suggests, much less requires, this result. The court therefore finds that Judge Shadur's dismissal of Defendant's counterclaims in December 1997 does not prevent Defendant from now raising that issue as a defense.

III. Copyright Protection for Plaintiff's Derivative Work

Having determined that the court may entertain Defendant's defense to the copyright infringement claim, the court turns to the more complicated issue of whether that defense defeats Plaintiff's claim as a matter of law. The parties do not dispute the facts surrounding the issue: They agree that Plaintiff's Symbol-guitar is a derivative work of Defendant's copyrighted Symbol; they agree that Plaintiff did not receive authorization from Defendant to use the Symbol; they agree that Defendant has been using another guitar that also incorporates the Symbol. The only point of dissension for the purposes of this motion is whether Plaintiff has a viable copyright infringement claim in such circumstances. Defendant contends that Plaintiff cannot put forth a prima facie case for copyright infringement because he did not have a valid copyright, which would have required permission from Defendant to use the Symbol. Plaintiff, on the other hand, argues for infringement on the theory that he holds a valid copyright for the derivative work, the Symbol-guitar, even without Defendant's authorization.

A. Prima Facie Case for Copyright Infringement

To establish a prima facie of copyright infringement, a plaintiff must prove two essential elements: (1) ownership of a valid copyright, and (2) copying of constituent elements of the work that are original. *Feist Publications, Inc. v. Rural Tel. Serv.*, 499 U.S. 340, 361,

111 S. Ct. 1282, 113 L. Ed. 2d 358 (1991). The registration of a copyright certificate creates a prima facie presumption of validity of a copyright. *See* 17 U.S.C. § 410(c). That presumption, however, is rebutted by evidence that disputes or rebuts the plaintiff's prima facie case. *See Mid America Title Co. v. Kirk,* 59 F.3d 719, 721 (7th Cir.1995). Therefore, Plaintiff's copyright registration will not be sufficient to demonstrate a valid copyright in light of contrary evidence.

Plaintiff does not dispute that his Symbol-guitar is a derivative work based on the copyrighted Symbol,[NOTE 10] (*see, e.g.,* Pl. Memo, at 1) but that does not necessarily deprive his creation of copyright protection. Section 103(a) of the Copyright Act explicitly provides that the subject matter of copyright, as specified by Section 102, includes "derivative works." 17 U.S.C. § 103(a). The court accordingly examines whether Plaintiff has an enforceable copyright in his Symbol-guitar.

B. Unauthorized Use

The exclusive right to prepare derivative works based on copyrighted material is as significant as the exclusive right to reproduce the copyrighted material. *See Atari, Inc. v. North Am. Philips Consumer Elec. Corp.,* 672 F.2d 607, 618 n. 12 (7th Cir. 1982) (the author's exclusive right to produce derivative works based on the original work "often can be more valuable than the right to the original work itself"). Defendant urges that in order to enjoy a copyright in his derivative work, Plaintiff must have received authorization from Defendant, the owner of the original copyrighted work upon which the derivative work was based. Plaintiff implicitly acknowledges that under this bright-line authorization standard for which Defendant argues, his copyright is invalid. Plaintiff contends, however, that courts have not adopted this bright-line standard for determining the validity of a copyright for a derivative work. In Plaintiff's view, his copyright is valid even without authorization from Defendant because Defendant's Symbol does not "pervade" Plaintiff's Symbol-guitar. Plaintiff's copyright, he maintains, is limited by section 103(a) to only those parts of his work that do not employ Defendant's Symbol. Whether the bright-line authorization standard or the more fact-based "pervades" standard controls is the central issue for the court. The statutory text is somewhat ambiguous, and the authorities contradictory as to which approach is appropriate. The court discusses the most pertinent cases here.

1. *Gracen*'s Bright-Line Authorization Standard

Defendant relies heavily on language from *Gracen v. Bradford Exchange,* 698 F.2d 300 (7th Cir.1983). In *Gracen,* the Seventh Circuit examined 17 U.S.C. § 106(2) to determine whether an artist had a valid copyright in derivative paintings and drawings based on the movie "The Wizard of Oz." The court affirmed the district court's grant of summary judgment on the grounds that the painting lacked sufficient originality to be copyrightable. *Id.* at 305. In *dicta,* the court discussed whether the preparer of the derivative works (in that case, the plaintiff) had the authority to use the underlying copyrighted movie. *Id.* at 302. According to the court, "[s]ince the copyright owner's bundle of exclusive rights includes the right 'to prepare derivative works based on the copyrighted work,' 17 U.S.C. § 106(2), even if Miss Gracen's paintings had enough originality to be copyrightable as derivative works she could not copyright them unless she had authority to use copyrighted materials from the movie." *Id.* [NOTE 11]

2. Plaintiff's "Pervades" Standard

Plaintiff emphasizes that this reference to authority for creation of a derivative work is *dicta.* He instead urges the court to adopt what he calls the "pervades" standard. Unfortunately, Plaintiff never articulates exactly what this standard consists of, resulting in some confusion on the part of both the Defendant and the court. The court understands Plaintiff's position on the copyrightability of derivative works to be as follows:

Copyright protection is available under section 103(a) for parts of the derivative work that do not employ the preexisting work regardless of whether permission was first obtained. Copyright protection is defined by section 103(a) independently of any authorization by the copyright owner.

(Mr. Pickett's Response to Defendant's Memorandum of Law in Support of Summary Judgment Submitted Pursuant to the Court's March 15, 1999 Request (hereinafter "Pl. Resp."), at 6.) Plaintiff does not cite to any courts that adhere to this "pervades" approach, which incidently does not even use the word "pervades." Rather, he relies on his interpretation of the statutory language and legislative history of section 103(a) to support the proposition that unauthorized derivative works are valid copyrightable works.

Section 103(a) covers copyright protection for derivative works and provides in pertinent part that "protection for a work employing preexisting material in which copyright subsists does not extend to any part of a work in which such material has been used unlawfully." 17 U.S.C. § 103(a). According to Plaintiff, this language establishes that Congress contemplated that some infringing derivative works would still receive copyright protection, but only covering those "original" parts not employing the pre-existing material. Plaintiff also relies on the legislative history to show that valid derivative works could be made that use a pre-existing copyrighted work without authorization. The House Report on section 103 explains:

The second part of the sentence that makes up section 103(a) deals with the status of a ... derivative work unlawfully employing preexisting copyrighted material. In providing that copyright protection does not extend to "any part of the work in which such material has been used unlawfully," the bill prevents an infringer from benefitting, through copyright protection, from committing an unlawful act, but preserves protection for those parts of the work that do not employ the preexisting work.

H.R.REP. No. 94-1476, at 57 (1976).

Plaintiff reads three expressions of Congress's intent here. First, Congress maintained that an individual unlawfully using pre-existing copyrighted matter in a derivative work could not be shielded from a copyright infringement suit by the owner of the pre-existing work. Second, Congress would not extend copyright protection to parts of the work using pre-existing material unlawfully. Finally, Congress preserved protection for those parts of the derivative work "that do not employ the pre-existing work" irrespective of unlawful use. (*See* Pl. Memo, at 2-3.) Plaintiff concludes from these principles that copyright protection will extend to any part of the derivative work that is not "pervaded" by the pre-existing copyrighted material, whether or not the holder of the copyright for the original work has granted permission.

3. The Second Circuit's "Pervades" Standard

There is yet a third approach, combining the bright-line authorization and "pervades" tests, though the parties have not identified it as such. Under this third approach, the creator of a derivative work would not require authorization if the preexisting work does not "pervade" the derivative work, but would require authorization if the pre-existing work does "pervade." The fact that the parties have not separately recognized this third approach has created some difficulties because Defendant, on the one hand, presumed that this was actually the approach being advocated by Plaintiff. Plaintiff's response brief, however, made clear that this was not the case.[NOTE 12] (*See* Pl.Resp., at 5.) Plaintiff, on the other hand, dismisses this approach as another misinterpretation of the requirement for copyright protection of derivative works, yet relies on cases following this approach.

The approach was first mentioned by the Second Circuit in *Eden Toys, Inc. v. Florelee Undergarment Co.*, 697 F.2d 27 (2d Cir.1982)[NOTE 13] as a model for determining whether derivative works are copyrightable. In *Eden Toys,* the holder of a license to manufacture and sell products based on the copyrighted "Paddington Bear" sued a manufacturer selling nightshirts featuring a print of a bear nearly identical to Paddington Bear. 697 F.2d at 30-31. Eden Toys, the plaintiff-license holder, had granted a sub-license to another manufacturer to produce a derivative work, namely a Paddington Bear gift wrap based on certain drawings created by Eden Toys. *Id.* The district court nonetheless found that Eden's use of the preexisting material copyrighted by Paddington was without permission, making the derivative drawings invalid and the sublicense inappropriate. *Id.* at 33 n. 6. Concluding otherwise, the Second Circuit observed, in a footnote, that "if Eden did not have Paddington's consent to produce a derivative work based on Paddington's copyrighted illustrations, its derivative copyrights would be invalid, since the pre-existing illustrations used without permission would 'tend... to pervade the entire derivative work.'" *Id.* (quoting 1 M. NIMMER & D. NIMMER, NIMMER ON COPYRIGHT § 3.06, at 3-21 (1982) (alteration in original)). The Second Circuit, however, determined that in this case permission was actually granted to Eden Toys such that the derivative works were valid. *Id.*

This "pervades" language was extended by the Southern District of New York in *Dynamic Solutions, Inc. v. Planning & Control, Inc.*, 646 F. Supp. 1329 (S.D.N.Y. 1986), in which a computer software writer brought a copyright infringement action against a business training program provider for a computer program derived from an earlier work. The defendant attacked the validity of the plaintiff's copyrights, contending they constituted unauthorized derivative works. *Id.* at 1340. Rejecting that argument, the court suggested that even when the author of a derivative work uses an underlying copyright without the permission of its owner, copyright protection for the derivative work should be denied only when the preexisting material "tends to pervade the entire derivative work." *Id.* (citing 1 M. NIMMER & D. NIMMER, NIMMER ON COPYRIGHT § 3.06, at 3-22 (1985); *Eden Toys*, 697 F.2d at 34 n. 6).[NOTE 14]

The Second Circuit's "pervades" approach thus differs from Plaintiff's in that the Second Circuit's standard acknowledges that authorization from the owner of the pre-existing work is required for a valid copyright when the pre-existing work "pervades" the derivative work. In contrast, under Plaintiff's interpretation, authorization is never necessary for a valid copyright in original parts of the derivative work (i.e., those parts not "pervaded" by the pre-existing work). For Plaintiff, a derivative work is *only* unlawful if the original work "pervades" it entirely; whether or not the creator of the original work has authorized it is irrelevant. In other words, Plaintiff finds no circumstances in which authorization would be an issue.

4. Proper Standard for Copyrightability of Derivative Works

In urging rejection of bright-line authorization standard in *Gracen*, Plaintiff makes much of the fact that it appeared by way of *dicta*. His argument is contrary to the salutary rule that "[i]n the absence of a controlling Supreme Court ruling, a federal district court is required to give great weight to the pronouncements of its Court of Appeals, even though those pronouncements appear by way of dictum." *Max M. v. Thompson*, 585 F. Supp. 317, 324 (N.D.Ill.1984). "While not excused from making an independent examination of the precise issue presented, we cannot presume that our Court of Appeals writes merely for intellectual exercise." *Id.* (internal quotes omitted) (citations omitted). This court is therefore unwilling to ignore the Seventh Circuit's reasoning in *Gracen*, even where that reasoning is arguably not a basis for the court's holding in that case.

Plaintiff's argument that *Gracen* is factually distinguishable from this matter is unpersuasive, as well. Plaintiff contends that he created an "original" work while the plaintiff in *Gracen* did not exercise any creativity in reproducing the original two-dimensional movie still in a two-dimensional painting. The court finds this distinction insufficient to distinguish *Gracen*. First, the conclusion that Plaintiff's Symbol-guitar was an "original" work belongs solely to Plaintiff. Indeed, as discussed below, Defendant urges the contrary.[NOTE 15] Additionally, even if such a factual distinction exists, it is immaterial to determining whether authorization from the copyright author is required for a valid copyright for a derivative work. Plaintiff conflates two separate issues, originality with valid copyright. [NOTE 16]

Plaintiff also stresses that courts in this district have rejected the *Gracen dictum* in favor of a "pervades" analysis. Plaintiff cites two cases in particular. In *Theotokatos v. Sara Lee Personal Prods.*, 971 F. Supp. 332 (N.D.Ill.1997) (Castillo, J.), the plaintiff had designed a t-shirt for the 1996 Summer Olympics employing the Olympic torch and rings. After registering his designs for copyright protection, plaintiff submitted his designs to Sara Lee, a major sponsor and licensee of the Olympic games, for possible use on t-shirts. *Id.* at 336. Sara Lee rejected his designs, but advised him to contact some of its sublicensees. *Id.* The plaintiff alleged that Andazia, one of the sublicensees, later submitted a substantially similar design to Sara Lee, which was ultimately approved and printed on t-shirts. *Id.* He also claimed that another Sara Lee t-shirt design infringed one of his designs. *Id.* at 337. On the motion to dismiss, the court first found that the plaintiff's designs possessed the requisite level of originality for copyright protection. *Id.* at 338. The court next discussed whether plaintiff's copyrights for derivative works were invalid because he failed to obtain authorization to use the Olympic rings, a protected design owned by the United States Olympic Committee. Finding other grounds for dismissal, the court did not reach the "difficult question" of whether the Olympic rings pervade the works as a whole. *Id.* at 340. Based on that discussion, Plaintiff claims that *Theotokatos* rejected the language of *Gracen* as merely *dicta* and instead indicated that whether the original design "pervaded" the derivative work was the significant question.

In *Liu v. Price Waterhouse L.L.P.*, No. 97 C 3093, 1999 WL 47025 (N.D.Ill. Jan. 25, 1999) (Holderman, J.), the plaintiff filed a complaint for copyright infringement of a computer software program. The plaintiff, one of a group of Chinese programmers, had been hired by Price Waterhouse to prepare a derivative work based on one of its programs. *Id.* at *1. The parties disputed the extent to which Price Waterhouse authorized the Chinese programmers to use the original computer program. *Id.* Notably, however, a June 7, 1995 letter between the parties authorized the Chinese programmers to prepare a derivative work, although it did not explicitly authorize them to copyright that derivative work. *Id.* at *3. The court also found that the letter did not explicitly prohibit them from copyrighting their derivative work. *Id.* On its motion for summary judgment, Price Waterhouse argued that the absence of any authorization to copyright the derivative work necessarily rendered the plaintiff's copyright invalid pursuant to *Gracen. Id.* Disagreeing, the court instead apparently declined to follow the *Gracen* doctrine as mere *dictum. Id.* at *3 - *4. Plaintiff thus interprets *Liu* also to reject the dicta in *Gracen* as an incorrect statement of law.

Plaintiff's view on both cases is mistaken on several fronts. First, in *Theotokatos,* while the court did perceive the language in *Gracen* to be *dicta,* the court did not reach the question of whether the pre-existing work pervaded the derivative work as a whole because it dismissed the case on other grounds. 971 F. Supp. at 340. In other words, as Defendant notes, the adoption of the "pervades" standard in *Theotokatos* is itself *dictum.* Additionally, the court acknowledged that the result in *Gracen* and its progeny would have been decided the same way under a standard that considered whether the original design "pervades" the new one. *Id.* at 341 n. 2. That acknowledgment, combined with the lack of explanation as to why a "pervades" standard should apply, makes *Theotokatos* weak authority for rejecting *Gracen's* bright-line authorization approach. Finally, *Theotokatos* actually undermines Plaintiff's position because *Theotokatos* supports the Second Circuit's interpretation of the "pervades" analysis, which Plaintiff himself has rejected as a misinterpretation of section 103(a). (*See* Pl.Resp., at 5.)

Furthermore, *Liu* is factually distinguishable from the case at hand because the plaintiff there did have authorization to prepare a derivative work. *See* 1999 WL 47025, at *3. The dispute instead centered on whether the same letter that granted authorization to prepare the work also granted authorization to copyright that derivative work. *Id. Liu's* rejection of *Gracen* therefore disagreed only with the suggestion in *Gracen* that one who obtains a license (i.e., authorization) from the author of the copyrighted work to prepare a derivative work must also receive explicit authorization to copyright that derivative work. As further support that *Liu* was not a rejection of the bright-line authorization test, the court notes that *Liu* did not adopt a "pervades" standard as the correct approach; in fact, *Liu* never mentions the competing "pervades" analysis.

The *Gracen* bright-line authorization standard also garners some support from the oft-quoted Professor Nimmer. In explaining the nature of a derivative work, Professor Nimmer explains:

A work is not derivative unless it has *substantially* copied from pre-existing works. If that which is borrowed consists merely of ideas and not of the expression of ideas, then although the work may have in part been derived from prior works, it is not a derivative work. Put another way, a work will be considered a derivative work only if it would be considered an infringing work if the material that it has derived from a pre-existing work had been taken without the consent of a copyright proprietor of such pre-existing work. *It is saved from being an infringing work only because the borrowed or copied material was taken with the consent of the copyright owner of the prior work,* or because the prior work has entered the public domain.

1 M. NIMMER & D. NIMMER, NIMMER ON COPYRIGHT § 3.01, at 3-3 (1997) (second emphasis added). In this court's view, if a derivative work needs the consent of the copyright owner of the pre-existing work to avoid infringement, a valid copyright would certainly not adhere in a case where consent was not obtained.[NOTE 17] It seems highly unlikely that a valid copyright could attach to such an infringing work. *See Harris Custom Builders, Inc. v. Hoffmeyer,* 92 F.3d 517, 521 (7th Cir.1996) (intimating that the unauthorized act of an infringer would not receive protection under the Copyright Act); *Anderson v. Stallone,* No. 87-0592, 1989 WL 206431, at *10 (C.D.Cal. Apr. 25, 1989) ("generally no part of an infringing derivative work should be granted copyright protection");

H.R.REP. No. 94-1476, at 57-58 (1976) (section 103(a) of the Copyright Act prevents an infringer from benefitting from an unlawful act through copyright protection).

Lastly, the court notes that *Gracen* need not be read to be conflicting with the Second Circuit's interpretation. It is possible to harmonize the two standards: the bright-line authorization standard may apply in all cases where the pre-existing work clearly "pervades" the derivative work; indeed, unless the pre-existing work "pervades" the new one, arguably the newer work is not "derivative" at all.[NOTE 18] The court does recognize that no Seventh Circuit case has addressed this matter specifically. Plaintiff has not, however, presented any compelling support for adoption of his "pervades" approach. Neither has any court followed Plaintiff's version of the "pervades" approach. The court is therefore willing to rest its findings on the *dicta* of *Gracen* and hold that Plaintiff's copyright in the Symbol-guitar is invalid because he lacks the necessary authorization from Defendant for use of the Symbol. Without deciding the issue as a matter of law, the court notes it is not certain that the result in this case would be different under the alternative analysis urged by Plaintiff. Notably, Plaintiff contends that he holds a valid copyright in those parts of his work that do not employ Defendant's symbol, even if no permission was obtained, because the Symbol does not "pervade" the derivative work. Plaintiff repeatedly insists that he has copyright protection under section 103(a) in the added original "parts" not found in the Symbol. (*See* Pl. Memo, at 3-4.) After urging adoption of the "pervades" analysis as the correct test, Plaintiff submits that "Defendant's two-dimensional symbol does not 'pervade' Mr. Pickett's three-dimensional guitar. The guitar has more than sufficient additional creative aspects to it that are not present in the symbol, but are above and beyond the symbol." (*Id.,* at 8.) Notably, he never explains what those original, creative parts are. Defendant argues that Plaintiff cannot do so "without conceding that the only elements added to Defendant's Symbol are the functional necessities associated with a guitar." (Def. Reply, at 9.) The court finds the argument persuasive.

Merriam Webster's Collegiate Dictionary defines "pervade" as "to become diffused throughout every part of." A comparison of the Symbol and Plaintiff's Symbol-guitar shows that all aspects of the Symbol appear to be incorporated by the guitar, from the arrowhead point, to the crossbow and horn-shaped pieces in the middle, to the round body. (*Compare* Symbol, Figure 2 *with* Plaintiff's Symbol-guitar, Figure 4.) The shape of the guitar itself is in the shape of Defendant's Symbol. The only arguably "original" aspects of the Symbol-guitar would include those things considered functional to a guitar, such as the strings or the neck of the instrument. Such utilitarian aspects are outside the protection of copyright law. 17 U.S.C. § 101; *cf. American Dental Assoc. v. Delta Dental Plans Assoc.,* 126 F.3d 977, 980 (7th Cir.1997) ("[a] lamp may be entirely original, but if the novel elements are also functional the lamp cannot be copyrighted").

Finally, as a matter of policy, the court is sympathetic to Defendant's concern that the court should not support creation of a *de facto* monopoly on derivative works to the detriment of the owner of the copyright in the preexisting work. *See Entertainment Research Group,*

Inc. v. Genesis Creative Group, Inc., 122 F.3d 1211, 1224 (9th Cir.1997) (denying copyright protection to derivative works on the ground that the rights of the holder of the underlying copyrighted product would be affected), *cert. denied,* ___ U.S. ___, 118 S. Ct. 1302, 140 L. Ed. 2d 468 (1998); *Ets-Hokin v. Skyy Spirits Inc.*, No. C 96-3690, 1998 WL 690856, at *8 (N.D.Cal. Sept. 28, 1998) (same). In *Entertainment Research Group,* the plaintiff designed and manufactured three-dimensional inflatable costumes to be purchased by companies and used at publicity events. 122 F.3d at 1214. The costumes were based on the companies' cartoon characters and were recognized as derivative works. *Id.* The plaintiff sued for copyright infringement when his former marketer and another manufacturer started selling allegedly substantially similar costumes. *Id.* at 1215. The Ninth Circuit affirmed the district court in denying copyright protection to the derivative works on the grounds that the rights of the holder of the underlying copyrighted characters would be affected. *Id.* at 1224. The court acknowledged that the costumes were so similar to the copyrighted cartoon characters that granting a copyright in the costumes would have the practical effect of providing ERG with a de facto monopoly on all inflatable costumes depicting the copyrighted characters also in ERG's costumes. Indeed, if ERG had copyrights for its costumes, any future licensee who was hired to manufacture costumes depicting these characters would likely face a strong copyright infringement suit from ERG.

Id. This, the court concluded, would be inappropriate.

Similarly, granting copyright protection to Plaintiff's Symbol-guitar in this case may effectively deprive Defendant of his exclusive right to produce additional derivative works based on the Symbol. For example, as Defendant points out, Plaintiff may well then possess the exclusive right to produce certain additional derivative works based on the Symbol, such as a Symbol-shaped bass guitar or a Symbol-shaped violin. That would undoubtedly dilute Defendant's rights in his own copyright in the Symbol, which includes the exclusive right to prepare derivative works based on the copyrighted work. Such a dilution would be an inappropriate result under the Copyright Act. *See* 17 U.S.C. § 103(b); *Entertainment Research Group,* 122 F.3d at 1219 ("In deciding whether to grant copyright protection to a derivative work, courts must be concerned about the impact such a derivative copyright will have on the copyright privileges and rights of the owner of the underlying work.").

Following the bright-line authorization standard in *Gracen,* the court therefore holds that Plaintiff's copyright in the Symbol-guitar is invalid because it is uncontested that Plaintiff lacked authorization. Although it need not reach the issue, the court notes Defendant's strong evidence that the Symbol pervades Plaintiff's derivative work, the Symbol-guitar, such that even under the Second Circuit's "pervades" standard, Plaintiff needed Defendant's permission for a valid copyright. Because that permission was not obtained, Plaintiff's copyright in the derivative work is not valid, and he is unable to establish a prima facie case of copyright infringement. Summary judgment is therefore granted in favor of Defendant, who now has good reason to "go crazy" and "party like it's 1999." After five long years of litigation, this court does not doubt that will be the case.

CONCLUSION

For the reasons discussed above, the court grants summary judgment for Defendant and dismisses the case.

NOTES:

NOTE 1: Defendant's law firm was able to program the actual symbol into their computers, resulting in court filings that use the Symbol to refer to him. The court's technical resources are unfortunately more limited. Rather than refer to the Artist as "Nelson," as Judge Shadur did, this court will call him simply "Defendant."

NOTE 2: All lyrics used in the opinion were transcribed by the Prince Lyric Transcription Team and were found at *http://members.aol.com/WhosPrince/lyrics/purple.html.*

NOTE 3: Because the motion was specially requested by the court, the parties have not submitted the normally requisite Rule 12(M) and 12(N) statements of undisputed facts. The court therefore gleans the facts from the statement of facts in the briefs and additional documents submitted thereto.

NOTE 4: Defendant's popularity is evidenced by various publications and fan clubs devoted to him. One such magazine is *Uptown,* an "independent and uncensored magazine exploring the world of the Artist formerly known as Prince." *http://www. uptown.se/99/uptown/html.* Another is prince.org, an unauthorized, unofficial, independent fansite that includes, among other things, the latest news about Defendant, events, and links to other fan associations around the world. *See http:// www. prince.org./main/html.*

NOTE 5: Defendant's fans were perhaps not surprised by Defendant's eventual adoption of this symbol, with its prototype combining the male and female signs. For example, the then-Prince wrote in his 1984 "I Would Die 4 U": "I'm not a woman. I'm not a man. I am something that you'll never understand."

NOTE 6: The record does not disclose whether the name change was accomplished through legal proceedings or informal adoption.

NOTE 7: Neither party devotes much attention to the fact that Mr. Yould created a guitar using Defendant's First Symbol back in 1991. (*See* Yould Dep., at 25.) Considering that copyright inheres in authorship and not registration, *see infra* note 8, if Mr. Yould first registered his copyright, Plaintiff's Symbol-guitar itself would arguably be subject to an action for copyright infringement. *See* 17 U.S.C. §§ 411(a), 501(b).

NOTE 8: That Defendant had not yet registered his copyright when Plaintiff registered his Symbol-guitar is irrelevant. Under the Copyright Act, "registration is not a condition of copyright protection." 17 U.S.C. § 408(a). Rather, "[c]opyright inheres in authorship and exists whether or not the work is ever registered." *Arthur Rutenberg Homes, Inc. v. Drew Homes, Inc.,* 29 F.3d 1529, 1531 (11th Cir.1994).

NOTE 9: The determination of whether an action is time-barred and the effects of such a decision involves an area of law that "has precipitated more ambiguity and caused more theoretical and practical snarls" than any other area of law. *Reinke v. Boden,* 45 F.3d 166, 169 (7th Cir.1995). It remains unsettled whether statutes of limitations extinguish the claim and destroy the right itself or whether they do no more than cut off resort to the courts for enforcement of a claim. *See Chase,* 325 U.S. at 313, 65 S. Ct. 1137 (noting the debate, but not settling those arguments). Likewise, it is unclear how to distinguish between those statutes of limitations whose expiration results in a "procedural" decision versus those that amount to a decision "on the merits." *See Reinke,* 45 F.3d at 169-170 (indicating the two categories, but not explaining how to determine which category applies to which statute of limitations). The parties do not discuss the ambiguities in this area, and the court accordingly does not focus its discussion on delineating the impact of rulings based on expired statutes of limitations.

NOTE 10: According to the Copyright Act:

> A "derivative work" is a work based upon one or more preexisting works, such as a translation, musical arrangement, dramatization, fictionalization, motion picture version, sound recording, art reproduction, abridgement, condensation, or any other form in which a work may be recast, transformed, or adapted. A work consisting editorial revisions, annotations, elaborations, or other modifications which, as a whole, represent an original work of authorship, is a "derivative work."

17 U.S.C. § 101.

NOTE 11: Other courts have followed *Gracen* in holding that the preparer of a derivative work can obtain a valid copyright only if certain conditions are met. *See, e.g., Fred Riley Home Building Corp. v. Cosgrove,* 864

F. Supp. 1034, 1037 (D.Kan.1994) ("the copyright claimant of the derivative work must have the consent of the holder of the copyright in the preexisting work for the creation of the derivative work.") (citing *Gracen*); *Gallery House, Inc. v. Yi,* 582 F. Supp. 1294, 1297 (N.D.Ill. 1984) ("It is well settled that where a subsequent work is 'derived' from an underlying design, that maker has no right to claim copyright (1) unless specifically licensed to do so by the author of the underlying design, and (2) unless the alleged derivative work comprises an original artistic addition to the underlying design.") (citing *Gracen*).

NOTE 12: Plaintiff's response brief quotes verbatim from Defendant's brief and then rejects it as the wrong interpretation of the meaning of "pervades." In this court's view, as discussed *infra,* this is the approach that has been adopted in the Second Circuit.

NOTE 13: The standard of review employed by *Eden Toys* has been superceded by statute. *See Weissmann v. Freeman,* 868 F.2d 1313, 1322 (2d Cir.1989). The former rule, followed by *Eden Toys,* allowed for the appellate court to evaluate *de novo* originality of a work when it could be determined entirely by reference to documentary evidence. *Id.* But in 1985, the Federal Rules of Civil Procedure were amended so that findings of fact based on documentary evidence are not to be set aside unless clearly erroneous. *Id.; see* FED.R.CIV.P. 52(a).

NOTE 14: Courts have followed the Second Circuit's "pervades" analysis in evaluating whether authorization was required for a valid copyright in derivative works. *See., e.g., JBJ Fabrics, Inc. v. Brylane, Inc.,* 714 F. Supp. 107, 110 (S.D.N.Y.1989) ("even if plaintiff's use of the underlying design were unlawful, it would be entitled to protection for its original contributions absent some showing by defendant that the unlawful use pervaded the entire work"). Plaintiff offers two cases as evidence that courts in this district have also rejected *Gracen* in favor of the "pervades" approach, namely *Theotokatos v. Sara Lee Personal Prods.,* 971 F. Supp. 332 (N.D.Ill.1997), and *Liu v. Price Waterhouse L.L.P.,* No. 97 C 3093, 1999 WL 47025 (N.D.Ill. Jan. 25, 1999). They are discussed more fully *infra.*

NOTE 15: Defendant insists that Plaintiff's work is, in fact, not sufficiently original to merit copyright protection. Plaintiff responds that transforming a two-dimensional drawing (the Symbol) into a three-dimensional sculpture (the Symbol-guitar) exhibits sufficient creativity and originality to merit copyright protection. The court need not decide the issue here, but notes that courts have fallen on both sides of the debate of whether converting a two-dimensional design to a three-dimensional object constitutes a copyrightable effort. *Compare Entertainment Research Group, Inc. v. Genesis Creative Group, Inc.,* 122 F.3d 1211, 1223 (9th Cir.1997) (originality of three-dimensional costumes from two-dimensional drawings upon which they were based not sufficient to maintain a copyright because any differences that existed were functional considerations not to be considered), *and Gallery House, Inc. v. Yi,* 582 F. Supp. 1294, 1297 (N.D.Ill.1984) (simply converting a two-dimensional design to a three-dimensional bronze statue does not constitute a copyrightable effort without sufficient original artistic contribution) *with W. Goebel Porzellanfabrik v. Action Indus., Inc.,* 589 F. Supp. 763, 767 (S.D.N.Y.1984) (translation of sketches into three-dimensional art works, including figurines, plaques, plates, bells, and dolls, adds sufficient creative effort to make the "Hummel figures" protected under copyright laws).

Common to all these cases is the fact that the derivative work consisted of transforming the two-dimensional drawing directly into a three-dimensional figure. For example, a costume of the Pillsbury Doughboy was based on a drawing of the Doughboy. *See Entertainment Research Group,* 122 F.3d at 1214 n. 2. None of the cases involved a derivative work that *incorporated* the two-dimensional drawing into a different three-dimensional work. The amount of original artistic contribution ascribed to the former is arguably less than that found in the latter. Plaintiff here did not merely convert the two-dimensional Symbol into a three-dimensional sculpture. He instead incorporated the Symbol into an entirely new creation, a Symbol-guitar. Whether this exhibits the requisite originality to merit copyright protection is not a question that this court need answer, however, for reasons discussed in the text.

NOTE 16: Plaintiff's argument is simply his reading of *Gracen*'s facts under the lens of his version of the "pervades" standard. He seemingly contends that a derivative work that is sufficiently original, which Plaintiff implies is one where the pre-existing work does not pervade the derivative work, would not suffer from an invalid copyright. Therefore, he is not arguing so much that the facts of *Gracen* are distinguishable from this case as he is advocating for his proposed standard to apply.

NOTE 17: Admittedly, even Professor Nimmer's treatise, cited ubiquitously as authority in copyright cases, does not answer this matter conclusively. Professor Nimmer addresses what he calls the "lawful use of the underlying work as a condition to a derivative copyright." He states that if the pre-existing work upon which a given derivative work is based is protected by copyright, its unauthorized incorporation in a derivative work will constitute an act of copyright infringement. NIMMER, *supra,* § 3.06, at 3-34.21. When considering whether without consent of the copyright owner of the pre-existing work the author of a derivative work still may claim copyright, he concludes that section 103(a) permits copyright in that which was originally contributed to such work even though the derivative author may be an infringer as to that which was borrowed from the pre-existing work. *Id.* at 3-34.21 - 3-34.22. Thus, "only that portion of a derivative ... work that employs the preexisting work would be denied copyright." *Id.* at 3-34.22. This seems to negate a bright-line authorization standard because it suggests that even without consent, a valid copyright may be maintained in original contributions. The court does note, however, that the statutory language does not require this result.

On the meaning of section 103(a) of the Copyright Act, Professor Nimmer explains, "[t]he effect generally would be to deny copyright to derivative works, in which the preexisting work *tends to pervade* the entire derivative work, but not to collective works, where the infringement arises from the copying of the selection and arrangement of a number of preexisting works, and not *per se* from the reproduction of any particular prior work." *Id.* at 3-34.22 - 3-34.23 (emphasis added). Curiously, though, he cites as support for this proposition *both* the cases following the Second Circuit's "pervades" standard and *Gracen* and its progeny. *See id.* at 3-34.22 n. 12.

Professor Nimmer also looks to the House Report, which comments on section 103(a) as conditioning copyright in a derivative work upon the pre-existing material not having been used "unlawfully" rather than merely without the consent of the copyright owner of such pre-existing material. *Id.* at 3-34.23. The two situations where use could be lawful, even without consent, are under the doctrine of fair use or an applicable foreign law. *Id.* Plaintiff does not attempt to fit his case into the two exceptions; in any event, it is clear that neither case would apply here.

NOTE 18: This conclusion is consistent with Professor Nimmer's observations. Significantly, Plaintiff concedes that the Symbol-guitar is a derivative work and may not now argue the differences between his guitar and Defendant's Symbol precludes that characterization.

STUDY QUESTIONS

- What was the issue in *Pickett v. Prince*? How did the court resolve the question of what constitutes a "derivative work"? Do you agree?
- Can you think of ways in which "derivative works" might arise in the museum context?
- What other intellectual property issues apart from copyrights might also be at stake in this case? How did the court address the plaintifff's claim that the three-dimensional aspects of the Symbol-guitar were subject to copyright? See NOTE 15 at the end of the case.

PART II: ELEMENTS OF COPYRIGHT

As discussed above, U.S. copyright law gives the copyright owner the exclusive right to control the distribution and exploitation of the work for a limited period of time. If a work is under copyright, you must obtain permission from the copyright owner to use the work or risk being sued for copyright infringement. If you do not or cannot obtain permission from the copyright owner, you should not use the work unless you can rely on one of the exceptions to copyright. In this section we will discuss how to determine whether a work is under copyright. In the next section we will discuss the exceptions to copyright protection. And finally, we will look at the application of copyright law through the lens of appropriation art.

COPYRIGHT DURATION

The duration of copyright is set by federal statute. Once the term of copyright expires, the work is no longer subject to copyright and is said to be "in the public domain." Works that were never under copyright, either because the work lacks originality or is otherwise not eligible for copyright protection, are also referred to as being "in the public domain." Works that are in the public domain can be freely used without permission from the copyright owner.

Due to changes in U.S. copyright law, the rules for determining whether copyright has expired are extremely technical. The current applicable U.S. copyright statute is the Copyright Act of 1976, as amended. Works created prior to the implementation of the 1976 Copyright Act must be analysed under the copyright law that was in effect at the time the work was created.

Pre-1972 sound-recordings present a special case—sound-recordings were not brought within the scope of federal copyright protection until 1972. Recent legislation, the Music Modernization Act (MMA), Pub.L. 115-264, has clarified the protected status of pre-1972 sound-recordings under federal copyright law. In addition, certain works created outside the territory of the United States, which had entered the public domain under prior copyright law, have had their copyright "restored" through an amendment to the Copyright Act. The restoration of copyright in these foreign works is addressed in the *Golan v. Holder* case included in the readings below.

Determining whether a given work is under copyright is a fact-based inquiry requiring extrinsic information about the copyrighted work and its ownership and history—its "provenance" to use a fancy museum term. As with provenance in other contexts, such as determining title to a work,[NOTE 1] crucial information may not be readily available. Key issues include: (i) when and where the work was created; (ii) who it was created by or for; (iii) whether and when a work was "published:" and (iv) whether the applicable formalities (copyright notice and registration and renewal) were followed. As a result, calculating the length of copyright can be a difficult process. Fortunately, there are several rules of thumb, and some excellent resources to help with the task. Even so, determining the copyright status of a given work can be a time-consuming and expensive process.

For recently created and new works—those works created in the United States after January 1, 1978—the copyright lasts for the life of the creator plus 70 years. For jointly created works, the copyright runs from the life of the longest surviving creator for 70 years. For employer-owned works and those created by an independent contractor as a work-for-hire, and for anonymous works, copyright lasts for the shorter of 95 years from the date of publication or 120 years from the date of creation.

For works created prior to January 1, 1978, duration depends on the law in effect at the time federal copyright protection was first secured. This may be either the date the work was first published or the date the work was registered with the U.S. Copyright Office. The copyright law also provides a "safe harbor" for older works: as of the writing of this book, works that were published prior to 1924 are in the public domain.

The date of publication is crucial to determining copyright duration because in most circumstances this is the date on which the term of copyright begins to toll. A work is "published" when copies of the work are distributed to the public by sale or other transfer of ownership, or by rental, lease, or lending. "Publication" also includes offering to distribute copies to a group of persons for the purpose of further distribution, public performance, or display. Importantly, a public performance or display of a work does not of itself constitute publication.

Ideally the date of publication will be found on the work itself as part of a copyright notice. The notice is often in the form of the symbol © or "copr." or the word "copyright" followed by the name of the author and the date of publication. However, for many 20th Century works of art this may not be the case. A date was not required by the prior copyright law (first enacted in 1909) for works of art, so many artworks which do have a copyright notice on them do not include a date. In addition, unpublished works of art were rarely registered under the prior copyright law. Furthermore, the term "publication" for works of art generally means the date an image of the work was reproduced and distributed publicly—in a catalogue or magazine for example—or the year the work was first sold or offered for sale, usually by a gallery, dealer or by way of a public auction. As a result, with respect to works of art created in the last century, detailed provenance research including the exhibition history and chain of title may be necessary before the copyright status of the work can be determined.

The copyright in a work may also be terminated by operation of law if the applicable statutory formalities—notice and registration—were not followed. As noted, under current copyright law no copyright notice or registration is required—copyright arises on creation. However, under the 1909 Copyright Act which applies to most 20th Century works, there were specific notice and registration requirements. Failure to comply with those copyright formalities resulted in the work entering the public domain.

The length of initial registration and subsequent renewal periods during most of the 20th Century was 28 years. In many cases works that were initially registered were not renewed within the applicable period. To complicate things further, in the later part of the 20th Century, Congress passed a series of amendments to the 1909 Copyright Act which extended the renewal period for certain already registered works. As a result, information about a work's copyright registration may need to be obtained before the copyright status of the work can be determined.

Additionally, before January 1, 1978, a copyright notice was required on all published works. If a work was published without the required notice, copyright in the work was waived and the work is now in the public domain. The 1976 Copyright Act included a transitional set of rules for copyright notices, which further complicates things. Between January 1, 1978 and March 1, 1989, the copyright notice requirement still applied, but copyright owners could correct an oversight during a grace period. As a result, works published between January 1, 1978 and March 1, 1989 without a copyright notice may still be under copyright. The notice requirement was completely abolished effective as of March 1, 1989. So information about a work itself may be necessary to determine its copyright status.

Foreign works (those created or first published outside the United States) may or may not have been required to carry a copyright notice, depending on when and where the work was first published. Works that failed to comply with these notice and registration formalities are now in the public domain. Information about where a work was created may also be needed before the copyright status can be determined.

As you can see, determining the status of copyright in a work is no easy task. Fortunately, copyright duration tables are a helpful tool in determining whether a work is still under copyright. The copyright duration chart maintained by the Cornell University Library, labelled "Copyright Term and the Public Domain in the United States" (https://copyright.cornell.edu/publicdomain) is perhaps the best of these copyright duration tables. Even so, there often is simply not enough information to definitively determine the copyright status of a particular work. In such cases, it is often necessary to rely on an "educated guess."

In some cases, it may be clear that the work remains under copyright, but the copyright owner cannot be identified. In other cases, the copyright owner is known but cannot be located. If the copyright owner is a company, for example, it may no longer be in business and no successor business can be identified. Similarly, an individual copyright owner may be deceased, and his or her heirs are not known or cannot be located. These works are sometimes referred to as "orphaned works."

As with other works that are known to be protected by copyright, in the case of orphaned works, reliance on one of the exceptions to copyright is the safest course to avoid a claim of copyright infringement. However, in certain circumstances, it may be that the risk of a copyright infringement claim is low enough that using the work without permission may be warranted. For example, if the copyright owner is a company that has been out of business for a long time and has no successor, the risk that the copyright owner will bring an infringement claim may be very low or non-existent. In such cases, a careful assessment of the risks and potential liabilities should be conducted, and consideration should be given to obtaining insurance coverage including protection against any copyright infringement claims. Although there is no "good faith" defense to copyright infringement, carefully documenting the research, analysis and reasoning behind the determination of the copyright status and attempts to locate copyright owners and obtain permission, is a good practice and may be helpful if a copyright owner later objects to your use.

CASES AND OTHER READINGS

Reading Note: The following case involves the copyright status of certain works created outside the United States. At issue is interpretation of a 1994 statute which amended the U.S. Copyright Act to clarify that such foreign works were entitled to the same term of copyright as U.S. works. As a result of this decision, the copyright in certain foreign works which had fallen into the public domain were restored.

GOLAN V. HOLDER

132 S.Ct. 873 (2012).

Justice GINSBURG delivered the opinion of the Court.

The Berne Convention for the Protection of Literary and Artistic Works (Berne Convention or Berne), which took effect in 1886, is the principal accord governing international copyright relations. Latecomer to the international copyright regime launched by Berne, the United States joined the Convention in 1989. To perfect U.S. implementation of Berne, and as part of our response to the Uruguay Round of multilateral trade negotiations, Congress, in 1994, gave works enjoying copyright protection abroad the same full term of protection available to U.S. works. Congress did so in § 514 of the Uruguay Round Agreements Act (URAA), which grants copyright protection to preexisting works of Berne member countries, protected in their country of origin, but lacking protection in the United States for any of three reasons: The United States did not protect works from the country of origin at the time of publication; the United States did not protect sound recordings fixed before 1972; or the author had failed to comply with U.S. statutory formalities (formalities Congress no longer requires as prerequisites to copyright protection).

The URAA accords no protection to a foreign work after its full copyright term has expired, causing it to fall into the public domain, whether under the laws of the country of origin or of this country. Works encompassed by § 514 are granted the protection they would have enjoyed had the United States maintained copyright relations with the author's country or removed formalities incompatible with Berne. Foreign authors, however, gain no credit for the protection they lacked in years prior to § 514's enactment. They therefore enjoy fewer total years of exclusivity than do their U.S. counterparts. As a consequence of the barriers to U.S. copyright protection prior to the enactment of § 514, foreign works "restored" to protection by the measure had entered the public domain in this country. To cushion the impact of their placement in protected status, Congress included in § 514 ameliorating accommodations for parties who had exploited affected works before the URAA was enacted.

Petitioners include orchestra conductors, musicians, publishers, and others who formerly enjoyed free access to works § 514 removed from the public domain. They maintain that the Constitution's Copyright and Patent Clause, Art. I, § 8, cl. 8, and First Amendment both decree the invalidity of § 514. Under those prescriptions of our highest law, petitioners assert, a work that has entered the public domain, for whatever reason, must forever remain there.

In accord with the judgment of the Tenth Circuit, we conclude that § 514 does not transgress constitutional limitations on Congress' authority. Neither the Copyright and Patent Clause nor the First Amendment, we hold, makes the public domain, in any and all cases, a territory that works may never exit.

I

A

Members of the Berne Union agree to treat authors from other member countries as well as they treat their own. Berne Convention, Sept. 9, 1886, as revised at Stockholm on July 14, 1967, Art. 1, 5(1), 828 U.N.T.S. 221, 225, 231-233. Nationals of a member country, as well as any author who publishes in one of Berne's 164 member states, thus enjoy copyright protection in nations across the globe. Art. 2(6), 3. Each country, moreover, must afford at least the minimum level of protection specified by Berne. The copyright term must span the author's lifetime, plus at least 50 additional years, whether or not the author has complied with a member state's legal formalities. Art. 5(2), 7(1). And, as relevant here, a work must be protected abroad unless its copyright term has expired in either the country where protection is claimed or the country of origin. Art. 18(1)-(2).[NOTE 2] A different system of transnational copyright protection long prevailed in this country. Until 1891, foreign works were categorically excluded from Copyright Act protection. Throughout most of the 20th century, the only eligible foreign authors were those whose countries granted reciprocal rights to U.S. authors and whose works were printed in the United States. See Act of Mar. 3, 1891, § 3, 13, 26 Stat. 1107, 1110; Patry, The United States and International Copyright Law, 40 Houston L.Rev. 749, 750 (2003).[NOTE 3] For domestic and foreign authors alike, protection hinged on compliance with notice, registration, and renewal formalities.

The United States became party to Berne's multilateral, formality-free copyright regime in 1989. Initially, Congress adopted a "minimalist approach" to compliance with the Convention. H.R.Rep. No. 100-609, p. 7 (1988) (hereinafter BCIA House Report). The Berne Convention Implementation Act of 1988 (BCIA), 102 Stat. 2853, made "only those changes to Ameri-

Dmitri Dmitriyevich Shostakovich, a Russian composer and pianist, is regarded as one of the major composers of the 20th century. He had a complex and difficult relationship with Stalin and the communist government of the Soviet Union. Copyright in Shostakovich's work, and those of many other well-known works which had been in the public domain, including Prokofief's Peter and the Wolf, *were restored by an act of Congress in 1994. Copyright restoration was upheld by the Supreme Court in* Golan v. Holder.

can copyright law that [were] clearly required under the treaty's provisions," BCIA House Report, at 7. Despite Berne's instruction that member countries—including "new accessions to the Union"—protect foreign works under copyright in the country of origin, Art. 18(1) and (4), 828 U.N.T.S., at 251, the BCIA accorded no protection for "any work that is in the public domain in the United States," § 12, 102 Stat. 2860. Protection of future foreign works, the BCIA indicated, satisfied Article 18. See § 2(3), 102 Stat. 2853 ("The amendments made by this Act, together with the law as it exists on the date of the enactment of this Act, satisfy the obligations of the United States in adhering to the Berne Convention...."). Congress indicated, however, that it had not definitively rejected "retroactive" protection for preexisting foreign works; instead it had punted on this issue of Berne's implementation, deferring consideration until "a more thorough examination of Constitutional, commercial, and consumer considerations is possible." BCIA House Report, at 51, 52.[NOTE 4]

The minimalist approach essayed by the United States did not sit well with other Berne members.[NOTE 5] While negotiations were ongoing over the North American Free Trade Agreement (NAFTA), Mexican authorities complained about the United States' refusal to grant protection, in accord with Article 18, to Mexican works that remained under copyright domestically. See Intellectual Property and International Issues, Hearings before the Subcommittee on Intellectual Property and Judicial Administration, House Committee on the Judiciary, 102d Cong., 1st Sess., 168 (1991) (statement of Ralph Oman, U.S. Register of Copyrights).[NOTE 6] The Register of Copyrights also reported "questions" from Turkey, Egypt, and Austria. *Ibid.* Thailand and Russia balked at protecting U.S. works, copyrighted here but in those countries' public domains, until the United States reciprocated with respect to their authors' works. URAA Joint Hearing 137 (statement of Ira S. Shapiro, General Counsel, Office of the U.S. Trade Representative (USTR)); *id.,* at 208 (statement of Professor Shira Perlmutter); *id.,* at 291 (statement of Jason S. Berman, Recording Industry Association of America (RIAA)).[NOTE 7] Berne, however, did not provide a potent enforcement mechanism. The Convention contemplates dispute resolution before the International Court of Justice. Art. 33(1). But it specifies no sanctions for noncompliance and allows parties, at any time, to declare themselves "not ... bound" by the Convention's dispute resolution provision. Art. 33(2)-(3) 828 U.N.T.S., at 277. Unsurprisingly, no enforcement actions were launched before 1994. D. Gervais, The TRIPS Agreement 213, and n.134 (3d ed.2008). Although "several Berne Union Members disagreed with [our] interpretation of Article 18," the USTR told Congress, the Berne Convention did "not provide a meaningful dispute resolution process." URAA Joint Hearing 137 (statement of Shapiro). This shortcoming left Congress "free to adopt a minimalist approach and evade Article 18." Karp, Final Report, Berne Article 18 Study on Retroactive United States Copyright Protection for Berne and other Works, 20 Colum.-VLA J.L. & Arts 157, 172 (1996).

The landscape changed in 1994. The Uruguay round of multilateral trade negotiations produced the World Trade Organization (WTO) and the Agreement on Trade-Related

Aspects of Intellectual Property Rights (TRIPS).[NOTE 8] The United States joined both. TRIPS mandates, on pain of WTO enforcement, implementation of Berne's first 21 articles. TRIPS, Art. 9.1, 33 I.L.M. 1197, 1201 (requiring adherence to all but the "moral rights" provisions of Article 6*bis*). The WTO gave teeth to the Convention's requirements: Noncompliance with a WTO ruling could subject member countries to tariffs or cross-sector retaliation. See Gervais, *supra,* at 213; 7 W. Patry, Copyright § 24:1, pp. 24-8 to 24-9 (2011). The specter of WTO enforcement proceedings bolstered the credibility of our trading partners' threats to challenge the United States for inadequate compliance with Article 18. See URAA Joint Hearing 137 (statement of Shapiro, USTR) ("It is likely that other WTO members would challenge the current U.S. implementation of Berne Article 18 under [WTO] procedures.").[NOTE 9]

Congress' response to the Uruguay agreements put to rest any questions concerning U.S. compliance with Article 18. Section 514 of the URAA, 108 Stat. 4976 (codified at 17 U.S.C. § 104A, 109(a)),[NOTE 10] extended copyright to works that garnered protection in their countries of origin,[NOTE 11] but had no right to exclusivity in the United States for any of three reasons: lack of copyright relations between the country of origin and the United States at the time of publication; lack of subject-matter protection for sound recordings fixed before 1972; and failure to comply with U.S. statutory formalities (*e.g.,* failure to provide notice of copyright status, or to register and renew a copyright). See § 104A(h)(6)(B)-(C).[NOTE 12]

Works that have fallen into the public domain after the expiration of a full copyright term—either in the United States or the country of origin—receive no further protection under § 514. *Ibid.*[NOTE 13] Copyrights "restored"[NOTE 14] under URAA § 514 "subsist for the remainder of the term of copyright that the work would have otherwise been granted ... if the work never entered the public domain." § 104A(a)(1)(B). Prospectively, restoration places foreign works on an equal footing with their U.S. counterparts; assuming a foreign and domestic author died the same day, their works will enter the public domain simultaneously. See § 302(a) (copyrights generally expire 70 years after the author's death). Restored works, however, receive no compensatory time for the period of exclusivity they would have enjoyed before § 514's enactment, had they been protected at the outset in the United States. Their total term, therefore, falls short of that available to similarly situated U.S. works.

The URAA's disturbance of the public domain hardly escaped Congress' attention. Section 514 imposed no liability for any use of foreign works occurring before restoration. In addition, anyone remained free to copy and use restored works for one year following § 514's enactment. See 17 U.S.C. § 104A(h)(2)(A). Concerns about § 514's compatibility with the Fifth Amendment's Takings Clause led Congress to include additional protections for "reliance parties"—those who had, before the URAA's enactment, used or acquired a foreign work then in the public domain. See § 104A(h)(3)-(4).[NOTE 15] Reliance parties may continue to exploit a restored work until the owner of the restored copyright gives notice of intent to enforce—either by filing with the U.S. Copyright Office within two years of restoration, or by actually notifying the reliance party. § 104A(c), (d)(2)(A)(i), and (B)(i). After that, reliance parties may continue to exploit existing copies for a grace period of one year. § 104A(d)(2)(A)(ii), and (B)(ii). Finally, anyone who, before the URAA's enactment, created a "derivative work" based on a restored work may indefinitely exploit the derivation upon payment to the copyright holder of "reasonable compensation," to be set by a district judge if the parties cannot agree. § 104A(d)(3).

B

In 2001, petitioners filed this lawsuit challenging § 514. They maintain that Congress, when it passed the URAA, exceeded its authority under the Copyright Clause and transgressed First Amendment limitations.[NOTE 16] The District Court granted the Attorney General's motion for summary judgment. *Golan v. Gonzales,* No. Civ. 01-B-1854, 2005 WL 914754 (D.Colo., Apr. 20, 2005). In rejecting petitioners' Copyright Clause argument, the court stated that Congress "has historically demonstrated little compunction about removing copyrightable materials from the public domain." *Id.,* at *14. The court next declined to part from "the settled rule that private censorship via copyright enforcement does not implicate First Amendment concerns." *Id.,* at *17.

The Court of Appeals for the Tenth Circuit affirmed in part. *Golan v. Gonzales,* 501 F.3d 1179 (2007). The public domain, it agreed, was not a "threshold that Congress" was powerless to "traverse in both directions." *Id.,* at 1187 (internal quotations marks omitted). But § 514, as the Court of Appeals read our decision in *Eldred v. Ashcroft,* 537 U.S. 186, 123 S.Ct. 769, 154 L.Ed.2d 683 (2003), required further First Amendment inspection, 501 F.3d, at 1187. The measure "'altered the traditional contours of copyright protection,'" the court said—specifically, the "bedrock principle" that once works enter the public domain, they do not leave. *Ibid.* (quoting *Eldred,* 537 U.S., at 221, 123 S.Ct. 769). The case was remanded with an instruction to the District Court to address the First Amendment claim in light of the Tenth Circuit's opinion.

On remand, the District Court's starting premise was uncontested: Section 514 does not regulate speech on the basis of its content; therefore the law would be upheld if "narrowly tailored to serve a significant government interest." 611 F.Supp.2d 1165, 1170-1171 (D.Colo.2009) (quoting *Ward v. Rock Against Racism,* 491 U.S. 781, 791, 109 S.Ct. 2746, 105 L.Ed.2d 661 (1989)). Summary judgment was due petitioners, the court concluded, because § 514's constriction of the public domain was not justified by any of the asserted federal interests: compliance with Berne, securing greater protection for U.S. authors abroad, or remediation of the inequitable treatment suffered by foreign authors whose works lacked protection in the United States. 611 F.Supp.2d, at 1172-1177.

The Tenth Circuit reversed. Deferring to Congress' predictive judgments in matters relating to foreign affairs, the appellate court held that § 514 survived First Amendment scrutiny. Specifically, the court determined that the law was narrowly tailored to fit the important government aim of protecting U.S. copyright holders' interests abroad. 609 F.3d 1076 (2010).

We granted certiorari to consider petitioners' challenge to § 514 under both the Copyright Clause and the First Amendment, 562 U.S. ___, 131 S.Ct. 1600, 179 L.Ed.2d 516 (2011), and now affirm.

II

We first address petitioners' argument that Congress lacked authority, under the Copyright Clause, to enact § 514. The Constitution states that "Congress shall have Power ... [t]o promote the Progress of Science ... by securing for limited Times to Authors ... the exclusive Right to their ... Writings." Art. I, § 8, cl. 8. Petitioners find in this grant of authority an impenetrable barrier to the extension of copyright protection to authors whose writings, for whatever reason, are in the public domain. We see no such barrier in the text of the Copyright Clause, historical practice, or our precedents.

A

The text of the Copyright Clause does not exclude application of copyright protection to works in the public domain. Symposium, Congressional Power and Limitations Inherent in the Copyright Clause, 30 Colum. J.L. & Arts 259, 266 (2007). Petitioners' contrary argument relies primarily on the Constitution's confinement of a copyright's lifespan to a "limited Tim[e]." "Removing works from the public domain," they contend, "violates the 'limited [t]imes' restriction by turning a fixed and predictable period into one that can be reset or resurrected at any time, even after it expires." Brief for Petitioners 22.

Our decision in *Eldred* is largely dispositive of petitioners' limited-time argument. There we addressed the question whether Congress violated the Copyright Clause when it extended, by 20 years, the terms of existing copyrights. 537 U.S., at 192-193, 123 S.Ct. 769 (upholding Copyright Term Extension Act (CTEA)). Ruling that Congress acted within constitutional bounds, we declined to infer from the text of the Copyright Clause "the command that a time prescription, once set, becomes forever 'fixed' or 'inalterable.'" *Id.,* at 199, 123 S.Ct. 769. "The word 'limited,'" we observed, "does not convey a meaning so constricted." *Ibid.* Rather, the term is best understood to mean "confine[d] within certain bounds," "restrain[ed]," or "circumscribed." *Ibid.* (internal quotation marks omitted). The construction petitioners tender closely resembles the definition rejected in *Eldred* and is similarly infirm.

The terms afforded works restored by § 514 are no less "limited" than those the CTEA lengthened. In light of *Eldred,* petitioners do not here contend that the term Congress has granted U.S. authors—their lifetimes, plus 70 years—is unlimited. See 17 U.S.C. § 302(a). Nor do petitioners explain why terms of the same duration, as applied to foreign works, are not equally "circumscribed" and "confined." See *Eldred,* 537 U.S., at 199, 123 S.Ct. 769. Indeed, as earlier noted, see *supra,* at 878, 882-883, the copyrights of restored foreign works typically last for fewer years than those of their domestic counterparts.

The difference, petitioners say, is that the limited time had already passed for works in the public domain. What was that limited term for foreign works once excluded from U.S. copyright protection? Exactly "zero," petitioners respond. Brief for Petitioners 22 (works in question "received a specific term of protection ... sometimes expressly set to zero"; "at the end of that period," they "entered the public domain"); Tr. of Oral Arg. 52 (by "refusing to provide any protection for a work," Congress "set[s] the term at zero," and thereby "tell[s] us when the end has come"). We find scant sense in this argument, for surely a "limited time" of exclusivity must begin before it may end.[NOTE 17]

Carried to its logical conclusion, petitioners persist, the Government's position would allow Congress to institute a second "limited" term after the first expires, a third after that, and so on. Thus, as long as Congress legislated in installments, perpetual copyright terms would be achievable. As in *Eldred,* the hypothetical legislative misbehavior petitioners posit is far afield from the case before us. See 537 U.S., at 198-200, 209-210, 123 S.Ct. 769. In aligning the United States with other nations bound by the Berne Convention, and thereby according equitable treatment to once disfavored foreign authors, Congress can hardly be charged with a design to move stealthily toward a regime of perpetual copyrights.

B

Historical practice corroborates our reading of the Copyright Clause to permit full U.S. compliance with Berne. Undoubtedly, federal copyright legislation generally has not affected works in the public domain. Section 514's disturbance of that domain, petitioners argue, distinguishes their suit from Eldred's. In adopting the CTEA, petitioners note, Congress acted in accord with "an unbroken congressional practice" of granting preexpiration term extensions, 537 U.S., at 200, 123 S.Ct. 769. No comparable practice, they maintain, supports § 514.

On occasion, however, Congress has seen fit to protect works once freely available. Notably, the Copyright Act of 1790 granted protection to many works previously in the public domain. Act of May 31, 1790 (1790 Act), § 1, 1 Stat. 124 (covering "any map, chart, book, or books already printed within these United States"). Before the Act launched a uniform national system, three States provided no statutory copyright protection at all.[NOTE 18] Of those that did afford some protection, seven failed to protect maps;[NOTE 19] eight did not cover previously published books;[NOTE 20] and all ten denied protection to works that failed to comply with formalities.[NOTE 21] The First Congress, it thus appears, did not view the public domain as inviolate. As we have recognized, the "construction placed upon the Constitution by [the drafters of] the first [copyright] act of 1790 and the act of 1802 ... men who were contemporary with [the Constitution's] formation, many of whom were members of the convention which framed it, is of itself entitled to very great weight." *Burrow-Giles Lithographic Co. v. Sarony,* 111 U.S. 53, 57, 4 S.Ct. 279, 28 L.Ed. 349 (1884).[NOTE 22]

Subsequent actions confirm that Congress has not understood the Copyright Clause to preclude protection for existing works. Several private bills restored the copyrights of works that previously had been in the public domain. See Act of Feb. 19, 1849 (Corson Act), ch. 57, 9 Stat. 763; Act of June 23, 1874 (Helmuth Act), ch. 534, 18 Stat. 618; Act of Feb. 17, 1898 (Jones Act), ch. 29, 30 Stat. 1396. These bills were unchallenged in court.

Analogous patent statutes, however, were upheld in litigation.[NOTE 23] In 1808, Congress passed a private bill restoring patent protection to Oliver Evans' flour mill. When Evans sued for infringement, first Chief Justice Marshall in the Circuit Court, *Evans v. Jordan,* 8 F.Cas. 872 (No. 4,564) (Va.1813), and then Justice Bushrod Washington for this Court, *Evans v. Jordan,* 9 Cranch 199, 3 L.Ed. 704 (1815), upheld the restored patent's validity. After the patent's expiration, the Court said, "a general right to use [Evans'] discovery was not so vested in the public" as to allow the defendant to continue using the machinery, which he had constructed between the patent's expiration and the bill's passage. *Id.,* at 202. See also *Blanchard v. Sprague,* 3 F.Cas. 648, 650 (No. 1,518) (C.C.D.Mass.1839) (Story, J.) ("I never have entertained any doubt of the constitutional authority of congress" to "give a patent for an invention, which ... was in public use and enjoyed by the community at the time of the passage of the act.").

This Court again upheld Congress' restoration of an invention to protected status in *McClurg v. Kingsland,* 1 How. 202, 11 Led. There we enforced an 1839 amendment that recognized a patent on an invention despite its prior use by the inventor's employer. Absent such dispensation, the employer's use would have rendered the invention unpatentable, and therefore open to exploitation without the inventor's leave. *Id.,* at 206-209.

Congress has also passed generally applicable legislation granting patents and copyrights to inventions and works that had lost protection. An 1832 statute authorized a new patent for any inventor whose failure, "by inadvertence, accident, or mistake," to comply with statutory formalities rendered the original patent "invalid or inoperative." Act of July 3, § 3, 4 Stat. 559. An 1893 measure similarly allowed authors who had not timely deposited their work to receive "all the rights and privileges" the Copyright Act affords, if they made the required deposit by March 1, 1893. Act of Mar. 3, ch. 215, 27 Stat. 743.[NOTE 24] And in 1919 and 1941, Congress authorized the President to issue proclamations granting protection to foreign works that had fallen into the public domain during World Wars I and II. See Act of Dec. 18, 1919, ch. 11, 41 Stat. 368; Act of Sept. 25, 1941, ch. 421, 55 Stat. 732.[NOTE 25]

Pointing to dictum in *Graham v. John Deere Co. of Kansas City,* 383 U.S. 1, 86 S.Ct. 684, 15 L.Ed.2d 545 (1966), petitioners would have us look past this history. In *Graham,* we stated that "Congress may not authorize the issuance of patents whose effects are to remove existent knowledge from the public domain, or to restrict free access to materials already available." *Id.,* at 6, 86 S.Ct. 684; *post,* at 907. But as we explained in *Eldred,* this passage did not speak to the constitutional limits on Congress' copyright and patent authority. Rather, it "addressed an invention's very eligibility for patent protection." 537 U.S., at 202, n. 7, 123 S.Ct. 769.

Installing a federal copyright system and ameliorating the interruptions of global war, it is true, presented Congress with extraordinary situations. Yet the TRIPS accord, leading the United States to comply in full measure with Berne, was also a signal event. See *supra,* at 880-881; cf. *Eldred,* 537 U.S., at 259, 264-265, 123 S.Ct. 769 (BREYER, J., dissenting) (acknowledging importance of international uniformity advanced by U.S. efforts to conform to the Berne Convention). Given the authority we hold Congress has, we will not second-guess the political choice Congress made between leaving the public domain untouched and embracing Berne unstintingly. Cf. *id.,* at 212-213, 123 S.Ct. 769.

C

Petitioners' ultimate argument as to the Copyright and Patent Clause concerns its initial words. Congress is empowered to "promote the Progress of Science and useful Arts" by enacting systems of copyright and patent protection. U.S. Const., Art. I, § 8, cl. 8. Perhaps counterintuitively for the contemporary reader, Congress' copyright authority is tied to the progress of science; its patent authority, to the progress of the useful arts. See *Graham,* 383 U.S., at 5, and n. 1, 86 S.Ct. 684; *Evans,* 8 F.Cas., at 873 (Marshall, J.).

The "Progress of Science," petitioners acknowledge, refers broadly to "the creation and spread of knowledge and learning." Brief for Petitioners 21; accord *post,* at 899-900. They nevertheless argue that federal legislation cannot serve the Clause's aim unless the legislation "spur[s] the creation of ... new works." Brief for Petitioners 24; accord *post,* at 899-900, 903, 908. Because § 514 deals solely with works already created, petitioners urge, it "provides no plausible incentive to create new works" and is therefore invalid. Reply Brief 4.[NOTE 26]

The creation of at least one new work, however, is not the sole way Congress may promote knowledge and learning. In *Eldred,* we rejected an argument nearly identical to the one petitioners rehearse. The *Eldred* petitioners urged that the "CTEA's extension of existing copyrights categorically fails to 'promote the Progress of Science,' ... because it does not stimulate the creation of new works." 537 U.S., at 211-212, 123 S.Ct. 769. In response to this argument, we held that the Copyright Clause does not demand that each copyright provision, examined discretely, operate to induce new works. Rather, we explained, the Clause "empowers Congress to determine the intellectual property regimes that, overall, in that body's judgment, will serve the ends of the Clause." *Id.,* at

222, 123 S.Ct. 769. And those permissible ends, we held, extended beyond the creation of new works. See *id.,* at 205-206, 123 S.Ct. 769. (rejecting the notion that "'the only way to promote the progress of science [is] to provide incentives to create new works'" (quoting Perlmutter, Participation in the International Copyright System as a Means to Promote the Progress of Science and Useful Arts, 36 Loyola (LA) L.Rev. 323, 332 (2002))). [NOTE 27]

Even were we writing on a clean slate, petitioners' argument would be unavailing. Nothing in the text of the Copyright Clause confines the "Progress of Science" exclusively to "incentives for creation." *Id.,* at 324, n. 5 (internal quotation marks omitted). Evidence from the founding, moreover, suggests that inducing *dissemination*—as opposed to creation—was viewed as an appropriate means to promote science. See Nachbar, Constructing Copyright's Mythology, 6 Green Bag 2d 37, 44 (2002) ("The scope of copyright protection existing at the time of the framing," trained as it was on "publication, not creation," "is inconsistent with claims that copyright must promote creative activity in order to be valid." (internal quotation marks omitted)). Until 1976, in fact, Congress made "federal copyright contingent on publication[,] [thereby] providing incentivesnot primarily for creation," but for dissemination. Perlmutter, *supra,* at 324, n. 5. Our decisions correspondingly recognize that "copyright supplies the economic incentive to create *and disseminate* ideas." *Harper & Row, Publishers, Inc. v. Nation Enterprises,* 471 U.S. 539, 558, 105 S.Ct. 2218, 85 L.Ed.2d 588 (1985) (emphasis added). See also *Eldred,* 537 U.S., at 206, 123 S.Ct. 769.[NOTE 28]

Considered against this backdrop, § 514 falls comfortably within Congress' authority under the Copyright Clause. Congress rationally could have concluded that adherence to Berne "promotes the diffusion of knowledge," Brief for Petitioners 4. A well-functioning international copyright system would likely encourage the dissemination of existing and future works. See URAA Joint Hearing 189 (statement of Professor Perlmutter). Full compliance with Berne, Congress had reason to believe, would expand the foreign markets available to U.S. authors and invigorate protection against piracy of U.S. works abroad, S.Rep. No. 103-412, pp. 224, 225 (1994); URAA Joint Hearing 291 (statement of Berman, RIAA); *id.,* at 244, 247 (statement of Smith, IIPA), thereby benefitting copyright-intensive industries stateside and inducing greater investment in the c reative process.

The provision of incentives for the creation of new works is surely an essential means to advance the spread of knowledge and learning. We hold, however, that it is not the sole means Congress may use "[t]o promote the Progress of Science." See Perlmutter, *supra,* at 332 (United States would "lose all flexibility" were the provision of incentives to create the exclusive way to promote the progress of science).[NOTE 29] Congress determined that exemplary adherence to Berne would serve the objectives of the Copyright Clause. We have no warrant to reject the rational judgment Congress made.

III

A

We next explain why the First Amendment does not inhibit the restoration authorized by § 514. To do so, we first recapitulate the relevant part of our pathmarking decision in *Eldred.* The petitioners in *Eldred,* like those here, argued that Congress had violated not only the "limited Times" prescription of the Copyright Clause. In addition, and independently, the *Eldred* petitioners charged, Congress had offended the First Amendment's freedom of expression guarantee. The CTEA's 20-year enlargement of a copyright's duration, we held in *Eldred,* offended neither provision.

Concerning the First Amendment, we recognized that some restriction on expression is the inherent and intended effect of every grant of copyright. Noting that the "Copyright Clause and the First Amendment were adopted close in time," 537 U.S., at 219, 123 S.Ct. 769, we observed that the Framers regarded copyright protection not simply as a limit on the manner in which expressive works may be used. They also saw copyright as an "engine of free expression[:] By establishing a marketable right to the use of one's expression, copyright supplies the economic incentive to create and disseminate ideas." *Ibid.* (quoting *Harper & Row,* 471 U.S., at 558, 105 S.Ct. 2218 (internal quotation marks omitted)); see *id.,* at 546, 105 S.Ct. 2218 ("rights conferred by copyright are designed to assure contributors to the store of knowledge a fair return for their labors").

We then described the "traditional contours" of copyright protection, i.e., the "idea/expression dichotomy" and the "fair use" defense.[NOTE 30] Both are recognized in our jurisprudence as "built-in First Amendment accommodations." *Eldred,* 537 U.S., at 219, 123 S.Ct. 769; see *Harper & Row,* 471 U.S., at 560, 105 S.Ct. 2218 (First Amendment protections are "embodied in the Copyright Act's distinction between copyrightable expression and uncopyrightable facts and ideas," and in the "latitude for scholarship and comment" safeguarded by the fair use defense).

The idea/expression dichotomy is codified at 17 U.S.C. § 102(b): "In no case does copyright protec[t] … any idea, procedure, process, system, method of operation, concept, principle, or discovery … described, explained, illustrated, or embodied in [the copyrighted] work." "Due to this [idea/expression] distinction, every idea, theory, and fact in a copyrighted work becomes instantly available for public exploitation at the moment of publication"; the author's expression alone gains copyright protection. *Eldred,* 537 U.S., at 219, 123 S.Ct. 769; see *Harper & Row,* 471 U.S., at 556, 105 S.Ct. 2218 ("idea/expression dichotomy strike[s] a definitional balance between the First Amendment and the Copyright Act by permitting free communication of facts while still protecting an author's expression" (internal quotation marks omitted)).

The second "traditional contour," the fair use defense, is codified at 17 U.S.C. § 107: "[T]he fair use of a copyrighted work, including such use by reproduction in copies …

for purposes such as criticism, comment, news reporting, teaching (including multiple copies for classroom use), scholarship, or research, is not an infringement of copyright." This limitation on exclusivity "allows the public to use not only facts and ideas contained in a copyrighted work, but also [the author's] expression itself in certain circumstances." *Eldred,* 537 U.S., at 219, 123 S.Ct. 769; see *id.,* at 220, 123 S.Ct. 769 ("fair use defense affords considerable latitude for scholarship and comment, ... even for parody" (internal quotation marks omitted)).

Given the "speech-protective purposes and safeguards" embraced by copyright law, see *id.,* at 219, 123 S.Ct. 769, we concluded in *Eldred* that there was no call for the heightened review petitioners sought in that case.[NOTE 31] We reach the same conclusion here. [NOTE 32] Section 514 leaves undisturbed the "idea/expression" distinction and the "fair use" defense. Moreover, Congress adopted measures to ease the transition from a national scheme to an international copyright regime: It deferred the date from which enforcement runs, and it cushioned the impact of restoration on "reliance parties" who exploited foreign works denied protection before § 514 took effect. See *supra,* at 882-883 (describing 17 U.S.C. § 104A(c), (d), and (h)). See also *Eldred,* 537 U.S., at 220, 123 S.Ct. 769 (describing supplemental allowances and exemptions available to certain users to mitigate the CTEA's impact).

B

Petitioners attempt to distinguish their challenge from the one turned away in *Eldred.* First Amendment interests of a higher order are at stake here, petitioners say, because they—unlike their counterparts in *Eldred*—enjoyed "vested rights" in works that had already entered the public domain. The limited rights they retain under copyright law's "built-in safeguards" are, in their view, no substitute for the unlimited use they enjoyed before § 514's enactment. Nor, petitioners urge, does § 514's "unprecedented" foray into the public domain possess the historical pedigree that supported the term extension at issue in *Eldred.* Brief for Petitioners 42-43.

However spun, these contentions depend on an argument we considered and rejected above, namely, that the Constitution renders the public domain largely untouchable by Congress. Petitioners here attempt to achieve under the banner of the First Amendment what they could not win under the Copyright Clause: On their view of the Copyright Clause, the public domain is inviolable; as they read the First Amendment, the public domain is policed through heightened judicial scrutiny of Congress' means and ends. As we have already shown, see *supra,* at 884-887, the text of the Copyright Clause and the historical record scarcely establish that "once a work enters the public domain," Congress cannot permit anyone—"not even the creator—[to] copyright it," 501 F.3d, at 1184. And nothing in the historical record, congressional practice, or our own jurisprudence warrants exceptional First Amendment solicitude for copyrighted works that were once in the public domain.[NOTE 33] Neither this challenge nor that raised in *Eldred,* we stress, allege Congress transgressed a generally applicable First Amendment prohibition; we are not faced, for example, with copyright protection that hinges on the author's viewpoint.

The Tenth Circuit's initial opinion determined that petitioners marshaled a stronger First Amendment challenge than did their predecessors in *Eldred,* who never "possessed unfettered access to any of the works at issue." 501 F.3d, at 1193. See also *id.,* at 1194 ("[O]nce the works at issue became free for anyone to copy, [petitioners] had vested First Amendment interests in the expressions, [thus] § 514's interference with [petitioners'] rights is subject to First Amendment scrutiny."). As petitioners put it in this Court, Congress impermissibly revoked their right to exploit foreign works that "belonged to them" once the works were in the public domain. Brief for Petitioners 44-45.

To copyright lawyers, the "vested rights" formulation might sound exactly backwards: Rights typically vest at the *outset* of copyright protection, in an author or rightholder. See, *e.g.,* 17 U.S.C. § 201(a) ("Copyright in a work protected... vests initially in the author...."). Once the term of protection ends, the works do not revest in any rightholder. Instead, the works simply lapse into the public domain. See, *e.g.,* Berne, Art. 18(1), 828 U.N.T.S., at 251 ("This Convention shall apply to all works which ... have not yet fallen into the public domain...."). Anyone has free access to the public domain, but no one, after the copyright term has expired, acquires ownership rights in the once-protected works.

Congress recurrently adjusts copyright law to protect categories of works once outside the law's compass. For example, Congress broke new ground when it extended copyright protection to foreign works in 1891, Act of Mar. 3, § 13, 26 Stat. 1110; to dramatic works in 1856, Act of Aug. 18, 11 Stat. 138; to photographs and photographic negatives in 1865, Act of Mar. 3, § 1, 13 Stat. 540; to motion pictures in 1912, Act of Aug. 24, 37 Stat. 488; to fixed sound recordings in 1972, Act of Oct. 15, 1971, 85 Stat. 391; and to architectural works in 1990, Architectural Works Copyright Protection Act, 104 Stat. 5133. And on several occasions, as recounted above, Congress protected works previously in the public domain, hence freely usable by the public. See *supra,* at 885-887. If Congress could grant protection to these works without hazarding heightened First Amendment scrutiny, then what free speech principle disarms it from protecting works prematurely cast into the public domain for reasons antithetical to the Berne Convention?[NOTE 34]

Section 514, we add, does not impose a blanket prohibition on public access. Petitioners protest that fair use and the idea/expression dichotomy "are plainly inadequate to protect the speech and expression rights that Section 514 took from petitioners, or ... the public"—that is, "the unrestricted right to perform, copy, teach and distribute the *entire* work, for any reason." Brief for Petitioners 46-47. "Playing a few bars of a Shostakovich symphony," petitioners observe, "is no substitute for performing the entire work." *Id.,* at 47.[NOTE 35] But Congress has not put petitioners in this bind. The question here, as in *Eldred,* is whether would-be users must pay for their desired use of the author's expression, or else limit their exploitation to "fair use" of that work. Prokofiev's *Peter and the Wolf* could once be performed free of charge; after § 514 the right to perform it must be obtained in the marketplace. This is the same marketplace, of course, that exists for the music of Prokofiev's U.S. contemporaries: works of Copland and Bernstein, for example, that enjoy copyright protection, but nevertheless appear regularly in the programs of U.S. concertgoers.

Before we joined Berne, domestic works and some foreign works were protected under U.S. statutes and bilateral international agreements, while other foreign works were available at an artificially low (because royalty-free) cost. By fully implementing Berne, Congress ensured that most works, whether foreign or domestic, would be governed by the same legal regime. The phenomenon to which Congress responded is not new: Distortions of the same order occurred with greater frequency—and to the detriment of both foreign and domestic authors—when, before 1891, foreign works were excluded entirely from U.S. copyright protection. See Kampelman, The United States and International Copyright, 41 Am. J. Int'l L. 406, 413 (1947) ("American readers were less inclined to read the novels of Cooper or Hawthorne for a dollar when they could buy a novel of Scott or Dickens for a quarter."). Section 514 continued the trend toward a harmonized copyright regime by placing foreign works in the position they would have occupied if the current regime had been in effect when those works were created and first published. Authors once deprived of protection are spared the continuing effects of that initial deprivation; § 514 gives them nothing more than the benefit of their labors during whatever time remains before the normal copyright term expires.[NOTE 36]

Unlike petitioners, the dissent makes much of the so-called "orphan works" problem. See *post,* at 904-907, 911-912. We readily acknowledge the difficulties would-be users of copyrightable materials may face in identifying or locating copyright owners. See generally U.S. Copyright Office, Report on Orphan Works 21-40 (2006). But as the dissent concedes, see *post,* at 906, this difficulty is hardly peculiar to works restored under § 514. It similarly afflicts, for instance, U.S. libraries that attempt to catalogue U.S. books. See *post,* at 905. See also Brief for American Library Association et al. as *Amici Curiae* 22 (Section 514 "exacerbated," but did not create, the problem of orphan works); U.S. Copyright Office, *supra,* at 41-44 (tracing orphan-works problem to Congress' elimination of formalities, commencing with the 1976 Copyright Act).[NOTE 37] Nor is this a matter appropriate for judicial, as opposed to legislative, resolution. Cf. *Authors Guild v. Google, Inc.,* 770 F.Supp.2d 666, 677-678 (S.D.N.Y.2011) (rejecting proposed "Google Books" class settlement because, *inter alia,* "the establishment of a mechanism for exploiting unclaimed books is a matter more suited for Congress than this Court" (citing *Eldred,* 537 U.S., at 212, 123 S.Ct. 769)). Indeed, the host of policy and logistical questions identified by the dissent speak for themselves. *Post,* at 905. Despite "longstanding efforts," see *Authors Guild,* 770 F.Supp.2d, at 678 (quoting statement of Marybeth Peters), Congress has not yet passed ameliorative orphan-works legislation of the sort enacted by other Berne members, see, *e.g.,* Canada Copyright Act, R.S.C., 1985, c. C-42, § 77 (authorizing Copyright Board to license use of orphan works by persons unable, after making reasonable efforts, to locate the copyright owner). Heretofore, no one has suggested that the orphan-works issue should be addressed through our implementation of Berne, rather than through overarching legislation of the sort proposed in Congress and cited by the dissent. See *post,* at 911-912; U.S. Copyright Office, Legal Issues in Mass Digitization 25-29 (2011) (discussing recent legislative efforts). Our unstinting adherence to Berne may add impetus to calls for the enactment of such legislation. But resistance to Berne's prescriptions surely is not a necessary or proper response to the pervasive question, what should Congress do about orphan works.

IV

Congress determined that U.S. interests were best served by our full participation in the dominant system of international copyright protection. Those interests include ensuring exemplary compliance with our international obligations, securing greater protection for U.S. authors abroad, and remedying unequal treatment of foreign authors. The judgment § 514 expresses lies well within the ken of the political branches. It is our obligation, of course, to determine whether the action Congress took, wise or not, encounters any constitutional shoal. For the reasons stated, we are satisfied it does not.

The judgment of the Court of Appeals for the Tenth Circuit is therefore *Affirmed.*

Justice KAGAN took no part in the consideration or decision of this case.

APPENDIX (Text of Title 17 U.S.C. § 104A OMITTED)

Justice BREYER, with whom Justice ALITO joins, dissenting.

In order "[t]o promote the Progress of Science" (by which term the Founders meant "learning" or "knowledge"), the Constitution's Copyright Clause grants Congress the power to "secur[e] for limited Times to Authors ... the exclusive Right to their ... Writings." Art. I, § 8, cl. 8. This "exclusive Right" allows its holder to charge a fee to those who wish to use a copyrighted work, and the ability to charge that fee encourages the production of new material. In this sense, a copyright is, in Macaulay's words, a "tax on readers for the purpose of giving a bounty to writers"—a bounty designed to encourage new production. As the Court said in *Eldred,* "'[t]he economic philosophy behind the [Copyright] [C]lause ... is the conviction that encouragement of individual effort by personal gain is the best way to advance public welfare through the talents of authors and inventors.'" *Eldred v. Ashcroft,* 537 U.S. 186, 212, n. 18, 123 S.Ct. 769, 154 L.Ed.2d 683 (2003) (quoting *Mazer v. Stein,* 347 U.S. 201, 219, 74 S.Ct. 460, 98 L.Ed. 630 (1954)). See T. Macaulay, Speeches on Copyright 25 (E. Miller ed.1913); E. Walterscheid, The Nature of the Intellectual Property Clause: A Study in Historical Perspective 125-126 (2002) (hereinafter Walterscheid).

The statute before us, however, does not encourage anyone to produce a single new work. By definition, it bestows monetary rewards only on owners of old works—works that have already been created and already are in the American public domain. At the same time, the statute inhibits the dissemination of those works, foreign works published abroad after 1923, of which there are many millions, including films, works of art, innumerable photographs, and, of course, books—books that (in the absence of the statute) would assume their rightful places in computer-accessible databases, spreading knowledge throughout the world. See *infra,* at 904-906. In my view, the Copyright Clause does not authorize Congress to enact this statute. And I consequently dissent.

I

The possibility of eliciting new production is, and always has been, an essential precondition for American copyright protection. The Constitution's words, "exclusive Right," "limited Times," "Progress of Science," viewed through the lens of history underscore the legal significance of what the Court in *Eldred* referred to as the "economic philosophy behind the Copyright Clause." 537 U.S., at 212, n. 18, 123 S.Ct. 769 (brackets omitted). That philosophy understands copyright's grants of limited monopoly privileges to authors as private benefits that are conferred for a public reason—to elicit new creation.

Yet, as the Founders recognized, monopoly is a two-edged sword. On the one hand, it can encourage production of new works. In the absence of copyright protection, anyone might freely copy the products of an author's creative labor, appropriating the benefits without incurring the nonrepeatable costs of creation, thereby deterring authors from exerting themselves in the first place. On the other hand, copyright tends to restrict the dissemination (and use) of works once produced either because the absence of competition translates directly into higher consumer prices or because the need to secure copying permission sometimes imposes administrative costs that make it difficult for potential users of a copyrighted work to find its owner and strike a bargain. See W. Landes & R. Posner, The Economic Structure of Intellectual Property Law 68-70, 213-214 (2003). Consequently, the original British copyright statute, the Constitution's Framers, and our case law all have recognized copyright's resulting and necessary call for balance.

At the time the Framers wrote the Constitution, they were well aware of Britain's 18th-century copyright statute, the Statute of Anne, 8 Anne, ch. 19 (1710), and they were aware of the legal struggles that produced it. That statute sought in part to control, and to limit, preexisting monopolies that had emerged in the book trade as a result of the Crown's having previously granted special privileges to royal favorites. The Crown, for example, had chartered the Stationers' Company, permitting it to regulate and to censor works on the government's behalf. The Stationers had thereby acquired control over the disposition of copies of published works, from which emerged the Stationers' copyright—a right conferred on company members, not authors, that was deemed to exist in perpetuity. See L. Patterson, Copyright in Historical Perspective 1-16, 114-150 (1968) (hereinafter Patterson); Walterscheid 59-65; Gómez-Arostegui, The Untold Story of the First Copyright Suit Under the Statute of Anne in 1710, 25 Berkeley Tech. L.J. 1247, 1250-1256 (2010).

To prevent the continuation of the booksellers' monopoly and to encourage authors to write new books, Parliament enacted the Statute of Anne. It bore the title: "An Act for the Encouragement of Learning, by vesting the Copies of printed Books in the Authors or Purchasers of such Copies, during the Times therein mentioned." And it granted authors (not publishers) and their assignees the "sole Right and Liberty of printing" their works for limited periods of time *in order to encourage them "to compose and write useful Books."* 8 Anne, ch. 19, § 1 (emphasis added). As one historian has put it, "[t]he central plank of the . . . Act was . . . a cultural *quid pro quo.* To encourage 'learned Men to compose and write useful Books' the state would provide a guaranteed, if temporally limited, right to print and reprint those works." Deazley, The Myth of Copyright at Common Law, 62 Camb. L.J. 106, 108 (2003). At first, in their attempts to minimize their losses, the booksellers argued that authors had a perpetual common-law copyright in their works deriving from their natural rights as creators. But the House of Lords ultimately held in *Donaldson v. Beckett,* 1 Eng. Rep. 837 (1774), that the Statute of Anne had transformed any such perpetual common-law copyright into a copyright of a limited term designed to serve the public interest. Patterson 15-16, 153, 158-179; Deazley, *supra,* at 114-126.

Many early colonial copyright statutes, patterned after the Statute of Anne, also stated that copyright's objective was to encourage authors to produce new works and thereby improve learning. See U.S. Copyright Office, Copyright Enactments, Bulletin No. 3, pp. 1, 6, 10, 11, 17, 19 (rev.1963) (statutes of Connecticut, New Jersey, Pennsylvania, South Carolina, Georgia, and New York); Walterscheid 74-75; Bracha, The Adventures of the Statute of Anne in the Land of Unlimited Possibilities: The Life of a Legal Transplant, 25 Berkeley Tech. L.J. 1427, 1444-1450 (2010).

At least, that was the predominant view expressed to, or by, the Founders. Patterson 93. Thomas Jefferson, for example, initially expressed great uncertainty as to whether the Constitution should authorize the grant of copyrights and patents at all, writing that "the benefit even of limited monopolies is too doubtful" to warrant anything other than their "suppression." Letter from Thomas Jefferson to James Madison (July 31, 1788), in 13 Papers of Thomas Jefferson 440, 443 (J. Boyd ed.1956). James Madison also thought that "Monopolies . . . are justly classed among the greatest nu[i]sances in Government." Letter from James Madison to Thomas Jefferson (Oct. 17, 1788), in 14 *id.,* at 16, 21 (J. Boyd ed.1958). But he argued that "in certain cases" such as copyright, monopolies should "be granted" ("with caution, and guarded with strictness against abuse") to serve as "*compensation for a benefit actually gained to the community* . . . which the owner might otherwise withhold from public use." Monopolies. Perpetuities. Corporations. Ecclesiastical Endowments. in J. Madison, Writings 756 (J. Rakove ed.1999) (emphasis added). Jefferson eventually came to agree with Madison, supporting a limited conferral of monopoly rights but only "*as an encouragement to men to pursue ideas which may produce utility.*" Letter from Thomas Jefferson to Isaac McPherson (Aug. 13, 1813), in 6 Papers of Thomas Jefferson, at 379, 383 (J. Looney ed.2009) (emphasis added). This utilitarian view of copyrights and patents, embraced by Jefferson and Madison, stands in contrast to the "natural rights" view underlying much of continental European copyright law—a view that the English booksellers promoted in an effort to limit their losses following the enactment of the Statute of Anne and that in part motivated the enactment of some of the colonial statutes. Patterson 158-179, 183-192. Premised on the idea that an author or inventor has an inherent right to the fruits of his labor, it mythically stems from a legendary 6th-century statement of King Diarmed "'to every cow her calf, and accordingly to every book its copy.'" A. Birrell, Seven Lectures on the Law and History of Copyright in Books 42 (1899). That view, though perhaps reflected in the Court's opinion, *ante,* at 893, runs contrary to the more utilitarian views that influenced the writing of our own Constitution's Copyright Clause. See S. Ricketson, The Berne Convention for the Protection of Literary and Artistic Works: 1886-1986, pp. 5-6 (1987) (The first French copyright laws "placed authors' rights on a more elevated basis than the Act of Anne had done," on the understanding that they were "simply according formal recognition to what was already inherent in the 'very nature of things'"); S. Stewart, International Copyright and Neighbouring Rights 6-7 (2d ed.1989) (describing the European system of *droit d'auteur*).

This utilitarian understanding of the Copyright Clause has long been reflected in the Court's case law. In *Mazer,* for example, the Court refers to copyright as embodying the view that "*encouragement of individual effort by personal gain* is the best way to advance public welfare through the talents of authors and inventors." 347 U.S., at 219, 74 S.Ct. 460 (emphasis added). In *Twentieth Century Music Corp. v. Aiken,* 422 U.S. 151, 95 S.Ct. 2040, 45 L.Ed.2d 84 (1975), the Court says that underlying copyright is the understanding that "*[c]reative work is to be encouraged and rewarded, but private motivation must ultimately serve the cause of promoting broad public availability of literature, music, and the other arts.*" *Id.,* at 156, 95 S.Ct. 2040 (emphasis added). And in *Sony Corp. of America v. Universal City Studios, Inc.,* 464 U.S. 417, 104 S.Ct. 774, 78 L.Ed.2d 574 (1984), the Court, speaking of both copyrights and patents, points out that the "monopoly privileges that Congress may authorize are. . . [not] primarily designed to provide a special private benefit. Rather, the limited grant is a means by which an important public purpose may be achieved. It is intended *to motivate the creative activity of authors . . . by the provision of a special reward.*" *Id.,* at 429, 104 S.Ct. 774 (emphasis added); see also, *e.g., Graham v. John Deere Co. of Kansas City,* 383 U.S. 1, 6, 86 S.Ct. 684, 15 L.Ed.2d 545 (1966) (The "constitutional command . . . '[to] promote the Progress [of Science]' . . . is the *standard* expressed in the Constitution and it may not be ignored"); *Fox Film Corp. v. Doyal,* 286 U.S. 123, 127, 52 S.Ct. 546, 76 L.Ed. 1010 (1932) ("The sole interest of the United States . . . lie[s] in the general benefits derived by the public from the labors of authors"). Congress has expressed similar views in congressional Reports on copyright legislation. Thus, for example, an 1892 House Report states:

> "The object to be attained and the reason for the constitutional grant of power are imbedded in the grant itself. They are 'to promote the progress of science and the useful arts.' . . . [The Clause says] nothing . . . about any desire or purpose to secure to the author or inventor his 'natural right to his property.'"

H.R.Rep. No. 1494, 52d Cong., 1st Sess., 2. Similarly, the congressional authors of the landmark 1909 Copyright Act wrote:

> "The Constitution . . . provides that Congress shall have the power to grant [copyrights] . . . [n]ot primarily for the benefit of the author, . . . but because the policy is believed to be for the benefit of the great body of people, *in that it will stimulate writing and invention,* to give some bonus to authors and inventors."

H.R.Rep. No. 2222, 60th Cong., 2d Sess., 7 (1909). And they went on to say:

> "Congress must consider . . . two questions: First, how much will the legislation stimulate the producer and so benefit the public; and, second, how much will the monopoly granted be detrimental to the public? The granting of such exclusive rights, under the proper terms and conditions, confers a benefit upon the public that outweighs the evils of the temporary monopoly."

Ibid. The upshot is that text, history, and precedent demonstrate that the Copyright Clause places great value on the power of copyright to elicit new production. Congress in particular cases may determine that copyright's ability to do so outweighs any concomitant high prices, administrative costs, and restrictions on dissemination. And when it does so, we must respect its judgment. See *Eldred,* 537 U.S., at 222, 123 S.Ct. 769. But does the Clause empower Congress to enact a statute that withdraws works from the public domain, brings about higher prices and costs, and in doing so seriously restricts dissemination, particularly to those who need it for scholarly, educational, or cultural purposes—all *without providing any additional incentive* for the production of new material? That is the question before us. And, as I have said, I believe the answer is no. Congress in this statute has exceeded what are, under any plausible reading of the Copyright Clause, its permissible limits.

II

The Act before us says that it "restores" American copyright to a set of works, which, for the most part, did not previously enjoy American copyright protection. These works had fallen into America's public domain, but as of the "restoration" date, they had not yet fallen into the public domain of the foreign country where they originated.

The statute covers works originating almost anywhere outside the United States. See 17 U.S.C. § 104A(h)(3) (setting out eligibility criteria); U.S. Copyright Office, Circular No. 38A: International Copyright Relations of the United States (2010). The relevant set of works consists primarily of works originating abroad that did not obtain, or at some point lost, American copyright protection because (1) the author failed to comply with applicable American copyright formalities (such as notice or renewal), or (2) the nation in which they were first published then lacked copyright relations with the United States, or (3) they are sound recordings fixed before February 15, 1972. § 104A(h)(6)(C). A work must also satisfy other technical requirements: It must have had a rightholder who was a national or resident of an eligible country on the day it was created; and it cannot have been published in the United States within 30 days of its first publication. § 104A(h)(6)(D). The Act grants these works a copyright that expires at the time it would have expired had the author obtained a full American copyright term starting from the date on which the work was first published (in the foreign country). § 104A(a)(1)(B).

The Act mainly applies to works first published abroad between 1923 and 1989. It does not apply significantly to earlier works because any work published before 1921 would have fallen into the public domain before 1977 had it received a full American copyright term, while works published between 1921 and 1923 obtained a "restored" copyright that expired before the 1998 Sonny Bono Copyright Term Extension Act, and so could have lasted two years at most. See Tit. I, § 101, 90 Stat. 2574 (extending the copyright term of works still under copyright in 1977 to 75 years); 17 U.S.C. § 304(b) (extending the copyright term of works still under copyright in 1998 to 95 years). It has less impact on more recent works because in 1989 the United States became a Berne member, abolished the copyright notice requirement, and thenceforth provided prospective copyright protection throughout the Berne Union. See R. Schechter & J. Thomas, Intellectual Property: The Law of Copyrights, Patents and Trademarks 75-77 (2003); § 7, 102 Stat. 2857-2858 (codified as amended at 17 U.S.C. §§ 401-406).

Despite these temporal limitations, the Act covers vast numbers of works. The first category includes works published in countries that had copyright relations with the United States during this time period, such as most of Western Europe and Latin America, Australia, and Japan, see Circular No. 38A, *supra,* at 878-883, whose authors did not satisfy American copyright formalities, perhaps because the author, who may not have sought an American copyright, published the book abroad without proper American notice, or perhaps because the author obtained a valid American copyright but failed to renew it.

The second category (works that entered the public domain due to a lack of copyright relations) includes, among others, all works published in Russia and other countries of the former Soviet Union before May 1973 (when the U.S.S.R. joined the Universal Copyright Convention (UCC)), all works published in the People's Republic of China before March 1992 (when bilateral copyright relations between the People's Republic and the United States were first established), all South Korean works published before October 1987 (when South Korea joined the UCC), and all Egyptian and Turkish works published before March 1989 (when the United States joined Berne). See *id.,* at 878-883, and 883, nn. 2, 5, 6.

The third category covers all sound recordings from eligible foreign countries published after February 15, 1972. The practical significance of federal copyright restoration to this category of works is less clear, since these works received, and continued to receive, copyright protection under state law. See 17 U.S.C. § 301(c).

Apparently there are no precise figures about the number of works the Act affects, but in 1996 the then-Register of Copyrights, Marybeth Peters, thought that they "probably number in the millions." The Year in Review: Accomplishments and Objectives of the U.S. Copyright Office, 7 Ford. Intellectual Property Media & Entertainment L.J. 25, 31 (1996).

A

The provision before us takes works from the public domain, at least as of January 1, 1996. See § 104A(h)(2)(A) (setting "restoration" dates). It then restricts the dissemination of those works in two ways.

First, "restored copyright" holders can now charge fees for works that consumers previously used for free. The price of a score of Shostakovich's Preludes and Fugues Op. 87, for example, has risen by a multiple of seven. Brief for Conductors Guild et al. as *Amici Curiae* 11. And, as the Court recognizes, an orchestra that once could perform "*Peter and the Wolf*. . . free of charge" will now have to buy the "right to perform it . . . in the marketplace." *Ante,* at 893. But for the case of certain "derivative" works, § 104A(d)(3), the "restored copyright" holder, like other copyright holders, can charge what the market will bear. If a school orchestra or other nonprofit organization cannot afford the new charges, so be it. They will have to do without—aggravating the already serious problem of cultural education in the United States. See Brief for Conductors Guild et al. as *Amici Curiae* 4-5, 7-8 (describing the inability of many orchestras to pay for the rental of sheet music covered by "restored copyright[s]").

Second, and at least as important, the statute creates administrative costs, such as the costs of determining whether a work is the subject of a "restored copyright," searching for a "restored copyright" holder, and negotiating a fee. Congress has tried to ease the administrative burden of contacting copyright holders and negotiating prices for those whom the statute calls "reliance part[ies]," namely those who previously had used such works when they were freely available in the public domain. § 104A(h)(4). But Congress has done nothing to ease the administrative burden of securing permission from copyright owners that is placed upon those who want to use a work that they did not previously use, and this is a particular problem when it comes to "orphan works"—older and more obscure works with minimal commercial value that have copyright owners who are difficult or impossible to track down. Unusually high administrative costs threaten to limit severely the distribution and use of those works—works which, despite their characteristic lack of economic value, can prove culturally invaluable.

There are millions of such works. For example, according to European Union figures, there are 13 million orphan books in the European Union (13% of the total number of books in-copyright there), 225,000 orphan films in European film archives, and 17 million orphan photographs in United Kingdom museums. A. Vuopala, Assessment of the Orphan works issue and Costs for Rights Clearance 19, 25 (2010), online at http://ec.europa.eu/information_ society/activities/digital_libraries/doc/ reports_orphan/anna_ report.pdf (all Internet materials as visited Jan. 13, 2012, and available in Clerk of Court's case file). How is a university, a film collector, a musician, a database compiler, or a scholar now to obtain permission to use any such lesser known foreign work previously in the American public domain? Consider the questions that any such individual, group, or institution usually must answer: Is the work eligible for restoration under the statute? If so, who now holds the copyright—the author? an heir? a publisher? an association? a long-lost cousin? Whom must we contact? What is the address? Suppose no one answers? How do we conduct a negotiation?

To find answers to these, and similar questions, costs money. The cost to the University of Michigan and the Institute of Museum and Library Services, for example, to determine the copyright status of books contained in the HathiTrust Digital Library that were published in the United States from 1923 to 1963 will exceed $1 million. Brief for American Library Assn. et al. as *Amici Curiae* 15.

It is consequently not surprising to learn that the Los Angeles Public Library has been unable to make its collection of Mexican folk music publicly available because of problems locating copyright owners, that a Jewish cultural organization has abandoned similar efforts to make available Jewish cultural music and other materials, or that film preservers, museums, universities, scholars, database compilers, and others report that the administrative costs associated with trying to locate foreign copyright owners have forced them to curtail their cultural, scholarly, or other work-preserving efforts. See, e.g., Comments of the Library Copyright Alliance in Response to the U.S. Copyright Office's Inquiry on Orphan Works 5 (Mar. 25, 2005), online at http://www.arl.org/bm~doc/1 cacomment0305.pdf; Comments of Creative Commons and Save The Music in Response to the U.S. Copyright Office's Inquiry on Orphan Works (Mar. 25, 2005), online at http:// www.copyright.gov/orphan/ comments/OW0643-STM-Creative Commons.pdf; General Agreement on Tariffs and Trade (GATT): Intellectual Property Provisions, Joint Hearing before the Subcommittee on Intellectual Property and Judicial Administration of the House Committee on the Judiciary and the Subcommittee on Patents, Copyrights and Trademarks of the Senate Committee on the Judiciary, 103d Cong., 2d Sess., 131, 273 (1994) (hereinafter Joint Hearing) (statement of Larry Urbanski, Chairman of the Fairness in Copyright Coalition and President of Moviecraft, Inc.); Brief for American Library Assn. et al. as *Amici Curiae* 6-23; Brief for Creative Commons Corp. as *Amicus Curiae* 7-8; Brief for Project Petrucci, LLC, as *Amicus Curiae* 10-11.

These high administrative costs can prove counterproductive in another way. They will tempt some potential users to "steal" or "pirate" works rather than do without. And piracy often begets piracy, breeding the destructive habit of taking copyrighted works without paying for them, even where payment is possible. Such habits ignore the critical role copyright plays in the creation of new works, while reflecting a false belief that new creation appears by magic without thought or hope of compensation.

B

I recognize that ordinary copyright protection also comes accompanied with dissemination-restricting royalty charges and administrative costs. But here the restrictions work special harm. For one thing, the foreign location of restored works means higher than ordinary administrative costs. For another, the statute's technical requirements make it very difficult to establish whether a work has had its copyright restored by the statute. Gard, In the Trenches with § 104A: An Evaluation of the Parties' Arguments in *Golan v. Holder* as It Heads to the Supreme Court, 64 Vand. L.Rev. En Banc 199, 216-220 (2011) (describing difficulties encountered in compiling the information necessary to create an online tool to determine whether the statute applies in any given case).

Worst of all, "restored copyright" protection removes material from the public domain. In doing so, it reverses the payment expectations of those who used, or intended to use, works that they thought belonged to them. Were Congress to act similarly with respect to well-established property rights, the problem would be obvious. This statute analogously restricts, and thereby diminishes, Americans' preexisting freedom to use formerly public domain material in their expressive activities.

Thus, while the majority correctly observes that the dissemination-restricting harms of copyright normally present problems appropriate for legislation to resolve, *ante,* at 893-894, the question is whether the Copyright Clause permits Congress seriously to exacerbate such a problem by taking works out of the public domain without a countervailing benefit. This question *is* appropriate for judicial resolution. Indeed, unlike *Eldred* where the Court had to decide a complicated line-drawing question—when is a copyright term too long?—here an easily administrable standard is available—a standard that would require works that have already fallen into the public domain to stay there. The several, just mentioned features of the present statute are important, for they distinguish it from other copyright laws. By removing material from the public domain, the statute, in literal terms, "abridges" a preexisting freedom to speak. In practical terms, members of the public might well have decided what to say, as well as when and how to say it, in part by reviewing with a view to repeating, expression that they reasonably believed was, or would be, freely available. Given these speech implications, it is not surprising that Congress has long sought to protect public domain material when revising the copyright laws. See *infra,* at 909 (listing instances). And this Court has assumed the particular importance of public domain material in roughly analogous circumstances. See *Graham,* 383 U.S., at 6, 86 S.Ct. 684 ("Congress may not authorize the issuance of patents whose effects are to remove existent knowledge from the public domain"); *Kewanee Oil Co. v. Bicron Corp.,* 416 U.S. 470, 484, 94 S.Ct. 1879, 40 L.Ed.2d 315 (1974) (trade secret protection is not incompatible with "policy that matter once in the public domain must remain in the public domain"); *Cox Broadcasting Corp. v. Cohn,* 420 U.S. 469, 496, 95 S.Ct. 1029, 43 L.Ed.2d 328 (1975) (First Amendment prohibits sanctioning press for publishing material disclosed in public court documents); see also *Dastar Corp. v. Twentieth Century Fox*

Film Corp., 539 U.S. 23, 33, 123 S.Ct. 2041, 156 L.Ed.2d 18 (2003) ("The right to copy . . . once a copyright has expired . . . passes to the public" (internal quotation marks omitted)).

Moreover, whereas forward-looking copyright laws tend to benefit those whose identities are not yet known (the writer who has not yet written a book, the musician who has not yet composed a song), when a copyright law is primarily backward looking the risk is greater that Congress is trying to help known beneficiaries at the expense of badly organized unknown users who find it difficult to argue and present their case to Congress. In *Eldred,* I thought this problem was severe. See generally 537 U.S., at 243-266, 123 S.Ct. 769 (dissenting opinion). And in light of the fact that Congress, with one minor exception, heard testimony only from the representatives of existing copyright holders, who hoped that passage of the statute would enable them to benefit from reciprocal treatment of American authors abroad, *infra,* at 910, I cannot say that even here the problem, while much diminished, was nonexistent.

I agree with the majority that, in doing so, this statute does not discriminate among speakers based on their viewpoints or subject matter. *Ante,* at 891-892. But such considerations do not exhaust potential First Amendment problems. Cf. *Sorrell v. IMS Health Inc.*, 564 U.S. ___, ___, 131 S.Ct. 2653, 2663, 180 L.Ed.2d 544 (2011) (finding First Amendment problem in statute that prohibits drug manufacturers from using publicly available prescriber-identifying information in their marketing efforts in part because it "disfavor[ed] specific speakers"); *Turner Broadcasting System, Inc. v. FCC,* 512 U.S. 622, 659, 114 S.Ct. 2445, 129 L.Ed.2d 497 (1994) ("Regulations that discriminate among media, or among different speakers within a single medium, often present serious First Amendment concerns").

Taken together, these speech-related harms (e.g., restricting use of previously available material; reversing payment expectations; rewarding rent-seekers at the public's expense) at least show the presence of a First Amendment interest. And that is enough. For present purposes, I need not decide whether the harms to that interest show a violation of the First Amendment. I need only point to the importance of interpreting the Constitution as a single document—a document that we should not read as setting the Copyright Clause and the First Amendment at cross-purposes. Nor need I advocate the application here of strict or specially heightened review. I need only find that the First Amendment interest is important enough to require courts to scrutinize with some care the reasons claimed to justify the Act in order to determine whether they constitute reasonable copyright-related justifications for the serious harms, including speech-related harms, which the Act seems likely to impose.

C

1

This statute does not serve copyright's traditional public ends, namely the creation of monetary awards that "motivate the creative activity of authors," *Sony,* 464 U.S., at 429, 104

S.Ct. 774, "encourag[e] individual effort," *Mazer,* 347 U.S., at 219, 74 S.Ct. 460, and thereby "serve the cause of promoting broad public availability of literature, music, and the other arts," *Twentieth Century Music,* 422 U.S., at 156, 95 S.Ct. 2040. The statute grants its "restored copyright[s]" *only* to works *already produced.* It provides no monetary incentive to produce anything new. Unlike other American copyright statutes from the time of the Founders onwards, including the statute at issue in *Eldred,* it lacks any significant copyright-related *quid pro quo.*

The majority seeks to avoid this awkward fact by referring to past congressional practice that mostly suggests that Congress may provide new or increased protection *both* to newly created *and* to previously created, works. *Ante,* at 885-886, 886-887; Act of May 31, 1790, § 1, 1 Stat. 124 (conferring its new federal copyright on new works as well as old); Act of July 3, 1832, § 3, 4 Stat. 559 (authorizing new patents for past and future inventors who inadvertently failed to comply with applicable statutory formalities); *McClurg v. Kingsland,* 1 How. 202, 11 L.Ed. 102 (1843) (applying an act deeming a past or future inventor's patent valid despite it being briefly used by, for example, the inventor's employer). I do not dispute that copyright power. Insofar as such a statute does the former, *i.e.,* extends protection to newly created material, it embodies copyright's traditional justification—eliciting new production. And I do not doubt that Congress may then also include existing works within the scope of, say, increased protection for equitable and administrative reasons. See *Eldred,* 537 U.S. at 204, 214-215, 123 S.Ct. 769 (describing equitable reasons for applying newly extended copyright terms to future and existing copyrights alike). The statute before us, however, does not directly elicit any new production. Compare *id.,* at 204-208, 123 S.Ct. 769; (majority opinion) (noting that statute's extended term would apply to newly created material, and finding that the determination of the likelihood of its eliciting new production in practice was a matter for Congress to determine), with *id.,* at 243-267, 123 S.Ct. 769 (BREYER, J., dissenting) (expressing the view that there is little likelihood, in practice, that the statute would elicit new material). See also Walterscheid 219 (the 1790 Congress likely thought it was substituting federal protection for preexisting state common-law protections); Maher, Copyright Term, Retrospective Extension, and the Copyright Law of 1790 in Historical Context, 49 J. Copyright Soc. USA 1021, 1023-1024, and n. 8 (2002) (numerical estimate suggesting that 1790 Act removed only a small number of books from public domain). The other statutes to which the majority refers are private bills, statutes retroactively granting protection in wartime, or the like. *Ante,* at 885-887; Act of Feb. 19, 1849, ch. 57, 9 Stat. 763 (Levi Corson); Act of June 23, 1874, ch. 534, 18 Stat., pt. 3, p. 618 (Tod Helmuth); Act of Feb. 17, 1898, ch. 29, 30 Stat. 1396 (Judson Jones); Act of Dec. 18, 1919, ch. 11, 41 Stat. 368; Act of Sept. 25, 1941, ch. 421, 55 Stat. 732; see also *Evans v. Jordan,* 9 Cranch 199, 3 L.Ed. 704 (1815) (upholding a private bill restoring patent protection to a flour mill). But special circumstances, like wars, hurricanes, earthquakes, and other disasters, prevent the realization in practice of a reasonable expectation of securing or maintaining a preexisting right. Private bills are designed to provide special exceptions for comparable equitable reasons. See also Act of Mar. 3, 1893, ch. 215, 27 Stat. 743 (similar, as far as I can tell). To find in these laws an important analogy to the present law, which for the most part covers works that the author did not expect to protect in America (and often did not particularly want to protect), seems somewhat farfetched.

In fact, Congressional practice shows the contrary. It consists of a virtually unbroken string of legislation preventing the withdrawal of works from the public domain. See, *e.g.,* Berne Convention Implementation Act of 1988, § 12, 102 Stat. 2860 (the Act "does not provide copyright protection for any work that is in the public domain in the United States"); Copyright Act of 1976, Tit. I, § 101, 90 Stat. 2573 (declining to extend copyright protection to any work that is in the public domain prior to the Act taking effect); Copyright Act of 1909, § 7, 35 Stat. 1077 ("[N]o copyright shall subsist in the original text of any work which is in the public domain, or in any work which was published in this country or any foreign country prior to the going into effect of this Act and has not been already copyrighted in the United States"); Act to Amend the Several Acts Respecting Copy Rights § 16, 4 Stat. 439 (the Act "shall not extend to any copyright heretofore secured, the term of which has already expired"); see also H.R.Rep. No. 1742, 87th Cong., 2d Sess., 3 (1962) (expressing concern that because "it is not possible to revive expired terms of copyright, it seems to the committee to be desirable to suspend further expiration of copyright for a period long enough to enable the working out of remaining obstacles to the overall revision of the copyright law").

2

The majority makes several other arguments. First, it argues that the Clause does not require the "creation of at least one new work," *ante,* at 888, but may instead "promote the Progress of Science" in other ways. And it specifically mentions the "dissemination of existing and future works" as determinative here. *Ante,* at 887-890, and n. 25. The industry experts to whom the majority refers argue that copyright protection of already existing works can help, say, music publishers or film distributers raise prices, produce extra profits and consequently lead them to publish or distribute works they might otherwise have ignored. But ordinarily a copyright—since it is a *monopoly* on copying—*restricts* dissemination of a work once produced compared to a competitive market. And simply making the industry richer does not mean that the industry, when it makes an ordinary *forward-looking* economic calculus, will distribute works not previously distributed. The industry experts might mean that temporary extra profits will lead them to invest in the development of a market, say, by advertising. But this kind of argument, which can be made by distributers of all sorts of goods, ranging from kiwi fruit to Swedish furniture, has little if anything to do with the nonrepeatable costs of initial creation, which is the special concern of copyright protection. See *supra,* at 878-879.

Moreover, the argument proves too much. It is the kind of argument that the Stationers' Company might well have made and which the British Parliament rejected. Cf. Patterson 154-155 (describing failed booksellers' bill seeking protection from foreign competition through an extension of the copyright term). It is the kind of argument that could justify a legislature's withdrawing from the public domain the works, say, of Hawthorne or of Swift or for that matter the King James Bible in order to encourage further publication of those works; and, it could even more easily justify similar action in the case of lesser known early works, perhaps those of the Venerable Bede. The Court has not, to my knowledge, previously accepted such a rationale—a rationale well removed from the special economic circumstances that surround the nonrepeatable costs of the initial creation of a "Writing." *Supra,* at 878. And I fear that doing so would read the Copyright Clause as if it were a blank check made out in favor of those who are not themselves creators.

It is not surprising that the copyright holders' representatives who appeared before Congress did not emphasize this argument. (With one minor exception only those representatives appeared, see generally Joint Hearing; the Copyright Office did not testify, *id.,* at 239.) Rather, they focused on the Berne Convention itself. By that time, Congress had already protected all *new* works of Berne members. But it had not provided additional protection to preexisting foreign works that were then in the American public domain. Industry witnesses testified that withdrawing such works from the American public domain would permit foreign copyright owners to charge American consumers more for their products; and that, as a result, the United States would be able to persuade foreign countries to allow American holders of preexisting copyrights to charge foreign customers more money for their products. See *id.,* at 241 (statement of Eric Smith, Executive Director and General Counsel, International Intellectual Property Alliance) ("[F]ailure to [comply with Article 18] will . . . undermine the ability of the United States to press other countries to implement the same sort of protection in their implementing legislation currently pending in many legislatures around the globe"); *id.,* at 253 (statement of Matt Gerson, Vice President for Congressional Affairs, Motion Picture Assn. of America) (similar). See also *id.,* at 85 (statement of Xavier Becerra, House Judiciary Committee member) ("[R]etroactivity . . . is probably the best way to ensure that some of our older American works, anything from Motown, to *Star Trek,* to *The Hardy Boys* get the protection in some of these emerging foreign markets. It is important to ensure that countries no longer use our U.S. law as an excuse for not extending retroactive copyright protections to some of our own works"). But see *id.,* at 272-279 (statement of Larry Urbanski, Chairman of the Fairness in Copyright Coalition and President of Moviecraft Inc.) (testifying against restoration on grounds similar to those set out, *supra,* at 882-884). This argument, whatever its intrinsic merits, is an argument that directly concerns a private benefit: how to obtain more money from the sales of existing products. It is not an argument about a public benefit, such as how to promote or to protect the creative process.

Third, the majority points out that the statute "gives [authors] nothing more than the benefit of their labors during whatever time remains before the normal copyright term expires." *Ante,* at 893. But insofar as it suggests that copyright should in general help authors obtain greater monetary rewards than needed to elicit new works, it rests upon primarily European, but not American, copyright concepts. See *supra,* at 879-880.

Fourth, the majority argues that this statutory provision is necessary to fulfill our Berne Convention obligations. *Ante,* at 879-881. The Treaty, in Article 18, says that the "Convention shall apply to all works which, at the moment of its coming into force [*i.e.,* 1989 in the case of the United States] have not yet fallen into the public domain in the country of origin through the expiry of the term of protection." Berne Convention for the Protection of Literary and Artistic Works, Art. 18(1), Sept. 9, 1886, as revised at Stockholm on July 14, 1967, 828 U.N.T.S. 221, 251. The majority and Government say that this means we must protect the foreign works at issue here. And since the Berne Convention, taken as a whole, provides incentives for the creation of new works, I am willing to speculate, for argument's sake, that the statute might indirectly encourage production of new works by making the United States' place in the international copyright regime more secure.

Still, I cannot find this argument sufficient to save the statute. For one thing, this is a dilemma of the Government's own making. The United States obtained the benefits of Berne for many years despite its failure to enact a statute implementing Article 18. But in 1994, the United States and other nations signed the Agreement on Trade-Related Aspects of Intellectual Property Rights, which enabled signatories to use World Trade Organization dispute resolution mechanisms to complain about other members' Berne Convention violations. But at that time the Government, although it successfully secured reservations protecting other special features of American copyright law, made no effort to secure a reservation permitting the United States to keep some or all restored works in the American public domain. And it made no effort to do so despite the fact that Article 18 explicitly authorizes countries to negotiate exceptions to the Article's retroactivity principle. See Art. 18(3), *ibid.* ("The application of [the retroactivity] principle *shall be subject to any provisions contained in special conventions to that effect* existing or to be concluded between countries of the Union" (emphasis added)); Gervais, *Golan v. Holder*: A Look at the Constraints Imposed by the Berne Convention, 64 Vand. L.Rev. En Banc 147, 151-152 (2011); Gard, 64 Vand. L.Rev. En Banc, at 206.

For another thing, the Convention does not require Congress to enact a statute that causes so much damage to public domain material. Article 18(3) also states that "the respective countries shall determine, each in so far as it is concerned, *the conditions of application of this principle.*" 18 U.N.T.S., at 251 (emphasis added). Congress could have alleviated many of the costs that the statute imposes by, for example, creating forms of compulsory licensing, requiring "restored copyright" holders to provide necessary administrative information as a condition of protection, or insisting upon "reasonable royalties." Cf. S. 2913, 110th Cong., 2d Sess. (2008) (legislation that would have limited judicial remedies against users of orphan works); H.R. 5889, 110th Cong., 2d Sess. (2008) (House version of same); American Society of Composers, Authors and Publishers, http://www.ascap.com/licensing/ termsdefined.aspx (society of music copyright owners offering blanket licenses that give users the unlimited right to perform any of its members' songs for a fixed fee, thus reducing negotiation and enforcement costs).

To say this is not to criticize the Convention or our joining it. Rather, it is to argue that the other branches of Government should have tried to *follow* the Convention and in particular its provisions offering compliance flexibility. The fact that the statute has significant First Amendment costs is relevant in this respect, for that Amendment ordinarily requires courts to evaluate less restrictive, alternative possibilities. Doing so here, reveals that neither Congress nor the Executive took advantage of less-restrictive methods of compliance that the Convention itself provides. And that fact means that the Convention cannot provide the statute with a constitutionally sufficient justification that is otherwise lacking.

III

The fact that, by withdrawing material from the public domain, the statute inhibits an important preexisting flow of information is sufficient, when combined with the other features of the statute that I have discussed, to convince me that the Copyright Clause, interpreted in the light of the First Amendment, does not authorize Congress to enact this statute.

I respectfully dissent from the Court's contrary conclusion.

NOTES:

NOTE 1: For a discussion of title and provenance, see Chapter 5: Title, Provenance and Authenticity.

NOTE 2: Article 18 of the Berne Convention provides:

"(1) This Convention shall apply to all works which, at the moment of its coming into force, have not yet fallen into the public domain in the country of origin through the expiry of the term of protection.

"(2) If, however, through the expiry of the term of protection which was previously granted, a work has fallen into the public domain of the country where protection is claimed, that work shall not be protected anew.

"(3) The application of this principle shall be subject to any provisions contained in special conventions to that effect existing or to be concluded between countries of the Union. In the absence of such provisions, the respective countries shall determine, each in so far as it is concerned, the conditions of application of this principle.

"(4) The preceding provisions shall also apply in the case of new accessions to the Union and to cases in which protection is extended by the application of Article 7 or by the abandonment of reservations." 828 U.N.T.S. 251.

NOTE 3: As noted by the Government's *amici,* the United States excluded foreign works from copyright not to swell the number of unprotected works available to the consuming public, but to favor domestic publishing interests that escaped paying royalties to foreign authors. See Brief for International Publishers Association et al. as *Amici Curiae* 8-15. This free-riding, according to Senator Jonathan Chace, champion of the 1891 Act, made the United States "the Barbary coast of literature" and its people "the buccaneers of books." S.Rep. No. 622, 50th Cong., 1st Sess., p. 2 (1888).

NOTE 4: See also S.Rep. No. 103-412, p. 225 (1994) ("While the United States declared its compliance with the Berne Convention in 1989, it never addressed or enacted legislation to implement Article 18 of the Convention."); Memorandum from Chris Schroeder, Counselor to the Assistant Attorney General, Office of Legal Counsel, Dept. of Justice (DOJ), to Ira S. Shapiro, General Counsel, Office of the U.S. Trade Representative (July 29, 1994), in W. Patry, Copyright and the GATT, p. C-15 (1995) ("At the time Congress was debating the BCIA, it reserved the issue of removing works from the public domain."); General Agreement on Tariffs and Trade (GATT): Intellectual Property Provisions, Joint Hearing before the Subcommittee on Intellectual Property and Judicial Administration of the House Committee on the Judiciary and the Subcommittee on Patents, Copyrights and Trademarks of the Senate Committee on the Judiciary, 103d Cong., 2d Sess., p. 120 (1994) (URAA Joint Hearing) (app. to statement of Bruce A. Lehman, Assistant Secretary of Commerce and Commissioner of Patents and Trademarks (Commerce Dept.)) ("When the United States adhered to the Berne

Convention, Congress ... acknowledged that the possibility of restoring copyright protection for foreign works that had fallen into the public domain in the United States for failure to comply with formalities was an issue that merited further discussion.").

NOTE 5: The dissent implicitly agrees that, whatever tentative conclusion Congress reached in 1988, Article 18 requires the United States to "protect the foreign works at issue," at least absent a special convention the United States did not here negotiate. *Post,* at 911. See also *post,* at 911 (citing Gervais, *Golan v. Holder*: A Look at the Constraints Imposed by the Berne Convention, 64 Vand. L.Rev. En Banc 147, 151-152 (2011)); *id.,* at 152 ("[T]he Convention clearly requires that *some* level of protection be given to foreign authors whose works have entered the public domain (other than by expiration of previous copyright)."). Accord S. Ricketson, The Berne Convention for the Protection of Literary and Artistic Works 1886-1986, p. 675 (1987) ("There is no basis on which [protection of existing works under Article 18] can be completely denied. The conditions and reservations," authorized by Article 18(3) [and stressed by the dissent, *post,* at 911-912] are of "limited" and "transitional" duration and "would not be permitted to deny [protection] altogether in relation to a particular class ... of works.").

NOTE 6: NAFTA ultimately included a limited retroactivity provision—a precursor to § 514 of the URAA—granting U.S. copyright protection to certain Mexican and Canadian films. These films had fallen into the public domain, between 1978 and 1988, for failure to meet U.S. notice requirements. See North American Free Trade Agreement Implementation Act, § 334, 107 Stat. 2115; Brief for Franklin Pierce Center for Intellectual Property as *Amicus Curiae* 14-16. One year later, Congress replaced this provision with the version of 17 U.S.C. § 104A at issue here. See 3 M. Nimmer & D. Nimmer, Copyright § 9A.03, 9A.04, pp. 9A-17, 9A-22 (2011) (hereinafter Nimmer).

NOTE 7: This tension between the United States and its new Berne counter parties calls into question the dissent's assertion that, despite the 1988 Act's minimalist approach, "[t]he United States obtained the benefits of Berne for many years." *Post,* at 910-911. During this six-year period, Congress had reason to doubt that U.S. authors enjoyed the *full* benefits of Berne membership.

NOTE 8: Marrakesh Agreement Establishing the World Trade Organization, Apr. 15, 1994, 1867 U.N.T.S. 154.

NOTE 9: Proponents of prompt congressional action urged that avoiding a trade enforcement proceeding—potentially the WTO's first—would be instrumental in preserving the United States' "reputation as a world leader in the copyright field." URAA Joint Hearing 241 (statement of Eric Smith, International Intellectual Property Alliance (IIPA)). In this regard, U.S. negotiators reported that widespread perception of U.S. noncompliance was undermining our leverage in copyright negotiations. Unimpeachable adherence to Berne, Congress was told, would help ensure enhanced foreign protection, and hence profitable dissemination, for existing and future U.S. works. See *id.,* at 120 (app. to statement of Lehman, Commerce Dept.) ("Clearly, providing for [retroactive] protection for existing works in our own law will improve our position in future negotiations."); *id.,* at 268 (statement of Berman, RIAA).

NOTE 10: Title 17 U.S.C. § 104A is reproduced in full in an appendix to this opinion.

NOTE 11: Works from most, but not all, foreign countries are eligible for protection under § 514. The provision covers only works that have "at least one author or rightholder who was, at the time the work was created, a national or domiciliary of an eligible country." 17 U.S.C. § 104A(h)(6)(D). An "eligible country" includes any "nation, other than the United States, that—(A) becomes a WTO member country after the date of the enactment of the [URAA]; [or] (B) on such date of enactment is, or after such date of enactment becomes, a nation adhering to the Berne Convention." § 104A(h)(3). As noted above, see *supra,* at 878-879, 164 countries adhere to the Berne Convention. World Intellectual Property Organization, Contracting Parties: Berne Convention, www.wipo.int/treaties (as visited Jan. 13, 2012, and in Clerk of Court's case file).

NOTE 12: From the first Copyright Act until late in the 20th century, Congress conditioned copyright protection on compliance with certain statutory formalities. The most notable required an author to register her work, renew that registration, and affix to published copies notice of copyrighted status. The formalities drew criticism as a trap for the unwary. See, *e.g.,* 2 Nimmer § 7.01[A], p. 7-8; Doyle, Cary, McCannon, & Ringer, Notice of Copyright, Study No. 7, p. 46 (1957), reprinted in 1 Studies on Copyright 229, 272 (1963).

In 1976, Congress eliminated the registration renewal requirement for future works. Copyright Act of 1976, § 302, 408, 90 Stat. 2572, 2580. In 1988, it repealed the mandatory notice prerequisite. BCIA § 7, 102 Stat. 2857. And in 1992, Congress made renewal automatic for works still in their first term of protection. Copyright Amendments Act of 1992, 106 Stat. 264-266. The Copyright Act retains, however, incentives for authors to register their works and provide notice of the works' copyrighted status. See, *e.g.,* 17 U.S.C. § 405(b) (precluding actual and statutory damages against "innocent infringers" of a work that lacked notice of copyrighted status); § 411(a) (requiring registration of U.S. "work[s]," but not foreign works, before an owner may sue for infringement). The revisions successively made accord with Berne Convention Article 5(2), which proscribes application of copyright formalities to foreign authors. Berne, however, affords domestic authors no escape from domestic formalities. See Art. 5(3) (protection within country of origin is a matter of domestic law).

NOTE 13: Title 17 U.S.C. § 104A(h)(6)(B) defines a "restored work" to exclude "an original work of authorship" that is "in the public domain in its source country through expiration of [its] term of protection." This provision tracks Berne's denial of protection for any work that has "fallen into the public domain in the country of origin through the expiry of the term of protection." Art. 18(1), 828 U.N.T.S., at 251.

NOTE 14: Restoration is a misnomer insofar as it implies that all works protected under § 104A previously enjoyed protection. Each work in the public domain because of lack of national eligibility or subject-matter protection, and many that failed to comply with formalities, never enjoyed U.S. copyright protection. See, *e.g.*, 3 Nimmer § 9A.04[A][1][b][iii], at 9A-26, and n. 29.4.

NOTE 15: A reliance party must have used the work in a manner that would constitute infringement had a valid copyright been in effect. See § 104A(h)(4)(A). After restoration, the reliance party is limited to her previous uses. A performer of a restored work, for example, cannot, post-restoration, venture to sell copies of the script. See 3 Nimmer § 9A.04[C][1][a], at 9A-45 to 9A-46.

NOTE 16: Petitioners' complaint also challenged the constitutionality of the Copyright Term Extension Act, 112 Stat. 2827, which added 20 years to the duration of existing and future copyrights. After this Court rejected a similar challenge in *Eldred v. Ashcroft*, 537 U.S. 186, 123 S.Ct. 769, 154 L.Ed.2d 683 (2003), the District Court dismissed this portion of petitioners' suit on the pleadings, *Golan v. Ashcroft*, 310 F.Supp.2d 1215 (D.Colo.2004). The Tenth Circuit affirmed, *Golan v. Gonzales*, 501 F.3d 1179 (2007), and petitioners do not attempt to revive that claim in this Court, Pet. for Cert. 7, n. 2. Neither have petitioners challenged the District Court's entry of summary judgment for the Government on the claim that § 514 violates the substantive component of the Due Process Clause.

NOTE 17: Cf. 3 Nimmer § 9A.02[A][2], at 9A-11, n. 28 ("[I]t stretches the language of the Berne Convention past the breaking point to posit that following 'expiry of the zero term' the ... work need not be resurrected.").

NOTE 18: See B. Bugbee, Genesis of American Patent and Copyright Law 123-124 (1967) (hereinafter Bugbee) (Delaware, Maryland, and Pennsylvania).

NOTE 19: See 1783 Mass. Acts p. 236; 1783 N.J. Laws p. 47; 1783 N.H. Laws p. 521; 1783 R.I. Laws pp. 6-7; 1784 S.C. Acts p. 49; 1785 Va. Acts ch. VI; 1786 N.Y. Laws p. 298.

NOTE 20: 1783 Conn. Pub. Acts no. 617; 1783 N.J. Laws p. 47; 1785 N.C. Laws p. 563; 1786 Ga. Laws p. 323. In four States, copyright enforcement was restricted to works "not yet printed" or "hereinafter published." 1783 Mass. Acts p. 236; 1783 N.H. Laws p. 521; 1783 R.I. Laws pp. 6-7; 1784 S.C. Acts p. 49.

NOTE 21: See Bugbee 109-123.

NOTE 22: The parties debate the extent to which the First Congress removed works from the public domain. We have held, however, that at least some works protected by the 1790 Act previously lacked protection. In *Wheaton v. Peters*, 8 Pet. 591, 8 L.Ed. 1055 (1834), the Court ruled that before enactment of the 1790 Act, common-law copyright protection expired upon first publication. *Id.*, at 657, 663. Thus published works covered by the 1790 Act previously would have been in the public domain unless protected by state statute. Had the founding generation perceived the constitutional boundary petitioners advance today, the First Congress could have designed a prospective scheme that left the public domain undisturbed. Accord *Luck's Music Library, Inc. v. Gonzales*, 407 F.3d 1262, 1265 (C.A.D.C.2005) (Section 514 does not offend the Copyright Clause because, *inter alia*, "evidence from the First Congress," as confirmed by *Wheaton*, "points toward constitutionality.").

NOTE 23: Here, as in *Eldred*, "[b]ecause the Clause empowering Congress to confer copyrights also authorizes patents, congressional practice with respect to patents informs our inquiry." 537 U.S., at 201, 123 S.Ct. 769.

NOTE 24: Section 514 is in line with these measures; like them, it accords protection to works that had lapsed into the public domain because of failure to comply with U.S. statutory formalities. See *supra*, at 882, and n. 11.

NOTE 25: Legislation of this order, petitioners argue, is best understood as an exercise of Congress' power to remedy excusable neglect. Even so, the remedy sheltered creations that, absent congressional action, would have been open to free exploitation. Such action, according to petitioners' dominant argument, see *supra*, at 884-885, is ever and always impermissible. Accord *Luck's Music Library*, 407 F.3d, at 1265-1266 ("Plaintiffs urge that [the 1790 Act and the wartime legislation] simply extended the time limits for filing and [did] not purport to modify the prohibition on removing works from the public domain. But to the extent that potential copyright holders failed to satisfy procedural requirements, such works"—like those protected by § 514 "would necessarily have already entered the public domain....").

NOTE 26: But see Brief for Motion Picture Association of America as *Amicus Curiae* 27 (observing that income from existing works can finance the creation and publication of new works); *Eldred,* 537 U.S., at 208, n. 15, 123 S.Ct. 769 (noting that Noah Webster "supported his entire family from the earnings on his speller and grammar during the twenty years he took to complete his dictionary" (internal quotation marks omitted)).

NOTE 27: The dissent also suggests, more tentatively, that at least where copyright legislation extends protection to works previously in the public domain, Congress must counterbalance that restriction with new incentives to create. *Post,* at 903. Even assuming the public domain were a category of constitutional significance, contra *supra,* at 884-887, we would not understand "the Progress of Science" to have this contingent meaning.

NOTE 28: That the same economic incentives might also induce the dissemination of futons, fruit, or Bibles, see *post,* at 909-910, is no answer to this evidence that legislation furthering the dissemination of literary property has long been thought a legitimate way to "promote the Progress of Science."

NOTE 29: The dissent suggests that the "utilitarian view of copyrigh[t]" embraced by Jefferson, Madison, and our case law sets us apart from continental Europe and inhibits us from harmonizing our copyright laws with those of countries in the civil-law tradition. See *post,* at 901-902, 910-911. For persuasive refutation of that suggestion, see Austin, Does the Copyright Clause Mandate Isolationism? 26 Colum. J.L. & Arts 17, 59 (2002) (cautioning against "an isolationist reading of the Copyright Clause that is in tension with ... America's international copyright relations over the last hundred or so years").

NOTE 30: On the initial appeal in this case, the Tenth Circuit gave an unconfined reading to our reference in *Eldred* to "traditional contours of copyright." 501 F.3d, at 1187-1196. That reading was incorrect, as we here clarify.

NOTE 31: See *Eldred,* 537 U.S., at 221, 123 S.Ct. 769 ("Protection of [an author's original expression from unrestricted exploitation] does not raise the free speech concerns present when the government compels or burdens the communication of particular facts or ideas.").

NOTE 32: Focusing narrowly on the specific problem of orphan works, the dissent overlooks these principal protections against "the dissemination-restricting harms of copyright." *Post,* at 906.

NOTE 33: "[R]equir[ing] works that have already fallen into the public domain to stay there" might, as the dissent asserts, supply an "easily administrable standard." *Post,* at 906. However attractive this bright-line rule might be, it is not a rule rooted in the constitutional text or history. Nor can it fairly be gleaned from our case law. The dissent cites three decisions to document its assertion that "this Court has assumed the particular importance of public domain material in roughly analogous circumstances." *Post,* at 907. The dictum in *Graham v. John Deere Co. of Kansas City,* 383 U.S. 1, 6, 86 S.Ct. 684, 15 L.Ed.2d 545 (1966), noted earlier, did not treat the public domain as a constitutional limit—certainly not under the rubric of the First Amendment. See *supra,* at 887. The other two decisions the dissent cites considered whether the federal Patent Act preempted a state trade-secret law, *Kewanee Oil Co. v. Bicron Corp.,* 416 U.S. 470, 479-484, 94 S.Ct. 1879, 40 L.Ed.2d 315 (1974), and whether the freedom of the press shielded reporters from liability for publishing material drawn from public court documents, *Cox Broadcasting Corp. v. Cohn,* 420 U.S. 469, 495-497, 95 S.Ct. 1029, 43 L.Ed.2d 328 (1975). Neither decision remotely ascribed constitutional significance to a work's public domain status.

NOTE 34: It was the Fifth Amendment's Takings Clause—not the First Amendment—that Congress apparently perceived to be a potential check on its authority to protect works then freely available to the public. See URAA Joint Hearing 3 (statement of Rep. Hughes); *id.,* at 121 (app. to statement of Lehman, Commerce Dept.); *id.,* at 141 (statement of Shapiro, USTR); *id.,* at 145 (statement of Christopher Schroeder, DOJ). The reliance-party protections supplied by § 514, see *supra,* at 882-883, were meant to address such concerns. See URAA Joint Hearing 148-149 (prepared statement of Schroeder).

NOTE 35: Because Shostakovich was a pre-1973 Russian composer, his works were not protected in the United States. See U.S. Copyright Office, Circular No. 38A: The International Copyright Relations of the United States 9, 11, n. 2 (2010) (copyright relations between the Soviet Union and the United States date to 1973).

NOTE 36: Persistently deploring "'restored copyright' protection [because it] removes material from the public domain," *post,* at 906, the dissent does not pause to consider when and why the material came to be lodged in that domain. Most of the works affected by § 514 got there after a term of zero or a term cut short by failure to observe U.S. formalities. See *supra,* at 903-904.

NOTE 37: The pervasive problem of copyright piracy, noted *post,* at 906, likewise is scarcely limited to protected foreign works formerly in the public domain.

STUDY QUESTIONS

- What was the copyright issue in front of the court in *Golan*? How did the court rule? Why did the dissent disagree?
- Both the majority and dissenting opinions contain lengthy discussions on the history of U.S. copyright law. Why is the historical context iimportant to their conclusions? Explain the key difference between the majority and the dissent on the purpose of the Constitution's copyright clause and how that affects their decision.
- What are the implications of the *Golan* case for copyright owners? How about for copyright users?

EXCEPTIONS TO COPYRIGHT

As noted above, if a work is subject to copyright, the copyright owner has the exclusive right to reproduce, distribute copies, prepare derivative works, and (for certain works) the right to display or perform the work in public. The U.S. Copyright Act provides several exceptions to this exclusive right which are relevant to museums. These include the exceptions for libraries and archives (Section 108), the first sale and public display exceptions (Section 109) and the doctrine of fair use (Section 107). Each of these will be covered in turn, with particular emphasis on the doctrine of fair use. It is important to note that the specific exemptions contained in Sections 108 and 109 do not limit the application of fair use under Section 107. In other words, one or more exceptions to copyright may be applicable in a given situation, and reliance on one exception does not preclude reliance on another exception as well.

Exceptions for Libraries and Archives

Section 108 of the U.S. Copyright Act permits libraries and archives to use copyrighted material in specific ways without first obtaining permission from the copyright owner. Libraries and archives are permitted to make one copy of an item in their collection for the purpose of making loans. They may also make up to three copies of a published work for the purposes of preservation or replacement if a copy of the work is not available at a fair price or if the work is out of print. A library or archive may also make up to three copies of an unpublished work for preservation purposes. If the copy is a digital copy, it must not be circulated outside the library or archive. Libraries and archives may also reproduce, distribute, display, or perform a published work that is in its last twenty years of copyright for the purposes of preservation, research, or scholarship if the work is not available at a fair price or subject to commercial exploitation. Libraries and archives may also make one copy of an entire work for a user who requests it if the work is not available at a fair price.

The exceptions contained in Section 108 apply only to libraries and archives that are open to the public, and to unaffiliated researchers in a specialized field. Section 108 does not specifically apply to museums, but many museums also function as libraries or archives. The Copyright Office has said that Section 108 is "stuck in time"—it did not anticipate and no longer addresses the ways in which copyrighted works are created, distributed, preserved, and accessed in the 21st Century. (See Revising Section 108 Copyright Exceptions for Libraries and Archives, available at: www.copyright.gov/policy/SECTION108) Legislation is periodically introduced to specifically add museums to Section 108, and to make other changes to the copyright law, but as of this writing none of these proposals have been enacted.

First Sale and Public Display Exceptions

Section 109 of the U.S. Copyright Act provides several exceptions to the copyright owner's exclusive rights. In the museum context, the most important of these exceptions are referred to as the first sale and public display exceptions. These exceptions reflect the fact that ownership of the copyright in a work can be, and often is, separated from ownership of a particular tangible copy of that work. For example, you may purchase a copy of this textbook, but in doing so you are not purchasing the copyright in it—the author owns that.

Section 109 (a) allows the owner of a tangible copy of a work, including a tangible copy of an audio recording (remember records and CDs [Compact Discs]?), to sell that copy without first obtaining permission from the copyright owner. It is this exception which allows for the resale of used books, phonograph records, tapes and CDs, DVDs, artwork, and the like. Under the first sale exception, a museum may buy and sell works of art without first obtaining the permission of the copyright owner. In some jurisdictions the sale of art may be subject to the payment of a resale royalty—a payment to the artist due on each sale of the work—but that is a separate matter. The point is that a particular copy of a copyrighted work may be freely transferable. In the digital age, ownership of tangible copies may become obsolete—increasingly, as with computer software for example, you are merely purchasing a license to use a digital work, not acquiring a tangible copy that you can buy and sell.

Paragraph (c) of Section 109 allows the owner of a tangible copy of a copyrighted work to exhibit its copy of the work in public without first obtaining the copyright owner's permission. This is very important for museums. Under the public display exception, the owner of a painting, sculpture, photograph, print, or other creative work may exhibit it in public without first obtaining permission from the copyright owner.

To be exempt from copyright under Section 109 the work must be "lawfully made." In *Kirtsaeng v. John Wiley & Sons*, 568 U.S. 519 (2013), the Supreme Court held that the first sale doctrine applies to copies of copyrighted works lawfully made abroad. In that case, the plaintiff imported and resold used textbooks that were published abroad, competing with the publisher's market in the United States. The implications of a contrary ruling—that the first sale exception only applies to works "lawfully made" in the United States—raised serious concerns in the museum community because it could limit the application of the first sale and public display exceptions to works of art made in the United States. A copy of an Amicus brief outlining these concerns is included in the Cases and Other Readings below.

In some jurisdictions (but not current in the United States) the sale of art may be subject to the payment of a "resale royalty"—a payment to the artist due on each sale of the work—but that is a separate matter. The point is that a particlar copy of a copyrighted work may be freely transferable. In the digital age, ownership of tangible copies may become obsolete—increasingly, as with computer software for example, you are merely purchasing a license to use a digital work, not acquiring a tangible copy that you can buy and sell. Recent technological developments, including the increasing popularity of "Non-Fungible Tokens" or NFTs, present many interesting questions about the ownership and sale of digital works of art.

Paragraph (c) of Section 109 allows the owner of a tangible copy of a copyrighted work to exhibit its copy of the work in public without first obtaining the copyright owner's permission. This is very important for museums. Under the public display exception, the owner of a painting, sculpture, photograph, print, or other creative work may exhibit it in public without first obtaining permission from the copyright owner.

The public display exception also specifically allows the showing of photographic transparencies (slides) of a copyrighted work—"projection of no more than one image at a time"—without permission from the copyright owner of the work appearing in the photograph. However, importantly this exception does not permit the screening of a motion picture or other audio-visual work as they involve projecting more than one image at a time. To screen an audio-visual work in public, you must get permission from the copyright owner or rely on another exception to copyright (most likely fair use).

The public display exception is limited to tangible copies of works—it specifically refers to display "where the copy is located." The applicability of the public display exception in the digital world—when there is no tangible copy—is problematic at best.

Fair Use

The doctrine of "fair use" is by far the most important exception to copyright. It can apply regardless of whether another exception may also apply. As noted above, the term of copyright—the period during which the copyright owner has the exclusive right to control exploitation of the copyrighted work—has increased dramatically over the past forty-plus years since the Copyright Act of 1976 was enacted. Creative works now remain under copyright for very long periods of time. Today very few new works enter the public domain except intentionally (through voluntary terms of use, Creative Commons, and similar proactive licensing, etc.) This has had a serious impact on freedom of expression.

The use of existing copyright-protected works is sometimes essential to creating new works and to fostering cultural and intellectual exchange. In many cases, it may be impossible to determine who is the owner of the copyrighted work (ironically due in large part to the elimination of the copyright notice requirement) or to locate a known copyright owner due to the passage of time or a lack of information (see the discussion of "orphan works" in the preceding section). In other cases, the copyright owner may refuse to give permission to use copyrighted material, regardless of the purpose.

As a result, the notion of "fair use" has become increasingly important. At its core, the doctrine of fair use recognizes that the exclusive rights granted to "inventors and creators" in the U.S. Constitution and implementing statutes are limited by the competing constitutional right to freedom of expression embodied in the First Amendment.

Traditionally fair use has been understood as a statutory defense to a claim of copyright infringement. As a practical matter, fair use arises in the context of risk-assessment ("may I rely on fair use to use an otherwise copyrighted work without permission?") as well as an affirmative defense to a copyright infringement lawsuit. The doctrine of fair use focuses on the context in which a copyrighted work is used—if the use can be considered a "fair use" under the statute, then the work may be used without obtaining permission from the copyright owner. Central to a fair use analysis is the question of *how* and *why* the work is being used without permission.

Section 107 of the U.S. Copyright Act includes a four-factor balancing test for fair use. The four factors are:

- the purpose and character of the use, including whether the use is commercial or noncommercial and whether the work is being used for the purposes of comment and criticism, parody and satire, scholarship and research, news reporting, or teaching;
- the nature of the copyrighted work, including the degree of creativity and originality and whether the work is published or unpublished;
- the amount and substantiality of the use, including whether the amount used is reasonably related to the purpose of the use (i.e., no more of the copyrighted work is used than is necessary to accomplish the purpose of the use) and to what degree the portion used represents the core of the copyrighted work;
- the impact of the unpermitted use on the market for the copyrightable work, including the extent to which the use may or has harmed the market or potential market for the copyrighted work.

While all four factors of the fair use test must be considered, judges tend to focus on two key considerations when applying fair use to artistic works. The first consideration is whether the use is "transformative"—that is, does the use change or "transform" the material taken from the copyrighted work either by using it for a different purpose than the original or presenting the work in a fundamentally different way. The second consideration is whether the amount and the kind of material taken from the copyrighted work was reasonable considering the nature of the copyrighted work and the way in which it is used in the new work. If the user is seen to be "free-riding"—benefiting financially—from the creative work of another, and not adding any new expression, the use is unlikely to be considered fair use.

Fair use is ultimately a judicially applied "rule of reason." Fundamental to fair use is the fact-specific nature of the analysis. Each time a copyrighted work is used in reliance on fair use, the particular facts surrounding that specific use—the context of use—must be carefully analyzed in light of the four-factor test as interpreted by case law. Judicial decisions applying fair use are notoriously subjective and may turn on key facts unique to a given case. As a result, it can be very difficult to reconcile the case law on fair use. The best way to understand fair use is to become familiar with many fact situations and how the courts have applied fair use in such cases. The U.S. Copyright Office has begun compiling a searchable database of fair use court decisions. The goal of the *Copyright Office Fair Use Index* is to make it easier to understand and apply the doctrine of fair use. The Index is available on the U.S. Copyright Office website.

Several voluntary guidelines and codes of best practices have also been developed to help practitioners assess whether a particular use may be considered "fair use." Two useful guidelines created specifically for museums are the Association of Art Museum Directors (AAMD) *Guidelines for the Use of Copyrighted Materials* and the College Art Association's (CAA) *Code of Best Practices for Fair Use in the Visual Arts.* These guidelines can be useful tools and a helpful shorthand, but they are not a substitute for a thorough fair use analysis based on the specific facts of a particular use.

CASES AND OTHER READINGS

Reading Note: The following Amicus ("friend of the court") brief was submitted to the Supreme Court by the Association of Art Museum Directors (AAMD) and a group of prestigious American museums. The museums were concerned that a ruling for the defendant publishing company would have serious implications for museums buying, selling, loaning, and displaying foreign works of art.

KIRTSAENG V. JOHN WILEY & SONS

United States Supreme Court

On Writ of Certiorari to the United States Court of Appeals for the Second Circuit

BRIEF OF THE ASSOCIATION OF ART MUSEUM DIRECTORS, THE ART INSTITUTE OF CHICAGO, THE J. PAUL GETTY TRUST, MUSEUM ASSOCIATES DBA LOS ANGELES COUNTY MUSEUM OF ART, THE MUSEUM OF MODERN ART, THE SAN FRANCISCO MUSEUM OF MODERN ART, THE SOLOMON R. GUGGENHEIM FOUNDATION, THE WHITNEY MUSEUM OF AMERICAN ART, *ET AL.* AS *AMICI CURIAE* IN SUPPORT OF PETITIONER

[Table of Contents Omitted]

[Table of Authorities Omitted]

The Association of Art Museum Directors, the Art Institute of Chicago, the J. Paul Getty Trust, Museum Associates dba Los Angeles County Museum of Art, the Museum of Modern Art, the San Francisco Museum of Modern Art, the Solomon R. Guggenheim Foundation, the Whitney Museum of American Art, and twenty-two other United States museums of art submit this *amicus* brief in support of Petitioner.[NOTE 1]

INTEREST OF *AMICI CURIAE*

Amici are art museums and an organization of art museum directors.[NOTE 2] The mission of art museums is to serve the public through art and art education by making available, to a wide audience, works that convey the full range of human artistic expression. The decision below threatens this mission. Art museums have long depended on Section 109 of the Copyright Act to develop and display their permanent collections and to assemble and present special exhibitions of art. In particular, Section 109(c) allows museums to publicly display artwork "lawfully made under this title" without having to obtain the copyright owner's permission. Section 109(a) similarly allows museums to acquire "lawfully made" works of art for their permanent collections and to borrow and loan such works for display in special exhibitions. Displaying, acquiring, borrowing, and loaning art are at the core of what museums do. The Second Circuit, however, by ruling that "lawfully made under this title" means lawfully made in the United States, set a precedent that could end Section 109's application to works of art of foreign origin. The copyrighted works potentially affected—modern, postwar, and contemporary artwork created outside of this country—are crucial to museum collections and exhibitions. Under the Second Circuit's reasoning, merely hanging a foreign-made painting on the walls of a museum, buying and importing a sculpture that was created outside the country, or loaning either to another institution for exhibition to the public, could give rise to claims of copyright infringement. The decision below has the potential to disrupt the mission of American museums and interfere with the public's access to art.

SUMMARY OF ARGUMENT

The decision below should be reversed for two reasons.

1. The decision below could have serious repercussions for American museums and their ability to exhibit art. Most U.S. art museums have permanent collections that were acquired through purchases, gifts, and bequests, and on which they draw for exhibitions to the public. Museums also present special exhibitions, largely made up of works not in their collections, through loans from private collectors, galleries, and other institutions. For all these activities museums depend on the protections afforded by Section 109. Section 109(c) provides that the owner of a particular copy "lawfully made under this title" is entitled to *display* that copy publicly without the copyright owner's permission. Section 109(a) similarly allows museums to buy, borrow, loan, and sell such "lawfully made" artworks.

   By confining Section 109(a)'s "lawfully made under this title" to copies manufactured in the United States, the Second Circuit set a precedent that, if extended, could limit Section 109(c) and cause museums to lose their ability to display foreign-made, copyrighted works of art to the public. Museums could also lose the ability under Section 109(a) to acquire, borrow, loan, and sell such artwork. The decision below potentially affects large swaths of modern, postwar, and contemporary art on display in American museums today.

   As a result, the decision below could harm the viewing public and the museum community. Every museum that hangs a painting of foreign origin in its galleries potentially is a copyright infringer. The most basic of museum functions—exhibiting art—could give rise to infringement claims. Museums would have to fall back on untested defenses like fair use, but would lose the certainty that Section 109 has long provided. To avoid the risk of liability, museums could be forced to seek licenses from copyright owners. But clearing rights will be expensive and in many cases impossible. The cost of having to find copyright owners and negotiate individual licenses will be high, and museums likely will be unable to locate the copyright owner in every instance even after a diligent search. Copyright owners, who have no obligation to grant licenses, could demand sizeable royalty payments and non-monetary concessions like control over curatorial decisions. Where museums are unable to secure permissions, they would face an untenable choice: running the risk of copyright infringement liability or not making art available to the public or even acquiring art, whether by gift, bequest, or purchase. Reversal is warranted to avoid these unintended consequences for the viewing public and the museum community.

2. The Second Circuit overlooked a fundamental point of law. Section 104 of the Copyright Act provides that all works eligible for protection under U.S. law are "subject to protection under this title." The text of the statute must be given effect. A work that is "subject to protection under this title" is subject to the full range of rights *and* limitations that the statute affords—including Section 109's limitations on copyright. The lower court erred by finding the statute ambiguous. It is not. A work that is eligible for Section 104 protection, and any copy of that work, is subject to Section 109's limitations on the exclusive distribution and public display rights regardless of where they were made.

Amici's reading has broad applicability. It would maintain effective Section 109 protections for museums with respect to foreign-made works of art and, more broadly, would ensure that the limitations of Section 109 apply to *every* work in which there is U.S. copyright protection without regard to where a copy of the work may have been manufactured.

At a minimum, the proper construction of Section 109 is one that treats works of U.S. and foreign origin the same. Absent clear statutory language to the contrary, a party that seeks to avail itself of the benefits of U.S. copyright law protections must also be subject to all the limitations of that law, regardless of where it made copies of the works at issue.

ARGUMENT

I. THE DECISION BELOW THREATENS THE ABILITY OF MUSEUMS TO EXHIBIT ART CREATED OUTSIDE THE UNITED STATES

A. Foreign-Made Art Plays an Essential Role in the Mission of this Nation's Museums

The mission of museums in this country is to serve the public through art and art education. Museums do this in a number of ways. Most art museums have permanent collections, which they acquire through purchases, gifts, and bequests, and from which they draw for exhibitions and educational programs. Art museums also present special exhibitions, which can be drawn from a museum's permanent collection, works owned by others, or a combination of both. Museums regularly borrow works of art from other institutions, private collectors, and galleries, and they rely on one another for loans of art. [NOTE 3] All these activities allow art museums to reach a large audience. In 2008, an estimated 51.1 million visitors, or 23% of American adults, attended an art museum or gallery in the United States.[NOTE 4]

American museums believe that art conveys the rich complexity of human experience, and they are committed to selecting and presenting works of art across a broad range of time periods, geographies, and artistic perspectives. Showing modern, postwar, and contemporary art is essential to this.[NOTE 5] Such works are a significant part of museum collections and exhibitions in this country. Many modern, postwar, and contemporary works originate from outside the United States. *Amici* hold works created by Constantin Brancusi, Alexander Calder, Marc Chagall, Salvador Dalí, Lucian Freud, Alberto Giacometti, Frida Kahlo, Anselm Kiefer, Yves Klein, Yayoi Kusama, René Magritte, Henri Matisse, Joan Miró, Piet Mondrian, Pablo Picasso, Gerhard Richter, Diego Rivera, Rachel Whiteread, and other influential artists of the twentieth and twenty-first centuries. Foreign-made art is not exclusively made by foreigners. American artists working abroad have created many influential works. Cy Twombly, for example, settled in Italy in 1957 where he worked for decades and became one of the most important painters of the postwar era.[NOTE 6]

Many works created outside the United States are iconic and have shaped the history of art as we know it. Picasso's *Les Demoiselles d'Avignon*, with its then-scandalous subject matter and radical break from traditional composition and perspective, broke norms of artistic expression and was crucial to the genesis of modern art.[NOTE 7] Brancusi's *Bird in Space*, a series of sixteen marble and bronze sculptures, is a work of inspired abstraction that strips away a bird's individualizing features to realize the artist's intent of capturing "the essence of flight."[NOTE 8] Brancusi's work was instrumental in expanding what courts at the time accepted as "art."[NOTE 9] Richter's *Woman Descending the Staircase*, which the artist created by projecting a photograph on a canvas and rendering the image with paint, addresses the way photography and painting create impressions of beauty, elegance, and glamour.[NOTE 10]

Brancusi's sculpture Bird in Space, *1923*.

For years, these and many other works of foreign origin have engaged viewers and challenged their perceptions of aesthetics, society, and what it means to be art. American museums curate and present exhibitions of countless foreign-made works of art every day. In addition to showing such works through their permanent collections, *amici* recently have exhibited or will exhibit:

- *Art of Another Kind: International Abstraction and the Guggenheim, 1949–1960*, which features works drawn from the museum's collection and explores the affinities and differences between artists working continents apart in a period of great transition and rapid creative development.[NOTE 11]
- *The Last Harvest: Paintings of Rabindranath Tagore*, which followed one of the most important cultural icons in India and Bangla- desh who helped shape the modern Indian identity.[NOTE 12]
- The works of Yayoi Kusama, who is among Japan's most prominent contemporary artists and whose art spans a variety of media including painting, drawing, sculpture, film, performance, and immersive installation; the photographs of Daido Moriyama, whose gritty depictions of Japanese urban life incorporate high contrast, graininess, and tilted vantages to convey the

fragmentary nature of modern realities; and *Tokyo 1955-1970*, which follows Tokyo's transformation from the capital of a war-torn nation into an international center for arts, culture, and commerce, eventually becoming home to some of the most important art being made at the time.[NOTE 13]

- *The Steins Collect: Matisse, Picasso, and the Parisian Avant-Garde*, which explored the collections of Gertrude, Leo, Michael, and Sarah Stein, American expatriates living in Paris whose art collections and social networks were instrumental in shaping Modernism.[NOTE 14]

Foreign-made modern, postwar, and contemporary works of art are an essential part of American museum collections and exhibitions. They are crucial to the mission of museums to make a wide range of art available to the public. If the decision below stands, museums in the United States that display these works are at risk.

B. The Decision Below Threatens the Section 109 Limitations on which Museums Depend

The decision below impacts more than foreign- made editions of textbooks. It establishes a precedent that could eliminate the express limitations in Section 109 with respect to all foreign-made copy- righted works, including large swaths of modern, postwar, and contemporary art on display in this nation's museums.

As a general matter, museums do not own the copyrights to the works and objects in their collections. That is because ownership of a copyright is distinct from ownership of any material object in which the work is embodied. 17 U.S.C. § 202. The artists who created those works, the artists' heirs, or foundations typically control those rights. Moreover, many works of art are embodied in only one object—a singular painting, drawing, or sculpture. For purposes of the copyright law, the "original" of a work of art is deemed a "copy." *See* 17 U.S.C. § 101 ("'Copies' are material objects . . . in which a work is fixed by any method now known or later developed, and from which the work can be perceived, reproduced, or otherwise communicated, either directly or with the aid of a machine or device. *The term 'copies' includes the material object . . . in which the work is first fixed.*") (emphasis added).

Museums then depend on Section 109 in two respects. Section 109(c), which the decision below does not discuss, provides that "the owner of a particular copy lawfully made under this title . . . is entitled, without the authority of the copyright owner, *to display that copy publicly*, either directly or by the projection of no more than one image at a time, to viewers present at the place where the copy is located." 17 U.S.C. § 109(c) (emphasis added). Section 109(c) thus expressly limits a copyright owner's right to control a museum's public display of artwork in its possession. *See* 17 U.S.C. § 106(5) ("the owner of copyright under this title has the exclusive rights . . . in the case of . . . pictorial, graphic, or sculptural works, . . . to display the copyrighted work publicly"). Section 109(c) "adopts the general principle that the lawful owner of a copy of a work should be able to put his copy on public display with- out the consent of the copyright owner." H.R. Rep. No. 94-

1476, at 79 (1976).[NOTE 15] As a result, a museum ordinarily does not need permission to show the public a copyrighted painting, drawing, sculpture, or any other object in its collection or in a special exhibition.

Museums also rely on Section 109(a). This provision allows museums to make uses that otherwise would implicate copyright owners' exclusive rights of distribution. Museums acquire works of art for their permanent collections through purchases, either with their own funds or funds given by others, or through donations or bequests. Museums also regularly borrow and loan works that are incorporated into special exhibitions. Many loaned works of art travel internationally. All these uses implicate copyright owners' distribution rights because of the Copyright Act's Section 106(3), which provides that "the owner of copyright under this title has the exclusive rights . . . to distribute copies . . . of the copyrighted work to the public by sale or other transfer of ownership, or by rental, lease, or lending." Section 109(a) then expressly limits the distribution right: museums need not obtain copyright permissions to buy, borrow, loan, or sell works of art because of the protections that Section 109(a) affords.[NOTE 16]

Together, Section 109(a) and Section 109(c) enable essential museum functions—the development and public display of permanent collections and special exhibitions of art. The decision below however confines Section 109(a)'s "lawfully made under this title" to works made in the United States. By doing so, it sets a precedent for similarly limiting Section 109(c). If "lawfully made under this title" means only copies lawfully made in the United States, museums could lose their ability under Section 109(c) to display foreign-made copyrighted works of art to the public, and under Section 109(a) to acquire, borrow, loan, and sell foreign-made works.

C. The Decision Below Puts at Risk Museums' Ability to Exhibit Foreign-Made Works of Art to the Public

The lower court's construction of Section 109 could have serious unintended consequences: if the decision below is upheld, every museum that exhibits a foreign-made painting, drawing, or sculpture under copyright is a potential infringer. To be clear, museums would not concede liability if infringement claims were brought.[NOTE 17] But the decision below could open museums across the country to copyright infringement lawsuits and claims for damages, attorneys' fees, and injunctions—costs that would have a chilling effect on how museums, already operating under tight budgets, manage their collections and exhibitions.

Without the protection of Section 109's limitations on the exclusive rights of public display and distribution, museums will be forced to decide whether to seek permission to exhibit, acquire, borrow, lend, and sell foreign-made artwork in order to avoid claims that they are infringing the copyright owners' exclusive rights. Having to clear rights for these basic museum functions will be extremely time-consuming, costly, and burdensome. As a practical matter it will be difficult, and in many cases impossible, to secure the rights. Leaving aside the question of how much a license would cost, museums would be forced to spend a great deal of time and energy locating copyright owners and negotiating rights, diverting scarce resources from other important museum functions and potentially delaying acquisitions, loans, and exhibitions. In many instances, it may be impossible for museums to locate copyright owners. Many artworks and objects are "orphan" works whose copyright owners cannot be found even after a reasonably diligent search, as they lack clear facts about their authorship, country of origin, date of creation, publication, and copyright duration.[NOTE 18] If the copyright owner's identity or a work's ownership status cannot be ascertained, museums will be left in legal limbo.

Even where the copyright owner of a work of art can be found, there is no guarantee the museum would be able to secure a license. A copyright owner could decide not to grant a license for any reason—for example, because he or she objected to the venue or curatorial aspects of the exhibition—or for no reason at all. Alternatively, the copyright owner could demand a sizeable royalty payment to allow the use to occur. What is the price a museum would have to pay for a copyright license to publicly display a work of art? To borrow, purchase, or receive a donated work? There is no precedent. The price is entirely at the discretion of the copyright owner: it will be as low or as high as he or she is willing to accept. With such bargaining power, the copyright owner could demand non-monetary compensation, like control over how the work is displayed, the content of the exhibition, or to whom the work is sold.

As such, the Second Circuit's decision places museums' curatorial freedom at risk. Regardless of the amount of a fee or the conditions attached to a license, this much is clear: today, American museums pay no copyright fees to exhibit, purchase, borrow, lend, or sell art, and they exercise broad freedom to make curatorial decisions. If the decision below is allowed to stand, museums conceivably could be forced to divert significant portions of their budgets—now spent on paying staff, running educational programs, and acquiring art—to clearing rights that never before existed. Museums may be forced to change what art they exhibit and how, to comply with copyright demands.

Ultimately, the cost of clearing rights in foreign-made works may be beyond what museums can afford. This places museums in an untenable position. They could, on the one hand, proceed with unlicensed uses of their collections. That opens them up to copyright infringement lawsuits and potentially devastating awards of damages and attorneys' fees. Or museums could avoid exhibiting or acquiring foreign-made works entirely, focusing their efforts instead on those works in which they have rights. Either way, the public loses. Spurring a cottage industry of litigation against this nation's museums hardly serves the public. The alternative—withholding art from public view—likewise serves no benefit.

The lower court's construction of "lawfully made under this title" has the potential to disrupt core museum functions, undermine the mission of this nation's museums to make art of all kinds widely available, and deprive the American public of access to foreign-made modern, postwar, and contemporary art. Reversal is warranted to avoid these consequences.

II. ALL WORKS PROTECTED BY U.S. COPYRIGHT, AND THEIR COPIES, ARE SUBJECT TO SECTION 109'S LIMITATIONS ON RIGHTS

A. Section 104 Expressly Makes Works "Subject to Protection under this Title" Regardless of Where their Copies Were Manufactured

Section 104 sets forth the criteria under which a work of authorship is protected under the copyright law of the United States.[NOTE 19] All works that satisfy the criteria of Section 104 are "subject to protection under this title." 17 U.S.C. § 104. The words of the statute must be given effect and are crucial here. A work that is "subject to protection under this title" is subject to all the contours of copyright protection—all the rights that attach to it under Section 106 of the Copyright Act, all the remedies available to the copyright owner for infringement of that work under Sections 501 through 513, and all the limitations on those rights and remedies under Sections 107 through 122. Section 104 makes the full range of U.S. copyright protections and limitations applicable to *all* eligible works, and it makes no distinction based on where a work or a copy of it was manufactured. All works eligible for protection under U.S. law, and all copies of those works, are subject to the limitations on the distribution and public display rights set forth in Section 109, regardless of where they were made.

The Second Circuit erred by not embracing this statutory reading. The court acknowledged that the wording of Section 104(b)(2) made it "possible to interpret § 109(a)'s 'lawfully made under this title' language to mean, in effect, 'any work that is subject to protection under this title.'" *John Wiley & Sons, Inc. v. Kirtsaeng*, 654 F.3d 210, 219-20 (2d Cir. 2011). The court further recognized that Petitioner here would prevail if it adopted this definition of Section 109(a). *Id.* at 220 n.38. But rather than apply Section 104 as determinative of the issue, the court instead treated Section 104 as only one aspect of the statute that could be used to interpret the meaning of Section 109(a)'s "lawfully made under this title." Finding that alternative readings were possible, the court concluded that the text of Section 109(a) was "utterly ambiguous." *Id.* at 220. Confronted with what it viewed as ambiguous text, the court then relied on two arguments, not grounded in the text of the Copyright Act, to find for Respondent: it found that Section 602(a)(1) would have no force in the vast majority of cases if Petitioner's argument were adopted, and it relied on dicta found in *Quality King*. *Id.* at 221.

The court erred in its first step when it found Section 109 ambiguous. The statute is not ambiguous. Section 104 establishes that all eligible works—and by extension, all copies thereof—are subject to all the protections, remedies, and limitations of the U.S. copyright law, including Section 109. The Second Circuit should have ended its analysis there. *See*

Conn. Nat'l Bank v. Germain, 503 U.S. 249, 254 (1992) ("When the words of a statute are unambiguous, then, this first canon is also the last: 'judicial inquiry is complete.'") (quoting *Rubin v. United States*, 449 U.S. 424, 430 (1981)). Simply put, if a work is eligible for protection under U.S. law, and the copyright owner seeks to enforce its rights under U.S. law, the works at issue—and all copies thereof—are subject to the same limitations imposed by the law regardless of where they were manufactured.[NOTE 20]

B. *Amici's* Reading Preserves Museums' Ability to Rely on Section 109 and Comports with *Quality King*

Amici's reading of Section 104 has broad applicability. It is coterminous with U.S. copyright law protection: every work that is protected under the Copyright Act is also subject to the *limitations* of Section 109. To use artwork as an example, if a painting is "unpublished," it is "subject to protection under this title" including the limitations of Section 109. *See* 17 U.S.C. § 104(a). If the painter who created the work was a national or domiciliary of the United States or of a "treaty party," the painting is subject to protection under this title and Section 109. *See* 17 U.S.C. § 104(b)(1). (A treaty party includes any country that is a party to the Berne Convention, the Universal Copyright Convention, the WTO Agreement, the WIPO Copyright Treaty, and any other copyright treaty to which the United States is party[NOTE 21]—virtually every country on Earth.) If the painting was first published in the United States or in a foreign nation that is a treaty party, once again, it is subject to protection under the Copyright Act and the limitations of Section 109. *See* 17 U.S.C. § 104(b)(2). Indeed, a work that falls outside of Section 104 has no U.S. rights for its owner to enforce, making moot the question whether Section 109 would apply in such a circumstance.

Amici's reading of the statute also accords with *Quality King*. There, the Court ruled that the importation right granted in Section 602(a) is limited by Section 109 (and indeed Sections 107 through 120). *Quality King Distribs., Inc. v. L'anza Research Int'l, Inc.*, 523 U.S. 135, 150 (1998). While the concurrence opined that the Court was not resolving cases in which the allegedly infringing imports were manufactured abroad, *Quality King*, 523 U.S. at 154, the majority opinion certainly left open the possibility that all copies of works protected under U.S. law are subject to Section 109's limitations regardless of where they were made. There is no reason to carve out a judicial exception from the rule that every work protected under the Copyright Act is subject to all the limitations on copyright contained in the statute.

C. Section 109 Must Be Construed to Give Effect to Section 104's Equal Treatment of Foreign and Domestic Works

Further highlighting the problems with the ruling below is that the Second Circuit failed to give effect to Section 104's mandate to treat foreign and domestic works equally. At a minimum, the text of Section 104 establishes the proper analytic framework for interpreting Section 109's "lawfully made under this title." Courts have recognized that the wording of Section 104 supports a construction that applies Section 109 to foreign-made copies. *See John Wiley & Sons*, 654 F.3d at 219-20 & n.38; *Pearson Educ., Inc. v. Liu*, 656 F. Supp. 2d 407, 412 (S.D.N.Y. 2009). More than that, Section 104 sets the principle that all copyright owners whose works are eligible for protection under U.S. law should receive the same copyright protections and limitations, and that eligible foreign works should receive no more or less favorable treatment unless there is clear language in the statute to the contrary.

Congress uses explicit language in the few instances where it has decided to treat foreign works differently than domestic works. When Congress implemented the WIPO Copyright and Performances and Phonograms Treaties, it exempted foreign works from the requirement that they be registered as a prerequisite for filing an infringement action. Congress amended Section 411(a) to provide that "no civil action for infringement of the copyright in any *United States work* shall be instituted until preregistration or registration of the copyright claim has been made in accordance with this title." 17 U.S.C. § 411(a) (emphasis added).[NOTE 22] Section 109(a) does not so clearly give preferential treatment for foreign- made copies, even though Congress could have chosen the words "lawfully made in the United States" instead of "lawfully made under this title." Indeed when it enacted the 1976 Act, Congress confirmed the principle of general applicability embodied in the text of the Section 109.[NOTE 23]

Absent a clear Congressional statement to the contrary, the words of Section 109(a) should be construed to give foreign- and U.S.-made copies the equal treatment that Section 104 contemplates. *See Pearson*, 656 F. Supp. 2d at 413 ("[w]hen Congress considered the place of manufacture to be important, . . . the statutory language clearly expresses that concern") (quoting *Sebastian Int'l, Inc. v. Consumer Contacts (Pty) Ltd.*, 847 F.2d 1093, 1098 n.1 (3d Cir. 1988)). "Lawfully made under this title" must refer to the lawfulness of a copy's manufacture as a function of United States copyright law, not to the place the copy was manufactured. *Id.* at 412.

CONCLUSION

The Court should reverse the decision below and find that a copy that was made and acquired abroad and then imported into the United States can always be distributed and publicly displayed within the United States without permission so long as the copyright owner authorized the first distribution abroad.

Respectfully submitted,

Counsel for Amici Curiae

NOTES:

NOTE 1: No counsel for any party authored this brief in whole or in part, and no counsel for a party or any party made a monetary contribution intended to fund the preparation or submission of this brief. All parties have consented to filing this brief, and letters reflecting their consent have been filed with the Clerk.

NOTE 2: A description of *amici* is set forth in the attached Appendix.

NOTE 3: Occasionally, a museum will deaccession a work—i.e., permanently remove it from the museum's collection—and dispose of it by transferring ownership. AAMD and its members have developed policies and procedures to govern the deaccessioning of works. *See* Association of Art Museum Directors, *AAMD Policy on Deaccessioning* (June 9, 2010), *available at* http://aamd.org/papers/documents/FinalDeaccessioning_Report_6_25_10.pdf.

NOTE 4: Nat'l Endowment for the Arts, *2008 Survey of Public Participation in the Arts*, 25-26 (Nov. 2009), *available at* http://www.nea.gov/research/2008-SPPA.pdf (measuring the number of Americans over the age of eighteen who visit museums).

NOTE 5: *Amici* emphasize these works because older works are likely to have fallen into the public domain and no longer are protected by copyright.

NOTE 6: *See* Randy Kennedy, *American Artist Who Scribbled a Unique Path*, N.Y. TIMES, July 5, 2011.

NOTE 7: *See Les Demoiselles d'Avignon*, MUSEUM OF MODERN ART, http://www.moma.org/collection/object.php?object_id=79766 (last visited July 3, 2012).

NOTE 8: *See Bird in Space*, METROPOLITAN MUSEUM OF ART, http://www.metmuseum.org/Collections/search-the-collections/210006 973 (last visited July 3, 2012); *Bird in Space*, LOS ANGELES COUNTY MUSEUM OF ART, http://collectionsonline.lacma. org/mwebcgi/mweb.exe?request=record;id=159125;-type=101 (last visited July 3, 2012); *Bird in Space*, GUGGENHEIM MUSEUM, http://www.guggenheim.org/new-york/collections/collection-online/ show-full/piece/?object=76.2553.51&search=&page=&f=Title (last visited July 3, 2012); *Bird in Space*, MUSEUM OF MODERN ART, http://www.moma.org/collection/object.php?object_id=81033 (last visited July 3, 2012).

NOTE 9: When a number of Brancusi's works, including *Bird in Space*, were shipped to the United States in 1926 for display at an exhibition in New York, customs officials refused to allow the works to enter duty-free because they considered the works "manufactures of metal" subject to an importation tax, rather than art. On appeal, the Customs Court ruled that the pieces were works of art despite the fact that they did not strictly imitate natural objects. *Brancusi v. United States*, 54 Treas. Dec. 428 (Cust. Ct. 1928).

NOTE 10: *See Woman Descending the Staircase*, ART INSTITUTE OF CHICAGO, http://www.artic.edu/aic/collections/artwork/147003 (last visited July 3, 2012).

NOTE 11: *Art of Another Kind: International Abstraction and the Guggenheim, 1949-1960*, GUGGENHEIM MUSEUM, http://www. guggenheim.org/new-york/exhibitions/on-view/art-of-another- kind (last visited July 3, 2012).

NOTE 12: *The Last Harvest Paintings of Rabindranath Tagore*, ART INSTITUTE OF CHICAGO, http://www.artic.edu/aic/collections/ exhibitions/Tagore/index (last visited July 3, 2012).

NOTE 13: *Yayoi Kusama*, WHITNEY MUSEUM OF AMERICAN ART, http://whitney.org/Exhibitions/YayoiKusama (last visited July 3, 2012); *Fracture: Daido Moriyama*, LOS ANGELES COUNTY MUSEUM OF ART, http://www.lacma.org/art/exhibition/fracture-daido-moriyama (last visited July 3, 2012); *Tokyo 1955-1970*, MUSEUM OF MODERN ART, http://www.moma.org/visit/ calendar/exhibitions/1242 (last visited July 3, 2012).

NOTE 14: Press Release, *The Steins Collect*, SAN FRANCISCO MUSEUM OF MODERN ART, http://www.sfmoma.org/about/press/press_ exhibitions/releases/862 (last visited July 3, 2012). The exhibition originated at SFMOMA and then traveled to Paris and the Metropolitan Museum of Art in New York.

NOTE 15: As a general principle, we believe that anyone who owns a copy of a work should be free to put that copy on public display without first obtaining authorization from the owner of copyright in that work. Thus, for example: the owner of a painting should be able to hang it in a public gallery . . .."

> STAFF OF H. COMM. ON THE JUDICIARY, 89TH CONG., COPYRIGHT LAW REVISION PART 6—SUPPLEMENTARY REPORT OF THE REGISTER OF COPYRIGHTS ON THE GENERAL REVISION OF THE U.S. COPYRIGHT LAW: 1965 REVISION BILL 30 (Comm. Print 1965).

NOTE 16: Museums would argue that a museum that borrows a work of art from another institution, collector, or gallery, or that lends a work to another museum, is not engaged in a distribution of "copies . . . to the public." *See* 17 U.S.C. § 106(3). Regardless of whether such uses are distributions for purposes of Section 106(3), Section 109(a) permits them without the copyright owner's permission.

NOTE 17: Museums would assert all meritorious defenses—for example, that their display of art is fair use. *See, e.g.*, 17 U.S.C. § 107.

NOTE 18: *See* J. Paul Getty Trust, *et al.*, *Initial Comments to Orphan Works Notice of Inquiry* (Mar. 24, 2005), *available at* http:// www.copyright.gov/orphan/comments/OW0610-ArtMuseums.pdf; Los Angeles County Museum of Art, *Initial Comments to Orphan Works Notice of Inquiry* (Mar. 25, 2005), *available at* http:// www.copyright.gov/orphan/comments/OW0644-LACMA.pdf. Whitney Museum of American Art, *Initial Comments to Orphan Works Notice of Inquiry* (May 6, 2005), *available at* http:// www.copyright.gov/orphan/ comments/reply/OWR0090-Whitney Museum.pdf.

NOTE 19: Section 104 provides, in relevant part:

(a) *Unpublished Works.*—The works specified by sections 102 and 103, while unpublished, *are subject to protection under this title* without regard to the nationality or domicile of the author.

(b) *Published Works.*—The works specified by sections (and 103, when published, *are subject to protection under this title* if—

(1) on the date of first publication, one or more of the authors is a national or domiciliary of the United States, or is a national, domiciliary, or sovereign authority of a treaty party, or is a stateless person, wherever that person may be domiciled; or

(2) the work is first published in the United States or in a foreign nation that, on the date of first publication, is a treaty party ....

17 U.S.C. § 104 (emphasis added). Subsections (3), (4), (5), and (6), which are not repeated here for the sake of brevity, make subject to U.S. copyright protection, respectively, sound recordings first fixed in a treaty party, works incorporated into buildings and structures located in the United States and treaty parties, works first published by the United Nations or the Organization of American States, and works within the scope of a Presidential proclamation. 17 U.S.C. § 104(b)(3), (4), (5), (6).

NOTE 20: Under this reading, Respondent's foreign editions are subject to the limitations of Section 109. Each of Respondent's eight copyrighted works at issue were first published in the U.S. Special Joint Appendix 1, 3, 5, 8, 10, 12, 14, 16. By operation of Section 104(b)(2), the works "are subject to protection under this title."

NOTE 21: 17 U.S.C. § 101 (definitions of "treaty party" and "inter- national agreement").

NOTE 22: The Copyright Act as enacted in 1976 provided that "no action for infringement of the copyright in any work shall be instituted until registration of the copyright claim has been made in accordance with this title." 17 U.S.C. § 411(a) (1976). The Berne Convention Implementation Act of 1988, Pub. L. No. 100-568, 102 Stat. 2853, 2859, amended this provision of the 1976 Act, which, in turn, was amended by the WIPO Copyright and Performances and Phonograms Treaties Implementation Act of 1998, Pub. L. No. 105-304, 112 Stat. 2860, 2863.

NOTE 23: "Section 109(a) *restates and confirms the principle that*, where the copyright owner has transferred ownership of a particular copy or phonorecord of a work, the person to whom the copy or phonorecord is transferred is entitled to dispose of it by sale, rental, or other means." H.R. Rep. No. 94-1476, at 79 (emphasis added). "Section 109(b) [subsequently renumbered 109(c)] *adopts the general principle* that the lawful owner of a copy of a work should be able to put his copy on public display without the consent of the copyright owner." *Id.* (emphasis added). Moreover, there is no indication that Congress intended to exempt foreign-made copies from Section 109. Congress has often considered and has thus far failed to enact a resale royalty right—that is, the right of a copyright owner to receive royalties from the resale of a work of art. *See* Visual Artists' Residual Rights Act of 1978, H.R. 11403, 95th Cong. (1978); Visual Artists Rights Amendment of 1986, H.R. 5722, 99th Cong. (1986); Visual Artists Rights Amendment of 1986, S. 2796, 99th Cong. (1986); Visual Artists Rights Act of 1987, H.R. 3221, 100th Cong. (1987). Such a right arguably could arise if foreign-made artwork were exempted from Section 109. The legislature's consideration of such legislation, and the absence in the debates with respect thereto of any assertion that such a right already exists in the Copyright Act (if only for non-United States works), suggests that the Congress understood that no such right exists.

[APPENDIX Omitted]

STUDY QUESTIONS

- *Kirtsaeng* involved the sale of used textbooks that were purchased by the plaintiff overseas and imported into the United States. The Supreme Court concluded that the books were "lawfully made" within the meaning of the U.S. Copyright Act, and that their resale was permissible under the first sale exception in Section 109 of the Copyrights Act.
- Why did a group of museums file an Amicus brief? What was the potential impact of *Kirtsaeng* on museums and museum collections?
- How do you think the "lawfully made" requirement in Section 109 affects the public display and first sale of graffiti and street art? Appropriation art (i.e., art that contains material that potentially infringes on another's copyright)?

Reading Note: The *Bill Graham Archives* case below is one of a line of cases exploring the scope and application of the fair use doctrine. It involved the incorporation of iconic rock concert posters in a coffee table book detailing the history of the San Francisco rock band the Grateful Dead. This case was one of the first court decisions to articulate the concept of "transformative use" in the context of artwork.

BILL GRAHAM ARCHIVES V. DORLING KINDERSLEY LTD.

448 F.3d 605 (2nd Cir. 2006)

Before: KEARSE and RAGGI, Circuit Judges, and RESTANI, Judge.

This appeal concerns the scope of copyright protection afforded artistic concert posters reproduced in reduced size in a biography of the musical group the Grateful Dead. Asserted copyright holder Bill Graham Archives, LLC ("BGA" or "Appellant") appeals from a judgment of the District Court for the Southern District of New York dismissing, on motion for summary judgment, its copyright infringement action against Dorling Kindersley Limited, Dorling Kindersley Publishing, Inc., and R.R. Donnelley & Sons Company (collectively "DK" or "Appellees"). We review the district court's grant of summary judgment *de novo,* and we agree with the court that DK's reproduction of BGA's images is protected by the fair use exception to copyright infringement.

BACKGROUND

In October of 2003, DK published *Grateful Dead: The Illustrated Trip* ("*Illustrated Trip*"), in collaboration with Grateful Dead Productions, intended as a cultural history of the Grateful Dead. The resulting 480-page coffee table book tells the story of the Grateful Dead along a timeline running continuously through the book, chronologically combining over 2000 images representing dates in the Grateful Dead's history with explanatory text. A typical page of the book features a collage of images, text, and graphic art designed to simultaneously capture the eye and inform the reader. Plaintiff BGA claims to own the copyright to seven images displayed in *Illustrated Trip,* which DK reproduced without BGA's permission.

Initially, DK sought permission from BGA to reproduce the images. In May of 2003, the CEO of Grateful Dead Productions sent a letter to BGA seeking permission for DK to publish the images. BGA responded by offering permission in exchange for Grateful Dead Productions' grant of permission to BGA to make CDs and DVDs out of concert footage in BGA's archives. Next, DK directly contacted BGA seeking to negotiate a license agreement, but the parties disagreed as to an appropriate license fee. Nevertheless, DK proceeded with publication of *Illustrated Trip* without entering a license fee agreement with BGA. Specifically, DK reproduced seven artistic images originally depicted on Grateful Dead event posters and tickets.[NOTE 1] BGA's seven images are displayed in significantly reduced form and are accompanied by captions describing the concerts they represent.

When DK refused to meet BGA's post publication license fee demands, BGA filed suit for copyright infringement. BGA sought to enjoin further publication of *Illustrated Trip,* the destruction of all unsold books, and actual and statutory damages. The parties cross-moved for summary judgment, with the primary issue before the district court being whether DK's use of BGA's images constituted fair use under the Copyright Act of 1976, 17 U.S.C. § 101 et seq. ("Copyright Act"). After applying the statutory fair use balancing test, the district court determined that DK's reproduction of the images was fair use and granted DK's motion for summary judgment.

DISCUSSION

Section 106 of the Copyright Act grants copyright holders a bundle of exclusive rights, including the right to "repro-

This iconic psychedelic rock concert poster designed by Jim Blashfield incorporates a Herb Greene photograph of Jefferson Airplane band members. The Grateful Dead appeared at the Hollywood Bowl with Jefferson Airplane in September 1967. Big Brother & The Holding Company, although listed on the poster, did not play this event due to a contractual dispute with Bill Graham. The poster is one of the seven copyrighted images at issue in the Bill Graham Archives *case.*

duce the copyrighted work in copies," and the right "to prepare derivative works based upon the copyrighted work." 17 U.S.C. § 106. For purposes of the motion, the district court assumed plaintiff possessed these rights in the contested images and there is no dispute that copying the images was not authorized by plaintiff. The issue before us on appeal, as it was in the district court, is whether DK's unauthorized use of BGA's copyrighted images is fair use. The fair use doctrine is a statutory exception to copyright infringement. Section 107 of the Copyright Act permits the unauthorized use or reproduction of copyrighted work if it is "for purposes such as criticism, comment, news reporting, teaching ..., scholarship, or research." 17 U.S.C. § 107. Whether such "fair use" exists involves a case-by-case determination using four non-exclusive, statutorily provided factors in light of the purposes of copyright. *Harper & Row, Publishers, Inc. v. Nation Enters.*, 471 U.S. 539, 549, 105 S.Ct. 2218, 85 L.Ed.2d 588 (1985). The factors are: (1) "the purpose and character of the use;" (2) "the nature of the copyrighted work;" (3) "the amount and substantiality of the portion used in relation to the copyrighted work as a whole;" and (4) "the effect of the use upon the potential market for or value of the copyrighted work." 17 U.S.C. § 107. "The ultimate test of fair use ... is whether the copyright law's goal of promoting the Progress of Science and useful Arts would be better served by allowing the use than by preventing it." *Castle Rock Entm't, Inc. v. Carol Publ'g Group*, 150 F.3d 132, 141 (2d Cir.1998) (internal citations and quotation marks omitted).

In this case, the district court concluded that the balance of fair use factors weighs in favor of DK. Although the issue of fair use is a mixed question of law and fact, the court may resolve issues of fair use at the summary judgment stage where there are no genuine issues of material fact as to such issues. *Wright v. Warner Books, Inc.*, 953 F.2d 731, 735 (2d Cir. 1991). As there are no genuine issues of material fact here, we review the district court's legal conclusions *de novo*. *New Era Publ'ns Int'l, ApS v. Carol Publ'g Group*, 904 F.2d 152, 155 (2d Cir.1990). We agree with the district court that DK's use of the copyrighted images is protected as fair use.

I. Purpose and Character of Use

We first address "the purpose and character of the use, including whether such use is of a commercial nature or is for nonprofit educational purposes." 17 U.S.C. § 107(1).[NOTE 2] Most important to the court's analysis of the first factor is the "transformative" nature of the work. *See* Pierre N. Leval, *Toward a Fair Use Standard*, 103 Harv. L.Rev. 1105, 1111 (1990). The question is "whether the new work merely supersede[s] the objects of the original creation, or instead adds something new, with a further purpose or different character, altering the first with new expression, meaning, or message." *Campbell v. Acuff–Rose Music, Inc.*, 510 U.S. 569, 579, 114 S.Ct. 1164, 127 L.Ed.2d 500 (1994) (internal citations and quotation marks omitted) (alteration in original).

Here, the district court determined that *Illustrated Trip* is a biographical work, and the original images are not, and therefore accorded a strong presumption in favor of DK's use.

In particular, the district court concluded that DK's use of images placed in chronological order on a timeline is transformatively different from the mere expressive use of images on concert posters or tickets. Because the works are displayed to commemorate historic events, arranged in a creative fashion, and displayed in significantly reduced form, the district court held that the first fair use factor weighs heavily in favor of DK.

Appellant challenges the district court's strong presumption in favor of fair use based on the biographical nature of *Illustrated Trip.* Appellant argues that based on this purported error the district court failed to examine DK's justification for its use of each of the images. Moreover, Appellant argues that as a matter of law merely placing poster images along a timeline is not a transformative use. Appellant asserts that each reproduced image should have been accompanied by comment or criticism related to the artistic nature of the image.

We disagree with Appellant's limited interpretation of transformative use and we agree with the district court that DK's actual use of each image is transformatively different from the original expressive purpose. Preliminarily, we recognize, as the district court did, that *Illustrated Trip* is a biographical work documenting the 30–year history of the Grateful Dead. While there are no categories of presumptively fair use, *see Campbell v. Acuff–Rose Music, Inc.,* 510 U.S. at 584, 114 S.Ct. 1164, courts have frequently afforded fair use protection to the use of copyrighted material in biographies, recognizing such works as forms of historic scholarship, criticism, and comment that require incorporation of original source material for optimum treatment of their subjects. *See* 17 U.S.C. § 107 (stating that fair use of a copyrighted work "for purposes such as criticism, comment... [or] scholarship... is not an infringement of copyright"); *Am. Geophysical Union v. Texaco, Inc.,* 60 F.3d 913, 932 (2d Cir.1994) (Jacobs, J., dissenting) (noting that "[m]uch of our fair use case law has been generated by the use of quotation in biographies, a practice that fits comfortably within the statutory categories of uses illustrative of uses that can be fair") (internal quotation marks omitted) (alteration in original); *Salinger v. Random House, Inc.,* 811 F.2d 90, 96 (2d Cir.1987) (holding that quotation of Salinger's letters in a biography could be considered criticism, scholarship, and research, which are among the illustrative statutory categories of fair use enumerated in 17 U.S.C. § 107). No less a recognition of biographical value is warranted in this case simply because the subject made a mark in pop culture rather than some other area of human endeavor. *See Twin Peaks Prods., Inc. v. Publ'ns Int'l, Ltd.,* 996 F.2d 1366, 1374 (2d Cir.1993) (noting that a work that comments about "pop culture" is not removed from the scope of Section 107 simply because it is not erudite).

In the instant case, DK's purpose in using the copyrighted images at issue in its biography of the Grateful Dead is plainly different from the original purpose for which they were created. Originally, each of BGA's images fulfilled the dual purposes of artistic expression and promotion. The posters were apparently widely distributed to generate public interest in the Grateful Dead and to convey information to a large number of people about the band's forthcoming concerts. In contrast, DK used each of BGA's images as historical artifacts to document and represent the actual occurrence of Grateful Dead concert events featured on *Illustrated Trip* 's timeline. In some instances, it is readily apparent that DK's image display enhances the reader's understanding of the biographical text.[NOTE 3] In other instances, the link between image and text is less obvious; nevertheless, the images still serve as historical artifacts graphically representing the fact of significant Grateful Dead concert events selected by the *Illustrated Trip* 's author for inclusion in the book's timeline.[NOTE 4] We conclude that both types of uses fulfill DK's transformative purpose of enhancing the biographical information in *Illustrated Trip,* a purpose separate and distinct from the original artistic and promotional purpose for which the images were created. *See Elvis Presley Enters., Inc. v. Passport Video,* 349 F.3d 622, 628–29 (9th Cir.2003) (finding the use of television clips to be transformative where "the clips play for only a few seconds and are used for reference purposes while a narrator talks over them or interviewees explain their context in Elvis' career," but not to be transformative where the clips "play without much interruption, [and t]he purpose of showing these clips likely goes beyond merely making a reference for a biography, but instead serves the same intrinsic entertainment value that is protected by Plaintiffs' copyrights"); *see also Hofheinz v. A & E Television Networks, Inc.,* 146 F.Supp.2d 442, 446–47 (S.D.N.Y.2001) (ruling that unauthorized inclusion of copyrighted film clips in actor's biographical film was protected fair use because the biography "was not shown to recreate the creative expression reposing in plaintiff's [copyrighted] film, [but] for the transformative purpose of enabling the viewer to understand the actor's modest beginnings in the film business"). In sum, because DK's use of the disputed images is transformative both when accompanied by referencing commentary and when standing alone, we agree with the district court that DK was not required to discuss the artistic merits of the images to satisfy this first factor of fair use analysis.

This conclusion is strengthened by the manner in which DK displayed the images. First, DK significantly reduced the size of the reproductions. *See Kelly v. Arriba Soft Corp.,* 336 F.3d 811, 818–20 (9th Cir. 2003) (finding online search engine's use of thumbnail-sized images to be highly transformative). While the small size is sufficient to permit readers to recognize the historical significance of the posters, it is inadequate to offer more than a glimpse of their expressive value. In short, DK used the minimal image size necessary to accomplish its transformative purpose.

Second, DK minimized the expressive value of the reproduced images by combining them with a prominent timeline, textual material, and original graphical artwork, to create a collage of text and images on each page of the book. To further this collage effect, the images are displayed at angles and the original graphical artwork is designed to blend with the images and text. Overall, DK's layout ensures that the images at issue are employed only to enrich the presentation of the cultural history of the Grateful Dead, not to exploit copyrighted artwork for commercial gain. *See Hofheinz,* 146 F.Supp. at 446.

Third, BGA's images constitute an inconsequential portion of *Illustrated Trip.* The extent to which unlicensed material is used in the challenged work can be a factor in determining whether a biographer's use of original materials has been sufficiently transformative to constitute fair use. *See Craft v. Kobler,* 667 F.Supp. 120, 129 (S.D.N.Y.1987) (Leval, J.) (finding biography of Stravinsky to be unfair in part because the takings were numerous and were the "liveliest and most entertaining part of the biography"). Although our circuit has counseled against considering the percentage the allegedly infringing work comprises of the copyrighted work in conducting *third-factor* fair use analysis, *see NXIVM Corp. v. Ross Inst.,* 364 F.3d 471, 480 (2d Cir.2004), several courts have done so, *see, e.g., Harper,* 471 U.S. at 565– 66, 105 S.Ct. 2218 (finding the fact that quotes from President Ford's unpublished memoirs played a central role in the allegedly infringing magazine article, constituting 13% of that article, weighed against a finding of fair use); *Salinger,* 811 F.2d at 98–99 (finding the fact that letters are quoted or paraphrased on approximately 40% of the book's 192 pages weighs against fair use). We find this inquiry more relevant in the context of *first-factor* fair use analysis.

In the instant case, the book is 480 pages long, while the BGA images appear on only seven pages. Although the original posters range in size from 139 x 199 to more than 199 x 27,9 the largest reproduction of a BGA image in *Illustrated Trip* is less than 39 x 41/2,9 less than 1/20 the size of the original. And no BGA image takes up more than one-eighth of a page in a book or is given more prominence than any other image on the page. In total, the images account for less than one-fifth of one percent of the book. This stands in stark contrast to the wholesale takings in cases such as those described above, and we are aware of no case where such an insignificant taking was found to be an unfair use of original materials.

Finally, as to this first factor, we briefly address the commercial nature of *Illustrated Trip. See Harper,* 562, 105 S.Ct. 2218 (stating that the fact that the purpose of a new use is commercial weighs against finding fair use). Even though *Illustrated Trip* is a commercial venture, we recognize that "nearly all of the illustrative uses listed in the preamble paragraph of § 107... are generally conducted for profit...." *Campbell,* 510 U.S. at 584, 114 S.Ct. 1164 (internal quotation marks omitted). Moreover, "[t]he crux of the profit/nonprofit distinction is not whether the sole motive of the use is monetary gain but whether the user stands to profit from exploitation of the copyrighted material without paying the customary price." *Harper,* 471 U.S. at 562, 105 S.Ct. 2218. Here, *Illustrated Trip* does not exploit the use of BGA's images as such for commercial gain. Significantly, DK has not used any of BGA's images in its commercial advertising or in any other way to promote the sale of the book. *Illustrated Trip* merely uses pictures and text to describe the life of the Grateful Dead. By design, the use of BGA's images is incidental to the commercial biographical value of the book.

Accordingly, we conclude that the first fair use factor weighs in favor of DK because DK's use of BGA's images is transformatively different from the images' original expressive purpose and DK does not seek to exploit the images' expressive value for commercial gain.

II. Nature of the Copyrighted Work

The second factor in a fair use determination is "the nature of the copyrighted work." 17 U.S.C. § 107(2). To resolve this inquiry the court considers "the protection of the reasonable expectations of one who engages in the kinds of creation/authorship that the copyright seeks to encourage." Leval, *supra,* at 1122. "[C]reative expression for public dissemination falls within the core of the copyright's protective purposes." *Campbell,* 510 U.S. at 586, 114 S.Ct. 1164.

The district court determined that the second factor weighs against DK because the images are creative artworks, which are traditionally the core of intended copyright protection. Nevertheless, the court limited the weight it placed on this factor because the posters have been published extensively. Appellant agrees that the district court properly weighed the second factor against DK, although it questions the lesser protection given to published works. Appellees counter that because the images are mixed factual and creative works and have been long and extensively published, the second factor tilts toward fair use.

We agree with the district court that the creative nature of artistic images typically weighs in favor of the copyright holder. We recognize, however, that the second factor may be of limited usefulness where the creative work of art is being used for a transformative purpose. *See Campbell,* 510 U.S. at 586, 114 S.Ct. 1164 (stating that the second factor is not "likely to help much in separating the fair use sheep from the infringing goats" in cases involving transformative copying of "publicly known, expressive works"). This is not a case such as *Ringgold v. Black Entm't Television, Inc.,* 126 F.3d 70 (2d Cir.1997), in which we held that the creative work was being used for the same decorative purpose as the original. Here, we conclude that DK is using BGA's images for the transformative purpose of enhancing the biographical information provided in *Illustrated Trip.* Accordingly, we hold that even though BGA's images are creative works, which are a core concern of copyright protection, the second factor has limited weight in our analysis because the purpose of DK's use was to emphasize the images' historical rather than creative value.

III. Amount and Substantiality of the Portion Used

The third fair use factor asks the court to examine "the amount and substantiality of the portion used in relation to the copyrighted work as a whole." 17 U.S.C. § 107(3). We review this factor with reference to the copyrighted work, not the infringing work. *New Era,* 904 F.2d at 159. The court must examine the quantitative and qualitative aspects of the portion of the copyrighted material taken. *Campbell,* 510 U.S. at 586, 114 S.Ct. 1164.

The district court determined that even though the images are reproduced in their entirety, the third fair use factor weighs in favor of DK because the images are displayed in reduced size and scattered among many other images and texts. In faulting this conclusion, Appellant contends that the amount used is substantial because the images are copied in their entirety. Neither our court nor any of our sister circuits has ever ruled that the copying of an entire work *favors* fair use. At the same time, however, courts have concluded that such copying does not necessarily weigh against fair use because copying the entirety of a work is sometimes necessary to make a fair use of the image. *See Kelly,* 336 F.3d at 821 (concluding that images used for a search engine database are necessarily copied in their entirety for the purpose of recognition); *Nunez v. Caribbean Int'l News Corp.,* 235 F.3d 18, 24 (1st Cir.2000) (concluding that to copy any less than the entire image would have made the picture useless to the story). Adopting this reasoning, we conclude that the third-factor inquiry must take into account that the "the extent of permissible copying varies with the purpose and character of the use." *Campbell,* 510 U.S. at 586–87, 114 S.Ct. 1164.

Here, DK used BGA's images because the posters and tickets were historical artifacts that could document Grateful Dead concert events and provide a visual context for the accompanying text. To accomplish this use, DK displayed reduced versions of the original images and intermingled these visuals with text and original graphic art. As a consequence, even though the copyrighted images are copied in their entirety, the visual impact of their artistic expression is significantly limited because of their reduced size. *See Kelly,* 336 F.3d at 821 (concluding that thumbnails are not a substitute for full-size images). We conclude that such use by DK is tailored to further its transformative purpose because DK's reduced size reproductions of BGA's images in their entirety displayed the minimal image size and quality necessary to ensure the reader's recognition of the images as historical artifacts of Grateful Dead concert events. Accordingly, the third fair use factor does not weigh against fair use.

IV. Effect of the Use upon the Market for or Value of the Original

The fourth factor is "the effect of the use upon the potential market for or value of the copyrighted work." 17 U.S.C. § 107(4). The court looks to not only the market harm caused by the particular infringement, but also to whether, if the challenged use becomes widespread, it will adversely affect the potential market for the copyrighted work. *Harper,* 471 U.S. at 568, 105 S.Ct. 2218. This analysis requires a balancing of "the benefit the public will derive if the use is permitted and the personal gain the copyright owner will receive if the use is denied." *MCA, Inc. v. Wilson,* 677 F.2d 180, 183 (2d Cir.1981).

In the instant case, the parties agree that DK's use of the images did not impact BGA's primary market for the sale of the poster images. Instead, we look to whether DK's unauthorized use usurps BGA's potential to develop a derivative market. Appellant argues that DK interfered with the market for licensing its images for use in books. Appellant contends that there is an established market for licensing its images and it suffered both the loss of royalty revenue directly from DK and the opportunity to obtain royalties from others.

"It is indisputable that, as a general matter, a copyright holder is entitled to demand a royalty for licensing others to use its copyrighted work, and that the impact on potential licensing revenues is a proper subject for consideration in assessing the fourth factor." *Texaco,* 60 F.3d at 929 (citations omitted). We have noted, however, that "were a court automatically to conclude in every case that potential licensing revenues were impermissibly impaired simply because the secondary user did not pay a fee for the right to engage in the use, the fourth fair use factor would *always* favor the copyright holder." *Id.* at 930 n. 17 (emphasis added); *see Princeton Univ. Press v. Mich. Document Servs.,* 99 F.3d 1381, 1387 (6th Cir.1996) (stating that a copyright holder must have a right to copyright revenues before finding that a failure to pay a license fee equals market harm); Leval, *supra,* at 1124 (stating that "[b]y definition every fair use involves some loss of royalty revenue because the secondary user has not paid royalties"); 4 Melville B. Nimmer & David Nimmer, *Nimmer on Copyright* § 13.05[A][4] (2005) (stating that "it is a given in every fair use case that plaintiff suffers a loss of a potential market if that potential is defined as the theoretical market for licensing the very use at bar"). Accordingly, we do not find a harm to BGA's license market merely because DK did not pay a fee for BGA's copyrighted images.

Instead, we look at the impact on potential licensing revenues for "traditional, reasonable, or likely to be developed markets." *Texaco,* 60 F.3d at 930. In order to establish a traditional license market, Appellant points to the fees paid to other copyright owners for the reproduction of their images in *Illustrated Trip.* Moreover, Appellant asserts that it established a market for licensing its images, and in this case expressed a willingness to license images to DK. Neither of these arguments shows impairment to a traditional, as opposed to a transformative market.[NOTE 5] *See* Leval, *supra,* at 1125 (explaining that "[t]he fourth factor disfavors a finding of fair use only when the market is impaired because the . . . material serves the consumer as a substitute, or, . . . supersedes the use of the original") (internal quotation marks omitted).

Here, unlike in *Texaco,* we hold that DK's use of BGA's images is transformatively different from their original expressive purpose.[NOTE 6] In a case such as this, a copyright holder cannot prevent others from entering fair use markets merely "by developing or licensing a market for parody, news reporting, educational or other transformative uses of its own creative work." *Castle Rock,* 150 F.3d at 146 n. 11. "[C]opyright owners may not preempt exploitation of transformative markets...." *Id.* Moreover, a publisher's willingness to pay license fees for reproduction of images does not establish that the publisher may not, in the alternative, make fair use of those images. *Campbell,* 510 U.S. at 585 n. 18, 114 S.Ct. 1164 (stating that "being denied permission to use [or pay license fees for] a work does not weigh against a finding of fair use"). Since DK's use of BGA's images falls within a transformative market, BGA does not suffer market harm due to the loss of license fees.

V. Balance of Factors

On balance, we conclude, as the district court did, that the fair use factors weigh in favor of DK's use. For the first factor, we conclude that DK's use of concert posters and tickets as historical artifacts of Grateful Dead performances is transformatively different from the original expressive purpose of BGA's copyrighted images. While the second factor favors BGA because of the creative nature of the images, its weight is limited because DK did not exploit the expressive value of the images. Although BGA's images are copied in their entirety, the third factor does not weigh against fair use because the reduced size of the images is consistent with the author's transformative purpose. Finally, we conclude that DK's use does not harm the market for BGA's sale of its copyrighted artwork, and we do not find market harm based on BGA's hypothetical loss of license revenue from DK's transformative market.

CONCLUSION

For the foregoing reasons, we conclude that DK's use of BGA's copyrighted images in its book *Illustrated Trip* is fair use. Accordingly, we AFFIRM.

NOTES:

NOTE 1: The disputed images appear as follows: (1) on page 76, a concert poster for the Grateful Dead, Jefferson Airplane, and Big Brother and the Holding Company playing at the Hollywood Bowl; (2) on page 103, a concert poster for the Grateful Dead, Jefferson Airplane, and Sons of Champlin playing at the Winterland Arena; (3) on page 130, a picture of the front and back of a concert ticket for a show at the Fillmore Theatre, reused for a Grateful Dead concert at the Winterland Arena; (4) on page 254, a concert poster for Grateful Dead shows at the Warfield Theatre; (5) on page 361, a concert poster for a Grateful Dead show at the Oakland Coliseum; (6) on page 397, a concert poster for a Grateful Dead show on New Year's Eve; and (7) on page 421, a fake in-house poster for a New Year's Eve 1993 concert.

NOTE 2: Obviously, the use here is of a general commercial nature rather than a nonprofit nature, but the inquiry is both a broader one and a narrower one than may appear at first glance as will be explained.

NOTE 3: For example, BGA claims copyright infringement of a concert poster image, reproduced on page 254 of *Illustrated Trip,* depicting two skeletons flanking the Warfield Theatre. The reader is expected to view this image together with the text on pages 254 and 255 under the caption, "The Warfield/ Radio City Shows," and with a noncontested image on page 255, depicting two skeletons flanking the Radio City Music Hall. In this instance, the text specifically comments on the poster image, explaining:

> The Dead's real 15th anniversary celebration in 1980 spanned two months, two coasts, and eventually two albums.... The bicoastal settings for the shows were very different—San Francisco's Warfield Theatre was an intimate house of 2,400 seats, while New York City's Radio City Music Hall was, well, Radio City—but the Dead's performances in both produced some of the most treasured moments of the band's early '80s period. . . . The [Dead's] otherwise brilliant Radio City run was marred by a bizarre dispute between the band and Radio City's management. The latter objected to promotional posters showing the inevitable skeletons flanking the venerable venue. Evidently not well versed in Grateful Dead iconography, the Radio City execs interpreted the posters as a coded message that the band thought that Radio City's days were numbered, and they slapped the band with a million-dollar lawsuit. The misunderstanding was quickly cleared up.

The author uses images to enhance the reader's understanding of the statement that Radio City Music Hall executives were unfamiliar with Grateful Dead iconography by displaying nearly identical concert promotion posters for the Warfield Theatre and the Radio City Music Hall.

NOTE 4: For example, BGA claims copyright infringement of a concert poster image, reproduced on page 103 of *Illustrated Trip,* promoting a concert at the Winterland Arena. The reader is expected to view this image together with an entry on the timeline for October 24, 25, and 26, accompanying text describing the shows, and a quotation from Bill Graham to the audience on Saturday, October 25. The text describes the show as follows: Hot Tuna, Jefferson Airplane, and Sons of Champlin play all three nights. On Saturday Stephen Stills may have played on "Turn on Your Lovelight." Sunday marks the last "Doin' that Rag." While the concert poster image does not necessarily enhance the reader's understanding of the text, it serves as a recognizable representation of the concert. It also documents concert information and provides notable historic details, such as the fact that, at this relatively early stage of its career, the Grateful Dead received second billing to Jefferson Airplane.

NOTE 5: To the contrary, had the book been commercially successful—which it was not—it might have garnered interest in the original images in full size because the reduced images have such minimal expressive impact. An afficionado might seek more than a "peek."

NOTE 6: *Texaco* may also be distinguished because in that case we found that scientific researchers' copying of scientific journal articles caused those journals to lose license revenues, because the researchers were looking to their own copies of the articles rather than downloading them from online databases such as Lexis, which paid the journals a license fee. *See* 60 F.3d at 929–32. In other words, *Texaco* involved direct evidence that the allegedly infringing use would cause the owner to lose license revenues derived from a substantially similar use.

Here, in contrast, BGA's direct evidence of its license revenues involves a use that is markedly different from the use by DK. The licenses BGA sold to other publishers were for substantially less transformative uses of its posters: full-page, prominently displayed reproductions of BGA's images, with little discussion of the images or their historical context, much less any compilation of other related works into a coherent whole. Indeed, one of the images BGA points to was used as the cover of a book. DK's use of BGA's images is markedly more original than the other uses that BGA has licensed and BGA thus has not shown direct evidence of significant lost license revenue from the uses at issue here.

STUDY QUESTIONS

- What was the court's ruling in *Bill Graham*? Does the size of the image matter? What other factors are important?
- How does this case apply in the museum context?

Reading Note: The Davidson case reprinted below is one of several copyright infringement lawsuits brought against the U.S. Postal Service for using artwork on postage stamps without permission from the copyright owner. In addition to applying the doctrine of fair use, the case discusses the monetary damages available to the plaintiff in a copyright infringement suit.

ROBERT S. DAVIDSON V. THE UNITED STATES

No. 13-942C (Fed. Cl. June 29, 2018)

OPINION

BRUGGINK, *Judge*.

This is an action for copyright infringement brought by Robert Davidson, the sculptor of the Lady Liberty replica statue in front of the New York-New York Hotel & Casino in Las Vegas, Nevada, against the United States, acting through the United States Postal Service ("Postal Service," or "USPS"). A two week trial was held in September 2017. Post-trial briefing is now complete, and post-trial argument was held on May 1, 2018. Because we find that Mr. Davidson's work was original and because the Postal Service's use of it was not permitted by statute, he is entitled to compensation in the amount of $3,554,946.95, plus interest.

BACKGROUND

Plaintiff fabricated a replica of the Statue of Liberty on the grounds of the New York-New York Hotel & Casino in Las Vegas in 1996. He applied for and obtained a copyright for the replica in 2013, too late for the statutory presumption of validity. It is also undisputed that the Postal Service used a photograph of that work on a stamp released in December 2010 without permission or attribution ("Lady Liberty stamp"). Plaintiff now seeks compensation for that use under 28 U.S.C. § 1498(b) (2012).

Defendant answers that plaintiff's work is too similar to the original in New York Harbor and that the government's use copied nothing original to plaintiff. Defendant also presents the defense of fair use under 17 U.S.C. § 107 (2012). We rejected on summary judgment a defense under section 120(a), which exempts pictorial representations of architectural works. *Davidson v. United States*, No. 13-942C, 2017 WL 3033774 (Fed. Cl. July 18, 2017). The questions for trial were thus whether the Las Vegas Lady Liberty is sufficiently original to be afforded copyright protection, whether the government's use was infringing, and, if so, whether it was otherwise excused as fair use under 17 U.S.C. § 107. The final question, if there was originality, infringement, and no fair use, is the measure of compensation owed plaintiff.

Trial told the story of how Mr. Davidson was contracted to create the replica and then his actual process of creating the statue that sits on the corner of Las Vegas and Tropicana Boulevards in Las Vegas, Nevada. The narrative then shifted to the Postal Service's selection and use of that image for its new 2011 "workhorse" Forever Stamp, followed by the events that happened after the use of Davidson's statue was discovered in 2011. The third act consisted of the presentations of experts who offered opinions on the merits of the stamp among collectors and, most centrally, what the government would have paid for such a use of plaintiff's work had the parties negotiated beforehand at arm's length under normal market conditions. We received testimony from the following witnesses:

This Statue of Liberty Forever stamp was issued by the United States Post Office on December 1, 2010. The stamp shows the replica of the Statue of Liberty (Liberty Enlightening the World) *located at the New York-New York Hotel and Casino on the Las Vegas Strip rather than the original Statue of Liberty in New York. The mistake was not recognized until March 2011. Ten and a half billion of the erroneous stamps were produced—the largest run of an error on a postage stamp. In 2013, sculptor Robert S. Davidson sued the Postal Service for copyright infringement and in July 2018, a judge ordered the United States Postal Service to pay Davidson $3.5 million.*

1. Plaintiff Robert Davidson primarily testified about his background in working with large-scale plaster work and sculpting, including his actual means and method when sculpting the Las Vegas Lady Liberty at issue.

2. Roy Betts is a USPS senior public relations representative. He testified regarding his public statements after the identity of the Lady Liberty image was publically discovered, and other internal communications regarding that issue.

3. Shawn Quinn is the USPS program manager for technology acquisition. He testified regarding his experience at the Postal Service, the process of manufacturing the stamps at issue, USPS's decision to continue using the Lady Liberty stamp after the identity of the sculpture was discovered, and other background information.

4. Joe Stratton is the Postal Service's manager of technical analysis, accounting, and finance. He testified regarding his postal experience as it relates to the sale of stamps, USPS accounting procedures as they relate to the sale of stamps, and any profits derived therefrom. He also testified more specifically about the sale of the stamps at issue in this case and how they were accounted for.

5. Terry McCaffrey was the former manager of stamp development at USPS. His testimony was heard via taped video deposition. He testified about the Postal Service's process in selecting the image of Mr. Davidson's work as well as the approval and finalization of that image. He was also asked why a flag-bearing stamp was married to the Lady Liberty stamp, about stamp classifications, and to provide other background information about relevant Postal Service processes and contractors.

6. William Gicker is the Postal Service's current manager of stamp development and was, at the time of the events discussed during trial, the "creative director for stamps." Tr. 812. He testified regarding the selection of the image of Mr. Davidson's statue, the process in finalizing that selection and placing it on the stamp, and the expected sales of such a stamp. He was also asked about USPS policies and procedures regarding the intellectual property of the images that the Postal Service uses on its stamps and any resulting licenses.

7. Amity Kirby is the USPS senior licensing specialist. She testified regarding her experience licensing out stamp images for third party use.

8. Jim Timmins is a business valuation expert with particular expertise in the valuation of intellectual property. He testified as plaintiff's expert on the proper measure of damages, offering his prior experience in valuing the licensing of intellectual property and his valuation of a hypothetical license between plaintiff and USPS.

9. Bruce Isaacson is an expert in market research and public surveys. He informed the court of the results of a 2016 survey that he conducted related to public customer behavior in retaining, or not, the Lady Liberty stamp.

10. David Keller is the supervisory park ranger for the National Park Service at the National Mall in Washington, DC, and was a park ranger at the Statue of Liberty from 2004 to 2011. He was offered as a records custodian for photographs of the New York statue. Those photographs ultimately were not admitted into evidence.

11. Daniel Piazza is an assistant curator of philately at the Smithsonian National Postal Museum. He is an expert in stamp collecting and the use and history of stamps. He testified about stamp collecting generally and his opinion regarding the popularity of the Lady Liberty stamp among collectors.

12. Christopher Bokhart is an independent financial expert in accounting and damages relating to intellectual property. He shared his opinions regarding the value of a hypothetical license between plaintiff and USPS, had one been agreed to before the events in question.

13. Sarah Handwerger is general counsel to RightsAssist, LLC, a contractor for the Postal Service. Her testimony was accepted into evidence by way of agreed-upon designations and counter-designations of deposition excerpts. She testified regarding the selection of the image on the Lady Liberty stamp and her and RightsAssist's role in that process. That testimony is in evidence as Joint Exhibit 12.

14. Sidney Brown is the Executive Director of PhotoAssist, a Postal Service contractor. She testified regarding her efforts for USPS in obtaining rights to images that it uses on stamps. Her testimony was presented in the form of designated deposition transcript excerpts, which are in evidence as Joint Exhibit 13.

I. Mr. Davidson And The Las Vegas Lady Liberty

Mr. Davidson began working with plaster in the early 1970s, initially in building construction, primarily on the outside of buildings being built in the Las Vegas area, where he has lived his entire life. He started at a company called Valley Plastering as a water boy—hosing down stucco exteriors plastered the previous day. He worked his way up the ranks over a 16 year period, reaching the rank of executive vice president before he left the company in 1987. He then started his own plastering business in 1988, called PlasterTech.

PlasterTech was at first primarily subcontracted on custom residential jobs. As he gained skill and reputation, plaintiff was tasked with interior plaster work as well. He recalled one home in which he finished 13 fireplaces, including one that had a lion's head design. *See* PX 4 (picture of lion fireplace).[NOTE 1] Thus began his experience as a sculptor and designer of plaster work.

Plaintiff sold his business and equipment to Ford Contracting in 1993 and began working directly for that company. Ford was a much bigger contractor, working on large-scale commercial projects such as hotels. As his career progressed, Mr. Davidson shifted focus to the custom design and sculpting of plaster pieces. He explained that he used foam to create the general contours of the finished pieces, which was easier to shape and refine with a high degree of precision. Additional materials were placed on top of the foam, including the plaster or equivalent material for the top finished layer.

One large project on which plaintiff worked at Ford Contracting was the Luxor Hotel in Las Vegas. Mr. Davidson described his role of using plaster and stucco, both on the interior and exterior, as "theming work." In that case, it involved finishing the plaster and stucco surfaces to match the Egyptian theme of the hotel. Tr. 67. He and his crew finished many of these walls to mimic giant precut limestone blocks. In doing so, he built wire templates and cutters to make the lines uniform in appearance. Also part of the theme at the Luxor was a 110-foot-tall replica of the Sphinx in Egypt.

Mr. Davidson testified that Ford Contracting's original Sphinx sculpting subcontractor was unable to complete the face of the statue, and so plaintiff volunteered to finish it. No finishing had been done on the face when plaintiff took over that project; only the frame stood where the face would be. He described his finishing process. It began with another firm making a maquette[NOTE 2] based on the face of the architect, Veldon Simpson, who designed the Luxor Hotel. After establishing some reference points on the frame, Mr. Davidson and his crew began adhering blocks of foam, precut to roughly match the dimensions that were needed to form the face. From there, the foam blocks were filed, rasped, shaped, and sculpted as best Mr. Davidson could to match the face of the Simpson maquette. When he was satisfied with one side of the face, he would take measurements to try to match the opposite side of the face as closely as possible. He changed the face somewhat, however, to avoid an unnatural symmetry in the face. After the form was correct, the plaster and other finish materials were layered on, and the statue was painted.

It took three months to finish the face of the Sphinx with the majority of the work being done at night. During the project Davidson became acquainted with the Western Architecture firm and an individual named Tracy Jones. Plaintiff testified that it was this relationship that led him to be selected as the sculptor of the Lady Liberty statue outside of the New York-New York Hotel in Las Vegas. Mr. Jones connected plaintiff with a company known as Recreation Development Company ("RDC"), which had need of a sculptor as a subcontractor to create the statue in front of the hotel and casino. After his success with the Sphinx, Mr. Davidson was eager to take on the even larger task of the Lady Liberty.

Plaintiff bid $385,000 to do the finish work on the Statue of Liberty replica. His was the winning bid. RDC was responsible for building the structure up until the point at which the foam would be applied by Mr. Davidson. Plaintiff testified that, per the contract, RDC was supposed to have supplied a scale model for plaintiff to follow. No such model was provided to plaintiff, however. Instead he was provided only some photographs of the original, a 12-inch curio, and the architect's outline of the general shape and form of the statue, which plaintiff used for rough dimensioning. The Las Vegas statue was intended to be approximately two-thirds of the size of the original Statue of Liberty.

Davidson took many trips to his local library to view pictures of the New York statue, but no picture he found provided "the three-dimensional feel of the statue." Tr. 130. The differences in shadow and vantage point meant that no one photograph was sufficient as a working guide. Plaintiff was thus left to construct his own maquette as a guide for the larger statue, which he did. *See* PX 234 at 83-86, 7-50, 56-57 (pictures of the plaintiff sculpting the maquette). He did so by making cross-sectional slices, stacking them up and gluing them together. The maquette was finished with the same cementitious acrylic-based coating as the final large statue. The maquette was built inside a jig, which allowed plaintiff to transfer the dimensions, scaled up, to the larger statue. Mr. Davidson also created a dimensioning graph to further aid in getting the dimensions right.

Plaintiff began the construction of the outside of the large statue before the maquette was finished. Although the maquette was his guide, it could not be perfectly replicated, nor did he try to copy it precisely. The process of forming the Lady Liberty was similar to that used in building the face of the Sphinx. Large blocks of foam were cut to rough dimension. Plaintiff then used finer tools to sculpt the form and image he desired. The finish materials–plaster mud and the acrylic-based coating–were also to be used to give shape to the statue. These could be layered to supply extra depth or used to fill in unwanted negative space. The very finest details were added by using hand rasps.

Plaintiff described the process of finishing the 12-foot-high face in this manner:

> Then it comes to the point where I go in with those fine hand rasps . . . and start to rasp it down. That's when the face starts to get some life to it and it really starts to speak to you and kind of tells you which way it's got to go. And it tells you if you do it wrong. It really does. You just start getting to that point to where you are satisfied with the results and you just stop.

Tr. 160. He went on to describe how the statue began to take life for him and to evoke an emotional response:

> But then you get to this point, this is where you start giving the eyes a little life, little subtle touches on the lips and every part of it. . . . Like I said, this is the part of the sculpture, really the only part of the sculpture, that . . . starts to speak to you.

Tr. 162.

He was asked what he had in mind when creating the face:

> Well, I felt since this was going to be for a new hotel in Las Vegas, I felt it just needed to be a little more appropriate for the hotel. I knew that the facade of the hotel would look similar to the skyline of New York, but it wouldn't duplicate it. Everything is out of proportion. . . . It was just a feel. And I just thought that this needed a little more modern, a little more contemporary face, definitely more feminine, just something that I thought was more appropriate for Las Vegas.

Tr. 162-63. He further testified that he looked for guidance at a picture of his mother-in-law every day and that her face was a large influence in the final form of his Lady Liberty's visage. No direction was given to him nor did anyone sign off on his design decisions. He was given free rein to sculpt the statue so long as the theme of the New York City skyline was maintained. His final product was, in his own words, "a little more modern, a little more feminine." Tr. 169. He thought that the original statue's face was "a little harsher. It wasn't as welcoming. It was a little more masculine." Tr. 175. He wanted an end result that was "softer" and "more contemporary." *Id.* "It's hard for me to use adjectives. It's one of those things, you sculpt it and you do it until you think you got it right." *Id.*

He was asked whether he made these changes to differentiate his work from the original or whether they were "just a byproduct of your design." Tr. 174. He replied that it was a byproduct of his design and that the specific features—"more defined eyes and eyelids or a pronounced cupid's bow shape of an upper lip"—were not specifically intended.[NOTE 3] Tr. 173.

On October 4, 1996, Mr. Davidson completed his work. He dedicated his achievement by placing a small plaque in memory of his mother-in-law on the crown of the statue. [NOTE 4] Tr. 179; PX 233 at 296 (photograph of plaque). The parties stipulated that Mr. Davidson's material and labor costs to build the statue totaled about $152,000, leaving him an approximate profit of $233,000 ($385,000 bid minus the $152,000 in costs). The $385,000 that plaintiff received for the project is comparable to other large projects that Mr. Davidson completed subsequent to the Lady Liberty.[NOTE 5]

II. The Postal Service's Use

The Postal Service introduced the first Forever Stamp in 2007, bearing the image of the Liberty Bell in Philadelphia. A Forever Stamp is purchased at the price of first-class postage at the time of purchase, but its value in use is always equal to the current price of one-ounce first-class postage. Upon introduction, it quickly became the main "workhorse" stamp for USPS. A workhorse stamp is one printed by USPS and used by the public primarily to send first class mail. It is a high volume stamp with a high percentage being redeemed for postage.

In 2008, the Postal Service began to work on updating the image of its Forever Stamp. Terry McCaffrey, the manager of stamp development at the time, was in charge of selecting the new image. Both he and William Gicker, McCaffrey's eventual replacement, testified that the public was tiring of the Liberty Bell image. Tr. 735. McCaffrey was looking for something "different and unique." Tr. 764. Because the new Forever Stamp was to be a workhorse stamp, the Postal Service and the Citizens' Stamp Advisory Committee intended it to be of another patriotic icon.[NOTE 6] Mr. McCaffrey testified that the committee liked the idea of a U.S. flag stamp but that such an image had been used so many times for workhorse stamps that the Postal Service and committee did not want to issue the flag stamp by itself. Ultimately a flag stamp was issued contemporaneously with the Lady Liberty stamp, and they were sold together.

Mr. McCaffrey began the search for a new image by asking a contractor, PhotoAssist, to give him access to several photo repositories to look for images of the flag and the Statue of Liberty. He testified that, at the time, the Postal Service had already used at least 20 different images of the Statue of Liberty on different stamps in one form or another. He thus searched the sites himself because he was looking for something "different and unique." Tr. 764. Of all of those images, only two or three were isolated on the face, which is what he was drawn to for the focus of the stamp. *Id.* at 765.

McCaffrey initially narrowed his selection to 24 images of the statue and the flag. These were then narrowed to three images of each, one of which was of plaintiff's statue, a photograph of the face taken by Raimund Linke. Mr. McCaffrey made these selections and did the subsequent culling by himself over the course of a single afternoon. He then contacted Mike Owens at PhotoAssist and asked him to obtain digital image files that he could work with to make his final selection. The photograph of plaintiff's sculpture came from Getty Images ("Getty"). Mr. McCaffrey did not realize that it was not of the New York statue. The other two pictures, from other vendors, were of the original statue.

Mr. McCaffrey selected the photograph of plaintiff's creation for use on the new stamp. In June 2010, he purchased from Getty on behalf of the Postal Service a nonexclusive three-year license for Mr. Linke's photograph, which authorized USPS to print over one million copies of the image. PX 57 (Getty license agreement). USPS paid Getty $1,500 for the license.[NOTE 7] Mr. McCaffrey stated that he would not have selected the image had he known it was not of the real Statue of Liberty. Tr. 805. That testimony was echoed by Sidney Brown, whose deposition testimony was admitted in written form. *See* JX 13 at 317-18.

After receiving the rights and the image, Mr. McCaffrey sized and cropped the picture to make it appropriate for a first-class stamp. Other than the addition of the typical Forever Stamp text superimposed on the face of the stamp, no further alteration was made to the photograph. The design had been generally approved for use on a workhorse stamp by the advisory committee and the Postmaster General in 2008. The committee also approved the pairing of the Lady Liberty stamp with the newly designed flag stamp on which Mr. McCaffrey had been working.

With the rights to the image secured and finalized stamp designs approved, the Postal Service made the decision to issue the two new workhorse stamps on December 1, 2010. According to Mr. Gicker that schedule was accelerated from the normal practice. Tr. 828-29. USPS was anxious to move on from the Liberty Bell stamp because the several-year run of that stamp created accounting difficulties for the Postal Service. As the price of first-class postage rose over time, it became more difficult for the Postal Service to account for the value of stamps that were sold but unredeemed. A new issue allows the Postal Service to mark all outstanding new stamps at a minimum value on the new stamp issue date. [NOTE 8] This internal pressure, in conjunction with the external demand for a new stamp design, drove the Postal Service to move quickly from the Liberty Bell stamp. In addition, the Postal Service hoped to put the new stamps in circulation in time for the holiday mailing season. The two new stamps, Lady Liberty and the flag stamp, were released for public sale on or about December 1, 2010, and went into full production as workhorse stamps. A press release was issued on that same day that attributed the photograph of the statue to Mr. Linke. PX 76. Plaintiff was given no attribution.

On March 18, 2011, USPS was made aware that the image on the stamp was that of plaintiff's work when an individual from a stock photography company, Sunipix, emailed the Postmaster General's inbox with that information. PX 37 at 3. The Postal Service and PhotoAssist quickly confirmed the facts and USPS began working internally on what its response would be. Layne Owens, the manager of stamp development, noted in an email to Stephen Kearney of USPS that, although PhotoAssist had failed to properly identify the subject of the photograph, after looking at it, "it's quite apparent that it had to be" of the Las Vegas replica. PX 85. In response to an inquiry from Mr. Kearney, Mr. Owens represented on March 21, 2011, that, had stamp development "known the origin of the photograph, we would have attributed the photograph as having been taken of the statue in Las Vegas; however, we would still have used this photo." PX 37 at 2. He went on to explain that the Statue of Liberty had appeared on 23 stamps prior to this one and that Mr. McCaffrey selected the image he did because it "was very different from anything we've done before. That was its appeal.... There are only so many ways to continue to reinterpret an iconic image." *Id.* Mr. Kearney then promised to pass along this information to Roy Betts, a USPS spokesperson, who had also received notice of the error from Sunipix. *Id.*

Mr. Owens confirmed that information to Roy Betts later that same day in a separate email: USPS "still love[s] the stamp design and would have selected this photograph anyway. We were looking for a different treatment of this icon that has been on 23 different stamps." PX 244 at 1. Mr. Owens further represented that corrections to future materials regarding the stamp would be made but that he did not think the Postal Service needed to issue a stand-alone correction. That was the public position Mr. Betts disseminated when asked by media and stamp collecting groups. He repeated the representation of Mr. Owens that the Postal Service loved the image, that it was looking for something different, and that it would have selected the image even if the facts had been known in 2010. *See* Tr. 420-21

(Betts); *see also* PX 109; PX 110. He made the same statements to other USPS personnel. PX 108; PX 121

In an internal memo dated March 23, 2011, Mr. Kearney detailed the error, stating that three billion of the paired stamps had been printed to date and that the legal department had been tasked with determining "what licenses must be executed." PX 95. The memo also reflected that USPS was examining what the contractual relationship between the sculptor of the Las Vegas statue and the New York-New York Hotel was, concluding that "it [was] too early to determine whether any liability exists or how much compensation may be required." *Id.* Mr. Owens informed the Citizens' Stamp Advisory Committee on April 14, 2011, that the stamp would continue to be used until supplies were exhausted and that the "image is a bold graphic that works well at stamp size and is immediately recognizable as Lady Liberty." PX 104. He reported that the stamp was "very popular." *Id.*

Several months later, in response to an inquiry by a member of Congress, the Postal Service stated that it should have correctly attributed the image to Mr. Davidson and that new procedures had been put in place to avoid such errors in the future. PX 151 at 2 (June 8, 2011 letter from the Deputy Postmast General to Congressman Elliot Engel). The Postal Service's letter also indicates that $8 million had been invested in printing these stamps and that withdrawing and reissuing a new one would have been cost prohibitive. *Id.*

USPS continued to ship and sell the Lady Liberty stamp. As of June 2011, USPS had printed 10.5 billion of the stamps, 4.4 billion of which were already in the field for sale or had been sold. It was anticipated that the remaining stamps would ship later that year. *See* PX 148 (email from Charles Delaney to Roy Betts). Mr. Quinn testified that, as of September 2011, an additional 1.125 billion stamps were issued. Tr. 539-40. As Mr. Quinn explained, given the production already completed, it would have been impossible for USPS to have produced another one billion stamps to replace those already printed and ready for distribution. Tr. 529-32.

In January 2014, the Lady Liberty stamp was retired along with the paired flag stamp. Ultimately, 4.9 billion of the Lady Liberty stamps were sold, amounting to just over $2.1 billion in sales for that stamp alone. Equal figures were sold and collected for the paired or "convoyed" flag stamp.[NOTE 9]

USPS employs a firm called Synovate to track and calculate how many stamps will not be used to send mail. This percentage is known as retention or breakage. Tr. 546-51 (Quinn). The Postal Service tracks these numbers because it accounts for stamps that will never be redeemed differently from those likely to be used as postage. Stamps retained by collectors or otherwise never redeemed represent virtually pure profit for USPS. Tr. 551. The higher the retention rate, the better for USPS, and Mr. Quinn stated that exploiting breakage and retention was always of interest to USPS management. Tr. 551, 611.

To that end, Synovate provided quarterly surveys on retention of stamps to the Stamp Services Department at USPS, which tracks such information to glean which stamps consumers were attracted to. Tr. 610-11. Mr. Quinn created a spreadsheet in 2011 that reflected a retention rate for the Lady Liberty and flag stamps at nearly 4.69% for that year, which amounted to nearly $75 million in value to USPS.[NOTE 10] Tr. 577-78, 582; PX 154; PX 154A. Mr. Quinn further explained, that although that retention rate is not high, those figures represented a high degree of profitability since the volume of workhorse stamps is very high.[NOTE 11] The final official USPS estimate for retention of the two stamps was 3.24%. Tr. 632-33 (Stratton). That figure was adopted in the Postal Service's financial statements. Tr. 633. The Postal Service's final estimate for profitability from the Lady Liberty stamp is $70,969,419 with an equal number for the flag stamp. *See* PX 212 (interrogatory answers).

III. Legal History

After the successful and profitable completion of the Las Vegas Lady Liberty statue, Mr. Davidson took a photograph of the face of the statue and used it as a logo for his Plaster-Tech business and for a new concrete cutting business that he started. Tr. 189-90; PX 233 at 313 (photograph). He testified that beginning around 1997 or 1998 he used the image on letterhead, business cards, equipment, and on the side of trucks. Tr. 189-90.

Plaintiff reports discovering the use of his statue by the Postal Service one day after his wife returned from a trip to a local post office. She had purchased a book of Forever Stamps and excitedly notified her husband that "our statue is on the stamp."[NOTE 12] Tr. 192. Sometime thereafter, plaintiff contacted an attorney regarding copyrighting his work. She agreed to file a copyright application on his behalf and did so in January 2012. *See* JX 1 (copyright application). Mr. Davidson also contacted a litigation firm based in Minneapolis, Minnesota, concerning his rights in his work. According to plaintiff, after several years working with Mr. Davidson, that firm withdrew from representation based on an asserted conflict of interest. *See* Tr. 194. Plaintiff then found local counsel who performed some additional work regarding the copyright registration. Mr. Davidson's copyright eventually was issued with an effective date of November 15, 2013. *See* JX 2 (Copyright Registration No. VA 1-882-070).

Mr. Davidson has never sought to license or otherwise monetize his copyright in the Las Vegas statue nor has he attempted to enforce his copyright against any party other than the United States. He was asked why he sought compensation from the government in this lawsuit:

> I don't know how they would acknowledge me. I don't believe after the fact that they would put my name on the stamp. If my name was on the stamp, then everybody would immediately recognize that it was me. And it was just a very tough, very demanding project. And I'm very proud of her, and it's just something I didn't think lightly of.

Tr. 200. He was also asked what he would have done had the Postal Service approached him prior to producing the stamp and asked permission to use an image. He responded that he would have sought advice on what the value of an image of his statue would have been. Tr. 200.

Plaintiff filed suit here in November 2013. After three years of discovery, the parties filed cross-motions for summary judgment in March and April 2017. Plaintiff sought a ruling that his work was original and protected and that the government was liable for infringing his copyright; defendant asserted the defenses of non-originality, fair use, and that plaintiff's statue was not eligible for copyright protection because it was an architectural work for which pictorial representations are exempted from copyright protection. We denied both parties' motions by an order dated July 17, 2018, in which we rejected defendant's argument regarding the pictorial representation of architectural works exception. We set the matter for trial on all unresolved issues.

DISCUSSION

There is no dispute that defendant used an image of plaintiff's statue without permission. Although the Postal Service paid for a license from Getty Images for the photograph, Getty had no rights to the underlying subject of the photograph. 28 U.S.C. § 1498(b) waives sovereign immunity for claims of copyright infringement against the federal government "for the recovery of his reasonable and entire compensation as damages for such infringement." *Id.*

The Copyright Act specifically protects "pictorial, graphic, and sculptural works." 17 U.S.C. § 102(a)(5) (2012). These works must be original. *Id.* § 102(b). We previously held that Mr. Davidson's statue was a sculpture rather than a building but did not reach the question of originality. *Davidson v. United States*, No. 13-942C, 2017 WL 3033774, *3 (Fed. Cl. July 18, 2017). The Copyright Act protects the "the form but not [the] mechanical or utilitarian aspects" of "artistic craftsmanship." *Id.* § 101. Plaintiff must prove a valid copyright, that it was infringed, and his damages.

Defendant has asserted that the statue is a replica and contains no truly original work, meaning that plaintiff's copyright is invalid and the government owes nothing for its use of an image of plaintiff's statue. As a related argument, defendant contends that it copied no original elements. Defendant also pleads the statutory defense of fair use under 17 U.S.C. § 107, which excuses certain uses of copyrighted work. Defendant bears the burden of proof on the statutory defense.

We begin with the question of whether Mr. Davidson's statue is entitled to copyright protection. If it is, we must decide whether defendant's use was infringing and, if so, excused as fair under the statue. If not, we turn to what damages are owed. We answer the first three questions in favor of plaintiff and thus must also consider damages. We take each issue in turn.

I. Infringement

The infringement issue presents the court with two questions: 1) is Mr. Davidson's copyright valid and, if so, 2) was it infringed? The parties disagree as to the correct answer to each.

There is no question that plaintiff was tasked with creating a replica of the Statue of Liberty in New York Harbor, but plaintiff testified that he was given artistic license and that he both intended and achieved a more contemporary and feminine face in the end. Defendant argues that there is insufficient evidence to establish that he accomplished his aim and that the idea of a softer and feminine appearance is not subject to copyright protection. Defendant also avers that it did not infringe because nothing it copied was original. It is the face, which plaintiff points to as the discriminator between the two statues, that was copied by defendant.

A. Mr. Davidson's Statue Is Original

Plaintiff's copyright registration was not within five years of the public availability of his work, and thus his work is not entitled to a statutory presumption of eligibility. *See* 17 U.S.C. § 410(c) (2012). He therefore bears the burden of proving that his copyright is valid, which is to say that he must prove his work to be original. *See Feist Publ'ns, Inc. v. Rural Tel. Serv. Co.*, 499 U.S. 340, 345 (1991) ("The *sine qua non* of copyright is originality."). This requires only a showing of "some minimal degree of creativity" and that it was his own independent creation of those original elements. *Id.* The Supreme Court described this level of required creativity as "extremely low" and stated that "even a slight amount will suffice." *Id.* The focus is on the expression of an original idea and not the idea itself. *Oracle Am., Inc. v. Google Inc.*, 750 F.3d 1339, 1354 (Fed. Cir. 2014). It is thus the case that a work of art need not be wholly original to be copyrightable; it need only be a new and original expression of some previous work or idea. *See Feist*, 499 U.S. at 345 (stating that "originality does not signify novelty" in discussing the protection afforded to compilations). Derivative works and compilations are specifically afforded protection by the act. 17 U.S.C. § 103(a) (2012). The protection applies, however, "only to material contributed by the author of such work, as distinguished from the preexisting material employed in the work." *Id.* § 103(b). As the Seventh Circuit stated, plaintiff must show "nontrivial expressive variation" between the original and the derived work and that any such differences "distinguish from the underlying work in some meaningful way." *Shrock v. Learning Curve Int'l, Inc.*, 586 F.3d 513, 521 (7th Cir. 2009). This is not meant to be a different or higher standard; the court need only find the same level of "originality . . . in a derivative work . . . as that required for copyright in any other work.[NOTE 13] *Id.* at 520. Here, we find that burden met.

Mr. Davidson's testimony establishes that his intent was not to merely copy the Statue of Liberty. Although he was hired to clearly invoke the iconic New York image, it was his testimony that he intended to give the face a "fresh" look, updating and making her appearance more feminine. He contrasted his result with the "harsher" and "more masculine" look of the original. He also testified that he envisioned his mother-in-law as inspiration for the new look and viewed her picture every night during the construction of the face of the statue. Though he could not give detail as to specific elements of the face, such as the lips or eyes, that he set out to change, he believed that he achieved a "softer" and more feminine final appearance.

Defendant makes much of the lack of contemporaneous statements made by Mr. Davidson to media or elsewhere of this currently-expressed intent.[NOTE 14] Defendant also argues that plaintiff's statements about the feminine and contemporary appearance that he sought to evoke are mere ideas unprotected by the Copyright Act. In the absence of definable features alien to the original, defendant finds the necessary modicum of originality missing. Defendant also makes much of the fact that plaintiff could not identify the specific features that he intended to change in order to render his statue's face more feminine and softer. We find no such requirement in the law, however. The finder of fact need only be able to observe a nontrivial expression of artistic creativity.

We are satisfied that plaintiff succeeded in making the statue his own creation, particularly the face. A comparison of the two faces unmistakably shows that they are different. Although the record does not contain many pictures of the original, the magazine cover provided by plaintiff which bears a picture of the original Statue of Liberty's face is sufficient. The differences are plainly visually observable, can be articulated, and are not merely "ideas." *Compare* PX 233-301 *with* PX 231-17. We agree that Mr. Davidson's statue evokes a softer and more feminine appeal. The eyes are different, the jaw line is less massive and the whole face is more rounded. It was these characteristics that drew Mr. McCaffrey to the image. *See Eden Toys, Inc. v. Florelee Undergarment Co.*, 697 F.2d 27, 34-35 (2d Cir. 1982) (finding that minor changes in the illustration of Paddington Bear, described as giving the bear a "different, cleaner look," were nontrivial). We note as well that Layne Owens, the manager of stamp development, was of the view that "it's quite apparent that it had to be" of the Las Vegas replica. PX 85. His statement that "[w]e were looking for a different treatment of this icon that has been on 23 different stamps," PX 244 at 1, along with Mr. Betts' similar comments, indicate that there are evident differences from the original.

Defendant argues that such apparent differences are but the result of camera angle, lighting, shadowing, and weathering and should be ignored for the purposes of the originality inquiry. We disagree. To the court, the differences in the faces are meaningful and not trivial. Nor do we find any secondary evidence to support defendant's assertion. In contrast, the record is replete with statements from the actors involved reaching the opposite conclusion: the two faces are distinct and these new facial features were appealing enough to have induced Mr. McCaffrey to select the image of plaintiff's statue and for the Postal

Service to have publically affirmed its decision to feature Mr. Davidson's statue as a new take on a classic icon. We view such statements and testimony as secondary evidence of what our own comparison reveals. Mr. Davidson's statue, although invoking an existing world-famous statue, is an original, creative work, and as such is the subject of a valid copyright registration.

B. The Postal Service Copied Original Elements

Having determined that the face of plaintiff's sculpture is distinct, original, and protected, we find that defendant's use was infringing. A necessary element to any infringement claim is not just that the work as a whole is original but also that the part copied by the defendant actually be original. *Harper & Row v. Nation Enterprises*, 471 U.S. 539, 548 (1985). Defendant argues that infringement cannot be assumed simply because the two works are found to be different. The government points to the fact that the Postal Service did not notice the difference between the two faces itself until notified months after producing many millions of stamps. The conclusion for defendant is that nothing original must have been copied. This is nonsense.

It is the face of the Las Vegas statue that is displayed on the offending stamp. It is the face that distinguishes the two statues. All of the testimony revolves around the two faces and whether the Las Vegas lady's face is different. Having found that it is, the conclusion that defendant's use infringed is inescapable. Mr. McCaffrey did no editing to the image other than sizing it for display on a stamp and adding the normal stamp copy. We find that the Postal Service's use of the image copied all of the original elements described above. We next turn to the question of whether defendant's infringing use was otherwise allowed as fair use under the statue.

II. Fair Use

Some copying of protected material is characterized by the Copyright Act as being fair use and thus excepted from the definition of infringement. This defense is laid out in 17 U.S.C. § 107 (2012):

> Notwithstanding the provisions of sections 106 and 106A, the fair use of a copyrighted work . . . is not an infringement of copyright. In determining whether the use made of a work in any particular case is a fair use the factors to be considered shall include—(1) the purpose and character of the use, including whether such use is of a commercial nature or is for nonprofit educational purposes; (2) the nature of the copyrighted work; (3) the amount and substantiality of the portion used in relation to the copyrighted work as a whole; and (4) the effect of the use upon the potential market for or value of the copyrighted work.

There is no generally applicable definition of fair use, and therefore each case must be decided on its own facts and unique circumstances. *Campbell v. Acuff-Rose Music, Inc.*, 510

U.S. 569, 577-78 (1994). The courts have generally considered each of the four elements listed in the statue as applicable in any particular case, and our review of the case law reveals that the law has not strayed far from those four considerations. In any event, the parties have limited themselves to arguing the four enumerated factors, and we are not aware of any other unique considerations to apply here.

A. Purpose and Character of the Use

The purpose and character of the use is often the dispositive factor in the fair use analysis. This factor embraces both how the work is used and to what end, i.e., whether the work is somehow transformed by the new use and what is the user of the work doing with it. If the work is transformed by the new use, the law will generally allow it under the fair use doctrine. *See Campbell*, 510 U.S. at 579 ("the goal of copyright, to promote science and the arts, is generally furthered by the creation of transformative works"). The Court posed the question as "whether the new work merely supersede[s] the objects of the original creation or instead adds something new, with a further purpose or different character, altering first with new expression, meaning, or message." *Id.* Further, the statute requires courts to consider whether the end use of the new work is "of a commercial nature or is for nonprofit or educational purposes." 17 U.S.C. § 107. The former suggesting that the use is not protected by the statute.

The government does not argue that nature of its use was transformative. Instead it argues that the nature and character of its use favors a finding of fair use "because, as a workhorse stamp, the vast majority of the revenues to the Postal Service represent payment of postage for the universal required service of mail" and "not as payment for the art shown on the stamp." Def.'s Post-Trial Br. 23.

Plaintiff disagrees, pointing to the fact that USPS sold over $4 billion worth of the stamps bearing plaintiff's work. Even using defendant's expert's numbers, the Postal Service made $140 million in pure profit from breakage from the Lady Liberty stamp and the flag stamp combined sales. This, in plaintiff's view, is a purely commercial use not intended to be protected by section 107's fair use defense.

We agree. As the Federal Circuit found in the *Gaylord* decision, where the Postal Service had sold $17 million in stamps, $5.4 million of which were retained by collectors and represented pure profit to the government, "the stamp clearly has a commercial purpose." *Gaylord v. United States*, 595 F.3d 1364, 1374 (Fed. Cir. 2010). The fact that a smaller percentage of the overall sales total represented breakage or retainage does not make the use noncommercial. Despite the fact that it regularly operates at a loss, the Postal Service is in business and seeks to operate at a profit, or at least seeks to fully fund its operations through its own revenues received from sales. It offers the service of delivering mail, which is, in a broad sense, in competition with private vendors offering similar services. The testimony of the Postal Service's own employees made clear that the attractiveness of the image played a key role in selecting it in hopes of attracting both overall higher sales and higher retention rates. The first factor strongly favors a finding of infringement.

B. Nature of the Copyrighted Work

The nature of the copyrighted work factor considers, to borrow a phrase from Justice Story, "the value of the materials used" to decide whether copyright protection should be extended despite a claim of fair use. *Folsom v. Marsh*, 9 F. Cas. 342, 348 (Cir. Court, D. Mass. 1841) (cited by the Supreme court when considering this factor in *Campbell*, 510 U.S. at 586). Some copyrighted works will receive less protection in the face of a fair use claim than others, such as when a work is derivative, as it is here. *See Campbell*, 510 U.S. at 586 ("some works are closer to the core of intended copyright protection than others, with the consequence that fair use is more difficult to establish when the former works are copied"). The courts consider questions such as "'(1) whether the work is factual or informational, and (2) whether the work is published or unpublished, with the scope of fair use involving unpublished works being considerably narrower.'" *Blanch v. Koons*, 467 F.3d 244, 256 (2d Cir. 2006) (quoting Howard B. Abrams, *The Law of Copyright*, § 15:52 (2006)). If a work is expressive or creative, a use by another is less likely to be considered fair. *See Gaylord*, 595 F.3d at 1374 (citing *Blanch*, 467 F.3d at 257).

Here, defendant claims that the derivative nature of Mr. Davidson's replica statue means that it is afforded only a "thin copyright." Def.'s Post- Trial Br. 23. Defendant points to the fact that the Postal Service was itself confused and did not recognize that plaintiff's work was not the original New York statue and that the public did not immediately recognize the difference.

The suggestion that the image added nothing to the postage aspect of the stamp is not credible, however. If that were the case the Postal Service would simply issue characterless stamps with nothing but the amount of postage. Nor would the Postal Service invest so much effort in the images it utilizes. More particularly, in this case, it is clear that the creative elements of plaintiff's work are precisely what attracted the Postal Service's interest.

Plaintiff counters that the creative elements employed by Davidson that we cited above in finding originality are precisely what mitigate against fair use here. Plaintiff also suggests that the fact that statue has been a publicly displayed monument since 1996, i.e., has been widely published, cuts against fair use.

This factor favors neither party. Although we did find that the original elements of plaintiff's statue were creative and expressive, its intended use as a replica mitigates in favor of defendant. Further, plaintiff's argument that his work had been publically displayed for over 10 years before the use is not well founded. When a work is published, a subsequent use is more likely to be considered fair use. *See Blanch*, 467 F.3d at 256. In sum, we find this factor favors neither party.[NOTE 15]

C. The Portion Used

Also relevant to this inquiry is the substantiality and portion of the original work used. This is self explanatory. The more of the original work copied, the less likely the new use will be considered fair, and, if the portion copied is of the critical core of expressive material, that use will not be fair. *See, e.g., Harper & Row Publishers, Inc. v. Nation Enters*, 471 U.S. 539, 564- 66 (1985) (affirming that copying 300 words from President Ford's memoirs was infringing because those words went to "the heart of the book").

Here we find that this factor favors plaintiff. The original and expressive portion of plaintiff's statue was the face, which was almost entirely captured (at least as from the vantage of the photograph) by the stamp. This factor mitigates against the government's asserted defense.

D. The Effect of the Use

The fourth inquiry looks at the "effect of the use upon the potential market for or value of the copyrighted work." 17 U.S.C. § 107. Plaintiff admits that this factor tilts in the government's favor as plaintiff could cite no harm to Mr. Davidson's business from the Postal Service's use, and he has shown no other interest in exploiting the work. We find this factor favors defendant.

E. The Use Was Not Fair

On balance, we find that defendant has not proven its use to have been fair. The Postal Service's use of the image on its "ship of the line" or workhorse stamp, printing billions of copies and selling them to the public as part of a business enterprise—whether for use to send mail or to be retained in collections—so overwhelmingly favors a finding of infringement that no fair use can be found. The government's citation to the fact that it only used the image on its workhorse stamp is ironic given that, although proportionally the profit is low as compared to that cited in *Gaylord*, the overall numbers are vastly higher. Defendant collected over $4 billion in revenue (both stamps, Lady Liberty and flag) from the use of Mr. Davidson's statue, and, even though a very low portion of the revenue represents profit, that number is over $70 million for the Lady Liberty stamp alone. Some portion of that is owed to plaintiff as damages. Further, the portion used was entirely of what we consider to have been the original work contributed by Mr. Davidson. The government's only real defense is that its use did not particularly harm plaintiff's business as an industrial sculptor. That may be true, but we also note that it certainly did not benefit him. The Postal Service offered neither public attribution nor apology.[NOTE 16]

III. Damages

Having reached the conclusions above, we consider the extent of compensation owed Mr. Davidson under 28 U.S.C. §1498(b). The statute states that, when the court finds infringement, it should award "reasonable and entire compensation as damages for such infringement." The Federal Circuit explained in its second *Gaylord* opinion that this measure is the same as under the Copyright Act's provision for actual damages, 17 U.S.C. § 405.17 678 F.3d 1339, 1343 (2012). The court found in that case that the measure of damages was the fair market value of a license to use plaintiff's work as defendant did. *Id.* This assumes a willing buyer and a willing seller negotiating at arm's length. *Id.* Assuming this framework, the matter is left to the trial court's discretion to craft an appropriate remedy. *Gaylord v. United States*, 777 F.3d 1363, 1369 (Fed. Cir. 2015).

Much of the trial testimony consisted of the respective experts' opinions on the value of a non-exclusive license for work such as the sculpture infringed here, as well as testimony of fact witnesses as to what the Postal Service's practice was in valuing, paying and selling licenses when it did so properly. Defendant also offered a survey expert whose work sought to dim the impact of the retention numbers (those stamps representing pure profit to USPS). We begin with the relevant fact testimony and then consider that of the experts.

A. USPS's Own Licensing Practices

The Postal Service has both an art department for acquiring the rights to images used on its stamps ("in-licensing") and a separate department for selling the rights to use the image of stamps (out-licensing). Both are relevant to our inquiry.

1. What USPS Pays for Art

Defendant's overall approach to a hypothetical negotiation was that, because it has never paid more than token amounts for the use of images, the court should cap damages at the most the Postal Service ever voluntarily pays, i.e., $5,000. The testimony of Mr. Gicker, Ms. Brown, and Ms. Handwerger was unequivocal that USPS never paid more than $5,000 for an image to be used on stamp. The amount was typically in the $1,000 to $2,000 range. Mr. McCaffrey testified that in 2008 the average was $3,000 if an artist was commissioned to illustrate an image for use on a stamp, and the cap was $5,000. Tr. 751-52. And it is the case that some entities will give USPS a no-fee license for use of their art on stamps. Two such examples given at trial were that of the Walt Disney Corporation and the estate of Andy Warhol. As plaintiff points out, however, such use comes with attribution, which amounts to free publicity. Mr. Gicker explained that most artists consider it an honor to have their work used on a stamp and view the visibility and publicity to be a highly valuable intangible benefit. Tr. 908-909; *see also* JX 13 at 217 (Sidney Brown's testimony). Plaintiff, of course, was not given that option.

Ms. Brown testified that the market for art and photos available to the Postal Service is ample. *See* JX 13 at 111-12. This is especially so for patriotic images because they are widely available from stock photography companies. Tr. 980 (Gicker). This presumably helps keep the price down for any single image desired by USPS. Even if the Postal Service cannot find the exact image it desires, it can commission photographers to produce the image. These arrangements also do not exceed $5,000. Tr. 761-63 (McCaffrey); Tr. 904-906 (Gicker). All the relevant USPS witnesses stated that a running royalty rate was unheard of and a "non-starter." JX 12 at 857 (stating that such an arrangement was a non-starter).

2. What USPS Demands to License Its Own Art

We heard the testimony of Amity Kirby, who is the senior licensing specialist at USPS. She has worked there for approximately 10 years, of which two or three have been as the senior licensing specialist. She currently is responsible for all of the licensing that the Postal Service does of its intellectual property. Prior to this position she worked in licensing for the Smithsonian Institute. She told the court about her experience out-licensing images of stamps for commercial usage by other entities and testified that it is USPS practice to copyright its stamps and stamp booklet covers. When an entity approaches USPS wanting to use the image of a stamp commercially, the Postal Service requires a license agreement, either fixing a flat fee or a running royalty. *See* Tr. 1036. If, for example, an author or group wanted to use the image of a stamp in a textbook and the run was limited to 100,000 copies, the Postal Service would likely ask for a flat fee. Tr. 1037. On the other hand, if a company approached Ms. Amity with a request to use a stamp on one million tee shirts for sale to the public, she would seek a running royalty.[NOTE 18] Tr. 1037-38. The higher the distribution, both as to total units and channels of distribution, the likelier that USPS would demand a running royalty.[NOTE 19] She also testified that nonprofit uses have in the past resulted in non- fee agreements. Tr. 1042. Her department considers stamp images to be art. Tr. 1047.

It was her testimony that, during the relevant time period, USPS practice was to license out its own intellectual property at a rate of 8% of total gross sales by the manufacturer of the product[NOTE 20] Tr. 1057 (referencing 2006). Today that number is 10%. Tr. 1060-61. USPS might deviate from that number, but 10% is the rate that it tries to achieve today.

Ms. Kirby also explained that companies frequently seek to buy a package of images from USPS to use on what she called a "program" organized around some theme. For example, Ms. Kirby stated that one frequent subject of out-licensing is the Postal Service's popular "love" stamps with romantically themed images. A license covering several images would typically involve a running royalty. Tr. 1063. She further testified that a license for a single image was more likely to result in a flat fee agreement. *Id.* The example she used was again a textbook displaying the image of a single stamp. That sort of a license would, however, be calculated on the total anticipated images being produced by the licensee. Tr. 1068. In that sense, it is an attempt to reverse engineer the result of what a running royalty rate might ultimately produce. It was her general observation that the Postal Service would try to "negotiate the best that we can get," because her job is to make the Postal Service money. Tr. 1070.

B. Expert Testimony on the Value of a Hypothetical License

Both parties presented testimony from business valuation experts whose expertise is in the valuation of intellectual property. Plaintiff's expert considered the market for artwork broadly speaking, while defendant's expert centered on USPS's own history in buying the rights to art. Predictably, the results are disparate. Defendant also presented testimony from an expert on public surveys. This individual conducted such a survey regarding the retention of the Lady Liberty stamp and attached flag stamp, inquiring as to the numbers retained and the reasons for retention. We outline each expert's testimony below.[NOTE 21]

1. Mr. Timmins

Plaintiff presented the testimony of Jim Timmins, an expert in valuing intellectual property, including copyrights. He is currently the owner and managing partner of Teknos Associates, a Silicon Valley business valuation and financial advisory firm. His firm's primary work is to "provide . . . business valuation services to companies, venture capital firms and others interested in the field for tax compliance, financial reporting, transaction support, and occasionally litigation support." Tr. 1138. His firm specializes in "technology-driven companies," valuing their securities and other intangible assets, such as patents, copyrights, and trademarks. He has provided opinions in roughly 60 court cases around the country.

Prior to nine years with his own company, Mr. Timmins worked for 10 years on Wall Street doing investment banking. It was at these firms that he began valuing businesses. He then moved to Silicon Valley, where he spent the next 15 years at a venture capital firm, working on bringing companies to initial public offering. In this position, he again valued business assets, including intellectual property and was involved in negotiating the purchase and sale of such rights. Tr. 1142. Included in that experience was the licensing of copyrights. Tr. 1143. He holds a bachelors degree from the University of Toronto and a masters of business administration ("MBA") from Stanford University. He does not have any prior experience valuing a copyright for art.

His ultimate conclusion was that the license for Mr. Davidson's statue should have generated a running royalty rate of 1.5% for the Lady Liberty stamps used to send mail and a 5% rate for stamps retained and not redeemed as postage. He also opined that the convoyed sales of the flag stamp should be covered by a 0.75% rate for flag stamps used to send mail and 2.5% for those not redeemed as postage. Philatelic products, sold strictly for collectors, according to Mr. Timmins, were entitled to a 10% royalty rate.[NOTE 22] He applied these rates against USPS's own recorded sales and estimated retention/breakage figures. The end result of which was a license valued at approximately $53,013,154.[NOTE 23]

In reaching these conclusions, Mr. Timmins considered the factors influencing both sides' positions, such as timing, duration, exclusivity, and territory. It was his opinion that the Postal Service in 2010 was under pressure to release a new Forever workhorse stamp and that viable alternatives, considering both time and cost, were not available to USPS. See Tr. 1177-83. Mr. Timmins then considered comparable licenses in the marketplace to inform his opinion, centering on licenses for artwork. That search revealed running royalty rates ranging from 2.5% to 10%, with an average of 6.5%. Tr. 1211-21.

Mr. Timmins did not consider USPS's own policy of not paying more than $5,000 to be a relevant fact and did not view it as a reflection of the bargaining positions of the parties. Tr. 1207. He thus did not factor it into his conclusion other than to reject it as a comparator in his basket of similar transactions. He did, however, consider Mr. Davidson's lack of history licensing his artwork. This, he concluded, put plaintiff in a weaker negotiating position, Tr. 1261, although it would not preclude Mr. Davidson from insisting on a running royalty. It simply drove down the rates Mr. Davidson might have achieved to below the market averages he found in his research. Mr. Timmins also assumed that the license agreement would provide no attribution to Mr. Davidson, which presumably would be worth something to Mr. Davidson.

2. Mr. Bokhart

Defendant offered the opinions of Christopher Bokhart. He was offered and accepted as an expert in the valuation of intellectual property. He holds a bachelor of science degree in management, with an emphasis in accounting from Purdue University. He is currently a certified public accountant and is also certified in financial forensics and fraud examining. He began his career in 1982 doing business valuation and litigation support at a firm called Peterson Consulting, a spin-off from Arthur Anderson. He quickly became the "IP go-to" at his firm as he gained experience valuing intellectual property. Tr. 1548. He stayed at Peterson for six years, after which he and several others from the firm started their own business, the IPC Group. The IPC Group grew over the years and eventually merged with former partners of Peterson Consulting to form InteCap, which employed about 200 people. Mr. Bokhart's work at both firms focused on valuing intellectual property as part of business valuation and financial consulting.

InteCap has since been acquired by another larger consulting conglomerate, Charles Rivers Associates, where Mr. Bokhart is currently a vice president. He continues to work in valuing intellectual property, including copyrights, trademarks, trade secrets, and patents. His work involves both litigation support and negotiation of license agreements and negotiations for purchase or sale of intellectual property. He testified that he has provided hundreds of opinions of valuation in litigation. Tr. 1551. He characterized his negotiation experience as "more than a handful of times." *Id.* His work valuing copyrights has been primarily outside of court. As an exception, he provided opinion and expert testimony for the government in the Gaylord case in this court.

Mr. Bokhart's conclusion was that Mr. Davidson's hypothetical license would have been worth no more than $10,000. This conclusion was informed by the facts that plaintiff has no history of making commercial use of his artwork and that the Postal Service's comparable licenses were all below $5,000. He testified that he examined hundreds of such licenses. He also thought that USPS had viable alternatives if an agreement for less than $10,000 could not be reached. In essence, he thought the comparable market was only what USPS paid for similar licenses and that Mr. Davidson had suffered little harm because "he never made an attempt to earn a profit on or commercialize himself." Tr. 1657.

3. Dr. Isaacson

Defendant also offered the testimony of Dr. Bruce Isaacson, an expert in the field of consumer surveys. Dr. Isaacson has a bachelor of science degree in engineering from Northwestern University, a MBA from Harvard Business School, and a doctor of business administration also from Harvard Business School. Dr. Isaacson's career has focused on marketing research regarding consumer behavior. His tool is the consumer survey. He has provided surveys and testimony for litigation in various federal and state courts and the Trademark Trial and Appeal Board. He has also testified before the Federal Trade Commission and the Better Business Bureau. He is currently the president of MMR Strategy Group, a marketing research and consulting firm. He has been with MMR for 12 years. One of this firm's specialities is providing litigation surveys. He estimated that his firm has conducted close to 500 surveys while he has been with the company, "the vast majority of which [he] would have been either involved with either directly managing or supervising those who were managing the survey." Tr. 1273.

After familiarizing himself with the particulars of this case, reading court documents, deposition transcripts, and doing some research on the business of USPS generally, he conducted a survey. His survey looked at three different areas of inquiry: 1) whether a respondent had ever purchased the Lady Liberty stamp; 2) what percentage of those who had purchased a stamp intended to retain the stamp (i.e., not use it to send mail) and how many they intended to retain; and 3) why they intended to keep it and not redeem it for postage. Tr. 1294. He testified that he was unsatisfied with the Postal Service's own research as to retention rates because it either did not look specifically at this stamp "or it was conducted in ways that were not necessarily consistent with those for a litigation survey." Tr. 1295. He did not explain the inconsistency other than that USPS retention figures often represent retention across all stamps for a single year. [NOTE 24] *Id.*

There were 1,790 respondents who responded to Dr. Isaacson's survey. He testified that he used a "control stamp" to weed out people who might have been mis-remembering the particular stamp referenced by the survey, Tr. 1302-03, the results of which were to remove 3% to 4% of the responses from the final tally. After controlling for the false positives, the results were: 43% of respondents reported purchasing the Lady Liberty stamp; 18.5% of that group have retained some of these stamps; 15.4% of respondents said that they still planned to use those stamps to send mail; 3.6% said that they intended to collect them; and approximately just over 1% intended to give them away, sell them, or make other use of the stamps. Tr. 1318-20. He did not provide any data as to the flag stamp.

These figures were examined in some detail on cross-examination. Using the same survey results but employing a method suggested by plaintiff's counsel on cross-examination resulted in 46% of respondents still holding the Lady Liberty stamp. *See* Tr. 1350-52. That result was reached by comparing the number of respondents who indicated that they had purchased the stamp and the number of persons who indicated that they still retained at least one of the stamps. Tr. 1351. Dr. Isaacson stated that "you could do that" and that he did not dispute that percentage. *Id.* That figure was then applied to the total United States stamp-buying population to estimate the number of people still holding this stamp: just under 50 million. Tr. 1351-52 (Dr. Isaacson in response to plaintiff's counsel posting approximately 50 million: "That would be right. . . ."). The total number of stamps still retained was on average 10.1 per person. Tr. 1352. Multiplying those two numbers resulted in about 494 million of these stamps still outstanding (still retained by purchasers and not redeemed) after five years. *Id.* Taking that figure and comparing it to the total of the Lady Liberty stamps sold, resulted in a retention rate of about 10%. Tr. 1355-56 ("Do you agree with that?. . . . The Witness: Yes.").

C. Plaintiff Has Proven Entitlement to Damages

The court is left to craft a remedy that best reflects what the fair market value of a non-exclusive license for plaintiff's artwork would have been in 2010. The Federal Circuit has endorsed the use of patent law tools to value licenses in the copyright context. *See Gaylord*, 777 F.3d at 1367. These include the factors enumerated in *Georgia-Pacific Corp. v. United States Plywood Corp.*, 318 F. Supp. 1116, 1120-21 (S.D.N.Y. 1970). Courts are encouraged to consider objective indicia of the value of similar work in the market. *See, e.g., Jarvis v. K2 Inc.*, 486 F.3d 526, 533-34 (9th Cir. 2007) (also cited in the third Federal Circuit *Gaylord* decision). These considerations may be informed by the licensor's and licensee's own history in similar transactions, but these will not be employed as an artificial inflator nor deflator of the fair market value at the time the negotiation would have taken place. *Gaylord*, 777 F.3d at 1368 (citing *Oracle Corp. v. SAP AG*, 765 F.3d 1081, 1093 (9th Cir. 2014)). The court is not foreclosed, however, from considering information that comes to light after the hypothetical negotiation. *See Lucent Techs., Inc. v. Gateway, Inc.*, 580 F.3d 1301, 1331 (Fed. Cir. 2009). These facts are what the Supreme Court long-ago dubbed the "book of wisdom." *Sinclair Refining Co. v. Jenkins Petroleum Process Co.*, 289 U.S. 689, 698 (1933).

The value reached by the court must assume a willing buyer and a willing seller. *Gaylord*, 678 F.3d at 1343. The Federal Circuit applied this axiom in affirming this court's damages award after remand in *Gaylord*, explaining that "the basic premise of the hypothetical negotiation . . . would have been the opportunity for making substantial profits if the two sides were willing to join forces, which we must assume that they were." 777 F.3d at 1368. We find that principle particularly apt in this case where the government, just as it did in *Gaylord*, relies on its unique history in paying only $5,000 for the rights to images on its stamps. As the Federal Circuit stated in the second *Gaylord* decision and then later explained in its third decision, such a holding would ignore the other side of the bargain: plaintiff's evidence of the value of such a license. Having infringed the copyright billions of times, defendant cannot now shield itself from liability by claiming that it would have walked away from the deal. *Gaylord*, 678 F.3d at 1343. We have to assume a *willing* buyer as well as a willing seller. This means that the government cannot avoid accountability by arbitrarily imposing limits on what it would have been willing to pay. *Id.* (citing *Rite-Hite Corp. v. Kelley Co.*, 56 F.3d 1538, 1555 (Fed. Cir. 1995) ([W]hat an infringer would prefer to pay is not the measure of damages.")). The rule is rationality in view of the evidence presented. *See Gaylord*, 777 F.3d at 1368.

We conclude that the most appropriate measure of damages is a mixed license which employees a flat fee for the Lady Liberty stamps used to send mail and a running royalty for retained stamps and philatelic products. *See id.* at 1344 ("The trial court's analysis of a hypothetical negotiation between [plaintiff] and the Postal Service may lead it to conclude that different license fees are appropriate for the three categories of infringing goods. . . .").

Given the sheer weight of the number of these stamps anticipated to be produced and used as postage, it would have made no economic sense for the Postal Service to have paid a running royalty for such use, nor do we think Mr. Davidson would have been in a position to demand one. As Mr. Stratton explained, the Postal Service's revenues do not meet its expenditures. The cost of carrying mail and maintaining the workforce to do so exceeds the stamp sales and other revenue earned. In essence, each stamp redeemed for service is a small contract on which USPS will lose money. We thus conclude that paying a running royalty on top of the loss already baked into each stamp redeemed for service is economically unreasonable and that fact would have been obvious to both parties at the time of the hypothetical negotiation. In this respect we think it relevant that other images could have readily been obtained that would perform the basic function of producing a workhorse stamp for actual postal use. Thus we find the nominal and historically accurate sum paid by the Postal Service, namely $5,000, to be an appropriate flat rate for this use.

There is, however, a portion of stamps sold on which the Postal Service makes money. The law presumes, as noted above, that both parties would have entered the negotiation looking to maximize profit. USPS makes almost entirely pure profit from stamps never redeemed for postage. It was USPS employee testimony that maximizing retainage and breakage was always a goal. It was also the testimony of USPS employees that the public expected new stamps and desired attractive images. To that end, Mr. McCaffrey selected the image of Mr. Davidson's work because it was just that: new, fresh, and attractive and thus likely to attract buyer interest. Although a bevy of patriotic images was available, market considerations drew Mr. McCaffrey to use Mr. Davidson's image. USPS was using his image to maximize its own profit, and it is not unreasonable to conclude that plaintiff would have demanded some percentage of those stamps, and other philatelic products, representing profit to defendant. It is also reasonable to conclude that the Postal Service would have been willing to pay such a percentage since it reflects no real additional risk. The royalty only attaches to purchases of stamps that would not engender additional cost. As in *Gaylord*, the market incentives were aligned on both sides of the deal to agree on a running royalty on retained stamps. *Gaylord*, 777 F.3d at 1370. Other than the Postal Service itself, neither party presented evidence of a similar transaction where billions of copies of an image were produced for commercial sale without a per-use royalty. We thus conclude that a running royalty is appropriate for these items because it balances the risks and rewards for both parties. *Id.* at 1369.

We find that a 5% running royalty on unredeemed and philatelic products is the correct figure. That figure is supported by Mr. Timmins' work in researching comparable art licenses, Ms. Kirby's testimony of the rates charged by USPS when it out-licenses its own art, and the USPS licenses introduced into evidence. Although Mr. Timmins opined that, if the base was made smaller by excluding stamps against which a running royalty would be applied, the rate would be higher, we find that Mr. Davidson would not likely have achieved a higher rate given his lack of experience in selling his own intellectual property. 5% is a reasonable figure supported by the average rates presented by Mr. Timmins and USPS's own out-licensing.

We do not, however, find that it is appropriate to apply this rate against the attached flag stamps. We heard no evidence as to why those stamps should be included in the base of stamps against which the royalty should be applied nor did we hear any legal reason why they need be included. In the patent context, convoyed sales are often included in the base, but the test is generally whether the convoyed item is functionally part of the same assembly or machine as the patented item. *See generally Rite-Hite Corp. v. Kelley Co., Inc.*, 56 F.3d 1538, 1550 (Fed. Cir. 1995). Here, the stamps are printed and sold side by side in a single booklet of stamps, but they are in essence entirely separate entities. The factors leading to the desirability of the Lady Liberty image do not automatically translate into retention of the flag stamp and we were presented with no evidence of such a phenomenon. We thus do not include the flag stamps in the base.

We are thus left with only the question of the quantum of base for the retainage and breakage rate to be applied against. We choose the Postal Service's own 2015 estimates as the most reasonable measure for total sales and its estimate for breakage rates. The parties stipulated that 4,948,761,166 of the Lady Liberty stamps were sold. The final year of sales was 2014. Total amount collected for those sales is $2,190,414,155. Stip. of Facts ¶ 28. The Postal Service estimated the breakage rate for all workhorse stamps during this time period to be 3.24%. *Id.* ¶ 29. Thus plaintiff applies 3.24% against $2,190,414,155 to arrive at a figure of $70,969,419 for breakage and retention. This is similar to, and actually lower than, the figures that Dr. Isaacson's survey data might suggest.[NOTE 25] We find that to be a conservative estimate and appropriate for use here. We thus apply a 5% royalty rate against that figure, which results in a $3,548,470.95 sum.

The parties agreed that the total revenue of philatelic products sold amounted to $29,515. Applying a 5% rate, the royalty for those products equals $1,476. That number is added to the $3,548,470.95 along with the $5,000 flat fee for redeemed stamps, for a total unadjusted damages figure of $3,554,946.95.

We note that plaintiff cites various contemporaneous or *post facto* circumstances as "book of wisdom" indicators that the government would have paid at least $10,000,000 for this license. They are primarily the cost to produce these stamps and the need to rush them into print in time for the 2010 Christmas mailing season. Defendant counters with its own example of a 9/11 commemorative stamp that was rushed to production as suggesting that Mr. Davidson would not have had USPS over the barrel, and thus the Postal Service would have had viable alternatives given the large selection of patriotic images available at stock photography repositories. We do not find the cost to produce the stamps or the concern about rushing production as telling on what USPS would have paid. That cost, in the hypothetical world of the negotiation, would have been incurred after an agreement would have been reached. As to the need to hurry the production, given defendant's own counterexample of viable alternatives available in short order, we find that these circumstances do not suggest a license fee higher than the one we have adopted. Nor, however, do we find that the government's viable alternatives scenario necessitates a finding that it would not have paid more than $5,000 in total for all usage. The economic incentives and realities cited above would have driven both parties towards a running royalty in the range that we have found.

CONCLUSION

Plaintiff has proven its entitlement to actual damages of $3,554,946.95, plus interest. The parties are directed to consult regarding the quantum of interest and to file a joint status report on or before July 27, 2018, informing the court of their agreed-upon amount or their respective positions as to that figure.

ERIC G. BRUGGINK, Judge

NOTES:

NOTE 1: "PX" stands for plaintiff's exhibit; "DX" stands for defendant's exhibit; and "JX" stands for joint exhibit.

NOTE 2: A maquette is a much reduced scale model of the eventual statue.

NOTE 3: Those adjectival descriptions of the face of his statue were quoted from plaintiff's copyright application file (JX 7) and were not endorsed by him on the stand. Defendant argues that these descriptions are not evidence because they constitute attorney advocacy. In any event, we do not rely on those statements because plaintiff did not endorse them on the stand.

NOTE 4: It reads: "In loving memory of Lucille Schwartz . . . 'This one is for you, mom.' Sculpting completed October 4, 1996, Robert Spencer Davidson." Tr. 180.

NOTE 5: Mr. Davidson testified that he also built the Joan of Arc at the Paris Hotel in Las Vegas and a Mount Rushmore-styled sculpture featuring Dudley Do-Right characters at Universal Studios in Orlando, Florida. He stated that he received about $350,000 gross for these works.

NOTE 6: The Citizens' Stamp Advisory Committee is made up of a maximum of 12 non-USPS employed individuals who serve at the Postmaster General's pleasure to assist in selecting images and artwork for stamps. *See* Tr. 679. Hundreds of ideas for stamp subjects are also submitted to the Postal Service by the general public. Mr. McCaffrey also testified that it is an unwritten rule that there must be a patriotic icon in circulation at all times. Tr. 676.

NOTE 7: Mr. Gicker, the current head of stamp design testified that the stamp development group has an annual budget of approximately $3.3 million, $400,000 of which is designated for the purchase of art and images to be used on stamps. This budget has remained largely static for the past 10 years. Mr. Stratton testified regarding the overall financial picture of the Postal Service, stating that costs have exceeded revenue each year since 2006, meaning that USPS operates at a loss. *See* Tr. 647-48. Nevertheless, annual revenues have exceeded $60 billion since 2008. Pretrial Stips. of Fact ¶ 2. If USPS were a private firm, it would be a Fortune 500 company. Tr. 1003 (Gicker)

NOTE 8: As Mr. Stratton explained, a postage stamp is evidence of payment for future services to be rendered by USPS. Therefore USPS cannot simply book unredeemed stamps as, in essence, profit, without accounting for the likelihood that some of those stamps will be called and the Postal Service required to provide service in exchange. *See* Tr. 634. As will be further explained, some amount of stamps sold by USPS will never be redeemed. These then can be accounted for as pure profit.

NOTE 9: It is not clear what happened to the remaining 4.5 billion stamps that were printed but not sold or distributed for retail sale.

NOTE 10: Other lower rates were also offered at trial by defendant's expert Bruce Isaacson based on his own survey work conducted for trial. We will discuss those numbers in greater detail below.

NOTE 11: He also stated that, by contrast, a commemorative stamp, which is usually of greater interest to collectors, might have a retention rate as high as 20 percent. The gross numbers of total sales of commemorative stamps would be much lower, however.

NOTE 12: It is not clear from his testimony when precisely this occurred, but it must have been sometime prior to January 2012 given that an attorney filed a copyright application on his behalf at that time.

NOTE 13: The Ninth Circuit has cautioned, however, that when the derivative work is "instantly identifiable" as embodying the "underlying copyrighted [material] in "'yet another form," the conclusion that nontrivial differences exist could not be reached by a jury. *Entm't Research Grp., Inc. v. Genesis Creative Grp., Inc.*, 122 F.3d 1211, 1223 (9th Cir. 1997) (quoting *Durham Indus., Inc. v. Tomy Corp.*, 630 F.2d 905, 909 (2d Cir. 1980)). In that case, the claimed copyright was in inflatable costumes of separately copyrighted cartoon characters. The circuit affirmed the district court's finding that the only differences between the two were attributable to the form as an inflatable costume rather than some new original expression of creativity. *Id.* at 1222. It was thus only utilitarian aspects of rendering a two-dimensional image into a three dimensional inflatable plastic costume that constituted any difference. *Id.* at 1223. Utilitarian aspects are not copyrightable. *Id.*; 17 U.S.C. § 101.

NOTE 14: Defendant also attempted to introduce at trial an article from a trade publication, Walls & Ceilings, in which out of court statements from Mr. Davidson were referenced. Plaintiff's hearsay objection was sustained and the article was not admitted. We note now, even if it had been admitted, it would not change our analysis.

NOTE 15: In the *Gaylord* case, the Federal Circuit affirmed this court's holding that the use of an image of the Korean War Memorial was not fair use. Both courts found for plaintiff on the second factor. The case is distinguishable, however, because Mr. Gaylord's monument was not a derivative work.

NOTE 16: The Postal Service issues public information notices when a new stamp is offered to the public with information about the art used on the stamp. Even after the error was found, USPS declined to update its informational bulletin with Mr. Davidson's name.

NOTE 17: Other types of damages, such as punitive, are not available against the government.

NOTE 18: She also testified that, if a group wanted to print a small run of tee shirts bearing the image of a stamp for an event, that would result in a flat fee arrangement. Tr. 1039 (stating that the average was $3,000 to $5,000).

NOTE 19: As Ms. Amity explained, a "running royalty" refers to a per-use royalty and is employed for extended periods of use. Tr. 1054.

NOTE 20: PX 157 is an example of just one such license agreement with an 8% running royalty fee based on total gross sales of vintage metal signs bearing images of USPS stamps. Plaintiff also introduced an example of an agreement with a puzzle manufacturer in which USPS negotiated a 5% running royalty on images of its own work and 3% if the image included someone else's intellectual property; the example being a stamp bearing the image of a Disney character. PX 158. PX 159 was an example of a license for the manufacture of gold foil stamp replicas. The rate was again 5%, but the contract included a minimum guarantee of $50,000 to the Postal Service.

NOTE 21: Defendant also offered the testimony of Daniel Piazza, a curator of philately at the Smithsonian National Postal Museum, his "dream job." Although he is extremely knowledgeable and a fascinating expert in the history of postage and stamp collecting in general, we did not find his testimony particularly helpful in reaching a conclusion as to what the market value of a license would have been for Mr. Davidson's copyright in 2010. Mr. Piazza's most relevant testimony was that the Lady Liberty stamp was not highly sought after as a collectible. That fact was not seriously disputed, and plaintiff's expert made no attempt at specially capturing dollars associated with collectors other than by assigning a royalty rate to unredeemed stamps generally, of which the number of stamps retained in collections is but a subset.

NOTE 22: Philatelic products are collectible items produced for sale other than for use as stamps. The parties agreed that $29,515 of such products had been sold by USPS associated with the two stamps at issue.

NOTE 23: As an alternative, plaintiff's post-trial brief suggests a mixed license of $1,000,000 for mail use stamps, a running royalty of 10% for unredeemed stamps, and 5% for the flat stamps not redeemed. Plaintiff offered $11,645,411 as the sum that those numbers would generate. *See* Pl.'s Post- Trial Br. 35.

NOTE 24: It is unclear whether Dr. Isaacson was asserting that USPS had no figures regarding only this stamp's retention rates. He did state that he checked his own work against the Postal Service's figures as a general check on the reasonableness of his results.

NOTE 25: It is unclear from the record precisely how defendant wished the court to have used Dr. Isaacson's retention rate estimate. The 3.6% figure he posited is higher than USPS's own breakage rate (3.24%) across all workhorse stamps for the years at issue, which was the figure used by Mr. Timmins in crafting his damages figure. Presumably the government does not wish us to apply the 3.6% rate against the $70 million in unredeemed stamps. To be fair, we assume this testimony was offered as a more general way of disputing any claim that Mr. Davidson's work drove above-normal collection of the stamp. That ultimately did not end up playing into plaintiff's damage theory.

STUDY QUESTIONS

- What mistake did the U.S. Postal Service make in *Davidson*? Why did the court reject the USPS's fair use defense?
- The court refers repeatedly to *Gaylord v. United States*, 595 F.3d 1364, 1374 (Fed. Cir. 2010), which also found copyright infringement by the U.S. Postal Service in its use of a photograph of a Korean War memorial statute on a postage stamp. Although it got permission from the photographer, the USPS failed to get permission from the artist who created the statute that was the subject of the photograph. How does the *Davidson* court's fair use analysis compare with that of *Gaylord*?
- How did the *Davidson* court determine the amount of the judgment?
- What lessons can you draw from the *Davidson* case about commissioning a work of art? What recommendations would you give a museum that wants to hire an artist to create a work of art?

FAIR USE AND APPROPRIATION ART

The term "appropriation art" refers to the practice of incorporating preexisting images and objects (photographs, artwork, etc.) in new works of art. The purpose of appropriation art is to engage viewers in a debate about the nature of freedom of expression. Often the appropriated images reflect our mass-media culture and are intended as a social commentary on mass production, high art versus low art, ownership of culture, etc. For some artists, the appropriation of other artists' work without permission is also part of an "artistic statement" about who gets to control their output and expression. (Ironically, some of the most outspoken appropriation artists are also highly protective of their own intellectual property rights.) Whatever the purpose, when the appropriated work is protected by copyright law, there is a risk that the owner of the appropriated work will sue for copyright infringement. In the art world, this sometimes occurs when a work of appropriation art is bought for a very high price and the owner of the underlying work seeks to share in the profits. Often the infringing artist defends the use of the underlying work as "fair use."

The court decisions included in the Cases and Other Readings section below include three lawsuits alleging copyright infringement by appropriation artist Jeff Koons. In each case, Koons asserted that his use of preexisting copyright protected material without permission was "fair use" under the U.S. copyright law; his claim of fair use was rejected in the first two cases and was accepted by the court in the third. The final case included in the readings involved a claim of copyright infringement by the appropriation artist Richard Prince in connection with a series of paintings. In that case, the appellate court concluded that in some of the paintings, the use was "fair use" but not in others. As you read these cases, consider the role the artist's stated intent in appropriating the preexisting material plays in the court's analysis in each case. Why do you think Jeff Koons was successful in claiming fair use in the *Blanch v. Koons* case? How did Richard Prince's lack of intent play a role in *Cariou v. Prince*? Both Koons and Prince have been the defendants in numerous copyright infringement lawsuits over the years. The four cases included below are just a few examples of the evolving jurisprudence on appropriation art and fair use. They are intended to illustrate a few of the many ways that copyright and "fair use" concepts arise in the museum context.

For museums that acquire and exhibit works of appropriation art, the use of copyrighted material without permission presents several problems. Due to legal concepts of "vicarious" and "contributory" infringement, a museum that acquires or displays appropriation art may be held liable for aiding in the infringement and may find itself a party to a copyright infringement lawsuit. This can be a very real concern. In *Blanch v. Koons* included in the readings below, Deutsche Bank AG and the Solomon R. Guggenheim Foundation commissioned and exhibited the painting that was the subject of the copyright infringement claim. And in the *Cariou v. Prince* copyright infringement case, also included in the readings below, the Gagosian, a renown art gallery in New York, was named as a defendant along with the appropriation artist.

Does this mean a museum that acquires appropriation art (either by purchase or donation) must conduct a fair use analysis before completing the acquisition? Perhaps. Also, does the potential fact that the work may be found to have infringed on another's copyright affect the museum's ability to display the work? Will it also affect the ability to sell or otherwise deaccession and dispose of the work? Recall that the First Sale and Public Display exceptions apply only to works "lawfully made." Is a work of art that includes material that infringes on someone's copyright "lawfully made"?

What about foreign intellectual property rights? And what about intellectual property rights that may be embodied in the work other than copyright? It is conceivable, for example, that a photograph of a clearly identifiable person may raise privacy and/or publicity rights concerns.

The collection of appropriation art may also raise ethical issues for museums. For example, under what circumstances is it appropriate for a museum to acquire or exhibit works that may violate the intellectual property rights of others? How does a museum balance respect for the exclusive rights of artists to their creative content with appreciation for democratic principles of artistic freedom of expression? Given this tension, how does a museum decide whose intellectual property rights should be recognized and protected, and to what extent? This may ultimately be answered by considering the museum's mission and values. These are all things a museum must consider when collecting works of appropriation art.

CASES AND OTHER READINGS

Reading Note: *Rogers v. Koons*, reprinted below, is one of several copyright infringement lawsuits involving works created by appropriation artist Jeff Koons for an exhibit he called *The Banality Show*. In this case, the court considered whether a painted, three-dimensional sculpture created by Koons infringed on a photographer's copyright in a black and white postcard photograph on which the sculpture was based.

ROGERS V. KOONS

960 F.2d 301 (2d Cir. 1992).

CARDAMONE, Circuit Judge:

The key to this copyright infringement suit, brought by a plaintiff photographer against a defendant sculptor and the gallery representing him, is defendants' borrowing of plaintiff's expression of a typical American scene—a smiling husband and wife holding a litter of charming puppies. The copying was so deliberate as to suggest that defendants resolved so long as they were significant players in the art business, and the copies they produced bettered the price of the copied work by a thousand to one, their piracy of a less well-known artist's work would escape being sullied by an accusation of plagiarism.

BACKGROUND FACTS

We think it helpful to understanding this appeal to set forth the principals' professional backgrounds. Plaintiff, Art Rogers, a 43-year-old professional artist-photographer, has a studio and home at Point Reyes, California, where he makes his living by creating, exhibiting, publishing and otherwise making use of his rights in his photographic works. Exhibitions of his photographs have been held in California and as far away as Maine, Florida and New York. His work has been described in French ("Le Monde"), British ("The Photo") and numerous American publications, including the Journal of American Photography, Polaroid's Close-Up Magazine and the Popular Photography Annual. Rogers' photographs are part of the permanent collection of the San Francisco Museum of Modern Art, the Center for Creative Photography at the University of Arizona and Joseph E. Seagrams and Sons in New York City. He has taught photography at the San Francisco Museum of Modern Art.

B. Creating The Photograph "Puppies"

In 1980 an acquaintance, Jim Scanlon, commissioned Rogers to photograph his eight new German Shepherd puppies. When Rogers went to his home on September 21, 1980 he decided that taking a picture of the puppies alone would not work successfully, and chose instead to include Scanlon and his wife holding them. Substantial creative effort went into both the composition and production of "Puppies," a black and white photograph. At the photo session, and later in his lab, Rogers drew on his years of artistic development. He selected the light, the location, the bench on which the Scanlons are seated and the arrange-

Artist Jeff Koons hired Italian artisans to create the painted wooden sculpture, String of Puppies *(1988) (right), based on a postcard version of a black and white photograph by Art Rogers (left). Koons called the sculpture exhibit* Banality Show.

ment of the small dogs. He also made creative judgments concerning technical matters with his camera and the use of natural light. He prepared a set of "contact sheets," containing 50 different images, from which one was selected.

After the Scanlons purchased their prints for $200, "Puppies" became part of Rogers' catalogue of images available for further use, from which he, like many professional photographers, makes his living. "Puppies" has been used and exhibited a number of times. A signed print of it has been sold to a private collector, and in 1989 it was licensed for use in an anthology called "Dog Days." Rogers also planned to use the picture in a series of hand-tinted prints of his works. In 1984 Rogers had licensed "Puppies", along with other works, to Museum Graphics, a company that produces and sells notecards and postcards with high quality reproductions of photographs by well-respected American photographers including, for example, Ansel Adams. Museum Graphics has produced and distributed the "Puppies" notecard since 1984. The first printing was of 5,000 copies and there has been a second similar size printing.

Defendant Jeff Koons is a 37-year-old artist and sculptor residing in New York City. After receiving a Bachelor of Fine Arts degree from Maryland Institute College of Art in 1976, he worked at a number of jobs, principally membership development at the Museum of Modern Art in New York. While pursuing his career as an artist, he also worked until 1984 as a mutual funds salesman, a registered commodities salesman and broker, and a commodities futures broker. In the ten years from 1980 to 1990 Koons has exhibited his works in approximately 100 Group Exhibitions and in eleven one-man shows. His bibliography is extensive. Koons is represented by Sonnabend Gallery, New York, Donald Young Gallery, Chicago, and Galerie Max Hetzler, Cologne, Germany. His works sell at very substantial prices, over $100,000. He is a controversial artist hailed by some as a "modern Michelangelo," while others find his art "truly offensive." A New York Times critic complained that "Koons is pushing the relationship between art and money so far that everyone involved comes out looking slightly absurd."

D. Creating the Sculpture "String of Puppies"

After a successful Sonnabend show in 1986, Koons began creating a group of 20 sculptures for a 1988 exhibition at the same gallery that he called the *Banality Show*. He works in an art tradition dating back to the beginning of the twentieth century. This tradition defines its efforts as follows: when the artist finishes his work, the meaning of the original object has been extracted and an entirely new meaning set in its place. An example is Andy Warhol's reproduction of multiple images of Campbell's soup cans. Koons' most famous work in this genre is a stainless steel casting of an inflatable rabbit holding a carrot. During 1986 and 1987 the sculptor traveled widely in Europe looking at materials and workshops where he might fabricate materials for the *Banality Show*. He decided to use porcelain, mirrors and wood as mediums. Certain European studios were chosen to execute his porcelain works, other studios chosen for the mirror pieces, and the small Demetz Studio, located in the northern hill country town of Ortessi, Italy, was selected to carve the wood sculptures.

Koons acknowledges that the source for "String of Puppies" was a Museum Graphics notecard of "Puppies" which he purchased in a "very commercial, tourist-like card shop" in 1987. After buying the card, he tore off that portion showing Rogers' copyright of "Puppies." Koons saw certain criteria in the notecard that he thought made it a workable source. He believed it to be typical, commonplace and familiar. The notecard was also similar to other images of people holding animals that Koons had collected. Thus, he viewed the picture as part of the mass culture—"resting in the collective sub-consciousness of people regardless of whether the card had actually ever been seen by such people."

Appellant gave his artisans one of Rogers' notecards and told them to copy it. But in order to guide the creation of a three-dimensional sculptural piece from the two-dimensional photograph, Koons communicated extensively with the Demetz Studio. He visited it once a week during the period the piece was being carved by the workers and gave them written instructions. In his "production notes" Koons stressed that he wanted "Puppies" copied faithfully in the sculpture. For example, he told his artisans the "work must be just like photo—features of photo must be captured;" later, "puppies need detail in fur. Details—Just Like Photo!;" other notes instruct the artisans to "keep man in angle of photo—mild lean to side & mildly forward—same for woman," to "keep woman's big smile," and to "keep [the sculpture] very, very realistic;" others state, "Girl's nose is too small. Please make larger as per photo;" another reminds the artisans that "The puppies must have variation in fur as per photo—not just large area of paint—variation as per photo." (emphasis supplied).

To paint the polychromed wood "String of Puppies" sculptures, Koons provided a chart with an enlarged photocopy of "Puppies" in the center; painting directions were noted in the margin with arrows drawn to various areas of the photograph. The chart noted, "Puppies, painted in shades of blue. Variation of light-to-dark as per photo. Paint realistic as per photo, but in blues." and "Man's hair, white with shades of grey as per black and white photo!" (emphasis supplied).

When it was finished, "String of Puppies" was displayed at the Sonnabend Gallery, which opened the *Banality Show* on November 19, 1988. Three of the four copies made were sold to collectors for a total of $367,000; the fourth or artist's copy was kept by Koons. Defendant Koons' use of "Puppies" to create "String of Puppies" was not authorized by plaintiff. Rogers learned of Koons' unauthorized use of his work through Jim Scanlon, the man who had commissioned Rogers to create "Puppies." A friend of Scanlon's, who was familiar with the photograph, called to tell him that what she took to be a "colorized" version of "Puppies" was on the front page of the calendar section of the May 7, 1989 Sunday Los Angeles Times. In fact, as she and Scanlon later learned, the newspaper actually depicted Koons' "String of Puppies" in connection with an article about its exhibition at the Los Angeles Museum of Contemporary Art.

PRIOR PROCEEDINGS

Rogers brought this action against Koons and Sonnabend Gallery on October 11, 1989, alleging copyright infringement and unfair competition under § 43(a) of the Lanham Act and under state law. Both sides advised the district court at an early stage of the proceedings that, at least as to copyright infringement, disputed factual issues were unlikely and disposition on summary judgment would probably be appropriate. After completion of discovery, both sides moved for that relief on July 5, 1990. Rogers' motion was limited to the copyright infringement claim. Koons and the Sonnabend Gallery sought summary judgment dismissing all counts in plaintiff's complaint.

The district court held oral argument on November 26, 1990. In a December 10, 1990 decision, described more fully below, it found that Koons copied "Puppies" in "String of Puppies" and that this copying was not a fair use. It therefore found infringement, 751 F. Supp. 474. Rogers' motion for an infringing profits award was denied because the trial court believed there were disputed questions of fact concerning their computation. As to Sonnabend Gallery, the district court concluded on February 22, 1991 that the record showed Sonnabend's as well as Koons' liability for infringing profits. On March 27, 1991 it entered a permanent injunction enjoining Koons and Sonnabend Gallery from making, selling, lending or displaying any copies of, or derivative works based on, "Puppies," and, pursuant to 17 U.S.C. § 503, requiring defendants to deliver all infringing articles to plaintiff within 20 days, including the fourth or artist's copy of "String of Puppies."

When defendants failed to comply with the turn-over order, Rogers moved to hold defendant Koons in contempt. The proceedings on that motion revealed that nine days after the injunction was issued, Koons had loaned the fourth copy of "String of Puppies" to a museum in Germany and arranged for its shipment out of the United States. After a hearing on May 8, 1991 the district court held Koons in contempt, directed him to do whatever was necessary to effect the sculpture's return from Germany, and imposed a daily fine for continued non-compliance to commence eight days later.

On May 28, 1991 we denied Koons' motion to stay the injunction and the contempt penalty pending appeal, but delayed the commencement of the daily fine until June 7, 1991. From the finding of copyright infringement, the granting of a permanent injunction, and the turn-over order appellants Koons and Sonnabend appeal. Rogers cross-appeals from the denial of an award prior to trial for infringing profits. We affirm.

DISCUSSION

I. Ownership of Copyright in an Original Work of Art

One of the powers given Congress under Art. I, § 8 of the United States Constitution is: "To promote the Progress of Science and useful Arts, by securing for limited Times to

Authors and Inventors, the exclusive Right to their respective Writings and Discoveries." Madison noted that "[T]he utility of this power will scarcely be questioned." The Federalist No. 43 (Madison) at 279. He further observed that copyright for authors was their right under common law. Id.; see 2 Blackstone, Commentaries on the Laws of England 407 (Univ. of Chicago ed. 1979). As a result, Congress enacted a copyright law, 17 U.S.C. § 101 et seq. (1976), under which the instant litigation was instituted.

To establish an infringement of a copyright, a plaintiff must show both ownership of a copyright and that defendant copied the protected material without authorization. See *Weissmann v. Freeman*, 868 F.2d 1313, 1320 (2d Cir.), *cert. denied*, 493 U.S. 883, 110 S. Ct. 219, 107 L. Ed. 2d 172 (1989). The Copyright Act makes a certificate of registration from the U.S. Register of Copyrights prima facie evidence of the valid ownership of a copyright, see 17 U.S.C. § 410(c), though that presumption of ownership may be rebutted, see *Hasbro Bradley, Inc. v. Sparkle Toys, Inc.*, 780 F.2d 189, 192 (2d Cir. 1985). Protection under the copyright statute extends to pictorial works, 17 U.S.C. § 102(a)(5). For more than a century photographs have been held to be copyrightable "writings" under Article I, § 8 of the Constitution. *Burrow-Giles Lithographic Co. v. Sarony*, 111 U.S. 53, 4 S. Ct. 279, 28 L. Ed. 349 (1884) (photograph of Oscar Wilde an original work of art).

Of the several issues before us, the first concerns the originality of "Puppies." Defendants do not challenge plaintiff's ownership of a valid copyright, but assert instead that the portion of Rogers' work allegedly infringed was not an original work of authorship protected under the 1976 Copyright Act. Since the law protects authors' exclusive rights to their works, the cornerstone of that law is that the work protected must be original. See *Feist Publications, Inc. v. Rural Telephone Service Co., Inc.*, —— U.S. ——, 111 S. Ct. 1282, 1287, 113 L. Ed. 2d 358 (1991). Thus, that a whole work is copyrighted does not mean that every element of it is copyrighted; copyright protection extends only to those components of the work that are original to the creator. *Id.* 111 S. Ct. at 1289. But the quantity of originality that need be shown is modest—only a dash of it will do. *Id.* at 1287; 1 M. Nimmer & D. Nimmer, Nimmer on Copyright § 1.08 [C] (1991) (Nimmer).

Elements of originality in a photograph may include posing the subjects, lighting, angle, selection of film and camera, evoking the desired expression, and almost any other variant involved. See *Burrow Giles*, 111 U.S. at 60, 4 S. Ct. at 282. 1 Nimmer, § 2.08 [E]. To the extent that these factors are involved, "Puppies" is the product of plaintiff's artistic creation. Rogers' inventive efforts in posing the group for the photograph, taking the picture, and printing "Puppies" suffices to meet the original work of art criteria. Thus, in terms of his unique expression of the subject matter captured in the photograph, plaintiff has established valid ownership of a copyright in an original work of art.

II. Unauthorized Copying by Defendant

Plaintiff next must demonstrate that defendant Koons copied his protected work without authorization. The district court granted summary judgment to Rogers on this issue, finding Koons' sculpture "String of Puppies" an unauthorized copy of Rogers' photograph. Summary judgment may be an appropriate remedy in copyright infringement suits. See, e.g., *Peter Pan Fabrics, Inc. v. Dan River Mills, Inc.*, 295 F. Supp. 1366, 1369 (S.D.N.Y.), *aff'd*, 415 F.2d 1007 (2d Cir. 1969). Yet, such relief will be denied when the question of substantial similarity is one on which reasonable minds could differ. See, e.g., *Twentieth Century-Fox Film Corp. v. MCA, Inc.*, 715 F.2d 1327, 1329 (9th Cir. 1983).

Here, the trial court found original elements of creative expression in the copyrighted work were copied and that the copying was so blatantly apparent as not to require a trial. We agree that no reasonable juror could find that copying did not occur in this case. First, this case presents the rare scenario where there is direct evidence of copying. Koons admittedly gave a copy of the photograph to the Italian artisans with the explicit instruction that the work be copied. Moreover, the importance of copying the very details of the photograph that embodied plaintiff's original contribution—the poses, the shading, the expressions—was stressed by Koons throughout the creation of the sculpture. His instructions invariably implored that the creation must be designed "as per photo." This undisputed direct evidence of copying is sufficient to support the district court's granting of summary judgment.

Further, even were such direct evidence of copying unavailable, the district court's decision could be upheld in this case on the basis that defendant Koons' access to the copyrighted work is conceded, and the accused work is so substantially similar to the copyrighted work that reasonable jurors could not differ on this issue. See *Warner Brothers, Inc. v. American Broadcasting Cos., Inc.*, 654 F.2d 204, 207 (2d Cir. 1981).

Substantial similarity does not require literally identical copying of every detail. See 3 Nimmer, § 13.03 [A]. See also *Comptone Company Ltd. v. Rayex Corp.*, 251 F.2d 487, 488 (2d Cir. 1958). Such similarity is determined by the ordinary observer test: the inquiry is "whether an average lay observer would recognize the alleged copy as having been appropriated from the copyrighted work." *Ideal Toy Corp. v. Fab-Lu Ltd.*, 360 F.2d 1021, 1022 (2d Cir. 1966). Or, stated another way, whether "the ordinary observer, unless he set out to detect the disparities, would be disposed to overlook them, and regard their aesthetic appeal as the same." *Peter Pan Fabrics, Inc. v. Martin Weiner Corp.*, 274 F.2d 487, 489 (2d Cir. 1960). Thus, Koons' allegation that a trial judge uneducated in art is not an appropriate decision-maker misses the mark; the decision-maker, whether it be a judge or a jury, need not have any special skills other than to be a reasonable and average lay person.

We recognize that ideas, concepts, and the like found in the common domain are the inheritance of everyone. What is protected is the original or unique way that an author expresses those ideas, concepts, principles or processes. Hence, in looking at these two works of art to determine whether they are substantially similar, focus must be on the similarity of the expression of an idea or fact, not on the similarity of the facts, ideas or concepts themselves. See *Durham Industries, Inc. v. Tomy Corp.*, 630 F.2d 905, 912 (2d Cir. 1980). It is not therefore the idea of a couple with eight small puppies seated on a bench that is protected, but rather Roger's expression of this idea—as caught in the placement, in the particular light, and in the expressions of the subjects—that gives the photograph its charming and unique character, that is to say, makes it original and copyrightable.

Thus, had appellant simply used the idea presented by the photo, there would not have been infringing copying. But here Koons used the identical expression of the idea that Rogers created; the composition, the poses, and the expressions were all incorporated into the sculpture to the extent that, under the ordinary observer test, we conclude that no reasonable jury could have differed on the issue of substantial similarity. For this reason, the district court properly held that Koons "copied" the original.

Moreover, no copier may defend the act of plagiarism by pointing out how much of the copy he has not pirated. See *Sheldon v. Metro-Goldwyn Pictures Corp.*, 81 F.2d 49, 56 (2d Cir.) (L. Hand, J.), *cert. denied*, 298 U.S. 669, 56 S. Ct. 835, 80 L. Ed. 1392 (1936). Thus, where substantial similarity is found, small changes here and there made by the copier are unavailing. It is only where the points of dissimilarity exceed those that are similar and those similar are—when compared to the original work—of small import quantitatively or qualitatively that a finding of no infringement is appropriate. See 3 Nimmer § 13.03 [B] [a]. This is not the case here. Koons' additions, such as the flowers in the hair of the couple and the bulbous noses of the puppies, are insufficient to raise a genuine issue of material fact with regard to copying in light of the overwhelming similarity to the protected expression of the original work.

Because of Koons' extensive use of the same expression of the idea that Rogers' created, it was properly held that he "copied" the protected features of the original. No genuine issue of material fact exists with respect to this finding; "String of Puppies" was copied from the photograph "Puppies" based either on the direct evidence of copying or on proof of access and substantial similarity. In light of this summary judgment was properly granted on this issue.

III. The Fair Use Doctrine

Defendant Koons further defends his use of Rogers' work "Puppies" to craft "String of Puppies" under a claim of a privilege of "fair use." This equitable doctrine permits other people to use copyrighted material without the owner's consent in a reasonable manner for certain purposes. Codified in § 107 of the 1976 Copyright Act, it is of ancient lineage. Section 107 states that an original work copied for purposes such as criticism or comment may not constitute infringement, but instead may be a fair use. The section provides an illustrative—but not exhaustive—list of factors for determining when a use is "fair." These factors include (1) the purpose and character of the use, (2) the nature of the copyrighted work, (3) the amount and substantiality of the work used, and (4) the effect of the use on the market value of the original. 17 U.S.C. § 107.

The fact that the test envisioned by the Act is dependent on the circumstances of each case, see 3 Nimmer, § 13.05 [A], might suggest summary judgment is unavailable when fair use is the issue, but such relief may be granted when appropriate. See e.g., *Stewart v. Abend*, 495 U.S. 207, 110 S. Ct. 1750, 109 L. Ed. 2d 184 (1990) (summary judgment granted upon finding of no fair use). The trial court found no genuine issues of fact present regarding the fair use exception and granted summary judgment to plaintiff on this issue also. We proceed therefore to analyze the fair use factors in the circumstances of the case at hand. Our examination of these factors leads us to conclude that the district court properly granted summary judgment in favor of plaintiff.

The first factor, purpose and character of the use, asks whether the original was copied in good faith to benefit the public or primarily for the commercial interests of the infringer. See *MCA, Inc. v. Wilson*, 677 F.2d 180, 182 (2d Cir. 1981). Knowing exploitation of a copyrighted work for personal gain militates against a finding of fair use. And—because it is an equitable doctrine—wrongful denial of exploitative conduct towards the work of another may bar an otherwise legitimate fair use claim. See 3 Nimmer, § 13.05 [A]. Relevant to this issue is Koons' conduct, especially his action in tearing the copyright mark off of a Rogers notecard prior to sending it to the Italian artisans. This action suggests bad faith in defendant's use of plaintiff's work, and militates against a finding of fair use.

The Supreme Court has held that copies made for commercial or profit-making purposes are presumptively unfair. See *Sony Corp. of America v. Universal City Studios, Inc.*, 464 U.S. 417, 449, 104 S. Ct. 774, 792, 78 L. Ed. 2d 574 (1984). The Court explained in a subsequent case that the "crux of the profit/nonprofit distinction is not whether the sole motive of the use is monetary gain but whether the user stands to profit from exploitation of the copyrighted material without paying the customary price." *Harper & Row, Publishers, Inc. v. Nation Enterprises*, 471 U.S. 539, 562, 105 S. Ct. 2218, 2231, 85 L. Ed. 2d 588 (1985). We have stated that, though it is a significant factor, whether the profit element of the fair use calculus affects the ultimate determination of whether there is a fair use depends on the totality of the factors considered; it is not itself controlling. See *Maxtone-Graham v. Burtchaell*, 803 F.2d 1253, 1262 (2d Cir. 1986), *cert. denied*, 481 U.S. 1059, 107 S. Ct. 2201, 95 L. Ed. 2d 856 (1987). Thus, while we note that Koons' substantial profit from his intentionally exploitive use of Rogers' work also militates against the finding of fair use, we turn next to consider his contention that the primary purpose of the use was for social comment.

Parody or Satire as Fair Use: The Act expressly provides that comment on or criticism of a copyrighted work may be a valid use under the fair use doctrine. We must analyze therefore whether "String of Puppies" is properly considered a comment on or criticism of the photograph "Puppies." Koons argues that his sculpture is a satire or parody of society at large. He insists that "String of Puppies" is a fair social criticism and asserts to support that proposition that he belongs to the school of American artists who believe the mass production of commodities and media images has caused a deterioration in the quality of society, and this artistic tradition of which he is a member proposes through incorporating these images into works of art to comment critically both on the incorporated object and the political and economic system that created it. These themes, Koons states, draw upon the artistic movements of Cubism and Dadaism, with particular influence attributed to Marcel Duchamp, who in 1913 became the first to incorporate manufactured objects (readymades) into a work of art, directly influencing Koons' work and the work of other contemporary American artists. We accept this definition of the objective of this group of American artists.

To analyze Koons' parody defense, we must first define it. Parody or satire, as we understand it, is when one artist, for comic effect or social commentary, closely imitates the style of another artist and in so doing creates a new art work that makes ridiculous the style and expression of the original. Under our cases parody and satire are valued forms of criticism, encouraged because this sort of criticism itself fosters the creativity protected by the copyright law. See *Warner Bros., Inc. v. American Broadcasting Cos., Inc.*, 720 F.2d 231, 242 (2d Cir. 1983). We have consistently held that a parody entitles its creator under the fair use doctrine to more extensive use of the copied work than is ordinarily allowed under the substantial similarity test. See *Elsmere Music, Inc. v. National Broadcasting Co.*, 623 F.2d 252, 253 (2d Cir. 1980) (*per curiam*).

Hence, it must first be determined whether "String of Puppies" is a parody of Rogers' work for purposes of the fair use doctrine. We agree with the district court that it is not. It is the rule in this Circuit that though the satire need not be only of the copied work and may, as appellants urge of "String of Puppies," also be a parody of modern society, the copied work must be, at least in part, an object of the parody, otherwise there would be no need to conjure up the original work. See *MCA, Inc. v. Wilson*, 677 F.2d at 185; 3 Nimmer, § 13.05 [C] n. 60.9.

We think this is a necessary rule, as were it otherwise there would be no real limitation on the copier's use of another's copyrighted work to make a statement on some aspect of society at large. If an infringement of copyrightable expression could be justified as fair use solely on the basis of the infringer's claim to a higher or different artistic use—without insuring public awareness of the original work—there would be no practicable boundary to the fair use defense. Koons' claim that his infringement of Rogers' work is fair use solely because he is acting within an artistic tradition of commenting upon the commonplace thus cannot be accepted. The rule's function is to insure that credit is given where credit is due. By requiring that the copied work be an object of the parody, we merely insist that the audience be aware that underlying the parody there is an original and separate expression, attributable to a different artist. This awareness may come from the fact that the copied work is publicly known or because its existence is in some manner acknowledged by the parodist in connection with the parody. Of course, while our view of this matter does not necessarily prevent Koons' expression, although it may, it does recognize that any such exploitation must at least entail "paying the customary price." *Harper & Row Publishers, Inc.*, 471 U.S. at 562, 105 S. Ct. at 2231.

The problem in the instant case is that even given that "String of Puppies" is a satirical critique of our materialistic society, it is difficult to discern any parody of the photograph "Puppies" itself. We conclude therefore that this first factor of the fair use doctrine cuts against a finding of fair use. The circumstances of this case indicate that Koons' copying of the photograph "Puppies" was done in bad faith, primarily for profit-making motives, and did not constitute a parody of the original work.

The next fair use factor asks what is the nature of the work that has been copied. Where the original work is factual rather than fictional the scope of fair use is broader. See *New Era Publications, Int'l. v. Carol Publishing Group*, 904 F.2d 152, 157 (2d Cir.), cert. denied, —— U.S. ——, 111 S. Ct. 297, 112 L. Ed. 2d 251 (1990). Whether the original is creative, imaginative, or represents an investment of time in anticipation of a financial return also should be considered. *MCA, Inc. v. Wilson*, 677 F.2d at 182. Here "Puppies" was a published work of art. As an original expression it has more in common with fiction than with works based on facts, such as, for example, biographies or telephone directories. Since "Puppies" was creative and imaginative and Rogers, who makes his living as a photographer, hopes to gain a financial return for his efforts with this photograph, this factor militates against a finding of fair use.

Where the amount of copying exceeds permissible levels, summary judgment has been upheld. *Walt Disney Productions v. Air Pirates*, 581 F.2d 751, 758 (9th Cir. 1978), cert. denied, 439 U.S. 1132, 99 S. Ct. 1054, 59 L. Ed. 2d 94 (1979). To a large degree, this factor involves the same analysis as that used when determining if the copy is substantially similar to the original. Sometimes wholesale copying may be permitted, while in other cases taking even a small percentage of the original work has been held unfair use. See *Maxtone-Graham*, 803 F.2d at 1263. "[W]hat is relevant is the amount and substantiality of the copyrighted expression that has been used, not the factual content of the material in the copyrighted works." *Salinger v. Random House, Inc.*, 811 F.2d 90, 97 (2d Cir.) (emphasis in original), *reh'g denied*, 818 F.2d 252, *cert. denied*, 484 U.S. 890, 108 S. Ct. 213, 98 L. Ed. 2d 177 (1987). It is not fair use when more of the original is copied than necessary. Even more critical than the quantity is the qualitative degree of the copying: what degree of the essence of the original is copied in relation to its whole. *Id.* at 98; see also *New Era Publications Int'l.*, 904 F.2d at 159.

Appellants claim that under a parody defense their use of Rogers' work did not exceed the level permitted under the fair use doctrine. As discussed previously, this Circuit has traditionally afforded parodists significant leeway with respect to the extent and nature of their copying. See *Elsmere*, 623 F.2d at 253, n. 1; *Berlin v. E.C. Publications, Inc.*, 329 F.2d 541,

545 (2d Cir.), *cert. denied*, 379 U.S. 822, 85 S. Ct. 46, 13 L. Ed. 2d 33 (1964). Yet, even under such a defense there are limitations on what constitutes fair use. See *MCA v. Wilson*, 677 F.2d at 185. Here, the essence of Rogers' photograph was copied nearly in toto, much more than would have been necessary even if the sculpture had been a parody of plaintiff's work. In short, it is not really the parody flag that appellants are sailing under, but rather the flag of piracy. Moreover, because we have already determined that "String of Puppies" is not a parody of Rogers' work, appellants cannot avail themselves of this heightened tolerance under a parody defense.

Nor does *Sony Corp. of America*, 464 U.S. at 449-50, 104 S. Ct. at 792-93, bear the weight that appellants place on it for the proposition that even 100 percent copying does not preclude a fair use finding. Although correct as a general statement, it applied in *Sony* to a narrow set of circumstances. Sony's copying equipment (Betamax VCRs) was used by members of the public to record television programs—the copyright of which was owned by plaintiffs. The question was whether Sony's selling of the copying equipment violated plaintiffs' rights under the Copyright Act. The Supreme Court said "no" because "time-shifting" for those watching a television program enlarges the viewing audience, and does not impair plaintiffs' commercial right in the value of the copyright. Hence, no basis existed under the Act upon which plaintiffs could hold Sony liable for selling VCR's to the general public. *Id.* at 421, 104 S. Ct. at 778.

Those are not the facts found here. Instead, Koons' copying of Rogers' work was the essence of the photograph, and designedly done as the notes to the Italian artisans conclusively reveal. Koons went well beyond the factual subject matter of the photograph to incorporate the very expression of the work created by Rogers. We find that no reasonable jury could conclude that Koons did not exceed a permissible level of copying under the fair use doctrine.

IV. Effect of the Use on the Market Value of the Original

The fourth factor looks at the effect of the use on the market value of the original. The Supreme Court in *Stewart,* 495 U.S. 207, 110 S. Ct. 1750, 109 L. Ed. 2d 184, stated that the fourth factor "is the 'most important, and indeed, central fair use factor.'" *Id.* at 238, 110 S. Ct. at 1769 (quoting 3 Nimmer § 13.05 [A]; see also *Harper & Row*, 471 U.S. at 566, 105 S. Ct. at 2233. Under this factor a balance must be struck between the benefit gained by the copyright owner when the copying is found an unfair use and the benefit gained by the public when the use is held to be fair. The less adverse impact on the owner, the less public benefit need be shown to sustain non-commercial fair use. It is plain that where a use has no demonstrable impact on a copyright owners' potential market, the use need not be prohibited to protect the artist's incentive to pursue his inventive skills. Yet where the use is intended for commercial gain some meaningful likelihood of future harm is presumed. See *Sony Corp. of America*, 464 U.S. at 451, 104 S. Ct. at 793.

A critical inquiry under this factor then is whether defendants Koons and Sonnabend planned to profit from their exploitation of "Puppies" without paying Rogers for their use of his photo—that is, whether Koons' work is primarily commercial in nature. We have already concluded that it is. In this case, of course, the copy was in a different medium than the original: one was a three-dimensional piece of sculpture, and the other a two-dimensional black and white photo. But the owner of a copyright with respect to this market-factor need only demonstrate that if the unauthorized use becomes "widespread" it would prejudice his potential market for his work. See *id.*; *Harper & Row*, 471 U.S. at 568, 105 S. Ct. at 2234. The reason for this rule relates to a central concern of copyright law that unfair copying undercuts demand for the original work and, as an inevitable consequence, chills creation of such works. Hence the inquiry considers not only harm to the market for the original photograph, but also harm to the market for derivative works. It is obviously not implausible that another artist, who would be willing to purchase the rights from Rogers, would want to produce a sculpture like Rogers' photo and, with Koons' work extant, such market is reduced. Similarly, defendants could take and sell photos of "String of Puppies," which would prejudice Rogers' potential market for the sale of the "Puppies" notecards, in addition to any other derivative use he might plan.

Further, in discussing this fourth factor, the leading scholar in this area of the law uses an example that closely parallels the facts of the present case and demonstrates the irrelevance of copying in a different medium when analyzing this factor: a movie adaptation is made of a book. Even though the movie may boost book sales, it is an unfair use because of the effect on the potential sale of adaptation rights. 3 Nimmer, § 13.05 [B]. The function of demand for each original work of art is a relevant facet in this factor's analysis; that is, fair use permits lyrics or music to be copied in a literary magazine, but where the same material is published in a song sheet magazine, purchased for playing and not simply for reading, it is an unfair use. *Id.*

Here there is simply nothing in the record to support a view that Koons produced "String of Puppies" for anything other than sale as high-priced art. Hence, the likelihood of future harm to Rogers' photograph is presumed, and plaintiff's market for his work has been prejudiced.

V. Infringing Profits

The next issue concerns Rogers' claim for infringing profits in the amount of $367,000. Under 17 U.S.C. § 504(b) a copyright owner is entitled to recover actual damages suffered as a result of the infringement as well as apportioned profits. The section states: "In establishing the infringer's profits, the copyright owner is required to present proof only of the infringer's gross revenue, and the infringer is required to prove his or her deductible expenses and the elements of profit attributable to factors other than the copyrighted work." Alternatively, in place of actual damages and apportioned profits, a copyright owner may elect to recover an award of statutory damages. See 17 U.S.C. § 504(c).

In Rogers' cross-appeal he asserts, in response to defendants' argument that we lack appellate jurisdiction over this issue, that jurisdiction exists on two independent bases. He further contends that there are no issues of fact and that the matter should be remanded simply to enter an award in his favor. Although we agree with Rogers that jurisdiction over this aspect of the judgment appealed from exists, we are unable to grant the award he seeks.

The district court stated that deposition and documentary evidence regarding the deductible expenses referred to in § 504(b) are present in the record. We are satisfied that defendants have incurred deductible expenses in some amount and that they should have an opportunity to prove them as an offset to plaintiff's evidence of infringing damages. Further, the amount of actual damages incurred by Rogers, as well as the proper apportionment of Koons' profits between Rogers and Koons, remain to be determined on remand. With respect to the calculation of actual damages, "the primary measure of recovery is the extent to which the market value of the copyrighted work at the time of the infringement has been injured or destroyed by the infringement." *Fitzgerald Pub. Co., Inc. v. Baylor Pub. Co., Inc.*, 807 F.2d 1110, 1118 (2d Cir. 1986). While we leave the ascertainment of damages to the district court, under the circumstances of this case, we think that a reasonable license fee for the use of "Puppies" best approximates the market injury sustained by Rogers as a result of Koons' misappropriation. See *Deltak, Inc. v. Advanced Systems, Inc.*, 767 F.2d 357, 360-61 (7th Cir. 1985) ("The value of the infringer's use is a permissible basis for estimating actual damages."); *Sid & Marty Krofft Television Productions, Inc. v. McDonald's Corp.*, 562 F.2d 1157, 1174 (9th Cir. 1977) (same).

On the subject of apportioning profits, the copyright law requires that Koons have the opportunity to establish those "elements of profit attributable to factors other than the copyrighted work." 17 U.S.C. § 504(b). These "elements" may include Koons' own notoriety and his related ability to command high prices for his work. See *Sheldon v. Metro-Goldwyn Corp.*, 309 U.S. 390, 407-09, 60 S. Ct. 681, 687-88, 84 L. Ed. 825 (1940) (considering "the drawing power of the 'motion picture stars' ... the artistic conceptions ... and ... the expert supervision and direction of the various processes which made possible the composite result"); *Frank Music Corp. v. Metro-Goldwyn-Mayer Inc.*, 886 F.2d 1545, 1549 (9th Cir. 1989), *cert. denied*, 494 U.S. 1017, 110 S. Ct. 1321, 108 L. Ed. 2d 496 (1990) ("Where a defendant alters infringing material to suit its own unique purposes, those alterations and the creativity behind them should be taken into account in apportioning the profits of the infringing work."); *Abend v. MCA, Inc.*, 863 F.2d 1465, 1478, *aff'd sub nom. Stewart v. Abend*, 495 U.S. 207, 110 S. Ct. 1750, 109 L. Ed. 2d 184 (1990) (considering outstanding performances and brilliant direction); *ABKCO Music, Inc. v. Harrisongs Music*, 508 F. Supp. 798, 801 (S.D.N.Y. 1981), *modified*, 722 F.2d 988 (2d Cir. 1983) (considering "international 'name'" of infringing recording artist). See also 3 Nimmer § 14.03 [C]. To the extent that Koons is able to prove that the profits at issue derive solely from his own position in the art world, he should be allowed to retain them.

Finally, we note that Rogers remains at liberty to elect statutory damages in lieu of an award of actual damages and apportioned profits. See 17 U.S.C. § 504(c). In fact, given Koons' wilful and egregious behavior, we think Rogers may be a good candidate for enhanced statutory damages pursuant to 17 U.S.C. § 504(c) (2). See Fitzgerald Pub. Co., 807 F.2d at 1115. Of course, that determination remains for the district court to make in the first instance.

The case must be remanded therefore for the district court to determine the amount of the award, a matter which it had reserved to itself prior to the institution of this appeal.

VI. The Turn-Over Order

Finally, the turn-over order of the artist's copy is an equitable remedy issued under the broad powers vested in a trial judge under 17 U.S.C. § 503(b) (court may order destruction or other reasonable disposition of infringing copies). In this case, after Judge Haight issued his turn-over order, Koons arranged to ship the fourth or artist's copy of "String of Puppies" from the United States to Germany. We see no abuse of the district court's discretion in directing turn-over and, under the circumstances, the contempt order for the direct violation of the turn-over order was entirely proper.

CONCLUSION

Accordingly, the judgment of the district court is affirmed in all respects.

Reading Note: The following case also involved a sculpture incorporating a three-dimensional rendition of a two-dimensional cartoon strip character placed in relation with two other toy characters. The work was also created as part of Koon's *Banality Show.* Again, the court was faced with determining whether the allegedly infringing use could be considered "fair use."

UNITED FEATURE SYNDICATE, INC. V. KOONS

817 F. Supp. 370 (S.D.N.Y. 1993)

OPINION AND ORDER. LEISURE, District Judge:

This is an action for copyright infringement, dilution, and unfair competition based upon defendant Jeff Koons' ("Koons") production of four identical sculptures entitled *Wild Boy and Puppy* which allegedly contain unauthorized copies of the Garfield comic strip character "Odie." Plaintiff United Feature Syndicate, Inc. ("UFS") has moved for partial summary judgment, pursuant to Rule 56(c) of the Federal Rules of Civil Procedure, as to defendant Koons' liability on the copyright infringement claims. For the reasons stated below, the motion is granted in its entirety.

BACKGROUND

Plaintiff UFS owns all right, title and interest in the copyrights covering the Garfield comic strip, which focuses on the life of *Garfield the Cat* and his interaction with several other characters. The Garfield comic strip was created in 1978 by James R. Davis and, since that time, has become one of the most famous comic strips in the United States. The Garfield comic strip currently appears in over 2,000 newspapers in the United States and around the world. In addition to the comic strip, plaintiff also possesses approximately 400 licenses for products or uses of the various Garfield characters, including the television production of the Garfield animation programs.

By virtue of its ownership of the copyright interest covering the Garfield comic strip, UFS also owns the copyright in the various characters. Among the most prominent and well-known of the Garfield comic strip characters is the dog "Odie" which has been regularly featured in the comic strip, in both likeness and name, since the strip's inception. It is the alleged unauthorized use of the "Odie" character in one of defendant's sculptures which forms the basis of the instant action.

Defendant Koons is an accomplished visual artist whose primary activities are in the creation of sculptural works of art. Koons is part of a contemporary artistic movement which takes images from popular culture and "re-contextualizes" them in a work of art in an effort to convey a certain message or idea to the viewer. This movement is sometimes categorized as "Pop Art" with Andy Warhol's reproduction of multiple images of Campbell's soup cans being a widely recognized example of this artistic tradition.

In October, 1986, after a successful presentation of certain stainless steel sculptures at the Sonnabend Gallery in New York City, Koons began working on his next set of sculptural works of art which would further develop the thoughts and themes expressed in the October exhibition. During the remainder of 1986 and throughout 1987, Koons travelled throughout the world looking for exotic materials, such as porcelain, which could be used for his next exhibition at the Sonnabend Gallery and also choosing workshops that were skilled at crafting such materials. Koons ultimately decided to use three types of materials for his next set of works: mirrors, wood, and porcelain. During this same period, Koons also collected the popular images and ideas which he could transform into works of sculpture. According to Koons, he would accumulate images from popular culture by cutting out items that he read or by purchasing objects during the course of his travels and then, at some later point, would begin the process of "re-contextualizing" these images into sculptures.

Jeff Koons' Wild Boy and Puppy (1988), *a ceramic sculpture which includes a three-dimensional representation of a dog based directly on a character from the popular syndicated comic strip Garfield by Jim Davis, was part of Koon's* Banality Series.

Koons decided that the unifying theme of this upcoming exhibition would be "banality." The exhibition focused on popular attitudes toward objects and facts of everyday life which were commonplace and Koons referred to this exhibition as the *Banality Show*. Koons did not physically make any of the sculptures for this Banality Show. Instead, Koons was the "producer" of the sculptures that is, he thought of the ideas for the sculptures and made the decision as to the materials to be used, as well as the sculpture's form, shape, size, and color. While he had absolute control over the production of the sculptures, the sculptures were physically manufactured by artisans who made the sculptures to Koons' specifications. During 1988, Koons worked with the studios and artisans who were commissioned by him to produce 20 separate sculptural works for the Sonnabend exhibition. Koons commissioned the artisans to create three "editions," or copies, of each sculpture, as well as an "artist's proof" which is not offered for sale but rather is kept by Koons as documentation of his work. On November 19, 1988, the "Banality" exhibition opened at the Sonnabend Gallery.

One of the twenty sculptures produced by Koons for this exhibition is entitled *Wild Boy and Puppy* and is the subject of this lawsuit.[NOTE 1] UFS contends that the "Puppy" in the sculpture is an unauthorized copy of the "Odie" character from the Garfield comic strip. In his deposition, Koons admits that the "Puppy" in the sculpture is based on a picture of the "Odie" character. According to Koons, he designed the sculpture by cutting out a color picture of "Odie" (the "Puppy") and placing it next to a cut-out image of a stuffed doll (the "Wild Boy") to form a collage which was used as the design for the sculpture. Deposition of Jeff Koons, sworn to on July 2, 1990 ("Koons Deposition"), at 63-64, 66-67, 91-94, annexed as Exhibit B to the Affidavit of John D. Parker, Esq., in Support of Plaintiff's Motion for Partial Summary Judgment, sworn to on January 15, 1991 ("Parker Affidavit"); *see also* Exhibit H to the Parker Affidavit (collage of *Wild Boy and Puppy*). Koons was unable to recall with certainty where he obtained the image of "Odie" used in the collage, but stated that he obtained it from some media source, such as a postcard or magazine. Koons Deposition, at 67, 92. The image of the "Wild Boy" is based on a stuffed toy doll that Koons found in Europe. Affidavit of Jeff Koons, sworn to on February 8, 1991 ("Koons Affidavit"), at ¶ 19.

According to Koons, he instructed the artisan who physically constructed the sculpture to reproduce the pictures of "Odie" and the doll contained in the collage as closely as possible.

Koons Deposition, at 93-94. Koons explained that he had the artisan copy the pictures as closely as possible so that he could maintain control over the end product. *Id.* Thus, the only deviation between the sculpture of the "Odie" character and the copyrighted picture of the "Odie" character used by Koons was the three-dimensional nature of the sculpture, as well as a technical change in the relative length of "Odie's" tongue which was made to give the sculpture additional structural stability. In addition, the sculpture of "Odie" was obviously larger than the picture of "Odie" contained in the collage, but the scale of the character, in relation to the other image (the "Wild Boy"), remained virtually the same. *Id.* at 93-94 and Exhibit H. At some later point, Koons instructed the artisan to add a third image, the butterfly-bee figure, to the sculpture. *Id.* at 62.

At Koons' direction, four identical porcelain sculptures of *Wild Boy and Puppy* were produced. Sonnabend Gallery displayed the *Wild Boy and Puppy* sculpture as part of the Banality Show which opened on November 19, 1988. Two of the four sculptures of the *Wild Boy and Puppy* were sold to collectors by Sonnabend Gallery for $125,000 each. The ownership of the third sculpture was retained by Ileana Sonnabend for her private collection. Koons owns the fourth copy of the sculpture which is referred to as the "artist's proof." The various sculptures displayed in the *Banality Show* attracted substantial media coverage, including a feature in *People* magazine, annexed as Exhibit G to the Parker Affidavit, which displayed a large picture of Koons surrounded by the three images contained in the *Wild Boy and Puppy* sculpture. Neither Koons nor Sonnabend Gallery sought UFS's permission to use "Odie" in the sculpture or informed UFS of their intended use of "Odie."

Plaintiffs filed the instant action on December 6, 1989, alleging several causes of action based upon the alleged unauthorized use of the "Odie" character in the *Wild Boy and Puppy* sculpture including: (1) unfair competition under the Lanham Act, 15 U.S.C. § 1051, *et seq.;* (2) copyright infringement under the Copyright Act of 1976, 17 U.S.C. § 101, *et seq.;* (3) dilution under Section 368-d of New York's General Business Law; and (4) common-law unfair competition under New York law. The complaint seeks both injunctive relief and monetary damages. Sonnabend Gallery was originally named as a defendant in this action along with Koons. However, Sonnabend Gallery and plaintiff subsequently reached a Settlement Agreement and, on January 19, 1993, the Court, by stipulation of the parties, ordered that the claims in the instant action as to Sonnabend Gallery be dismissed with prejudice. Thus, the only remaining defendant is Jeff Koons.

Plaintiff has moved for partial summary judgment against defendant Koons on the issue of liability with respect to the copyright claims, contained in Counts II and III, which allege that the manufacture and sale of these sculptures infringe upon UFS's copyrights in the comic strip character "Odie." Defendant Koons contends, *inter alia,* that the *Wild Boy and Puppy* sculpture is protected under the fair use doctrine as a parody and that there are disputed issues of material fact which preclude summary judgment in plaintiff's favor on the issue of liability.[NOTE 2]

DISCUSSION

I. STANDARD FOR SUMMARY JUDGMENT

Rule 56(c) of the Federal Rules of Civil Procedure provides that summary judgment "shall be rendered forthwith if the pleadings, depositions, answers to interrogatories, and admissions on file, together with the affidavits, if any, show that there is no genuine issue as to any material fact and that the moving party is entitled to a judgment as a matter of law." Fed.R.Civ.P. 56(c); *see Celotex Corp. v. Catrett,* 477 U.S. 317, 322, 106 S. Ct. 2548, 2552, 91 L. Ed. 2d 265 (1986); *Anderson v. Liberty Lobby, Inc.,* 477 U.S. 242, 247, 106 S. Ct. 2505, 2509, 91 L. Ed. 2d 202 (1986); *Lang v. Retirement Living Publishing Co.,* 949 F.2d 576, 580 (2d Cir. 1991). Summary judgment "is appropriate only 'after adequate time for discovery and upon motion, against a party who fails to make a showing sufficient to establish the existence of an element essential to that party's case, and on which that party will bear the burden of proof at trial.'" *Thornton v. Syracuse Sav. Bank,* 961 F.2d 1042, 1046 (2d Cir.1992) (quoting *Celotex,* 477 U.S. at 322, 106 S.Ct. at 2552).

"In deciding whether to grant summary judgment all inferences drawn from the materials submitted to the trial court are viewed in a light most favorable to the party opposing the motion. The nonmovant's allegations are taken as true and it receives the benefit of the doubt when its assertions conflict with those of the movant."

Cruden v. Bank of New York, 957 F.2d 961, 975 (2d Cir.1992). "Only when no reasonable trier of fact could find in favor of the nonmoving party should summary judgment be granted." *Id.; accord Taggart v. Time Inc.,* 924 F.2d 43, 46 (2d Cir.1991); *see also Lang,* 949 F.2d at 580 ("In determining how a reasonable jury would decide, the court must resolve all ambiguities and draw all inferences against the moving party."); *Binder v. Long Island Lighting Co.,* 933 F.2d 187, 191 (2d Cir.1991) ("Viewing the evidence produced in the light most favorable to the nonmovant, if a rational trier could not find for the nonmovant, then there is no genuine issue of material fact and entry of summary judgment is appropriate.").

The substantive law governing the case will identify those facts that are material, and "[o] nly disputes over facts that might affect the outcome of the suit under the governing law will properly preclude the entry of summary judgment." *Anderson,* 477 U.S. at 248, 106 S. Ct. at 2510. "[T]he judge's function is not himself to weigh the evidence and determine the truth of the matter but to determine whether there is a genuine issue for trial." *Anderson,* 477 U.S. at 249, 106 S. Ct. at 2510.

The party seeking summary judgment "bears the initial responsibility of informing the district court of the basis for its motion," and identifying which materials "it believes demonstrate the absence of a genuine issue of material fact." *Celotex,* 477 U.S. at 323, 106 S. Ct. at 2552. Once a motion for summary judgment is properly made, however, the burden then shifts to the non-moving party, which "'must set forth specific facts showing that there is a genuine issue for trial.'" *Anderson,* 477 U.S. at 250, 106 S. Ct. at 2511 (quoting Fed.R.Civ.P. 56(e)). "[T]he mere existence of *some* alleged factual dispute between the parties will not defeat an otherwise properly supported motion for summary judgment; the requirement is that there be no *genuine* issue of *material* fact." *Anderson,* 477 U.S. at 247-48, 106 S. Ct. at 2509-10 (emphasis in original). "Conclusory allegations will not suffice to create a genuine issue. There must be more than a 'scintilla of evidence,' and more than 'some metaphysical doubt as to the material facts.'" *Delaware & Hudson Railway Co. v. Consolidated Rail Corp.,* 902 F.2d 174, 178 (2d Cir.1990) (quoting *Anderson,* 477 U.S. at 252, 106 S. Ct. at 2512 and *Matsushita Electric Indus. Co. v. Zenith Radio Corp.,* 475 U.S. 574, 586, 106 S. Ct. 1348, 1355, 89 L. Ed. 2d 538 (1986)), *cert. denied,* ___ U.S. ___, 111 S. Ct. 2041, 114 L. Ed. 2d 125 (1991). "The non-movant cannot escape summary judgment merely by vaguely asserting the existence of some unspecified disputed material facts, or defeat the motion through mere speculation or conjecture." *Western World Ins. Co. v. Stack Oil, Inc.,* 922 F.2d 118, 121 (2d Cir.1990) (quotations omitted); *see also Gnazzo v. G.D. Searle & Co.,* 973 F.2d 136, 138 (2d Cir.1992) ("[The Court must] consider the record in the light most favorable to the nonmovant. However, the non-movant may not rest upon the mere allegations or denials of her pleading, but must set forth specific facts showing that there is a genuine issue for trial.") (quotation and citations omitted).

II. THE SECOND CIRCUIT'S DECISION IN *ROGERS v. KOONS*

In a recent decision, *Rogers v. Koons,* 960 F.2d 301 (2d Cir.), *cert. denied,* ___ U.S. ___, 113 S. Ct. 365, 121 L. Ed. 2d 278 (1992), the Second Circuit addressed a copyright claim against Koons with respect to another sculpture, entitled *String of Puppies,* which Koons also produced and displayed at the Banality Show. The factual circumstances in *Rogers* are very similar to the instant case and many of the same legal issues are involved. I n that case, Koons designed the *String of Puppies* sculpture at issue by using an Art Rogers' copyrighted photograph *Puppies* contained on a Museum Graphics notecard which Koons purchased in a card shop in 1987. Koons tore off the portion of the card bearing the copyright notice of *Puppies,* sent the card to his artisans and instructed them to copy the photograph as closely as possible. Koons had four copies of the *String of Puppies* sculpture made. Three of the copies were sold by Sonnabend Gallery to collectors for a total of $367,000, and Koons retained the fourth copy of the sculpture as an "artist's proof." *Id.* 960 F.2d at 305.

The plaintiff moved for summary judgment in *Rogers* and, in his opposition papers, Koons argued, *inter alia,* that his transformation of the *Puppies* photograph into the "String of Puppies" sculpture constituted a work of art which fell within the protection of the fair use doctrine as a parody or social comment on society at large. *Id.* at 309. In granting summary judgment in plaintiff's favor on the copyright claim, the District Court held that the *String of Puppies* sculpture was copied from the *Puppies* photograph without authorization and that such use was not protected under the fair use doctrine. The Second Circuit upheld the Court's summary judgment determination and emphasized that "it is not really the parody flag that appellants are sailing under, but rather the flag of piracy." 960 F.2d at 311. In reaching this decision, the Second Circuit rejected virtually every legal argument which Koons has asserted in the instant case in opposition to UFS's similar motion for summary judgment.

The *Rogers* decision involved a different work of art than the sculpture at issue here and this Court will obviously base its decision on UFS's summary judgment motion solely on the record developed in the instant case. Nevertheless, given the factual similarities between the cases, the *Rogers* decision does provide a helpful framework in which the Court can examine the legal issues presented by the parties in the instant motion. Defendant Koons argues that there are differences between the sculpture in *Rogers* and the *Wild Boy and Puppy* sculpture at issue in the instant case which make *Rogers* inapposite and require the Court to deny UFS's summary judgment motion in its entirety. However, as explained below, the Court has examined the record in the instant case and finds that summary judgment in UFS's favor is appropriate on the issue of liability with respect to the copyright claims.

III. ELEMENTS OF COPYRIGHT INFRINGEMENT

The copyright laws have long recognized that copyright protection is available for cartoon and comic strip characters. *See, e.g., Warner Bros. Inc. v. American Broadcasting Cos.,* 720 F.2d 231, 240 (2d Cir.1983) (Superman); *Walt Disney Productions v. Air Pirates,* 581 F.2d 751, 754-55 (9th Cir. 1978), *cert. denied,* 439 U.S. 1132, 99 S. Ct. 1054, 59 L. Ed. 2d 94 (1979) (Mickey Mouse and other Disney characters); *Detective Comics v. Bruns Publications,* 111 F.2d 432, 433 (2d Cir.1940) (Superman); *King Features Syndicate v. Fleischer,* 299 F. 533, 535 (2d Cir.1924) (Barney Google's horse, Spark Plug). In order to establish a claim for copyright infringement for a protected work, a plaintiff must show both ownership of a valid copyright and that defendant copied the protected work without authorization. *See Computer Assocs. Int'l, Inc. v. Altai, Inc.,* 982 F.2d 693, 701 (2d Cir.1992); *Rogers v. Koons,* 960 F.2d at 306; *Weissmann v. Freeman,* 868 F.2d 1313, 1320 (2d Cir.), *cert. denied,* 493 U.S. 883, 110 S. Ct. 219, 107 L. Ed. 2d 172 (1989); *Hasbro Bradley, Inc. v. Sparkle Toys, Inc.,* 780 F.2d 189, 192 (2d Cir.1985).

A. OWNERSHIP OF VALID COPYRIGHT

UFS has submitted Certificates of Registration from the Registrar of Copyrights which cover the "Odie" comic strip character. *See* Parker Affidavit, at Exhibit D. In addition, UFS also possesses the Certificate of Registration for three-dimensional representations of "Odie" with respect to "plush toys" or "soft sculptures." *Id.* Pursuant to the Copyright Act, 17 U.S.C. § 410(c), a certificate of registration is *prima facie* evidence of the valid ownership of a copyright and the burden then shifts to the defendant to rebut that presumption of ownership. *See Rogers,* 960 F.2d at 306; *Hasbro Bradley, Inc.,* 780 F.2d at 192; *Eckes v. Card Prices Update,* 736 F.2d 859, 861 (2d Cir. 1984). Defendant Koons has offered no proof to rebut the presumption of ownership created by UFS's possession of certificates of registration covering the "Odie" character. Thus, UFS has established that it is the owner of the valid copyrights to the "Odie" character and there are no issues of material fact to be resolved on that issue.

B. UNAUTHORIZED COPYING BY KOONS

To prevail on the summary judgment motion, plaintiff UFS must also demonstrate that no issues of fact exist as to the issue of Koons' unauthorized copying. It is well-established that "[t]he plaintiff may prove defendant's copying either by direct evidence or, as is most often the case, by showing that (1) the defendant had access to the plaintiff's copyrighted work and (2) that defendant's work is substantially similar to the plaintiff's copyrightable material." *Computer Assocs. Int'l, Inc.,* 982 F.2d at 701; *see also Walker v. Time Life Films, Inc.,* 784 F.2d 44, 48 (2d Cir.), *cert. denied,* 476 U.S. 1159, 106 S. Ct. 2278, 90 L. Ed. 2d 721 (1986).

In the instant case, defendant Koons' unauthorized copying of the "Odie" character is so obvious that no reasonable factfinder could conclude otherwise. First, the Court finds that there is uncontroverted direct evidence of copying. In his deposition, Koons admits that the original design for *Wild Boy and Puppy* came from a color picture of "Odie" that he obtained from an accessible media source, such as a postcard or magazine, and combined with a picture of a stuffed doll. Koons Deposition, at 63-64, 66-67, 91-94.[NOTE 3] Koons instructed the artisan that the sculpture should be made "as close as possible" to the pictures in the collage, which included the "Odie" character. *Id.* at 93-94. Koons explained that, when he provided the artisan with a picture, he wanted him to treat the picture as "factual" and reproduce that picture as closely as possible so that Koons could maintain control of the final product. *Id.* Koons also admitted that he did not seek UFS's permission to use the "Odie" character in his sculpture. *Id.* at 52. Thus, the Court determines that this undisputed direct evidence of copying, by itself, is sufficient to support granting summary judgment in plaintiff's favor on the issue of unauthorized copying.

Even assuming *arguendo* that there was insufficient direct evidence of copying, summary judgment would be warranted based upon the fact that Koons' admittedly had access to the copyrighted work and that Koons' sculpture is substantially similar to the copyrighted work. The Second Circuit has held that substantial similarity is determined by "'whether an average lay observer would recognize the alleged copy as having been appropriated from the copyrighted work.'" *Rogers,* 960 F.2d at 307 (quoting *Ideal Toy Corp. v. Fab-Lu Ltd.,* 360 F.2d 1021, 1022 (2d Cir.1966)). The test also has been defined as "whether 'the ordinary observer, unless he set out to detect the disparities, would be disposed to overlook them, and regard their aesthetic appeal as the same.'" *Rogers,* 960 F.2d at 307-08 (quoting *Peter Pan Fabrics, Inc. v. Martin Weiner Corp.,* 274 F.2d 487, 489 (2d Cir.1960)).

In the instant case, the Court finds that even the most casual observer would recognize the "Puppy" in the *Wild Boy and Puppy* sculpture as the "Odie" character. The "Puppy" is virtually an exact reproduction of the "Odie" character. While Koons' changed the relative length of "Odie's" tongue in his sculpture, that alteration was such a minor component of the "Odie" character that it would be unnoticed by the casual observer and, in any event, would not alter the observer's ability to recognize the "Puppy" in the sculpture as being "Odie." Thus, no significance can be placed on this minor variation. The Court finds that no reasonable factfinder could view the "Puppy" in *Wild Boy and Puppy* and conclude that the "Puppy" is not the "Odie" character.

Koons contends that the *Wild Boy and Puppy* sculpture contains two other separate images, the boy and butterfly-bee, and that this grouping of images is a work of art that is a completely distinct and different work from the copyrighted "Odie" character. It is well established that "no plagiarist can excuse the wrong by showing how much of his work he did not pirate." *Sheldon v. Metro-Goldwyn Pictures Corp.,* 81 F.2d 49, 56 (2d Cir.) (L. Hand, J.), *cert. denied,* 298 U.S. 669, 56 S. Ct. 835, 80 L. Ed. 1392 (1936); *see also Stewart v. Abend,* 495 U.S. 207, 238, 110 S. Ct. 1750, 1769, 109 L. Ed. 2d 184 (1990) ("[A] taking may not be excused merely because it is insubstantial with respect to the *infringing* work.") (quoting *Harper & Row, Publishers, Inc. v. Nation Enterprises,* 471 U.S. 539, 565, 105 S. Ct. 2218, 2233, 85 L. Ed. 2d 588 (1985); 3 Nimmer § 13.03[B], at 13-51 ("It is entirely immaterial that in many respects plaintiff's and defendant's works are dissimilar if in other respects similarity as to a substantial element of plaintiff's work can be shown."). Thus, "[i]f substantial similarity is found, the defendant will not be immunized from liability by reason of the addition in his work of different characters or additional and varied incidents, nor generally by reason of his work proving more attractive or saleable than the plaintiffs." 3 Nimmer § 13.03[B], at 13-51, 52.

While the Court recognizes that this general rule must be applied with caution in the context of graphic or three-dimensional works as distinguished from literary works, *see Warner Bros. v. American Broadcasting Cos., supra,* 720 F.2d at 241-42, the Court finds that the grouping of the "Odie" character with two other images does not create a material issue of fact as to the question of substantial similarity. In *Warner Bros.,* the Second Circuit held that an issue of substantiality similarity exists when significant differences exist between the character in defendant's work and the copyrighted character:

Ultimately, care must be taken to draw the elusive distinction between a substantially similar character that infringes a copyrighted character despite slight differences in appearance, behavior, or traits, and a somewhat similar though non-infringing character whose appearance, behavior, or traits, and especially their combination, significantly differ from those of a copyrighted character, even though the second character is reminiscent of the first one.

720 F.2d at 242. However, in the instant case, the Court is not faced with this "elusive distinction" because this is not a situation, as in *Warner Bros.,* where the defendant's character

has significant dissimilarities to the copyrighted character. Instead, the "Puppy" in Koons' sculpture is a virtual reproduction of the "Odie" character in both its appearance and expression. The addition of the two other images does not, in any way, affect the ability of a lay observer to recognize the "Puppy" as "Odie." Under such circumstances, the use of two other images in the sculpture in conjunction with the wholesale pirating of the "Odie" character does not create a factual dispute which precludes summary judgment in favor of plaintiff on the issue of substantial similarity. In light of the overwhelming similarity of the "Puppy" in the *Wild Boy and Puppy* to the "Odie" character and the undisputed proof of Koons' access to the copyrighted material, a reasonable factfinder must conclude that Koons copied the protected features of the original character even if there were no evidence of direct copying.

IV. FAIR USE

Defendant Koons argues that his use of the "Odie" character is protected by the fair use doctrine. This equitable doctrine, which is codified in Section 107 of the 1976 Copyright Act, allows others to use copyrighted material without the owner's consent, under certain circumstances, for purposes such as "criticism, comment, news reporting, teaching … scholarship, or research." 17 U.S.C. § 107. Section 107 enumerates four factors which the Court should consider in assessing whether the use of a work in any particular case is a fair use:

(1) the purpose and character of the use, including whether such use is of a commercial nature or is for nonprofit educational purposes;

(2) the nature of the copyrighted work;

(3) the amount and substantiality of the portion used in relation to the copyrighted work as a whole; and

(4) the effect of the use upon the potential market for or value of the copyrighted work.

17 U.S.C. § 107. This list is not intended to be exhaustive, but rather simply sets forth examples of the types of factors which the Court should consider in the application of the fair use doctrine. While the factual nature of this inquiry might suggest that summary judgment is inappropriate when fair use is the issue, it is well established that the general standard of summary judgment applies in such cases and, thus, the granting of summary judgment is proper when there are no genuine issues of fact present regarding the applicability of the fair use doctrine. *See, e.g., Stewart,* 495 U.S. at 236-38, 110 S.Ct. at 1768-69; *Rogers,* 960 F.2d at 308-09; *Maxtone-Graham v. Burtchaell,* 803 F.2d 1253, 1258-59 (2d Cir.1986), *cert. denied,* 481 U.S. 1059, 107 S. Ct. 2201, 95 L. Ed. 2d 856 (1987). In other words, when the historical facts underlying the factors are not in dispute, summary judgment on the issue of fair use is appropriate:

"the essential character of the fair use doctrine as an equitable rule of reason makes it all the more appropriate for the court itself to decide whether the fair use defense applies when the historical facts underlying each of the four factors are not disputed."

Maxtone-Graham, 803 F.2d at 1258 (quoting *Hustler Magazine, Inc. v. Moral Majority, Inc.,* 606 F. Supp. 1526, 1532 (C.D.Cal.1985), *aff'd,* 796 F.2d 1148 (9th Cir.1986) (quotation and citation omitted)). In the instant case, while Koons has attempted to raise issues of fact to avoid summary judgment, the Court finds that the material historical facts are not in dispute. Instead, the real dispute focuses on the ultimate conclusions to be drawn from the admitted facts. As noted below, based upon an analysis of these facts, the Court finds that summary judgment in plaintiff's favor on the fair use issue is warranted.

A. THE FAIR USE FACTORS

(1) *Purpose and Character of the Unauthorized Use*

The first factor in the fair use analysis focuses on "whether the original was copied in good faith to benefit the public or primarily for the commercial interests of the infringer." *Rogers,* 960 F.2d at 309 (citing *MCA, Inc. v. Wilson,* 677 F.2d 180, 182 (2d Cir.1981)). A finding that the defendant knowingly exploited the copyrighted work for personal gain militates against a finding of fair use. *Rogers,* 960 F.2d at 309. The Supreme Court has noted that "[t]he crux of the profit/nonprofit distinction is not whether the sole motive of the use is monetary gain but whether the user stands to profit from exploitation of the copyrighted material without paying the customary price." *Harper & Row, Publishers, Inc. v. Nation Enterprises,* 471 U.S. 539, 562, 105 S. Ct. 2218, 2231, 85 L. Ed. 2d 588 (1985). Therefore, when the unauthorized copies are made for a commercial or profit-making purpose, the use is presumptively unfair. *Stewart,* 495 U.S. at 237, 110 S. Ct. at 1768; *Sony Corp. of America v. Universal City Studios, Inc.,* 464 U.S. 417, 449, 104 S. Ct. 774, 792, 78 L. Ed. 2d 574 (1984); *Rogers,* 960 F.2d at 309.

In the instant case, it is undisputed that two of the *Wild Boy and Puppy* sculptures were sold for $125,000 each and that, after subtracting the costs associated with producing such sculptures, Koons expected to make a profit. Koons Deposition, at 57, 85-87; *see also* Koons' Response to Plaintiff's Rule 3(g) Statement, dated February 15, 1991, at ¶ 2. While Koons does not concede that profit is the motivation for his work, he admits that there are "business aspects" to his work and "the main objective ... in the business aspect of the endeavor would be to make a profit on it." Koons Deposition, at 23. There is also undisputed evidence that Koons advertised the 1988 Banality Show, which included the *Wild Boy and Puppy* sculpture, in at least four magazines. Koons Deposition, at 29-33.

The Court finds this undisputed evidence strongly indicates that Koons' use of the copyrighted "Odie" character was "of a commercial nature" and that Koons stands to profit from his exploitation of the copyrighted material without paying the customary price. The fact that the infringing copy can be classified as "art" or as being part of an "artistic tradition" cannot be used as a shield to salvage an otherwise defective fair use defense. The creation of musical compositions, films, plays, and literature can all be characterized as "art" or "artistic expression." If the subjective classification of an otherwise infringing work as "art" automatically immunized such work under the fair use doctrine, the doctrine would virtually eviscerate the protection afforded by the Copyright Act. Instead, the fair use analysis properly focuses, *inter alia,* on whether the work is "of a commercial nature" which looks primarily at whether the defendant stands to profit from the use of the copyrighted material without paying for such usage.

In *Rogers v. Koons, supra,* the Second Circuit noted that, with respect to the "String of Puppies" sculpture at issue in that case, "there is simply nothing in the record to support a view that Koons produced *String of Puppies* for anything other than sale as high-priced art." *Rogers,* 960 F.2d at 312. The Court has examined the record in the instant case and reaches the same conclusion with respect to *Wild Boy and Puppy.* While such evidence militates against finding fair use, it is not a controlling factor. Instead, such evidence must be considered in conjunction with the remaining statutory factors. *Id.,* 960 F.2d at 309.[4]

(2) *Nature of the Copyrighted Work*

The second fair use factor requires an analysis of the nature of the copyrighted work. As the Supreme Court has noted, "[t]he law generally recognizes a greater need to disseminate factual works than works of fiction or fantasy." *Harper & Row,* 471 U.S. at 563, 105 S. Ct. at 2232. Thus, fair use is less likely to be found when the original copyrighted work is fictional, rather than a factual or informational work such as a biography, a telephone directory, a textbook, or a "how to" book. *See Stewart,* 495 U.S. at 237-38, 110 S.Ct. at 1768-69; *Harper & Row,* 471 U.S. at 563, 105 S. Ct. at 2232. In making this assessment, other factors such as "[w]hether the original is creative, imaginative, or represents an investment of time in anticipation of a financial return also should be considered." *Rogers,* 960 F.2d at 310. In the instant case, it is undisputed that "Odie" is a fictional character created by James R. Davis as part of the Garfield comic strip, in anticipation of financial return. Moreover, "Odie" clearly must be classified as a creative and imaginative character and, thus, the second factor weighs heavily in plaintiff's favor.

While recognizing that the "Odie" character falls within the realm of the "creative," Koons argues that, as a result of the commercial success of the Garfield characters (including "Odie") and their pervasive presence in our society, these characters, to a certain extent, have become "public figures." *See* Koons' Memorandum of Law in Opposition to the Motion for Partial Summary Judgment ("Koons' Opposition Memorandum"), at 21-22. In other words, the contention is that, due to plaintiffs placement of the Garfield characters in the public eye, these characters have "a factual existence as such" which entitles them to less protection under the copyright laws. *Id.* at 22. The Court finds that this argument is without merit and fails to create a material issue of fact with respect to the second factor under the fair use doctrine. The popularity and commercial success of the Garfield characters cannot transform them into the "factual" realm any more than Mickey Mouse, Snoopy, Superman, or Bart Simpson could be said to have acquired a "factual existence" which results in a loss of their copyright protection. In other words, unlike a trade name that loses its protection under the Lanham Act when it becomes generic, these imaginative characters do not lose copyright protection as a result of their incorporation into American culture. *See Warner Bros.,* 720 F.2d at 242. No matter how popular a character may become, the copyright owner is entitled to guard against the unauthorized commercial exploitation of that character. *Id.* [NOTE 5] To hold otherwise would thwart a fundamental purpose of the Copyright Act which is to foster creativity by assuring the creator of an original work that he or she will reap the exclusive benefits generated from the commercial success of the work.

Accordingly, since the "Odie" character is a fictional, imaginative work, the second factor strongly militates against finding the Koons' use of that character in his sculpture constituted a fair use. Moreover, the Court finds that Koons' has failed to raise any genuine issues of material fact with respect to this second factor.

(3) *The Amount and Substantiality of the Unauthorized Use*

In *Rogers v. Koons, supra,* the Second Circuit noted that "[w]here the amount of copying exceeds permissible levels, summary judgment has been upheld" in favor of plaintiff on the fair use issue. 960 F.2d at 310-11. To a large extent, this third factor "involves the same analysis as that used when determining if the copy is substantially similar to the original." 960 F.2d at 311. At issue is "the amount and substantiality of the portion used in relation to the copyrighted work, not to the allegedly infringing work." *New Era Publications Int'l, ApS v. Carol Publishing Group,* 904 F.2d 152, 158 (2d Cir.1990), *cert. denied,* 498 U.S. 921, 111 S. Ct. 297, 112 L. Ed. 2d 251 (1990). In assessing this factor, "'[t]here are no absolute rules as to how much of a copyrighted work may be copied and still be considered a fair use.'" *Id.* (quoting *Maxtone-Graham,* 803 F.2d at 1263). While this determination has a quantitative element, the Second Circuit has emphasized that "[e]ven more critical than the quantity is the qualitative degree of the copying: what degree of the essence of the original is copied in relation to its whole." *Rogers,* 960 F.2d at 311.

Applying this factor in the instant case, the undisputed facts clearly demonstrate that the *Wild Boy and Puppy* sculpture, designed by Koons, copies the "Odie" character virtually in its entirety. Under the circumstances of the instant case, no reasonable factfinder could conclude that Koons' use of the copyrightable components of the "Odie" character did not exceed a permissible level of copying under the fair use doctrine. *See, e.g., Rogers,* 960 F.2d at 311 (where Koons' sculpture copied "nearly *in toto*" the essence of plaintiff Rogers' "Puppies" photograph, "no reasonable jury could conclude that Koons did not exceed a permissible level of copying under the fair use doctrine").

(4) *Effect of the Use on the Market Value of the Original*

The fourth factor, which examines the effect of the defendant's use on the market value of the original work, "is the 'most important, and indeed, central fair use factor.'" *Stewart,* 495 U.S. at 238, 110 S. Ct. at 1769 (quoting 3 Nimmer § 13.05[A], at 13-81); *see also Harper & Row,* 471 U.S. at 566, 105 S. Ct. at 2233. Under this factor, the less adverse the impact on the copyright owner's potential market, the less public benefit need be shown to sustain a non-commercial fair use. *Rogers,* 960 F.2d at 312. However, where the use of the copyrighted work is commercial in nature, future harm to the potential markets for the copyright owner's work is presumed. *Sony Corp. of America,* 464 U.S. at 451, 104 S. Ct. at 793; *Rogers,* 960 F.2d at 312. Thus, as recognized in *Rogers,* a critical inquiry under this factor is whether Koons planned to profit from the exploitation of the "Odie" character without paying UFS for such use. *Id.* The Court has already found, based upon the undisputed historical facts, that the use of the "Odie" character in the *Wild Boy and Puppy* sculpture was primarily commercial in nature and that Koons intended to profit from the sale of as many as three copies of the sculpture. Under such circumstances, harm to UFS's ability to market the "Odie" character is presumed and the fourth factor strongly favors finding no fair use.

Koons argues that his representation to the public that there would only be three editions of the sculpture made, as well as one "artist's proof," is ethically and legally binding. [NOTE 6] Thus, Koons contends that, since he is prohibited from producing any more than the three copies plus the one "artist's proof' of *Wild Boy and Puppy* which are already in existence, this limited edition work does not harm UFS's ability to market the "Odie" character. However, UFS need not show actual harm. Instead, the Second Circuit has held that "the owner of a copyright with respect to this market-factor need only demonstrate that if the unauthorized use becomes 'widespread' it would prejudice his potential markets for his work." *Rogers,* 960 F.2d at 312. Applying this principle in *Rogers,* the Court found likelihood of future harm to the marketing of Rogers' photograph even though the *String of Puppies* sculpture, like the sculpture in the instant case, was limited to an edition of three copies. *Id.* Moreover, the variations in the medium in which the copy is made does not, in any way, diminish the copyright owner's ability to protect potential markets. Thus, in assessing this fourth factor, "courts do not focus solely on the market for the work itself, but also on the 'harm to the market for derivative works.'" *New Era Publications,* 904 F.2d at 159 (quoting *Harper & Row,* 471 U.S. at 568, 105 S.Ct. at 2234).

Even in the absence of the presumption of harm which arises from the commercial nature of Koons' sculpture, there is no question that if the unauthorized use of the "Odie" character in sculptures became widespread it would prejudice UFS's potential market with respect to sculptures, as well as other three-dimensional representations of "Odie." UFS currently has approximately 400 licenses for products or uses of various "Garfield" characters, including "Odie." It is clear that UFS's rights in the "Odie" character would allow it to license the manufacture of porcelain statutes of "Odie" or other three-dimensional representations of that character. The widespread sale of unauthorized sculptures of "Odie," such as in *Wild Boy and Puppy*, would obviously have an adverse impact on the potential market for such products.

Similarly, the Court notes that the existence of even three of these sculptures would prejudice UFS's ability to exploit this potential market. For example, the creator of the *Garfield* comic strip, James Davis, is an accomplished artist and may, at some point, decide to create artistic sculptures of his characters for commercial sale. The existence of Koons' work would certainly have a negative impact on the ability to market such a work. Moreover, to the extent that UFS would sell the rights to produce such sculptures to another artist, the market for such sculptures has been reduced by the unauthorized use of the "Odie" character.

Finally, Koons' *Wild Boy and Puppy* sculptures also have the ability to affect other markets of the "Odie" character well beyond the realm of sculptures, statues, or other three-dimensional representations of the character. As commonly done by artists when a work is particularly successful, Koons could decide to license the use of *Wild Boy and Puppy* in posters, cards, T-shirts, calendars and other derivative works. Thus, there is the potential that Koons' use of the "Odie" character would impact licenses granted by UFS in these markets to the extent such licenses already exist or, at the very least, would affect UFS's ability to exploit these markets in the future.

In sum, given the commercial nature of Koons' sculpture, future harm to the market value of the copyright in "Odie" is presumed. Even in the absence of this presumption, the circumstances clearly indicate Koons' use of the copyrighted character has prejudiced UFS's ability to exploit potential markets for its character. Defendant Koons has failed to raise any material issues of fact which would allow a reasonable factfinder to find in his favor with respect to this fourth factor.

B. PARODY OR SATIRE

It is well recognized that there is a branch of the fair use doctrine which deals specifically with the use of a copyrighted work for purpose of parody or satire. In *Rogers v. Koons, supra,* the Second Circuit defined parody or satire and explained the underlying rationale for its incorporation into the fair use doctrine under the general theme of "comment or criticism" of a copyrighted work:

Parody or satire, as we understand it, is when one artist, for comic effect or social commentary, closely imitates the style of another artist and in so doing creates a new art work that makes ridiculous the style and expression of the original. Under our cases parody and satire are valued forms of criticism, encouraged because this sort of criticism itself fosters the creativity protected by the copyright law.

Rogers, 960 F.2d at 309; *see also Warner Bros.,* 720 F.2d at 242-43. Thus, if a defendant's work is determined to be a parody of the copyrighted work, the defendant is entitled to "more extensive use of the copied work than is ordinarily allowed under the substantial similarity test." *Rogers,* 960 F.2d at 310.

Koons argues that the "Odie" character is being used as a parody to symbolize the cynical and empty nature of society. In his affidavit, Koons explains the meaning behind the *Wild Boy and Puppy* work of art is that the Puppy is making a cynical, gagging gesture toward the Wild Boy and such a gesture shows that the Puppy "has lost the ability to find beauty in the most simple things; he cannot embrace the love of life." Koons Affidavit, at ¶ 15. Koons is trying to convey to the viewer that the Puppy's ridicule and cynicism towards the Wild Boy reveals the Puppy's banality. Thus, Koons is exposing the emptiness of the Puppy's scorn and, in so doing, praising the Boy for his sense of freedom. *Id.* at ¶ 16. Koons is using the Puppy as an object of modern mass culture to emphasize that modern culture has become dangerously empty and cynical. *See* Reply Memorandum of Law in Opposition to the Motion by Plaintiff for Partial Summary Judgment, at 15.

In *Rogers,* Koons made virtually the identical argument with respect to his *String of Puppies* sculpture which copied the "Puppies" photograph. Koons contended in *Rogers* that his sculpture was a satire or parody of society at large which showed that mass production of commodities and images had led to a deterioration of the quality of society. *Rogers,* 960 F.2d at 309. In affirming the granting of summary judgment in plaintiff's favor, the Second Circuit emphatically rejected that argument and held that "though the satire need not be only of the copied work and may, as appellants urge of *String of Puppies*, also be a parody of modern society, the copied work must be, at least in part, an object of the parody, otherwise there would be no need to conjure up the original work." *Rogers,* 960 F.2d at 310. Applying this rule, the Second Circuit found that "even given that *String of Puppies* is a satirical critique of our materialistic society, it is difficult to discern any parody of the photograph 'Puppies' itself." *Id.* Thus, the Court found, as a matter of summary judgment, that Koons' *String of Puppies* did not constitute a parody of the original work under the fair use doctrine. In reaching this decision, the Second Circuit articulated the policies which support the rule that the copied work must, at least in part, be an object of the parody:

We think this is a necessary rule, as were it otherwise there would be no real limitation on the copier's use of another's copyrighted work to make a statement on some aspect of society at large. If an infringement of copyrightable expression could be justified as fair use solely on the basis of the infringer's claim to a higher or different artistic usewithout insuring public awareness of the original workthere would be no practicable boundary to the fair use defense. Koons' claim that his infringement of Rogers' work is fair use solely because he is acting within an artistic tradition of commenting upon the commonplace thus cannot be accepted. The rule's function is to insure that credit is given where credit is due. By requiring that the copied work be an object of the parody, we merely insist that the audience be aware that underlying the parody there is an original and separate expression, attributable to a different artist.

Rogers, 960 F.2d at 310; *see also MCA, Inc.,* 677 F.2d at 185 ("We are not prepared to hold that a commercial composer can plagiarize a competitor's copyrighted song, substitute dirty lyrics of his own, perform it for commercial gain, and then escape liability by calling the end result a parody or satire on the mores of society. Such a holding would be an open-ended invitation to musical plagiarism.").

In the instant case, the *Wild Boy and Puppy* sculpture cannot qualify as a parody or satire because, as in *Rogers,* the sculpture is, at best, a parody of society at large, rather than a parody of the copyrighted "Odie" character. In the wake of the *Rogers* decision, Koons attempts to argue that the sculpture is, indeed, a parody of the "Odie" figure itself and that there are factual disputes with respect to this issue which preclude summary judgment. This position is in complete contradiction to the undisputed evidence in the case. In fact, Koons concedes this point in his initial memorandum of law in opposition to UFS's motion, prior to the Second Circuit's decision in *Rogers:*

Defendants recognize that the *Wild Boy and Puppy* sculpture was not intended to be a parody or a satire of the comic strip character "Odie." Indeed Koons has testified that he was not even aware of the identity of the Puppy when he chose it as a source for his sculpture (although he was using it in a satirical fashion). It is the use of the comic strip character as a social comment in the sculpture that brings the Koons use within the same line of reasoning or approach as the parody cases.

Koons' Opposition Memorandum, at 32-33; *see also* Koons Affidavit, at ¶ 19 ("I never had the slightest intention (or even knowledge) that I was including a special dog named 'Odie'. If I had thought there would be a strong public reaction to the Puppy as 'Odie' I would not have selected it for the piece."); Koons Deposition, at 63 ("I found the image of the puppy, which I had no idea was OdieI didn't even find out it was Odie by name until I exhibited the piece. . . ."). Thus, Koons has admitted that the sculpture is not a parody of the "Odie" character. In addition, Koons also conceded that he could have used other images or figures to make the same point. *See* Koons Deposition, at 63-64. Given that Koons admits that other images or figures could have been used in the sculpture besides "Odie," it becomes even more obvious that the sculpture cannot be a comment, criticism, or parody directed, in any way, at "Odie" and there is no justification for the parody defense under such circumstances. Accordingly, since "Odie" is not an object of the parody but merely is claimed to be "an animal figure" that is part of a more general parody on the banality of life or criticism of the mass media culture at large, the teachings of *Rogers* requires that Koons' parody argument be rejected as a matter of law.

In any event, even if Koons' use of the "Odie" character could be classified as a parody, his claim of fair use still would fail. The classification of a work as a parody does not automatically immunize such work from an infringement claim, but rather the parody must be examined in light of the statutory factors. *See, e.g., Fisher v. Dees,* 794 F.2d 432, 435 (9th Cir.1986) (parody is not presumptively classified as a fair use, but rather "must be considered individually, in light of the statutory factors, reason, experience, and, of course, the general principles developed in past cases"); *see also New Line Cinema Corp. v. Bertlesman Music Group, Inc.,* 693 F. Supp. 1517, 1525 (S.D.N.Y.1988). Thus, while parodists are provided significant leeway with respect to the extent and nature of their copying, there are limitations on how much of the original work the parodists can use. *Rogers,* 960 F.2d at 311; *MCA, Inc.,* 677 F.2d at 184-85. When a parody is directed at the copyrighted work being used, the parody falls within the scope of fair use only if the unauthorized user takes no more of the copyrighted work than is necessary for purposes of the parody. In the instant case, Koons appropriated virtually the entire "Odie" character which certainly was much more than would have been necessary if *Wild Boy and Puppy* had been a parody of "Odie." Therefore, assuming *arguendo* that Koons' sculptures could be viewed as a parody of "Odie," the fair use defense would still be unavailable because the use was "so substantial as to be unfairly excessive." *MCA, Inc.,* 677 F.2d at 185.

Considering all of the aforementioned fair use factors, the Court finds that summary judgment in plaintiffs favor on the issue of liability is warranted. The record clearly indicates that Koons intentionally copied the "Odie" character, virtually *in toto,* in his *Wild Boy and Puppy* sculpture and two editions of that sculpture were sold at $125,000 each. Koons stands to profit from his commercial exploitation of the "Odie" character without paying the customary price for such use and, at the same time, has harmed potential markets for the "Odie" character. Moreover, based upon the record in this case, no reasonable factfinder could conclude that Koons' sculpture constitutes a parody of the "Odie" character. All of the fair use factors strongly militate against a finding of fair use and defendant has failed to raise any material issues of fact which would preclude a summary judgment determination in plaintiff's favor.[NOTE 7] In sum, drawing all reasonable inferences in defendant's favor, there is no evidence which would allow a reasonable factfinder to rule for the defendant on the issue of copyright liability in the instant case.

CONCLUSION

For the reasons stated above, the Court hereby grants plaintiffs motion for partial summary judgment on the issue of copyright liability as to Counts Two and Three in the complaint. The parties shall appear for a pre-trial status conference on April 23, 1993, at 3:00 p.m., in Courtroom 318.

SO ORDERED.

NOTES:

NOTE 1: A photograph of the *Wild Boy and Puppy* sculpture is annexed as an Appendix to this Opinion and Order.

NOTE 2: Defendant Koons filed a cross-motion for partial summary judgment, dated February 15, 1991, seeking to dismiss the copyright claims. On June 3, 1991, the Court stayed the cross-motions for summary judgment pending a decision by the Second Circuit in *Rogers v. Koons,* 89 Civ. 6707 (CSH), which was a copyright action involving similar motions with respect to another sculpture produced by Koons as part of the Banality Show. On April 2, 1992, the Second Circuit issued its decision in *Rogers v. Koons,* 960 F.2d 301 (2d Cir.), *cert. denied,* ___ U.S. ___, 113 S. Ct. 365, 121 L. Ed. 2d 278 (1992), granting summary judgment for plaintiff. On May 22, 1992, at a conference before the Court, counsel for defendant Koons indicated that the cross-motion for summary judgment was withdrawn. *See* Affirmation of John B. Koegel, Esq., dated July 16, 1992. The parties, at the request of the Court, submitted supplemental memoranda of law addressing the effect of the *Rogers* decision on plaintiff's motion for summary judgment.

NOTE 3: Similarly, in his affidavit, Koons concedes that the particular "Puppy" in the sculpture "happens to be "Odie."" Koons Affidavit, at ¶ 19.

NOTE 4: Koons argues that, unlike in *Rogers,* there is no evidence of bad faith in Koons' use of the plaintiff's work and, thus, summary judgment is inappropriate on this first factor. In *Rogers,* the Court found that Koons had torn the copyright mark off of the plaintiff's copyrighted notecard prior to sending it to the Italian artisans and, thus, exhibited bad faith. 960 F.2d at 309. While the copyright notice appears to have also been missing from the cut-out of the "Odie" character used as a basis for *Wild Boy and Puppy* in the instant case, Koons argues that there is no evidence that he tore off the copyright notice and, thus, there is a factual dispute on the bad faith issue which precludes summary judgment. The Court finds this argument to be without merit. The finding of bad faith in *Rogers* was simply one of many factors considered by the Court and was not a prerequisite to the summary judgment determination. Assuming *arguendo* that in the instant case Koons did not tear off the copyright notice and did not intend to hide such notice from others, the Court finds that, based upon all of the other factors, summary judgment in plaintiff's favor is appropriate. Thus, even if this factual dispute on this particular issue was resolved in defendant's favor, it would not affect the outcome. *See Anderson,* 477 U.S. at 248, 106 S. Ct. at 2510 ("Only disputes over facts that might affect the outcome of the suit under the governing law will properly preclude the entry of summary judgment.").

NOTE 5: The Court recognizes that such characters, like other types of copyrighted works, can be the subject of a parody which is protected by the fair use doctrine. However, as noted *infra,* Koons' use of "Odie" does not fall within the parody branch of the fair use doctrine.

NOTE 6: The Court notes that this legal and ethical obligation, at best, prevents Koons from producing any more editions of the *Wild Boy and Puppy* sculpture, and would not prevent him from continued commercial exploitation of the "Odie" character and other Garfield characters in new sculptures or the licensing of the *Wild Boy and Puppy* sculpture for derivative uses.

NOTE 7: Defendant Koons argues that the "artist's proof" of the *Wild Boy and Puppy* sculpture is not offered for sale and, therefore, must be considered separately. In addition, Koons argues that there are factual disputes regarding the legal treatment of the "artist's proof" which preclude summary judgment. The Court finds this argument unpersuasive. The dispute regarding the status of the "artist's proof" relates to the issue of damages and, in no way, impacts on this Court's summary judgment determination on the issue of liability. *See Rogers,* 960 F.2d at 313.

Reading Note: This third Jeff Koons case involved a painting in which Koons incorporated a blown-up portion of an advertising photograph featuring a woman's legs and sandal-clad feet. The photograph was one of several appropriated elements in the painting, which, according to Koons, was intended to "comment on the ways in which some of our most basic appetites... are mediated by popular images".

BLANCH V. KOONS

467 .3d 244 (2d Cir.2006)

SACK, Circuit Judge:

> This appeal presents the question whether an artist's appropriation of a copyrighted image in a collage painting is, under the circumstances, protected "fair use" under the copyright law. See 17 U.S.C. §107.

On commission from defendants Deutsche Bank AG, a German corporation ("Deutsche Bank"), and The Solomon R. Guggenheim Foundation, a New York not-for-profit corporation ("Guggenheim"), defendant Jeff Koons created a collage painting, initially for display in Berlin, Germany, in which he copied, but altered the appearance of, part of a copyrighted photograph taken by the plaintiff Andrea Blanch. After seeing the painting on subsequent display at Guggenheim's museum in New York City, Blanch brought this action for copyright infringement. The district court (Louis L. Stanton, Judge) granted summary judgment to the defendants on the ground that Koons's appropriation of Blanch's photograph was fair use. We affirm.

BACKGROUND

Jeff Koons is a visual artist. His work has been exhibited widely in museums and commercial galleries and has been the subject of much critical commentary. He is known for incorporating into his artwork objects and images taken from popular media and consumer advertising, a practice that has been referred to as "neo-Pop art" or (perhaps unfortunately in a legal context) "appropriation art." His sculptures and paintings often contain such easily recognizable objects as toys, celebrities, and popular cartoon figures.

Koons has been the subject of several previous lawsuits for copyright infringement. In the late 1980s, he created a series of sculptures for an exhibition entitled the *Banality Show* ("*Banality*"). In doing so, he commissioned large three-dimensional reproductions of images taken from such sources as commercial postcards and syndicated comic strips. Although many of the source images were copyrighted, Koons did not seek permission to use them. In separate cases based on three different sculptures from *Banality*, this Court and two district courts concluded that Koons's use of the copyrighted images infringed on the rights of the copyright holders and did not constitute fair use under the copyright law. See *Rogers v. Koons*, 960 F.2d 301 (2d Cir.), *cert. denied*, 506 U.S. 934, 121 L. Ed. 2d 278, 113 S. Ct. 365 (1992); *Campbell v. Koons*, No. 91 Civ. 6055, 1993 WL97381, 1993 U.S. Dist. LEXIS 3957 (S.D.N.Y. Apr. 1, 1993); *United Feature Syndicate v. Koons*, 817 F. Supp. 370 (S.D.N.Y. 1993).

The present action arises in connection with a later series of Koons's work entitled *Easyfun-Ethereal.* It was commissioned in 2000 by Deutsche Bank in collaboration with Guggenheim. Deutsche Bank and Guggenheim have jointly established the "Deutsche Gug-

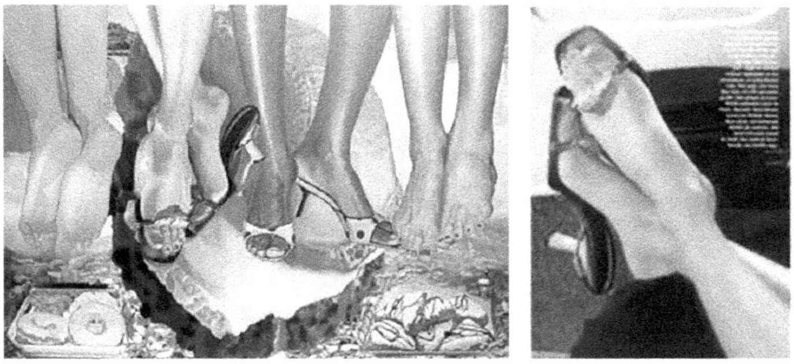

In 2000, artist Jeff Koons made a series of large collage paintings using appropriated images which were scanned, enlarged and incorporated into the work. One of the Easyfun-Ethereal *paintings,* Niagara *(2000), included part of a copyrighted photograph of a woman's feet and legs resting on a man's lap. The photograph,* Silk Sandals *by fashion photographer Andrea Blanch, appeared in the August 2000 issue of the fashion magazine Allure. Blanch sued Koons for copyright infringement in 2003.*

genheim Berlin," an art exhibition space housed in a Deutsche Bank building in Berlin, Germany. Under their collaboration agreement, Deutsche Bank provides space, underwrites exhibition expenses, and pays for the commission of new works of art. Guggenheim curates the exhibitions and advises as to which work should be commissioned. Pursuant to a separate agreement, Deutsche Bank donates a fifty percent interest in each commissioned work to Guggenheim.

Koons's Painting

To create the *Easyfun-Ethereal* paintings, Koons culled images from advertisements or his own photographs, scanned them into a computer, and digitally superimposed the scanned images against backgrounds of pastoral landscapes. He then printed color images of the resulting collages for his assistants to use as templates for applying paint to billboard-sized, 10' x 14' canvasses. The *Easyfun-Ethereal* paintings, seven in all, were exhibited at the Deutsche Guggenheim Berlin from October 2000 to January 2001.

One of the *Easyfun-Ethereal* paintings, *Niagara*, is the subject of this action. Like the other paintings in the series, *Niagara* consists of fragmentary images collaged against the backdrop of a landscape. The painting depicts four pairs of women's feet and lower legs dangling prominently over images of confections—a large chocolate fudge brownie topped with ice cream, a tray of donuts, and a tray of apple danish pastries—with a grassy field and Niagara Falls in the background. The images of the legs are placed side by side, each pair pointing vertically downward and extending from the top of the painting approximately two-thirds of the way to the bottom. Together, the four pairs of legs occupy the entire horizontal expanse of the painting. A black-and-white reproduction of *Niagara* is included in the Appendix to this opinion.

In an affidavit submitted to the district court, Koons states that he was inspired to create *Niagara* by a billboard he saw in Rome, which depicted several sets of women's lower legs. By juxtaposing women's legs against a backdrop of food and landscape, he says, he intended to "comment on the ways in which some of our most basic appetites—for food, play, and sex—are mediated by popular images." "By re-contextualizing these fragments as I do, I try to compel the viewer to break out of the conventional way of experiencing a particular appetite as mediated by mass media."

Blanch's Photograph

Koons drew the images in *Niagara* from fashion magazines and advertisements. One of the pairs of legs in the painting was adapted from a photograph by the plaintiff Andrea Blanch, an accomplished professional fashion and portrait photographer. During her career of more than twenty years, Blanch has published her photographs in commercial magazines, including Details, G.Q., Vogue, and Allure; in photography periodicals and collections; and in advertisements for clients selling products under such widely recognized names as Revlon, Universal Films, Johnny Walker, and Valentino. She is also the author of a book of photographs and interviews entitled *Italian Men: Love & Sex.*

The Blanch photograph used by Koons in *Niagara* appeared in the August 2000 issue of Allure magazine. Entitled "Silk Sandals by Gucci" ("Silk Sandals"), it depicts a woman's lower legs and feet, adorned with bronze nail polish and glittery Gucci sandals, resting on a man's lap in what appears to be a first-class airplane cabin. The legs and feet are shot at close range and dominate the photograph. Allure published "Silk Sandals" as part of a six-page feature on metallic cosmetics entitled "Gilt Trip." A black-and-white reproduction of the photograph is also in the Appendix.

Blanch photographed "Silk Sandals" at a "shoot" organized by Conde Nast Publications, Allure's publisher. According to Blanch's deposition testimony, Paul Cavaco, the creative director of Allure, suggested the model, sandals, and nail polish to be used in the photograph. Blanch participated in their selection and retained control over the camera, the film, the lighting, and the composition of the photographs. She testified that it was her idea to use an airplane interior as a backdrop and to place the female model's feet on the male model's lap. She explained that she wanted to "show some sort of erotic sense[;] . . . to get . . . more of a sexuality to the photographs."

Koons's Use of Blanch's Photograph

While working on the *Easyfun-Ethereal* series, Koons saw "Silk Sandals" in Allure. According to Koons, "certain physical features of the legs [in the photograph] represented for me a particular type of woman frequently presented in advertising." He considered this typicality to further his purpose of commenting on the "commercial images . . . in our consumer culture."

Koons scanned the image of "Silk Sandals" into his computer and incorporated a version of the scanned image into *Niagara.* He included in the painting only the legs and feet from the photograph, discarding the background of the airplane cabin and the man's lap on which the legs rest. Koons inverted the orientation of the legs so that they dangle vertically downward above the other elements of *Niagara* rather than slant upward at a 45-degree angle as, they appear in the photograph. He added a heel to one of the feet and modified the photograph's coloring. The legs from "Silk Sandals" are second from the left among the four pairs of legs that form the focal images of *Niagara*. Koons did not seek permission from Blanch or anyone else before using the image.

The Parties' Economic Gains and Losses

Deutsche Bank paid Koons $ 2 million for the seven *Easyfun-Ethereal* paintings. He reports that his net compensation attributable to *Niagara* was $ 126,877. Deutsche Bank received gross revenues of approximately $ 100,000 from the exhibition of the "Easyfun-Ethereal" paintings at the Deutsche Guggenheim Berlin, a total that includes admission fees and catalogue and postcard sales. The record does not reflect Deutsche Bank's expenses for that exhibition other than the commission of the paintings.

The subsequent exhibition of the paintings at the Solomon R. Guggenheim Museum in New York sustained a net loss, although when profits from catalogue and postcard sales are taken into account, Guggenheim estimates that it earned a profit of approximately $2,000 from *Niagara*. In 2004, the auction house Sotheby's reportedly appraised *Niagara* at $ 1 million. The work has not, however, been sold, nor does the record indicate that it or any other painting commissioned by Deutsche Bank has been offered for sale or been the subject of a bid.

Allure paid Blanch $ 750 for "Silk Sandals." Although Blanch retains the copyright to the photograph, she has neither published nor licensed it subsequent to its appearance in Allure. Indeed, Blanch does not allege that she has ever licensed any of her photographs for use in works of graphic art or other visual art. At her deposition, Blanch testified that Koons's use of the photograph did not cause any harm to her career or upset any plans she had for "Silk Sandals" or any other photograph in which she has rights. She also testified that, in her view, the market value of "Silk Sandals" did not decrease as the result of Koons's alleged infringement.

This Lawsuit

After the initial exhibition of the *Easyfun-Ethereal* painting at the Deutsche Guggenheim Berlin, *Niagara* was exhibited in other museums and public galleries. Blanch did not see the painting until it was on display at the Guggenheim Museum in New York during the summer of 2002. On October 10, 2003, she filed this lawsuit asserting that Koons infringed her copyright in "Silk Sandals" in violation of the Copyright Act of 1976, 17 U.S.C. §101 et seq. On August 20, 2004, Blanch amended her complaint to add Deutsche Bank and Guggenheim as defendants and later served them with the amended complaint. She alleges that they "participated in, facilitated, and caused the acts of infringement by Koons" by commissioning the work despite knowing, based on Koons's history with, among other things, the "*Banality*" cases, that Koons was likely to infringe the copyrights of others.

On November 1, 2005, the district court granted summary judgment to the defendants. The court concluded that Koons's *Niagara* did not infringe Blanch's "Silk Sandals" because its use of the image from "Silk Sandals" constituted fair use. Considering the four non-exclusive statutory factors upon which a fair-use determination is made, see 17 U.S.C. §107, the court determined that: (1) the purpose and character of Koons's use was "transformative" and therefore favored by copyright law; (2) Blanch's copyrighted work was "banal rather than creative," and therefore the nature of the copyrighted work weighed in favor of the defendants; (3) although the women's legs are the "focal point of interest" in Blanch's photograph, the image is of limited originality, so the statutory factor concerning "the amount and substantiality of the portion used in relation to the copyrighted work as a whole," was neutral between the parties; and (4) Blanch's photograph could not have captured the market occupied by *Niagara*, so that the final factor, the effect of the use upon the potential market for the copyrighted work, favored the defendants. See *Id.* Based on its conclusion that, as a matter of law, each of the statutory factors concerning fair use either favored the defendants or was neutral between the parties, the court concluded that the defendants were entitled to summary judgment.

Blanch appeals.

DISCUSSION

Standard of Review

We review a district court's grant of summary judgment de novo. Summary judgment should be granted if "there is no genuine issue as to any material fact and . . . the moving party is entitled to a judgment as a matter of law." Fed. R. Civ. P. 56(c). "Although '[f]air use is a mixed question of law and fact,' this court has on a number of occasions resolved fair use determinations at the summary judgment stage where . . . there are no genuine issues of material fact."

Fair Use

The Supreme Court, in its landmark decision addressing the fair-use defense, *Campbell v. Acuff-Rose Music, Inc.*, 510 U.S. 569 (1994), remarked: "From the infancy of copyright protection, some opportunity for fair use of copyrighted materials has been thought necessary to fulfill copy- right's very purpose, 'To promote the Progress of Science and useful Arts.'" *Id.* at 575.

As Judge Leval observed in his seminal law review article on the subject, the law of copyright "is intended to motivate the creative activity of authors and inventors by the provision of a special reward .... The monopoly created by copyright thus rewards the individual author in order to benefit the public." Pierre N. Leval, *Toward a Fair Use Standard*, 103 Harv. L. Rev. 1105, 1108 (1990).

At the same time, though, "excessively broad protection would stifle, rather than advance, the [law's] objective." *Id.* at 1109. "Monopoly protection of intellectual property that impeded referential analysis . . . would strangle the creative process." *Id.* at 1108. Fair use should therefore be perceived as an "integral part of copyright, whose observance is necessary to achieve the objectives of that law." *Id.* at 1107.

Copyright law thus must address the inevitable tension between the property rights it establishes in creative works, which must be protected up to a point, and the ability of authors, artists, and the rest of us to express them or ourselves by reference to the works of others, which must be protected up to a point. The fair-use doctrine mediates between the two sets of interests, determining where each set of interests ceases to control.

The fair-use doctrine was first codified in the Copyright Act of 1976, which describes four non- exclusive factors that must be considered in determining fair use.

> [T]he fair use of a copyrighted work . . . for purposes such as criticism, comment, news. reporting, teaching (including multiple copies for classroom use), scholarship, or research, is not an infringement of copyright. In determining whether the use made of a work in any particular case is a fair use the factors to be considered shall include—
>
> - the purpose and character of the use, including whether such use is of a commercial nature or is for nonprofit educational purposes;
> - the nature of the copyrighted work;
> - the amount and substantiality of the portion used in relation to the copyrighted work as a whole; and
> - the effect of the use upon the potential market for or value of the copyrighted work.
>
> The fact that a work is unpublished shall not itself bar a finding of fair use if such finding is made upon consideration of all the above factors.

17 U.S.C. §107.

As the words of section 107 indicate, the determination of fair use is an open-ended and context-sensitive inquiry. In *Campbell*, the Supreme Court warned that the task

> is not to be simplified with bright-line rules, for the statute, like the doctrine it recognizes, calls for case-by-case analysis. The text employs the terms "including" and

"such as" in the preamble paragraph to indicate the illustrative and not limitative function of the examples given, which thus provide only general guidance about the sorts of copying that courts and Congress most commonly had found to be fair uses. Nor may the four statutory factors be treated in isolation, one from another. All are to be explored, and the results weighed together, in light of the purposes of copyright.

"The ultimate test of fair use . . . is whether the copyright law's goal of 'promoting the Progress of Science and useful Arts,' U.S. Const., art. I, §8, cl. 8, 'would be better served by allowing the use than by preventing it.'"

A. First Factor: The Purpose and Character of the Use

The first statutory factor in the fair-use inquiry is "the purpose and character of the use, including whether such use is of a commercial nature or is for nonprofit educational purposes." 17 U.S.C. §107(1).

1. "Transformative" Use. We have, post-*Campbell,* addressed and applied this first factor many times. In *Davis v. The Gap, Inc.,* 246 F.3d 152, 174 (2d Cir. 2001), we described it this way:

> The heart of the fair use inquiry is into the first specified statutory factor identified as "the purpose and character of the use." 17 U.S.C. §107 (1). This formulation, as the Supreme Court observed in *Campbell,* 510 U.S. at 578, draws on Justice Story's famous reference in *Folsom v. Marsh,* 9 F. Cas. 342, 348, F. Cas. No. 4901 (C.C.D. Mass. 1841) (No. 4901), to "the nature and objects of the selections made." As the *Campbell* Court explained,
>
>> The central purpose of this investigation is to see, in Justice Story's words, whether the new work merely "supersedes the objects" of the original creation, or instead adds something new, with a further purpose or different character, altering the first with new expression, meaning, or message . . . , in other words, whether and to what extent the new work is "transformative." Although such transformative use is not absolutely necessary for a finding of fair use, the goal of copyright, to promote science and the arts, is generally furthered by the creation of transformative works. Such transformative works thus lie at the heart of the fair use doctrine's guarantee of breathing space. *Campbell,* 510 U.S. at 579 (emphasis added [in Davis])(alteration in original) (citations omitted).

Id. If "'the secondary use adds value to the original—if [copyrightable expression in the original work] is used as raw material, transformed in the creation of new information, new aesthetics, new insights and understandings—this is the very type of activity that the fair use doctrine intends to protect for the enrichment of society.'"[NOTE 1]

Koons does not argue that his use was transformative solely because Blanch's work is a photograph and his a painting, or because Blanch's photograph is in a fashion magazine and his painting is displayed in museums. He would have been ill advised to do otherwise. We have declined to find a transformative use when the defendant has done no more than find a new way to exploit the creative virtues of the original work.[NOTE 2] See *Davis,* 246 F.3d at 174 (use of plaintiff's eyewear in a clothing advertisement not transformative because it was "worn as eye jewelry in the manner it was made to be worn"); *Castle Rock Entm't,* 150 F.3d at 142-43 (quiz book called the "Seinfeld Aptitude Test" not transformative when its purpose was "to repackage [the television show] Seinfeld to entertain Seinfeld viewers"); *Ringgold v. Black Entm't Television, Inc.* 126 F.3d 70, 79 (2d Cir. 1997) (copy of plaintiff's painting used as decoration for a television program's set not transformative because it was used for "the same decorative purpose" as the original).

But Koons asserts—and Blanch does not deny—that his purposes in using Blanch's image are sharply different from Blanch's goals in creating it. Compare Koons Aff. at P4 ("I want the viewer to think about his/her personal experience with these objects, products, and images and at the same time gain new insight into how these affect our lives.") with Blanch Dep. at 112-113 ("I wanted to show some sort of erotic sense[;] . . . to get . . . more of a sexuality to the photographs."). The sharply different objectives that Koons had in using, and Blanch had in creating, "Silk Sandals" confirms the transformative nature of the use. See *Bill Graham Archives,* 448 F.3d at 609 (finding transformative use when defendant's purpose in using copyrighted concert poster was "plainly different from the original purpose for which they were created").

Koons is, by his own undisputed description, using Blanch's image as fodder for his commentary on the social and aesthetic consequences of mass media. His stated objective is thus not to re- package Blanch's "Silk Sandals," but to employ it "'in the creation of new information, new aesthetics, new insights and understandings.'" When, as here, the copyrighted work is used as "raw material," in the furtherance of distinct creative or communicative objectives, the use is transformative.

The test for whether *Niagara*'s use of "Silk Sandals" is "transformative," then, is whether it "merely supersedes the objects of the original creation, or instead adds something new, with a further purpose or different character, altering the first with new expression, meaning, or message." The test almost perfectly describes Koons's adaptation of "Silk Sandals": the use of a fashion photograph created for publication in a glossy American "lifestyles" magazine—with changes of its colors, the background against which it is portrayed, the medium, the size of the objects pictured, the objects' details and, crucially, their entirely different purpose and meaning—as part of a massive painting commissioned for exhibition in a German art-gallery space. We therefore conclude that the use in question was transformative.

2. Commercial Use. Koons made a substantial profit from the sale of *Niagara.* And "whether [the] use [in question] is of a commercial nature or is for nonprofit

educational purposes" is an explicit part of the first fair-use factor. In *American Geophysical Union v. Texaco Inc., 60 F.3d 913 (2d Cir. 1994), we said:*

> The commercial/nonprofit dichotomy concerns the unfairness that arises when a secondary user makes unauthorized use of copyrighted material to capture significant revenues as a direct consequence of copying the original work.

Consistent with these principles, courts will not sustain a claimed defense of fair use when the secondary use can fairly be characterized as a form of commercial exploitation, i.e., when the copier directly and exclusively acquires conspicuous financial rewards from its use of the copyrighted material. Conversely, courts are more willing to find a secondary use fair when it produces a value that benefits the broader public interest. The greater the private economic rewards reaped by the secondary user (to the exclusion of broader public benefits), the more likely the first factor will favor the copyright holder and the less likely the use will be considered fair.

But the use at issue in *American Geophysical Union* was photocopying—"an untransformed duplication" of the copyrighted works. And we later observed in *NXIVM Corp. v. Ross Inst.*, 364 F.3d 471 (2d Cir. 2004), that

> The Supreme Court in Campbell rejected the notion that the commercial nature of [a] use could by itself be a dispositive consideration. The *Campbell* opinion observes that "nearly all of the illustrative uses listed in the preamble paragraph of §107, including news reporting, comment, criticism, teaching, scholarship, and research … 'are generally conducted for profit,'" *Campbell*, 510 U.S. at 584 (quoting *Harper & Row*, 471 U.S. at 592) (Brennan, J., dissenting), and that Congress "could not have intended" a rule that commercial uses are presumptively unfair. *Id.* The commercial objective of the secondary work is only a subfactor within the first factor. "The more transformative the new work, the less will be the significance of other factors, like commercialism, that may weigh against a finding of fair use." *Id.* at 579.

Finding the work substantially transformative, the district court properly discounted the secondary commercial nature of the use. We agree.

We do not mean to suggest that the commercialism of the use by the secondary user of the original is not relevant to the inquiry. But here, since the "new work" is "substantially transformative," "the significance of other factors, [including] commercialism[,] are of [less significance]."

It can hardly be said, moreover, that the defendants' economic gains from *Niagara* were "to the exclusion of broader public benefits." Notwithstanding the fact that artists are sometimes paid and museums sometimes earn money, the public exhibition of art is widely and we think properly considered to "have value that benefits the broader public interest." See also 20 U.S.C. §951 (stating that "access to the arts and the humanities" fosters "wisdom and vision" and makes citizens "masters of their technology and not its unthinking servants").

3. Parody, Satire, and Justification for the Copying.

The secondary work in *Campbell* was a parody, and some of the language in the opinion, and some of the cases following it are specifically about parody. *Niagara*, on the other hand, may be better characterized for these purposes as satire—its message appears to target the genre of which "Silk Sandals" is typical, rather than the individual photograph itself. See *Rogers*, 960 F.2d at 310 (concluding that a previous work by Koons was not a parody because "the copied work must be, at least in part, an object of the parody" and it was "difficult to discern in Koons's work] any parody of the photograph . . . itself").

We have applied *Campbell* in too many non-parody cases to require citation for the proposition that the broad principles of *Campbell* are not limited to cases involving parody. But the satire/parody distinction may nevertheless be relevant to the application of these principles. As the *Campbell* Court observed, "[p]arody needs to mimic an original to make its point, and so has some claim to use the creation of its victim's (or collective victims') imagination, whereas satire can stand on its own two feet and so requires justification for the very act of borrowing."

It is not, of course, our job to judge the merits of *Niagara*, or of Koons's approach to art. The question is whether Koons had a genuine creative rationale for borrowing Blanch's image, rather than using it merely "to get attention or to avoid the drudgery in working up something fresh." Although it seems clear enough to us that Koons's use of a slick fashion photograph enables him to satirize life as it appears when seen through the prism of slick fashion photography, we need not depend on our own poorly honed artistic sensibilities. Koons explained, without contradiction, why he used Blanch's image:

> Although the legs in the Allure Magazine photograph ["Silk Sandals"] might seem prosaic, I considered them to be necessary for inclusion in my painting rather than legs I might have photographed myself. The ubiquity of the photograph is central to my message. The photograph is typical of a certain style of mass communication. Images almost identical to them can be found in almost any glossy magazine, as well as in other media. To me, the legs depicted in the Allure photograph are a fact in the world, something that everyone experiences constantly; they are not anyone's legs in particular. By using a fragment of the Allure photograph in my painting, I thus comment upon the culture and attitudes promoted and embodied in Allure Magazine. By using an existing image, I also ensure a certain authenticity or veracity that enhances my commentary—it is the difference between quoting and paraphrasing—and ensure that the viewer will understand what I am referring to.[NOTE 3]

We conclude that Koons thus established a "justif[ication for] the very act of [his] borrowing." Whether or not Koons could have created *Niagara* without reference to "Silk Sandals," we have been given no reason to question his statement that the use of an existing image advanced his artistic purposes.

4. "Bad Faith." Much has been written about whether good faith was de-emphasized by the advent of *Campbell or essentially written out of the first part of the fair-use test. The question was thoroughly explored by the majority and concurring opinions in NXIVM Corp., 364 F.3d at 478-79; id. at 483-87 (Jacobs, J., concurring). In any event, the only act of bad faith alleged here is that Koons used Blanch's photograph without first asking her permission. We are aware of no controlling authority to the effect that the failure to seek permission for copying, in itself, constitutes bad faith and the cases addressing bad faith tend to arise in circumstances strikingly different from* the situation here. See *Harper & Row, 471 U.S. at 562-63 (purloined manuscript); NXIVM Corp., 364 F.3d at 478 (breach of confidentiality agreement); Rogers, 960 F.2d at 309 (tearing off of copyright mark); Weissmann v. Freeman, 868 F.2d 1313, 1324 (2d Cir. 1989) ("total deletion of the original author's name and substitution of the copier's"). And as the Campbell Court noted by way of dictum, "If the use is otherwise fair, then no permission need be sought or granted." In light of that statement by the Supreme Court and ours based upon it, it can hardly be said to have been an act of bad faith for Koons to have neither "sought [n]or [been] granted" permission for the use of "Silk Sandals" so long as, as we conclude here, the use is "otherwise fair."*

5. Conclusions as to the First Factor. Because Koons's appropriation of Blanch's photograph in *Niagara* was intended to be—and appears to be—"transformative," because the creation and exhibition of the painting cannot fairly be described as commercial exploitation and the "commerciality" of the use is not dispositive in any event, and because there is insufficient indication of "bad faith," we agree with the district court that the first fair-use factor strongly favors the defendants.

B. Second Factor: Nature of the Copyrighted Work

The second statutory factor is "the nature of the copyrighted work." 17 U.S.C. §107(2). It "calls for recognition that some works are closer to the core of intended copyright protection than others, with the consequence that fair use is more difficult to establish when the former works are copied."

> Two types of distinctions as to the nature of the copyrighted work have emerged that have figured in the decisions evaluating the second factor: (1) whether the work is expressive or creative, such as a work of fiction, or more factual, with a greater leeway being allowed to a claim of fair use where the work is factual or informational, and (2) whether the work is published or unpublished, with the scope for fair use involving un- published works being considerably narrower.

2 Howard B. Abrams, The Law of Copyright, §15:52 (2006).

As noted, Blanch's "Silk Sandals" was published. Under the second of the two considerations mentioned by Abrams, that fact favors the defendants.[NOTE 4]

As for the first consideration, we disagree with the district court's characterization of Blanch's photograph as "banal rather than creative." Accepting that "Silk Sandals" is a creative work, though, it does not follow that the second fair-use factor, even if it somewhat favors Blanch, has significant implications for on our overall fair-use analysis. As we recently explained, although "the creative nature of artistic images typically weighs in favor of the copyright holder," "the second factor may be of limited usefulness where the creative work of art is being used for a transformative purpose." To paraphrase *Bill Graham Archives*, the second fair-use factor has limited weight in our analysis because Koons used Blanch's work in a transformative manner to comment on her image's social and aesthetic meaning rather than to exploit its creative virtues. See *Bill Graham Archives*, 448 F.3d at 612-13.

C. Third Factor: Amount and Substantiality of the Portion Used

The third factor bearing on fair use is "the amount and substantiality of the portion used in relation to the copyrighted work as a whole." 17 U.S.C. §107(3). The question is whether "'the quantity and value of the materials used,' are reasonable in relation to the purpose of the copying."

As we have discussed in part A.1.3 of this opinion, above, Koons asserts that his artistic goals led him to incorporate preexisting images such as Blanch's photograph into his paintings in order to reference certain "fact[s] in the world." The issue here is not "justification," which we addressed in part A.1.3. The question is whether, once he chose to copy "Silk Sandals," he did so excessively, beyond his "justified" purpose for doing so in the first place—whether the use was "reasonable in relation to the purpose of the copying."

It seems to us that Koons's copying of "Silk Sandals" was indeed reasonable when measured in light of his purpose, to convey the "fact" of the photograph to viewers of the painting, and in light of the quantity, quality, and importance of the material used. He did not copy those aspects of "Silk Sandals" "whose power lies in [Blanch's] individualized expression." As Blanch testified in her deposition, her key creative decisions in the shoot were the choice of an airplane cabin as a setting and her placement of the female model's legs on the male model's lap. But neither the airplane background nor the man's lap appear in *Niagara*. It depicts only the woman's legs and sandal-clad feet. In light of Koons's choice to extract the legs, feet, and sandals in "Silk Sandals" from their background, we find his statement that he copied only that portion of the image necessary to evoke "a certain style of mass communication," to be persuasive. We conclude that the amount and substantiality of Koons's copying was "reasonable in relation to the purpose of the copying." The district court said that "[t]he third factor is neutral as between the parties"; we think that it weighs distinctly in Koons's favor. This modest difference in our views, however, does not alter our ultimate conclusion on fair use.

D. Fourth Factor: Market Effects

The fourth and final statutory factor is "the effect of the use upon the potential market for or value of the copyrighted work." 17 U.S.C. §107(4).[NOTE 5] "In considering. the fourth factor, our concern is not whether the secondary use suppresses or even destroys the market for the original work or its potential derivatives, but whether the secondary use usurps the market of the original work." "The market for potential derivative uses includes only those that creators of original works would in general develop or license others to develop."

Blanch acknowledges that she has not published or licensed "Silk Sandals" subsequent to its appearance in Allure, that she has never licensed any of her photographs for use in works of graphic or other visual art, that Koons's use of her photograph did not cause any harm to her career or upset any plans she had for "Silk Sandals" or any other photograph, and that the value of "Silk Sandals" did not decrease as the result of Koons's alleged infringement. In light of these admissions, it is plain that *Niagara* had no deleterious effect "upon the potential market for or value of the copyrighted work." 17 U.S.C. §107(4). [NOTE 6] The fourth fair-use factor greatly favors Koons.

CONCLUSION

Having explored the statutory factors and weighed them together in light of the purposes of copyright, *Campbell*, 510 U.S. at 578, we think that the district court's conclusion was correct—that copyright law's goal of "promoting the Progress of Science and useful Arts," U.S. Const., art. I, §8, cl. 8, would be better served by allowing Koons's use of "Silk Sandals" than by preventing it, see *Castle Rock Entm't*, 150 F.3d at 141. We therefore conclude that neither he nor the other defendants engaged in or are liable for copyright infringement. We affirm the judgment of the district court.

KATZMANN, Circuit Judge, concurring:

I concur in the disposition of this case and appreciate the very considerable thinking in the majority opinion. I agree that Koons' work is highly transformative of Blanch's, using it as raw material for an entirely different type of art, and that his use of Blanch's work furthered a purpose (art that comments on existing images by juxtaposing them against others) that can make a finding of fair use appropriate. In both respects, the facts of this case are quite distinguishable from those of *Rogers v. Koons*, 960 F.2d 301 (2d Cir. 1992), in which Koons slavishly recreated a copyrighted work in a different medium without any objective indicia of transforming it or commenting on the copyrighted work. Moreover, the fourth factor of the fair-use analysis dramatically favors Koons, in that Blanch failed to show that Koons' use of her work actually harmed her in any way. She thus stands in stark contrast to the plaintiff in *Rogers*, for whom licensing of his work in general, and the appropriated work in particular, yielded considerable revenue. On the facts of this case, it is easy to conclude that the copyright law's goals are better served by a finding of fair use.

I respectfully part company with the majority opinion, however, because I believe it sweeps more broadly in several places than is necessary to decide this simple case. For example, I see no need to state that we "discount[] the secondary commercial nature of the use." This language was taken from *NXIVM Corp. v. Ross Inst.*, 364 F.3d 471, 478 (2d Cir. 2004), which used it in the context of applying our presumption that the first factor favors the defendant where the use is for one of the purposes specifically listed in 17 U.S.C. §107. Here, where Koons' use is not for one of the archetypal purposes specifically contemplated by Congress and such a presumption does not apply, it is uncertain whether we have license to "discount" its commercial nature, as opposed to balancing that consideration against the use's transformativeness and other countervailing concerns—particularly because consideration of a use's commercial nature (unlike its "transformativeness") is explicitly part of our statutory mandate. See 17 U.S.C. §107(1).

Rather than reaching this question, I would simply apply our established analysis for weighing commercialism, see Am. *Geophysical Union v. Texaco, Inc.*, 60 F.3d 913, 922-23 (2d Cir. 1994). As in *Am. Geophysical Union*,"the link between [the defendant's] commercial gain and [the defendant's] copying is somewhat attenuated," in that the copying of Blanch's work was simply one small part of what made Koons' work so valuable rather than the heart of the enterprise.

Similarly, there seems to be no need to rely so heavily on what the majority acknowledges is a sentence of dictum in a footnote in *Campbell v. Acuff-Rose Music, Inc.*, 510 U.S. 569 (1994), to the effect that failure to seek authorization, even where doing so would have been feasible, is not relevant to the fair-use inquiry. I see no reason, on these facts, to wade into, the contentious battle over the role of good faith in the post-*Campbell* fair use inquiry. Instead, I would simply conclude that whatever bad faith Koons may have exhibited in this case, as well as the limited commercial nature of his use, would not outweigh the much stronger considerations pointing toward a finding of fair use.

To be clear, I do not argue with the majority's thoughtful discussion of these points, except to question whether its conclusions are compelled by precedent. If and when I encounter a case that requires me to do so, I may well adopt them. I merely believe that this is not such a case, and so I do not now join what I regard as dicta as applied to these facts.

This is our Circuit's second encounter with Koons' work. His work, like that of other appropriation artists, inherently raises difficult questions about the proper scope of copyright protection and the fair-use doctrine. I would continue to answer those questions as necessary to decide particular cases, mindful that the fair-use inquiry is a fact-specific one that is "not to be simplified with bright-line rules."

NOTES:

NOTE 1: As the Supreme Court noted in *Campbell*, however, a finding of transformativeness "is not absolutely necessary for a finding of fair use." *Campbell*, 510 U.S. at 579 (citing *Sony Corp. of Am. v. Universal City Studios, Inc.*, 464 U.S. 417, 455 n.40, 104 S. Ct. 774, 78 L. Ed. 2d 574 (1984)); see also 17 U.S.C. §107 (listing "multiple copies for classroom use" as among the categories of potentially fair uses); Rebecca Tushnet, *Copy This Essay: How Fair Use Doctrine Harms Free Speech and How Copying Serves It*, 114 Yale L.J. 535, 555 (2004) (noting that historically some forms of "pure copying" were "at the core of fair use"). Nor is transformativeness necessarily the only important factor. See *Campbell*, 510 U.S. at 578 ("[T]he four statutory factors . . . [a]re all to be explored, and the results weighed together, in light of the purposes of copyright.").

NOTE 2: It has been suggested that the exploitation of new, complementary markets is the hallmark of fair use. See *Ty, Inc. v. Publ'ns Int'l*, 292 F.3d 512, 517 (7th Cir. 2002) ("[C]opying that is complementary to the copyrighted work (in the sense that nails are complements of hammers) is fair use, but copying that is a substitute for the copyrighted work (in the sense that nails are substitutes for pegs or screws), or for derivative works from the copyrighted work, is not fair use." (citation omitted)); see also 4-13 Melville B. Nimmer & David Nimmer, Nimmer on Copyright §13.05[B][1] (2006) ("[I]f . . . the defendant's work, although containing substantially similar material, performs a different function than that of the plaintiff's, the defense of fair use may be invoked."). But as the Seventh Circuit recognized, this reasoning is in tension with the Copyright Act's express grant to copyright holders of rights over derivative works. See *Ty, Inc.*, 292 F.3d at 518 ("Were control of derivative works not part of a copyright owner's bundle of rights, it would be clear that [defendant's] books fell on the complement side of the divide and so were sheltered by the fair-use defense."). A derivative use can certainly be complementary to, or fulfill a different function from, the original.

NOTE 3: Koon's clear conception of his reasons for using "Silk Sandals," and his ability to articulate those reasons, ease our analysis in this case. We did not mean to suggest, however, that either is a sine *qua non* for a finding of fair use—as to satire or more generally.

NOTE 4: We have said that when "'the copyrighted [material is] unpublished, the second [fair use] factor weighs heavily in favor'" of the plaintiff. *New Era Publ'ns Int'l, ApS v. Henry Holt and Co., Inc.*, 873 F.2d 576, 583 (2d Cir. 1989) (quoting *Salinger v. Random House, Inc.*, 811 F.2d 90, 97 (2d Cir.), *cert. denied*, 484 U.S. 890, 98 L. Ed. 2d 177, 108 S. Ct. 213 (1987)), *cert. denied*, 493 U.S. 1094, 110 S. Ct. 1168, 107 L. Ed. 2d 1071(1990). "In 1992, however, Congress amended §107 to state that: ‹The fact that a work is unpublished shall not itself bar a finding of fair use if such finding is made upon consideration of all the above factors.'" *Sundeman v. Seajay Soc'y, Inc.*, 142 F.3d 194, 204 (4th Cir. 1998) (quoting 17 U.S.C. §107). We have not had occasion to address the published/unpublished distinction since that amendment. But see *NXIVM Corp.*, 364 F.3d at 480 (the parties did not dispute that because the copyrighted work was unpublished, the second fair-use factor favored the plaintiffs).

NOTE 5: The Supreme Court has recently retreated from its earlier cases suggesting that the fourth statutory factor is the most important element of fair use, see *Harper & Row*, 471 U.S. at 566, recognizing instead that "all [factors] are to be explored, and the results weighed together, in light of the purposes of copyright," *Campbell*, 510 U.S. at 578.

NOTE 6: We have sometimes found that the fourth factor favors the plaintiff even in the absence of evidence that the plaintiff has tapped, or even intends to tap, a derivative market. See, e.g.,*Castle Rock Entm't*, 150 F.3d at 145-46 ("Although Castle Rock has evidenced little if any interest in exploiting this market for derivative works . . . the copyright law must respect that creative and economic choice."). But nothing in the record here suggests that there was a derivative market for Blanch to tap into that is in any way related to Koons's use of her work, even if she dearly wanted to. And it is of course circular to assert simply that if we were to hold in her favor she could then charge Koons for his further use of "Silk Sandals." See *Am. Geophysical Union*, 60 F.3d at 929 n.17 ("By definition every fair use involves some loss of royalty revenue because the secondary user has not paid royalties." (quoting Leval, supra, 103 Harv. L. Rev. at 1124)).

STUDY QUESTIONS

- *Rogers v. Koons* and *United Features Syndicate v. Koons* involved sculptures created by Jeff Koons for his *Banality Show* exhibition at the Sonnabend Gallery. A third case, *Campbell v. Koons*, No. 91 Civ. 6055, 1993 WL97381, 1993 U.S. Dist. LEXIS 3957 (S.D.N.Y. Apr. 1, 1993), also involved a sculpture created for that exhibition—*Ushering in Banality*—which was based on a pre-existing photograph by Barbara Campbell. Discuss the similarities and differences between these arts works and the source material appropriated in each.

Artist Jeff Koons included this sculpture of a pig with a green ribbon being pushed by two young angels with a young boy dressed in a tracksuit behind it as part of his Banality Show. *In Campbell v, Koons,* Ushering in Banality *(1988) was ruled to have "deliberately and exactly copied" a photograph by Barbara Campbell. As he had done with* String of Puppies, *Koons had instructed his Italian studio to replicate Campbell's* Boys with Pig *using it as a model for the three-dimensional sculpture.*

- Assess the court's application of "parody/satire" in *Rogers* and *United Features Syndicate.*
- What do you make of the "public figure" argument raised in *United Features Syndicate*?
- Compare and contrast the issues and outcomes in the three Jeff Koons fair use cases—*Rogers, United Features Syndicate* and *Blanch* cases. What similarities and differences affected the results in these three cases?
- What role did "bad faith" play in the decision in these Koons cases?
- What were the key differences from the other two cases which affected the outcome in *Blanch*?
- The concurring judge in *Blanch* states: "This is our Circuit's second encounter with Koons' work. His work, like that of other appropriation artists, inherently raises difficult questions about the proper scope of copyright protection and the fair-use doctrine. I would continue to answer those questions as necessary to decide particular cases, mindful that the fair-use inquiry is a fact-specific one that is "not to be simplified with brightline rules. What are the implications of this approach to fair use?

Reading Note: The last fair use case included in these Appropriation Art readings involved a claim of copyright infringement brought by a photographer against appropriation artist Richard Prince. The photographer claimed that Prince had used portions of photographs published in a book of photography in a series of large collage-paintings without his permission. In a feat of judicial line-drawing, the appeals court determined that in some of the paintings, the use was fair use, but remanded others for further consideration by the trial court.

CARIOU V. PRINCE ET AL.

714 F.3d 694 (2013)

BARRINGTON D. PARKER, Circuit Judge:

In 2000, Patrick Cariou published *Yes Rasta*, a book of classical portraits and landscape photographs that he took over the course of six years spent living among Rastafarians in Jamaica. Richard Prince altered and incorporated several of Cariou's *Yes Rasta* photographs into a series of paintings and collages, called Canal Zone, that he exhibited in 2007 and 2008, first at the Eden Rock hotel in Saint Barthélemy ("St. Barth's") and later at New York's Gagosian Gallery.[NOTE 1] In addition, Gagosian published and sold an exhibition catalog that contained reproductions of Prince's paintings and images from Prince's workshop.

Cariou sued Prince and Gagosian, alleging that Prince's Canal Zone works and exhibition catalog infringed on Cariou's copyrights in the incorporated *Yes Rasta* photographs. The defendants raised a fair use defense. After the parties cross-moved for summary judgment, the United States District Court for the Southern District of New York (Batts, J.) granted Cariou's motion, denied the defendants', and entered a permanent injunction. It compelled the defendants to deliver to Cariou all infringing works that had not yet been sold, for him to destroy, sell, or otherwise dispose of.

Prince and Gagosian principally contend on appeal that Prince's work is transformative and constitutes fair use of Cariou's copyrighted photographs, and that the district court imposed an incorrect legal standard when it concluded that, in order to qualify for a fair use defense, Prince's work must "comment on Cariou, on Cariou's Photos, or on aspects of popular culture closely associated with Cariou or the Photos." *Cariou v. Prince*, 784 F. Supp.2d 337, 349 (S.D.N.Y.2011). We agree with Appellants that the law does not require that a secondary use comment on the original artist or work, or popular culture, and we conclude that twenty-five of Prince's artworks do make fair use Cariou's copyrighted photographs. With regard to the remaining five artworks, we remand to the district court, applying the proper standard, to consider in the first instance whether Prince is entitled to a fair use defense.[NOTE 2]

BACKGROUND

The relevant facts, drawn primarily from the parties' submissions in connection with their cross-motions for summary judgment, are undisputed. Cariou is a professional photographer who, over the course of six years in the mid-1990s, lived and worked among Rastafarians in Jamaica. The relationships that Cariou developed with them allowed him to take a series of portraits and landscape photographs that Cariou published in 2000 in a book titled *Yes Rasta*. As Cariou testified, *Yes Rasta* is "extreme classical photography [and] portraiture," and he did not "want that book to look pop culture at all." Cariou Dep. 187:8-15, Jan. 12, 2010.

Cariou's publisher, PowerHouse Books, Inc., printed 7,000 copies of *Yes Rasta*, in a single printing. Like many, if not most, such works, the book enjoyed limited commercial success. The book is currently out of print. As of January 2010, PowerHouse had sold 5,791 copies, over sixty percent of which sold below the suggested retail price of sixty dollars. PowerHouse has paid Cariou, who holds the copyrights to the *Yes Rasta* photographs, just over $8,000 from sales of the book. Except for a handful of private sales to personal acquaintances, he has never sold or licensed the individual photographs.

Prince is a well-known appropriation artist. The Tate Gallery has defined appropriation art as "the more or less direct taking over into a work of art a real object or even an existing work of art." J.A. 446. Prince's work, going back to the mid-1970s, has involved taking photographs and other images that others have produced and incorporating them into paintings and collages that he then presents, in a different context, as his own. He is a leading exponent of this genre and his work has been displayed in museums around the world, including New York's Solomon R. Guggenheim Museum and Whitney Museum, San Francisco's Museum of Modern Art, Rotterdam's Museum Boijmans van Beuningen, and Basel's Museum fur Gegenwartskunst. As Prince has described his work, he "completely tr[ies] to change [another artist's work] into something that's completely different." Prince Dep. 338:4-8, Oct. 6, 2009.

Prince first came across a copy of *Yes Rasta* in a bookstore in St. Barth's in 2005. Between December 2007 and February 2008, Prince had a show at the Eden Rock hotel in St. Barth's that included a collage, titled Canal Zone (2007), comprising 35 photographs torn out of *Yes Rasta* and pinned to a piece of plywood. Prince altered those photographs significantly, by among other things painting "lozenges" over their subjects' facial features and using only portions of some of the images. In June 2008, Prince purchased three additional copies of *Yes Rasta*. He went on to create thirty additional artworks in the Canal Zone series, twenty-nine of which incorporated partial or whole images from *Yes Rasta*. [NOTE 3] The portions of *Yes Rasta* photographs used, and the amount of each artwork that they constitute, vary significantly from piece to piece. In certain works, such as James Brown Disco Ball, Prince affixed headshots from *Yes Rasta* onto other appropriated images,

Artist Richard Prince's 2008 Canal Zone *series included 29 paintings which incorporated copyrighted photographs by Patrick Cariou taken from his 2000 book* Yes Rasta, *including* Graduation *(2008) (right).* Canal Zone *was exhibited at the Gagosian Gallery and eight paintings sold for more than one million dollars apiece. In 2009 Cariou brought a copyright infringement suit against Prince, the Gagosian Gallery, Lawrence Gagosian, and catalogue publisher Rizzoli. In March 2011, U.S. District judge Deborah Batts ruled against Prince and ordered the defendants to destroy all remaining copies of the catalogue and the unsold paintings which made use of Cariou's photographs. Prince appealed the decision and Cariou petitioned the Supreme Court, which denied cert. The case was eventually settled.*

all of which Prince placed on a canvas that he had painted. In these, Cariou's work is almost entirely obscured. The Prince artworks also incorporate photographs that have been enlarged or tinted, and incorporate photographs appropriated from artists other than Cariou as well. *Yes Rasta* is a book of photographs measuring approximately 9.5" × 12". Prince's artworks, in contrast, comprise inkjet printing and acrylic paint, as well as pasted-on elements, and are several times that size. For instance, Graduation measures 72 3/4" × 52 1/2" and James Brown Disco Ball 100 1/2" × 104 1/2". The smallest of the Prince artworks measures 40" × 30", or approximately ten times as large as each page of *Yes Rasta.*

In other works, such as Graduation, Cariou's original work is readily apparent: Prince did little more than paint blue lozenges over the subject's eyes and mouth, and paste a picture of a guitar over the subject's body.

Between November 8 and December 20, 2008, the Gallery put on a show featuring twenty-two of Prince's Canal Zone artworks, and also published and sold an exhibition catalog from the show. The catalog included all of the Canal Zone artworks (including those not in the Gagosian show) except for one, as well as, among other things, photographs showing *Yes Rasta* photographs in Prince's studio. Prince never sought or received permission from Cariou to use his photographs.

Prior to the Gagosian show, in late August, 2008, a gallery owner named Cristiane Celle contacted Cariou and asked if he would be interested in discussing the possibility of an exhibit in New York City. Celle did not mention *Yes Rasta*, but did express interest in photographs Cariou took of surfers, which he published in 1998 in the aptly titled Surfers. Cariou responded that Surfers would be republished in 2008, and inquired whether Celle might also be interested in a book Cariou had recently completed on gypsies. The two subsequently met and discussed Cariou's exhibiting work in Celle's gallery, including prints from *Yes Rasta.* They did not select a date or photographs to exhibit, nor did they finalize any other details about the possible future show.

At some point during the Canal Zone show at Gagosian, Celle learned that Cariou's photographs were "in the show with Richard Prince." Celle then phoned Cariou and, when he did not respond, Celle mistakenly concluded that he was "doing something with Richard Prince.... [Maybe] he's not pursuing me because he's doing something better, bigger with this person.... [H]e didn't want to tell the French girl I'm not doing it with you, you know, because we had started a relation and that would have been bad." Celle Dep. 88:15-89:7, Jan. 26, 2010. At that point, Celle decided that she would not put on a "Rasta show" because it had been "done already," and that any future Cariou exhibition she put on would be of photographs from Surfers. Celle remained interested in exhibiting prints from Surfers, but Cariou never followed through.

According to Cariou, he learned about the Gagosian Canal Zone show from Celle in December 2008. On December 30, 2008, he sued Prince, the Gagosian Gallery, and Lawrence Gagosian, raising claims of copyright infringement. See 17 U.S.C. §§ 106, 501. The defendants asserted a fair use defense, arguing that Prince's artworks are transformative of Cariou's photographs and, accordingly, do not violate Cariou's copyrights. See, e.g., *See, e.g., Campbell v. Acuff-Rose Music, Inc.*, 510 U.S. 569, 578-79 (1994). Ruling on the parties' subsequently-filed cross-motions for summary judgment, the district court (Batts, J.) "impose[d] a requirement that the new work in some way comment on, relate to the historical context of, or critically refer back to the original works" in order to be qualify as fair use, and stated that "Prince's Paintings are transformative only to the extent that they comment on the Photos." *Cariou v. Prince*, 784 F.Supp.2d 337, 348-49 (S.D.N.Y.2011). The court concluded that "Prince did not intend to comment on Cariou, on Cariou's Photos, or on aspects of popular culture closely associated with Cariou or the Photos when he appropriated the Photos," id. at 349, and for that reason rejected the defendants' fair use defense and granted summary judgment to Cariou. The district court also granted sweeping injunctive relief, ordering the defendants to "deliver up for impounding, destruction, or other disposition, as [Cariou] determines, all infringing copies of the Photographs, including the Paintings and unsold copies of the Canal Zone exhibition book, in their possession." *Id.* at 355.[NOTE 4] This appeal followed.

DISCUSSION

I.

We review a grant of summary judgment de novo. See *Blanch v. Koons*, 467 F.3d 244, 249-50 (2d Cir.2006). The well known standards for summary judgment set forth in Rule 56(c) apply. See Fed.R.Civ.P. 56. "Although fair use is a mixed question of law and fact, this court has on numerous occasions resolved fair use determinations at the summary judgment stage where ... there are no genuine issues of material fact." Blanch, 467 F.3d at 250 (quotation marks and brackets omitted); see also *Harper & Row, Publishers, Inc. v. Nation Enters.*, 471 U.S. 539, 560, 105 S.Ct. 2218, 85 L.Ed.2d 588 (1985); *Castle Rock Entm't, Inc. v. Carol Publ'g Grp., Inc.*, 150 F.3d 132, 137 (2d Cir.1998). This case lends itself to that approach.

II.

The purpose of the copyright law is "[t]o promote the Progress of Science and useful Arts...." U.S. Const., Art. I, § 8, cl. 8. As Judge Pierre Leval of this court has explained, "[t]he copyright is not an inevitable, divine, or natural right that confers on authors the absolute ownership of their creations. It is designed rather to stimulate activity and progress in the arts for the intellectual enrichment of the public." Pierre N. Leval, *Toward a Fair Use Standard*, 103 Harv. L.Rev. 1105, 1107 (1990) (hereinafter "Leval"). Fair use is "necessary to fulfill [that] very purpose." *Campbell*, 510 U.S. at 575, 114 S.Ct. 1164. Because "'excessively broad protection would stifle, rather than advance, the law's objective,'" fair use doctrine "mediates between" "the property rights [copyright law] establishes in creative works, which must be protected up to a point, and the ability of authors, artists, and the rest of us to express them—or ourselves by reference to the works of others, which must be protected up to a point." *Blanch*, 467 F.3d at 250 (brackets omitted) (quoting Leval at 1109).

The doctrine was codified in the Copyright Act of 1976, which lists four non-exclusive factors that must be considered in determining fair use. Under the statute,

[T]he fair use of a copyrighted work … for purposes such as criticism, comment, news reporting, teaching (including multiple copies for classroom use), scholarship, or research, is not an infringement of copyright. In determining whether the use made of a work in any particular case is a fair use the factors to be considered shall include—

(1) the purpose and character of the use, including whether such use is of a commercial nature or is for nonprofit educational purposes;

(2) the nature of the copyrighted work;

(3) the amount and substantiality of the portion used in relation to the copyrighted work as a whole; and

(4) the effect of the use upon the potential market for or value of the copyrighted work.

17 U.S.C. § 107. As the statute indicates, and as the Supreme Court and our court have recognized, the fair use determination is an open-ended and context-sensitive inquiry. *Campbell*, 510 U.S. at 577-78, 114 S.Ct. 1164; *Blanch*, 467 F.3d at 251. The statute "employs the terms 'including' and 'such as' in the preamble paragraph to indicate the illustrative and not limitative function of the examples given, which thus provide only general guidance about the sorts of copying that courts and Congress most commonly had found to be fair uses." *Campbell*, 510 U.S. at 577-78, 114 S.Ct. 1164 (quotation marks and citation omitted). The "ultimate test of fair use ... is whether the copyright law's goal of 'promoting the Progress of Science and useful Arts' … would be better served by allowing the use than by preventing it." *Castle Rock*, 150 F.3d at 141 (brackets and citation omitted).

The first statutory factor to consider, which addresses the manner in which the copied work is used, is "[t]he heart of the fair use inquiry." *Blanch*, 467 F.3d at 251. We ask

> whether the new work merely 'supersedes the objects' of the original creation, or instead adds something new, with a further purpose or different character, altering the first with new expression, meaning, or message[,] … in other words, whether and to what extent the new work is transformative.... [T]ransformative works … lie at the heart of the fair use doctrine's guarantee of breathing space….

Campbell, 510 U.S. at 579, 114 S.Ct. 1164 (citations and some quotation marks omitted) (quoting *Folsom v. Marsh*, 9 F.Cas. 342, 348) (C.C.D.Mass.1841) (Story, J.). "If 'the secondary use adds value to the original—if [the original work] is used as raw material, transformed in the creation of new information, new aesthetics, new insights and understandings—this is the very type of activity that the fair use doctrine intends to protect for the enrichment of society.'" *Castle Rock*, 150 F.3d at 142 (quoting Leval 1111). For a use to be fair, it "must be productive and must employ the quoted matter in a different manner or for a different purpose from the original." Leval at 1111.

The district court imposed a requirement that, to qualify for a fair use defense, a secondary use must "comment on, relate to the historical context of, or critically refer back to the original works." *Cariou*, 784 F.Supp.2d at 348. Certainly, many types of fair use, such as satire and parody, invariably comment on an original work and/or on popular culture. For example, the rap group 2 Live Crew's parody of Roy Orbison's "Oh, Pretty Woman" "was clearly intended to ridicule the white-bread original." *Campbell*, 510 U.S. at 582, 114 S.Ct. 1164 (quotation marks omitted). Much of Andy Warhol's work, including work incorporating appropriated images of Campbell's soup cans or of Marilyn Monroe, comments on consumer culture and explores the relationship between celebrity culture and advertising. As even Cariou concedes, however, the district court's legal premise was not correct. The law imposes no requirement that a work comment on the original or its author in order to be considered transformative, and a secondary work may constitute a fair use even if it serves some purpose other than those (criticism, comment, news reporting, teaching, scholarship, and research) identified in the preamble to the statute. *Id.* at 577, 114 S.Ct. 1164; *Harper & Row*, 471 U.S. at 561, 105 S.Ct. 2218. Instead, as the Supreme Court as well as decisions from our court have emphasized, to qualify as a fair use, a new work generally must alter the original with "new expression, meaning, or message." *Campbell*, 510 U.S. at 579, 114 S.Ct. 1164; see also *Blanch*, 467 F.3d at 253 (original must be employed "in the creation of new information, new aesthetics, new insights and understandings"(quotation marks omitted)); *Castle Rock*, 150 F.3d at 142.

Here, our observation of Prince's artworks themselves convinces us of the transformative nature of all but five, which we discuss separately below. These twenty-five of Prince's artworks manifest an entirely different aesthetic from Cariou's photographs. Where Cariou's serene and deliberately composed portraits and landscape photographs depict the natural beauty of Rastafarians and their surrounding environs, Prince's crude and jarring works, on the other hand, are hectic and provocative. Cariou's black-and-white photographs were printed in a 9 1/2" × 12" book. Prince has created collages on canvas that incorporate color, feature distorted human and other forms and settings, and measure between ten and nearly a hundred times the size of the photographs. Prince's composition, presentation, scale, color palette, and media are fundamentally different and new compared to the photographs, as is the expressive nature of Prince's work. See *Campbell*, 510 U.S. at 579, 114 S.Ct. 1164.

Prince's deposition testimony further demonstrates his drastically different approach and aesthetic from Cariou's. Prince testified that he "[doesn't] have any really interest in what [another artist's] original intent is because ... what I do is I completely try to change it into something that's completely different.... I'm trying to make a kind of fantastic, absolutely hip, up to date, contemporary take on the music scene." Prince Dep. 338:4-339:3, Oct. 6, 2009. As the district court determined, Prince's Canal Zone artworks relate to a "post-apocalyptic screenplay" Prince had planned, and "emphasize themes [of Prince's planned screenplay] of equality of the sexes; highlight 'the three relationships in the world, which are men and women, men and men, and women and women'; and portray a contemporary take on the music scene." *Cariou*, 784 F.Supp.2d at 349; see Prince Dep. 339:3-7, Oct. 6, 2009.

The district court based its conclusion that Prince's work is not transformative in large part on Prince's deposition testimony that he "do[es]n't really have a message," that he was not "trying to create anything with a new meaning or a new message," and that he "do[es]n't have any ... interest in [Cariou's] original intent." *Cariou*, 784 F.Supp.2d at 349; see Prince Dep. 45:25-46:2, 338:5-6, 360:18-20, Oct. 6, 2009. On appeal, Cariou argues that we must hold Prince to his testimony and that we are not to consider how Prince's works may reasonably be perceived unless Prince claims that they were satire or parody. No such rule exists, and we do not analyze satire or parody differently from any other transformative use.

It is not surprising that, when transformative use is at issue, the alleged infringer would go to great lengths to explain and defend his use as transformative. Prince did not do so here. However, the fact that Prince did not provide those sorts of explanations in his deposition—which might have lent strong support to his defense—is not dispositive. What is critical is how the work in question appears to the reasonable observer, not simply what an artist might say about a particular piece or body of work. Prince's work could be transformative even without commenting on Cariou's work or on culture, and even without Prince's stated intention to do so. Rather than confining our inquiry to Prince's explanations of his artworks, we instead examine how the artworks may "reasonably be perceived" in order to assess their transformative nature. *Campbell*, 510 U.S. at 582, 114 S.Ct. 1164; *Leibovitz v. Paramount Pictures Corp.*, 137 F.3d 109, 113-14 (2d Cir.1998) (evaluating parodic nature of advertisement in light of how it "may reasonably be perceived"). The focus of our infringement analysis is primarily on the Prince artworks themselves, and we see twenty-five of them as transformative as a matter of law.

In this respect, the Seventh Circuit's recent decision in *Brownmark Films, LLC v. Comedy Partners*, 682 F.3d 687 (7th Cir.2012), is instructive. There, the court rejected the appellant's argument that copyright infringement claims cannot be disposed of at the motion-to-dismiss stage, and affirmed the district court's dismissal of such a claim under Fed.R.Civ.P. 12(b)(6). *Brownmark Films*, 682 F.3d at 690. Considering whether an episode of the animated television show *South Park* presented a parody (and therefore a protected fair use) of a viral internet video titled "What What (In The Butt)," the court concluded that "[w]hen the two works ... are viewed side-by-side, the *South Park* episode is clearly a parody of the original ... video." *Id.* at 692. For that reason, "the only two pieces of evidence needed to decide the question of fair use in [*Brownmark* were] the original version of [the video] and the episode at issue." *Id.* at 690.

Here, looking at the artworks and the photographs side-by-side, we conclude that Prince's images, except for those we discuss separately below, have a different character, give Cariou's photographs a new expression, and employ new aesthetics with creative and communicative results distinct from Cariou's. Our conclusion should not be taken to suggest, however, that any cosmetic changes to the photographs would necessarily constitute fair use. A secondary work may modify the original without being transformative. For instance, a derivative work that merely presents the same material but in a new form, such as a book of synopses of televisions shows, is not transformative. See *Castle Rock*, 150 F.3d at 143; *Twin Peaks Prods., Inc. v. Publ'ns Int'l, Ltd.*, 996 F.2d 1366, 1378 (2d Cir.1993). In twenty-five of his artworks, Prince has not presented the same material as Cariou in a different manner, but instead has "add[ed] something new" and presented images with a fundamentally different aesthetic. *Leibovitz*, 137 F.3d at 114.

The first fair use factor—the purpose and character of the use—also requires that we consider whether the allegedly infringing work has a commercial or nonprofit educational purpose. See, e.g., *Blanch*, 467 F.3d at 253. That being said, "nearly all of the illustrative uses listed in the preamble paragraph of § 107, including news reporting, comment, criticism, teaching, scholarship, and research... are generally conducted for profit." *Campbell*, 510 U.S. at 584, 114 S.Ct. 1164 (quotation marks omitted). "The commercial/nonprofit dichotomy concerns the unfairness that arises when a secondary user makes unauthorized use of copyrighted material to capture significant revenues as a direct consequence of copying the original work." *Am. Geophysical Union v. Texaco Inc.*, 60 F.3d 913, 922 (2d Cir.1994). This factor must be applied with caution because, as the Supreme Court has recognized, Congress "could not have intended" a rule that commercial uses are presumptively unfair. *Campbell*, 510 U.S. at 584, 114 S.Ct. 1164. Instead, "[t]he more transformative the new work, the less will be the significance of other factors, like commercialism, that may weigh against a finding of fair use." *Id.* at 579, 114 S.Ct. 1164. Although there is no question that Prince's artworks are commercial, we do not place much significance on that fact due to the transformative nature of the work.

We turn next to the fourth statutory factor, the effect of the secondary use upon the potential market for the value of the copyrighted work, because such discussion further demonstrates the significant differences between Prince's work, generally, and Cariou's. Much of the district court's conclusion that Prince and Gagosian infringed on Cariou's copyrights was apparently driven by the fact that Celle decided not to host a *Yes Rasta* show at her gallery once she learned of the Gagosian Canal Zone show. The district court determined that this factor weighs against Prince because he "has unfairly damaged both the actual and potential markets for Cariou's original work and the potential market for derivative use licenses for Cariou's original work." *Cariou*, 784 F.Supp.2d at 353.

Contrary to the district court's conclusion, the application of this factor does not focus principally on the question of damage to Cariou's derivative market. We have made clear that "our concern is not whether the secondary use suppresses or even destroys the market for the original work or its potential derivatives, but whether the secondary use usurps the market of the original work." *Blanch*, 467 F.3d at 258 (quotation marks omitted) (emphasis added); *NXIVM Corp. v. Ross Inst.*, 364 F.3d 471, 481-82 (2d Cir.2004). "The market for potential derivative uses includes only those that creators of original works would in general develop or license others to develop." *Campbell*, 510 U.S. at 592, 114 S.Ct. 1164. Our court has concluded that an accused infringer has usurped the market for copyrighted works, including the derivative market, where the infringer's target audience and the nature of the infringing content is the same as the original. For instance, a book of trivia about the television show *Seinfeld* usurped the show's market because the trivia book "substitute[d] for a derivative market that a television program copyright owner ... would in general develop or license others to develop." *Castle Rock*, 150 F.3d at 145 (quotation marks omitted). Conducting this analysis, we are mindful that "[t]he more transformative the secondary use, the less likelihood that the secondary use substitutes for the original," even though "the fair use, being transformative, might well harm, or even destroy, the market for the original." *Id.*

As discussed above, Celle did not decide against putting on a *Yes Rasta* show because it had already been done at Gagosian, but rather because she mistakenly believed that Cariou had collaborated with Prince on the Gagosian show. Although certain of Prince's artworks contain significant portions of certain of Cariou's photographs, neither Prince nor the Canal Zone show usurped the market for those photographs. Prince's audience is very different from Cariou's, and there is no evidence that Prince's work ever touched—much less usurped—either the primary or derivative market for Cariou's work. There is nothing in the record to suggest that Cariou would ever develop or license secondary uses of his work in the vein of Prince's artworks. Nor does anything in the record suggest that Prince's artworks had any impact on the marketing of the photographs. Indeed, Cariou has not aggressively marketed his work, and has earned just over $8,000 in royalties from *Yes Rasta* since its publication. He has sold four prints from the book, and only to personal acquaintances.

Prince's work appeals to an entirely different sort of collector than Cariou's. Certain of the Canal Zone artworks have sold for two million or more dollars. The invitation list for a dinner that Gagosian hosted in conjunction with the opening of the Canal Zone show included a number of the wealthy and famous such as the musicians Jay-Z and Beyonce Knowles, artists Damien Hirst and Jeff Koons, professional football player Tom Brady, model Gisele Bundchen, Vanity Fair editor Graydon Carter, Vogue editor Anna Wintour, authors Jonathan Franzen and Candace Bushnell, and actors Robert DeNiro, Angelina Jolie, and Brad Pitt. Prince sold eight artworks for a total of $10,480,000, and exchanged seven others for works by painter Larry Rivers and by sculptor Richard Serra. Cariou on the other hand has not actively marketed his work or sold work for significant sums, and nothing in the record suggests that anyone will not now purchase Cariou's work, or derivative non-transformative works (whether Cariou's own or licensed by him) as a result of the market space that Prince's work has taken up. This fair use factor therefore weighs in Prince's favor.

The next statutory factor that we consider, the nature of the copyrighted work, "calls for recognition that some works are closer to the core of intended copyright protection than others, with the consequence that fair use is more difficult to establish when the former works are copied." *Campbell*, 510 U.S. at 586, 114 S.Ct. 1164. We consider "'(1) whether the work is expressive or creative, ... with a greater leeway being allowed to a claim of fair use where the work is factual or informational, and (2) whether the work is published or unpublished, with the scope for fair use involving unpublished works being considerably narrower.'" *Blanch*, 467 F.3d at 256 (quoting 2 Howard B. Abrams, The Law of Copyright, § 15:52 (2006)).

Here, there is no dispute that Cariou's work is creative and published. Accordingly, this factor weighs against a fair use determination. However, just as with the commercial character of Prince's work, this factor "may be of limited usefulness where," as here, "the creative work of art is being used for a transformative purpose." *Bill Graham Archives v. Dorling Kindersley Ltd.*, 448 F.3d 605, 612 (2d Cir.2006).

The final factor that we consider in our fair use inquiry is "the amount and substantiality of the portion used in relation to the copyrighted work as a whole." 17 U.S.C. § 107(3). We ask "whether the quantity and value of the materials used ... are reasonable in relation to the purpose of the copying." *Blanch*, 467 F.3d at 257 (quotation marks omitted). In other words, we consider the proportion of the original work used, and not how much of the secondary work comprises the original.

Many of Prince's works use Cariou's photographs, in particular the portrait of the dreadlocked Rastafarian at page 118 of *Yes Rasta*, the Rastafarian on a burro at pages 83 to 84, and the dreadlocked and bearded Rastafarian at page 108, in whole or substantial part. In some works, such as Charlie Company, Prince did not alter the source photograph very much at all. In others, such as Djuana Barnes, Natalie Barney, Renee Vivien and Romaine Brooks take over the Guanahani, the entire source photograph is used but is also heavily obscured and altered to the point that Cariou's original is barely recognizable. Although "[n]either our court nor any of our sister circuits has ever ruled that the copying of an entire work favors fair use[,].... courts have concluded that such copying does not necessarily weigh against fair use because copying the entirety of a work is sometimes necessary to make a fair use of the image." *Bill Graham*, 448 F.3d at 613. "[T]he third-factor inquiry must take into account that the extent of permissible copying varies with the purpose and character of the use." *Id.* (internal quotation marks omitted).

The district court determined that Prince's "taking was substantially greater than necessary." *Cariou*, 784 F.Supp.2d at 352. We are not clear as to how the district court could arrive at such a conclusion. In any event, the law does not require that the secondary artist may take no more than is necessary. See *Campbell*, 510 U.S. at 588, 114 S.Ct. 1164; *Leibovitz*, 137 F.3d at 114. We consider not only the quantity of the materials taken but also "their quality and importance" to the original work. *Campbell*, 510 U.S. at 587, 114 S.Ct. 1164. The secondary use "must be [permitted] to 'conjure up' at least enough of the original" to fulfill its transformative purpose. *Id.* at 588, 114 S.Ct. 1164 (emphasis added); *Leibovitz*, 137 F.3d at 114. Prince used key portions of certain of Cariou's photographs. In doing that, however, we determine that in twenty-five of his artworks, Prince transformed those photographs into something new and different and, as a result, this factor weighs heavily in Prince's favor.

As indicated above, there are five artworks that, upon our review, present closer questions. Specifically, Graduation, Meditation, Canal Zone (2008), Canal Zone (2007), and Charlie Company do not sufficiently differ from the photographs of Cariou's that they incorporate for us confidently to make a determination about their transformative nature as a matter of law. Although the minimal alterations that Prince made in those instances moved the work in a different direction from Cariou's classical portraiture and landscape photos, we cannot say with certainty at this point whether those artworks present a "new expression, meaning, or message." *Campbell*, 510 U.S. at 579, 114 S.Ct. 1164.

Certainly, there are key differences in those artworks compared to the photographs they incorporate. Graduation, for instance, is tinted blue, and the jungle background is in softer focus than in Cariou's original. Lozenges painted over the subject's eyes and mouth—an alteration that appears frequently throughout the Canal Zone artworks—make the subject appear anonymous, rather than as the strong individual who appears in the original. Along with the enlarged hands and electric guitar that Prince pasted onto his canvas, those alterations create the impression that the subject is not quite human. Cariou's photograph, on the other hand, presents a human being in his natural habitat, looking intently ahead. Where the photograph presents someone comfortably at home in nature, Graduation combines divergent elements to create a sense of discomfort. However, we cannot say for sure whether Graduation constitutes fair use or whether Prince has transformed Cariou's work enough to render it transformative.

We have the same concerns with Meditation, Canal Zone (2007), Canal Zone (2008), and Charlie Company. Each of those artworks differs from, but is still similar in key aesthetic ways, to Cariou's photographs. In Meditation, Prince again added lozenges and a guitar to the same photograph that he incorporated into Graduation, this time cutting the subject out of his background, switching the direction he is facing, and taping that image onto a blank canvas. In Canal Zone (2007), Prince created a gridded collage using 31 different photographs of Cariou's, many of them in whole or significant part, with alterations of some of those photographs limited to lozenges or cartoonish appendages painted or drawn on. Canal Zone (2008) incorporates six photographs of Cariou's in whole or in part, including the same subject as Meditation and Graduation. Prince placed the subject, with lozenges and guitar, on a background comprising components of various landscape photographs, taped together. The cumulative effect is of the subject in a habitat replete with lush greenery, not dissimilar from many of Cariou's *Yes Rasta* photographs. And Charlie Company prominently displays four copies of Cariou's photograph of a Rastafarian riding a donkey, substantially unaltered, as well as two copies of a seated nude woman with lozenges covering all six faces. Like the other works just discussed, Charlie Company is aesthetically similar to Cariou's original work because it maintains the pastoral background and individual focal point of the original photograph—in this case, the man on the burro. While the lozenges, repetition of the images, and addition of the nude female unarguably change the tenor of the piece, it is unclear whether these alterations amount to a sufficient transformation of the original work of art such that the new work is transformative.

We believe the district court is best situated to determine, in the first instance, whether such relatively minimal alterations render Graduation, Meditation, Canal Zone (2007), Canal Zone (2008), and Charlie Company fair uses (including whether the artworks are transformative) or whether any impermissibly infringes on Cariou's copyrights in his original photographs. We remand for that determination.

III.

In addition to its conclusion that Prince is liable for infringing on Cariou's copyrights, the district court determined that the Gagosian defendants are liable as vicarious and contributory infringers. Cariou, 784 F.Supp.2d at 354. With regard to the twenty-five of Prince's artworks, which, as we have held, do not infringe on Cariou's copyrights, neither Lawrence Gagosian nor the Gallery may be liable as a vicarious or contributory infringer. See *Faulkner v. Nat'l Geographic Enters., Inc.*, 409 F.3d 26, 40 (2d Cir.2005). If the district court concludes on remand that Prince is liable as a direct infringer with regard to any of the remaining five works, the district court should determine whether the Gagosian defendants should be held liable, directly or secondarily, as a consequence of their actions with regard to those works. See Copyright Act, 17 U.S.C. § 106(1), (2), (3), (5).

CONCLUSION

For the reasons discussed, we hold that all except five (Graduation, Meditation, Canal Zone (2007), Canal Zone (2008), and Charlie Company) of Prince's artworks make fair use of Cariou's photographs. We express no view as to whether the five are also entitled to a fair use defense. We REMAND with respect to those five so that the district court, applying the proper standard, can determine in the first instance whether any of them infringes on Cariou's copyrights or whether Prince is entitled to a fair use defense with regard to those artworks as well. The judgment of the district court is REVERSED in part and VACATED in part.[NOTE 5] The case is REMANDED for further proceedings consistent with this opinion.

WALLACE, J., Senior Circuit Judge, concurring in part and dissenting in part:

I agree with the bulk of the majority decision as to the law, including the majority's determination that the district court incorrectly imposed a requirement that the allegedly infringing works comment on the original works to be entitled to a fair use defense. See *Cariou v. Prince*, 784 F.Supp.2d 337, 348-49 (S.D.N.Y.2011). I nevertheless part company with the majority.

While we may, as an appellate court, determine that secondary works are fair use in certain instances, see *Harper & Row, Publishers, Inc. v. Nation Enters.*, 471 U.S. 539, 560, 105 S.Ct. 2218, 85 L.Ed.2d 588 (1985), in the usual case, after correcting an erroneous legal standard employed by the district court, we would remand for reconsideration. This standard, I suggest, should apply here where factual determinations must be reevaluated—and perhaps new evidence or expert opinions will be deemed necessary by the fact finder—after which a new decision can be made under the corrected legal analysis. But the majority short-circuits this time-tested search for a just result under the law. I would not apply the shortcut but would set aside the summary judgment, remand the entire case to the district court, and allow the district court to analyze material evidence under the proper standard.

Unlike the majority, I would allow the district court to consider Prince's statements in reviewing fair use. While not the sine qua non of fair use, see *Blanch v. Koons*, 467 F.3d 244, 255 n. 5 (2d Cir. 2006), I see no reason to discount Prince's statements as the majority does. While it may seem intuitive to assume that a defendant claiming fair use would typically give self-serving *ex post facto* testimony to support a defense, this Court has nevertheless relied on such statements when making this inquiry—even if just to confirm its own analysis. See *id.* at 252-53, 255; see also *Castle Rock Entm't, Inc. v. Carol Publ'g Grp., Inc.*, 150 F.3d 132, 142 (2d Cir.1998) (looking to statements of the allegedly infringing work's creators when analyzing the purpose and character of the secondary work). Thus, I view Prince's statements—which, as Prince acknowledges, consist of "his view of the purpose and effect of each of the individual [p]aintings"—as relevant to the transformativeness analysis.

The majority relies on the Seventh Circuit's decision in *Brownmark Films, LLC v. Comedy Partners*, 682 F.3d 687 (7th Cir.2012), for the proposition that all the Court needs to do here to determine transformativeness is view the original work and the secondary work and, apparently, employ its own artistic judgment. In my view, *Brownmark* cannot be extended so far. *Brownmark* arose under an unusual procedural posture: a motion to dismiss based on a non-pleaded fair use affirmative defense converted into a motion for summary judgment on appeal. See id. The court in *Brownmark* determined that it needed only to review the allegedly infringing video against the original to determine that the secondary work was permissible parody. Id. at 692-93. It appears to me, however, that *Brownmark* left open the possibility that additional evidence could be relevant to the fair use inquiry in a different procedural context. See id. at 692 n. 2 (identifying that the defendant could have put forth additional evidence to bolster its fair use defense if the case arose from a typical summary judgment motion); *id.* at 692 (stating that the district court was only required to consider the original and secondary videos, "especially in light of [the plaintiff's] failure to make any concrete contention" as to the secondary video's potential market impact).

Further, *Brownmark* apparently arose in the context of a clear case of parody—so obvious that the appeals court affirmed the district court's conclusion that fair use was evident from even a «fleeting glance» at the original and secondary works. *Id.* at 689-90. I do not believe that the transformativeness of Prince's works—which have not been presented as parody or satire—can be so readily determined. Because this case arises after extensive discovery and argument by the parties, I disagree that we must limit our inquiry to our own artistic perceptions of the original and secondary works.

Indeed, while I admit freely that I am not an art critic or expert, I fail to see how the majority in its appellate role can "confidently" draw a distinction between the twenty-five works that it has identified as constituting fair use and the five works that do not readily lend themselves to a fair use determination. This, mind you, is done on a summary judgment review with no understanding of what additional evidence may be presented on remand. I also fail to see a principled reason for remanding to the district court only the five works the majority identifies as close calls, although I agree that they must be sent back to the trial court. If the district court is in the best position to determine fair use as to some paintings, why is the same not true as to all paintings? Certainly we are not merely to use our personal art views to make the new legal application to the facts of this case. Cf. *Campbell v. Acuff-Rose Music, Inc.*, 510 U.S. 569, 582, 114 S.Ct. 1164, 127 L.Ed.2d 500 (1994) ("'[I] t would be a dangerous undertaking for persons trained only to the law to constitute themselves final judges of the worth of [a work], outside of the narrowest and most obvious limits'"), quoting *Bleistein v. Donaldson Lithographing Co.*, 188 U.S. 239, 251, 23 S.Ct. 298, 47 L.Ed. 460 (1903). It would be extremely uncomfortable for me to do so in my appellate capacity, let alone my limited art experience.

In my view, because the district court takes the primary role in determining the facts and applying the law to the facts in fair use cases, after which we exercise our appellate review if called upon to do so, I conclude that as to each painting, "the district court is best situated to determine, in the first instance," whether Prince is entitled to a fair use defense in light of the correct legal standard. See majority opinion at 711-12. I mean no disrespect to the majority, but I, for one, do not believe that I am in a position to make these fact- and opinion-intensive decisions on the twenty-five works that passed the majority's judicial observation. I do not know what additional facts will become relevant under the corrected rule of law, nor am I trained to make art opinions *ab initio*.

I would thus remand the entire case—all thirty of Prince's paintings—for further proceedings in the district court on an open record to take such additional testimony as needed and apply the correct legal standard. On this basis, therefore, I respectfully dissent.

NOTES:

NOTE 1: We refer to Gagosian Gallery and its owner Lawrence Gagosian collectively as "Gagosian" or the "Gallery."

NOTE 2: The district court's opinion indicated that there are twenty-nine artworks at issue in this case. See *Cariou*, 784 F.Supp.2d at 344 nn. 5, 6. There are actually thirty.

NOTE 3: Images of the Prince artworks, along with the *Yes Rasta* photographs incorporated therein, appear in the Appendix to this opinion. The Appendix is available at http://www.ca2.uscourts.gov/11-1197apx.htm.

NOTE 4: At oral argument, counsel for Cariou indicated that he opposes the destruction of any of the works of art that are the subject of this litigation.

NOTE 5: Because we reverse the district court with regard to the twenty-five of the artworks, and leave open the question of fair use with regard to the remaining five, we vacate the district court's injunction. In the event that Prince and Gagosian are ultimately held liable for copyright infringement, and in light of all parties' agreement at oral argument that the destruction of Prince's artwork would be improper and against the public interest, a position with which we agree, the district court should revisit what injunctive relief, if any, is appropriate. See *eBay, Inc. v. MercExchange, L.L.C.*, 547 U.S. 388, 391, 126 S.Ct. 1837, 164 L.Ed.2d 641 (2006); *Salinger v. Colting*, 607 F.3d 68, 77 (2d Cir.2010).

STUDY QUESTIONS

- In *Cariou* the artist Richard Prince refused to explain his artistic intent—essentially saying that as a "postmodern" artist he simply had no intent at all. What other "extenuating factors" were at play here? Did these factors have an impact on the trial court's ruling? How about on appeal? How does the concept of pre-existing material as "raw ingredients" affect the application of fair use?
- In what ways did the dissenting judge agree and disagree with the majority opinion?
- After the appellate court issued its ruling, Cariou filed a Petition for a Writ of Certiorari with the U.S. Supreme Court, but it did not accept the petition. After remand to the trial court, the case was settled. Why do you think the parties decided to settle?
- What role does "artistic intent" play in these four appropriation art cases?
- To what degree do you think "judicial aesthetics" play in these cases? Is that appropriate?
- Where copyright infringement was found in these cases, how did the court approach the question of remedies?
- Consider the vicarious liability of the artist's gallery or commissioning entity in each of these four cases. What implications can you foresee for museums that collect and exhibit appropriation art?

PART III: MUSEUMS AND INTELLECTUAL PROPERTY

Museums routinely create and use intellectual property as part of every functional aspect of museum activity. Museums are content creators, content users, and content managers. It is important to remember that intellectual property rights can be lost or waived through improper use. And museums can be held liable not only directly for their own actions but also for the actions of others through the concepts of vicarious and contributory liability. A basic understanding of intellectual property concepts (outlined above) is necessary to protect the museum's interest in its own intellectual property, and to avoid liability for infringing on the intellectual property rights of others. An integrated approach to the management of a museum's intellectual property also enables the museum to effectively leverage its assets to further the museum's mission and public purpose. As museum consultants John Falk and Beverly Sheppard wrote in *Thriving in the Knowledge Age*: "Understanding how to manage and exploit intellectual property assets… should be an important part of any museum's business model."

Conducting an audit of the museum's intellectual property can be a strategic part of managing a museum's assets. A museum intellectual property audit will enable the museum to identify the many types of intellectual property under its control. The audit is an assessment of both the museum's intellectual property assets and its management practices in connection with those assets. The audit should focus on how best to manage those assets to further the museum's mission, values, and goals.

Typically, an audit will be performed by a committee composed of representatives from each of the museum's functional departments—collections management, programs and exhibits, marketing and development, human resources, museum enterprises and shops, etc. The committee's audit report should include recommendations to minimize risks and maximize the value associated with the creation, custody, and care of the museum's intellectual property assets. The audit may disclose areas where museum policies and procedures need to be established or revised.

Developing intellectual property policies to address the museum's management of its intellectual property assets and those of other intellectual property owners helps to ensure that these assets are properly managed. The adoption of appropriate clearance procedures for using works protected under intellectual property laws will help to reduce the risks of infringing on other people's intellectual property rights.

Establishing best practices for clearing rights is also important. Documenting efforts to determine whether a work is under copyright, for example, and whether reliance on fair use is warranted, should be standard operating procedure.

Obtaining insurance coverage providing protection against copyright infringement can be a prudent practice, particularly when questions about the copyright status of the work and the application of exceptions to copyright are present. Errors and omissions (E&O) insurance coverage protects against intellectual property claims, including copyright infringement and privacy-based claims such as defamation. At the end of the day, clearing intellectual property rights involves an analysis of applicable laws and the assessment of the potential risks involved with the intended use.

Museum's should adopt a "mission-driven" approach to managing the museum's intellectual property. This means using the museums intellectual property assets to further the museum's mission and public purpose. An intellectual property development cycle can aid the museum's sustainability. By creating, managing, and marketing the museum's intellectual property, the museum can engage its audience, capture audience information, and cultivate that audience to generate support for the museum. This in turn allows the museum to create more intellectual property. In this way, effective management of the museums intellectual property assets will reinforce the museum's brand, demonstrate effective stewardship, minimize disputes with vendors and partners, reduce risks, and enhance development opportunities.

ONLINE ACTIVITY

Research museum intellectual property policies and professional codes and best practices guidelines. Is a museum IP audit required for accreditation by the AAM?

NOTES:

NOTE 1: Falk and Sheppard, *Thriving in the Knowledge Age: New Business Models for Museums and Other Cultural Institutions,* AltaMira Press (2006), p. 129.

CHAPTER 5: MUSEUM COLLECTIONS

This chapter is all about museum collections. We first explore some of the many legal and ethical issues raised in connection with collections management, including acquisitions, loans, and disposal of museum collections. We then focus on cultural property and special collection issues relating to museum collections, including a review of U.S. and international laws governing the movement and display of museum collections; restitution and repatriation claims; and laws regarding special collections.

LEGAL AND ETHICAL OBLIGATIONS REGARDING COLLECTIONS

Stewardship of museum collections is a core function of all museums that have collections. It is also an important concern for museums that borrow and display the collections of others. Collections stewardship is part of proper museum governance and is a core duty of the museum's board of trustees. Museums have a legal duty to provide for the adequate care and management of their collections. This includes establishing comprehensive collections management policies and providing appropriate staff and resources to properly preserve and maintain the museum's collections.

Museum collections are not "owned" in the traditional sense of property ownership. Rather, they are held in trust for the public. Caring for collections is a core fiduciary duty and museum board members are held to the highest duty of care in managing the museum's collections. In *Parkinson v. Murdock*, 332 P.2d 273 (Kan. 1958), the court identified a legal duty to provide for collections care. In that case, a charitable trust had been established to acquire an art collection for the city of Wichita, Kansas. The stated purpose of the bequest establishing the charitable trust was "to provide an art collection" for the city. The bequest did not contain any express authority to use trust funds for any purpose other than acquiring artwork. The trustees of the charitable trust petitioned the court to approve the expenditure of trust funds for the purposes of collections care, including hiring a conservator and to prepare and publish a catalogue of the collection. The court approved the use of funds for these purposes, stating that "it is essential to the fulfillment of [the stated purpose of the trust] that the paintings and object of art be properly housed and cared for." The court added, "After the trust was set up the city of Wichita had the continuing obligation to maintain suitable housing for the objects..."

Museums also have an ethical obligation to provide adequate care for their collections. Ethical duties are imposed by museum professional codes. The American Alliance of Museums (AAM) has adopted an extensive series of professional codes regarding collections stewardship. Among these is the obligation to prepare a comprehensive management plan. The AAM's *Standards and Best Practices for Collections Stewardship* require that "[a] current, approved, comprehensive collections management policy is in effect and actively used to guide the museum's stewardship of its collections." AAM professional codes of ethics also govern various aspects of acquisition, loan, exhibition, and deaccessioning and disposal of collections objects, as well as guidelines on handling various types of special collections. Other museum associations, including the American Association of Museum Directors (AAMD) and the American Association for State and Local History (AASLH), have published numerous policy guidelines and best practices for the management of collections by their member organizations.

Collections management policies vary widely. There are different types of museums and different types of collections. The collections management policy must adequately address the individual museum and its own collections. It is also important that the collections management policy be reviewed and updated regularly to accurately reflect the museum and its collections.

A well-drafted collections management policy can serve several valuable purposes. These include reducing risks of legal liability, demonstrating compliance with applicable ethical codes, and establishing institutional best practices. The collections management policy is useful in educating board, members, staff, volunteers, donors and the public about museum procedures and practices. It is also helpful in explaining museum practices to the general public and in guiding and defending the museum's decision-making. Collection management policies can also be misused, particularly to shield the museum from legitimate criticism regarding questionable museum practices. At times, these policies are enacted in response to public outcry and may consist of arbitrary rules to avoid difficult decisions. The temptation to do so should be avoided.

In developing the museum's collections management policy, external and internal factors must be considered. The policy must comply with applicable legal laws and regulations affecting the museum's collections and collections practices. It must also be consistent with current applicable professional codes, guidelines, and best practices. The museum's collecting practices as reflected in its collections management policy should also be able to withstand public scrutiny. The policy should clearly support the museum's mission and values as well as accurately reflect the museum's collecting practices and other institutional factors.

A comprehensive collections management policy should begin with a description of the museum and its collections. Recitation of the museum's mission, vision and a brief summary of its collecting history, a statement of governance authority, and a summary of applicable museum ethical codes are helpful to provide context. A description of the scope of the museum's collections and the various categories of collection objects it contains can also provide helpful background.

The collections management policy should include a description of specific practices and procedures regarding the museum's collections. These will include procedures relating to acquisitions and accessioning, deaccessioning and disposal, loans, and for handling objects that are placed in the temporary custody of the museum.

The policy should address related issues concerning the collections, including collections care and conservation, insurance and risk management, records-keeping including documentation regarding provenance and collections inventories. Provisions should be included to address access to the collections, appraisals, ownership of intellectual property, and any legal and ethical considerations, including those raised by particular culturally sensitive objects and special collections.

ONLINE ACTIVITY

- Find and critique a museum collections management policy.

ACQUISITIONS AND ACCESSIONS

While there are museums which do not have collections *per se*—a children's museum, for example—for most museums, collecting objects (whether artworks, historical artifacts, natural history specimens, or other things) is a core part of the museum's mission. As a result, museums have formal procedures for adding objects to their collections.

In the museum world, there are really two steps to placing a work in the museum's permanent collection. This two-step process is reflected in terminology that is unique to museums. In the museum context, the term "acquisition" is used in connection with the purchase or donation of a work for the museum. The term "accession" is a term that denotes the acquisition of a work for the museum with the *intent* to retain the object permanently. "Accessioning" is the formal process for putting objects into the museum's permanent collection. A museum should not "accession" a work that it does not intend to keep permanently. Works that are accessioned are documented in the museum's collections records and given a unique identifier such as an inventory number.

The distinction between acquired and accessioned objects reflects an important difference in the museum's obligations for care of the object, as well as the museum's obligations regarding any subsequent disposal of the object. Once an object has been accessioned, it should not be disposed of without first being "de-acessioned"—that is, being formally removed from the permanent collection. (Deaccessioning will be discussed in detail later in this chapter.)

A museum may "acquire" an object without intending to "accession" it. For example, a museum may accept a donation—of an antique desk for example—as an acquisition, but may decide not to "accession" the desk but instead use it as a functional piece of furniture, in the director's office for example. Similarly, an object may be acquired for resale, or for use as part of an educational collection (to be used but not conserved).

In some cases, a museum may acquire a group of objects and then after carefully reviewing them, decide to accession only some of the objects—a process sometimes referred to as "culling." Rather than acquiring the objects and then "cull" them, the better practice is to hold the objects in temporary custody while determining which objects to acquire and which to accession. (Temporary custody is discussed in more detail below.)

While there is no legal requirement to do so, it is generally considered a best practice to inform the donor if the museum does not intend to accession a donated work. In some cases, the museum may offer to return to the donor any objects it subsequently decides not to accession. Returning a donated object may raise tax issues for the donor if they have already taken a tax deduction. (The tax implications of gifts are discussed in more detail below.)

Considerations that go into whether to acquire and/or accession an object or a collection of objects vary depending on the type of museum and the museum's particular collecting practices. Strict adherence to the museum's collections management plan regarding acquisitions and accessioning is essential.

Some museums establish a collections committee made up of board members and/or members from various stakeholder communities, often with special expertise in relevant collections. The collection committee is charged with reviewing acquisition proposals (usually submitted by the museum's curator in accordance with a formal process) and making recommendations to the museum director regarding potential acquisitions. Museum staff are often sensitive to relations with their donors and are afraid to turn down object donations even when appropriate. Properly maintaining inappropriate collections objects is an expense most museums cannot afford. Use of a collections committee can give the museum director a degree of cover when faced with turning down donations. To avoid offending the would-be donor, the director can point to the recommendation of the collections committee as the reason for her decision.

Costs of conservation and care for the object should be part of the acquisition decision-making process. Certain objects may require extensive conservation or may present unique storage or display problems which should be factored into deciding whether the museum is willing and able to provide adequate care for the object. Afterall, once an object is accessioned into the museum's collection, the museum has a duty to preserve and care for that object for the foreseeable future.

GIFTS

Museum collections may be acquired by purchase or by gift. Gifts made through a will are often referred to as "bequests." In the case of unsolicited bequests of collections objects, the museum should consider carefully whether accepting the bequest conforms with its collection management policies and collecting goals. A museum is not legally obligated to accept all bequests of objects. If the bequest does not further the museum's collecting goals, it may be possible to arrange to sell the object and use the proceeds for collections purposes, unless the bequest specifically prohibits this.

In accepting a gift, the museum should be careful to make sure that the donor actually owns—"holds title to"—the object, and has the authority to make the donation. Particularly in the case of a bequest, or in other situations where there may be more than one owner—a husband and wife, for example, or the heirs of an estate—the museum should make sure that all owners agree to making the gift. There is always a risk that a partial owner may appear later and object to the making of the gift. Before accepting a gift, the museum should consider the same questions regarding title and provenance addressed below regarding acquisitions in general.

Donors often want to impose restrictions on the gift of an object or collection. Typical gift restrictions include requirements for exhibiting the work, such as making the gift contingent on it being displayed in the museum's galleries, often on a permanent basis. Complying with such gift restrictions can easily become problematic and usurps the museum's role of curating and caring for its collections. A well-drafted bequest with restrictions would include procedures for altering the restrictions or include time limits on restrictions. It is best to negotiate the terms of a bequest with the museum to ensure that the interests of both the donor and the museum are taken into consideration.

Restrictions imposed as part of a bequest are often interpreted based on whether the restriction was intended by the decedent to be binding, or rather was merely "precatory"—that is, just reflecting the decedent's wishes or preferences with respect to the bequest. Central to the inquiry is interpreting the donor's intent regarding the bequest. The extent to which a deceased donor can influence how the museum manages a bequest is sometimes referred to as "the dead hand"—that is, by imposing restrictions, the deceased donor maintains control of the bequest from beyond the grave.

The courts have a role in overseeing and interpreting bequests through the legal concept of "equitable relief." There are two general types of equitable relief which may be employed in altering a restrictive bequest. The legal doctrine of *cy pres*—Latin for "as near as may be"—is applied in situations where it is impossible, impracticable or illegal to carry out the purpose of the bequest. In such cases, a court may determine that the restriction should be lifted. Alternatively, under the doctrine of equitable deviation, the court may approve a change in the means or method for achieving the purpose of the bequest.

While in the past gift restrictions were relatively more commonplace, particularly in bequests (wealthy donors were particularly fond of the "dead hand"), most museums now have a policy of not accepting gifts with restrictions except in rare situations. Often donors concerns can be adequately addressed through "precatory" language expressing the donor's wishes, rather than absolute requirements. For example, a donor can express a wish that the object be displayed instead of conditioning the gift on the requirement that it be displayed. The museum's collections management policy should address gift restrictions and establish a procedure for considering exceptions when warranted.

While a binding gift can be made orally or in writing, acquisitions made by gift should, whenever possible, be documented with a written "deed of gift" signed by the donor. The deed of gift is a contract between the donor and the museum, and must comply with basic principles of offer, acceptance, and consideration to be enforceable. The Deed of Gift should clearly identify the object being donated. The Deed of Gift should also ask the donor to provide copies of all title and provenance information relevant to the gifted object and contain appropriate language with respect to the assignment of any related intellectual property owned by the donor as part of the gift. A description of how the gifted object will be used—will it be accessioned? used for educational purposes? or resold?—should also be included in a Deed of Gift. The written deed of gift can take a variety of forms. Two examples of deed of gift agreements are included the readings below.

While the inclusion of representations and warranties, as well as indemnification language, can be included in a written Deed of Gift, museums are often hesitant to impose any legal liability on their donors. The extent to which the Deed of Gift addresses these issues may depend on the museum's intuitional tone. Ideally a gift transaction should be treated with the same level of due diligence as all other acquisitions, but often museums approach gifts with a much lower standard of care. This can come back to haunt the museum later.

Gifts raise tax considerations, most of which are only of concern to the donor. Depending on her particular financial situation, a donor may be entitled to a charitable contribution deduction for gifts to certain nonprofit organizations or governmental entities, including museums. The issues that may involve the museum include the completion of the gift (that is, when and how the complete donation has occurred), and whether the donation is accepted for a related or unrelated use (that is, is the museum accessioning the gift, or perhaps reselling it).

It is important for the museum to inform the donor of how the museum intends to use the donated object—will it be accessioned, be part of an educational collection, or sold to raise funds for the collection?—because this may impact the donor's ability to take a tax deduction for the gift. Use for a purpose that furthers the museum's mission is called a "related use."

For donations valued at over $5,000, donors are required to obtain an appraisal from a "qualified appraiser" and submit documentation to the Internal Revenue Service (IRS).

While museums generally should avoid playing a role in valuing or appraising the gifted work, the museum may play an indirect role in this process because it may be required to prepare a "substantiation letter" verifying receipt of the gift and signing off on the donor's IRS Form 8283 to confirm receipt of the gift and indicate whether it will be used for a purpose related to the museum's mission. The museum is not required to verify the appraised value of the gift, but this can raise a potential ethical dilemma when it is obvious the donor is inflating the value of the gift to obtain a larger than warranted deduction—a form of tax fraud.

TEMPORARY CUSTODY

Often as part of the process of considering an offered gift, the work is placed in the temporary custody of the museum so that the museum can examine the object, determine its authenticity and provenance, and consider whether it wants to accept the gifted work. While the work is in the temporary custody of the museum, it is held in trust for the owner under the legal concept of "bailment." The standard of care with which the museum is obligated to treat the object varies depending on who is benefitting from the bailment.

When an object is placed in the temporary custody of a non-owner, whether for the purposes of examination, authentication, conservation, consideration for acquisition, or loaned for exhibition, a bailment relationship is formed. The object is held in trust for the owner and the relationship between the owner and the possessor is that of bailor and bailee. The duty of care that a possessor-bailee owes to the owner-bailor depends on who is benefiting from the bailment. If the bailment is for the benefit of the owner-bailor, the possessor-bailee's duty of care is minimal: The possessor-bailee would only be liable for acts of gross negligence involving the object. If, on the other hand, the bailment is for the benefit of the possessor-bailee, then the possessor-bailee is held to a duty of great care and may be held liable for even slight acts of negligence. Where the bailment is for the mutual benefit of both parties, the possessor-bailee is held to an ordinary duty of care and may be liable for an ordinary degree of negligence.

As a best practice, museums should treat objects under temporary custody with the same degree of care as they would their own collections. It is also important to document the temporary custody of an object with a written "temporary custody" receipt. Policies and practices for handling objects in temporary custody can be addressed in the museum's collections management policy, including designating a staff member responsible for overseeing objects in temporary custody and establishing termination and return procedures. What the museum can do with the object while it is in its temporary custody—such as examining, researching and conserving it—should be discussed with the owner, carefully documented, and strictly followed, to avoid any misunderstandings.

PLEDGES AND PROMISED GIFTS

Sometimes a donor makes a promise to donate an object to the museum at some time in the future. Such a promise is sometimes called a "pledge" or a "promised gift." Whether a promised gift is binding on the donor and can be enforced by the museum depends on applicable state law. Putting the pledge in writing is essential. Many states have so-called "dead man" statutes that prohibit testimony on oral pledges made by a deceased donor. The written pledge or promised gift agreement should express the entire agreement of the parties—like the "dead man" rule, the "parole evidence" rule prevents testimony which contradicts the terms of the written agreement.

To be enforceable as a contract, the pledge must include an offer, acceptance, and consideration. The offer should be unconditional or conditioned on the occurrence of a specific event. To demonstrate offer and acceptance, the pledge should be signed by both the person promising the gift and someone with authority to act for the museum. Consideration should go both ways—the donor's consideration is the promise to make the donation, while the donee's consideration is the benefit conferred or agreed to be conferred on the donor. A description of how the gift is intended to be used by the museum may be enough in this regard.

Reliance on a promise is a substitute for consideration. If the museum relies on a promised gift and reneging on that promise would result in harm to the museum, the courts may find "detrimental reliance" and may enforce the promise based on the theory of "promissory estoppel." For this reason, a well-drafted pledge agreement states what action(s) the museum is taking or will take in reliance on the donor's promised gift. For example, the museum may agree to build a new gallery to house the promised gift. By taking steps in reliance on the gift, the promise may become enforceable.

A promised gift of a high value object like a painting by a famous artist may be encumbered (or may later become encumbered) by a security interest or other lien. Art collectors are increasingly using works in their collection as collateral for bank loans, either to buy more art or to pay other debts. For this reason, in some pledge situations, a museum may want to consider a Uniform Commercial Code (UCC) filing to ensure that the terms of the promised gift are not undermined. It is also good practice to check for UCC filings when accepting a gift or a promised gift of artwork to ensure that the work is not already encumbered by a lien.

Sometimes, after a donor makes a pledge or promised gift, his or her circumstances change such that the donor is either unable or unwilling to complete the gift. While a museum may have an enforceable pledge, in many situations the museum may be hesitant to sue the donor to enforce it. Whether such drastic action should be taken may depend on the circumstances surrounding the broken pledge as well as the extent to which the museum has relied on the promised gift. These are tricky situations where the museum's ongoing relationships with donors and potential donors, and the museum's reputation are at stake.

There are five main areas where disputes with pledges and gifts commonly arise. These include issues surrounding: the mental capacity of the donor to make the donation; the donor's authority to make the donation; the intent and purpose of the gift or promised gift; restrictions placed on the gift; and unanticipated changes in the circumstances of the donor. Any of these situations may result in a lawsuit regarding the enforceability of the gift and the museums rights and obligations with respect to the gift.

Once a gift is made, it is absolute and, barring a legal challenge to the validity of the gift, cannot be rescinded by the donor or anyone else. Except to the extent that the museum has agreed to any restrictions on the gift, the museum is the putative owner of the donated object. As with all its collections, the museum holds the donated object in trust for the public. While some museums have a policy of notifying donors (or the donor's heirs) if later the museum decides to dispose of, or "deaccession", the object, there is no legal obligation to do so.

ARTIST COMMISSIONS

Another way some museums acquire new works is by commissioning their creation by an artist. A typical commission arrangement involves the museum advancing funds to the artist to create a work that is then exhibited by the museum. Commissioning agreements take a variety of forms, and their contractual terms are often subject to detailed negotiations between the parties. An example of an artist commissioning agreement is included in the Cases and Other Readings section below.

Artist commissions can raise numerous complex contractual issues. Ownership and intellectual property rights in the commissioned work may be retained by the artist or acquired by the museum, depending on how the commission agreement is structured. Needless to say, care must be taken to clearly set out the expectations and obligations of each party to a commission agreement.

The lack of a written commissioning agreement can and often does, lead to dis-agreements and other problems. Recall the *Community for Creative Nonviolence* case discussed in the previous chapter: the central issue in that case involved ownership of the copyright in the completed work, which should have been addressed with "work-for-hire" language included in a written commissioning agreement. In *Massachusetts Museum of Contemporary Art v. Büchel*, included in the readings below, the artist never signed a commissioning agreement with the museum. Disagreements about the scope and budget for the project arose, and the museum went to court to seek clarification about its right to exhibit the unfinished work.

CASES AND OTHER READINGS

Reading Note: There are a variety of forms and templates used in connection with managing museum collections. Often it is the museum registrar who is responsible for keeping track of museum collections. The sample deed of gift and commissioning agreements below are just some of the many "boilerplate" agreements used by museum registrars to document transactions and other issues involving museum collections.

SAMPLE DEED OF GIFT

I (we) give, transfer, and assign to [INSERT NAME AND ADDRESS OF MUSEUM], irrevocably and unconditionally, with no restrictions, all right, title, and interests (including all copyright and related interests), which I (we) have, to the object(s) described below. I (we) affirm that I (we) own said object(s) and that to the best of my(our) knowledge I (we) have good and complete right, title, and interests to give.

Description of Gift: [DESCRIBE THE OBJECT(S) HERE OR ATTACH A LIST]

I/We wish that the gift be identified as:

"Gift of____________________________ 202__"

To the best of my/our belief, this gift is free and clear of all encumbrances and restrictions, and the object(s) has/have not been imported or exported into or from any country contrary to its laws.

Signature of Donor: ______________________________ (date) _______________

Signature of Donor: ______________________________ (date) _______________

Address of Donor(s): ____

The [INSERT NAME OF MUSEUM] hereby accepts the above described gift and acknowledges receipt of the same.

___________________________ (date) _______________

[INSERT NAME], Executive Director

Please complete this deed of gift and return one copy to:

Registrar

[MUSEUM NAME]

[MUSEUM ADDRESS]

Thank you for your generous gift to the [INSERT NAME OF MUSEUM].

SAMPLE MUSEUM COLLECTION GIFT AGREEMENT

This Museum Collection Gift Agreement is entered into this ____ day of __________, 202_ ("Effective Date") by and between [INSERT DONOR'S NAME AND ADDRESS] ("Donor") and [INSERT MUSEUM NAME AND ADDRESS]. For good and valuable consideration, the receipt and sufficiency of which is acknowledged, the parties agree as follows:

1. **Collection**. Donor hereby donates to Museum a collection consisting of [INSERT BRIEF DISCRIPTION OF OBJECTS BEING DONATED] ("Collection"). The Collection is more particularly described on the attached inventory, Attachment A, which is incorporated herein by reference. [OR: The accession record to be prepared by Museum will serve as evidence of the materials in the Collection.] Any additional materials that Donor gives to Museum will be governed by the terms of this Agreement unless Donor and Museum agree upon different terms in a writing made in advance of such additional gift.

2. **Copyright.** Donor hereby dedicates to the public domain such intellectual property as Donor may own in the Collection. [OR: Donor hereby transfers and assigns to Museum such intellectual property as Donor may own in the Collection.] [OR: Donor hereby dedicates to the public domain such intellectual property as Donor may own in the Collection.] [OR: Donor hereby transfers and assigns to Museum such intellectual property as Donor may own in the Collection], subject to the following exceptions: [LIST EXCEPTIONS HERE.] [OR: Donor reserves all rights in such intellectual property as Donor may own in the Collection, subject to the uses identified in Attachment __ hereto, which is incorporated herein by reference.]

3. **Warranties.** Donor warrants that, to the best of Donor's knowledge, Donor owns the physical property in the Collection, free and clear of any liens, and Donor has the full right, power and authority to transfer the Collection to Museum.

4. **Name of the Collection.** The Collection is to be known as ________________________.

5. **Use by Donor.** The following conditions govern use of the Collection by Donor for so long as the Collection is held by Museum: (a) Donor may access the Collection during Museum's normal business hours, consistent with Museum practices and procedures governing access by the general public; and, (b) In the event that Donor wishes to borrow materials from the Collection [for the purpose of [DESCRIBE THE PURPOSE HERE]], the parties will enter into an agreement of loan specifying such details as the materials to be borrowed, the term of the loan, shipping, and the care to be taken of the borrowed materials. Donor shall pay all shipping, insurance, and handling costs for borrowed materials, shall assume full responsibility for such materials, and shall reimburse Museum, for loss or damage to such materials. In the event of loss or damage to materials, the Donor and the Museum shall attempt to agree upon the replacement or repair value of the materials; if the parties cannot agree, however, Museum's valuation will control. If Donor wishes to borrow original materials from the Collection for which the Museum does not have a preservation copy, Museum may require that Donor pay for such a copy for inclusion in Museum's collections.

6. **Disposal.** Should Museum determine that any part of the Collection is inappropriate for retention but may be of interest to Donor or another museum, the Museum will provide Donor with sixty (60) days' prior written notice to elect return of the materials to Donor or to another museum selected by Donor. Museum shall provide such notice both by e-mail and by a method evidencing receipt (such as facsimile or certified mail, return receipt requested), to Donor as follows: [INSERT DONOR'S MAILING ADDRESS HERE]. Donor shall promptly notify Museum of any changes to Donor's contact information. Notice is effective when given. If Museum does not receive a response from Donor within sixty days of providing notice to Donor using Donor's most recent contact information as provided by Donor, Museum may proceed at its discretion.

7. **Choice of Law and Jurisdiction.** This agreement is to be governed by, and construed in accordance with, the law of [INSERT STATE]. Any action in regard to the agreement or arising out of its terms and conditions is to be instituted and litigated in the courts for [INSERT STATE].

In witness whereof, the authorized representatives of the parties have signed this agreement effective as of the last date of signature:

Donor

By: ____ (date) _______________

For the Museum

By: [INSERT NAME AND TITLE] _________________ (date) _______________

SAMPLE ART MUSEUM COMMISSION, INSTALLATION, AND EXHIBITION AGREEMENT

This Commission, Installation and Exhibition Agreement ("Agreement") is made effective as of [INSERT DATE] ("Effective Date"), by and between [INSERT NAME AND ADDRESS OF MUSEUM], ("Museum") and [INSERT NAME AND ADDRESS OF ARTIST] ("Artist") regarding an exhibition at the Museum of original work by the Artist, entitled _________________ ("Exhibition"). The Exhibition is scheduled for presentation to the public at the Museum from [INSERT START AND END DATES] ("Exhibition Period").

1. PROJECT DESCRIPTION

1.1 The Artist will conceive, produce, and participate in the fabrication and installation of an artwork [DESCRIBE HERE OR IN AN ATTACHEMENT] ("Artwork") to be installed in the Museum's [INSERT GALLERY/LOCATION] and exhibited throughout the Exhibition Period.

1.2 The Artwork shall be completed and installed no later than [INSERT DATE].

2. RESPONSIBILITIES OF THE ARTIST

2.1 The Artist shall be wholly responsible, at Artist's sole expense, for the production and fabrication of the Artwork.

2.2 The Artist will collaborate with representatives of the Museum [INSERT NAMES/TITLES OR INCLUDE IN AN ATTACHEMENT] during the preparation and installation of the Artwork.

2.3 The Artist will attend an opening reception for the Exhibition, scheduled for [INSERT DATE, TIME AND LOCATION], and will also be available for such additional events as may be arranged by the Museum.

2.4 The Artist agrees to give interviews and speak with selected members of the press concerning the Exhibition and the Artwork, if so requested by the Museum.

2.5 The Artist will participate in public programs and other events and will speak to the Museum docents and staff, if requested by the Museum. The format and scheduling will be mutually agreed upon by the Artist and the Museum.

2.6 The Artist hereby assigns the Museum the irrevocable right to create, publish, and to circulate for publication by the Museum or the media, reproductions or derivative works of any and all existing works by the Artist, and views of the Artwork in progress as well as views of the finished Artwork for any Museum purpose, in any and all formats or media including, but not limited to the Exhibition catalogue, the Museum's membership magazine, annual report, press releases, brochures, advertisements, and website; and reviews and features in newspaper and periodical articles, broadcast television reports, and internet websites. Such photographic documentation carried out by the Museum, and any copyright therein, shall be the sole property of the Museum.

2.7 Any reproduction or subsequent exhibition of the Artwork produced as a result of this Agreement shall include the following exhibition credit: [INSERT CREDIT LINE].

2.8 The final disposition of the Artwork will be decided jointly by the Artist and the Museum in time to arrange for its transfer at the conclusion of the Exhibition, subject to the terms and conditions of this Agreement.

2.9 Unless otherwise expressly agreed by the parties in writing, the Museum shall have no obligation to retain the Artwork at the Museum facility or in storage at the end of the Exhibition.

3. RESPONSIBILITIES OF THE MUSEUM

[INSERT IF APPLICABLE WHERE FOUNDATION/THIRD PARTY IS PAYING THE COSTS] shall be solely responsible for all financial obligations of the Museum under this Agreement.

3.1 The Museum will provide a per diem of [INSERT AMOUNT] for the Artist during the installation period, tentatively scheduled to begin [INSERT DATE] through [INSERT DATE] ("Installation Period") to enable the Artist to complete the project and then attend the opening events referred to in Section 2.3 above. Notwithstanding the above, the Artist shall complete and install the Artwork no later than [INSERT DATE].

3.2 The Museum will arrange and pay for the Artist's lodging (room and tax only): 1 room for approximately [INSERT #] nights during the installation period.

3.3 The Museum will pay for one roundtrip coach class airfare for the Artist from [INSERT TO/FROM LOCATIONS IF APPLICABLE].

3.4 The Museum will provide technical assistance and personnel to facilitate installation of the Artwork in conjunction with the Artist. The Artist shall comply with the Museum's requirements and staff instructions regarding installation and shall not use any materials or supplies that the Museum determines, in its sole discretion, would damage the Museum's assets or facilities or otherwise pose a risk to persons or property.

3.5 The Museum will prepare and publish an Exhibition Catalogue in connection with the Exhibition, the look and scale of which will be determined by the Museum. In accordance with the Museum's standard Exhibition Catalogue distribution guidelines, the Museum will give the Artist [INSERT NUMBER] free copies of the Exhibition Catalogue. Additional copies may be purchased by Artist at a [INSERT DISCOUNT] percent discount off the retail price, or at Museum's actual cost, whichever is greater.

3.6 The Museum and/or its affiliated support groups plan to arrange a public artist reception scheduled for [INSERT DATE, TIME AND LOCATION]. The time and nature of museum events is subject to change, any such changes to be communicated to the Artist.

3.7 The Artist and the Museum will agree to a maintenance schedule for the installation/Artwork prior to the Exhibition's opening.

3.8 The Museum will not restore, conserve, or otherwise alter the Artwork without notifying the Artist unless the Museum determines that the immediate safety of the Artwork, the Museum, or the public is involved. Any emergency alterations will be recorded and forwarded to the Artist. The Museum may, at any time and at its sole discretion modify, relocate or remove all or any part of the Artwork if it is deemed by the Museum to be hazardous to other artworks, the building, or visitors or because of any other legal requirements or accessibility issues. The Museum, in its sole discretion, may also relocate or remove parts of the Artwork temporarily or for repairs, if needed. With respect to the Artwork produced under this Agreement for exhibition in the Museum's facility and any reproductions of such Artwork made for any Museum purpose, and notwithstanding any other provision of this Agreement, the Artist hereby waives any and all claims against the Museum [INSERT ANY OTHER AFFILIATED INDIVIDUALS/ENTITIES] arising at any time and under any circumstances, under the under the federal Visual Artists Rights Act (17 U.S.C. §§ 106A and 113(d)), the California Art Preservation Act (Cal. Civil Code §§ 987 et seq.), and other local, state, federal and international laws that convey rights of the same nature.

3.9 The Museum agrees that people responsible for the security of the Exhibition shall be present in the Exhibition area whenever it is open to the public and that the Exhibition area will be secured and alarmed at all other times. The Museum shall take the same precautionary measures to protect and conserve the Exhibition objects, including the Artwork, from possible disasters, including earthquakes, as it does for like objects in its own collection.

4. PACKING, SHIPPING, AND INSTALLATION

4.1 Packing and shipping of the Artwork from [INSERT ORIGINAL LOCATION] to and from the Museum shall be arranged by the Museum's Registrar in conjunction with the Artist, with the assistance of professional fine art packers and shippers.

4.2 The Museum, represented by the Museum Registrar, and the Artist will determine mutually convenient dates for the inbound and outbound shipments of the Artwork.

4.3 The Artist certifies that the objects lent are in such condition as to withstand ordinary strains of packing, transportation, and handling.

4.4 Costs of professional fine art packers and shippers will be paid for by the Museum, who will be billed directly for those services, subject to Museum's prior written approval. The Museum will provide qualified packers for unpacking and repacking.

4.5 The Museum agrees to de-install and have the Artwork packed and ready for shipping after the Exhibition closes, according to the mutually agreed-upon schedule. All of the objects will be repacked in the same crates and in the same manner in which they are received.

4.6 The Artist agrees to meet all Museum requirements and schedules required for the safety of the installation and Artwork, and its timely shipment to and from the Museum.

4.7 The Artwork will be returned only to the Artist, and not a third party, at the address stated at the beginning of this Agreement or to a new location within the same or a shorter geographic range. Any such parts that the Artist does not wish returned to him shall be disposed of at the discretion of the Museum.

4.8 If the legal ownership of the Artwork should change during the Exhibition period, whether by reason of death, sale, insolvency, gift or otherwise, the Artist or the

Artist's agent will, prior to its return, be required to establish its legal right to receive or redirect the delivery of the Artwork by proof satisfactory to the Museum. The new owner shall be responsible to pay any difference in the shipment charges due to the change of the address. If the Artist wishes to send materials to a third party, the Artist must absorb all costs associated with the shipping and insurance.

5. INSURANCE AND PROCEDURES IN THE EVENT OF LOSS OR DAMAGE

5.1 Insurance coverage for the Artwork while in transit to and from the Museum and while on display will be provided by the Museum.

5.2 Prior to shipping of the Artwork, the Museum will provide the Artist with a Loss Payee coverage document naming Artist as Loss Payee under the Museum's fine arts insurance policy. The Museum's insurance will provide "all risks," wall-to-wall fine arts insurance coverage, subject to standard exclusions, including coverage in the event of an earthquake, and shall be in such amount and subject to such conditions as are reasonably satisfactory to the Museum. Prior to the shipment of the Artwork, the Artist shall provide Museum with reasonable insurance value that reflects the fair market value for the Artwork.

5.3 If any loss or damage appears to have occurred in transit, the Museum will preserve all packing materials for inspection by the shipper and will photograph the packing materials, crate and art objects.

5.4 If the installation/Artwork suffers damage to a part or parts, which have been industrially fabricated and can be replaced to Artist's specifications, the amount of such insurance shall be limited to the cost of such replacement.

5.5 Any disputes concerning the value of the damages and losses shall be resolved by a committee that includes a representative of the Museum, a representative of the Artist, and an independent expert appointed by both parties or as otherwise required by the Museum's fine arts insurance policy.

5.6 Notwithstanding any other provisions in this Agreement, the Museum's total liability under this Agreement for the Artwork shall not exceed the total insurance coverage for the Artwork. In the event of loss or damage, the amount payable by the insurance secured by the Museum under this Agreement, if any, shall be the sole recovery available to the Artist from the Museum [INSERT OTHER AFFILIATED ENTITIES]. Any recovery for depreciation of loss of value of an object shall be calculated as a percentage of the insured value of the object. The Artist agrees to comply with the procedures and requirements of the Museum's insurance policy and providers in the event of a claim.

5.7 With respect to losses or damages to persons or property other than the Artwork, Artist agrees to assume the risk for any injuries, damages or losses ("Losses") by Artist, Artist's employees, agents, invitees or contractors, while creating or installing the Artwork under this Agreement and hereby releases the Museum [INSERT OTHER AFFILIATED ENTITIES] for any and all related claims and liability for such Losses.

6. APPLICABLE LAW AND DISPUTE RESOLUTION

6.1 Matters relating to the subject matter hereof, but not specifically covered by the Agreement shall be resolved between parties in good faith.

6.2 Both parties hereby consent to the jurisdiction of the State of [INSERT STATE WHERE EITHER MUSEUM OR ARTIST IS LOCATED] with respect to all matters governed hereunder.

7. INABILITY TO PERFORM

7.1 If the Artist is unable, for any reason, to conceive, produce or set up the Artwork as agreed upon, the Artist shall return all monies paid to him.

8. FORCE MAJEURE

8.1 Neither party shall be liable in damages or have the rights to terminate this Agreement for any delay or default in performing hereunder if such delay or default is caused by conditions beyond its control including, but not limited to Acts of God, Government restrictions (including the denial or cancellation of any export or other necessary license), wars, insurrections and/or any other cause beyond the reasonable control of the party whose performance is affected.

9. UNDERSTANDING OF AGREEMENT

9.1 This Agreement contains the final terms, conditions and financial arrangements as entered into both parties. Any amendments to the Agreement will be with the written mutual consent of both parties.

9.2 The Agreement shall be effective from the Effective Date set forth above.

IN WITNESS WHEREOF, both parties shall each make and possess the original Agreements signed by the authorized signatories.

[INSERT APPROPRIATE SIGNATURE BLOCK—NAMES/TITLES, OTHER REQUIRED APPROVALS]

_______________________________ _______________________________

For the Artist *Date*

_______________________________ _______________________________

For the Museum *Date*

STUDY QUESTIONS

- Assess the sample Deed of Gift and Museum Collection Deed of Gift. What recommendations would you make to improve these agreements? How would the terms of a purchase agreement differ from those of these gift agreements? What other form agreements do you think should a museum prepare and have on hand with regard to managing its museum collections?

Reading Note: The case below raises a number of issues involving an art installation commissioned by the Massachusetts Museum of Contemporary Art (Mass MoCA). While the museum negotiated a written commissioning agreement, the artist never signed it. After disagreements arose over the scope and budget for the project, the museum initiated this lawsuit, seeking a "declaratory judgement" regarding its rights to display the unfinished work. The artist counter-sued, asserting that his "moral rights" under the Visual Artist's Rights Act (VARA) included the right to control exhibition of the work. For more on VARA, see chapter 4.

MASSACHUSETTS MUSEUM OF CONTEMPORARY ART FOUNDATION V. BÜCHEL

593 F.3d 38 (2010) Before LIPEZ and HOWARD, Circuit Judges, and WOODCOCK, District Judge. LIPEZ, Circuit Judge.

As one observer has noted, this case, which raises important and unsettled legal issues under the Visual Artists Rights Act ("VARA"), may well serve as "the ultimate how-not-to guide in the complicated world of installation art." Geoff Edgers, *Dismantled,* The Boston Globe, Oct. 21, 2007, at 1N. Artist Christoph Büchel conceived of an ambitious, football-field-sized art installation entitled *Training Ground for Democracy*, which was to be exhibited at the Massachusetts Museum of Contemporary Art ("MASS MoCA," or "the Museum"). Unfortunately, the parties never memorialized the terms of their relationship or their understanding of the intellectual property issues involved in the installation in a written agreement. Even more unfortunately, the project was never completed. Numerous conflicts and a steadily deteriorating relationship between the artist and the Museum prevented the completion of *Training Ground for Democracy* in its final form.

In the wake of this failed endeavor, the Museum went to federal court seeking a declaration that it was "entitled to present to the public the materials and partial constructions" it had collected for *Training Ground for Democracy*. Büchel responded with several counterclaims under VARA and the Copyright Act,[NOTE 1] seeking an injunction that would prevent MASS MoCA from displaying the unfinished installation and damages for the Museum's alleged violations of his rights under both VARA and the general Copyright Act.

On cross-motions for summary judgment, the district court assumed that VARA applies to unfinished works of art, but it nonetheless ruled for the Museum in all respects because, even granting VARA's applicability, it found no genuine issues of material fact. *Massachusetts Museum of Contemporary Art Found., Inc. v. Büchel*, 565 F. Supp. 2d 245 (D.Mass. 2008). Büchel appeals. Because we find that, if VARA applies, genuine issues of material fact would foreclose summary judgment on one of Büchel's VARA claims—that MASS MoCA violated his right of artistic integrity by modifying the installation—we cannot assume that VARA applies to unfinished works but instead must decide its applicability. We conclude that the statute does apply to such works.

We further conclude that, in addition to his VARA claim, Büchel asserts a viable claim under the Copyright Act that MASS MoCA violated his exclusive right to display his work publicly. Accordingly, we reverse in part the grant of summary judgment for MASS MoCA and remand for further proceedings.

I.

A. The Parties

MASS MoCA opened in 1999 as a center for the creation and display of contemporary art. The Museum "seeks to catalyze and support the creation of new art, expose [its] visitors to bold visual and performing art in all stages of production, and re-invigorate the life of a region in socioeconomic need." Massachusetts Museum of Contemporary Art, Mission Statement, http://www.massmoca.org/mission.php (last visited Jan. 13, 2010). In its expansive facility in North Adams, Massachusetts, the Museum strives to "make the whole cloth of art making, presentation and public participation a seamless continuum." *Id.* Over the last decade, the Museum has hosted the production and presentation of over sixty exhibits of visual art, including over 600 works of art by more than 250 individual artists. Some of

In 2006, Mass MoCA commissioned an installation by Swiss artist Christoph Büchel. Entitled Training Ground for Democracy, *the work was intended to be an experiential statement about life in the post-911 world. A dispute soon developed, with Mass MoCA expressing concern over the growing cost and scope of the project, and Büchel objecting to the museum's handling of the installation.*

these works have been displayed in Building 5, the Museum's signature exhibition space, which spans the length of a football field. The Museum strives to "offer visual artists the tools and time to create works of a scale and duration impossible to realize in the time and space-cramped conditions of most museums," and MASS MoCA prides itself on exposing its audiences to "all stages of art production: rehearsals, sculptural fabrication, and developmental workshops are frequently on view, as are finished works of art." *Id.*

Christoph Büchel is a Swiss visual artist who lives and works in Basel, Switzerland. He is "known for building elaborate, politically provocative environments for viewers to wander, and sometimes to crawl, through." Randy Kennedy, *The Show Will Go On, but the Art Will Be Shielded,* N.Y. Times, May 22, 2007, at E1 ("*The Show Will Go On*"). One critic has stated that "Mr. Büchel's environments are huge in scale," "like bristling three-dimensional history paintings," yet are "so obsessively detailed that they might best be described as panoramic collage." Roberta Smith, *Is It Art Yet? And Who Decides?,* N.Y. Times, Sept. 16, 2007, at 21.

B. Factual Background

Focusing first on those facts that are undisputed, we sketch the course of dealings between Büchel and MASS MoCA to put this appeal in context.[NOTE 2] MASS MoCA became interested in planning a new installation with Büchel. The artist visited the North Adams facility in October 2005 to begin preliminary discussions regarding the project, and those discussions continued into 2006. At some point during this time, Büchel proposed, and the Museum agreed to, a project entitled "*Training Ground for Democracy.*" As Museum Director Joseph Thompson indicated in a letter to Büchel's gallery representatives, MASS MoCA understood that "Büchel's projects typically require a lengthy period of installation and preparation," and that, given the gallery space of Building 5, "this project [would] be his largest venture to date."

Büchel conceived of the exhibit as "essentially a village, ... contain[ing] several major architectural and structural elements integrated into a whole, through which a visitor could walk (and climb)." According to an affidavit submitted to the district court, Büchel envisioned the work in the following way:

> It was to adopt the role-play of U.S. military training for its visitors, who would be given the opportunity to "virtually" change their own various iden-

> tities in relation to the collective project called "democracy": training to be an immigrant, training to vote, protest, and revolt, training to loot, training iconoclasm, training to join a political rally, training to be the objects of propaganda, training to be interrogated and detained and to be tried or to judge, training to reconstruct a disaster, training to be in conditions of suspended law, and training various other social and political behavior.

In August 2006, Büchel spent ten days in residence at MASS MoCA. During this time, he and a partner prepared a basic schematic model of the proposed installation. MASS MoCA agreed to acquire, at Büchel's direction but its own expense, the materials and items necessary for the project.

Unfortunately, the parties never formalized the contours of their relationship or firmly established the project's financial scope and precise specifications by executing any written instrument. Although MASS MoCA's curator, Nato Thompson (no relation to the Museum Director),[NOTE 3] sent Büchel's gallery sales representative in the United States a letter on September 14, 2006 that was designed to "formalize [the parties'] relationship on this project," there is no indication that Büchel himself ever saw, much less signed, this proposal.[NOTE 4] The gallery responded with a proposed contract of its own, providing that MASS MoCA should bear the costs of transporting and organizing the various materials for the installation. The Museum did not respond to this proposal. Additionally, it is undisputed that Büchel never signed a document waiving any rights to which he would otherwise be entitled under VARA. The parties did apparently agree, however, that once the planned installation was finished, and after the public exhibition period had concluded, MASS MoCA would not contest Büchel's sole title to any copyright in the completed work. The parties set an opening date of December 16, 2006 for the exhibit.

Over the course of the fall, tensions began to develop between the artist and MASS MoCA employees, particularly Joseph Thompson. "In summary, the museum felt the artist's directions were vague, and his financial and logistical demands were increasingly unreasonable; the artist felt the museum was compromising his artistic integrity and failing to follow his instructions." *MASS MoCA,* 565 F.Supp.2d at 247. One frequent source of conflict between the parties was the budget, with the Museum understandably concerned about keeping its costs for the massive project under control, and Büchel understandably insistent that his vision for *Training Ground* be fully realized. But as the district court correctly noted, "[t]he dispute about these financial understandings is not material" to whether Büchel has presented triable claims under either VARA or the Copyright Act, *id.* at 250, and we therefore need not focus on its messy details.

Instead, for our purposes, the key conflict between MASS MoCA and the artist involved Büchel's dissatisfaction with the way in which the Museum was implementing his instructions and procuring the items necessary for the installation. Büchel himself was not present in North Adams for the first several months of work on the project. Instead, he conducted much of his work on the installation throughout the fall of 2006 remotely, by providing Museum personnel with detailed instructions as to the particular materials he required and their placement within the exhibition space.

In the words of the district court, "[a]t various points in the development of the installation, Büchel proposed several major components," some but not all of which later became part of the installation "as its elements evolved through discussions with MASS MoCA during the construction process." *Id.* These major components included a movie theater, a house, a bar, a mobile home, various sea containers, a bomb carousel, and an aircraft fuselage. *Id.* The Museum had begun seeking out some of these materials and others for potential use in the installation as soon as Büchel left North Adams at the end of August 2006, and continued to do so throughout the fall. One of the Museum's curators described the search for these items (at Büchel's direction) as "the ultimate scavenger hunt." However, problems soon arose, especially between Thompson and Büchel, as to the progress of the project, particularly when, as Thompson explained in an internal Museum email dated October 28, 2006, he had tried to "move the project along" by "making a few decisions in [Büchel's] stead." Thompson noted that Büchel, whom he described as having "clear vision" and "rock solid integrity," had taken "extreme, mortal … offense" to Thompson's efforts.

On October 29, 2006, Büchel returned to North Adams to complete *Training Ground for Democracy*, and three of his assistants from Switzerland arrived shortly thereafter. Unhappy with some of the work that had been done by the Museum in his absence, Büchel felt that certain logistical and organizational failures by the Museum had endangered the timely opening of the show. Büchel wrote in an email to Thompson that he would not allow the Museum to open an "unfinished show in my name, since you are responsible for this major delay." By early December 2006, Büchel insisted that the Museum postpone the opening of the show and asserted that he would not "accept an opening of a work in progress or other compromise." During the first week of the month, MASS MoCA agreed to delay the opening, posting the following message on its website: "Due to logistical complexities encountered by the museum in preparing galleries for Christoph Büchel's vast installation, the exhibition's official opening date… will be re-scheduled."

Büchel remained onsite at the Museum working on *Training Ground* until December 17, 2006, when he left for the holidays. In Büchel's estimation, *Training Ground* was then only about 40% complete. At the time, he planned to return on January 8, 2007, in order to finish the work in time for a March 3 opening. When he left North Adams, the artist was obviously disappointed with the progress of *Training Ground.* He called the Museum disorganized and faulted it for underestimating the scope of his project. He felt that Museum employees, by failing to precisely carry out his detailed instructions and making artistic decisions in his stead, had generated even more work for his crew, as numerous components of the installation had to be reworked to Büchel's specifications. In general, he felt that the Museum was trying to scale back his artistic vision without consulting him.

Meanwhile, the Museum was running out of money for the project. In an attempt to secure further funding, it disregarded Büchel's express wishes and, in late December 2006, asked for money from his galleries. Angry and frustrated, the artist wrote that he would not move forward with the installation until "all financial problems are solved, regarding ALL elements of the show and until my crew is being sure that they [are] getting paid." By mid-January 2007, tensions had escalated to the point where Büchel informed the Museum that he would not return to continue work on *Training Ground* unless certain conditions, both financial and artistic, were met.

In Büchel's absence, MASS MoCA staff continued to work on the installation. The parties disagree as to whether the employees were merely executing instructions left by the artist or whether their actions represented independent artistic judgment, exercised in direct contravention of Büchel's express wishes. The parties also disagree as to whether, in the spring of 2007, while negotiations had stalled but work on the installation was ongoing, the Museum promoted—and even showed—the unfinished work to numerous visitors without Büchel's consent, in one form or another.

As the vitriolic exchanges between the parties continued, and negotiations over the project's eventual completion became hopeless, *Training Ground* languished in its unfinished state. It became clear that Büchel would not complete the installation. On May 22, 2007, MASS MoCA announced the cancellation of *Training Ground,* and contemporaneously publicized the opening of a new exhibit entitled *Made at MASS MoCA*, which was to be "a documentary project exploring the issues raised in the course of complex collaborative projects between artists and institutions." Massachusetts Museum of Contemporary Art, Press Release, *Presentation of Training Ground for Democracy Cancelled; New Exhibition, Made at MASS MoCA, to Open on Saturday, May 26* (Press Release), available at http://www.massmoca.org/event_details.php?id=144 (May 22, 2007). The press release noted that this lawsuit had been filed the previous day; it also highlighted the Museum's desire to use its "other experiences working with artists" to "provide [its] audience with thought-provoking insights into the complexities of the art-making process." *Id.* The release further explained that, due to "space constraints imposed by the materials assembled for *Training Ground for Democracy,*" the exhibition would be presented in the Museum's "only remaining available gallery space"; therefore, in order to enter the exhibit, visitors would have to pass through Building 5, "housing the materials and unfinished fabrications that were to have comprised elements of *Training Ground for Democracy.*" *Id.* The Museum represented that "[r]easonable steps [had] been taken to control and restrict the view of these materials, pending a court ruling."

When *Made at MASS MoCA* opened, many in the art world disagreed with the Museum's handling of its dispute with Büchel, though the parties have different views on whether the Museum's actions ultimately tarnished the artist's reputation. Moreover, the parties differ on whether the "reasonable steps ... taken to control and restrict the view of the materials"—the placement of yellow tarpaulins over the unfinished work—actually concealed all of the individual components and vital design elements of *Training Ground*, or whether the tarpaulins simply "hid an elephant behind a napkin," effectively inviting individuals to peek behind the cloth coverings and view the unfinished work. *See* Charles Giuliano, *Christoph Buchel's Tarp Art at Mass MoCA: Crap Under Wrap* (July 31, 2007) (*Crap Under Wrap*), *available at* http://www.berkshirefinearts.com/show_article.php?article_id=368 & category=finearts.

C. Procedural Background

The Museum sued Büchel on May 21, 2007, in the United States District Court for the District of Massachusetts. The complaint asserted a single claim for declaratory relief under VARA. The Museum sought a declaration that it was "entitled to present to the public the materials and partial constructions assembled in connection with an exhibit planned with the Swiss artist Büchel." Büchel responded by asserting five counterclaims against the Museum. The first sought a declaratory judgment and an injunction under VARA prohibiting the Museum from publicly displaying "the unfinished Work of Art or any of its component elements." The second sought damages for MASS MoCA's alleged violations of Büchel's VARA rights by "intentionally distort[ing] and modif[ying] the Work of Art" and allowing members of the public to "see and pass through" the unfinished work, both with and without the yellow tarpaulins. The third, fourth and fifth counterclaims sought damages and injunctive relief under the Copyright Act based on alleged violations of Büchel's right to publicly display and create derivative works from his work.

On MASS MoCA's motion, the court ordered an expedited discovery schedule that included a private viewing by the district court of Building 5 and the unfinished installation. After the close of discovery, both sides filed cross-motions seeking summary judgment on the complaint and all counterclaims. On September 21, 2007, the court held oral argument on the cross-motions and ruled from the bench. That decision addressed only the Museum's original complaint seeking declaratory relief to allow public display of the partially completed project and Büchel's corresponding counterclaim seeking to prevent the Museum from showing the then-existing work. The court ruled in favor of the Museum, noting that nothing in VARA prevented MASS MoCA from showing the incomplete project. Therefore, MASS MoCA was "entitled to present" the unfinished installation to the public as long as it posted a disclaimer that would "inform anyone viewing the exhibit that the materials assembled in Building 5 constitute an unfinished project that [did] not carry out the installation's original intent." The court correspondingly denied the artist's request for injunctive relief barring public display of the unfinished installation, ruling that he had failed to prove a likelihood of success on the merits of his VARA claim. The court stated that it would "in the coming weeks" issue a detailed memorandum explaining its oral rulings and addressing the remaining claims.

However, several days after obtaining the ruling in its favor, MASS MoCA changed course. The Museum posted an announcement on its website stating that it had "begun removing materials gathered for *Training Ground for Democracy* and [would] not permit the public to enter the planned installation.» MASS MoCA Blog, "We'll Remove *Training Ground,*" http://blog.massmoca.org/2007/09/28/well-remove-training-ground/ (Sept. 28, 2007) (last visited Jan. 13, 2010).

On July 11, 2008, the district court issued its written opinion, recognizing that some of the issues presented in the case were now moot, but nevertheless wishing to explain its holding and to address the VARA and Copyright Act claims remaining in the case. The court summarized its holding this way:

> When an artist makes a decision to begin work on a piece of art and handles the process of creation long-distance via e-mail, using someone else's property, someone else's materials, someone else's money, someone else's staff, and, to a significant extent, someone else's suggestions regarding the details of fabrication—with no enforceable written or oral contract defining the parties' relationship—and that artist becomes unhappy part-way through the project and abandons it, then nothing in the Visual Artists Rights Act or elsewhere in the Copyright Act gives that artist the right to dictate what that "someone else" does with what he has left behind, so long as the remnant is not explicitly labeled as the artist's work. No right of artistic "attribution" or "integrity," as those terms are conceived by VARA, is implicated, let alone violated in these circumstances. Similarly, the Copyright Act provides no mechanism for relief, legal or equitable, to an artist such as Defendant Büchel here, based on the decision of an exhibitor such as Plaintiff MASS MoCA to allow patrons to walk past covered components of an unfinished installation.

565 F.Supp.2d at 248-29. The court therefore granted MASS MoCA's motion for summary judgment and denied Büchel's, entering judgment for the Museum on its claim for declaratory relief as well as on all five of Büchel's counterclaims. Büchel appeals.

II.

Passed in 1990, the Visual Artists Rights Act, 17 U.S.C. § 106A, was an amendment to the Copyright Act that protects the "moral rights" of certain visual artists in the works they create, consistent with Article 6*bis* of the Berne Convention. *Phillips v. Pembroke Real Estate, Inc.,* 459 F.3d 128, 133 (1st Cir.2006); *Carter v. Helmsley-Spear, Inc.,* 71 F.3d 77, 83 (2d Cir.1995) (citing H.R.Rep. No. 101-514, at 5 (1990) ("House Report"), *as reprinted in* 1990 U.S.C.C.A.N. 6915, 6917).[NOTE 5] The "rubric of moral rights encompasses many varieties of rights," but the two most widely recognized are attribution and integrity. *Id.* at 81 (citing Ralph E. Lerner & Judith Bresler, *Art Law* 417, 420 (1989)). We will discuss both of these in detail below, but note briefly now that the right of attribution protects the author's right to be identified as the author of his work and also protects against the use of his name in connection with works created by others. *Id.* The right of integrity "allows the author to prevent any deforming or mutilating changes to his work."

Id. Although these moral rights "exist independent[ly] of the economic rights" granted to all authors under the Copyright Act, 5 William F. Patry, *Patry on Copyright* § 16:1 (2009), they are part of the same statutory framework.

A. The Copyright Act

Under the Copyright Act, "[c]opyright protection subsists ... in original works of authorship fixed in any tangible medium of expression." 17 U.S.C. § 102(a). A copyright owner has certain exclusive rights to the work, which are enumerated in 17 U.S.C. § 106. *T-Peg, Inc. v. Vermont Timber Works, Inc.,* 459 F.3d 97, 108 (1st Cir.2006). Of particular relevance to this litigation, the copyright holder has the exclusive right to publicly display the copyrighted work and to prepare derivative works based upon it. 17 U.S.C. § 106(5), (2). "One infringes a copyright when he or she violates one of the exclusive rights to a work held by a copyright owner, and the owner has the right to sue for infringement." *T-Peg, Inc.,* 459 F.3d at 108 (citing 17 U.S.C. § 501). The remedies provided by the Copyright Act include injunctive relief and actual or statutory damages. *See* 17 U.S.C. §§ 502, 504. [NOTE 6]

B. VARA

Beyond the Copyright Act's protections of certain economic rights, VARA provides additional and independent protections to authors of works of visual art. *See Carter,* 71 F.3d at 81-83. A work of visual art is defined to include "a painting, drawing, print, or sculpture,[NOTE 7] existing in a single copy" or in a limited edition. 17 U.S.C. § 101. The definition specifically excludes a number of works that are otherwise copyrightable, including motion pictures and other audiovisual works, books, posters, periodicals, works made for hire, and merchandising, advertising, promotional, or packaging materials. *Id.*

VARA provides that, in addition to the exclusive rights provided by section 106 of the Copyright Act, but subject to certain limitations, the author of a work of visual art

(1) shall have the right—

(A) to claim authorship of that work, and

(B) to prevent the use of his or her name as the author of any work of visual art which he or she did not create;

(2) shall have the right to prevent the use of his or her name as the author of the work of visual art in the event of a distortion, mutilation, or other modification of the work which would be prejudicial to his or her honor or reputation; and

(3) subject to the limitations set forth in section 113(d), shall have the right—

(A) to prevent any intentional distortion, mutilation, or other modification of that work which would be prejudicial to his or her honor or reputation, and any intentional distortion, mutilation, or modification of that work is a violation of that right, and

(B) to prevent any destruction of a work of recognized stature, and any intentional or grossly negligent destruction of that work is a violation of that right.

17 U.S.C. § 106A(a).

VARA's passage reflected Congress's belief that the art covered by the Act "meet[s] a special societal need, and [its] protection and preservation serve an important public interest." House Report at 5-6, *as reprinted in* 1990 U.S.C.C.A.N. at 6915-16. To encourage the creation of such art, VARA protects the "moral rights" of its creators. These are "rights of a spiritual, non-economic and personal nature" that exist "independently of an artist's copyright in his or her work" and "spring from a belief that an artist in the process of creation injects his spirit into the work and that the artist's personality, as well as the integrity of the work, should therefore be protected and preserved." *Carter,* 71 F.3d at 81. The recognition of moral rights fosters a "'climate of artistic worth and honor that encourages the author in the arduous act of creation.'" *Id.* at 83 (quoting House Report at 6, *as reprinted in* 1990 U.S.C.C.A.N. at 6915). Although an artist may not transfer his VARA rights (as they are considered an extension of his personality), he may waive those rights by "expressly agree[ing] to such waiver in a written instrument." 17 U.S.C. § 106A(e)(1). Also, "[a]ll remedies available under copyright law, other than criminal remedies, are available in an action for infringement of moral rights." *Carter,* 71 F.3d at 83 (citing 17 U.S.C. § 506); *see also* 17 U.S.C. § 501(a).[NOTE 8] More specifically, by guaranteeing the moral rights of "attribution" and "integrity," VARA "'protects both the reputations of certain visual artists and the works of art they create.'" *Carter,* 71 F.3d at 83 (quoting House Report at 6, *as reprinted in* 1990 U.S.C.C.A.N. at 6915). Before discussing the precise contours of these rights, we consider whether, as a threshold matter, the indisputably unfinished *Training Ground for Democracy* was a "work of visual art" within the meaning of VARA.

C. Does VARA Apply to Unfinished Works of Art?

Büchel argues that the district court erred by failing to recognize that VARA applies with equal force to incomplete artistic endeavors that would otherwise be subject to VARA protection. He asserts that the Act's plain language compels such a conclusion, which he claims is confirmed by the legislative history and sparse case law interpreting the statute. The Museum, for its part, does not argue that unfinished works are excluded from VARA's scope. Instead, it interprets the district court's opinion as "expressly assum[ing]" that VARA applied to *Training Ground for Democracy* in its incomplete state, and then concluding that Büchel had failed to put forth sufficient evidence to raise a triable issue regarding the violation of his rights under the statute.

We do not read the district court's ruling to conclude categorically that VARA does not apply to unfinished works. Rather, the court held that, if the statute applied, "display of th[e] unfinished installation would have violated neither Büchel's right of attribution nor his right of integrity." 565 F. Supp. 2d at 259. Nonetheless, the court repeatedly expressed skepticism about Büchel's claim that the incomplete *Training Ground* fell within VARA's scope, observing at one point in its opinion that "unfinished art may not be covered by VARA at all." *Id.* at 258; *see also id.* at 259 ("[I]t is doubtful that VARA even covered the assembled materials that constituted this unfinished installation."). Moreover, the court qualified the statute's application to unfinished works: "To the extent that an artist seeks protection for an uncompleted work, a violation of one of VARA's two explicitly recognized rights must be demonstrated with special clarity." *Id.* at 258.

Our review of the district court's interpretation of VARA is de novo. *Phillips,* 459 F.3d at 139. "'As in all statutory construction cases, we begin with the language of the statute,'" *id.* (quoting *Barnhart v. Sigmon Coal Co.,* 534 U.S. 438, 450, 122 S. Ct. 941, 151 L. Ed. 2d 908 (2002)), and "[i]f the meaning of the text is unambiguous our task ends there as well," *United States v. Godin,* 534 F.3d 51, 56 (1st Cir. 2008). "If the statute's language is plain, the sole function of the courts—at least where the disposition required by the text is not absurd—is to enforce it according to its terms." *In re Rudler,* 576 F.3d 37, 44 (1st Cir.2009) (quotation marks and citations omitted).

The definition of a "work of visual art" for VARA purposes is stated "in terms both positive (what it is) and negative (what it is not)." *Carter,* 71 F.3d at 84. An unfinished sculptural installation such as *Training Ground for Democracy* is not one of the items specifically excluded from VARA protection,[NOTE 9] and MASS MoCA wisely does not attempt to argue otherwise. Instead, we must determine whether the "positive" aspect of the definition of "work of visual art" includes an *unfinished* version of a «sculpture existing in a single copy." 17 U.S.C. § 101.

The text of VARA itself does not state when an artistic project becomes a work of visual art subject to its protections. However, VARA is part of the Copyright Act, and that Act's definition section, which defines "work of visual art," specifies that its definitions, unless otherwise provided, control throughout Title 17. *See* 17 U.S.C. § 101. That general definitional section of the Copyright Act states that a work is "created" when it "is fixed in a copy ... for the first time." Further, "where a work is prepared over a period of time, *the portion of it that has been fixed at any particular time constitutes the work as of that time.*" 17 U.S.C. § 101 (emphasis added). A work is "fixed" when it has been formed, "by or under the authority of the author," in a way that is "sufficiently permanent or stable to permit it to be perceived, reproduced, or otherwise communicated for a period of more than transitory duration." *Id.*

Not surprisingly, based on section 101's general definitions, courts have held that the Copyright Act's protections extend to unfinished works. *See, e.g., Dumas v. Gommerman,* 865 F.2d 1093, 1097 (9th Cir.1989), *rejected on other grounds by Community for Creative Non-Violence v. Reid,* 490 U.S. 730, 739, 742 n. 8, 109 S. Ct. 2166, 104 L. Ed. 2d 811 (1989); *Zyware, Inc. v. Middlegate, Inc.,* No. 96 Civ. 2348(SHS), 1997 WL 685336, at *4 (S.D.N.Y. Nov.4,

1997) (noting that there is "no requirement that a work be complete before it is protected by the Copyright Act"); *Playboy Enters. Inc. v. Dumas,* 831 F. Supp. 295, 314 (S.D.N.Y.1993) ("[T]he [Copyright] Act protects works in progress."), *modified on other grounds by* 840 F. Supp. 256 (S.D.N.Y.1993), *aff'd in part, rev'd in part by* 53 F.3d 549 (2d Cir.1995).

Reading VARA in accordance with the definitions in section 101, it too must be read to protect unfinished, but "fixed," works of art that, if completed, would qualify for protection under the statute.[NOTE 10] To conclude otherwise would be "contrary to the rule that provisions of a single act should be construed in as harmonious a fashion as possible." *United States v. Maravilla,* 907 F.2d 216, 231 (1st Cir.1990) (citation omitted). At least one circuit has previously assumed VARA's applicability to unfinished works. *See Carter,* 71 F.3d at 83-88 (discussing VARA claims stemming from an unfinished, walk-through sculpture being installed in the lobby of a building).[NOTE 11]

Our conclusion that the statute's plain language extends its coverage to unfinished works makes it unnecessary to delve into VARA's legislative history. We nonetheless note that we have looked closely at that history, and it fully supports our reading of the plain language. Common sense points in the same direction. Moral rights protect the personality and creative energy that an artist contributes to his or her work. That convergence between artist and artwork does not await the final brush stroke or the placement of the last element in a complex installation. *See, e.g.,* Monica Pa & Christopher J. Robinson, *Making Lemons out of Lemons: Recent Developments in the Visual Artists Rights Act,* 3 Landslide 22, 24 (Jan./Feb. 2009) ("[T]he history of art is full of sublime 'unfinished' works of art, such as Leonardo da Vinci's *Statue of a Horse* (begun 1488), Michelangelo's *Tomb of Pope Julius II* (begun 1505), or El Greco's The *Vision of St. John* (1608-14)."); Laura Flahive Wu, *Massachusetts Museum of Contemporary Art v. Büchel: Construing Artists' Rights in the Context of Institutional Commissions,* 32 Colum. J.L. & Arts 151, 163 (2008) (noting that "many works are considered 'art' even though they capture creative expression short of an artist's ultimate realization of that expression").

We thus hold that VARA protects the moral rights of artists who have "created" works of art within the meaning of the Copyright Act even if those works are not yet complete. [NOTE 12]

III.

Given Büchel's right to protection under VARA for his artistic investment in a partially completed artwork, we must now assess the district court's ruling that Büchel failed to raise a genuine issue of material fact with respect to any of his claims. We review the district court's grant of summary judgment de novo. *Insituform Techs., Inc. v. Am. Home Assur. Co.,* 566 F.3d 274, 276 (1st Cir.2009). "The presence of cross-motions neither dilutes nor distorts this standard of review." *Scottsdale Ins. Co. v. Torres,* 561 F.3d 74, 77 (1st Cir.2009) (quotation marks and citations omitted); *see also Littlefield v. Acadia Ins.*

Co., 392 F.3d 1, 6 (1st Cir. 2004) ("Cross motions simply require us to determine whether either of the parties deserves judgment as a matter of law on facts that are not disputed.") (quotation marks and citation omitted). Summary judgment is appropriate where "there is no genuine issue as to any material fact" and "the movant is entitled to judgment as a matter of law." Fed.R.Civ.P. 56(c)(2); *see also Sullivan v. City of Springfield,* 561 F.3d 7, 14 (1st Cir.2009). "A dispute is 'genuine' if the evidence about the fact is such that a reasonable jury could resolve the point in favor of the non-moving party. A fact is 'material' if it has the potential of determining the outcome of the litigation." *Scottsdale Ins. Co.,* 561 F.3d at 77 (citation omitted).

We first consider Büchel's claims asserting violations of his attribution and integrity rights under VARA and then address his claims under other provisions of the Copyright Act, which assert violations of his rights to control the display of the installation and to create derivative works based on it.

A. The Scope of VARA's Integrity and Attribution Rights

1. The Right of Integrity

VARA's right of integrity, codified at 17 U.S.C. § 106A(a)(3)(A), provides that an artist shall have the right "to prevent any intentional distortion, mutilation, or other modification of [his or her] work which would be prejudicial to his or her honor or reputation, and [that] any intentional distortion, mutilation, or modification of that work is a violation of that right." It thus allows artists to protect their works against intentional modifications that would be prejudicial to their honor or reputations. House Report at 6, *as reprinted in* 1990 U.S.C.C.A.N. at 6915.[NOTE 13]

There is arguably some uncertainty about the plaintiff's burden of proof in a case such as this because the second part of section (a)(3)(A)—stating that "any intentional distortion, mutilation, or modification of th[e] work is a violation" of the right of integrity—does not explicitly require a showing of prejudice when the alteration already has occurred and damages, rather than injunctive relief, would be the appropriate remedy. *See* 5 Patry, *supra,* § 16:22 (noting the ambiguity). Because those VARA cases that make it to court are "generally ... decided on threshold questions such as whether the artist's work is a work of visual art within the scope of the Act," Pa & Robinson, *supra,* at 26, courts have had little occasion to give content to the rights that VARA guarantees. *See* Wu, *supra,* at 159 ("[C]ourts avoid construing the extent of VARA protection by finding that works do not meet the threshold requirements for 'visual art' protected by VARA."). Unsurprisingly, therefore, we have found no case law discussing a possible difference in the showing required for injunctive relief and damages for right-of-integrity claims.

Some courts, however, have assumed without analysis that the prejudice showing is necessary for both injunctive relief and damages. See, e.g., *Hanrahan v. Ramirez,* No. 2:97-

CV-7470, 1998 WL 34369997, at *3 (C.D.Cal. June 3, 1998) (citing 17 U.S.C. § 106A(a)(3)); *Carter v. Helmsley-Spear, Inc.*, 861 F. Supp. 303, 329-30 (S.D.N.Y.1994), *aff'd in part, vacated in part, and rev'd in part by Carter*, 71 F.3d at 77. At least one commentator likewise accepts, without discussion, that the damages remedy requires a showing of prejudice. *See* Melville B. Nimmer, 3-8D *Nimmer on Copyright* § 8D.06[C][1] (noting that "an intentional and prejudicial mutilation is an integrity violation, remediable through not only an injunction, but damages as well"). Interestingly, Nimmer raises, and dismisses, a different imprecision in section (a)(3)(A):

> The statutory language—"distortion, mutilation, or other modification of the work which would be prejudicial to his or her honor or reputation"—is susceptible of a reading whereby the requisite prejudice applies only to "modification," not to the antecedents of "distortion" or "mutilation." Though not without ambiguity, the better view under the Berne Convention, from which this language is drawn, is that prejudice applies in all three instances.

Id.

We agree with Nimmer's view of the provision, including the application of the prejudice requirement to a claim for damages, and consider that construction soundly grounded in VARA's legislative history. Under the heading "Purpose of the Legislation," the House Report notes that the right of integrity "allows artists to protect their works against modifications and destructions that are prejudicial to their honor or reputations." House Report at 6, *as reprinted in* 1990 U.S.C.C.A.N. at 6915. The Report also notes that the rights provided by VARA are "analogous to those protected by Article 6*bis* of the Berne Convention," *id.*, which in turn describes the right of integrity as applicable to «certain modifications and other derogatory actions» that would be prejudicial to the artist's honor or reputation.[NOTE 14] Given the stated purpose of the legislation and the similar depiction of the integrity right in the Berne Convention, we conclude that Congress intended the prejudice requirement to apply to the right of integrity whether the remedy sought is injunctive relief or damages.[NOTE 15]

Although VARA does not define the terms "prejudicial," "honor," or "reputation," the House Report recommended that the prejudice inquiry "focus on the artistic or professional honor or reputation of the individual as embodied in the work that is protected," and "examine the way in which a work has been modified and the professional reputation of the author of the work." House Report at 15, *as reprinted in* 1990 U.S.C.C.A.N. at 6925-26 (footnotes omitted). Relying on dictionary definitions of prejudice, honor and reputation, the district court in *Carter* concluded that it should "consider whether [the proposed] alteration would cause injury or damage to plaintiffs' good name, public esteem, or reputation in the artistic community." 861 F. Supp. at 323. We think this a useful approach, but emphasize that the focus is on the artist's reputation in relation to the altered work of art; the artist need not have public stature beyond the context of the creation at issue. *See* House Report at 15, *as reprinted in* 1990 U.S.C.C.A.N. at 6925 ("[A]n author need not prove a preexisting standing in the artistic community.").

2. The Right of Attribution

VARA's right of attribution grants the author of a work of visual art the right, in part, (1) "to claim authorship of that work"; (2) "to prevent the use of his or her name as the author of any work of visual art which he or she did not create"; and (3) "to prevent the use of his or her name as the author of the work of visual art in the event of a distortion, mutilation, or other modification of the work which would be prejudicial to his or her honor or reputation." 17 U.S.C. § 106A(a)(1),(2). The right "ensures that artists are correctly identified with the works of art they create, and that they are not identified with works created by others." House Report at 6, *as reprinted in* 1990 U.S.C.C.A.N. at 6915. In addition, if a work of visual art has been distorted or modified (and, unlike the integrity right, the original distortion or modification need not be intentional), associating the author's name with the distorted work against his wishes would violate his right of attribution.

The right of attribution under VARA thus gives an artist a claim for injunctive relief to, inter alia, assert or disclaim authorship of a work. Whether VARA entitles an artist to damages for violation of the right of attribution is a separate question. We find the answer in the difference between the statutory language on the right of integrity and the language on the right of attribution. Subsection (a)(3) of section 106A, which codifies the right of integrity, is further divided into two subsections: (A) confers the right to protect the work against intentional alterations that would be prejudicial to honor or reputation, and (B) confers the right to protect a work of "recognized stature" from destruction.[NOTE 16] Although both subsections are framed as rights "to prevent" certain conduct, they both also contain an additional clause stating that the occurrence of that conduct is, at least in certain circumstances, "a violation of th[e] right" to prevent the conduct from happening. *See* 17 U.S.C. § 106A(a)(3)(A) ("any intentional distortion, mutilation, or modification of that work is a violation of that right"); *id.* at § 106(a)(3)(B) ("any intentional or grossly negligent destruction of that work is a violation of that right").

No such "violation" clause is included in the sections codifying the right of attribution. *See* Nimmer, *supra,* at § 8D.06[B][1] ("The statute does not make any provision to redress *violation* of any of the foregoing three attribution rights."). The legislative history sheds no light on this difference, but Nimmer speculates as follows:

> Perhaps the implication is that whereas an integrity violation could give rise to a monetary recovery, failure to attribute is remediable solely through injunction. If that conclusion were intended, Congress certainly could have expressed its intent less obliquely.

Id.

We agree with Nimmer's surmise that VARA does not provide a damages remedy for an attribution violation. Where the statutory language is framed as a right "to prevent" conduct, it does not necessarily follow that a plaintiff is entitled to damages once the conduct occurs. The question is whether "doing" the act the artist has a right to prevent also triggers a damages remedy, and the statutory language indicates that Congress answered that question for the attribution right differently from the integrity right.

It is also noteworthy that Congress crafted a damages remedy for the destruction of a work of recognized stature that is narrower than the right to prevent destruction of such works. While an artist may "prevent *any* destruction of a work of recognized stature," only an "intentional or grossly negligent destruction of that work is a violation of that right." 17 U.S.C. § 106A(a)(3)(B) (emphasis added). This narrowing further indicates that Congress did not intend a damages remedy to arise automatically from the right to prevent conduct. In failing to provide a damages remedy for any type of violation of the moral right of attribution, Congress may have concluded that artists could obtain adequate relief for the harms of false attribution by resorting to the Copyright Act and other traditional claims.

B. Büchel's VARA Claims

With this legal framework in mind, we turn to the record before the district court. By dismantling *Training Ground*, the Museum prevented the further use of Büchel's name in connection with the work, eliminating any basis for injunctive relief, and we therefore do not address the attribution claim in our VARA analysis. We thus consider the evidence in the light most favorable to Büchel in determining whether there are genuine issues of material fact regarding the alleged violations of his right of integrity.

As noted above, the district court concluded that Büchel's right of integrity was not implicated by MASS MoCA's conduct. The court found that "nothing in MASS MoCA's planned display of the unfinished installation would have violated Büchel's right of integrity, for the simple reason that no completed work of art ever existed on these facts for the museum to distort, mutilate or modify." 56 F. Supp. 2d at 260. Although the court stated that it would assume that VARA applied to unfinished works, its analysis appears to be influenced by a more limited view of the statute's scope. The court stated that "[t]o suggest that the display of an unfinished and abandoned work somehow constitutes a distortion, mutilation, or modification of that non-existent work is simply inconsistent with the ordinary usage of those terms." *Id.* Having concluded that VARA applies with full force to unfinished works, however, we cannot accept the district court's reliance on the unfinished state of "Training Ground" to minimize the rights of its creator.

It cannot be disputed that, at least by the time Büchel left North Adams in December 2006, *Training Ground* was "fixed" within the meaning of the Copyright Act—i.e., materials had been placed in Building 5 "by or under the authority of the author" in a "sufficiently permanent or stable" manner to allow the work to be "communicated for a period of more than transitory duration." 17 U.S.C. § 101. The elements of the installation had been chosen by Büchel, and his assistants and the Museum workers had put numerous components of the project in place under his direct supervision. Although far from complete, the work by the end of 2006 included parts of the "Saddam Compound" and the cinema, and Büchel and his assistants had begun detailing several of the containers intended to house elements such as a jail, museum and voting booths. With this substantial work in place, the sculpture had an established presence in Building 5. Büchel thus had rights in the work that were protected under VARA, notwithstanding its unfinished state.

Büchel alleges that MASS MoCA violated his right to integrity in three distinct ways: first, by continuing to work on the installation without his authorization, particularly in early 2007, and by then exhibiting the distorted artwork to the public; second, by using tarpaulins to "partially cover"—and thus modify and distort—the installation, and allowing Museum visitors to see it in that condition; and third, merely by showing Büchel's work in its unfinished state, which he claims was a distortion. Büchel asserts that these actions caused prejudice to his honor or reputation.

As we shall explain, we conclude that summary judgment was improperly granted to MASS MoCA because material disputes of fact exist concerning the first of Büchel's integrity claims—i.e., that MASS MoCA modified *Training Ground* over his objections, to his detriment. We further conclude that the record contains sufficient evidence to allow a jury to find that MASS MoCA's actions caused prejudice to Büchel's honor or reputation. The other integrity claims, however, are unavailing.

1. Continuing Work on *Training Ground*

Büchel asserts that, in the months following his departure from North Adams in December 2006, the Museum encroached on his artistic vision by making modifications to the installation that in some instances were directly contrary to his instructions. In rejecting Büchel's VARA claims, the district court described the Museum's actions as perhaps "occasionally misguided" attempts "to implement Büchel's long-distance instructions." 565 F. Supp. 2d at 260. The court found that these "[f]umbled efforts to assist in creating, or failing to create, a work of art are not equivalent to distortion, modification, or mutilation of the art." *Id.* at 260-61.

Although a jury might agree with the court's assessment, the evidence viewed in the light most favorable to Büchel would allow a finding that at least some of the Museum's actions violated VARA. The record permits the inference that, even during his time as an artist-in-residence at MASS MoCA, Museum staff members were disregarding his instructions and intentionally modifying *Training Ground* in a manner that he did not approve. For example, on December 14, 2006, just before he left for the holidays, Büchel complained to Thompson that in "many cases people just do stuff without checking back if its ok to do s[omething], when they think by themselves the plan has to be changed." Büchel expressed further concerns in an email to Thompson later that month: "I don't [k]now if this is really a great opportunity when you get an invitation to do a show, where you have to make constantly tons of compromises, where you have to fight constantly against stubborn[n]ess as well [as] against the institution and work with people that think they know my art better than I do as well [as] try to sabotage the project...."

In early 2007, when he was no longer on-site, Büchel again accused the Museum of "sabotage acts" and, in a January 16 letter, issued an ultimatum: he would return to North Adams to complete *Training Ground* only if the Museum assented to a number of specific conditions. Aside from certain budgetary concerns irrelevant here, Büchel included the following among his list of demands:

> There is NO negotiation about the scope of the project.
>
> There are no elements to be eliminated as you propose and I don't accept any orders and any more pressure or compromises how things have to be done, neither from you or your crew....
>
> I will not give you any permission to show an unfinished project nor will I show nor let you show any work in progress, as you proposed already earlier.
>
> I will not accept without consequences any additional sabotage acts, as done to artworks of mine and as well done to the installation in progress[.]

The letter also identified several points of disagreement with the Museum concerning the content of the project, including Büchel's insistence that there be "no transport street through the exhibition" and that he did not "need to be told if an airplane fuselage section fits in the show or not. I don't negotiate constantly my art with you or Nato...." Accusing the Museum director of showing "little respect towards [his] plans," he told Thompson "please don't tell me all the time how I have to do my project regarding its scope and it's [sic] methods that needs [sic] to be applied."

Unsatisfied with the Museum's response to his list of demands, Büchel wrote to Thompson again on January 27, 2007. He warned that, based on the information he had been provided, "there [was] a lot of stuff not being done according to my instructions." Again, he noted several elements of the work that had been installed against his wishes.[NOTE 17] Thompson and Büchel traded emails during the first few days of February, with Büchel stating that he would "not negotiate further this matter... because almost any of the main conditions are simply not fulfilled" and Thompson writing that he believed the Museum had "responded to [Büchel's] main issues."

After that, direct communication between Büchel and the Museum became sparse. It was during this time, Büchel alleges, that the Museum developed a "Plan B"[NOTE 18] to be implemented in the event—which was looking increasingly likely—that he did not return to finish the exhibit. Plan B, which involved publicly exhibiting the unfinished installation without the artist's permission, called for completing various elements of the installation in a way the Museum knew might differ from Büchel's artistic concept. Büchel cites an email chain on February 14 that included Joseph Thompson and Dante Birch, in which Thompson, stating that the Museum "seem[ed] to be getting closer and closer to Plan B," gave specific instructions on various elements of the installation. Thompson suggested that Museum staff do "[a]nything else Dante and Nato feel is known with 80% certainty."

At least some Museum staff members recognized that continuing to work on the installation without Büchel's input might be problematic. Later in the February 14 email chain, Dante Birch noted that he was "interested in protecting the museum from intellectual property issues." Pointing out that the show was advertised as a Büchel in the Museum's schedule, he stated that when reviewers came, "the question will be 'what is it?' ... and if it's reviewed as a Buchel we're in deep shit." Thompson's plans also raised concern among other MASS MoCA employees, including curator Susan Cross, who cautioned Thompson in a January 31 email that "we tend to forget that whether we're doing the welding or not, there is an 'author'—an artist for whom we shouldn't make decisions.... At what point, if at all, does an artist lose his right to owning the idea and his/her 'intellectual property?' ... I think it is still art and still belongs to Buchel."

Both in his deposition and in his affidavit, Büchel described ways in which he felt the Museum had knowingly disregarded his specific instructions. For example, MASS MoCA's decision to build a cinderblock wall through the Cape Codstyle house in the installation, despite Büchel's expressed desire that the construction await his return, resulted in what Büchel considered a "big distortion of the meaning of that element." The record is replete with similar allegations concerning other components of the installation, including the cinema, the bomb carousel, the Saddam spiderhole, the police car and the mobile home. Indeed, even the Museum, in its August 31, 2007 memorandum of law in support of its motion for summary judgment, admitted that the installation "[m]aterials as they now stand *reflect significant aesthetic and design choices by MASS MoCA personnel,* including with respect to the layout of the [m]aterials, and with respect to the selection and procurement of pre-existing buildings and vehicles that have been modified and incorporated into the [m]aterials.» (Emphasis added.)[NOTE 19]

MASS MoCA argues that the evidence, taken in its entirety, does not add up to a triable issue with respect to a violation of Büchel's right of integrity, but shows only that Museum personnel were attempting to carry out Büchel's vision based on his instructions. Indeed, the Museum notes that the work slowed as Büchel's instructions became unavailable.[NOTE 20] MASS MoCA specifically disputes Büchel's reading of the February 14 email chain as demonstrating the Museum's disregard of his creative rights over the installation, asserting that the discussion among its staff members in fact reflects a conscious effort to determine how far the Museum could appropriately go in light of the remaining instructions left by the artist. In one email, for example, Thompson noted that "we are putting the correct objects in the spaces cb indicated. ... That's not 'doing a buechel [sic]' that's prepping for buechel [sic] assuming, as we still are, that there is some chance we'll see him here again." Other communications in the record also could be interpreted as showing the Museum doing its best to carry out Büchel's concept for the art work.

As we have noted, a jury may well accept the Museum's depiction of its intention and its actions. At this juncture, however, the record must be viewed in the light most favorable to Büchel. The evidence we have described would permit a jury to find that the Museum forged ahead with the installation in the first half of 2007 knowing that the continuing construction in Büchel's absence would frustrate—and likely contradict—Büchel's artistic vision. We thus conclude that a jury issue exists as to whether these actions effected an intentional distortion or other modification of *Training Ground* that subjected MASS MoCA to liability under VARA.

The record also contains evidence from which a jury could conclude that the Museum's alterations had a detrimental impact on Büchel's honor or reputation. An article in the Boston Globe reported that, in February, Museum officials had shown the unfinished project to a group of Museum directors and curators who were attending an arts conference in the area. *See* Geoff Edgers, *Behind doors, a world unseen: Dispute cloaks massive installation at MASS MoCA,* Boston Globe (March 28, 2007), *available at* www.boston.com/ae/theater_arts/articles/2007/03/28/behind_doors_a_world_unseen/ ("*Behind doors, a world unseen*"). Another journalist reported on observing the unfinished (and still untarped) work. *See The Show Will Go On, supra.*

Although the commentary generated by these visits is not all negative,[NOTE 21] there was sufficient evidence for a jury to find that the changes to *Training Ground* caused prejudice to Büchel. The New York Times noted that the exhibition would "certainly give people unfamiliar with his obsessive, history-driven aesthetic an inaccurate sense of his art, and this is indeed a form of damage." *Is It Art Yet?, supra.* A critic for the Boston Globe similarly observed that "many people are going to judge [Büchel] and his work on the basis of this experience." Ken Johnson, *No admittance: MASS MoCA has mishandled disputed art installation,* Boston Globe, July 1, 2007, at 1N. One viewer, writing in *Commentary* magazine, observed that "I am not sure that it suffers from being enveiled." Michael J. Lewis, *The Cost of Transgression,* http://www.commentarymagazine.com/blogs/index.php/lewis/499 (June 4, 2007). A review published in *Berkshire Fine Arts*—subtitled "Crap Under Wrap"—concluded that it would be a "huge mistake" to uncover the installation, which offered "virtually nothing of substance or interest." *Crap Under Wrap, supra.*

The record thus shows that some viewers of the installation reacted unfavorably to the work in its allegedly modified and distorted form. A factfinder might conclude, of course, that it was Büchel's underlying concept (notwithstanding its unfinished state) rather than MASS MoCA's actions that elicited the negative reactions. However, a jury could also reasonably infer that the negative impressions resulted from the Museum's unauthorized modifications to *Training Ground*, diminishing the quality of the work and thereby harming Büchel's professional honor or reputation as a visual artist.

In concluding that Büchel has adduced sufficient evidence to support a right-of-integrity claim, we reject the Museum's assertion that to find a violation of Büchel's right of integrity in these circumstances would make it impossible for parties to collaborate on large-scale artistic works. The Museum warns that, under Büchel's interpretation, "no one other than the artist himself ... may *ever* perform any work in fabricating visual art unless that specific task has been authorized by the artist." We disagree. Although the artist's vision must govern, that principle does not prevent collaboration at the implementation level so long as the artist's vision guides that implementation. Here, Büchel alleges a campaign of intentional distortion and modification to his work in which Museum personnel repeatedly ignored his express wishes. Our holding that the summary judgment record precludes an affirmance of the district court on this claim may serve as a cautionary tale to museums contemplating similar installations in the future—guiding them to document the terms of their relationship and obtain VARA waivers where necessary—but it does not prevent museums or other collaborators from working cooperatively with artists on such non-traditional artworks.

2. Showing *Training Ground* Covered with Tarpaulins

Büchel also claims that MASS MoCA improperly modified and distorted "Training Ground" when it partially covered it with the yellow tarpaulins and displayed it in that condition. He asserts that the record shows beyond dispute that visitors looked behind the tarps, that the tarp-adorned installation was "judged by others to be Büchel's work, and that his honor and reputation were harmed by it." In response, the Museum argues that the yellow tarpaulins were merely functional—a way of keeping people "out" of the installation—rather than an aesthetic modification of the artwork that gave MASS MoCA patrons a distorted view of it.

Although the tarpaulins did prevent visitors to the Museum from seeing the entire unfinished installation, the record shows that a number of people were able to form an impression of *Training Ground* despite the partial covering. For example, according to one observer,

> [the tarps] don't reach the floor, and they rise only about two feet above eye level, so they don't cover much. You can easily crouch down to slip your head underneath or peek through the slits between the vinyl sheets. Beyond the passageway formed by the tarps, the monumental elements of the installation rise all around you, plain as day—the cinderblock walls, the two-story house, the guard tower, the trailers, the carnival ride, all compacted together in a claustrophobic, politically surreal borough of hell, George Orwell by way of David Lynch.

Thomas Micchelli, *Christoph Büchel Training Ground for Democracy,* The Brooklyn Rail (September 2007), *available at* http://www.brooklynrail.org/2007/09/artseen/buchel. Another critic noted that the installation "under all the tarps is really kind of a conceptual peep show. It doesn't take much effort or imagination to see most of the work.... Mass MoCA is hiding an elephant behind a napkin," and called it a "wink, wink, wrap show." *Crap Under Wrap, supra.* Photographs in the record confirm that the covers did not obscure the general path and layout of the installation. Indeed, given the location of

Training Ground, visitors to *Made at MASS MoCA* could not avoid seeing the unfinished *Training Ground* bedecked in tarpaulins.

Nonetheless, although the installation unquestionably looked different with the tarpaulins partially covering it, we agree with the district court that the mere covering of the artwork by the Museum, its host, cannot reasonably be deemed an intentional act of distortion or modification of Büchel's creation. To conclude otherwise would be to say that, even if all had gone well, the Museum would have been subject to a right-of-integrity claim if it had partially covered the work before its formal opening to prevent visitors from seeing it prematurely.

This is not to say that MASS MoCA was necessarily acting with pure intentions when it created *Made at MASS MoCA* in close proximity to the tarped *Training Ground*. It might be a fair inference that the Museum was deliberately communicating its anger with Büchel by juxtaposing his unfinished work with the successful artistic collaborations depicted in its new exhibition. The partial covering of *Training Ground* may have been intended to highlight, rather than hide, the failed collaboration. [NOTE 22] The right of integrity under VARA, however, protects the artist from distortions of his work, not from disparaging commentary about his behavior. In our view, a finding that the Museum's covering of the installation constituted an intentional act of distortion or modification of Büchel's artistic creation would stretch VARA beyond sensible boundaries.

3. Exhibiting *Training Ground* in Its Unfinished State

Büchel maintains that, even aside from the alleged modifications to *Training Ground*, merely exhibiting the work of art in its unfinished state, without the artist's consent, constitutes a distortion. We reject this claim. A separate moral right of disclosure (also known as the right of divulgation) protects an author's authority to "prevent third parties from disclosing [his or her] work to the public without the author's consent," and is not covered by VARA. *See* Cyrill P. Rigamonti, *Deconstructing Moral Rights,* 47 Harv. Int'l L.J. 353, 373, 405 (2006) ("[T]he VARA ignores the rights of disclosure and withdrawal and instead focuses on the rights of attribution and integrity....").

Although Büchel proffered an expert who opined that showing an unfinished work without the artist's permission is inherently a distortion, we decline to interpret VARA to include such a claim where a separate moral right of disclosure is widely recognized in other jurisdictions and Congress explicitly limited the statute's coverage to the rights of attribution and integrity. *See* Amy M. Adler, *Against Moral Rights,* 97 Cal. L.Rev. 263, 268 (2009) (noting that most European countries "recognize a right of divulgation, giving the artist the right to decide when (and whether) the work is complete and can be shown"); Rigamonti, *supra,* at 356 ("The standard set of moral rights recognized in the literature consists of the author's right to claim authorship (right of attribution), the right to object to modifications of the work (right of integrity), the right to decide when and how the work in question will be published (right of disclosure), and the right to withdraw a work after publication (right of withdrawal)." (footnotes omitted)); 5 *Patry on Copyright* § 16:23 (noting that VARA does not give the artist "a right to prohibit display of mutilated versions of his or her work, only the right to prohibit the mutilation itself"). Any right Büchel possesses to withhold display of his artwork must be found outside VARA. We consider below his claim to such a right under section 106(5) of the Copyright Act. *See infra* Section IV.

4. Summary of VARA Claims

After careful review of the record, we are persuaded that a reasonable jury could find that Büchel is entitled to relief under VARA based on the Museum's continuing work on *Training Ground* over his objections. Genuine disputes of material fact foreclose summary judgment for either Büchel or MASS MoCA on that claim. We find no merit, however, in Büchel's claim that MASS MoCA intentionally modified or distorted *Training Ground* by covering it with tarpaulins, and we reject as outside the scope of the statute Büchel's claim that the Museum violated VARA by displaying the installation over his objections. We affirm the district court's grant of summary judgment for the Museum on Büchel's right-of-attribution claim, which became moot when MASS MoCA dismantled the installation in 2007.

IV.

We now assess Büchel's challenge to the grant of summary judgment for MASS MoCA on his Copyright Act claims.

A. Public Display

The owner of a copyrighted work has the exclusive right to "display the copyrighted work publicly." 17 U.S.C. § 106(5). Displaying a work is defined as "show[ing] a copy of it, either directly or by means of a film, slide, television image, or any other device or process." 17 U.S.C. § 101. A "copy" includes the original. *Id.* Büchel argued below, as he does on appeal, that the Museum's repeated public exhibitions of *Training Ground for Democracy* constituted a public display of his work in violation of his exclusive right under section 106(5). The district court gave no explicit reason for its dismissal of this claim, remarking only that "[f]or the reasons already stated," presumably in its discussion of VARA, MASS MoCA was "entitled to judgment on this count." 565 F. Supp. 2d at 261.

The court also remarked, however, that since Büchel "would have suffered a violation of no right recognized by this statute, this messy situation simply fell outside the boundary of VARA and, *a fortiori*, outside the more general provisions of the Copyright Act." *Id.* at 260. This statement reflects a misreading of the Copyright Act. As we have explained, the moral rights granted to specific artists under VARA are separate and independent from the economic rights guaranteed by section 106. 17 U.S.C. § 106A(a) (providing that rights of attribution and integrity are "independent of the exclusive rights provided in section 106"). Thus, the inadequacy of claims under VARA does not, on its own, signify the inadequacy of more traditional copyright claims. *See* Wu, *supra,* at 164 (observing that VARA has "acquired the attributes of a false talisman," both because artists overly rely on it in "instances where economic rights, including traditional rights of copyright provided by Section 106 ... would more effectively protect their interests" and also because courts tend to view VARA claims as "devalu[ing] entitlements to economic rights pleaded in tandem with VARA claims").

We thus turn specifically to this claim. The Museum argues that Büchel has failed to present a triable issue of fact on his claim under section 106(5) because the unfinished work was never publicly displayed. However, as we have described in the context of our VARA discussion, there is significant record evidence suggesting that the work was repeatedly and deliberately exhibited to numerous individuals.[NOTE 23]

MASS MoCA also asserts an affirmative defense under section 109(c), which provides that "the owner of a particular copy lawfully made under this title, or any person authorized by such owner, is entitled, without the authority of the copyright owner, to display that copy publicly." 17 U.S.C. § 109(c). The Museum argues that it owned the physical copy of *Training Ground*, and that section 109(c) therefore permitted it to display the unfinished work. Here again, however, the record reveals disputed issues of fact with respect to whether the Museum's copy was "lawfully made," as it may have been created in violation of the artist's rights under VARA. Moreover, Büchel introduced evidence to rebut the Museum's assertion that "the installation's various components" all belonged to, or were purchased by, MASS MoCA. Finally, Büchel presented evidence that the Museum understood that the physical copy of the installation belonged to him.[NOTE 24] Accordingly, viewing the evidence in the light most favorable to Büchel, we cannot say that a reasonable jury could not conclude that the Museum violated his exclusive right to publicly display *Training Ground for Democracy.*

B. Derivative Works

The Copyright Act also grants artists the exclusive right to "prepare derivative works based upon the copyrighted work." 17 U.S.C. § 106(2). A derivative work is defined as one "based upon one or more preexisting works," such as a translation, musical arrangement, fictionalization, "or any other form in which a work may be recast, transformed, or adapted." 17 U.S.C. § 101. A derivative work includes any work "consisting of editorial revisions, annotations, elaborations, or other modifications which, as a whole, represent an original work of authorship." *Id.* Büchel brought two claims based on this provision, asserting that MASS MoCA created unauthorized derivative works based on the installation itself and on the work's models and plans.

The district court ruled that, "[e]ven assuming that the stumbling, and eventually abandoned, process of collaboration during 2006 produced an original work of art subject to copyright protection, which is highly doubtful, clearly no 'derivative' work of art was created by MASS MoCA's attempt (however flawed) to play its part in this process." 565 F. Supp. 2d at 261. It further rejected Büchel's argument that, by placing tarpaulins over the unfinished installation, the Museum created a separate, unauthorized derivative work. *Id.*

On appeal, Büchel summarily argues that what the Museum displayed in Building 5, both with and without the yellow tarpaulins, "recast" or "transformed" the work that he had originally set out in his plans and left behind in December 2006, thus creating derivative works under the Copyright Act.[NOTE 25] In response, MASS MoCA again argues that its staff was following Büchel's instructions when working on *Training Ground* in his absence, and that the Museum therefore was merely executing Büchel's vision rather than exercising its own artistic judgment to create a new, derivative artwork.

A derivative work within the meaning of the Copyright Act "consists of a contribution of original material to a pre-existing work so as to recast, transform or adapt the pre-existing work," and the variation from the original must be "sufficient to render the derivative work distinguishable from its prior work in any meaningful manner." Nimmer, *supra,* § 3.03[A]; *see also Schrock v. Learning Curve Int'l, Inc.,* 586 F.3d 513, 520-21 (7th Cir.2009); *Woods v. Bourne Co.,* 60 F.3d 978, 990 (2d Cir.1995). As we have held, Büchel's contention that his work was modified without his permission and to his detriment gives rise to a right-of-integrity claim under VARA. Every modification of a work of art does not, however, result in the creation of a derivative work.

In Büchel's 52-page opening brief, there is one paragraph that purports to analyze the derivative work claim, and that paragraph itself is largely descriptive rather than analytical. Büchel cites no cases and does not explain how the modified *Training Ground* was sufficiently original and distinctive within the meaning of the Copyright Act to qualify as a derivative work. His reply brief adds another paragraph, citing cases, but he again asserts in summary fashion that the modifications resulted in a derivative work. He states that the degree of creativity needed for a derivative work is minimal, but does not explain how the Museum's alterations create a new work that, as a whole, meets the Copyright Act's originality requirement. The law applicable to derivative work claims, particularly as it intersects with VARA's protection for works of visual art, is complex. See, e.g., *Lee v. A.R.T. Co.,* 125 F.3d 580, 582-83 (7th Cir.1997); Henry Hansmann, *Authors' and Artists' Moral Rights: A Comparative Legal and Economic Analysis,* 26 J. Legal Stud. 95, 114-116 (1997). Büchel's undeveloped argument is so perfunctory that we deem the claim waived. *See United States v. Zannino,* 895 F.2d 1, 17 (1st Cir.1990) (stating that, on appeal, "issues adverted to in a perfunctory manner, unaccompanied by some effort at developed argumentation, are deemed waived").

V.

We summarize our holdings:

1. VARA's protection of an artist's moral rights extends to unfinished creations that are "works of art" within the meaning of the Copyright Act;

2. The right of integrity under VARA protects artists from distortions, mutilations or modifications of their works that are prejudicial to their reputation or honor, and prejudice must be shown for both injunctive relief and damages;

3. Büchel has adduced sufficient evidence to raise a genuine issue of material fact as to whether MASS MoCA violated his right of integrity on one of his three asserted bases for liability, namely, by modifying *Training Ground* over his objections in a manner that harmed his honor or reputation. His right-of-integrity claims based on the yellow tarpaulins and the mere display of *Training Ground* lack merit;

4. Büchel's right-of-attribution claim is moot, as VARA provides only injunctive relief to protect the right of attribution and the installation no longer exists;

5. The record reveals a genuine issue of material fact as to whether MASS MoCA violated Büchel's exclusive right under section 106(5) of the Copyright Act to display his work publicly;

6. Büchel fails to adequately develop his claim that MASS MoCA violated his exclusive right under section 106(2) to prepare derivative works based on *Training Ground*, and that claim is therefore waived.

We thus remand the case for further proceedings on Büchel's remaining right-of-integrity claim under VARA and his public display claim under section 106 of the Copyright Act.

Affirmed in part, vacated in part, and remanded for further proceedings consistent with this decision. Each party is to bear its own costs.

NOTES:

NOTE 1: VARA was enacted as an amendment to the Copyright Act. *See infra* Section II.

NOTE 2: We consider the parties' conflicting accounts of the key evidence in our summary judgment analysis, *infra.*

NOTE 3: Throughout the opinion, any reference to "Thompson" without a first name will refer to Museum Director Joseph Thompson. Nato Thompson will be identified by his full name.

NOTE 4: The letter, signed by Museum Director Joseph Thompson, was attached to an email sent by Nato Thompson. The proposal did not lay out a definitive budget for the project, although in a separate letter to Büchel the following day, Joseph Thompson stated "we think we've got a $160,000 project on our hands in direct costs." In a reply email dated September 24, 2006, Büchel did not explicitly agree to or reject the $160,000 figure, but suggested that MASS MoCA get in touch with his two galleries, which might provide information regarding "potential sponsors like foundations" for the installation.

NOTE 5: The Berne convention, developed at the instigation of Victor Hugo and first adopted in Berne, Switzerland in 1886, is "'an international copyright treaty providing that works created by citizens of one signatory nation will be fully protected in other signatory nations, without the need for local formalities.'" *Phillips*, 459 F.3d at 133 n. 3 (quoting *Black's Law Dictionary*, 8th ed. (1999)).

NOTE 6: Under the Copyright Act, a plaintiff may elect to recover statutory damages instead of actual damages for each work infringed "in a sum of not less than $750 or more than $30,000 as the court considers just." 17 U.S.C. § 504(c)(1). If the copyright owner proves that the infringement was committed willfully, the court "in its discretion" may increase the award of statutory damages to "a sum of not more than $150,000." *Id.* at 504(c)(2). The award may also be reduced to $200 if the infringer proves that he or she was not aware "and had no reason to believe that his or her acts constituted an infringement of copyright." *Id.*

NOTE 7: The parties do not dispute that, if completed, *Training Ground for Democracy* would have been a sculpture and therefore a qualified "work of visual art" under VARA. Furthermore, VARA's legislative history states that "[t]he term 'sculpture' includes, but is not limited to, castings, carvings, modelings, and *constructions.*" House Report at 11 (1990), *as reprinted in* 1990 U.S.C.C.A.N. at 6921 (emphasis added). The Second Circuit in *Carter* similarly considered VARA's application to a "very large 'walk-through sculpture' occupying most, but not all, of [a] building's lobby." 71 F.3d at 80; *see also id.* at 84 ("Concededly, considered as a whole, the work is a sculpture and exists only in a single copy.").

NOTE 8: Section 501(a) states, in relevant part, that "[a]nyone who violates any of the exclusive rights of the copyright owner ... or of the author as provided in section 106A(a) [VARA]... is an infringer of the copyright or right of the author, as the case may be." The provision further states that, with the exception of the criminal penalties provided under section 506, "any reference to copyright shall be deemed to include the rights conferred by section 106A(a)."

NOTE 9: As provided in 17 U.S.C. § 106A(c)(3), VARA specifically excludes certain categories of artwork listed in section 101 of the Copyright Act:

> (A) (i) any poster, map, globe, chart, technical drawing, diagram, model, applied art, motion picture or other audiovisual work, book, magazine, newspaper, periodical, data base, electronic information service, electronic publication, or similar publication;
> (ii) any merchandising item or advertising, promotional, descriptive, covering, or packaging material or container;
> (iii) any portion or part of any item described in clause (i) or (ii);
> (B) any work made for hire

17 U.S.C. § 101.

NOTE 10: Nothing in the language of VARA or the definitions provision of the Copyright Act permits distinct treatment for the rights of copyright owners whose works are complete and those whose works are still in progress. We therefore reject the "special clarity" standard articulated by the district court for proving a violation of an artist's VARA rights in an unfinished work of art.

NOTE 11: The Second Circuit ultimately found that the sculpture was exempted from VARA protections because it was a "work for hire." *See* 71 F.3d at 86-88.

NOTE 12: Our decision in *Phillips* is not inconsistent with this holding. In *Phillips*, we held that VARA did not apply to site-specific works of art, in which the particular location of the artwork is one of its physical elements and removal of the artwork destroys it. 459 F.3d at 140. We observed that VARA does not explicitly address protection for site-specific works despite the impact of such works on real property interests, *id.* at 142, and we declined to interpret VARA in a way that was neither supported by the statutory language nor sensible as policy. *See id.* at 142-43. Here, the plain language controls, and there is no conflict with "'long-established and familiar principles'" of the common law. *Id.* at 142 (quoting *United States v. Texas*, 507 U.S. 529, 534, 113 S. Ct. 1631, 123 L. Ed. 2d 245 (1993)).

NOTE 13: In some jurisdictions, the right of integrity also generally protects artwork from destruction. *See Carter*, 71 F.3d at 81. In the United States, however, VARA protects only works of "recognized stature" from destruction. 17 U.S.C. § 106A(a)(3)(B). That right is not implicated in this case.

NOTE 14: Article 6*bis* of the Berne Convention, which is titled "Moral Rights," includes a heading that lists among those rights "to object to certain modifications and other derogatory actions." The provision itself states, in relevant part:

> (1) Independently of the author's economic rights, and even after the transfer of the said rights, the author shall have the right... to object to any distortion, mutilation or other modification of, or other derogatory action in relation to, the said work, which would be prejudicial to his honor or reputation.

Berne Convention for the Protection of Literary and Artistic Works art. *6bis,* Sept. 9, 1986, S. Treaty Doc. No. 99-27, 1161 U.N.T.S. 30.

NOTE 15: Based on revisions to the statutory language made during the legislative process, Patry concludes that "where an intentional distortion, mutilation, or other modification has already occurred, the plaintiff need not prove harm to his or her honor or reputation." 5 Patry, *supra,* § 16:22. He further states, without supporting citation, that "[i]t was understood informally" that the final version of the provision was designed "to permit a cause of action ... without the need for proof that the artist's honor or reputation was harmed." *Id.* To the extent Patry's conclusion is that no evidence of harm is necessary, we reject it as inconsistent with the available legislative history, as discussed above. It may be, however, that Congress's concern was only that a plaintiff not be required to prove the actual amount of damage to reputation, but could opt for the statutory damages remedy upon showing prejudice. *See* 17 U.S.C. §§ 501(a), 504(c) (stating that a VARA plaintiff may elect to recover statutory damages instead of actual damages and profits).

NOTE 16: Section 106A(a)(3) states that the author of a work of visual art shall have the right "(A) to prevent any intentional distortion, mutilation, or other modification of that work which would be prejudicial to his or her honor or reputation" and the right "(B) to prevent any destruction of a work of recognized stature."

NOTE 17: "I wrote very clearly immediately to [Dante Birch, the Museum's production manager] not to use the method we talked about and stop it ..., as well cinder block walls have to be partly redone that have been built without my instruction...."

NOTE 18: The term "Plan B" appears in the record in a February 14, 2007 email from Thompson to other Museum staff.

NOTE 19: This assertion by MASS MoCA was made to support its contention, rejected by the district court and halfheartedly renewed on appeal, that the unfinished installation might constitute a joint work of Büchel and the Museum. A claim of joint authorship requires proof that the parties "entertain in their minds the concept of joint ownership." *Thomson v. Larson,* 147 F.3d 195, 201 (2d Cir.1998) (quotation marks and citation omitted). Here, multiple facts indicate that the parties' understanding from the outset was that *Training Ground* was solely a Christoph Büchel work of art. The Museum's December 6, 2006 postponement announcement described the work as "Christoph Büchel's vast installation" and, as reflected in the emails described above, Museum personnel internally recognized Büchel as the artist, at least as *Training Ground* was originally conceived. It is also undisputed that, at the outset of their relationship, the parties had agreed that Büchel alone would hold the copyright in the finished work. These facts negate any claim of joint authorship.

NOTE 20: In his deposition, Thompson testified as follows:

> [T]here was a whole long list of things for which we had adequate direction and understanding that we could continue forward to a certain point. When the work began to get very detailed and would require input from Christoph, if we could get the input from him, we would continue, and if we didn't, we would stop.

NOTE 21: Thompson told an outside consultant for the Museum in March 2007 that a curator at the New Museum in New York had just viewed the installation "and said it was one of the best works he's seen in the past three years."

NOTE 22: Indeed, the Boston Globe's art critic, Ken Johnson, described the exhibit as a "self-serving photo and text display" that implicitly conveys criticism of Büchel for the failure of *Training Ground for Democracy. See MASS MoCA has Mishandled Disputed Art Installation, supra.* The juxtaposition left Johnson with the impression that MASS MoCA was "exacting revenge" against the artist "by turning his project into a show that misrepresents, dishonors, vilifies, and even ridicules him." *Id.*

NOTE 23: In addition to the journalists and Museum personnel noted earlier, a newspaper reported that the mayor of North Adams had seen the exhibit twice, once with Governor Deval Patrick. *See Behind doors, a world unseen, supra.*

NOTE 24: For example, in an email sent on September 11, 2006 to curator Nato Thompson, the Museum's director (Joseph Thompson) said: "I assume you've already laid out the general idea [to Büchel] (we build it, and it belongs to you)," and also noted that Büchel had the right to "sell all or part of it." The Museum's proposed contract, which was never signed, would have conferred ownership on Büchel. It stated that, "[u]pon termination of the exhibition, the fabricated work shall be owned outright by you, including all copyrights and related preparatory materials."

NOTE 25: Our analysis of the right-of-integrity tarpaulin claim disposes as well of Büchel's contention that covering the installation constituted a modification of the original work that resulted in the creation of a derivative work.

STUDY QUESTIONS

- In *MASS MoCA v. Büchel*, the museum initiated the lawsuit. Why do you think they did this? Describe the relationship between the museum and the artist. Why wasn't a written agreement executed by the parties? What intellectual property issues were at stake?
- The Visual Artists Rights Act (VARA) allows an artist to waive their VARA rights through a written waiver—termed a "VARA waiver." How would a VARA waiver have avoided this conflict? Why do you think museums are hesitant to insist that commissioned artists execute a VARA waiver?
- The district court in *MASS MoCA v. Büchel*, issued a bench ruling granting declaratory judgement for the museum on the issue of whether it could display the unfinished work. Instead of continuing to exhibit the unfinished work, the museum decided instead to close the exhibit. Why do you think the museum did this?
- What advice would you give the museum to avoid problems with commissioned artists in the future?

TITLE, PROVENANCE, AND AUTHENTICITY

Questions regarding title and provenance may arise at the time a work is being acquired through a gift or a purchase, or later as the result of a claim alleging theft or seeking repatriation. Title and provenance questions may also be encountered as part of a collections inventory, when a work is loaned, in connection with insurance coverage, or when a work is being considered for deaccessioning.

When we use the term "title" in the legal sense, we are not talking about the name of the work. Title in a work refers to the rights of ownership in the work. The term is often used in connection with real estate and personal property. If you own title to a piece of real property—your house for example—that means you are its owner. You are the "title owner of record." Similarly, if you own a car, your ownership is recorded by way of a document called a vehicle title. When you sell the car, you also assign or transfer the title to it to the new owner. In the museum context, the concept of "title" to a work similarly involves aspects of ownership.

While museums do not actually "own" the works in their collections in the traditional sense, but rather hold them in trust for the public, as trustees they are considered to hold legal title to the works in their collections. When used in connection with museum collections, two aspects of title must be considered—completeness of title, and quality of title.

Completeness of title involves an assessment of the rights in the work that are owned or being acquired. In addition to ownership of the physical work, ownership of intellectual property rights in the work and any restrictions or limitations on ownership, as well as the rights of any beneficiaries, must be considered.

Quality of title, on the other hand, involves an assessment of the work's provenance and authenticity. "Good title" refers to a work that is not subject to any liens, encumbrances, or claims affecting current ownership in the work. "Chain of title" refers to the record of ownership in the work overtime. The "provenance" of a work refers not only to completeness of title, but more broadly to all information on the history of an object. In addition to information on ownership, the provenance of a work includes information on its creation, exhibition, loan, publication, and other aspects of the work's history. For archeological works, the object's "provenience" or "find spot"—that is, the place where the work was found—is an important part of the provenance of the work.

When acquiring a work, the museum should exercise due diligence regarding both the completeness and quality of title to the work. Before acquiring a work, the museum should request all provenance information that the donor or seller has. The museum may ask the transferor to complete a "provenance questionnaire" and provide all documentation in his possession. The museum should also conduct its own independent research about both the object and the transferor.

The status of the transferor of the work—which may be a donor or a seller—should be carefully assessed. Does the person offering to transfer the work have the authority to do so? Legal disputes involving the person giving or selling the work may arise in several ways. Disputes involving ownership may be brought by a spouse, or in the case of a bequest, by one of the heirs, or because the owner (knowingly or unknowingly) is in the possession of stolen art. The financial status of the owner can also impact the transfer. A transfer of property by an owner who subsequently files for bankruptcy may be deemed a fraudulent transfer. Under bankruptcy law, a sale or other transfer may be voided up to six years after the transaction has occurred. For these reasons, due diligence should include consideration of the transferor's reputation, financial situation, marital status, and any other relevant information that may impact the transferor's authority to transfer ownership in the work.

Research about the object should include a check for any Uniform Commercial Code (UCC) filings that might indicate liens or encumbrances; a search of art loss registries and databases of lost or stolen art; and, if applicable, research into the origin of the work) and its movement from its country of origin ("source country") to its present location. When acquiring antiquities and ancient art and other cultural property, it is always important to ask "where did the object come from and how did it get here?" and in particular "were all applicable export and import laws followed?" Any information that may affect the museum's right to own the object ("enjoy quiet title") should be carefully assessed. These questions will be explored later in this chapter.

In the case of a purchase, the purchase agreement may include representations and warranties regarding the status of the transferor and about the object being purchased. In the process of negotiating the scope of the representations and warranties, the museum may learn valuable information from the transferor. For example, if the transferor refuses to make a representation about a particular aspect of the work (regarding its provenance or authenticity, for example), this can raise a red flag. The purchase agreement may also include an indemnification provision requiring the transferor to be responsible for any claims or lawsuits arising from the transfer. These contractual provisions may help to reduce the risks associated with the acquisition, but they are not a substitute for the museum's own independent research and assessment.

Stolen art presents particular problems. Under American law, a thief cannot convey good title. As a result, the victim of a theft may—often at a much later date—bring a claim to recover a work that has been stolen. In legal parlance, these are referred to as "replevin actions" or "restitution claims." Fundamentally, these replevin and restitution cases involve disputes over who properly holds title to the artwork. Given the particular facts, did the previous owner retain title, or was title lost due to some intervening event? Defenses to a claim of superior ownership include the statute of limitations, adverse possession, and laches (the failure to assert one's possessory rights). Stolen art cases often involve a "good faith purchaser"—that is, the person who has acquired the work does not know the work has been stolen and, as a result, is as much a victim of the theft as the owner of the stolen work.

Statutes of limitations and laches defenses can cut off claims to artwork that disappeared a long time ago. A key issue in cases involving a statute of limitations defense concerns when the clock started ticking on the obligation to initiate the lawsuit. Some jurisdictions apply the so-called "Discovery Rule," which states that the cause of action accrues at the time the victim of the theft, acting with reasonable due diligence, discovers or should have discovered the location of the missing property. Other jurisdictions apply the "Demand and Refusal Rule," which says that the statute begins to run when a demand for the return of the stolen object is refused by the current possessor.

A successful laches defense must show that the delay by claimant in asserting their claim was unreasonable and unfairly prejudiced the possessor. The *Georgia O'Keeffe* case reprinted below considers these title issues in the context of several paintings that resurfaced over thirty years after they first went missing.

In assessing whether to order the return (restitution) of the work, the courts consider equitable considerations, including what efforts the owner took to recover the stolen property, the extent of the buyer's due diligence in assessing whether the work might be stolen, and the extent to which the court's decision may prejudice a good faith purchaser.

Ethical considerations weigh heavily in cases involving a good faith purchaser of stolen art. A museum may have an ethical obligation to "right a wrong" even when the museum may be on the winning side of the legal argument. The major museum associations have promulgated ethical guidelines regarding particular collecting areas—including works with Nazi-era provenance and antiquities—to address the problem of stolen and looted objects. The International Foundation for Art Research (IFAR) has compiled a list of these guidelines on their website (www.ifar.org). Museum trustees should carefully consider these ethical obligations and the evidentiary basis of the claim before developing a litigation strategy. (See discussion below regarding "requests for return.")

Often an appraisal of a work is performed as part of acquiring a work. An appraisal is an assessment of the economic value of the work. An appraisal may be required for tax purposes or for insurance purposes. Since the value of a work is highly dependent on the authenticity of the work, conducting an appraisal requires an assessment of the work's authenticity.

The essence of "authenticity" is whether the work is what it purports to be. With artwork, often this involves questions regarding attribution—that is, is the work by the artist to whom it is being attributed? For antiquities, the issues may revolve around the object's history, including where it was found. Authentication of a work involves careful consideration of the work's provenance (ownership history), provenience ("find spot"), connoisseurship, and scientific and technical analysis. Some artists or their estates convene "authentication boards" which opine on the authenticity of a given artist's oeuvre. Some of these authentication boards have become contentious in recent years, attracting lots of litigation brought by disgruntled art owners. As a result a number of prominent artists' estates have discontinued the practice.

Disputes regarding appraisals and authentication frequently result in lawsuits. Legal claims may be based on misrepresentation (either intentionally or negligently representing that work is not what it is); disparagement or defamation (harm suffered from the devaluation of a work or of one's reputation); breach of contract. (the purchaser did not get the benefit of its bargain), or other legal theories.

Dealing with unsolicited gifts and unclaimed objects left in the temporary custody of the museum is a perennial problem which also involves title issues. It is not unusual in conducting a collections inventory to find objects which lack documentation of ownership. Sometimes works were loaned to the museum and forgotten. In other cases, the owners cannot be located, or are unresponsive. These objects are sometimes referred to as "old loans" or "objects found in the collection." If the object had been on loan to the museum, the object is subject to bailment—the museum as bailee has an obligation to care for the object unless the bailment relationship can be terminated. Because there is no documentation demonstrating a clear transfer of ownership, the museum cannot establish good title to the object. This becomes a particular issue when the museum wants to deaccession and dispose of these objects. For further discussion of these abandoned or "orphaned" objects, see the discussion in the Deaccessioning and Disposal section below.

CASES AND OTHER READINGS

Reading Note: The case reprinted below addresses questions regarding title to artwork. Several paintings from an art gallery that went missing in 1946 resurfaced over thirty years later at another art gallery. At issue was whether the present holder had acquired title to the works. Before the court could address who owned the artwork, it had to clarify the applicable law. As a result, the case contains a detailed discussion of title to works of art.

GEORGIA O'KEEFFE V. BARRY SNYDER D/B/A PRINCETON GALLERY OF FINE ART

416 A.2d 862 (N.J. 1980).
The opinion of the Court was delivered by POLLOCK, J.

This is an appeal from an order of the Appellate Division granting summary judgment to plaintiff, Georgia O'Keeffe, against defendant, Barry Snyder, d/b/a Princeton Gallery of Fine Art, for replevin of three small pictures painted by O'Keeffe. *O'Keeffe v. Snyder,* 170 *N.J. Super.* 75 (1979). In her complaint, filed in March, 1976, O'Keeffe alleged she was the owner of the paintings and that they were stolen from a New York art gallery in 1946. Snyder asserted he was a purchaser for value of the paintings, he had title by adverse possession, and O'Keeffe's action was barred by the expiration of the six-year period of limitations provided by *N.J.S.A.* 2A:14-1 pertaining to an action in replevin. Snyder impleaded third party defendant, Ulrich A. Frank, from whom Snyder purchased the paintings in 1975 for $35,000.

The trial court granted summary judgment for Snyder on the ground that O'Keeffe's action was barred because it was not commenced within six years of the alleged theft. The Appellate Division reversed and entered judgment for O'Keeffe. *O'Keeffe, supra,* 170 *N.J. Super.* at 92. A majority of that court concluded that the paintings were stolen, the defenses of expiration of the statute of limitations and title by adverse possession were identical, and Snyder had not proved the elements of adverse possession. Consequently, the majority ruled that O'Keeffe could still enforce her right to possession of the paintings. The dissenting judge stated that the appropriate measurement of the period of limitation was not by analogy to adverse possession, but by application of the "discovery rule" pertaining to some statutes of limitation. He concluded that the six-year period of limitations commenced when O'Keeffe knew or should have known who unlawfully possessed the paintings, and that the matter should be remanded to determine if and when that event had occurred. *Id.* at 96-97.

We granted certification to consider not only the issues raised in the dissenting opinion, but all other issues. 81 *N.J.* 406 (1979). We reverse and remand the matter for a plenary hearing in accordance with this opinion.

I

The record, limited to pleadings, affidavits, answers to interrogatories, and depositions, is fraught with factual conflict. Apart from the creation of the paintings by O'Keeffe and their discovery in Snyder's gallery in 1976, the parties agree on little else.

O'Keeffe contended the paintings were stolen in 1946 from a gallery, An American Place. The gallery was operated by her late husband, the famous photographer Alfred Stieglitz. An American Place was a cooperative undertaking of O'Keeffe and some other American artists identified by her as Marin, Hardin, Dove, Andema, and Stevens. In 1946, Stieglitz arranged an exhibit which included an O'Keeffe painting, identified as Cliffs. According to O'Keeffe, one day in March, 1946, she and Stieglitz discovered Cliffs was missing from the wall of the exhibit. O'Keeffe estimates the value of the painting at the time of the alleged theft to have been about $150.

About two weeks later, O'Keeffe noticed that two other paintings, Seaweed and Fragments, were missing from a storage room at An American Place. She did not tell anyone, even Stieglitz, about the missing paintings, since she did not want to upset him. Before the date when O'Keeffe discovered the disappearance of Seaweed, she had already sold it (apparently for a string of amber beads) to a Mrs. Weiner, now deceased. Following the grant of the motion for summary judgment by the trial court in favor of Snyder, O'Keeffe submitted a release from the legatees of Mrs. Weiner purportedly assigning to O'Keeffe their interest in the sale.

O'Keeffe testified on depositions that at about the same time as the disappearance of her paintings, 12 or 13 miniature paintings by Marin also were stolen from An American Place. According to O'Keeffe, a man named Estrick took the Marin paintings and "maybe a few other things." Estrick distributed the Marin paintings to members of the theater world who, when confronted by Stieglitz, returned them. However, neither Stieglitz nor O'Keeffe confronted Estrick with the loss of any of the O'Keeffe paintings.

This photograph by Alfred Stieglitz documents a 1931 exhibition of Georgia O'Keefe paintings at An American Place, a cooperative gallery operated by Stieglitz in New York City. The gallery was on the seventeenth floor of a newly constructed skyscraper on Madison Avenue. In 1946, three small O'Keeffe's paintings— Cliffs, Fragments, and Seaweed*—disappeared from the gallery. Thirty years later, O'Keeffe sued art dealer Barry Synder and the Princeton Art Gallery for their return in O'Keeffe v. Synder.*

There was no evidence of a break and entry at An American Place on the dates when O'Keeffe discovered the disappearance of her paintings. Neither Stieglitz nor O'Keeffe reported them missing to the New York Police Department or any other law enforcement agency. Apparently the paintings were uninsured, and O'Keeffe did not seek reimbursement from an insurance company. Similarly, neither O'Keeffe nor Stieglitz advertised the loss of the paintings in Art News or any other publication. Nonetheless, they discussed it with associates in the art world and later O'Keeffe mentioned the loss to the director of the Art Institute of Chicago, but she did not ask him to do anything because "it wouldn't have been my way."

O'Keeffe does not contend that Frank or Snyder had actual knowledge of the alleged theft. Stieglitz died in the summer of 1946, and O'Keeffe explains she did not pursue her efforts to locate the paintings because she was settling his estate. In 1947, she retained the services of Doris Bry to help settle the estate. Bry urged O'Keeffe to report the loss of the paintings, but O'Keeffe declined because "they never got anything back by reporting it." Finally, in 1972, O'Keeffe authorized Bry to report the theft to the Art Dealers Association of America, Inc., which maintains for its members a registry of stolen paintings. The record does not indicate whether such a registry existed at the time the paintings disappeared.

In September, 1975, O'Keeffe learned that the paintings were in the Andrew Crispo Gallery in New York on consignment from Bernard Danenberg Galleries. On February 11, 1976, O'Keeffe discovered that Ulrich A. Frank had sold the paintings to Barry Snyder, d/b/a Princeton Gallery of Fine Art. She demanded their return and, following Snyder's refusal, instituted this action for replevin.

Frank traces his possession of the paintings to his father, Dr. Frank, who died in 1968. He claims there is a family relationship by marriage between his family and the Stieglitz family, a contention that O'Keeffe disputes. Frank does not know how his father acquired the paintings, but he recalls seeing them in his father's apartment in New Hampshire as early as 1941-1943, a period that precedes the alleged theft. Consequently, Frank's factual contentions are inconsistent with O'Keeffe's allegation of theft. Until 1965, Dr. Frank occasionally lent the paintings to Ulrich Frank. In 1965, Dr. and Mrs. Frank formally gave the paintings to Ulrich Frank, who kept them in his residences in Yardley, Pennsylvania and Princeton, New Jersey. In 1968, he exhibited anonymously Cliffs and Fragments in a one day art show in the Jewish Community Center in Trenton. All of these events precede O'Keeffe's listing of the paintings as stolen with the Art Dealers Association of America, Inc. in 1972.

Frank claims continuous possession of the paintings through his father for over thirty years and admits selling the paintings to Snyder. Snyder and Frank do not trace their provenance, or history of possession of the paintings, back to O'Keeffe.

As indicated, Snyder moved for summary judgment on the theory that O'Keeffe's action was barred by the statute of limitations and title had vested in Frank by adverse possession.

For purposes of his motion, Snyder conceded that the paintings had been stolen. On her cross motion, O'Keeffe urged that the paintings were stolen, the statute of limitations had not run, and title to the paintings remained in her.

II

In general, cross motions for summary judgment do not "obviate a plenary trial of disputed issues of fact, where such exists; nor do cross-motions constitute a waiver by the litigants to such a trial." *Rotwein et al. v. General Accident Group & Cas. Co.,* 103 *N.J. Super.* 406, 424-425 (Law Div. 1968). Cross motions do not warrant granting summary judgment unless one of the moving parties is entitled to judgment as a matter of law. 6 *Moore's Federal Practice* (2d ed. 1976), § 56.13 at 341. Cross motions for summary judgment do not preclude the existence of issues of fact. *Id.* at 345. Although a defendant may assert that, according to his theory of the case, the material facts are undisputed, he must be allowed to show that if plaintiff's theory is adopted there remains a genuine issue of material fact. *See Walling v. Richmond Screw Anchor Co.,* 154 *F.*2d 780, 784 (2d Cir.1946), *cert.* den. 328 *U.S.* 870, 66 *S.Ct.* 1383, 90 *L.Ed.* 1640 (1946). Where there are cross motions for summary judgment, a party may make concessions for the purposes of his motion that do not carry over and support the motion of his adversary. 6 *Moore's, supra,* § 56.13 at 344. *Eagle v. Louisiana and Southern Life Insurance Company,* 464 *F.*2d 607, 608 (10th Cir.1972); *Begnaud v. White,* 170 *F.*2d 323, 327 (6th Cir.1948).

The Appellate Division accepted O'Keeffe's contention that the paintings had been stolen. However, in his deposition, Ulrich Frank traces possession of the paintings to his father in the early 1940's, a date that precedes the alleged theft by several years. The factual dispute about the loss of the paintings by O'Keeffe and their acquisition by Frank, as well as the other subsequently described factual issues, warrant a remand for a plenary hearing. *See Judson v. Peoples Bank & Trust Co. of Westfield,* 17 *N.J.* 67 (1954).

In reversing the cross motions for summary judgment, the Appellate Division erred in accepting one of two conflicting versions of material fact: the theft of the paintings in March, 1946 as asserted by O'Keeffe as against the possession of the paintings by the Frank family since the early 1940's. Instead of recognizing the existence of this controversy, the Appellate Division misconstrued Snyder's concession that the paintings had been stolen. That concession was made to enable the trial court to determine Snyder's motion for summary judgment that title had passed by adverse possession. The concession was not available to resolve O'Keeffe's cross motion for summary judgment. Hence, there is an issue of material fact, whether the paintings were stolen, that compels remand for trial.

Without purporting to limit the scope of the trial, other factual issues include whether (1) O'Keeffe acquired title to Seaweed by obtaining releases from the legatees of Mrs. Weiner;

(2) the paintings were not stolen but sold, lent, consigned, or given by Stieglitz to Dr. Frank or someone else without O'Keeffe's knowledge before he died; and (3) there was any business or family relationship between Stieglitz and Dr. Frank so that the original possession of the paintings by the Frank family may have been under claim of right.

III

On the limited record before us, we cannot determine now who has title to the paintings. That determination will depend on the evidence adduced at trial. Nonetheless, we believe it may aid the trial court and the parties to resolve questions of law that may become relevant at trial.

Our decision begins with the principle that, generally speaking, if the paintings were stolen, the thief acquired no title and could not transfer good title to others regardless of their good faith and ignorance of the theft. *Joseph v. Lesnevich,* 56 *N.J. Super.* 340, 346 (App.Div. 1959); *Kutner Buick, Inc. v. Strelecki,* 111 *N.J. Super.* 89, 97 (Ch.Div. 1970); *see Ashton v. Allen,* 70 *N.J.L.* 117, 119 (Sup.Ct. 1903). Proof of theft would advance O'Keeffe's right to possession of the paintings absent other considerations such as expiration of the statute of limitations.

Another issue that may become relevant at trial is whether Frank or his father acquired a "voidable title" to the paintings under *N.J.S.A.* 12A:2-403(1). That section, part of the Uniform Commercial Code (U.C.C.), does not change the basic principle that a mere possessor cannot transfer good title. 2 *Anderson, Uniform Commercial Code* (2d ed. 1971) § 2-403:6 at 41 (*Anderson*). Nonetheless, the U.C.C. permits a person with voidable title to transfer good title to a good faith purchaser for value in certain circumstances. *N.J.S.A.* 12A:2-403(1). If the facts developed at trial merit application of that section, then Frank may have transferred good title to Snyder, thereby providing a defense to O'Keeffe's action. No party on this appeal has urged factual or legal contentions concerning the applicability of the U.C.C. Consequently, a more complete discussion of the U.C.C. would be premature, particularly in light of our decision to remand the matter for trial.

On this appeal, the critical legal question is when O'Keeffe's cause of action accrued. The fulcrum on which the outcome turns is the statute of limitations in *N.J.S.A.* 2A:14-1, which provides that an action for replevin of goods or chattels must be commenced within six years after the accrual of the cause of action. The trial court found that O'Keeffe's cause of action accrued on the date of the alleged theft, March, 1946, and concluded that her action was barred. The Appellate Division found that an action might have accrued more than six years before the date of suit if possession by the defendant or his predecessors satisfied the elements of adverse possession. As indicated, the Appellate Division concluded that Snyder had not established those elements and that the O'Keeffe action was not barred by the statute of limitations.

Since the alleged theft occurred in New York, a preliminary question is whether the statute of limitations of New York or New Jersey applies. The New York statute, *N.Y. Civ. Prac. Law* § 214 (McKinney), has been interpreted so that the statute of limitations on a cause of action for replevin does not begin to run until after refusal upon demand for the return of the goods. *Menzel v. List,* 49 *Misc.*2d 300, 267 *N.Y.S.*2d 804 (Sup.Ct. 1966), aff'd as modified, 28 *A.D.*2d 516, 279 *N.Y.S.*2d 608 (App.Div. 1966), third party claim reversed on other grounds, 24 *N.Y.*2d 91, 246 *N.E.*2d 742, 298 *N.Y.S.*2d 979 (Ct. App. 1969). Here, O'Keeffe demanded return of the paintings in February, 1976. If the New York statute applied, her action would have been commenced within the period of limitations.

The traditional rule to determine which of two statutes of limitations is applicable is that the statute of the forum governs unless the limitation is a condition of the cause of action. *See Marshall v. Geo. M. Brewster & Son, Inc.,* 37 *N.J.* 176 (1962). However, this Court has discarded the mechanical rule that the statute of limitations of the forum must be employed in every suit on a foreign cause of action. *Heavner v. Uniroyal, Inc.,* 63 *N.J.* 130, 140-141 (1973). *Heavner* set out five requirements for barring an action by applying a statute of limitations other than the appropriate New Jersey statute: (1) the cause of action arose in the other state; (2) the parties are all present in and amenable to jurisdiction in the other state; (3) New Jersey has no substantial interest in the matter; (4) the substantive law of the other jurisdiction is applicable, and (5) the limitations' period of the other jurisdiction has expired at the time of the commencement of the suit in New Jersey. *Id.* at 141. The *Heavner* rule provides a limited and special exception to the general rule that the rule of the forum determines the applicable period of limitations. *Raskulinecz v. Raskulinecz,* 141 *N.J. Super.* 148, 153 (Law Div. 1976). In the present case, none of the parties resides in New York and the paintings are located in New Jersey. On the facts before us, it would appear that the appropriate statute of limitations is the law of the forum, *N.J.S.A.* 2A:14-1. On remand, the trial court may reconsider this issue if the parties present other relevant facts.

IV

On the assumption that New Jersey law will apply, we shall consider significant questions raised about the interpretation of *N.J.S.A.* 2A:14-1. The purpose of a statute of limitations is to "stimulate to activity and punish negligence" and "promote repose by giving security and stability to human affairs." *Wood v. Carpenter,* 101 *U.S.* 135, 139, 25 *L.Ed.* 807, 808 (1879); *Tevis v. Tevis,* 79 *N.J.* 422, 430-431 (1979); *Fernandi v. Strully,* 35 *N.J.* 434, 438 (1961). A statute of limitations achieves those purposes by barring a cause of action after the statutory period. In certain instances, this Court has ruled that the literal language of a statute of limitations should yield to other considerations. *Compare, e.g., Velmohos v. Maren Engineering Corp.,* 83 *N.J.* 282, 293 (1980) *with Galligan v. Westfield Centre Service, Inc.,* 82 *N.J.* 188, 192-193 (1980).

To avoid harsh results from the mechanical application of the statute, the courts have developed a concept known as the discovery rule. *Lopez v. Swyer,* 62 *N.J.* 267, 273-275 (1973); *Prosser, The Law of Torts* (4 ed. 1971), § 30 at 144-145; 51 *Am.Jur.*2d, *Limitation of Actions,* § 146 at 716. The discovery rule provides that, in an appropriate case, a cause of action will not accrue until the injured party discovers, or by exercise of reasonable diligence and intelligence should have discovered, facts which form the basis of a cause of action. *Burd v. New Jersey Telephone Company,* 76 *N.J.* 284, 291-292 (1978). The rule is essentially a principle of equity, the purpose of which is to mitigate unjust results that otherwise might flow from strict adherence to a rule of law. *Lopez, supra,* 62 *N.J.* at 273-274.

This Court first announced the discovery rule in *Fernandi, supra,* 35 *N.J.* at 434. In *Fernandi,* a wing nut was left in a patient's abdomen following surgery and was not discovered for three years. *Id.* at 450-451. The majority held that fairness and justice mandated that the statute of limitations should not have commenced running until the plaintiff knew or had reason to know of the presence of the foreign object in her body. The discovery rule has since been extended to other areas of medical malpractice. *See, e.g., Lopez, supra* (alleged negligent radiation therapy following a radical mastectomy for breast cancer); *Yerzy v. Levine,* 108 *N.J. Super.* 222 (App.Div.), aff'd per curiam as modified, 57 *N.J.* 234 (1970) (negligent severance by surgeon of bile duct).

Increasing acceptance of the principle of the discovery rule has extended the doctrine to contexts unrelated to medical malpractice. *See, e.g., Diamond v. New Jersey Bell Telephone Co.,* 51 *N.J.* 594, 596-597 (1968) (discovery rule applicable in negligent installation of an underground conduit causing flooding of plaintiff's property); *New Mkt. Poultry Farms, Inc. v. Fellows,* 51 *N.J.* 419, 425 (1968) (discovery rule applicable to negligently prepared survey discovered eleven years after the act); *Brown v. College of Medicine and Dentistry,* 167 *N.J. Super.* 532, 536-537 (Law Div. 1979) (dicta would permit action for lost wages pursuant to breach of union's duty to represent fairly bargaining unit even though action instituted beyond period of limitations); *McCoy Co., Inc. v. S.S. "Theomitor III",* 133 *N.J. Super.* 308 (Law Div. 1975) (discovery rule permits untimely amendment of complaint to include subsidiary corporations where parent company had been sued within limitations' period); *Gibbins v. Kosuga,* 121 *N.J. Super.* 252 (Law Div. 1972) (cause of action allowed under *N.J.S.A.* 2A:14-1 when plaintiffs discovered nine years after closing that well was not located on their property). *See also Rosenau v. City of New Brunswick,* 51 *N.J.* 130, 139-140 (1968) (discovery rule discussed as applying to cause of action under *N.J.S.A.* 2A:14-1 for damage to plaintiff's home fourteen years after installation of defective water meter).

The statute of limitations before us, *N.J.S.A.* 2A:14-1, has been held subject to the discovery rule in an action for wrongful detention of shares of stock. *Federal Insurance Co. v. Hausler,* 108 *N.J. Super.* 421, 426 (App.Div. 1970). In *Hausler,* the defendant purchased preferred stock of a corporation through a stockbroker. On March 9, 1961, the broker erroneously sent to the customer a certificate for common stock of greater value. The broker discovered the error in December, 1961, but did not learn the identity of the customer's account in which the error was made until November, 1962. Defendants refused to exchange the common stock for the preferred stock. Plaintiff, a bonding company subrogated to the broker's rights, instituted an action on July 2, 1968, within six years of the date on which the broker learned the identity of the defendants as the customers who wrongfully received the common stock, but more than six years after the broker knew it had a cause of action. Judge Goldmann, writing for a unanimous court, reversed the grant of a summary judgment for defendants and remanded the matter for a full trial to determine whether (1) the broker knew or reasonably should have known of the error and the defendants' identity in December, 1961 and (2) defendants knew of the mistake from the beginning and fraudulently concealed it. Overruling the trial court which had concluded "[t]his is not a good case in which to apply the discovery rule," Judge Goldmann found the discovery rule applicable. *Id.* at 424, 426. Similarly, we conclude that the discovery rule applies to an action for replevin of a painting under *N.J.S.A.* 2A:14-1. O'Keeffe's cause of action accrued when she first knew, or reasonably should have known through the exercise of due diligence, of the cause of action, including the identity of the possessor of the paintings. *See* N. Ward, *Adverse Possession of Loaned or Stolen Objects Is Possession Still 9/10ths of the Law?*, published in *Legal Problems of Museum Administration* (ALI-ABA 1980) at 89-90.

We leave to the discretion of the trial judge whether to conduct a preliminary hearing to determine whether O'Keeffe is entitled to the benefit of the discovery rule. Ordinarily that determination would be made in a preliminary hearing out of the presence of the jury. *Lopez, supra,* 62 *N.J.* at 275. But if much of the evidence adduced at the hearing will be the same as that adduced at trial, the judge may elect to receive the evidence in the course of the trial and decide the limitations question at the end of the plaintiff's case or at the conclusion of all evidence. If that procedure is adopted, the trial judge should exclude the jury when the anticipated evidence relates only to the limitations issue, as receipt of that evidence in the presence of the jury might prejudice another party. *Id.* at 275 n. 3.

In determining whether O'Keeffe is entitled to the benefit of the discovery rule, the trial court should consider, among others, the following issues: (1) whether O'Keeffe used due diligence to recover the paintings at the time of the alleged theft and thereafter; (2) whether at the time of the alleged theft there was an effective method, other than talking to her colleagues, for O'Keeffe to alert the art world; and (3) whether registering paintings with the Art Dealers Association of America, Inc. or any other organization would put a reasonably prudent purchaser of art on constructive notice that someone other than the possessor was the true owner.

V

The acquisition of title to real and personal property by adverse possession is based on the expiration of a statute of limitations. R. Brown, *The Law of Personal Property* (3d ed. 1975), § 4.1 at 33 (Brown). Adverse possession does not create title by prescription apart from the statute of limitations. Walsh, *Title by Adverse Possession,* 17 *N.Y.U.L.Q.Rev.* 44, 82 (1939) (Walsh); *see Developments in the Law Statutes of Limitations,* 63 *Harv.L.Rev.* 1177 (1950) (*Developments*).

To establish title by adverse possession to chattels, the rule of law has been that the possession must be hostile, actual, visible, exclusive, and continuous. *Redmond v. New Jersey Historical Society,* 132 *N.J. Eq.* 464, 474 (E. & A. 1942); 54 *C.J.S. Limitations of Actions* § 119 at 23. *Redmond* involved a portrait of Captain James Lawrence by Gilbert Stuart, which was bequeathed by its owner to her son with a provision that if he should die leaving no descendants, it should go to the New Jersey Historical Society. The owner died in 1887, when her son was 14, and her executors delivered the painting to the Historical Society. The painting remained in the possession of the Historical Society for over 50 years, until 1938, when the son died and his children, the legatees under his will, demanded its return. The Historical Society refused, and the legatees instituted a replevin action.

The Historical Society argued that the applicable statute of limitations, the predecessor of *N.J.S.A.* 2A:14-1, had run and that plaintiffs' action was barred. The Court of Errors and Appeals held that the doctrine of adverse possession applied to chattels as well as to real property, *Redmond, supra,* 132 *N.J. Eq.* at 473, and that the statute of limitations would not begin to run against the true owner until possession became adverse. *Id.* at 475. The Court found that the Historical Society had done nothing inconsistent with the theory that the painting was a "voluntary bailment or gratuitous loan" and had "utterly failed to prove that its possession of the portrait was 'adversary,' 'hostile.'" *Id.* at 474-475. The Court found further that the Historical Society had not asserted ownership until 1938, when it refused to deliver the painting to plaintiff, and that the statute did not begin to run until that date. Consequently, the Court ordered the painting to be returned to plaintiffs.

The only other New Jersey case applying adverse possession to chattels is *Joseph v. Lesnevich,* 56 *N.J. Super.* 340 (App.Div. 1949). In *Lesnevich,* several negotiable bearer bonds were stolen from plaintiff in 1951. In October, 1951, Lesnevich received an envelope containing the bonds. On October 21, 1951, Lesnevich and his business partner pledged the bonds with a credit company. They failed to pay the loan secured by the bonds and requested the credit company to sell the bonds to pay the loan. On August 1, 1952, the president of the credit company purchased the bonds and sold them to his son. In 1958, within one day of the expiration of six years from the date of the purchase, the owner of the bonds sued the credit company and its president, among others, for conversion of the bonds. The Appellate Division found that the credit company and its president held the bonds "as openly and notoriously as the nature of the property would permit." *Lesnevich, supra,* 56 *N.J. Super.* at 355. The pledge of the bonds with the credit company was considered to be open possession.

As *Lesnevich* demonstrates, there is an inherent problem with many kinds of personal property that will raise questions whether their possession has been open, visible, and notorious. In *Lesnevich,* the court strained to conclude that in holding bonds as collateral, a credit company satisfied the requirement of open, visible, and notorious possession. Other problems with the requirement of visible, open, and notorious possession readily come to mind. For example, if jewelry is stolen from a municipality in one county in New Jersey, it is unlikely that the owner would learn that someone is openly wearing that jewelry in another county or even in the same municipality. Open and visible possession of personal property, such as jewelry, may not be sufficient to put the original owner on actual or constructive notice of the identity of the possessor.

The problem is even more acute with works of art. Like many kinds of personal property, works of art are readily moved and easily concealed. O'Keeffe argues that nothing short of public display should be sufficient to alert the true owner and start the statute running. Although there is merit in that contention from the perspective of the original owner, the effect is to impose a heavy burden on the purchasers of paintings who wish to enjoy the paintings in the privacy of their homes.

In the present case, the trial court and Appellate Division concluded that the paintings, which allegedly had been kept in the private residences of the Frank family, had not been held visibly, openly, and notoriously. Notwithstanding that conclusion, the trial court ruled that the statute of limitations began to run at the time of the theft and had expired before the commencement of suit. The Appellate Division determined it was bound by the rules in *Redmond* and reversed the trial court on the theory that the defenses of adverse possession and expiration of the statute of limitations were identical. Nonetheless, for different reasons, the majority and dissenting judges in the Appellate Division acknowledged deficiencies in identifying the statute of limitations with adverse possession. The majority stated that, as a practical matter, requiring compliance with adverse possession would preclude barring stale claims and acquiring title to personal property. *O'Keeffe, supra,* 170 *N.J. Super.* at 86. The dissenting judge feared that identifying the statutes of limitations with adverse possession would lead to a "handbook for larceny." *Id.* at 96. The divergent conclusions of the lower courts suggest that the doctrine of adverse possession no longer provides a fair and reasonable means of resolving this kind of dispute. The problem is serious. According to an affidavit submitted in this matter by the president of the International Foundation for Art Research, there has been an "explosion in art thefts" and there is a "worldwide phenomenon of art theft which has reached epidemic proportions."

The limited record before us provides a brief glimpse into the arcane world of sales of art, where paintings worth vast sums of money sometimes are bought without inquiry about their provenance. There does not appear to be a reasonably available method for an owner of art to record the ownership or theft of paintings. Similarly, there are no reasonable means readily available to a purchaser to ascertain the provenance of a painting. It may be time for the art world to establish a means by which a good faith purchaser may reasonably obtain the provenance of a painting. An efficient registry of original works of art might better serve the interests of artists, owners of art, and bona fide purchasers than the law of adverse possession with all of its uncertainties. L. DuBoff, *The Deskbook of Art Law* at 470-472 (Fed. Pub.Inc. 1977). Although we cannot mandate the initiation of a registration system, we can develop a rule for the commencement and running of the statute of limitations that is more responsive to the needs of the art world than the doctrine of adverse possession.

We are persuaded that the introduction of equitable considerations through the discovery rule provides a more satisfactory response than the doctrine of adverse possession. The discovery rule shifts the emphasis from the conduct of the possessor to the conduct of the owner. The focus of the inquiry will no longer be whether the possessor has met the tests of adverse possession, but whether the owner has acted with due diligence in pursuing his or her personal property. For example, under the discovery rule, if an artist diligently seeks the recovery of a lost or stolen painting, but cannot find it or discover the identity of the possessor, the statute of limitations will not begin to run. The rule permits an artist who uses reasonable efforts to report, investigate, and recover a painting to preserve the rights of title and possession.

Properly interpreted, the discovery rule becomes a vehicle for transporting equitable considerations into the statute of limitations for replevin, *N.J.S.A.* 2A:14-1. In determining whether the discovery rule should apply, a court should identify, evaluate, and weigh the equitable claims of all parties. *Lopez, supra,* 62 *N.J.* at 274. If a chattel is concealed from the true owner, fairness compels tolling the statute during the period of concealment. *See Lopez, supra,* 62 *N.J.* at 275 n. 2; *Developments, supra,* 1220 (1950). That conclusion is consistent with tolling the statute of limitations in a medical malpractice action where the physician is guilty of fraudulent concealment. *See Tortorello v. Reinfeld,* 6 *N.J.* 58, 67 (1950); *Bauer v. Bowen,* 63 *N.J. Super.* 225 (App.Div. 1960).

It is consistent also with the law of replevin as it has developed apart from the discovery rule. In an action for replevin, the period of limitations ordinarily will run against the owner of lost or stolen property from the time of the wrongful taking, absent fraud or concealment. Where the chattel is fraudulently concealed, the general rule is that the statute is tolled. 51 *Am.Jur.*2d, *Limitation of Actions,* § 124 at 693; 54 *C.J.S. Limitations of Actions,* § 119 at 23; Annotation, "When statute of limitations commences to run against action to recover, or for conversion of, property stolen or otherwise wrongfully taken," 136 *A.L.R.* 658, 661-665 (1942); *see* Dawson, *Fraudulent Concealment and Statutes of Limitation,* 31 *Mich.L.Rev.* 875 (1933); Annotation, "What constitutes concealment which will prevent running of statutes of limitations," 173 *A.L.R.* 576 (1948); Annotation, "When statute of limitations begins to run against action for conversion of property by theft," 79 *A.L.R.*3d 847, § 3 at 853 (1975); *see also* Dawson, *Estoppel and Statutes of Limitation,* 34 *Mich.L.Rev.* 1, 23-24 (1935).

A purchaser from a private party would be well-advised to inquire whether a work of art has been reported as lost or stolen. However, a bona fide purchaser who purchases in the ordinary course of business a painting entrusted to an art dealer should be able to acquire good title against the true owner. Under the U.C.C. entrusting possession of goods to a merchant who deals in that kind of goods gives the merchant the power to transfer all the rights of the entruster to a buyer in the ordinary course of business. *N.J.S.A.* 12A:2-403(2). In a transaction under that statute, a merchant may vest good title in the buyer as against the original owner. *See Anderson, supra,* § 2-403:17 *et seq.* The interplay between the statute of limitations as modified by the discovery rule and the U.C.C. should encourage good faith purchases from legitimate art dealers and discourage trafficking in stolen art without frustrating an artist's ability to recover stolen art works.

The discovery rule will fulfill the purposes of a statute of limitations and accord greater protection to the innocent owner of personal property whose goods are lost or stolen. Accordingly, we overrule *Redmond v. New Jersey Historical Society, supra,* and *Joseph v. Lesnevich, supra,* to the extent that they hold that the doctrine of adverse possession applies to chattels.

By diligently pursuing their goods, owners may prevent the statute of limitations from running. The meaning of due diligence will vary with the facts of each case, including the nature and value of the personal property. For example, with respect to jewelry of moderate value, it may be sufficient if the owner reports the theft to the police. With respect to art work of greater value, it may be reasonable to expect an owner to do more. In practice, our ruling should contribute to more careful practices concerning the purchase of art.

The considerations are different with real estate, and there is no reason to disturb the application of the doctrine of adverse possession to real estate. Real estate is fixed and cannot be moved or concealed. The owner of real property knows or should know where his property is located and reasonably can be expected to be aware of open, notorious, visible, hostile, continuous acts of possession on it.

Our ruling not only changes the requirements for acquiring title to personal property after an alleged unlawful taking, but also shifts the burden of proof at trial. Under the doctrine of adverse possession, the burden is on the possessor to prove the elements of adverse possession. *Wilomay Holding Co. v. Peninsula Land Co.,* 36 *N.J. Super.* 440, 443 (App.Div. 1955), certif. den. 19 *N.J.* 618 (1955). Under the discovery rule, the burden is on the owner as the one seeking the benefit of the rule to establish facts that would justify deferring the beginning of the period of limitations. *See Lopez, supra,* 62 *N.J.* at 276.

VI

Read literally, the effect of the expiration of the statute of limitations under *N.J.S.A.* 2A:14-1 is to bar an action such as replevin. The statute does not speak of divesting the original owner of title. By its terms the statute cuts off the remedy, but not the right of title. Nonetheless, the effect of the expiration of the statute of limitations, albeit on the theory of adverse possession, has been not only to bar an action for possession, but also to vest title in the possessor. There is no reason to change that result although the discovery rule has replaced adverse possession. History, reason, and common sense support the conclusion that the expiration of the statute of limitations bars the remedy to recover possession and also vests title in the possessor. Professor Brown explains the historical reason for construing the statute of limitations as barring the right of title as well as an action for possession:

> The metamorphosis of statutes simply limiting the time in which an action may be commenced into instrumentalities for the transfer of title may be explained perhaps by the historical doctrine of disseisin which, though more customarily applied to land, was probably originally controlling as to chattels also. By this doctrine the wrongful possessor as long as his possession continued, was treated as the owner and the dispossessed occupant considered merely to have a personal right to recapture his property if he could. [Brown, *supra,* § 4.1 at 34]

See 3 *Am.Jur.*2d, *Adverse Possession,* § 202 at 290-292; 3 *American Law of Property,* § 15.16 at 834. Before the expiration of the statute, the possessor has both the chattel and the right to keep it except as against the true owner. The only imperfection in the possessor's right to retain the chattel is the original owner's right to repossess it. Once that imperfection is removed, the possessor should have good title for all purposes. Ames, *The Disseisin of Chattels,* 3 *Harv. L.Rev.* 313, 321 (1890) (Ames). As Dean Ames wrote: "An immortal right to bring an eternally prohibited action is a metaphysical subtlety that the present writer cannot pretend to understand." *Id.* at 319. Recognizing a metaphysical notion of title in the owner would be of little benefit to him or her and would create potential problems for the possessor and third parties. The expiration of the six-year period of *N.J.S.A.* 2A:14-1 should vest title as effectively under the discovery rule as under the doctrine of adverse possession.

Our construction of *N.J.S.A.* 2A:14-1 is consistent with the construction of *N.J.S.A.* 2A:14-6, one of the statutes pertaining to title by adverse possession of real estate. That statute recites that one with right or title of entry into real estate shall make such entry within 20 years after the accrual of the right or be barred. It does not expressly state that the expiration of 20 years vests title in the possessor. Two other statutes pertaining to the adverse possession of real estate, *N.J.S.A.* 2A:14-30 and 31, expressly state that adverse possession for the statutory period shall vest title in the possessor. Notwithstanding the difference in wording between *N.J.S.A.* 2A:14-6 and *N.J.S.A* 2A:14-30 and 31, the former statute has always been construed as vesting title in the adverse possessor at the end of the statutory period. *See, e.g., Braue v. Fleck,* 23 *N.J.* 1, 16 (1956).

To summarize, the operative fact that divests the original owner of title to either personal or real property is the expiration of the period of limitations. In the past, adverse possession has described the nature of the conduct that will vest title of a chattel at the end of the statutory period. Our adoption of the discovery rule does not change the conclusion that at the end of the statutory period title will vest in the possessor.

VII

We next consider the effect of transfers of a chattel from one possessor to another during the period of limitation under the discovery rule. Under the discovery rule, the statute of limitations on an action for replevin begins to run when the owner knows or reasonably should know of his cause of action and the identity of the possessor of the chattel. Subsequent transfers of the chattel are part of the continuous dispossession of the chattel from the original owner. The important point is not that there has been a substitution of possessors, but that there has been a continuous dispossession of the former owner. Professor Ballantine explains:

> Where the same claim of title has been consistently asserted for the statutory period by persons in privity with each other, there is the same reason to quiet and establish the title as where one person has held. The same flag has been kept flying for the whole period. It is the same ouster and disseisin. If the statute runs, it quiets a title which has been consistently asserted and exercised as against the true owner, and the possession of the prior holder justly enures to the benefit of the last.

H. Ballantine, *Title by Adverse Possession,* 32 *Harv.L. Rev.* 135, 158 (1919).

The same principle appears in the *Restatement (Second) of Torts*: In some cases, the statute of limitations begins to run before the defendant took possession as when a previous taker converted the chattel and later transferred possession to the defendant. *Restatement (Second) of Torts* 2d § 899 at 442 (1977).

For the purpose of evaluating the due diligence of an owner, the dispossession of his chattel is a continuum not susceptible to separation into distinct acts. Nonetheless, subsequent transfers of the chattel may affect the degree of difficulty encountered by a diligent owner seeking to recover his goods. To that extent, subsequent transfers and their potential for frustrating diligence are relevant in applying the discovery rule. An owner who diligently seeks his chattel should be entitled to the benefit of the discovery rule although it may have passed through many hands. Conversely an owner who sleeps on his rights may be denied the benefit of the discovery rule although the chattel may have been possessed by only one person.

We reject the alternative of treating subsequent transfers of a chattel as separate acts of conversion that would start the statute of limitations running anew. At common law, apart from the statute of limitations, a subsequent transfer of a converted chattel was considered to be a separate act of conversion. In his dissent, Justice Handler seeks to extend the rule so that it would apply even if the period of limitations had expired before the subsequent transfer. Nonetheless, the dissent does not cite any authority that supports the position that the statute of limitations should run anew on an act of conversion already barred by the statute of limitations. Adoption of that alternative would tend to undermine the purpose of the statute in quieting titles and protecting against stale claims. Brown, *supra,* § 4.3 at 38.

The majority and better view is to permit tacking, the accumulation of consecutive periods of possession by parties in privity with each other. *Lesnevich, supra,* 56 *N.J. Super.* at 357; *see also O'Connell v. Chicago Park Dist.,* 376 *Ill.* 550, 34 *N.E.*2d 836 (1941); Brown, *supra,* § 18-39; Walsh, *supra* at 84; Comment, 14 *Rut.L.Rev.* 443, 444-445 (1960). As explained by Professor Walsh:

> The doctrine of tacking applies as in corresponding cases of successive adverse possessions of land where privity exists between such possessors. Uncertainty is created by cases which hold that each successive purchaser is subject to a new cause of action against which the statute begins to run from that time, in this way indefinitely extending the time when the title will be quieted by operation of the statute. It should be entirely clear that the purposes of statutes of limitation are the same whether they relate to land or chattels, and therefore the same reasons exist for tacking successive possessions as the prevailing cases hold. Nevertheless, under the cases, new actions in conversion arise against successive purchases of the converted property, and there is strong reason back of the argument that the statute runs anew against each succeeding cause of action. No doubt the prevailing rule recognizing privity in these cases may be based upon the argument that the possessory title is transferred on each successive sale of the converted chattel, subject to the owner's action to recover the property, and the action of replevin which is his proprietary action, continues in effect against succeeding possessors so that the statute bars the action after the successive possessions amount to the statutory period.

Walsh, *supra* at 83-84. In New Jersey tacking is firmly embedded in the law of real property. *O'Brien v. Bilow,* 121 *N.J.L.* 576, 578-579 (E. & A. 1938). The rule has been applied also to personal property. *Lesnevich, supra,* 56 *N.J. Super.* at 357. In *Lesnevich,* the pledge of the bonds with the credit company and the subsequent purchase by the company's president were separate acts of conversion. The pledge was beyond the period of the statute of limitations and the purchase was within the period. *Id.* at 353. The Appellate Division permitted tacking of the two periods, with the result that the second act of conversion did not alter the running of the period. *Id.* at 357.

The dissent by our colleague Justice Handler seeks to distinguish *Lesnevich* because it involved negotiable instruments. However, the law of negotiable instruments was irrelevant to the decision since the court held the credit company and its president were not holders in due course. *Lesnevich, supra,* 56 *N.J. Super.* at 352.

Treating subsequent transfers as separate acts of conversion could lead to absurd results. As explained by Dean Ames:

> The decisions in the case of chattels are few. As a matter of principle, it is submitted this rule of tacking is as applicable to chattels as to land. A denial of the right to tack would, furthermore, lead to this result. If a converter were

> to sell the chattel, five years after its conversion, to one ignorant of the seller's tort, the disposed owner's right to recover the chattel from the purchaser would continue five years longer than his right to recover from the converter would have lasted if there had been no sale. In other words, an innocent purchaser from a wrong-doer would be in a worse position than the wrong-doer himself, a conclusion as shocking in point of justice as it would be anomalous in law.

Ames, *supra* at 323, footnotes omitted. It is more sensible to recognize that on expiration of the period of limitations, title passes from the former owner by operation of the statute. Needless uncertainty would result from starting the statute running anew merely because of a subsequent transfer. 3 *American Law of Property*, § 15.16 at 837. It is not necessary to strain equitable principles, as suggested by the dissent, to arrive at a just and reasonable determination of the rights of the parties. The discovery rule permits an equitable accommodation of the rights of the parties without establishing a rule of law fraught with uncertainty.

VIII

We recognize the possible relevancy of claims of common law and statutory copyright and related questions of infringement. The parties have not raised any copyright issue in the pleadings, on the motion for summary judgment, or on this appeal. On the limited record before us, we cannot evaluate the existence or merit of copyright claims. Depending on the evidence adduced at trial, copyright claims may arise under federal statutes or the common law. For present purposes, it is sufficient to note that there are valuable rights in a work of art, apart from the right to title and possession; such as, the rights of reproduction, distribution, and display. Those rights, assembled under the rubric of a copyright, are not involved in this appeal.

Shortly before and after oral argument, various motions were filed with the Court. A motion by O'Keeffe for acceleration is now moot. Motions to supplement the record by O'Keeffe and Snyder, as well as a petition by the Art Dealers Association of America to file a brief *amicus curiae,* raise essentially factual matters. Because we remand this matter for trial, those motions also are rendered moot.

O'Keeffe is a distinguished American artist, now 92 years old and living in New Mexico. In this proceeding, she has been deposed in her attorney's office in New York City. At oral argument, we were informed that she had visited New York recently for reasons unrelated to the litigation. Nonetheless, if, because of her age, O'Keeffe is unable to travel to New Jersey for trial, an appropriate application may be made to the trial court to perpetuate her testimony. Furthermore, we direct the trial court to expedite both discovery proceedings and the trial.

We reverse the judgment of the Appellate Division in favor of O'Keeffe and remand the matter for trial in accordance with this opinion.

SULLIVAN, J., dissenting.

I do not see the need for a remand. We have plaintiff Georgia O'Keeffe's affidavit and deposition concerning the paintings, defendant Barry Snyder's affidavit as to the circumstances under which he acquired possession of them and the deposition of third party defendant Ulrich A. Frank. Apparently, the parties felt that there was nothing further needed, as cross-motions for summary judgment were made.

Plaintiff is a famous artist and the creator of the three paintings in suit. These paintings were in her possession located in an art studio run by her husband Alfred Stieglitz. In 1946 she and her husband noticed that one of the paintings, then on display, was missing from the wall on which it was hung. Plaintiff recalled that she and Stieglitz talked about "the picture being gone" although she did not remember exactly what was said. Plaintiff also testified that Stieglitz spoke "a good deal" about the missing picture to everyone who came into the studio.

Shortly thereafter plaintiff discovered that two other paintings of hers, not on display, were also missing. She did not notify the police as she was certain that they could not or would not do anything as the paintings had small monetary value at the time, but she and Stieglitz did speak to friends and acquaintances in art circles about the theft. She said that since "the word was out" in art circles in New York about the stolen paintings she and her husband hoped that some clue as to the identity of the thief would be known. She felt that all she could do was wait and see if some information would come concerning the paintings' whereabouts. In 1972, shortly after the Art Dealers Association of America, Inc. (Association) came into existence and established a registry of stolen paintings, the loss of the three paintings was reported to the Association which listed them as stolen on its registry. In late 1975, plaintiff learned that the paintings were on consignment to an art gallery in New York and in February 1976 she discovered that they were in the possession of defendant Barry Snyder, a Princeton art dealer. She immediately demanded their return and, following refusal, instituted the present suit.

Snyder had purchased the pictures from Ulrich A. Frank, the third party defendant, in March 1975. In his affidavit filed in the cause, Snyder, although a professional art dealer, stated that he was unaware of the registry of stolen paintings maintained by the Association which showed the paintings as stolen at the time he purchased them. Although he paid $35,000 for them, Snyder made no attempt to authenticate the paintings or verify ownership—this in spite of the fact that Frank, who had acquired possession of them by gift from Dr. Frank, his late father, did not know how his father had come by the paintings.

Now that his motion for summary judgment has been lost, defendant Snyder suggests speculative possibilities that he says merit inquiry even though there is nothing in the record to support them. I see no substance in any of them, and a remand as prejudicial to plaintiff who is now more than 92 years of age. She created these paintings. They were in her possession when they disappeared from her husband's art gallery in 1946. She did not learn of their whereabouts until late 1975 when they were offered for sale. She immediately started suit to recover them as soon as she was able to identify the person who had possession of them. Under these circumstances the six-year statute of limitations for bringing an action in replevin, *N.J.S.A.* 2A:14-1, was tolled and plaintiff, as the rightful owner, is entitled to a judgment in her favor.

I have no quarrel with most of the legal principles set forth in the majority opinion. We part company in the manner in which they have been applied to the undisputed facts of this case. I would affirm the Appellate Division ruling in its entirety.

HANDLER, J., dissenting.

The Court today rules that if a work of art has been stolen from an artist, the artist's right to recover his or her work from a subsequent possessor would be barred by the statute of limitations if the action were not brought within six years after the original theft. This can happen even though the artist may have been totally innocent and wholly ignorant of the identity of the thief or of any intervening receivers or possessors of the stolen art. The Court would grudgingly grant some measure of relief from this horrendous result and allow the artist to bring suit provided he or she can sustain the burden of proving "due diligence" in earlier attempting to retrieve the stolen artwork. No similar duty of diligence or vigilance, however, is placed upon the subsequent receiver or possessor, who, innocently or not, has actually trafficked in the stolen art. Despite ritualistic disavowals, the Court's holding does little to discourage art thievery. Rather, by making it relatively more easy for the receiver or possessor of an artwork with a "checkered background" to gain security and title than for the artist or true owner to reacquire it, it seems as though the Court surely will stimulate and legitimatize art thievery.

I believe that there is a much sounder approach in this sort of case than one that requires the parties to become enmeshed in duplicate or cumulative hearings that focus on the essentially collateral issues of the statute of limitations and its possible tolling by an extended application of the discovery doctrine. The better approach, I would suggest, is one that enables the parties to get to the merits of the controversy. It would recognize an artist's or owner's right to assert a claim against a newly-revealed receiver or possessor of stolen art as well as the correlative right of such a possessor to assert all equitable and legal defenses. This would enable the parties to concentrate directly upon entitlement to the artwork rather than entitlement to bring a lawsuit. By dealing with the merits of the claims instead of the right to sue, such an approach would be more conducive to reconciling the demands for individual justice with societal needs to discourage art thievery. In addition, such a rule would comport more closely with traditional common law values emphasizing the paramountcy of the rights of a true owner of chattels as against others whose possession is derived from theft. Simultaneously, it would acknowledge that the claims of the true owner as against subsequent converters may in appropriate circumstances be counterbalanced by equitable considerations.

I therefore dissent.

I

By virtue of cross-motions for summary judgment, the posture of the case as it comes to us is that the paintings were stolen from their true owner, plaintiff O'Keeffe, and that defendant Snyder acted in good faith in purchasing the paintings. Hence, we are presented for purposes of this appeal with the classic confrontation between a true owner of property and a subsequent bona fide purchaser for value, each of whom is relatively innocent and each of whom has been victimized by a thief. The true owner here is the artist who created the paintings, and she seeks to recover them through an action for replevin.

An action brought for replevin is a proper means for an owner to regain possession of chattels lost through conversion. *Baron v. Peoples National Bank of Secaucus,* 9 *N.J.* 249, 255-256 (1952); D. Dobbs, *The Law of Remedies* § 5.13 at 399 *et seq.* (1973); 20 *N.J. Practice* (Ackerson & Fulop, *Skills and Methods*) § 1711 at 490 (2 ed. 1973); 66 *Am.Jur.*2d, *Replevin,* § 39 at 860 (1973); see also *Plummer v. Kingsley,* 190 *Or.* 378, 384-385, 226 *P.*2d 297, 300-301 (Sup.Ct. 1951); J. Darlington, *The Law of Personal Property* 4 (1891). The statute of limitations applicable to replevin actions is six years. *N.J.S.A.* 2A:14-1. A fundamental miscalculation by the majority, however, is its assumption that this six-year limitations statute is applicable to O'Keeffe's claims. The statute of limitations defense was raised by defendant Snyder, but it is not available here because Snyder's acts of conversion—his purchase of the paintings from third-party defendant Frank and his refusal to return them to plaintiff O'Keeffe upon demand—constituted independent tortious acts each of which occurred well within six years of the commencement of plaintiff's lawsuit. Hence, there is no reason not to permit O'Keeffe's lawsuit and allow the parties to proceed to the heart of the controversy. [NOTE 1]

In averting a direct confrontation with the merits of the dispute, the majority ignores some rather fundamental law. It rejects the doctrine that the acquisition of a stolen chattel, or a refusal to return it upon demand, itself constitutes a tortious conversion as against the true owner. *Ante* at 489-490. It has not come to this position easily. The majority opinion recognizes the New York rule which clearly and dispositively treats a subsequent possessor's refusal to return goods upon a demand from the owner as an act of conversion that triggers the running of the statute of limitations applicable to replevin actions. *Ante* at 502-504. See *Menzel v. List,* 49 *Misc.*2d 300, 304-305, 267 *N.Y.S.*2d 804, 809 (Sup.Ct. 1966), aff'd as modified 28 *A.D.*2d 516, 279 *N.Y.S.*2d 608 (App.Div. 1967), rev'd in part on other grounds, 24 *N.Y.*2d 91, 246 *N.E.*2d 742, 298 *N.Y.S.*2d 979 (Ct.App. 1969). But the Court, relying upon *Heavner v. Uniroyal, Inc.,* 63 *N.J.* 130, 140-141 (1973), declines to follow the New York law on the theory that the New York law is a statute of limitations and that the New Jersey statute of limitations, rather than that of New York, should be applied. The issue, however, is not whether the New Jersey statute of limitations should be followed rather than that of New York. The New York rule of subsequent conversions, rejected by the majority, is not a "statute of limitations," but rather is a *substantive* principle of the law of torts. The majority simply sidesteps the question of which state's *tort* law ought to be applied to this case.

Nevertheless, in the context of this case, that misstep should not be significant since it does not appear that New York law with respect to actionable conversion is truly at variance with the law of this jurisdiction. See, *e.g., Joseph v. Lesnevich*, 56 *N.J. Super.* 340, 346 (App.Div. 1959). It is clearly the predominant view that subsequent transfers of a stolen chattel constitute separate acts of conversion. R. Bowers, *The Law of Conversion* § 40 at 31 (1917); R. Brown, *The Law of Personal Property* § 6.6 at 58 (3 ed. 1975); F.V. Harper and F. James, Jr., *The Law of Torts* § 2.35 at 188-189 (1956); W. Prosser, *The Law of Torts* § 15 at 84 (4 ed. 1971); *Restatement (Second) of Torts* § 229, Comments e and g (1965); Annot., "When Statute of Limitations Begins to Run against Action for Conversion of Property by Theft," 79 *A.L.R.*3d 847, § 4 at 855 (1975). Indeed, in authority used today in the majority opinion (*ante* at 492-493), it does not appear to be questioned even by institutions clothed with probity—*e.g.,* art museums—that an acquisition of stolen art constitutes a separate conversionary act which starts the statute of limitations running either initially or "anew." Ward, "Adverse Possession of Loaned and Stolen Objects: Is Possession Still 9/10ths of the Law?," in *Legal Problems of Museum Administration* 83, 96-97 (ALI-ABA 1980) (as to acquisition of stolen art, "the principle would be that the statute of limitations would start to run on the date of our [*i.e.,* the museum's,] innocent acquisition").

The Court seems to harbor the view that a subsequent transfer of stolen property does not, in effect, constitute a separate conversionary act. As a tortious act, a subsequent conversion known to the injured owner of the goods would constitute the accrual of a cause of action and would trigger the running of the statute of limitations. Nevertheless, according to the Court, a second or subsequent act of conversion does not constitute a separate cause of action because it does not start the "statute of limitations running anew," this position being allegedly consistent with "[t]he majority and better view [which] permit[s] tacking." *Ante* at 503. The majority's reliance here on *Joseph v. Lesnevich, supra,* for this proposition is unconvincing. While the court in that case did allow a "tacking" of wrongful possession, it did so only with regard to negotiable instruments, a long-established exception to the general rule. 56 *N.J. Super.* at 346, 357. See *Shaw v. R.R. Co.,* 101 *U.S.* 557, 564, 25 *L.Ed.* 892, 894 (1880); Bowers, *supra,* § 41 at 31-32; Darlington, *supra* at 357; Dobbs, *supra,* § 4.7 at 286-288; Prosser, *supra,* § 15 at 84-85.

The Court further observes in this case that a cause of action for conversion accrued with the original theft of the paintings in 1946; it assumes that the statute of limitations commenced to run from the date of that theft, at least absent any tolling of the limitations period by the application of the discovery rule. The reasoning then jumps. According to the Court, unless there were "tacking," *i.e.,* a refusal to allow or require the statute of limitations to run "anew" from the occurrence of the second and separate act of conversion, we would in effect be allowing a stale claim. Since "stale claims" are to be discouraged through statutes of limitations, "tacking" must be invoked to bar the old claim. *Ante* at 503. In this elliptical fashion, the majority effectively obliterates the tortious character of a subsequent conversion. *Ante* at 504.

There are several weaknesses in the Court's position. The most fundamental is the contention that O'Keeffe's claim against Snyder is "stale." Another is the assumption that the policies of repose and the like can be fulfilled in this case only by eliminating a legitimate cause of action, namely, that based on a subsequent conversion. Still another is the majority's view, derived from an affidavit, that stability of possession and title is as important in the world of art as it is in the field of commercial sales and, indeed, is so important that it requires a rule that will, more often than not, settle title to stolen art in the hands of an ultimate possessor whether he or she be truly innocent, simply lucky, just plain cunning, or actually larcenous. *Ante* at 503. No persuasive reasons are advanced for the view that this notion of "stability," which would serve in many cases actually to legitimatize art theft, is more important than is the return of stolen unique, artistic creations to their creator or true owner when this is justified by equitable considerations.

II

The holding of the majority, which involves a convoluted rendition of the law of statutes of limitations and adverse possession, in my respectful opinion, not only espouses an erroneous perception of the proper public policy to be achieved, but is actually unneeded even to secure the values endorsed by the Court. There is no reason why the concerns of the majority cannot be reasonably and fully accommodated by traditional doctrines that would, in a case such as this, lead us to a thorough consideration and careful balancing of all the equities as they bear directly upon the merits of the controversy.

It is the general rule that "a bona fide purchaser of personal property taken tortiously or wrongfully, as by trespass or theft, does not acquire a title good against the true owner." *Kutner Buick, Inc. v. Strelecki,* 111 *N.J. Super.* 89, 97 (Ch.Div. 1970) (purchaser of stolen motor vehicle); accord, *Joseph v. Lesnevich, supra,* 56 *N.J. Super.* at 346; see *Ashton v. Allen,* 70 *N.J.L.* 117, 119 (Sup.Ct. 1903); Bowers, *supra,* § 40 at 30-31; Darlington, *supra* at 359. This principle is recognized by the majority, *ante* at 488-489 and was embraced both by the Appellate Division majority, *O'Keeffe v. Snyder,* 170 *N.J. Super.* 75, 82 (App.Div. 1979), and in the dissent of Judge Fritz, *id.* at 93.

This rule is not a recent development. As noted by Judge Fritz in his dissenting opinion below, *id.* at 94, it has a long and distinguished history and was recognized by Lord Blackstone as a fundamental principle of English law with respect to chattels or personal property. 2 W. Blackstone, *Commentaries* [*]449; 3 *Blackstone, supra* at [*]145. This basic rule as to nonpassage of title to stolen personalty, *viz,* "[i]f a person steal [*sic*] goods and sell [*sic*] them, the title is not transferred, but remains in the original owner, and he may reclaim them," was adopted in this country. J. Elliott, *New Jersey Law of Sales* 369 n. 14 (1909); see Bowers, *supra,* § 40 at 31. Early cases in the United States followed this rule that good title could not be acquired from a thief, even by a bona fide purchaser. *E.g., Shaw v. R.R. Co., supra,* 101 *U.S.* at 564-565, 25 *L.Ed.* at 894; *Heckle v. Lurvey,* 101 *Mass.* 344, 345 (Sup.Jud.Ct. 1869) ("[t]he principle is well settled, that, when a thief sells chattels, even to an honest purchaser, no title passes"); *Dame v. Baldwin,* 8 *Mass.* 518, 521 (1812); *Williams v. Merle,* 11 *Wend.* 80, 81-82 (N.Y. Sup. Ct. 1831); *Mowrey v. Walsh,* 8 *Cowen* 238, 241 (N.Y. Sup. Ct. 1826).

This legal axiom was not altered by the codification and adoption of the Uniform Commercial Code (hereinafter Code or U.C.C.), which has been described as "deriv[ing] from the common law" and as "assum[ing] the continuing existence of a large body of pre-Code and non-Code law on which it rests for support, which it displaces to the least possible extent, and without which it could not survive." Gilmore, "Article 9: What it Does for the Past," 26 *La.L.Rev.* 285, 285-286 (1966). See J. White & R. Summers, *Handbook of the Law Under the Uniform Commercial Code* § 2 at 6 (1972). On the topic of acquisition of title to chattels from a wrongdoer, the Code states that "[a] purchaser of goods acquires all title which his transferor had or had power to transfer...." *N.J.S.A.* 12A:2-403(1) (*U.C.C.* § 2-403(1)). Therefore, if the wrongdoer has no title, he or she cannot convey title; the purchaser acquires only that title reposing in the transferor. As noted in the New Jersey Study Comments to the U.C.C. as enacted, "[n]othing in this portion of the subsection [*N.J.S.A.* 12A:2-403(1)] would change the law that a purchaser from a thief gains no interest in the goods." Study Comment 2 to *N.J.S.A.* 12A:2-403(1). See *Lieber v. Mohawk Arms, Inc.,* 64 *Misc.*2d 206, 208, 314 *N.Y.S.*2d 510, 512 (Sup.Ct. 1970) (plaintiff entitled under U.C.C. to recover possession from bona fide purchaser certain of Adolf Hitler's personal effects to which plaintiff had title and which had been stolen from plaintiff); 67 *Am.Jur.*2d, *Sales,* § 257 at 392 (1973).

It follows from this well-established principle that, generally, as between the true owner who has lost personal property through theft and a subsequent good faith purchaser for value, the former is entitled to the goods over the latter. Title remains in the true owner rather than flowing to the bona fide purchaser when "'the wrongdoer sells the chattel to [such] innocent purchaser ... because the wrongdoer had [no title] to give.'" *Kutner Buick, Inc. v. Strelecki, supra,* 111 *515 *N.J. Super.* at 97 (quoting from *National Retailers Mut. Ins. Co. v. Gambino,* 1 *N.J. Super.* 627, 629 (Law Div. 1948)). Accord, *Joseph v. Lesnevich, supra,* 56 *N.J. Super.* at 346; see, *e.g., Barry Industries, Inc. v. Aetna Casualty & Surety Co.,* 302 *A.*2d 61, 63 (D.C. 1973) ("The law is well settled that a possessor of stolen goods can never convey good title.") (sale of stolen automobile); *Jordan v. Kancel,* 188 *Kan.* 292, 294, 361 *P.*2d 894, 896 (Sup.Ct. 1961) (replevin action to recover television sets sold without title or authority by rental agent; "[i]t is a general rule with regard to personal property that title, like a stream, cannot rise higher than its source" (citation omitted)); *Linwood Harvestore, Inc. v. Cannon,* 427 *Pa.* 434, 437, 235 *A.*2d 377, 380 (Sup.Ct. 1967) (good faith purchase of farm equipment from converter; "[t]he general rule for chattels is that a bona fide purchaser from a thief gets nothing"); Prosser, *supra* § 15 at 87; *Restatement (Second) of Torts, supra,* § 229, Comment e at 448.

These basic tenets are fully applicable to creative works of art and govern ownership claims in the case of the theft or wrongful appropriation of artistic creations such as those involved in this case. *E.g., Porter v. Wertz,* 68 *A.D.*2d 141, 149, 416 *N.Y.S.*2d 254, 259 (App.Div. 1979) (true owners of a painting by Maurice Utrillo, entitled *Chateau de Lion-sur-Mer,* could recover either the painting or damages as against defendant gallery which purchased the painting from an individual who had acquired it wrongfully from another person who was not authorized by the owner to sell it); *cf. Lieber v. Mohawk Arms, Inc., supra,* 64 *Misc.*2d at 208, 314 *N.Y.S.*2d at 512 (owner of personal effects of Adolf Hitler entitled to recover these unique items stolen from him by transferor of defendant bona fide purchaser).

Consequently, if we were to view this record as presenting only the undisputed fact that the paintings were stolen and could thus not be validly transferred thereafter to Snyder as a bona fide purchaser, plaintiff O'Keeffe would clearly be entitled to prevail. And, in that posture, I would subscribe to the result urged in the dissenting opinion of Justice Sullivan, *ante* at 506-507, namely, a reversal and entry of judgment in favor of plaintiff. Under all of the circumstances, however, I do not believe that such a disposition would be appropriate and would instead counsel a remand, albeit with a focus and under guidelines very different from those expressed in the majority opinion.[NOTE 2]

III

"As a general rule, a defendant in a replevin action may interpose any defense which questions the plaintiff's title or right to possession, or upholds his own taking or unlawful detention." 66 *Am.Jur.*2d, *Replevin,* § 47 at 864 (1973) (footnotes omitted). See 20 *N.J. Practice, supra,* § 1739 at 509-510. While the fundamental principle is that a wrongdoer cannot, as against the true owner, convey good title even to a bona fide purchaser, that precept is not absolute. Some exceptions to this common law rule are derived from judicial rulings, others, from statutes. Dobbs, *supra,* § 4.7 at 282, 286; *N.J.S.A.* 12A:2-403(2) (*U.C.C.* § 2-403(2)) (U.C.C. codifies the common law notion of voidable or equitable title where goods have been "entrusted" by the owner "to a merchant who deals in goods of that kind").

Aside from specialized defenses peculiar to sales transactions, there are also general equitable defenses—such as laches, unclean hands, estoppel or mistake—cognizable in equity actions or in other actions in which such defenses may be raised. Dobbs, *supra,* § 2.4 at 45 *et seq.* Notwithstanding in this case a failure to denominate each and every equitable defense which might be available to him, defendant Snyder has adequately invoked the defenses which would be germane in addressing plaintiff's claim for the return of the paintings. He has asserted his own ownership of the paintings, implying thereby that, under all of the circumstances surrounding the original disappearance of the paintings, their subsequent possession by others, and his eventual purchase for value, his own entitlement to possession of them exceeds that of O'Keeffe. He has also alleged laches as against plaintiff, undoubtedly intending to establish that she delayed unduly in bringing an action to recover her paintings against those whom she knew or ought to have known were in possession thereof and that, as a result, he ultimately stands to suffer a loss.

Our courts have taken an expansive and flexible approach in the application of equitable defenses. See, *e.g., Journeymen Barbers, Hairdressers & Cosmetologists' Int'l Union v. Pollino,* 22 *N.J.* 389, 401 (1956); see also *Johnson v. Yellow Cab Transit Co.,* 321 *U.S.* 383, 387-388, 64 *S.Ct.* 622, 625, 88 *L.Ed.* 814, 819 (1944). For example, in *Untermann v. Untermann,* 43 *N.J. Super.* 106, 109 (App.Div. 1956), certif. den. 23 *N.J.* 363 (1957), while the court stated that the doctrine of unclean hands may bar a cause of action for separate maintenance, it also observed that this defense was an aspect or application of the broader equitable principle that "he who seeks equity must do equity"; hence, the defendant in such an action could under certain circumstances be estopped to raise the defense. The *Untermann* court further noted that the "doctrines of unclean hands and estoppel ... are somewhat akin.... They are flexible in their application, turning largely on the circumstances involved in the ... 'total situation.' ... They may turn, too, upon the relative innocence or culpability of the plaintiff and defendant, for the law may aid the one who is comparatively the more innocent." 43 *N.J. Super.* at 109 (citations omitted). We recently recognized this principle in *Kazin v. Kazin,* 81 *N.J.* 85, 94 (1979). *Cf. Union Beach Bd. of Educ. v. New Jersey Educ. Ass'n,* 96 *N.J. Super.* 371, 386-389 (Ch.Div. 1967) (doctrine of unclean hands was not available to defendants whose conduct was in violation of the Constitution and where the imposition of the doctrine would be contrary to public policy), aff'd 53 *N.J.* 29, 43 (1968) (Weintraub, C.J.) ("the doctrine will not be invoked when to do so will injure the public").

Similarly, equitable estoppel has been applied flexibly "as a general principle, used as a means of preventing [one] from taking an inequitable advantage of a predicament in which his own conduct had placed his adversary." Prosser, *supra,* § 105 at 691; see *Kazin v. Kazin, supra,* 81 *N.J.* at 94. Sometimes referred to as estoppel *in pais,* this doctrine "has been defined as 'an impediment or bar, by which a man is precluded from alleging, or denying, a fact, in consequence of his own previous act, allegation or denial to the contrary.'" Prosser, *supra,* § 105 at 691 (footnote omitted).

These estoppel-based equitable defenses have been applied in actions involving conflicting ownership claims to chattels. *E.g., Nelson v. Wolf,* 4 *N.J.* 76, 79-80 (1950) (an "owner may be estopped from setting up his own title and the lack of title in the vendor as against a *bona fide* purchaser for value where the owner has clothed the vendor with possession and other indicia of title"); see *James Talcott, Inc. v. Associates Discount Corp.,* 302 *F.*2d 443, 447 (8 Cir.1962) (Blackmun, J.) (under Arkansas law estoppel is defense to action to recover for wrongful resale of goods initially transferred to vendor by conditional sale); *Zendman v. Harry Winston, Inc.,* 305 *N.Y.* 180, 184-188, 111 *N.E.*2d 871, 873-875 (Ct.App. 1953) (under New Jersey law, estoppel defense invocable by purchaser where owner vested vendor with apparent authority to dispose of or sell the particular chattel); *Hertz Corp. v. Hardy,* 197 *Pa.Super.* 466, 471-476, 178 *A.*2d 833, 836-838 (Super.Ct. 1962) (estoppel is an affirmative defense to an action for replevin of rented automobile which has been wrongfully sold to defendants; here, however, defendant bona fide purchaser had not relied on anything that plaintiff did and thus the equitable estoppel defense must fail).

A thorough balancing of the equities has been followed specifically to adjudicate the competing claims for misappropriated works of art. In *Porter v. Wertz, supra,* plaintiffs had loaned a Utrillo painting to a potential purchaser thereof pending a decision as to whether or not to purchase it; that individual, however, proceeded to sell the painting to a delicatessen employee who in turn sold it to a gallery which then resold it to a buyer who took the painting to Venezuela. 68 *A.D.*2d at 142-145, 416 *N.Y.S.*2d at 255-256. The court considered all of defendant's affirmative statutory and equitable defenses as well as its factual assertions of ownership based upon good faith. It ruled that defendant art gallery was not entitled to statutory estoppel under *U.C.C.* § 2-403(2), finding, first, that the delicatessen employee, the gallery's vendor, was not an art dealer, *i.e.,* was not "a person in the business of selling goods of that kind" (*U.C.C.* § 1-201(9)); and, second, that the gallery was not "a person [acting] ... in good faith" (*U.C.C.* § 1-201(9)) in the purchase of the Utrillo since it had not exercised the conjunctive statutory requirements of "honesty in fact and the observance of reasonable commercial standards of fair dealing in the trade," *U.C.C.* § 2-103(1)(b), *viz,* the gallery's indifference as to the "provenance"[NOTE 3] of the painting. 68 *A.D.*2d at 145-146, 416 *N.Y.S.*2d at 257. The *Porter* court also rejected the gallery's equitable estoppel defense, observing "that although one may not be a buyer in the ordinary course of business as defined in the Uniform Commercial Code, he may be a good-faith purchaser for value and enjoy the protection of precode [*sic*] estoppel." *Id.* at 147, 416 *N.Y.S.*2d at 258 (citation omitted). Nevertheless, the court concluded that plaintiffs had vested in the bailee (who sold to the delicatessen employee) nothing more than possession, which "without more is insufficient to create an estoppel." *Id.* at 148, 416 *N.Y.S.*2d at 259 (citation omitted). Finally, in assessing defendant's ownership claims in that case, the *Porter* court concluded that the gallery did not qualify as a "good faith purchaser," since it had not investigated the provenance of the Utrillo painting. *Id.* at 149, 416 *N.Y.S.*2d at 259. The language of the court is instructive in this regard:

> The ... claim that the failure to look into Wertz's authority to sell the painting was consistent with the practice of the trade does not excuse such conduct. This claim merely confirms the observation of the trial court that "in an industry whose transactions cry out for verification of... title... it is deemed poor practice to probe...." Indeed, commercial indifference to ownership or the right to sell facilitates traffic in stolen works of art. Commercial indifference diminishes the integrity and increases the culpability of the apathetic merchant. In such posture, [the gallery] cannot be heard to complain.

Ibid.

Equitable considerations have special pertinency in the instant proceedings. They appropriately require the fullest exposure of all facets of the controversy: the uniqueness of the chattels—paintings created by a renowned artist whose artworks have in general grown greatly in value; the theft or mysterious disappearance of these paintings several decades ago; the subsequent possession and enjoyment of the paintings by the Frank family; Frank's subsequent attempts to sell the paintings, and their eventual acquisition by Snyder; the experience and status of Snyder in the art world, and whether he sufficiently investigated the provenance of the O'Keeffe paintings and acted with commensurate due care and reasonable prudence when he purchased them.[NOTE 4] The difficulties caused by the lengthy interim between the original disappearance of the paintings and their ultimate surfacing in Snyder's gallery also has a definite bearing upon the equities in this case.[NOTE 5] These considerations, I believe, should be given direct application as constituent elements of the primary claims and the affirmative defenses of the parties rather than be given at most, as required by the majority opinion, oblique application as an aspect of the discovery rule relevant only as to whether O'Keeffe is entitled to assert a claim for the stolen paintings.

IV

I am mindful that the majority is concerned with the importance of the policy of repose and the discouragement of stale claims. At times, however, these policies must yield to other equally important policies. Compare, for example, *Velmohos v. Maren Engineering Corp.*, 83 *N.J.* 282, 293 (1980), with *Galligan v. Westfield Centre Service, Inc.*, 82 *N.J.* 188, 192-193 (1980). The majority has in this case gone well beyond a simple and understandable desire for quietude in litigation. It has actually placed the entire burden of proof as to the absence of comparative fault upon the original owner-artist, albeit in the sheep's clothing of the discovery rule. *Ante* at 492-494, 499-500. I see no justification for removing that burden from the defendant, who may assert equities in his favor to establish his entitlement to the artwork. Ward, *supra* at 96. I respectfully repeat that the Court's anxiety in this regard can be fully and properly accommodated in this case without first fictionalizing the tortious character of Snyder's conversion and then applying as the only pertinent statute of limitations that which was triggered as of the date of the original theft, subject to an artificial and novel extension of the discovery rule, all of which does not really allow the parties to get to the heart of the matter.

All of the factors which trouble the majority, I suggest, can and should be addressed in the context of a remand directing the trial court to consider the defendant's affirmative defenses, to recognize that defendant bears the burden of proof with respect to those defenses, and, ultimately, to weigh the respective interests of the parties by balancing the equities in order to determine who should bear the loss of the paintings.

For these reasons, I dissent.

For reversal and remandment—Chief Justice WILENTZ and Justices PASHMAN, CLIFFORD, SCHREIBER and POLLOCK—5.

For affirmance—Justices SULLIVAN and HANDLER—2.

NOTES:

NOTE 1: It is understandable that both lower courts in addressing the merits of the controversy dealt with the defenses of the statute of limitations and adverse possession since those courts were bound by *Redmond v. New Jersey Historical Society*, 132 *N.J. Eq.* 464 (E. & A. 1942), and at least constrained by *Joseph v. Lesnevich*, 56 *N.J. Super.* 340 (App.Div. 1959). This Court, however, is not required to follow either decision; it is, therefore, less explicable as to why the Court has permitted itself to become entangled in these abstruse doctrines as applied to stolen or lost works of art. At any rate, I do not believe that *Lesnevich* is a persuasive decision as to the necessity for "tacking" in the application of the statute of limitations to chattels. *Post* at 511. Also I agree with the dissenting view below of Judge Fritz, 170 *N.J. Super.* at 93, 95 that the doctrine of adverse possession should not be applied to personalty and, to that extent, I join the Court in overruling *Redmond,* which had found the doctrine to be applicable to conflicting ownership claims to a painting (132 *N.J. Eq.* at 473). *Ante* at 498-499.

NOTE 2: I am constrained to agree with the Court that the cross-motions for summary judgment have not satisfactorily eliminated all disputes as to material facts. It seems manifest that the parties brought their respective motions in order to obtain dispositive rulings as to the defenses of the statute of limitations and the doctrine of adverse possession. If defendants were entitled to prevail under either of these defenses, this would have terminated the litigation (the result actually reached by the trial court). Since, in my view, these defenses are not available, rulings in favor of plaintiff would have the effect only of a partial summary judgment under *R.* 4:46-2 because other issues remain unresolved in the case. Such a result would require a remand to decide such remaining issues. See *Rotwein v. General Accident Group,* 103 *N.J. Super.* 406, 424-425 (Law Div. 1968).

NOTE 3: The "history of ownership or the right to possess or sell an object [*sic*] d'art." 68 *A.D.*2d at 146, 416 *N.Y.S.*2d at 257.

NOTE 4: Authority relied on here by the majority recognizes the responsibilities of experienced and knowledgeable persons in the art world, *viz*: "If the object is a work of a living artist [,] it may be that no one can be an innocent purchaser from a seller who lacks a provenance without at least calling the artist." Ward, "Adverse Possession of Loaned and Stolen Objects: Is Possession Still 9/10ths of the Law?," in *Legal Problems of Museum Administration* 83, 96 (ALI-ABA 1980). Moreover, "[a]s experts[,] the court will expect [museums] to be more familiar with how to go about this [(checking the "usual sources" to see if the work of art is stolen)] than the average innocent purchaser." *Ibid.*

NOTE 5: There is no compelling reason why courts or parties should suffer the "Ames anomaly" referred to by the majority in support of its thesis. Ames, "The Disseisin of Chattels," 3 *Harv.L.Rev.* 313, 323 (1890). *Ante* at 504. To the extent that it appears that O'Keeffe's claims against any person in possession prior to Snyder would have been barred under the statute of limitations, this factor would constitute a potent, if not dispositive, equity in favor of Snyder.

STUDY QUESTIONS

- The *O'Keeffe* case exemplifies the problems of a "good faith purchaser for value." Summarize the relevant facts. What steps did O'Keeffe take to recover her paintings? According to the majority opinion, what facts were in dispute?
- What legal theories did the defendants rely on for their defense? Why is adverse possession problematic when personal property is involved?
- Explain the "discovery rule"? What are the obligations of the owner under the discovery rule? How does this affect the tolling of the statute of limitations? What are the obligations of the purchaser of art? How did the dissents differ in their legal analysis and conclusions?
- O'Keeffe reported the loss of her paintings to the International Foundation for Art Research (IFAR) in 1972. IFAR was established in 1969 but did not formally launch the Art Loss Register until 1991. What is the role of art registries such as the Art Loss Registry in art theft cases? What other purposes do art registries serve? In what ways do you think the development of digital technology and online databases have affected the ability to recover stolen artwork?

Reading Note: The case reprinted below involves questions of authenticity in a work of art. The Andy Warhol Authentication Board denied a collector's request for authentication of a Warhol print. The collector sued, alleging a variety of claims against the Authentication Board. As a result of lawsuits such as this, many artists authentication boards have scaled back or abandoned their authentication activities.

SIMON-WHELAN V. ANDY WARHOL FOUNDATION FOR THE VISUAL ARTS

No. 07 Civ. 6423 (LTS) (US Dist. Ct., S.D. New York 2009)

OPINION AND ORDER

LAURA TAYLOR SWAIN, District Judge.

Plaintiff Joe Simon-Whelan ("Simon-Whelan" or "Plaintiff") brings this action against the Andy Warhol Foundation for the Visual Arts, Inc. (the "Foundation"), the Estate of Andy Warhol (the "Estate"), Vincent Fremont ("Fremont"), individually and in his capacity as Successor Executor of the Estate, Vincent Fremont Enterprises ("VFE"), the Andy Warhol Authentication Board, Inc. (the "Board"), John Does 1-20, Jane Does 1-10 and Richard Roes 1-10 (collectively, "Defendants"). Plaintiff claims, on behalf of himself and a putative class of art buyers who have allegedly purchased Warhol works at artificially inflated prices, that the defendants have violated the federal Sherman Anti-Trust Act and New York's Donnelly Act by engaging in a conspiracy to restrain and monopolize trade in the market for Warhol works. Plaintiff asserts a further individual and class claim for unjust enrichment (relating to the allegedly artificially high prices of Warhol works), individual claims for false advertising and publicity in violation of the federal Lanham Act (relating to the denial of the authenticity of a work owned by Plaintiff), fraud (based on allegations that certain defendants induced Plaintiff to submit his work to the Board and to sign a general

In 1989, Joe Simon-Whelan paid $195,000 for a 24 x 20in Warhol self-portrait from a London dealer who said it had been acquired directly from the artist and had been authenticated by the Andy Warhol Art Authentication Board as a 1964 Warhol silkscreen. In 2001 its value was estimated at £2m-3m and Simon-Whelan decided to sell it. To enhance its commercial value, he submitted it to the Authentication Board again to ensure inclusion in Warhol's catalogue raisonné. However, on submission, and again on resubmission, the Board concluded it was a fake. The presence of two "Denied" stamps—that Simon-Whelan believes has ended any hope of the picture ever being accepted as genuine—has led him to refer to it as "Double Denied."

release and convenant not to sue in connection with such submissions (the "Submission Agreement")), and an individual and class claim for a declaratory judgment invalidating the Submission Agreement.

Defendants move to dismiss all of Plaintiff's claims. The Court has reviewed thoroughly all of the parties' submissions and arguments in connection with the claims. For the reasons stated below, Defendants' motion to dismiss is granted in part and denied in part.

BACKGROUND

The Amended Class Action Complaint (the "Complaint") includes the following relevant allegations.

The Estate is located in New York and was determined to have a fair market value just below four hundred million dollars. (Compl. at ¶¶ 19, 43.) The Estate originally owned close to 100,000 works of art by Andy Warhol. (Id. at ¶ 38.) Originally, the Estate's executor was Frederick Hughes ("Hughes") and Fremont was named as alternate executor. (Id. at ¶¶ 28, 36.) The Foundation is a not-for-profit charitable trust incorporated in the State of New York. (Id. at ¶ 18.) Prior to the creation of the Foundation, Freemont oversaw the sale of Warhol's paintings. (Id. at ¶ 3.) Currently, Fremont is the exclusive sales agent for the Foundation's Warhol paintings. (Id. at ¶ 51.) VFE is a New York corporation, with its principal place of business being in New York. (Id. at ¶ 21.) The Board is a not-for profit New York corporation, with its principal place of business in New York. (Id. at ¶ 22.) The Board is responsible for authenticating the works of Andy Warhol. (See id. at ¶ 68.) John Does 1-20 are past and present officers of the Foundation. (Id. at ¶ 23.) Jane Does 1-10 are past and present members of the Board. (Id. at ¶ 24.) Richard Roes 1-10 are past and present agents of the Foundation and/or Board. (Id. at ¶ 25.)

The Conspiracy

Plaintiff alleges that the Defendants have, for a period of twenty years, conspired to control the market for Andy Warhol artwork. (Compl. at ¶ 1.) The Foundation and the Board are allegedly the central actors in the conspiracy. (Id. at ¶ 9.) According to Plaintiff, Defendants have complete control over the authentication of Warhol artwork by virtue of the Board's status as sole recognized authentication authority for Warhol works and the Foundation's publication of an official catalogue of Warhol works. (Id. at ¶ 17.) Defendants employ two methods for authenticating Warhol artwork. (Id. at ¶ 65.) The first is a system of Board ratings of individual works as by Warhol, not by Warhol, or works as to which the Board expresses no opinion at the time. (Id. at ¶ 64-65.) The second is informal authentication by virtue of inclusion in the Warhol Catalogue Raisonné (the "Catalogue"). (Id.) The Catalogue, published by the Foundation, is an allegedly comprehensive listing of all authentic Warhol artwork in existence.[NOTE 1] (Id.)

According to Plaintiff, the Board has denied the authenticity of works that were previously owned by the Estate and stamped with serial numbers from the Estate (id. at ¶ 86), routinely denies the authenticity of a certain percentage of Warhols, particularly when several from the same series are submitted (id. at ¶ 87), has denied authentication as a means of retaliation (id. at ¶¶ 83-85), has approached owners of Warhols to "lure" them into submitting their works for authentication (id. at ¶¶ 119, 185), and changes its authentication policies when the change suits the Board's financial interests (id. at ¶ 89). Plaintiff alleges that Defendants use their control over the authentication methods to create a scarcity in the market for Warhol artwork and inflate the value of the Warhol works in the Foundation's possession. (Id. at ¶¶ 17, 214.)

At some time between 1988 and July 1990, the Estate implemented a policy requiring persons seeking authentication of works to sign a "Submission Agreement." (Id. at ¶ 91.) The Board has continued the Estate's policy of requiring persons submitting works for authentication to sign the Submission Agreement. (Id. at ¶ 97.) The Submission Agreement includes the following clause:

By signing this letter Owner:

> . . .
>
> (iii) hereby indemnifies the Authentication Board, the Foundation, the Estate of Andy Warhol (the "Estate"), and all members of and officers, directors, agents, representatives, employees and others at any time acting for the Authentication Board, the Foundation or the Estate (collectively, the "Indemnitees"), and agrees to defend and hold each Indemnitee harmless and releases, waives and covenants not to sue any Indemnitee, based upon any claim or liability asserted (a) by Owner or by any person or entity acquiring the Work, or any interest in the Work from Owner (a "Buyer") or any person or entity from whom Owner or any predecessor in interest acquired the Work which is based directly or indirectly on the legend or endorsement, if any, affixed to the Work, or on any letter herein referred to, or any other action by the Authentication Board or any other Indemnitee in connection herewith, including without limitation any claim that the opinion expressed therein is not correct, or (b) by any other person to whom Owner or the Buyer has made any statement or representation respecting the authenticity the Work or any action of the Authentication Board or any other Indemnitee in connection therewith, and hereby agrees to pay or reimburse each Indemnitee for all costs and expenses incurred by the Indemnitee in connection with any such asserted claim or liability, including without limitation the fees and expenses of legal counsel. (Compl. at ¶ 99, Ex. B at 3.)

Double Denied

Plaintiff originally purchased a painting (referred to herein and in the Complaint as Double Denied) for $195,000 in 1989. (Id. at ¶ 19.) According to Plaintiff, the painting is one of several created in August 1965 at Warhol's direction from an acetate personally created and chosen by Warhol. (Id.) Plaintiff alleges that the painting had previously been authenticated by the Foundation and the Estate, including by Hughes and Fremont, and had passed through several major dealers, each of whom had carefully vetted the painting's provenance. (Id.)

Plaintiff offered to sell his painting in or about July 2001. (Id. at ¶ 148.) Plaintiff alleges that, from July through December 2001, Fremont repeatedly urged Plaintiff, by telephone, email and in a face-to-face meeting in Los Angeles, to submit his painting to the Board. (Id. at ¶ 149.) An interested buyer was also informed by the Board that it would not stand by the prior authentications; the painting would have to be submitted to the Board. (Id. at ¶ 151.) Plaintiff submitted Double Denied for authentication on December 20, 2001, and signed a copy of the Submission Agreement dated December 21, 2001, in connection with the submission. (Compl. at ¶ 153, Ex. B.) The Board stamped the painting "Denied." (Id. at ¶¶ 20, 155.) After the Board's initial determination, Plaintiff was informed that he was welcome to resubmit the painting with additional documentation. (Id. at ¶ 158.) Fremont urged him to resubmit the painting with additional documentation. (Id. at ¶ 159.) Plaintiff spent more than a year documenting the painting's origin and history and resubmitted the painting with additional documentation in February 2003. (Id. at ¶¶ 161-62.)

Plaintiff alleges that, on or about February 12, 2003, he was informed by Paul Morissey that Fremont had told Morissey that the painting had been denied again. (Id. at ¶ 163.) By letter dated July 14, 2003, the Board notified plaintiff that it had rejected Double Denied a second time. (Id. at ¶ 165.) The Board subsequently issued a letter, dated May 18, 2004, purporting to explain the basis of the Board's denial. (Id. at ¶¶ 168-72; Compl. Ex. E.) Plaintiff alleges that the Board fraudulently denied the authenticity of Double Denied and that the denials were a foregone conclusion. (Id. at ¶¶ 247, 249.) Plaintiff alleges that, as a result of this second rejection, Plaintiff was unable to sell any of the Warhols that he owned without first submitting them to the Board and that he was ultimately forced to sell his Warhols through third-parties at a fraction of the price. (Id. at ¶ 166.) Further, Plaintiff alleges that, by excluding Double Denied from the Catalogue, the Defendants have represented that the painting is a fake, thus depressing its market value. (Id. at ¶ 237.)

Plaintiff brings this action requesting a declaratory judgment that the Submission Agreement is unenforceable, as well as injunctive, declaratory and monetary relief in respect of his claims under Section One and Two of the Sherman Act, the New York Donnelly Act, the Lanham Act, and for fraud and unjust enrichment. Defendants seek dismissal of Plaintiff's claims pursuant to Rule 12(b)(6) of the Federal Rules of Civil Procedure, arguing that the claims are barred by the release and covenant not to sue provisions of the Submission Agreements, that the allegations of the Complaint are insufficient to plead plausibly Plaintiff's antitrust claims because, inter alia, the claims are time barred and Plaintiff lacks standing to assert them, that the Complaint's Lanham Act and fraud allegations are likewise insufficient to meet the applicable pleading standards, and that the Complaint fails to state a claim for relief for unjust enrichment as against Fremont as "successor executor."

DISCUSSION

Rule 12(b)(6) and 9(b) Standards

In deciding a motion to dismiss a complaint for failure to state a claim pursuant to Rule 12(b)(6) of the Federal Rules of Civil Procedure, the Court must "accept as true all factual statements alleged in the complaint and draw reasonable inferences in favor of the non-moving party." *McCarthy v. Dunn & Bradstreet Corp.*, 483 F.3d 184, 191 (2d Cir. 2007) (internal citations omitted). The issue is whether the plaintiff is entitled to offer evidence to support his claims. *Hudson Valley Black Press v. Internal Revenue Service*, 307 F. Supp. 2d 543, 545 (S.D.N.Y. 2004). Nevertheless, "[t]o survive a motion to dismiss, a complaint must contain sufficient factual matter, accepted as true, to 'state a claim to relief that is plausible on its face.'" *Ashcroft v. Iqbal*, ___ S.Ct. ___, 2009 WL 1361536, at *12 (May 18, 2009) quoting *Bell Atlantic Corp. v. Twombly*, 550 U.S. 544, 570 (2007). "Where a complaint pleads facts that are merely consistent with a defendant's liability, it stops short of the line between possibility and plausibility of entitlement to relief." *Iqbal*, 2009 WL 1361536, at *12 (internal quotations and citations omitted). This Twombly standard applies to all civil actions. *Id.* at *16.

Rule 9(b) of the Federal Rules of Civil Procedure requires that "[i]n alleging fraud or mistake, a party must state with particularity the circumstances constituting fraud or mistake." FED. R. CIV. P. 9(b). Particularity requires the plaintiff to "(1) specify the statements that the plaintiff contends were fraudulent, (2) identify the speaker, (3) state where and when the statements were made, and (4) explain why the statements were fraudulent." *Stevelman v. Alias Research, Inc.*, 174 F.3d 79, 84 (2d Cir. 1999) (internal citations omitted). The issue is whether the allegations provide fair and reasonable notice of the time, place, speaker, and content of the alleged misrepresentation or omission. *Shields v. Citytrust Bancorp, Inc.*, 25 F.3d 1124, 1128-29 (2d Cir. 1994).

Validity of the Submission Agreements

Defendants argue that Plaintiff has failed to state a claim for invalidation of the Submission Agreements he signed in connection with the Board's reviews of Double Denied, and that his entire Complaint should be dismissed, because the Submission Agreements include, *inter alia*, a provision in which Plaintiff "releases, waives and covenants not to sue any Indemnitee . . . based upon any claim or liability asserted (a) by [Plaintiff] or by any person or entity acquiring the Work, or any interest in the Work from [Plaintiff] . . . which is based directly or indirectly on the legend or endorsement, if any, affixed to the Work, or on any letter herein referred to, or any other action by the Authentication Board or any other Indemnitee in connection herewith, including without limitation any claim that the opinion is not correct." (Compl., Ex. B, at 3.)

The Complaint's allegations of fraud and wrongdoing in connection with the solicitation of the Submission Agreements are sufficient to state plausibly his claim for declaratory relief invalidating the exculpatory provisions of the agreements. A party may not invoke such an agreement to insulate itself from intentional wrongdoing, such as that alleged in this action. See *Kalisch-Jarcho, Inc. v. City of New York* 58 N.Y.2d 377, 384-85 (N.Y. 1983) ("[A]n exculpatory agreement, no matter how flat and unqualified its terms, will not exonerate a party from liability under all circumstances. Under announced public policy, it will not apply to exemption of willful or grossly negligent acts . . . [and] an exculpatory clause is unenforceable when, in contravention of acceptable notions of morality, the misconduct for which it would grant immunity smacks of intentional wrongdoing. This can be explicit, as when it is fraudulent, malicious or prompted by the sinister intention of one acting in bad faith." (internal citations omitted)). Plaintiff has sufficiently alleged that he was fraudulently induced into signing the submission agreements. See *Nurnberg v. Hobo Corp.*, 30 A.D.3d 359, 360 (1st Dep't 2006) ("A party asserting fraudulent inducement is required to identify a material representation, known to be false and made with the intention of inducing reliance, and actual reliance resulting in damages."); see also *Merrill Lynch, Pierce, Fenner & Smith, Inc. v. Wise Metals Group, LLC*, 19 A.D.3d 273, 275 (1st Dep't 2005) ("A contract induced by fraud, however, is subject to rescission, rendering it unenforceable by the culpable party."). The Complaint includes allegations that the Submission Agreements were utilized in an effort to conceal, and to protect Defendants from recriminations arising from, intentional, illegal action. Taking all inferences in Plaintiff's favor, he has sufficiently alleged facts in support of his claim for declaratory relief at this stage of the proceedings and Defendants' motion must be denied insofar as it seeks the dismissal of Plaintiff's declaratory judgment claim concerning the Submission Agreements.

Sherman Antitrust Act and New York Donnelly Act Claims

Plaintiff asserts claims under Section One of the Sherman Act, which prohibits combinations in restraint of trade,[NOTE 2] and under Section Two of that Act, which prohibits monopolization.[NOTE 3] Plaintiff also asserts a claim under New York State's antitrust statute—the Donnelly Act—which prohibits contracts or agreements in restraint of trade and monopolization. See N.Y. Gen. Bus. Law §§ 340 et seq. Defendants argue that Plaintiff has failed plausibly to plead a conspiracy and that the Complaint must therefore be dismissed under *Twombly*, and further argue that Plaintiff lacks standing, and that his antitrust claims are time-barred.

The New York Court of Appeals has held that the New York Donnelly Act should generally be construed in light of Sherman Act precedents. *X.L.O. Concrete Corp. v. Rivergate Corp.*, 83 N.Y.2d 513, 518 (1994) ("This Court has held that the Donnelly Act, having been modelled on the Federal Sherman Act of 1890, should generally be construed in light of Federal precedent and given a different interpretation only where State policy, differences in the statutory language or the legislative history justify such a result." (internal quotations omitted)). Accordingly, the Court analyzes Plaintiff's Sherman Act and New York Donnelly Act claims together.

Plausibility of Plaintiff's Antitrust Allegations

Defendants argue that Plaintiff has failed to plead plausibly his antitrust allegations. Having considered carefully all of Defendants' arguments, the Court disagrees. Plaintiff has alleged a conspiracy involving the only two entities authenticating Warhol works, the Foundation (through the Catalogue Raisonné) and the Board (through direct authentication), to restrict artificially competition in the market for authentic Warhols. This unreasonable restraint in violation of Section One of the Sherman Act, it is alleged, raises the prices of the Foundation's Warhol works and ensures that galleries and museums choose Foundation works (so as to limit the risk that their authenticity will later be denied by the Board). Plaintiff has also alleged facts indicative of anticompetitive conduct with a specific intent to monopolize and a dangerous probability of achieving monopoly power in violation of Section Two of the Sherman Act.

Plaintiff asserts that the Board is completely dominated and controlled by the Foundation (Compl. at ¶ 66), and that the Foundation uses the Board to remove competing Warhols from the market in an attempt to monopolize the market (Compl. at ¶¶ 13-16). Plaintiff has alleged sufficient facts in support of the illegal restraint on trade and monopolization claims to satisfy the plausibility standard. For example, Plaintiff alleges that the Board has made unsolicited suggestions that owners of purported Warhol works submit their works for authentication; that the Board's authentication policies, to the extent that they exist, are applied inconsistently and allow the Board to reverse prior determinations when doing so would further the conspiracy; that the Board has refused to authenticate works that the Foundation previously attempted, unsuccessfully, to purchase; that the Board has denied the authenticity of works that others associated with the Estate and the Foundation have previously authenticated; and that, unlike other authentication boards, which are composed of well-qualified and well-known independent experts, the Board is populated by individuals who lack expertise in the authentication of Warhol works and who are not independent of the Foundation. (Compl. at ¶¶ 8, 74-5, 82-85, 126, 130, 155.)

Plaintiff has also sufficiently identified a relevant geographic and product market in which trade was allegedly unreasonably restrained or monopolized, as required to state a claim under Sections One and Two of the Sherman Act. See *Kramer v. Pollock-Krasner Foundation*, 890 F. Supp. 250, 254 (S.D.N.Y. 1995). "In determining the relevant market, the general rule is that commodities reasonably interchangeable by consumers for the same purposes make up that part of the trade or commerce monopolization of which may be illegal." *Vitale v. Marlborough Gallery*, No. 93 Civ. 6276, 1994 WL 654494, at *3 (S.D.N.Y. July 5, 1994) (internal quotations omitted). A narrowly defined submarket can be a relevant geographic product market. *Kramer*, 890 F. Supp. at 254. Plaintiff's allegations of a distinct submarket in the offering and sale, at auction or otherwise, of Andy Warhol works within the modern and contemporary art market are sufficient in this regard. See *Vitale*, 1994 WL 654494, at *4 ("Examining plaintiff's assertion of a submarket in light of the above criteria, the Court finds, for the purposes of this motion to dismiss, that Jackson Pollock paintings may constitute a submarket, the monopolization of which may be unlawful under 15 U.S.C. § 1 or § 2.").

Plaintiff's Antitrust Injury

Defendants argue that Plaintiff does not have standing to assert his antitrust claims because he has not suffered an antitrust injury in connection with either his purchase of Double Denied or the Board's denial of the work. "An antitrust injury is an 'injury of the type the antitrust laws were intended to prevent and that flows from that which makes defendants' acts unlawful.'" *Paycom Billing Services, Inc. v. Mastercard Intern., Inc.*, 467 F.3d 283, 290 (2d Cir. 2006), quoting *Brunswick Corp. v. Pueblo Bowl-O-Mat, Inc.*, 429 U.S. 477, 489 (1977).

Plaintiff's allegation that the double-stamping of "Denied" on his artwork in furtherance of the alleged antitrust conspiracy has prevented him from competing as a seller in the lucrative market for authentic Warhols is sufficient to frame an antitrust injury. See, e.g., *Daniel v. American Bd. of Emergency Medicine*, 428 F.3d 408, 439 (2d Cir. 2005) (although plaintiffs lacked standing in that case, the Second Circuit recognized that it is possible that a would-be competitor could demonstrate standing to challenge an exclusionary scheme that precludes him from entering the market).

Plaintiff has not, however, alleged that he has suffered any injury arising from the alleged price-inflationary aspects of the conspiracy. Plaintiff did not purchase Double Denied from the Foundation, and nowhere in the Complaint does Plaintiff allege that Double Denied was ever sold by the Foundation or recognized by the Board as authentic. Plaintiff has thus failed to plead facts sufficient to demonstrate that he has standing to complain of any price-inflation aspect of the alleged antitrust conspiracy and the Complaint will be dismissed to the extent Plaintiff's claims are premised on allegations that Defendants' actions have artificially inflated prices for Warhol works. Those claims will be dismissed for the further reason that, as explained below, any claim that Plaintiff might possess for damages in connection with his purchase of Double Denied is time barred.

Statute of Limitations

The statute of limitations for federal antitrust claims is four years. See 15 U.S.C. § 15b. The statute of limitation for New York Donnelly Act claims is also four years. N.Y. Gen. Bus. Law §§ 340(5); *Matter of Crowley Foods, Inc. V. Lefkowitz*, 75 A.D.2d 940, 942 (3d Dep't 1980). Defendants argue that Plaintiff's antitrust claim must be dismissed in its entirety as time barred because, to the extent it is premised on his 1989 purchase of Double Denied, it was brought some 14 years too late and, to the extent it is premised on exclusion of Double Denied from the market for authentic Warhol works, it accrued in 2002 when the painting's authenticity was first denied.

As explained above, Plaintiff's allegations are insufficient to demonstrate that he has any claim against Defendants relating to the purchase price of his painting. Nor has he alleged facts that would warrant a finding of fraudulent concealment that would defeat the limitations bar even if he were able to articulate an antitrust claim premised on the price he paid for Double Denied. In order to toll the statute of limitations on the basis of fraudulent concealment, Plaintiff must show that: "(1) the defendant wrongfully concealed material facts relating to defendant's wrongdoing; (2) the concealment prevented plaintiff's discovery of the nature of the claim within the limitations period; and (3) plaintiff exercised due diligence in pursuing the discovery of the claim during the period plaintiff seeks to have tolled." *Corcoran v. N.Y. Power Auth.*, 202 F.3d 530, 543 (2d Cir. 1999) (internal quotation marks omitted). The plaintiff has the burden of demonstrating the appropriateness of equitable tolling, *Boos v. Runyon*, 201 F.3d 178, 185 (2d Cir. 2000), and "must plead each of these elements with particularity as required by Rule 9(b) of the Federal Rules of Civil Procedure," *National Group for Communications and Computers Ltd. v. Lucent Techs. Inc.*, 420 F. Supp. 2d 253, 265 (S.D.N.Y. 2006). "[I]n order to toll the statute of limitations under the fraudulent concealment doctrine, Plaintiffs must also allege that they were ignorant of the antitrust violation and that their ignorance was not the result of a lack of due diligence." *In re Issuer Plaintiff Initial Public Offering Antitrust Litigation*, No. 00 Civ. 7804, 2004 WL 487222, *4 (S.D.N.Y. March 12, 2004); see also *Klehr v. A.O. Smith Corp.*, 521 U.S. 179, 194 (1997) ("a plaintiff who is not reasonably diligent may not assert 'fraudulent concealment.'"). Plaintiff's Complaint does not proffer facts sufficient to demonstrate that his discovery of a price-related claim was prevented by Defendants' concealment of wrongful actions during the limitation period, nor does it demonstrate the exercise of due diligence during the period for which Plaintiff seeks to have the limitations bar tolled. Accordingly, this aspect of Plaintiff's antitrust claim will be dismissed.

However, the Court finds that Plaintiff's antitrust monopolization and market restraint allegations, insofar as they are based on the allegedly exclusionary impact of the Board's second denial of Double Denied, are not time-barred. Although the Board's original denial of Plaintiff's painting occurred more than five years before Plaintiff brought this action, Plaintiff has alleged facts sufficient, at this stage, to invoke the continuing conspiracy exception based on the Board's second denial. To come within the continuing conspiracy exception, "a plaintiff must allege that she has been injured by continued, separate antitrust violations within the limitations period." *Vitale v. Marlborough Gallery*, No. 93 Civ. 6276, 1994 WL 654494, at *5 (S.D.N.Y. July 5, 1994) (internal quotations omitted). The continuing conspiracy exception will start the statute of limitations anew if the plaintiff alleges "an overt act which (1) is a new and independent act that is not merely a reaffirmation of a previous act; and (2) inflicts new and accumulating injury on the plaintiff." Id. (internal quotations omitted). Construing the allegations in the light most favorable to Plaintiff, the Court finds that Plaintiff has alleged sufficiently that the second denial was not a mere reaffirmation of the first. Plaintiff alleges that Defendants not only permitted, but encouraged, him to resubmit the painting with additional documentation and that he suffered additional, distinct injury as a result of the second denial.

Therefore, Plaintiff's individual Sherman Antitrust and New York Donnelly Act claims are dismissed with prejudice to the extent that they are based on his purchase of Double Denied because they are time barred, but Defendants' motion is denied to the extent that Plaintiff's federal and Donnelly Act monopolization and market restraint claims are based on the Board's rejection of Double Denied as an authentic Warhol.

Lanham Act Claim

Plaintiff asserts a violation of section 43(a) of the Lanham Act, which prohibits the use of false designation of origin, false or misleading description of fact or false or misleading representation of fact that is likely to cause confusion in commerce or in commercial advertising. [NOTE 4] In addition to arguing that Plaintiff is barred from bringing these claims insofar as they are based on Defendants' stamping of Plaintiff's painting "Denied" because the Submission Agreements included an acknowledgment that such a stamp could be affixed, Defendants argue that Plaintiff cannot assert a Lanham Act claim because the Act does not impose liability for statements of opinion, and that Plaintiff has not alleged a false statement in connection with commercial advertising as required by the "commercial advertising or promotion" prong of the Section 1125(a)(1).

As explained above, Plaintiff has alleged facts sufficient to state a claim for a declaration that the Submission Agreements are not enforceable. Thus, dismissal of Plaintiff's Lanham Act claims on the basis of the acknowledgment in those agreements is not appropriate at this stage.

Plaintiff has also alleged sufficient facts to state a claim under the Lanham Act in connection with Defendants' letters. Although it is well established that a "statement of opinion is not actionable under the Lanham Act if it could not reasonably be seen as stating or implying provable facts about a competitor's goods or services," *Boule v. Hutton*, 328 F.3d 84, 93 (2d Cir. 2003), it is not clear, at this stage, that Defendants' letters were such mere statements of opinion. The Court cannot determine at this stage of the proceeding whether the Defendants' letters, although purporting to be opinions, could reasonably be seen as stating or implying provable facts about the authenticity of Double Denied. The Second Circuit's decision in *Boule*, which involved the resolution of such issues based on factual findings after a bench trial, is not to the contrary.

Additionally, to the extent that Defendants argue that Plaintiff has no claim based on Defendants' May 18, 2004, letter because he has conceded that descriptive statements in that letter were "literally true," Plaintiff has sufficiently alleged that the statements were nonetheless fraudulent and misleading. See *Groden v. Random House, Inc.*, 61 F.3d 1045 (2d Cir. 1995) ("In order to be actionable under the Lanham Act, a challenged advertisement must be literally false or, though literally true, likely to mislead or confuse consumers." (emphasis added)).

Plaintiff has not, however, proffered allegations sufficient to frame a violation of the "commercial advertising or promotion" prong of the Lanham Act. "In this circuit, to constitute 'commercial advertising or promotion' under the Lanham Act, a statement must be: (1) commercial speech, (2) made for the purpose of influencing consumers to buy defendant's goods or services, and (3) although representations less formal than those made as part of a classic advertising campaign may suffice, they must be disseminated sufficiently to the relevant purchasing public." *Gmurzynska v. Hutton*, 355 F.3d 206, 210 (2d Cir. 2004) (internal quotations omitted). Although Plaintiff alleges that the Catalogue, which is published by the Foundation, is the only recognized means of authentication other than direct authentication by the Board, the Complaint does not proffer allegations as to Defendants' use of the Catalogue in connection with the commercial offer of their goods and services.

Thus, the Court finds that Plaintiff has sufficiently alleged violations of Section 43(a) of the Lanham Act in connection with Defendants' letters, but has failed to allege sufficient facts to plead a Lanham Act claim in connection with the exclusion of Double Denied from the Catalogue.

Fraud

Defendants contend that Plaintiff has failed to plead his fraud claim with particularity as required by Rule 9(b) and, thus, it should be dismissed. See Fed. R. Civ. P. 9(b). Particularity requires the plaintiff to "(1) specify the statements that the plaintiff contends were fraudulent, (2) identify the speaker, (3) state where and when the statements were made, and (4) explain why the statements were fraudulent." *Stevelman v. Alias Research, Inc.*, 174 F.3d 79, 84 (2d Cir. 1999). The issue is whether the allegations provide fair and reasonable notice of the time, place, speaker, and content of the alleged misrepresentation or omission. *Shields v. Citytrust Bancorp, Inc.*, 25 F.3d 1124, 1128-29, 1130 (2d Cir. 1994).

Plaintiff has alleged fraud sufficiently in connection with the repudiation of Double Denied. Plaintiff alleges that, in July 2001 and continuing through December 2001, Fremont intervened in Plaintiff's attempts to sell Double Denied and fraudulently induced Plaintiff to submit his painting to the Board for authentication. Plaintiff further alleges Fremont was aware at the time that the Board would deny the authenticity of Double Denied. Plaintiff also alleges that, in February 2002, Fremont once again induced the Plaintiff to resubmit Double Denied, after conducting additional research, to the Board. The Complaint alleges that Fremont made these statements with the knowledge that Plaintiff would rely on Fremont's statements and that a rejection by the Board was certain. The Complaint also alleges that in February of 2002 the Board's agent, Claudia Defendi, urged Plaintiff to resubmit Double Denied despite knowing that a rejection from the Board was predetermined. See *International Motor Sports Group v. Gordon*, No. 82709, 98 Civ. 5611, 1999 WL 619633, at *3 (S.D.N.Y. Aug. 16, 1999) (Rule 9(b) does not require "a plaintiff [to] plead dates, times and places with absolute precision, so long as the complaint gives fair and reasonable notice to defendants of the claim and the grounds upon which it is based"). Plaintiff's allegations of fraud in connection with the repudiation of Double Denied are sufficient under Rule 9(b) and Defendants' motion to dismiss Plaintiff's fraud claim is denied.

Unjust Enrichment Claim

Defendants' motion is denied as to Plaintiff's claim of unjust enrichment. The claim is not implausibly pled, in that the Complaint includes allegations concerning, inter alia, Defendants' profiting at Plaintiff's expense.

Fremont's Official Capacity

Defendants' motion is also denied as to Plaintiff's claims against Fremont in his official capacity. The Complaint alleges that Fremont is the "successor" executor of the Estate. Defendants' arguments regarding the naming and appointment of the Estate's executor and Fremont's actual status can be addressed in an appropriate evidentiary context at a later stage of the proceeding.

CONCLUSION

For the foregoing reasons, Defendants' motion to dismiss the Complaint is granted in part and denied in part. Plaintiff's antitrust claims are dismissed for lack of standing to the extent that they are premised on inflamation of the prices of Warhol artwork. Plaintiff's Lanham Act claim is dismissed insofar as it is premised on the exclusion of Double Denied from the Catalogue Raisonné. Defendant's motion is denied in all other respects. The stay of discovery is lifted and the parties are directed to confer and to file an updated Joint Preliminary Pre-Trial Statement one week before the next conference in this action, which the Court will hold on Tuesday, June 30, 2009, at 3:00 p.m. The Clerk of Court is respectfully requested to terminate docket entry no. 21.

SO ORDERED.

NOTES:

NOTE 1: The Catalogue Raisonné recites that a fourth volume is reserved for newly found works, revised, updated and newly found information. (Reply Brief at 18, n.2).

NOTE 2: "Every contract, combination in the form of trust or otherwise, or conspiracy, in restraint of trade or commerce among the several States . . . is declared to be illegal." 15 U.S.C.A. § 1 (West 2009).

NOTE 3: "Every person who shall monopolize, or attempt to monopolize, or combine or conspire with any other person or persons, to monopolize any part of the trade or commerce . . . shall be deemed to be guilty of a felony. . . ." 15 U.S.C.A, § 2 (West 2009).

NOTE 4: "Any person who, on or in connection with any goods or services, or any container for goods, uses in commerce any word, term, name, symbol, or device, or any combination thereof, or any false designation of origin, false or misleading description of fact, or false or misleading representation of fact, which— (A) is likely to cause confusion, or to cause mistake, or to deceive as to the affiliation, connection, or association of such person with another person, or as to the origin, sponsorship, or approval of his or her goods, services, or commercial activities by another person, or (B) in commercial advertising or promotion, misrepresents the nature, characteristics, qualities, or geographic origin of his or her or another person's goods, services, or commercial activities, shall be liable in a civil action by any person who believes that he or she is or is likely to be damaged by such act." 15 U.S.C.A, § 1125 (a)(1)(A) & (B) (West 1998).

STUDY QUESTIONS

- In the *Andy Warhol Foundation* case who was the plaintiff and what claims did he make?
- How did the Authentication Board go about authenticating Warhol's works?
- What is the role of a catalogue raisonne?
- Why did the Board require an indemnification letter as part of the authentication process?
- What is the impact on a work of being denied by the Board?
- Assess plaintiff's antitrust, statute of limitations, trademark and fraud claims.
- The court's ruling in the *Andy Warhol Foundation* case gave the plaintiff's legal team access to the foundation to gain witness depositions and other evidence. However, Simon-Whelan was forced to drop the case in October 2010 when he ran out of money. While the defendants denied any scheme, saying the Authentication Board rejected only 15 to 18 per cent of applications each year, it has since been disbanded and the Warhol Foundation no longer authenticates Warhol works. What are the implications for art collectors, including museums from the curtailing of authentication board practices?

LOANS

Collecting museums routinely loan out objects from their collections to other institutions. Museums also borrow objects from collectors and other owners. Policies and practices regarding loans should be part of the museum's collections management loan policies.

When a museum borrows objects, whether from a private collector or another institution, the loan is a "bailment," and the borrowing museum is in the position of a bailee. The museum holds the loaned object in trust for the owner (the "bailor"). The law recognizes varying duties of care for bailments depending on the relationship between the bailor and bailee. (See discussion about bailments in Temporary Custody section above.) These duties are imposed when there is no express contract between the parties.

To avoid ambiguity, a well drafted loan agreement will include language establishing the standard of care that will be applied to the object while it is on loan. Often the borrowing museum expressly agrees to exercise the same level of care for the borrowed object as it does for its own collections.

Insurance coverage is an important consideration with respect to loans and is often the subject of considerable negotiation in loan agreements. Who will obtain insurance coverage, who will pay for it, who will be covered and for what amount, are just some of the many issues that need to be addressed in the loan agreement. Often the greatest risks to an object arise while it is transit, so details about how an object will be transported to the museum and returned to the lender should also be part of the loan agreement. Working out all of these details on behalf of the museum is usually the responsibility of the museum registrar.

The cost of insurance for a major exhibition can be considerable. In some cases, artwork may be so valuable that insurance coverage cannot be obtained. Risks such as terrorism may also make it difficult or impossible to obtain insurance coverage. To encourage cultural exchanges and facilitate museum loans, Congress enacted the Art and Artifacts Indemnity Act [note 1] under which the U.S. government guarantees to pay any loss or damage claims arising out of international exhibitions. The program proved so successful that it has been expanded to cover domestic exhibitions as well.

Loans can pose a variety of ethical considerations. Sometimes collectors view museums as convenient places to store their collections. Particularly when a loan is coupled with a promise of a future donation, it may become hard for the museum to resist accepting the loan. An object loaned to a prestigious museum as part of a well-publicized exhibit may increase in value—sometimes referred to as "the museum effect." A lender may hope to benefit from this by making the loan. When the lender is a board member or employee of the museum, these situations may pose potential conflicts of interest. These issues should be addressed as part of the museum's collections management and ethics policies.

Some of the most interesting issues involving loaned objects result from incomplete or missing provenance. Care must be taken to verify that the lender has the authority to make the loan and otherwise has good title. If a claim for replevin or restitution of a work is made while it is in the custody of the museum, the museum may find itself in the middle of a lawsuit.

International loans—whether from an individual lender or a foreign museum—pose a set of unique issues. One particular problem involves the risk that a valuable work of art may be seized, either to satisfy a debt owed by the artworks's owner unrelated to the work itself, or because the work becomes the subject of a repatriation or restitution claim. In the latter case, the U.S. Government may assert that the work is "stolen" within the meaning of the National Stolen Property Act and seize the work pursuant to that Act. [note 2]

The *Portrait of Wally* case, which was settled after years of litigation, initially involved seizure of an Egon Schiele painting that was on loan to the Museum of Modern Art

(MoMA). The painting was seized under both New York and federal forfeiture statutes. The case is one of many restitution claims involving Nazi-era artwork. A press release announcing the settlement is reprinted in the Cases and Other Readings below.

The risk of seizure can be a substantial deterrent to cultural exchange. To address this, Congress enacted an "immunity from seizure" statute which exempts certain works of cultural significance imported into the United States by a cultural organization for non-commercial temporary exhibition.[note 3] A museum may apply for a declaration of immunity from the U.S. State Department under this statute.

Another law, the Federal Immunity from Seizure Act (FISA), grants immunity from U.S. court jurisdiction to foreign governments except in certain limited situations. In other words, a foreign government cannot be sued in American courts except under certain circumstances. A key exception to this sovereign immunity is when the sovereign is engaged in taking property in violation of international law and is involved in a commercial activity in the United States with respect to that property. In response to a restitution lawsuit brought by the heirs of a Russian artist whose artwork was loaned by the City of Amsterdam to two major U.S. museums,[note 4] Congress has amended FISA to clarify that loans by foreign governments for temporary museum exhibitions do not constitute "commercial activity" for the purposes of the statute. (For more on restitution and repatriation claims, see "*Requests for Return*" below.)

NOTES:

NOTE 1: Art and Artifacts Indemnity Act, 20 U.S.C. Section 971 et. seq.

NOTE 2: National Stolen Property Act, 18 U.S.C. §§ 2314

NOTE 3: The Immunity from Seizure Act, 22 U.S.C. Section 2459

NOTE 4: *Malewicz v. City of Amsterdam*, 362 F. Supp. 2d 298 (D.D.C. 2005) aff'd by 517 F. Supp. 2d 322 (D.D.C. 2007)

CASES AND OTHER READINGS

Reading Note: The press release reprinted below announces the settlement of a civil forfeiture action involving Egon Schiele's painting *Portrait of Wally.* The painting was seized while on loan to a New York museum and subject to over a decade of litigation surrounding a Nazi-era restitution claim. The case is an example of how the National Stolen Property Act (NSPA) is used to aid in the return of cultural property to its rightful owners.

UNITED STATES ANNOUNCES $19 MILLION SETTLEMENT IN CASE OF PAINTING STOLEN BY NAZI

Press Release. July 20, 2010

PREET BHARARA, the United States Attorney for the Southern District of New York, and JOHN T. MORTON, the Director of the Department of Homeland Security's United States Immigration and Customs Enforcement ("ICE"), announced today that the United States has entered into a settlement agreement with the Leopold Museum Privat-Stiftung (the "Foundation") and LEA BONDI JARAY's estate (the "Estate") to resolve the civil forfeiture action against *Portrait of Wally* (*"Wally"*), an oil painting by EGON SCHIELE that a Nazi stole from a Jewish woman in 1939. According to the terms of the settlement agreement, the Leopold Museum will pay BONDI's Estate $19 million in exchange for the painting.

EGON SCHIELE painted *Wally* in 1912. The painting depicts WABURGA "WALLY" NEUZIL, SCHIELE's primary model and his lover from about 1911 until he married EDITH ANNA HARMS in 1915. In the decades following World War II, SCHIELE became one of the most prominent Austrian artists of the twentieth century. BONDI, an Austrian Jew and owner of an art gallery (the "Würthle Gallery") in Vienna, acquired *Wally* some time before 1925. In March of 1938, in what is known as the Anschluss, German troops occupied Austria and annexed it to Germany.

Pursuant to German Aryanization laws prohibiting Jews from owning businesses, the Würthle Gallery was designated as "non-Aryan" and subject to confiscation. BONDI thereafter sold the Würthle Gallery to a Nazi art collector named FRIEDRICH WELZ. In 1939, on the eve of BONDI's escape to England, WELZ went to BONDI's apartment to discuss the gallery. He saw *Wally* hanging on the wall and demanded that BONDI give it to him. She resisted, as *Wally* was part of her private collection and had never been part of the

Egon Schiele's Portrait of Wally *(1912) depicts Walburga "Wally" Neuzil, Schiele's lover and model for several years. The painting, acquired by Rudolf Leopold in 1954, became part of the collection of the Leopold Museum when it was established by the Austrian government. Near the end of a 1997-1998 exhibit of Schiele's work at the Museum of Modern Art in New York, the painting's provenance was revealed in an article published in the* New York Times. *The heirs of Lea Bondi Jaray, to whom the work had belonged before World War II, contacted the New York County District Attorney who issued a subpoena forbidding its return to Austria. The work was tied up in litigation for years by Bondi's heirs, who claimed that the painting had been stolen and should be returned to them. In 2010, the Leopold Museum agreed to pay $19 million to Bondi's heirs as part of a settlement agreement.*

Würthle Gallery. BONDI ultimately relented at the behest of her husband, however, who reminded her that they intended to flee Austria and that WELZ could prevent their escape.

After the war, United States military forces in Austria arrested WELZ and seized *Wally* and other artworks. These artworks were transferred to the Austrian Government, in accordance with the policy and practice of the United States military to return property seized from Nazis to the governments of the countries of origin. *Wally* was ultimately delivered to the government-owned Austrian National Gallery in the Belvedere Palace (the "Belvedere").

In 1953, Dr. RUDOLPH LEOPOLD, an Austrian collector of artwork by SCHIELE, visited BONDI during a trip to London. During this visit, BONDI told LEOPOLD that the painting belonged to her and asked him to go to the Belvedere and recover it on her behalf. LEOPOLD agreed to help her. Instead of helping BONDI recover her painting, however, LEOPOLD entered into an agreement with the Belvedere whereby he exchanged a SCHIELE painting from his own collection for *Wally*. When BONDI later discovered that LEOPOLD had acquired *Wally* for himself, she retained lawyers to attempt to convince LEOPOLD to return the painting to her, to no avail. BONDI continued to fight to recover her beloved painting until her death in 1969.

In 1994, LEOPOLD's art collection, including *Wally*, became part of the newly formed Leopold Museum. In 1997, the Leopold Museum loaned part of its SCHIELE collection, including *Wally*, to New York's Museum of Modern Art (the "MoMA"). *Wally* was shipped to New York in September 1997. On September 21, 1999, United States Magistrate Judge JAMES C. FRANCIS IV issued a federal seizure warrant for *Wally* based upon a finding of probable cause that the painting was stolen property imported into the United States in violation of federal law. Pursuant to the warrant, the United States Customs Service seized the painting.

The next day, the United States commenced a civil action in order to forfeit *Wally* and return it to its rightful owner, BONDI's estate. The United States Attorney's Office for the Southern District of New York filed a civil Complaint in Manhattan federal court and alleged that *Wally* was forfeitable as stolen property knowingly imported into, and about to be exported from, the United States in violation of the National Stolen Property Act, 18 U.S.C. § 2314. The Estate, the Leopold Museum, and MoMA filed claims to the painting in the forfeiture proceeding. During the litigation, the Museum maintained that WELZ did not steal the painting and that LEOPOLD did not know it was stolen property when it was imported into the United States.

On September 30, 2009, United States District Judge LORETTA A. PRESKA issued a 109-page decision on the parties' summary judgment motions. The Court rejected the Museum's position that *Wally* was not stolen property, and concluded that the painting was BONDI's personal property, that WELZ had stolen it, and that the property remained stolen when it was imported into the United States. The Court further ruled that the

Government had made a probable cause showing that LEOPOLD knew *Wally* was stolen property when it was imported into the United States. Thus, the only issue to be resolved at trial was whether the Leopold Museum could overcome the Government's evidence and prove that Leopold did not know that *Wally* was stolen property when it was imported into the United States. The Court scheduled a trial for July 26, 2010, to decide this single issue.

Today, the Government, the Estate, and the Leopold Museum reached a settlement agreement that resolves the litigation. Under the terms of the agreement, the Leopold Museum will pay the Estate $19 million in exchange for *Wally*. The civil forfeiture action brought public attention to the struggle of victims of Nazi crimes to recover art and other property stolen by the Nazis.

United States Attorney PREET BHARARA stated: "More than 70 years after *Portrait of Wally* was stolen, today's settlement marks another small step towards justice for victims of property crimes during WWII. Lea Bondi Jaray and her family were steadfast in their long battle to restore their rightful ownership of *Portrait of Wally*. Their determination provides hope for others who lost precious property and art to Nazi theft. Without the hard work and dedication of this Office's Asset Forfeiture Unit and ICE, the true provenance of *Portrait of Wally* would not have been uncovered nor justice done after so many years."

ICE Director JOHN T. MORTON stated: "A seven-decade-old injustice was made right today by this settlement. Thanks to the intrepid investigative work of ICE agents in our New York office and the years of unwavering legal work by the U.S. Attorney for the Southern District of New York, the heirs of an art dealer robbed of this exquisite painting by the Nazis will be compensated. We are proud that this case has caused those who deal in art to be extremely vigilant about works caught up in the Holocaust and to join us in trying to rectify the past."

Mr. BHARARA praised the investigative work of ICE. He also thanked the Treasury Executive Office for Asset Forfeiture, the United States Customs and Border Protection, and the Manhattan District Attorney's Office for their assistance in this case.

Assistant United States Attorneys SHARON COHEN LEVIN, ANNA E. ARREOLA, and BARBARA A. WARD are in charge of the forfeiture proceeding.

STUDY QUESTIONS

- Egon Schiele's painting *Portrait of Wally* was caught up in many years of litigation. What triggered this litigation? What role did the U.S. government play? What authority did the government rely on to seize the painting?

- Summarize the underlying facts of the dispute. What issue was left for trial? Why do you think the parties finally settled? Do you think the settlement agreement was a good solution?

DEACCESSIONING AND DISPOSAL

"Deaccessioning" is the process used to permanently remove an object from a museum's collection. The term can also be used in connection with documenting the involuntary removal of an object from the collection by operation of law, in the case of a successful restitution or repatriation claim for example, or due to circumstances not controlled by the museum, such as theft of the object. Deaccessioning presupposes that the object in question was once "accessioned"—that is, it was formally accepted into the museum's collection with the intent to keep it on a permanent basis. An object that has not been accessioned need not be formally deaccessioned unless the museum's collections management policy requires it. "Disposal" refers to the act of getting rid of an object—by sale or other transfer of ownership, destruction, or otherwise. It presumes the object has already been deaccessioned if necessary.

While accessioned museum collections are presumed to be held on a permanent basis, there are a variety of reasons why a museum might want to deaccession and dispose of a collection or a particular object. A collections inventory may identify objects that were inadvertently accessioned but are not deemed appropriate to be part of the museum's permanent collection. The museum may find that it has duplicates or multiples of a certain type of object. An object may become damaged to a degree that it is no longer able to be property conserved. Or the museum may determine that it is unable to properly care for an object. In other cases, the museum may determine that certain museum objects no longer align with its mission and collecting goals. Most controversially, the museum may face financial problems or be unable to maintain its facilities: It may look to selling high-value objects from its collection as a way to solve problems unrelated to the objects themselves.

Some deaccessioning controversies arise when the museum is part of a larger institution which is facing financial or other difficulties—a college or university for example. The board of the parent organization may not always understand and appreciate the special status of the museum's collections.

Deaccessioning of a museum object raises both legal and ethical issues. From a legal perspective, deaccession can raise issues regarding museum governance, and may require compliance with applicable state and possibly local law. In *Wilstach Estate*, 1 Pa. D. & C.2d 197 (Pa. Orph. Ct. 1954), a Pennsylvania court acknowledged that museum trustees have the authority to deaccession collections objects. The court opined that a trustee of a charitable trust can exercise such powers as are necessary and appropriate to carry out the purpose of the trust and which are not expressly forbidden by the terms of the trust. The board-level responsibility to manage the museum's collections includes the authority to deaccession and dispose of those collections, so long as in doing so the board is in full compliance with its fiduciary duties.

The decision to deaccession an object is a board-level decision because it involves disposing of an asset of the trust. In matters involving the museum's collections, including deaccessioning, the museum trustees are judged using the traditional trust standard—the highest duty of care. This is because collections management is a core function of the museum as a charitable trust. (See the discussion of trustee fiduciary duties in chapter 1: *Museum Organization and Governance*).

As with other issues involving the museum as a charitable trust, the state attorney general has a role in overseeing the deaccessioning process. The state attorney general has the right to investigate and bring legal actions against charitable organizations to enforce the fiduciary duties of the charity's trustees. A state attorney general may also revoke a museum's charitable status for misuse or abuse of its charitable privilege. The state attorney general can issue advisory opinions on deaccessioning proposals. It may also represent the public in cases involving the interpretation or alteration of the charitable trust, including in declaratory judgement, *cy pres* and equitable deviation cases.

Depending on the jurisdiction, there may be other laws affecting a museum's ability to deaccession objects from its collections. Provisions of state corporate and charitable trust laws may also apply when assessing the conduct of museum trustees with respect to deaccessioning. For example, state charitable laws may require trustees to consider the impact on the community as a result of their decisions regarding a charitable trust. The disposal of a large percentage of the museum's collection at one time may trigger state corporate governance statutes that require approval by the corporate shareholders for any substantial disposal of the corporation's assets; if the museum has voting members, it may be necessary, or at least prudent, to obtain their approval. Local "cultural property" laws that require consideration of an object's historic or cultural significance to the community may also apply. In response to perceived abuses regarding deaccessioning have led some states, most notably New York, to consider enacting state laws regulating the process of deaccessioning by museums under their jurisdiction.

In addition to issues concerning governmental oversight, when considering whether to deaccession a museum object, the possibility of third-party rights in the object must also be carefully analyzed. Under the Visual Artist Rights Act (VARA) (17 U.S.C. Section 106A) and state equivalents, a living artist may have certain "moral rights" in an object which may be implicated in a decision to deaccession the object. Depending on the circumstances, notice and the opportunity to remove a work may be required to be given to the artist or his estate before a protected work can be removed or destroyed. If the artist signed a "VARA waiver" as provided in the federal statute, there may be no legal need to contact the artist before disposing of the work, although other legal requirements may still apply. Out of respect for the artist, many museums consult with artists and their estates before making the decision to deaccession the artist's work, regardless of whether there is a legal obligation to do so.

If the object is subject to donor-imposed restrictions on its disposal, these also must be addressed. Depending on the terms of the gift, the restrictions may be binding and enforceable, or be merely "precatory"—that is, only expressing the wishes or desires of the donor. A review of the Deed of Gift and any other relevant documentation relating to the gift are an important part of the deaccessioning process. Depending on the nature of the gift restrictions, the museum may need to obtain a declaratory court order addressing the gift restrictions before it can proceed with deaccessioning the work.

Where documentation is lacking, consideration must be given to whether the donor intended to donate the object, or whether it was intended to be a loan. In cases where donor intent is unclear, transfer of the object to another museum or charitable institution—rather than an outright sale—may be an acceptable solution, so long as the donor's intent is honored.

In some cases, the museum's title to the object may need to be established before it can be deaccessioned. So-called "old loans" or "objects found in the collection" are those objects where there is no clear evidence that the object was acquired by gift or purchase. Sometimes objects are left at the museum anonymously with no explanation—like an unwanted baby left on the steps of an orphanage. More often, however, the objects are intentionally left with the museum for review and consideration as a proposed gift. While such "deposits" should be documented with a temporary custody receipt (see the discussion in chapter 4, *Temporary Custody*), this is not always done. In some cases, months or even years may go by before a decision on whether to acquire and accession the objects is made, and during that time contact with the owner may be lost. Records documenting the status of the object as a loan or a gift may also be lost. In these situations, establishing the museum's title to the object can be problematic.

Some states have enacted statutes to address the problem of establishing the museum's title to these abandoned or "orphaned" objects. These statutes typically set out a procedure for establishing the museum's title in the work, including public notice and a waiting period, after which the museum is deemed to be the owner with good title to the object. These statutes may also include procedures for handling claims made for the return of collections objects to the owner's successors or other claimants. The Minnesota Museum Property Act included in the Cases and Other Readings below is an example of these types of statutes.

In addition to the forgoing legal considerations, museums must also take museum association ethical guidelines on deaccessioning into account. The American Alliance of Museum (AAM) guidelines on deaccessioning require all member museums to have a written policy on deaccessioning works from their collections (See AAM, *Direct Care of Collections: Ethics,*

Guidelines and Recommendations (April 2016)). The American Association of Museum Directors (AAMD) imposes similar requirements on its members (See AAMD, *Policy on Deacessioning* (amended October 2015)). In making the decision to deaccession an object, the museum should weigh the interest of the public the museum serves and give due consideration to the museum community in general as well as to the needs of the individual museum. While the governing board is ultimately responsible for the deaccessioning decision, it should give weight to the recommendations of its professional curatorial staff.

Procedures for deciding to deaccession an object from the museum's collection should be formalized as part of the museum's collections management policy. The first step is to establish clear and unrestricted title to the object. The provenance of the object should be researched and documented as fully and completely as possible. If there are any encumbrances or restrictions which may impact disposal, these must be addressed. Authority to make the deaccessioning decision must also be established. Normally this authority should be equal to or higher than the authority required to accession the object. Often the authority to deaccession rests in the board of directors, but this authority may be delegated depending on the value and significance of the objects to be deaccessioned. The process and decision to deaccession should be thoroughly documented and that record preserved along with other collections records.

While some museums maintain a practice of notifying the donor or the donor's heirs when a donated object is being considered for disposal, if the gift was unrestricted the donor retained no legal interest in the object and there is no legal obligation to give notice about the disposition of the object. The practice of notifying a donor is more of a "goodwill" policy intended to maintain relations with the donor, but the practice can also backfire if the donor or its heir mistakenly believe they retained rights in the object.

As noted above, where there are legally binding restrictions on an object which affect its disposal, the museum may need to seek court approval to dispose of the object. In highly controversial situations, the museum may also want to seek approval from the state's attorney general and/or a declaratory ruling from a court before proceeding with a deaccessioning plan. Even in such cases, the museum's relationship with its donors and its reputation with the public at large may be harmed.

There are a variety of methods for disposing of museum objects—the object can be sold by auction, through a private sale, or through a dealer. Collections objects can also be exchanged or given to another museum. As a charitable trust, once an object has been removed from the collections, the museum has a fiduciary obligation to obtain the best price for the object. However, because the museum holds the object in the public trust, the museum has a competing duty to ensure the object remains available to the public. This creates a tension regarding the ultimate disposition of the object. Any transaction must be arms-length and any potential conflicts of interest or self-dealing by board members, employees, and anyone else with a special relationship to the museum, must be avoided.

The method of disposal may depend on the type of collection, the museum's applicable policies, ethical guidelines, and the like. Anthropological collections, for example, are typically only disposed of through exchange with another museum—commercial transactions involving these types of collections are generally frowned upon.

The museum's mission may also have some bearing on how disposal of the work is accomplished. Some museums have a policy that works must remain in the public sphere. If a work is to be sold, public auction is generally considered the best way to demonstrate an arms-length transaction and avoid potential conflicts of interest. However, there may be reasons why a private sale or sale through a dealer may be preferable and, in some cases, may be a better choice for maximizing proceeds from a sale.

How the proceeds from the sale of museum objects are used can be highly controversial. Museum collections are generally not considered financial assets for accounting purposes (See FASB *Accounting Standards Update 2019-03* (2019)), and museum professional codes discourage museums from selling their collections for financial gain. The way in which proceeds from deaccessioning can be used may depend on the type of museum and the kind objects being deaccessioned. Generally speaking, museum professional and ethical guidelines prohibit the use of proceeds from deaccessioning for purposes other than maintaining the collections. The American Alliance of Museums (AAM) *Guidelines on Deaccessioning Activity* allows proceeds to be used for "acquisition or direct care," while the American Association of Museum Directors (AAMD) *Policy on Deaccessioning* (applicable mainly to art museums) restricts the use of proceeds for acquisitions of new works. The American Association for State and Local History (AASLH) guidelines prohibit the sale of collections "in order to provide financial support for institutional operations, facilities maintenance, or any other reason other than the preservation or acquisition of collections." (AASLH *Statement of Professional Standards and Ethics*)

When considering deaccessioning of museum objects, the museum must be aware of the impact of disposing of its collections on public perceptions of its public trust responsibility. In highly controversial situations, the museum's reputation and credibility are at stake. The importance of approaching deaccessioning in a carefully considered and transparent manner cannot be overstated.

CASES AND OTHER READINGS

Reading Note: The statute reprinted below is an example of how some states have addressed the problem of establishing title to objects found in museum collections for which there is a lack of ownership documentation. The act provides a notification process which, if followed, will result in the presumption that the museum holds title to the object. It also includes a process for resolving competing claims of ownership in an object.

MINNESOTA MUSEUM PROPERTY ACT

Minnesota Statutes Chapter 345,
Sections 345.70 to 345.74 (2019)

345.70 MINNESOTA MUSEUM PROPERTY ACT; DEFINITIONS.

(a) As used in this section, the terms defined in this subdivision have the meanings given them.

(b) "Archives repository" means a nonprofit organization or a public agency whose primary functions include selecting, preserving, and making available records of historical or enduring value, and that is open to the public on a regular basis. Archives repository does not include a public library.

(c) "Loan" means the placement of property with a museum or archives repository that is not accompanied by a transfer of title of the property to the museum or archives repository and for which there is some record that the owner intended to retain title to the property. Loan does not include transfers between museums, between archives repositories, or between museums and archives repositories unless the transferring institution specifically provides in writing that the transfer is a loan under this section.

(d) "Museum" means a nonprofit organization or a public agency that is operated primarily for the purpose of collecting, cataloging, preserving, or exhibiting property of educational, scientific, historic, cultural, or aesthetic interest and that is open to the public on a regular basis. Museum does not include a public library.

(e) "Property" means personal property.

345.71 LOANS OF PROPERTY TO A MUSEUM OR ARCHIVES REPOSITORY.

Subdivision 1. **Ownership records.**

Each museum or archives repository shall keep accurate records of all property on loan to the museum or archives repository, including the name and address of the owner, if known, and the beginning and ending date of the loan period. At the time that a person makes a loan to a museum or archives repository, the museum or archives repository shall give the owner of the property a copy of this section. If a museum or archives repository is notified of a change in the ownership of any property loaned to a museum or archives repository, the museum or archives repository shall inform the new owner of the provisions of the loan agreement and shall send the new owner a copy of this section. Not less than 90 days before a museum or archives repository changes its address or dissolves, the museum or archives repository shall notify all owners of that change of address or dissolution. If a museum or archives repository becomes the owner of property under section

345.72 or 345.73, the museum or archives repository shall maintain any records that the museum or archives repository has regarding the property for not less than two years after the date on which the museum or archives repository becomes the owner of the property.

Subd. 2. **Change in address or ownership.**

The owner of property loaned to a museum or archives repository shall provide the museum or archives repository with written notice of any change of the owner's address, of the owner's designated agent, of the designated agent's address, and of the name and address of the new owner if there is a change in the ownership of the property loaned to the museum or archives repository.

345.72 ACQUIRING TITLE TO ABANDONED PROPERTY.

Subdivision 1. **Acquisition.**

Property loaned to a museum or archives repository whose loan has an expiration date is abandoned when there has not been written contact between the owner and the museum or archives repository for at least seven years after that expiration date. If the loan has no expiration date, the property is abandoned when there has not been written contact between the owner and the museum or archives repository for at least seven years after the museum or archives repository took possession of the property.

Subd. 2. **Notice.**

(a) If a museum or archives repository wishes to acquire title to abandoned property, the museum or archives repository shall, not less than 60 days after property is abandoned under subdivision 1, send a notice by certified mail with return receipt requested to the owner's last known address. The notice shall contain all of the following:

(1) a statement that the loan is terminated and that the property is abandoned;

(2) a description of the property;

(3) a statement that the museum or archives repository will become the owner of the property if the present owner does not submit a written claim to the property to the museum or archives repository within 60 days after receipt of the notice; and

(4) a statement that the museum or archives repository will make arrangements with the owner to return the property to the owner or dispose of the property as the owner requests if the owner submits a written claim to the property to the museum or archives repository within 60 days after receipt of the notice.

(b) The notice in paragraph (a) shall be substantially in the following form:

NOTICE OF ABANDONMENT OF PROPERTY

To: (name of owner) ____________________________

(address of owner) ____________________________

Please be advised that the loan agreement is terminated for the following property (describe the property in sufficient detail to identify the property): __________

The above described property that you loaned to (name and address of museum or archives repository) __________ will be considered abandoned by you and will become the property of __________ (name of museum or archives repository) if you fail to submit to the museum or archives repository a written claim to the property within 60 days after receipt of this notice.

If you do submit a written claim to the property within 60 days after receipt of this notice, __________ (name of museum or archives repository) will arrange to return the property to you or dispose of the property as you request. The cost of returning the property to you or disposing of the property is your responsibility unless you have made other arrangements with the museum or archives repository.

__________ (name of person to contact at museum or archives repository and address of museum or archives repository)

Subd. 3. **Publication.**

If the notice sent by the museum or archives repository under subdivision 2 is returned to the museum or archives repository undelivered, the museum or archives repository shall give notice of the abandoned property by publication, and the organization's website, if applicable, containing the following:

(1) the name and last known address of the present owner;

(2) a description of the property;

(3) a statement that the property is abandoned and that the museum or archives repository will become the owner of the property if no person can prove their ownership of the property;

(4) a statement that a person claiming ownership of the property shall notify the museum or archives repository in writing of that claim within 60 days after publication of the last legal notice; and

(5) the name and mailing address of the person who may be contacted at the museum or archives repository if a person wants to submit a written claim to the property.

Subd. 4. **Claims for the property.**

(a) If the museum or archives repository receives a timely written claim for the property from the owner or the owner's agent in response to the notice sent under subdivision 2 or 3, the museum or archives repository shall return the property to the owner or dispose of the property as the owner requests. The owner shall advise the museum or archives repository in writing as to how the property shall be disposed of or returned to the owner. Costs of returning the property or disposing of the property shall be the responsibility of the owner unless the owner and the museum or archives repository have made other arrangements.

(b) If the museum or archives repository receives a timely written claim for the property from a person other than the person who loaned the property to the museum or archives repository in response to the notice sent under subdivision 2 or 3, the museum or archives repository shall, within 60 days after receipt of the written claim, determine if the claim is valid. A claimant shall submit proof of ownership with the claim. If more than one person submits a timely written claim, the museum or archives repository may delay its determination of ownership until the competing claims are resolved by agreement or legal action. If the museum or archives repository determines that the claim is valid, or if the competing claims are resolved by agreement or judicial action, the museum or archives repository shall return the property to the claimant submitting the valid claim or dispose of the property as the valid claimant requests. Costs of returning the property or disposing of the property shall be the responsibility of the valid claimant.

(c) If the museum or archives repository does not receive a timely written claim to the property or if the museum or archives repository determines that no valid timely claim to the property was submitted, the museum or archives repository becomes the owner of the property. The museum or archives repository becomes the owner of the property on the day after the period for submitting a written claim ends or on the day after the museum or archives repository determines that no valid timely written claim was submitted. The museum or archives repository owns the property free from all claims.

345.73 ACQUIRING TITLE TO UNDOCUMENTED PROPERTY.

Subdivision 1. **Acquisition.**

Property in the possession of a museum or archives repository which the museum or archives repository has reason to believe may be on loan and, for which the museum or archives repository does not know the owner, or have any reasonable means of determining the owner, becomes the property of the museum or archives repository if no person has claimed the property within seven years after the museum or archives repository took possession of the property. The museum or archives repository becomes the owner of the property on the day after the seven-year period ends, and after following the notification process outlined in subdivision 2, free from all claims.

Subd. 2. **Notification.**

The museum or archives repository that wishes to acquire title to undocumented property described in subdivision 1 shall provide public notice in the manner described in section 345.72.

Subd. 3. **Presumption of gift to museum.**

Effective August 1, 2004, property that: (1) is found in or on property controlled by the museum; (2) is from an unknown source; and (3) might reasonably be assumed to have been intended as a gift to the museum, is conclusively presumed to be a gift to the museum if ownership of the property is not claimed by a person within 90 days of its discovery.

345.74 CONSERVATION OF MUSEUM PROPERTY.

Subdivision 1. **Protection of loaned property.**

Unless there is a written loan agreement to the contrary, a museum may apply conservation measures to property on loan to the museum without the lender's permission or formal notice if action is required to protect the property on loan or other property in the custody of the museum, or the property on loan is a hazard to the health and safety of the public or the museum staff, and either:

(1) the museum is unable to reach the lender at the lender's last known address within three days before the time the museum determines action is necessary; or

(2) the lender does not respond or will not agree to the protective measures the museum recommends and does not terminate the loan and retrieve the property within three days.

Subd. 2. **Lien.**

If a museum applies conservation measures to property under this section, or with the agreement of the lender, unless the agreement provides otherwise, the museum acquires a lien on the property in the amount of the costs incurred by the museum.

Subd. 3. **Liability.**

The museum is not liable for injury to or loss of the property if the museum:

(1) had a reasonable belief at the time the action was taken that the action was necessary to protect the property on loan or other property in the custody of the museum, or that the property on loan was a hazard to the health and safety of the public or the museum staff; and

(2) exercised reasonable care in the choice and application of conservation measures.

STUDY QUESTIONS

- How does the Minnesota Museum Property Act (MMPA) address the problem of "old loans" and "objects found in the collections"?
- Compare the notice requirements in cases where there is evidence of a loan with cases where there is a presumption of a gift. Does the statue encourage sound record-keeping?
- The MMPA was enacted in 2004. Assess the notice requirements in light of today's digital technology. Can you see any problems for museums with complying with the Act?

Reading Note: The propriety of deaccessioning museum collections can arise in a variety of contexts. In July 2013, the City of Detroit, Michigan, filed for bankruptcy. Prior to the filing, the emergency manager explored ways of avoiding defaulting on the City's pension obligations. One proposal—termed "Art for Pensions"—was to sell the Detroit Institute of Art's collections, which were valued at as much as $4.6 billion. The Michigan State Attorney General opinion reprinted below was issued in response to this proposal.

STATE OF MICHIGAN
OPINION OF THE ATTORNEY GENERAL

Opinion No. 7272 (June 13, 2013)

Subject: Conveyance or transfer of Detroit Institute of Arts collection.

Opinion: The art collection of the Detroit Institute of Arts is held by the City of Detroit in charitable trust for the people of Michigan, and no piece in the collection may thus be sold, conveyed, or transferred to satisfy City debts or obligations.

To: Honorable Randy Richardville
State Senator

You have asked whether the art collected and displayed at the Detroit Institute of Arts may be sold, transferred, or otherwise disposed for the purpose of satisfying debts or obligations of the City of Detroit (City) unrelated to the operation or purpose of the Detroit Institute of Arts.

The Detroit Institute of Arts (museum) is an encyclopedic museum with an expansive collection of art. "The [museum's] collection is among the top six in the United States, comprising a multicultural and multinational survey of human creativity from prehistory through the 21st century."[NOTE 1] The museum is located in the City's Cultural Center Historic District, which is listed in the National Register of Historic Places.[NOTE 2] The museum is operated by a nonprofit corporation, the Detroit Institute of Arts Founders Society (Founders Society).

The City itself is presently under the administration of an emergency manager as provided for in the Local Financial Stability and Choice Act, 2012 PA 436, MCL 141.1541 et seq. That act allows the emergency manager to sell, convey, or otherwise transfer assets of the City, if such is provided for in the manager's financial and operating plan,[NOTE 3] or otherwise with the prior written approval of the Governor. MCL 141.1552(r).[NOTE 4] As your request notes, some have suggested that the museum's art collection, to which the City has legal title, could be sold under this act in order to satisfy debts or obligations owed by the City, but unrelated to the art collection or the museum.[NOTE 5]

Before addressing your question, it is helpful to provide an overview of the museum's creation and present operations.

I. HISTORICAL OVERVIEW OF THE DETROIT INSTITUTE OF ARTS.

The museum was incorporated by its founding members as a nonprofit charitable corporation 128 years ago pursuant to legislation enacted in 1885. In that year, the Michigan Legislature enacted 1885 PA 3, an "[a]ct for the formation of corporations for the cultivation of art." The act provided that a group of individuals could "become a body corporate" for "the purpose of founding a public art institute" "in the manner and for the purposes . . . set forth" in the act. Section 1, CL 1915, S 10759. The act stated that the corporation must have articles of incorporation setting forth its purpose, Section 2, CL 1915, 10760, and further provided that:

> Such corporations shall have power . . . to receive, acquire, collect, and own paintings, sculpture, engravings, drawings, pictures, coins, and other works of art, and to institute, maintain, or assist schools for the teaching of art.
>
> The public exhibition of its collection of works of art shall be the duty of every such corporation, and, as soon as it shall be prepared to do so, it shall, under reasonable regulations, and without any improper discriminations, open its buildings and art collection to the general public. [1885 PA 3, Sections 3 and 4, CL 1915, 10761, 10762; emphasis added.]

The property of the corporation would be tax exempt, Section 18, CL 1915, § 10776, and the corporation would be managed by a board of trustees who served without compensation. Sections 6 through 11, CL 1915, 10764 - 10769. The act required that "all gifts, devises, or requests" be "faithfully used for the purposes" of the corporation, and "no dividend in money or property" could be made among the corporation's members. Section 15, CL 1915, 10773. The corporation was prohibited from changing its "character and purposes," and from selling "its general art collection." Section 16, CL 1915, 10774. And the corporation could only wind up its affairs if provided for by law. *Id.*

The museum, then known as the Detroit Museum of Art, was incorporated on April 16, 1885, pursuant to these requirements, and set forth its purpose in its articles of incorporation as "for the founding of a public art institute in the City of Detroit, which may . . . receive and use such gifts, contributions, devises and bequests as may be made for art purposes: receive, acquire, collect and own paintings, sculpture, engravings, drawings, pictures, coins and other works of art, and may do all things authorized by said Act. (1885 Articles of Incorporation, Detroit Museum of Art).[NOTE 6] The museum immediately thereafter began acquiring pieces of art for its collection through purchases, gifts, donations, and bequests.

Not long after the museum's incorporation, the Legislature passed various acts empowering the City to appropriate money to support the museum, and to issue bonds for the construction of buildings. This expenditure of public money on behalf of the museum, a private nonprofit corporation, raised concerns and a lawsuit was filed. See *Detroit Museum of Art v Engel*, 187 Mich 432, 434-435; 153 NW 700 (1915). During this time period, the museum had conveyed its buildings and real estate to the City. (No art was conveyed to the City given the express prohibition in the incorporating legislation). However, the museum retained control of its collection and operation. *Detroit Museum of Art*, 187 Mich at 435.

The Michigan Supreme Court ultimately concluded that these appropriations violated the 1908 Constitution's restrictions on a city's lending of credit to an entity other than a public or "municipal agency." *Id.* at 439-443. The Court agreed that the museum served a "public purpose," but did not find that fact or the fact that the museum had conveyed its buildings and real property to the City dispositive since it did "not change the museum's character as a private corporation." *Id.* at 440. Presumably, after this decision, the museum no longer received appropriations from the City, and the museum apparently began to struggle financially. In response, in 1919 the Legislature amended 1885 PA 3, as amended by 1913 PA 245, to allow corporations formed under that act to convey their property. 1919 PA 67 provided that a "corporation organized under [1885 PA 3] situated in a city empowered to maintain a public art institute ... may convey all or any of its property to said city ... and said property so conveyed shall ... be faithfully used for the purposes for which such corporation was organized. Section 20. 1885 PA 3, 1913 PA 245, and 1919 PA 67 were subsequently repealed by 1921 PA 84, as part of the consolidation of corporations law, but were subject to the savings provision in that act.

Pursuant to this statutory authorization and the City's 1918 Charter, which authorized the City to operate an art institute and to acquire art for the institute, Charter XIX, Sections

1, 7, the museum, in its corporate capacity as the Detroit Museum of Art, conveyed its buildings and art collection to the City in 1919. With the legal transfer of the properties and art collection to the City, the City was now free to support the museum; and it did so by funding both museum operations and by purchasing new art for the collection. The nonprofit corporation, however, did not wind up its affairs but rather continued to exist to assist the museum with gifts of art and with support of museum operations and their costs. That nonprofit corporation exists today as the Founders Society, as noted above.

Over the ensuing years, the museum's structure and funding sources changed as needed based on changing circumstances. By 1955, the City began to encounter financial problems, and its acquisitions for the museum collection largely ceased. In 1973, the museum temporarily closed due to lack of funding. Shortly thereafter, in 1977, the State began granting money to the City so that the museum could continue operating. In 1983, the City claimed greater control over the museum's operations: museum employees became employees of the City. These events led to the issuance of an opinion by Attorney General Frank Kelley, which confirmed the validity of State appropriations or grants to the City for the benefit of the museum. In confirming State support for the museum, Attorney General Kelley recognized the museum's state or "public purpose" and status as a unique, cultural treasure of the people of Michigan:

> Unquestionably, and uniquely in Michigan, the Detroit Institute of Arts, as a widely acclaimed cultural facility, is utilized by the citizens of this state without regard to residency in the city. The facility is an outstanding tourist attraction utilized by tourists and their families. Its vast displays and cultural facilities are readily and regularly available to Michigan students. Both the Governor in his Executive Budget, and the Legislature in the enactment of appropriations for the support of the Detroit Institute of Arts, have recognized its place in the cultural life of this state. [OAG, 1983-1984, No 6225, pp 303, 308 (May 7, 1984).]

Following the Attorney General's opinion, state grants for the museum continued; though by the 1990s, these grants began decreasing. From 1977 through 2011, state funding for the museum totaled roughly $300 million.

In 1997, the structure and operation of the museum changed again. Under a 1997 Operating Agreement, the City maintained its legal title to the art collection, but transferred operations—and their entire cost back to the Founders Society. From 1997 to the present, the museum has operated under this Agreement. And despite the Founders Society's best efforts to support the museum with charitable dollars, it continued to face financial difficulties. In 2010, the Legislature enacted the Art Institute Authorities Act, 2010 PA 296, MCL 123.1201 et seq. This act authorized the establishment of an art institute authority for the levying of property taxes to support "art institute [s]" like the museum. MCL 123.12053.[NOTE 7]

In November 2012, voters of Oakland, Macomb, and Wayne Counties passed the millage to help support the museum. This millage supplements the museum's charitable endowment and regular charitable contributions.

II. PRESENT OPERATIONS.

To address your question, a closer examination of the 1997 Operating Agreement is also required. Other helpful documents include the Museum's Collections Management Policy, which is referenced in the Operating Agreement; the ethical policies governing both American and international museums; and the accounting practices that apply to museum art collections.

A. 1997 Operating Agreement.

The 1997 Operating Agreement, which expires in 2018, currently governs the relationship between the Founders Society and the City. The Operating Agreement is referenced explicitly in the City's charter: "The Arts Department shall maintain and operate the Detroit Institute of Arts directly or pursuant to an operating agreement." 2012 Charter for the City of Detroit, S 7-301.

Several sections of the Operating Agreement are relevant to the ownership and disposition of the art collection.

Section E. of the Operating Agreement specifies that the City retains ownership of the art collection, the museum properties, and any newly acquired art. And Section F. 12. requires the Founders Society to use best efforts to solicit gifts and donations of works of art for the benefit of the museum.

Section F.2.(a) of the Operating Agreement cedes responsibility for managing the City's art collection to the Founders Society in accord with the museum's Collections Management Policy, which is discussed below. In addition, Section F.2.(b) cedes the right to acquire and dispose of the museum's works of art to the Founders Society; providing that any funds it receives from any sale must be used solely to purchase other works of art for the art collection. In consideration for exclusive right to manage the museum and control the artwork, subject to the terms of the agreement, the Founders Society assumed full responsibility for all operating expenses of the museum, as well as other obligations that had previously been the responsibility of the City, including "management of the art collections; presentation of exhibitions and other events; maintenance of the museum building, the Frederick lot ... and the employee parking lot; collection and expenditure of income; fundraising; marketing; acquisition/disposition of works of art; and all other financial operations...." Section D.3. Although the City retains legal title to the museum and its artwork, the sale of the artwork by the City is not permitted under the Operating Agreement and would seriously undermine the ability of the Founders Society to fulfill its contractual responsibilities.

B. Collections Management Policy.

The museum's Collections Management Policy, to which Section F.2.(a) of the Operating Agreement requires the Founders Society to adhere, includes language restricting the disposition of the art collection. Section V.A. states: "In considering objects or groups of objects, the Museum must be ever aware of its role as trustee of the collection for the benefit of the public." Section V.E. similarly states: "The manner of disposition should be in the best interest of the Museum, the public it serves, the public trust it represents, and the scholarly and cultural communities it serves." Section V.F. limits the use of the disposition proceeds: "Net proceeds derived from the sale of a deaccessioned object (i.e., the proceeds of the disposition less all related expenses) shall not be used as operating funds. Such net proceeds shall be placed in the selling curatorial department's Art Acquisition Fund . . ."

C. Professional Codes of Ethics.

The museum's Collections Management Policy, which views museum assets as being held in "public trust"[NOTE 8] and which strictly limits deacquisition of art, is in accord with the professional codes of ethics adopted by the American Alliance of Museums and the International Council of Museums.[NOTE 9] Relevant sections from these ethical codes follow.

The American Alliance of Museum's Code of Ethics (adopted 1991, amended 2000) states:

> Taken as a whole, museum collections and exhibition materials represent the world's natural and cultural common wealth. As stewards of that wealth, museums are compelled to advance an understanding of all natural forms and of the human experience. It is incumbent on museums to be resources for humankind and in all their activities to foster an informed appreciation of the rich and diverse world we have inherited. It is also incumbent upon them to preserve that inheritance for posterity.
>
> Museums in the United States are grounded in the tradition of public service. They are organized as public trusts, holding their collections and information as a benefit for those they were established to serve. . . .
>
> [D]isposal of collections through sale, trade or research activities is solely for the advancement of the museum's mission. Proceeds from the sale of nonliving collections aye to be used consistent with the established standards of the museum's discipline, but in no event shall they be used for anything other than acquisition or direct care of collections.[NOTE 10]

The International Council of Museums' Code of Ethics (adopted 1986, amended 2001, and revised 2004) gives similar principles:

> Principle 2: Museums that maintain collections hold them in trust for the benefit of society and its development.
>
> Principle 2.16: Museum collections are held in public trust and may not be treated as a realizable asset. Money or compensation received from the deaccessioning and disposal of objects and specimens from a museum collection should be used solely for the benefit of the collection and usually for acquisitions to that same collection.[NOTE 11]

D. Accounting Practices.

In accord with the view that museum art collections are held in trust for the public and are not financial assets of the museum, neither the City nor the Founders Society have capitalized the art collection. In other words, the art collection is not considered on either the City's or the Founders Society's books as an asset with a monetary value because, though these assets have substantial monetary value, they are not assets that can simply be sold; rather, they are subject to the strict deaccessioning policies discussed above.

The decision not to capitalize the art collection accords with the American Association for State and Local History's policy against capitalization of museum collections. It also accords with the accounting principles of both the Financial Accounting Standards Board and the Governmental Accounting Standards Board, which each allow the non-capitalization of museum collections. See FASB, No. 116, ¶¶11-1B; GASB No. 34. By contrast, the City has capitalized other City works of art that are outside the museum's collection; the City's 2012 Comprehensive Annual Financial Report lists these works of art as capital assets valued at $29.8 million.[NOTE 12] It is understood that such works of art include the City's "Spirit of Detroit" statue, the Joe Louis "fist," and other works of art in City buildings.

III. THE ART COLLECTION IS HELD IN CHARITABLE TRUST AND MAY NOT BE SOLD TO SATISFY CITY DEBTS.

Against this backdrop, you ask whether the art collected and displayed at the museum may be sold or transferred for purposes of satisfying debts or obligations of the City unrelated to the collection or the museum. The answer to this question is no. As explained below, this question is governed by the law of charitable trusts.

A. Michigan law favors the creation of charitable trusts.

Michigan charitable trust law is rooted in the common law. Much of that law is now codified in various statutes, such as the Supervision of Trustees for Charitable Purposes Act, 1961 PA 101, MCL 14.251 seq., the Charitable Gifts Act, 1915 PA 280, MCL 554.351 et seq., the Nonprofit Corporation Act, 1982 PA 162, MCL 450.2101 et seq., and the Estates and Protected Individuals Code (EPIC), 1998 PA 386, MCL 700.1101 et seq.

Though the museum was incorporated before many of these statutes were enacted, the basic principles of charitable trust law are uniform and longstanding.

A Michigan court observed decades ago that "'[c]haritable gifts and trusts are favorites of the law and of the courts, and the courts will declare valid, and give effect to, such gifts and trusts where it is possible to do so. . . .'" *In re Rood's Estate*, 41 MIch App 405, 422; 200 NW2d 728 (1972), quoting 14 CJS, Charities, S 6, p 427. The Supervision of Trustees for Charitable Purposes Act echoes this sentiment, providing that "[i]t is hereby declared to be the policy of the state that the people of the state are interested in the administration, operation and disposition of the assets of all charitable trusts in the state." MCL 14.251. That act further provides that the "act, in all of its provisions, in the interests of society and in conformity with public policy is intended to protect the rights and interest of the people of the state and the uncertain and indefinite beneficiaries of all charitable trusts... MCL 14.265.[NOTE 13]

The EPIC defines the word "trust" in the following way:

> "Trust" includes, but is not limited to, an express trust, private or *charitable*, with additions to the trust, wherever and however created. Trust includes, but is not limited to, a trust created or determined by judgment or decree under which the trust is to be administered in the manner of an express trust. [MCL '700.1107(n); emphasis added.]

Case law confirms this, concluding that the term "trust" is not limited to express trusts and extends to corporations created to administer trusts. See *In re Americana Foundation*, 145 Mich App 735; 378 NW2d 586 (1985).

The EPIC defines a "charitable trust" as "a trust . . . created for a charitable purpose described in section 7405(1)." MCL 700.7103(c). Section 7405(1), MCL 700.7405(1), in turn, provides that a charitable trust "may be created for the relief of poverty, the advancement of education or religion, the promotion of health, scientific, literary, benevolent, governmental, or municipal purposes, . . . or other purposes the achievement of which is beneficial to the community." See also Restatement (Third) of Trusts 27-28 (2003); 15 Am Jur 2d, Charities, 5 and 32. Section 2(b), MCL 14.252(b), of the Supervision of Trustees for Charitable Purposes Act similarly defines "charitable trust" as "the relationship where a trustee holds property for a charitable purpose." While neither of these Acts expressly mention art museums, the public exhibition of art is generally considered a charitable purpose. See 15 Am Jur 2d, Charities, 49. See also *Hardntan v Feinstein*, 240 Cal Rptr 483, 486 (Cal Ct App 1987) ("Art museums advance education and therefore serve a charitable purpose."). In fact, charitable trusts and nonprofit corporations are the organizational structures generally available to private museums." Sara Tam, Note, *In Museums We Trust: Analyzing the Mission of Museums, Deaccessioning Policies, and the Public Trust*, 39 Fordham Urb L J 849, 855-856 (2012).

These more recent statutory iterations of the term "charitable trust" are consistent with the Michigan Supreme Court's past descriptions. In *Scarney v. Clarke*, 282 Mich 56, 63-64; 275 NW 765 (1937), the Court observed:

> In 2 Restatement of the Law of Trusts, p 1096, S 349, it is said:
>
> > "A charitable trust may be created by (a) a declaration by the owner of property that he holds it upon a charitable trust; or (b) a transfer *inter vivos* by the owner of property to another person to hold it upon a charitable trust."
>
> In charitable trusts, the public is the beneficiary. A distinguishing characteristic of such a trust is that the prospective beneficiary is undetermined and unknown, and while such a trust need not be for the benefit of the entire public, yet it must be public in nature and for unascertained beneficiaries. [See also *Scudder v Security Trust Co*, 238 Mich 318; 213 NW 131 (1927) (discussing requirements for creation of charitable trust).]

Historically, to create a charitable trust, no specific words needed to be used, rather "'[i]t [was] sufficient . . . to show [ ] an intention that the property should be held subject to a legal obligation to devote it to purposes which are charitable.'" *Knights of Equity Mentorial Scholarships Conun v University of Detroit*, 359 Mich 235, 242-243; 102 NW2d 463 (1960) (affirming that agreement between voluntary association and university created a charitable trust), quoting 4 Scott, Trusts (2d ed.) S 351, at 2574. See also *In re Rood's Estate*, 41 Mich App at 413 ("A determination that a charitable trust is created needs only a finding that 'some charitable purpose' exists.") and *In re Americana Foundation*, 145 Mich App at 738739. The EPIC similarly does not require any particular words be used to create a trust, MCL 700.7401(1) and MCL 700.7402, and a trust may even be created through oral statements, MCL 700.7407.

In general, any legal entity, including a municipality, may serve as trustee of a charitable trust. Restatement (Third) of Trusts, S 33; 15 Am Jur 2d, Charities § 83. The Supervision of Trustees for Charitable Purposes Act defines "[t]rustee" to "mean [ ] any individual, group of individuals, association, foundation, trustee corporation, or other legal entity holding property for any *charitable* purpose." MCL 14.252(a) (emphasis added). See also *Harcbnan*, 240 Cal Rptr at 485-486 (Fine Arts Museums of San Francisco is charitable trust administered by City of San Francisco as trustee). A city may thus act as trustee of a charitable trust established for the purpose of maintaining and operating an art museum.

A "trustee shall administer the trust in good faith, [ ] in accordance with its terms and purposes, for the benefit of the trust beneficiaries." MCL 700.7801. See also MCL 700.7802. With a trust, whether charitable or otherwise, the trustee holds the legal interest—or legal title—in the assets, but the beneficiary holds the equitable interest. *Apol-*

linari v Johnson, 104 Mich App 673, 675, 305 NW2d 565 (1981) ("The separation of legal and equitable title is one of the distinctive features of the trust relationship. Legal title vests in the trustee to be held for the benefit of the beneficiary."). See also *In re Americana Foundation*, 145 Mich App at 740 (Trustee foundation "held the legal estate whereas the public received the benefit and enjoyment."); Restatement (Third) of Trusts, S 2, comment d, see also id., S 42. Thus, while a trustee has legal title to the trust assets, a trustee may not dispose of trust assets as the trustee wishes; instead, a trustee is limited to using the assets for the designated purposes of the trust. MCL 700.7801. See also *In re Friends for Long Island's Heritage*, 911 NYS2d 412 (NY App Div 2010) (nonprofit corporation could not sell assets donated for purpose of public exhibition and display to pay off corporate debts upon dissolution.).

B. The art collection is held in charitable trust for the people of Michigan and cannot be sold for purposes other than the acquisition of art.

With its incorporation in 1885, the museum was created as a nonprofit corporation with a specific charitable purpose: "the public exhibition of its collection of works of art." 1885 PA 3, Section 4, CL 1915, S 10762. The museum's 1885 Articles of Incorporation reflect this purpose. The museum was authorized to acquire art for that specific purpose, 1885 PA 3, Section 3, CL 1915, 10761, and was required to "faithfully use[l" "[a]ll gifts, devises, or bequests made to" the museum for that purpose. *Id.*, Section 15, CL 1915, 10773. The museum could not change its "character and purposes" or sell "its general art collection" unless authorized by the Legislature. *Id.*, Section 16, CL 1915, 10774.

Thus, as a legal entity holding assets for a charitable purpose, the museum was founded as a charitable trust. The museum's charitable purpose was the exhibition of art for the public; the art collection thereafter acquired by the museum became the res or assets of the trust. And as the charitable trustee, the Founders Society was limited to using its assets—the art collection—for its dedicated charitable purpose.

Moreover, the Legislature's intent was plain: once an art institution like the museum incorporated and began collecting art and dutifully exhibiting its collection for the public, it was do so in perpetuity if possible. Hence, the Legislature created restrictions on a change to the character or purpose of the art institution, and the disposition of its general collection; and it required that any winding up be provided for by law so as to "best promote and perpetuate" "the purposes" of the institution. 1885 PA 3, Section 10774, CL 1915, S 10774.

In 1919, in the wake of the Michigan Supreme Court's ruling in *Detroit Museum of Art v Engel*, the Legislature determined that the best method to "promote and perpetuate" "the purposes" of the museum was to authorize the conveyance of all property to a "city empowered to maintain a public art institute." 1919 PA 67, Section 20. This conveyance would allow the City directly to support the museum consistent with the Supreme Court's ruling. The law also required the City to "faithfully[ ] use[ ]" the art conveyed "for the purposes for which" the institution was organized, which was to operate a "public art institute" and exhibit art to the "general public." No provision was included for a city to change or modify the purpose, sell the art conveyed, or wind up or dissolve its public art institute.

Pursuant to these express statutory authorizations, the Founders Society transferred its art collection to the City in 1919. When the City accepted the transfer, it was bound by the language of 1919 PA 67 to perpetuate and "maintain a public art institute" that would exhibit art to the general public, and to "faithfully[ ] use[ ]" the art conveyed for that purpose. Under charitable trust law, this transfer was a transfer of the Founders Society's legal interest or legal title in its charitable assets to a new charitable trustee—the City. Under those circumstances, the equitable interest in the art collection remained with the people of Michigan, the ultimate beneficiaries of the museum's or Founders Society's charitable purpose. *Appollinari*, 104 Mich App at 675. See also *Hardynan*, 240 Cal Rptr at 486 ("[A]lthough the Fine Arts Musuems [ ] is administered by City officials [as trustee], the trust assets do not constitute public assets but rather the *res* of a charitable trust.").[NOTE 14]

In accepting the trust, consistent with the statute, the City agreed at its own cost and expense to maintain and operate the trust, which by City Charter included the mandate that the City "[s]hall acquire, collect, own and exhibit, in the name of the city, works of art, books and other objects such as are usually incorporated in Museums of Art." 1918 City Charter, Chapter XIX, Section 7(c).[NOTE 15] Over the years, the museum's art collection grew through charitable donations of art and direct purchases by the City. As new pieces were added to the collection, the entire collection continued to be dedicated towards the museum's initial charitable purpose: the public display of its art collection. See MCL 700.1107(n) (term "trust includes . . . an express trust, private or charitable, with additions to the trust, wherever and however created.") (Emphasis added). Thus, the entire collection—to this day—continues to be held in charitable trust for this same charitable purpose, including the pieces acquired by the City with City money that were purchased and added to the museum collection.[NOTE 16]

This conclusion is consistent with Michigan trust law, and restrictions found in the Nonprofit Corporation Act, the statute under which charitable, nonprofit corporations incorporate today. See MCL 450.2301(5) ("This act shall not be deemed to permit assets held by a corporation for charitable purposes to be used, conveyed or distributed for noncharitable purposes.") Moreover, the museum's current operations and policies under the 1997 Operating Agreement, the museum's Collections Management policies, the ethical policies of the various museum associations, and the Founders Society's and the City's accounting practices, confirm this result. Rather, these documents, discussed above, expressly state that the entire collection is held in trust for the public and strictly limit the use of the art to its public exhibition, and any disposition of art or proceeds from the disposition of art can only be used to acquire additional art for the museum's collection. Based on these facts and charitable trust law, the City, as charitable trustee, cannot sell art from the trust for the purpose of satisfying debts owed to its creditors.

CONCLUSION

It is my opinion, therefore, that the art collection of the Detroit Institute of Arts is held by the City of Detroit in charitable trust for the people of Michigan, and no piece in the collection may thus be sold, conveyed, or transferred to satisfy City debts or obligations. In issuing this opinion, I recognize the serious financial hardships that face the City, the difficulties that the people who live and work in the City have endured for decades, and the many challenges facing the citizens of the City of Detroit and the State in the future. Yet, in the 128 years since the creation of the Detroit Institute of Arts, at no time have the people demanded that their most precious cultural resources be sold in order to satisfy financial obligations. To the contrary, the citizens of this State recognize that abandoning or selling the public's artwork would damage not only the City's but the State's cultural commonwealth. In Michigan, we not only appreciate our cultural treasures, we guard them zealously in charitable trust for all state residents, present and future.

BILL SCHUETTE, Attorney General

NOTES:

NOTE 1: See www.dia.org/about/history.aspx

NOTE 2: See http://nrhp.focus.nps.gov/natregsearchresult.do?fullresult=true&recordid=55.

NOTE 3: MCL 141.1551 requires an emergency manager to develop a written financial and operating plan addressing various issues, and to submit the plan to the State Treasurer.

NOTE 4: An emergency manager must first submit any proposed sale of assets to the local government unit's governing body for approval. MCL 141.1559(1). If the governing body disapproves the proposed sale, the governing body must present an alternative plan that yields a similar financial result. The local emergency financial assistance loan board then chooses between the options. MCL 141.1559(2).

NOTE 5: Because this opinion concludes that the art collection is held in charitable trust, it is unnecessary to address whether the collection is the type of asset that could be sold for purposes of MCL 141.1552(r). But arguably, the Legislature, in enacting the Local Financial Stability and Choice Act, did not intend that unique cultural assets of a local unit of government be sold since such a sale would not be in the best interests of the health, safety, and welfare of the citizens of this State. MCL 141.1543

NOTE 6: The museum's corporate documents are available at www.dleg.state.mi.us/bcs corp/sr corp.asp.

NOTE 7: The act defines "art institute" as "an encyclopedic art museum whose primary art collection and facility, at the date an authority is established, are owned by a municipality located in this state." MCL 123.1203(a).

NOTE 8: The term "public trust" as used by museums and their associations should not be equated with the "public trust doctrine" that Michigan and other courts have applied to navigable waterways. See, e.g., *Glass v Goeckel*, 473 Mich 667, 694; 703 NW2d 58 (2005) (finding that the shores of the Great Lakes below the ordinary high water mark were held in public trust.). See also *Netweg v Wallace*, 237 Mich 14, 17; 208 NW 51 (1926) and *State v Venice of America Land Co*, 160 Mich 680, 702; 125 NW 770 (1910). While there has been debate in other states for extending this doctrine to apply to cultural resources, like museums, see Sara Tam, Note, 39 Fordham Urb L J 849, 861-863 (2012), In *Museums We Trust: Analyzing the Mission of Museums, Deaccessioning Policies, and the Public Trust*, research discloses no Michigan cases that have applied the public trust doctrine outside of the natural resources context.

NOTE 9: Museums and professional organizations began promulgating ethical codes regarding deaccessioning and museum practices, after the Metropolitan Museum of Art in New York planned to sell several significant pieces in 1972. Tam, *In Museums We Trust*, 39 Fordham Urb LJ at 864865.

NOTE 10: Available at www.aam-us.org/regources/ethics-standards-and-begt-practices/code-of-ethics-formuseums.

NOTE 11: Available at http://icom.museum/the-vision/code.of.ethics/.

NOTE 12: See City of Detroit's 2012 Comprehensive Annual Financial Report, pp 29, 95, available at http://www.detroitmi.gov/DepartmentsandAgenciee/Finance/AccountgDivision.aspx.

NOTE 13: The Supervision of Trustees for Charitable Purposes Act provides that "[t]he attorney general ... shall represent the people of the state and the uncertain or indefinite beneficiaries in all charitable trusts in this state, and may enforce such trusts by proper proceedings in the courts of this state." MCL 14.254(a). see also MCL 554.352 and MCL 700.7405(3).

NOTE 14: While the entire art collection is held in charitable trust, the plain language of 1919 PA 67 further protects any piece of art acquired from 1885 through the 1919 transfer from sale for a non-museum related purpose because the City of Detroit can only "use[l" that art "for the purposes for which" the museum was organized, which was to operate a "public art institute" and display art to the "general public." 1919 PA 67, Section 20; 1885 PA 3, Sections 1, 3, and 4, CL 1915, 10759, 10761, and 10762. This language precludes a sale of artwork obtained through this transfer for the purpose of satisfying City debts unrelated to the art collection or the museum. And other Michigan laws add protection to those works of art that were gifts from charitable donors. See, e.g., MCL 554.352 (gifts for charitable purposes create a charitable trust that "shall be liberally construed by the court so that the intentions of the creator thereof shall be carried out whenever possible.").

NOTE 15: Notably, while the 1918 City Charter empowered the Arts Commission, subject to the approval of the city council, to sell, convey, and lease any real property, Id., Section 7(g), no express provision was made for the sale or disposal of the art work.

NOTE 16: A contrary conclusion that some of the art collection is held in charitable trust and other art is not—for instance, the art purchased by the City is neither consistent with trust law nor reasonable. If this were the case, assets held in charitable trust would necessarily reside in the same collection as non-charitable assets, despite the fact that the whole collection exists for the singular charitable purpose of the public exhibition of art. See MCL 700.7811(2) (A trustee shall keep trust property separate from the trustee's property.") Moreover, under that view, as substantial charitable contributions continued to be made over the years both directly to the collection and in support of the collection, the commingling of charitable assets with non-charitable assets could be viewed as a breach of charitable trust. See MCL 700.7901. That untenable result further supports the conclusion that the entire collection existed—and continues to exist—in charitable trust.

STUDY QUESTIONS

- The Michigan Attorney General's Opinion was an important factor in resolution of the City of Detroit's bankruptcy case. A plan to sell paintings from the Detroit Museum of Art to fund the city's pension obligations was described at the time as an "art-for-pensions" deal.
- What does the opinion tell us about the role of the Attorney General in the oversight of charitable trusts?
- A Michigan State Senator requested the opinion. Why did he want to know whether the Detroit Institute of Arts could deaccession its collection?
- Is the Detroit museum's collection held in trust for the public or is it a saleable asset owned by the City of Detroit?
- Why was the provenance of the museum's collections important? What legal principles and precedents did the AG rely on in forming this opinion? What counter arguments could be made?

- What other reasons (apart from questions of legality addressed in the opinion) might have factored in the decision not to sell the museum's art collection?
- What does the Michigan Attorney General's Opinion say about the ownership of museum collections? About the management of charitable trusts? And the obligations of trustees of charitable trusts?
- What lessons for public museums can you drawn from the Michigan Attorney General's Opinion?

Reading Note: The American Alliance of Museums (AAM) provides accreditation—a stamp of approval—to museums that meet and maintain certain standards established by the AAM. It is rare for the AAM to revoke accreditation, but as the press release below demonstrates, it has done so for violations of its Code of Ethics provisions on deaccessioning.

STATEMENT ON THE DEACCESSIONING BY THE DELAWARE ART MUSEUM AND THE ACTION TAKEN BY THE AAM ACCREDITATION COMMISSION

Press Release (June 18, 2014)

Accreditation conferred by the American Alliance of Museums designates a museum's credibility to donors, funders and the public. Accredited museums have a fundamental fiduciary and ethical responsibility to care for and maintain their collections and determine their disposition following national standards. The collections of accredited museums must be unencumbered and cannot be treated as disposable financial assets. As the accrediting body the AAM Accreditation Commission has a responsibility to take action when violations to standards occur.

On June 17, 2014, the AAM Accreditation Commission unanimously voted to remove the Delaware Art Museum's accredited status in response to the board's decision of March 26, 2014, to deaccession and to sell works from the collections for purposes other than acquisitions or direct care of collections. The action of the Delaware Art Museum is in direct violation of museum standards and ethics.

The American Alliance of Museums Code of Ethics for Museums says, "disposal of collections through sale, trade or research activities is solely for the advancement of the museum's mission. Proceeds from the sale of nonliving collections are to be used in a manner consistent with the established standards of the museum's discipline, but in no event shall they be used for anything other than acquisition or direct care of collections."

The Accreditation Commission is the appointed seven-member body of museum professionals responsible for making independent decisions regarding AAM accreditation.

Media Contact, Alliance Communication

STUDY QUESTIONS

- What was the American Alliance of Museums (AAM) concern with the Delaware Museum of Art's deaccessioning plan? What enforcement action did the AAM take? Why do you think the AAM took the action that it did?
- How would you advise the Delaware Museum board of trustees (or any museum board) with respect to deaccessioning objects from their collections?

THEFT

Another way that objects leave museum collections is through theft. Sometimes the theft is obvious and dramatic, as in the case of the still unsolved March 18, 1990, theft of thirteen works of art valued at $500 million from the Isabella Stewart Gardner Art Museum in Boston. More commonly, however, works disappear while in storage and the theft is only discovered at a later date when the museum collection is inventoried, sometimes many years later.

As noted in the earlier discussion concerning title and stolen art, under U.S. law good title cannot be acquired from a thief. As a result, even a good faith purchaser—someone who bought the work without knowing that it was stolen—may later be required to give up possession of a stolen work.

The lapse of time between when a work is stolen and when it reappears in public can be quite long. A typical scenario involves an unwitting heir—a son or daughter perhaps—who finds a work of art in a deceased person's possession, takes it to an art dealer with the idea of selling it, and only then discovers that the work was stolen.

At what point does the owner of a stolen work have an obligation to notify the good faith purchaser and to assert a claim to the stolen work? When does the statute of limitations begin to toll in cases involving stolen art? What steps must the victim of a theft take to assert its rights in a work that has been stolen? These were some of the issues at the heart of the *Georgia O'Keeffe* case reprinted above, and are just some of the questions the courts regularly must address in considering cases involving stolen art.

Insurance may also play a role in the ownership of a stolen work. Where an insurance company has paid out on a theft claim, the insurance company may be the one entitled to ownership of the recovered work. If a work stolen from a museum is later recovered, the museum may need to repay the insurance company for any compensation it received under its insurance policy.

REQUESTS FOR RETURN

Another way an object may leave the museum's collection is as the result of a request for return. As discussed previously, once a donor gifts a work to the museum, absent any restrictions, the transfer is complete, and the museum is deemed to have title to the work. Donor remorse is not a reason to return a gift. However, if the transfer is the result of an invalid gift—perhaps the donor did not have the exclusive authority to make the gift or did not have good title—it is possible that the gift could be rescinded, in which case the museum would be obligated to return the object to the rightful owner.

A request for return may also result from additional provenance research into an object that raises questions about its title. The museum may discover after it has acquired a work that it does not have good title, either because the work has been stolen or due to some other defect in the chain of title. Such cases are referred to as "restitution" claims. Restitution claims often involve questions of standing and jurisdiction, as well as defenses including statutes of limitations, laches, and estoppel. While restitution claims involving works of art with Nazi-era provenance are perhaps the most publicized, requests for return can take many forms and can involve claims to works taken in many different eras and contexts.

Requests for return from source countries (the country where the work originated or was first found) are referred to as "repatriation" claims. A repatriation claim may arise from the illegal excavation and/or removal of a work from the country of origin. Repatriation claims often involve complex questions concerning international treaties, import and export restrictions, and national patrimony (state ownership) laws. Repatriation claims will be discussed in more detail in the section below dealing with cultural property.

National laws may also require the return of cultural property to source communities. The Native American Graves Protection and Repatriation Act (NAGPRA) (25 U.S.C. 3001 et seq.), for example, requires American museums to research their collections to identify objects subject to the Act, including human remains, funerary and sacred objects, and objects of cultural patrimony, and to arrange to return these objects to the native tribes from which they were taken. NAGPRA sets out procedures for adjudicating repatriation claims and established a review committee composed of representatives from Native American tribes and from the museum and scientific committee to oversee the law's implementation. NAGPRA has served as an example to other countries of an effective method for the restitution and repatriation of cultural objects to source communities.

Regardless of whether the claim is for restitution or repatriation, the question is essentially one of whether the work has been "stolen" in the broadest sense of being improperly taken, and the goal is to return the work to its rightful owner. In some cases, as previously mentioned and more fully discussed below, the National Stolen Property Act is used as a basis for seizing the object and returning it to its proper owner. This is what happened in the *Portrait of Wally* (a restitution case) discussed above, and *McClain and Schultz* (both repatriation cases) included in the Cases and Other Readings below. In repatriation claims, patrimony laws and import and export laws may also be implicated.

Barriers to return can be and are often raised, including asserting the legal defenses of statute of limitations, laches, and equitable estoppel, among others. Claims to return may also involve jurisdictional issues such as standing to sue, sovereign immunity (including application of the U.S. Federal Sovereign Immunity Act), and issues involving seizure and immunity from seizure. Asserting such defenses raises ethical issues for museums. (See *Cultural Property and Special Collections* below for more on this topic.)

Increasingly museums are committed to addressing bona fide restitution claims and agree to waive available defenses in an effort to ensure an equitable resolution. The American Alliance of Museums takes the position that "museums should address claims of ownership asserted in connection with objects in their custody openly, responsively and with respect for the dignity of all parties involved. Each claim should be considered on its own merits." (See AAM guidelines on *Unlawful Appropriation of Objects During the Nazi Era.*) Most museum professional organizations hold similar positions.

CULTURAL PROPERTY AND SPECIAL COLLECTIONS

The term "cultural property" has been defined to mean those products of human creativity (tangible or intellectual) that, on religious or secular grounds, are designated by a nation as being of unique importance to the nation for reasons relating to archeology, prehistory, history, literature, art or science. Put another way, cultural property refers to the tangible manifestations of a nation or community's cultural heritage.

Inherent in the concept of cultural property is the relationship between the object and national, ethnic or tribal identity. Consequently, the concept of cultural property poses the fundamental question of who owns culture? Are the products of human creativity owned by all humans collectively, or are they "owned" or controlled by a particular nation or group? In his seminal article on the subject, "Two Ways of Thinking About Cultural

Property," Professor John Merriman described the relationship between "source" counties where cultural property originates, and "market" countries which serve as marketplaces for transactions involving cultural property.[NOTE 1]

Disputes regarding cultural property often arise when objects—art or antiquities for example—are transported across national borders or are otherwise "appropriated" by those not associated with the group claiming ownership by virtue of their cultural heritage. Trade in cultural property raises both legal and ethical issues for museums.

There are several basic types of cultural property laws. Certain cultural property laws address a nation or group's claim to ownership or "patrimony" of objects found or created within a particular country or by groups associated with that country. These are often referred to as "patrimony laws." Closely associated with patrimony laws are laws restricting the movement of cultural property across national boundaries, including export laws and import restrictions. In addition, a variety of international laws and treaties govern the movement and trade in certain types of cultural property.

While as a general rule, the United States will not enforce the laws of another country, there are a number of ways in which U.S. laws work in relationship with foreign patrimony and export laws to in effect further their purpose of protecting a source country's cultural property. For example, the National Stolen Property Act (NSPA) (18 U.S.C. Sections 2314 and 2315),[NOTE 2] administered by the U.S. Department of Justice, has been used to "enforce" foreign patrimony laws, by in effect declaring that an object removed from a source country in violation of that country's patrimony laws or export laws is "stolen" property under the NSPA and therefore subject to forfeiture and return to the source country. The *McClain* and *Schultz* cases reprinted in the Cases and Other Readings below involve application of the NSPA and its relationship to foreign patrimony and import/export laws.

In response to the 1970 UNESCO Convention on the Means of Prohibiting and Preventing the Illicit Import, Export and Transfer of Ownership of Cultural Property, in 1983 the U.S. enacted the Cultural Property Implementation Act (CPIA) (19 U.S.C. Section 2601 et seq.). Broadly speaking, the 1970 UNESCO Convention contemplates that governments will enter into agreements to enforce each other's cultural property laws. Through CPIA, the U.S. Senate ratified the 1970 UNESCO Convention subject to reservations intended to preserve the "independent judgment" of the United States as to when and how to impose import restrictions on cultural artifacts when requested by "State Parties" to the Convention. CPIA also established the Cultural Property Advisory Committee (CPA) which is housed in the State Department and advises the President on requests from other countries to protect their cultural heritage. CPAC periodically issues "Memoranda of Understanding" or MOUSs respecting import restrictions on specific types of works as well as mutual agreements to address illicit markets and other specific concerns regarding the trade in cultural property.[NOTE 3]

The major museum associations, including the American Alliance of Museums (AAM) and the American Association of Museum Directors (AAMD) have promulgated guidelines to address various aspects of cultural property in museum collections. The primary goal of these guidelines is to prevent looting of archeological sites by restricting the licit (legitimate) market for antiquities. Both the AAM and AAMD guidelines discourage museums from acquiring ancient art and antiquities unless it can be demonstrated that the particular object in question was outside the country of origin before enactment of the UNESCO treaty in 1970.[NOTE 4] Given the nature of provenance research, and the paucity of information about many of these objects, this is a high bar indeed.

Preservation laws seek to protect specific cultural property deemed to embody important aspects of a country's national heritage. Preservation laws can take a wide variety of forms. U.S. laws involving the preservation of cultural property include laws protecting historic buildings and properties such as the Historic Preservation Act (16 U.S.C. 470, Section 106) (see discussion on *Historic Preservation* in chapter 2 above) and laws protecting archeological sites on federal lands, including the Antiquities Act (54 U.S.C. 3203) and the Archeological Resources Protection Act (16 U.S.C. 470). Most states have state-equivalents to these federal preservation laws.

The American approach to protecting antiquities and archeological sites is very different from that of other countries. In the U.S., the focus is on protecting objects found on federal and state-owned public lands. Objects found on private land are generally considered to be private property owned by the owner of the private land. In England, on the other hand, antiquities found on public or private lands are considered to be owned by the sovereign, and finders are required to report their finds to the government in accordance with so-called "Treasure Trove" laws.

Still another set of treaties, laws and ethical guidelines regulate the ownership, movement and use of particular types of objects—often referred to as "special collections." A variety of laws and international treaties affecting the trade, transportation and use of certain plants and animals. For example, the Convention on International Trade in Endangered Species (CITES) protects more than 37,000 species of endangered and threatened wildlife. To date, 183 countries have voluntarily agreed to adhere to CITES, adopting their own laws to implement the terms of the Convention.

In the U.S., the Lacey Act (16 U.S.C. Sections 3371–3378) is an omnibus statute that restricts interstate transportation of wildlife (including specimens) in violation of applicable federal laws and treaties. Under the Lacey Act it is unlawful to import, export, sell, acquire, or purchase fish, wildlife or plants that are taken, possessed, transported, or sold in violation of U.S. or Native American tribal law, or in interstate or foreign commerce involving any fish, wildlife, or plants taken possessed or sold in violation of state or foreign law.

The Endangered Species Act (16 U.S.C. Section 1531 et seq. (1973)) established a program for the conservation of threatened and endangered species and the habitats in which they are found. The ESA provides criteria for listing species as endangered or threatened and prohibits any action that causes a "taking" of a listed species of endangered fish or wildlife. Other federal laws regulating the trade in specific species of wildlife, including the Marine Mammal Protection Act (16 U.S.C. Chapter 31), the Migratory Bird Act (16 U.S.C. Sections 703 to 712), the Bald and Golden Eagle Protection Act (16 U.S.C. Sections 668 et. seq.), the Wild Exotic Bird Conservation Acy (16 U.S.C. Chapter 69), the African Elephant Conservation Act (16 U.S.C. Section 4201), and the Antarctic Conservation Act (16 U.S.C. Sections 2401 to 2413).

Museum associations have promulgated a variety of guidelines and best practices covering many of these types of special collections. Museums that have special collections—those that include animal, bird and fish specimens in particular—need to be aware of these international treaties, laws and ethical codes. A well-drafted collections management plan will include guidance on those laws that impact a particular museum's special collections.

Cultural property, preservation, and special collections laws may affect a variety of museum activities, including collecting (especially field collecting), lending or borrowing, accepting donations, acquisitions, and deaccessioning, and transporting objects across U.S. state lines and foreign boundaries, and on the high seas. In some instances, permits will be required before these activities can lawfully occur. Failure to comply with the requirements of these treaties and laws can result in seizure of the subject object(s), personal liability, civil and criminal penalties, and damage to personal, professional, and institutional reputations.

NOTES:

NOTE 1: John Merryman, "Two Ways of Thinking About Cultural Property", The American Journal of International Law, Vol. 80, No. 4 (October 1986) pp. 831—853.

NOTE 2: It is a criminal violation of the National Stolen Property Act to knowingly possess, conceal, sell, or dispose of any goods of the value of $5,000 or more, which have crossed a State or *U.S. boundary* after being "stolen" (emphasis added).

NOTE 3: For a current list, see Cultural Property Advisory Council, *Current Import Restrictions.*

NOTE 4: See AAM *Guidelines on Archeological Material and Ancient Art* and AAMD *Guidelines on the Acquisition of Archeological Material and Ancient Art.*

CASES AND OTHER READINGS

Reading Note: In the *McClain* case reprinted below, the appellate court reviewed the application of the National Stolen Property Act and Mexican patrimony law in criminal convictions for illegally trafficking in pre-Columbian antiquities. The case is one of a number of important cases involving cultural property.

UNITED STATES V. MCCLAIN

593 F.2d 658 (5th Cir. 1979). GEE, Circuit Judge:

Again before us come Patty McClain, Mike Bradshaw, Ada Simpson and William Simpson, challenging their second round of convictions for having received, concealed and/or sold stolen goods in interstate or foreign commerce and also for conspiracy to do the same, violations of 18 U.S.C. §§ 371, 2314 and 2315. The goods in which they dealt are pre-Columbian artifacts, and in neither this nor the prior trial was there evidence that the appellants or anyone else had taken the items from the personal possession of another. The legal theory under which the case was tried was that the artifacts were "stolen" only in the sense that Mexico generally has declared itself owner of all pre-Columbian artifacts found within its borders. Thus, anyone who digs up or finds such an item and deals in it without governmental permission has unlawfully converted the item from its proper owner. [NOTE 1]

By various formulations, appellants and the amicus curiae, the American Association of Dealers in Ancient, Oriental Primitive Art, raise basically three issues in this appeal. They challenge: (1) the propriety of the application of the National Stolen Property Act (N.S.P.A.), 18 U.S.C. §§ 2314, 2315, to dealings in pre-Columbian artifacts; (2) the correctness and sufficiency of the jury instructions regarding the Mexican law of pre-Columbian artifacts; and (3) the sufficiency of the evidence to support the convictions as measured under their view of the Mexican law. Though in raising these issues the appellants did not distinguish between their convictions on the substantive count and their convictions on the conspiracy count, we find that their arguments regarding jury instructions compel reversal of the substantive count only. On the conspiracy charges, we find the shortcomings below merely harmless error and thus affirm the convictions on that count for the reasons expressed below. This mixed disposition requires a more detailed account of the facts than is present in the earlier opinion. We first review, therefore, the evidence adduced at trial, cast in the light most favorable to the government's verdict.

I. THE APPELLANTS' DEALINGS IN PRE-COLUMBIAN ARTIFACTS.

In May 1973, Joseph Rodriguez, a resident of Calexico, California, arrived at a Dallas motel with a collection of pre-Columbian artifacts for display and sale. [NOTE 2] He sold pieces at least to a local art dealer and to a law professor who was staying in the same motel. He thereafter moved his wares to a San Antonio motel, apparently as a result of his dealings with the professor, who taught in San Antonio. From the new location Rodriguez contacted prospective buyers, including Alberto Mejangos, who unbeknownst to Rodriguez was director of the Mexican Cultural Institute, an educational outpost of the Mexican government located in San Antonio. Suspecting Rodriguez of illicit dealings, Mejangos and Adalina Diaz-Zambrano, the librarian at the institute, visited Rodriguez to see the collection, without identifying themselves as officials of the Mexican government.

Rodriguez showed them a large collection of fine artifacts, many of which were caked with mud and straw. When he was asked how it was possible that he had all these ancient artifacts, Rodriguez said that he had five squads working in various Mexican archaeological zones and that the objects were passed, a few at a time "by contraband" to his Calexico store, which served as a front for his operation. When he amassed enough objects, he said, he would sell them in different localities. He priced the items he showed Mr. Mejangos and Ms. Diaz-Zambrano at figures ranging between $5,000 and $20,000, explaining that the prices had gone up as a result of the February 1972 presidential agreement between the United States and Mexico. He said he now had to give more money to the people who were passing the objects to him.

At some time after these meetings in San Antonio, Rodriguez returned to Calexico, leaving the collection behind with appellants William and Ada Simpson who were authorized to sell the items. The next known transaction regarding the Rodriguez artifacts occurred in early December 1973. Simpson and appellant Mike Bradshaw contacted William Maloof of Cleveland, Ohio, a college friend of Bradshaw, in an effort to raise money for an oil importation venture. They offered Maloof several of the artifacts as collateral for the loan Maloof considered making. Simpson, Bradshaw, and a third man whom Maloof spoke with only by phone,[NOTE 3] told Maloof that the items had been "stolen" or "smuggled" out of Mexico. They said that a man named Rodriguez was "chief of the Mexican Secret Service" and had gotten the artifacts from "a vault" in Mexico. Patty McClain was mentioned as an appraiser who knew the value of the artifacts. Simpson and Bradshaw told Maloof that they planned to take most of the objects to Europe, "auction" them off, and then return them to the United States. This process would yield bills of sale from European art dealers, which would facilitate later resale. Maloof, suspecting he was being swindled, contacted the FBI and showed the objects to them. After being alerted by the Cleveland office, the Houston office of the FBI delegated Special Agent John McGauley, to determine whether stolen pre-Columbian artifacts were being sold by the group. To assist in the covert investigation, McGauley brought in Travis Benkendorfer, who had proven to be a reliable informant on other occasions.

In February 1974, after failing to contact Harry McClain, Benkendorfer succeeded in reaching the Simpson residence by telephone. Identifying himself as a Mr. Benks, Benkendorfer told Mrs. Simpson a cover story that he was interested in acquiring stolen treasury bills, stocks, bonds, or other stolen or illegal merchandise for resale. He said that he represented an international combine with Mafia or other underworld connections and that any stolen merchandise they purchased would immediately be flown out of the country by private plane. Mrs. Simpson replied that her husband and his partner Patty McClain were then in California, waiting for a shipment of pre-Columbian artifacts to cross the border. She said that she would have her husband and Mrs. McClain contact Benkendorfer. When Simpson called Benkendorfer the next morning, Benkendorfer repeated his story. He explained that he had gotten Simpson's name through a Long Island man with Mafia connections and had been instructed to discover for his principal whether Simpson had any artifacts for sale. Simpson replied that he had approximately 150 pieces already in San Antonio and was in Calexico awaiting a new shipment from the diggings. He described a "conduit" by which the items were taken from the diggings to the archaeological institute in Mexico, where documents or permits were forged or backdated. The items were then trucked in disguise to the border at Calexico before distribution to various cities in the United States, particularly San Antonio. Simpson stated that what they were doing "is illegal, but really not illegal, because if the Mexican authorities knew basically what we were doing, they would take them away from us, because the Mexicans really claim all of the items belong to them." Simpson explained further that the backdating of the papers was due to a new "presidential law" that had gone into effect in Mexico, prohibiting private ownership of artifacts after its effective date. He said that the group had planned to ship the items to Europe for sale but that they could save shipping and breakage costs if Benkendorfer and his principal bought the new shipment right at the border. Simpson said that Rodriguez and Patty McClain each had collections that also would be available. Benkendorfer said he would discuss the offer with his principal. He later relayed the message through Mrs. Simpson that he would prefer to have all the items shipped to San Antonio for a single viewing and purchase decision. Simpson agreed to this proposal, emphasizing that all of them would have to be extremely discreet. He said they would get into a lot of problems if the United States government caught them since what they were doing was against the law. He repeated that the Mexicans claimed ownership of the items. Simpson also mentioned during the conversation that his associate Mike Bradshaw was flying from Alabama to Calexico with money to pay for the items that were coming across the border.

Several days later, Benkendorfer received word from Mrs. Simpson that trouble had developed in the conduit or channel. Patty McClain confirmed this when she later contacted Benkendorfer to discuss terms for the sale of her collection. She said that the driveshaft of the truck carrying the artifacts had broken south of the border and that Simpson was sending a new truck to the interior to bring in the goods. In terms highly similar to Simpson's she also described the "channel" from the diggings and the system for getting backdated permits and trucking the items to Calexico developed by Joe and "staff." She said that she and Simpson were responsible for distributing the goods to various points away from Calexico, especially if they were bound for the European market. When Benkendorfer repeated his cover story, McClain gave him some of her artifacts to show to his principal, Mr. Dooley (Agent McGauley). McClain made Benkendorfer promise not to show the items to an art dealer or museum because a recent similar showing had caused the FBI to investigate. McClain agreed that Benkendorfer and McGauley might bring their own appraiser to the San Antonio showing, though she was anxious that the appraiser not come from Mexico City. She explained that she was afraid he might return and report their doings to the authorities because "what we are basically doing is against the law." A final topic during this meeting involved a mild expression of interest by Benkendorfer in purchasing Mexican gold. When Benkendorfer next spoke with Simpson, in addition to repeating the story of the broken driveshaft, Simpson offered to sell Benkendorfer some gold bars that were coming out of Mexico via the same conduit as the artifacts. Simpson then put "his partner" Joe Rodriguez on the phone to explain the gold deal, which Benkendorfer rejected after hearing the details.

During his next phone conversation with Simpson, who was still in Calexico, Benkendorfer spoke with appellant Mike Bradshaw for the first time. Bradshaw's comments evidenced his knowledge of the conduit and the planned sale, and he stressed the need for discretion due to the danger. Following this round of contacts the defendants seemed to grow even more cautious. Simpson interrogated Benkendorfer about where he had learned Simpson's name; McClain expressed concern about the amount of information Simpson and Bradshaw had conveyed to Benkendorfer by phone; several of the appellants sought to assure themselves that Benkendorfer was not with the FBI. McClain even tried to renegotiate the timetable of the showing and sale so that the new shipment would not be sold until after the in-country items had been successfully conveyed. Such a split timetable was ultimately agreed upon after Benkendorfer told Simpson that his New York connection had authorized the purchase of artifacts currently held by Simpson, Rodriguez, and McClain and that a decision whether to buy the next shipment would come later.[NOTE 4]

On the appointed date, March 4, 1974, Agent McGauley and Benkendorfer arrived at the San Antonio Holiday Inn, chosen by Simpson because it had a meeting room with an outside entrance that would be "discreet." Over supper with the four appellants and Mike Bradshaw's fiance, they discussed various aspects of the deal. McGauley repeated the cover story, adding that his New York syndicate was trying to corner the market on preColumbian artifacts. The defendants again voiced concern that McGauley's appraiser was coming from Mexico and might return to inform the Mexican government. McGauley assured them that the expert had been adequately paid and that he had methods of ensuring the man's silence. The defendants mentioned that the items were coming from a dig that the Mexican authorities did not know about. Simpson commented that if the FBI knew the artifacts were at the hotel they would seize them. McGauley assured them that he was not an FBI agent. At supper the defendants further suggested that McGauley also go to the west coast to buy some very valuable stelae and large figurines accumulated there by Clive Hollinshead. Because McGauley had obtained only a single certified bank draft for the "purchase," the parties worked out an escrow agreement to handle the need to inspect the items at separate locations.

After supper, Benkendorfer and McGauley briefly viewed the artifacts in the locked meeting room and retired for the night. The next morning the "appraiser," Dr. Eduardo Montes Moctezuma of the Mexican Department of Archaeology, arrived with his "interpreter," another undercover FBI agent. While these two men, Agent McGauley, William Simpson and Patty McClain examined the artifacts one by one, Benkendorfer, Bradshaw and Mrs. Simpson stayed in the coffee shop. During the wait, Bradshaw informed Benkendorfer that he had invested a great deal of time and money to make Rodriguez' conduit secure, that he had been to the diggings and followed the conduit all the way up through Calexico, California. Bradshaw confirmed earlier Simpson comments that the Indians who were stealing the artifacts had no idea of their worth and were paid only a small sum to get the artifacts from the diggings, to "rob the graves." He also stated that Rodriguez had paid off several customs inspectors along the border to pass the items across.

During the appraisal in the meeting room, McClain and Simpson confirmed that, in addition to the artifacts still located in California, Rodriguez was bringing more across the border and that they would be available to McGauley. These had not crossed yet because of the truck breakdown. McGauley arranged to purchase the goods he had just inspected, contingent upon inspection of the items available in California.

Over lunch McGauley negotiated the sale terms with appellants agreeing on a price of $115,000 for the San Antonio lot, including McClain's items. Bradshaw and Simpson then arranged to meet McGauley, the "appraiser" and the "interpreter" in Los Angeles the next day to view the Hollinshead artifacts. McClain and Mrs. Simpson agreed to remain behind and rewrap and store the items. The next day, March 6, 1974, Simpson and Bradshaw were arrested in Los Angeles during the course of negotiations to purchase the Hollinshead artifacts for $850,000. McClain and Mrs. Simpson were arrested in San Antonio the same day.

There was evidence at trial that none of the items "purchased" by Agent McGauley bore the indicia of registration with the Archaeological Registry maintained by the Mexican government since 1934—a permanent, coded number placed with indelible ink on an inconspicuous area of the piece. Nor were any documents of registration for these pieces in the names of either Rodriguez or any of the appellants found in the registry. Additionally, no export permits had been obtained for the items. In fact, since 1897 the Mexican government has issued only temporary export permits, and those are issued exclusively to cultural institutions or universities. Permits have never been issued to private individuals or for commercial purposes.

II. APPLICATION OF N.S.P.A. TO DEALINGS IN PRE-COLUMBIAN ARTIFACTS.

Appellants attack the application of the N.S.P.A. to their conduct under two different theories. They first argue that Congress never intended the N.S.P.A. to reach items deemed "stolen" only by reason of a country's declaration of ownership. In any event, they claim, the N.S.P.A. was superseded by the 1972 Law on Importation of Pre-Columbian Monumental or Architectural Sculpture or Murals, 19 U.S.C. §§ 2091- 95, which provides only the civil penalty of forfeiture[NOTE 5] for importation of certain types of pre-Columbian artifacts.[NOTE 6] Second, they and their amicus argue that due process is violated by imposing criminal penalties through reference to Mexican laws that are vague and inaccessible except to a handful of experts who work for the Mexican government.

We view appellants' first argument as foreclosed by our doctrine of law of the case. Under that doctrine it is our practice to apply a rule of law enunciated by the court to the same issues in subsequent proceedings and appeals in the same case. Unlike the rule of res judicata, the doctrine applies only to issues that were decided in the former proceeding but not to questions that might have been decided but were not. *Carpa, Inc. v. Ward Foods, Inc.*, 567 F.2d 1316, 1320 (5th Cir. 1978). Though appellants articulated their theories in a slightly different manner in the first appeal, they provoked a square holding that, in addition to the rights of ownership as understood by the common law, the N.S.P.A. also protects ownership derived from foreign legislative pronouncements, even though the owned objects have never been reduced to possession by the foreign government. *United States v. McClain*, 545 F.2d 988, 994-97 (5th Cir. 1977). Moreover, the earlier panel had considered evidence of the 1972 statute, its legislative history and UNESCO negotiations, holding nevertheless that neither statute nor treaty nor our historical policy of encouraging the importation of art more than 100 years old had the effect of narrowing the N.S.P.A. so as to make it inapplicable to artifacts declared to be the property of another country and illegally imported into this country. 545 F.2d at 996-97. Appellants' attempt to raise these points again on appeal is therefore foreclosed *unless*

> [1] the evidence on a subsequent trial was substantially different, [2] controlling authority has since made a contrary decision of the law applicable to such issues, or [3] the decision was clearly erroneous and would work manifest injustice.

Morrow v. Dillard, 580 F.2d 1284, 1290 (5th Cir. 1978), quoting *White v. Murtha*, 377 F.2d 428, 431-32 (5th Cir. 1967).

Of these customary heads of exception, only the third is even a colorable issue. Appellants attempt to identify clear error in the panel's decision largely by pointing to the legislative history of the 1972 statute. From stray congressional remarks, such as that of Representative Byrnes of Wisconsin that the legislation deals with "items stolen in the country of origin, and we are saying that if it is stolen it cannot be brought in,"[NOTE 7] coupled with the statute's noncoverage of movable artifacts such as ceramic pots or figurines and provision of civil forfeiture as the only penalty, appellants seek to establish a very specific legislative understanding and intent. They argue (1) that Congress believed that pre-Columbian artifacts were not forfeitable under preexisting laws such as the N.S.P.A.; (2) that Congress must have intended to allow importation of movable items like most of those in the Rodriguez/Simpson/McClain collections; and (3) that Congress intended that illegal importation of immovables be punished by forfeiture of the item and not by imprisonment or fine under the criminal laws.

Our study of the statute and its scant legislative history persuades us that appellants' reading of it is not correct. Both the Report by the House Ways and Means Committee and the Report by the Senate Finance Committee explicitly refer to the presence of other unspecified sanctions: "While legal remedies for the return of such objects are available in U.S. courts in some cases, these procedures can be extremely expensive and time consuming and do not provide a meaningful deterrent to the pillage of pre-Columbian sites now taking place."[NOTE 8] Moreover, the Act covers objects imported from all the countries of Latin America. These countries may have acted quite differently to protect their cultural heritages, some by declaring national ownership and others merely by enacting stringent export restrictions. Since it covers artifacts from such a large number of countries, the Act is better seen not as an indication that other available penalties were thereby precluded, but rather as a recognition that additional deterrents were needed. We cannot see in this congressional intent any desire to prevent application of criminal sanctions for dealing in items classified as stolen because a particular country has enacted national ownership of its patrimony.[NOTE 9]

Appellants' second challenge is not so easily resolved. It is elementary that criminal statutes must give notice of the acts they prohibit before valid penalties may be imposed thereunder. In their first appeal, appellants argued broadly that a reference to any foreign law for the purpose of determining what is or is not "stolen" would "inject an unacceptable degree of uncertainty into the administration" of the N.S.P.A. This argument also drew a firm holding—a ruling that application of the N.S.P.A. to foreign exportation did not render that statute void for vagueness. 545 F.2d at 1001, 1002 n. 30. The court reasoned that the statute's specific scienter requirement eliminates the possibility that a defendant is convicted for an offense he could not have understood to exist. In support, the court cited *Boyce Motor Lines v. United States*, 342 U.S. 337, 340, 72 S.Ct. 329, 331, 96 L.Ed. 367 (1952), for the proposition that it is not "unfair to require that one who deliberately goes perilously close to an area of proscribed conduct shall take the risk that he may cross the line." The court finally noted that it would have been impossible for the statute to have explicitly described every type of theft that might fall within its broad purview. Id.

In assessing whether the law of the case doctrine precludes further challenge under a void-for-vagueness theory, we first observe that the panel's holding was in response to a challenge about reference to foreign law generally and not to a challenge about the specific Mexican statutes. Moreover, we think it very significant that the panel's response was made in the context of its independent review of the relevant Mexican statutes. Its study of those statutes led the court to conclude that Mexico had not *unequivocally* declared national ownership of *all* artifacts until 1972. 545 F.2d at 997-1000. Entailed in the proposition that criminal penalties on the basis of the 1972 declaration of ownership are proper, is the probable corollary that criminal penalties on the basis of, for instance, the 1897 Mexican statute alone would have been improper because that statute did not declare the nation's ownership of movables with sufficient clarity.[NOTE 10] The panel's opinion is consistent with the view that, had there been no subsequent enactments that declared ownership with enough specificity to be accessible to and understandable by our citizenry, criminal penalties may well have violated our fundamental standards of due process. We are therefore convinced that, insofar as criminal liability in the second trial may possibly have been predicated on a conclusion that the 1897 Act declared Mexican ownership of all artifacts, appellants' precise due process challenge was not decided before and therefore survives. Because the due process challenge is so closely linked with the issue of the proper view of Mexican law, further discussion of this issue will be postponed until we have described and assessed the record on that point.

III. JURY INSTRUCTIONS REGARDING MEXICAN LAW, SUFFICIENCY OF EVIDENCE.

At appellants' first trial a deputy attorney general of Mexico testified as an expert witness, and the trial court subsequently instructed the jury that Mexico had, since 1897, vested itself with ownership of all pre-Columbian artifacts found in that country. As mentioned above, its independent review of translations of the various Mexican statutes convinced the earlier panel that Mexico had not unequivocally claimed ownership of all such artifacts until 1972. The earlier Mexican statutes seemed only to have claimed national ownership of immovable monuments and such movable artifacts as were found on, and possibly in, the immovable objects.[NOTE 11] Movable objects not in the above classes seemed capable of being privately owned and conveyed, though the Mexican government required that such objects be registered and retained the right to acquire items of great cultural or archaeological value by purchase at a fair price. Certain other provisions referred to in the petition for rehearing seem to have established a presumption against private ownership of any movable not registered within the applicable time limits.[NOTE 12] In view of the complicated and gradual nature of Mexico's apparent declarations of ownership, the earlier panel ruled that the defendants were entitled to a new trial because of the prejudice that may have resulted from the erroneous instruction that Mexico owned all artifacts as early as 1897. Its analysis of the changes in Mexican law convinced the panel that the jury should have been told to determine when the artifacts had been exported from Mexico and to "apply the applicable Mexican law to that exportation."

When the additional complication of the statutory presumptions was raised in the petition for rehearing, the court explained that its earlier discussion of Mexican law had not been "an exegesis of every relevant statutory clause or a holding on every issue that was or might have been raised." Rather, the court contemplated that on remand "objective testimony" on the meaning of the relevant Mexican enactments would be introduced, so as to lighten the burden both of the district court and reviewing court. The court reiterated that the earlier instructions had been "clearly in error" as to Mexican law but added that at any subsequent trial "experts will have an opportunity to correct any misconstruction of which this Court may have been guilty in venturing forth in the arcane field of the Mexican law of pre-Columbian artifacts." *United States v. McClain, on petition for rehearing*, 551 F.2d 52, 54 (5th Cir. 1977).

Pursuant to these instructions, at the second trial the judge admitted testimony from several government and defense witnesses about the relevant Mexican law. Only two of the witnesses were accepted by the court as experts specifically on the Mexican law of archaeological monuments. The first, Javier Andres Oropeza-Secura, is the Director of the Judicial Branch of the National Institute of Anthropology and History of Mexico, the office in charge of the official registry for ancient artifacts. The second was Ricardo de los Rios, an attorney who currently works at the Ministry of Labor and who formerly worked in the Attorney General's office, where he prosecuted about 150 cases under the Mexican laws regulating artifacts. Since each of these men is an employee of the Mexican government and was challenged by defendants as possibly biased, the government introduced other witnesses to corroborate their testimony. Carlos Schon, an attorney in Mexico City with a general practice and a heavily American clientele, was allowed to testify as a licensed practitioner of the general laws of Mexico from whom one may seek legal opinions. His testimony on archaeological law was based on his review of the various statutes and the Mexican Constitution. Though the testimony of these witnesses varied on a specific point here and there, the weight of their testimony as a whole indicated a general opinion that the Mexican government owned all pre-Columbian artifacts at least as early as 1897.[NOTE 13] Rights of private individuals were limited to the right of possession, but only if the particular artifact had been properly registered, and the mere right to possess does not confer the right to sell an item or to give it as security for a loan.

These views were further corroborated by two civilian witnesses, one Mexican and one American. Ms. DiazZambrano testified that she had learned in elementary school that the Mexican people own all vestiges of preHispanic civilizations found in the country. Dr. Richard E.W. Adams, Professor of Anthropology and Dean of Humanities and Social Science at The University of Texas in San Antonio, testified that he had participated in several archaeological excavations in Mexico. He stated that in 1953 at a class he attended at the School of Anthropology and History in Mexico City, he was told that all archaeological items are the property of the nation and cannot be exported. He also testified that, insofar as it affected his work and the difficulty of exporting legitimately excavated objects from Mexico, the Mexican law had not changed in the last twenty years. Against this massive record, appellants offered, in addition to their own views of Mexican law, the testimony of Ignacio Gomez Palacio, an attorney in Mexico who engages in legal research, writing, and a general practice. Like Mr. de los Rios, his opinion was based on independent review of the Mexican Constitution and relevant statutes, rather than on any long-held expertise on the particular subject of pre-Columbian artifacts. His testimony was similar to the conclusions reached earlier by the Fifth Circuit panel, and he seems to be the only witness to explain persuasively several passages in the statutes that are anomalous under the categorical views advanced by the government witnesses.[NOTE 14]

On this new record the trial judge faced a dilemma. The Fifth Circuit had ruled him in error for having concluded that Mexico had claimed ownership as early as 1897, and the panel had re-emphasized its ruling even while instructing him to allow experts to correct any error in the appellate opinion. Yet the great weight of the government's new expert testimony indicated that his earlier conclusion might still be the proper view of Mexican law—at least as interpreted by some of the few Mexican nationals qualified to express an authoritative opinion. Perhaps in view of this dilemma about the paths open to him and because none of the parties urged that it was his function to decide the question of applicable foreign law, the trial judge gave the jury the task of deciding whether and when Mexico *validly* enacted national ownership of the artifacts involved.[NOTE 15] In addition to now urging for the first time that the court erred in failing to make the determination of foreign law, the appellants argue that certain aspects of the instructions were erroneous and that the court erred in refusing to give the instructions they had offered.

Rule 26.1 of the Federal Rules of Criminal Procedure provides in part that "[t]he court, in determining foreign law, may consider any relevant material or source, including testimony, whether or not submitted by a party or admissible under [Rule 26.] The court's determination shall be treated as a ruling on a question of law." Despite appellants' fond hopes, Rule 26.1 does not itself mandate that the judge rather than the jury decide all questions of foreign law. Rather, it provides that any determination a judge does make shall be treated as a ruling on a question of law. This "functional approach," carefully side-stepping the issue of who is to decide the question, was deliberate on the part of the draftsmen.[NOTE 17]

Our pre-Rule cases make clear that the proper procedure is for the judge rather than the jury to determine questions of foreign law. *Daniel Lumber Co. v. Empresas Hondurenas,* S.A., 215 F.2d 465 (5th Cir. 1954), *cert. denied*, 348 U.S. 927, 75 S.Ct. 340, 99 L.Ed. 727 (1955); *Liechti v. Roche*, 198 F.2d 174 (5th Cir. 1952). To close the gap left in the Federal Rules of Criminal Procedure, we reaffirm that division of functions now, as we have done in the corresponding civil context. *First National City Bank v. Compania de Aquaceros, S.A.*, 398 F.2d 779, 782 (5th Cir. 1968). But it does not necessarily follow that putting the matter to the jury is reversible error. There is no automatic prejudice to the substantial rights of a defendant inherent in letting the jury decide the question on the basis of expert testimony. Indeed, the question whether the right to a jury trial in criminal matters requires submission of a question of foreign law to the jury, because it can be found as a matter of fact, has never been definitively laid to rest.[NOTE 18] In the absence of compelling evidence of prejudice, we would be loath to reverse a conviction such as this where the evidence of guilt and of intent to violate both foreign and domestic law is near overwhelming. We believe, nevertheless, that reversal of at least the substantive count is required here because the most likely jury construction of Mexican law upon the evidence at trial is that Mexico declared itself owner of all artifacts at least as early as 1897. And under this view of Mexican law, we believe the defendants may have suffered the prejudice of being convicted pursuant to laws that were too vague to be a predicate for criminal liability under our jurisprudential standards.

It may well be, as testified so emphatically by most of the Mexican witnesses, that Mexico has considered itself the owner of all pre-Columbian artifacts for almost 100 years. If so, however, it has not expressed that view with sufficient clarity to survive translation into terms understandable by and binding upon American citizens.[NOTE 19] Neither the early statutes nor the Constitution of 1917 clearly declare national ownership of the sort of pre-Columbian movable artifacts in which appellants dealt. One of the government experts testified that a literal translation of the Mexican statutes into English would mislead those not familiar with Mexican law into thinking that such movables had been capable of being privately owned.[NOTE 20] Another admitted that there were "confusions" in the 1934 statute caused by the lack of technical language and that subsequent statutes had been designed to clarify the legal situation.[NOTE 21]

The 1972 statute, on the other hand, is clear and unequivocal in claiming ownership of all artifacts.[NOTE 22] Deferring to this legitimate act of another sovereign, we agree with the earlier panel that it is proper to punish through the National Stolen Property Act encroachments upon legitimate and clear Mexican ownership, even though the goods may never have been physically possessed by agents of that nation. Nor does the infirmity of vagueness attach to the 1970 and possibly the 1934 statute insofar as they established presumptions that unregistered movables belong to the sovereign. Had these theories alone (either post-1972 exportation or post1934 appropriation, coupled with failure to register) been presented to the jury, our appellate task would have been much simpler.[NOTE 23] There is no doubt that the evidence is sufficient to have sustained convictions under either theory, and there would have been little prejudice involved in letting the jury decide the appropriate Mexican law to apply. But the expert testimony in the main allowed the jury to conclude that Mexico had long owned all these items outright. There was thus little need for the jury to consider legal and factual technicalities such as the probable date of exportation or the effect of the presumptions upon appellants' unregistered items. Unfortunately, under this broad view of Mexican law, our basic standards of due process and notice preclude us from characterizing the artifacts as "stolen." Though the National Stolen Property Act is not void for vagueness because the general class of offenses to which it is directed is plainly within its terms, it cannot properly be applied to items deemed stolen only on the basis of unclear pronouncements by a foreign legislature. The principle from *Boyce Motor Lines*, employed in the earlier appeal, cannot be used to deflect the vagueness charges directed at the early Mexican statutes. The basic premise of *Boyce*—the existence of an area of conduct that is proscribed in reasonably certain terms—is absent. *Boyce Motor Lines v. United States*, 342 U.S. at 340, 72 S.Ct. 329. The 1897 statute, the 1930 statute, and even the 1934 and 1970 statutes, unless there is specific focus on the presumption mechanism, do not clearly announce any line that appellants' willfulness can have led them to cross. As the Supreme Court observed in *Screws v. United States*, 325 U.S. 91, 105, 65 S.Ct. 1031, 1037, 89 L.Ed. 1495 (1945), "willful conduct cannot make definite that which is undefined." We therefore conclude that the convictions pursuant to the substantive count must be reversed.

By contrast, the requisite degree of prejudice for reversal is lacking as to the conspiracy count. The evidence presented to the jury amply showed that appellants' conspiracy was much broader than an intent to deal in the single collection already in the United States for an unspecified length of time. It is abundantly clear that they conspired to bring in at least one other load, and most likely a continuing stream of articles that, owing to a broken drive shaft and appellants' subsequent arrest, never arrived. Their plans regarding those loads—and the conduit itself—were clearly illegal under any view of Mexican law, including that presented by their own witnesses. The evidence is massive that appellants knew and deliberately ignored Mexico's post-1972 ownership claims. In addition, the continuing nature of their enterprise was highlighted in the closing arguments to the jury by the government and the defendants alike. Moreover, the instructions regarding the conspiracy count were separated from the instructions regarding the substantive count and, in outlining the required elements of the offense, the judge made no reference back to the jury's role regarding Mexican law. He correctly charged that the defendants need never have completed the illegal object of their conspiracy to be found guilty and also correctly instructed that none of the overt acts need themselves be illegal. The phone calls and meetings with McGauley and Benkendorfer and indeed the sale of the Rodriguez/Hollinshead/McClain collection can each be seen as overt acts in stringing along the "Mafia" buyers until the channel for regular importation of newly dug items was fully operational, as the buyers had requested.

Given the strength of this evidence regarding the continuing illegal purpose of appellants which, if effectuated, would necessarily entail dealing in "stolen" property under any view of Mexican law, we hold that the dubious shifting of the determination of Mexican law constituted harmless error as to the conspiracy count.[NOTE 25]

Accordingly, appellants' convictions on the conspiracy count are AFFIRMED, and the convictions on the substantive court are REVERSED.

NOTES:

NOTE 1: See generally *United States v. McClain*, 545 F.2d 988 (5th Cir.), rehearing denied, 551 F.2d 52 (5th Cir. 1977). Only one other reported conviction has resulted from application of the National Stolen Property Act to dealings in preColumbian artifacts. In *United States v. Hollinshead*, 495 F.2d 1154 (9th Cir. 1974), Clive Hollinshead of Los Angeles, California, was successfully prosecuted for transporting into the United States a known and cataloged Guatamalan stela. Hollinshead was on probation for this offense during the events leading to the instant prosecution. At least appellants Simpson and Bradshaw knew Hollinshead and were aware of his conviction and probation. Hollinshead was to have supplied several of the artifacts that appellants were selling when they were arrested.

NOTE 2: Rodriguez, a codefendant at the original trial, was not retried with the others because he was found mentally incompetent in the interim.

NOTE 3: The man identified himself as Harry McClain, who is appellant Patty McClain's husband.

NOTE 4: During one of the conversations to perfect details of the San Antonio meeting, Simpson asked whether Benkendorfer and McGauley would be interested in purchasing a three-ton stela from the Mexican interior. Simpson was contemplating a burro trip down to the monument so the buyers could inspect it before it was cut into three pieces for transportation out of the country. Benkendorfer declined the offer when he learned that the object was still in place.

NOTE 5: 19 U.S.C. § 2093 details the only penalties contained in the 1972 Importation Act. It provides that any object imported in violation of the Act shall be seized and subject to forfeiture under the customs laws.

NOTE 6: This statute prohibits importation into the United States, unless the country of origin has certified exportation, of "stone carvings and wall art which are pre-Columbian monumental or architectural sculpture or murals." The latter term is defined in § 2095(3) as any stone carving or wall art (or fragment or part thereof) that (1) is the product of pre-Columbian Indian culture of Mexico, Central America, South America, or the Caribbean Islands; (2) was an immobile monument or architectural structure or was a part of, or affixed to, any such monument or structure; and (3) is subject to export control by the country of origin. Though some of the artifacts seized in San Antonio and Los Angeles seem to come within this definition, the majority of the pieces are movable items such as ceramic dishes, pots, or figurines that may not have been part of or affixed to monuments or walls within the apparent meaning of the statute.

NOTE 7: 118 Cong.Rep. 37098 (1972) (emphasis added).

NOTE 8: H.R. Rep. No. 92-824, 92d Cong., 2d Sess. 3 (1972); S.Rep. No. 92-1221, 92d Cong., 2d Sess. 2 (1972).

NOTE 9: During the congressional debates, Rep. Byrnes also stated:

> The situation is that a narrow class of very valuable archaeological objects from the pre-Columbian period in South America are being taken out of that country [sic] illegally, and being brought into this country.
> There is no prohibition in this country about bringing in these articles, the prohibition is against taking these articles out of the country in which they are found, and this is an attempt to cooperate with these countries to avoid this exploitation that is taking place.

118 Cong.Rec. 37097 (1972).

Instead of reading into these remarks the specific and technical meaning attributed to them by appellants, we understand the congressman to be referring to the general state of American law regarding the importation of items illegally exported from another country. As the earlier panel observed, the fundamental rule, absent modification as by the 1972 statute, is that it is not a violation of law to import an item of art or anything else simply because it has been illegally exported from another country. 545 F.2d at 996. But that generalized principle does not preclude federal criminal liability for concealing, selling, or transporting across state or international borders items that are not only illegally exported from a country such as Mexico, but are also incapable of being privately owned or conveyed. Dealing in such items is dealing in stolen goods and may be punished accordingly, irrespective of import regulations.

NOTE 10: Article I of the Law on Archaeological Monuments, May 11, 1897 (Diaro Official de 11 de Mayo de 1897, see XIV Annario de Legislacion y Jurisprudencia [1897]), declared "archaeological monuments" to be the "property" ("propriedad") of the nation, but "archaeological monuments" were defined in article 2 as "ruins of cities, Big Houses [Casas Grandes], troglodytic dwellings, fortifications, palaces, temples, pyramids, sculpted rocks or those with inscriptions, and in general all the edifaces that in any aspect may be interesting for the study of civilization and history of the ancient settlers of Mexico." There was no corresponding declaration of ownership of movable artifacts such as codices, idols, amulets, though exportation of such items was forbidden unless legally authorized. Art. 6.

NOTE 11: For instance, the Law for the Protection and Preservation of Archaeological and Historical Monuments, Typical Towns and Places of Scenic Beauty, January 19, 1934 (82 Diario Official 152, 19 de enero de 1934), broadened the definition of "monuments" to include "all vestiges of the aboriginal civilizations dating from before the completion of the Conquest." Art. 3. But art. 4 clearly declared national ownership of artifacts in more limited categories—"immovable archaeological monuments" and "objects which are found [in or on] immovable archaeological monuments." See 545 F.2d at 998-99, including n. 20 that explains the dispute over movable items found in immobile monuments.

NOTE 12: Art. 9 of the 1934 statute, supra note 11, created a Register of Private Archaeological Property" ("Propriedad") with which private individuals were to register movable monuments in their "control" or "ownership." (Translation of any terms suggestive of private ownership was hotly disputed at trial.) Art. 12 of that statute prescribed that objects not registered within the period stipulated in the Act's transitory articles "shall be presumed to come from archaeological monuments which are real property." Because the Act had earlier declared national ownership of all immovable monuments, supra note 11, the force of this presumption seems to nationalize all movable artifacts not registered by the end of the transitory period. There is a similar presumption in the statute that superseded the 1934 Act, the Federal Law Concerning Cultural Patrimony of the Nation, December 16, 1970 (303 Diario Official 8, 16 de diciembre de 1970). See art. 55 thereof, which provides that movable objects not registered within the allowed time limits are presumed "the property of the nation." ("propriedad").

NOTE 13: The witnesses, though very emphatic in affirming their understanding of longstanding national ownership of all artifacts, were unable to identify specific passages (apart from the 1934 and 1970 presumptions) in the 1897, 1930, 1934, or 1970 statutes that claimed outright ownership of the sort of movables largely involved in this case. By contrast, those statutes contain several explicit declarations of ownership of immovables and smaller movable items found on, and possibly in, the immovable monuments. *Supra*, notes 10 and 11.

On cross-examination, appellants tried to lead the government witnesses to admit that the specific pronouncements of ownership of some objects indicated an obvious legislative intent to leave undistributed private ownership of other objects, especially since various provisions seem clearly to contemplate private ownership. For instance, art. 26 of the 1930 statute provides that "[i]n order to determine the ownership ('propriedad') of movable things of artistic, archaeological or historical value that are discovered in a casual manner and not as a result of archaeological excavation or exploration, the provisions of the Civil Code of the Federal District and Federal Territories related to treasures will apply, but the Federal Government may acquire the discovered objects for their fair price, when it deems this appropriate."

The witnesses stood their ground, however, arguing that the expressions of limited ownership did not preclude general ownership of all artifacts. Without succeeding in rationalizing the statutory provisions with his categorical view of government ownership, Carlos Schon at least attempted to identify an arguable source of national ownership by reference to art. 27 of the Mexican Constitution of 1917. That provision, as explained by Schon, provides that the property of the land and the water within the limits of the national territory belongs originally to the nation, which has the power to transmit them to private individuals as private property. He interpreted art. 27 as extending to manmade items buried in the land, in addition to the natural deposits of minerals and ores found therein. Under his view, unless the legislature acts to grant to individuals derived ownership rights regarding any of these things, national ownership is retained.

The testimony of Ricardo de los Rios also touched on art. 27, and there are indications he may have held similar views of its meaning. The questions he was asked did not cause him to focus on the issue with sufficient precision for us to determine his position, however.

NOTE 14: As observed in note 13, *supra*, it was difficult for the government witnesses to account for the statutory declarations of ownership of some items if the government supposedly owned all types of artifacts already. The declaratory passages made much more sense under Gomez' view that the government only gradually expanded its ownership claims. Contrary to Schon's analysis, Gomez read art. 27 of the 1917 Constitution as restricted to land, subsoil, and materials naturally occurring therein, such as minerals, precious stones, ores, oil. He classified manmade items that were found in the soil as "treasure trove" and noted that ownership claims to such items were regulated by provisions of the Civil Code of the Federal District. He analyzed art. 26 of the 1930 statute, set out in note 13, *supra*, as incorporating by reference the treasure trove statutes and as further evidence of the ability of private persons to own at least some artifacts under the earlier statutes.

NOTE 15: The judge instructed the jury as follows:

> Now, in order to find any one or more of the defendants guilty on one or more of the counts in the indictment, the government must prove three essential elements of the offense charged in this case beyond a reasonable doubt as follows: 1. That the Republic of Mexico was the owner of the alleged artifacts, if any, at the time such artifacts were exported if and only if you so find, from the Republic of Mexico into the United States of America; 2. That such artifacts, if any, were in fact exported from Mexico and thus imported into the United States of America from the Republic of Mexico; and 3. That such alleged artifacts were produced before the Spanish Conquest of Mexico and the government of the Republic of Mexico had not issued or granted a permit or license allowing and authorizing the defendants or any other person, firm, corporation, governmental agency or others to export such artifacts, if any, from Mexico to the United States of America or to any other country or place; and such artifacts, if any, had not been registered under Mexican law.
>
> As I have said, all three and each and every one of the essential elements that I have just given you must be proved and established to your satisfaction beyond a reasonable doubt before you can find the defendants guilty in this particular case.
>
> Now, there is absolutely no presumption that the defendants or any one of them knew the Mexican law. On the other hand, the United States of American is under no obligation to prove that the defendants knew the place from which the artifacts were allegedly stolen, if it is shown beyond a reasonable doubt that they were in fact stolen. What the United States must prove to your satisfaction beyond a reasonable doubt is that the defendants knew that the artifacts were in fact stolen under the laws of Mexico regardless of where they came or from where they were stolen *and that the Mexican government had in fact effectively adopted valid laws acquiring ownership of such artifacts*, if any, *which were in existence at the time of such theft*, if any, and that the defendants knew and understood such laws and that such laws had been violated.

(emphasis added).

NOTE 16: On numerous occasions during the trial the judge had clearly indicated his intent to give this issue to the jury. Beyond one tentative expression of doubt by an assistant prosecutor, none of the parties objected to putting this burden on the jury. The judge had also requested assistance from the parties in formulating the instructions on Mexican law, but none responded until the last moment, when they proffered handwritten requests in part tracking the earlier panel opinion. The judge thought his own set of instructions carefully followed the panel opinion because the jury was being told, in effect, to apply the applicable Mexican law to the defendants' behavior. In objecting to the charge, defendants' only points were that their proffered instructions were more precise renditions of the panel's legal conclusions than were the trial judge's. When, during the bench conference after the instructions had been given, the judge commented, "I put quite a burden on [the jury — to find whether the Mexican laws were valid enactments]," appellants' attorneys failed to comment on the procedure.

NOTE 17: The Advisory Committee Notes on the Fed.R.Civ.P. 44.1 to which we are referred by the draftsmen of the Rules of Criminal Procedure observe that Rule 44.1, to which Rule 26.1 is substantially identical, does not address itself to this problem because the rules generally refrain from allocating functions between judge and jury. The committee adds "It has long been thought, however, that the jury is not the appropriate body to determine issues of foreign law," citing, among other authorities, our pre-Federal Rules cases, *Daniel Lumber Co. v. Empresas Hondurenas*, S.A., 215 F.2d 465 (5th Cir. 1954), *cert. denied*, 348 U.S. 927, 75 S.Ct. 340, 99 L.Ed. 727 (1955), and *Liechti v. Roche*, 198 F.2d 174 (5th Cir. 1952). Advisory Committee Note to Rule 44.1, Fed.R.Civ.P., Title 28, U.S.C.A,

NOTE 18: See, e.g., Kaplan, "Continuing Work of the Civil Committee: 1966 Amendments of the Federal Rules of Civil Procedure (II)," 81 Harv. L.Rev. 591, 617 (1968). Because no one argues the point here, we express no opinion on the issue.

NOTE 19: Because of our disposition of the claims in this appeal largely on the ground of unconstitutional vagueness and harmless error, we need not now undertake the delicate task of deciding the meaning of the Mexican statutes and the manner in which the various provisions interact. We leave that task to subsequent courts should the government prosecute others by reference to pre-1972 Mexican statutes, either directly or as incorporated by art. 4 of the 1972 Transitory. *See* note 22 *infra*.

NOTE 20: Carlos Schon took issue with the translations offered in evidence by the defendants — the translations used by the earlier panel in assessing the Mexican statutes. He especially objected to translating the word "propriedad" as "ownership" or "property," though he conceded that that rendering was proper in some of the statutory passages. He said that only one familiar with the Mexican law could decide when to translate the word as "ownership" because in many instances regarding artifacts the law limits "propriedad" to connoting mere possessory rights. Translation of "propriedad" as "property" might incorrectly lead those unfamiliar with Mexican law to believe some artifacts could be "outright property." Mr. Schon further testified that "translation de dominion" could be translated as "acts of conveyance," provided the latter term was not understood to include "transfer of property or outright ownership." The literal translation, "transfer of dominion," would also be misleading, since the correct meaning of the law does not go beyond allowing "transfer of possession."

NOTE 21: As an instance of such "confusion" in the 1934 statute, Mr. Oropeza identified art. 10, which can be translated as requiring registration of private "transfers of ownership." In the original it reads: "Los proprietarios de objetos inscritos deberan dar conocimiento de las traslaciones de propriedad, para que se haga la anotacion correspondiente."

NOTE 22: The 1972 statute also contains a grandfather clause under which rights gained under previous statutes are preserved. Transitory, Article Fourth. Thus, if private persons were allowed ownership as opposed to mere possessory rights under the earlier laws, those rights would be retained provided the owner complied with the requirements of those laws.

NOTE 23: We express no opinion regarding the claim, made by amicus in its brief in the earlier appeal, that predicating criminal liability on a presumption contained in a foreign statute would also infringe due process.

NOTE 24: During closing arguments, William Simpson, who was defending himself, referred to the testimony about the continuing conspiracy and sought to turn it to his own advantage:

> Mr. Rodriguez, according to Mrs. Zambrano's testimony, . . . told her that there were five groups of Mexicans, peons, farmers, people trying to make money apparently digging in Mexico and supplying him with great quantities of artifacts.
>
> The same thing holds true with that story. It can't possibly be true. Mrs. Zambrano under my examination, cross examine [sic] stated emphatically that that was happening at the present time, that that was a continuing operation; yet we have an inventory and it has been established that these pieces are the same pieces that Mr. Rodriguez left with me at that time, May of 1973.
>
> If Mrs. Zambrano's testimony was accurate, and I'm not saying it wasn't told to her, I don't believe it was, but if it was accurate, by necessity, being a conspiracy as we are charged here today, that inven-

tory would have increased considerably. Five groups of Mexicans in a conduit as represented by Mrs. Zambrano channeling it into San Antonio, my goodness gracious, it would have filled up my house. We would not only have had the bedroom and the living room filled, it would have been added to and added to in great quantities.

NOTE 25: For these and additional reasons, we reject appellants' other challenges to the jury instructions. We can detect no affirmative errors in the statements about Mexican law made by the court. Nor did the judge err in refusing to give the instructions offered by appellants. The proffered summaries of Mexican law were fatally flawed in their treatment of the presumptions in the 1934 and 1970 statutes. Those presumptions, as part of statutes repealed by enactment of subsequent statutes, no longer have independent legal force. But they were not thereby rendered totally nugatory. The character of items excavated and held without registration for the statutory period may have been irrevocably impressed with a presumption of government ownership. In any event, no legal ownership of such items seems possible after the effective date of the 1972 statute. All items not legally owned by individuals were then nationalized, and it became impossible legally to own items without complying with the requirements of the earlier statutes. Transitory, Art. Fourth.

STUDY QUESTIONS

- How did the court in *McClain* apply the National Stolen Property Act (NSPA)?
- Do you agree with the court's conclusion about applying Mexican law?

Reading Note: Another important case involving cultural property is the *Schultz* case reprinted below. It also involves an appeal of a criminal conviction for illegally trafficking in antiquities. In this case, the conviction is based on the National Stolen Property Act and Egyptian patrimony laws. The court also considers various defenses, including one based on the enactment of the Cultural Property Implementation Act (CPIA).

UNITED STATES V. SCHULTZ

333 F.3d 393 (2nd Cir.2003)

MESKILL, Circuit Judge.

Defendant-appellant Frederick Schultz (Schultz) appeals from a judgment of conviction entered in the United States District Court for the Southern District of New York, Rakoff, J., after a trial by jury. Schultz was convicted of one count of conspiracy to receive stolen property that had been transported in interstate and foreign commerce, in violation of 18 U.S.C. § 371. The district court had jurisdiction pursuant to 18 U.S.C. § 3231. Appellate jurisdiction is appropriate because "[w]e have jurisdiction to consider appeals from final decisions of the district courts, which are judgments of conviction and sentence in criminal cases." *United States v. Ferguson*, 246 F.3d 129, 138 (2d Cir.2001). See also 28 U.S.C. § 1291.

BACKGROUND

Schultz was a successful art dealer in New York City. On July 16, 2001, he was indicted on one count of conspiring to receive stolen Egyptian antiquities that had been transported in interstate and foreign commerce, in violation of 18 U.S.C. § 371. The underlying substantive offense was violation of 18 U.S.C. § 2315, the National Stolen Property Act (NSPA).

Schultz moved to dismiss the indictment, asserting that the items he was charged with conspiring to receive were not stolen within the meaning of the NSPA. Specifically, Schultz contended that the Egyptian antiquities he allegedly conspired to receive were not owned by anyone, and therefore could not be stolen. The prosecution asserted that the antiquities were owned by the Egyptian government pursuant to a patrimony law known as "Law 117" which declared all antiquities found in Egypt after 1983 to be the property of the Egyptian government. After an evidentiary hearing, the district court denied the motion to dismiss in a written memorandum and order. See *United States v. Schultz*, 178 F.Supp.2d 445 (S.D.N.Y.2002). Schultz was tried before a jury in January and February 2002.

The following facts were adduced at trial.

In 1991, Schultz met Jonathan Tokeley Parry (Parry), a British national, through a mutual friend. Parry showed Schultz a photograph of an ancient sculpture of the head of Pharaoh Amenhotep III, and told Schultz that he had obtained the sculpture in Egypt earlier that year from a man who represented himself to be a building contractor. Parry had used an Egyptian middle-man named Ali Farag (Farag) to facilitate the deal. Parry had smuggled the sculpture out of Egypt by coating it with plastic so that it would look like a cheap souvenir, then removed the plastic coating once the sculpture was in England.

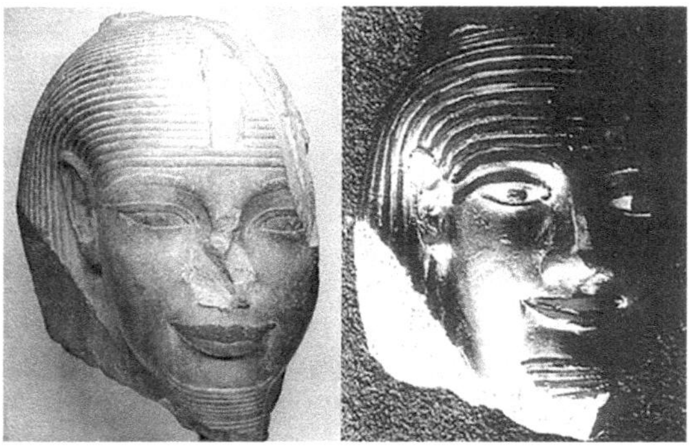

This sculptured head of the 18th Dynasty pharaoh Amenhotep III (ca. 1403-1354 B.C.) (left) was purchased by Johnathan Tokeley Parry in Cairo shortly after it had been looted. He dipped the sculpture in clear plastic and painted it to resemble a cheap tourist souvenir (right). Frederick Schultz, a well-known New York art dealer sold it for $1.2 million in 1993. For a decade Parry and Schultz smuggled artifacts out of Egypt and faked their provenance, telling potential buyers that they were collected by an Englishman named Thomas Alcock in the 1920s. In 2001, Schultz was charged with conspiracy to receive stolen Egyptian antiquities that had been transported in interstate and foreign commerce in violation of the National Stolen Property Act (NSPA). In United States v. Schultz, the court upheld Schultz's criminal conviction. He served 33 months in prison and was fined $50,000.

Schultz offered Parry a substantial fee to serve as the agent for sale of the Amenhotep sculpture, which Parry accepted. Parry and Schultz discussed the problems that might arise if they were discovered to have the piece, and set out to create a false provenance for the sculpture, so that they could sell it. They decided that they would claim that the sculpture had been brought out of Egypt in the 1920s by a relative of Parry and kept in an English private collection since that time. Parry and Schultz invented a fictional collection, the "Thomas Alcock Collection," and represented to potential buyers that the sculpture came from this collection. With Schultz's knowledge, Parry prepared fake labels, designed to look as though they had been printed in the 1920s, and affixed the labels to the sculpture. Parry also restored the sculpture using a method popular in the 1920s.

Acting as Parry's agent, Schultz attempted to sell the Amenhotep sculpture to various parties, using the "Thomas Alcock Collection" story, but was unsuccessful. Eventually, Parry sold the sculpture to Schultz for $800,000, and Schultz sold it to a private collector in 1992 for $1.2 million. In June 1995, Robin Symes (Symes), who then owned the Amenhotep sculpture, asked Schultz to provide him with more details about the sculpture's origin, because he had learned that the Egyptian government was pursuing the sculpture. Schultz responded by asking questions regarding the Egyptian pursuit, but did not provide Symes with any additional information regarding the Amenhotep sculpture.

Parry and Schultz became partners, in a sense. They endeavored to bring more Egyptian antiquities into America for resale, smuggling them out of Egypt disguised as cheap souvenirs, assigning a false provenance to them, and restoring them with 1920s techniques. Parry testified about six items or groups of items, in addition to the Amenhotep sculpture, that he and Schultz attempted to remove from Egypt and sell under the false provenance of the Thomas Alcock Collection.

In 1991, Parry smuggled a sculpture of Meryet Anum (a daughter of Pharoah Ramses II) out of Egypt and performed extensive restorations on it. Parry brought the sculpture to New York and showed it to experts who determined it to be a fake.

In 1992, Parry sold Schultz a black top vase for $672, informing Schultz that the vase had been brought out of Egypt. Parry affixed a Thomas Alcock Collection label to the vase. Schultz and Parry acquired this vase because they believed that including some less valuable pieces in the imaginary Thomas Alcock Collection would make the Collection more believable.

In 1992, Parry wrote to Schultz from Egypt, telling Schultz that he had obtained a sculpture he called "The Offeror." Parry smuggled The Offeror out of Egypt and performed extensive restoration work on it. Parry believed the sculpture was authentic until testing revealed it to be a fake. Parry delivered The Offeror to Schultz without informing him of either the extensive restorations or the fact that the sculpture was not authentic. However, when Schultz discovered the sculpture was a fake, he returned it to Parry. Later, when Parry was arrested, The Offeror was confiscated by British authorities. Schultz contacted the authorities attempting to claim The Offeror as his own, eventually sending a forged invoice purporting to show that Schultz had bought the sculpture from a New York art dealer and had given it to Parry only for restoration. Schultz did not succeed in claiming The Offeror.

In 1992, Parry and Farag learned that someone had reported them to the Egyptian authorities for dealing in antiquities. Due in part to the assistance of Farag's father, who was a powerful Egyptian government official, Parry and Farag were able to get their names removed from police records by paying a bribe to certain corrupt members of the Egyptian antiquities police. These same corrupt police officers then entered into a deal with Parry and Farag, offering them a variety of antiquities in police possession in exchange for Parry and Farag paying off some debts owed by the police officers. Parry chose three items from the "bran tub"[NOTE 1] full of items offered; he later sent those items to Schultz. Parry informed Schultz of how he had obtained the items. One of the items was marked with an Egyptian government registry number, which Parry succeeded in partially obliterating.

In 1992, Parry purchased the top half of a limestone sculpture of a striding figure, which he dubbed "George," from a group of Egyptian villagers. Apparently, when the sculpture had been found, it was in pieces, and the pieces were divided among rival groups of villagers. Parry wrote to Schultz telling him of the acquisition and informing Schultz that he was attempting to obtain George's bottom half. Parry also requested money to assist in the purchase of George and other items. Parry and Farag eventually succeeded in purchasing the bottom half of the sculpture, and reassembled the whole thing. Parry then coated George in plastic, and in plaster, and painted it to look like a tourist souvenir so it could be taken out of Egypt. Parry kept Schultz informed of his progress and eventually brought George to New York for Schultz to sell. When George was offered for sale, it was treated with 1920s restoration techniques and represented to be part of the Thomas Alcock Collection. Schultz was unable to sell George, and Parry requested that Schultz send George to Switzerland, where Parry planned to retrieve it. For reasons that are not clear from the record, Parry was not able to retrieve George.

In June 1994, Parry was arrested in Great Britain, and Farag was arrested in Egypt. Each was charged with dealing in stolen antiquities. Schultz was aware of the arrests and communicated extensively with Parry after his arrest about Parry's legal situation. Parry and Schultz also continued to correspond regarding plans for new acquisitions.

In December 1994, Parry wrote to Schultz describing three limestone "stelae," or inscribed slabs, which had been discovered by builders in Egypt and were being offered for sale. Parry had an expert review photographs of the stelae, and the expert determined that the pieces were newly discovered and not listed in any of the catalogs of antiquities known to the Egyptian government. By 1995, there were ten pieces available from this find, and although Parry had been taken into custody in Great Britain, he continued attempting, with Schultz, to obtain the stelae. Schultz sent money for this purpose, and Parry directed that the pieces be shipped to Switzerland for Parry to retrieve in 1996. However, neither Parry nor Schultz ever actually obtained the stelae.

Throughout their partnership, Parry and Schultz communicated regularly; many of their letters were introduced in evidence by the government. Their letters indicate an awareness that there was a great legal risk in what they were doing. This awareness is reflected both in the content of the letters and in Parry's and Schultz's use of "veiled terms," code, or even languages other than English.

The jury found Schultz guilty on the sole count of the indictment, and on June 11, 2002, Schultz was sentenced principally to a term of 33 months' imprisonment. This appeal followed.

On appeal, the Court received three amicus curiae briefs. The National Association of Dealers in Ancient, Oriental & Primitive Art, Inc.; International Association of Professional Numismatists; The Art Dealers Association of America; The Antique Tribal Art Dealers Association; The Professional Numismatists Guild; and The American Society of Appraisers filed a brief in support of Schultz. An ad hoc group called Citizens for a Balanced Policy with Regard to the Importation of Cultural Property, made up of politicians, academics, and art collectors, also filed a brief in support of Schultz. These briefs argue primarily that allowing Schultz's conviction to stand would threaten the ability of legitimate American collectors and sellers of antiquities to do business. The Archaeological Institute of America; The American Anthropological Association; The Society for American Archaeology; The Society for Historical Archaeology; and the United States Committee for the International Council on Monuments and Sites filed a brief in support of the United States. This brief argues primarily that sustaining Schultz's conviction and applying the NSPA to cases such as this one will help to protect archaeological and cultural sites around the world.

DISCUSSION

I. Application of the NSPA to Cases Involving Patrimony Laws

In order to preserve its cultural heritage, Egypt in 1983 enacted a "patrimony law" which declares all antiquities discovered after the enactment of the statute to be the property of the Egyptian government. The law provides for all antiquities privately owned prior to 1983 to be registered and recorded, and prohibits the removal of registered items from Egypt. The law makes private ownership or possession of antiquities found after 1983 illegal. Schultz's primary argument is that the NSPA does not apply to cases in which an object was "stolen" only in the sense that it was possessed or disposed of by an individual in violation of a national patrimony law, as opposed to "stolen" in the commonly used sense of the word, for instance, where an object is taken from a museum or a private collection. The government contends that the plain language of the NSPA indicates that the NSPA applies to any stolen property, regardless of the source of the true owner's title in the property. The question, in other words, is whether an object is "stolen" within the meaning of the NSPA if it is an antiquity which was found in Egypt after 1983 and retained by an individual (and, in this case, removed from Egypt) without the Egyptian government's consent.

The NSPA reads, in pertinent part, as follows:

> Whoever receives, possesses, conceals, stores, barters, sells, or disposes of any goods, wares, or merchandise, securities, or money of the value of $5,000 or more … which have crossed a State or United States boundary after being stolen, unlawfully converted, or taken, knowing the same to have been stolen, unlawfully converted, or taken … [s]hall be fined under this title or imprisoned not more than ten years, or both.

18 U.S.C. § 2315 (2000).

This statute is unambiguous. It applies to goods that are "stolen, unlawfully converted, or taken." Id. Goods that belong to a person or entity and are taken from that person or entity without its consent are "stolen" in every sense of that word. See, e.g., Black's Law Dictionary 989-90 (6th ed. abr.1991) (defining "stolen" as "[a]cquired or possessed, as a result of some wrongful or dishonest act or taking, whereby a person willfully obtains or retains possession of property which belongs to another, without or beyond any permission given, and with the intent to deprive the owner of the benefit of ownership (or possession) permanently"); Webster's Third New International Dictionary 2248 (1971) (defining "stolen" as "obtained or accomplished by theft, stealth, or craft"). Accordingly, Schultz's actions violated the NSPA if the antiquities he conspired to receive in the United States belonged to someone who did not give consent for Schultz (or his agent) to take them. That "someone" is the nation of Egypt.

In 1983, Egypt enacted Law 117. The law, which is entitled "The Law on the Protection of Antiquities," reads, in pertinent part, as follows:

> Article 1
>
> An "Antiquity" is any movable or immovable property that is a product of any of the various civilizations or any of the arts, sciences, humanities and religions of the successive historical periods extending from prehistoric times down to a point one hundred years before the present, so long as it has either a value or importance archaeologically or historically that symbolizes one of the various civilizations that have been established in the land of Egypt or that has a historical relation to it, as well as human and animal remains from any such period.

ARTICLE 6

All antiquities are considered to be public property — except for charitable and religious endowments.... It is impermissible to own, possess or dispose of antiquities except pursuant to the conditions set forth in this law and its implementing regulations.

ARTICLE 7

As of [1983], it is prohibited to trade in antiquities.

ARTICLE 8

With the exception of antiquities whose ownership or possession was already established [in 1983] or is established pursuant to [this law's] provisions, the possession of antiquities shall be prohibited as from [1983].

Law 117 includes a chapter entitled "Sanctions and Penalties" detailing the criminal penalties to be imposed on persons found to have violated the law. This section provides, inter alia, that a person who "unlawfully smuggles an antiquity outside the Republic or participates in such an act shall be liable to a prison term with hard labor and a fine of not less than 5,000 and not more than 50,000 pounds." A person who steals or conceals a state-owned antiquity faces a prison term of three to five years and a minimum fine of 3,000 pounds. A person who removes or detaches an antiquity from its place, counterfeits an antiquity, or unlawfully disposes of an antiquity faces a prison term of one to two years and a minimum fine of 100 pounds. A person who writes on, posts notices on, or accidentally defaces an antiquity faces a prison term of three to twelve months and/or a fine of 100 to 500 pounds.

Schultz moved in the district court to dismiss the indictment on the ground that Law 117 did not vest true ownership rights in the Egyptian government, and, accordingly, the items he conspired to smuggle out of Egypt were not "stolen" within the meaning of the NSPA. In response to Schultz's motion, the district court conducted an evidentiary hearing regarding Law 117 pursuant to Federal Rule of Criminal Procedure 26.1.[NOTE 2] At that hearing, two Egyptian officials testified as fact witnesses for the government: Dr. Gaballa Ali Gaballa and General Ali El Sobky.

Dr. Gaballa is Secretary General of Egypt's Supreme Council of Antiquities, which is a part of the Ministry of Culture. The Supreme Council employs more than 20,000 people. Dr. Gaballa was asked: "Who owns all newly discovered antiquities?" He responded: "The Egyptian government, of course." Dr. Gaballa clarified that people who owned antiquities prior to the adoption of Law 117 in 1983 are permitted to continue to possess the antiquities, but they may not transfer, dispose of, or relocate the antiquities without notifying the Egyptian government. Dr. Gaballa testified that pursuant to Law 117, when the Egyptian government learns that an antiquity has been discovered, agents of the government immediately take possession of the item. The item is then registered and given a number.

In response to questioning by the court, Dr. Gaballa asserted that there are no circumstances under which a person who finds an antiquity in Egypt may keep the antiquity legally. The person who found the antiquity is not compensated for the item, because it never belonged to the finder. The only time compensation is paid is when a person owns a plot of land on which an immovable structure is located, and the government takes possession of the entire plot of land in order to possess the structure; in such a case, only the value of the land itself, and not the value of the structure, is taken into account in determining the amount of payment.

The court also asked Dr. Gaballa whether Law 117 had been used to bring legal actions against persons in Egypt who did not comply with the law, but did not attempt to remove an antiquity from Egypt. Dr. Gaballa responded that he was aware of cases in which Law 117 had been applied to persons whose violations of the law took place entirely inside Egypt.

The government's second witness, General El Sobky, is the Director of Criminal Investigations for the Egyptian Antiquities Police. General El Sobky testified that his department, which employs more than 400 officers, regularly investigates and prosecutes people for violating Law 117. General El Sobky testified that most of the Law 117 investigations and prosecutions conducted by his department are of people who are trafficking in antiquities within Egypt, as opposed to exporting them out of Egypt. Furthermore, General El Sobky testified, even when a person is acquitted in such a prosecution, if the person is found to possess an antiquity, that antiquity is seized and retained by the government.

Schultz called one expert witness at the hearing, Khaled Abou El Fadl, a professor of Islamic and Middle Eastern law at the University of California—Los Angeles (UCLA) Law School. Professor Abou El Fadl opined that Law 117 was at times ambiguous and confusing. He further testified that the language of Law 117 did not make it clear whether the law "intended to keep the antiquities inside of Egypt or actually was asserting governmental ownership over the antiquities." Professor Abou El Fadl asserted that "nothing in Law 117 prevents the Antiquities Authority from leaving physical possession of even an antiquity discovered after 1983 in the hands of a private finder, so long as the private finder promptly notifies the Authority of his find."

On cross-examination, Professor Abou El Fadl stated that he had never practiced law in Egypt, nor was he licensed to practice law in Egypt. He testified that he had never read Law 117 prior to being requested to do so by Schultz's counsel, and that he had been unable to locate any treatises discussing Law 117.

Schultz contends that in spite of its plain language, Law 117 is not a "real" ownership law, and that Egypt does not truly claim ownership over all antiquities, but merely seeks to restrict their export. The district court disagreed, finding, based substantially on the testimony and other evidence presented at the hearing, that the plain language of Law 117 accurately reflects its purpose and effect: to vest absolute and true ownership of all antiquities found in Egypt after 1983 in the Egyptian government. See *Schultz*, 178 F.Supp.2d at 448.

"Issues of foreign law are questions of law," Fed.R.Crim.P. 26.1 (2003), and accordingly we review the district court's findings regarding Law 117 de novo. See *Curley v. AMR Corp.*, 153 F.3d 5, 11 (2d Cir.1998) ("[A] court's determination of foreign law is treated as a question of law, which is subject to de novo review." (citing parallel rule Fed.R.Civ.P. 44.1)).

Schultz failed to present any evidence at the hearing or at trial that Law 117 is not what its plain language indicates it is, that is, an ownership law. Professor Abou El Fadl's opinion that the law is ambiguous cannot overcome the combination of (1) the plain text of the statute, and (2) the testimony of two Egyptian government officials to the effect that the statute is a true ownership law and is enforced as such. Although Professor Abou El Fadl testified that he believed it would be possible for Egyptian authorities to leave antiquities in the possession of private individuals who discovered them, Schultz offered no evidence that the authorities ever actually had permitted an individual to retain an antiquity found after 1983. The Egyptian government officials testified that there was no legal way for a private individual to retain possession of an antiquity discovered after 1983, and that all such antiquities are seized by the government.

Law 117 defines "antiquity" and prescribes the procedure to be followed by persons in possession of antiquities at the time the Law takes effect, and by persons who discover antiquities thereafter. It sets forth serious criminal penalties for the violation of its provisions. It provides for licensure of certain foreign archaeological missions, and for circumstances under which antiquities may be donated by the government to foreign museums in appreciation of those missions' work. The Law's provisions are directed at activities within Egypt as well as export of antiquities out of Egypt. Law 117 makes it clear that the Egyptian government claims ownership of all antiquities found in Egypt after 1983, and the government's active enforcement of its ownership rights confirms the intent of the Law. Accordingly, we conclude that Law 117 is clear and unambiguous, and that the antiquities that were the subject of the conspiracy in this case were owned by the Egyptian government.

The question thus becomes whether Schultz's actions in conspiring to take antiquities owned by the Egyptian government pursuant to Law 117 out of Egypt violate the NSPA. Schultz argues that even if Law 117 does intend to vest true ownership of all antiquities with the Egyptian government, that sort of "ownership" should not be recognized by the United States for purposes of prosecution under the NSPA.

Schultz urges us to adopt a narrow reading of the NSPA. However, the Supreme Court and this Court have acknowledged that the NSPA has a "broad purpose," *McElroy v. United States*, 455 U.S. 642, 655, 102 S.Ct. 1332, 71 L.Ed.2d 522 (1982), and that "the statute should be broadly construed." *United States v. Wallach*, 935 F.2d 445, 469 (2d Cir.1991) (citing *Moskal v. United States*, 498 U.S. 103, 113, 111 S.Ct. 461, 112 L.Ed.2d 449 (1990)).

We have held that the language of the NSPA "is broad enough to justify the federal courts in applying the statute whenever they determine that the [property was] stolen in another country." *United States v. Greco*, 298 F.2d 247, 251 (2d Cir.1962); see also *United States v. Parness*, 503 F.2d 430, 440 n. 14 (2d Cir.1974) (citing Greco with approval). Accordingly, there can be no doubt that if the antiquities involved in the conspiracy were stolen in Egypt and then shipped to the United States, the NSPA would be violated.

Just as the property need not be stolen in the United States to bring the NSPA into play, the fact that the rightful owner of the stolen property is foreign has no impact on a prosecution under the NSPA. See *United States v. Frazier*, 584 F.2d 790, 794 (6th Cir.1978) ("The court ruled that even if it were conceded that the defendants would be able to prove beyond a reasonable doubt that" the victim was a foreign company, the NSPA would still apply. "This was clearly a correct interpretation of the statute."). Furthermore, this Court has held that the NSPA applies to stolen property even where the person from whom the property was stolen may not have been the true owner of the property, and that the validity of the victim's title in the property is sometimes "irrelevant." *United States v. Benson*, 548 F.2d 42, 46 (2d Cir.1977).[NOTE 3] Accordingly, it does not matter that the antiquities at issue here were stolen in a foreign country, or that their putative owner is a foreign entity.

Notwithstanding all of the above, Schultz insists that the antiquities are not "stolen" within the meaning of the NSPA because they were never truly owned by the Egyptian government. The leading opinion addressing this question was issued by the Fifth Circuit, over 25 years ago, in *United States v. McClain*, 545 F.2d 988 (5th Cir.1977). The parties frame the question on appeal as whether the Second Circuit should adopt the reasoning set forth by the Fifth Circuit in *McClain*.

Schultz asserts that we should reject the holding in *McClain* based on existing Second Circuit precedent, which he reads as being hostile to McClain. Schultz then raises several additional arguments in support of his position, namely: (1) that *McClain's* approach conflicts with United States policy, (2) that the enactment of the Convention on Cultural Property Implementation Act of 1983, 19 U.S.C. §§ 2601-2613 (CPIA), "confirms that Congress never intended [the] NSPA to reach ownership claims based upon national vesting laws when the property has not been reduced to the possession of the foreign state," and (3) that the common law definition of "stolen" would not reach the property at issue here. We address each of these arguments in turn.

A. *McClain* in the Second Circuit

The *McClain* defendants were convicted of conspiring to violate the NSPA by importing artifacts from Mexico that were covered by a Mexican law declaring all such artifacts to be owned by the Mexican government. See id. at 992. The defendants claimed, as Schultz does here, that the NSPA did not apply to "stolen" objects that were taken in violation of patrimony laws. See id. at 994. The Fifth Circuit concluded that the NSPA did apply to such objects.[NOTE 4] See id. at 996-97.

The *McClain* Court cited precedent according an expansive meaning to the term "stolen" in the NSPA, including *United States v. Handler*, 142 F.2d 351, 353 (2d Cir.1944), which held that embezzled property is "stolen" within the meaning of the NSPA. See *McClain*, 545 F.2d at 995 (citing cases). The *McClain* Court also cited *United States v. Bottone*, 365 F.2d 389, 393-94 (2d Cir.1966). In *Bottone*, the defendants photocopied documents detailing secret manufacturing processes, and transported the photocopies across state lines. See *Bottone*, 365 F.2d at 391. The original documents were taken from the rightful owner only briefly for copying, and were never transported in interstate or foreign commerce. See id. at 393. The Court found that the transport of the photocopies violated the NSPA, and the fact that the photocopies were "never possessed by the original owner should be deemed immaterial." Id. at 393-94.

The *McClain* Court also distinguished between mere unlawful export and actual theft, holding that "a declaration of national ownership is necessary before illegal exportation of an article can be considered theft, and the exported article considered 'stolen,' within the meaning of the [NSPA]." *McClain*, 545 F.2d at 1000-01. The court engaged in a close study of the Mexican patrimony law, including its language, history and purpose, and concluded that the Mexican government had made a declaration of national ownership satisfying this standard. See id. at 997-1000. As discussed above, Egypt has made a clear declaration of national ownership through Law 117, and has enforced that law accordingly.

Summarizing its decision in *McClain*, the Fifth Circuit stated:

> This conclusion is a result of our attempt to reconcile the doctrine of strict construction of criminal statutes with the broad significance attached to the word "stolen" in the NSPA. Were the word to be so narrowly construed as to exclude coverage, for example, with respect to pre-Columbian artifacts illegally exported from Mexico after the effective date of the 1972 [patrimony] law, the Mexican government would be denied protection of the [NSPA] after it had done all it reasonably could do [to vest] itself with ownership to protect its interest in the artifacts. This would violate the apparent objective of Congress: the protection of owners of stolen property. If, on the other hand, an object were considered "stolen" merely because it was illegally exported, the meaning of the term "stolen" would be stretched beyond its conventional meaning. Although "stealing" is not a term of art, it is also not a word bereft of meaning. It should not be expanded at the government's will beyond the connotation depriving an owner of its rights in property conventionally called to mind.

McClain, 545 F.2d at 1001-02 (footnotes omitted). We agree that the Fifth Circuit reached the proper balance between these competing concerns in *McClain*.

i. Hollinshead

Although *McClain* is often described as the only federal appeals court case to have considered the application of the NSPA to property deemed stolen under a foreign patrimony law, the issue was actually first encountered by the Ninth Circuit three years before *McClain* in *United States v. Hollinshead,* 495 F.2d 1154 (9th Cir.1974). The facts of *Hollinshead* are very similar to those in the case at hand. "Hollinshead, a dealer in pre-Columbian artifacts, arranged with one Alamilla, a co-conspirator, to procure such artifacts in Central America, and to finance Alamilla in doing so." Id. at 1155. Once the artifacts were obtained, they were shipped to Hollinshead in the United States. See id.

Hollinshead was convicted of conspiracy to transport stolen property in interstate and foreign commerce, in violation of 18 U.S.C. § 2314. See id. The trial centered on a particular artifact that had been found in a Mayan ruin in the jungle of Guatemala and eventually shipped to Hollinshead. See id. The artifact was "stolen" as defined by the NSPA because under Guatemalan law "all such artifacts are the property of the Republic, and may not be removed without permission of the government." Id. As occurred in this case, the district court had received testimony regarding the law of Guatemala as applied to such artifacts. See id.

The Ninth Circuit was not presented in *Hollinshead* with a direct attack on the application of the NSPA to cases involving patrimony laws; that was not the basis of the defendant's appeal. However, the Ninth Circuit's discussion indicates its acceptance of the prosecution's theory in *Hollinshead*: that an object is "stolen" within the meaning of the NSPA if it is taken in violation of a patrimony law. See id. at 1156. We are aware of no other federal appeals court that has reached this issue.

The Second Circuit has rarely addressed *McClain*, and has never decided whether the holding of *McClain* is the law in this Circuit. See *United States v. Long Cove Seafood,* 582 F.2d 159, 163, 165 (2d Cir.1978) (Long Cove); *United States v. An Antique Platter of Gold,* 184 F.3d 131, 134 (2d Cir.1999) (Steinhardt).[NOTE 5] Although Schultz asserts that these cases support his position, we disagree with his interpretation of these precedents.

ii. Long Cove

The defendants in *Long Cove* were charged with violating the NSPA by taking undersized clams from Long Island Sound and selling them to area restaurants. See *Long Cove,* 582 F.2d at 161, 162. There was no dispute that the practice of harvesting and selling undersized clams violated various environmental laws; the question was whether the transport of these clams across state lines constituted the interstate transport of "stolen" goods under the NSPA. See id. at 162-63. The government argued that the clams were "stolen" from the State of New York because of a New York law that provides:

> The State of New York owns all fish, game, wildlife, shellfish, crustacea and protected insects in the state, except those legally acquired and held in private

> ownership. Any person who kills, takes or possesses such fish, game, wildlife, shellfish, crustacea or protected insects thereby consents that title thereto shall remain in the state for the purpose of regulating and controlling their use and disposition.

Id. at 164 (quoting N.Y. Envtl. Conserv. Law § 11-0105).

The Court stated that the key question was "whether New York has asserted a true ownership interest in wildlife such as the Fifth Circuit, in [*McClain*], held that Mexico has done since 1972 with respect to pre-Columbian artifacts. We think not." Id. at 165. The Court emphasized that the New York statute stated that the purpose of asserting ownership was only to regulate and control the use and disposition of wildlife, not to actually take possession of it. See id. The Court further noted that while New York claimed to own the wildlife, it was not liable for an attack by any wild animal, as a private owner of such an animal would be. See id.

The distinctions between the facts of the *Long Cove* case and the facts of the case at hand are clear and require a different outcome here. First, as the testimony before the district court made clear, Egypt does assert a possessory interest in antiquities pursuant to Law 117. While the State of New York has never attempted to seize all wildlife found within its borders, Dr. Gaballa testified that the Egyptian government actively pursues any person found to have obtained an antiquity and takes immediate possession of all antiquities of which it becomes aware.

Second, both Dr. Gaballa and General El Sobky confirmed that the purpose of Law 117 is to bring all newly discovered antiquities within the direct possession and control of the Egyptian government in order to ensure that they are properly preserved and documented. Hundreds of antiquities police are employed by the Egyptian government solely to effectuate this purpose. To the contrary, the purpose of the New York law is simply to control the use and disposition of wildlife. See *Long Cove*, 582 F.2d at 164-65.

Third, the New York law explicitly excepts those wildlife "legally acquired and held in private ownership." Id. at 164. Law 117 provides for no exceptions for private ownership of antiquities discovered after the effective date of the law.[NOTE 6] It is legal under certain circumstances for a private person to obtain and dispose of wildlife in New York, for instance, by obtaining a hunting, fishing or trapping license. See, e.g., N.Y. Envtl. Conserv. Law § 11-0701(4) (McKinney 2003) ("A fishing license entitles the holder to take fish by angling, spearing, hooking, longbow and tipups, to take frogs by spearing, catching with the hands or by use of a club or hook, and to take bait fish for personal use."). When a licensed hunter or fisherman catches wildlife in New York, it is his to keep and dispose of as he chooses.

In Egypt, on the other hand, it is impossible for a private party to get a license to obtain, possess or dispose of antiquities. Law 117 does provide in Article 34 for "foreign missions" to receive archaeological exploration and excavation licenses. However, Article 35 states that "[a]ll antiquities discovered by foreign archaeological excavation missions shall be state owned." If the Antiquities Authority determines that the foreign mission is "outstanding," and has performed "important excavation and restoration work," the Authority may reward the mission by donating certain antiquities which "are expendable by reason of their similarity to other items excavated from the same location." Even then, the donated antiquities must be "thoroughly examined and fully recorded," and may only be donated to a museum, not to the excavators themselves.

We also note that in *Long Cove* we were not called upon to rule directly on the application of the NSPA to property owned pursuant to a patrimony law, and we did not question the correctness of *McClain*. *Long Cove* cited *McClain* more than once, in a positive light, which is significant in light of the considerable publicity the Fifth Circuit's controversial holding in *McClain* had generated at the time. See *Long Cove*, 582 F.2d at 163, 165. These citations give no indication that the Court disapproved of the outcome or analysis of McClain.

iii. Steinhardt

Schultz also contends that our decision in *Steinhardt* indicates that we have rejected the holding of *McClain*. In *Steinhardt*, the district court had found that an Italian antiquity should be forfeited by Steinhardt, who had imported it into the United States, because (1) Steinhardt had made material misrepresentations on a customs form or, (2) in the alternative, the antiquity was properly owned by the Italian government pursuant to a patrimony law and was therefore stolen property within the meaning of the NSPA and subject to forfeiture. See *Steinhardt*, 184 F.3d at 134. On appeal, we concluded that Steinhardt had made a material misstatement on a customs form when he represented that the antiquity was from Switzerland, not Italy. See id. at 137. Accordingly, the Court concluded that the antiquity was subject to forfeiture.[NOTE 7] See id. at 138. The Court declined to reach the alternative ground relied on below, stating: "We need not ... address whether the NSPA incorporates concepts of property such as those contained in the Italian patrimony laws." Id. at 134.

It is irrelevant that we previously reviewed a case in which it was not necessary to reach the question now before us. It is not at all uncommon for us to decline to reach an issue when the case before us can be resolved on other grounds. See, e.g., *Wexner v. First Manhattan Co.*, 902 F.2d 169, 174 (2d Cir.1990) ("[I]n light of our determination that the district court should be affirmed on other grounds, we find it neither necessary nor appropriate to reach this issue today."). Our failure to address a question that is not necessary to the outcome of a case is simply a wise exercise of our discretion. See *United States v. United States Gypsum Co.*, 333 U.S. 364, 402, 68 S.Ct. 525, 92 L.Ed. 746 (1948) (Frankfurter, J., concurring in part) ("Deliberate dicta, I had supposed, should be deliberately avoided. Especially should we avoid passing gratuitously on an important issue of public law where due consideration of it has been crowded out by complicated and elaborate issues that have to be decided.").[NOTE 8] We find Schultz's reliance on *Steinhardt* unpersuasive.

B. United States Policy

Schultz contends that it is United States policy not to enforce the export restrictions of foreign nations. Schultz offers no evidence in support of this assertion, but even if his assessment of United States policy is accurate, the outcome of this case is unaffected. We have already concluded, based on the plain language of Law 117 and the evidence in the record, that Law 117 is an ownership law, not an export-restriction law. Two Egyptian officials testified under oath that the law is used in Egypt to prosecute people for trafficking in antiquities within Egypt's borders. Law 117 provides for a minimum five-year prison term and a fine of 3,000 pounds for persons convicted of "[t]heft or concealment of a state owned antiquity." Persons convicted of smuggling an antiquity out of Egypt face "a prison term with hard labor and a fine of not less than 5,000 and not more than 50,000 pounds." Clearly, theft or concealment of an antiquity within Egypt is a different offense than smuggling an antiquity out of Egypt, and both are prohibited by Law 117. Accordingly, even if Schultz's interpretation of American policy is accurate, it is not relevant here. While Law 117 does restrict exportation of cultural objects, its scope is not limited to export restrictions. Law 117 is more than an export regulation—it is a true ownership law.

C. The CPIA

Schultz contends that the adoption of the CPIA shows that Congress did not intend the NSPA to apply to objects such as the ones he conspired to bring to the United States. The CPIA implements a United Nations convention that was ratified by the United States in 1982, the purpose of which was to achieve "greater international cooperation towards preserving cultural treasures that not only are of importance to the nations whence they originate, but also to greater international understanding of our common heritage." S.Rep. No. 97-564, at 21 (1982).

The CPIA provides a mechanism for the American government to establish import restrictions on "cultural property" at the request of another signatory nation and after a determination by the President that (1) "the cultural patrimony of [the requesting nation] is in jeopardy from the pillage of archaeological or ethnological materials of [that nation]," (2) the requesting nation "has taken measures ... to protect its cultural patrimony," (3) the import restrictions are necessary and would be effective in dealing with the problem, and (4) the restrictions are in the "general interest of the international community." 19 U.S.C. § 2602(a)(1)(A)-(D) (2003).

Schultz argues that the CPIA was intended to be the only mechanism by which the United States government would deal with antiquities and other "cultural property" imported into the United States. However, nothing in the language of the CPIA supports that interpretation, and the legislative history shows that exactly the converse is true. As the district court correctly noted, Schultz, 178 F.Supp.2d at 449, the Senate Report on the CPIA expressly states that the CPIA "neither preempts state law in any way, nor modifies any Federal or State remedies that may pertain to articles to which [the CPIA's] provisions ... apply." S.Rep. No. 97-564, at 22 (1982). Furthermore, the Senate Report states that the CPIA "affects neither existing remedies available in state or federal courts nor laws prohibiting the theft and the knowing receipt and transportation of stolen property in interstate and foreign commerce (e.g., National Stolen Property Act, Title 18, U.S.C. Sections 2314-15)." Id. at 33 (emphasis added).

The CPIA also bars the importation of items that have been stolen from a museum or other cultural institution in a foreign signatory nation. See 19 U.S.C. § 2607. Schultz argues that because only those items that are stolen from specified places are covered by the CPIA, Congress never intended in any way to limit the import of items "stolen" only in the sense that they were taken in violation of patrimony laws. This argument is unpersuasive. The CPIA does not state that importing objects stolen from somewhere other than a museum is legal. If, for instance, an artifact covered by the CPIA were stolen from a private home in a signatory nation and imported into the United States, the CPIA would not be violated, but surely the thief could be prosecuted for transporting stolen goods in violation of the NSPA.

The CPIA is an import law, not a criminal law; it is not codified in Title 18 ("Crimes and Criminal Procedure"), with the NSPA, but in Title 19 ("Customs Duties"). It may be true that there are cases in which a person will be violating both the CPIA and the NSPA when he imports an object into the United States. But it is not inappropriate for the same conduct to result in a person being subject to both civil penalties and criminal prosecution, and the potential overlap between the CPIA and the NSPA is no reason to limit the reach of the NSPA. See, e.g., *Hudson v. United States*, 522 U.S. 93, 98-99, 118 S.Ct. 488, 139 L.Ed.2d 450 (1997) (holding that a person may be subjected to civil and criminal penalties for the same conduct without violating the Double Jeopardy Clause).

For the reasons set forth above, we conclude that the passage of the CPIA does not limit the NSPA's application to antiquities stolen in foreign nations.[NOTE 9]

D. Common Law Definition of "Stolen"

Schultz argues that the Court must look to the common law definition of "stolen" to determine whether the antiquities at issue are covered by the NSPA.[NOTE 10] Schultz cites *United States v. Turley*, 352 U.S. 407, 77 S.Ct. 397, 1 L.Ed.2d 430 (1957), in which the Supreme Court considered the meaning of the term "stolen" in the context of the statute that served as the precursor and model for the NSPA. See id. at 410-11, 77 S.Ct. 397. The Supreme Court stated: "We recognize that where a federal criminal statute uses a common-law term of established meaning without otherwise defining it, the general practice is to give that term its common-law meaning." Id. at 411, 77 S.Ct. 397. Schultz contends that interpreting the NSPA to apply to items that are "stolen" in the sense that they are possessed by a defendant in violation of a foreign patrimony law would be in derogation of the common law. However, in *Turley*, the Supreme Court explicitly recognized that "'stolen' (or 'stealing') has no accepted common-law meaning." Id. If "stolen" has no common law meaning, we cannot look to the common law to assist us in interpreting that term.

The Supreme Court also stated in *Turley* that the term "stolen" included "all felonious takings … regardless of whether or not the theft constitutes common-law larceny." Id. at 417, 77 S.Ct. 397. In other words, according to the Supreme Court, the precursor to the NSPA—and by extension the NSPA—covers a broader class of crimes than those contemplated by the common law. Accordingly, we find this argument unpersuasive.

E. Summary

In light of our own precedents and the plain language of the NSPA, we conclude that the NSPA applies to property that is stolen in violation of a foreign patrimony law. The CPIA is not the exclusive means of dealing with stolen artifacts and antiquities, and reading the NSPA to extend to such property does not conflict with United States policy. We believe that, when necessary, our courts are capable of evaluating foreign patrimony laws to determine whether their language and enforcement indicate that they are intended to assert true ownership of certain property, or merely to restrict the export of that property. In this case, the district court carefully evaluated the language of Law 117. The court also heard testimony from one academic expert and two Egyptian government officials. This evidence was sufficient to inform the court of the nature of Egypt's interest in the antiquities that were the subject of the conspiracy.

Although we recognize the concerns raised by Schultz and the amici about the risks that this holding poses to dealers in foreign antiquities, we cannot imagine that it "creates an insurmountable barrier to the lawful importation of cultural property into the United States." Our holding does assuredly create a barrier to the importation of cultural property owned by a foreign government. We see no reason that property stolen from a foreign sovereign should be treated any differently from property stolen from a foreign museum or private home. The *mens rea* requirement of the NSPA will protect innocent art dealers who unwittingly receive stolen goods, while our appropriately broad reading of the NSPA will protect the property of sovereign nations.

II. Defense of Mistake of United States Law

Schultz argues on appeal that the district court erred in refusing to allow him to present a defense of mistake of law. Specifically, Schultz sought to argue to the jury that he did not know that importing antiquities owned by the Egyptian government pursuant to Law 117 violated the NSPA.[NOTE 11] The government contends that the district court was correct to bar this defense, relying on "the venerable principle that ignorance of the law generally is no defense to a criminal charge." *Ratzlaf v. United States*, 510 U.S. 135, 149, 114 S.Ct. 655, 126 L.Ed.2d 615 (1994).

Schultz concedes that this is the general rule, but asserts that certain exceptions exist. Schultz cites three cases in which he contends that the Supreme Court found a defense of mistake of law was proper: *Ratzlaf,* 510 U.S. at 137, 114 S.Ct. 655 ("To establish that a defendant 'willfully violat[ed]' the antistructuring law, the Government must prove that the defendant acted with knowledge that his conduct was unlawful."); *Cheek v. United States*, 498 U.S. 192, 200, 111 S.Ct. 604, 112 L.Ed.2d 617 (1991) (interpreting "the statutory term 'willfully' as used in the federal criminal tax statutes as carving out an exception to the traditional rule" that mistake of law is no defense); and *Liparota v. United States*, 471 U.S. 419, 426, 105 S.Ct. 2084, 85 L.Ed.2d 434 (1985) (reading food stamp fraud provision to include a requirement that the defendant knew that his actions were unlawful, where "to interpret the statute otherwise would be to criminalize a broad range of apparently innocent conduct").

In addition, Schultz cites two federal appellate decisions from other circuits. In *United States v. Lizarraga-Lizarraga*, 541 F.2d 826 (9th Cir.1976), the Ninth Circuit reversed a defendant's conviction for illegal export of ammunition to Mexico because the district court had failed to instruct the jury that the defendant could be convicted only if he knew it was illegal to transport ammunition to Mexico. See id. at 828. Similarly, in *United States v. Grigsby*, 111 F.3d 806 (11th Cir.1997), the Eleventh Circuit reversed the conviction of a defendant for illegally importing elephant tusks because the district court had failed to instruct the jury that the defendant could be convicted only if he knew importing the items was illegal. See id. at 821, 834. Each of the cases relied on by Schultz is inapposite, for two reasons.

First, these decisions involve specific intent statutes. For instance, the statute at issue in *Lizarraga-Lizarraga* (now repealed) made it unlawful "willfully" to export certain items to Mexico. See *Lizarraga—Lizarraga*, 541 F.2d at 827. The inclusion of the term "willfully," the court found, made it clear that Congress intended to punish only those who exported ammunition knowing it was unlawful to do so. See id. at 828. Likewise, the statute of conviction in *Grigsby* specified that "[w]hoever knowingly violates section 4223 of this title" would be subject to criminal penalties. 16 U.S.C. § 4224 (2000) (emphasis added). The tax statute at issue in *Cheek* and the antistructuring statute at issue in *Ratzlaf* each also specified that only defendants who "willfully" violated the law would be subject to prosecution. See 26 U.S.C. §§ 7201, 7203; 31 U.S.C. § 5322.

The NSPA does not include the term "willfully." The section of the NSPA applicable to Schultz reads as follows:

> Whoever receives, possesses, conceals, stores, barters, sells, or disposes of any goods, wares, or merchandise, securities, or money of the value of $5,000 or more ... which have crossed a State or United States boundary after being stolen, unlawfully converted, or taken, knowing the same to have been stolen, unlawfully converted, or taken ... [s]hall be fined under this title or imprisoned not more than ten years, or both.

18 U.S.C. § 2315 (2000) (emphasis added). The only knowledge requirement in the NSPA is knowledge that the goods were "stolen, unlawfully converted, or taken." Id.; see *United States v. Rosa*, 17 F.3d 1531, 1546 (2d Cir.1994) (noting that the NSPA does not require knowledge that an item traveled in interstate or foreign commerce, but "does include a *mens rea* element with respect to the status of the goods as having been stolen"); *Godwin v. United States*, 687 F.2d 585, 588 (2d Cir.1982) ("A violation of 18 U.S.C. § 2315 normally requires simply the act of receiving or disposing of stolen goods of the requisite value moving in interstate commerce, coupled with knowledge that the goods are stolen."). A defendant charged with violating the NSPA may argue that he did not know a certain fact that made his conduct criminal, that is, that he did not know the objects in question were stolen. Schultz's "mistake of Egyptian law" defense goes to that issue. However, if a jury finds that a defendant knew all of the relevant facts, the defendant cannot then escape liability by contending that he did not know the law.

Second, the cases cited by Schultz are inapposite because each concerns conduct that normally might not be considered unlawful. The *Lizarraga—Lizarraga* Court, for instance, emphasized that in enacting the statute of conviction, Congress "did not intend to criminally penalize innocent or negligent errors." *Lizarraga—Lizarraga*, 541 F.2d at 828. The Supreme Court's primary concern in *Liparota* was that the statute under consideration in that case not be read in such a way as "to criminalize a broad range of apparently innocent conduct." *Liparota*, 471 U.S. at 426, 105 S.Ct. 2084.

In addition, the record demonstrates that Schultz's actions were not "innocent" or merely "negligent." This is not a case in which the defendant believed that he was doing something lawful, and was surprised to find that his conduct could result in criminal sanctions. To the contrary, Schultz was conspiring to smuggle antiquities out of Egypt and into the United States. He was defrauding (or attempting to defraud) potential buyers; the Thomas Alcock Collection story was invented by Schultz and Parry for the sole purpose of deceiving people as to the origin of the antiquities and when they had been taken out of Egypt. Schultz continued to do business in this manner even after his partners, Parry and Farag, had been arrested. Furthermore, Schultz and Parry demonstrated a keen awareness of the illegality of their actions by communicating in "code," forging documents, and even explicitly discussing the possibility that one or more of them might end up imprisoned.[NOTE 12]

We conclude that the district court did not err in denying Schultz's request to present a defense of mistake of American law. The jury did not have to find that Schultz knew what he was doing was illegal. As long as the jury found beyond a reasonable doubt that Schultz knew the antiquities were "stolen," the jury, following the law, would have been required to convict Schultz even if it believed he had misunderstood American law.

III. Conscious Avoidance Jury Instruction

Prior to Schultz's trial, the government requested that the court charge the jury on the doctrine of conscious avoidance, and submitted a proposed jury instruction on that issue.

The district court included an instruction on conscious avoidance in its charge, which was provided to the parties prior to the charge conference, but the court's charge did not use the language suggested by the government. Schultz did not object to the use of a conscious avoidance charge or to the specific language proposed by the district court. On appeal, Schultz contends that the district court's instruction to the jury on the doctrine of conscious avoidance was erroneous.

A. Standard of Review

"Because defendant did not object to the charge at trial, our review is for plain error." *United States v. Bala*, 236 F.3d 87, 94 (2d Cir.2000); see also Fed.R.Civ.P. 56(b). The parties agree that this is the proper standard of review.

To establish plain error, a court must find 1) an error, 2) that is plain, 3) that affects substantial rights.... If an error meets these first three requirements, the Court engages in a fourth consideration: whether or not to exercise its discretion to correct the error. The plain error should be corrected only if it seriously affects the fairness, integrity, or public reputation of judicial proceedings.

United States v. Keigue, 318 F.3d 437, 441-42 (2d Cir.2003) (internal citations and quotation marks omitted); see also *United States v. Gore*, 154 F.3d 34, 43 (2d Cir.1998) ("A 'plain' error is an error so egregious and obvious as to make the trial judge and prosecutor derelict in permitting it, despite the defendant's failure to object."). Schultz "bears the burden of persuasion to show that the district court's charge amounts to plain error." *United States v. Vasquez*, 267 F.3d 79, 87 (2d Cir.2001).

"We do not review portions of [jury] instructions in isolation, but rather consider them in their entirety to determine whether, on the whole, they provided the jury with an intelligible and accurate portrayal of the applicable law." *United States v. Weintraub*, 273 F.3d 139, 151 (2d Cir.2001).

B. The District Court's Instruction

The district court charged the jury as follows:

> [A] defendant may not purposefully remain ignorant of either the facts or the law in order to escape the consequences of the law. Therefore, if you find that the defendant, not by mere negligence or imprudence but as a matter of choice, consciously avoided learning what Egyptian law provided as to the ownership of Egyptian antiquities, you may [infer], if you wish, that he did so because he implicitly knew that there was a high probability that the law of Egypt invested ownership of these antiquities in the Egyptian government.

> You may treat such deliberate avoidance of positive knowledge as the equivalent of such knowledge, unless you find that the defendant actually believed that the antiquities were not the property of the Egyptian government.

Schultz argues, correctly, that the Second Circuit has "repeatedly emphasized that, in giving the conscious avoidance charge, the district judge should instruct the jury that knowledge of the existence of a particular fact is established (1) if a person is aware of a high probability of its existence, (2) unless he actually believes that it does not exist." *United States v. Feroz*, 848 F.2d 359, 360 (2d Cir.1988) (per curiam). In Schultz's estimation, the charge given by the district court failed to convey these essential points to the jury. The government concedes that the language of the charge did not precisely mirror the language set out in prior Second Circuit cases, but contends that the charge as given was sufficiently clear and contained all of the necessary elements.

We have stated before that "no jury instruction is ever perfect." *United States v. Joyner*, 313 F.3d 40, 47 (2d Cir.2002). We do not review a jury instruction to determine whether it precisely quotes language suggested by Supreme or Appellate Court precedent. Instead, we review the court's instructions to determine whether "considered as a whole, [the instructions] adequately communicated [the essential] ideas to the jury." *United States v. Velez-Vasquez*, 116 F.3d 58, 61 (2d Cir.1997). "We cannot place the talismanic weight urged by [the defendant] on [the] exact wording [of a controlling opinion] and do not believe the district court needed to echo the opinion paragraph by paragraph to convey adequately its import to the jury." *United States v. Schatzle*, 901 F.2d 252, 255 (2d Cir.1990); see also *United States v. Beech-Nut Nutrition Corp.*, 871 F.2d 1181, 1196 (2d Cir.1989) (finding no error in conscious avoidance charge even though it "arguably" could have led the jury to draw an "unwarranted inference"); *United States v. McBride*, 786 F.2d 45, 51 (2d Cir.1986) (finding no error in conscious avoidance charge because "[t]he charge made reference to purposeful avoidance of the truth, awareness of a high probability of the fact at issue, and the absence of the defendant's actual belief in the nonexistence of the crucial fact"); cf. *DeFalco v. Bernas*, 244 F.3d 286, 312 n. 16 (2d Cir.2001) (finding no plain error where, "[a]lthough the language of the jury instruction [was] not ideal," the charge as a whole did not reveal "an error 'so serious and flagrant that it goes to the very integrity of the trial,' or one that 'deprived the jury of adequate legal guidance to reach a rational decision'"); *Owen v. Thermatool Corp.*, 155 F.3d 137, 139 (2d Cir.1998) (finding no error in jury charge that failed to use the "more precise and more typical" phrasing set forth in precedent, because charge "adequately stated the law").

Here, the charge given by the district court adequately stated the law of conscious avoidance. The court set forth both essentials required by Feroz. The charge informed the jury that it could find conscious avoidance only if it found both (1) that Schultz avoided gaining actual knowledge "because he implicitly knew that there was a high probability that the law of Egypt invested ownership of these antiquities in the Egyptian government" and (2) that Schultz did not "actually believe[ ] that the antiquities were not the property of the Egyptian government." The court also gave a "good faith" instruction and reiterated, immediately after giving the conscious avoidance charge, that Schultz could be found guilty only if the jury found that he had participated in the conspiracy "knowing that it contemplated the acquisition and/or sale of antiquities that had been stolen from Egypt." (emphasis added).

It is true that the district court's instructions on this point could "have been more precise." *United States v. Bonito*, 57 F.3d 167, 174 (2d Cir.1995). "At trial, had objection been lodged to the imprecision, the judge would have been well advised to correct it. But on appeal, and in light of the charge as a whole, we see no error so obvious and seriously prejudicial to [the defendant's] substantial rights as to constitute plain error." Id. The instruction as given was sufficient to inform the jury of the law of conscious avoidance, and did not constitute plain error.[NOTE 13]

IV. Admission of Testimony of Witnesses Other than Schultz Regarding Their Personal Knowledge of Law 117

Schultz contends that the district court erred in permitting the government to elicit testimony from five witnesses—James Romano and Edna Russman, curators of the Brooklyn Museum of Art; Edmund Pillsbury, head of the Kimbell Museum; Blake Woodruff, a former employee of Schultz; and Betsy Bryan, a professor of Egyptology—regarding those witnesses' personal knowledge of Law 117. Schultz objected to this testimony in the district court; it appears that the basis for the objection was that the testimony was irrelevant. "The standard of review applicable to the evidentiary rulings of the district court is abuse of discretion." *Old Chief v. United States*, 519 U.S. 172, 174 n. 1, 117 S.Ct. 644, 136 L.Ed.2d 574 (1997). "Unless a district court's determination of relevance is arbitrary or irrational, it will not be overturned." *Conway v. Icahn & Co.*, 16 F.3d 504, 511 (2d Cir.1994).

"'Relevant evidence' means evidence having any tendency to make the existence of any fact that is of consequence to the determination of the action more probable or less probable than it would be without the evidence." Fed.R.Evid. 401 (2002). There is no dispute that the fact of Schultz's knowledge of Law 117 "is of consequence to the determination of the action" at hand. Id. The only question is whether the district court abused its discretion in determining that this testimony had "any tendency" to make that fact "more probable or less probable."

The government contends that this testimony was relevant to the question whether Schultz was aware of Law 117 because evidence that the Law was widely known among those in Schultz's field tended to make it more probable that Schultz, who had worked in the field for decades, also knew about it. Furthermore, as the government emphasizes, each of the witnesses that was asked about his or her own knowledge of Law 117 had dealt directly with Schultz. Schultz had offered to sell "George" and the Amenhotep sculpture to James Romano and Edmund Pillsbury, respectively, using the Thomas Alcock Collection story. Schultz provided false information about the Amenhotep sculpture to Betsy Bryan, and showed "George" to Edna Russman, telling her it came from an old collection. Blake Woodruff had been employed by Schultz at Schultz's art gallery. The district court concluded that these witnesses' testimony tended to show that "even an ignoramus in this field would know at least about patrimony laws."

Schultz relies on *United States v. Patrisso*, 262 F.2d 194 (2d Cir.1958).[NOTE 14] In *Patrisso*, one of the defendants, Mankes, was convicted of knowingly possessing stolen property, in part on the strength of evidence that the person who sold the goods to Mankes knew the goods were stolen. See id. at 195, 197. The Court reversed the conviction, finding that the evidence admitted regarding Mankes' codefendants' knowledge that the property was stolen was prejudicial to Mankes. See id. at 198. *Patrisso* is not on point, for at least three reasons.

First, *Patrisso* is not a relevance case. The Court never held that the evidence admitted was irrelevant as to Mankes, only that it was so prejudicial to him as to be inadmissible. See id. at 197. Here, the defendant has argued that the evidence was not admissible because it was irrelevant, not because it was prejudicial.

Second, the factual circumstances of the *Patrisso* case differed materially from those present here. In *Patrisso*, the Court noted that Mankes' behavior was not consistent with consciousness of guilt; he made no effort to conceal the stolen property. See id. at 198. As noted above, Schultz's behavior indicated a consciousness that his actions were illegal in some way. Mankes, however, was at least four steps removed from the actual theft: Patrisso obtained the property from the person who stole it and sold the property to Ellis; Ellis sold the property to Postrel; Postrel sold the property to Mankes. See id. at 196. Schultz, on the other hand, was actively involved in obtaining the antiquities, smuggling them out of Egypt, and disguising their true origins. The nature of the property at issue in Patrisso—television tubes—was not such that a person would naturally inquire about its source, whereas the evidence in this case established that persons considering purchasing Egyptian antiquities make extensive inquiries into the provenance of the antiquities.

Third, and most important, the type of knowledge at issue in *Patrisso* is materially different than the type of knowledge at issue here. Schultz was an acknowledged expert in the field of Egyptian antiquities, with many years of experience. It would have been natural for Schultz to know about Law 117. To the contrary, it would not have been natural for Mankes' codefendants to tell him that the goods he was buying were stolen, and there was no other possible way for Mankes to have obtained that knowledge. Knowledge of a duly adopted, widely publicized, and vigorously enforced law such as Law 117 is quite different from knowledge of the specific theft of a specific product in *Patrisso*. Testimony from colleagues who worked with Schultz as to their own understanding of Egyptian law "was relevant both to explain the practice of the industry in which this prosecution arose and to establish what someone with [the defendant's] extended background in the industry probably would know." *United States v. Leo*, 941 F.2d 181, 197 (3d Cir.1991).

"Evidence need not be conclusive in order to be relevant." *Contemporary Mission v. Famous Music Corp.*, 557 F.2d 918, 927 (2d Cir.1977). "Nonconclusive evidence should still be admitted if it makes a proposition more probable than not; factors which make evidence less than conclusive affect only weight, not admissibility." *S.E.C. v. Singer*, 786 F.Supp. 1158, 1166 (S.D.N.Y.1992). Schultz's defense at trial was that he was unaware of the existence of Law 117. Evidence that those with whom Schultz dealt in the antiquities profession knew of Law 117, and particularly that Schultz's own employee knew of the Law, goes directly to the plausibility of Schultz's defense. "Determinations of relevance are entrusted to the sound discretion of the trial judge." *United States v. Quiroz*, 13 F.3d 505, 514 (2d Cir.1993). Here, we see no abuse of that discretion.

CONCLUSION

We conclude that the NSPA applies to property that is stolen from a foreign government, where that government asserts actual ownership of the property pursuant to a valid patrimony law. We find the remainder of Schultz's claims to be without merit. Accordingly, the judgment of the district court is hereby affirmed.

NOTES:

NOTE 1: A "bran tub" is a British term for a sort of "grab bag" selection of items.

NOTE 2: Rule 26.1 reads, in pertinent part, as follows: "Issues of foreign law are questions of law, but in deciding such issues a court may consider any relevant material or source—including testimony—without regard to the Federal Rules of Evidence." Fed.R.Crim.P. 26.1 (2003). The Advisory Committee Note to this Rule specifically acknowledges that the Rule may be applicable where "[t]he content of foreign law may ... be relevant in proceedings arising under 18 U.S.C. §§ 1201, 2312 to 2317." Fed.R.Crim.P. 26.1 advisory committee's note.

NOTE 3: *Benson* involved a prosecution under a different section of the NSPA, 18 U.S.C. § 2314, which prohibits the transport of stolen property, as opposed to the receipt of stolen property, which is prohibited by § 2315. Our precedent interpreting § 2314 is persuasive in considering § 2315, as the two sections merely address different aspects of the same type of criminal behavior, namely dealing in stolen property, and both are part of the same legislative scheme.

NOTE 4: The *McClain* Court reversed the convictions on other grounds. See id. at 1003.

NOTE 5: We also cited to *McClain*, without discussion, in *United States v. Bennett*, 665 F.2d 16, 22 (2d Cir.1981).

NOTE 6: Law 117 does provide an exception for antiquities "whose ownership or possession was already established at the time th[e] law came into effect." Schultz argues that this provision renders Law 117 ambiguous, because it suggests that the Egyptian government does not truly intend to own all antiquities; we cannot agree. Schultz's expert, Professor Abou El Fadl, testified that Egypt has a constitutional provision which, like the United States Constitution, prohibits the taking of private property by the government without compensation. Providing an exception to the general rule of government ownership for those who already had legal possession of antiquities prior to the adoption of Law 117 avoids the problem of having to pay compensation to those private owners. Viewed in this light, the exception actually supports the government's position that

Law 117 represents an effort to obtain true ownership and actual possession of all antiquities; if Law 117 were merely an export law, there would be no need to exempt existing owners, as their property rights would not be affected as long as they made no attempt to export their antiquities.

NOTE 7: *Steinhardt* involved the application of 18 U.S.C. § 545. As we explained:

> Section 545 prohibits the importation of merchandise into the United States "contrary to law" and states that material imported in such a manner "shall be forfeited." 18 U.S.C. § 545. The government claims that the importation of [the Italian antiquity] was illegal because it violated 18 U.S.C. § 542, which prohibits the making of false statements in the course of importing merchandise into the United States.

Steinhardt, 184 F.3d at 134-35 (internal footnote omitted).

NOTE 8: The dangers inherent in a court's reaching out to decide issues not essential to the outcome of the case before it were perhaps most colorfully described by the 19th century English jurist Lord Justice Bowen, who has been quoted by our Supreme Court as saying:

> I am extremely reluctant to decide anything except what is necessary for the special case, because I believe by long experience that judgments come with far more weight and gravity when they come upon points which the Judges are bound to decide, and I believe that obiter dicta, like the proverbial chickens of destiny, come home to roost sooner or later in a very uncomfortable way to the Judges who have uttered them, and are a great source of embarrassment in future cases.

Darr v. Burford, 339 U.S. 200, 214, 70 S.Ct. 587, 94 L.Ed. 761 (1950), overruled in part on other grounds by *Fay v. Noia*, 372 U.S. 391, 83 S.Ct. 822, 9 L.Ed.2d 837 (1963).

NOTE 9: Schultz notes that Senator Moynihan stated, after the adoption of the CPIA, that part of the compromise reached in passing that law included an agreement to later amend the NSPA to overrule *McClain*. See 131 Cong. Rec. S2598-03 (Mar. 6, 1985). Senator Moynihan introduced legislation on two occasions which would have done just that; however, neither bill passed. Accordingly, although it may have been Senator Moynihan's belief that the Congress intended to overrule *McClain* in separate legislation after the adoption of the CPIA, that never actually happened. We note that this history further supports our holding that the CPIA itself did nothing to overrule *McClain* or alter the effect of the NSPA with regard to foreign antiquities.

NOTE 10: Schultz also argues that because a thing can only be "stolen" if it is already owned, then the term "ownership" is implied in the NSPA (although that word never appears anywhere in the text of the NSPA), and accordingly, we must determine the common law meaning of "ownership." We decline to accept this invitation to delve into the meaning of a term that is not even present in an unambiguous statute.

NOTE 11: This argument is referred to by the parties as the "mistake of American law defense." Schultz was permitted to present a "mistake of Egyptian law defense" to the jury.

NOTE 12: The jury heard substantial evidence indicating that Schultz was actually aware that the NSPA had been applied to objects stolen in violation of a patrimony law. Specifically, it appears that Schultz was aware of the *McClain* decision.

In 1994, Schultz was contacted by the Turkish government. The Turkish government requested that Schultz detail the provenance of several items in his gallery that the Turkish authorities believed to be of Turkish origin. In this correspondence, the Turkish government noted that all antiquities found in Turkey are the property of the Turkish government under a patrimony law. Schultz, acting through counsel, refused to cooperate with Turkey in this inquiry, claimed that Schultz had no knowledge that any Turkish artifacts in his possession were stolen, and referred to the *McClain* case.

Schultz concedes in his appellate brief that the *McClain* decision was "well publicized." Schultz was an owner of a gallery dealing in antiquities, and was once the president of the National Association of Dealers in Ancient, Oriental and Primitive Art, suggesting that he would be aware of all significant developments in the field.

Accordingly, even if Schultz had been permitted to present this defense, it is unlikely that the jury would have credited it.

NOTE 13: Even if the instruction were plain error, it is not at all clear that Schultz could meet his weighty burden of establishing that the error affected the outcome of the trial, in light of the sufficient evidence introduced to permit a rational jury to infer that Schultz had actual knowledge of Law 117. Furthermore, permitting Schultz's conviction to stand would not seriously affect the fairness or integrity of judicial proceedings.

NOTE 14: Schultz also relies on *Cheek* and *Liparota*, contending that because the Supreme Court never suggested that it would have been possible for the government to call witnesses to testify to their own knowledge of the facts at issue, such testimony is not permissible. This argument is without merit.

STUDY QUESTIONS

- What illegal acts were alleged in *Schultz*? How did the court apply the NSPA in this case?
- What defenses did *Schultz* assert and how did the court rule?
- The court in *Schultz* reviews several other important cultural property cases including *McClain, Holinshead*, and *Steinhart*. Compare and contract these cases. What was the underlying basis for determining the property was "stolen" for the purposes of the NSPA in each of these cases? What other grounds for seizure under the NSPA might there be?

CHAPTER 6: MUSEUM FUNDING

In this final chapter, we address some of the many issues related to museum funding. We explore some of the laws and ethical issues regarding charitable donations, gifts, fundraising registration and disclosure requirements, and endowments. We also consider legal and ethical issues surrounding government funding for the arts, including controversial exhibits. And we discuss the role of affiliates and friends' groups, and museum lobbying and advocacy activities.

SOURCES OF FUNDING FOR MUSEUMS

American funding for the arts is a complex and evolving system of entrepreneurial incentives, philanthropic activities, and government support. The three broad categories of U.S. arts funding are: direct arts appropriations (from government entities such as the National Endowment for the Arts, and from regional, state, and local art agencies; other public subsidies (including direct and indirect support from a variety of governmental agencies and particular legislation); and private philanthropy (including donations from individuals, corporations, and foundations).

Arts organizations, including museums, receive financial support from a variety of sources: grants and donations, earned income, and endowment income. In its 2012 survey "How the United States Funds the Arts" the National Endowment for the Arts (NEA) reported that contributed income (private and public grants and donations) made up 44.9% of funding for the arts. Of this amount, the vast majority, 38.2%, consisted of grants and donations made by private individuals, corporations, and foundations. Public funding for the arts made up a modest 6.7% of this amount. Earned income—income from admissions fees, ticket sales and the like—made up 40.7% of funding for the arts. Income from endowments provided 14.4% of funding for the arts. As the NEA report demonstrates, private philanthropy is by far the largest source of contributed financial support for the arts in the United States.

For museums in particular, the four main categories of funding are government grants, private donations, earned revenue, and investment (endowment) income. Government support comes from federal, state, and local government agencies. According to a 2008 study by the Institute of Museum and Library Services (IMLS), "As a proportion of total revenue, government support to U.S. museums ranged between 7% and 33% by museum type. However, when government administered museums are removed from the analysis, the highest proportion of public support drops to 24%. A great deal of variation lies beneath this simple estimate. Because museums of different types have widely varied operating budgets, equivalent proportions represent radically different public dollar investments." [NOTE 1]

As with the arts in general, museums receive the largest share of their funding from private donors and corporate sponsors. Much of this funding is tied to a specific exhibit or program, often in connection with an educational purpose. Unlike the arts in general, earned income forms only a small part of museum income—5% according to the American Alliance of Museums (AAM). Admission fees (mostly from special exhibits and performances), income from museum shops and parking lots, and rental fees make up most of this portion of museum revenue. The final category is endowment income: on par with the arts in general, American museums generate on average about 12% of their revenue from endowment income. [NOTE 2]

Most U.S. museums are organized as nonprofit charitable organizations. As such they are eligible for designation as tax-exempt entities under Section 501 of the Internal Revenue Code—most commonly under Section 501(c)(3). Hence museums are often referred to as "501(c)(3) tax exempt organizations." Generally speaking, a tax-exempt entity does not have to pay tax on revenue it receives in the course of pursuing its mission, but it may be obligated to pay Unrelated Business Income Tax—or "UBIT"—on income generated from activities which are not directly related to its mission. State law may also exempt certain nonprofits, including museums, from state sales taxes and local property taxes.

CHARITABLE DONATIONS

Gifts of property, including pledges and promised gifts, were addressed in chapter 5. Gifts of money may raise some of the same issues. The charitable donation must be made voluntarily and without consideration. There must be an intent to make the gift (referred to as "donative intent"). There must be delivery and acceptance. There cannot be any *quid quo pro* (this for that) in exchange for the gift. Just as with promised gifts, pledges of financial support must be binding to be enforceable. This can be done by tying the pledge to an act in reliance on the pledge made by the museum.

Sometimes a donor wants to place restrictions on a monetary gift. In other cases, the museum offers to put restrictions on the use of the charitable donation. It is not unusual that the gift is made for a specific purpose, as part of a capital campaign for example, or to establish an endowment. (Endowments will be discussed further below). Although the museum will want to exercise caution in accepting restrictions on charitable donations, the issues they raise are usually not as problematic as restrictions placed on gifts of tangible property. Complying with restrictions placed on charitable donations may require expert legal counsel and at times may result in litigation with competing beneficiaries or require going to court to either alter or eliminate the restriction. (See chapter 5 for a discussion of cy pres and equitable deviation.)

Sometimes a donor will designate a cash donation to a museum in their will. These bequests can also raise issues that are similar to those involving object bequests. The museum may have to decide whether it is willing to accept restrictions included in a bequest.

Although often a donor will discuss designating a charity such as a museum in their will with the organization as part of estate planning, it is not unusual for a museum to learn that it is a beneficiary of a charitable bequest only after the donor dies. The *Portland Museum of Art* case included in the Cases and Other Readings below, involved an unusual will contest between a museum and the decedent's housekeeper. The museum, which would have been the residuary beneficiary under a prior will, alleged that the donor's housekeeper exerted undue influence and manipulated the decedent into changing her will to make the housekeeper the residuary beneficiary.

Some charitable donations are made in exchange for certain benefits offered by the museum. Enticements may be as nominal as a coffee mug or a discount in the museum shop. But they may also include potentially valuable concessions such as naming rights to a new gallery or museum building. Such agreements should be carefully negotiated and documented. Among the essential terms of a naming rights agreement, for example, is the museum's right to terminate the agreement in the event the person named becomes associated with improper or nefarious conduct which could harm the museum's reputation. Careful consideration of all aspects of the transaction, and anticipation of potential issues which may arise, sometimes at a much later date, is essential to a well-drafted gift agreement.

Like object gifts, financial donations to tax exempt nonprofit organizations may be deductible under federal tax laws. The charitable donation tax deduction has historically provided an incentive to make private donations to charities, including museums, but recent changes in the tax laws have reduced those incentives for many taxpayers. The deduction is now only available to taxpayers who itemize deductions on their tax returns. Since the standard deduction has been doubled under the new tax law enacted in 2017, the number of taxpayers who would benefit from itemizing their taxes has been substantially reduced. It is likely that some donors will apply strategies such as lumping together charitable donations or making larger donations in a tax year when they itemize and forego donations in other tax years when they use the standard deduction. Donor advised funds (DAFs), which allow for a large tax deduction for contributions to a charitable fund managed by a private foundation, which subsequently makes non-deductible donations to charitable organizations in consultation with the fund owner (the "donor-advisor"), may become even more attractive for some taxpayers. It remains to be seen how these changes to the tax code will impact charitable donations, particularly for museums. Since tax laws are constantly changing, it is important to develop good relationships with attorneys and accountants well-versed in nonprofit tax issues.

For those who do still itemize, there are special rules regarding the deductibility of certain contributions, including museum memberships, tickets for galas and special events, corporate sponsorships, and the like. If premiums and benefits are received in exchange for the donation, there must be "no substantial benefit" to the donor/taxpayer. Certain nominal benefits—think coffee cups, for example—that fall below a certain value threshold do not reduce the amount of the donation that can be deducted for tax purposes. Other benefits that are deemed "unsubstantial" include free admission, parking, museum store discounts, admission to member events, newsletters, and the like. The IRS provides guidance on what may be considered a gift for tax purposes and the extent to which the gift may be deductible for tax purposes.[NOTE 3] As IRS regulations change frequently, they should be reviewed regularly to ensure compliance.

Since the deductibility of a cash donation is primarily an issue for the donor and the donor's accountant, the museum's role is limited. For *quid pro quo* donations—those which are partly a contribution and partly payment for goods or services (such as food and drink at a gala) over a certain *de minimis* amount (in 2018 it was $75), the museum is obligated to send the donor a letter (sometimes referred to as a "substantiation letter") acknowledging the donation and stating the value of any substantial benefit received in connection with the donation. The donor will keep this letter with his tax records. Donors must retain substantiation letters from the charity for any contribution over $250 that the donor claims on its tax returns. For this reason, charities including museums routinely send out acknowledgement letters for contributions over this amount.

A museum's fundraising efforts may be subject to federal and state law. Federal regulation of fundraising is accomplished principally through the federal tax code and enforced by the Internal Revenue Service (IRS). Museums and other nonprofits that fail to comply with federal fundraising laws risk losing their tax-exempt status. Excessive payments to for-profit professional fundraisers can be a red flag. Although not involving a museum, the United Cancer Council case included in the readings below involved IRS scrutiny of an agreement between a charitable organization and a for-profit company which provided fundraising services. The IRS questioned the terms of the agreement, which favored the for-profit company, and raised concerns about whether the nonprofit board had conferred a "private benefit" to the for-profit company in violation of the nonprofit boards' fiduciary duties. (Recall the discussion of museum board fiduciary duties in chapter 1.) The charitable organization appealed the IRS decision to revoke the charities federal tax-exempt status.

Most states also regulate charitable fundraising through state charitable solicitations laws. There is no uniform law—each state regulates charities that operate within their state differently—which can make compliance difficult. State laws may impose registration, disclosure, and reporting requirements on charities and fundraisers. An increasing number of states require out-of-state ("foreign") charities engaged in fundraising in a state to register with the state's charities oversight board. For museums engaged in fundraising in multiple states or nationwide, compliance can be a challenge.

Internet fundraising has become commonplace. To address the problem of compliance, voluntary guidelines for internet fundraising, known as the Charleston Principles, have been established. The Charleston Principles mandate that charities must register in the state where they are physically located, in any state where they specifically target donors, in any state where they received repeated, ongoing, and substantial donations, and in any state where the organization's non-internet activities require registration. Mass email solicitations—like bulk mailing letters and mass facsimiles—may trigger reporting requirements.

NOTES:

NOTE 1: IMLS, "Exhibiting Public Value: Government Funding for Museums in the United States" (December 2008).

NOTE 2: See Ford Bell, "How are Museums Supported Financially in the United States?" Embassy of the United States of America (2012).

NOTE 3: See IRS Publication 1771, *Charitable Gifts: Substantiation and Disclosure Requirements.*

CASES AND OTHER READINGS

Reading Note: The case reprinted below involved a contested will. In a somewhat unusual move, the museum, which would have been the residuary beneficiary under a prior will, sued the housekeeper of the decedent, who received the residuary estate under the terms of a subsequent will that was executed under suspicious circumstances. The museum alleged that the housekeeper interfered with the museum's inheritance and asserted several related claims.

PORTLAND MUSEUM OF ART V. ANNEMARIE GERMAIN

CV-19-02 (ME Superior Ct. 2018)

ORDER ON DEFENDANT'S MOTION FOR SUMMARY JUDGMENT

Before the Court is Defendant Annemarie Germain's motion for summary judgment. Plaintiff Portland Museum of Art (the "PMA") has opposed this motion, and it is in order for decision. For the following reasons, the motion is denied.

1. BACKGROUND

The following facts are drawn from the parties' statements of material facts and are not in dispute except where otherwise indicated.

A. The Relationship Between Ms. Germain and Mrs. Potter

Newell Potter died in 2004, leaving all of his assets to his wife, Mrs. Eleanor Potter. (PL's S.M.F. 108.) Before he died, he asked Ms. Germain to "watch out for his wife and make sure nobody takes advantage of her." (*Id.*) After Mr. Potter's death, Ms. Germain would visit Mrs. Potter on the weekends and would also see her during the week while they were working together at Warren Furniture in Westbrook. (Def.'s S.M.F. 1.) Mrs. Potter broke her leg in March 2012. (Def.'s S.M.F. 2.) Ms. Germain stayed with Mrs. Potter while she was recuperating from her leg injury but maintained a home in Biddeford Pool. (Def.'s S.M.F. p. 3.) Ms. Germain teased Mrs. Potter one day by saying, "I have to go home" and "you'd probably love it if l was here 24/7," and Mrs. Potter answered, "Oh, will you?" (Def.'s S.M.F. p. 4; Pl.'s Resp. to Def.'s S.M.F. p, 4.) Ms. Germain moved in with Mrs. Potter in March 2012 at Mrs. Potter's request. (Def.'s S.M.F. p, 5.)

On occasion, Mrs. Potter asked Ms. Germain to proofread checks, or to write out a check for Mrs. Potter to sign. (Def.'s S.M.F. p. 10.) The only instances in which Ms. Germain wrote out the amount of the check were at Mrs. Potter's specific direction. (*Id.* p. 11.) Mrs. Potter never pre signed blank checks for Ms. Germain to complete, nor did she sign checks before the amount was written in. (*Id.* p. 12.) According to Ms. Germain, Mrs. Potter would write her a check "just because she likes the shirt you had on that day or the high heels you had on." (Pl.'s S.M.F. p. 126.)

After Ms. Germain was added to Mrs. Potter's TD Bank checking account in June of 2014, almost $100,000 was deposited into the account, which had never had checks issued out of it before. (*Id.* p. 127.) Ms. Germain also began receiving funds from this checking account. (*Id.*) In December 2014, Ms. Germain was added as a co-owner to all of Mrs. Potter's Bangor Savings Bank certificate of deposit accounts. (*Id.* p. 128.) By the time Mrs. Potter died, all of her funds belonged to Ms. Germain through joint accounts. (*Id.* p. 129.)

After she started working for Mrs. Potter, friends noticed paintings, jewelry, and other valuables in Ms. Germain's Biddeford Pool home. (*Id.* p. 130.) Ms. Germain also began driving a gold Cadillac that Mrs. Potter purchased for her. (*Id.* p. 131.) The next year, Mrs. Potter bought Ms. Germain a Jeep Wrangler, which Mrs. Potter had to use a stool to get into. (*Id.*) In December 2014, Mrs. Potter bought Ms. Germain a second Cadillac for her birthday. (*Id.*) Although Ms. Germain claims Mrs. Potter gifted her "thousands" of pieces of jewelry, Ms. Germain told her sister that she also found hidden jewelry in the house and kept it. (*Id* p, 132.)[NOTE 1] Mrs. Potter also funded Ms. Germain's extensive online shopping. (*Id* p. 133.) Between January 2011 and March 2012, Mrs. Potter charged less than $1,500 to her credit card. (*Id* p. 134.) In 2013, Mrs. Potter charged $29,692.96 to her credit card, and she charged $39,046.00 in 2014. (*Id* p. 135.)

Although Mrs. Potter's attorneys thought Mrs. Potter was paying Ms. Germain $5,000 per month, Ms. Germain received $111,500 from Mrs. Potter's Bangor Savings Bank checking account in 2014 alone. (*Id.* p. 136.) Darrell Perry, a contractor who was hired to make improvements to Mrs. Potter's home "for the benefit of Annemarie" which included adding a sunroom and renovating the kitchen, and who witnessed Mrs. Potter's October 2, 2014 Will, was paid $17,450.00 in 2013 and $46,040.56 in 2014. (*Id* p. 138.)

When Mrs. Potter visited with her step-grandchildren, Ms. Germain would not leave Mrs. Potter alone with them, and Mrs. Potter did not engage in their conversations and sounded "scared and nervous" when she spoke. (*Id.* at 115.) When Mrs. Potter was hospitalized in 2014, her family was not informed. (*Id.* p. 116.) [NOTE 2]

B. The March 2014 Will

In the mid-1990s, Mrs. Potter and her husband created reciprocal Wills and Trusts that would provide for Mr. Potter's grandchildren. (Pl.'s S.M.F. 139.) Mrs. Potter later executed another Will on November 28, 2005. (Def.'s S.M.F. 17.) The only bequest the 2005 Will made to the PMA was a gold necklace, and even then, only in the event Barbara Greenburg Harrison was not alive at the time of Mrs. Potter's death. (*Id.* p.19.) The next Will Mrs. Potter executed is dated December 11, 2007 and contained the same bequest to the PMA as the 2005 Will. (*Id.* pp. 20-21.)

Mrs. Potter first spoke with Attorney Kelley Young about the possibility of creating a trust for her sister, Barbara Coleman, in 2009. (Pl.'s S.M.F. 140.) [NOTE 3] The idea of revising her estate plan to include a trust was revisited with Attorney Young and Attorney Matthew Goldfarb, Mrs. Potter's longtime lawyer and friend of 45 years, in the spring of 2013. (*Id.* 141.) Ultimately, the only aspect to be determined was what to do about Mrs. Potter's residuary estate. (*Id.* 143.) After considering the matter for over two years, Mrs. Potter decided to name the PMA as the residuary beneficiary of her estate. (*See id.* 145; Def.'s Reply S.M.F. 145.)

Consistent with Mrs. Potter's expressed wishes, Attorney Young prepared a pour-over will that devised her estate to a trust that would be administered primarily for the benefit of Mrs. Coleman. (Pl.'s S.M.F. 149.) According to her trust agreement, upon her death, her trustees—Attorney Goldfarb and Hugh Judge of R.M. Davis, Inc.—were to retain $500,000 for Mrs. Coleman's benefit, distribute her home to Ms. Germain, make specific gifts to Mrs. Potter's step daughter, step-grandchildren and other charitable interests, and then distribute the balance to the PMA free and clear of trust, amounting to approximately $1.2 to $2 million, depending on how much was left after Mrs. Potter's passing. (*Id.* p. 150.) The PMA was also the remainder beneficiary of the funds set aside for Mrs. Coleman. (*Id.* p. 151.) Attorney Goldfarb did not believe the desired distribution of Mrs. Potter's home to Ms. Germain was the result of undue influence. (Def.'s S.M.F. 34.)

Ms. Germain was not present at the initial meeting to discuss changing the 2007 Will on September 18, 2013, and she did not bring Mrs. Potter to that meeting. (*Id* p.33.) Prior to execution, Attorneys Goldfarb and Young reviewed Mrs. Potter's estate plan alone with her paragraph-by-paragraph, and Attorney Young made Mrs. Potter aware of everything that was in her trust. (Pl.'s S.M.F. 153.) The attorneys then invited Ms. Germain into the room and reviewed the basic sketch of the estate plan with her. (*Id.* p. 155.) Although Mrs. Potter's trust specifically directed her trustees to deed her home to Ms. Germain, Ms. Germain complained "loudly and vociferously about the fact that her name wasn't mentioned in the will" and "that she was not happy with the will and trust." (*Id.* at 156.0[NOTE 4] Attorney Young then asked Ms. Germain to leave the room while Mrs. Potter executed the documents. (*Id.* p. 157.)

Mrs. Potter executed the Will and Trust on March 18, 2014. (Def.'s S.M.F. 23.) The process of changing the Will took two-and-a-half years. (*Id.* at 29; Pl.'s Resp. to Def.'s S.M.F. 29.) Attorney Young mailed Mrs. Potter a copy of her estate planning documents on April 25, 2014. (Pl.'s S.M.F. 161.)

On June 5, 2014, Mrs. Potter called Attorney Young out of the blue, saying she urgently wanted to make changes to her estate plan. (Pl.'s S.M.F. 164.) Prior to that date, Mrs. Potter had never expressed any concerns about her estate plan to Attorneys Young and Goldfarb. (*Id.* p. 165.) Troubled and suspicious of Ms. Germain, Attorney Young suggested a face-to-face meeting alone with Mrs. Potter, which she refused. (*Id.* p. 166.) A few days later, Mrs. Potter called again and insisted that Attorney Young "tear up her will." (*Id.* p. 167.) Attorney Young does not believe that Mrs. Potter's instruction to destroy her March 2014 Will and Trust reflected her personal desire or decision, but was the result of an idea "that Matt Goldfarb and Hugh Judge were stealing Eleanor's property… that Anna had planted." (*Id.* p. 169.) Concerned that Mrs. Potter was being influenced by Ms. Germain, Attorney Young responded that he would not tear up the will, but would deliver the documents to her or send them to her new lawyer. (*Id.* p. 170.) Mrs. Potter refused to reveal the identity of her new lawyer, would not allow Attorney Young to send her prior estate planning documents to her new lawyer, which was "unusual," and instead told Attorney Young to bring her the documents. (*Id.* p. 171.)

When Attorney Young hand-delivered Mrs. Potter's estate planning documents on June 10, 2014, Ms. Germain opened the door and, in front of Mrs. Potter, started "berat[ing]" Attorney Young. (*Id.* p. 172.) Ms. Germain called Attorney Young "a thief," and told him to "admit to Eleanor" that Attorneys Young and Goldfarb and Hugh Judge "were stealing from Eleanor" by placing her assets into a trust they would administer. (*Id.* p. 173.) Mrs. Potter asked Attorney Young, "Why are you stealing from me?" (*Id.* p. 174.) When Attorney Young tried to explain that this was not the case, Ms. Germain interjected and called Attorney Young a "pansy ass," claiming he forced Mrs. Potter "to sign something she didn't want when [they] asked Anna to leave the room." (*Id.* p. 175.) Ms. Germain again complained that "her name was not in the will" and that the house was not going to her, despite the clear language of Mrs. Potter's trust instrument. (*Id.* p. 176.) When Attorney Young tried to show Ms. Germain that she was in fact receiving the house, Ms. Germain threatened to put Attorney Young's name "all over the Old Port as a thief." (*Id.* at 177.) [NOTE 5]

The next day, Mrs. Potter fired Attorney Goldfarb. (*Id.*p. 178.) When Attorney Goldfarb called her to seek an explanation, Mrs. Potter refused to talk to him. (*Id.* p. 179.)

C. The October 2014 Will

On June 3, 2014, Ms. Germain and Mrs. Potter met with Attorney Richard LeBlanc. (Def.'s S.M.F. 50.) During the meeting, it was discussed that Donald Coleman's IRA of over $250,000 would pass directly to Mrs. Coleman, and that there seemed to be a number of joint accounts that now belonged to Mrs. Coleman alone, as well as a residence owned as tenants-in-common so that Mr. Coleman's 50% interest would pass to a trust to Mrs. Coleman. (*Id.* p. 51.)

Attorney Nelson Toner began representing Mrs. Potter during the summer of 2014. (*Id.* p. 59; Pl.'s Resp. to Def.'s S.M.F. 59.) Attorney Toner first learned of Mrs. Potter through Attorney LeBlanc, who had contacted Attorney Toner to ask for help with Mrs. Coleman. (Def.'s S.M.F. 61.) When introducing Attorney Toner to the situation with Mrs. Potter, Attorney LeBlanc told Attorney Toner that Ms. Germain was a caregiver for Mrs. Potter and lived with her at the home. (*Id.* p. 91.)

Attorney Young expected to hear from Mrs. Potter's new attorney to request a copy of his file and to discuss Mrs. Potter's prior estate plan, as is typical, but he was "baffled" when this "call never came." (Pl.'s S.M.F. 182.) Shortly after Mrs. Potter had retained Attorney Toner, Attorney LeBlanc called him to express his own concerns about Mrs. Potter's relationship with Ms. Germain, telling Attorney Toner that he had witnessed Mrs. Potter being "coach[ed]" by Ms. Germain. (*Id.*p. 183.)

Attorney Toner's first meeting with Mrs. Potter was sometime between July 9 and July 14, 2014. (Def.'s S.M.F. 64.) When Attorney Toner arrived for the meeting, he was greeted by Ms. Germain. (*Id.* at 67.) During the beginning of the meeting, Attorney Toner, Ms. Germain, and Mrs. Potter were all sitting at the dining room table. (*Id.* p. 68.) According to Attorney Toner's billing records, the initial meeting lasted 30 minutes. (*Id.* p. 71.) Attorney Toner met three times with Mrs. Potter for a combined total of little more than an hour. (Pl.'s S.M.F. 185.)

Mrs. Potter wanted to simplify her estate plan and write a new estate plan. (Def.' s S.M.F. 72.) Attorney Toner did not speak to Attorneys Goldfarb or Young about the prior estate plan because he felt that he could help execute her wishes without knowing why she was upset with Attorneys Goldfarb and Young. (*Id.* p. 79.) Attorney Toner's notes from the initial meeting read "Assets to Annemarie Germain" under the heading "Ellie's Will Discussion." (*Id.* p. 83.) During the meeting, Mrs. Potter also specifically discussed having Ms. Germain serve as her personal representative. (*Id.* p. __.) Attorney Toner was told that Mrs. Potter was unhappy with her estate plan because it reflected "someone else's goals and objectives" and did not leave all of her assets to Ms. Germain, but he did not learn any specifics about her prior estate plan, its beneficiaries, or the true extent of her assets. (Pl.'s S.M.F. 187.) He never saw or asked for a copy of the March 2014 Will and Trust, and he never thought to investigate whether Mrs. Potter had been given any misinformation about the Will and Trust; he simply "left it alone." (*Id.* p. 188.)

Mrs. Potter lived in the neighborhood where Attorney Toner grew up, but Attorney Toner did not know Mrs. Potter personally. (Def.'s S.M.F., 60.) Mrs. Potter was able to recall Attorney Toner's family living on Chenery Street, even though about 40 years had elapsed since they had lived on Chenery Street. (*Id.* at 90.)

Attorney Toner drafted a will in August 2014 that left Mrs. Potter's entire estate to Ms. Germain. (Pl.'s S.M.F., 190.) He also drafted documents naming Ms. Germain as Mrs. Potter's financial power of attorney. (*Id.* p. 191.) On September 2, 2014, Ms. Germain called Attorney Toner to request instructions on how Mrs. Potter could finalize her will. (*Id.* p. 198.) Attorney Toner spoke with Ms. Germain three times between September 2 and September 9, 2014 concerning Mrs. Potter's will. (*Id* p. 199.)

Mrs. Potter returned home from a stay in the hospital on September 24, 2014. (*Id.,* 202.) The will prepared by Attorney Toner was executed on October 2, 2014. (Def.'s S.M.F,. 100.) Mrs. Potter died on March 21, 2015 at the age of 90. (Pl.'s S.M.F., 211.) The October 2014 Will was filed with the Cumberland County Probate Court on April 20, 2015. (Def.'s S.M.F. at 101.) Mrs. Coleman died on August 6, 2018, and Ms. Germain is also the primary beneficiary of Mrs. Coleman's estate plan, which Attorney Toner drafted. (Pl.'s S.M.F. p. 215.)

The PMA filed its Complaint against Ms. Germain on August 2, 2017. The Complaint contains three counts: tortious interference with expected inheritance, undue influence/constructive trust, and demand for an accounting pursuant to 18-A M.R.S. § 5-916.

2. STANDARD OF REVIEW

Summary judgment is appropriate if, based on the parties' statements of material fact and the cited record, there is no genuine issue of material fact and the moving party is entitled to judgment as a matter of law. M.R. Civ. P. [Maine Rules of Civil Procedure] 56(c); *Dyer,* 2008 ME 106, at 14, 951 A.2d 821. "A material fact is one that can affect the outcome of the case. A genuine issue of material fact exists when the factfinder must choose between competing versions of the truth." *Dyer,* 2008 ME 106, at 14, 951 A.2d 821 (internal citation and quotation marks omitted). When deciding a motion for summary judgment, the court reviews the evidence in the light most favorable to the non-moving party. *Id.*

If the moving party's motion for summary judgment is properly supported, the burden then shifts to the non-moving party to respond with specific facts indicating a genuine issue for trial in order to avoid summary judgment. M.R. Civ. P. 56(e). When a defendant moves for summary judgment, the plaintiff must respond with evidence establishing a prima facie case. *Watt v. UniFirst Corp.*, 2009 ME 47, at 21, 969 A.2d 897. The evidence proffered by the plaintiff "need not be persuasive at that stage, but the evidence must be sufficient to allow a factfinder to make a factual determination without speculating." *Estate of Smith v. Cumberland Cnty.*, 2013 ME 13, at 19, 60 A.3d 759. If the plaintiff fails to present sufficient evidence, then the defendant is entitled to a summary judgment. *Watt*, 2009 ME 47, at 21, 969 A.2d 897.

3. DISCUSSION

In this fact-intensive case, despite the existence of some facts upon which the parties agree, the parties' motion papers present two very different accounts of the relationship between Mrs. Potter and Ms. Germain and the circumstances surrounding the making of Mrs. Potter's will. As a summary of the undisputed facts, it is clear that until the fall of 2014, multiple versions of Mrs. Potter's will included bequests to members of her family and to charities including the PMA, as well as a bequest to Ms. Germain of her house, yet the version of Mrs. Potter's will in existence at the time of her death left her entire estate to Ms. Germain. How and why Mrs. Potter decided to change her will in this manner is vigorously disputed. There are a number of disputed facts not recounted above pertaining to the relationship between Ms. Germain and Mrs. Potter; Mrs. Potter's relationship with, and Ms. Germain's treatment of, Mrs. Potter's step-grandchildren; Mrs. Potter's physical and mental state during the last year of her life; and the circumstances surrounding the signing of the October 2014 will.

A. Ms. Germain's evidentiary objections

As a threshold matter, Ms. Germain has objected to the admissibility of much of the PMA's summary judgment evidence. The Court agrees with Ms. Germain on this matter in some respects. For instance, the PMA has not properly authenticated Mrs. Potter's medical records. *See* M.R. Evid. 803(6), 901. Attorney Frawley's affidavit is not sufficient to authenticate these documents. *Cf Bank of Am., N A. v. Greenleaf*, 2014 ME 89, at 3, 34, 96 A.3d 700 (affirming order of sanctions for failure to comply with M.R. Civ. P. 56(e) when attorney inappropriately sought to create a foundation for admissibility of business records by submitting an affidavit regarding his own knowledge of the bank's recordkeeping practices and asserting facts about which he lacked personal knowledge). The Court agrees with Ms. Germain that the medical records, as presented by the PMA, are not admissible at this stage.

Ms. Germain further argues that the affidavit of Judith Montgomery should be excluded because the PMA's interrogatory responses only identified Ms. Montgomery as a "witness with knowledge of Defendant's relationship with Mrs. Potter" and did not provide her address or phone number as requested by the interrogatory. Ms. Germain alleges that "[f]rom the content of the [August 21, 2018] affidavit, PMA obviously knew more information than it disclosed at the Rule 26(g) conference" which was held on March 7, 2018 and in which the PMA represented that it had disclosed all responsive information it possessed at the time. Given that, according to her affidavit, Ms. Montgomery's property abuts Mrs. Potter's property, it seems likely the PMA knew Ms. Montgomery's address when responding to Ms. Germain's interrogatories and failed to disclose that address. Even if her address was not known at that time, it was obviously discovered by the PMA sometime between March 7, 2018 and August 21, 2018. While the duty to supplement discovery responses is quite limited in Maine, a party is nonetheless "under a duty seasonably to supplement the response with respect to any question directly addressed to ... the identity and location of persons having knowledge of discoverable matters...." M.R. Civ. P. 26(e)(l). The Court finds the PMA failed to seasonably supplement its discovery response. In doing so, Ms. Germain was prejudiced because she was not able to ascertain Ms. Montgomery's location in order to properly investigate her knowledge of the relationship between Ms. Germain and Mrs. Potter. The Court will exclude Ms. Montgomery's affidavit from its consideration of this motion.

Ms. Germain further argues that the PMA's affidavits are insufficient because the jurats are sworn on knowledge, information and belief. The jurat of Attorney Young, for example, states:

> Before me personally appeared the above-named, D. Kelley Young, who swore to the truth of the facts in the foregoing affidavit of his own knowledge or on information and belief and, to the extent on information and belief, he has reason to believe and does believe them to be true.

(Pl.'s Opp'n to Mot. Summ. J., Ex. 2.) While it is correct that "[a]ffidavits in support of a motion for summary judgment that are solely based upon information and belief are insufficient," such affidavit "may be considered ... if the affidavit otherwise shows that it was made from personal knowledge." *Dineen v. Star Press, Inc.,* 391 A.2d 834, 835 (Me. 1978). Rather than disregard all of the PMA' s affidavits in full, the Court has carefully considered the basis for personal knowledge in each affidavit relied upon in this Order.

While the PMA has failed to properly authenticate some of its evidence and the Court is excluding Judith Montgomery's affidavit, the Court nonetheless finds the PMA has proffered sufficient admissible evidence to create a prima facie case on each count of its Complaint.

B. Count I: Tortious interference with expected inheritance

A claim for tortious interference with expected inheritance requires proof of (1) the existence of an expectancy of inheritance; (2) an intentional interference by a defendant through tortious conduct, such as fraud, duress, or undue influence; (3) a reasonable certainty that the expectancy of inheritance would have been realized but for the defendant's interference; and (4) damage resulting from the interference. *Morrill v. Morrill,* 1998 ME 133, 7, 712 A.2d 1039. Ms. Germain contends the PMA cannot satisfy its burden to prove the second and third elements of this claim.

1. Undue influence

The parties first dispute whether the PMA has produced evidence of intentional interference through undue influence. '"Undue influence is defined as unfair persuasion of a party who is under the domination of the person exercising the persuasion or who by virtue of the relationship between them is justified in assuming that that person will not act in a manner inconsistent with his welfare."' *Cote v. Cote,* 2016 ME 94, at 14, 143 A.3d 117 (quoting *Theriault v. Burnham,* 2010 ME 82, at 6, 2 A.3d 324) (internal alteration omitted).

a. Confidential relationship

"A presumption of undue influence arises 'if the plaintiff shows by a preponderance of the evidence that a confidential relationship existed between the defendant and the decedent.'" *Id.* "'A confidential relationship is one in which an individual placed trust and confidence in the defendant and there was a great disparity of position and influence in the relationship."' *Id.* The PMA argues undue influence may be presumed in this case because Mrs. Potter and Ms. Germain were engaged in a confidential relationship.

The existence of a confidential relationship is a question of fact, *Cote,* 2016 ME 94, at 14, 143 A.3d 117, and a number of disputed facts inform the question in this case. Ms. Germain testified she did "[w]hatever she wanted, whatever she needed, whatever I felt needed to be done" for Mrs. Potter, including sometimes taking her to doctors' appointments and cooking meals, as well as verifying Mrs. Potter filled out checks correctly. (Germain Dep. 37:15-38:6.) Ms. Germain was taking care of Mrs. Potter in the last years of her life, during which time Mrs. Potter repeatedly required hospitalization and was likely physically vulnerable. Ms. Germain insisted that she never helped Mrs. Potter with her finances and that Mrs. Potter "did her own finances." (Germain Dep. 37:23-38:6.) Despite this assertion, there is no dispute that Ms. Germain was added as a co-owner to all of Mrs. Potter's Bangor Savings Bank certificate of deposit accounts, and by the time Mrs. Potter died, all of her funds belonged to Ms. Germain through joint accounts. There is also evidence in the record that Ms. Germain had use of Mrs. Potter's credit cards and contracted for over $60,000 worth of improvements to Mrs. Potter's home. A strong inference can be made based on the evidence presented by the PMA that Ms. Germain made liberal use of her access to Mrs. Potter's credit cards. Regardless of how Ms. Germain defines "doing one's finances," the PMA has presented evidence that Mrs. Potter was not managing her money independently.

The Court also finds it notable that Ms. Germain describes the relationship as: "her and I lived as a mother and a daughter" and testified that when someone erroneously referred to Ms. Germain as Mrs. Potter's daughter, Mrs. Potter "would not correct them.... She would never say that's not my daughter." (Germain Dep. 39:14-15; 150:6-20.) While Ms. Germain and Mrs. Potter were not familial relations, confidential relationships are not confined to familial relationships. However, the Law Court has referred to familial relationships to describe characteristics of confidential relationships as follows:

> That the parties are related by blood or marriage may lead a court to find that a confidential relation exists, where there is evidence as to trusting and where the blood or family relationship is in a close degree so that the imposition of great trust and the letting down of all guards and bars is natural. But mere kinship itself does not establish a confidential relation; often relatives are hostile to each other or deal at arm's length and act independently and so are held not to have been a confidential relation.

Ruebsamen v. Maddocks, 340 A.2d 31, 35 (Me. 1975). Based on Ms. Germain's testimony, an inference could be drawn that she and Mrs. Potter regarded each other as familial relations and consequently, rather than deal with one another at arm's length, their relationship involved "great trust and the letting down of all guards and bars." *Id.* The Court finds a genuine issue of material fact as to whether Ms. Germain and Mrs. Potter shared a confidential relationship.

Assuming the factfinder were to conclude a confidential relationship existed, a presumption of undue influence would be raised, and Defendant would have the burden to come forward with "evidence tending to affirmatively show entire fairness on his part and freedom of the other from undue influence." *Id* at 37. The Court finds there is likewise a genuine issue of material fact as to whether Ms. Germain's dealings with Mrs. Potter were entirely fair and free from undue influence.

b. Evidence of undue influence

The PMA contends that even if Ms. Germain and Mrs. Potter did not have a confidential relationship, the facts support a finding of undue influence. The Court agrees and finds the PMA has proffered sufficient evidence to demonstrate a genuine issue of material fact as to whether Mrs. Potter was unduly influenced to sign the October 2014 Will.

A summary of some of the facts indicating the existence of undue influence follows: Ms. Germain would not leave Mrs. Potter alone with her step-grandchildren, who were beneficiaries of Mrs. Potter's prior wills. Ms. Germain was not initially involved in the decision to change Mrs. Potter's 2007 Will, and Mrs. Potter spent two-and-a-half years working with her attorneys to create a new estate plan. Mrs. Potter signed the March 2014 Will and Trust after reviewing it paragraphby-paragraph with Attorneys Goldfarb and Young, out of the presence of Ms. Germain. When the attorneys reviewed the estate plan with Ms. Germain, she verbally expressed that she was not happy with it. When Attorney

Young hand-delivered the estate planning documents to Mrs. Potter's home, Ms. Germain answered the door, berated Attorney Young in front of Mrs. Potter, and again complained about the contents of the Will. Mrs. Potter was under the impression, almost certainly erroneous, that Attorneys Young and Goldfarb were stealing from her.

Ms. Germain and Mrs. Potter together met with Attorney LeBlanc, who put them in contact with Attorney Toner. Ms. Germain was also present for at least a portion of the first meeting with Attorney Toner. After three brief meetings, Attorney Toner drafted a will leaving Mrs. Potter's entire estate to Ms. Germain and documents appointing Ms. Germain as Mrs. Potter's financial power of attorney. Ms. Germain spoke to Attorney Toner at least three times before Mrs. Potter signed the October 2014 Will. The October 2014 Will was signed during the last few months of Mrs. Potter's life, ten days after she returned home from a stay in the hospital. There is evidence, albeit at least partially disputed by Ms. Germain, that Mrs. Potter signed her final Will when Ms. Germain was present and Attorney Toner was not. (*See* PL's S.M.F. 203-206.) Attorneys Young and LeBlanc at least suspected Ms. Germain was coaching Mrs. Potter.

Ms. Germain insists the PMA cannot prove undue influence because Mrs. Potter's decision to change her will was made independently, and she secured independent counsel to carry out her wishes. At this point, it is not entirely clear how Mrs. Potter came to be represented by Attorney Toner; however, viewing the evidence in the light most favorable to the PMA, there is some evidence that Attorney Toner was not truly independent. For instance, it is suspicious that Attorney Toner also drafted Mrs. Coleman's will, of which Ms. Germain is also the primary beneficiary. Ms. Germain also had multiple conversations with Attorney Toner, some of which appear to have occurred outside of Mrs. Potter's presence. These facts raise an inference that Ms. Germain was instrumental in establishing the relationship between Attorney Toner and Mrs. Potter which ultimately led to the execution of the will leaving Mrs. Potter's entire estate to Ms. Germain. This evidence is not conclusive proof of Attorney Toner's lack of independence, but it supports more than mere speculation. *See Estate of Smith,* 2013 ME 13, at 19, 60 A.3d 759.

Considering the facts recounted above in conjunction with the many disputed facts the parties have alleged surrounding the creation of the October 2014 Will, the Court concludes the PMA has proffered sufficient evidence of undue influence to survive summary judgment.

2. Causation

The causation element of tortious interference requires a plaintiff to show "a reasonable certainty that the expectancy of inheritance would have been realized but for the defendant's interference." *Morrill,* 1998 ME 133, __, 712 A.2d 1039. Viewing the facts in the light most favorable to the PMA, there is ample evidence in the record that Ms. Germain's interference was the "but for" cause of the changes to Mrs. Potter's estate plan which resulted in the PMA's loss of its expected inheritance. Ms. Germain openly expressed her displeasure over the March 2014 will and berated Attorney Young in front of Mrs. Potter. When Attorney Young came to Mrs. Potter's house to deliver her estate planning documents, Mrs. Potter asked him, "Why are you stealing from me?" and a reasonable inference can be drawn that Ms. Germain was the source of this belief. There is also evidence that Ms. Germain may have orchestrated the relationship between Mrs. Potter and Attorney Toner and may have coached Mrs. Potter into changing her will to leave her entire estate to Ms. Germain. This evidence is sufficient for this claim to survive a motion for summary judgment.

What Ms. Germain has offered with this motion is one interpretation of the facts of this case. The PMA, however, has put forth sufficient evidence to support an alternative interpretation which would warrant a finding of tortious interference with expected inheritance. Many disputed facts color each interpretation, and factfinding in this case will depend heavily on a number of credibility determinations. Summary judgment cannot be granted "when the factfinder must choose between competing versions of the truth," *Dyer*, 2008 ME 106,, 14, 951 A.2d 821, and therefore summary judgment must be denied on this count.

C. Count II: Undue influence/constructive trust

Ms. Germain argues that, as with the PMA's claim for tortious interference, it also cannot support its claim for undue influence and constructive trust because it has not proffered evidence of undue influence or other tortious conduct. Ms. Germain notes, further, that this claim must be proven by clear and convincing evidence, and that the heightened standard of proof should be taken into consideration at the summary judgment stage. *See Anderson v. Liberty Lobby, Inc.*, 477 U.S. 242, 254-55 (1986). The PMA counters that, regardless of the standard of proof, it has made a prima facie case for this claim. The Court agrees with the PMA.

Similarly to the undue influence element of tortious interference, in order to support a claim for undue influence and imposition of a constructive trust, a plaintiff must show that "it was highly probable that defendants exerted unfair persuasion on the plaintiff while she was (1) under defendant's domination or (2) justified in assuming that defendants would not act in a manner inconsistent with her welfare by virtue of the relationship between them." *Dolloff v. Dolloff*, 593 A.2d 1044, 1046 (Me. 1991). "[A] party's weakness, infirmity, or advanced age" as well as "family relationships such as parent-child" may be factored into the determination of whether there was undue influence. *Id.* As explained at length above regarding the PMA's claim for tortious interference, the PMA has submitted sufficient evidence of undue influence to generate a genuine issue of material fact to be resolved by a factfinder, even considering the PMA's heightened standard of proof required by this claim.

D. Count III: Accounting under 18-A M.R.S. §5-916

The Court also declines to enter summary judgment on Count III of the Complaint, which demands an accounting of all assets held or formerly held by Mrs. Potter and all financial transactions conducted by Mrs. Potter or by Ms. Germain on Mrs. Potter's behalf since the date Ms. Germain became Mrs. Potter's power of attorney and the date of Mrs. Potter's death.

Ms. Germain argues the Maine Uniform Power of Attorney Act, 18-A M.R.S. 5-901 *et seq.,* does not apply to this case because there is no longer a principal-agent relationship between Mrs. Potter and Ms. Germain due to Mrs. Potter's death. Ms. Germain contends this conclusion is supported by the language of the statute, which provides a petition may be filed in the county " in which either the principal or the agent resides." 18-A M.R.S. § 5-916(a). Specifically, Ms. Germain argues "there was no principal or agent when the petition was filed; Mrs. Potter was deceased, terminating the power of attorney and the principal/agent relationship." (Def.'s Mot. Summ. J. 17.) The PMA counters that the statute does not require the petition to be filed during the life of the principal.

The parties both cite authority from other jurisdictions to support their opposing interpretations of the applicability of the Uniform Power of Attorney Act following the death of the principal. *Compare In re Edward J Burke Estate,* No. 10768- MA, 2016 Del. Ch. LEXIS 121, at *15-17 (Aug. 10, 2016) (finding petition for accounting should have been filed prior to principal's death) *with Smith v. Smith,* No. 45313, 2018 Ida. LEXIS 216, pp. *21-23 (Dec. 18, 2018) (finding statute's plain language does not expressly require petition to be made before principal's death). This Court generally agrees with the Idaho Supreme Court that while some of the statutory language could support the interpretation proposed by Ms. Germain, a time limit should not be read into the statute when the text does not expressly contain one. The Court finds Mrs. Potter's death does not bar the PMA's petition for an accounting pursuant to 18 A.M.R.S. § 5-916.

Ms. Germain also argues summary judgment should be granted on this Count because she never invoked the power of attorney granted by Mrs. Potter and therefore there are no transactions to be reviewed. Ms. Germain has not submitted an affidavit to support this contention, and based on the record before the Court, it is unclear whether this statement is accurate. The Court thus declines to grant summary judgment on this ground as well.

4. CONCLUSION

For the foregoing reasons, Defendant Annemarie Germain's Motion for Summary Judgment is DENIED.

NOTES:

NOTE 1: Defendant admits Plaintiffs Statements of Material Facts No. 132, subject to the objection that the affidavit of Ms. Germain's sister is noncompliant with M.R. Civ. P. 56(e)'s requirement that affidavits be made on personal knowledge and shall show affirmatively that the affiant is competent to testify to the matters stated therein. As discussed more fully below, the Court has considered the extent to which Plaintiffs affidavits appear to be based on personal knowledge.

NOTE 2: Defendant admits Plaintiffs Statements of Material Facts No. 115 and 116, subject to the objection that the affidavits of Mrs. Potter's step-grandchildren are noncompliant with M.R. Civ. P. 56(e)'s. As discussed below, the Court has considered the extent to which Plaintiffs affidavits appear to be based on personal knowledge.

NOTE 3: Defendant qualifies this statement and Statement No. 141 to the extent they are drafted to make it appear as if Mrs. Potter approached the attorneys specifically about creating a trust. It is clear Mrs. Potter engaged Attorneys Young and Goldfarb for the purpose of revising her estate plan, and the issue of creating a trust for her sister was discussed.

NOTE 4: Citing Attorney Goldfarb's deposition testimony, Ms. Germain qualifies this statement by noting: "Attorney Goldfarb went on to testify that he responded 'I am directed to see that you get the house and a generous stipend,' and that 'that was basically it.'" (Def.'s Reply S.M.F. p. 156.)

NOTE 5: Curiously, Defendant admits to the entirety of this confrontation without qualification in her reply statement of material facts, despite denying most of the substance of this interaction during her deposition. (*Compare* Def.'s Reply S.M.F. pp. 172-177 *with* Germain Dep. 209:3-212:23.)

Reading Note: In this appeal of an Internal Revenue Service (IRS) revocation of a charity's tax-exempt status, the court reviews the IRS decision, which was based on the terms of a fundraising services agreement. The agreement was highly favorable to the for-profit fundraiser and, in the IRS's opinion, improperly inured to the benefit of the private company.

UNITED CANCER COUNCIL V. COMMISSIONER OF INTERNAL REVENUE

109 T.C. 326 (1997)

Before POSNER, Chief Judge, and COFFEY and KANNE, Circuit Judges.

The United Cancer Council is a charity that seeks, through affiliated local cancer societies, to encourage preventive and ameliorative approaches to cancer, as distinct from searching for a cure, which has been the emphasis of the older and better-known American Cancer Society, of which UCC is a splinter. The Internal Revenue Service revoked UCC's charitable exemption and the Tax Court upheld the revocation, precipitating this appeal.

So far as relates to this case, a charity, in order to be entitled to the charitable exemption from federal income tax, and to be eligible to receive tax-exempt donations, must be "organized and operated exclusively for [charitable] purposes" and "no part of the net earnings of [the charity may] inure[ ] to the benefit of any private shareholder or individual." 26 U.S.C. §§ 501(c)(3) (exemption); 170(c)(2)(B), (C) (receipt of donations); 26

C.F.R. § 1.501(a)-1(c), 1.501(c)(3)-1(d)(1)(i), (ii). The IRS claims that UCC (which is defunct) was not operated exclusively for charitable purposes, but rather was operated for, or also for, the private benefit of the fundraising company that UCC had hired, Watson & Hughey Company (W & H). The Service also claims that part of the charity's net earnings had inured to the benefit of a private shareholder or individual-W & H again. The Tax Court upheld the Service's second ground for revoking UCC's exemption-inurement-and did not reach the first ground, private benefit. The only issue before us is whether the court clearly erred, *Fund for the Study of Economic Growth & Tax Reform v. IRS*, 161 F.3d 755, 758-59 (D.C.Cir.1998); *Church of Scientology v. Commissioner*, 823 F.2d 1310, 1317 (9th Cir.1987); see also *Walgreen Co. v. Commissioner*, 68 F.3d 1006, 1009-10 (7th Cir.1995); *Williams v. Commissioner*, 1 F.3d 502, 505 (7th Cir.1993), in finding that a part of UCC's net earnings inured to the benefit of a private shareholder or individual.

It is important to understand what the IRS does not contend. It does not contend that any part of UCC's earnings found its way into the pockets of any members of the charity's board; the board members, who were medical professionals, lawyers, judges, and bankers, served without compensation. It does not contend that any members of the board were owners, managers, or employees of W & H, or relatives or even friends of any of W & H's owners, managers, or employees. It does not contend that the fundraiser was involved either directly or indirectly in the creation of UCC, or selected UCC's charitable goals. It concedes that the contract between charity and fundraiser was negotiated at an arm's length basis. But it contends that the contract was so advantageous to W & H and so disadvantageous to UCC that the charity must be deemed to have surrendered the control of its operations and earnings to the noncharitable enterprise that it had hired to raise money for it.

The facts are undisputed. In 1984, UCC was a tiny organization. It had an annual operating budget of only $35,000, and it was on the brink of bankruptcy because several of its larger member societies had defected to its rival, the American Cancer Society. A committee of the board picked W & H, a specialist in raising funds for charities, as the best prospect for raising the funds essential for UCC's survival. Another committee of the board was created to negotiate the contract. Because of UCC's perilous financial condition, the committee wanted W & H to "front" all the expenses of the fundraising campaign, though it would be reimbursed by UCC as soon as the campaign generated sufficient donations to cover those expenses. W & H agreed. But it demanded in return that it be made UCC's exclusive fundraiser during the five-year term of the contract, that it be given co-ownership of the list of prospective donors generated by its fundraising efforts, and that UCC be forbidden, both during the term of the contract and after it expired, to sell or lease the list, although it would be free to use it to solicit repeat donations. There was no restriction on W & H's use of the list. UCC agreed to these terms and the contract went into effect.

Over the five-year term of the contract, W & H mailed 80 million letters soliciting contributions to UCC. Each letter contained advice about preventing cancer, as well as a pitch for donations; 70 percent of the letters also offered the recipient a chance to win a sweepstake.

The text of all the letters was reviewed and approved by UCC. As a result of these mailings, UCC raised an enormous amount of money (by its standards)—$28.8 million. But its expenses—that is, the costs borne by W & H for postage, printing, and mailing the letters soliciting donations, costs reimbursed by UCC according to the terms of the contract—were also enormous: $26.5 million. The balance, $2.3 million, the net proceeds of the direct-mail campaign, was spent by UCC for services to cancer patients and on research for the prevention and treatment of cancer. The charity was permitted by the relevant accounting conventions to classify $12.2 million of its fundraising expenses as educational expenditures because of the cancer information contained in the fundraising letters.

Although UCC considered its experience with W & H successful, it did not renew the contract when it expired by its terms in 1989. Instead, it hired another fundraising organization—with disastrous results. The following year, UCC declared bankruptcy, and within months the IRS revoked its tax exemption retroactively to the date on which UCC had signed the contract with W & H. The effect was to make the IRS a major creditor of UCC in the bankruptcy proceeding. The retroactive revocation did not, however, affect the charitable deduction that donors to UCC since 1984 had taken on their income tax returns. See *Bob Jones University v. Simon*, 416 U.S. 725, 728-29, 94 S.Ct. 2038, 40 L.Ed.2d 496 (1974); Rev. Proc. 82-39, § 3.01, 1982-1 Cum. Bull. 759, 1982 WL 196338 (July 6, 1982).

The term "any private shareholder or individual" in the inurement clause of section 501(c)(3) of the Internal Revenue Code has been interpreted to mean an insider of the charity. *Orange County Agricultural Society, Inc. v. Commissioner*, 893 F.2d 529, 534 (2d Cir.1990); *Church of Scientology v. Commissioner*, supra, 823 F.2d at 1316-19; *Church by Mail, Inc. v. Commissioner*, 765 F.2d 1387, 1392 (9th Cir.1985); *American Campaign Academy v. Commissioner*, 92 T.C. 1053, 1066, 1989 WL 49678 (1989). A charity is not to siphon its earnings to its founder, or the members of its board, or their families, or anyone else fairly to be described as an insider, that is, as the equivalent of an owner or manager. The test is functional. It looks to the reality of control rather than to the insider's place in a formal table of organization. The insider could be a "mere" employee-or even a nominal outsider, such as a physician with hospital privileges in a charitable hospital, *Harding Hospital, Inc. v. United States*, 505 F.2d 1068, 1078 (6th Cir.1974); John E. Burke, "Hospital-Physician Joint Ventures," GCM 39862, 1991 WL 776308 (IRS Dec. 2, 1991), a licensor, *Est of Hawaii v. Commissioner*, 71 T.C. 1067, 1078-81, 1979 WL 3604 (1979), aff'd, 647 F.2d 170 (9th Cir.1981) (realistically, a case involving a founder's siphoning of charitable donations), or for that matter a fundraiser, *National Foundation, Inc. v. United States*, 13 Cl.Ct. 486, 494-95 (1987) although the court in that case rejected the argument that the fundraiser controlled the charity.

The Tax Court's classification of W & H as an insider of UCC was based on the fundraising contract. Such contracts are common. Fundraising has become a specialized professional activity and many charities hire specialists in it. If the charity's contract with the fundraiser makes the latter an insider, triggering the inurement clause of section 501(c)(3) and so destroying the charity's tax exemption, the charity sector of the economy is in trouble. The

IRS does not take the position that every such contract has this effect. What troubles it are the particular terms and circumstances of UCC's contract. It argues that since at the inception of the contract the charity had no money to speak of, and since, therefore, at least at the beginning, all the expenses of the fundraising campaign were borne by W & H, the latter was like a founder, or rather refounder (UCC was created in 1963), of the charity. The IRS points out that 90 percent of the contributions received by UCC during the term of the contract were paid to W & H to defray the cost of the fundraising campaign that brought in those contributions, and so argues that W & H was the real recipient of the contributions. It argues that because W & H was UCC's only fundraiser, the charity was totally at W & H's mercy during the five-year term of the contract-giving W & H effective control over the charity. UCC even surrendered the right to rent out the list of names of donors that the fundraising campaign generated. The terms of the contract were more favorable to the fundraiser than the terms of the average fundraising contract are.

Singly and together, these points bear no relation that we can see to the inurement provision. The provision is designed to prevent the siphoning of charitable receipts to insiders of the charity, not to empower the IRS to monitor the terms of arm's length contracts made by charitable organizations with the firms that supply them with essential inputs, whether premises, paper, computers, legal advice, or fundraising services.

Take the Service's first point, that W & H defrayed such a large fraction of the charity's total expenses in the early stages of the contract that it was the equivalent of a founder. Pushed to its logical extreme, this argument would deny the charitable tax exemption to any new or small charity that wanted to grow by soliciting donations, since it would have to get the cash to pay for the solicitations from an outside source, logically a fundraising organization. We can't see what this has to do with inurement. The argument is connected to another of the Service's points, that W & H was UCC's only fundraiser during the period of the contract. If UCC had hired ten fundraisers, the Service couldn't argue that any of them was so large a recipient of the charity's expenditures that it must be deemed to have controlled the charity. Yet in terms of the purposes of the inurement clause, it makes no difference how many fundraisers a charity employs. W & H obtained an exclusive contract, and thus was the sole fundraiser, not because it sought to control UCC and suck it dry, but because it was taking a risk; the exclusive contract lent assurance that if the venture succeeded, UCC wouldn't hire other fundraisers to reap where W & H had sown.

And it was only at the beginning of the contract period that W & H was funding UCC. As donations poured into the charity's coffers as a result of the success of the fundraising campaign, the charity began paying for the subsequent stages of the campaign out of its own revenues. True, to guarantee recoupment, the contract with W & H required UCC to place these funds in an escrow account, from which they could be withdrawn for UCC's charitable purposes only after W & H recovered the expenses of the fundraising campaign. But this is a detail; the important point is that UCC did not receive repeated infusions of capital from W & H. All the advances that W & H had made to UCC to fund the fundraising campaign were repaid. Indeed, it is an essential part of the government's case that W & H profited from the contract.

The other point that the Service makes about the exclusivity provision in the contract—that it put the charity at the mercy of the fundraiser, since if W & H stopped its fundraising efforts UCC would be barred from hiring another fundraiser until the contract with W & H expired—merely demonstrates the Service's ignorance of contract law. When a firm is granted an exclusive contract, the law reads into it an obligation that the firm use its best efforts to promote the contract's objectives. *Wood v. Duff-Gordon*, 222 N.Y. 88, 118 N.E. 214 (N.Y.1917) (Cardozo, J.); *Advent Systems Ltd. v. Unisys Corp.*, 925 F.2d 670, 679-80 (3d Cir.1991); E. Allan Farnsworth, Contracts § 7.17, pp. 509-11 (3d ed.1999). If W & H folded its tent and walked away, it would be in breach of this implied term of the contract and UCC would be free to terminate the contract without liability.

The Service also misses the significance of the contract's asymmetrical treatment of the parties' rights in the donor list. The charitable-fundraising community distinguishes between "prospect files" and "housefiles." A prospect file is a list of people who have not given to the charity in question but are thought sufficiently likely to do so to be placed on the list of addressees of a direct-mail fundraising campaign. If the prospect responds with a donation, his or her name is transferred to the housefile, that is, the list of people who have made a donation to the charity. A housefile is very valuable, because people who have already donated to a particular charity are more likely to donate to it again than mere prospects are likely to donate to it for the first time. The housefile's value to the charity is thus as a list of people who are good prospects to respond favorably to future solicitations. Its value to the fundraiser is quite different. The fundraiser is not a charity. The value to it of a housefile that it has created is the possibility of marketing it (as a prospect file—but as a prospect file in which all the prospects are charitable donors rather than a mere cross-section of potential donors) to another charity that hires it. So it made perfect sense for the contract to give the fundraiser the exclusive right to use the UCC housefile that it created in raising money for other charities, while reserving to UCC the right to use the housefile to solicit repeat donations to itself.

The Service's point that has the most intuitive appeal is the high ratio of fundraising expenses, all of which went to W & H because it was UCC's only fundraiser during the term of the contract, to net charitable proceeds. Of the $28-odd million that came in, $26-plus million went right back out, to W & H. These figures are deceptive, because UCC got a charitable "bang" from the mailings themselves, which contained educational materials (somewhat meager, to be sure) in direct support of the charity's central charitable goal. A charity whose entire goal was to publish educational materials would spend all or most of its revenues on publishing, but this would be in support rather than in derogation of its charitable purposes.

Even if this point is ignored, the ratio of expenses to net charitable receipts is unrelated to the issue of inurement. For one thing, it is a ratio of apples to oranges: the gross expenses of the fundraiser to the net receipts of the charity. For all that appears, while UCC derived a net benefit from the contract equal to the difference between donations and expenses plus the educational value of the mailings, W & H derived only a modest profit; for we know what UCC paid it, but not what its expenses were. The record does contain a table showing that W & H incurred postage and printing expenses of $12.5 million, but there is nothing on its total expenses.

To the extent that the ratio of net charitable proceeds to the cost to the charity of generating those proceeds has any relevance, it is to a different issue, one not presented by this appeal, which is whether charities should be denied a tax exemption if their operating expenses are a very high percentage of the total charitable donations that they receive. To see that it's a different issue, just imagine that UCC had spent $26 million to raise $28 million but that the $26 million had been scattered among a host of suppliers rather than concentrated on one. There would be no issue of inurement, because the Service would have no basis for singling out one of these suppliers as being in "control" of UCC (or the suppliers as a group, unless they were acting in concert). But there might still be a concern either that the charity was mismanaged or that charitable enterprises that generate so little net contribution to their charitable goals do not deserve the encouragement that a tax exemption provides. Recall that most of UCC's fundraising appeals offered the recipient of the appeal a chance to win a sweepstake, a form of charitable appeal that, we are told, is frowned upon. There may even be a question of how reputable W & H is (or was). See *Commonwealth v. Watson & Hughey Co.*, 128 Pa.Cmwlth. 484, 563 A.2d 1276 (Pa. Commw.1989). But these points go to UCC's sound judgment, not to whether W & H succeeded in wresting control over UCC from the charity's board.

UCC's low net yield is no doubt related to the terms of the fundraising contract, which were more favorable to the fundraiser than the average such contract. But so far as appears, they were favorable to W & H not because UCC's board was disloyal and mysteriously wanted to shower charity on a fundraiser with which it had no affiliation or overlapping membership or common ownership or control, but because UCC was desperate. The charity drove (so far as the record shows) the best bargain that it could, but it was not a good bargain. Maybe desperate charities should be encouraged to fold rather than to embark on expensive campaigns to raise funds. But that too is a separate issue from inurement. W & H did not, by reason of being able to drive a hard bargain, become an insider of UCC. If W & H was calling the shots, why did UCC refuse to renew the contract when it expired, and instead switch to another fundraiser?

We can find nothing in the facts to support the IRS's theory and the Tax Court's finding that W & H seized control of UCC and by doing so became an insider, triggering the inurement provision and destroying the exemption. There is nothing that corporate or agency law would recognize as control. A creditor of UCC could not seek the satisfaction of his claim from W & H on the ground that the charity was merely a cat's paw or alter ego of W & H, as in *Pepper v. Litton*, 308 U.S. 295, 311-12, 60 S.Ct. 238, 84 L.Ed. 281 (1939), or *Freeman v. Complex Computing Co.*, 119 F.3d 1044, 1051-53 (2d Cir.1997). The Service and the Tax Court are using "control" in a special sense not used elsewhere, so far as we can determine, in the law, including federal tax law. It is a sense which, as the amicus curiae briefs filed in support of UCC point out, threatens to unsettle the charitable sector by empowering the IRS to yank a charity's tax exemption simply because the Service thinks the charity's contract with its major fundraiser too one-sided in favor of the fundraiser, even though the charity has not been found to have violated any duty of faithful and careful management that the law of nonprofit corporations may have laid upon it. The resulting uncertainty about the charity's ability to retain its tax exemption-and receive tax-exempt donations—would be a particular deterrent to anyone contemplating a donation, loan, or other financial contribution to a new or small charity. That is the type most likely to be found by the IRS to have surrendered control over its destiny to a fundraiser or other supplier, because it is the type of charity that is most likely to have to pay a high price for fundraising services. "Developments in the Law-Nonprofit Corporations," 105 Harv. L.Rev. 1578, 1649-51 (1992). It is hard enough for new, small, weak, or marginal charities to survive, because they are likely to have a high expense ratio, and many potential donors will be put off by that. The Tax Court's decision, if sustained, would make the survival of such charities even more dubious, by enveloping them in doubt about their tax exemption.

We were not reassured when the government's lawyer, in response to a question from the bench as to what standard he was advocating to guide decisions in this area, said that it was the "facts and circumstances" of each case. That is no standard at all, and makes the tax status of charitable organizations and their donors a matter of the whim of the IRS.

There was no diversion of charitable revenues to an insider here, nothing that smacks of self-dealing, disloyalty, breach of fiduciary obligation or other misconduct of the type aimed at by a provision of law that forbids a charity to divert its earnings to members of the board or other insiders. What there may have been was imprudence on the part of UCC's board of directors in hiring W & H and negotiating the contract that it did. Maybe the only prudent course in the circumstances that confronted UCC in 1984 was to dissolve. Charitable organizations are plagued by incentive problems. Nobody owns the right to the profits and therefore no one has the spur to efficient performance that the lure of profits creates. Donors are like corporate shareholders in the sense of being the principal source of the charity's funds, but they do not have a profit incentive to monitor the care with which the charity's funds are used. Maybe the lack of a profit motive made UCC's board too lax. Maybe the board did not negotiate as favorable a contract with W & H as the board of a profit-making firm would have done. And maybe tax law has a role to play in assuring the prudent management of charities. Remember the IRS's alternative basis for yanking UCC's exemption? It is that as a result of the contract's terms, UCC was not really operated exclusively for charitable purposes, but rather for the private benefit of W & H as well. Suppose that UCC was so irresponsibly managed that it paid W & H twice as much for fundraising services as W & H would have been happy to accept for those services, so that of UCC's $26 million in fundraising expense $13 million was the equivalent of a gift to the fundraiser. Then it could be argued that UCC was in fact being operated to a significant degree for the private benefit of W & H, though not because it was the latter's creature. That then would be a route for using tax law to deal with the problem of improvident or extravagant expenditures by a charitable organization that do not, however, inure to the benefit of insiders.

That in fact is the IRS's alternative ground for revoking the exemption, the one the Tax Court gave a bye to. It would have been better had the court resolved that ground as well as the inurement ground, so that the case could be definitively resolved in one appeal. But it did not, and so the case must be remanded to enable the court to consider it. We shall not prejudge the proceedings on remand. The usual "private benefit" case is one in which the charity has dual public and private goals, see, e.g., *Better Business Bureau v. United States*, 326 U.S. 279, 283, 66 S.Ct. 112, 90 L.Ed. 67 (1945); *Living Faith, Inc. v. Commissioner*, 950 F.2d 365 (7th Cir.1991); *American Campaign Academy v. Commissioner*, supra, 92 T.C. at 1064-65, and that is not involved here. However, the board of a charity has a duty of care, just like the board of an ordinary business corporation, see, e.g., *Riss v. Angel*, 131 Wash.2d 612, 934 P.2d 669, 680-81 and n. 5 (Wash.1997); *Fairhope Single Tax Corp. v. Rezner*, 527 So.2d 1232, 1236 (Ala.1987); *Frances T. v. Village Green Owners Ass'n*, 42 Cal.3d 490, 229 Cal.Rptr. 456, 723 P.2d 573, 582 n. 13 (Cal.1986), and a violation of that duty which involved the dissipation of the charity's assets might (we need not decide whether it would—we leave that issue to the Tax Court in the first instance) support a finding that the charity was conferring a private benefit, even if the contracting party did not control, or exercise undue influence over, the charity. This, for all we know, may be such a case.

Reversed and Remanded.
POSNER, Chief Judge.

STUDY QUESTIONS

- Although not involving a museum, the *United Cancer Council* case addresses some important aspects of fundraising agreements. What were the legal and ethical concerns at issue here?
- Why did the UCC hire a professional fundraiser? What did the Internal Revenue Service think of the agreement between the fundraising consultant and the organization? Does the court share the IRS' opinion?
- What does the case tell us about general contract law and tax-exempt nonprofit organizations?
- What was the board's role in overseeing the organization's fundraising efforts? Did the UCC board properly exercise its fiduciary responsibilities?
- Explain the alternative "private benefit" theory raised by the court that resulted in the case being remanded to the Tax Court.

ENDOWMENTS

Endowments are a special type of investment fund in which the principal is preserved and only the investment income is expended. Endowments are essentially a special form of restricted gift. The money in an endowment fund can only be used for the purposes for which the fund was established. A donor can establish an endowment fund on behalf of a museum. An endowment fund can also be set up by the museum's board. Often an endowment fund is established as part of a capital campaign or to provide ongoing funding for a particular program, initiative, or staff position.

Endowments are governed by the Uniform Prudent Management of Institutional Funds Act (UPMIFA) in most states. UPMIFA sets forth standards of conduct in managing and investing institutional funds, including endowments. The choice of investments made in a regulated endowment fund must meet the "prudent person" standard of care. The traditional rule on spending from an endowment fund was to maintain the fund principal—calculated at the fair market value at the time the funds were received. The so-called "Massachusetts Rule" imposes a ceiling above which spending from an endowment is considered "imprudent." This is usually expressed as a percentage—that is, for example no more that 5% of the endowment may be expended each year. UPMIFA requires that endowment funds be managed with specific considerations but does not impose a ceiling on how much can be withdrawn from the endowment each year.

A museum's investments, including endowment funds, are usually managed through a board-level investment committee, or delegated to an external financial advisor overseen by a committee of the board. Museums should adopt an investment policy consistent with applicable law and institutional goals. The policy not only sets out the relevant legal framework for making investment decisions, but also describes how the museum meets those requirements. The investment policy should be specific to the museum and take into account the museum's strategic plan, assets, and resources. Common elements of an investment policy include investment objectives; asset allocations; benchmarks for asset classes; payout rates; financial manager selection, compensation and review; reporting and monitoring; and periodic review of the policy itself.

GOVERNMENT FUNDING

Government funding for the arts, including museums, comes in a variety of forms. As discussed above, the largest form of government funding is the result of the charitable donation tax deduction. The tax-deductibility of charitable donations is an indirect government subsidy to encourage scientific, educational, and artistic activities. In addition to tax incentives, specific government programs are established to encourage or support certain arts-related activities. Examples of specific government arts programs include the Works Project Administration (WPA), which was established during the Great Depression of the

1930s to provide financial support to unemployed artists. More recent similar programs such as the Comprehensive Employment and Training Act (CETA) also provided employment and training for artists (and others) after the financial crisis in the first decade of the 21st century.

A third form of government support for the arts is in the form of public endowments that provide grants to support the arts. On the federal level, the best known are the National Endowment for the Humanities (NEH) and the National Endowment for the Arts (NEA). The NEH and the NEA are part of a nationwide network of funding for the arts.

The NEH is governed by a board appointed by the President and approved by the U.S. Senate. It has seven program divisions and offices. The NEH works closely with state humanities councils. It also oversees the Institute for Museum and Library Services (IMLS). IMLS provides grants for a variety of museum-related purposes. State humanities councils are funded by NEH and through private, foundation, corporate, and sometimes state government support.

The NEA provides grants for arts-related projects which further its mission to "supports arts learning, affirms and celebrates America's rich and diverse cultural heritage, and extends its work to promote equal access to the arts in every community across America." The NEA employs a peer review system with three independent levels of review to consider grants. Grant proposals are vetted by a panel of artists and arts experts in specific disciplines including literature, museums and visual arts, dance, musical theater, and arts education. The National Council on the Arts (NCA), which is composed of 14 artists, scholars, and arts patrons appointed by the President and confirmed by the Senate, reviews recommendations from the peer review panels and votes on the proposals to be funded. The NEA Chairperson, who is appointed by the President for a four-year term, reviews the NCA recommendations and makes the final decision on grant awards.

Regional and state arts agencies and state humanities councils also provide grant support for the arts. These entities are structured like the NEA and the NEH. Expert panels review proposals and make recommendations. An arts council or commission—typically appointed by the state's governor—sets funding policies and priorities. Funding comes from state revenue and from NEA and NEH allocations, as well as from private and foundation support. State arts boards tend to support smaller and more local organizations, and younger, less established artists than the NEA and NEH do.

Another level of government support for the arts comes from local arts agencies. There are over 4,000 local arts agencies at the city and county level in the United States. Historically all arts-related financial support was local. After the Chicago World's Fair in 1893 many cities set up arts commissions as part of their urban planning efforts. Today local art commissions often receive funding from state arts agencies (which in turn receive funding from the NEA and NEH). They often oversee commissioned works for public buildings, municipal orchestras and museums, and regional and local arts centers. Many cities mandate private developers to include public art projects as part of their development plans.

In addition to this network of federal, state, and local agencies supporting the arts, other governmental entities also provide support for the arts. On the federal level, there are a wide variety of governmental and quasi-governmental entities involved in supporting the arts through specific programs. These include the Smithsonian Institution, the Corporation for Public Broadcasting, the National Gallery of Art, the Department of the Interior (Save America's Treasures), the Kennedy Center for the Performing Arts, the Department of Education (Arts in Education), the National Capital Planning Commission, the General Services Commission (Arts in Architecture), the Advisory Council on Historic Preservation, the State Department (Cultural Affairs exchanges, presentations, etc.), and the Commission on Fine Arts. Support for arts programming also comes from the Library of Congress (American Folklife Center), the National Parks Service, the U.S. Department of Agriculture, and the U.S. military. Legislative earmarks may also be focused on support for the arts. Internationally, the U.S. State Department conducts a variety of programs aimed at supporting and promoting the arts, including the Voice of America, the U.S. Information Agency, Radio and Television MARTI and World Net.

CONTROVERSIAL EXHIBITS

Government support for the arts raises broad questions about the appropriate role of government in a democratic society; different types of support that governments can provide to the arts; and the conditions under which artistic creativity is best nurtured. They also underscore the tension between blasphemous, obscene, or hate-filled expression and the protections afforded by the First Amendment.

Controversial art exhibits which have received government funding and support bring these difficult questions into focus. Among some of the better-known controversies regarding government support include the exhibition of the Enola Gay at the Smithsonian Air and Space Museum in 1994; the *Sensation* exhibit which was organized by the Royal Academy of Art in 1997 and which travelled first to Berlin and then to Brooklyn in 1999; and, more recently, the *Hide/Seek* exhibit at the Smithsonian (2010) and the Brooklyn Museum (2011).

CASES AND OTHER READINGS

Reading Note: *National Endowment for the Arts v. Finley*, reprinted below, involved a 1990 amendment to the federal law establishing the National Endowment for the Arts (NEA), which required consideration of "general standards of decency and respect for the diverse beliefs and values of the American public" as part of the NEA's grant funding decisions. The amendment was enacted during the highly politicized "culture wars" of the 1990s and posed a number of difficult questions of constitutional law. The case exemplifies the highly controversial nature of government funding for the arts.

NATIONAL ENDOWMENT FOR THE ARTS V. FINLEY

524 U.S. 569 (1998)

JUSTICE O'CONNOR delivered the opinion of the Court.

JUSTICE GINSBURG joins all but Part II-B of this opinion.

The National Foundation on the Arts and the Humanities Act of 1965, as amended in 1990, 104 Stat. 1963, requires the Chairperson of the National Endowment for the Arts (NEA) to ensure that "artistic excellence and artistic merit are the criteria by which [grant] applications are judged, taking into consideration general standards of decency and respect for the diverse beliefs and values of the American public." 20 U. S. C. § 954(d)(1). In this case, we review the Court of Appeals' determination that § 954(d)(1), on its face, impermissibly discriminates on the basis of viewpoint and is void for vagueness under the First and Fifth Amendments. We conclude that § 954(d)(1) is facially valid, as it neither inherently interferes with First Amendment rights nor violates constitutional vagueness principles.

I

A

With the establishment of the NEA in 1965, Congress embarked on a "broadly conceived national policy of support for the … arts in the United States," see § 953(b), pledging federal funds to "help create and sustain not only a climate encouraging freedom of thought, imagination, and inquiry but also the material conditions facilitating the release of… creative talent." § 951(7). The enabling statute vests the NEA with substantial discretion to award grants; it identifies only the broadest funding priorities, including "artistic and cultural significance, giving emphasis to American creativity and cultural diversity," "professional excellence," and the encouragement of "public knowledge, education, understanding, and appreciation of the arts." See §§ 954(c)(1)-(10).

Applications for NEA funding are initially reviewed by advisory panels composed of experts in the relevant field of the arts. Under the 1990 amendments to the enabling statute, those panels must reflect "diverse artistic and cultural points of view" and include "wide geographic, ethnic, and minority representation," as well as "lay individuals who are knowledgeable about the arts." §§ 959(c)(1)-(2). The panels report to the 26-member National Council on the Arts (Council), which, in turn, advises the NEA Chairperson. The Chairperson has the ultimate authority to award grants but may not approve an application as to which the Council has made a negative recommendation. § 955(f).

Since 1965, the NEA has distributed over $3 billion in grants to individuals and organizations, funding that has served as a catalyst for increased state, corporate, and foundation support for the arts. Congress has recently restricted the availability of federal funding for individual artists, confining grants primarily to qualifying organizations and state arts agencies, and constraining subgranting. See Department of the Interior and Related Agencies Appropriations Act, 1998, § 329, 111 Stat. 1600. By far the largest portion of the grants distributed in fiscal year 1998 were awarded directly to state arts agencies. In the remaining categories, the most substantial grants were allocated to symphony orchestras, fine arts museums, dance theater foundations, and opera associations. See National Endowment for the Arts, FY 1998 Grants, Creation & Presentation 5-8, 21,20,27.

Throughout the NEA's history, only a handful of the agency's roughly 100,000 awards have generated formal complaints about misapplied funds or abuse of the public's trust. Two provocative works, however, prompted public controversy in 1989 and led to congressional revaluation of the NEA's funding priorities and efforts to increase oversight of its grant-making procedures. The Institute of Contemporary Art at the University of Pennsylvania had used $30,000 of a visual arts grant it received from the NEA to fund a 1989 retrospective of photographer Robert Mapplethorpe's work. The exhibit, entitled *The Perfect Moment*, included homoerotic photographs that several Members of Congress condemned as pornographic. See, e.g., 135 Congo Rec. 22372 (1989). Members also denounced artist Andres Serrano's work *Piss Christ*, a photograph of a crucifix immersed in urine. See, e.g., id., at 9789. Serrano had been awarded a $15,000 grant from the Southern Center for Contemporary Art, an organization that received NEA support.

When considering the NEA's appropriations for fiscal year 1990, Congress reacted to the controversy surrounding the Mapplethorpe and Serrano photographs by eliminating $45,000 from the agency's budget, the precise amount contributed to the two exhibits by NEA grant recipients. Congress also enacted an amendment providing that no NEA funds "may be used to promote, disseminate, or produce materials which in the judgment of [the NEA] may be considered obscene, including but not limited to, depictions of sadomasochism, homoeroticism, the sexual exploitation of children, or individuals engaged in sex acts and which, when taken as a whole, do not have serious literary, artistic, political, or scientific value." Department of the Interior and Related Agencies Appropriations Act, 1990, 103 Stat. 738-742. The NEA implemented Congress' mandate by instituting a requirement that all grantees certify in writing that they would not utilize federal funding to engage in projects inconsistent with the criteria in the 1990 appropriations bill. That certification requirement was subsequently invalidated as unconstitutionally vague by a Federal District Court, see *Bella Lewitzky Dance Foundation v. Frohnmayer,* 754 F. Supp. 774 (CD Cal. 1991), and the NEA did not appeal the decision.

In the 1990 appropriations bill, Congress also agreed to create an Independent Commission of constitutional law scholars to review the NEA's grant-making procedures and assess the possibility of more focused standards for public arts funding. The Commission's report, issued in September 1990, concluded that there is no constitutional obligation to provide arts funding, but also recommended that the NEA rescind the certification requirement and cautioned against legislation setting forth any content restrictions. Instead, the Commission suggested procedural changes to enhance the role of advisory panels and a statutory reaffirmation of "the high place the nation accords to the fostering of mutual respect for the disparate beliefs and values among us." See Independent Commission, Report to Congress on the National Endowment for the Arts 83-91 (Sept. 1990), 3 Record, Doc. No. 51, Exh. K (hereinafter Report to Congress).

Immersion (Piss Christ) *(1987) by Andres Serrano is a photograph of a small plastic crucifix submerged in a small glass tank of the artist's urine. The work was a winner of the Southeastern Center for Contemporary Art's "Awards in the Visual Arts" competition, which was sponsored in part by the National Endowment for the Arts (NEA). The work generated a large amount of controversy based on assertions that it was blasphemous. Serrano himself said of the controversy: "I had no idea* Piss Christ *would get the attention it did, since I meant neither blasphemy nor offense by it. I've been a Catholic all my life, so I am a follower of Christ." The photograph is mentioned in* Finley v. NEA.

Informed by the Commission's recommendations, and cognizant of pending judicial challenges to the funding limitations in the 1990 appropriations bill, Congress debated several proposals to reform the NEA's grant-making process when it considered the agency's reauthorization in the fall of 1990. The House rejected the Crane Amendment, which would have virtually eliminated the NEA, see 136 Congo Rec. 28656-28657 (1990), and the Rohrabacher Amendment, which would have introduced a prohibition on awarding any grants that could be used to "promote, distribute, disseminate, or produce matter that has the purpose or effect of denigrating the beliefs, tenets, or objects of a particular religion" or "of denigrating an individual, or group of individuals, on the basis of race, sex, handicap, or national origin," id., at 28657-28664. Ultimately, Congress adopted the

Williams/Coleman Amendment, a bipartisan compromise between Members opposing any funding restrictions and those favoring some guidance to the agency. In relevant part, the Amendment became § 954(d)(1), which directs the Chairperson, in establishing procedures to judge the artistic merit of grant applications, to "tak[e] into consideration general standards of decency and respect for the diverse beliefs and values of the American public." *

*Title 20 U. S. C. § 954(d) provides in full that:

"No payment shall be made under this section except upon application therefor which is submitted to the National Endowment for the Arts in accordance with regulations issued and procedures established by the Chairperson. In establishing such regulations and procedures, the Chairperson shall ensure that:

"(1) artistic excellence and artistic merit are the criteria by which applications are judged, taking into consideration general standards of decency and respect for the diverse beliefs and values of the American public; and "(2) applications are consistent with the purposes of this section. Such regulations and procedures shall clearly indicate that obscenity is without artistic merit, is not protected speech, and shall not be funded."

The NEA has not promulgated any official interpretation of the provision, but in December 1990, the Council unanimously adopted a resolution to implement § 954(d)(1) merely by ensuring that the members of the advisory panels that conduct the initial review of grant applications represent geographic, ethnic, and esthetic diversity. See Minutes of the Dec. 1990 Retreat of the National Council on the Arts, reprinted in App. 12-13; Transcript of the Dec. 1990 Retreat of the National Council on the Arts, reprinted in id., at 3233. John Frohnmayer, then Chairperson of the NEA, also declared that he would "count on [the] procedures" ensuring diverse membership on the peer review panels to fulfill Congress' mandate. See id., at 40.

B

The four individual respondents in this case, Karen Finley, John Fleck, Holly Hughes, and Tim Miller, are performance artists who applied for NEA grants before § 954(d)(1) was enacted. An advisory panel recommended approval of respondents' projects, both initially and after receiving Frohnmayer's request to reconsider three of the applications. A majority of the Council subsequently recommended disapproval, and in June 1990, the NEA informed respondents that they had been denied funding. Respondents filed suit, alleging that the NEA had violated their First Amendment rights by rejecting the applications on political grounds, had failed to follow statutory procedures by basing the denial on criteria other than those set forth in the NEA's enabling statute, and had breached the confidentiality of their grant applications through the release of quotations to the press, in violation of the Privacy Act of 1974, 5 U. S. C. § 552(a). Respondents sought restoration of the recommended grants or reconsideration of their applications, as well as damages for the alleged Privacy Act violations. When Congress enacted § 954(d)(1), respondents, now joined by the National Association of Artists' Organizations (NAAO), amended their complaint to challenge the provision as void for vagueness and impermissibly viewpoint based. First Amended Complaint ~ 1.

The District Court denied the NEA's motion for judgment on the pleadings, 795 F. Supp. 1457, 1463-1468 (CD Cal. 1992), and, after discovery, the NEA agreed to settle the individual respondents' statutory and as-applied constitutional claims by paying the artists the amount of the vetoed grants, damages, and attorney's fees. See Stipulation and Settlement Agreement, 6 Record, Doc. No. 128, pp. 3-5.

The District Court then granted summary judgment in favor of respondents on their facial constitutional challenge to § 954(d)(1) and enjoined enforcement of the provision. See 795 F. Supp., at 1476. The court rejected the argument that the NEA could comply with § 954(d)(1) by structuring the grant selection process to provide for diverse advisory panels. *Id.,* at 1471. The provision, the court stated, "fails adequately to notify applicants of what is required of them or to circumscribe NEA discretion." *Id.,* at 1472. Reasoning that "the very nature of our pluralistic society is that there are an infinite number of values and beliefs, and correlatively, there may be no national 'general standards of decency,'" the court concluded that § 954(d)(1) "cannot be given effect consistent with the Fifth Amendment's due process requirement." *Id.,* at 1471-1472 (citing *Grayned v. City of Rockford,* 408 U. S. 104, 108-109 (1972)). Drawing an analogy between arts funding and public universities, the court further ruled that the First Amendment constrains the NEA's grant-making process, and that because § 954(d)(1) "clearly reaches a substantial amount of protected speech," it is impermissibly overbroad on its face. 795 F. Supp., at 1476. The Government did not seek a stay of the District Court's injunction, and consequently the NEA has not applied § 954(d)(1) since June 1992.

A divided panel of the Court of Appeals affirmed the District Court's ruling. 100 F.3d 671 (CA9 1996). The majority agreed with the District Court that the NEA was compelled by the adoption of § 954(d)(1) to alter its grant-making procedures to ensure that applications are judged according to the "decency and respect" criteria. The Chairperson, the court reasoned, "has no discretion to ignore this obligation, enforce only part of it, or give it a cramped construction." *Id.,* at 680. Concluding that the "decency and respect" criteria are not "susceptible to objective definition," the court held that § 954(d)(1) "gives rise to the danger of arbitrary and discriminatory application" and is void for vagueness under the First and Fifth Amendments. *Id.,* at 680-681. In the alternative, the court ruled that § 954(d)(1) violates the First Amendment's prohibition on viewpoint-based restrictions on protected speech. Government funding of the arts, the court explained, is both a "traditional sphere of free expression," *Rust v. Sullivan,* 500 U. S. 173, 200 (1991), and an area in which the Government has stated its intention to "encourage a diversity of views from private speakers," *Rosenberger v. Rector and Visitors of Univ. of Va.,* 515 U. S. 819, 834

(1995). 100 F. 3d, at 681-682. Accordingly, finding that § 954(d)(1) "has a speech-based restriction as its sole rationale and operative principle," *Rosenberger, supra,* at 834, and noting the NEA's failure to articulate a compelling interest for the provision, the court declared it facially invalid. 100 F. 3d, at 683.

The dissent asserted that the First Amendment protects artists' rights to express themselves as indecently and disrespectfully as they like, but does not compel the Government to fund that speech. *Id.,* at 684 (opinion of Kleinfeld, J.). The challenged provision, the dissent contended, did not prohibit the NEA from funding indecent or offensive art, but merely required the agency to consider the "decency and respect" criteria in the grant selection process. *Id.,* at 689690. Moreover, according to the dissent's reasoning, the vagueness principles applicable to the direct regulation of speech have no bearing on the selective award of prizes, and the Government may draw distinctions based on content and viewpoint in making its funding decisions. *Id.,* at 684-688. Three judges dissented from the denial of rehearing *en banc,* maintaining that the panel's decision gave the statute an "implausible construction," applied the "'void for vagueness' doctrine where it does not belong," and extended "First Amendment principles to a situation that the First Amendment doesn't cover." 112 F.3d 1015, 1016-1017 (CA9 1997).

We granted certiorari, 522 U. S. 991 (1997), and now reverse the judgment of the Court of Appeals.

II

A

Respondents raise a facial constitutional challenge to § 954(d)(1), and consequently they confront "a heavy burden" in advancing their claim. *Rust, supra,* at 183. Facial invalidation "is, manifestly, strong medicine" that "has been employed by the Court sparingly and only as a last resort." *Broadrick v. Oklahoma,* 413 U. S. 601, 613 (1973); see also *FW/PBS, Inc. v. Dallas,* 493 U. S. 215, 223 (1990) (noting that "facial challenges to legislation are generally disfavored"). To prevail, respondents must demonstrate a substantial risk that application of the provision will lead to the suppression of speech. See *Broadrick, supra,* at 615.

Respondents argue that the provision is a paradigmatic example of viewpoint discrimination because it rejects any artistic speech that either fails to respect mainstream values or offends standards of decency. The premise of respondents' claim is that § 954(d)(1) constrains the agency's ability to fund certain categories of artistic expression. The NEA, however, reads the provision as merely hortatory, and contends that it stops well short of an absolute restriction. Section 954(d)(1) adds "considerations" to the grant-making process; it does not preclude awards to projects that might be deemed "indecent" or "disrespectful," nor place conditions on grants, or even specify that those factors must be given any particular weight in reviewing an application. Indeed, the agency asserts that it has adequately implemented § 954(d)(1) merely by ensuring the representation of various backgrounds and points of view on the advisory panels that analyze grant applications. See Declaration of Randolph McAusland, Deputy Chairman for Programs at the NEA, reprinted in App. 79 (stating that the NEA implements the provision "by ensuring that the peer review panels represent a variety of geographical areas, aesthetic views, professions, areas of expertise, races and ethnic groups, and gender, and include a lay person"). We do not decide whether the NEA's view—that the formulation of diverse advisory panels is sufficient to comply with Congress' command—is in fact a reasonable reading of the statute. It is clear, however, that the text of § 954(d)(1) imposes no categorical requirement. The advisory language stands in sharp contrast to congressional efforts to prohibit the funding of certain classes of speech. When Congress has in fact intended to affirmatively constrain the NEA's grant-making authority, it has done so in no uncertain terms. See § 954(d)(2) ("[O]bscenity is without artistic merit, is not protected speech, and shall not be funded").

Furthermore, like the plain language of § 954(d), the political context surrounding the adoption of the "decency and respect" clause is inconsistent with respondents' assertion that the provision compels the NEA to deny funding on the basis of viewpoint discriminatory criteria. The legislation was a bipartisan proposal introduced as a counterweight to amendments aimed at eliminating the NEA's funding or substantially constraining its grant-making authority. See, e.g., 136 Congo Rec. 28626, 28632, 28634 (1990). The Independent Commission had cautioned Congress against the adoption of distinct viewpoint-based standards for funding, and the Commission's report suggests that "additional criteria for selection, if any, should be incorporated as part of the selection process (perhaps as part of a definition of 'artistic excellence'), rather than isolated and treated as exogenous considerations." Report to Congress 89. In keeping with that recommendation, the criteria in § 954(d)(1) inform the assessment of artistic merit, but Congress declined to disallow any particular viewpoints. As the sponsors of § 954(d)(1) noted in urging rejection of the Rohrabacher Amendment: "[I]f we start down that road of prohibiting categories of expression, categories which are indeed constitutionally protected speech, where do we end? Where one Member's aversions end, others with different sensibilities and with different values begin." 136 Congo Rec. 28624 (statement of Rep. Coleman); see also id., at 28663 (statement of Rep. Williams) (arguing that the Rohrabacher Amendment would prevent the funding of Jasper Johns' flag series, *The Merchant of Venice*, *Chorus Line*, *Birth of a Nation*, and the *Grapes of Wrath*). In contrast, before the vote on § 954(d)(1), one of its sponsors stated: "If we have done one important thing in this amendment, it is this. We have maintained the integrity of freedom of expression in the United States." *Id.*, at 28674.

That § 954(d)(1) admonishes the NEA merely to take "decency and respect" into consideration and that the legislation was aimed at reforming procedures rather than precluding speech undercut respondents' argument that the provision inevitably will be utilized as a tool for invidious viewpoint discrimination. In cases where we have struck down legislation as facially unconstitutional, the dangers were both more evident and more substantial. In *R. A. V. v. St. Paul,* 505 U. S. 377 (1992), for example, we invalidated on its face a municipal ordinance that defined as a criminal offense the placement of a symbol on public or private property" 'which one knows or has reasonable grounds to know arouses anger, alarm or resentment in others on the basis of race, color, creed, religion or gender.'" See id., at 380. That provision set forth a clear penalty, proscribed views on particular "disfavored subjects," id., at 391, and suppressed "distinctive idea[s], conveyed by a distinctive message," id., at 393.

In contrast, the "decency and respect" criteria do not silence speakers by expressly "threaten[ing] censorship of ideas." See ibid. Thus, we do not perceive a realistic danger that § 954(d)(1) will compromise First Amendment values. As respondents' own arguments demonstrate, the considerations that the provision introduces, by their nature, do not engender the kind of directed viewpoint discrimination that would prompt this Court to invalidate a statute on its face. Respondents assert, for example, that "[o]ne would be hard-pressed to find two people in the United States who could agree on what the 'diverse beliefs and values of the American public' are, much less on whether a particular work of art 'respects' them"; and they claim that" '[d]ecency' is likely to mean something very different to a septegenarian in Tuscaloosa and a teenager in Las Vegas." Brief for Respondents 41. The NEA likewise views the considerations enumerated in § 954(d)(1) as susceptible to multiple interpretations. See Department of the Interior and Related Agencies Appropriations for 1992, Hearing before the Subcommittee on Interior and Related Agencies of the House Committee on Appropriations, 102d Cong., 1st Sess., 234 (1991) (testimony of John Frohnmayer) ("[N]o one individual is wise enough to be able to consider general standards of decency and the diverse values and beliefs of the American people all by him or herself. These are group decisions"). Accordingly, the provision does not introduce considerations that, in practice, would effectively preclude or punish the expression of particular views. Indeed, one could hardly anticipate how "decency" or "respect" would bear on grant applications in categories such as funding for symphony orchestras.

Respondents' claim that the provision is facially unconstitutional may be reduced to the argument that the criteria in § 954(d)(1) are sufficiently subjective that the agency could utilize them to engage in viewpoint discrimination. Given the varied interpretations of the criteria and the vague exhortation to "take them into consideration," it seems unlikely that this provision will introduce any greater element of selectivity than the determination of "artistic excellence" itself. And we are reluctant, in any event, to invalidate legislation "on the basis of its hypothetical application to situations not before the Court." *FCC v. Pacifica Foundation,* 438 U. S. 726, 743 (1978).

The NEA's enabling statute contemplates a number of indisputably constitutional applications for both the "decency" prong of § 954(d)(1) and its reference to "respect for the diverse beliefs and values of the American public." Educational programs are central to the NEA's mission. See § 951(9) ("Americans should receive in school, background and preparation in the arts and humanities"); § 954 (5) (listing "projects and productions that will encourage public knowledge, education, understanding, and appreciation of the arts" among the NEA's funding priorities); National Endowment for the Arts, FY 1999 Application Guidelines 18-19 (describing "Education & Access" category); Brief for Twentysix Arts, Broadcast, Library, Museum and Publishing *Amici Curiae* 5, n. 2 (citing NEA Strategic Plan FY 1997-FY 2002, which identifies children's festivals and museums, art education, at-risk youth projects, and artists in schools as examples of the NEA's activities). And it is well established that "decency" is a permissible factor where "educational suitability" motivates its consideration. *Board of Ed., Island Trees Union Free School Dist. No. 26 v. Pico,* 457 U. S. 853, 871 (1982); see also *Bethel School Dist. No. 103 v. Fraser,* 478 U. S. 675, 683 (1986) ("Surely it is a highly appropriate function of public school education to prohibit the use of vulgar and offensive terms in public discourse"). Permissible applications of the mandate to consider "respect for the diverse beliefs and values of the American public" are also apparent. In setting forth the purposes of the NEA, Congress explained that "[i]t is vital to a democracy to honor and preserve its multicultural artistic heritage." § 951(10). The agency expressly takes diversity into account, giving special consideration to "projects and productions ... that reach, or reflect the culture of, a minority, inner city, rural, or tribal community," § 954(c)(4), as well as projects that generally emphasize "cultural diversity," § 954(c)(1). Respondents do not contend that the criteria in § 954(d)(1) are impermissibly applied when they may be justified, as the statute contemplates, with respect to a project's intended audience.

We recognize, of course, that reference to these permissible applications would not alone be sufficient to sustain the statute against respondents' First Amendment challenge. But neither are we persuaded that, in other applications, the language of § 954(d)(1) itself will give rise to the suppression of protected expression. Any content-based considerations that may be taken into account in the grant-making process are a consequence of the nature of arts funding. The NEA has limited resources, and it must deny the majority of the grant applications that it receives, including many that propose "artistically excellent" projects. The agency may decide to fund particular projects for a wide variety of reasons, "such as the technical proficiency of the artist, the creativity of the work, the anticipated public interest in or appreciation of the work, the work's contemporary relevance, its educational value, its suitability for or appeal to special audiences (such as children or the disabled), its service to a rural or isolated community, or even simply that the work could increase public knowledge of an art form." Brief for Petitioners 32. As the dissent below noted, it would be "impossible to have a highly selective grant program without denying money to a large amount of constitutionally protected expression." 100 F. 3d, at 685 (opinion of Kleinfeld, J.). The "very assumption" of the NEA is that grants will be awarded according to the "artistic worth of competing applicants," and absolute neutrality is simply "inconceivable." *Advocates for the Arts v. Thomson,* 532 F.2d 792, 795-796 *(CA1),* cert. denied, 429 U. S. 894 (1976).

Respondents' reliance on our decision in *Rosenberger v. Rector and Visitors of Univ. of Va.,* 515 U. S. 819 (1995), is therefore misplaced. In *Rosenberger,* a public university declined to authorize disbursements from its Student Activities Fund to finance the printing of a Christian student newspaper. We held that by subsidizing the Student Activities Fund, the University had created a limited public forum, from which it impermissibly excluded all publications with religious editorial viewpoints. *Id.*, at 837. Although the scarcity of NEA funding does not distinguish this case from *Rosenberger*, see *id.*, at 835, the competitive process according to which the grants are allocated does. In the context of arts funding, in contrast to many other subsidies, the Government does not indiscriminately "encourage a diversity of views from private speakers," id., at 834. The NEA's mandate is to make esthetic judgments, and the inherently content-based "excellence" threshold for NEA support sets it apart from the subsidy at issue in *Rosenberger*—which was available to all student organizations that were" 'related to the educational purpose of the University,'" id., at 824—and from comparably objective decisions on allocating public benefits, such as access to a school auditorium or a municipal theater, see *Lamb's Chapel v. Center Moriches Union Free School Dist.*, 508 U. S. 384, 386 (1993); *Southeastern Promotions, Ltd. v. Conrad*, 420 U. S. 546, 555 (1975), or the second class mailing privileges available to "all newspapers and other periodical publications," see *Hannegan v. Esquire, Inc.*, 327 U. S. 146, 148, n. 1 (1946).

Respondents do not allege discrimination in any particular funding decision. (In fact, after filing suit to challenge § 954(d)(1), two of the individual respondents received NEA grants. See 4 Record, Doc. No. 57, Exh. 35 (Sept. 30, 1991, letters from the NEA informing respondents Hughes and Miller that they had been awarded Solo Performance Theater Artist Fellowships).) Thus, we have no occasion here to address an as-applied challenge in a situation where the denial of a grant may be shown to be the product of invidious viewpoint discrimination. If the NEA were to leverage its power to award subsidies on the basis of subjective criteria into a penalty on disfavored viewpoints, then we would confront a different case. We have stated that, even in the provision of subsidies, the Government may not "ai[m] at the suppression of dangerous ideas," *Regan v. Taxation with Representation of Wash.*, 461 U. S. 540, 550 (1983) (internal quotation marks omitted), and if a subsidy were "manipulated" to have a "coercive effect," then relief could be appropriate. See *Arkansas Writers' Project, Inc. v. Ragland*, 481 U. S. 221, 237 (1987) (SCALIA, J., dissenting); see also *Leathers v. Medlock*, 499 U. S. 439, 447 (1991) ("[D]ifferential taxation of First Amendment speakers is constitutionally suspect when it threatens to suppress the expression of particular ideas or viewpoints"). In addition, as the NEA itself concedes, a more pressing constitutional question would arise if Government funding resulted in the imposition of a disproportionate burden calculated to drive "certain ideas or viewpoints from the marketplace." *Simon & Schuster, Inc. v. Members of N.Y. State Crime Victims Bd.*, 502 U. S. 105, 116 (1991); see Brief for Petitioners 38, n. 12. Unless § 954(d)(1) is applied in a manner that raises concern about the suppression of disfavored viewpoints, however, we uphold the constitutionality of the provision. Cf. *Red Lion Broadcasting Co. v. FCC*, 395 U. S. 367, 396 (1969) ("[W]e will not now pass upon the constitutionality of these regulations by envisioning the most extreme applications conceivable, but will deal with those problems if and when they arise" (citation omitted)).

B

Finally, although the First Amendment certainly has application in the subsidy context, we note that the Government may allocate competitive funding according to criteria that would be impermissible were direct regulation of speech or a criminal penalty at stake. So long as legislation does not infringe on other constitutionally protected rights, Congress has wide latitude to set spending priorities. See *Regan, supra,* at 549. In the 1990 amendments that incorporated § 954(d)(1), Congress modified the declaration of purpose in the NEA's enabling Act to provide that arts funding should "contribute to public support and confidence in the use of taxpayer funds," and that "[p]ublic funds ... must ultimately serve public purposes the Congress defines." § 951(5). And as we held in *Rust,* Congress may "selectively fund a program to encourage certain activities it believes to be in the public interest, without at the same time funding an alternative program which seeks to deal with the problem in another way." 500 U. S., at 193. In doing so, "the Government has not discriminated on the basis of viewpoint; it has merely chosen to fund one activity to the exclusion of the other." *Ibid.;* see also *Maher v. Roe,* 432 U. S. 464, 475 (1977) ("There is a basic difference between direct state interference with a protected activity and state encouragement of an alternative activity consonant with legislative policy").

III

The lower courts also erred in invalidating § 954(d)(1) as unconstitutionally vague. Under the First and Fifth Amendments, speakers are protected from arbitrary and discriminatory enforcement of vague standards. See *NAACP v. Button,* 371 U. S. 415, 432-433 (1963). The terms of the provision are undeniably opaque, and if they appeared in a criminal statute or regulatory scheme, they could raise substantial vagueness concerns. It is unlikely, however, that speakers will be compelled to steer too far clear of any "forbidden area" in the context of grants of this nature. Cf. *Board of Airport Comm'rs of Los Angeles v. Jews for Jesus, Inc.,* 482 U. S. 569, 574 (1987) (facially invalidating a flat ban on any "First Amendment" activities in an airport); *Hoffman Estates v. Flipside, Hoffman Estates, Inc.,* 455 U. S. 489, 499 (1982) ("prohibitory and stigmatizing effect" of a "quasicriminal" ordinance relevant to the vagueness analysis); *Grayned v. City of Rockford,* 408 U. S., at 108 (requiring clear lines between "lawful and unlawful" conduct). We recognize, as a practical matter, that artists may conform their speech to what they believe to be the decision making criteria in order to acquire funding. See Statement of Charlotte Murphy, Executive Director of NAAO, reprinted in App. 2122. But when the Government is acting as patron rather than as sovereign, the consequences of imprecision are not constitutionally severe.

In the context of selective subsidies, it is not always feasible for Congress to legislate with clarity. Indeed, if this statute is unconstitutionally vague, then so too are all Government programs awarding scholarships and grants on the basis of subjective criteria such as "excellence." See, e.g., 2 U. S. C. § 802 (establishing the Congressional Award

Program to "promote initiative, achievement, and excellence among youths in the areas of public service, personal development, and physical and expedition fitness"); 20 U. S. C. § 956(c)(1) (providing funding to the National Endowment for the Humanities to promote "progress and scholarship in the humanities"); § 1134h(a) (authorizing the Secretary of Education to award fellowships to "students of superior ability selected on the basis of demonstrated achievement and exceptional promise"); 22 U. S. C. § 2452(a) (authorizing the award of Fulbright grants to "strengthen international cooperative relations"); 42 U. S. C. § 7382c (authorizing the Secretary of Energy to recognize teachers for "excellence in mathematics or science education"). To accept respondents' vagueness argument would be to call into question the constitutionality of these valuable Government programs and countless others like them. Section 954(d)(1) merely adds some imprecise considerations to an already subjective selection process. It does not, on its face, impermissibly infringe on First or Fifth Amendment rights. Accordingly, the judgment of the Court of Appeals is reversed, and the case is remanded for further proceedings consistent with this opinion.

It is so ordered.

JUSTICE SCALIA, with whom JUSTICE THOMAS joins, concurring in the judgment.

"The operation was a success, but the patient died."

What such a procedure is to medicine, the Court's opinion in this case is to law. It sustains the constitutionality of 20 U. S. C. § 954(d)(1) by gutting it. The most avid congressional opponents of the provision could not have asked for more. I write separately because, unlike the Court, I think that § 954(d)(1) must be evaluated as written, rather than as distorted by the agency it was meant to control. By its terms, it establishes content- and viewpoint-based criteria upon which grant applications are to be evaluated. And that is perfectly constitutional.

I. THE STATUTE MEANS WHAT IT SAYS

Section 954(d)(1) provides:

> "No payment shall be made under this section except upon application therefor which is submitted to the National Endowment for the Arts in accordance with regulations issued and procedures established by the Chairperson. In establishing such regulations and procedures, the Chairperson shall ensure that:
>
> "(1) artistic excellence and artistic merit are the criteria by which applications are judged, taking into consideration general standards of decency and respect for the diverse beliefs and values of the American public."

The phrase "taking into consideration general standards of decency and respect for the diverse beliefs and values of the American public" is what my grammar-school teacher would have condemned as a dangling modifier: There is no noun to which the participle is attached (unless one jumps out of paragraph (1) to press "Chairperson" into service). Even so, it is clear enough that the phrase is meant to apply to those who do the judging. The application reviewers must take into account "general standards of decency" and "respect for the diverse beliefs and values of the American public" when evaluating artistic excellence and merit. One can regard this as either suggesting that decency and respect are elements of what Congress regards as artistic excellence and merit, or as suggesting that decency and respect are factors to be taken into account *in addition to* artistic excellence and merit. But either way, it is entirely, 100% clear that decency and respect are to be taken into account in evaluating applications.

This is so apparent that I am at a loss to understand what the Court has in mind (other than the gutting of the statute) when it speculates that the statute is merely "advisory." *Ante,* at 581. General standards of decency and respect for Americans' beliefs and values *must* (for the statute says that the Chairperson "shall ensure" this result) be taken into account, see, e.g., American Heritage Dictionary 402 (3d ed. 1992) ("consider ... [t]o take into account; bear in mind"), in evaluating all applications. This does not mean that those factors must always be dispositive, but it *does* mean that they must always be considered. The method of compliance proposed by the National Endowment for the Arts (NEA) selecting diverse review panels of artists and nonartists that reflect a wide range of geographic and cultural perspectives-is so obviously inadequate that it insults the intelligence. A diverse panel membership increases the odds that, *if and when* the panel takes the factors into account, it will reach an accurate assessment of what they demand. But it in no way increases the odds that the panel *will* take the factors into consideration—much less *ensures* that the panel will do so, which is the Chairperson's duty under the statute. Moreover, the NEA's fanciful reading of § 954(d)(1) would make it wholly superfluous. Section 959(c) already requires the Chairperson to "issue regulations and establish procedures ... to ensure that all panels are composed, to the extent practicable, of individuals reflecting ... diverse artistic and cultural points of view."

The statute requires the decency and respect factors to be considered in evaluating *all* applications—not, for example, just those applications relating to educational programs, *ante,* at 584, or intended for a particular audience, *ante,* at 585. Just as it would violate the statute to apply the artistic excellence and merit requirements to only select categories of applications, it would violate the statute to apply the decency and respect factors less than universally. A reviewer may, of course, give varying weight to the factors depending on the context, and in some categories of cases (such as the Court's example of funding for symphony orchestras, *ante,* at 583) the factors may rarely if ever affect the outcome; but § 954(d)(1) requires the factors to be considered in every case.

I agree with the Court that § 954(d)(1) "imposes no categorical requirement," *ante,* at 581, in the sense that it does not require the denial of all applications that violate general standards of decency or exhibit disrespect for the diverse beliefs and values of Americans. Cf. § 954(d)(2) ("[O]bscenity ... shall not be funded"). But the factors need not be conclusive to be discriminatory. To the extent a particular applicant exhibits disrespect for the diverse beliefs and values of the American public or fails to comport with general standards of decency, the likelihood that he will receive a grant diminishes. In other words, the presence of the "tak[e] into consideration" clause "cannot be regarded as mere surplusage; it means something," *Potter v. United States,* 155 U. S. 438, 446 (1894). And the "something" is that the decision maker, all else being equal, will favor applications that display decency and respect, and disfavor applications that do not.

This unquestionably constitutes viewpoint discrimination. [NOTE 1] That conclusion is not altered by the fact that the statute does not "compe[l]" the denial of funding, *ante,* at 581, any more than a provision imposing a five-point handicap on all black applicants for civil service jobs is saved from being race discrimination by the fact that it does not compel the rejection of black applicants. If viewpoint discrimination in this context is unconstitutional (a point I shall address anon), the law is invalid unless there are some situations in which the decency and respect factors *do not constitute viewpoint discrimination.* And there is none. The applicant who displays "decency," that is, "[c]onformity to prevailing standards of propriety or modesty," American Heritage Dictionary, at 483 (def. 2), and the applicant who displays "respect," that is, "deferential regard," for the diverse beliefs and values of the American people, *id.,* at 1536 (def. 1), will *always* have an edge over an applicant who displays the opposite. And finally, the conclusion of viewpoint discrimination is not affected by the fact that what constitutes "'decency'" or "'the diverse values and beliefs of the American people'" is difficult to pin down, *ante,* at 583—any more than a civil service preference in favor of those who display "Republican-Party values" would be rendered nondiscriminatory by the fact that there is plenty of room for argument as to what Republican-Party values might be.

The "political context surrounding the adoption of the 'decency and respect' clause," which the Court discusses at some length, *ante,* at 581, does not change its meaning or affect its constitutionality. All that is proved by the various statements that the Court quotes from the Report of the Independent Commission and the floor debates is (1) that the provision was not meant categorically to exclude any particular viewpoint (which I have conceded, and which is plain from the text), and (2) that the language was not meant to do anything that is unconstitutional. That in no way propels the Court's leap to the countertextual conclusion that the provision was merely "aimed at reforming procedures," and cannot be "utilized as a tool for invidious viewpoint discrimination," *ante,* at 582. It is evident in the legislative history that § 954(d)(1) was prompted by, and directed at, the public funding of such offensive productions as Serrano's *Piss Christ,* the portrayal of a crucifix immersed in urine, and Mapplethorpe's show of lurid homoerotic photographs. Thus, even if one strays beyond the plain text it is perfectly clear that the statute was meant to disfavor—that is, to discriminate against—such productions. Not to ban their funding absolutely, to be sure (though as I shall discuss, that also would not have been unconstitutional), but to make their funding more difficult.

More fundamentally, of course, all this legislative history has no valid claim upon our attention at all. It is a virtual certainty that very few of the Members of Congress who voted for this language both (1) knew of, and (2) agreed with, the various statements that the Court has culled from the Report of the Independent Commission and the floor debate (probably conducted on an almost empty floor). And it is wholly irrelevant that the statute was a "bipartisan proposal introduced as a counterweight" to an alternative proposal that would directly restrict funding on the basis of viewpoint. See *ante,* at 581-582. We do not judge statutes as if we are surveying the scene of an accident; each one is reviewed, not on the basis of how much worse it could have been, but on the basis of what it says. See *United States v. Estate of Romani,* 523 U. S. 519, 535 (1998) (SCALIA, J., concurring in part and concurring in judgment). It matters not whether this enactment was the product of the most partisan alignment in history or whether, upon its passage, the Members all linked arms and sang, "The more we get together, the happier we'll be." It is "not consonant with our scheme of government for a court to inquire into the motives of legislators." *Tenney v. Brandhove,* 341 U. S. 367, 377 (1951). The law at issue in this case is to be found in the text of § 954(d)(1), which passed both Houses and was signed by the President, U. S. Const., Art. I, § 7. And that law unquestionably disfavors—discriminates against—indecency and disrespect for the diverse beliefs and values of the American people. I turn, then, to whether such viewpoint discrimination violates the Constitution.

II. WHAT THE STATUTE SAYS IS CONSTITUTIONAL

The Court devotes so much of its opinion to explaining why this statute means something other than what it says that it neglects to cite the constitutional text governing our analysis. The First Amendment reads: "Congress shall make no law ... *abridging* the freedom of speech." U. S. Const., Amdt. 1 (emphasis added). To abridge is "to contract, to diminish; to deprive of." T. Sheridan, A Complete Dictionary of the English Language (6th ed. 1796). With the enactment of § 954(d)(1), Congress did not *abridge* the speech of those who disdain the beliefs and values of the American public, nor did it *abridge* indecent speech. Those who wish to create indecent and disrespectful art are as unconstrained now as they were before the enactment of this statute. *Avant-garde artistes* such as respondents remain entirely free to *epater les bourgeois;*[NOTE 2] they are merely deprived of the additional satisfaction of having the bourgeoisie taxed to pay for it. It is preposterous to equate the denial of taxpayer subsidy with measures "aimed at the *suppression* of dangerous ideas." *Regan v. Taxation with Representation of Wash.,* 461 U. S. 540, 550 (1983) (emphasis added) (quoting *Cammarano v. United States,* 358 U. S. 498, 513 (1959), in turn quoting *Speiser v. Randall,* 357 U. S. 513, 519 (1958)). "The reason that denial of participation in a tax exemption or other subsidy scheme does not necessarily 'infringe' a fundamental right is that—unlike direct restriction or prohibition—such a denial does not, as a general rule, have any significant coercive effect." *Arkansas Writers' Project, Inc. v. Ragland,* 481 U. S. 221, 237 (1987) (SCALIA, J., dissenting). One might contend, I suppose, that a threat of rejection by the only available source of free money would constitute coercion and hence "abridgment" within the meaning of the First Amendment. Cf. *Norwood v. Harrison,* 413 U. S. 455, 465 (1973). I would not agree with such a contention, which would make the NEA the mandatory patron of all art too indecent, too disrespectful, or even too *kitsch* to attract private support. But even if one accepts the contention, it would have no application here. The NEA is far from the sole source of funding for art—even indecent, disrespectful, or just plain bad art. Accordingly, the Government may earmark NEA funds for projects it deems to be in the public interest without thereby abridging speech. *Regan v. Taxation with Representation of Wash., supra,* at 549. Section 954(d)(1) is no more discriminatory, and no less constitutional, than virtually every other piece of funding legislation enacted by Congress. "The Government can, without violating the Constitution, selectively fund a program to encourage certain activities it believes to be in the public interest, without at the same time funding an alternative program...." *Rust v. Sullivan,* 500 U. S. 173, 193 (1991). As we noted in *Rust,* when Congress chose to establish the National Endowment for Democracy it was not constitutionally required to fund programs encouraging competing philosophies of government—an example of funding discrimination that cuts much closer than this one to the core of *political* speech which is the primary concern of the First Amendment. See *id.*, at 194. It takes a particularly high degree of chutzpah for the NEA to contradict this proposition, since the agency itself discriminates—and is required by law to discriminate—in favor of artistic (as opposed to scientific, or political, or theological) expression. Not all the common folk, or even all great minds, for that matter, think that is a good idea. In 1800, when John Marshall told John Adams that a recent immigration of Frenchmen would include talented artists, "Adams denounced all Frenchmen, but most especially 'schoolmasters, painters, poets, &C.' He warned Marshall that the fine arts were like germs that infected healthy constitutions." J. Ellis, After the Revolution: Profiles of Early American Culture 36 (1979). Surely the NEA itself is nothing less than an institutionalized discrimination against that point of view. Nonetheless, it is constitutional, as is the congressional determination to favor decency and respect for beliefs and values over the opposite because such favoritism does not "abridge" anyone's freedom of speech.

Respondents, relying on *Rosenberger v. Rector and Visitors of Univ. of Va.,* 515 U. S. 819, 833 (1995), argue that viewpoint-based discrimination is impermissible unless the government is the speaker or the government is "disburs[ing] public funds to private entities to convey a governmental message." *Ibid.* It is impossible to imagine why that should be so; one would think that directly involving the government itself in the viewpoint discrimination (if it is unconstitutional) would make the situation even worse. Respondents are mistaken. It is the very business of government to favor and disfavor points of view on (in modern times, at least) innumerable subjects—which is the main reason we have decided to elect those who run the government, rather than save money by making their posts hereditary. And it makes not a bit of difference, insofar as either common sense or the

Constitution is concerned, whether these officials further their (and, in a democracy, our) favored point of view by achieving it directly (having government-employed artists paint pictures, for example, or government-employed doctors perform abortions); or by advocating it officially (establishing an Office of Art Appreciation, for example, or an Office of Voluntary Population Control); or by giving money to others who achieve or advocate it (funding private art classes, for example, or Planned Parenthood). [NOTE 3] None of this has anything to do with abridging anyone's speech. *Rosenberger,* as the Court explains, *ante,* at 586, found the view-point discrimination unconstitutional, not because funding of "private" speech was involved, but because the government had established a limited public forum—to which the NEA's granting of highly selective (if not highly discriminating) awards bears no resemblance.

The nub of the difference between me and the Court is that I regard the distinction between "abridging" speech and funding it as a fundamental divide, on this side of which the First Amendment is inapplicable. The Court, by contrast, seems to believe that the First Amendment, despite its words, has some ineffable effect upon funding, imposing constraints of an indeterminate nature which it announces (without troubling to enunciate any particular test) are not violated by the statute here—or, more accurately, are not violated by the quite different, emasculated statute that it imagines. "[T]he Government," it says, "may allocate competitive funding according to criteria that would be impermissible were direct regulation of speech or a criminal penalty at stake," *ante,* at 587-588. The Government, *I* think, may allocate both competitive and noncompetitive funding *ad libitum,* insofar as the First Amendment is concerned.

Finally, what is true of the First Amendment is also true of the constitutional rule against vague legislation: it has no application to funding. Insofar as it bears upon First Amendment concerns, the vagueness doctrine addresses the problems that arise from government *regulation* of expressive conduct, see *Grayned v. City of Rockford,* 408 U. S. 104, 108-109 (1972), not government grant programs. In the former context, vagueness produces an abridgment of lawful speech; in the latter it produces, at worst, a waste of money. I cannot refrain from observing, however, that if the vagueness doctrine *were* applicable, the agency charged with making grants under a statutory standard of "artistic excellence"—and which has itself thought that standard met by everything from the playing of Beethoven to a depiction of a crucifix immersed in urine—would be of more dubious constitutional validity than the "decency" and "respect" limitations that respondents (who demand to be judged on the same strict standard of "artistic excellence") have the humorlessness to call too vague.

• • • •

In its laudatory description of the accomplishments of the NEA, *ante,* at 574, the Court notes with satisfaction that "only a handful of the agency's roughly 100,000 awards have generated formal complaints," *ibid.* The Congress that felt it necessary to enact § 954(d)(1) evidently thought it much *more* noteworthy that *any* money exacted from American taxpayers had been used to produce a crucifix immersed in urine or a display of homoerotic photographs. It is no secret that the provision was prompted by, and directed at, the funding of such offensive productions. Instead of banning the funding of such productions absolutely, which I think would have been entirely constitutional, Congress took the lesser step of requiring them to be disfavored in the evaluation of grant applications. The Court's opinion today renders even that lesser step a nullity. For that reason, I concur only in the judgment.

JUSTICE SOUTER, dissenting.

The question here is whether the italicized segment of this statute is unconstitutional on its face: "[A]rtistic excellence and artistic merit are the criteria by which applications [for grants from the National Endowment for the Arts (NEA)] are judged, *taking into consideration general standards of decency and respect for the diverse beliefs and values of the American public.*" 20 U. S. C. § 954(d) (emphasis added). It is.

The decency and respect proviso mandates viewpoint-based decisions in the disbursement of Government subsidies, and the Government has wholly failed to explain why the statute should be afforded an exemption from the fundamental rule of the First Amendment that viewpoint discrimination in the exercise of public authority over expressive activity is unconstitutional. The Court's conclusions that the proviso is not viewpoint based, that it is not a regulation, and that the NEA may permissibly engage in viewpoint-based discrimination, are all patently mistaken. Nor may the question raised be answered in the Government's favor on the assumption that some constitutional applications of the statute are enough to satisfy the demand of facial constitutionality, leaving claims of the proviso's obvious invalidity to be dealt with later in response to challenges of specific applications of the discriminatory standards. This assumption is irreconcilable with our longstanding and sensible doctrine of facial overbreadth, applicable to claims brought under the First Amendment's speech clause. I respectfully dissent.

I

"If there is a bedrock principle underlying the First Amendment, it is that the government may not prohibit the expression of an idea simply because society finds the idea itself offensive or disagreeable." *Texas v. Johnson,* 491 U. S. 397, 414 (1989). "[A]bove all else, the First Amendment means that government has no power to restrict expression because of its message [or] its ideas," *Police Dept. of Chicago v. Mosley,* 408 U. S. 92, 95 (1972), which is to say that "[t]he principle of viewpoint neutrality ... underlies the First Amendment," *Bose Corp. v. Consumers Union of United States, Inc.,* 466 U. S. 485, 505 (1984). Because this principle applies not only to affirmative suppression of speech, but also to disqualification for government favors, Congress is generally not permitted to pivot discrimination against otherwise protected speech on the offensiveness or unacceptability of the views it expresses. See, e.g., *Rosenberger v. Rector and Visitors of Univ. of Va.,* 515 U.

S. 819 (1995) (public university's student activities funds may not be disbursed on viewpoint-based terms); *Lamb's Chapel v. Center Moriches Union Free School Dist.*, 508 U. S. 384 (1993) (after-hours access to public school property may not be withheld on the basis of viewpoint); *Leathers v. Medlock,* 499 U. S. 439, 447 (1991) ("[D]ifferential taxation of First Amendment speakers is constitutionally suspect when it threatens to suppress the expression of particular ideas or viewpoints"); *Pacific Gas & Elec. Co. v. Public Util. Comm'n of Cal.*, 475 U. S. 1 (1986) (government-mandated access to public utility's billing envelopes must not be viewpoint based); *Members of City Council of Los Angeles v. Taxpayers for Vincent,* 466 U. S. 789, 804 (1984) ("[T]he First Amendment forbids the government to regulate speech in ways that favor some viewpoints or ideas at the expense of others").

It goes without saying that artistic expression lies within this First Amendment protection. See, e.g., *Hurley v. Irish-American Gay, Lesbian and Bisexual Group of Boston, Inc.*, 515 U. S. 557, 569 (1995) (remarking that examples of painting, music, and poetry are "unquestionably shielded"); *Ward v. Rock Against Racism,* 491 U. S. 781, 790 (1989) ("Music, as a form of expression and communication, is protected under the First Amendment"); *Schad v. Mount Ephraim,* 452 U. S. 61, 65 (1981) ("Entertainment, as well as political and ideological speech, is protected; motion pictures, programs broadcast by radio and television, and live entertainment, such as musical and dramatic works, fall within the First Amendment guarantee"); *Kaplan v. California,* 413 U. S. 115, 119-120 (1973) ("[P]ictures, films, paintings, drawings, and engravings ... have First Amendment protection"). The constitutional protection of artistic works turns not on the political significance that may be attributable to such productions, though they may indeed comment on the political,[NOTE 1] but simply on their expressive character, which falls within a spectrum of protected "speech" extending outward from the core of overtly political declarations. Put differently, art is entitled to full protection because our "cultural life," just like our native politics, "rest[s] upon [the] ideal" of governmental viewpoint neutrality. *Turner Broadcasting System, Inc. v. FCC,* 512 U. S. 622, 641 (1994).

When called upon to vindicate this ideal, we characteristically begin by asking "whether the government has adopted a regulation of speech because of disagreement with the message it conveys. The government's purpose is the controlling consideration." *Ward v. Rock Against Racism, supra,* at 791 (citation omitted). The answer in this case is damning. One need do nothing more than read the text of the statute to conclude that Congress's purpose in imposing the decency and respect criteria was to prevent the funding of art that conveys an offensive message; the decency and respect provision on its face is quintessentially viewpoint based, and quotations from the Congressional Record merely confirm the obvious legislative purpose. In the words of a cosponsor of the bill that enacted the proviso, "[w]orks which deeply offend the sensibilities of significant portions of the public ought not to be supported with public funds." 136 Congo Rec. 28624 (1990).[NOTE 2] Another supporter of the bill observed that "the Endowment's support for artists like Robert Mapplethorpe and Andre[s] Serrano has offended and angered many citizens," behooving "Congress ... to listen to these complaints about the NEA and make sure that exhibits like [these] are not funded again." *Id.,* at 28642. Indeed, if there were any question at all about what Congress had in mind, a definitive answer comes in the succinctly accurate remark of the proviso's author, that the bill "add[s] to the criteria of artistic excellence and artistic merit, a shell, a screen, a viewpoint that must be constantly taken into account." *Id.,* at 28631.[NOTE 3]

II

In the face of such clear legislative purpose, so plainly expressed, the Court has its work cut out for it in seeking a constitutional reading of the statute. See *Edward J. DeBartolo Corp. v. Florida Gulf Coast Building & Constr. Trades Council,* 485 U. S. 568, 575 (1988).

A

The Court says, first, that because the phrase "general standards of decency and respect for the diverse beliefs and values of the American public" is imprecise and capable of multiple interpretations, "the considerations that the provision introduces, by their nature, do not engender the kind of directed viewpoint discrimination that would prompt this Court to invalidate a statute on its face." *Ante,* at 583. Unquestioned case law, however, is clearly to the contrary.

"Sexual expression which is indecent but not obscene is protected by the First Amendment," *Sable Communications of Cal., Inc. v. FCC,* 492 U. S. 115, 126 (1989), and except when protecting children from exposure to indecent material, see *FCC v. Pacifica Foundation,* 438 U. S. 726 (1978), the First Amendment has never been read to allow the government to rove around imposing general standards of decency, see, e.g., *Reno v. American Civil Liberties Union,* 521 U. S. 844 (1997) (striking down on its face a statute that regulated "indecency" on the Internet). Because "the normal definition of 'indecent' ... refers to nonconformance with accepted standards of morality," *FCC v. Pacifica Foundation, supra,* at 740, restrictions turning on decency, especially those couched in terms of "general standards of decency," are quintessentially viewpoint based: they require discrimination on the basis of conformity with mainstream mores. The Government's contrary suggestion that the NEA's decency standards restrict only the "form, mode, or style" of artistic expression, not the underlying viewpoint or message, Brief for Petitioners 39-41, may be a tempting abstraction (and one not lacking in support, cf. *Bolger v. Youngs Drug Products Corp.,* 463 U. S. 60, 83-84 (1983) (STEVENS, J., concurring in judgment)). But here it suffices to realize that "form, mode, or style" are not subject to abstraction from artistic viewpoint, and to quote from an opinion just two years old: "In artistic ... settings, indecency may have strong communicative content, protesting conventional norms or giving an edge to a work by conveying otherwise inexpressible emotions ... Indecency often is inseparable from the ideas and viewpoints conveyed, or separable only with loss of truth or expressive power." *Denver Area Ed. Telecommunications Consortium, Inc. v. FCC,* 518 U. S. 727,805 (1996) (KENNEDY, J., joined by GINSBURG, J., concurring) (citation and internal quotation marks omitted); see also *Cohen v. California,* 403 U. S. 15, 26 (1971)

("[W]e cannot indulge the facile assumption that one can forbid particular words without also running a substantial risk of suppressing ideas in the process"). "[T]he inextricability of indecency from expression," *Denver Area Ed. Telecommunications Consortium, supra,* at 805, is beyond dispute in a certain amount of entirely lawful artistic enterprise. Starve the mode, starve the message.

Just as self-evidently, a statute disfavoring speech that fails to respect America's "diverse beliefs and values" is the very model of viewpoint discrimination; it penalizes any view disrespectful to any belief or value espoused by someone in the American populace. Boiled down to its practical essence, the limitation obviously means that art that disrespects the ideology, opinions, or convictions of a significant segment of the American public is to be disfavored, whereas art that reinforces those values is not. After all, the whole point of the proviso was to make sure that works like Serrano's ostensibly blasphemous portrayal of Jesus would not be funded, see *supra,* at 603, while a reverent treatment, conventionally respectful of Christian sensibilities, would not run afoul of the law. Nothing could be more viewpoint based than that. Cf. *Rosenberger,* 515 U. S., at 831 (a statute targeting a "prohibited perspective, not the general subject matter" of religion is viewpoint based); *United States v. Eichman,* 496 U. S. 310, 317 (1990) (striking down anti-flagburning statute because it impermissibly prohibited speech that was "disrespectful" of the flag). The fact that the statute disfavors art insufficiently respectful of America's "diverse" beliefs and values alters this conclusion not one whit: the First Amendment does not validate the ambition to disqualify many disrespectful viewpoints instead of merely one. See *Rosenberger, supra,* at 831-832.

B

Another alternative for avoiding unconstitutionality that the Court appears to regard with some favor is the Government's argument that the NEA may comply with § 954(d) merely by populating the advisory panels that analyze grant applications with members of diverse backgrounds. See *ante,* at 577, 581. Would that it were so easy; this asserted implementation of the law fails even to "reflec[t] a plausible construction of the plain language of the statute." *Rust v. Sullivan,* 500 U. S. 173, 184 (1991).

The Government notes that § 954(d) actually provides that "[i]n establishing ... regulations and procedures, the Chairperson [of the NEA] shall ensure that (1) artistic excellence and artistic merit are the criteria by which applications are judged, taking into consideration general standards of decency and respect for the diverse beliefs and values of the American public." According to the Government, this language requires decency and respect to be considered not in judging applications, but in making regulations. If, then, the Chairperson takes decency and respect into consideration through regulations ensuring diverse panels, the statute is satisfied. But it would take a great act of will to find any plausibility in this reading. The reference to considering decency and respect occurs in the subparagraph speaking to the "criteria by which applications are judged," not in the preamble directing the Chairperson to adopt regulations; it is in judging applications that decency and respect are most obviously to be considered. It is no surprise, then, that the Government's reading is directly contradicted by the legislative history. According to the provision's author, the decency and respect proviso "mandates that in the awarding of funds, in the award process itself, general standards of decency must be accorded." 136 Congo Rec. 28672 (1990). Or, as the cosponsor of the bill put it, "the decisions of artistic excellence must take into consideration general standards of decency and respect for the diverse beliefs and values of the American public." *Id.,* at 28624.

The Government offers a variant of this argument in suggesting that even if the NEA must take decency and respect into account in the active review of applications, it may satisfy the statute by doing so in an indirect way through the natural behavior of diversely constituted panels. This, indeed, has apparently been the position of the Chairperson of the NEA since shortly after the legislation was first passed. But the problems with this position are obvious. First, it defies the statute's plain language to suggest that the NEA complies with the law merely by allowing decency and respect to have their way through the subconscious inclinations of panel members. "[T]aking into consideration" is a conscious activity. See Webster's New International Dictionary 2570 (2d ed. 1949) (defining "take into consideration" as "[t]o make allowance in judging for"); *id.*, at 569 (defining "consideration" as the "[a]ct or process of considering; continuous and careful thought; examination; deliberation; attention"); *id.*, at 568 (defining "consider" as "to think on with care ... to bear in mind"). Second, even assuming that diverse panel composition would produce a sufficient response to the proviso, that would merely mean that selection for decency and respect would occur derivatively through the inclinations of the panel members, instead of directly through the intentional application of the criteria; at the end of the day, the proviso would still serve its purpose to screen out offending artistic works, and it would still be unconstitutional. Finally, a less obvious but equally dispositive response is that reading the statute as a mandate that may be satisfied merely by selecting diverse panels renders § 954(d)(1) essentially redundant § 959(c), which provides that the review panels must comprise "individuals reflecting a wide geographic, ethnic, and minority representation as well as individuals reflecting diverse artistic and cultural points of view." Statutory interpretations that "render superfluous other provisions in the same enactment" are strongly disfavored. *Freytag v. Commissioner,* 501 U. S. 868, 877 (1991) (internal quotation marks omitted).

C

A third try at avoiding constitutional problems is the Court's disclaimer of any constitutional issue here because "[§] 954(d)(1) adds 'considerations' to the grant-making process; it does not preclude awards to projects that might be deemed 'indecent' or 'disrespectful,' nor place conditions on grants, or even specify that those factors must be given any particular weight in reviewing an application." *Ante,* at 580-581. Since "§ 954(d)(1) admonishes the NEA merely to take 'decency and respect' into consideration," *ante,* at 582, not to make funding decisions specifically on those grounds, the Court sees no constitutional difficulty.

That is not a fair reading. Just as the statute cannot be read as anything but viewpoint based, or as requiring nothing more than diverse review panels, it cannot be read as tolerating awards to spread indecency or disrespect, so long as the review panel, the National Council on the Arts, and the Chairperson have given some thought to the offending qualities and decided to underwrite them anyway. That, after all, is presumably just what prompted the congressional outrage in the first place, and there was nothing naive about the Representative who said he voted for the bill because it does "not tolerate wasting Federal funds for sexually explicit photographs [or] sacrilegious works." 136 Congo Rec. 28676 (1990). But even if I found the Court's view of "consideration" plausible, that would make no difference at all on the question of constitutionality. What if the statute required a panel to apply criteria "taking into consideration the centrality of Christianity to the American cultural experience," or "taking into consideration whether the artist is a communist," or "taking into consideration the political message conveyed by the art," or even "taking into consideration the superiority of the white race"? Would the Court hold these considerations facially constitutional, merely because the statute had no requirement to give them any particular, much less controlling, weight? I assume not. In such instances, the Court would hold that the First Amendment bars the government from considering viewpoint when it decides whether to subsidize private speech, and a statute that mandates the consideration of viewpoint is quite obviously unconstitutional. Cf. *Dawson v. Delaware,* 503 U. S. 159, 167 (1992) (holding that the First Amendment forbids reliance on a defendant's abstract beliefs at sentencing, even if they are considered as one factor among many); *Ozonoff v. Berzak,* 744 F.2d 224, 233 (*CA1* 1984) (Breyer, J.) (holding that an Executive Order which provided that a person's political associations *"may* be considered" in determining security clearance violated the First Amendment). Section 954(d)(1) is just such a statute.

III

A second basic strand in the Court's treatment of today's question, see *ante,* at 585-587, and the heart of JUSTICE SCALIA'S, see *ante,* at 595-599, in effect assume that whether or not the statute mandates viewpoint discrimination, there is no constitutional issue here because government art subsidies fall within a zone of activity free from First Amendment restraints. The Government calls attention to the roles of government-as-speaker and government-as-buyer, in which the government is of course entitled to engage in viewpoint discrimination: if the Food and Drug Administration launches an advertising campaign on the subject of smoking, it may condemn the habit without also having to show a cowboy taking a puff on the opposite page;[NOTE 4] and if the Secretary of Defense wishes to buy a portrait to decorate the Pentagon, he is free to prefer George Washington over George the Third.[NOTE 5]

The Government freely admits, however, that it neither speaks through the expression subsidized by the NEA,[NOTE 6] nor buys anything for itself with its NEA grants. On the contrary, believing that "[t]he arts ... reflect the high place accorded by the American people to the nation's rich cultural heritage," § 951(6), and that "[i]t is vital to a democracy … to provide financial assistance to its artists and the organizations that support their work," § 951(10), the Government acts as a patron, financially underwriting the production of art by private artists and impresarios for independent consumption. Accordingly, the Government would have us liberate government-as-patron from First Amendment strictures not by placing it squarely within the categories of government-as-buyer or government-as-speaker, but by recognizing a new category by analogy to those accepted ones. The analogy is, however, a very poor fit, and this patronage falls embarrassingly on the wrong side of the line between government-as-buyer or -speaker and government-as- regulator-of-private-speech.

The division is reflected quite clearly in our precedents. Drawing on the notion of government-as-speaker, we held in *Rust v. Sullivan,* 500 U. S., at 194, that the Government was entitled to appropriate public funds for the promotion of particular choices among alternatives offered by health and social service providers (e.g., family planning with, and without, resort to abortion). When the government promotes a particular governmental program, "it is entitled to define the limits of that program," and to dictate the viewpoint expressed by speakers who are paid to participate in it. *Ibid.*[NOTE 7] But we added the important qualifying language that "[t]his is not to suggest that funding by the Government, even when coupled with the freedom of the fund recipients to speak outside the scope of the Government-funded project, is invariably sufficient to justify Government control over the content of expression." *Id.,* at 199. Indeed, outside of the contexts of government-as-buyer and government-as-speaker, we have held time and time again that Congress may not "discriminate invidiously in its subsidies in such a way as to aim at the suppression of … ideas." *Regan v. Taxation with Representation of Wash.,* 461 U. S. 540, 548 (1983) (internal quotation marks and brackets omitted); see also *Lamb's Chapel,* 508 U. S., at 394 (when the government subsidizes private speech, it may not "favor some viewpoints or ideas at the expense of others"); *Hannegan v. Esquire, Inc.,* 327 U. S. 146, 149 (1946) (the Postmaster General may not deny subsidies to certain periodicals on the ground that they are "morally improper and not for the public welfare and the public good").

Our most thorough statement of these principles is found in the recent case of *Rosenberger v. Rector and Visitors of Univ. of Va.,* 515 U. S. 819 (1995), which held that the University of Virginia could not discriminate on viewpoint in underwriting the speech of student-run publications. We recognized that the government may act on the basis of viewpoint "when the State is the speaker" or when the State "disburses public funds to private entities to convey a governmental message." *Id.,* at 833. But we explained that the government may not act on viewpoint when it "does not itself speak or subsidize transmittal of a message it favors but instead expends funds to encourage a diversity of views from private speakers." *Id.,* at 834. When the government acts as patron, subsidizing the expression of others, it may not prefer one lawfully stated view over another.

Rosenberger controls here. The NEA, like the student activities fund in *Rosenberger,* is a subsidy scheme created to encourage expression of a diversity of views from private speakers. Congress brought the NEA into being to help all Americans "achieve a better understanding of the past, a better analysis of the present, and a better view of the future." § 951(3). The NEA's purpose is to "support new ideas" and "to help create and sustain ... a climate encouraging freedom of thought, imagination, and inquiry." §§ 951(10), (7); see also S. Rep. No. 300, 89th Cong., 1st Sess., 4 (1965) ("[T]he intent of this act should be the encouragement of free inquiry and expression"); H. R. Rep. No. 99-274, p. 13 (1985) (Committee Report accompanying bill to reauthorize and amend the NEA's governing statute) ("As the Preamble of the act directs, the Endowment['s] programs should be open and richly diverse, reflecting the ferment of ideas which has always made this Nation strong and free"). Given this congressional choice to sustain freedom of expression, *Rosenberger* teaches that the First Amendment forbids decisions based on viewpoint popularity. So long as Congress chooses to subsidize expressive endeavors at large, it has no business requiring the NEA to turn down funding applications of artists and exhibitors who devote their "freedom of thought, imagination, and inquiry" to defying our tastes, our beliefs, or our values. It may not use the NEA's purse to "suppres[s] ... dangerous ideas." *Regan v. Taxation with Representation of Wash., supra,* at 548 (internal quotation marks omitted).

The Court says otherwise, claiming to distinguish *Rosenberger* on the ground that the student activities funds in that case were generally available to most applicants, whereas NEA funds are disbursed selectively and competitively to a choice few. *Ante,* at 586. But the Court in *Rosenberger* anticipated and specifically rejected just this distinction when it held in no uncertain terms that "[t]he government cannot justify viewpoint discrimination among private speakers on the economic fact of scarcity." 515 U. S., at 835. Scarce money demands choices, of course, but choices "on some acceptable [viewpoint] neutral principle," like artistic excellence and artistic merit;[NOTE 9] "nothing in our decision[s] indicate[s] that scarcity would give the State the right to exercise viewpoint discrimination that is otherwise impermissible." *Ibid.;* see also *Arkansas Ed. Television Comm'n v. Forbes,* 523 U. S. 666, 676 (1998) (scarcity of air time does not justify viewpoint-based exclusion of candidates from a debate on public television; neutral selection criteria must be employed). If the student activities fund at issue in *Rosenberger* had awarded competitive, merit-based grants to only 50%, or even 5%, of the applicants, on the basis of "journalistic merit taking into consideration the message of the newspaper," it is obvious beyond peradventure that the Court would not have come out differently, leaving the University free to refuse funding after considering a publication's Christian perspective.[NOTE 10]

A word should be said, finally, about a proposed alternative to this failed analogy. As the Solicitor General put it at oral argument, "there is something unique ... about the Government funding of the arts for First Amendment purposes." Tr. of Oral Arg. 27. However different the governmental patron may be from the governmental speaker or buyer, the argument goes, patronage is also singularly different from traditional regulation of speech, and the limitations placed on the latter would be out of place when applied to viewpoint discrimination in distributing patronage. To this, there are two answers. The first, again, is *Rosenberger,* which forecloses any claim that the NEA and the First Amendment issues that arise under it are somehow unique. But even if we had no *Rosenberger,* and even if I thought the NEA's program of patronage was truly singular, I would not hesitate to reject the Government's plea to recognize a new, categorical patronage exemption from the requirement of viewpoint neutrality. I would reject it for the simple reason that the Government has offered nothing to justify recognition of a new exempt category.

The question of who has the burden to justify a categorical exemption has never been explicitly addressed by this Court, despite our recognition of the speaker and buyer categories in the past. The answer is nonetheless obvious in a recent statement by the Court synthesizing a host of cases on viewpoint discrimination. "The First Amendment presumptively places this sort of discrimination beyond the power of the government." *Simon & Schuster, Inc. v. Members of N.Y. State Crime Victims Bd.,* 502 U. S. 105, 116 (1991). Because it takes something to defeat a presumption, the burden is necessarily on the Government to justify a new exception to the fundamental rules that give life to the First Amendment. It is up to the Government to explain why a sphere of governmental participation in the arts (unique or not) should be treated as outside traditional First Amendment limits. The Government has not carried this burden here, or even squarely faced it.

IV

Although I, like the Court, recognize that "facial challenges to legislation are generally disfavored," *FW/PBS, Inc. v. Dallas,* 493 U. S. 215, 223 (1990), the proviso is the type of statute that most obviously lends itself to such an attack. The NEA does not offer a list of reasons when it denies a grant application, and an artist or exhibitor whose subject raises a hint of controversy can never know for sure whether the decency and respect criteria played a part in any decision by the NEA to deny funding. Hence, the most that we could hope for in waiting for an as-applied challenge would be (a) a plaintiff whose rejected proposal raised some risk of offense and was not aimed at exhibition in a forum in which decency and respect might serve as permissible selection criteria, or (b) a plaintiff who sought funding for a project that had been sanitized to avoid rejection. But no one has denied here that the institutional plaintiff, the National Association of Artists' Organizations (NAAO), has representative standing on behalf of some such potential plaintiffs. See App. 21-25 (declaration of NAAO's Executive Director, listing examples of the potentially objectionable works produced by several member organizations). We would therefore gain nothing at all by dismissing this case and requiring those individuals or groups to bring essentially the same suit, restyled as an as-applied challenge raising one of the possibilities just mentioned.

In entertaining this challenge, the Court finds § 954(d)(1) constitutional on its face in part because there are "a number of indisputably constitutional applications" for both the "decency" and the "respect" criteria, *ante,* at 584, and it is hard to imagine "how 'decency' or 'respect' would bear on grant applications in categories such as funding for symphony orchestras," *ante,* at 583. There are circumstances in which we have rejected facial challenges for similar reasons. "A facial challenge to a legislative Act is, of course, the most difficult challenge to mount successfully, since the challenger must establish that no set of circumstances exists under which the Act would be valid." *United States v. Salerno,* 481 U. S. 739, 745 (1987). But quite apart from any question that might be raised about that statement as a general rule,[NOTE 11] it is beyond question, as the Court freely concedes, that it can have no application here, it being well settled that the general rule does not limit challenges brought under the First Amendment's speech clause.

There is an "exception to the [capable-of-constitutional application] rule recognized in our jurisprudence [for] facial challenge[s] based upon First Amendment free-speech grounds. We have applied to statutes restricting speech a so-called 'overbreadth' doctrine, rendering such a statute invalid in all its applications (i.e., facially invalid) if it is invalid in any of them." *Ada v. Guam Society of Obstetricians* & Gynecologists, 506 U. S. 1011, 1012 (1992) (SCALIA, J., dissenting from denial of certiorari);[NOTE 12] see, e.g., *Reno v. American Civil Liberties Union,* 521 U. S. 844 (1997) (striking down decency provision of Communications Decency Act as facially overbroad); *id.*, at 893-894 (O'CONNOR, J., concurring in judgment in part and dissenting in part) (declining to apply the rule of *Salerno* because the plaintiffs' claim arose under the First Amendment); *Schad v. Mount Ephraim,* 452 U. S., at 66 ("Because appellants' claims are rooted in the First Amendment, they are entitled to ... raise an overbreadth challenge") (internal quotation marks omitted); *Gooding v. Wilson,* 405 U. S. 518, 521-522 (1972).[NOTE 13] Thus, we have we have routinely understood the overbreadth doctrine to apply where the plaintiff mounts a facial challenge to a law investing the government with discretion to discriminate on viewpoint when it parcels out benefits in support of speech. See, e.g., *City of Lakewood v. Plain Dealer Publishing Co.,* 486 U. S. 750, 759 (1988) ("[A] facial challenge lies whenever a licensing law gives a government official or agency substantial power to discriminate based on the content or viewpoint of speech by suppressing disfavored speech or disliked speakers"); *Forsyth County v. Nationalist Movement,* 505 U. S. 123 (1992) (applying overbreadth doctrine to invalidate on its face an ordinance allowing for content-based discrimination in the awarding of parade permits).

To be sure, such a "facial challenge will not succeed unless the statute is 'substantially' overbroad," *New York State Club Assn., Inc. v. City of New York,* 487 U. S. 1, 11 (1988), by which we mean that "a law should not be invalidated for overbreadth unless it reaches a substantial number of impermissible applications," *New York v. Ferber,* 458 U. S. 747, 771 (1982). But that is no impediment to invalidation here. The Court speculates that the "decency" criterion might permissibly be applied to applications seeking to create or display art in schools[NOTE 14] or children's museums, whereas the "respect" criterion might permissibly be applied to applications seeking to create art that celebrates a minority, tribal, rural, or inner-city culture. But even so, this is certainly a case in which the challenged statute "reaches a substantial number of impermissible applications," not one in which the statute's "legitimate reach dwarfs its arguably impermissible applications." *Id.,* at 771, 773. On the contrary, nothing in the record suggests that the grant scheme administered under the broad authorization of the NEA's governing statute, see §§ 951, 954(c), devotes an overwhelming proportion of its resources to schools and ethnic commemoration. Since the decency and respect criteria may not be employed in the very many instances in which the art seeking a subsidy is neither aimed at children nor meant to celebrate a particular culture, the statute is facially overbroad. Cf. *City of Lakewood,* supra, at 766 ("[I]n a host of ... First Amendment cases we have ... considered on the merits facial challenges to statutes or policies that embodied discrimination based on the content or viewpoint of expression, or vested officials with open-ended discretion that threatened the same, even where it was assumed that a properly drawn law could have greatly restricted or prohibited the manner of expression or circulation at issue"). Accordingly, the Court's observation that there are a handful of permissible applications of the decency and respect proviso, even if true, is irrelevant.[NOTE 15]

The Government takes a different tack, arguing that overbreadth analysis is out of place in this case because the "prospect for 'chilling' expressive conduct," which forms the basis for the overbreadth doctrine, see, e.g., *Massachusetts v. Oakes,* 491 U. S. 576, 584 (1989) (plurality opinion of O'CONNOR, J.), "is not present here." Brief for Petitioners 20-21, n. 5. But that is simply wrong. We have explained before that the prospect of a denial of government funding necessarily carries with it the potential to "chil[l] ... individual thought and expression." *Rosenberger,* 515 U. S., at 835. In the world of NEA funding, this is so because the makers or exhibitors of potentially controversial art will either trim their work to avoid anything likely to offend, or refrain from seeking NEA funding altogether. Either way, to whatever extent NEA eligibility defines a national mainstream, the proviso will tend to create a timid esthetic. And either way, the proviso's viewpoint discrimination will "chill the expressive activity of [persons] not before the court." *Forsyth County, supra,* at 129. See App. 22-24 (declaration of Charlotte Murphy, Executive Director of respondent NAAO) (recounting how some NAAO members have not applied for NEA grants for fear that their work would be found indecent or disrespectful, while others have applied but were "chilled in their applications and in the scope of their projects" by the decency and respect provision). Indeed, because NEA grants are often matched by funds from private donors, the constraining impact of § 954(d)(1) is significantly magnified:

> "[T]he chilling effect caused by [the NEA's viewpoint-based selection criteria] is exacerbated by the practical realities of funding in the artistic community. Plainly stated, the NEA occupies a dominant and influential role in the financial affairs of the art world in the United States. Because the NEA provides much of its support with conditions that require matching or co-funding from private sources, the NEA's funding involvement in a project necessarily has a multiplier effect in the competitive market for funding of artistic endeavors.... [In addition,] most non-federal funding sources regard the NEA award as an imprimatur that signifies the recipient's artistic merit and value. NEA grants lend prestige and legitimacy to projects and are therefore critical to the ability of artists and companies to attract non-federal funding sources. Grant applicants rely on the NEA well beyond the dollar value of any particular grant." *Bella Lewitzky Dance Foundation v. Frohnmayer,* 754

F. Supp. 774, 783 (CD Cal. 1991) (footnote and internal quotation marks omitted).[NOTE 16]

Since the decency and respect proviso of § 954(d)(1) is substantially overbroad and carries with it a significant power to chill artistic production and display, it should be struck down on its face.[NOTE 17]

V

The Court does not strike down the proviso, however. Instead, it preserves the irony of a statutory mandate to deny recognition to virtually any expression capable of causing offense in any quarter as the most recent manifestation of a scheme enacted to "create and sustain ... a climate encouraging freedom of thought, imagination, and inquiry." § 951(7).

NOTES:

SCALIA DISSENT:

NOTE 1: If there is any uncertainty on the point, it relates only to the adjective, which is not at issue in the current discussion. That is, one might argue that the decency and respect factors constitute *content* discrimination rather than *viewpoint* discrimination, which would render them easier to uphold. Since I believe this statute must be upheld in either event, I pass over this conundrum and assume the worst.

NOTE 2: Which they do quite well. The *oeuvres d'art* for which the four individual plaintiffs in this case sought funding have been described as follows:

> "Finley's controversial show, 'We Keep Our Victims Ready,' contains three segments. In the second segment, Finley visually recounts a sexual assault by stripping to the waist and smearing chocolate on her breasts and by using profanity to describe the assault. Holly Hughes' monologue 'World Without End' is a somewhat graphic recollection of the artist's realization of her lesbianism and reminiscence of her mother's sexuality. John Fleck, in his stage performance 'Blessed Are All the Little Fishes,' confronts alcoholism and Catholicism. During the course of the performance, Fleck appears dressed as a mermaid, urinates on the stage and creates an altar out of a toilet bowl by putting a photograph of Jesus Christ on the lid. Tim Miller derives his performance 'Some Golden States' from childhood experiences, from his life as a homosexual, and from the constant threat of AIDS. Miller uses vegetables in his performances to represent sexual symbols." Note, 48 Wash. & Lee L. Rev. 1545, 1546, n. 2 (1991) (citations omitted).

NOTE 3: I suppose it would be unconstitutional for the government to give money to an organization devoted to the promotion of candidates nominated by the Republican Party—but it would be just as unconstitutional for the government itself to promote candidates nominated by the Republican Party, and I do not think that that unconstitutionality has anything to do with the First Amendment.

SOUTER DISSENT:

NOTE 1: Art "may affect public attitudes and behavior in a variety of ways, ranging from direct espousal of a political or social doctrine to the subtle shaping of thought which characterizes all artistic expression." *Joseph Burstyn, Inc. v. Wilson,* 343 U. S. 495, 501 (1952).

NOTE 2: There is, of course, nothing whatsoever unconstitutional about this view as a general matter. Congress has no obligation to support artistic enterprises that many people detest. The First Amendment speaks up only when Congress decides to participate in the Nation's artistic life by legal regulation, as it does through a subsidy scheme like the NEA. If Congress does choose to spend public funds in this manner, it may not discriminate by viewpoint in deciding who gets the money.

NOTE 3: On the subject of legislative history and purpose, it is disturbing that the Court upholds § 954(d) in part because the statute was drafted in hope of avoiding constitutional objections, with some Members of

Congress proclaiming its constitutionality on the congressional floor. See *ante,* at 581582. Like the Court, I assume that many Members of Congress believed the bill to be constitutional. Indeed, Members of Congress must take an oath or affirmation to support the Constitution, see U. S. Const., Art. VI, cl. 3, and we should presume in every case that Congress believed its statute to be consistent with the constitutional commands, see, e.g., *United States v. X-Citement Video, Inc.,* 513 U. S. 64, 73 (1994) ("[W]e do not impute to Congress an intent to pass legislation that is inconsistent with the Constitution"); *Yates v. United States,* 354 U. S. 298, 319 (1957). But courts cannot allow a legislature's conclusory belief in constitutionality, however sincere, to trump incontrovertible unconstitutionality, for "[i]t is emphatically the province and duty of the judicial department to say what the law is." *Marbury v. Madison,* 1 Cranch 137, 177 (1803).

I recognize, as the court explains, *ante,* at 581, that the amendment adding the decency and respect proviso was a bipartisan counterweight to more severe alternatives, and that some Members of Congress may have voted for it simply because it seemed the least among various evils. See, e.g., 136 Congo Rec. 28670 (1990) ("I am not happy with all aspects of the Williams-Coleman substitute.... It ... contains language concerning standards of decency that I find very troubling. But I applaud Mr. WILLIAMS for his efforts in achieving this compromise under very difficult circumstances.... I support the Williams-Coleman substitute"). Perhaps the proviso was the mildest alternative available, but that simply proves that the bipartisan push to reauthorize the NEA could succeed only by including at least some viewpoint-based limitations. An appreciation of alternatives does not alter the fact that Congress passed decency and respect restrictions, and it did so knowing and intending that those restrictions would prevent future controversies stemming from the NEA's funding of inflammatory art projects, by declaring the inflammatory to be disfavored for funding.

NOTE 4: See *Rust v. Sullivan,* 500 U. S. 173, 194 (1991) ("When Congress established a National Endowment for Democracy to encourage other countries to adopt democratic principles, 22 U. S. C. § 4411 (b), it was not constitutionally required to fund a program to encourage competing lines of political philosophy such as communism and fascism").

NOTE 5: On proposing the Public Works Art Project (PWAP), the New Deal program that hired artists to decorate public buildings, President Roosevelt allegedly remarked: "I can't have a lot of young enthusiasts painting Lenin's head on the Justice Building." Quoted in Mankin, Federal Arts Patronage in the New Deal, in America's Commitment to Culture: Government and the Arts 77 (K. Mulcahy & M. Wyszomirski eds. 1995). He was buying, and was free to take his choice.

NOTE 6: Here, the "communicative element inherent in the very act of funding itself," *Rosenberger v. Rector and Visitors of Univ. of Va.,* 515 U. S. 819, 892-893, n. 11 (1995) (SOUTER, J., dissenting), is an endorsement of the importance of the arts collectively, not an endorsement of the individual message espoused in a given work of art.

NOTE 7: In *Rust,* "the government did not create a program to encourage private speech but instead used private speakers to transmit specific information pertaining to its own program. We recognized that when the government appropriates public funds to promote a particular policy of its own it is entitled to say what it wishes." *Rosenberger, supra,* at 833 (citing *Rust, supra,* at 194).

NOTE 8: The Court's attempt to avoid *Rosenberger* by describing NEA funding in terms of competition, not scarcity, will not work. Competition implies scarcity, without which there is no exclusive prize to compete for; the Court's "competition" is merely a surrogate for "scarcity."

NOTE 9: While criteria of "artistic excellence and artistic merit" may raise intractable issues about the identification of artistic worth, and could no doubt be used covertly to filter out unwanted ideas, there is nothing inherently viewpoint discriminatory about such merit-based criteria. We have noted before that an esthetic government goal is perfectly legitimate. See *Metromedia, Inc. v. San Diego,* 453 U. S. 490, 507-508 (1981) (plurality opinion). Decency and respect, on the other hand, are inherently and facially viewpoint based, and serve no legitimate and permissible end. The Court's assertion that the mere fact that grants must be awarded according to artistic merit precludes "absolute neutrality" on the part of the NEA, *ante,* at 585, is therefore misdirected. It is not to the point that the Government necessarily makes choices among competing applications, or even that its judgments about artistic quality may be branded as subjective to some greater or lesser degree; the question here is whether the Government may apply patently viewpoint-based criteria in making those choices.

NOTE 10: JUSTICE SCALIA suggests that *Rosenberger* turned not on the distinction between government-as-speaker and government-as-facilitator-of-private-speech, but rather on the fact that "the government had established a limited public forum." *Ante,* at 599. Leaving aside the proper application of forum analysis to the NEA and its projects, I cannot agree that the holding of *Rosenberger* turned on characterizing its metaphorical forum as public in some degree. Like this case, *Rosenberger* involved viewpoint discrimination, and we have made it clear that such discrimination is impermissible in all forums, even nonpublic ones, *Cornelius v.*

NAACP Legal Defense & Ed. Fund, Inc., 473 U. S. 788,806 (1985), where, by definition, the government has not made public property generally available to facilitate private speech, *Perry Ed. Assn. v. Perry Local Educators' Assn.*, 460 U. S. 37,46 (1983) (defining a nonpublic forum as "[p]ublic property which is not by tradition or designation a forum for public communication"). Accordingly, *Rosenberger's* brief allusion to forum analysis was in no way determinative of the Court's holding.

NOTE 11: Cf., e.g., *Planned Parenthood of Southeastern Pa. v. Casey*, 505 U. S. 833, 895 (1992) (statute restricting abortion will be struck down if, "in a large fraction of the cases in which [the statute] is relevant, it will operate as a substantial obstacle to a woman's choice to undergo an abortion").

NOTE 12: We have, however, recognized that "the overbreadth doctrine does not apply to commercial speech." *Hoffman Estates v. Flipside, Hoffman Estates, Inc.*, 455 U. S. 489, 497 (1982).

NOTE 13: Cf. *United States v. Salerno*, 481 U. S. 739, 745 (1987) ("The fact that the Bail Reform Act might operate unconstitutionally under some conceivable set of circumstances is insufficient to render it wholly invalid, since we have not recognized an 'overbreadth' doctrine outside the limited context of the First Amendment").

NOTE 14: In placing such emphasis on the potential applicability of the decency criterion to educational programs, the Court neglects to point out the existence of § 954a, entitled "[a]ccess to the arts through support of education," which is concerned specifically with funding for arts education, especially in elementary and secondary schools. It seems that the NEA's "mission" to promote arts education, *ante*, at 584, is carried out primarily through § 954a, not § 954. While the decency standard might be constitutionally permissible when applied to applications for grants under § 954a, that standard does not appear to be relevant to such applications at all; the decency and respect provision appears in § 954(d), which governs grant applications under § 954, not under § 954a.

NOTE 15: The Court seemingly concedes that these isolated constitutional applications are in fact of little matter. For after speaking of specific applications that may be valid, the Court goes on to admit that these "would not alone be sufficient to sustain the statute." *Ante*, at 585. The Court nonetheless upholds the statute because it is not "persuaded that, in other applications, the language of § 954(d)(1) itself will give rise to the suppression of protected expression." *Ibid.* This conclusion appears to rest on some combination of (a) the Court's competition rationale as distinguishing *Rosenberger* and justifying the discrimination, (b) the Court's reading of the decency and respect proviso as something other than viewpoint based, and (c) the Court's treatment of "taking into consideration" as establishing no firm mandate subject to constitutional scrutiny. As already explained, however, fair reading of the text and attention to case law foreclose reliance on any, let alone all, of these arguments.

NOTE 16: See also, e.g., 131 Congo Rec. 24808 (1985) ("[S]upport from the Endowmen[t] has always represented a 'Good Housekeeping Seal' of approval which has helped grantees generate non-Federal dollars for projects and productions").

NOTE 17: I agree with the Court that § 954(d) is not unconstitutionally vague. Any chilling that results from imprecision in the drafting of standards (such as "artistic excellence and artistic merit") by which the Government awards scarce grants and scholarships is an inevitable and permissible consequence of distributing prizes on the basis of criteria dealing with a subject that defies exactness. The necessary imprecision of artistic-merit-based criteria justifies tolerating a degree of vagueness that might be intolerable when applying the First Amendment to attempts to regulate political discussion. Cf. *Arkansas Ed. Television Comm'n v. Forbes*, 523 U. S. 666, 694-695 (1998) (STEVENS, J., dissenting). My problem is not with the chilling that may naturally result from necessarily open standards; it is with the unacceptable chilling of "dangerous ideas," *Speiser v. Randall*, 357 U. S. 513, 519 (1958), that naturally results from explicitly viewpoint-based standards.

STUDY QUESTIONS

- What prompted Congress to amend the National Endowment for the Arts (NEA) Act, which was the subject of the lawsuit in *NEA v. Finley*?
- What was the issue before the Supreme Court and how did the majority rule?

- To what extent does Justice Scalia agree with the majority opinion? How do the Scalia and Souter dissents differ?
- Judging from Scalia's comments, what do you think is his personal view about *avant garde* art?
- Summarize the different interpretations on whether the NEA grant-making process represents "viewpoint" discrimination? What is the importance of the Justice's perspective on the federal government's role as "buyer," "speaker," and "patron"? What do these three opinions tell us about the issues surrounding public funding for the arts?

Reading Note: Also emblematic of the "culture wars," the following case arose from attempts by the Mayor of New York City to prevent the *Sensation* exhibit from being shown at the Brooklyn Institute of Arts. The case is another example of the politically charged legal and ethical issues that can arise in connection with controversial exhibits.

BROOKLYN INSTITUTE OF ARTS V. CITY OF NEW YORK

64 F. Supp. 2d 184 (E.D.N.Y. 1999)

Opinion and Order

GERSHON, District Judge.

The Mayor of the City of New York has decided that a number of works in the Brooklyn Museum's currently showing temporary exhibit *Sensation: Young British Artists from the Saatchi Collection* are "sick" and "disgusting" and, in particular, that one work, a painting entitled *The Holy Virgin Mary* by Chris Ofili, is offensive to Catholics and is an attack on religion. As a result, the City has withheld funds already appropriated to the Museum for operating expenses and maintenance and, in a suit filed in New York State Supreme Court two days after the Museum filed its suit in this court, seeks to eject the Museum from the City-owned land and building in which the Museum's collections have been housed for over one hundred years.

The Museum seeks a preliminary injunction barring the imposition of penalties by the Mayor and the City for the Museum's exercise of its First Amendment rights. The City and the Mayor move to dismiss the Museum's suit in this court, insofar as it seeks injunctive and declaratory relief, on the ground that this court must abstain from exercising jurisdiction in favor of the New York court action, in which, they argue, the Museum may assert, by way of defense and counterclaim, its First Amendment claims. For the reasons that follow, defendants' motion is denied, and plaintiff's motion is granted.

BACKGROUND

An examination of the history of the Brooklyn Museum and its relationship to the City of New York will illuminate the current controversy.

I. The History of the Brooklyn Museum

The Brooklyn Museum traces its origin to the Brooklyn Apprentices' Library, founded in 1823, whose book collection was first permanently housed in a Brooklyn Heights building constructed in 1825, reportedly after General Lafayette laid its cornerstone on the Fourth of July. A successor entity, the Brooklyn Institute, incorporated in 1843, expanded its holdings of books, natural history specimens and, to a lesser extent, art objects during the ensuing decades of the nineteenth century. By the late 1880's, prominent citizens and public figures of the then independent City of Brooklyn conceived an ambitious plan to vastly expand the Brooklyn Institute's collections in a mammoth new building, which would rival the combined collections of New York City's Metropolitan Museum of Art and Museum of Natural History.

The City of New York had already established in the 1870's a relationship with the Metropolitan Museum of Art and the Museum of Natural History that would serve as a prototype for the City's relationship with other designated cultural institutions, and for the relationship of the Brooklyn Museum with the cities of Brooklyn and later New York. That relationship is described in the official "Procedures Manual for New York City's Designated Cultural Institutions," at 3, as "joint partnerships between the City and a group of private citizens." The Procedures Manual describes that state legislation was passed to

Sensation *was a 1997 exhibition of contemporary art owned by advertising magnate Charles Saatchi, including many works by Young British Artists, (YBAs). The exhibit was first shown at the Royal Academy of Arts in London. The exhibition later toured to the Hamburger Bahnhof in Berlin and the Brooklyn Museum in New York City. The show generated controversy in both London and New York City due to the inclusion of controversial images of convicted English murder Myra Hindley and a painting of the Virgin Mary which used elephant dung and contained images of female genitalia. The exhibition was also criticized as an attempt to inflate the value of the Saatchi collection. A proposed showing at the National Gallery of Australia was cancelled when the gallery's director decided the exhibition was "too close to the market."*

incorporate those two museums, authorizing the City to construct the museums' facilities and to lease those facilities and the City-owned parkland on which they were located to the new corporations. The museums, in turn, "became responsible for programming the facilit[ies] and acquiring and exhibiting [their] collections. The leases ... contemplate that the City will maintain the building[s] while the [museums oversee] the display of [their] collection[s] to the general public."

In keeping with this historical precedent, the New York State Legislature in 1889 authorized the City of Brooklyn to reserve a portion of Prospect Park as "building sites for museums of art and science and libraries," and to lease such sites at nominal rent for up to one hundred years to corporations "created for educational purposes," provided that "such museums and libraries shall at all reasonable times be free, open and accessible to the public and private schools of the said city, and open and accessible to the general public on such terms of admission as the said mayor and commissioners shall approve...." L. 1889, c. 372, § 2.

The Brooklyn Institute was reorganized into the Brooklyn Institute of Arts and Sciences, the formal name of the plaintiff in this action (now known as the "Brooklyn Museum of Art" or "Brooklyn Museum" and sometimes referred to here as the "Museum"), by the New York State Legislature in 1890. The Act formally incorporating the Brooklyn Institute of Arts and Sciences, L. 1890, c. 172, designated by name approximately fifty private individuals as the original trustees of the Institute, and authorized the Institute to adopt its own constitution, bylaws, and all appropriate rules and regulations for its self-governance. *Id.* §§ 4, 5. Subsequent laws added public officials as *ex officio* members of the Board of Trustees, including the Mayor, Comptroller, Park Commissioner and Borough President. L. 1893, c. 579, *as amended,* L.1934, c. 87 and L.1949, c. 127. The 1890 Act further provides:

> *Section 2.* The purposes of said corporation shall be the establishment and maintenance of museums and libraries of art and science, the encouragement of the study of the arts and sciences and their application to the practical wants of man, and the advancement of knowledge in science and art, and in general to provide the means for popular instruction and enjoyment through its collections, libraries and lectures.
>
> *Section 3.* The museums and libraries of said corporation shall be open and free to the public and private schools of said city, at all reasonable times, and open to the general public on such terms of admission as shall be approved by the mayor and park commission of said city.

On December 23, 1893, as authorized by state law, the City of Brooklyn leased the land to the Institute for a term of one hundred years (the "Lease"), tracking the language of the 1889 Act as to the use of the property and the requirements for access by schools and the general public. The Lease further provides that "if and when such museums ... shall cease to be maintained according to the true intent and meaning of said act, and of this lease, then this lease shall be forfeited, and the said lands, and buildings thereon erected shall revert to the City of Brooklyn." Pursuant to other Acts of the New York State Legislature (L. 1891, c. 89; L. 1894, c. 577; L. 1896, c. 406), the City of Brooklyn funded construction of a building on the site designed by the noted architectural firm of McKim, Mead & White (although only a fraction of the original ambitious building plan was ever completed), to be leased to the Institute.

Upon completion of construction of a wing of the new building, the City of Brooklyn entered into a building lease and contract (the "Contract") with the Institute, for a term coextensive with the Lease, to house the Institute's collections. The City of New York is the successor to the City of Brooklyn under the Lease and the Contract. The parties agree that, upon the expiration of the original term of the Lease agreement in December 1993, the Museum remained a tenant in possession of the land and the building on the same terms and conditions as contained in the Lease and Contract.

The Contract provides that:

> The Brooklyn Institute of Arts and Sciences ... shall place on exhibition in said Museum Building collections of paintings and other works of art and collections and books representing or illustrating each and all of the Departments of the arts and sciences named in the constitution of said Institute, and shall cause to be properly arranged, labelled and catalogued all such collections and books as may be open to public exhibition or for public use, for the instruction and benefit of the residents of Brooklyn or the general public.

The Contract is unequivocal that the City has no ownership rights with respect to any of the collections in the Museum. It provides:

> That the collections of books and other objects in art and sciences placed in the Museum Building for purposes of exhibition, instruction, or to enable the Brooklyn Institute of Arts and Sciences to carry out its purposes as authorized in its charter, shall continue to be and shall remain absolutely the property of the [Institute], and that neither the [Mayor nor the City of Brooklyn] by reason of said property being placed in said building or continuance therein, have any title, property or interest therein.

The Museum established, as a branch, the first children's museum in the world in 1899. Throughout the first decades of this century, the Museum's collections greatly expanded, with Departments of Fine Arts, Natural Sciences, and a newly-established Department of Ethnology. The Museum decided in the 1930's to focus on its collections of fine art and cultural history, and to abandon its mission as a science museum. The Museum's natural history specimens were sent to other institutions. In 1934, the State legislature amended the description of the Institute's purpose quoted above, by adding reference to establishment and maintenance of "botanical gardens" and the provision of popular instruction and enjoyment through "musical and other performances." L.1934, c. 87. In the 1970's, various components of the Brooklyn Institute of Arts and Sciences became independent institutions, including the Brooklyn Children's Museum, the Brooklyn Academy of Music and the Brooklyn Botanic Garden.

The Museum today describes itself as having the second largest art collection in the United States, with approximately one and a half million objects. Its collections are divided into the following departments: (1) Egyptian, classical and ancient middle eastern art; (2) painting and sculpture; (3) arts of Africa, the Pacific and the Americas; (4) Asian art; (5) decorative arts, costumes and textiles; and (6) prints, drawings and photography. The Museum also has two research libraries and an archive. The Museum's permanent collection includes secular as well as numerous non-secular objects. Materials submitted to the court confirm the following description by the Museum's Chief Curator: "The collections include Catholic and Protestant religious works of art, Jewish religious objects, objects representing many Eastern religions, African spiritual objects, native American tribal objects, pre-Colombian objects, Islamic religious objects, as well as religious objects from numerous other cultures." These include many paintings and other objects which are reverential of the Madonna and other figures and symbols important to Christianity.

In addition to displaying works from its permanent collection to the public, the Museum regularly mounts temporary exhibits, and has done so throughout its history. Some of these exhibits involve well-known artists and their works. Others display little-known artists or obscure or esoteric works. The current temporary exhibit, *Sensation: Young British Artists from the Saatchi Collection* (the *Sensation Exhibit* or the *Exhibit*) is not the first controversial exhibit the Museum has mounted. Past controversial exhibits include art and performance exhibits in 1990 and 1991, respectively entitled, *The Play of the Unmentionable: The Brooklyn Museum Collection*, and *Too Shocking to Show*, which, to judge from contemporaneous news articles and materials prepared by the Museum, were provocative responses to protests over exhibits and performances at other institutions. Neither party to this litigation is aware of any past objection by the City to any Museum exhibit, or any prior effort by the City to stop an exhibit because of the content of any works included.

Undisputed documentary evidence establishes the Museum's commitment, throughout its history and continuing to date, to extensive educational programs for children, teachers, families, members of surrounding communities, and the general public. The Museum's Education Division serves over fifty thousand children and thirty-five thousand adults each year, with a staff of twenty-six full-time employees, nine full-time paid interns, thirty-five part-time instructors, and forty volunteer tour guides.

II. CITY FUNDING OF THE BROOKLYN MUSEUM

The Contract provides that "[the City] shall pay to the [Institute] each year such sum as may be necessary for the maintenance of said Museum Building, or as may be authorized by law or be apportioned or appropriated by [the City]." The Contract specifically defines "maintenance" to include: (1) repairs and alterations; (2) fuel; (3) waste removal; (4) wages of employees providing essential maintenance, custodial, security and other basic services; (5) cleaning and general care; (6) tools and supplies; and (7) insurance for the building, furniture and fixtures.

Consistent with the applicable statutes, the Lease, and the Contract, as well as with historical practices, the City's Procedures Manual specifies that public funds are provided to designated cultural institutions to help meet costs for general maintenance, security and energy, and in some instances to support education programs. City funds generally "are not used for direct curatorial or artistic services." Procedures Manual at 12. The City also approves certain capital expenditures as part of its program "to protect and ensure the continued existence of New York City's most precious assets, its cultural institutions, for local communities, the general public and the artistic community." *Id.* at 14. The City's Fiscal Year 2000 appropriation of approximately $5.7 million to the Museum specifies that the funding contributes to "maintenance, security, administration, curatorial, educational services and energy costs." The City was not asked to fund the controversial exhibit giving rise to this action. The City's Fiscal Year 2000 appropriation to the Brooklyn Children's Museum is approximately $1.6 million.

Nothing in the City's lengthy annual final report and budget request form, which each institution must supply, asks for detailed information concerning the individual works in exhibits. Instead, the form is designed to determine, among other things: the general purposes and plans of the institution; "brief descriptions" (emphasis in original) of immediate past and future programming; accomplishments and plans for educational programs for children, educators and the general public; and detailed financial information.

III. THE CONTROVERSY OVER THE SENSATION EXHIBIT

The Sensation Exhibit was first shown in 1997 at the Royal Academy of Art in London, where it drew record crowds for a contemporary art exhibit and generated controversy and some protest demonstrations. The Brooklyn Museum's Director, Arnold Lehman, viewed the Exhibit in London and decided to attempt to bring it to New York after its scheduled showing at a museum in Berlin. The Exhibit includes approximately ninety works of some forty contemporary British artists, a number of whom have received recognition by the artistic community. Chris Ofili, Damien Hirst, and Rachel Whiteread, for example, have received the Turner Award from the Tate Gallery. After being shown in Brooklyn, the Exhibit is scheduled to be shown at the National Gallery of Australia, and the Toyota City Museum outside of Tokyo.

Mr. Lehman's efforts to bring the Exhibit to Brooklyn continued through 1998, and plans were finalized in April 1999. Mr. Lehman, starting in 1998, kept the Museum's Board of Trustees informed of his efforts, and of the Exhibit's controversial nature. The Mayor of the City is an *ex officio* member of the Board, but his representative did not attend certain meetings at which the Exhibit was discussed, although minutes of the meetings were sent to him. The Commissioner of the City's Department of Cultural Affairs, Schuyler Chapin, also is an *ex officio* member of the Board of Trustees. His designated representative did attend meetings regularly and receive minutes of Board meetings. On or about March 10, 1999, Mr. Lehman gave Commissioner Chapin a copy of the catalog for the Exhibit and discussed its content. The catalog includes photographs and descriptions of virtually all of the works in the Exhibit, including every work that the City now finds objectionable. For example, it contains a full page color photograph of *The Holy Virgin Mary* and a description of the materials of which it is made, including elephant dung. On or about April 6, 1999, Mr. Lehman sent letters to members of the Board of Trustees, including Commissioner Chapin and other public officials, stating that the Exhibit was controversial, and he set forth the Museum's plans to charge an admission fee for the Exhibit and to require that all children be accompanied by an adult. The letters specifically described the work of the artist Damien Hirst, recognized "for his sections of various animals (sharks, lambs, etc.) individually preserved and presented in sealed, formaldehyde-filled glass containers." The Museum issued a similar press release on about the same date. A *New York Times* article on April 8, 1999, entitled "British Outrage Heads for Brooklyn," described reactions of shock and condemnation, together with protests, that the Exhibit had generated in London, as well as accusations by detractors that the Exhibit promoted the commercial interests of Charles Saatchi, owner of all of the works in the Exhibit. The article described some of the controversial works in the Exhibit, including that of Hirst.

Commissioner Chapin, in a letter dated April 14, thanked Mr. Lehman for his "fascinating letter" about the Exhibit, which, he wrote, seemed designed to "shake up New York's art world." Commissioner Chapin voiced no objection to the Museum's planned admission policies and promised to convey "any thoughts about funding he might have." There is no evidence that the Mayor himself was personally aware of the specific contents of the Exhibit.

The Exhibit was scheduled to open to the public at the Museum on October 2, 1999. City officials first began raising objections to the Exhibit on September 22. On that date, Commissioner Chapin, stating that he was acting on behalf of the Mayor, advised Mr. Lehman by telephone that the City would terminate all funding to the Museum unless it canceled the Exhibit. Commissioner Chapin specifically referred to the fact that the Mayor found objectionable *The Holy Virgin Mary* by Chris Ofili. (All of the five Ofili works in the Exhibit use elephant dung together with other materials. In addition, on the painting entitled *The Holy Virgin Mary*, there are small photographs of buttocks and female genitalia scattered on the background.) The Mayor explained his position publicly that day, taking particular exception to *The Holy Virgin Mary*. The Mayor stated that this work "offends me" and "is sick," and he explained his decision to terminate City funding as follows:

> You don't have a right to a government subsidy to desecrate someone else's religion. And therefore we will do everything that we can to remove funding from the [Museum] until the director comes to his senses. And realizes that if you are a government subsidized enterprise then you can't do things that desecrate the most personal and deeply held views of the people in society.

The Mayor also referred to a Hirst work of two pigs in formaldehyde as "sick stuff" to be exhibited in an art museum.

The following day, the Mayor accused the Museum of violating the Lease by mounting an exhibit which was inaccessible to schoolchildren and by failing to obtain his permission to restrict access to the Exhibit, which he made clear he would not give because of his view that taxpayer-funded property should not be used to "desecrate religion" or "do things that are disgusting with regard to animals." In a letter from New York City Corporation Counsel Michael D. Hess to Mr. Lehman, dated September 23, 1999, Mr. Hess stated that "[t]he Mayor will not approve a modification of the Contract to allow [the Museum] to restrict admission to the museum. In light of the fact that [the Museum] has already determined that it would be inappropriate for those under 17 years of age to be admitted to the exhibit without adult supervision (a determination with which the City does not disagree), [the Museum] cannot proceed with the exhibit as planned."

The Mayor and other senior City officials continued, and escalated, their attacks on the Exhibit and their threats to the Museum, vowing to cut off all funding, including construction funding, to seek to replace the Board of Trustees, to cancel the Lease, and to assume possession of the Museum building, unless the Exhibit were canceled. The Mayor asserted on September 24 that he would not "have any compunction about trying to put them out of business, meaning the board." On September 28, the Mayor publicly stated that taxpayer dollars should not "be used to support the desecration of important national or religious symbol, of any religion." A City press release that day denounced "an exhibit which besmirches religion and is an insult to the community." The press release announced that, in response to the Museum Board's formal decision that day to proceed with the Exhibit, the City would end its funding of the Museum immediately. In his deposition, Deputy Mayor Joseph Lhota acknowledged that he had earlier told the Chairman of the Museum's Board of Trustees, Robert Rubin, that all City funding to the Museum would be canceled unless the Museum agreed to remove *The Holy Virgin Mary* from the Exhibit.

In response to the City's threats, including explicit statements by senior officials that the City would withhold its monthly payment of $497,554 due on October 1, 1999, the Museum commenced this action against the City and the Mayor on September 28, 1999, pursuant to 42 U.S.C. § 1983, seeking declaratory and injunctive relief, to prevent the defendants from punishing or retaliating against the Museum for displaying the Exhibit, in violation of the Museum's rights under the First and Fourteenth Amendments, including cutting off funding, terminating the lease, seizing the building or attempting to fire the Board of Trustees. The City has in fact withheld the scheduled October payment to the Museum. Plaintiff filed an amended complaint on October 1, 1999, adding claims for damages against the defendants, and claims of violation of the Equal Protection Clause and state and local law.

Meanwhile, on September 30, 1999, shortly before a conference scheduled by this court began, the City filed an action for ejectment against the Museum in New York State Supreme Court, Kings County. On the basis of that suit, the City invoked the abstention principles of *Younger v. Harris,* 401 U.S. 37, 91 S. Ct. 746, 27 L. Ed. 2d 669 (1971), and asked this court to dismiss plaintiff's claims for injunctive and declaratory relief. At the conference, plaintiff was directed to file its contemplated preliminary injunction motion on October 4, and defendants were directed to file their abstention motion on the same date; limited document and deposition discovery was authorized; an exchange of affidavits, documents and briefs responding to the respective motions was scheduled for October 7; and a hearing was scheduled for October 8. Neither plaintiff nor defendants chose to present witnesses at the October 8 hearing. The parties' requests for an opportunity to present additional materials, including documents, affidavits, and supplemental briefs, were granted. The parties filed their respective supplemental materials on October 15; defendants filed a final responding declaration on October 21, and plaintiff filed a clarifying letter in response to that declaration on October 22. Numerous individuals and organizations have filed briefs *amicus curiae*; they are identified in the Appendix. Based upon agreements between the parties made in open court on October 20, certain allegations regarding financial hardship in plaintiff's supplemental submissions are not being considered on the motion for a preliminary injunction.

The City's state court ejectment action alleges that the Museum forfeited its right to occupy the premises by violating the Lease, the Contract, and the Museum's enabling legislation, in the following respects: (1) imposing a $9.75 admission charge for the Exhibit, without the Mayor's approval; (2) violating the Museum's obligation to "educate and enlighten school children and the public" and to serve a public purpose, in that the Museum intended to proceed with the Exhibit, which the City contends contains inappropriate, "sensational" matter that is "offensive to significant segments of the public;" and (3) improperly furthering "the commercial interests of private parties," rather than public purposes, because the works in the Exhibit come from the private collection of Charles Saatchi, who is a client of Christie's, the auction house, which also gave financial support to the Exhibit.

As described above, City officials had also claimed that the Museum's decision to restrict admission of children to the Exhibit violated the terms of the Lease, which, they claimed, requires open and equal access to the Museum by schoolchildren. Two days before the City initiated its ejectment action, the Museum's Board responded to this complaint by rescinding the requirement that children under seventeen be accompanied by adults, and instead posted warning notices.

At oral argument on October 8, the City announced that it was abandoning two of the three grounds for its ejectment action. The abandoned grounds are that the City is entitled to eject the Museum based upon the admission charge, and upon a perceived impropriety in the relationship among Mr. Saatchi, Christie's and the Museum. The City also abandoned any claim based upon the initial restriction on the admission of minors. The City now claims a right to eject the Museum based solely on its perception of the content of works in the *Sensation Exhibit*. The defendants' supplemental memorandum, filed after oral argument, asserts that the First Amendment does not prohibit the City from refusing to subsidize displays of art that are offensive and foster religious intolerance; it does not rely upon either of the grounds abandoned in the ejectment action.

ABSTENTION: THE MOTION TO DISMISS

The City and the Mayor seek dismissal of this action, insofar as it seeks injunctive or declaratory relief, in deference to a state court ejectment action filed by the City two days after this action was filed. The City, recognizing that the damages claim cannot be dismissed under abstention principles, *see Quackenbush v. Allstate Ins. Co.,* 517 U.S. 706, 116 S. Ct. 1712, 135 L. Ed. 2d 1 (1996), also requests this Court to stay determination of the damages claim in deference to the state ejectment action. The motion is denied.

"Federal courts have an unflagging obligation to adjudicate cases brought within their jurisdiction. It is now black-letter law that abstention from the exercise of federal jurisdiction is the narrow exception, not the rule." *Cecos International, Inc. v. Jorling,* 895 F.2d 66, 70 (2d Cir. 1990); *see Quackenbush,* 517 U.S. at 716, 116 S. Ct. 1712. The City cannot oust the federal courts of jurisdiction over a fundamental First Amendment dispute by asserting in state court a landlord-tenant issue, especially one that, as will be seen, is purely pretextual. There is no federal constitutional issue more grave than the effort by government officials to censor works of expression and to threaten the vitality of a major cultural institution, as punishment for failing to abide by governmental demands for orthodoxy. The defendants have not shown that the plaintiff, having properly invoked this court's jurisdiction, must instead assert its First Amendment claims as counterclaims to an ejectment action.

I. Principles of *Younger* Abstention

Younger v. Harris, 401 U.S. 37, 91 S. Ct. 746 (1971), relying on principles of federalism and comity, required the federal courts to abstain from interfering with an ongoing state criminal proceeding, even though the defense was that the statute under which the prosecution was brought violated the First Amendment. Nothing in that case, or in the cases since *Younger* which have applied the doctrine to certain types of civil actions, requires abstention here. *Younger* abstention requires that *each* of the following requirements be satisfied: 1) there is an ongoing state proceeding that will be disrupted by the federal suit; 2) an important state interest is implicated; and 3) the plaintiff has an avenue open for review of its constitutional claims in the ongoing state proceeding. *See, e.g., Hansel v. Town Court,* 56 F.3d 391, 393 (2d Cir.), *cert. denied,* 516 U.S. 1012, 116 S. Ct. 572, 133 L. Ed. 2d 496 (1995). None of these requirements is met here.

To begin with, there simply was no ongoing state proceeding at the time the Museum brought its federal suit. "A federal court need not stay its jurisdictional hand when there is no state action pending at the time the federal suit is filed, even if there is a substantial likelihood that a state proceeding will be instituted in the future to vindicate the state's interests." *Cecos International,* 895 F.2d at 72; *see Steffel v. Thompson,* 415 U.S. 452, 462, 94 S. Ct. 1209, 39 L. Ed. 2d 505 (1974). *Hicks v. Miranda,* 422 U.S. 332, 349, 95 S. Ct. 2281, 45 L. Ed. 2d 223 (1975), upon which defendants rely, applied *Younger* where state criminal proceedings had not yet begun against the federal plaintiffs when the federal complaint was filed, but no proceedings of substance had taken place in federal court. It has no application here. In *Hicks,* extensive criminal proceedings in an obscenity case involving a theater owned by, and employees of, the federal plaintiffs were in progress, and the federal plaintiffs had appeared in those proceedings. Thus, an ongoing state criminal process was disrupted by the federal court's intervention. The Museum's federal action did not threaten to disrupt an ongoing state proceeding, much less a criminal proceeding.

Second, the City cannot establish the important state interest necessary to apply *Younger* in this civil case. As the Supreme Court stated in *New Orleans Pub. Service, Inc. v. Council of City of New Orleans,* 491 U.S. 350, 109 S. Ct. 2506, 105 L. Ed. 2d 298 (1989), in rejecting a claim that the federal court should abstain in deference to a state court action in a rate-making proceeding:

> Although our concern for comity and federalism has led us to expand the protection of *Younger* beyond state criminal prosecutions, to civil enforcement proceedings ... and even to civil proceedings involving certain orders that are uniquely in furtherance of the state courts' ability to perform their judicial functions ... it has never been suggested that *Younger* requires abstention in deference to a state judicial proceeding reviewing legislative or executive action. Such a broad abstention requirement would make a mockery of the rule that only exceptional circumstances justify a federal court's refusal to decide a case in deference to the States.

Id. at 367-68, 109 S. Ct. 2506 (citations omitted). An ejectment action is neither a "civil enforcement proceeding" nor one "uniquely in furtherance of the state courts' ability to perform their judicial functions." It is a landlord-tenant action that is routinely available in disputes between private parties. And the proper inquiry is "the importance of the generic proceedings to the State," *id.* at 365, 109 S. Ct. 2506, not the importance of the state's interest in the particular case.

In *Philip Morris, Inc. v. Blumenthal,* 123 F.3d 103 (2d Cir.1997), the Court held that *Younger* abstention was not warranted where the State had sued tobacco companies in state court seeking injunctive relief and damages under Connecticut's unfair trade practices law ("CUTPA"), state antitrust law, and state common law for the costs of treating tobacco-related illnesses. The Court rejected the State's argument that an important state interest was involved in the state court litigation, on the ground that "the state action does not appear to differ greatly from a private action under CUTPA, and the mere fact that the state is involved as a party does not transform the action into a 'sovereign enforcement' proceeding." *Id.* at 107. Similarly, that the City is involved as a party does not transform an ejectment action into an enforcement proceeding.

The City argues that this case, unlike a private landlord-tenant dispute, involves important questions regarding proper use of public property and public funds. Use of "public funds," however, is not an issue in an ejectment action, and there is nothing inherently significant in a government landlord's claim of a lease violation by a tenant, even one which is publicly chartered and publicly subsidized. To be sure, this is no ordinary landlord-tenant dispute. But the importance of this litigation arises from the significance of the First Amendment issues involved; and it is precisely for that reason that the federal interests are supreme and that the federal courts should not be ousted of jurisdiction.

Finally, the state ejectment action will not give the Museum the kind of opportunity to present its constitutional claims that *Younger* abstention requires. Unlike the situation in *Younger* and cases relying on *Younger,* resolution of the City's claimed right to evict the Museum will not necessarily require determination of any First Amendment issues. For example, the Museum could be successful on the claim of a lease violation without the state court ever reaching First Amendment issues. Even if it did reach them, the ejectment claim does not encompass the Museum's additional claims regarding actual and threatened termination of funding and efforts to remove its Board of Trustees. Thus, the defendants' argument that plaintiff's federal claims will be central to resolution of the ejectment action is rejected.

The defendants' further argument, that the Museum can, in any event, obtain resolution of its First Amendment claims by filing counterclaims to the ejectment action, fundamentally misapprehends the limits of abstention. The mere fact that a state court of general jurisdiction can entertain any claim between two parties properly before it is too insubstantial a basis for compelling a party which wishes to bring federal constitutional claims in federal court to present those claims to a state court instead. There is little difference between what the defendants seek here and compelling a plaintiff to bring a federal civil rights claim in state court in the first instance simply because a state forum is always available to hear it. Defendants' reliance on a footnote in *Moore v. Sims,* 442 U.S. 415, 430 n. 12, 99 S. Ct. 2371, 60 L. Ed. 2d 994 (1979), which rejected "mere semantical" distinctions between a "defense" and a "counterclaim," is misplaced. The Court viewed the state child abuse proceedings involved in *Moore* as implicating an important state interest closely analogous to the state's enforcement of its criminal laws. In addition, unlike here, the federal court was asked to interfere with an ongoing state proceeding, and one which involved a complex state statutory scheme. The Court's confidence, in *Moore,* that all of the federal plaintiffs' constitutional claims, however labeled, would be resolved in the state court action does not mean that every time a plaintiff seeks to vindicate federal constitutional rights in federal court, the governmental defendant can force the plaintiff into state court by filing a different lawsuit there.

II. The *Younger* Exception

Even if the three required elements for *Younger* abstention were established, abstention nevertheless is inappropriate if the state proceedings were initiated in bad faith, for purposes of harassment, retaliation or other improper motive, or in other extraordinary circumstances. *Cullen v. Fliegner,* 18 F.3d 96, 103-04 (2d Cir.1994); *see Moore,* 442 U.S. at 432-33, 99 S. Ct. 2371; *Huffman v. Pursue, Ltd.,* 420 U.S. 592, 611-12, 95 S. Ct. 1200, 43 L. Ed. 2d 482 (1975); *Younger,* 401 U.S. at 53-54, 91 S. Ct. 746. Generally, such a showing can be made if the party bringing the state action can "have no reasonable expectation of obtaining a favorable outcome." *Cullen,* 18 F.3d at 103; *cf. Allee v. Medrano,* 416 U.S. 802, 819 & n. 14, 94 S. Ct. 2191, 40 L. Ed. 2d 566 (1974). It can also be made, even if there is a reasonable expectation of success, if the state action "has been brought to retaliate for or to deter constitutionally protected conduct." *Cullen,* 18 F.3d at 103.[NOTE 1] Here, both such circumstances exist.

The City's attempt to distinguish *Cullen,* by arguing that "the state action is not punishment for something else plaintiff did in the past nor is it a sham intended to deter future speech" is unpersuasive. The ejectment action *is* "punishment for something else" the Museum's refusal to stop the Exhibit and it *is* a "sham intended to deter future speech." The undisputed record demonstrates that the Mayor and other senior City officials were offended by the content of the Exhibit, as they stated from the beginning, and then sought to find a basis in the pertinent legal instruments which could plausibly justify their determination to compel the Museum to remove certain offending works from the Exhibit or cancel the Exhibit, or, failing that, to deprive the Museum of funding and seek replacement of its Board.[NOTE 2] The City's rapid abandonment of two of the three grounds of its action, *see supra* at 193, supports this conclusion, as does the absence of evidence in the record for the one remaining ground in the ejectment action. *See infra* at 203-04.

Thus, the state court action was conceived and initiated as an instrument to pressure the Museum and to compel it to cancel the Exhibit or remove specific objectionable works, without any reasonable expectation by the City that it could prevail on the merits of an action for ejectment, and it is part of an ongoing effort to retaliate against and deter plaintiff's exercise of First Amendment rights. The federal courts are not divested of jurisdiction in deference to such governmental purposes, nor to a municipality's preference to litigate federal constitutional issues in state court.

THE FIRST AMENDMENT CLAIM: THE MUSEUM'S MOTION FOR A PRELIMINARY INJUNCTION

I. Standard for Issuing a Preliminary Injunction

A party seeking a preliminary injunction must ordinarily demonstrate (a) irreparable harm and (b) either (1) likelihood of success on the merits or (2) sufficiently serious questions going to the merits to make them a fair ground of litigation and a balance of hardships tipping decidedly in its favor. *Time Warner Cable of New York City v. Bloomberg L.P.,* 118 F.3d 917, 923 (2d Cir.1997). The defendants argue that the second, lesser standard is inapplicable to them as governmental actors, but the kind of governmental conduct entitled to a "higher degree of deference" and therefore requiring a showing of a likelihood of success on the merits, *see Able v. United States,* 44 F.3d 128, 131 (2d Cir.1995) (per curiam), is not involved in this case, where defendants essentially rely on the Lease, which restates the purposes of the enabling legislation, and the Contract.[NOTE 3] In any event, as will be seen, the Museum easily establishes a likelihood of success on the merits.

II. Irreparable Harm

The Museum is suffering and will continue to suffer irreparable harm if an injunction is not granted. "The loss of First Amendment freedoms, for even minimal periods of time, unquestionably constitutes irreparable injury." *Elrod v. Burns,* 427 U.S. 347, 373, 96 S. Ct. 2673, 49 L. Ed. 2d 547 (1976) (plurality opinion); *Bery v. City of New York,* 97 F.3d 689, 693 (2d Cir.1996), *cert. denied* 520 U.S. 1251, 117 S. Ct. 2408, 138 L. Ed. 2d 174 (1997). Because of this, it is sometimes said that "when an injunction is sought to protect First Amendment rights, likelihood of success on the merits and irreparable harm merge into a single threshold requirement." *801 Conklin St. Ltd. v. Town of Babylon,* 38 F. Supp. 2d 228, 235 (E.D.N.Y. 1999) (citations omitted); *Blum v. Schlegel,* 830 F. Supp. 712, 723 (W.D.N.Y.1993), *aff'd,* 18 F.3d 1005 (2d Cir.1994) (citations omitted). *See also Beal v. Stern,* 184 F.3d 117, 123-124 (2d Cir.1999).

The City and the Mayor argue that there is no irreparable injury because the Museum has not shown that the withholding of funding prevented it from showing the Sensation Exhibit or that the loss of its operating and maintenance subsidy will force the imminent closing of the Museum. Counsel for defendants further stated at oral argument that the City's own ejectment suit cannot be a sound basis for a preliminary injunction motion because the suit has just begun and, "in the event that that particular action gets to a critical stage," the motion can be renewed. These arguments ignore the very reason that interference with First Amendment rights constitutes irreparable injury.

This is not a case involving the mere assertion of an incidental infringement of First Amendment rights insufficient to establish irreparable harm. *See e.g. Hohe v. Casey,* 868 F.2d 69, 72-73 (3d Cir.), *cert. denied* 493 U.S. 848, 110 S. Ct. 144, 107 L. Ed. 2d 102 (1989). Nor does the Museum rely on remote or speculative fears of future retaliation. *See, e.g., Latino Officers Association v. Safir,* 170 F.3d 167, 171 (2d Cir.1999); *Alvarez v. City of New York,* 2 F. Supp. 2d 509, 513 (S.D.N.Y.1998). The Museum has already suffered direct and purposeful penalization by the City in response to its exercise of First Amendment rights. First, the City has cut off appropriated funding. Second, the City has sued in state court to evict the Museum from the property which it has occupied for over one hundred years and in which it houses its enormous collections of ancient and modern art. In its abstention motion, the City asks the court to treat its ejectment suit as brought in good faith, that is, as brought with the goal of ejecting the Museum. It cannot on the one hand seek so serious a penalty (it could, after all, have brought only a declaratory judgment action) and on the other hand claim that no harm is imminent. For a museum of the magnitude of the Brooklyn Museum, planning for a move of one and a half million art objects would obviously be a monumental task. Given the finding of a likelihood of success on the merits of the Museum's claim of a First Amendment violation, the Museum should not have to wait until a City sheriff is at the door to seek equitable relief.

In addition, the facts establish an ongoing effort by the Mayor and the City to coerce the Museum into relinquishing its First Amendment rights. On September 24, the Mayor stated that "since they [the Museum Board members] seem to have no compunction about putting their hands in the taxpayers' pockets ... and throwing dung on important religious symbols, I'm not going to have any compunction about trying to put them out of business, meaning the board." Then, on September 28, the Mayor went on to state that "[t]he Corporation Counsel told them what we're going to do, the lease tells us what we're required to do, which is to evict them and to stop dealing with them as a board. We'll do that over a period of time. We'll hold back their funds because they are not a properly constituted board at this point and then over a period of time there will be a substitute board put in place."

That the Museum has so far stood up to these efforts does not deprive it of the right to injunctive relief. The prospect of money damages does not cure the irreparable injury of an already existing, purposeful penalization for the exercise of First Amendment rights. Nor must the Museum endure ongoing efforts to coerce the relinquishment of those rights, including the continuing threat of ejectment, because money damages are available at the conclusion of the suit. Irreparable injury has been established.

III. The Museum's Likelihood of Success on its First Amendment Claim

"If there is any fixed star in our constitutional constellation, it is that no official, high or petty, can prescribe what shall be orthodox in politics, nationalism, religion, or other matters of opinion...." *West Virginia State Bd. of Educ. v. Barnette,* 319 U.S. 624, 642, 63 S. Ct. 1178, 87 L. Ed. 1628 (1943). In keeping with that principle, the First Amendment bars government officials from censoring works said to be "offensive," *Texas v. Johnson,* 491 U.S. 397, 414, 109 S. Ct. 2533, 105 L. Ed. 2d 342 (1989), "sacrilegious," *Joseph Burstyn, Inc. v. Wilson,* 343 U.S. 495, 531, 72 S. Ct. 777, 96 L. Ed. 1098 (1952), "morally improper," *Hannegan v. Esquire,* 327 U.S. 146, 149, 66 S. Ct. 456, 90 L. Ed. 586 (1946), or even "dangerous," *Regan v. Taxation with Representation of Washington,* 461 U.S. 540, 548, 103 S. Ct. 1997, 76 L. Ed. 2d 129 (1983). "If there is a bedrock principle underlying the First Amendment, it is that the government may not prohibit the expression of an idea simply because society finds the idea itself offensive or disagreeable." *Texas v. Johnson,* 491 U.S. at 414, 109 S. Ct. 2533.

In *Hannegan,* for example, the Supreme Court held that the Postmaster General could not deny second-class postal privileges to a magazine, admittedly not containing material that was obscene and therefore illegal, because it was found by him not to be conducive to the "public good." *Hannegan,* 327 U.S. at 149, 66 S. Ct. 456. In *Joseph Burstyn, Inc.,* 343 U.S. at 531, 72 S. Ct. 777, the Supreme Court found the First Amendment violated by a New York statute authorizing denial of a license to motion pictures found to be "sacrilegious." While noting the "substantial questions" that might be raised under the religion clauses of the First Amendment if a censor had to determine what fell within the standard, the Court said:

> However, from the standpoint of freedom of speech and the press, it is enough to point out that the state has no legitimate interest in protecting any or all religions from views distasteful to them which is sufficient to justify prior restraints upon the expression of those views. It is not the business of government in our nation to suppress real or imagined attacks upon a particular religious doctrine, whether they appear in publications, speeches, or motion pictures.

343 U.S. at 505, 72 S. Ct. 777.

Similarly, in *Spence v. Washington,* 418 U.S. 405, 94 S. Ct. 2727, 41 L. Ed. 2d 842 (1974), the Supreme Court struck, on First Amendment grounds, a flag misuse statute as applied to a college student who hung an American flag with a peace symbol on it upside down out of his window. Among the grounds considered and rejected for upholding the judgment against the student, the Court noted: "that the State may have desired to protect the sensibilities of passersby" is not a basis for suppressing ideas, and that "[a]nyone who might have been offended could easily have avoided the display." *Spence,* 418 U.S. at 412, 94 S.

Ct. 2727. Thus, "[u]nder our system of government there is an accommodation for the widest varieties of tastes and ideas. What is good literature, what has educational value, what is refined public information, what is good art, varies with individuals as it does from one generation to another." *Hannegan,* 327 U.S. at 157, 66 S. Ct. 456 (footnote omitted).

The City and the Mayor acknowledge that the art being shown at the Museum and the ideas which they find that art to express are within the protections of the First and Fourteenth Amendments. Contrary to their assertions, however, although they did not physically remove the art objects from the Museum, they are not insulated from a claim that they are violating the overwhelming body of First Amendment law establishing that government cannot suppress ideas indirectly any more than it can do so directly.

Governmental efforts to suppress expression can take many forms, and the courts have not hesitated to invalidate those efforts, no matter how indirect the form. In *Speiser v. Randall,* 357 U.S. 513, 78 S. Ct. 1332, 2 L. Ed. 2d 1460 (1958), for example, the Supreme Court noted that "[t]o deny an exemption to claimants [of property tax exemptions] who engage in certain forms of speech is in effect to penalize them for such speech. Its deterrent effect is the same as if the State were to fine them for this speech." 357 U.S. at 518, 78 S. Ct. 1332. In *Hannegan,* the Court recognized that "[t]he second-class [mail] privilege is a form of subsidy," 327 U.S. at 151, 66 S. Ct. 456 (footnote omitted), and found that the denial of the privilege based on the immorality of a publication amounted to illegal censorship. *Id.* at 157, 66 S. Ct. 456.

In yet another line of cases illustrating that freedom of speech cannot be subjected to indirect violations, the Supreme Court has held that the First Amendment protects government employees and those who have independent contracts with the government from termination based solely on speech found offensive to the government. *See, e.g., Bd. of County Commissioners, Wabaunsee County, Kansas v. Umbehr,* 518 U.S. 668, 116 S. Ct. 2342, 135 L. Ed. 2d 843 (1996); *Perry v. Sindermann,* 408 U.S. 593, 92 S. Ct. 2694, 33 L. Ed. 2d 570 (1972). For example, in *Perry,* the Supreme Court held that a professor at a State college who lacked any contractual or tenure right to re-employment could not be denied renewal of his contract on the ground that he had publicly criticized the policies of the college administration. The Court stated:

> For at least a quarter-century, this Court has made clear that even though a person has no "right" to a valuable governmental benefit and even though the government may deny him the benefit for any number of reasons, there are some reasons upon which the government may not rely. It may not deny a benefit to a person on a basis that infringes his constitutionally protected interests especially, his interest in freedom of speech. For if the government could deny a benefit to a person because of his constitutionally protected speech or associations, his exercise of those freedoms would in effect be penalized and inhibited. This would allow the government to "produce a result

which (it) could not command directly." Such interference with constitutional rights is impermissible.

408 U.S. at 597, 92 S. Ct. 2694 (citation omitted).

In many different contexts, then, the Supreme Court has made clear that, although the government is under no obligation to provide various kinds of benefits, it may not deny them if the reason for the denial would require a choice between exercising First Amendment rights and obtaining the benefit. That is, it may not "discriminate invidiously in its subsidies in such a way as to 'aim … at the suppression of dangerous ideas.'" *Regan,* 461 U.S. at 548, 103 S. Ct. 1997 (citation omitted).

The decision to withhold an already appropriated general operating subsidy from an institution which has been supported by the City for over one hundred years, and to eject it from its City-owned building, because of the Mayor's objection to certain works in a current exhibit, is, in its own way, to "discriminate invidiously in its subsidies in such a way as to 'aim … at the suppression of dangerous ideas.'" *Id.* "The Government's purpose is the controlling consideration" in determining whether a restriction on speech is viewpoint discriminatory. *Ward v. Rock Against Racism,* 491 U.S. 781, 791, 109 S. Ct. 2746, 105 L. Ed. 2d 661 (1989). By its own words, the City here threatened to withhold funding if the Museum continued with its plans to show the Exhibit. When the Museum resisted, the City withheld its funding and filed a suit for ejectment. While initially the City engaged in various claims of a violation of its Lease and Contract, unrelated to the content of the Exhibit, the City has now admitted the obvious; it has acknowledged that its purpose is directly related, not just to the content of the Exhibit, but to the particular viewpoints expressed. There can be no greater showing of a First Amendment violation.

In a case remarkably similar to this one, *Cuban Museum of Arts and Culture, Inc. v. City of Miami,* 766 F. Supp. 1121 (S.D.Fla.1991), the City of Miami was enjoined from refusing to renew an expired lease with the Cuban Museum because the Court held that the City had violated the museum's First Amendment rights, in that the refusal to renew was motivated by the City's opposition to the museum's exhibition of works of Cuban artists who were either living in Cuba or who had not denounced Fidel Castro. These works were highly offensive to a large segment of the Cuban population of Miami. The Court found that the exhibition was fully protected by the First Amendment, that the absence of a "right" to renewal did not defeat the First Amendment claim, and that the claimed lease violations were pretextual. *See Cuban Museum,* 766 F. Supp. at 1126-27 ("the Conduct of the City Commission with respect to the asserted grounds for the denial of continued possession reveals that the reasons asserted were either minor concerns or a pretextual basis upon which to remove the Cuban Museum and its present directors"). It found that the "City would not have acted to deny the plaintiffs' continued use and possession of the premises but for the plaintiffs' controversial exercise of their First Amendment rights." *Id.* at 1129. The same is true here.

The cases establishing the principle that the government cannot avoid the reach of the First Amendment by acting indirectly rather than directly also illustrate the fallacy in the claim of the Mayor and the City that, while the Exhibit can be shown privately, "the taxpayers don't have to pay for it." Federal taxpayers in effect pay for the mailing of periodicals that many of them find objectionable; and they subsidize all manner of views with which they do not agree, indeed, which they may abhor, through tax exemptions and deductions given to other taxpayers. State taxpayers pay the salary for the professor whom the State wants to fire for speaking out against the State college. In sum, where the denial of a benefit, subsidy or contract is motivated by a desire to suppress speech in violation of the First Amendment, that denial will be enjoined. That is all that is involved here.

This of course does not mean that the taxpayers are being required to "support" a particular viewpoint. On the contrary, the Supreme Court has rejected similar justifications for the suppression of ideas. For example, in *F. C. C. v. League of Women Voters,* 468 U.S. 364, 104 S. Ct. 3106, 82 L. Ed. 2d 278 (1984), the Supreme Court struck as unconstitutional a statutory provision that forbade noncommercial stations, which receive a grant from the Corporation for Public Broadcasting, to "engage in editorializing." With the following language, the Court rejected the contention that the provision could be defended on the ground that it was "intended to prevent the use of taxpayer moneys to promote private views with which taxpayers may disagree":

> This argument is readily answered by our decision in *Buckley v. Valeo,* 424 U.S. 1, 90-93, 96 S. Ct. 612, 46 L. Ed. 2d 659, ... *passim* (1976) (per curiam). As we explained in that case, virtually every congressional appropriation will to some extent involve a use of public money as to which some taxpayers may object.... Nevertheless, this does not mean that those taxpayers have a constitutionally protected right to enjoin such expenditures. Nor can this interest be invoked to justify a congressional decision to suppress speech.

468 U.S. at 385 n. 16, 104 S. Ct. 3106 (citations omitted).

Clarifying what the case at bar is *not* about will further illustrate the distinction between requiring the taxpayer to support a particular point of view, which is not involved here, and barring government officials from invidiously discriminating against ideas they find offensive, either to themselves or to members of the community.

First, there is no issue presented here about the City's right to itself take positions, even controversial ones. The Museum does not challenge the principle that government may choose, through its funding, to espouse a viewpoint on a matter of public concern without, as a result, being required to give equal time to an opposing view. *See Rust v. Sullivan,* 500 U.S. 173, 111 S. Ct. 1759, 114 L. Ed. 2d 233 (1991). Thus, the doctrine of *Rust,* upon which defendants rely, has no relevance here. That is, the Mayor and the City are permitted to foster the values that they claim to be seeking to foster, such as respect for the most dearly held beliefs of others and lack of vulgarity in art. As the Court stated in *Barnette,* 319 U.S.

at 640, 63 S. Ct. 1178, however, "[n]ational unity as an end which officials may foster by persuasion and example is not in question. The problem is whether under our Constitution compulsion as here employed is a permissible means for its achievement." Indeed, the notion that government officials can stifle expression in order to protect the public good reverses our most basic principles. As Justice Jackson so compellingly described in *Barnette,* in striking a compulsory flag salute and pledge of allegiance statute:

> Government of limited power need not be anemic government. Assurance that rights are secure tends to diminish fear and jealousy of strong government, and by making us feel safe to live under it makes for its better support. Without promise of a limiting Bill of Rights it is doubtful if our Constitution could have mustered enough strength to enable its ratification. To enforce those rights today is not to choose weak government over strong government. It is only to adhere as a means of strength to individual freedom of mind in preference to officially disciplined uniformity for which history indicates a disappointing and disastrous end.

Id. at 636-37, 63 S. Ct. 1178.

Second, the City and the Mayor argue that, if they are not allowed to cut off all financial support to the Museum as a result of its display of the Sensation Exhibit, there will be no limit on what the public is required to support in the name of the First Amendment. This is incorrect. The Museum makes no claim in this case that government has an obligation to fund particular forums of expression such as museums. *See generally Regan,* 461 U.S. at 540, 103 S. Ct. 1997 (citations omitted). Nor is there an issue in this case as to whether the City could be required to provide funding to support the *Sensation Exhibit* or any other particular exhibit, if the Museum had sought funding on an exhibit-by-exhibit basis. The City has not in fact provided the funding some $2 million to cover the various expenses involved in presenting the *Sensation Exhibit.* Thus, the issue is not whether the City could have been required to provide funding for the *Sensation Exhibit,* but whether the Museum, having been allocated a general operating subsidy, can now be penalized with the loss of that subsidy, and ejectment from a City-owned building, because of the perceived viewpoint of the works in the Exhibit. The answer to that question is no.

The reliance of the City and the Mayor on *National Endowment for the Arts v. Finley,* 524 U.S. 569, 118 S. Ct. 2168, 141 L. Ed. 2d 500 (1998), as support for their claim that viewpoint discrimination in arts funding is permissible, is misplaced. In *Finley,* the Supreme Court rejected a facial challenge to a provision adding "general standards of decency and respect for the diverse beliefs and values of the American public" to the "considerations" to be applied by the NEA in the awarding of grants to individual artists and arts organizations. The Court described the provision's legislative history, including Congress's rejection of language that would have prohibited awards of grants that would have the purpose or effect of denigrating particular religions, or of denigrating people on the basis of race, sex, handicap, or national origin. 118 S. Ct. at 2173. It noted that, ultimately, "[t]he legislation was a bipartisan proposal introduced as a counterweight to amendments aimed at eliminating the NEA's funding or substantially constraining its grant-making authority." *Id.* at 2176. The Court also noted that "Congress declined to disallow any particular viewpoints," *id.,* and it went on to hold the challenged provision facially constitutional upon finding that it "[did] not preclude awards to projects that might be deemed 'indecent' or 'disrespectful' nor place conditions on grants..." and, further, because the Court did "not perceive a realistic danger" that it will be used "to effectively preclude or punish the expression of particular views." *Id.* at 2175-77. Thus, even in *Finley,* where the issue was the "considerations" that could apply in the awarding of grants, unlike here, where funding has already been appropriated for general operating expenses, the Supreme Court upheld the "decency" and "respect" considerations only by reading them, on their face, as not permitting viewpoint discrimination.

When questioned on oral argument whether the City could direct a publicly supported library to remove particular books on pain of a loss of financial support, counsel for defendants responded that the visual art in the Exhibit has a greater impact than do books. Counsel for the Museum, in reply, noted that books like *Mein Kampf* have done enormous harm, but are still protected by the First Amendment. The relative power of books and visual art is of course immaterial. The communicative power of visual art is not a basis for restricting it but rather the very reason it is protected by the First Amendment. As recently stated by the Court of Appeals for the Second Circuit, "[v]isual art is as wide ranging in its depiction of ideas, concepts and emotions as any book, treatise, pamphlet or other writing, and is similarly entitled to full First Amendment protection." *Bery,* 97 F.3d at 695. *See also Ward,* 491 U.S. at 790, 109 S. Ct. 2746 (citations omitted), where the Supreme Court, speaking of music, said:

> From Plato's discourse in the *Republic* to the totalitarian state in our own times, rulers have known its capacity to appeal to the intellect and to the emotions, and have censored musical compositions to serve the needs of the state.... The Constitution prohibits any like attempts in our own legal order.

In their supplemental memorandum, the Mayor and the City argue that libraries are different from art museums because they are less selective; unlike the works in museums, they say, the inclusion of a book in a library carries "no connotation of worthiness or endorsement of its content." On the contrary, public libraries are, of physical and fiscal necessity, selective; they do not contain every book published. And there is no basis in the record for concluding that the Brooklyn Museum, with its one and a half million art objects, any more than a public library, endorses the perceived content of every work it makes available to the public. Whether or not the City and the Mayor agree with the Museum's judgment that a particular exhibit is worthy of showing is no different, in constitutional terms, from whether or not they agree that particular books are worthy of being made available to the public in a public library.

The City and the Mayor argue that they can avoid an injunction based upon the First Amendment because the showing of the *Sensation Exhibit* violates the Museum's statutory purposes and the terms of its Lease and Contract with the City. According to defendants, the withholding of financial support does not reflect a violation of the First Amendment but only an effort to vindicate the City's contractual rights. As in the *Cuban Museum* case, this claim is pretextual. *See supra* at 200-01. In addition, it is without evidentiary basis. The language of the statutes, the Lease and the Contract, and the undisputed evidence as to how the City itself has viewed these documents, shows a high likelihood that the Museum will defeat any claims that it is acting in violation of its statutory and contractual purposes as an art museum providing the public with enjoyment and education about art.

Whether the art shown is perceived as offensive or respectful, vulgar or banal, "good" art or "bad" art, the Mayor and the City offer no basis for the court to conclude that the Exhibit falls outside the broad parameters of the enabling legislation.[NOTE 4] Nor is there any basis for the City's accusation that the Museum has failed in its duty to educate.[NOTE 5] As for the defendants' emphasis on the unsuitability of the *Sensation Exhibit* for children, they acknowledge that there is nothing in the Lease or Contract which requires that every exhibit be suitable for schoolchildren of all ages. Nor is there anything which prevents the Museum from imposing reasonable restrictions on the access of schoolchildren to certain exhibits, in order to accommodate the Museum's undisputed right to display what Deputy Mayor Lhota called "mature" works of art.[NOTE 6]

There is also no language in the Lease or Contract that gives the Mayor or the City the right to veto works chosen for exhibition by the Museum. The Contract provides for the City to make maintenance payments to the Museum, without stating any conditions regarding the content of the Museum's artworks. The inability of the City and the Mayor to identify any standard for what constitutes a Lease or Contract violation, other than the Mayor and Deputy Mayor's personal views, reinforces the conclusion that it has never been contemplated that the City or the Mayor would have veto power over the Museum's decisions as to what to display.[NOTE 7] Deputy Mayor Lhota testified that there are no rules, regulations or procedures or even an *ad hoc* method for determining whether the City would view a particular work as inappropriate. The City's Procedures Manual confirms this.

That the advertising for the Exhibit cautions viewers that "the contents of the exhibition may cause shock, vomiting, confusion, panic, euphoria and anxiety" is not, as the City urges, an admission by the Museum that the Exhibit violates the Lease and Contract. Taking the advertising at face value (although the City has also argued that it is a crude effort to attract attention to the Exhibit), the City fails to show that art that is considered shocking, provocative, or disturbing gives rise to a violation of the Lease or the Contract.

The City and the Mayor argue that, if the court enjoins the withholding of its subsidy, the Museum will be free, under the protection of the First Amendment, to do anything at all, even transform itself into, for example, a museum of pornography. That, of course, is absurd. The Museum has been publicly supported for over one hundred years as a broad-based *art* museum. If it now sold its collections and became a pornography museum, the withholding of operating subsidies and the claims of a lease or contract violation would arise under vastly different facts from those presented here. The City and the Mayor have not shown that the funding provided has not been spent for the purpose authorized.

Finally, the City and the Mayor argue that they have a "duty" to withdraw support for the Museum because it showed paintings that are offensive and that desecrate religion in a public building. Given the Mayor's emphasis on the anti-Catholic sentiment he finds in the Ofili work, and despite the defendants' explicit disavowal of reliance on the Establishment Clause on oral argument, it is important to note the requirement that government remain neutral with regard to religious expression, whether "it manifest a religious view, an antireligious view, or neither." *Rosenberger v. Rector and Visitors of University of Virginia,* 515 U.S. 819, 841, 115 S. Ct. 2510, 132 L. Ed. 2d 700 (1995). In *Rosenberger,* the Supreme Court held unconstitutional a state university's denial of funding to a student journal solely because the journal espoused a Christian viewpoint. *See generally Joseph Burstyn, Inc.,* 343 U.S. 495, 72 S. Ct. 777, 96 L. Ed. 1098.

It is undisputed that the Museum's permanent collections contain many reverential depictions of the Madonna as well as other religious paintings and ritual objects. Just as there is no suggestion that the Museum is violating the Establishment Clause and endorsing religion by showing these works, see, e.g., *Agostini v. Felton,* 521 U.S. 203, 117 S. Ct. 1997, 138 L. Ed. 2d 391 (1997) and *Lemon v. Kurtzman,* 403 U.S. 602, 91 S. Ct. 2105, 29 L. Ed. 2d 745 (1971), there can equally be no suggestion that the Museum is violating the Establishment Clause by showing Mr. Ofili's work. The question of endorsement is evaluated from the perspective of the "objective observer." *See Wallace v. Jaffree,* 472 U.S. 38, 76, 105 S. Ct. 2479, 86 L. Ed. 2d 29 (1985) (O'Connor, J., concurring). The Brooklyn Museum contains art from all over the world, from many traditions and many centuries. No objective observer could conclude that the Museum's showing of the work of an individual artist which is viewed by some as sacrilegious constitutes endorsement of anti-religious views by the City or the Mayor, or for that matter, by the Museum, any more than that the Museum's showing of religiously reverential works constitutes an endorsement by them of religion. The suggestion that the Mayor and the City have an obligation to punish the Museum for showing the Ofili work turns well-established principles developed under the Establishment Clause on their head. If anything, it is the Mayor and the City who by their actions have threatened the neutrality required of government in the sphere of religion.

CONCLUSION

The City's motion to dismiss is denied. As the Museum has established irreparable harm and a likelihood of success on its First Amendment claim, its motion for a preliminary injunction is granted. An injunction, in the following form, will issue:

> The court having granted plaintiff's motion for a preliminary injunction pursuant to Federal Rule of Civil Procedure 65 by opinion and order dated November 1, 1999:
>
> Defendants the City of New York and Rudolph W. Giuliani, individually and in his official capacity as Mayor of the City of New York, and all those acting in concert with them are hereby enjoined, during the pendency of this action, from inflicting, or taking any steps to inflict, any punishment, retaliation, discrimination, or sanction of any kind against the Brooklyn Institute of Arts and Sciences, doing business as the Brooklyn Museum of Art as well as against any of the Brooklyn Museum of Art's directors, officers or representatives, as a result of the Brooklyn Museum of Art's displaying the Exhibit *SENSATION: Young British Artists from the Saatchi Collection* (the Exhibit), including but not limited to:
>
> 1) withholding or otherwise failing to provide the Brooklyn Museum of Art any sums of money appropriated, allocated, promised or otherwise payable to the Brooklyn Museum of Art;
>
> 2) denying, delaying, or otherwise discriminatorily treating pending or future funding requests of any type as the result of the Exhibit;
>
> 3) evicting or seeking to evict the Brooklyn Museum of Art from its premises at 200 Eastern Parkway, Brooklyn, or otherwise directly or indirectly interfering with the Brooklyn Museum of Art's occupancy and use of those premises, including prosecuting against the Brooklyn Museum of Art the action styled *The City of New York v. The Brooklyn Institute of Arts and Sciences,* filed September 30, 1999 in the Supreme Court of the State of New York, Kings County, Index No. 35376/99;
>
> 4) interfering in any manner, directly or indirectly, with the composition of the Board of Trustees of the Brooklyn Museum of Art, other than those members of the Board of Trustees who are the designees of the defendants, or interfering with the Board of Trustees' exercise of its authority.

The parties are directed to confer and to submit their positions, in writing, on the giving of security pursuant to Rule 65(c), by the close of business today.

SO ORDERED.

STUDY QUESTIONS

- In the *Brooklyn Museum* case, what actions and threats by the city prompted the museum to bring the lawsuit?
- Explain the relationship the city and the Brooklyn Museum. What changes to the parties positions during the course of the lawsuit?
- How did the museum's plan to manage visitors to the *Sensation* exhibit play a role in the lawsuit?
- Why did the court view the city's threat to evict the museum as "pretextual"? How is withholding a benefit different from a government providing benefits as was the case in NEA *v. Finley*? How does this affect the court's First Amendment analysis in this case?
- Do you think the court's comparison of a museum to a public library makes sense?
- What advice would you have given the Brooklyn Museum in dealing with this controversy?
- In 1990, the Cincinnati Contemporary Art Center (CAC) and its executive director, Dennis Barre, were indicted on criminal obscenity charges related to an exhibition of Robert Mapplethorpe's *The Perfect Moment* photographs. After a two-week trial featuring expert witnesses from across the country, both the CAC and Barre were acquitted on all counts. The trial and its outcome challenged perceptions about contemporary art, public funding for the arts, and what constitutes "obscenity."

The Perfect Moment *was the most comprehensive retrospective of works by New York photographer Robert Mapplethorpe. The show spanned twenty-five years of his career, featuring celebrity portraits, self-portraits, interracial figure studies, floral still lifes, homoerotic images, and collages. The exhibition, organized by the Institute of Contemporary Arts in Philadelphia, opened in the winter of 1988 just months before Mapplethorpe's death from AIDS complications. On tour, in the summer of 1989, the exhibition became the centerpiece of a controversy concerning federal funding of the arts and censorship when the City of Cincinnati indicted the Contemporary Arts Center and its Director for obscenity. Mapplethorpe's photographs are also referenced in* Finley v. NEA.

- American jurisprudence does not recognize a legal cause of action for "blasphemy"—disrespect of the sacred—but a number of other countries, including a number of European and most Muslim countries do. How do you think the types of controversial exhibits discussed in the foregoing section would be handled in a country that does have a law prohibiting blasphemy?

PRIVATE GRANT FUNDING

In addition to governmental support for the arts, there are a wide variety of charitable foundations and other organizations which offer grants to artists and arts-related nonprofits, including museums. Some of these grants are for general support for the organization, while others are for specific programs or purposes. Identifying grant opportunities, and applying for and obtaining grants, can constitute a large part of a museum's development efforts. Full-time staff or outside professional grant writers are often employed to seek grant funding for various aspects of museum activities. In some cases, grants to individual artists require that the grant be managed through a nonprofit organization, often referred to as a "fiscal agent." Some museums serve as fiscal agents or otherwise participate with individual artists in obtaining grant funding.

The requirements of a particular grant are set out in a grant agreement. The specific requirements and conditions of a grant can vary widely. Typically, they include detailed reporting requirements to demonstrate how the grant funds were used. Sometimes questions about ownership of intellectual property created under the grant arise. Strict compliance with grant requirements is very important, not only to limit liability for misuse of grant funds, but also to maintain an ongoing positive relationship with granting organizations and the museum's reputation within the granting community.

EARNED INCOME

In addition to private philanthropic and government grant support, museums generate income from admission fees, merchandising and retail sales, rental fees, and the like. These sources of income are referred to as "earned income." A variety of legal issues can arise in connection with activities that generate earned income for museums. Some of these involve contractual relationships; for example, a museum may rent out its facilities for private events such as weddings or receptions. Museum retail shops which sell merchandize may have to deal with variety of contracting and licensing agreements relating to the objects it sells. And while not normally a source of legal controversy, even a museum's admissions fees can be the subject of litigation, as exemplified by the settlement agreement with the Metropolitan Museum of Art in New York reprinted in the reading below. Federal, state, and local laws and regulations, as well as museum professional practices and codes of ethics, may be involved. Many of the issues museums face in connection with earned income are the same or similar to those which would be faced by any business or organization engaging in these types of activities.

Earned income may also raise tax issues unique to nonprofit entities. As a charitable organization, a museum must be organized and operated primarily for exempt purposes but may engage in a certain amount of income-producing activity that is unrelated to its exempt purpose. The income derived from the unrelated purpose is subject to tax as "Unrelated Business Taxable Income" or UBTI.

The IRS employs two tests to determine whether income is taxable as UBTI. Under the "organizational test" the question is whether the entity is organized for a tax-exempt purpose. Under the "operational test" the question is whether the income producing activities of the organization promote the organization's tax-exempt purpose. To be taxable as UBTI, the activity of the tax-exempt entity must constitute (i) a trade or business, (ii) regularly carried on, and (iii) not substantially related to the tax-exempt purpose of the organization.

For-profit businesses often provide funding for specific museum activities including sponsoring museum exhibits or programs. Often the sponsor is given promotional or marketing opportunities in exchange for funding. Corporate sponsorships are generally not considered UBTI so long as no substantial return benefit or *quid pro quo* is given to the sponsor other than the use or acknowledgement of the business name and logo. Promotion that could be considered advertising, however, may result in the funding being considered UBTI and subject to tax.

There are many exceptions and rules regarding UBTI. Among the exceptions and rules relevant to museums are certain museum shop items that arguably further the museum's mission; museum café revenues; volunteer-run museum shops; museum-owned parking lots; revenues from licensing of donor lists; certain travel tours sponsored by museums; passive income from museum investments (including endowments); revenues from rentals of museum facilities; and royalties from certain museum intellectual property.

The IRS rules are very case dependent. IRS Revenue Rulings can be helpful in assessing whether a specific revenue-generating activity will be considered UBTI. IRS Revenue Rulings 73-104 (exceptions to UBTI) and 73-105 (items sold in museum shops) indicate that payments that are contingent on attendance, ratings, etc., regular publication, or trade show or convention activity may result in the sponsorship being taxed as UBTI.

Corporate sponsorships can also raise ethical considerations. Exhibits or programs that are too closely aligned with a company's goods or services, or where the company has had a major influence on how they are portrayed, may raise the appearance of a conflict of interest. The American Alliance of Museums (AAM) and other museum professional organizations, have established policies, guidelines, and codes of ethics specifically addressing corporate sponsorships.

CASES AND OTHER READINGS

Reading Note: The settlement agreement reprinted below resolved a dispute with the Metropolitan Museum of Art in New York over its admission fee policies. The class action plaintiffs had alleged that the museum's admission practices and the way they were communicated to the public, violated applicable law.

SASKA V. THE METROPOLITAN MUSEUM OF ART

Civil Action No. 650775/2013

SETTLEMENT AGREEMENT

This Settlement Agreement is made and entered into as of the 26th day of February, 2016 by and among Filip Saska, Tomas Nadrchal, and Stephen Michelman (collectively "Class Plaintiffs") and The Metropolitan Museum of Art (the "Museum"), a New York nonprofit corporation.

WHEREAS the Museum currently operates pursuant to a "pay what you wish" admission system under which visitors to the Museum's exhibition halls may pay an admission fee of their choice; and

WHEREAS the Class Plaintiffs in March 2013 commenced a civil action against the Museum (the "Action") in the Supreme Court of the State of New York (the "Court") asserting that the Museum's admission practices, and the manner in which they are communicated to the public, violate New York law and the Museum's lease with the City of New York; and

WHEREAS the Complaint in the Action asserts claims on behalf of a putative class for both injunctive and other relief; and

WHEREAS the Class Plaintiffs intend to prosecute the Action vigorously if it cannot be resolved by agreement; and

WHEREAS the Museum denies the material allegations of the Complaint and intends to defend the Action vigorously if it cannot be resolved by agreement; and

WHEREAS the Museum and Class Plaintiffs now wish to resolve the claims and defenses asserted or which could have been asserted in the Action on the terms set forth herein and to stipulate to the entry of an order providing for disposition of all such claims and defenses, without otherwise admitting any issue of fact or law;

NOW, THEREFORE, in consideration of the foregoing and the mutual promises and covenants hereinafter set forth, and for other good and valuable consideration, the receipt and sufficiency of which are hereby acknowledged, and with intent to be legally bound, it is hereby agreed by the Parties, subject to the final approval of the Court and any review of such approval by the appellate courts, as follows:

With 6,479,548 visitors to its three locations in 2019, the Metropolitan Museum of Art in New York City was the fourth most visited art museum in the world. The main building at 1000 Fifth Avenue, along the Museum Mile on the eastern edge of Central Park in Manhattan's Upper East Side, (pictured here) is by area one of the world's largest art galleries. Its permanent collection contains over two million works, divided among 17 curatorial departments. In the years after the financial crisis of 2007-2008, the Met's admission policies were the subject of years of debate and litigation.

Settlement Class

1. For the purposes of this settlement only, Class Plaintiffs will seek, and the Museum will not oppose, the Court's certification of a class (the "Settlement Class") defined as follows:

   All persons who, at any time from March 5, 2007 to the date of final approval of the Settlement Agreement, purchased either (i) admission to the exhibition halls of The Metropolitan Museum of Art (in person, online, or through a third party vendor, in any location, using any form of payment) or (ii) a Metropolitan Museum of Art membership.

2. The Parties stipulate and agree that the definition of the proposed class in paragraph 101 of the Complaint in the Action shall be amended to be the same as the Settlement Class, and that the Court's orders preliminarily and finally approving this Settlement Agreement shall so amend the Complaint.

3. Plaintiffs will seek, and the Museum will not oppose, the Court's appointment of Emery Celli Brinckerhoff & Abady LLP as counsel for the Settlement Class ("Class Counsel"), and the appointment of Plaintiffs Filip Saska, Tomas Nadrchal, and Stephen Michelman as representatives of the Settlement Class.

Settlement Consideration

4. Subject to the termination rights and other conditions stated in this Settlement Agreement, Class Plaintiffs and the Museum agree, as consideration for the settlement of the Action as described herein, that they will jointly propose to the Court the entry of a Judgment in substantially the form annexed hereto as Exhibit A.

Release of Claims

5. The "Releasing Parties" in this Settlement Agreement include the (i) Class Plaintiffs and their respective heirs, executors, administrators, trustees, successors, assigns, and representatives, and (ii) all other members of the Settlement Class and their respective heirs, executors, administrators, trustees, successors, assigns, and representatives.

6. The Releasing Parties hereby, upon the Court's final approval of this Settlement Agreement, expressly and irrevocably waive and fully, finally, and forever settle, discharge, and release the Museum from any and all manner of claims, demands, actions, snits, and causes of action, whether individual, class, representative, or otherwise in nature, whether known or unknown, suspected or unsuspected, for injunctive relief as to all Releasing Parties and for all forms of relief as to the Class Plaintiffs, that any Releasing Party ever had, now has, or hereafter can, shall, or may have, arising out of or relating in any way to the Museum's admission practices or its communications with the public concerning those practices, as follows:

    a. The three Class Plaintiffs release all claims of any nature, whether for equitable relief, money damages, or attorneys' fees and expenses.

    b. All other members of the Settlement Class release only claims for equitable relief and for attorneys' fees and expenses, and shall not be deemed to have settled, discharged or released the Museum from any claim for monetaiy damages. The claims released pursuant to this subparagraph and subparagraph a. are collectively referred to as "Released Claims."

7. Each Releasing Party further expressly and irrevocably waives and fully, finally, and forever settles and releases, upon the Court's final approval of this Settlement Agreement, any and all defenses, rights, and benefits that the Releasing Party may have or that may be derived from the provisions of applicable law which, absent such waiver, may limit the extent or effect of the release contained in the preceding paragraph.

8. The Releasing Parties hereby covenant and agree that they shall not hereafter seek to establish liability against the Museum based, in whole or in part, upon any of the Released Claims.

Preliminary Court Approval

9. Class Plaintiffs and the Museum agree to use reasonable and good faith efforts to effectuate preliminary Court approval of this Settlement Agree-

ment, including filing necessary motion papers and scheduling a date and time for any necessary hearings that are mutually convenient for the Court, Class Plaintiffs, and the Museum.

10. Class Plaintiffs and the Museum agree to effectuate the Court's entry of an order (the "Preliminary Approval Order"), in the form of Exhibit B hereto, to:

    a. Preliminarily approve this Settlement Agreement.

    b. Approve the provisional certification of the Settlement Class for settlement purposes only, and declare that in the event of termination of this Settlement Agreement as provided below, certification of the Settlement Class shall automatically be vacated and the Museum may fully contest certification of any class as if no Settlement Class had been certified.

    c. Appoint Emery Celli Brinckerhoff & Abady LLP as Class Counsel.

    d. Determine that the Publication Notice in the form of Exhibit C and Notice Plan described in Exhibit D are fair, adequate, and sufficient, constituting the best practicable notice under the circumstances, and are reasonably calculated to reach members of the Settlement Class and apprise them of this Action, the terms and conditions of the Settlement Agreement, and their rights under the Settlement Agreement.

    e. Approve the procedures described in the Notice for members of the Settlement Class to object to this Settlement Agreement.

    f. Schedule a final approval hearing (the "Final Approval Hearing"), for a time, date, and place mutually convenient for the Court, Class Plaintiffs, and the Museum and at least 95 days after the Court's entry of the Preliminary Approval Order, at which the Court will conduct an inquiry into the fairness of this Settlement Agreement and determine whether the settlement should be finally approved.

    g. Stay all proceedings in the Action as between Class Plaintiffs and the Museum, except those related to effectuating and complying with the Settlement Agreement, pending the Court's determination of whether the Settlement Agreement should be finally approved.

Notice Procedures

11. As soon as practicable following entry of the Court's Preliminary Approval Order, Class Counsel shall cause the Publication Notice to be placed on the dedicated website for this Action, www.metfees.com (the "Settlement Website"), and the Museum shall (i) cause the Publication Notice to be placed in such publications and with such frequency as is described in Exhibit D hereto, in accordance with the Plan for Publication Notice, and (ii) concurrently place on the home page of the Museum's public website a banner with a link to the Settlement Website in the form attached as Exhibit E. The Settlement Website will provide notice of the date and time that the Court sets for a hearing on final approval of this Settlement Agreement, and clearly displayed links to complete copies of the following materials:

    a. This Settlement Agreement and its exhibits.
    b. The Court's order granting preliminary approval of this Settlement Agreement.
    c. The Complaint.
    d. The October 30, 2013 decision of the Court.
    e. The February 5, 2015 decision of the Appellate Division.

12. As explained in the Publication Notice, any member of the Settlement Class may object to this Settlement Agreement. Any member of the Settlement Class who wishes to assert such an objection (an "Objector") must file with the Court and send to Class Counsel and counsel for the Museum, by first class mail and postmarked not later than 45 days prior to the date set for the Final Approval Hearing, a written statement of objections. That statement must (i) state the full name and address and telephone number of the Objector, (ii) provide information sufficient to establish that the Objector is a member of the Settlement Class, (iii) state the full name and address and telephone number of any counsel representing the Objector in connection with the objections, (iv) describe all objections of the Objector and the specific reasons therefor (including legal support that the Objector wishes to bring to the Court's attention), and (v) attach any affidavits or other evidence relied upon in support of the objection.

13. At or before the time when a motion for final approval is filed, Class Counsel and counsel for the Museum shall notify the Court in writing that the Notice Plan was carried out and that the website notice, publication notice, and any other notice was provided in the manner directed by the Court.

Final Court Approval

14. Class Counsel and counsel for the Museum will move for the Court to enter a Judgment and Order Granting Final Approval of Settlement (the "Judgment" and the "Order Granting Final Approval"), in the form of Exhibits A and F hereto, which will:

a. Determine that the Court has personal jurisdiction over Defendants and all members of the Settlement Class, and jurisdiction to finally approve this Settlement Agreement.

b. Finally approve this Settlement Agreement, including its release provisions, and find that the Settlement Agreement was made in good faith, following aim's-length negotiations, and was not collusive, and further find that the Settlement Agreement is fair, reasonable, and adequate for the Settlement Class.

c. Define the Settlement Class and finally certify it for settlement purposes only, and declare that in the event of termination of this Settlement Agreement, certification of the Settlement Class shall automatically be vacated and the Museum may fully contest certification of any class as if no Settlement Class had been certified.

d. Approve the notice provided to the Settlement Class as fair, adequate, and sufficient, as the best practicable notice under the circumstances, aiid as reasonably calculated to appiise members of the Settlement Class of the Action, this Settlement Agreement, and their objection rights, and as fully satisfying the requirements of CPLR 904, and any other applicable laws or rules of the Court, and due process.

e. Incorporate all terms and conditions of this Settlement Agreement by reference, and state the settlement consideration and full terms of the release.

f. Provide that the Court retains continuing jurisdiction over the Settlement Class and the Museum to implement, administer, consummate, and enforce this Settlement Agreement, and the Judgment and the Order Granting Final Approval.

g. Dismiss the claims for money damages asserted in the First Cause of Action with prejudice as to the Class Plaintiffs but without prejudice as to all other members of the Settlement Class, and without costs except as provided herein.

h. Direct that the Released Claims asserted in the Action on behalf of either the Class Plaintiffs or members of the Settlement Class are otherwise dismissed with prejudice and without costs except as provided herein.

i. Enter a final injunction incorporating the terms of the consent decree stated in paragraph 15, below.

Terms of Consent Decree

15. In consideration of and subject to all other terms of this Settlement Agreement, and without admission of liability, the parties agree to consent to the entry of a final injunction (the "Consent Decree") as follows:

a. Disclosures of "pay what you wish" admissions policy: During the term of the Consent Decree, the Museum shall provide disclosures ("Pay What You Wish Disclosures") of its "pay what you wish" admissions policy in the following manner:

i. The Museum will maintain a sign or signs plainly visible to visitors approaching the ticket cashiers informing visitors of the Museum's "pay what you wish" admissions policy and the suggested admission amounts by each category of visitor. Such sign(s) will disclose the Museum's "pay what you wish" admissions policy in a manner substantially similar to Exhibit G hereto, it being agreed that signage with identical content in the same order and spacing, and in the same relative type font sizes, and with the same prominence of display and prominence of placement as disclosures currently in use, shall be "substantially similar" regardless of other changes in the design or presentation.

ii. The Museum's website will disclose the Museum's "pay what you wish" admissions policy in a manner substantially similar to Exhibit H hereto, it being agreed that disclosure of the admissions policy with identical content in the same order and spacing, and in the same relative type font sizes, with the same prominence of display and prominence of placement as disclosures currently in use, shall be "substantially similar" regardless of other changes in the design or presentation.

iii. The Museum's on-site ticket kiosks and the first screens of the transaction pages will disclose the Museum's "pay what you wish" admissions policy in a manner substantially similar to Exhibit I hereto, it being agreed that disclosure of the admissions policy with identical content in the same order and spacing, and in the same relative type font sizes, with the same prominence of display and prominence of placement as disclosures currently in use, shall be "substantially similar" regardless of other changes in the design or presentation.

b. Third party websites: The Museum will include a provision in its contracts with CityPass, New York Pass, Explorers Pass and NYCitAll Pass ("Third Party Vendors") that each Third Party Vendor shall disclose the Museum's "pay what you wish" admissions policy, such that purchasers can reasonably have been notified of such policy prior to purchasing a product which includes admission to the Museum. The Museum will use commercially reasonable efforts to enforce such contract provisions.

c. Future changes in suggested admission amounts: The Museum may change the amounts of the suggested admission amounts under the existing "pay what you wish" admissions policy. If it does so, it may change the amounts of the suggested prices shown on its Pay What You Wish Disclosures. Any such change, if limited to changing the amounts of the suggested prices, will not require the consent of the Class Plaintiffs or the approval of the Court.

d. Staff training/ evaluation: The Museum will continue its existing policies of (i) not evaluating Visitor Services staff according to individual sales amounts, and (ii) providing Visitor Services staff with introductory training and quarterly refresher training programs on the "pay what you wish" policy and procedures for explaining that policy to visitors. Such procedures shall require that each cashier either ask how much visitors would like to pay or state that visitors may pay any amount they choose, and that, in accordance with training procedures currently in place, Visitor Services staff working as "line-busters" explain to visitors that they may pay less than the full suggested admission amount at the cashier's desk if they continue waiting in line.

e. Future changes in Museum admission policy: The Museum may, without seeking consent of the Class Plaintiffs or approval of the Court, change its admissions policy to charge some or all visitors mandatory admission fees (*i.e.,* fees charged on a basis other than the "pay what you wish" system), subject to any required governmental approvals. Any such change shall be deemed an "Admissions Policy Change." The Museum will announce any Admissions Policy Change by means of a press release, with a copy provided simultaneously to Class Counsel, at least 30 days before the effective date of the Admissions Policy Change.

f. Revised disclosures following changes in Museum admission policy: Immediately upon the effective date of any Admissions Policy Change, the Museum may revise the signs at the entrances to the Museum, the Museum's web site, and communications with Third Party vendors (all such revisions being referred to as "Revised Disclosures") to reflect the Admissions Policy Change.

g. Court review and approval of Revised Disclosures: Within 30 days after the effective date of any Admissions Policy Change, the Museum will apply to the Court, with notice to Class Counsel, for an order concerning application of the Consent Decree to the Revised Disclosures describing such Admissions Policy Change. If the Admissions Policy Change provides for a "pay what you wish" policy for some class or classes of visitors, the Court will review the Revised Disclosures and shall approve them if they disclose the availability of "pay what you wish" admission to such visitors in a manner substantially similar to the terms of paragraphs 15.a.i.-iii., above, governing Pay What You Wish Disclosures. On any such motion the Museum, as movant, shall bear the burden of persuading the Court that no such conflict or incompatibility exists. If the Admissions Policy Change does not provide for a "pay what you wish" policy for any class of visitors, the Court will enter an order stating that the Consent Decree is inapplicable to such Revised Disclosures.

h. Availability of "pay what you wish" admission: During the term of the Consent Decree, so long as the Museum's admissions policy permits some or all visitors to enter the Museum's exhibition halls on a "pay what you wish" basis, the Museum will ensure that eligible visitors are provided with a reasonable opportunity to purchase admission at the public entrance to the Museum for less than the full suggested admission fee if they choose.

i. Duration of consent decree: The Consent Decree, once entered, shall remain in effect until 78 months after the date of execution of this Settlement Agreement. Upon the expiration of that time, the Consent Decree shall, without further order of the Court, expire and be of no further force or effect.

Attorneys' Fees and Expenses

16. Upon entry of Final Approval of this Settlement Agreement by the Court, Class Counsel may apply to the Court for an award of attorneys' fees and expenses to be paid by the Museum. So long as the total aggregate amount sought does not exceed $350,000, the Museum agrees not to oppose such application or to argue that the amount sought is unreasonable. The Museum shall not be required to pay any attorneys' fees and expenses until either (i) all deadlines for any person to seek appellate review of the order granting Final Approval of this Settlement Agreement have elapsed without such review having been sought, or (ii) all possible appeals from such order have been concluded and the order has been affirmed without substantial modification.

Incentive Payments to Class Plaintiffs

17. The Museum agrees to make an incentive payment of $1,000 each ($3,000 total) to the three Class Plaintiffs in consideration for their services as Class Plaintiffs and their release of their individual claims for damages. Payment shall be made by check payable to Class Counsel as attorneys for each Class Plaintiff and shall be delivered to Class Counsel. The Museum shall not be required to pay such incentive payments until either (i) all deadlines for any person to seek appellate review of the order granting Final Approval of this Settlement Agreement have elapsed without such review having been sought, or (ii) all possible appeals from such order have been concluded and the order has been affirmed without substantial modification.

Termination

18. This Settlement Agreement may be terminated only as provided below.

Termination shall be effected by written notice to all parties and the Court within ten business days after the event giving rise to the termination:

a. Any party may terminate if the Court does not enter any of the following in substantially the form attached, or subsequently seeks to modify significantly any such documents: (i) the Preliminary Approval Order attached as Exhibit B hereto, and (ii) the Judgment and the Order Granting Final Approval attached as Exhibits A and F hereto.

b. Any party may terminate this Settlement Agreement if the Court's Preliminary Approval Order, the Court's Judgment, or the Court's Order Granting Final Approval are not substantially affirmed or arc significantly modified on any appeal.

19. In the event of termination of this Settlement Agreement:

a. This Settlement Agreement shall be null and void, and of no force and effect, except as provided in this paragraph 19 and in paragraphs 24, 25, and 26 below.

b. Any certification of the Settlement Class by the Court for settlement purposes will automatically be vacated. The Class Plaintiffs, and all members of the putative class, will retain all claims as if this Settlement Agreement had not been entered into. Museum will retain all defenses to certification and its non-opposition to the Settlement Class for settlement purposes only shall not be used as evidence, and shall not be admissible as such, in support of class certification in the Action or any other civil action or proceeding.

c. Class Plaintiffs and the Museum shall revert to their positions prior to the execution of the original Settlement Agreement, including with respect to the appropriateness of class certification, as if no Settlement Agreement in this Action had been reached or executed.

Continuing Jurisdiction

20. During the term of the Consent Decree, the Court will retain continuing jurisdiction over the Class Plaintiffs, the Settlement Class, and the Museum to implement, administer, consumate, and enforce this Settlement Agreement and the Judgment and the Order Granting Final Approval.

21. Class Plaintiffs, the Settlement Class, and the Museum hereby irrevocably submit to the exclusive jurisdiction of the Court for any suit, action, proceeding, or dispute arising out of or relating to this Settlement Agreement or the Judgment and the Order Granting Final Approval.

22. In the event that the provisions of this Settlement Agreement or the Judgment and the Order Granting Final Approval are asserted by the Museum as a defense in whole or in part to any claim or cause of action or otherwise raised as an objection in any other suit, action, or proceeding by a Class Plaintiff or member of the Settlement Class, it is hereby agreed

that the Museum may seek, and that Class Plaintiffs will not oppose, a stay of that suit, action, or proceeding until the Court has entered an order or judgment determining any issues relating to the defense or objections based on such provisions.

Additional Terms and Conditions

23. Plaintiffs, the Settlement Class, the Museum, and their respective counsel shall execute all documents and perform any additional acts reasonably necessary and proper to effectuate the terms of this Settlement Agreement and to obtain the benefit of this Settlement Agreement for Plaintiffs, the Settlement Class, and Defendants.

24. The Museum specifically denies any and all liability in this Action. It is expressly understood and agreed that the Museum, by entering into this Settlement Agreement, is not admitting any liability or wrongdoing and is not admitting the truth of any allegations or circumstances, and is not waiving any defense or affirmative defense.

25. This Settlement Agreement, and all negotiations, documents, and discussions associated with it, shall not be construed as, or deemed to be, evidence of any admission of any liability or wrongdoing on the part of the Museum or any of the Released Parties, or of the truth or merit of any allegations or claims in the Action, or evidence of any admission on the part of Class Plaintiffs and the Settlement Class that their potential claims lack merit, and shall not be offered or accepted as evidence of such in any litigation, arbitration, or other proceeding; provided, however, that nothing contained herein shall preclude use of this Settlement Agreement in any proceeding to enforce this Settlement Agreement.

26. At any time prior to the Final Approval of this Settlement Agreement, the Museum may in its discretion change its practices with respect to admission fees and the communication of those practices to conform to all or part of the provisions of the proposed Consent Decree. The patties agree that in the event the Settlement Agreement does not receive Final Approval (or such Final Approval is reversed on appeal) or is terminated for any reason, the Museum's decision to adopt such changes prior to Final Approval will not be admissible in evidence to prove that the Museum's prior practices were unlawful or toıtious.

27. If any notice is required to be given under the terms of this Settlement Agreement, it shall be provided in writing and sent via e-mail and overnight mail to the following: [addresses omitted]

28. This Settlement Agreement, together with its exhibits, constitutes the entire agreement between the parties with regard to the subject matter hereof.

This Settlement Agreement may not be modified or amended except by a writing signed by all signatories hereto or their successors-in-interest.

29. It is understood and agreed that this Settlement Agreement shall be construed without regard to any presumption or other rule requiring construction against the party causing the document to be drafted. Each Party is entering into this Settlement Agreement voluntarily, without duress, with the consultation and advice of its legal counsel, and with full understanding of its terms.

30. This Settlement Agreement shall be interpreted and construed in accordance with the laws of the State of New York, without regard to the conflict of laws jurisprudence of the State of New York that would result in the application of the laws of any other jurisdiction.

31. This Settlement Agreement shall bind and inure to the benefit of the respective heirs, personal representatives, successors and assigns of the Parties.

32. This Settlement Agreement may be executed in any number of counterparts, each of which shall be deemed to be an original but all of which shall constitute one and the same Agreement. Executed signature pages for this Settlement Agreement may be delivered by facsimile or email and such facsimiles or emails shall be deemed as if actual signature pages had been delivered.

IN WITNESS WHEREOF, the signatories have read and understood this Settlement Agreement, have executed it, represent that the undersigned are authorized to execute this Settlement Agreement on behalf of their respectively represented parties, have agreed to be bound by its terms, and have duly executed this Settlement Agreement.

[Signatures omitted]
[Exhibits omitted]

STUDY QUESTIONS

- Who were the plaintiffs in *Saska v. Metropolitan Museum of Art*? Why did they sue the museum?
- What did the museum agree to as part of the Settlement Agreement? Do you think the outcome was appropriate?
- What advice would you give to museum's about their admission fee policies?

FRIENDS GROUPS

Affiliated nonprofit organizations are often used for fundraising purposes. Sometimes the affiliated group has a specific development focus, such as engaging younger museum audiences, or is active in purchasing art or other collections which the group then donates to the museum.

Often referred to as "Friends Groups" these entities typically are set up as separate nonprofit organizations and have separate boards, but they often have varying degrees of autonomy from the principal organization. In some cases, there is a great deal of overlap between individuals serving on the governing board of each organization.

A number of governmental and quasi-governmental organizations, including historical societies and parks and recreational agencies, use private nonprofit friends groups to enable fundraising activities. The National Park Service, for example, has many affiliated friends groups. Many art museums also have affiliated organizations.

While friends groups may have advantages, they also have the potential to create misunderstandings, conflicts or worse. The key to the effective use of friends groups is in managing the relationship so that the roles of the two entities is clearly understood and the autonomy of each organization is respected. One best practice is to negotiate a written affiliation agreement setting out the relationship between the two entities, and the responsibilities and obligations of each.

The NPS has developed a set of best practices in a document entitled *Best Practices in Friends Groups and National Parks.* Among the best practices identified in the NPS report are:

a. Parks and Friends must have a shared mission and similar goals for long term collaboration to work.

b. Mutual trust, necessary for the completion of large-scale projects, is earned over time.

c. Both partners must contribute equally to the relationship and be aware of park priorities and nonprofit needs.

d. Clear and constant communication between Parks and Friends, both in meetings or informal lunches, leads to understanding.

e. Both partners should commit to the relationship for the long term and work toward institutionalizing the partnership so that it is sustained beyond staff changes on both sides.

f. Create a culture of sharing and collaboration amongst Park and Friends staff members to create staff "buy-in."

g. Mutual respect between the park Superintendent and the Friends Executive Director facilitates success.

LOBBYING AND ADVOCACY

Lobbying by nonprofit institutions, including museums, is regulated primarily through the federal tax code. Lobbying activities are also regulated through federal and state registration and disclosure laws.

On the federal level, legal restrictions on political advocacy depend first and foremost on the nature of the nonprofit organization's tax-exempt status. Charitable organizations can qualify as tax-exempt under several different provisions of the tax code. Those that are tax-exempt under Section 501(c)(3) of the Internal Revenue Code—as are most private museums and museum associates or "friends groups"—are prohibited from taking part in political campaigns and from devoting "a substantial part" of their activities on activities defined as "lobbying." Organizations that violate these rules risk losing their tax-exempt status.

Federal tax law relies on a distinction between "advocacy" and "lobbying" activities. Advocacy encompasses a wide range of activities intended to influence public policy. Lobbying, on the other hand, is narrowly defined by the IRS Code as "attempts to influence legislation." Lobbying includes direct communications with legislators or government officials ("direct lobbying") as well as indirect attempts to influence legislation by affecting the opinions of the general public ("indirect" or "grassroots" lobbying). In either case, the activities must involve specific legislation and reflect an opinion on that legislation. In the case of grassroots lobbying, there must also be a "call to action"—that is, the communication must direct the recipient to contact a legislator or identify one or more legislators who will vote on the legislation.

Many museum boards and staff mistakenly believe that their organization cannot engage in public policy debates and advocacy activities without jeopardizing their tax-exempt status or otherwise running afoul of the law. While a museum should remain true to its mission and beware of the impact of its activities on its reputation and its public trust status, there are in fact a great many activities that a museum can engage in that are neither considered political campaigning nor lobbying under federal law. Presenting non-partisan research and analysis on a legislative issue and responding to requests from a legislative body for technical advice on specific legislation is not considered lobbying. Communicating with museum membership about pending legislation is not lobbying, so long as the organization does not encourage its members or others to lobby. For example, a museum could send out a public affairs bulletin to its members, and even take a position in support of or against the legislation, and it would not count as lobbying so long as it did not include a "call to action." Perhaps most importantly, self-defense activity—that is, seeking to influence legislators (but not the general public) on matters that may affect the organization's own existence, powers, tax-exempt status, and similar matters—does not constitute lobbying under federal tax law.

When a museum does engage in activities that may constitute lobbying under the IRS rules, the organization must track its expenditures on these activities to ensure that it does not run afoul of IRS spending restrictions. The spending restrictions have traditionally been defined through a vague "no substantial part" test which requires the organization to demonstrate that "no substantial part of the activities of the organization constitute lobbying. However, nonprofits, including museums, may elect instead to track their lobbying activities using a predefined "expenditure" test. The rules provide a sliding scale of permissible lobbying expenditure limits based on the size of the organization's budget.

Nonprofits that engage in advocacy and lobbying activities may also be required to register under federal and state lobbying disclosure laws, and file periodic reports on those activities under certain circumstances. Under the federal Lobbying Disclosure Act, 2 U.S.C. Section 160, a nonprofit organization is required to register and report on its lobbying activities if it employs at least one "lobbyist" and spends more than $20,000 in a semi-annual period on lobbying activities. An employee who engages in certain lobbying activities, such as meeting with federal executive or legislative officials, which constitute more than 20 percent of that employee's total work time, is considered a lobbyist under the federal law. Nonprofits which make the Section 501(h) election may use the broader tax law definition of "lobbying" activities and submit IRS Form 990 to satisfy the reporting requirements of the federal disclosure law. State disclosure and reporting laws vary.

Federally funded nonprofits, including museums, that engage in lobbying activities need to take care to organize their legislative work such so that no federal funds are used for that purpose. If a museum is actively engaged in public policy and advocacy activities, it should consider adopting a written policy clarifying the scope of the work and the time and resources that will be allocated to those activities.

These rules only apply to the nonprofit organization itself and not to individuals acting in their own capacity and not as representatives of the organization. Staff or board members can advocate individually or join volunteer advocacy groups as long as the group has no connection to the nonprofit with which the individual is associated. In doing so, it is important to avoid using the name or letterhead of the nonprofit museum. Where an individual is closely associated in the public's mind with a particular nonprofit, it may be advisable to treat the activity as part of the organization's advocacy activities.

Many nonprofit organizations prepare an advocacy handbook to assist their members with effectively pursuing the organization's advocacy goals. The handbook sets out the organization's policy initiatives and provides suggestions on how to contact government officials and conduct advocacy activities.

LIST OF IMAGES

Page 224: James Earl Reid, "Third World America" (1985). (Fair Use).

Page 237: Prince Rogers Nelson, "Love Symbol #2" (1992). (Fair Use).

Page 259: Roger & Renate Rössing, "Dmitri Shostakovich's portrait, in the audience at the Bach Celebration of July 28, 1950" (1950). (Creative Commons Attribution-Share Alike 3.0 Germany license/Fair Use).

Page 298: Constantin Brâncuşi, *Bird in Space* (1926). Image—Seattle Art Museum. (Fair Use).

Page 308: Bill Graham Archives LLC, Jefferson Airplane/Grateful Dead/Big Brother and the Holding Company concert poster (1967). (Fair Use).

Page 318: Robert S. Davidson/US Postal Service, Statue of Liberty Forever Stamp/Liberty Enlightening the World (2010). (Fair Use).

Page 348: Art Rogers, *Puppies* (1980)/Jeff Koons, *String of Puppies* (1988). (Fair Use).

Page 363: Jeff Koons, *Wild Boy and Puppy* (1988). (Fair Use).

Page 381: Jeff Koons, *Niagara* (2000)/Andrea Blanch, *Silk Sandals* (2000). (Fair Use).

Page 395: Jeff Koons, *Ushering in Banality* (1988). (Fair Use).

Page 397: Patrick Cariou, photograph from *Yes Rasta* (2000)/Richard Prince, *Graduation* (2008). (Fair Use).

Page 433: Mass MOCA, press photograph documenting installation of *Training Ground for Democracy* (2006). (Fair Use).

Page 464: Alfred Stieglitz, "Georgia O'Keeffe—Exhibition at American Place Gallery" (1931-1932). Alfred Stieglitz Collection, National Gallery of Art. (Public Domain/Fair Use).

Page 490: Possibly Andy Warhol, "Self Portrait—Double Denied" (1964). (Fair Use).

Page 506: Egon Schiele, *Portrait of Wally* (1912). Leopold Museum. (Public Domain/Fair Use).

Page 554: Before and after photographs of Head of Amenhotep III. Source unknown, possibly U.S. Customs court evidence. (Fair Use).

Page 609: Andres Serrano, *Piss Christ* (1987). (Fair Use).

Page 639: Brooklyn Museum, photograph of *Sensation* exhibit gallery (1997). (No Restrictions/Fair Use.)

Page 662: Museum of Contemporary Art Chicago, Installation view, Robert Mapplethorpe: *The Perfect Moment* (1989). (Fair Use).

Page 666: The Metropolitan Museum of Art, photograph of Fifth Street entrance. (Press Photo/Fair Use.)

INDEX

Page references for figures are italicized.

ACKNOWLEDGMENTS

With special thanks to:

My museum law colleagues,
from whom I have learned so much;

My students at Johns Hopkins,
George Washington University,
Mitchell Hamline Law School and
Case Western University Law School,
who studied various versions of this textbook;

My friend Scott, for helping to put this all together;

My daughter Emelia, for her encouragement and
proofreading skills; and

The pandemic, without which this textbook would
likely never have been completed.

www.ingramcontent.com/pod-product-compliance
Ingram Content Group UK Ltd.
Pitfield, Milton Keynes, MK11 3LW, UK
UKHW050649200926
475560UK00005BA/353

9 781538 166352